Fourth Edition

Children's Books in Children's Hands

An Introduction to Their Literature

Charles Temple
Hobart and William Smith Colleges

Miriam Martinez
University of Texas at San Antonio

Junko Yokota
National-Louis University

With Contributions by
Evelyn B. Freeman
The Ohio State University at Mansfield

PEARSON

Boston Columbus Indianapolis New York San Francisco Upper Saddle River
Amsterdam Cape Town Dubai London Madrid Milan Munich Paris Montreal Toronto
Delhi Mexico City Sao Paulo Sydney Hong Kong Seoul Singapore Taipei Tokyo

Vice President, Editor-in-Chief, Literacy: Aurora Martínez Ramos
Associate Sponsoring Editor: Barbara Strickland
Editorial Assistant: Meagan French
Vice President, Director of Marketing: Quinn Perkson
Executive Marketing Manager: Krista Clark
Production Editor: Paula Carroll
Editorial Production Service: Publishers' Design and Production Services, Inc./Kathy Smith
Manufacturing Buyer: Megan Cochran
Electronic Composition: Publishers' Design and Production Services, Inc.
Interior Design: Anne Flanagan
Photo Researcher: Annie Pickert
Cover Designer: Linda Knowles

Credits and acknowledgments borrowed from other sources and reproduced, with permission, in this textbook appear on appropriate page within text (or on page 571–572).

Illustrations from pages i, vii–xix, xxiii–xxvii, 1,3,27,54, 105, 148 and in all the Teaching Idea, Top Shelf, Issue to Consider, Recommended Books, and Teacher/Librarian Partnerships features copyright © 2009 by Frané Lessac. Illustrations from pages ix, xii–xv, xxii, 167, 169, 208, 255, 293, 329, 355, and all Technology in Practice features are copyright © 2004 by Frané Lessac. Illustrations from pages 389, 391, 411, 434, and 473 copyright © 2000 by Frané Lessac. All other credits for reproduction of book covers and interiors are credited where they appear.

Book plate #22 (From *Ella Sarah Gets Dressed* copyright © 2003 by Margaret Chodos-Irvine, reprinted by permission of Houghton Mifflin Harcourt Publishing Company.)

Book plate #23 ("Book Cover" from *Cook-A-Doodle-Doo!* by Janet Stevens and Susan Stevens Crummel, Illustrations copyright © 1999 by Janet Stevens, reprinted by permission of Houghton Mifflin Harcourt Publishing Company.)

Cataloging-in-Publication Data is on file at the Library of Congress.

10 9 8 7 6 5 4 3 2   (EB)   14 13 12 11

www.pearsonhighered.com

ISBN-10: 0-13-704877-7
ISBN-13: 978-0-13-704877-9

To the memory of Frances, and with gratitude to our readers—
may you follow your dreams and do good work.

C.T.

To Elena and Emma and all the stories we will share.

M.M.

To Alyssa and Jeremy, Mia and Reid

J.Y.

About the Authors

The authors of this text were drawn together by a love of children's books and a fascination with the people who make them and by the hope that another generation of students, teachers, librarians, and parents could be inspired to take up the challenge of getting those works into the hands of children.

Charles Temple is a banjo-picking storyteller and teacher educator at Hobart and William Smith Colleges. He has co-authored many books in the field of reading and language arts, including *All Children Read, Understanding Reading Problems,* and *The Beginnings of Writing.* He has also published several books for children. Dr. Temple has worked over the years with teachers in Europe, Asia, Africa, and Central and South America who are using literacy and literature to better students' lives.

Favorite books as a child included *The Broad Highway* by Jeffery Farnol, Uncle Wiggily Stories and Dr. Doolittle, and also Tom Swift, and the *All-About Books*.

Miriam Martinez is a teacher educator at the University of Texas at San Antonio who loves nothing more than getting lost in good books, including children's books, of course! She is recipient of the International Reading Association's Arbuthnot Award, which honors outstanding university teachers of children's literature. Dr. Martinez coedited *Book Talk and Beyond: Children and Teachers Respond to Literature* (1995) and *What a Character! Character Study as a Gateway to Literary Understanding* (2005), both published by the International Reading Association. She served for seven years as the coeditor of "Bookalogues," a children's book review column in the journal *Language Arts.* She is publicity chair for the Children's Literature Assembly. The focus of her research and writing is on ways of bringing children and books together to foster students' literary and literacy development.

Favorite books as a child included *Horton Hatches the Egg* by Dr. Seuss, *The Four-Story Mistake* by Elizabeth Enright, *Then There Were Five* by Elizabeth Enright, *Dangerous Island* by Helen Mather-Smith Mindlin, and *The Bobbsey Twins in Mexico* by Laura Lee Hope.

Junko Yokota is a professor and director of the Center for Teaching through Children's Books at National-Louis University in Chicago, Illinois. She was a classroom teacher and a school librarian during the first ten years of her career. Her publications include articles and review columns in a wide variety of reading/language arts and children's literature journals, chapters in professional books, and *Kaleidoscope: A Multicultural Booklist for Grades K–8* published by the National Council of Teachers of English. She has served on the Caldecott and Newbery Award Committees, chaired the Batchelder Award Committee, and

been a judge on the Audies Awards. Dr. Yokota is past president of the United States Board on Books for Young People (the U.S. national section of IBBY and a recipient of the Virginia Hamilton Award for Contribution to Multicultural Literature and of the Reading the World Award. She served on the Hans Christian Andersen Jury to select the 2006 and 2008 author and illustrator winners of the highest international award for children's literature.

Having grown up in Japan, her favorite childhood books were in her first language, including picture songbooks from which her mother sang to her.

Brief Contents

Contents

4 Literature Representing Diverse Perspectives   105

5 International Literature   148

Part Two   Exploring the Genres of Children's Literature   167

8 Modern Fantasy and Science Fiction   255

9 Contemporary Realistic Fiction   293

10 Historical Fiction   329

11   Informational Books and Biography   355

Part Three Creating the Literature-Based Classroom   389

15   Literary and Content Units   473

Preface

In a bookseller's booth at a reading conference a few years back, we noticed the literary critic, Louise Rosenblatt, standing by herself in a lull between book signings. We fell into conversation with her and were immediately impressed by her energy and her strong convictions. "Good books shouldn't be used for anything!" the nonagenarian critic declared. "They should be appreciated for what they are!" Those of you who know her famous description of aesthetic reading—in which the reader brings to bear on a book her emotions, associations, prior reading experiences, and literary knowledge—will understand that to Rosenblatt "appreciation" was an engaging thing, not a casual activity.

Yet there are people who would strongly disagree with her position. Take the fourth-grade teacher who is planning a unit on the voyage of Columbus, a unit that would not be complete without reading Pam Conrad's *Pedro's Journal*. Or the fifth-grade teacher who wants his students to understand more about Central America than its countries, capitals, and major exports—so he puts Ann Cameron's *The Most Beautiful Place in the World* on their reading list. Or the sixth-grade class exploring the immigrant experience that devours Karen Hesse's *Letters from Rifka* and Pam Muñoz Ryan's *Esperanza Rising*.

Think of those two positions for a moment. The critic says the rewards of reading come most abundantly to the child who learns to bring the full range of her intelligence and her experiences to the reading act. The teacher says that may be true, but there is a lot to learn about living in the world, too, and we are blessed with riches of books whose pages bring knowledge to life for children.

Then comes the literacy activist, who adds that it is also important that children become readers because children who develop the habit of reading derive so many benefits. Their knowledge of the world is broader, their vocabularies richer, their insights into human situations more nuanced, their empathy for people from other neighborhoods deeper, and their ability to reflect on themselves more profound. Up and down the hallways of any school, highly skilled teachers are doing their best to teach children to read; but unless children want to read, and unless they do read, that instruction counts for little.

Those three observations—the critic's, the teacher's, and the literacy activist's—nicely set the agenda for this book.

To become knowledgeable about children's literature means that you should understand how literature works, what literary dynamics are, and how children read and respond to literature. In other words, you will need the critic's perspective.

But you will also need to be familiar with the huge range of good books available for children—the folktales, poems, multicultural books, novels about the range of human experiences, information books, and biographies. In other words, you will need the resourceful teacher's perspective, too.

Nothing we do will matter, though, unless children read—unless they gain the habit of reading and immerse themselves in books. For that to happen, you must become a Pied Piper (in a good sense!)—a person who knows how to lure children into books and help them have a wonderful experience once they are there. You will need to adopt the stance of the literacy activist.

New to This Edition

- New to this edition most importantly are the new books we are reviewing and presenting—dozens of new titles and many new authors in each chapter. The UPS drivers in Geneva, New York; San Antonio; and Chicago can find our houses with their eyes closed. They have been stopping by almost daily for decades delivering new books.

- Just as in previous editions, there is a strong emphasis in *Children's Books in Children's Hands*, *Fourth Edition*, on books from many cultural groups. New to this edition is a new chapter on international books (Chapter 5). Just as children's books provide a vivid and engaging way to take the perspectives of people from many cultures, children's books can take us beyond our national borders to experience lives under very different circumstances.

- The book has a modified organization that casts the chapters on literary elements and picture books as the foundation for chapters on the literary genres.

- This edition helps readers understand ways they can draw directly on their understandings of literary and visual elements and of literary genres to organize literature study for students.

- A special four-color insert helps the reader appreciate the visual elements of picture books.

- Last but not least, we consider it good news when a children's book is issued in paperback, becoming more accessible to more readers. Thus it is with some excitement that we send out this paperback fourth edition of *Children's Books in Children's Hands*, in hopes that it will reach still more readers, too.

How This Book Is Organized

Part One, "Understanding Literature and the Child Reader," orients the reader to the study of children's literature, and gives you the critic's perspective. **Chapter 1**, "Children's Books in Children's Hands," introduces the child reader and the reading process, focusing on children's intellectual and personality development and on the nature of children's responses to literature. **Chapter 2**, "Literary Elements in Works for Children," introduces a set of literary concepts with which to approach children's books, describing how plots are organized, how characters are drawn, and how themes are developed. **Chapter 3**, "Picture Books," focuses on how art and text combine to form unique works. **Chapter 4**, "Literature Representing Diverse Perspectives," reflects this book's strong emphasis on multicultural literature. It investigates the ways various cultural groups are depicted in children's literature, highlights the progress that has been made in publishing children's books that represent various cultural groups more extensively and fairly, surveys the multicultural books that are available, and sets out guidelines for selecting high-quality multicultural books for children. **Chapter 5**, "International Literature," is a new chapter recognizing the importance of reading books from around the world. It investigates important issues, surveys the books that are available, and sets out guidelines for selecting high-quality international books for children.

Part Two, "Exploring the Genres of Children's Literature," surveys the books that have been written for children, type by type or genre by genre. Each of the chapters in this part outlines the historical development of a particular genre, examines the literary qualities that distinguish the genre and the reading demands those qualities place on the child, reviews outstanding examples of works from the genre, and sets out criteria for selecting good works in the genre. Each chapter closes with an extensive annotated list of recommended books in the genre. **Chapter 6**, "Poetry for Children," surveys the genre from nursery rhymes to contemporary multicultural poetry for children. **Chapter 7**, "Traditional Literature," looks at folk literature from many times and cultures. **Chapter 8**, "Modern Fantasy and Science Fiction," considers the artistry that enables readers to enter hypothetical worlds. **Chapter 9,** "Contemporary Realistic Fiction," looks at ways authors create believable books that are set in the "here and now" and that address the wide-ranging problems and delights of today's children. Books set in times that may be many generations removed from our own are discussed in **Chapter 10,** "Historical Fiction," which explains the origins of the current emphasis on meticulous accuracy in this genre. **Chapter 11,** "Informational Books and Biography," surveys a growing area of children's literature in which talented writers present the real world and its people to young readers in skillfully focused works that can be as riveting as fiction.

Part Three, "Creating the Literature-Based Classroom," was written for current and future teachers and librarians and anyone else who wants to share literature with children in ways that ensure that they will get the most from the encounters. **Chapter 12,** "Literary Meaning-Making and Children's Responses to Literature," discusses reader response theory and its implications for the study and sharing of children's literature. **Chapter 13,** "Inviting Children into Literature: Classroom Libraries, Read-Alouds, and Storytelling," explains how to entice children into literature through the creation of classroom libraries and through activities such as reading aloud, storytelling, readers' theater, and journal writing. Conducting book discussions with children so that they are empowered to say what they feel and are encouraged to grow through the discussions is the topic of **Chapter 14,** "Encouraging Response to Literature." Constructing literature units and literature-based content area units and guiding children through them is the focus of **Chapter 15,** "Literary and Content Units." This chapter, like the others in this part, provides extensive lists of recommended books for use in the literature-based classroom.

The appendix offers a list of the recipients of major children's book awards.

In addition, you can find the following updated appendixes on the book's MyEducationKit (www.myeducationkit.com): Children's Magazines, Professional Organizations, Children's Book Publishers' Addresses, Book Selection Aids, and Children's Literature Web Sites.

Pedagogical Enrichment and Features of This Book

The richly illustrated fourth edition is packed with practical applications and unique pedagogical features:

Top Shelf 4.1

Multiracial Characters

Aneesa Lee and the Weaver's Gift by Nikki Grimes. Illustrated by Ashley Bryan.

black is brown is tan by Arnold Adoff. Illustrated by Emily Arnold McCulley.

Habibi by Naomi Shihab Nye.

I Love Saturdays y domingos by Alma Flor Ada. Illustrated by Elivia Savadier.

Molly Bannaky by Alice McGill. Illustrated by Chris Soentpiet.

"Top Shelf" book lists in every chapter list our best picks of titles that exemplify a particular concept discussed in the chapter (e.g., Humorous Picture Books or Multicultural Audiobooks.)

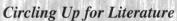

Teaching Idea 15.4

Circling Up for Literature

Creating links between literature and content area instruction enriches learning in the content area. For a study of living things in science, get multiple copies of the following titles: *Stone Fox*, *The Midnight Fox*, *Stranded*, and *Shiloh*. Allow your students to choose the book they want to read and then organize students into literature circles. These groups can meet to set their reading pace and to decide whether they will read as partners, as a group, or alone. They can respond to the books in writing or through discussion. Many teachers include the choice of a culminating activity by offering responses such as designing a book jacket complete with the author's biography and recommendations by their peers or creating a commercial for the book that is taped à la the PBS series, *Reading Rainbow*.

"Teaching Ideas" provide valuable, practical lessons and activities for sharing literature with children in the classroom.

Technology in Practice 7.1

Resources on the Web

There are several excellent web sites devoted to folktales and folklore. Kay E. Vandergrift maintains a site useful for its access to variations of common tales at **http://www.scils .rutgers.edu/~kvander/swlinks.html**.

Professor D. L. Ashliman's web site contains links to a host of folk stories and other resources, including instruction in storytelling at **http://www.pitt.edu/~dash/ashliman .html**. Once you are there, you can explore the web sites from the main page.

The de Grummond Children's Literature Collection of the University of Southern Mississippi has a site at **http://www.lib.usm.edu/~degrum/html/aboutus-welcome.shtml**, especially biographies of children's authors. There are three domains devoted to collections of scores of versions of "Jack and the Beanstalk," "Cinderella," and "Little Red Riding Hood." Many of the texts and illustrations can be viewed online.

Heidi Anne Heiner's *Sur la Lune* has annotated fairy tales—forty-nine of them as of this writing— and there are links to the versions of the tales that are still in print and available from Amazon.com. The address of her site is **http://www.surlalunefairytales.com**.

"Technology in Practice" teaching tips in each chapter reflect our collective experience with the intersection of electronics and print, and provide activities for the classroom utilizing new media technology (e.g., how to create a student book referral database).

Ask the Author . . .   Bruce Coville

Favorite Books As a Child

The Dr. Dolittle Books
by Hugh Lofting

The Mushroom Planet Books
by Eleanor Cameron

Tom Swift in the City of Gold

When I began producing audiobooks, it seemed natural to focus on fantasy, since that was what I wrote, and also the bulk of what I read. But as it turns out, there are numerous reasons why fantasy works particularly well on audio—especially in the full cast form that I produce in, where we use a separate actor for each major character.

To begin with, fantasy grows out of the oral tradition. The roots of most fantasy novels can be found in myth, legend, and folklore—all things that were originally meant to be heard. Whether consciously or not, I think this has an effect on the writing of fantasy. Good fantasy, especially good children's fantasy, is just plain fun to listen to. It's also fun to read aloud, since the characters tend to be large (sometimes larger than life), vividly realized, and vocally interesting. So we usually have a great time in the studio!

Of course, this also represents a challenge. What, for example, does a dragon sound like? The recording is made or lost in the casting process, and over the years I have had to find actors to play everything from bunnies to dragons, with stops in th

them a chance to go places more realistic fiction doesn't allow for. But it does mean we spend a lot of time trying to work out how each of these creatures should sound!

One of the real joys of this form is that it allows us to bring a book to life for the child listener in a way that still leaves room for imaginative participation. Unlike film and television, where the images are set and finished, with audio the child has to engage, and create the images in his or her head. Film and television do all the work for you, and can dull the imagination. Audiobooks engage and stimulate it.

After all, no matter how good special effects become, nothing will ever beat the dragon you create in your own imagination!

Bruce Coville is the author of 90 books for children and young adults, including the international bestseller *My Teacher Is an Alien*, and the wildly popular *Unicorn Chronicles* series. He has been, at various times, a teacher, a toymaker, a magazine editor, a gravedigger, and a cookware salesman. He is also the founder of *Full Cast Audio*, an audiobook publishing

Each chapter includes an "Ask the Author" (or Illustrator, Editor, or Educator) box, in which a prominent children's author, illustrator, editor, or educator responds to a question related to the chapter content.

Issue to Consider

Are Themes Really There?

As we have just said, the theme of a contemporary literary work is more often implied than explicitly stated. Not surprisingly, the identification and interpretation of themes that are not explicitly stated give rise to lively debates. Critics argue not only about what the theme of a specific work really is, but also about whether it is possible to say definitively what a book's theme is. While some critics claim that skilled readers are adept at discovering themes that less skilled readers will miss, others (known as "deconstructionists" or "transactionalists" in the field of literary theory) insist that what a book means—its theme—lies to a large degree in the experience, background, and personality of each reader who encounters it.

These differing opinions certainly do not prevent literary critics, authors, and book lovers from discussing themes. Readers often have different ideas about the theme of a particular book. And authors sometimes even disagree with what the critics identify as the themes of their books!

Can ten readers agree on what the theme of a book is? Can we ask children to say what a particular book's theme is?

What do you think?

"Issue to Consider" boxes in each chapter present a highly debated issue in children's literature.

Experiences for Further Learning

1. Compile your own anthology of poems for children. Organize it around a theme or an issue—for example, poems for choral reading, poems from many cultures, or poems to celebrate holidays. So that you can become acquainted with contemporary poetry, use ten different sources, choose no more than two poems per source, and make sure they were published within the last fifteen years. (Thanks to Linnea Henderson for this suggestion.)

2. A good poem may sound natural, but on examination it is likely to turn out to have been very carefully crafted. Take a poem such as A. A. Milne's "Happiness" (from ***When We Were Very Young***). Try substituting other words for any of Milne's. Does the poem sound as good?

3. Put together a collection of rhymes that accompany activities—jump-rope rhymes, work poems, poems to accompany explorations, poems that accompany science study. Ask for examples from friends and fellow students. Be especially attuned to rhymes from different cultures: Mexican American, Asian American, African American, and Appalachian.

"Experiences for Further Learning" are end-of-chapter activities that help readers deepen their own understanding of the chapter content.

 ## *Recommended Books*

I indicates interest level by age (P = preschool, YA = young adult)

The picture books in this chapter are not marked with an asterisk since all are picture books. The picture books that are listed within the genre chapters that follow are marked with an asterisk.

Toy Books

Ahlberg, Janet, and Allan Ahlberg. *The Jolly Postman or Other People's Letters*. Little, Brown, 1986. A postman delivers letters to and from various fairy tale characters. Miniature letters, cards, and postcards are included. (**I:** P–8)

Cousins, Lucy. *Maisy's Pop-Up Playhouse*. Candlewick, 1995. Pages of this book fold down to create rooms in a playhouse. (**I:** P)

Ehlert, Lois. *Color Zoo*. HarperCollins, 1989. As they turn the pages, children see various shapes that unlayer to reveal different animal faces. Shape names and animal names are

Gravett, Emily. *Meerkat Mail*. Simon, 2007. Postcards are used as a toy component to both offer information and to advance the story of a meerkat who leaves home and travels the world. (**I:** K–7)

Hill, Eric. *Where's Spot?* Putnam, 1980. Sally looks for Spot, who has not eaten his dinner. Children lift flaps to help search for the missing puppy. Over twenty other books about Spot (with Spanish versions of some titles) are available. (**I:** P)

Hoban, Tana. *Black on White*. Greenwillow, 1993. This board book shows black shapes of familiar objects such as an elephant, a butterfly, and a leaf on a white background. Its companion book is *White on Black* (1993). *Black and White* (2007). (**I:** P)

Inkpen, Mick. *Where, Oh Where, Is Kipper's Bear?* Red Wagon Books/Harcourt, 1995. Kipper, the dog's teddy bear, is missing; flaps, pop-ups, and pull tabs help readers search for the

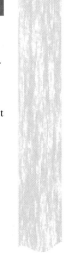

Each chapter concludes with extensive lists of "Recommended Books" that offer publication data, a brief annotation, and interest level by age for every book listed. These lists have been extensively updated for the fourth edition with scores of new entries.

Teacher/Librarian Partnership
Partnerships for Literacy

In decades past, teachers taught students how to read, and librarians provided access to the materials for reading. Teachers set the curriculum; librarians looked up the resources. The 1980s brought about the publication of Information Power (by the AASL), and librarians became the information literacy specialist—someone who helped students locate information, evaluate information, and use that information in their research. But still, the curriculum was classroom-driven and librarians were the support personnel.

What's the future for librarian/classroom teacher partnership as both work to support student learning? Redefining past roles and looking for new ways to partner depends on the commitment and engagement of each participant. The school librarian as instructional partner with the classroom teacher indicates more of an equal partnership, with both people taking on the role of teacher. When both parties recognize that such partnerships can facilitate each person's job and potentially result in better learning opportunities for students, the necessary planning time becomes a worthwhile investment.

"Teacher/Librarian Partnership" features in Chapters 5, 13, 14, and 15 offer suggestions for collaborations between teachers and librarians.

Supplements to Aid Teachers and Students

The following supplements provide an outstanding array of resources that facilitate learning about children's literature. For more information, ask your local Allyn & Bacon Merrill Education representative or contact the Allyn & Bacon Merrill Faculty Field Support Department at 1-800-526-0485. For technology support, please contact technical support directly at 1-800-677-6337 or *http://247.pearsoned.com*. Many of the supplements are available for download from the Instructor Resource Center at *www.pearsonhighered.com/irc*.

Instructor's Manual and Test Bank provides a variety of instructional tools, including chapter overviews, "pre-reading" directions, questions for class discussion, classroom activities, extending the reading assignments, plus multiple-choice and essay questions. (Available for download from the Instructor Resource Center at *www.pearsonhighered.com/irc*.)

Pearson MyTest is a powerful assessment generation program that helps instructors easily create and print quizzes and exams. Questions and tests are authored online, allowing ultimate flexibility and the ability to efficiently create and print assessments anytime, anywhere! Instructors can access Pearson MyTest and their test bank files by going to *www.pearsonmytest.com* to log in, register, or request access. Features of Pearson MyTest include:

Premium assessment content

- Draw from a rich library of assessments that complement your Pearson textbook and your course's learning objectives.
- Edit questions or tests to fit your specific teaching needs.

Instructor-friendly resources

- Easily create and store your own questions, including images, diagrams, and charts using simple drag-and-drop and Word-like controls.
- Use additional information provided by Pearson, such as the question's difficulty level or learning objective, to help you quickly build your test.

Time-saving enhancements

- Add headers or footers and easily scramble questions and answer choices—all from one simple toolbar.

- Quickly create multiple versions of your test or answer key, and when ready, simply save to Microsoft Word or PDF format and print!
- Export your exams for import to Blackboard 6.0, CE (WebCT), or Vista (WebCT)!

Dynamic Resources Meeting Your Needs

MyEducationKit is a dynamic web site that connects the concepts addressed in the text with effective teaching practice. Plus, it's easy to use and integrate into assignments and courses. Whenever the MyEducationKit logo appears in the text, follow the simple instructions to access a variety of multimedia resources geared to meet the diverse teaching and learning needs of instructors and students. Here are just a few of the features that are available:

- Online study plans, including self-assessment quizzes, and resource material.
- Gradetracker, an online grade book.
- A wealth of multimedia resources, including classroom video, expert video commentary, student and teacher artifacts, case studies, strategies, and lesson plans.
- Web links to important national organizations and sites in your field.

Study Plan

A MyEducationKit Study Plan is a multiple-choice assessment with feedback tied to chapter objectives. A well-designed Study Plan offers multiple opportunities to fully master required course content as identified by the objectives in each chapter:

- *Chapter Objectives* identify the learning outcomes for the chapter and give students targets to shoot for as they read and study.
- *Multiple-Choice Assessments* assess mastery of the content. These assessments are mapped to chapter objectives, and students can take the multiple-choice quiz as many times as they want. Not only do these quizzes provide overall scores for each objective, but they also explain why responses to particular items are correct or incorrect.

Children's Literature Database

A searchable database of thousands of excellent children's literature titles comes with the MyEducationKit for the Temple text. This database allows users to find books in every genre, by hundreds of authors and illustrators, by awards won, by year published, by topic and description, as well as many other search options. In the Activities and Applications section of the MyEducationKit site, users will learn how to use the database to

- Create text sets to accommodate lesson needs
- Develop an individualized reading list
- Pull together trade books to enrich a math, science, or social studies unit
- Prepare an author or illustrator study

Assignments and Activities

Designed to save instructors preparation time and enhance student understanding, these assignable exercises show concepts in action (through database use, video, cases, and/or student and teacher artifacts). They help students synthesize and apply concepts and strategies they read about in the book.

Multimedia Resources

The rich media resources you will encounter throughout MyEducationKit include

- *Videos*. The authentic classroom videos in MyEducationKit show how real teachers handle actual classroom situations. Discussing and analyzing these videos not only deepens understanding of concepts presented in the text, but also builds skills in observing children and classrooms.

- *Student and teacher artifacts*. Real K–12 student and teacher classroom artifacts—tied to the chapter topics in your text—offer practice in working with the different materials teachers encounter daily in their classrooms.

- *Web links*. On MyEducationKit you don't need to search for the sites that connect to the topics covered in your chapter. Here, you can explore web sites that are important in the field and that give you perspective on the concepts covered in your text.

- *Essay questions*. These questions encourage consideration of chapter topics. Hints and feedback are provided.

- *Extension activities*. These course assignments give teachers many options for valuable classroom activities.

General Resources on MyEducationKit

The Resources section on MyEducationKit is designed to help students pass their licensure exams, put together effective portfolios and lesson plans, prepare for and navigate the first year of their teaching careers, and understand key educational standards, policies, and laws. This section includes:

- *Licensure Exams:* Contains guidelines for passing the Praxis exam. The *Practice Test Exam* includes practice multiple-choice questions, case study questions, and video case studies with sample questions.

- *Lesson Plan Builder:* Helps students create and share lesson plans.

- *Licensure and Standards:* Provides links to state licensure standards and national standards.

- *Beginning Your Career:* Offers tips, advice, and valuable information on:
  - Resume Writing and Interviewing: Expert advice on how to write impressive resumes and prepare for job interviews.
  - Your First Year of Teaching: Practical tips on setting up a classroom, managing student behavior, and planning for instruction and assessment.
  - Law and Public Policies: Includes specific directives and requirements educators need to understand under the No Child Left Behind Act and the Individuals with Disabilities Education Improvement Act of 2004.

Visit www.myeducationkit.com *for a demonstration of this exciting new online teaching resource.*

Acknowledgments

Frances Temple and Nancy Roser helped shape our thinking early in the project; we are grateful to both. We also wish to thank Nancy for suggesting the title of the book, which so aptly captures our mission as the authors. Bird Stasz and her students at Wells College used the first edition in manuscript form and tried out many of the exercises with the children at Peachtown School in Aurora, New York, where Bill Schara is head teacher. We thank all these people for their encouragement and valuable feedback.

Joy Moss, teacher educator at the University of Rochester (New York) and an elementary school literature teacher, brought to bear her considerable experiences in sharing literature with children as she read and commented on the first edition of the book in its formative stages.

Thanks are due to Evelyn B. Freeman, who contributed and extensively revised Chapter 11, "Informational Books and Biography." Evie's delightful energy, enthusiasm for her field of specialty, and impressive bibliographic knowledge in that area resulted in what many reviewers deemed the most complete and authoritative discussion of informational books for children they've encountered in any survey text.

We have long admired the colorful and vibrant art of Frané Lessac, whose illustrations graced the first three editions of the book, so we were honored when she agreed to create new illustrations for this edition. And we are once again delighted with the results.

Thanks also go to the talented children's book authors, illustrators, editors, and educators who so generously shared their thoughts and experiences for "Ask the Author" features. In addition, several writer and illustrator friends gave us a look inside their craft: thanks to the Rochester Writers Group, especially Cynthia DeFelice, Ellen Stoll Walsh, M. J. Auch, Vivian Vande Velde, and Robin Pulver; also to Barbara Seuling and Bill Hooks. Several children's book editors did much the same thing; we wish to thank Matilda Welter, Refna Wilkin, Kent Brown, and Richard Jackson.

For invaluable insights, thanks go to Bill Teale and Gail Bush. For their expert knowledge of children's books, our thanks go to Toby Rajput, Ruth Quiroa, Shari Frost, Meg Pyterek, Claudia Katz, and Jacqui Kolar.

We gratefully acknowledge the thoughtful and expert suggestions of those who responded to questionnaires and reviewed the manuscript for the fourth edition: Barbara Thompson Book, Indiana University Southeast; Karla Broadus, University of Texas at San Antonio; Mary Jane Eisenhauer, Purdue University North Central; Pamela Jewett, University of South Carolina; Sharron L. McElmeel, University of Wisconsin-Stout; Margaret Mize, Chaminade University; Karen Phelan, Anne Arundel Community College.

We gratefully acknowledge those who reviewed the manuscript for the first, second, and third editions: Alma Flor Ada, University of San Francisco; Paulette Babner, Cape Cod Community College; Erin Banks, Eastern Michigan University; John Beach, University of Nebraska at Omaha; Jessica Bevans, Ohio State University; Celestine Cheeks, Towson University; Linda DeGroff, University of Georgia; Pat Farthing, Appalachian State University; Peter Fisher, National-Louis University; Esther Fusco, Hofstra University; Connie Golden, Marietta College; Ambika Gopalakrishnan, California State University,

Long Beach; M. Jean Greenlaw, University of North Texas; Dan Hade, Penn State University; Darwin L. Henderson, University of Cincinnati; Janet Hill, Kent State University; Judith Hillman, St. Michael's College; Miriam J. Johnson; Bridgewater State College; Nancy J. Johnson, Western Washington University; Linda Leonard Lamme, University of Florida; Barbara A. Lehman, The Ohio State University; Susan Lehr, Skidmore College; Diane L. Lowe, Framingham State College; Amy A. McClure, Ohio Wesleyan University; Dianne L. Monson, University of Minnesota; Maria Offer, Northern Michigan University; Richard Osterburg, California State University, Fresno; Patricia J. Pollifrone, Gannon University; T. Gail Pritchard, University of Alabama; Roxanne Reedyk, Lakeland College; Mary Kate Sableski, University of Dayton; Olivia Saracho, University of Maryland; Sam Sebesta, University of Washington; Lesley Shapiro, National-Louis University; Charlotte Skinner, Arkansas State University; Elizabeth A. Smith, Otterbein College; Jeff Smith, Roosevelt High School, Kent, Ohio; Karen J. Sweeney, Wayne State College; Ian W. Wojcik-Andrews, Eastern Michigan University.

The staff at Allyn and Bacon deserves much credit for helping us pull this off: Barbara Strickland, our managing editor; Meagan French, editorial assistant; and especially our editor, Aurora Martínez Ramos, who provided good cheer and good sense along the way.

Charles Temple
Miriam Martinez
Junko Yokota

Part One

Understanding Literature and the Child Reader

1

Children's Books in Children's Hands

> . . . and they tucked him in bed
> all soft and warm
> and they held his paw
> and they sang him a song.

A four-year-old child in her mother's lap hears Margaret Wise Brown's *Little Fur Family* and is filled with a secure feeling of being a special child, very much loved. In the coming months, the child picks up the book every now and then, and that same feeling of warmth and security comes over her each time she does.

Brown bear, brown bear, what do you see?
I see a yellow duck looking at me.

3

Brown Bear, Brown Bear, What Do You See? by Bill Martin, Jr., with illustrations by Eric Carle, has helped countless young children get off to a confident start as readers.

In a first-grade classroom on the South Pacific island of Fiji, the teacher has created a hand-lettered enlarged version of Bill Martin, Jr.'s ***Brown Bear, Brown Bear, What Do You See?*** She reads it to her assembled class, pointing with a ruler to each word. Even before she has finished the first reading, children are anticipating what she is going to say next. The second time through, the children, supported by the patterned text and the illustrations, are reading along with her. There are no bears on Fiji, though, and soon the children are writing their own book based on Bill Martin's pattern but featuring a mongoose, a mynah bird, an iguana, and other local animals. Martin's book has helped these children of Fiji learn to read and write.

Trip-trap, trip-trap, trip-trap, trip-trap.
"Who's that walking on my bridge?" roared the Troll.
"It is I, Little Billy Goat Gruff."

In a South Texas classroom, Jackie murmurs, "Oh, good," when Ms. Sloan sends her group to the library center, a favorite in the classroom. Some of her fellow students browse through the collection looking for particular books. Jackie says, "Let's do 'Three Billy Goats Gruff.'" Four other children agree and cut short their search. Now the five children—three goats, one troll, and a narrator—are acting out this folktale that is so well known to them from their teacher's reading it aloud. And of course one performance will not do. Everyone wants a chance to be the troll!

Again Prietita heard a faint crying sound . . . This time she was sure it was a woman crying. She wanted to run away, but she forced herself to walk toward the sound.
    Soon she came into an open area where the moon was reflected on the surface of a lagoon. Prietita looked across the lagoon and saw a flash of white in the trees. Then she saw a dark woman dressed in white emerge from the trees and float above the water. (Anzaldua, 1995, unpaged)

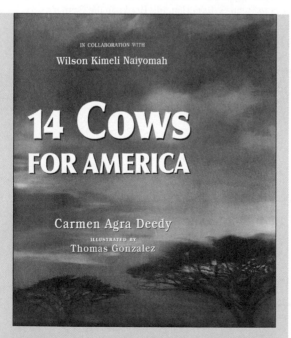

ILLUSTRATION 1.1. Generous Maasai herdsmen from Kenya donated cows to America as a gesture of solace after September 11, 2001, in this true story. (From *14 Cows for America* by Carmen Agra Deedy. Illustrated by Thomas Gonzalez, Peachtree Publishers, 2009.)

A teacher reads aloud from Gloria Anzaldua's ***Prietita and the Ghost Woman/Prietita y La Llorona***, a modern tale that features the "Weeping Woman," a ghostly character familiar among Hispanic children in Mexico and the American Southwest. "We tell about *la Llorona* down in the valley at my *abuela's* house," says Ana Margarita. "But she's not nice like this lady. She's the one who catches little kids if they go out at night, especially near the water." Then she politely provides the pronunciation of *Llorona*, "You pronounce the double L like a 'Y'," she says—and goes on to explain some of the other Spanish words such as *curandera* and *remedio* that are given in the book. She has a look on her face that says, "Isn't it great to discuss a book about things from *my* side of town?!"

. . . fourteen cows for America.
Because there is no nation so powerful it cannot be wounded,
Nor a people so small they cannot offer mighty comfort.

In a fourth-grade classroom in Atlanta, a teacher has just finished reading Carmen Deedy's ***Fourteen Cows for America*** (2009) with two-page spreads of lifelike illustrations of a Maasai community in East Africa.

"Look closely in the eye of the person in the picture," she says.
"Oh!" says a student. "It's a tiny reflection of a building. It's burning, and you can see the smoke!"
"So the young man can still see the attack on the twin towers. It's still in his eyes, even when he's so far away from it in Africa," says another student.
"Was that a true story?" asks another.

"Yes, it was. Let's turn the page." The next pages give an account of a young man from the Maasai tribe who was studying medicine in the United States when he happened to witness the attack on the World Trade Center in New York. When he returned to his village a year later, his people were so moved by his descriptions that they donated some of their most valuable possessions—fourteen cows—to America.

"But where are the cows?" a student asks. Later the class looks up the event on the Internet and finds newspaper accounts of the Maasai village's generous act, entries about the Maasai people, and an entry about Wislon Kimeli Naiyomah, the young man in the story.

> The shouts grow louder and someone's knocked the light again and it's throwing shadows off those dark juvy faces. I see Boo rise up with his stick and hack down. That squirrel skin cap ain't on his head no more and you can see the small dents in his clean skull. I rush towards those busting arms and you can see Hodge in the middle. He's got Coly Jo pinned down. Coly Jo is holding his squirrel-skin cap like you're holding onto that lucky rabbit's foot when you're slinging some craps. Someone is trying to crib it out of his hand. Boo just hacks down with that stick.
>
> Some juvies are cheering and others have backed away into their own private knots. Coly Jo's shirt has been ripped off and his skin is dark and shiny like a new street and there are marks on his soft belly that look like red crow feet. (Rapp, 1997, p. 12).

John Cunningham's sixth-grade class has finished Louis Sachar's **Holes** (2000), about a juvenile detention camp. Now he is reading them parts of Adam Rapp's **The Buffalo Tree** (1997), a book about "juvies," young people who are incarcerated in a juvenile detention home.

One student sighs, shakes her head, and remarks, "This is more like what it must really be like to be locked up in one of those places. I mean, I loved **Holes**, but that book seems kind of like a dream in comparison—not a good dream, but like nothing is quite real. But this, this—you can almost smell the anger, almost taste the blood in your mouth."

Good books—like good paintings, plays, movies, sculptures, and other creative works—merit appreciation in their own right. But good books serve children in some specific ways. Good children's books can evoke strong feelings and come to stand for childhood emotions, much in the way a security blanket does. Good books can give children reference points for understanding their own experiences, lessons that may last a lifetime. Good books may make children proud of and knowledgeable about their own culture and open windows onto other cultures. Good books may help children understand how others live, and how they face the same issues in their lives. Good books, and the sharing of them, cultivate children's capacity for empathy and compassion. Good books educate the imagination, as children stretch to visualize what it would be like to walk in the shoes of a character in a book.

> "All great things that have happened in the world, happened first of all in someone's imagination, and the aspect of the world of tomorrow depends largely on the extent of the power of imagination of those who are just now learning to read. That is why children must have books, and why there must be people . . . who really care what kind of books are put into the children's hands." (Astrid Lindgren, author of **Pippi Longstocking**, from her acceptance speech for the Hans Christian Andersen Award in 1958)

Good books may give children much of the motivation and even the concepts they need to learn to read and the models that show them how to write. Good books offer children delight, mystery, charm, an experience of awe, and companionship. Good books invite children to play with language. Good picture books cultivate children's visual literacy and their aesthetic sense. Good books nurture children's appreciation of the author's craft.

Teaching Idea 1.1

Ask the Children!

Have a conversation with a group of children about children's books. Ask these questions in a conversational way:

1. How do you know a book is a children's book?

2. What are three of your favorite children's books?

3. What makes them good—that is, if you met someone who was going to write a book for children, what advice would you tell her or him to make it a *good* book?

4. How do you feel after you've read a really good book? What are you thinking about?

Note carefully what the children say. Is there a difference in what children of different ages admire in books? How do their criteria for good children's books compare with those set out in this chapter?

Go to the Assignments and Activities section of Chapter 1 in the MyEducationKit and complete the activities. As you work through the activities and answer the accompanying questions, consider the importance of evaluating literature for children.

What Are Good Books for Children?

For the student of children's literature, there is a lot to learn about. Let's identify some key questions here, and relate them to the upcoming chapters, where you will find answers.

What Are Good Books for Each Child?

Answering that question that will require some criteria for quality in children's books. And since the answer depends partly on the age and interests of the child, we should consider ways in which readers respond to literature and how they differ in their responses at different ages. These issues will be the focus of this chapter.

Knowing what good books are for different children requires some intelligent way of talking about goodness and mediocrity in books—that is, we will need a serviceable set of terms to help us talk about literary features of children's books. Those will be the focus of Chapter 2.

Some of the most appealing books for children are illustrated books. Picture books are a unique art form, combining aspects of novels and movies. Appreciating the dynamics of picture books deserves its own focus, and that will be the topic of Chapter 3.

A huge contribution of children's literature is to help children understand themselves and appreciate people from other cultures. Multicultural books mostly written within North America will be the focus of Chapter 4. Because many good books are available to children from writers in other parts of the world, we will focus on international literature in Chapter 5.

Having considered those background issues, we will then look more closely at the books themselves: the kinds of books available (arranged by genre), the evolution of books over the years, and exemplary writers and illustrators of children's books. In the pages that follow, we will examine Poetry for Children (Chapter 6), Traditional Literature (Chapter 7), Modern Fantasy and Science Fiction (Chapter 8), Contemporary Realistic Fiction (Chapter 9), Historical Fiction (Chapter 10), and Informational Books and Biography (Chapter 11).

In the last section of the book, we provide readers with answers to some practical questions: What can I do to create a love of reading in every child, and how can I use books to expand children's knowledge? Answering those questions requires that we begin with a close look at ways children respond to what they read, which we do in Chapter 12. How do we put books into children's hands and invite them to step inside the covers and enjoy them? That is the focus of Chapter 13. How do we encourage and guide their responses to what they read? That is the focus of Chapter 14. Finally, teachers, present and future, often look for ways to organize books into teaching units, and that will be the focus of Chapter 15.

What Is Children's Literature?

It is surprisingly hard to define a children's book. In his own apology for not offering a straight answer to the question, "What *is* a children's book?" Peter Hunt writes,

> [T]he answer is that we all *know* what it is, but it is not very easy to *tell* what it is (or what it is not). . . . [I]t is everything from a Sixteenth Century chapbook to a twentieth century computer-based, interactive device. It is everything from the folk tale to the problem novel, from the picture book to the classroom poem, from the tract to the penny dreadful, from the classic to the comic. (Hunt, 1995, p. ix)

Children's literature is the collection of books that are read to and by children. That collection is enormous: There are hundreds of thousands of English-language children's titles in print. It is still growing: 50,000 new titles are published every year in the English language alone. And it is old: The tradition of publishing literature for English-speaking children dates back two and a half centuries, predating the founding of the American republic.

Issue to Consider
Even Comic Books?!

Although children who are now in school think of Superman, Spiderman, Batman, and Cat Woman as characters in action-packed movies, in previous generations young people knew the real score: These were characters from comic books, those pulpy-paged illustrated thrillers from the days before television, that cost only 10 cents—and then 15, and then 25, and then . . . they all but disappeared. Comic books were either a staple of life or a threat to civilization, depending on whom you asked. In the 1950s, during the McCarthy Era when people suspected that the moral fiber of our country was under attack from many quarters, a set of Congressional hearings were held in which comic books were accused of promoting amorality, lawlessness, and perversion. In 1954, the major comic book publishers agreed to police themselves and adopted the Comics Code Authority, which insists, among other things, that:

1. Crimes shall never be presented in such a way as to create sympathy for the criminal, to promote distrust of the forces of law and justice, or to inspire others with a desire to imitate criminals.

2. No comics shall explicitly present the unique details and methods of a crime.

3. Policemen, judges, government officials, and respected institutions shall never be presented in such a way as to create disrespect for established authority.

4. If crime is depicted it shall be as a sordid and unpleasant activity. (Comics Code Authority)

Source: Comix: A History of Comic Books in America, by Les Daniels, copyright 1971 by Les Daniels and Mad Peck Studios.

Many comic book publishers went out of business, and the rest quickly lost ground to the growing attraction of television—which, of course, some would argue has become an even greater threat to children's intellects and morals.

Now comic books are back in a new form, called *graphic novels*. They are being produced with some sophistication—printed on glossy paper and costing more money. Many graphic novels are reprints of comic books, several episodes strung together as one volume. Others are newly created as graphic novels. Notable among these are *manga*, graphic novels from Japan.

The American Library Association is taking graphic novels seriously, and they put out an annual list of the best graphic novels (see the home page at **http://www.ala.org**). Graphic novels are reviewed in *School Library Journal* and *Kirkus*.

Some advocates of graphic novels are enthusiastic about their exciting multimedia formats. Others note their appeal to reluctant readers—especially children from 11 or 12 and up. (You can, after all, "read" them by only occasionally looking at the words.) Educators we talked to in an unscientific survey weren't sure. When we asked to review the graphic novels in one middle school library recently, the librarian confided that it was not yet possible: The principal had taken them all into his office, and was still trying to decide if they should go on the shelves.

What do you think: Should they?

Children's literature spans the range from alphabet books and nursery rhyme collections for the very young through novels and informational books for adolescents (or young adults, as they are called in the book trade)—in other words, from birth to about age fifteen.

Today, most children's books are written expressly for children. But there are books written originally for adults that have become popular with children—from an earlier period, John Bunyan's ***Pilgrim's Progress*** and Daniel Defoe's ***Robinson Crusoe*** and, more recently, ***Platero and I (Platero y yo)*** by Juan Ramon Jimenez. Other works, such as Charles Perrault's "Sleeping Beauty in the Woods" and the anonymous ***Arabian Nights***—were written for adults but have been adapted for children. And the oral tradition—myths, ballads, epics, and folktales—makes up a large body of material that was told to adults and children alike, including the well-known stories "Jack and the Beanstalk," "Rapunzel," "Brer Rabbit and the Briar Patch," "Cucarachita Martina and Ratoncito Perez," and "Anansi the Spider."

Today, children's books are published by the juvenile books branches of large publishing houses such as Random House and Houghton Mifflin, as well as by publishers that serve the children's market exclusively, such as Orchard Books and Candlewick Press. Many publishers offer books published under imprints, which might, like Atheneum, be the name of an originally independent publisher that has been taken over by a larger house or, like Richard Jackson Books, Margaret K. McElderry Books, and Walter Lorraine Books, reflect arrangements by which publishers allow their most successful editors to publish books under their own names.

Sales of children's books have increased tremendously in recent years. Classroom teachers are using more children's literature than ever. And as more families have gotten the message about the importance of having children's books in the home, sales of these books to individuals have at last surpassed sales to schools and libraries. Major newspapers review books for children just as they review adult fare. Since the success of the **Harry Potter** series a few years ago, some papers now have a separate children's best-seller list.

Qualities of Children's Literature

As teachers of college courses on children's literature, we sometimes catch ourselves smiling to see an adult student smuggling **Frog and Toad Are Friends** to class between a copy of **War and Peace** and a thick tome on organic chemistry. That image sometimes makes us stop to ask: What is the study of children's literature doing in a college curriculum? Just how serious is the quality of children's books? There are several ways to answer these questions.

First, although children's books might seem simple, their simplicity is achieved through hard work by talented writers. Many people try to produce books for children, but the percentage of manuscripts that are actually published is unbelievably small. In a recent year, one major publishing house received five thousand unsolicited manuscripts and published two of them.

Award-winning author Katherine Paterson (1988) compares writing a children's book to composing music. She suggests that a good children's book is like a score for a chamber quartet, rather than a work for a full symphony. The work for the chamber quartet is less elaborate; but if its melodies are pleasing and its harmonies apt, it will have no less quality than a full orchestral work. In the same way, a good children's book will have fewer layers of complexity than a good book for adults, but if it is created with great care, it can also have excellence.

Second, because much of our contemporary children's literature grew out of the folktales from oral traditions, children's books contain many timeless stories that know no age boundaries. In **The Anatomy of Criticism**, Northrop Frye wrote that all literature is one fabric, woven of many strands of plot, image, and theme that have been told over and over in stories around the world, throughout all time. The most essential stories—those that tell of virtue rewarded, of straying into danger and struggling to get back out, of learning to distinguish the things of lasting value, of finding one's true qualities and putting them to the service of others—are the materials out of which all literature is made. They are found in their purest form in myths and folktales from around the world, and in books for children.

Third, children's books are worthy of serious study because the education of children warrants society's best energies. Good books will help children by making them literate, giving them knowledge of the world and empathy for those with whom they share it, offering them stories and images to furnish their minds and nurture their imaginations, and kindling their appreciation for language used well. Given its worthy goals, such literature deserves attention and respect.

What makes a book a children's book? A children's book usually has these qualities:

- **A child protagonist and an issue that concerns children.** A children's book usually has a central character that is the age of the intended audience. Children identify more easily with one of their own. Even when the central character is not a child—as in "Cinderella," for example—children need to feel that the central issues of a story concern them in some way.

Teaching Idea 1.2

Intertextuality!

"Intertextuality" is a term for the similarities between stories—the features like the problem situation (such as children being left at home alone), the plot structure (the hero as least-likely-to-succeed going on a quest and proving himself or herself a hero), the pattern of actions (such as one thing leading to another), the kinds of characters (such as a trickster spider), or even important details (such as a piece of clothing that identifies the true hero).

Read one of these collections of stories to children; then lead the class in completing a Venn Diagram (two interlocking circles) about them.

For kindergarten through grade 3:

- *Hattie and the Fox*, by Mem Fox
- *The Little Red Hen*, retold and illustrated by Paul Galdone

It's not just the chicken heroes! It's also the pattern of the chicken-hero going to one character after another, and having them give the same lazy response that makes these stories similar.

For older students:

- *The Children's Homer*, by Padraic Colum
- *The Homecoming*, by Cynthia Voigt
- *Bud, Not Buddy*, by Christopher Paul Curtis
- *Parvana's Journey*, by Deborah Ellis

Here the pattern to observe is *the journey*. What sends each character or set of characters on their way? What discouragements and distractions do they face along the way? What faith sustains them? How do they grow and change as they travel? What turns out to be more important: the arrival or the journey?

- **A straightforward story line, with a linear and limited time sequence in a confined setting.** Books for younger children usually focus on one or two main characters, cover short time sequences (they are usually—but not always—told straight through from problem to solution, without flashbacks), and most often are set in one place. When writing for older children, authors gradually take more license with time sequences and may interweave more than one plot strand, as Louis Sachar does in **Holes**.

- **Language that is concrete and vivid and not overly complex.** The words in children's books—especially in picture books—primarily name actors and actions. Books without pictures need to have more verbal description to help children visualize characters and settings. They use dialogue to move the story along. And they give glimpses of the characters' motives. In all these cases, readers see more of what characters do than of what they say, and certainly more of both than of what they think.

Qualities of Outstanding Children's Literature

What makes a good children's book? Qualities that make outstanding children's books apply to excellent literature for any age. If a book satisfies the following criteria, it is a good children's book:

- **Good books expand awareness.** Good books give children names for things in the world and for their own experiences. Good books take children inside other people's perspectives and let children "walk two moons" in their shoes. They broaden children's understanding of the world and their capacity for empathy.

- **Good books provide an enjoyable read that doesn't overtly teach or moralize.** Many children's books turn out to be about something—to have themes, in fact—and it is often possible to derive a lesson from them. But if a book seems too deliberately contrived so as to teach a lesson, children (and critics) will not tolerate it.

- **Good books tell the truth.** Outstanding children's books usually deal with significant truths about the human experience. Moreover, the characters in them are true to life, and the insights the books imply are accurate, perhaps even wise.

- **Good books embody quality.** The words are precisely chosen and often poetic in their sound and imagery; the plot is convincing, the characters believable, and the description telling.

- **Good books have integrity.** The genre, plot, language, characters, style, theme, and illustrations, if any, all come together to make a satisfying whole.

- **Good books show originality.** Excellent children's books introduce readers to unique characters or situations or show them the world from a unique viewpoint; they stretch the minds of readers, giving them new ways to think about the world and new possibilities to consider.

Children's Books and Childhood

The criteria for excellence just outlined have not always held true. That is because the life stage of childhood has evolved throughout history as adults changed their definition of *childhood* and their views of young people. Literature for children has changed, too, following the fortunes of childhood as a life stage. As Victor Watson writes, "Children's books reflect and are bound up in cultural changes; they are particularly susceptible to developing assumptions about the nature of childhood, adolescence, and education" (2001, p, vi).

Children in the Middle Ages

It has been said that until roughly five hundred years ago, childhood as we know it did not exist in the West (Aries, 1962). That is because up until the Renaissance, children's activities—the games they played and the stories they heard—were not separated from those of adults.

Ask the Critic . . .   Betsy Hearne

Betsy Hearne

Favorite Books As a Child

My favorite story growing up was "East of the Sun and West of the Moon," which may explain why my favorite children's books now are *Tuck Everlasting* by Natalie Babbitt and *Holes* by Louis Sachar—both novels with strong folktale and fantasy elements.

Some critics, such as Northrop Frye and E. D. Hirsch, Jr., maintain that there are some stories that all Western children could benefit from being exposed to. Do you agree? Do you believe there are some core stories or works that all children should know, or do you see the issue another way?

The idea of canonizing stories that all Western children should know is understandably controversial. On the one hand, this would solve problems in defining curriculum, testing educational achievement, and establishing cultural frames of reference in a multicultural environment. Yet realizing such an idea raises as many questions as it answers. Literature is not a science with objective, quantifiable standards of measurement. Who will decide which stories belong in the canon? How do we incorporate individual differences (both adults' and children's) into the subjective task of assessing a story's importance? Is it possible to reconcile myriad conflicting values in a small selection or, conversely, reflect representative values in a large selection? In terms of use, a core of "approved" stories is bound to take precedence over other texts. What are the implications for publishing new texts? And how long do we wait before inducting a story? Some books and stories that are now considered classics met with a negative reaction when they were first published. This includes traditional fairy tales, picture books such as **Where the Wild Things Are,** and many examples of fiction across two centuries.

On the practical front, what are the effects of mandating stories to creative teachers, who may find such a prescription stifling? Sometimes it is more effective to study one story in depth, establishing a process and a set of principles that can then be applied broadly, than to cover a predetermined core, which can easily become an exercise in superficial exposure. Certainly, the identification of a canon of stories, those that have appealed to both critics and children over a long period of time, would require a balanced emphasis on the often warring factors of high quality and general appeal.

Proponents of a clearly defined—and, by implication, required—body of stories common to all children either believe that these questions are answerable or believe that the disadvantages of compromise are worth the advantages of commonality. My own experience of reviewing, teaching, and storytelling over several decades has persuaded me that adult consensus on these issues is rare, if not impossible, and that children and stories are a quirky, unpredictable match depending on personality, peer group, family environment, and many other factors. Of course every child needs some stories. But selecting the same stories for "all Western children" involves the kind of generalized social and aesthetic assumptions that have plagued efforts to establish a literary canon in higher education. I would suggest that a buffet of stories, from which children and adults can choose together, is preferable to a set menu.

Betsy Hearne is a professor in the Graduate School of Library and Information Science at the University of Illinois at Urbana-Champaign, where she teaches children's literature and storytelling. She is the author of numerous articles and books, including *Choosing Books for Children: A Commonsense Guide*; the folktale anthology *Beauties and Beasts*; several novels for children (most recently *Listening for Leroy* and *Wishes, Kisses, and Pigs*); and a picture book, *Seven Brave Women*, which won the 1998 Jane Addams Children's Book Award. The former children's book editor of *Booklist* and of *The Bulletin of the Center for Children's Books*, she has reviewed books for thirty years and contributes regularly to the *New York Times Book Review*.

Children drank alcoholic beverages, smoked tobacco, and used coarse language. After the age of seven, most children were made to work in the kitchen, in the fields, or in shops. When the village storyteller could be persuaded to tell a tale, children and adults alike gathered around to hear it. In medieval England, games such as Red Rover could involve people of all ages in a village.

It is not surprising, then, that books were not written expressly for children in those times. The few children who could read had no choice but to turn to adult fare. The ballad "Robin Hood," for example, was known as far back as 1360 A.D., and three printed versions of the legend existed before 1534. Child readers, then as now, enjoyed and accepted the romantic concept of robbing the rich to help the poor. Other romantic stories circulating at the time were those about King Arthur and the Knights of the Round Table and about Bevis, a thirteenth-century hero who hacked his way out of dungeons and slew dragons.

In 1476, William Caxton established the first printing press in England, and in 1477, he published one of the earliest books expressly for children. Called ***A Booke of Curteseye,*** it was filled with do's and don'ts for an audience of aristocratic boys preparing for social engagements and military careers.

Children in Puritan Times

By the seventeenth century, more works were being written for children, but most did not make for enjoyable reading. The Puritans, the stern religious exiles who established the English colonies in America, infused early American children's works with their certainty that the devil could enter young bodies. They even wrote poems exalting death at an early age—better to die innocent than grow up and be corrupted. Given the didactic and fiery messages of Puritan authors, it is not surprising that most of their works are no longer read. Here is an example of Puritan prose written in 1702 by one Thomas Parkhurst:

> My dear Children, consider what comfort it will be unto you when you have come to dye, that when other children have been playing, you have been praying. The time will come, for ought you know very shortly, . . . when thou shalt be sick upon thy bed, and thou shalt be struggling for life, thy poor little body will be trembling, so that the very bed will shake under thee, thine eyestrings will break, and then thy heartstrings will break; . . . then, O then, the remembrance of thy holy life will give thee reassurance of the love of God.

Despite this bleak view, nonetheless, there were some bright moments. Books were generally instructional and religious in nature, but many writers did sugarcoat their instruction with rhymes, riddles, and good stories. Also, children continued to find adult fare to their liking. John Bunyan's Christian allegory, ***Pilgrim's Progress***, was read for centuries. What made it palatable to children was its portrayal of a sense of family. Children are presumed to have skipped over the lengthy religious commentary to savor the happy family life. Indeed, the story of Christian can still hold the imagination of children who read the adapted, abridged, and illustrated versions.

Children of the fifteenth to eighteenth centuries also turned to hornbooks and chapbooks for their reading fare. In both England and America, peddlers traveled from town to town selling items such as pots, pans, needles, medicine, and hornbooks—which looked like paddles, averaged two and a half by five inches, were usually made of wood, and often were attached to a leather thong so that children could hang them around the neck or wrist. The lesson sheet or story was pasted onto the flat surface, then covered with horn, a film of protective material similar to animal horn. Hornbooks were filled with lessons in religion, manners, the alphabet, and reading.

The same traveling salesmen who peddled hornbooks inspired the invention of chapbooks ("chap" is derived from the word "cheap"). Chapbooks were made of folded sheets of paper and so were inexpensive to produce and light to carry. They contained popular stories of the day, such as "Jack, the Giant Killer," "The History of Sir Richard Whittington," and "Saint George and the Dragon," and also large numbers of cautionary tales, illustrating the do's and don'ts of childhood. Contemporary author Gail E. Haley has written and illustrated ***Dream Peddler***, about a fictitious chapbook peddler who was proud of his profession because he gave children fairy tales and adventures to cultivate their dreams.

ILLUSTRATION 1.2. Hornbooks, the reading fare of many early American children, usually contained an alphabet and a prayer or psalm.

North Wind Picture Archive

Children in the Enlightenment

In 1693, John Locke published *Some Thoughts Concerning Education*, which influenced child-rearing practices on both sides of the Atlantic. The book's exhortation that "some easy pleasant book" be given to children was good for the circulation of children's books. Nonetheless, the books still promoted strict moralistic teachings, if in narrative form.

At the dawn of the eighteenth century, more playful and pleasurable literature began to emerge. The verses of Isaac Watts were popular, and although to a contemporary ear they sound overly moralistic and didactic, for their time they were less so than those of his predecessors. In 1743, Mary Cooper published *The Child's New Plaything, Being a Spelling Book Intended to Make the Learning to Read a Diversion*. An American edition of the book came out in 1750 with even more "diversions," reflecting a change in how stories for children were perceived. *The New England Primer*, which combined alphabet and catechism, was the most widely read book of the period, another indication of the instructive mindset of the eighteenth century.

During this period, children also continued to read books written for adults. Many of Daniel Defoe's works were popular with children. In fact, *The Life and Surprising Adventures of Robinson Crusoe of York, Marine*, with its fearless optimism and high adventure, proved popular with children for the better part of two centuries. Jonathan Swift's *Gulliver's Travels*, published in 1726, is another book that was written for adults but adopted by children. Although the book is filled with heavy satire that reflects Swift's quarrels with the imperfections of humankind in general and Englishmen in particular, its language and plot are irresistible.

Two and half centuries ago, an innovative entrepreneur named John Newbery (1713–1767) prepared the way for the blossoming of children's literature in the nineteenth and twentieth centuries. Newbery moved to London in 1744 and launched the first commercially successful company dedicated almost exclusively to publishing beautiful and pleasurable children's books. In his thirty-year career, Newbery published twenty titles for children in attractive, playful formats, including the accordion book, made of one long strip folded accordion-style to form "pages." He was the first to introduce illustrations by first-rate artists, and he published books in more permanent, attractive bindings than the popular, less expensive chapbooks.

In 1922, Frederick Melcher, the founder of *Publisher's Weekly*, made a donation to the American Library Association to establish an annual award for the most distinguished contribution to literature for children. Fittingly, the award was named after John Newbery. (A list of the award winners and the honor books over the past eight decades appears in the Appendix.)

Newbery is believed also to have written some of the books he published, including *A Little Pretty Pocket-Book* and *The History of Little Goody Two-Shoes*. Read for the better part of a century in England and the United States, *Little Goody Two-Shoes* was the first best-seller written for children (and one of the longest lasting). The book might not be familiar to you, but the phrase "goody two shoes" is still used to mean a person with overly refined behavior.

The "Golden Age of Children's Literature"

As the example of *Little Goody Two-Shoes* illustrates, children's books up until the 1800s were often strongly didactic—if not downright preachy. But in the 1800s, books for children became more entertaining. In the 1800s, delightful works written expressly for children emerged that still rank among the most popular books of all time. During the long reign of Queen Victoria from 1837 to her death in 1901, England enjoyed a period of stability. Parents began to sentimentalize childhood, creating what has been called "the cult of childhood." Some of the very best writers created books for children. Books written in nineteenth century that still circulate briskly include Clement Moore's *The Night Before Christmas* (1823), Hans Christian Andersen's *The Ugly Duckling* and *The Little Mermaid* (translated into English in 1846), Lewis Carroll's *Alice's Adventures in Wonderland* (1865), Louisa May Alcott's *Little Women* (1868), Mark Twain's *The Adventures of Tom Sawyer* (1876),

Randolph Caldecott's ***The House That Jack Built*** (1878), Carlo Collodi's ***The Adventures of Pinocchio*** (1881), Robert Louis Stevenson's ***Treasure Island*** (1883), Joel Chandler Harris' ***Uncle Remus: His Songs and Sayings*** (1883), and Rudyard Kipling's ***The Jungle Book*** (1894).

This "The Golden Age" of children's literature continued up until the 1920s. The early 1900s saw the publication of L. Frank Baum's ***The Wizard of Oz*** (1900), Beatrice Potter's ***The Tale of Peter Rabbit*** (1902), James Barrie's ***Peter Pan in Kensington Garden*** (1906), Kenneth Grahame's ***The Wind in the Willows*** (1908), Frances Hodgson Burnett's ***The Secret Garden*** (1910), Hugh Lofting's ***The Story of Dr. Dolittle*** (1920), Margery Williams' ***The Velveteen Rabbit*** (1922), and A.A. Milne's ***Winnie the Pooh*** (1926).

Although the "Golden Age" as a sort of distant period of excellence in children's literature may have ended with Milne, many other much-beloved books, especially picture books, emerged in the decades after. Hardie Grammtkie's ***Little Toot*** came out in 1931. Dr. Seuss (Theodore Geissel) published ***And to Think I Saw It on Mulberry Street*** and J. R. R. Tolkien published ***The Hobbit*** in 1937. Virginia Lee Burton's ***Mike Mulligan and His Steam Shovel*** dates from 1939, the same year Ludwig Bemmelmen's ***Madeleine*** appeared. Robert McCloskey's ***Make Way for Ducklings*** and H. A. Rey's ***Curious George*** both came out in 1941. Eleanor Estes won the Newbery Award with ***The Hundred Dresses*** in 1944. C. S. Lewis' ***The Lion, the Witch, and the Wardrobe*** was published in 1950, and E. B. White's ***Charlotte's Web*** followed two years later. All of these books are so popular with contemporary children that it may be hard to believe they delighted their great grandparents, too.

Contemporary Children's Books

There is one obvious distinction between most of the books published for children through the 1950s and those that followed. Up until the early 1960s, in the United States, children's literature featured white children almost exclusively. Then in the 1965, with the Civil Rights movement waking mainstream Americans to the realization that their conception of "us" was largely limited to white, English-speaking children, Nancy Larrick wrote a path-breaking article for the *Saturday Review* in which she pointed out the paucity of nonwhite characters in books for children. Shortly afterward, the Council on Interracial Books for Children was established, with the goal of persuading writers and artists of color to produce works for children. The American Library Association added to its Newbery and Caldecott Awards the Coretta Scott King Award in 1982, to celebrate books that honorably and accurately depict African American children (see Chapter 4).

These efforts opened the door to a wealth of talent. Not only has the representation of minority children in English-language children's literature increased substantially in the last thirty years, but the writers and artists of color who have broken into print are among the best we have. Children's books are written by, and feature, African Americans, Latinos, Asian Americans, and Native Americans, as well as children from families of limited means and those who otherwise depart from the older stereotype of white, middle-class, two-parent homes. Far more international literature is available for the American child reader—especially books from Latin America and Asia—and these books are written with greater sensitivity than in the past. Mostly gone are the stereotypical depictions of people from other continents; the norm is to have people from other cultures write their own books or be presented as they would present themselves. Indeed, a whole subfield of multicultural children's literature has emerged to help librarians, teachers, and parents take advantage of the multicultural works that are available. (Chapter 4 of this book is devoted to that subject.)

Even as the "Golden Age of Children's Literature" was in full flower, there were, as Prime Minister Benjamin Disraeli acknowledged, "Two Nations" in nineteenth century England.

Teaching Idea 1.3

Exploring Literature From the Golden Age

Authors writing children's literature a century ago often used more elaborate language than contemporary children's book authors do. Such writing had its own virtue. Here is an experiment. For students in third grade and above, read a section from Kenneth Grahame's original *The Wind in the Willows*—the chapter "Dulce Domus" will do fine. Tell the children a little bit about the characters: Ratty is a "Hail fellow, well met" type who has invited his new friend Mole for an outing in the countryside, and now they are making their way home. Mole, of course, is naturally timid, and might have preferred to stay home in the first place. Ask the students to listen carefully and try to picture the scene in their minds. After you have finished reading, have them tell you what they envisioned. It may help to have them draw the scene first.

Afterwards, ask if Grahame's writing "worked" for them.

The children of the aristocrats and the growing middle class were delving with delight into these wonderful new children's books, while the children of the poor from the age of five were working 16-hour days in the mines and factories. Today in North America, children's books are not experienced by all children, either—at least not in their homes. Although children's literature in America has exploded with color and diversity, many American children rarely see a children's book or hear one read aloud at home (Hart & Risley, 1995; Heath, 1984).

Go to the Extension Activities section of Chapter 1 in the MyEducationKit for your book and complete activity #1 to select developmentally appropriate titles.

Children's Development and Response to Literature

There is no doubt that books give children edification and delight. There is also no doubt that what children take from books changes as they pass from age to age and have experiences with books and with supportive adults who share books with them. In the sections that follow, to gain an understanding of children's book preferences at different levels of development, we look at the interplay of children's intellectual, social, and personality development as well as their developing ability to read. We begin with the period of early childhood.

Experiencing Books in Early Childhood

Children's books serve many purposes in early childhood, some of them emotional, some social, some intellectual, some linguistic, and some literary. Let's consider the contributions of children's books to young children's lives.

Reading aloud a favorite book occasions a closeness between a parent and a child. Good books for preschoolers may do this in two ways. Books for reading at bedtime, such as Margaret Wise Brown's *Goodnight Moon* and P. D. Eastman's *Are You My Mother?* often express a theme of security and closeness. But these books build closeness in another way: They invite reading and rereading at bedtime so often that they may become family rituals.

The importance of these rituals cannot be overstressed. Psychologists have long noted the importance of an intimate bond between parent and child to the child's later emotional well-being. Mary Ainsworth and her associates (1982) noted that starting in the first few weeks of life and culminating by age 2, a child may form a strong and positive attachment to one or both parents and to caregivers, and this attachment can provide a bedrock of well-being that prepares a child to form friendships with other children and to explore and learn from the world. Daniel Stern (1982) observed that parents and children learn each other through patterned interactions such as turn taking in face-to-face play. One important patterned interaction occurs when parents and preschool teachers share a book with a child: showing a picture, having the child name the picture, turning the page, and showing another picture. Indeed, researchers have shown that more securely attached infants have cozier and more interactive booksharing sessions with their parents (Bus & van Ijzendoorn, 1995; Zambo, 2007).

More than intimacy is involved in early encounters with books, however. For one thing, the child is also learning language from such exchanges. When a child sees a picture of an object at the same time as hearing his or her parent read the word for it, the child learns a concept. The parent reinforces the learning by pointing to the picture and asking, "What's that?" The child answers, and the parent affirms the child's answer or corrects it. Such a procedure becomes a kind of informal teaching routine, a form of scaffolding, an enjoyable moment of shared focus through which a parent helps a child learn language (Mol, Bus, & de Jong, 2009; Ninio & Bruner, 1978). Of course, not

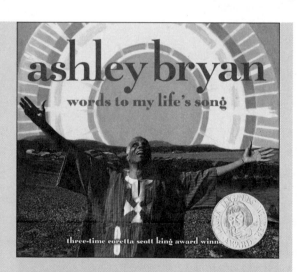

ILLUSTRATION 1.3. Many young children's most enjoyable moments with books were spent chanting the words and exploring the pictures in the many books by the exuberant poet and illustrator, Ashley Bryan. (Reprinted with permission of Simon & Schuster Books for Young Readers, an imprint of Simon & Schuster Children's Publishing Division from *Ashley Brian: Words to My Life's Song* by Ashley Bryan with photographs by Bill McGuinness. Jacket illustrations copyright © 2009 Ashley Bryan. Jacket photographs copyright © 2009 Bill McGuinness.)

just bedtime stories but also nursery rhymes and concept books lend themselves to these beneficial early reading transactions.

A child in a parent's lap learns important lessons about the ways books work. The child learns that books have fronts, backs, and pages. Pages have tops and bottoms, print and pictures. Eventually, the child will learn that even though pictures might seem more fun to look at, it is the print that "talks." A child may learn favorite authors, too: Dr. Seuss's books have the funny rhythms and rhymes; Rosemary Wells's books have the bunnies that have feelings; Eric Carle makes books with holes in the pictures.

In summary, during early childhood, children find a special closeness in being read to, and these reading-aloud episodes figure importantly in forming relationships that are necessary to children's emotional and cognitive well-being. The reading-aloud episode is also an enjoyable and important opportunity for learning language. Moreover, it is a time to learn about language: Language is real, it can be represented, it comes in certain patterns, and it calls pictures to mind. Early experiences with books show a child what books are for, how they are put together, how they work, and even who wrote and illustrated them. It is a fortunate child who learns these lessons early in life; she or he will be richer for them intellectually and linguistically and will find it natural to learn to read when she or he goes to school.

Experiencing Books in the Preschool and Early Primary School Years

As they approach kindergarten age, children are more actively following not only rhymes, but also books with plots. Children are imbibing story plots at this age. Stein and Glenn's (1979) research showed that just as children learn the grammar of their native language by speaking with adults, they also learn the "grammar" of stories from their exposure to them. By *grammar,* they meant elements such as a character in a setting who has a problem, makes attempts to solve it, and finally reaches some resolution that has a consequence: a new state of affairs. When Stein and Glenn told kindergarten children a story that had these elements rearranged out of order, the children spontaneously arranged them properly when they retold the story. Knowing the grammar of stories will go a long way toward preparing a child to understand them.

Children are clearly enthralled with the content of stories, too. Kieran Egan (1992) observed that strongly plotted stories—especially fairy tales and folktales—have a powerful appeal to children of this age, perhaps because they are concerned with the most basic dimensions of life. Stories, as Frank Kermode (2000) observed, give children frameworks for understanding what life means. After all, it is in stories that people and events are clearly good or bad and heroic or not, whereas in real life, it might be hard to tell. Real people act out of complex mixes of motives, and their actions may have both good and bad consequences.

Folktales, fairy tales, and other clearly plotted fiction for younger children show characters who are unambiguously good and bad, or, if they stray from what is the "right" path, the characters learn clear lessons from what happens. The young girls in both *The Talking Eggs* and *Mufaro's Beautiful Daughters* are kind and generous, and they are rewarded. The vain sisters are not. In both *Sylvester and the Magic Pebble* and *Strega Nona*, the characters use their new powers—in both these cases, magic—carelessly and suffer the consequences.

In later years, children might question whether life's choices are really so simple or virtue so easy to come by, but in the ages from 4 to 7, children seem to want some general reassurance that actions matter, that there is some connection between the way we behave and the way things turn out for us, and that we can tell what is good to do and what is not. The basic story plots that children like to hear at this age give them pointers for making sense of the actions and consequences they experience in their lives.

Children in the 4 to 7 age range are not given to long, interpretive discussions. Because they cannot easily tell fiction from nonfiction (Applebee, 1975), children are likely to accept stories as accounts of what really happened to someone somewhere. Susan Lehr's research (1988) did show that kindergarteners could recognize that two stories have the same theme, especially if the children had rich experiences with literature. It is still not likely to dawn on young children that a story can be an elaborate metaphor for a truth on a different plane. Piaget

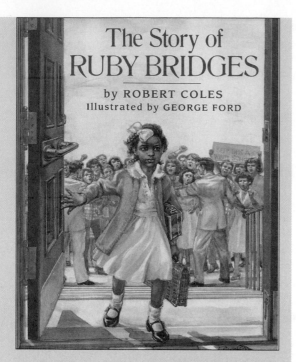

ILLUSTRATION 1.4. The real-life story of the six-year-old girl who helped integrate schools in New Orleans is a plot that engages young readers in *The Story of Ruby Bridges*. (Illustration copyright © 1995 by George Ford from *The Story of Ruby Bridges* by Robert Coles. Reprinted by permission of Scholastic Inc.)

demonstrated this point by asking children the meaning of statements such as "When the cat's away, the mice will play." Children in this age group thought the expression referred only to cats and mice; they didn't seem to get the connection to children's behavior when the teacher is out of the room (Piaget, 1955). From her observations of kindergarten-age children responding to a story without any special prompt from the teacher, Janet Hickman (1992) found that they tended to respond with their bodies—clapping, moving, and shouting refrains.

Given encouragement from a teacher, however, kindergarten and first-grade children can become quite involved in the moral dimensions of stories. Their thinking, though deeply felt, is sometimes one-sided. For example, a group of first-graders heard Norma Green's **The Hole in the Dike**, about a Dutch boy who saved Holland from a flood when he stuck his finger in a hole in the dike. Several were puzzled when, at the end of the book, the boy was called the Hero of Holland. "But he was naughty! He stayed out all night at the dike and he should have gone straight home!" said one. "He should be punished for breaking the rules . . . and making his mom worry!" said another. These children focused narrowly on one side of the problem—the rule infraction—rather than on the greater good the boy did.

Similarly, five-year-old Mirel was indignant when the vulnerable pig played tricks on the wolf in Susan Meddaugh's hilarious picture book **Hog-Eye**, even though the wolf had kidnapped the pig and intended to eat it. Mirel's thinking seems to have centered on the pig's playing tricks on the wolf, and she lost sight of the fact that the wolf had something far worse in mind for the pig.

Learning to Read

The period from ages 4 to 7 straddles what reading specialists call the periods of *emergent literacy* and *beginning reading* (Temple, Ogle, Crawford, & Freppon, 2010). Emergent literacy refers to the acquisition of a host of concepts about print, about language, and about the activities of reading and writing that provide the foundation for learning the skills of literacy. We have already mentioned some of these concepts: the fact that print, and not pictures, "talks" and the fact that books are read from front to back and pages from top to bottom. We described the insight that language is real, and that it not only accompanies events in the here-and-now but that it can call up a virtual reality that was not present—it makes pictures in our minds. Children must also discover that language comes to us in units of words (not always an obvious concept, since in speech, we run our words together) and that words are represented in print by groups of letters bound by spaces. Furthermore, spoken words can be divided into syllables and syllables into phonemes (for example, the three sounds that correspond to the C, A, and T in "cat"). In English, writing is based on the alphabetic principle, which (roughly) relates letters or groups of letters to phonemes in words.

Learning to read requires, among other things, that children understand the alphabetic principle and learn to negotiate the relationships between letters and sounds. A valuable source for learning the alphabetic principle and letter-sound relationships is rhymes: A child who learns to chant the lines in **The Cat in the Hat** is just a step away from realizing that the rhyming words "cat" and "hat" share a collection of sounds, -at (some call these shared sounds a *phonogram pattern*), and are distinguished only by their beginnings, the "kuh" and "huh" sounds. That child is ready to perceive the phonemes "kuh" and "huh" and will soon come to recognize that the letter C spells one of the sounds and H spells the other.

Of course, another source of knowledge of the alphabetic principle is alphabet books: books that call attention to one letter at a time and show children a group of objects that begin with the sound that is spelled by that letter. Together with some judicious teaching, rhyming books (such as **The Cat in the Hat** and **Sheep in a Jeep**) and alphabet books provide children with an enjoyable source of the information they will need to crack the code of English spelling.

Along with discovering the alphabetic principle, children learn to recognize words and store in memory a growing body of words they can recognize immediately. Building this sight vocabulary is helped along if children think of words in families, such as *bank, tank, sank, spank, thank*. Again, rhyming books such as **Sheep in a Jeep** and **The Cat in the Hat** provide sources of word families. Resourceful teachers will make word walls (Cunningham, 1999) of these word families—that is, make displays of them on the wall, grouped together. They may also invite children to use word sort activities with the words (Bear et al., 2007)— that is, play grouping games with the word patterns.

Children are learning to make meaning from books, too, at this age. As we noted, they are learning the patterns that structure the plots of stories and figuring out how to use those patterns to recognize the main characters, their goals, and their attempts to reach those goals. Resourceful teachers will structure their story talk with children around these story elements; ask children what the character's problem is and what she or he wants to do; and ask them to predict how the character will do it.

Kindergarten and first-grade children face a special dilemma when it comes to their own reading. Children at this age may have been listening to increasingly sophisticated fare, which may even include chapter books for some. Yet their own reading skills limit them to materials with only a few words per line and only a few syllables per word. Fortunately, a solution to this problem has been provided by many ingenious writers, from Dr. Seuss to Bill Martin, Jr., and many others who write *easy readers*. These books with short words and highly patterned language allow children to practice their fledgling reading skills. Some easy readers also offer content worth pondering. For instance, Arnold Lobel's many **Frog and Toad** books and James Marshall's **George and Martha** books have stories that are worth talking about.

Experiencing Books in the Primary Grades

As they advance from second grade toward the upper primary grades, children's thinking abilities change, allowing them to notice more, to think of several aspects of a problem at once, and to distinguish confidently between fact and fiction. Most children begin to read with real fluency, and they develop preferences for authors and styles of books. Although the prolific readers might prefer to "keep reading, keep reading," rather than to stop and ponder the meaning of what they have read, thoughtful teachers and parents who are able to engage these children in conversations about books are invariably rewarded with the surprising insights these children express.

The topics these children prefer to read about are widely varied. The children are enthralled by magic (note the phenomenal appeal of the **Harry Potter** books for third- and fourth-grade children and beyond), but the magic must be carefully developed and must conform to a consistent logic. The same goes for fantasy: Children are no longer so satisfied by the easy magic of fairy tales; they are concerned with the details of how things work (Egan, 1992).

Children in the 7 to 10 year age range like to read books that show possibilities for individual achievement. The personality theorist Erik Erikson (1968) noted that at this age, children are developing a sense of initiative and later of industry. A story like Rosemary Wells's **Hazel's Amazing Mother,** in which a heroic parent saves a child from many improbable situations, appeals less to this age group than to younger readers. Now the child wants to read about children who solve their problems themselves. For example, after hearing Jane Yolen's **The Emperor and the Kite**, Elizabeth Hillman's **Min-Yo and the Moon Dragon**, and Robert D. San Souci's **The Samurai's Daughter: A Japanese Legend**, a group of second-graders discussed the heroines in these tales: "I like stories about girls who go on adventures!" "Min-Yo and the emperor's daughter were so small . . . but they saved their kingdoms!" "Even though they were little . . . they did big things!" "And they didn't use magic . . . but they were very brave and smart." "The Samurai's daughter was a pearl diver . . . that's how she knew how to kill the sea monster. . . . She didn't need magic. . . . I bet her father was really surprised that she could do all that . . . even though she's a girl!"

Children's thinking becomes more flexible after age 7, and this makes possible deeper insights into literature. In their preschool years, children might have preferred books with clear moral orientations—stories that, like "Cinderella," unambiguously contrast good and

Top Shelf 1.1

Touchstone Books for Different Ages

Early Childhood Books

Cabrera, Jane (2005). *If You're Happy and You Know It Clap Your Hands*. Holiday House.

Dunrea, Olivier (2002). *Gossie and Gertie.* Houghton Mifflin.

Preschool

Bang, Molly. (2004). *When Sophie Gets Angry.* Scholastic.

Carle, Eric. (1981). *The Very Hungry Caterpillar.* Philomel.

Ehlert, Lois. (1993). *Eating the Alphabet.* Voyager.

Finch, Mary. (2001). *The Three Billy Goats Gruff.* Illustrated by Roberta Arenson. Barefoot Books.

Willems, Mo. (2004). *Knuffle Bunny*. Hyperion.

Primary (books for learning to read)

DiCamillo, Kate. (2007). *Mercy Watson: Princess in Disguise*. Illustrated by Chris Van Dusen. Candlewick.

Rylant, Cynthia. (2006). *Mr. Putter and Tabby Make a Wish*. Illustrated by Arthur Howard. Harcourt.

Seeger, Laura Vaccaro. (2007). *First the Egg*. Roaring Brook.

Shaw, Nancy. *Sheep in a Jeep*. Illustrated by Margot Apple. Houghton Mifflin.

Willems, Mo. (2007). *I Am Invited to a Party*. Hyperion.

Wood, Audrey. (1999). *Silly Sally*. Red Wagon.

Primary (books for reading aloud)

Avi. (2008). *The End of the Beginning: Being the Adventure of a Small Snail (and an Even Smaller Ant).* Harcourt.

Cronin, Doreen. (2000). *Click, Clack, Moo: Cows That Type.* Illustrated by Betsy Lewin. Simon and Schuster.

(continues)

Top Shelf 1.1

Primary (books for reading aloud cont.)

Henkes, Kevin. (1996). *Lilly's Purple Plastic Purse*. Greenwillow.

Steig, William. (1990). *Doctor Desoto*. Farrar, Straus, & Giroux.

Upper Elementary

Browne, Anthony. (2001). *Voices in the Park*. DK.

Creech, Sharon. (2002). *Love that Dog*. Joanna Cotler.

Sachar, Louis. 1998). *Holes.* Farrar, Straus, & Giroux.

Wiles, Deborah. (2001). *Love, Ruby Lavender*. Gulliver.

Middle School

Avi. (1991). *Nothing But the Truth*. Scholastic.

Bartoletti, Susan Campbell. (2005). *Hitler Youth.* Scholastic Nonfiction.

Curtis, Christopher Paul. (1999). *Bud, Not Buddy*. Delacorte.

Walker, Sally M. (2005). *Secrets of a Civil War Submarine*. Carolrhoda.

bad—but now they enjoy books with more complexity. For example, children in an advanced second-grade class were asked to respond to Aesop's fable "The Grasshopper and the Ant" and Leo Lionni's modern version, *Frederick*. After listening to Aesop's fable, most of the children agreed that the ant was right to let the grasshopper starve because the grasshopper didn't do the work to get food for the winter. However, after listening to *Frederick*, most of the children developed a new perspective. Frederick did not collect grain with the other, hard-working mice, but they tolerated his uniqueness and recognized his contribution as an artist. His poetry provided food for the mind and the imagination during the long, dark days of winter. The children contrasted the acceptance of individual differences in Lionni's story with the harsh justice of the ant in Aesop's fable: "I liked *Frederick* better. Everybody's different, and you shouldn't punish someone just because they're different." "I think the Ant should have read *Frederick*. . . . I bet Grasshopper's music could have made the Ant happier during the winter."

As children consider the moral dimensions of a story, they also may take the motives of a character into account, although this kind of sophistication doesn't happen all at once. For example, when William Steig's *The Real Thief* was read aloud to third- and fourth-graders, most of them empathized with the mouse, Derek, who stole a number of items from the royal treasury: "He's not a real villain . . . he's not really bad . . . he just wanted to make his place nicer so he could feel more special . . . and important." "He didn't mean to get Gawain in trouble." "And anyway, he put it back later when Gawain got accused. I feel sorry for Derek. I'm glad the author let him get a second chance." A few still held to their earlier way of seeing moral issues: "He stole, and that's wrong, and he should be punished!" "I didn't like the ending because he didn't really get punished."

Becoming Prolific Readers

By late second grade, children have reached the possibility of becoming readers. If they can find books and authors they enjoy, many will become prolific readers. It is important to guide children to the right books. Research shows that some of the best suggestions for books to read come from other children, but all children will need exposure to many, many interesting books, in many genres, by many authors. Ideas for sharing books with children are found in the third section of this book.

Children are developing their capacity to comprehend what they read, too. Research summarized by Temple et al. (2010) suggests that in children, comprehension consists of the ability to:

- relate what they already know to what they are reading. For example, in making sense of a story, a comprehending reader will summon up what she already knows about a particular setting, a specific historical period, or people who follow certain trades.

- follow the pattern set up by the genre. For example, a child who is reading a pour quoi tale will know that he or she is following a fanciful account of how something came to be. The child will expect some magic, but will look for a connection between the premise of the story and some phenomenon in the real world that the story seeks to explain.

- visualize or form images of what is being read. As a child reads Natalie Babbitt's description of the hot day in August in the beginning of *Tuck Everlasting*, she should be able to feel the stagnant stickiness and picture the hazy humidity of the air.

- recognize main ideas and supporting details. As a child reads a story, he should recognize important events that set up main problems and follow the successions of attempts and outcomes as the main character seeks to reach his or her goal.

- summarize. A child who can fill out a story map of a plot can be said to have this ability. The same can be said about a child who can compose a cinquain, a five-line descriptive poem, about a character or about the topic of an informational book.

Although they might not always initiate them, children flourish on discussions about what they read during the primary school years. The depths of children's insights about literature, as well as the critical tools they bring to discussion, grow rapidly, especially with the guidance of a teacher who is skilled at managing discussions. (The chapters in the last section of this book will help you to become such a teacher!) The exchanges transcribed in the preceding sections demonstrate the value of having open discussions of literature. As children who still think in less mature ways hear their more advanced classmates state their positions and their reasons for them, the less mature children are challenged to question their own thinking; eventually, they will advance to more sophisticated levels of reasoning.

Still, it is important for teachers to remember that talking about books with classmates is not done just to make students more skillful comprehenders—any more than talking with your classmates in the college cafe, or with the members of your own family around the dinner table is done to make you a more skillful conversationalist. Reading should be a joy, a pleasure, an adventure. Reading should also become a habit. We want students to become readers.

Experiencing Books in the Upper Elementary and Middle Grades

As children pass through the later primary and middle school years, developments in their ability to reason go hand in hand with their greater sense of seriousness about their life roles. Intellectually, children are more flexible in their reasoning and are accordingly able to enjoy stories with more complex plot structures. In the social realm, children can give consideration to more than one point of view at a time and hence develop a more sophisticated sense of fairness. In their personal development, as Erikson put it, children are driven to gain a sense of industry: On the one hand, they enjoy books about children who are or become good at doing things; on the other hand, they soak up books that will give them the information they need to become good at things.

As children advance into middle school, further cognitive and emotional changes take place that influence their responses to literature. Chroniclers of cognitive development note that young people's minds can more readily think about abstractions. They now enjoy ideas almost for their own sake. Hence, it is not surprising that Janet Hickman (1992) found many children in fifth grade who enjoyed analyzing the motives of characters and the themes and implications of stories. Older students do too.

With a growing ability to entertain abstractions comes a new focus on "-isms." Younger children can certainly understand issues of social justice and environmental protection, especially as they affect characters or places they care about, but early adolescent students

Issue to Consider

Should We Consider Reading a "Skill"?

The No Child Left Behind Act of 2002 has had a strong influence on reading instruction in the public schools. The Act, and the energetic campaigns from the government that have promoted it, have emphasized these aspects of reading:

■ Phonemic awareness instruction

■ Phonics instruction

■ Fluency instruction

■ Vocabulary instruction

■ Text comprehension instruction

(*Source:* Center for the Improvement of Early Reading Achievement (CIERA)/National Institute for Literacy (NIFL). *Put Reading First: The Research Building Blocks for Teaching Children to Read: Kindergarten Through Grade 3.* [http://www.nifl.gov/partnershipforreading/publications/reading_first1.html])

Defining reading in terms of these five abilities may have made reading instruction in the schools more manageable for government authorities, but it also may direct attention away from the joy of reading, the habit of reading, the goal that children will like to read and become readers.

How do we balance a concern for developing children's reading skills and a commitment to making sure they become readers?

engage these issues more easily and may care about issues themselves, such as racism, feminism, and environmentalism, as passionately as younger children care about the people and places that are affected by those issues.

Early adolescents are also more conscious of themselves than younger children. (The difference between younger and older children's awareness of themselves is a source of comedy in Beverly Cleary's books about Ramona Quimby.) Erikson suggests that adolescents are becoming preoccupied with developing a sense of identity: They are beginning to wonder who they are.

The interplay of the issues raised here is reflected in the literature that children enjoy in late childhood and early adolescence. It is not surprising that stories such as ***Shiloh*** and ***Hatchet*** appeal to children in the late elementary grades. They concern young people who, almost against their will, develop talents that help them to win in adult competition or to survive in the wilderness against heavy odds. Both books, in addition to their other qualities, appeal to young people who are concerned with being good at things, at developing a sense of industry. Jerry Spinelli's ***Maniac Magee***, a modern day pseudo-legend about a boy who breaks the color barrier with acts of skill and kindness, and Deborah Ellis's ***The Breadwinner***, which treats similar problems in a more realistic vein, add to the theme of developing a sense of industry and a concern with racism. Thus, both books also engage young people's growing ability to think about social justice issues, and appeal to their idealism.

Louis Sachar's ***Holes***, a surrealistic story about a boy who is falsely sentenced to a labor camp for early adolescents, satirizes any preoccupation with being good at tasks that adults set out for children. Instead, it stresses themes of social justice while encouraging the critical side of young people's idealism: skepticism about the motives of adults in authority.

A great many books about finding one's identity are written for early adolescents. The problems of adolescence are legion. Young people may lose themselves in the group. They may feel that they die many deaths as they are rejected by this or that companion or by this or that cohort. They may yield to the ever-present temptation to sell themselves short by falling into crime, drugs, or materialism. Self-definition can mean identifying with a nationality different from that of one's parents or coming to grips once and for all with one's racial identity. It certainly means defining one's sexual orientation. Books can help. Books reflect identities back to people. Whether in the form of biographies, essays, realistic fiction, or poetry, many books address young people's struggle for self-definition, their struggle against the problems of adolescence, and their suddenly awakened recognition of justice and hypocrisy.

Reading at This Age

With their greater mental flexibility, late elementary and early adolescent readers are able to follow more complex plot structures and devices. They can make a narrative emerge from the blank verse of Jacqueline Woodson's ***Locomotion***; at the older end of the spectrum, they can make a narrative come together from the weavings of memoranda, film scripts, and court records in Walter Dean Myers's ***Monster***. They can follow the intricate new realities of fantasy fiction such as Phillip Pullman's ***The Golden Compass***.

Reading at this age can, to a greater extent than before, involve deep and complex discussions. Young people can explore characters' motives, themes of works, authors' artistry, and even the treatment of the same theme in different books.

They can also read critically. They can "read against the grain," bringing to light implicit assumptions about the sexes and people of different social groups. As Alan Luke suggests (1998), they can begin to ask questions such as, "What other readings can be made of this text?", "Whose voice is at play in this text?", and "Whose voice is silenced?"

Before leaving the topic of children's development and children's literature, we should note that children's development does not take place like shifting through the gears of an automobile. When it comes to reading and responding to literature, development is not strictly a stage-by-stage process. Younger children often behave in ways that were ascribed here to older children and vice versa. Moreover, exposure to literature and the experience of discussing books can make an enormous difference in the sophistication of children's literary understanding, and these differences are detectable as early as kindergarten (Lehr, 1988). Data collected by Wilson, Fielding, and Anderson (see Stanovich, 1992) suggest that in the

At the middle school level, children begin reading more critically and often choose books that focus on issues of identity, mirroring their own struggle for a newly emerging identity.

typical fifth-grade class, the top group of students may read more than 200 times as many book pages in a year as the lowest group of students. The quantity of reading and the quality of the discussions children experience make significant differences in the sophistication with which they are able to read.

Censorship and Children's Literature

All teachers make decisions about what books to put into children's hands. Of course, teachers choose books that they think will interest children and that will appeal to the children's level of understanding. Of course, they choose books that they think have some sort of merit. But at the same time teachers make some books available, they deny children access to others. When teachers deny children access to books because they think those books are too risqué or controversial or when other adults put pressure on teachers to deny access to certain books, then we are dealing with the issue of censorship.

Simply put, censorship means to deny someone access to books or ideas (Naylor, 1991). The First Amendment of the Constitution of the United States reads, "Congress shall make no law respecting an establishment of religion, or prohibiting the free exercise thereof; or abridging the freedom of speech, or of the press. . . ." This language suggests that individual freedom is at issue whenever teachers or other school officials deny children's access to written materials. But many parents claim the right to expect teachers not to expose children to material on topics that the parents would rather handle more delicately at home or keep away from their children altogether. Teachers, for their part, may choose to introduce children to a book they know will stretch their minds and not to share books they consider trashy. Whose rights should prevail? And how should the issue of rights be squared with the requirements of responsible education?

Some topics seem to raise more pressures for censorship than others, and the controversial topics are not always the ones we might expect. In society at large, the areas in which the media feel the most pressure for censorship are sex and violence, especially in our entertainment. These topics seem to cause less controversy in schools, though (Traw, 1996), perhaps because there is something closer to a consensus among parents and teachers that books

ILLUSTRATION 1.5. Books like the popular *Captain Underpants* series that deal with bodily functions are, surprisingly, seldom censored in schools. (From *Captain Underpants and the Perilous Plot of Professor Poopypants* by Dav Pilkey. Scholastic Inc./The Blue Sky Press. Copyright © 2000 by Dav Pilkey. Reprinted by permission of Scholastic Inc.)

with more than trace amounts of sex and violence should not be circulated at school. It is true that there is the occasional book such as Judy Blume's *Forever* that describes sexual acts (and, sure enough, this book has suffered campaigns to get it off the shelves). But for the most part, in children's literature, sex is off limits, and few people want to argue about it. Other bodily functions seem to escape censorship, however. Taro Gomi's *Everyone Poops* and Shinto Cho's *The Gas We Pass* are sometimes found in school, and Dav Pilkey's *Captain Underpants* series, with titles such as *Captain Underpants and the Perilous Plot of Professor Poopypants*, is freely distributed during "Drop Everything and Read" time, even (especially!) in third grade.

The surprisingly difficult issue is religion. Religion seems to come up in two ways. We are familiar with the direct way, as exemplified by the state school board of Kansas's recent decision (later overturned) to require biology teachers to teach Creationism—the biblically based doctrine that God really did create man and woman in his own image—and not evolution—the theory that human beings descended from pre-human primates. Usually, religious censorship comes up in less direct ways, as groups of parents and other citizens campaign against books that they believe spread antireligious ideas. Especially vulnerable to censorship are books about magic and witches.

The *Harry Potter* books and even Tomie dePaola's *Strega Nona* books have evoked campaigns for removal from people who believe the descriptions of magic that permeate them are not harmless fun but suggestive of Satanism. Sometimes the criticisms miss the target entirely. For instance, the storyteller Joseph Bruchac described visiting a school district in South Dakota where a citizens' group had demanded that the school remove all books from the library having to do with Transcendentalism. (The parents apparently confused the nineteenth-century literary movement led by Ralph Waldo Emerson with a popular method of meditation.) But whether the groups bringing complaints about books have done their homework or not, schools and teachers need to be prepared to defend their choice of books.

Arguments over religion and alleged Satanism may deflect attention from another kind of passive censorship that is also serious: What are we leaving out? James Loewen filled a book with teachings that were either distorted in or missing altogether from the typical American school curriculum. He entitled his book *Lies My Teacher Taught Me: Everything Your American History Book Got Wrong* (Loewen, 1996). If our children are going to sharpen their minds and forge better ways of living in the future, they will need access to materials that challenge the status quo. But teachers who have been beleaguered by parents upset about Strega Nona or Harry Potter might not be very daring when it comes to looking at the true story of Christopher Columbus, the struggle to improve working conditions in America, or even the constructive role religion has played in U.S. life. Because censorship removes from consideration materials that might stretch children's minds, the American Library Association (ALA) has issued statements opposing it. Here is why:

Why is censorship harmful?

Censorship is harmful because it results in the opposite of true education and learning. In the process of acquiring knowledge and searching for truth, students can learn to discriminate—to make decisions rationally and logically in light of the evidence. By suppressing all materials containing ideas or themes with which they do not agree, censors produce a sterile conformity and a lack of intellectual and emotional growth in students. (ALA web page, November 2, 2000)

What seems clear is that in some districts, at least, there is less of a consensus about what schools should teach and less trust

Technology in Practice 1.1

Learning About Books Online

The online bookstore, **www.amazon.com**, is a valuable source of information about books. Click on "Books" from the menu of tabs arrayed horizontally across the top of the home page. When the window labeled "Books" opens on the left side of the page, immediately click "Advanced Search" underneath before entering other information. That will take you to another page where you can search for books by title, author, or subject. You can limit your search there to books for specific age groups, such as 4–8 or 9–12.

When you click on the title of a book, you will be taken to a page devoted to that book. If you click on the author's name at the top of the page, you will be taken to other titles by that author or illustrator. By scrolling down to the bottom of the page, you can usually find a publisher's description of the book and a review of the book, often by *School Library Journal, Publishers Weekly*, and others.

You may purchase books from Amazon, of course, or you can also purchase used copies of books, often at great reductions, through the used book dealers that Amazon links to its site.

on the part of the parents than there was before the drumbeat of critiques of U.S. schools that began in the 1980s. How should teachers conduct themselves in the face of the occasional demands for censorship of children's reading fare in the schools?

We recommend the following steps:

1. Stay aware of what is in your classroom library and the groups of books you assign, and know why they are there. You should be confident that the books you are making available have literary merit, are enjoyable, raise interesting and important themes, and broaden children's awareness of people and places and events. You should be confident that they are not mean-spirited, racist, or prurient.

2. Make sure that your school has responsible guidelines for choosing books. One source of such guidelines is the National Council of Teachers of English (NCTE). NCTE has a special section on their website devoted to the topic of censorship, including suggested guidelines for choosing materials for students to read. The web address is <**www.ncte.org/ censorship**>.

3. Be prepared to speak up for the contribution that good books make to children's education. Also be prepared to explain the benefit to individual children and to society as a whole when students learn to distinguish what is worthwhile from what is not worthwhile and to entertain ideas and points of view that are different from their own.

4. Realize that others may disagree with your choice of a certain book, for reasons they believe are right. Be prepared to recognize their concern for their child and to respect that concern.

5. Be aware that, should the choice of books in your classroom or school be criticized in ways that you believe are unfair or misguided, and should calm conversation not resolve the problem, there are resources that can help. One is the American Library Association (ALA), which has an Office for Intellectual Freedom. The website of the American Library Association is at <**www.ala.org**>; the Office for Intellectual Freedom is also found on the ALA website. Another source of help is the National Council of Teachers of English, whose website is found at <**www.ncte.org**>.

Resources for Children's Books

To check your comprehension on the content covered in this chapter, go to the MyEducationKit for your book and complete the Study Plan for Chapter 1. Here you will be able to take a chapter quiz and receive feedback on your answers.

Studying children's literature in college differs in many ways from studying other literature, especially in this way: The focus is turned as much or more toward contemporary books for children as it is toward great works of the past. That is because—with the explosion in the number of books published for children, improvements in the technology of color reproduction, and a growing diversity in the range of people children need to know and care about—many of the very best books for contemporary children have appeared in the past twenty years. And they continue to be published every year. Therefore, to be well read in children's books, you must read backwards and forwards: Read the best of the books already published, and read the best of those just coming out. For the best books already published, you can count on the Recommended Books section at the end of each chapter (especially those in Chapters 5–11). The most important books in the development of each genre are discussed in each chapter in the section on historical development. If you want a historical perspective on children's literature, you should read those books as well. But what of the new books? How can you find your way to those that are best?

Several journals review children's books and promote the best ones. These journals, which include *The Horn Book Magazine, School Library Journal, Booklist,* and *Bookbird* as well as the book review sections of several professional magazines such as *The Reading Teacher* and *Language Arts,* have slightly different emphases and target audiences. Journals published by other teachers' organizations such as the National Council for the Social Studies <**www.ncss.org**> and the National Science Teachers Association <**www.nsta.org**> also list children's books that are keyed to topics from those subject areas.

Experiences for Further Learning

1. Reread the vignettes on pages 3–5. Can you think of books that served you in each of those ways when you were a child? Are there other ways in which books appealed to you? Compare your answers with those of your classmates.

2. Pick a children's book. Evaluate it according to the criteria of a good children's book set out on page 9. How does it fare? Are there other criteria of excellence that you would propose?

3. This chapter stated that children's books have changed throughout history, roughly as views of childhood changed. What trends do you see at work in society that may change children's literature in the next twenty years? What qualities or values would you expect to remain the same in children's literature?

4. Interview three teachers of the elementary grades. Ask them how many different ways they use children's books with their students. Compare their answers with the vignettes found on pages 3–5.

5. Find a school librarian or a children's librarian who has worked in the field for thirty years or more. Ask her or him to talk about the ways in which books for children have changed, children's interests have changed, and parents' concerns about their children's reading materials have changed—and how these issues have remained the same. Prepare a two-column list of ways in which children's books have remained the same and ways in which they have changed. Share your list with your peers.

Now go to Chapter 1 in the MyEducationKit (www.myeducationkit.com) for your book, where you can:

- Find learning outcomes for Chapter 1.

- Access the Children's Literature Database for your own exploration.

- Complete Assignments and Activities that can help you more deeply understand the chapter content.

- Extend knowledge with content-specific Web Links.

- Deepen and apply content understanding with Extension Activities.

- Check your comprehension on the content covered in the chapter by going to the Study Plan. Here you will be able to take a chapter quiz and receive feedback on your answers.

- Find the following updated appendices: Major Children's Book Awards, Children's Magazines, Professional Organizations, Children's Book Publishers' Addresses, Book Selection Aids, and Children's Literature Web Sites.

 *References*

Ainsworth, Mary D. S. "Attachment: Retrospect and Prospect." *The Place of Attachment in Human Behavior.* Ed. C. M. Parkes and J. Stevenson-Hinde. Basic Books, 1982.

Alcott, Louisa May. *Little Women.* Questar, 1868/1991.

Ancona, George. *Pablo Remembers: The Fiesta of the Day of the Dead.* Lothrop, Lee & Shepard, 1993.

Anzaldua, Gloria. *Prietita and the Ghost Woman.* Illustrated by Maya Christina Gonzalez. Children's Book Press, 2001.

Andersen, Hans Christian. *The Little Mermaid.* Random House, 1892/1993.

———. *The Ugly Duckling.* Dover, 1914/1992.

Applebee, Arthur. *The Child's Concept of Story.* University of Chicago Press, 1975.

Aries, Phillippe. *Centuries of Childhood: A Social History of Family Life.* Knopf, 1962.

Asbjornsen, Peter, and J. E. Moe. *The Three Billy Goats Gruff.* Illustrated by Glen Rounds. Holiday House, 1993.

Avi. *Nothing but the Truth.* Orchard Books, 1991.

Babbit, Natalie. *Tuck Everlasting.* Farrar, 1975.

Bear, Donald, Marcia Invernizzi, Shane Templeton, and Francine Johnston. *Words Their Way: Word Study for Phonics, Vocabulary, and Spelling Instruction,* 4th Ed. Prentice Hall, 2007.

Blume, Judy. *Forever.* Pocket Books, 1996.

Brown, Margaret Wise. *Goodnight, Moon.* HarperCollins, 1991.

———. *Little Fur Family.* Illustrated by Garth Williams. HarperCollins, 1991.

Bunyan, John. *Pilgrim's Progress.* Dent, 1678/1911.

Bus, Adriana G., & Ijzendoorn, Marinus H. van. "Mothers Reading to Their 3-Year-Olds: The Role of Mother-Child Attachment Security in Becoming Literate." *Reading Research Quarterly 30* (October/November/December 1995), 998–1015.

Carroll, Lewis. *Alice's Adventures in Wonderland.* Castle Books, 1865/1978.

Caxton, William. *A Booke of Curteseye,* 1477.

Cho, Shinto. *The Gas We Pass.* Kane/Miller Book Publishers, 1994.

Collodi, Carlo. *The Adventures of Pinocchio.* Knopf, 1883/1988.

Cooper, Mary. *The Child's New Plaything, Being a Spelling Book Intended to Make the Learning to Read a Diversion,* 1743.

Creech, Sharon. *Walk Two Moons.* HarperCollins, 1994.

Cunningham, Patricia. *Phonics They Use.* Addison Wesley, 1999.

Daniels, Les. *Comix: A History of Comic Books in America.* Dutton, 1971.

Deedy, Carmen Agra, in association with Wilson Kimeli Naiyomah. *14 Cows for America.* Illustrated by Thomaz Gonzalez. Peachtree Publishers, 2009.

Defoe, Daniel. *Robinson Crusoe.* Running Press, 1719/1991.

dePaola, Tomie. *Strega Nona.* Simon & Schuster, 1979.

Dr. Seuss. *The Cat in the Hat.* Random House, 1957.

Eastman, P. D. *Are You My Mother?* Random House, 1988.

Egan, Kieran. "Individual Development in Literacy." *Stories and Readers.* Ed. Charles Temple and Patrick Collins. Christopher-Gordon, 1992.

Erikson, Erik. *Identity: Youth and Crisis.* Norton, 1968.

Frye, Northrop. *The Anatomy of Criticism.* Princeton University Press, 1957.

Gomi, Taro. *Everyone Poops.* Kane/Miller Book Publishers, 1993.

Green, Norma. *The Hole in the Dike.* Scholastic, 1993.

Haley, Gail E. *Dream Peddler.* Dutton, 1993.

Harris, Benjamin. *New England Primer.* 1686.

Hart, Betty, and Risley, Todd (1995). *Meaningful Differences in the Everyday Experience of Young American Children.* Baltimore: Brookes.

Heath, Shirley Brice. "What No Bedtime Story Means: Narrative Skills at Home and School." *Language in Society 11*(1) (April 1982): 49–76.

Hickman, Janet. "What Comes Naturally: Growth and Change in Children's Free Response to Literature." *Stories and Readers.* Ed. Charles Temple and Patrick Collins. Christopher-Gordon, 1992.

Hillman, Elizabeth. *Min Yo and the Moon Dragon.* Illustrated by John Wallner. Harcourt Brace, 1992.

http://www.ala.org/alaorg/oif/intellectualfreedomandcensorship .html "Intellectual Freedom and Censorship Q and A."

Hunt, Peter. *Children's Literature: An Illustrated History.* New York: Oxford University Press, 1995.

Jimenez, Juan Ramon. *Platero and I.* Translated by Antonio de Nicolas. Universe.com, 2000.

Kermode, Frank. *The Sense of an Ending.* Oxford University Press, 2000.

Larrick, Nancy. "The All-White World of Children's Books." *Saturday Review* (1965, September 11): 63–65.

Lehr, Susan. "The Child's Developing Sense of Theme as a Response to Literature." *Reading Research Quarterly 23*(3) (1988): 337–357.

Lionni, Leo. *Frederick.* Pantheon, 1967.

Locke, John. *Some Thoughts Concerning Education,* 1693.

Loewen, James. *Lies My Teacher Told Me: Everything Your American History Textbook Got Wrong.* Touchstone, 1996.

Luke, Alan. "Getting Over Method: Literacy Teaching as Work in New Times." *Language Arts 75*(4) (April 1998): 305–313.

Martin, Bill, Jr. *Brown Bear, Brown Bear, What Do You See?* Illustrated by Eric Carle. Henry Holt, 1983.

Meddaugh, Susan. *Hog-Eye.* Houghton Mifflin, 1995.

Mol, Suzanne E., Adriana G. Bus, and Maria T. de Jong. "Interactive Book Reading in Early Education: A Tool to Stimulate Print Knowledge as Well as Oral Language." *Review of Educational Research. 79*(2) (June 2009), 979–1008.

Myers, Walter Dean. *Harlem, A Poem.* Scholastic, 1997.

———. *Monster.* Amistad, 2001.

Naylor, Alice. "Censorship." *Children and Books.* 8th ed. Ed. Zena Sutherland and May Hill Arbuthnot. HarperCollins, 1991.

Naylor, Phyllis Reynolds. *Shiloh.* Atheneum, 1990.

Newbery, John. *The History of Little Goody Two-Shoes.* Singing Tree Press. 1766/1970.

———. *A Little Pretty Pocket-Book.* Harcourt, Brace & World, 1744/1967.

Ninio, Annette, and Jerome Bruner. "The Achievement and Antecedents of Labeling." *Journal of Child Language, 5* (1978): 5–15.

Paterson, Katherine. *The Gates of Excellence.* New York: Dutton, 1988.

Paulsen, Gary. *Hatchet*. Macmillan Publishing Company, 1986.

Perrault, Charles. "Sleeping Beauty in the Woods" (La belle au bois dormant). Mercure gallant, February 1696.

Piaget, Jean. *The Language and Thought of the Child*. World, 1955.

Pilkey, Dav. *Captain Underpants and the Perilous Plot of Professor Poopypants: The Fourth Epic Novel*. Scholastic, 2000.

Rapp, Adam. *The Buffalo Tree*. Front Street, 2007.

Sachar, Louis. *Holes*. Farrar, Straus, & Giroux, 1998.

San Souci, Robert D. *The Samurai's Daughter: A Japanese Legend*. Dial, 1992.

———. *The Talking Eggs: A Folktale from the American South*. Illustrated by Jerry Pinkney. Dutton, 1989.

Shaw, Nancy. *Sheep in a Jeep*. Illustrated by Margot Apple. Houghton Mifflin, 1997.

Spinelli, Jerry. *Maniac Magee*. Little, Brown & Company, 1991.

Stanovich, Keith. "Are We Overselling Literacy?" *Stories and Readers*. Ed. Charles Temple and Patrick Collins. Christopher-Gordon, 1992.

Steig, William. *The Real Thief*. Farrar, Straus, & Giroux, 1985.

———. *Sylvester and the Magic Pebble*. Simon and Schuster, 1969.

Stein, N. L., and C. G. Glenn. "An Analysis of Story Comprehension in Elementary School Children." *New Directions in Discourse Processing*. Ed. R. O. Freedle. Vol. 2. Ablex, 1979.

Steptoe, John. *Mufaro's Beautiful Daughters: An African Tale*. Lothrop, Lee, and Shepard, 1997.

Stern, Daniel. *The First Relationship*. Harvard University Press, 1977.

Swift, Jonathan. *Gulliver's Travels*. William Morrow, 1726/1983.

Temple, Charles. "What If 'Beauty' Had Been Ugly? Reading against the Grain of Gender Bias in Children's Books." *Language Arts 70*(2) (February 1993): 89–93.

Temple, Charles, Donna Ogle, Alan Crawford, and Penny Freppon. *All Children Read*. 3rd ed. Allyn and Bacon, 2010.

Traw, Rick. "Beware! Here There Be Beasties: Responding to Fundamentalist Censors." *The New Advocate, 9*(1) (Winter 1996): 35–56.

Twain, Mark. *The Adventures of Huckleberry Finn*. Webster, 1885.

———. *The Adventures of Tom Sawyer*. American Publishing, 1876.

Watson, Victor. *The Cambridge Guide to Children's Books in English*. Cambridge University Press, 2001.

Wells, Rosemary. *Hazel's Amazing Mother*. Dial, 1985.

Yolen, Jane. *The Emperor and the Kite*. Illustrated by Ed Young. Putnam, 1988.

Zambo, Debby. Love, Language, and Emergent Literacy. *YC Young Children 62*(3) (May, 2007) 32–37.

2

Literary Elements in Works for Children

Changeling: an ugly, stupid or strange child superstitiously believed to have been left by fairies in place of a pretty, charming child.

(Random House Dictionary, *Unabridged Edition*)

It was old Bess, the Wise Woman of the village, who first suspected that the baby at her daughter's house was a changeling.

For a time she held her peace. Many babies were ill-favored, she told herself. Many babies cried with what seemed fury against the world—though this little Saaski had not done so as a newborn. It even seemed to Old Bess that the child had not looked quite like this for its first few months, but somehow she could never quite remember. Likely the babe just had a worse than usual colic. No doubt her skin, dark as a gypsy tinker's so far, would lighten so as to look more fitting with that fluff of pale hair—or the hair might darken. It was even possible that the strange, shifting color of her eyes would settle down in good time. The parents both had blue eyes—Anwara's sky blue like Old Bess's own, big Yanno the blacksmith's deeper shade. The child's were cloud gray, or moss green, even a startling lilac—never blue.

Eloise McGraw, The Moorchild, *1998.*

Develop a text set of literature that could be used to demonstrate various literary elements by using the Children's Literature Database in Chapter 2 of the MyEducationKit for this book.

The Artistry of Literary Elements

Literature is a miracle. With words on a page, a writer can take readers to a place that never was, let them know people who never lived, and help them share adventures that never happened—and, in spite of the artifice, create something truer than life itself.

Is it possible to look closely at the magic of literature without destroying its ability to amaze us? We think so. It may actually enhance our appreciation of a work to have a vocabulary and a set of concepts to help us admire its wonders, or note the shortcomings of a less-than-satisfactory work.

In this chapter, we describe the literary qualities that critics and teachers most often refer to when they talk about texts. Knowing these characteristics will give us a vocabulary for exploring the elements of texts that move readers, and also for evaluating works for young readers.

The main elements of a literary work we will discuss are **the genre, the setting, the characterization, the plot, the theme, the stance of the implied reader, the point of view,** and **the author's style**. Let's first take a closer look at each of these literary elements. Later we will consider some special literary features of informational books and poetry.

Go to the Extension Activities section of Chapter 2 in the MyEducationKit for your book and complete activity #1 to consider the role of literary elements when comparing exemplary and awful children's books.

Genre: The "Rules of the Game"

Genre in literature corresponds to the rules of play in a game. Just as players need to know if they are to play with the hands, feet, or head; whether the play stops or keeps going when a player is down; or whether other players may substitute when a player is tired—writers and readers also play within understood rules. Those rules constitute the **genre** of the work. They let readers know what to expect, and how to evaluate what happens.

In virtually every work of fiction, the story begins with a title and an initial situation, and the reader implicitly appreciates the problem and begins to wonder about, and often predict, a solution. The range of possible solutions is controlled by the genre. If the work is realistic, we expect the solution to be possible in real life. If the work is a fairy tale, we know that the solution may be magical. If the work is fantasy, we are prepared for the story to take us into a kind of reality removed from our own, and then tell us something about our human nature or the world we live in.

Consider these lines from the beginning of the Grimm brothers' tale, "The Frog Prince." A princess has lost her ball in a deep well, and weeps bitterly. The story continues,

> As she was thus lamenting, someone called out to her, "What is the matter with you, princess? Your crying would turn a stone to pity." She looked around to see where the voice was coming from and saw a frog, who had stuck his thick, ugly head out of the water. "Oh, it's you, old water-splasher," she said. "I am crying because my golden ball has fallen into the well."

The princess considers it unremarkable to have a conversation with a frog, so the reader will not be surprised if the solution to the main problem in the story is equally supernatural.

But consider the problem in Kate DiCamillo's ***Because of Winn-Dixie***. Here a young girl who has been abandoned by her mother seeks to make friends after moving into a new community. She is helped by a disarmingly friendly dog; still, the genre leads readers to set their sights on small victories, drawn from the palette of real life. The dog won't talk. The mother may not even return. But ordinary strangers may show flickers of conviviality that eventually grow into a community of friends.

Sometimes, it is true, a work starts out in one genre, and then shifts to another. When it does, readers usually sense that a rule has been broken. Cornelia Funke's ***Thief Lord*** is an exciting read—but in the final chapters fantastic elements are worked into the plot, and some readers may feel a little bit misled. Or a work may straddle the line between realism and fantasy. Nearly everything in Louis Sachar's ***Holes*** *almost* could have happened—the rattlesnake juice fingernail polish and the incredible foot deodorizer are two items that are a little over the top—otherwise, the pattern of coincidences is unlikely but not really impossible. And the book stays realistic enough for the reader to identify with the characters and care about them. Because ***Holes*** is consistently surrealistic (just a little more magical than real life), readers settle into the work and are delighted but not thrown off by the pattern of amazing interlocking events.

Works may even keep the reader guessing as to what sort of genre they are reading. ***The Magician's Nephew***, the first volume in C.S. Lewis's *Narnia* series, keeps readers wondering what is so peculiar about Uncle Andrew—until the two children slip on a magical ring and are transported to another world. In those early moments before the magical ring works its power, readers' curiosity is aroused as much by the questions of what *kinds of things* can happen (that is, "What genre is this, anyway?") as by the question of what *will* happen.

The Genres of Children's Literature

The genres of children's books include various kinds of folktales, realistic fiction, fantasy, poetry, historical fiction, biography, and informational books. The genres are not all neat divisions. As we have already noted, some books blur the line between realistic fiction and fantasy. Others add fantastic elements to bring history to life. Others use seemingly historical settings to create a good adventure.

Note that **picture books** may be written in any of the genres: folktales, realistic fiction, poetry, informational books. Picture books are a kind of format rather than a genre; so they are not included in our list of genres.

Figure 2.1 describes the main genres of literature for children.

ILLUSTRATION 2.1 Newbery medal-winner *Shiloh* poses a thought-provoking ethical dilemma that pits animal rights—and a boy's love for a dog—against property rights. (Jacket Cover from Shiloh by Phyllis Reynolds Naylor. Used by permission of Bantam Books, a division of Random House, Inc.)

Genre	Definition	Subtype
Folktales	Works by anonymous authors that were passed on orally from generation to generation	**fairy tales:** tales in which magic is prominent **legends:** larger-than-life tales of famous people **fables:** stories with a moral **epics:** long rhymed works that relate a hero's exploits **myths:** ancient stories about the gods **pour quoi stories:** lighter stories than myths that explain, often delightfully, about the reasons for things
Realistic Fiction	Fictional stories that *might have happened.* In realistic fiction, events are plausible, and settings are usually drawn from actual geography.	**adventure stories:** works that tell of a character's struggles against nature or other people **humorous stories:** works that are funny **relationship stories** (or other problem stories): works that focus on relations between people or a character's struggles with her own self-doubts **historical fiction:** works with realistic characters and plots set in a historical time and place
Fantasy	Works with otherworldly or supernatural elements	**high fantasy:** works that create a parallel universe alongside the real world **low fantasy:** works in which a magical element intrudes into life in the real world, and makes possible a series of events which otherwise stay very true to life **science fiction:** works that create a fictionalized setting or set of events based on some projection of scientific knowledge
Poetry	Works in verse	**narrative poems:** works that tell a story in verse **lyric or expressive poems:** verses that convey observations or express feelings **humorous poems:** jokes, funny riddles, or humorous stories in verse **novels in verse:** book-length poems that tell a story

FIGURE 2.1 Genres of Children's Literature

Settings: How Do Authors Create Times and Places?

The setting is the time and place in which the events of a story occurred. An important part of any author's task is to help the reader visualize the events being narrated and the people who are living them. Because whatever is visualized must be seen in time and space, the setting of the story is an important part of the reader's invitation into an imaginary experience.

How explicitly the setting is described varies with the genre. In a folktale, the setting may get scant mention, yet it can still have symbolic significance. In realistic fiction, the setting can be used to add verisimilitude, or lifelikeness, to the story and make it easier for readers to believe in the events. In a survival story, the setting works against the main character or characters—almost as if it were a character itself. In historical fiction or in stories from other cultures, the setting may share center stage with the characters and events, since readers may be as curious about what life is or was like in that setting as they are about what happens in the story. The same can be said of science fiction or fantasy—genres in which the author is free to make up whole new worlds. Let's look, then, at how settings vary with some of these genres.

Settings in Folktales and Fairy Tales

The Grimms' story "The Frog Prince" (Grimm and Grimm, 1857/1972) has this setting:

> In olden times when wishing still helped one, there lived a king whose daughters were all beautiful, but the youngest was so beautiful that the sun itself, which had seen so much, was astonished whenever it shone in her face. Close by the king's castle lay a dark forest, and under an old lime-tree in the forest was a well, and when the day was very warm, the King's child went out into the forest and sat down beside the cool fountain. (p. 17)

Teaching Idea 2.1
Exploring Folktale Settings

Have the students think of the settings in folktales they know, such as "Puss 'n Boots," "The Old Lady Who Lived in a Vinegar Bottle," or "Hans Clodhopper." Who lives in each setting? What takes place there? Make a chart like the one in Figure 2.2 in which students record findings about different settings. What generalizations can they draw?

	Who lives at home in a cottage? What happens at home?	Who lives in the forest? What happens in the forest?	Who lives in a castle? What happens there?
"Puss 'n Boots"			
"Sleeping Beauty"			
"Little Red Riding Hood"			
"The Gunny Wolf"			

FIGURE 2.2 Settings in Folktales and Fairy Tales

Ask the Editor . . .   Richard W. Jackson

Favorite Books as a Child

- *The 500 Hats of Bartholomew Cubbins* by Dr. Seuss (which appealed to my theatrical instincts)
- *Alice's Adventures in Wonderland* by Lewis Carroll (because it is the only book I recall being read aloud to me)

What was the best manuscript you ever received, and what qualities do you look for in an author?

The best manuscript I've received? Ever? You might have asked me to choose between my children! There are several bests. Paula Fox's *Maurice's Room*—she'd written only three chapters at the time I first saw it but I remember reading them aloud to my wife and saying, "This woman will win the Newbery medal someday." And she did. Such vividness in the people, such kindness in the humor. And such a voice. Also a favorite—the text for *The Relatives Came* by Cynthia Rylant, for somewhat the same reasons. I believe we didn't change a word, though "best" for me doesn't mean word perfect. More important than immediate perfection is the breath of life in a piece. Frances Temple's *Taste of Salt* was another revelation—a "breathing" book about modern Haiti, about brave young people whose lives were, at the time, largely unimaginable by Americans (of any age). The book is written in two first-person teenage voices, and there is urgency in every word. For "I" stories, urgency is crucial.

Even "light" books, such as Avi's *S.O.R. Losers* or Judy Blume's *Are You There God? It's Me, Margaret,* depend on urgency for their success. In funny stories as well as serious, you need to sense the narrator's urge to bend your ear. *Toning the Sweep* by Angela Johnson is another unique example of urgent voice. It began as a collection of quick scenes, poetic impressions, snippets of conversation about a girl witnessing her grandmother's struggle with cancer; it grew into a novel over several years. Thrilling years.

I look for long-term associations with writers or illustrators and rarely take on anyone published by many houses—for snobbish reasons, I suppose. I look for loyalty and for brains. For devotion to hard work and a certain delicacy of touch. I listen for voice. Just this minute the phone rang and—speaking of voice—a cheery one said, "I've figured out how to do it, the whole book. It was our conversation yesterday that helped." The caller was Theresa Nelson, a superb novelist whose first book, *The 25-cent Miracle,* is another best. She's written four beauties since. My response to such calls has remained unchanging since 1962: gratitude and joy.

Richard W. Jackson is editor of Richard Jackson Books, an imprint of Orchard Books, which publishes some thirty new titles a year. His articles have appeared in *The Horn Book Magazine, School Library Journal,* and *The New Advocate.*

The first sentence introduces this "no-particular-time" when magical things happened. Japanese folktales often begin just as simply: "Once long ago in the middle of the mountains. . . ." Russian folk tales may open this way: "Sometime long, long ago, in a kingdom you wouldn't know . . . " Native American tales often say: "Many lifetimes ago, in the days of the Ancient Ones . . ." Arabic folktales sometimes begin: "There was, and there was not, in the fullness of time . . . "

Settings in folktales are described with few details. They represent everywhere and nowhere, but they often have particular associations. In European tales, *home* is where normal life is lived, securely. The *forest* is where one may be tested by sinister forces. The *country* is where simple but honest folk live, whereas the *town* is the place of sophisticated but possibly treacherous people. A *cottage* is a place one usually wants to rise above (but may have to learn to settle for), and a *palace* is the residence of those who were born privileged or who have had triumphant success. Because the genre of folk stories tends to use these same settings with the same connotations again and again, the mere mention of them usually cues the reader to make these associations.

Settings in Realistic Fiction

Settings in realistic fiction are usually described with great detail. Just as the genre of a work sets and limits our expectations for what can happen in it (magic can happen in fantasy books and fairy tales, but not realistic fiction), the way a setting is described in realistic fiction sets and limits our expectations for what can happen in that work. Aspects of a setting can include:

- the immediate social group (that is, the people immediately surrounding the character),
- the wider social setting (that is, the characters' nationality, race, and social class)
- the geography (including what kinds of activities typically happen there, as well as what has happened there in the past and how people feel about it), and
- the historical period (the current decade or earlier ones).

In the opening lines of her Newbery Award-winning children's novel *Shiloh*, Phyllis Reynolds Naylor uses 11-year-old Marty's voice, complete with his out-of-school grammar ("The day Shiloh come . . . ") to describe a "big Sunday dinner" scene. Marty, his two sisters, his mother, and his father are dining on a rabbit his father shot, and while everyone else is eating hungrily, Marty is having squeamish thoughts about eating an animal freshly killed. The opening lines reveal both kinds of social setting: the people with whom Marty shares his life (and with whom his sensitive personality makes him something of a misfit), and his race and social class—white Southern mountain people of limited means.

Two pages further into the book, Marty the narrator takes the reader for a walk around the physical setting. His words describe the Appalachian landscape that he sees from the hilltop near his family's small house, recount what he has learned from his Daddy about how it "used to be," and reveal how Marty feels about where he lives. Whatever happens in the story will happen among the rugged people who live in an economically strapped Southern rural mountain environment, in a time when many people have migrated to other places to live.

ILLUSTRATION 2.2 The setting of Alvarez' book is the Dominican Republic during the Trujillo dictatorship. Her adult novel, *In the Time of the Butterflies*, used the same setting. (Jacket cover by Edward G. Acker, copyright © 2002 by Julia Alvarez. Jacket illustration copyright © 2002 by Edward G. Acker, III, from *Before We Were Free* by Julia Alvarez. Used by permission of Alfred A. Knopf, an imprint of Random House Children's Books, a division of Random House, Inc.)

Settings as Important Features in Themselves

In some genres, settings can figure so strongly as to share attention with the characters in the story. The setting may produce challenges that characters must strive against. The grinding and desolate urban setting of Jerry Spinelli's **Maniac Magee** seems to have permeated people's attitudes with harshness, and Maniac must struggle against both in his quest for humanity.

Alternatively, the setting may become almost a metaphor for the meaning of the work. In Edward Bloor's **Tangerine**, the artificial gated community, Windsor Downs, was thrown together callously and dangerously over sinkholes and other natural threats in central Florida, a fact the residents try unsuccessfully to ignore. The setting finds a parallel in the life of protagonist Paul Fisher's family, with its veneer of normalcy built over terrible secrets.

In multicultural literature, details of the setting may seem commonplace to one group but appear striking to another. For example, Alma Flor Ada's **My Name Is Maria Isabel** begins:

> Maria Isabel looked at the cup of coffee with milk and the buttered toast in front of her. But she couldn't bring herself to eat.
>> Her mother said, "Maribel, cariño, hurry up."
>> Her father added, "You don't want to be late on your first day, do you?" (p. 1)

Children from Spanish American lineage will find that scene reassuringly familiar. But other readers might be surprised that a young girl would drink coffee for breakfast, moved

at the mother's affectionate shortening of the girl's name, and impressed that the mother speaks to her daughter in two languages. In effect, the setting is functioning almost as a character in the story.

In a historical novel, the details of the setting may also go a long way toward satisfying young readers' curiosity about a place that is far removed in time. The earthiness of English village life early in the fourteenth century is brought home in the first paragraph of Karen Cushman's *The Midwife's Apprentice*:

> When animal droppings and garbage and spoiled straw are piled up in a great heap, the rotting and moiling give forth heat. Usually no one gets close enough to notice because of the stench. But the girl noticed and, on that frosty night, burrowed deep into the warm, rotting muck, heedless of the smell. (p. 1)

Here again, although the characters also do much to impress themselves on readers, the setting of this historical novel continually surprises and informs them.

Characterization: How Do People Emerge from the Page?

Characterization is the art of creating people out of words on the page. When a writer has done a good job of characterization, readers feel as if they have gotten to know another person. How does a writer achieve that? Writers introduce characters to us in some of the same ways that we get to know people in real life: by showing us what they do, by showing their relationships with others, and by passing on what the characters say about themselves. Writers also give characters roles to play—protagonist, antagonist, helper, etc.—and this colors the way we feel about them. And, of course, writers sometimes come right out and describe characters. Let's look at each of these dimensions of characterization.

These ways of describing characters are displayed in Figure 2.3.

Actions	What characters do
Relations	Who the character's "people" are; how the character relates to them
Sense of themselves	How the characters describe themselves, especially their "epiphanies"
Roles characters play	Some characters are heroes (protagonists), some are rivals (antagonists), others are helpers, others are beneficiaries of the heroes' actions
Author's description	What the author says about them

FIGURE 2.3   How Characters Come to Life

Characters Are Developed through Their Actions

Skillful writers "show us, and don't tell us." In *The Breadwinner*, instead of showing us that Parvana's older sister is mean and insensitive, Deborah Ellis shows us the girl badgering Parvana with cruel insults, even when Parvana cuts her hair, puts on boy's clothes, and risks her life to get provisions for her family in Taliban-controlled Kabul, Afghanistan.

Instead of telling us that T.J. in *Roll of Thunder, Hear My Cry* is a deceiving egotist, Mildred Taylor shows us T.J. embarrassing Stacey by saying he looks like a preacher in his new overcoat; the result of this humiliation is Stacey giving his overcoat to T.J. It is left to the reader to interpret these actions and decide what kind of character we are dealing with— just as it is with the people we meet in real life.

Characters Are Developed through Their Relations with Others

Characters are also brought to life when readers see who "their people" are—and how they relate to those people. Marty in *Shiloh* is a member of a hard-working and frugal family in rural Appalachia. Jason in *The Giver* lives in a deliberately wholesome family in a bland, engineered society. Bud, in *Bud, Not Buddy*, is a member of the African American culture that conducts its affairs largely out of sight of the dominant white culture, unless they are thrown together in mixed race groups of poor people, as in a Hooverville or a soup line. But, as it turns out, his real people are a troupe of jazz musicians.

Often, book characters are portrayed as being out of harmony with their own group. In *Shiloh*, Marty is at home in the woods with a rifle in his hands; but unlike the rest of his family, he is sensitive to the suffering of animals. Esperanza, the namesake of Pam Muñoz Ryan's *Esperanza Rising*, is the slowest in her family to make the transition from Mexican aristocracy to American working class. Parvana, in *The Breadwinner*, is a member of an educated family who is quietly rebelling against the Taliban—but, as a girl who is still physically undeveloped, she can go out and work and interact with others, unlike her older sister and her mother.

Characters Are Developed through Their Sense of Themselves

Skillful authors sometimes have characters voice realizations about themselves. When they do, readers learn something from those realizations—we have identified with the character and have experienced the events of the story alongside the character, and now are reaping the

Brian Smith

When a writer creates well-developed characters—those whose thoughts, feelings, and attitudes are evident through what they think, say, and do in the story—readers feel they are getting to know other people.

benefits of the character's own enlightenment. Perhaps this dynamic explains why, as scholars have demonstrated, people who have the habit of reading show greater self-awareness than those who do not (Freire, 1965; Luria, 1976).

The central conflict in *Esperanza Rising* comes not just from the horrendous changes in circumstances in Esperanza's life, when she is smuggled away from her aristocratic heritage in Mexico to make a new life among migrant workers in California. Rather, it arises from her accepting those changes and crafting a sense of wholeness for her life. Ryan has Esperanza go up into the hills with her future husband and lie down and hug the earth so they can hear its heartbeat. Then Ryan writes:

> As the sun rose, Esperanza began to feel as if she rose with it. . . . She closed her eyes . . . and she glided above the earth, unafraid. She let herself be lifted into the sky, and knew that she would not slip away. She knew that she would never lose Papa, or El Rancho de las Rosas, or Abuelita or Mama, no matter what happened. . . . She had her family, a garden full of roses, her faith, and the memories of those who had gone before her. . . . Miguel had been right about never giving up, and she had been right, too, about rising above those who would hold them down. (pp. 249–250)

Readers get to know Esperanza all the better through this expression of her thoughts. As characters get to know themselves, readers not only gain insights into them but also learn from the author's language describing the jolts and epiphanies of this life. By comparing their own experiences to those of the characters that the author describes for them, readers gain some awareness of themselves, too.

Characters Are Developed through the Roles They Play in the Plot

If a character in a story is cast in the role of the protagonist, or the hero, readers are inclined to be sympathetic toward him or her. If the character is cast as the antagonist, the villain or the hero's rival, readers are disposed to "fill in the blanks" of that character's personality with bad qualities. (This happens in real life, too: Just listen to what emotional sports fans say about players on the opposing team!)

If the character is cast as the helper, readers might expect her or him to be loyal and generous, possibly amusing—but not more beautiful, brave, or admirable than the hero. If the character plays the role of receiver, the person whom the hero wants to rescue or otherwise help, readers expect that person to be deserving of that help (Scholes, 1975; Souriau, 1955).

Characters can change roles in stories, of course. In *Because of Winn-Dixie*, the other children Opal encounters are presented as rivals or antagonists at first, but then each is revealed with her or his own pain, and eventually each is transformed by Opal's inclusive caring. In *The Wednesday Wars,* Holling Hoodhood's teacher Mrs. Baker is described at first as his enemy ("She hates my guts"), but later she becomes his larger-than-life advocate.

Characters Are Displayed through the Author's Description

Teaching Idea 2.2
Character Webs

For a character in a book, have the students construct a character web. Write the character's name in the center of a piece of chart paper and draw a circle around it. Have the students think of a word that describes the character. Write that word as a "satellite" to the character's name, connected by a line. Next, have the students think of an **example** of something the character does that justifies the describing word (see Figure 2.4).

Authors sometimes give readers descriptions of their characters. J.K. Rowling introduces Dudley Dursley, the spoiled and overstuffed son of Harry Potter's guardians, this way:

> Dudley looked a lot like Uncle Vernon. He had a large pink face, not much neck, small, water blue eyes, and thick blond hair that lay smoothly on his thick, fat head. Aunt Petunia often said that Dudley looked like a baby angel—Harry often said that Dudley looked like a pig in a wig. (***Harry Potter and the Sorcerer's Stone,*** p. 21)

In case the reader needs more clues to Dudley's personality, he is immediately shown counting his Christmas presents—and finding that he's come up two short from last year. Then his fawning mother slips more presents into the pile—so we see his relationship to this overindulgent woman, as well.

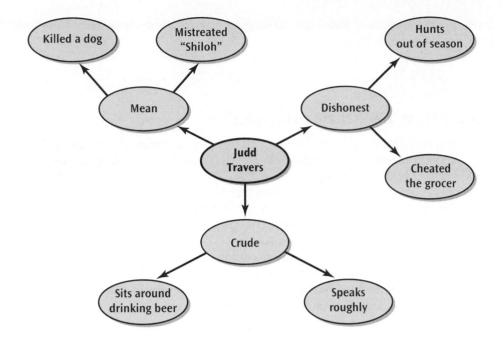

FIGURE 2.4   Character Map for Judd Travers from Phyllis Reynolds Naylor's *Shiloh*.

Rounded Characters and Flat Characters

Rounded characters are actors in a story whom we really get to know, along with their pasts, their relationships, their motives, their inner thoughts, and the changes they go through in the story. **Flat characters** are the opposite: They are introduced in a story and then they act predictably, as if they are needed as foils for the more prominent characters to play off. We learn little about them, except for their effects on other characters. For example, in ***Roll of Thunder, Hear My Cry***, the Wallace boys are mean and violent racists who prey on black people, and who hide behind the privileges of being white. The author, Mildred Taylor, doesn't explain why the Wallaces are racist—she doesn't need to. The Wallaces show up in several scenes in the book, and they are consistently mean—they are a threatening presence throughout the story. The Wallaces are flat characters. They are developed only enough to show what the other characters in the story are up against, but their own motives are not fully explained, and they don't go through significant changes in the story.

Contrasted with flat characters are rounded characters, whose motives are explained, who are seen from many points of view, and who usually develop and change as the story progresses. Cassie Logan, in ***Roll of Thunder, Hear My Cry***, is the protagonist of the story. We are let in on her thoughts. We see what she does, why she does it, and what she thinks about her actions. The reader often understands things that Cassie, as a young girl growing up in difficult circumstances, does not yet understand. Her awareness of herself and others expands as she goes through the story, so that she is wiser by the end. She is a rounded character.

Rounded Characters Undergo Changes

The protagonists in many books undergo changes as their stories progress. For example, in ***Because of Winn-Dixie***, Opal learns to move past her feelings of abandonment and become a provider of comfort to others. In ***The Lion, the Witch, and the Wardrobe***, Edmund learns to move from selfishness to loyalty and dependability, after having been transformed by a power bigger than he is. In Cynthia Lord's ***Rules***, Catherine learns that the way to cope with her brother's autism is to expand her own capacity to relate to people who are different, to become their ally.

In some ways, the point of any story is to demonstrate what happened to the main character and how the events that took place helped her or him to change. This is one of the main ways that stories teach, even when they do not appear to be didactic. Each of us has only one life to live, and we often learn the important lessons too late. With books, though, we have access to

ILLUSTRATION 2.3   As we allow ourselves to assume the role of the implied reader of *Roll of Thunder, Hear My Cry,* we may take on the emotional and intellectual perspective of those who have suffered painful racial oppression. (Cover from *Roll of Thunder, Hear My Cry* by Mildred Taylor, copyright © 1976 by Mildred D. Taylor. Used by permission of Dial Books for Young Readers, A division of Penguin Young Readers Group, A Member of Penguin Group (USA) Inc., 345 Hudson St., New York, NY 10014. All rights reserved.)

Top Shelf 2.2

Books with Memorable Characters

Curtis, Christopher Paul (2002). ***Bud, Not Buddy***. Yearling.

DiCamillo, Kate (2001). ***Because of Winn-Dixie***. Candlewick.

Jiménez, Francisco (1997). ***The Circuit: Stories From the Life of a Migrant Child***. University of New Mexico Press.

Lord, Cynthia (2006). ***Rules***. Scholastic.

Morgenstern, Susie (2003). *A **Book of Coupons***. Puffin.

Schmidt, Gary (2007). ***The Wednesday Wars***. Clarion.

hundreds and thousands of lives—and the struggles many characters have gone through and what they learned from them.

Plots: How Do Stories Happen?

A plot is a meaningful ordering of events with their consequences, a "who did what, and why." A plot is the conveyor belt that pulls a reader through the text, helping them get to know characters and scenes along the way, before arriving at a cumulative insight. Plots fascinate people. When you add up not just the literature people read, but also the films and videos they watch and the TV shows (don't forget the soap operas) they view during so many hours each day, it is clear that most people consider plots a staple of life.

In this section, we look at plots in several ways. We look first at the conflicts that give rise to plots; then we examine the structure of plots. Common plot types will be the next topic, followed by a consideration of some of the twists and turns of plots that authors have at their disposal—techniques such as episodes within plots, surface and underlying plots, and the interplay of genre with plots.

Plots and Conflicts

Plots unfold when a character is drawn toward a significant goal but faces some kind of conflict in reaching it. Conflicts in fiction usually take one of four different forms: between the character and some rival person, between the character and himself or herself, between the character and the environment, or between the character and society.

Conflict between Characters

In J. K. Rowling's ***Harry Potter and the Sorcerer's Stone,*** the ultimate conflict is between Harry Potter and Voldemort, the wicked sorcerer who killed Harry's parents and who is intent on doing further evil in the world. Along the way, there are other conflicts: between Harry and his stepfamily, the Dursleys, and between Harry and his friends and the residents of Slytherin Hall, a rival dormitory within Hogwarts School.

Roald Dahl's books often introduce conflicts between characters: between Danny and his father and Victor Hazlett, the wealthy landowner, in ***Danny the Champion of the World*** or between Matilda and her ghastly parents in ***Matilda***.

Posing conflict between characters is a surefire way for authors to engage readers. It is not surprising that so many action shows on television and in escape fiction use conflict between "good guys" and "bad guys." Sophisticated literature usually employs some other kinds of conflicts, often in combination with each other.

Conflict within a Character

In William Steig's ***Spinky Sulks***, problems arise because Spinky gets his feelings hurt too easily: Rather than rolling with punches that inevitably come from living with others, he withdraws and sulks. Thus, the conflict in the book is located within Spinky himself: It is a tension between his need to have friends and the fragile emotions that keep him from interacting. In Pam Muñoz Ryan's ***Esperanza Rising,*** the heroine struggles with accepting her lot and overcoming her social class prejudice and her sense of entitlement. She resolves the conflict when she realizes she can move into the future while keeping the core strengths and traditions her loved ones have always shared.

Conflict between a Character and Nature

Books with survival themes pit their protagonists against nature. Gary Paulsen's books do this brilliantly, as in ***Hatchet***, in which a boy learns to survive in the woods after an airplane crash, and ***The Voyage of the Frog***, in which a boy survives an ocean crossing on a sailboat. In Jean Craighead George's ***Julie of the Wolves***, the heroine survives in the Arctic tundra by adopting the ways of the wolves. In Theodore Taylor's ***The Cay,*** eleven-year-old Phillip survives on a desert island in the Caribbean with the help of Timothy, an older islander. In Frances Temple's *Grab Hands and Run,* the family learns to survive threats from both human and natural challenges, as undocumented aliens do.

Conflict between a Character and Society

Characters in books are often at odds with society. Sometimes society embraces some evil or some prejudice against which the character must struggle. Such is the case in Afghanistan under the rule of the Taliban in *The Breadwinner.* In other books, the struggle with society comes about not because society is particularly evil, but just because it is what it is. For example, in Gary Soto's sophisticated stories in *Baseball in April,* we meet well-drawn Mexican American characters struggling to get along in Fresno, California. Poverty and ethnic segregation shape the characters' actions and limit their possibilities; yet the point of the stories is not to complain about social evils, but rather to show how typical young people deal with the small and large issues of their lives in such a setting.

Plot Structures

Plots have universal features, which literary scholars tend to describe this way. A plot begins with an **exposition** or **introduction,** which provides the information necessary to understand the story. Then comes the **complication,** in which some conflict is introduced and the character or characters begin their attempts to resolve it. The **rising action** follows from the complication, as the characters work their way through the situation in which they find themselves and pursue their goal. Most of the way through the book comes the **climax**, the point of maximum tension, when the character tries to resolve the conflict and things seem to be most at stake. After the climax comes a rapid series of events that can be called the **falling action**, which culminate in the **dénouement** (French for "untying," because finally the tensions introduced in the story are relaxed). The dénouement can also be called the **resolution**. Either way, here is where the problem is solved and the conflict resolved (see Figure 2.5).

In Alma Flor Ada's *The Gold Coin*, the **exposition** is the part where Juan approaches a hut he plans to rob and spies an old woman inside holding a gold coin and saying, "I must be the richest person in the world." The **complication** comes when Juan breaks into the hut after the woman leaves and finds no gold coin. Now, in order to meet his goal of stealing her riches (or so he thinks), he must follow the old woman. Tensions mount (the **rising action**) throughout the story as Juan follows the old woman, Doña Josefa, to one farm after another—where he is told of a generous and helpful act she has just performed and is given work to do to pass the time before the farmers can take him to his next destination. The **climax** is the surprising events that befall Juan when he catches up with Doña Josefa alone on the road. And the **falling action** follows when Juan realizes that he has been transformed. The **dénouement** or **resolution** is tactfully left for the reader to imagine. How will Juan lead his life, now that he has learned the value of being trusted by others, of being generous?

Top Shelf 2.3

Books with Memorable Plots

Avi (2002). *Krispin, the Cross of Lead*. Hyperion.

Hiassen, Carl (2006). *Hoot!* Yearling.

Ryan, Pam Muñoz (2002). *Esperanza Rising*. Scholastic.

Skarmeta, Antonio (2003). *The Composition*. Illustrated by Alfonso Ruano. Groundwood.

Soto, Gary (2007). *Chato Goes Cruisin'*. Illustrated by Susan Guevara. Puffin.

Turner, Megan Whalen (2006). *The King of Attolia*. Greenwillow.

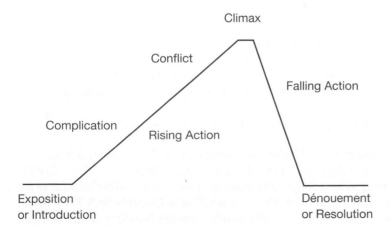

FIGURE 2.5 Typical Plot Structure

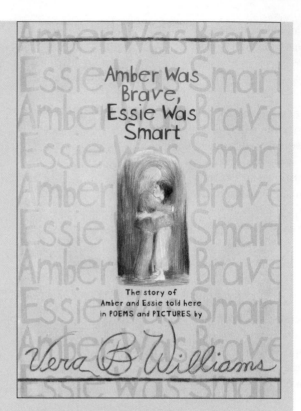

ILLUSTRATION 2.4 Caldecott Winner Vera B. Williams wrote this novel in verse about two girls' struggle to survive poverty in an urban environment. Children's authors like Williams continue to be more worried about children in poverty than politicians are. (*Amber Was Brave, Essie Was Smart*, by Vera B. Williams. Copyright © 2001 by Vera B. Williams. Used by permission of HarperCollins Publishers.)

Recurring Plots

Some plot forms are used again and again in stories. To lump them together by their common forms is to take nothing away from them; on the contrary, it may point out their larger psychic meaning and their contribution to our understanding of the human drama.

The Initiation Story

In traditional societies in which initiation rituals are still required of young people, a high price is exacted for reaching adulthood. In one anthropologist's account (Turnbull, 1982), initiates are commonly taken out of the tribe and into the woods, where they are exposed to extreme pain or danger. Their childhood is stripped from them as their old clothes and other possessions are confiscated and burned. They are taught weighty secrets and given new responsibilities, before finally being reintroduced to the tribe, where the community pays homage to them and recognizes their new state.

Children's literature is full of initiation stories, in which a young character is given some challenge to get through; having successfully met the challenge, she or he is recognized as being more mature or more worthy. "Jack and the Beanstalk" and "Hansel and Gretel" are initiation stories. Gary Paulsen's *Hatchet* is an initiation story of a boy's survival in the woods; Katherine Paterson's *Lyddie* is an initiation story about a girl's learning to stand up for herself in the harsh environment of early industrial Lowell, Massachusetts. Mary Hoffman's *Amazing Grace,* illustrated by Caroline Binch, is an initiation story about an African American girl's efforts to transcend the limits of race and sex and play the part of *Peter Pan* in a first-grade play.

Becoming initiated sometimes implies trade-offs: The protagonist must trade innocence for experience. Hansel and Gretel lost their childhood and experienced horror before they could be reunited with their father, in what must have been an uneasy relationship. In Roald Dahl's *Danny the Champion of the World,* Danny learns a terrible secret about his father and his father's family. The knowledge destroys his cozy domesticity with his father, but it also enables Danny to save his father from danger and eventually to become a family and community hero.

Growing up requires pain and struggle, embracing some things and giving up others—scary steps for a child. Initiation stories point the way, not by revealing the particular path a child will take, because that is necessarily unique to each person, but by offering the hope and assurance that there is sunlight up above the clouds.

The Journey

Another metaphor for arduous progress and change is the journey. People all over the world have been motivated by deep urges to uproot themselves and travel long distances. As hunter-gatherers, humans ranged widely over the landscape, following animals or seeking greener habitats. Since ancient times, different cultures have had the custom of making pilgrimages to religious places—to Canterbury, Mecca, Santiago de Compostela—a practice that survives today. Voyages of discovery, for trade, to make war or bring comfort to the suffering—all seem to follow some deep-seated human urge to go, to see, and to be changed along the way.

Frances Temple's *The Ramsay Scallop* goes to the roots of the tradition, as it recounts a young betrothed couple's pilgrimage from England to Spain in the year 1299. Cynthia Voigt's *The Homecoming* is an unforgettable example of the journey, as the children of the Tillerman family go in search of someone to raise them. Sharon Creech's *Walk Two Moons*, another story of a child's journey in search of family, won the Newbery Award in 1995. Christopher Paul Curtis won a Newbery Award in 1999 for *Bud, Not Buddy*, the story of an orphaned African American boy's odyssey across Michigan in the 1930s to find some remnants of his family. In *Parvana's Journey,* the sequel to *The Breadwinner* by Deborah Ellis, the children's travel across war-torn Afghanistan is fraught with land mines below, bombs raining from above, and uneasy relations among the children themselves. In all of these stories, with every challenge they meet along the way, the characters grow in their awareness of other people, the circumstances that surround them, and themselves.

Episodes: Stories within Stories

Many books, especially those for older children, give us patterns of episodes within larger plots. Francisco Jiménez' *The Circuit* is a series of small stories all framed by the reality of a childhood in an undocumented migrant worker family in California. In fact, two episodes from this book have been made into stand-alone picture books.

Beverly Cleary's *Ramona and Her Father* is another good example of a larger story framing several shorter ones. One main problem—the father's sudden loss of his job—leads logically to several smaller problems that pull the child reader through one, two, or three chapters, each with its own closure, until the main conflict of the book is resolved.

The "Real" Story versus the Story as Revealed

Suspense is created in many stories when the author reveals, bit by bit, what is "really going on." In such stories, there is a "real story" that finally becomes clear to the reader after all of the details have been brought to light in the story-as-written. For example, in the first pages of Louis Sachar's Newbery Award-winning book *Holes,* we meet the ne'er-do-well great-great-grandson of a ne'er-do-well prospector who, though innocent, is being sent to a juvenile detention camp. During the early chapters of the book, we follow the inmates at the camp as they are forced to dig holes on a dry lake bed, presumably as an exercise in penitence, under the heartless supervision of stern guards and a surrealistically sadistic warden. Bit by bit it becomes clear what is really going on: The great-great-grandfather had, indeed, found a treasure many years before, and the daily hole digging is not a penitential exercise after all, but an attempt by the warden to use the inmates at the camp to help her recover that treasure. It is as if *Holes* were two stories: the underlying "real" story (the great-great-grandfather's treasure and the warden's manipulation of the boys to find it), and the story-as-narrated (the boys' experiences at the detention camp), through which the "real" story is gradually revealed.

In *Holes*, and in most other mystery stories, there is a series of present events and references to past events that are fed to the reader page by page, and the underlying or "real" story that all of this points to (Barthes, 1974). Mystery and suspense are created as readers ask themselves what is really going on—that is, as the author uses his or her unfolding narrative to give hints about the underlying story, and the readers try to figure out what that story is.

EXCLUSIVE TEACHERS EDITION

A SINGLE SHARD

Linda Sue Park

ILLUSTRATION 2.5 A brilliantly crafted initiation story set many centuries ago in Korea, *A Single Shard* plausibly depicts a boy's apprenticeship on the way to becoming a master potter. (Jacket cover from *A Single Shard* by Linda Sue Park. Used by permission of Random House Children's Books, a division of Random House, Inc.)

Teaching Idea 2.3
Plotting the Story Journey

Students can make a kind of graph to plot a story journey. Drawing a line from left to right across a chart, they can make the line go up for events when morale is high and down for events when morale is low. Above the line, they can write in what happened. Below the line, they can write in how a character felt or what she or he learned.

Themes: How Do Stories Convey Meaning?

A theme is an issue or a lesson that a story brings to a reader's consciousness. Beyond the question "What happened to whom and why?" readers sometimes ask, "What is this work really about?" "What does it mean?" or even "Why did the author write this work?" Answers to those questions are usually statements of theme.

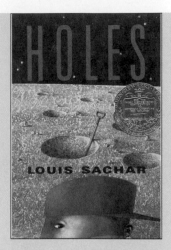

ILLUSTRATION 2.6 Louis Sachar won a Newbery Award for this tale about a boy sentenced to dig holes in the dry lake bottom of a work camp where he has an unforeseen opportunity to break the family curse. (Jacket design by Vladimir Radunsky from *Holes* by Louis Sachar. Jacket art and design copyright © 1998 by Vladimir Radunsky. Reprinted by permission of Farrar, Straus, & Giroux, LLC)

Explicit and Implicit Themes

Themes may be stated explicitly or suggested implicitly by the text. A good example of an explicit theme is found in the Zuñi story ***The Dragonfly's Tale,*** retold and illustrated by Kristina Rodanas. A community that has long been blessed by bounteous crops suddenly experiences famine when the people squander their food and callously offend the two goddesses who have been responsible for their bounty. When the village goes off in search of something to eat, a thoughtful and generous boy and girl again win the favor of the goddesses. The theme of the story, the virtues of conservation and kindness, is made explicit in the closing lines of the book:

> From then on, the people were careful not to take the Corn Maidens' gifts for granted. They respected the boy and his sister, and learned their ways of kindness. The cornfields thrived, and all the Ashiwi prospered. (n. pag.)

An implicit theme is an idea that is strongly suggested but not explicitly stated. In Alma Flor Ada's ***The Gold Coin,*** there is no explicit mention of the lesson that giving is better than taking or that the esteem of one's fellows is more valuable than gold. Readers have to infer those ideas from what happens in the story.

Especially in contemporary literature, stating themes is not always an easy or foolproof matter. Good writers rarely start with explicit themes in mind. Author Frances Temple (1994a) explained her approach to themes this way: "At first, I'm just getting out the story. Once it's written down, I can go through and see what the story is adding up to—and then as I rewrite I can make sure that what stays in the book pulls more or less in the same direction."

Many authors express surprise, however, at the themes others find in their works. For instance, author Charles Temple was surprised to read in a review of his ***Shanty Boat*** (illustrated by Melanie Hall) that the work was about the importance of respecting differences. Temple had thought it was just a rhyme about a quirky old guy who lived on a boat; he had created it as an exaggerated portrait of his own brother.

Themes are sometimes represented or symbolized by an image in a story. In Natalie Babbitt's ***Tuck Everlasting***, the image of the wheel is used again and again—presumably to symbolize the life cycle, and the sad consequences of stepping off it. In Cynthia Lord's ***Rules,*** the rules themselves come to stand for the girl protagonist's attempts to impose boundaries on her autistic brother; finally she realizes that it is she who has been too hemmed in by an overly ordered view of what behavior is acceptable, who is a friend, and in what form joy may come.

ILLUSTRATION 2.7 Natalie Babbitt uses the image of a wheel in the text of *Tuck Everlasting* to remind the reader of how important it is to accept that one is part of the life cycle. (Jacket design from *Tuck Everlasting* by Natalie Babbitt. Copyright © 1975 by Natalie Babbitt. Reprinted by permission of Farrar, Straus, & Giroux, LLC)

Reading against the Grain

The explicit and implicit themes described above were the sort many authors might have agreed were present in their work. But if we define a theme, as the critic Rebecca Lukens does, as a source of "insight into people and how they think and feel" (Lukens, 1990), then there are other layers of themes that we must take into account. These are layers of themes that the authors may not have intended.

Almost every work of literature takes some stance toward the social order: toward the relative roles and attributes of males and females, old and young, rich and poor, and so on. Of course, those stances are not always explicit. A work of literature may overtly argue for the status quo, may implicitly take the status quo for granted, or may argue for a different social order. Reading against the grain is a way to examine the unexamined, question the unquestioned, and hold up to scrutiny the unspoken assertions the text is making about the way lives are lived in society. Reading against the grain means asking, "Is this book a true portrait of how people behave? Is it a portrait of how they ought to behave?"

One fruitful way to read against the grain is to ask questions about differences in a text's portrayals of various characters:

- Males and females
- Old people and young people
- People of different social classes
- People of different races

Issue to Consider

Are Themes Really There?

A s we have just said, the theme of a contemporary literary work is more often implied than explicitly stated. Not surprisingly, the identification and interpretation of themes that are not explicitly stated give rise to lively debates. Critics argue not only about what the theme of a specific work really is, but also about whether it is possible to say definitively what a book's theme is. While some critics claim that skilled readers are adept at discovering themes that less skilled readers will miss, others (known as "deconstructionists" or "transactionalists" in the field of literary theory) insist that what a book means—its theme—lies to a large degree in the experience, background, and personality of each reader who encounters it.

These differing opinions certainly do not prevent literary critics, authors, and book lovers from discussing themes. Readers often have different ideas about the theme of a particular book. And authors sometimes even disagree with what the critics identify as the themes of their books!

Can ten readers agree on what the theme of a book is? Can we ask children to say what a particular book's theme is?

What do you think?

- Americans and Third World residents
- People who are differently abled

Another way to read against the grain is to list the characteristic actions taken by different people in the story and then to match those actions with the rewards the people receive. An examination of the story "Beauty and the Beast" to determine the ways in which males and females acted and the rewards or punishments they received revealed that males were rewarded for going after what they wanted—although they had to learn the hard way to be respectful of all sorts of people. Women, though, were rewarded for not going after what they wanted—for focusing on serving others and being pure (Temple, 1993).

Another way to examine the unexamined is to ask, "What would have been different if these events had happened to another character?" For example, in Phyllis Reynolds Naylor's **Shiloh,** what if Marty's little sister, Dara Lynn, had found the dog instead of Marty? Would her parents have taken her devotion to the dog as seriously? Would she have had the freedom to keep it secretly and arrange to give it food? What does this tell the reader about the range of activity boys and girls are permitted? What if Marty's well-to-do friend David Howard had found Shiloh? Would he have gone to so much trouble not to confront Judd with his mistreatment of animals—or would he simply have called the authorities? Would he and his family have been so careful not to make an enemy of Judd? What does this tell us about the range of options open to people from different social classes?

A text is a piece of virtual experience that can be held up and examined from many angles. As the questions above make clear, readers can find interesting meanings to talk about in almost any text, regardless of whether an author intended those meanings.

The Stance of the Implied Reader

The stance of the implied reader is one more device written into a work besides the plot, the setting, the characters, and the theme (Booth, 1961; Iser, 1974). The implied reader is the ideal interpreter of a work, as imagined by the author. The implied reader is not usually mentioned in the text, but his or her activity is essential if the text is to "work." If events or characters in a text are exciting, funny, sad, suspenseful, heroic, blameworthy, or even understandable, those events or characters must be perceived in those ways *by some reader*. Those qualities do not exist except as responses of a reader to a work. Therefore, in constructing a piece of literature, the writer must consciously or unconsciously keep an ideal reader in mind and arrange the details of the work in such a way as to evoke the desired responses from that reader.

Top Shelf 2.4

Books with Memorable Themes

Amado, Elisa (2007). *Tricycle.* Illustrated by Alfonso Ruano. Groundwood Books.

Browne, Anthony (2001). *Voices in the Park*. DK Children's Books.

Bunting, Eve (1999). *Smoky Night*. Illustrated by David Diaz. Voyager.

Howe, James (2003). *Horace and Boris but Mostly Dolores*. Illustrated by Amy Walrod. Aladdin.

Steig, William (1984). *The Real Thief*. Farrar, Straus, & Giroux.

Yumoto, Kuzumi (1998). *The Friends*. Translated by Cathy Hirano. Dell.

Ziefert, Harriet (1988). *A New Coat for Anna*. Illustrated by Anita Lobel. Dragonfly.

Top Shelf 2.5

Books That Emphasize the Implied Reader

Allard, Harry (1985). *Miss Nelson Is Missing.* Illustrated by James Marshall. Houghton Mifflin.

Blume, Judy (1976). *Blubber.* Yearling.

Estes, Eleanor (1974). *The Hundred Dresses.* Voyager.

Rathman, Peggy (1995). *Officer Buckle and Gloria.* Putnam.

Sendak, Maurice (1988). *Where the Wild Things Are.* HarperCollins.

Taylor, Mildred (1992). *Mississippi Bridge.* Skylark.

As they begin to read a work, actual readers implicitly take the perspective of the implied reader and begin to have emotional and intellectual reactions to the work in ways the author has scripted for them. Or else they don't: If a book is too silly, too "hard," or too far outside their usual way of seeing things, the actual readers might not be willing or able to take the stance of the implied reader, and the book will not work for them.

There are at least three ways in which an actual reader can take the stance of the implied reader. The first is by identifying with characters. The second is by taking a moral perspective on the story. The third is by filling in gaps to make the story "work."

Identifying with Characters

Identification with one or more characters in a text is an important function of the implied reader. When actual readers step into the shoes of a character, the reader suffers what that character suffers, faces the dilemmas that character faces, and feels the consequences of the choices they (the character and, vicariously, the reader) have made.

For example, the reader has ample opportunity to identify with the character of Esperanza in the beginning of *Esperanza Rising.* She is about to celebrate her birthday in a loving family, and is waiting for her father to return with the presents so the party can begin. Through this and other scenes, most readers find it easy to see themselves in Esperanza's shoes. But after the family has been forced from their homes and they are making their way north to the United States to start new lives as laborers, we are shown the scene in which Esperanza snatches her doll away from the hands of a barefoot peasant girl:

> Mama and Hortensia both stopped their needles and stared at Esperanza.
>
> Mama looked across at the girl's mother. "I am sorry for my daughter's bad manners."
>
> Esperanza looked at Mama in surprise. Why was she apologizing to these people? She and Mama shouldn't even be sitting in this car.
>
> Mama looked at Esperanza. "I don't think it would have hurt to let her hold it for a few minutes."
>
> "But, Mama, she is poor and dirty . . ." said Esperanza.
>
> "When you scorn these people, you scorn Miguel, Hortensia, and Alfonso [their former servants who are now leading them north]. And you embarrass me and yourself. As difficult as it is to accept, our lives are different now." (pp. 69–70)

Since the reader has already identified with Esperanza, the reader feels shame and embarrassment, as if the reader herself had simultaneously committed that hurtful act and then realized how misguided it was.

Another striking example of the way an author fosters identification is found in Mildred Taylor's *Roll of Thunder, Hear My Cry.* In the very first scene of the book, readers are walking along in Depression-era Mississippi with the Logan children, following an unpaved road with steep banks on either side and skirting deep-red muddy pools. A school bus careens along behind them. But it doesn't stop to pick them up. Instead, the driver veers into a puddle and raises a wave of thick red ooze that douses their clothes, hair, and bodies. The driver grins wildly, and the young passengers laugh and jeer as the bus roars on. The children wring out their clothes and keep walking. The bus driver and the passengers are white. The Logan children—and, through identifying with them, the readers—are black. For white readers, the effect of reading that scene can be as transforming as Mildred Taylor intended it to be—but only if they accept the stance of the implied reader.

Taking the Intended Moral Stance

Another way in which the text influences readers is by inviting them to take a moral stance on the story—a stance the author has staked out as part of the construction of the work. As we noted above, for a story to work, the author has to be able to count on readers to believe that some goals are worthwhile, that some events are exciting, that some things people say are funny or sad or shocking. If readers adopt these views—if only for the duration of the reading—the book will come together for them. If they don't, it won't. So far, so good.

But no readers hold precisely the orientations asked of them by all books. They occasionally have to stretch to accept a certain point of view for the time during which they participate in a certain book. This stretching has consequences. We have all had the experience of being told a joke that was so sexist, racist, or otherwise mean-spirited that we had to decide whether to keep listening, scold the teller, or walk away. It's the times we didn't quite muster the energy to do either of the latter two that are most bothersome. If, for the sake of the humor, we temporarily agree to take the stance the joke requires of us, we may give a polite laugh, but feel compromised. That is because we have just agreed to live the life of a bigot, if only for two minutes.

Author Mildred Taylor challenges readers to take a moral stance early in *Roll of Thunder, Hear My Cry.* Following the incident on the muddy road, the Logan children dig the bottom out of one of the puddles, so that when the driver again tries to douse the children he breaks the axle of the bus. Will readers go along with that? If they do, they will close ranks with the Logans for the duration of the book. If they don't, they have an uneasy reading experience ahead of them.

Many of the late Roald Dahl's very popular books, such as *Danny the Champion of the World, Matilda, George's Marvelous Medicine,* and *Charlie and the Chocolate Factory,* present unlikeable characters with no redeeming features. Sometimes they are other children, sometimes teachers, sometimes relatives, sometimes parents. Each of these characters harms the protagonist in some way, and each of them receives a bad outcome of one sort or another. In the meantime, we readers are invited to hate these characters and to delight in the terrible if quirky things that befall them. For many readers, though—especially those who try to respond to people who annoy us not with hatred but with understanding—Dahl's books raise moral challenges. The challenge is not in what Dahl says explicitly, but in the emotional stance he sets out for readers to take. Some readers are unwilling to take it.

Filling in the Gaps

The implied reader functions in one last way. A writer friend of ours says, "You have to trust your readers to figure some things out for themselves. They'll feel more like they're with you if you let them have the fun of figuring things out. Telling them too much spoils the fun." Writers leave gaps in their work to be filled in by the reader's realizations. In Maurice Sendak's *Where the Wild Things Are,* for example, a visual clue is given early in the book as to where the Wild Things came from. (Can you find it?)

In Harry Allard and James Marshall's *Miss Nelson Is Missing!,* readers are never told where Miss Viola Swamp, the no-nonsense substitute teacher, came from—or, for that matter, where she went. But at the end of the story the reader sees Miss Nelson reading in bed, next to a closet with an ugly black dress hanging in it—just like the one Viola Swamp wore. And there's a box on the shelf marked in upside-down letters that spell "wig."

In *Shiloh,* Marty's mother tells him she's afraid that if she doesn't tell his father that Marty has been hiding the dog, his father might wonder what other secrets she has been keeping from him. She doesn't come right out and say that she's afraid of creating suspicions of marital infidelity in her husband's mind. But that Marty's mother is thinking about sexual fidelity is strongly suggested by the very next scene. As she's washing dishes, she sings along with a sensuous song on the country music station, and blushes when Marty enters the kitchen and hears her singing.

Point of View

Point of view is the perspective from which the events in a story are perceived and narrated. The choices of point of view are first person (in which one of the characters in the work narrates the story, using the first-person pronoun "I") and third person (in which a narrator outside the story relates events that happened to those in it, using the third-person pronouns "she," "he" and "they"). When the author's knowledge of events shifts freely between different characters' points of view and the author describes events no one character could have known, he or she is writing from the point of view known as third-person omniscient ("all-knowing").

Stories in the First Person

Stories in the first person, such as *Shiloh,* tell the tale through a character's voice. Narration in the first person lends immediacy to the action and lets readers know what the character is feeling. But it also limits readers to that character's perspective.

Stories in the Third Person

Most of the time, authors describe the action as happening to someone else. This point of view is called narration in the **third person**. Pam Muñoz Ryan narrated *Esperanza Rising* in the third person. She did not narrate the story from Esperanza's voice, but she did stick strictly to Esperanza's point of view. The author never tells us anything that Esperanza herself did not know.

Third-person omniscient narration occurs when authors tell stories from the point of view of a narrator who knows more than any one character could. Louis Sachar narrated *Holes* in the third-person omniscient voice, as he was able to tell different stories from different time periods that only later came together in an explanatory whole.

Writing in the third person gives the author a broad range of choices of what to show the reader. Nonetheless, skilled writers usually narrate events as if from one character's point of view at a time. In *Harry Potter and the Sorcerer's Stone,* for example, in the opening scene when Dumbledore and his colleagues are lurking around the Dursleys' suburban home, they are described from the point of view of Mr. Dursley, who sees them but is only mildly puzzled by them, because it is not his nature to be either curious or observant. Soon, however, the scene switches to the Dursleys' kitchen, and now Mr. and Mrs. Dursley and their son Dudley are described from Harry Potter's point of view—we need to see through his eyes how grotesque they are.

When an author changes the perspective of the narration from one character to another, the results can change the meaning. Jon Scieszca's *The True Story of the Three Little Pigs by A. Wolf* is a tongue-in-cheek demonstration of the fact that the events in a story may look different from another character's perspective. Phillip Pullman's *I Was a Rat!* reminds us that even a bit player in a story—like a coachman Cinderella's fairy godmother left in human form—may have an entirely different take on events.

Teaching Idea 2.4

Retelling a Story From Another Perspective

Have the students retell a familiar story from a different character's perspective. They might retell "Hansel and Gretel" from the point of view of the father, or "Little Red Riding Hood" from the point of view of her mother.

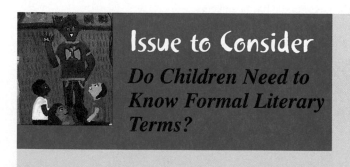

Issue to Consider

Do Children Need to Know Formal Literary Terms?

In this chapter on literary aspects of books for children we have used terms like *plot, theme, implied reader*, various kinds of *conflict*, and the like. We suspect there may be a few readers who are asking themselves, "Does anyone really need to know these technical things in order to appreciate a children's book? After all, you don't need to know how to take the engine apart to enjoy a nice car."

Will knowing literary terms help teachers teach? Will knowing literary terms add to children's appreciation of the books they read? There are many good answers to those questions. What are yours?

What do you think?

Style

Style is not what is said, but how it is said. When a book makes you hear a distinct voice in your head or when you find a passage so good you want to read it out loud to a friend, chances are you're responding to style. Style is not the same thing as talent. A talented writer may write in different styles and may have a gift for matching a style with the content of each book she or he writes.

Some of the elements of style are words, images, metaphors, sounds, and voice. Let's look at each.

Words

The poet William Carlos Williams wrote, "Each object in nature and each idea has an exact name." Good writers behave as if that were true, and they strive to name experiences exactly. Mark Twain wrote, "The difference between the right word, and almost the right word, is the difference between the lightning bug and the lightning."

But what makes a word "right"? Good word choices are concrete and vivid—they show, rather than sum up and judge. Or if they sum up and judge, they do so exactly. Good words create fresh images. Good writing crackles with insight.

Writing can be sparse or rich, as writers use few words or many to create impressions. Rich writing was more common in the nineteenth century and early in the twentieth. Note this passage from Kenneth Grahame's immortal *The Wind in the Willows*:

> Never in his life had he seen a river before—this sleek, sinuous, full-bodied animal, chasing and chuckling, gripping things with a gurgle and leaving them with a laugh, to fling itself on fresh playmates that shook themselves free, and were caught and held again. All was a-shake and a-shiver—glints and gleams and sparkles, rustle and swirl, chatter and bubble. (pp. 3–4)

Grahame's language consists of long sentences awash with colorful adjectives, images, and metaphors.

Spare writing can also be powerful. Frances Temple told *Grab Hands and Run* in the voice of twelve-year-old Felipe, and so the words she chose are simple and direct. Here is a scene from a parsonage in Guatemala, where refugees from the civil war in El Salvador find momentary protection:

> Another little girl comes in, a child with big dark eyes, younger than Romy. Father Ramon opens his arms to her and speaks gently, but at the sight of him she begins to scream and fastens herself around the leg of a table. Her screams are terrible, and no one can stop them.
> Father Ramon looks so upset that I follow him into the courtyard.
> "Why does she scream, Padre?" I ask him. "Can I help?"
> "Ask the soldiers why she screams, son," says Father Ramon. I have never heard anyone sound so sad. (p. 62)

Word choice doesn't depend on a fancy vocabulary—just on exact descriptions.

Images

Imagery is the art of making readers experience details as if through their own five senses. Alexander Carmichael had a good phrase for it: "bringing the different characters before the mind as clearly as the sculptor brings the figure before the eye" (quoted in Briggs, 1977, p. 10). That is the art of imagery—whether it is characters, settings, or actions that are illuminated for the mind's eye. The trick might be no more than mentioning sensory details: The writer mentions, however offhandedly, how things smelled, felt, tasted, sounded, and

Brian Smith

When a book makes you hear a distinctive voice in your head or when you find a passage so compelling you have to share it with a friend, chances are you're responding to an author's style.

ILLUSTRATION 2.8 Narrated in the voice of a twelve-year-old refugee, *Grab Hands and Run* uses simple syntax and vocabulary that nonetheless describe moving scenes and powerful events. (Cover from *Grab Hands and Run* by Frances Temple, 1993. Used by permission of the estate of Frances Temple.)

looked. But the effect is of living the moments described, rather than hearing a summary of them. Here is a moment from *Tuck Everlasting*:

> Shifting his position, he turned his attention to a little pile of pebbles next to him. As Winnie watched, scarcely breathing, he moved the pile carefully to one side, pebble by pebble. Beneath the pile, the ground was shiny wet. The boy lifted a final stone and Winnie saw a low spurt of water, arching up and returning, like a fountain, into the ground. He bent and put his lips to the spurt, drinking noiselessly, and then he sat up again and drew his shirt sleeve across his mouth. As he did this, he turned his face in her direction—and their eyes met. (p. 26)

Read that passage again, and see how many senses it appeals to. You feel the shifts of posture in your body and the quiet breathing in your chest. You relish the many visual images—the shiny wet ground, the spurt of water arching and returning. You hear the silence of the stealthy motions. You almost taste the water and feel the rough swipe of the shirt sleeve across your lips. With her skillful use of imagery, Babbitt has not so much described this scene as enacted it.

Metaphors

To use a metaphor is to describe one thing in terms of something else. Technically, there is a distinction between a simile, which is an overt comparison that says, "X is like Y"; a true metaphor, which talks about X as if it were Y; and personification, which ascribes human features, actions, or motives to something that isn't human.

Here is *Tuck Everlasting* again:

> The road that led to Treegap had been trod out long before by a herd of cows who were, to say the least, relaxed. It wandered along in curves and easy angles, swayed off and up in a pleasant tangent to the top of a small hill, ambled down again between fringes of bee-hung clover, and then cut sidewise across a meadow. (p. 5)

This isn't quite personification: The road is described as if it were not a person, but a cow—wandering, swaying, and ambling. To describe the road this way is to enliven the writing with unobtrusive magic.

Sounds

Aristotle advised writers to get the sounds of language right and the sense would take care of itself. In the voice of a good prose writer, the sounds of language speak almost as beautifully as they do in poetry.

You might think of poetry as rhyme and rhythm, but to catch the poetry of prose, you must widen your scope. Prose doesn't often rhyme, but its sounds speak to each other through *consonance* (a run of similar consonant sounds) and *assonance* (a run of similar vowel sounds). Prose doesn't scan into this meter or that, but there is a rhythm to the flow of the words: a sing-song cadence, a pell-mell dash, or a chant and refrain.

Listen to the sounds from a page of Patricia MacLachlan's prose text from her picture book *What You Know First*:

> We'll sleep in the hay with our eyes open
> Until they drop shut.
> Listening
>   to the rain on the tin roof
>   the wind rattling the windows
> Waking when the rooster crows
> In sunlight. (n. pag.)

Do you hear the *r*'s and the *w*'s echoing each other? Do you hear the words that begin with vowels, too ("eyes open"), as well as the similar vowel sounds ("windows" and "crows") speaking to each other? Both are examples of alliteration. Read the passage aloud and listen for the rhythm. Hear the flow of the words until the abrupt "drop shut." See how those choppy words break the flow, just as closed eyes signal that the flow of consciousness has been interrupted by sleep.

For more on rhythm, here is an excerpt from Bruce Brooks's ***The Moves Make the Man***:

> . . . cradling the ball and at the last minute pulling my left hand away like Oscar Robertson and snapping that lubricated right wrist and knowing, feeling it right straight through from the tips of the fingers that had let fly the ball and touched it all the way to the last, straight down the front edge of my body to my toes just before they hit the ground again, that the shot was true, feeling the swish and tickle of the net cords rushing quick down my nerves, and landing square and jaunty in time to watch, along with everybody else, as the ball popped through the net without a single bit of deceit, so clean it kicked the bottom of the cords back up and looped them over the rim, which is called a bottoms up and means you shot it perfect and some people even count them three points in street games. (p. 70)

That is one long sentence! The rhythm is the breathless tumble of an athlete's thoughts, which find expression in the equally breathless patter of sportscasters.

Voice

Go to the Extension Activities section of Chapter 2 in the MyEducationKit for your book and complete activity #2 to think about the importance of voice in *Roll of Thunder, Hear My Cry*.

Voice in literature has to do with the way the author comes across—from folksy to impersonal, from bold to timid, from expert to unreliable. Especially if the author writes in the first person, the voice of the piece may involve the narrator's dialect, personality, and slant on the world. Listen to Lucille Clifton's narrator in ***The Three Wishes***:

> My name is Zenobia, after somebody in the Bible. My name is Zenobia and everybody call me Nobie. Everybody but Victor. He call me Lena, after Lena Horne, and when I get grown I'm goin' to Hollywood and sing in the movies and Victorius is gonna go with me 'cause he's my best friend. That's his real name. (p. 1)

The voice is relaxed, informal, and optimistic.

But even if a book is written in the third person, the narrator can come across as someone to be reckoned with. Natalie Babbitt begins ***Tuck Everlasting*** with these words:

> The first week of August hangs at the very top of summer, the top of the live-long year, like the highest seat of a Ferris wheel when it pauses in its turning. The weeks that come before only climb from balmy spring, and those that follow drop to the chill of autumn, but the first week of August is motionless, and hot. It is curiously silent, too, with blank white dawns and glaring noons, and sunsets smeared with too much color. Often at night there is lightning, but it quivers all alone. There is no thunder, no relieving rain. These are strange and breathless days, the dog days when people are led to do things they are sure to feel sorry for after. (p. 3)

Listen to the tone she takes. Authoritative, knowledgeable, impersonal—maybe even a little bossy. (The weather's not like that where *we* live.) This is the voice of a storyteller who is fully in charge. Now listen to Roald Dahl's first words in ***Matilda***:

A good informational book—like good literature of any genre—has the capacity to engage young readers through humor, vivid imagery, and engaging style, while making accurate information readily accessible to them.

It's a funny thing about mothers and fathers. Even when their own child is the most disgusting little blister you could ever imagine, they still think that he or she is wonderful.

Some parents go further. They become so blinded by adoration they manage to convince themselves their child has qualities of genius.

Well, there is nothing very wrong with all this. It's the way of the world. It is only when the parents begin telling us about the brilliance of their own revolting offspring, that we start shouting, "Bring us a basin! We're going to be sick!" (p. 7)

Dahl's voice is outrageous, spicy, opinionated—but likely to be a lot of fun. Dahl seems to be out to undermine his own narrator's authority. Likely as not, children will feel compelled to talk back to him.

To check your comprehension on the content covered in this chapter, go to the MyEducation-Kit for your book and complete the Study Plan for Chapter 2. Here you will be able to take a chapter quiz and receive feedback on your answers.

Visual Literacy

Picture books have another set of features of their own. In Chapter 3 we will explore the visual language of picture books—or, to put it more properly, the verbal-and-visual language of picture books. The pictures have visual dynamics that communicate to readers: the colors that are used, the kinds of lines that are drawn, the placement of characters and objects on the page, the flow from page to page, the title page, the back cover, and the end papers—all are used by skillful illustrators and bookmakers to create a pleasing whole. Add to that the interaction of text and illustration—for example, often things are shown in the picture that complement or even contradict what is said in print—and there is a kind of language of expression used in picture books that needs to be explored in its own right.

Experiences for Further Learning

1. Think of two different characters in a book you've recently read—say, *The Gold Coin*. Prepare a Venn diagram, writing the features of personality and temperament the characters have in common in the overlapping area and those that separate them in the other parts of each circle. Compare your diagram with those of your classmates.
2. Make three columns on a piece of paper. In the left-hand column, list three male and three female characters in *Shiloh*. In the middle column, write two or three major actions these people took in the book. In the right-hand column, list the rewards or punishments they received at the end. Discuss these results. Can you formulate a statement that explains the pattern of who is rewarded and who is not in the story?
3. Choose a short but poignant scene from *Tuck Everlasting*. (Chapter 12 will work nicely.) Think through the scene from a different character's point of view—visualize the scene, for example, from Tuck's point of view rather than Winnie's. Which of Tuck's concerns come to the surface that do not emerge in the scene as written? How does Winnie appear?

Now go to Chapter 2 in the MyEducationKit (www.myeducationkit.com) for your book, where you can:

■ Find learning outcomes for Chapter 2.
■ Access the Children's Literature Database for your own exploration.
■ Extend knowledge with content-specific Web Links.
■ Deepen and apply content understanding with Extension Activities.
■ Check your comprehension on the content covered in the chapter by going to the Study Plan. Here you will be able to take a chapter quiz and receive feedback on your answers.
■ Find the following updated appendices: Major Children's Book Awards, Children's Magazines, Professional Organizations, Children's Book Publishers' Addresses, Book Selection Aids, and Children's Literature Web Sites.

Recommended Books

* indicates a picture book; **I** indicates interest level (P = preschool, YA = young adult)

Books with Striking Settings

Avi. *The True Confessions of Charlotte Doyle.* Orchard, 1990. Life on an eighteenth-century merchant ship, with Charlotte living "before the mast." (**I:** 11–YA)

Cameron, Ann. *The Most Beautiful Place in the World.* Knopf, 1988. What it's like to live as a peasant child in a Guatemalan village. (**I:** 8–10)

Erdich, Louise. *The Game of Silence.* HarperCollins, 2005. The rich lifestyle of the Ojibwes is brought to life in this story about Omakaya and her people. Beneath the peacefulness of the traditional way of life described in the book lies an undercurrent of dread as the white settlers draw ever nearer. (**I:** 9–12)

Farmer, Nancy. *The Sea of Trolls.* Atheneum, 2004. When Jack and his sister are captured by Vikings and swept away from their quiet Saxon home and life, Jack is caught up in adventures that lead him to the far north to the land of the trolls. (**I:** 9–12)

Holt, Kimberly Willis. *Dancing in Cadillac Light.* Putnam, 2001. It's 1968, and a time of wonder: The road in front of Jaynell's house is being paved; men will walk on the moon, and Grandpa buys a 1962 Cadillac. But the real wonder occurs after Grandpa dies and Jaynell is forced to face her own and her family's prejudices against members of the lower class. (**I:** 10 and up)

Soto, Gary. *Baseball in April and Other Stories.* Harcourt, 1990. Young life among mostly poor Mexican Americans in contemporary Fresno, California. (**I:** 11–YA)

Books with Interesting Characters

Bloor, Edward. *Tangerine.* Harcourt, 1997. A nearsighted soccer champ works for social justice in an artificial planned community in Florida in a novel with surrealistic overtones. (**I:** 12 and up)

Creech, Sharon. *Heartbeat.* HarperCollins, 2004. Annie has a best friend named Max, loves to run and draw, and has a grandfather suffering from dementia and a mother expecting a new baby. This novel, written in free verse, is rich with the "stuff of life." (**I:** 10 and up)

Crum, Shutta. *Spitting Image.* Clarion, 2003. Twelve-year-old Jessie wants to find her place in the world. She wants to make the world a better place—like the Vista volunteer in her Appalachian community—and she wants to know who her father is. Readers will meet a strong and memorable protagonist in Jessie Bovey. (**I:** 12 and up)

Dahl, Roald. *The BFG.* Farrar, 1982. The Big Friendly Giant comes across as a real person in this imaginative story. (**I:** 9–12)

Dowell, Frances O'Roark. *Chicken Boy.* Athenenum, 2005. Tobin McCauley has a lot on his plate. His mother has died, and he is caught in the ongoing feud between his grandmother and daddy. But a new friend and a school project begin Toby's transformation to wholeness. (**I:** 9–12)

Draanen, Wendelin Van. *Flipped.* Knopf, 2001. In second grade, Juli fell for Bryce, but for six years Bryce has avoided Juli. Then, in eighth grade, as both Juli and Bryce see their families in a new light, their perspectives on each other begin to shift. In alternating chapters Juli and Bryce relate their common experiences from vastly different perspectives. (**I:** 10–12)

Hiassen, Carl. *Hoot!* Yearling, 2006. A young "wild child" and his friends unravel the plans of unscrupulous developers in this environmental-themed book set in Florida. (**I:** 12 and up)

Weeks, Sarah. *So B. It: A Novel.* HarperCollins/Laura Geringer Books, 2004. Twelve-year-old Heidi's world revolves around her mother with the "bum brain" and their agoraphobic neighbor. But when Heidi discovers a roll of undeveloped film that discloses her mother's previous life, she sets out on a quest to discover her roots. (**I:** 9–12)

White, Ruth. *Buttermilk Hill.* Farrar, Straus, & Giroux, 2004. Surrounded by loving parents and a devoted extended family, Piper's life seems perfect—until her parents divorce. Piper finds healing through friendship, as well as through stories and poetry. (**I:** 9–12)

Books with Interesting Plots

Cleary, Beverly. *Ramona and Her Father.* Morrow, 1978. The problem of the father's unemployment gives rise to smaller problems, whetting the reader's curiosity for the long term and the short term. (**I:** 7–10)

DiCamillo, Kate. *The Tale of Despereaux: Being the Story of a Mouse, a Princess, Some Soup, and a Spool of Thread.* Illustrated by Timothy B. Ering. Candlewick, 2003. The story features the heroic exploits of a tiny mouse named Despereaux who strives to save the princess he loves from the destructive schemes of a dungeon rat and a dim-witted servant girl. (**I:** 9–12)

Funke, Cornelia. *Inkheart.* Translated by Anthea Bell. Scholastic/ Chicken House, 2003. When Meggie was three, her father, Mo, read aloud from a book, and as he read, an evil ruler, Capricorn, escaped from the book and came to life while Meggie's mother disappeared into the world of that book. Years later, when Capricorn captures Mo, Meggie sets out on a quest to save her father. (**I:** 10 and up)

Ritter, John H. *The Boy Who Saved Baseball.* Philomel, 2003. Threatened by the loss of their local baseball field (and an accompanying way of life), the local team accepts a challenge to save the field by playing a game against their archrivals. (**I:** 9 and up)

Sachar, Louis. *Holes.* Farrar, Straus, & Giroux, 1998. Newbery Award-winning tale of young Stanley Yelnats's arduous days digging holes in the dry lake bottom at a reformatory where the digging is said to be for penitence, but there may be another purpose, connected to a treasure. (**I:** 9–12)

*Steig, William. *The Amazing Bone.* Farrar, 1976. This book, like Steig's *Sylvester and the Magic Pebble, Caleb and Kate,* and *Roland, the Minstrel Pig,* has a straightforward plot that follows the pattern described in this chapter: conflict, rising action, climax, resolution, denouement. (**I:** 5–10)

Temple, Frances. *Grab Hands and Run.* Orchard, 1993. A journey story about the flight of a Salvadoran refugee family from their homeland through the United States to Canada. (**I:** 10–13)

Turner, Megan Whelan. *The Thief.* Greenwillow, 1996. A Newbery Honor Book, in which Gen, a thief and a prisoner for life, is promised his freedom if he will steal a precious jewel for the king's magus. (**I:** 9–12)

Books with Interesting Themes

*Bercaw, Edna Coe. *Halmoni's Day.* Illustrated by Robert Hunt. Dial, 2000. Jennifer is embarrassed to take her Korean-speaking grandmother to the school's Grandparents' Day until Halmoni shares a story with the class that shows how love can reach over generational and language barriers. (**I:** 7–10)

*Demi. *The Donkey and the Rock.* Holt, 1999. When the towns-people attend a trial between a donkey and a rock, they dis-cover the folly of yielding to idle curiosity. (**I:** 5–8)

Fleming, Candace. *Boxes for Katje.* Illustrated by Stacey Dressen-McQueen. Farrar, Straus, & Giroux, 2003. Following World War II, a young American girl sends a care package to Holland, initiating a two-way correspondence between two girls and a bond between two towns. (**I:** 8–12)

Grimes, Nikki. *Dark Sons.* Hyperion, 2005. In this free verse narrative, Grimes explores the relationship between fathers and sons: The biblical Ishmael struggles to understand why his father Abraham exiles him when his wife Sarah gives birth to a son. Sam, a contemporary boy, sees his father leave his mother for a white woman. (**I:** 10 and up)

Harrington, Janice. *Going North.* Illustrated by Jerome Lagarrigue. Farrar, Straus, & Giroux, 2004. The North holds promise for an African American family, but Jessie doesn't want to leave her home in Alabama. Only on the trip north does Jessie begin to understand the racism of her native state and the promise offered by life up North. (**I:** 8–12).

*Hoffman, Mary. *Amazing Grace.* Illustrated by Caroline Binch. Dial, 1991. Grace's grandmother helps her realize she can do anything she wants to. (**I:** 5–9)

Mack, Tracy. *Birdland.* Scholastic, 2003. With his fragile family posed on the verge of collapse, Jed and his best friend create a documentary to capture the same images recorded in the poetry notebook of Jed's dead brother. (**I:** 11 and up)

*Shange, Ntozake. *Whitewash.* Illustrated by Michael Sporn. Walker, 1997. A young child of color is assaulted by a street gang, who spray paint her face white. Her mixed race class helps her deal with the consequences. (**I:** 8 and up)

Smith, Hope Anita. *The Way a Door Closes.* Illustrated by Shane W. Evans. Henry Holt, 2003. This is the story of a family and how it changes when the father loses his job and leaves the family. This story, told through a series of poems, features rich characterization. (**I:** 10 and up)

Van Draanen, Wendelin. *Swear to Howdy.* Alfred A. Knopf, 2003. When his family moves to Lost River, Rusty finds a new best friend in Joey and soon finds himself caught up in adventures and misadventures with his prankster friend. When one of their pranks ends in a tragedy, Rusty must grapple with what a true friend is. (**I:** 10 and up)

*Williams, Vera B. *A Chair for My Mother.* Mulberry, 1982. A little girl and her family pull together to make a new home when theirs is destroyed by fire. (**I:** 6–10)

Woodson, Jacqueline. *Locomotion.* Putnam, 2003. Lonnie Motion's parents died when he was seven. At eleven, his teacher has invited him to write poetry—a medium through which he explores a range of emotions and experiences that include being a foster child who is separated from his little sister. (**I:** 9–12)

Resources

Egoff, Sheila, G. T. Stubbs, and L. F. Ashley. *Only Connect: Readings on Children's Literature.* 2nd ed. Oxford University Press, 1980.

Frye, Northrop. *The Educated Imagination.* Indiana University Press, 1964.

Hearne, Betsy, and Marilyn Kaye. *Celebrating Children's Literature.* Lothrop, Lee, & Shepard, 1981.

Hunt, Peter. *Children's Literature: The Development of Criticism.* Routledge, 1990.

Lukens, Rebecca. *A Critical Handbook of Children's Literature.* 4th ed. HarperCollins, 1990.

May, Jill. *Children's Literature and Critical Theory.* Oxford University Press, 1995.

Nodleman, Perry, ed. *Touchstones: Reflections on the Best in Children's Literature.* Children's Literature Association, 1985.

Sale, Roger. *Fairy Tales and After: Snow White to E. B. White.* Harvard University Press, 1978.

Scholes, Robert. *Structuralism in Literature.* Yale University Press, 1974.

Temple, Charles, and Patrick Collins, eds. *Stories and Readers.* Christopher-Gordon, 1992.

References

Allard, Harry. *Miss Nelson Is Missing!* Illustrated by James Marshall. Houghton Mifflin, 1977.

Barthes, Roland. *S/Z.* Trans. Richard Miller. Hill & Wang, 1974.

Booth, Wayne. *The Rhetoric of Fiction.* University of Chicago Press, 1961.

Briggs, Katherine. *British Folktales.* Pantheon, 1977.

Brooks, Bruce. *The Moves Make the Man.* HarperCollins, 1984.

Clifton, Lucille. *The Three Wishes.* Yearling, 1994.

Creech, Sharon. *Walk Two Moons.* HarperCollins, 1994.

Dahl, Roald. *Charlie and the Chocolate Factory.* Knopf, 1985.

———. *George's Marvelous Medicine.* Knopf, 1982.

———. *Matilda.* Viking, 1988.

George, Jean Craighead. *Julie of the Wolves.* HarperCollins, 1974.

Grahame, Kenneth. *The Wind in the Willows.* Scribner's, 1908/1953.

Grimm, Jacob, and Wilhelm Grimm. *The Complete Grimms' Fairy Tales.* Pantheon, 1972.

Iser, Wolfgang. *The Implied Reader: Patterns of Communication in Prose Fiction from Bunyan to Beckett.* Johns Hopkins University Press, 1974.

Levine, Gail Carson. *Ella Enchanted.* HarperTeen, 2004.

Lowry, Lois. *The Giver.* Houghton Mifflin, 1993.

Lukens, Rebecca. *A Critical Handbook to Children's Literature.* 4th ed. HarperCollins, 1990.

MacLachlan, Patricia. *What You Know First.* Illustrated by Barry Moser. HarperCollins, 1995.

McGraw, Eloise. *The Moorchild,* Aladdin, 1998.

Paterson, Katherine.. *Lyddie.* Lodestar, 1991.

Pullman. Phillip. *I Was a Rat!* Yearling, 2002.

Scieszca, Jon. *The True Story of the Three Little Pigs, by A. Wolf.* Illustrated by Lane Smith. Dutton, 1995.

Sendak, Maurice. *Where the Wild Things Are.* Harper & Row, 1963.

Souriau, Etienne. *Les Deux Cent Milles Situations Dramatiques.* Flammarion, 1955.

Spinelli, Jerry. *Maniac Magee.* Little, Brown, 1990.

Steig, William. *Spinky Sulks.* Sunburst, 1991.

Temple, Charles. *Shanty Boat.* Illustrated by Melanie Hall. Houghton Mifflin, 1993a.

———. "'What If Beauty Had Been Ugly?' Reading against the Grain of Gender Bias in Children's Books." *Language Arts 70* (February 1993b): 89–93.

Temple, Frances. Personal communication. 1994a.

———. *The Ramsey Scallop.* Orchard, 1994b.

Turnbull, Colin. *The Human Cycle.* HarperCollins, 1982.

3

Picture Books

> *The gratifying thing* about good art is the longer one looks at it the more one sees, the more one sees, the deeper one feels, and the deeper one feels the more profoundly one thinks. Looking at art is everything!
>
> —*from* **Picture Books for Children**, *4th ed.*
> *by Patricia J. Cianciolo*

What Are Picture Books?

Today's picture books are filled with good art—art that invites repeated lingering, elicits a depth of feeling, and promotes profound thinking. A picture book in the purest sense is one that relies solely on illustrations to convey its message; a broader definition includes books in which the illustrations combine with text to create a message. A picture book can take many forms. It can be a wordless book, which tells a story solely through illustrations. It can be an illustrated book, in which the words carry most of the message, but illustrations either depict what is stated in the text or decorate the page. It can be a picture storybook, in which a tale is told through a combination of illustrations and text, each amplifying the other to create a unified whole. Much of the discussion in this chapter focuses on the picture storybook.

Picture books are also characterized by a unique use of language. *Wordless books* are marked by the absence of written language; however, language is implied through the illustrations, so it exists within the book, but not in a visible text. *Concept books* have language that is unique in its ability to convey the meaning of concepts such as the alphabet, numbers, shapes, or colors. *Beginning Readers* are books that use controlled language to enable children to practice reading independently. The best *picture storybooks* have language that is rich in its ability to tell the story well. They may include vocabulary that is beyond the child's independent reading level, but is valuable in helping nurture a depth of understanding achievable only by precise language use.

Picture books are types of books, and there are picture books as a book type within each of the genres discussed in later chapters: picture books that are historical fiction, picture books that are fantasies, and so on. This chapter focuses on building a depth of understanding about picture books as a form rather than concentrating on the content, which will be addressed within the genre chapters.

The Evolution of Picture Books

Since the publication of the first picture book in 1658, many factors have influenced the evolution of these books for children. Picture books have changed as their creators have explored the interplay of text and illustrations and refined their concepts of picture books. Developments in printing technology have influenced the technical as well as the artistic aspects of creating picture books.

The Development of the Concept of the Picture Book

What is generally considered the first picture book is **Orbis Sensualium Pictus** (**The Visible World in Pictures**), published in 1658 by Johannes Amos Comenius (1592–1670), a visionary educator from what is now the Republic of Slovakia. Comenius believed that children should be taught about practical matters in the language they used daily, in addition to being taught the "dead" languages, history, and catechisms, as was popular at the time. He added illustrations to informational text to increase children's understanding and pleasure. Following the lead of Comenius, most picture books of the seventeenth and eighteenth centuries were created to educate children and guide their moral behavior.

Children's book publishing advanced dramatically under the leadership of John Newbery (1713–1767). In 1744, Newbery established a company in London dedicated almost exclusively to publishing beautiful children's books. He created books for children in attractive, playful formats, including the accordion book, which was a long strip folded accordion-like to form "pages." He was the first to introduce illustrations by accomplished artists, and his books had permanent, attractive bindings.

Picture books flourished in England during the nineteenth century. Much of the credit for changes in picture books is given to Edmund Evans, an artist, publisher, and printer. Evans advanced the development of picture books by recognizing the importance of the relationship

PEARSON
my education kit

Go to the Assignments and Activities section of Chapter 3 in the MyEducationKit and complete the activities. As you work through the activities and answer the accompanying questions, consider the importance of evaluating picture books for children.

between illustration and book design. In addition, using photographic techniques, he created copies that closely resembled the original illustrations to improve the color printing process. Evans persuaded artists such as Randolph Caldecott (1846–1886), Walter Crane (1845–1915), and Kate Greenaway (1846–1901) to create books for children (Kiefer, 1995).

Walter Crane is known for his careful attention to his books' designs and for synchronizing text and illustrations. He was among the first to attend to the overall effect of double-page spreads and to the use of color and beautifully designed pages. Some of the books Crane illustrated in the 1860s are still being reproduced, including his *Sing a Song of Sixpence* and *The House That Jack Built.*

Another notable creator of picture books from the late nineteenth century was Kate Greenaway, whose portrayal of an idealized childhood can be seen in *A—Apple Pie.* Greenaway's enchantment with the Victorian world is evident in her illustrations, which are filled with flowers, gardens, and happy, prettily dressed children.

The picture book form made the greatest leap toward its modern manifestation in the hands of English illustrator Randolph Caldecott, of whom Maurice Sendak (1990) wrote:

> He devised an ingenious juxtaposition of picture and word, a counterpoint that never happened before. Words are left out—but the picture says it. Pictures are left out—but the word says it. In short, it is the invention of the picture book. (p. 21)

Caldecott built on Crane's ideas about book design, perfecting the unification of text and illustration and allowing illustrations to interpret and extend the text beyond what the words implied. Also, Caldecott created illustrations that were not contained within borders, so characters virtually bounced off the pages.

Later, another English illustrator, Beatrix Potter (1866–1943), recognized the need to consider the audience when creating children's books. She insisted that her books be appropriately sized for little hands. Potter's stories of woodland animals are endearing not only because of the well-written text, but also because of the meticulously drawn illustrations.

By the 1930s, the concept of the modern picture book had basically taken shape. The illustrations extended the text, the text and illustrations were interdependent, and the importance of the book's entire design was recognized (Schwartz, 1982).

Changes in Printing Technology

Improvements in printing technology over the years account for great changes in the appearance of picture books. Paper, the use of color, printing quality, and art styles have contributed to the evolution of the picture book.

Illustrations in early picture books were created using a relief method such as woodblock printing. Artists carved illustrations on wood blocks by cutting away the background. The resulting images, which stood above the rest of the block, were inked and impressed on paper by printing machines. Comenius created *Orbis Sensualium Pictus* on wood blocks and included elaborate illustrations and designs in the page borders, a carryover from the hand-decorated manuscripts that were created before the advent of the printing press. Each illustration had to be painstakingly carved on a separate block. John Newbery, who was the first to produce books whose primary purpose was to amuse children, used wood engravings for most of his publications. Thomas Bewick perfected wood engraving in the late eighteenth century and is best known for being the first to add color to illustrations. Every book was colored by hand; ironically, some of those hands belonged to children who worked under sweatshop conditions.

In the late nineteenth century, metal plates and metal engravings were used. William Blake used etchings on metal plates to illustrate his *Songs of Innocence.* Walter Crane's illustrations in *Absurd ABC* were hand-colored, and the typography in that book was considered to be as excellent as the pictures. John Tenniel's illustrations of *Alice's Adventures in Wonderland* were printed by letterpress from metal engravings.

Lithography, a process invented in the late eighteenth century, allowed artists to work on flat stones that had a very hard, smoothly polished surface. Images were drawn on the stone with wax crayons or touche, a crayonlike liquid material. The ink adhered to the waxed portions of the stone; images were then printed on dampened paper using enormous pressure.

One example of fine lithography can be seen in Hans Fischer's 1958 illustrations for Charles Perrault's *Puss in Boots.* (See color plate ILL.6.)

The use of photography and letterpress printing revolutionized the printing of picture books in the early twentieth century. At first, colors had to be separated by hand, and the process was both tedious and expensive. It was not until illustrators could turn color separation over to machines that the number of full-color illustrations in picture books increased. Photography and later the laser scanner made the greatest impact on the quality of art reproduction.

In the twentieth century, printing technology improved tremendously, and art can now be reproduced so that it closely resembles its original form. Picture books have become objects of great beauty. The use of computer technology to create picture books may lead to a new era of book illustration. Since the advent of the laser scanner, the printing process imposes few limitations on the artist. It is amazing what illustrators have been able to use: Imaginative picture books have been made with collages of cardboard, cereal, and plastic, as David Diaz did in illustrating Eve Bunting's *Smoky Night,* the 1995 Caldecott-winning book, or even wood veneers, which is what Paul O. Zelinsky used to illustrate Anne Isaacs's *Swamp Angel,* a 1995 Caldecott Honor Book.

Computer technology itself offers illustrators a new medium. Artists have different reactions to the use of computers to create art. Some suggest that technology separates the artist from the reader and that children will always prefer illustrations in which "the hand of the artist" is recognizable. On the other hand, some highly regarded and established illustrators have made such a complete transition to computer-generated art that they have given up paintbrushes entirely. More recently, a new generation of digital art illustrators who create their art solely digitally have emerged. Others have merged their work as painters, manipulating their hand painted or drawn images by scanning and manipulating them on-screen.

Authors and Illustrators Who Have Defined the Field

The work of many early authors and illustrators has contributed to the shaping and defining of the field of picture books. Many are mentioned in the previous sections on the development of the concept of the picture book and changes in printing technology. Some early works continue to be enjoyed by children today—evidence of the timeless appeal of these creations.

Beatrix Potter's 1902 publication of *The Tale of Peter Rabbit* is celebrated as her debut as a creator of children's books, although her first book was published earlier. This story originally appeared in a series of letters in 1893 to Noel, the son of her former governess, and was intended to cheer him up when he was ill with scarlet fever. Potter included black-and-white drawings to accompany the story. Years later, after several publication rejections, she used her own funds to have the book published. Frederick Warne & Co. agreed to publish this "little book for little hands" on the condition that Potter provide color illustrations. More than twenty other books followed. The tales of such animal characters as Pigling Bland, Squirrel Nutkin, Jemima Puddleduck, Benjamin Bunny, Hunca Munca, and Jeremy Fisher are known by children all around the world.

Before the 1930s, the picture books that were available to children in the United States were typically imported from England and other European countries. However, between 1930 and 1960, many authors and illustrators came from Europe and joined those working in the United States to establish a solid foundation of American picture books. Ludwig Bemelmans, Roger Duvoisin, Feodor Rojankovsky, and Tomi Ungerer were among those who emigrated from Europe. American picture book creators of that time were Robert McCloskey, Wanda Gág, Robert Lawson, Virginia Lee Burton, Marie Hall Ets, and Margaret Wise Brown. Many of the books created during that era continue to be popular with children.

Wanda Gág's 1929 book *Millions of Cats* still delights readers with the repeated phrases "Hundreds of cats, Thousands of cats, Millions and billions and trillions of cats." The lonely man who sets out to find a cat to keep him and his wife company simply cannot choose from among the millions of cats, each with unique qualities. The lines of the hills and roads in the black-and-white illustrations show the long distance the man travels in search of a cat and echo the long line of cats that follow him home.

Many adults today remember reading Virginia Lee Burton's 1939 story of **Mike Mulligan and His Steam Shovel** as they grew up. When new electric and diesel shovels take jobs away from steam shovels, Mike takes his steam shovel, Mary Anne, to Popperville and proves that she can dig "as much in one day as a hundred men could dig in a week." The house in Burton's 1942 **The Little House** was said to be so well built that the "great-great-grandchildren's great-great-grandchildren" would live there. Although both of these works are much more than a half-century old, they meet contemporary criteria for good picture books.

Of the many books written by Margaret Wise Brown, the one most cherished by millions of readers over the years is **Goodnight Moon.** In this bedtime story, published in 1947, a little rabbit is in bed, saying goodnight to each item in the bedroom and outside the window. Gradually, the lights dim until it is dark in the room, and the rabbit falls asleep.

Robert McCloskey's 1942 Caldecott-winning **Make Way for Ducklings** made Boston Public Garden famous all over the world to children who read and reread the endearing story of a duck family in search of a place to live. Among McCloskey's other books from the 1940s and 1950s that continue to enjoy wide popularity are **Blueberries for Sal** and **Time of Wonder,** both depicting life in rural Maine.

Marcia Brown's first book was published in 1946, and only one year later she produced her first Caldecott Honor Book, **Stone Soup: An Old Tale.** Her interest in folktales and fairy tales continued in the many books that followed. She values the passing down of stories through generations and enjoys helping to preserve traditional tales. In fact, all three of Brown's Caldecott Medal books are folktales or fairy tales: **Cinderella** in 1955, **Once a Mouse** in 1962, and **Shadow** in 1983. Each is illustrated with a different medium: **Cinderella** (written by Charles Perrault) was created with watercolors; **Once a Mouse** has woodcut-style illustrations; **Shadow** mixes collage, paint, and print.

Ezra Jack Keats is known for his distinctive collages, but it is his depictions of the daily life of inner-city children that was ground breaking for the 1960s. In the 1963 Caldecott winner, **The Snowy Day,** Keats used a variety of papers—gift wrap, wallpaper, and other printed papers—to add color and texture to his illustrations. In this story, Peter wakes up, sees a snowy scene outside his window, and spends the day playing in the snow. Keats continued to depict Peter's experiences in subsequent books. Although the experiences depicted are often universal—getting a new baby sister in **Peter's Chair** and playing in the neighborhood in **Apt. 3**—the details of the setting clearly place these stories in city neighborhoods. Keats's picture books are enjoyed in translation by children in many countries.

John Steptoe knew from the time he was in high school that he wanted to write and illustrate books for African American children; he realized there was a great need for books these children could relate to. Immediately after high school, Steptoe published his first book, **Stevie.** Although the theme—a boy's jealousy at having to share his mother's attention with a younger boy—is universal and can be appreciated by all children, regardless of race, the book uses language to which African American children can relate directly. Steptoe continued to write and illustrate books that met his goal of providing for the literary needs of African American children, winning wide acclaim and numerous book awards, including the Coretta Scott King Award for illustrations.

Tomie dePaola has written over one hundred and illustrated over two hundred books for children. His artwork is characteristically done in watercolor in a folk art style. dePaola's loving family relationships are the root of many of his books, including **Nana Upstairs & Nana Downstairs, Now One Foot, Now the Other,** and **Tom,** which depict an intergenerational affection and bond, as well as a child dealing with the loss brought about by death. His Italian and Irish heritages are the source of his interest in those cultures, which several of his books reflect. Perhaps the best known is **Strega Nona,** a Caldecott Honor Book in which an Italian "Grandma Witch" with a magical touch leaves her helper, Big Anthony, home alone with a magic pot that can cook pasta by itself. dePaola's years in a Benedictine monastery influenced the eventual creation of books with religious stories or themes. In the early 1970s, **The Cloud Book, Charlie Needs a Cloak,** and **The Popcorn Book** made Tomie dePaola an early leader in writing narrative informational books—books with the intent of offering information to children, but that are set to a story. After years of creating picture books, dePaola has turned to writing chapter books. The first in his autobiographical series, **26 Fairmount Avenue,** was named a 2000 Newbery Honor Book. Published in the same year, Barbara Elleman's comprehensive biography, *Tomie dePaola: His Art & His Stories,* offers readers an in-depth look at the life and work of this popular author and illustrator.

Leo Lionni's career as a children's book author and illustrator began when he told a story to his grandchildren to pass the time while they were traveling together by train. Later published as a book, the story was about two children depicted as colors—blue and yellow—who hug and become green. *Little Blue and Little Yellow* was illustrated with torn-paper collage, which portrayed human emotions abstractly. Lionni continued to write and illustrate many books whose characters embodied concepts important in human relationships; perhaps this accounts for their continued popularity today. *Inch by Inch,* Lionni's second book, was named a Caldecott Honor Book (one of three of his books to win that award). In this story, an inchworm outwits predators and survives by measuring them "inch by inch." For this book, Lionni mixed crayon with collage. In another story of survival, *Swimmy*, a school of fish gathers into a formation resembling a large fish to fend off predators who have eaten Swimmy's family. The combination of sponge printing and watercolor in this book effectively depicts the underwater world. *Frederick* is particularly well known for both its collage artwork and the story: As a family of mice gathers supplies to prepare for the coming winter, Frederick "stores up" stories and poetry as his contribution.

Categories of Picture Books

Picture books have a range of purposes, from introducing rhymes and serving as manipulative toys to helping children learn concepts. In this section, we organize picture books into five groups: early childhood books, wordless books, picture books with minimal text, beginning readers' books, and picture storybooks. Early childhood books are primarily intended for very young children and include board books, books of Mother Goose and nursery rhymes, concept books, alphabet books, counting books, and toy books. (Mother Goose and nursery rhyme books are discussed in Chapter 7, "Traditional Literature.") Wordless books vary more in intended age. Their primary purpose is to allow readers to create the text mentally while looking at the pictures. Picture books with minimal text are closely related to wordless books. Beginning readers' books give children a start at reading independently. Picture storybooks comprise the largest subgroup of picture books. The stories are written specifically to be embellished by illustrations and are told through the marriage of text and illustrations. Picture books from various genres are predominantly discussed in the specific chapters that cover those genres, including historical fiction (Chapter 10) and informational books (Chapter 11).

Early Childhood Books

Many children enjoy books from the moment they are held in an adult's lap and have a book shared with them or are able to hold them on their own. Some books are particularly appropriate for young children, because of both their form and their content. The novelty of toy books sustains children's curiosity, and the durable format of board books stands up to rough treatment from little hands (and teeth). The rhythmic rhymes of Mother Goose make it easy for little ones to chant along. Concept books introduce young children to informational books; alphabet books help them to explore the language in its written form, and counting books provide opportunities to practice math concepts.

Toy Books

Preschoolers can become acquainted with books very early, thanks to cloth, vinyl, and board books. These books usually have a sturdy or washable construction and simple pictures, showing one object per page. They are typically eight to ten pages long. If there are any words, they may simply label objects on the page. For slightly older children, pop-ups, pull-tabs, flaps to lift, half-pages, and other gadgets invite playful manipulation. Classic toy books include Dorothy Kunhardt's *Pat the Bunny,* a tactile and participatory book that is still in print seventy years after its first edition, and *The Nutshell Library,* a boxed set of miniature books by Maurice Sendak that generations of children have enjoyed for over forty years.

Among books for the very youngest are board books by noted author/illustrators such as Nancy Tafuri, Lucy Cousins, and Helen Oxenbury. Board books often come in series of three to four titles centered on topics of immediate interest to very young children, such as animals, things babies do, or family members. Tana Hoban created two books for newborns: *Black on White* and *White on Black.* Both books show shadows of objects on solid backgrounds, creating high contrast between black and white. John Steptoe's *Baby Says* features African American babies, as do books by Eloise Greenfield with Jan Spivey Gilchrist, Angela Shelf Medearis, and Andrea Pinkney with Brian Pinkney. In another board book series, Rosemary Wells humorously chronicles the antics of Max. Other board books are reproductions of picture books originally published in hardcover for older children, such as the board book version of Eric Carle's *The Very Busy Spider* or Peggy Rathmann's *Good Night, Gorilla.*

Some books are not quite board books, but have pages that are thicker and glossier than usual book pages. Cut-out shapes layer and unlayer on sixteen boldly colored pages to create various animal faces in *Color Zoo,* by Lois Ehlert, which was a Caldecott Honor Book. She used the same method to create her *Color Farm.* In addition to the heavy card stock paper versions of the original volumes, these books are now available as board books.

Some pop-up books are fairly straightforward, with single-fold pop-ups; other paper-engineered pop-ups are more elaborate, often with moving parts. One particularly popular series is the lift-the-flap series by Eric Hill about a dog named Spot. In *Where's Spot?,* children lift flaps to help mother dog Sally open the door, look inside a wardrobe, and peek under the bed to search for her pup Spot. In Mark Inkpen's *Where, Oh Where, Is Kipper's Bear?,* Kipper the dog searches for his bear. Young readers delight in finding the bear under the covers, reading a book by flashlight—which turns on when they lift up the quilt.

Laura Vaccaro Seeger has created a well-designed concept book entitled *Black? White! Day? Night! A Book of Opposites.* With cutouts and lift-the-flap features, the concept of opposites is explored in clever but clearly defined ways. Particularly fine examples of complex paper-engineered books are created by Robert Sabuda. For the most part, they are intended for an older audience than toddlers—in fact, the elaborate and complex designs appeal to all ages. *Cookie Count* is a counting book that features all types of cookies—from fortune cookies with mice pulling the fortunes out to the cookies that form the gingerbread house at the end. Some books combine pop-ups with pull tabs, flaps, and other parts to be manipulated. One example is Paul Zelinsky's *The Wheels on the Bus.* In addition to wheels that turn, the book has a bus door that swings open, passengers who board, wipers that swish, babies who cry open-mouthed, and mothers who shake their fingers.

Eric Carle's picture books have toy components that are integral to the story line. In *The Very Hungry Caterpillar,* actual holes in a series of illustrations of food indicate where the caterpillar dined. *The Very Quiet Cricket* searches for a friend until he finally meets another cricket; at that point, readers hear the sound of a cricket (produced by a computer chip embedded in the book). The raised surface of the spider's web in *The Very Busy Spider* becomes increasingly larger as the spider continues to spin. When the firefly meets friends in *The Very Lonely Firefly,* they light up.

Dan Harper's *Telling Time with Big Mama Cat* is an example of a toy book in which the reader is allowed to manipulate the hands of the clock (the toy) while reading the story. Some books are toys themselves. *Maisy's Pop-Up Playhouse,* by Lucy Cousins, looks like a book but opens up to create a doll house for Maisy the mouse. The house has a bedroom, a kitchen, and a bathroom, and includes cutouts of dishes, pots and pans, and toys for the tub. Can David Pelham's *Sam's Sandwich* be called a book? Sam smirks as he creates an unusual sandwich for his sister—filled with the usual sandwich fillings as well as surprise creatures from the garden. Each page folds out in the shape of the filling, and the covers are the bread. These toy books are artistic creations that stimulate children to create their own stories as they play with them.

Some books with toy components are for a little older audience, but they still include the toy component in a manner that best utilizes the device to contribute to the book's overall experience. For example, Emily Gravett's *Meerkat Mail* effectively includes postcards throughout the book, showing both sides of the postcard in "lift-the-flap" style. In the story, a meerkat living in the Kalahari Desert ventures away from home and sends a series of postcards to her family. Through the device of the postcard format, information about each place in the world that the meerkat travels to is included, and the text written on it contributes to the story. Visual humor and anticipation is implied through the image of the jackal that lurks in the background, with its potential prey, the meerkat, completely oblivious to it.

Concept Books

Concept books convey knowledge, answering the question "What's that?" They cover a wide range of topics—the alphabet, numbers, colors, shapes, and opposites, to name a few. To appreciate the contribution of these picture books, you need only think about how difficult it is sometimes to describe and convey the meaning of concepts in words alone. Because of their significance and abundance, alphabet and counting books are discussed separately in this section. The important thing to remember when evaluating concept books is how clearly the information is presented and how appropriate it is to the reader's conceptual development.

Tana Hoban is a prolific creator of concept books, and hers rely on photographs to relay information. One book, *26 Letters and 99 Cents*, introduces the alphabet when it is read from one end and the concept of money when it is turned over and read from the other end. Bruce McMillan also creates photographic concept and information books. *One, Two, One Pair* shows objects that come in pairs: hands, feet, socks, mittens, boots, and skates. We see a child prepare to go skating and follow along as pairs are introduced—but surprise! The child is also part of a pair, and a twin is introduced at the skating pond.

Two concept books that explore the primary colors and how colors mix are Ann Jonas's *Color Dance* and Ellen Stoll Walsh's *Mouse Paint*. Both concepts are explored in the context of a story. In *Color Dance*, three girls dance with red, yellow, and blue sheets of sheer fabric. As they dance and their sheets cross, new colors are made. In *Mouse Paint*, three mice splash around in red, yellow, and blue paint. When they dance around in each other's puddles, new colors are made.

Sometimes, concepts are introduced within the context of a simple story. In Donald Crews's Caldecott Honor Book *Freight Train*, children are introduced to colors and the names of types of cars in a freight train. The book does much more than merely label objects, however. It shows the movement of the train in darkness and daylight by blurring the colors of the cars and introduces children to words such as "tunnel" and "trestle." Lois Ehlert's books also introduce concepts within a storyline. In *Planting a Rainbow,* the story

Children enjoy perusing picture books with their classmates at the school library.

Lindfors Photography

begins, "Every year, Mom and I plant a rainbow." It goes on to describe how bulbs are planted in the fall and seedlings and seeds in the spring, and then they watch the rainbow grow. The next six pages are cut so that a strip of color shows in staggered form along the end of each page. As you flip each colored strip in rainbow order, the flowers in the featured color are shown in full bloom. For example, a tulip, a zinnia, a tiger lily, and a poppy are shown as orange flowers. The concept of color is made clear through this straightforward story line that ends with the child and mother picking all colors of flowers throughout the summer.

Alphabet Books

Alphabet books are one of the oldest and most popular varieties of concept books. Preschoolers are often first exposed to the alphabet through picture books, and such books are available in large numbers. A traditional alphabet book shows a one-to-one correspondence between a letter and an object whose name begins with that letter. Typically, there is one letter and one object per page. One example is Bert Kitchen's *Animal Alphabet.* Each page of this book has a clearly printed letter and a picture of an animal, some that are familiar or ones that are not as familiar. More complex alphabet books show more objects per page to illustrate the featured letter; the "B" may be represented by a bicycle as a central picture, but birds, bells, and beans may be found in the border. *Anno's Alphabet* is subtitled "An Adventure in Imagination." For each letter, an intricate, unusual object beginning with that letter is pictured. For the beginner, these pictures are often too sophisticated for simple letter-sound associations. This kind of book is for children who know the alphabet and are willing to extend their knowledge of its application. Finally, some alphabet books challenge readers to discover as many objects as they can find hidden within a very busy illustration that includes numerous objects with names that begin with the featured letter. *Animalia* by Graeme Base is an example of such a book. The text on one page says, "Beautiful Blue Butterflies Basking by a Babbling Brook," and objects that begin with the letter "B"—baboon, bassoon, bee, beetle, book, bear, bonnet—are hidden on the page.

Many books play with the sounds of language while introducing the alphabet. A popular one is Bill Martin, Jr., and John Archambault's *Chicka Chicka Boom Boom.* Children especially enjoy the rhythmic, rhyming text that tells the story of alphabet letters vying to see which can climb to the top of the coconut tree first. A similar rhyming book featuring the letters of the alphabet is Jane Bayer's *A, My Name Is Alice,* whose alphabet rhymes are illustrated by Steven Kellogg. The rhymes are traditional accompaniments to playground games such as jump rope or ball bouncing games: "A, my name is Alice and my husband's name is Alex. We come from Alaska and we sell ants. Alice is an Ape. Alex is an Anteater." A different way of playing with the sounds of language is through alliteration. Maurice Sendak's *Alligators All Around* has "Alligators all around / bursting balloons / catching colds / doing dishes." Crescent Dragonwagon's *Alligator Arrived with Apples,* illustrated by José Aruego and Ariane Dewey, has various animals arriving for a Thanksgiving feast, each bringing foods beginning with the same letter as its name: "Bear Brought Banana Bread, Biscuits, and Butter."

A large variety of themed alphabet books are also available. One book with a food theme is *Eating the Alphabet: Fruits and Vegetables from A to Z,* by Lois Ehlert, which shows a variety of fruits and vegetables in alphabetical order. Another alphabet book with a food theme is Arnold Lobel's *On Market Street,* illustrated by Anita Lobel, in which each page depicts a letter composed of fruits, vegetables, and other market items that begin with that letter. *The Handmade Alphabet,* by Laura Rankin, introduces the hand and finger positions used by the American Sign Language Association for the letters of the alphabet. Each page also shows an object that begins with the featured letter.

The alphabet is used to organize all kinds of information at many conceptual levels; there is a rich array of alphabet books for all ages. *The Z Was Zapped,* by Chris Van Allsburg, is an alphabet book that is suitable for intermediate-grade students. Each letter establishes a rather dark theatrical scene within a larger drama of what happens to each letter from A to Z. Leo and Diane Dillon won the Caldecott Medal for their illustrations for Margaret Musgrove's *Ashanti to Zulu: African Traditions,* in which each letter introduces a paragraph of text about a tribe on the African continent. In George Shannon's *Tomorrow's Alphabet,* the alphabet is the organizing sequence to help children predict what things will become in the future. For example, "A is for seed—tomorrow's APPLE/ B is for eggs—tomorrow's BIRDS."

It is clear that some alphabet books are meant for children who are old enough to understand complex ideas. David Pelletier's Caldecott Honor Book *The Graphic Alphabet* takes alphabet letters and artistically places them in graphic art that depicts the word: The "i" of iceberg is nearly submerged beneath the water level, but a shadow of the lower portion of the letter can be seen below the surface, and the "h" is seen "hovering" in midair. Another alphabet book that is more artistic than practical in its rendition of the concept is Suse MacDonald's *Alphabatics.* Each letter of the alphabet transforms from its block letter presentation by twisting, turning, and changing its shape to become part of the featured object that represents the letter. The "A" turns upside down with the tip submerged in water, and the bottom half of the letter becomes the boat represented by "Ark." In *Alphabet Under Construction* by Denise Fleming, Mouse is busily "airbrushing the A, buttoning the B," and using words like "dye, quilt, and weld" to construct the alphabet.

Counting Books

Counting books introduce children to a mathematical concept. The most basic counting books clearly show a number along with easily identifiable objects to count, without much background clutter to confuse children. Eric Carle's *1, 2, 3 to the Zoo* is about animals aboard a train on their way to the zoo. Each double-page spread shows a number on the upper left and a boxcar with the correct number of a particular animal on board. The eleventh page is a foldout in which children can see all the animals in their zoo home and the empty train.

Denise Fleming's *Count!* encourages children to count from one to ten vibrantly colored, action-oriented creatures. Then the book continues counting by tens to fifty. Diana Pomeroy's *One Potato: A Counting Book of Potato Prints* features fruits and vegetables from one to ten, then by tens to fifty, and ends with 100 sunflower seeds. All of the art in this book is created with potato prints, and potato-printing instructions for adult readers are included at the end of the book.

Lois Ehlert's *Fish Eyes: A Book You Can Count On* encourages children to count the fish on a page, then add one more by counting the narrator fish. The illustrations have cutout eyes for children to count. *Ten Black Dots,* by Donald Crews, shows dots placed in a child's world—"2/Two dots can make the eyes of a fox" or "5/Five dots can make buttons on a coat." The solid black dots are easy to find and count on all the backgrounds.

Books like Eric Carle's *The Very Hungry Caterpillar* offer children an opportunity to count numbers within a story line. Children can count the fruit the caterpillar eats, while listening to the story being read. Inspired by a hole in the road that caused a traffic back-up during its repair, Nikola-Lisa tells the story in *One Hole in the Road.* Dan Yaccarino illustrates the numbers of flagmen, barricades, stoplights, engineers, and hammers needed to fix that hole.

Wordless Books

The pictures tell everything in wordless books, and it is an artistic feat to make the stories intriguing, understandable, and satisfying. The text resides in the mind of the reader, who must interpret the pictures to understand the story. Wordless books give children the opportunity to be flexible in their interpretation of a story: They can discuss possibilities for the text, look for clues in the illustrations, and practice storytelling. Wordless books have been popular for years; Pat Hutchins's *Changes, Changes* remains, after nearly forty years, one of the best wordless picture books. The characters and setting are established with images made from wood blocks. The story line of two wooden figures resourcefully creating objects to fit varying dilemmas is action packed, and the theme is easily grasped, yet thought-provoking.

Peter Spier created numerous wordless books. In *Rain,* the story opens on the endpapers as a brother and sister play outside in the sun. An approaching dark cloud brings a sudden rainstorm, and the children don rain gear so that they can delight in the changes that rain brings. Spier alters the pace—from a single picture taking up the entire double spread to a series of ten smaller pictures—to create a sequence that moves the story along. Emily Arnold McCully's *Picnic* tells the story of a mouse family whose picnic is interrupted when they

Teaching Idea 3.1

Observing Details in Wordless Books

The pictures in wordless books are often full of detailed information, presented in a holistic, intricately woven artistic style. To hone children's visual observation skills, have them find as much pictorial information as they can in a variety of wordless books. In *Animalia*, children can look for items beginning with the featured alphabet letter; in *Anno's U.S.A.*, older children can look for pictures of cultural artifacts, historical events, famous people, and the like. In wordless books that tell a story, children can look for ways in which the details of the illustration add to the main story line.

realize that one child is missing. They drive back along the bumpy road and then continue their picnic once they have been reunited with the mouse who had gotten bumped out of the truck.

David Wiesner's *Tuesday* won the Caldecott Medal in 1992. The only text is the notation about time of day on Tuesday. The hilarious exploits of a community of frogs who fly hither and yon on lily pads linger in the reader's visual memory as the many shades of green immerse the reader in the frog world. Another book by Wiesner, *Sector 7,* is seemingly a story told in illustration rather than through words. However, a closer look at the book reveals that much of what is to be interpreted from this presentation is found in the words embedded within the illustrations. Readers discover what happens at Sector 7—creating and dispatching clouds according to schedule, waiting for other clouds to return to the station—through a double spread in which words on the departures and arrivals board as well as signs for "Waiting Room" and "Assignment Station" clue them in.

Sisters Jacqueline Preiss Weitzman and Robin Preiss Glasser teamed up to create *You Can't Take a Balloon into The Metropolitan Museum.* Careful observers will note that there are parallel stories within this book: the one that depicts the little girl and her grandmother observing the art in the museum and the one that depicts the city life outside the museum as the balloon passes scenes that parallel what is being seen in the museum. The question for readers to ponder is "Does art reflect life, or does life reflect art?"

Wordless storybooks such as these offer children many opportunities to imagine what the text could be. Note, however, that not all wordless books contain stories. Some wordless books are simply a themed set of pictures.

Picture Books with Minimal Text

Books with minimal text are related to the category to wordless books. The story is told predominantly through the illustrations, as in wordless books, but a few words are strategically included. In some cases, those few words are critical to the story; in other cases, they amplify the story, but are not critical to its success. In Peggy Rathmann's *Good Night, Gorilla,* the zookeeper walks from cage to cage wishing the animals good night, oblivious to the fact that the gorilla has taken his keys and is letting each animal out. The animals follow the zookeeper home and into the bedroom, where his wife discovers the animals. She then leads them back to the zoo. The only text is the repeated refrain, "Good night _____." This story would work even without the text, because the humor is obvious in the illustrations alone. Chris Raschka's *Yo! Yes?* shows two boys encountering each other and using minimal dialogue to communicate: "Yo!" exclaims the first, and the second responds, "Yes?" With continued one- and two-word exclamations, utterances, and questions, one tries to strike up a friendship and the other considers the possibility. Although the text is minimal, it is critical to the story. In addition to the words used, the text size, color, and use of punctuation marks add to the fullness of the story. In David Shannon's *No, David!,* mother is always having to tell her rambunctious son, "No, David, no!" "No! No! No!" "I said no, David!" The other lines in the book are all cautionary commands—that is, all except the last line of the story.

Molly Bang's story of Sophie's anger at being required to share her toy with her sister is expressed precisely in the minimal text that accompanies the expressive illustrations in *When Sophie Gets Angry—Really, Really Angry.* Her explosive anger is vividly portrayed in the illustrations, and the accompanying text endorses the emotion. *Sometimes I'm Bombaloo* offers an interesting emotional comparison to this book but with more text.

In Jane Simmons's *Come Along, Daisy!*, Mama Duck urges her duckling to keep up, but Daisy is distracted playing and gets separated from her mother. Although there is more than minimal text in this book, it is quite simple and the story can be understood just by viewing the illustrations, which show Daisy happily in the midst of the pond while playing and then starkly alone when she realizes that her mother is no longer in sight.

Emotions are clearly expressed through the art even with minimal text, and the plot is also clear in books such as Mélanie Watts' *Scaredy Squirrel*, in which an ever-timid squirrel who keeps an emergency kit and never leaves his own tree is forced to leap into action and discovers that he is a flying squirrel. Likewise, Jeremy Tankard's *Grumpy Bird* shows a very grumpy bird's change of mood as his friends play along with him in follow-the-leader, even flying off at the end with him.

Beginning Readers' Books

Children need books they can read independently as they practice their emerging reading abilities. Some books are more likely to be a success with beginning readers because of their predictable format. Other books are more likely to be accessible to beginning readers because of their controlled vocabulary.

Predictable Books

Predictable books have highly structured or repetitive texts that are easy for fledgling readers to read independently. For children, being able to predict what will happen serves as a motivation to read and provides great satisfaction. Predictable books often use rhythms and rhymes or simple story structures to make it easy for the young reader to perceive the pattern of the text and use it to guess upcoming words. Such factors encourage emerging readers to take risks—and the reward is being in on what is happening.

As you will see in Chapter 7 on "Traditional Literature," rhythms and rhymes and story structure are what helped people recite songs, poems, and folktales from memory before literacy was widespread. Predictable books also use these devices from oral language to support beginning readers. Predictable books have been available for many years. Some, like Marjorie Flack's *Ask Mr. Bear* and Charles Shaw's *It Looked Like Spilt Milk,* have become classics. However, since the 1980s, there has been a tremendous increase in the availability of predictable books, largely because of the role these books play in beginning reading instruction in schools.

A pioneer writer in this format is children's author and educator Bill Martin, Jr. Over three decades ago, Martin set out to write a series of books that would be easy for beginners to read. Of these Instant Readers, perhaps the best known is *Brown Bear, Brown Bear, What Do You See?* On one page, the text says, "Brown Bear, Brown Bear, what do you see?" The next page reads, "I see a yellow duck looking at me," and on that page readers find a yellow duck created by illustrator Eric Carle. The language pattern and illustrations work together so nicely that countless beginning readers have been able to recite/read the book after a brief introduction.

Uri Shulevitz's *One Monday Morning* uses a cumulative pattern and supportive illustrations to enumerate the important people who come to visit the young narrator in his urban apartment. *The Napping House,* by Audrey and Don Wood, repeats the phrase "In a napping house, where everyone is sleeping" and builds a story by adding a new sleepy character on each page—along with an array of interesting words about sleeping, such as "dozing," "napping," and "snoring."

Although not all books that are enlarged are predictable books, many of the "big books" used for beginning reading instruction are three-foot-high versions of predictable books. Children can watch as the teacher points to the words as they are read. The numerous instructional possibilities that arise from allowing children to see the text make big books especially popular for shared reading in primary classrooms (Holdaway, 1979). Teachers of young children often use big books in front of a class or small group as students read in unison. Big books that are not predictable books are used in library story times or classroom read-aloud sessions. The advantage of big books in these situations is that the illustrations are large enough for all the children to see.

Easy Readers

Easy readers are often among the first books that children read independently. Although they are not strictly picture storybooks as described later in this chapter, they have a formula that

Read the interview where James Howe discusses his Pinky and Rex and his Bunnicula books by going to the Conversations section of Chapter 3 in the MyEducationKit for your book.

includes a generous amount of illustration throughout the book. They typically have some kind of controlled vocabulary; that is, the number of words, the types of words, and the sentence structure and length are determined by a formula that estimates the relative reading level of a book. The controlled vocabulary can result in poor writing, and some easy reader books are reminiscent of basal readers of the past. However, many easy readers combine literary merit with an opportunity for beginning readers to read on their own successfully. Roser, Martinez, McDonnold and Fuhrken (2004) use the term "beginning chapter books" to describe books whose text is divided into chapters and whose readability is at approximately the first-, second-, or third-grade level. These books have pictorial support and typically have a problem-centered plot structure. Roser and colleagues also found that children make their book choices predominantly because they like the series; fortunately, many of these beginning chapter books have been written in series.

One of the most innovative and famous writers of easy reader books was Dr. Seuss (a pseudonym for Theodor Seuss Geisel). In the 1930s, Dr. Seuss wrote such children's books as *The Five Hundred Hats of Bartholomew Cubbins* and *And to Think That I Saw It on Mulberry Street.* In 1957, convinced that beginning readers were being given uninteresting stories stifled by controlled vocabulary in basal readers of the time, Dr. Seuss changed the outlook on easy reader books when he published *The Cat in the Hat.* With a limited number of words, he tells the story of a cat whose outlandish behavior stuns two well-behaved children who have been left alone in their house for a short while. Dr. Seuss went on to delight generations of beginning readers with more outrageous characters and out-of-the-ordinary events told in easy-reading verse in *Hop on Pop* and *Green Eggs and Ham,* among others. His impact in the field of beginning readers is so significant that the American Library Association has named the (Theodor Seuss) Geisel award in his honor.

Since then, many easy readers have been written. *Henry and Mudge: The First Book of Their Adventures,* by Cynthia Rylant, is the first of a series of easy readers by this award-winning author. The text uses limited vocabulary, yet has the qualities of poetry, as this excerpt about Mudge the dog shows:

> He couldn't smell Henry.
> He couldn't smell
> his front porch.
> He couldn't smell
> the street he lived on.
> Mudge looked all around
> and didn't see anything
> or anyone
> he knew.

The friendly crayon line drawings by Sucie Stevenson enliven the text and encourage fledgling readers by giving visual clues to what the words must be.

Arnold Lobel is another writer who has written brilliantly within the constraints of limited numbers of words and simple sentence structures. In 1971, his *Frog and Toad Are Friends* was named a Caldecott Honor Book for its illustrations. And *Frog and Toad Together* was a 1973 Newbery Honor Book for its text.

James Marshall's wit and creativity are evident in his many humorous easy-reading books. His text and illustrations are seemingly simple, yet the character and plot development is rich and complete. In *Three by the Sea* (written under the pseudonym Edward Marshall), readers meet Lolly, Spider, and Sam, who are having a picnic at the beach. Children are propelled to continue reading as they anticipate what will happen when a rat buys a cat to be his friend or when a monster comes out of the sea and finds three children on a beach. Young readers are equally motivated to read about Fox attempting to make money at various jobs so that he can buy a new bike in *Fox on the Job.*

Mo Willems creates the Elephant and Piggie books in which the two humorously interact through engaging and entertaining dialogue, even on such seemingly mundane subjects as the weather. Piggie considers the weather and is undecided about playing outside as Gerald continuously wonders, *Are You Ready to Play Outside?*

Denys Cazet's *Minnie and Moo Go Dancing* and *Minnie and Moo Go to the Moon* are humorous short stories that describe the antics of two cows. When they go dancing, they are horrified at the thought that the hamburgers served as refreshments are made from cows—Could they be former friends? Watercolor illustrations maintain the lighthearted appeal of these humorous stories.

Betsy Byars's *My Brother, Ant* offers beginning readers a chance to practice reading text that is humorous in the way it portrays two brothers and their relationship. Likewise, Laura Kvasnosky's *Zelda and Ivy* series offers stories of two sisters (portrayed as foxes). Both series are likely to appeal to child readers in that they portray sibling relationships at the age level of the readers.

Some easy readers are more advanced, to meet the needs of children's developing reading ability. Although these "transitional chapter books" (Roser, Martinez, McDonnold & Fuhrken, 2004) are longer and include more complex words, the qualities that make easy readers readable are still present. Tomie dePaola's Newbery Honor Book *26 Fairmount Avenue* is the beginning of a series of easy reader chapter books that are based on his life. dePaola maintains a child's voice as he describes the events of his childhood. The stories continue in *Here We All Are* and *On My Own.* The engaging text is likely to make readers feel that they are hearing a friend relate the events of his daily life. Other more complex easy readers include the *Mr. Putter and Tabby* series by Cynthia Rylant and the *Pinky and Rex* series by James Howe. Mother-daughter team Monika Bang-Campbell and Molly Bang created *Little Rat Sets Sail,* in which Little Rat's parents sign her up for sailing lessons so she can learn to overcome her fear of water. Detailed information of sailboats is presented through visual diagrams; sailing jargon is contextualized so it is easy to understand; and the division into chapters makes this book an appealing step into early chapter books.

Some books "play" with the use of text and illustration in a way that directly gets at the close examination of words. In *One Boy*, Seeger uses a clever format of covering most of the previous page's text, but leaving open a "mask" as a hole, allowing readers to see that part of each second set of lines is taken from words in the first line. For example, the book begins, "One boy, all alone" with the "one" showing through the box. The closing, "All done" allows adults to convey to beginning readers the notion of words that look alike but don't sound alike.

Books like these fill a vital need. Many preschoolers have grown accustomed to having their parents and teachers read fascinating and eloquent books to them, and when children reach school age, we hope parents and teachers will continue to read to them, for it will take much time and hard practice before they will be able to read such books for themselves. Easy readers, though, can be interesting and pithy books in highly readable language. It can be difficult to maintain quality in a format in which simplicity is paramount, but the continued efforts of such authors as Tomie dePaola, Laura Seeger, and Mo Willems are rewarded when young readers can enjoy interesting content in well-crafted language.

Picture Storybooks

There are more picture storybooks than any other type of picture book. As defined earlier, a picture storybook is one in which the text and the illustrations work together to amplify each other; in other words, part of the story is told through the illustrations and part is told through the text. Text and illustrations do not merely reflect each other; rather, combined, they tell a story that goes beyond what each one tells alone. The text of picture storybooks is best when it is rich in language use. Examples of rich language can be found in books by William Steig, Kevin Henkes, or Patricia Polacco, as well as many others. One sure way to tell whether a book has rich language use is if we particularly enjoy reading it aloud for its rich language and if children perceive the book as "coming alive" when listening.

Visual Literacy

Since the days of cave paintings, communicating through visual images has been important, and it is an ability that everyone must continuously develop. Because most people can see relatively well, the need to develop the ability to comprehend visual images has not been emphasized as much as that of comprehending text. Yet children are constantly being asked to rely on their visual comprehension skills, whether it is overtly stated or merely implied. Just as there are components of written communication that readers must know how to interpret, there are also parallel components of visual communication that must be interpreted. Teachers who directly address these important elements as they work with children are able to incorporate the teaching and scaffolding children need as they learn and grow in their visual literacy. It could begin as easily as talking about a book such as *Duck! Rabbit!,* in which a central figure's drawn head is interpreted as a duck by one voice, and as a rabbit by the other.

In this section, we present an overview of some of the major artistic elements of design; later, we explore them in more detail and apply them to comprehending the illustrations in picture books in the section "How Picture Storybooks Work." Elements that apply to visual literacy in informational books are examined in Chapter 11.

Elements of Design

Artists rely on various elements of design to communicate with their audience. When artwork is done well, the reader can enjoy the aesthetics of the illustrations and appreciate the emotions conveyed through the manipulation of artistic elements. The elements of design are line, shape, color, light, and texture. The combination of line, shape, color, light, and texture is called *composition*.

Let's examine one book in some depth and look at the use of these elements. (See color plate ILL. 11, 12, and 13.) In *The Paperboy,* Dav Pilkey presents the story of a paperboy's morning. As the story begins, the paperboy is asleep in his bed; readers see him rising, eating breakfast, folding papers, delivering on his route, returning home, and getting back into bed for some "time for dreaming." Throughout all of this, he is accompanied by his dog.

Line

Lines can be thin and light or heavy and bold; they can be straight, jagged, or curved. Line is used effectively in *The Paperboy* to create the rolling shapes of the hills in the background, which give a sense of long distances. Line also conveys the sense of fast movement when the paperboy and his dog are returning home: The dog's tail is horizontal, and the paperboy's empty bag is flying behind him.

Shape

Shape is created when spaces are contained by a combination of lines. The triangular roof, the side-by-side arrangement of the rectangular doors in the hallway, the two square windows in the kitchen, and the big rectangular work table in the garage all combine with the center gutter of the book to give the house in *The Paperboy* a symmetrical feel—one that creates a sense of solid security in the paperboy's home. In the opening double-page spread, the predictable shapes of the houses give a sense of a solid community life. The rolling shapes of the land separate the houses and give a sense of distance between them, even though they are painted close together on the page. The sense of distance and spaciousness leads the reader to think that this is more a rural area than an urban one.

Color

Color can range over the full spectrum, or it can be limited to a defined range—for example, black and white and the various shades of gray in between that characterize what "value" means. One instance of dramatic use of color in *The Paperboy* is the single beam of the yellow headlight from the paperboy's bicycle, seen against the dark colors of the neighborhood before dawn.

Light

Pilkey uses light to show the time of day in **The Paperboy.** When the lamp beside the boy's bed is turned on, his room lights up, but it is dark outside. Only a nightlight gives light in the hallway when the paperboy is getting up in the morning. By the time he returns from his route, though, light is peeking from underneath his parents' door, and the light in his sister's room can be seen beyond the doorway.

Texture

Texture is the illusion of a tactile surface created in an illustration. In **The Paperboy,** texture in the wood boards of the ceiling and floor is created through the use of lines and shading. The shading of the trees also contributes texture.

Technology in Practice 3.1
Digitized Picture Books

Find a website that has picture books online, for example Tumble Books (www.tumblebooks.com) or One More Story (www.onemorestory.com) (they have a trial book for free, or your public library website may give you access through your library card). Once you are familiar with the numerous ways in which readers can interact with digitized books, weigh the pros and cons of each type of interaction. Consider which outcomes are educational and which ones focus on entertainment or motivation. Decide how you will introduce such books to your students, what parameters you will set, and how you will promote the most positive features of digitized picture books. Introduce the digitized book to students along with the traditional book version and engage students in discussions of what each type of "reading experience" has to offer.

Appreciating the Artistic Craft of the Picture Book

The illustrations in picture books for children have become increasingly sophisticated over the years as the picture book has developed as a format. In addition, changes in printing technology have made it possible to reproduce a much greater range of artwork. This section focuses on two aspects of art in picture books: artistic media and artistic style.

Artistic Media

The artists who create picture books rely on a number of media to express their visions of the stories. Some illustrators use a "signature" medium almost exclusively; others select different media depending on how they want to express their views of the particular story. The examples in this section vary from informational books to various genres of fiction and are not necessarily picture storybooks.

Painting: Watercolor, Gouache, Oil, and Other Paints

More children's books are illustrated with watercolor than with any other medium. Watercolors allow illustrators to convey many emotions. Watercolor paintings can be solidly intense or watery and fluid-looking, depending on the amount of water used. Gouache is a type of watercolor paint that contains an added white powder to create a more opaque finished product. Artists who desire an opaque look may also use acrylic paints or oil paints.

Allen Say is a noted illustrator who works in watercolor. In his Caldecott-winning book **Grandfather's Journey**, Say tells the story of how his grandfather left Japan and made the United States his home. When the grandfather visited Japan years later, World War II prohibited him from returning to the United States. Now his grandson has followed in his path and says, "The funny thing is, the moment I am in one country, I am homesick for the other." The natural beauty of each country is depicted in watercolor views of ocean, mountains, and greenery. The prequel to this story is Say's **Tree of Cranes.**

Frané Lessac uses gouache to create vividly colorful images of the Caribbean Islands in many books, such as **The Chalk Doll** by Charlotte Pomerantz, in which a mother reminisces about her childhood in Jamaica. In **Caribbean Alphabet,** she uses the alphabet to list unique qualities of the islands—for example, breadfruit, hibiscus, reggae, and steel bands. In Susan Guevara's illustrations in acrylic paint on scratchboard for Gary Soto's **Chato and**

Read the interview where Susan Guevara discusses how she creates illustrations by going to the Conversations section of Chapter 3 in the MyEducationKit for your book.

Listen to Susan Guevara discuss what inspires her as an artist by going to the Conversations section of Chapter 3 in the MyEducationKit for your book.

the Party Animals, readers see the lines that mark the movement of the paintbrush. These marks, and the heavy use of color, add to the vibrancy and energy of the book.

Thomas Locker characteristically uses oil paintings that give viewers a sense of wide landscapes, such as those in Lenny Hort's *The Boy Who Held Back the Sea.* Paul Zelinsky's *Rumpelstiltskin* is also rendered in oil paint, an appropriate medium to complement the medieval setting. Floyd Cooper employs a variation on oil painting in which he applies a very thin layer of paint to a surface and, when it dries, creates areas of light by using an eraser; he then adds color at the end. He used this technique to create the illustrations in *I Have Heard of a Land* by Joyce Carol Thomas, as well as in all of his other works.

Some illustrators paint on surfaces other than paper. Baba Wagué Diakité's *The Hatseller and the Monkeys,* a West African story about monkeys who steal hats from a hatseller while he naps, is painted on ceramic tiles. Paul Zelinsky's illustrations in the Caldecott Honor Book *Swamp Angel* by Anne Isaacs were painted on wood veneers.

Pencil Drawing

Stephen Gammell uses pencils to convey a range of emotions, from the happy, nostalgic feel of Karen Ackerman's *Song and Dance Man* to the sinister, gory tone of Alvin Schwartz's *Scary Stories* series. Pencils can be used to create strong lines, shaded areas, smudged shadows, and fine details. Readers sense the warmth of relationships in various books depicting family events, illustrated by Gammell with colored pencils. For instance, in *Song and Dance Man,* pastel hues against the white background give a soft glow to the attic in which the grandfather and his grandchildren share a moment from the past, as the grandfather dances and reminisces about the time when he was a song and dance man. Few areas are solidly shaded; rather, visible lines help guide the reader's eyes to areas of focus and give dimension to objects. Gammell's work in *Scary Stories to Tell in the Dark,* by Alvin Schwartz, seems a far cry from *Song and Dance Man,* even though both are pencil illustrations. In the *Scary Stories* book, the black-and-white images have unfinished lines, supporting the sense of the haunted as being unpredictably present and only partially visible. Even without color, we can clearly visualize the blood dripping. The jagged lines create feelings of horror. In these two examples, Gammell shows the range of artistic expression possible with one medium.

Paper Crafts: Collage, Papermaking, Cut Paper

Various forms of paper crafts are used by illustrators of children's books. The most commonly used form is collage, in which, traditionally, various types of paper are cut or torn and pieced together onto a background to create a picture, as in the art of Ezra Jack Keats, Eric Carle, and Leo Lionni. The papers may be of varying weights and colors—anything from giftwrap to wallpaper to handmade paper. To create the art for *Saint Valentine,* Robert Sabuda cut marbleized and handmade paper into tiny squares and created a mosaic for each illustration, using over a thousand paper bits for each full-page illustration. To create the art for *Wings,* Christopher Myers used magazine pictures, paper of varying types, and even paper that presumably comes from an envelope on which the U.S. Post Office had printed the coding for mail. Holly Meade was inspired by Thai art forms to create the collage work in *Hush!,* by Minfong Ho, a lullaby story set in Thailand. Steve Jenkins and wife Robin Page team up to create various books of cut and torn-paper collage. In *Move!,* animal motions—such as swing, slither, and slide—are effectively depicted.

Australian author/illustrator Jeannie Baker's books such as *Where the Forest Meets the Sea* are focused on the theme of taking care of the environment for future generations. Appropriately, she creates her illustrations with relief collages of amazing details, using natural materials like stone, plaster from old walls, grass, leaves, cracked paint, earth, knitted wool, natural vegetation, hair. She has learned how to preserve and add permanent color to natural plants in order to combine the naturalness in texture while offering a wider range of color with which to illustrate.

British author/illustrator Lauren Child has created many books in collage media. She draws the characters and collages them onto backgrounds that are created with paper, fabric, photographs, and other drawn materials. The seeming simplicity of the way she depicts her characters has an informality and childlike appeal. These illustrations match her storytelling style well. Her books have a strong child perspective and are humorously presented. In *Who's Afraid of the Big, Bad Book?*, Child introduces a boy who has mischievously drawn on, cut out, and mistreated his book of fairy tales. One day, he falls into his book and encounters the characters whose lives he has tampered with. Upon his return to the real world, he works to erase the princess's mustache, return the prince he had cut out for his Mother's Day card, and otherwise correct the damages he had previously inflicted on the lives of his storybook characters.

Illustrator Denise Fleming creates vibrant illustrations by making a sheet of handmade paper for each illustration. She makes a pulp out of cotton rag fiber and water, adds color, and spreads the pulp out on a framed wire screen to create a background. The framed screen allows the excess water to drip out. Using plastic squeeze bottles filled with colored pulp, she pours shapes on the background or fills in her hand-cut stencils. For *Barnyard Banter,* she added various items: hair from her horse's mane created interesting dimensions and textures; pieces of burlap potato sacks became part of a wire pen for peacocks; and coffee grounds helped to create the image of soil. The completed piece is dried through a special process. Fleming's book *In the Small, Small Pond* was named a Caldecott Honor Book. The illustrations show the creatures of a small pond in their daily environment. Fleming captures their movements and activities with alliterative and rhyming phrases—for example, "lash, lunge, herons plunge" and "sweep, swoop, swallows scoop."

David Wisniewski used cut paper to create the illustrations for his 1997 Caldecott Medal winner, *The Golem,* as well as for his other books. He uses an X-Acto knife to cut intricate designs and layers pieces to achieve a three-dimensional effect. Robert Sabuda created the art for *The Paper Dragon,* by Marguerite W. Davol, in the style of Chinese paper-cut art, by making precise and detailed cuts in tissue paper he painted. Each illustration is three pages long; the double spreads have a page that folds out, thereby creating a scroll-like effect.

Three-Dimensional Art

As book production technology advanced, the possibilities of artistic media became much less limited. Just about anything of any size can now be photographed, copied, or digitally manipulated for reproduction in a picture book. Thus, in recent times, there has been an increase in the use of three-dimensional art.

Many illustrators do not limit themselves to paper when creating collages, but employ a wide range of materials, including three-dimensional objects. For his 1995 Caldecott-winning book *Smoky Night,* written by Eve Bunting, David Diaz used matches, plastic bags, hangers, cereal, bubble wrap, and shoe soles, in addition to a variety of papers, to create collage backgrounds to frame his acrylic paintings and the text in this book depicting the 1992 Los Angeles riots. Lois Ehlert's *Snowballs* shows a family of snowpeople—complete with dog and cat—created with birdseed, a knit hat, seashells, a compass, a cinnamon stick, a pinecone, luggage claim checks, plastic forks, and toy fish, among other things. In another collage book, *Red Leaf, Yellow Leaf,* about a sugar maple tree, Ehlert used a kite, twine, ribbon, birdseed, burlap, twigs, and roots to create the illustrations.

In Joan Steiner's *Look-Alikes,* the double spreads look, at first glance, like scenes such as a train station, a playground, or a street. Closer inspection reveals that the picture is made entirely by using real objects to create a world of miniature scale; cinnamon sticks serve as logs, and a razor blade is converted into a vacuum cleaner. Her book for younger children is entitled *Look-Alikes Jr.: Find More Than 700 Hidden Everyday Objects*.

Scratchboard

Brian Pinkney is known for using scratchboard as his signature medium. Scratchboard pictures are created by using sharp instruments to scratch away the top surface of a board, leaving precise lines on the surface. Pinkney believes that his passion for carving and painting come together in scratchboard: He both carves the pictures and paints them when creating his book illustrations. For Robert D. San Souci's *Sukey and the Mermaid,* the story of how Sukey's luck changes when she meets a black mermaid, Pinkney created a black-and-white scratchboard. A photographic technique made it possible for him to add color to a print of the original scratchboard piece to produce the finished product. He used a similar technique

Top Shelf 3.2

Picture Books that Raise Issues of Social Justice

Smoky Night by Eve Bunting. Illustrated by David Diaz.

Baseball Saved Us by Ken Mochizuki. Illustrated by Dom Lee.

Old Henry by Joan Blos. Illustrated by Stephen Gammell.

The Composition by Antonio Skarmeta. Illustrated by Alfonso Ruano.

Freedom Summer by Deborah Wiles. Illustrated by Jerome Lagarrigue.

to illustrate *Duke Ellington: The Piano Prince and His Orchestra,* by Andrea Davis Pinkney, but with a vivid use of colors to give a more painted effect.

Beth Krommes won the Caldecott Award for her scratchboard illustrations in *The House in the Night*. In it, she effectively created a world at nighttime in black and white scratchboard with golden highlights to show moonlight, stars, and other featured spaces.

Printmaking

Printmaking was the original method by which books for children were illustrated. Originals have been made on stone, metal, wood, sponge, potato, and a range of materials. Ink is added to the raised surface, pressed against a sheet of paper, and a reverse image appears on the paper.

Woodcut illustrations were particularly common in books of the past, but are still used today. Marcia Brown's *Once a Mouse,* rendered in woodcut, was awarded the 1962 Caldecott Medal. Ed Emberley used woodcuts to illustrate Barbara Emberley's *Drummer Hoff,* which won a Caldecott Medal in 1968. Gail E. Haley's *A Story, a Story,* the 1971 Caldecott winner, has illustrations carved on wood blocks. Keizaburo Tejima gives readers a sense of connection to the natural world through his woodcuts in *Swan Sky,* which tells the story of the migration of swans. One year, a swan, ill and unable to go to the summer home, is left behind by her family. The woodcut illustrations fully use the natural effect of the wood grain to illustrate the ripples in the lake, the reflections of the mountains, and the feathers of the swans. Barry Moser used a synthetic wood engraving medium to create the illustrations for Madeline Moser's *Ever Heard of an Aardwolf?* The images were printed in black and white, laser-scanned and enlarged, then hand-colored with watercolors.

Margaret Chodos-Irvine used a variety of print-making techniques, including linoleum blocks, to create her Caldecott Honor-winning book, *Ella Sarah Gets Dressed*. Ella Sarah is a little girl who asserts her independence by choosing the clothes she wants to wear. She announces, "I want to wear my pink polka-dot pants, my dress with orange-and-green flowers, my purple-and-blue striped socks, my yellow shoes, and my red hat." Chodos-Irvine, whose own daughter Ella Sarah served as the inspiration for the book, employs several different print-making methods to visually tell this story.

Photography

Several children's book illustrators use photography to create visual images. Tana Hoban and Bruce McMillan have created many books that use photographs to communicate basic concepts to young children. In *Shapes, Shapes, Shapes,* Hoban's photographs of scenes and objects that children see in their everyday environment exemplify the concepts of various shapes. In McMillan's *Counting Wildflowers,* readers are presented with a numeral, the number word, and a photograph of the corresponding number of wildflowers. George Ancona relies on photographs in books such as *Carnaval* to lend an air of immediacy to stories focused on particular groups of people and their celebration. Walter Dean Myers collected old photographs for *Brown Angels: An Album of Pictures and Verse* and for *Glorious Angels: A Celebration of Children.* The photographs provided the impetus for poetry; he created the poetry while imagining the lives of the people the photographs portrayed. In all of the books just described, the illustrator is the photographer, and photography itself is the art form. Photography has also been used to capture images of original three-dimensional art; in such cases, photography serves as the vehicle for exhibiting the original art. One example is the cut-paper art that David Wiesnewski creates for his books and then has photographed by a professional. The photographer gets name credit for his role in bringing the original images to the book form, but it is Wiesnewski who is considered the illustrator.

Computer-Generated Art

Many newcomers to the field of book illustrating are generating art on the computer, along with veteran illustrators who are trying this new medium. J. Otto Siebold illustrated the *Mr. Lunch* books entirely with computer-generated art. Nina Crews created *You Are Here* by taking original photographs and manipulating them digitally on the computer to create a collage. In the book, two sisters embark on a magical journey, shrinking small enough to ride a toy airplane throughout their dining room. The computer allowed Crews to adjust the proportions of the objects she had photographed so that readers could see how the sisters could ride a toy airplane and call a cat a "monster." Veteran illustrators Don Wood and Audrey Wood gave up their paintbrushes and turned completely to their computers to create drawings for their books since 1996 when they began creating digital illustration by collaborating with their son, Bruce Wood. Janet Stevens relies on a computer to embellish her art in *Cook-a-Doodle-Doo!,* a humorous twist on the "Little Red Hen" story. Along the sidebars that border the main story, cooking tips are included. Her detailed explanation of how she creates her books can be found at her website. Jane Wattenberg's *Henny-Penny* was created by using Adobe Photoshop. Wattenberg photographed her own fowls and then manipulated the images on the computer to create her photo-compositions. David Diaz also used Adobe Photoshop to create his illustrations in *The Pot that Juan Built.* Some, like South African illustrator Niki Daley, use the computer only in the planning stages of their work. He uses a stylus and pad to draft his preliminary sketches and finds the ability to easily manipulate the proportions and positions (he says, without all that "rubbing and erasing") to be helpful in planning his final artwork, which he completes in watercolor.

Mixed Media

Illustrators often combine different media in creating their work. Many illustrators combine pen and ink with watercolor washes. Patricia Polacco uses pencil to create initial sketches and then finishes them with watercolors, but the original pencil markings are often visible as part of the final product. Eric Carle paints on his tissue papers and then pencils in details on his collages. Ruth Heller combined a large number of media—magic markers, paints, colored pencils, and others. In his 2000 Caldecott-winning book, *Joseph Had a Little Overcoat,* Simms Taback used watercolor, gouache, pencil, ink, and collages—of photographs of people, handmade paper, and pictures of textured items like braided rugs and sweaters. For Arnold Adoff's *Love Letters,* Lisa Desimini used photographs, sculptured models, oil paint, collages of three-dimensional objects, and computer graphics. Lauren Child uses drawing, coloring with various mediums, and collaging to create her final artwork. Increasingly often, we see digital media as part of "mixed media" as artists such as Jeremy Tankard use a combination of photography, paints, and digital media to create his finished images in *Grumpy Bird*. Similarly, *Knuffle Bunny* has photographs that have been digitally included (and enhanced / cleaned up!) that Mo Willems uses as background, but he paints the characters and the focal point of the story.

Artistic Style

The artistic style used by the illustrator conveys much of the aesthetic impact on the reader/ viewer's understanding as well as his or her emotional engagement and response. When we refer to *style,* we mean the impression created by the combined effect of visual elements discussed previously: line, shape, color, light, and texture. Style is important in conveying the mood of the story and in contextualizing the setting, as well as in defining characters. In well-crafted picture books, the style amplifies the text and works in harmony with it. The styles that are most frequently found in picture books for children are realism, impressionism, expressionism, cartoon, folk art, naïve art, surrealism, abstract art, romanticism, and postmodernism. It is important to remember that just as texts can cross genres and include elements of multiple genres, illustrations can have elements of more than one style. Some artists have created a personal style that is so distinct that their work is instantly recognizable: The illustrations of Tomie dePaola, Lois Ehlert, and Gerald McDermott remain consistent throughout the body of their work. Others, like David Shannon or Ed Young, tend to vary their styles to match each book.

Teaching Idea 3.3

Interpreting the Story as Told through Illustration

Select some books that have a strong story line that can be interpreted through the illustrations. Have children examine the illustrations without reading the text and ask them to tell the story as they see it. Some teachers call this prereading strategy of predicting the text by previewing the illustrations a "picture walk." Then read the text, and discuss how the story is similar to or different from the story they interpreted through illustration alone. Go back through the illustrations and check whether they see things differently or find additional ways of interpreting the story after hearing the text.

Realism

Perhaps the most commonly used style in illustrated books for children, realism presents the world as realistically as possible. Artists do research to make their work as accurately representative as possible, especially in depicting historical settings or culturally specific ones. Allen Say's images of Japan and of Asians in America have a near-photographic quality to them. In *Grandfather's Journey,* the characters are represented as if in real life, including the details of the setting of each illustration. Many pages have a portrait-like quality to them.

Impressionism

The style of Impressionism began with a group of painters who wanted to work in less restrictive ways than realism permitted, desiring to capture the moment in which they painted. Often working with looser interpretations and with less defined lines than realism, these artists did not labor over details as long as the overall effect—the impression—worked. An example of impressionism can be found in the work of Jerry Pinkney. In his interpretation of *The Ugly Duckling,* more emphasis is placed on the interplay of light and color—particularly on the endpapers where the images depict the ducks swimming and how they appear above/below waterlines—rather than near-exact representations of details such as all of the duck feathers. Impressionism works particularly well in representing this story, as the viewer interprets the spontaneity of living creatures in motion.

Expressionism

In expressionistic art, emotions are shown in the ways in which the artist portrays different aspects of the illustration to communicate feelings or mood. Things may be slightly out of proportion or given emphasis through devices that include placement or more detail of certain elements. The artist draws the attention of the viewer through such devices. In David Shannon's work in *Encounter,* he focuses the viewer's attention on specific elements that guide the reader on an emotional path through the book.

Cartoon

Many children find cartoon art appealing for its liveliness and playfulness, often expressing humor and fast-paced action along with rapidly changing moods. Line is used to effectively portray emotion, and proportions are sometimes exaggerated to emphasize story elements. Kevin Henkes masterfully pairs cartoon art with his text to tell a complete story. Readers will quickly realize how Henkes manipulates line to show readers the emotions of characters in the story. In *Lilly's Purple Plastic Purse,* Lilly's emotions change from disappointment to fury to sadness, sometimes by mere changes in eyebrows and head position. He also uses proportion to show how Lilly feels about the earlier attitude she displayed toward her teacher when she discovers a note from him in her purse.

Folk Art

Illustrators rely on folk art to partner with a story that is steeped in heritage—one that projects generations of traditions and cultural roots being passed down. Often, the culture portrayed is isolated from others in time or place so that the motifs, colors, and symbols remain specific and pure, and not influenced by others. Sometimes, there is a primitive quality to folk art. Barbara Cooney's illustrations in *The Ox-Cart Man* by Donald Hall do just that. They clearly set a time and place through both overall impression and details so that viewers understand the setting completely. Details that show what he packs on his wagon (barrel of apples, bag of goose feathers, and cabbages, for example), or big impressions of the life that was led on the farm (carving a new yoke, making flax into linen, and tapping the sugar maple trees) all contribute to assisting readers in understanding the setting.

Naïve Art

Flat, two-dimensional art that has a child-like quality to it is referred to as naïve art. Sometimes, it is self-taught artists who use naïve art; at other times, illustrators employ naïve art style to match the mood of a book's text. Figures are usually depicted from the front, back, or side, but always without a three-dimensional quality. Illustrator Frané Lessac's work can be seen on the cover of our textbook and throughout the book, and is an example of naïve art.

Surrealism

Unreal, unexpected, and sometimes even bizarre elements are part of surrealistic art. The illustrator may manipulate these "never could happen" aspects of the imagination in order to express internal feelings or thoughts; it may represent symbolism for the viewer to ponder, or it may be used to move the action of the story along. Anthony Browne's books are examples of surrealism. Gorillas float in the air, trunks of trees in wooded forests disappear, and humans turn into pigs. Likewise, Chris Van Allsburg's work represents surrealism as ships and trains fly through the air and weather changes unexplainably.

Abstract Art

Images are recognizable, but altered from realism in works of abstract art. Illustrators portray images in ways that create ambience and evoke mood. Chris Raschka's work often employs abstract art. He uses shapes and colors that evoke images and represent feelings. Valdimir Radunsky uses shapes in vaguely representational ways, but they are not accurate representations of objects or human bodies as we know them.

Romanticism

Often used with realism or impressionism, romanticism ignores the blemishes in the world and flourishes the best of what might be. Rich palettes of color are used to enhance the feeling of luxurious extravagance. Traditional tales with "happily ever after" endings are often the candidates for romanticized style. (Kinuko) K. Y. Craft sets her **Cinderella** book in seventeenth-eighteenth century France and employs a romanticized style. Colors almost glitter and glow on the pages, and details like lace, flowers, and billowing fabric softly accentuate all edges so they are flowing and rounded.

Examples of Artistic Style	Title	Illustrator
Realism	Mufaro's Beautiful Daughters	John Steptoe
Impressionism	Mirette on the High Wire	Emily Arnold McCully
Expressionism	Hiroshima no Pika	Toshi Maruki
	Chato's Kitchen (by Gary Soto)	Susan Guevara
Cartoon	Click Clack Moo (by Doreen Cronin)	Betsy Lewin
	Officer Buckle and Gloria	Peggy Rathmann
	Sylvester and the Magic Pebble	William Steig
Folk Art	The Magic Gourd	Baba Wagué Diakité
Naïve Art	A Chair for My Mother	Vera Williams
	Two of Everything	Lily Toy Hong
	Three Cheers for Catherine the Great! (by Cari Best)	Giselle Potter
Surrealism	Tuesday	David Wiesner
	My Name is Yoon (by Helen Recorvits)	Gabi Swiatkowska
	Frida	Ana Juan
Abstract Art	The Maestro Plays (by Bill Martin, Jr.)	Vladimir Radunsky
	The Green Frogs: A Korean Folktale	Yumi Heo
Romanticism	The Tale of the Firebird	Gennady Spirin
Postmodernism	And the Dish Ran Away With the Spoon	Janet Stevens and Susan Stevens Crummel
	Black and White	David Macaulay

Postmodernism

In recent times, illustrators have moved from traditional notions of artwork in picture books to break new ground. McCallum (1996) describes postmodernism as having the following features: "narrative fragmentation and discontinuity, disorder and chaos, code mixing and absurdity." These illustrators have mixed styles, borrowed from others' works, and they push the viewer to make sense of illustrations that are out of traditional bounds. *The Three Pigs* by Wiesner is an example of such a book. This book breaks the rules for how picture books typically develop by having the characters "fly" out of their story on a paper airplane, only to enter other stories of traditional literature that have related characters. Readers are required to bring their knowledge of these stories into play in order to make the transition along with the characters.

How Picture Storybooks Work

When we read a story that moves us deeply, we often speak of how the setting, characters, plot, and other elements of the book contributed to its effect. But if a picture moves us, most of us do not have a set of terms readily available to describe what caused the picture's effect. Picture books afford readers the opportunity to deepen their understanding of visual communication—their visual literacy. Knowing some terms can help teachers and parents talk as knowledgeably about pictures as they do about texts and better appreciate the principles that govern how picture book illustrations communicate meaning. The following elements of visual communication will concern us here:

- Design: book size and shape, book covers and jackets, endpapers, page turns, borders, text layout and typeface, and the number and placement of frames on a page
- Characterization, which refers to the consistent visual identity of the characters
- Perspective, settings, and other repeated phenomena
- Backgrounds
- Color, especially as it relates to mood
- Picture/text relationships—that is, which aspects of the communication are carried by the text and which are conveyed by the pictures and how the pictures and text interact

Ellen Handler Spitz (1999) refers to picture books as relying on accepted conventions of style and design and likens a picture book's spatial use to that of a theatre stage. Taking that analogy further, we believe that a picture book brings together the visual images in a defined space, includes language to combine with those images, and offers viewers a merged experience in which they cannot readily separate the influence of one on the other.

Clearly, much goes into the creation of picture books. Many people besides the author and illustrator are involved in creating the final product. Editors, art directors, designers, and printers all have professional roles. Decisions about the book size, paper type, endpapers, font, and book jacket all contribute to the visual impact of the finished book.

Design

Children's books are printed in multiples of eight pages, and picture books are typically thirty-two pages long. One page is taken up by the title page, a second by the copyright information, and often another by the dedication—leaving the illustrator of most picture books a little less than thirty pages to work with. Within these few pages, the illustrator creates a visual world. By laying out the illustrations in a particular way, the illustrator controls the readers' journey through that world, much as a tour guide leads a group through a city or a landscape. Like a tour guide, the illustrator can move readers quickly from place to place and happening to happening or cause readers to pause in one spot and let impressions settle in.

Book Size and Shape

The size and shape of a book has impact both in conveying content information and in eliciting the reader/viewer's emotional and aesthetic response. Tall books like Jon Agee's *Milo's Hat Trick* allow a viewer's perspective that shows the bear jumping in and out of the magician's hat at Rabbit's command. A wide book with pages shown as double-spread units often gives a sense of the horizon and its vastness. In *Freight Train,* Donald Crews effectively used the wide double-spread to show a train in movement, colors bleeding from one train to another in fast motion to form the new colors. Maurice Sendak's *Nutshell Library* was made to fit in the palms of young children's hands. Four slip-cased books fit tidily in a box. Creating illustrations in large books like *Make Way for Ducklings* allowed author/illustrator Robert McCloskey to show readers Mr. and Mrs. Mallard flying over Boston, and also show all eight of the ducklings following their mother, while the height of the book allows us to see Michael halting oncoming traffic.

Book Covers and Jackets

Readers are first introduced to a book by its cover and jacket, and they serve as an invitation into the book. Covers on picture books offer a sample of what's inside—somewhat of a "window" to what lies within the covers. This may be particularly important for children who engage with pictures even before they consider the text, and for those who form a physical engagement with the book through its cover (Powers, 2003). As an atypical but very appropriate example, in *The Lion and the Mouse*, the cover does not include the title and author/illustrator information. The wordless cover matches the interior of the book, where nearly wordlessly, the illustrations convey and carry the story. Book jackets often provide a lot of information beyond the book cover: They may include additional information about the author and illustrator; they typically include a write-up to "hook" a reader into the book; and they may include information on other books the author or illustrator has created and even some excerpts of reviews.

Endpapers

In function, the endpapers connect the pages of the book to the cover. Many also serve as prologues/epilogues to the content of the pages. Kevin Henkes created the opening endpapers for *Old Bear* using dark brown on medium brown outlines of leaves, suggesting the autumn season that leads into a bear's hibernation cycle. The closing endpaper for the book shows purple outlines of flowers, implying the arrival of spring. Both endpapers are subtly single toned and effective without attracting inordinate attention, adding to the overall "satisfying wholeness" of the reader's experience with the book.

Single Pages and Double-Page Spreads

As a rule, putting a picture on each page propels readers through the story at an even pace, whereas putting more than one picture on a page is a way to depict a series of actions or the rapid occurrence of actions. Spreading a single picture across two facing pages (a double-page spread) can signal a pause—a moment to ponder the events.

In *The Amazing Bone,* written and illustrated by William Steig, a succession of one-page illustrations shows Pearl's quick progress through the bustle of town life. A double-page spread showing Pearl sitting on the ground in the woods under trees raining wild cherry blossoms conveys a sense of her being overwhelmed by the beauty (and the seeming innocence) of nature.

In Sherley Anne Williams's *Working Cotton,* illustrator Carole Byard created a series of double-page spreads. These spreads communicate the boundless flatness of the migrant workers' world, where the child works from dark to dark in a field that appears to go on forever. This landscape is emphasized by the horizontally wide shape of the book.

Philipe Dupasquier's book *Dear Daddy* has an unusual layout: Pictures covering the lower halves of the pages show the events in the girl's life, while pictures across the top halves of the pages show her father's activities as a merchant seaman aboard a ship steaming around the world. Toward the end of the story, the pictures converge; finally, with Daddy's return, father and daughter occupy the visual space together.

Borders

Borders around pictures offer a means for the illustrator to control how intimately readers feel involved with the pictures. Some illustrators put decorative borders around four sides. These may put the action at some distance, sentimentalize it, or make it clear that the time period or place depicted is remote.

Trina Schart Hyman uses borders in an interesting way in Margaret Hodges's *St. George and the Dragon.* Each border suggests a stained glass window, and she reinforces this impression by sometimes drawing smaller images in the border panels in a way that embellishes the images in the center panel, but this also makes it seem as if the images were painted on the glass, rather than viewed through a window. On other pages, though, the images in the center intrude into the borders, and then we get the impression that we are looking not at static images in a stained glass window but through clear leaded glass at real figures just on the other side.

In *Where the Wild Things Are,* author and illustrator Maurice Sendak uses borders in a striking way. The sizes of the borders wax and wane with the crescendo and decrescendo of Max's wild adventures. In the opening pages, plain white borders contain relatively small pictures of Max. As his fantasy grows, though, so do the pictures—first filling a page, then spilling onto the opposite page, until the "wild rumpus" in the middle of the book pushes margins and words off the double-page spreads. As order returns, so do the borders—until, on the last page, the pictures are gone, leaving nothing but text.

In other books, the lack of borders conveys informality and communicates a sense of the picture going beyond the pages of the book. Jerry Pinkney's illustrations for Hans Christian Andersen's *The Ugly Duckling* bleed off the edges of the paper, and readers suppose that they were cut off from the world beyond the pages, restricted by the page size. This format seems especially fitting for a glimpse of the natural world.

Page Turns

Page turns allow an illustrator to create and relieve suspense. William Moebius (1986) called this phenomenon "the drama of the turning page." Many illustrators make use of this technique to add dramatic interest. One such example can be found in the pacing of Nancy Winslow Parker's illustrations of John Langstaff's text *Oh, A-Hunting We Will Go*. With each verse, children are implicitly challenged to guess where each animal will be put before they turn the page and read the completed rhyme (i.e., fox-box). Sometimes, an illustrator will include clues that lead readers to the next page. In the Australian book, *I Went Walking* by Mem Fox, Julie Vivas gives readers a glimpse of a portion of the animal on the following page in the background of the previous page. And sometimes, it challenges readers to contemplate the content being presented in a guessing game format. In *Tomorrow's Alphabet* by George Shannon, illustrated by Donald Crews, readers are told that that *A* is for *seed*. The subsequent page shows that seeds are tomorrow's apples. While imagining the real-world answer to the question, the alphabet organization offers clues to the reader as to what each page turn might reveal.

Text Layout and Typeface

The visual aspect of text can convey messages to the reader. Typically, text is presented in a straightforward, horizontal manner with most line breaks determined by the side margins. Easy readers use larger fonts and employ line breaks as a way of helping emerging readers pace their reading to have a more natural flow. Sometimes, illustrators use the text layout in ways that integrate the text into the illustrations. Some of those instances include speech bubbles within the illustration (as in the *Magic School Bus* books by Joanna Cole and illustrated by Bruce Degen) or letters or journal entries printed as the illustration as well as the text on a given page. At other times, the artistic placement, font, and color of the text is visually integrated into the illustration in such a way that the text is an important part of the visual presentation. Peter Sís creates books that do just that, as does Chris Raschka. In *The Maestro Plays,* Vladimir Randusky places Bill Martin's words in ways that emulate the movements of various circus actors. Similarly, in Lloyd Moss's *Zin! Zin! Zin! A Violin*, Marjorie Priceman incorporates text into illustrations in fluid ways. The typeface design, color, and size also communicate as part of the artistic style and mood of the text.

The Last Page

The last page of a picture book is often used for something of an afterword. Many illustrators reserve this last page for an epilogue, a comment on what has gone before. Maurice Sendak used the last page of **Where the Wild Things Are** to tell the reader that Max's supper was still hot after he returned from his antics with the Wild Things. Dav Pilkey used the last page of **The Paperboy** to show readers that after finishing his route, the paperboy went back to bed and entered a dream world. At times, authors and illustrators create an explicit epilogue. Kevin Henkes creates such a statement in **Chrysanthemum,** so readers know "what happened" beyond the denouement concluding Chrysanthemum's name dilemma.

Characterization

Characterization refers to the way in which an illustrator helps readers identify a particular character and continue to recognize that character throughout the changes of scene or status in the whole book. This is not easy. Leonardo da Vinci painted only one *Mona Lisa*, but would we always recognize the *Mona Lisa* if da Vinci had depicted her fifteen or twenty times, in different perspectives and in different circumstances? This is the challenge faced by the illustrator of virtually every picture book. To meet that challenge, some artists, such as Ted Lewin, hire models to pose for their drawings in different settings. Others, such as Jerry Pinkney, rely on family members to serve as models. He has them don various costumes and pose so that he can photograph them and use the photographs as reference as he draws. When artists work purely from the imagination, though, they must decide on identifying features by which readers will immediately know their characters. When reading Arnold Lobel's books, for instance, we can keep Frog and Toad straight in our minds because Frog is always green and Toad is always brown.

Features of a character may become so recognizable that even a part of a character may serve to identify the whole. In James Marshall's **Fox and His Friends,** for example, readers can recognize little sister Louise just from the tip of her tail hanging down into the frame from her perch atop a telephone pole. Similarly, in Mem Fox's **Hattie and the Fox,** just the presence of a nose in the bushes signals that a fox is stalking the barnyard animals.

Rosemary Wells's rabbits are wonderfully endearing. She draws them with large faces, big eyes, and small mouths. Max seems to be passively suffering his plight, and Ruby is manipulating things to her liking; either way, they evoke sympathy. A researcher of animal behavior, Iraneus Eibl-Eibesfeldt (1975), observed that among the higher animal species (including humans), adults are hereditarily conditioned to accept a certain array of features as "cute"—and when they see this array, their nurturant behavior is triggered. The array includes a head that is large in proportion to the body, a large forehead, big eyes, and a small mouth. The pictures of Max and Ruby in **Bunny Cakes,** by Rosemary Wells, show many of these features.

Mo Willems masterfully creates characterization, largely evident through illustration. In **Knuffle Bunny**, readers can clearly understand preschooler Trixie's emotional journey despite the fact that her verbal expressions are all babbling. Likewise, in **Don't Let the Pigeon Drive the Bus**, the pigeon's emotional range from pleading to conniving to angry outbursts are all depicted through the illustrations.

Perspective

Illustrators use a variety of perspectives to give readers different vantage points from which to view the situation. In Chris Van Allsburg's **Two Bad Ants,** two ants decide to stay behind in a kitchen when their fellow ants return to the colony with crystals requested by the queen. The two ants find themselves being scooped out of the bed of crystals into a boiling lake of brown bitter water. Thus begins their dangerous adventure, which moves from coffee cup to toaster to garbage disposal to electrical outlet. Readers watch the ants' adventure from various perspectives—looking down to see the ants on the ground and up to see them on the kitchen counter. When the ants are in the coffee cup being rushed toward the mouth of the coffee drinker, the perspective is from directly behind the ants, and readers see the mouth just as the ants see it. Then the view is from inside the toaster, and the ants are seen sitting on top of the bread crust. The close-up view of the water faucet makes it easy to see why the ants might mistake it for a waterfall.

In Istvan Banyai's *Zoom,* readers first see an up-close picture; with each page turn, the lens is pulled back so that more of the object shows until, finally, the earth is but a speck on the page. The pattern is repeated in *Rezoom.* Readers are challenged to look closely and consider the perspective of the illustration compared to that of the previous page and the page that follows. Steve Jenkins's *Looking Down* follows a similar format as it allows readers to imagine being an astronaut in space looking down, focusing closer and closer to see land mass, streets, homes, and yards, and finally focusing on one ladybug.

In Mordicai Gerstein's Caldecott-winning *The Man Who Walked Between the Towers,* the reader is shown the story from shifting perspectives that heighten each illustration's impact on how the reader understands the experience. From the cover art, Gerstein invites readers to stand and balance with Philippe on the wire, looking down on the city below. Readers also see the towers from the ground up, so they understand the height; they are shown the towers from the side so they understand the distance between the two. But in the most dramatic spread that is four pages wide, readers join Philippe a quarter mile high and experience the awe he must have felt.

Perspective can also be inclusive of understanding whose point of view is expressed in telling a story. In Mark Teague's *Dear Mrs. LaRue,* Ike's perspective is made abundantly clear to readers through both text and illustration. Mrs. LaRue sends Ike to Obedience School for his exuberant behavior that often gets him into trouble, and Ike manages to make the plush doggy spa-like place appear more like a jail. The color illustrations reveal the truthful images of a spa-like ideal world, while black and white images on the same double-spread pages show the situation (jail-like) as Ike portrays it to Mrs. LaRue.

Backgrounds

Characters are often identified by the objects that surround them. In William Steig's *The Amazing Bone,* Pearl seems most at home in the spring forest, gently showered by cherry blossoms. In spite of his dapper appearance, the loathsome wolf that accosts her lives in a ramshackle cottage with the screen door hanging from one hinge and trash scattered about the overgrown front yard. His slovenly surroundings indicate an uncaring heart. In *Where the Wild Things Are,* Max's room becomes overgrown with trees and bushes, a signal that wildness is taking hold of him.

In *A New Coat for Anna,* written by Harriet Ziefert and illustrated by Anita Lobel, piles of urban wreckage, peopled by maimed veterans with palms outstretched, dramatize the state of want, sadness, and shock in which Anna and her mother are living. The wilderness that surrounds Sylvester-turned-rock, in William Steig's *Sylvester and the Magic Pebble,* conveys his terrible state of loneliness and isolation—a state that will surely last forever unless he finds some spectacular solution to his problem.

White space is a negative space use of background, or the absence of a specific background in order to achieve focus on the illustration within the white space. Emily Gravett is especially masterful in employing white space effectively, as evidenced in *Orange Pear Apple Bear*. In this book, the four words and the corresponding items illustrated within an expanse of white space are combined in different ways to show a playful approach to the words and items. In *Monkey and Me*, the little girl plays with her stuffed monkey as they describe having been to see various animals that they pretend to be. The spacing of illustrations on the double spread and the amount of white space invites readers to enter the story and participate.

Color

Color is often used to reflect emotions and communicate moods. Both particular colors and their intensity are used to convey a mood to readers. Janice Del Negro's spooky storytelling in *Lucy Dove* is perfectly partnered with Leonid Gore's acrylic paintings. The colors establish the setting as they are appropriately dark and somber, reflecting the mood in the eerie graveyard and the scary monster. Even the light in the illustrations casts an unnatural aura.

Arnold Lobel portrays Frog and Toad in greens and browns and uses the same colors for his backgrounds. This reminds readers of the natural camouflage of frogs and toads, whose skins blend into the landscape. The muted colors also prepare readers for plots that are more inwardly directed and thoughtful than overt and active.

James Marshall uses color symbolically even in the seemingly light cartoon-style illustrations of his *Hansel and Gretel.* The sky—looming beyond the trees that are disorienting the lost children and behind the witch's gingerbread house—is pure black. The illustrations are completely free of this ominous color only when Hansel and Gretel cross the lake on a duck's back and arrive at home, where their father waits.

An especially skillful use of color is found in Anita Lobel's illustrations for *A New Coat for Anna.* Set in a European city after World War II, the book tells of Anna's mother, apparently widowed, who barters family heirlooms to a shepherd, a weaver, a dye maker, and a tailor—each of whom contributes something to making Anna a new coat. The story opens with the drab colors of a city in ruins, and the drabness is echoed by the bleak expression on the face of Anna's sad, exhausted mother. As each new character enters the story, a bit more color enters, too, until the story culminates in a festive Christmas celebration with greenery and yellow candles and Anna at the center of things in her brand-new bright red coat. By giving up bits of her past and reaching out to others, Anna's mother has created a community, and she and her new friends have brought color and joy back into each other's lives.

Even though the most obvious difference between children's books of the early twentieth century and those of the present is the quality and quantity of color used, black and white still remains a viable, and at times preferred, alternative for book illustrations. Black-and-white illustrations communicate mood primarily through the intensity of black tones used in shading, the boldness of lines, and the placement of the illustration against the amount of white space. Cross-hatching, or crisscrossing of lines, can add texture and depth. Wanda Gág used black-and-white pen-and-ink drawings in her first book, *Millions of Cats.* In some of his work, Chris Van Allsburg used a soft Conté pencil and pencil dust to create books that are entirely black and white; *The Garden of Abdul Gasazi, The Mysteries of Harris Burdick,* and *Jumanji* all won awards. John Steptoe used black-and-white pencil drawings in *The Story of Jumping Mouse: A Native American Legend,* which was named a 1985 Caldecott Honor Book.

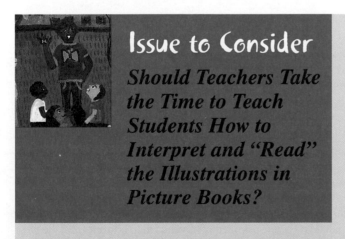

Issue to Consider

Should Teachers Take the Time to Teach Students How to Interpret and "Read" the Illustrations in Picture Books?

Illustrators take great care to do their part in telling the story within a book. Designers work with book elements to influence the overall effect on the viewer's understanding and experience with the book. All in all, there is a lot for students to consider as the visual literacy of understanding the book.

Whoever helps students to learn to become visually literate must also study how picture books work through the visual elements of art: design, medium, and style. This requires some basic understandings of the visual communication medium. Focusing on the text alone leaves out much that is presented to the reader that is only presented through the visual aspects of the illustration or book design. But does too much emphasis on the visual side take away from a focus on comprehending the text?

What do you think? Teachers are already challenged with teaching their students to read the text and to understand it. Is it their responsibility to also teach their students how to "read" the visual messages to be found in the illustrations? If so, how will teachers gain the background knowledge necessary to do so? If not, who will help students take steps toward visual literacy?

Teaching Idea 3.4

Try Your Hand at the Artist's Medium

Select an artistic medium described earlier in the chapter. Examine many books that employ that medium. Then provide students with the materials so that they, too, can try their hand at it. For example, studying the collage work of artists like Leo Lionni, Eric Carle, Ezra Jack Keats, Lauren Child, or Bryan Collier may lead to a creation out of materials like magazine cut outs, drawings, originally created paper, or many other items. Or, students may want to try a technique like dressing up as a book character, taking a digital photograph, and manipulating the image on a computer to add a background. Then they could use that printout as a reference point in drawing their own illustration. There are many professional resource books that describe the work of various illustrators in detail. See the Resource list in this chapter.

Go to the Extension Activities section of Chapter 3 in the MyEducationKit for your book and complete activity #1 to examine the importance of illustrations in picture books.

Sometimes, black-and-white images are used because they match the historical content of the book perfectly. In Avi's *Silent Movie,* the protagonist leaves Europe and arrives in America, but is unable to be reunited with his father. However, one day, he is offered a part in a silent movie and his father happens to see him—thereby making a reunion possible. Silent movies were filmed and played in black and white—thus, the author's creation of film style illustrations in black and white match the content of the book as well as the delivery.

Picture/Text Relationships

If the relationship between the illustrations and the text is handled skillfully, the illustrations support the text, but not in a completely predictable way. Children will be more actively engaged if part of the meaning of the story is left for them to infer from the illustrations.

In *Where the Wild Things Are,* the hand drawing of a Wild Thing "by Max" on the wall is a clue to the observant reader that the wild things Max encounters have been created out of his imagination. In the same vein, in Harry Allard's *Miss Nelson Is Missing!,* artist James Marshall drew a box marked "wig" in upside-down letters next to an ugly black dress in the open closet next to Miss Nelson's bed. Observant readers will pick up this clue to solve the mystery of the identity of Miss Viola Swamp, Miss Nelson's harsh alter ego. Author and illustrator Susan Meddaugh blurs the line between her two roles to produce interesting picture-text relationships in her recent works. In *Martha Speaks,* Meddaugh tells the story of a family dog that gains the gift of speech after eating alphabet soup. Martha, the suddenly loquacious dog, spews language all over the page. The reader soon tires of reading it all, just as the family tires of hearing it. Meanwhile, the text of the story proceeds in the print at the bottom of the page. In *Hog-Eye,* a story about a little pig that outwits a mean but illiterate wolf, the pig pretends to read from a book of magic spells. Those who can read can see what the hapless wolf cannot: The pig is reading from a tome entitled *Getting to Know Your Carburetor.*

The 1996 Caldecott Medal winner, *Officer Buckle and Gloria* by Peggy Rathmann, tells of a police officer who makes tiresome speeches about home and school safety. Interest in his presentations suddenly increases a hundredfold when he begins to take a police dog, Gloria, with him. Because Gloria stands just behind him, Officer Buckle doesn't see that the dog is pantomiming and generally cutting up while he gives his otherwise boring speech. The text doesn't mention Gloria's antics, either. We readers are in on a secret that Officer Buckle doesn't know, because we are informed by the pictures as well as the text. The most telling picture of all is the one in which Officer Buckle discovers, by way of television, what Gloria has been up to. In addition to depicting Officer Buckle's reaction and Gloria's response, the picture includes the large mirror that hangs on the wall behind the couch, which allows the reader to see what is showing on the television screen.

In *The Journey of Oliver K. Woodman,* Uncle Ray is unable to accept his niece Tamika's invitation to visit, so he creates a wooden man and sends it to her by way of "hitchhiking." Oliver K. Woodman is accompanied by a note asking that travelers help him get from the west coast to the east, and for them to send his creator, Ray, a postcard letting him know of his progress to his destination. What readers see is an interplay between text and illustration, with some of the text (the letters and postcards) being shown as the illustration itself. The illustrations offer much of the potential for children's emotional response to this book, along with their depth of understanding of the situations. In fact, Tamika is portrayed as a biracial child only through the illustrations.

Criteria for Evaluating Picture Books

Picture books are evaluated for their illustrations as well as for their text (except in cases of wordless books). But it is more than the sum of the two; it is the way that they are integrated to create a "satisfying whole" that is at the heart of evaluating picture books. The main points can be summarized as follows:

- Is the story well written according to the literary standards outlined in Chapter 2?
- Text (literary elements): Is the language of the text skillfully crafted?
- Illustrations (artistic elements): Do the illustrations communicate not just literally but symbolically through the use of colors, framing, shading, and other visual elements?
- Integration of text and illustrations: Do the pictures interplay with the text and do the text and the pictures seem to clarify, enhance, and extend each other?

Awards for Picture Books

Many awards honor high-quality picture books and their creators. Here, we highlight two of the most widely recognized awards given to illustrators: the Caldecott Medal and the Coretta Scott King Award for illustrations. In addition, we describe two awards for the text of picture books: the Charlotte Zolotow Award and the Theodor Seuss Geisel Award.

Caldecott Medal

The American Library Association's Association of Library Service to Children honored Randolph Caldecott in 1938 by giving his name to an annual award for the most distinguished picture book published in the United States in the previous year. Funds to establish the Caldecott Medal were donated to the ALA by Frederick Melcher, president of the Wilson Publishing Company. Books that have won the medal for their illustrations have a gold seal on the jackets, and honor books have a silver seal. A list of Caldecott winners and honor books appears in the Appendix.

Coretta Scott King Award

Each year, the American Library Association gives one Coretta Scott King Award for writing and one for illustrations, as well as honor book citations. The ALA's guidelines for the award state that "recipients are African American authors and illustrators whose distinguished books promote an understanding and appreciation of the culture and contribution of all people to the realization of the 'American dream.'" The Appendix lists all previous winners and honor books.

Charlotte Zolotow Award

The Charlotte Zolotow Award is presented to the author who is honored for having written the book that is chosen as the best picture book text published in the United States in the preceding year. The award was established in 1998 to honor editor and author Charlotte Zolotow, and it is administered by the Cooperative Children's Book Center at the University of Wisconsin-Madison. Appendix A lists all previous winners and honor books.

Theodor Seuss Geisel Award

First awarded in 2006, this new award is given for the most distinguished beginning reader published in English the previous year and is awarded by the American Library Association. ALA seeks recognition for "literary and artistic achievement that demonstrate creativity and imagination to engage children in reading," honoring the ways in which Dr. Seuss entertained and offered readable texts to generations of children as they learned to read.

Top Shelf 3.3

Picture Books that Show the Interplay of Text with Illustrations

Voices in the Park by Anthony Browne.

Come Away from the Water, Shirley by John Burningham.

Time to Get Out of the Bath, Shirley by John Burningham.

Rosie's Walk by Pat Hutchins.

Creators of Picture Books

Space limitations make it impossible to give a biographical sketch of every important picture book author or illustrator. We have chosen to highlight only a few; many others are mentioned in earlier discussions in this chapter in sections on artistic media and artistic style, and in discussions on how a picture storybook works; still others are included as featured authors and illustrators in other chapters.

Eric Carle

Eric Carle spent his first six years in the United States and has happy memories of kindergarten, freely creating art on large sheets of paper with big brushes and bright colors. However, most of his childhood was spent in his parents' homeland, Germany, during World War II. Carle's introduction to the world of children's book illustration came when a pink lobster he had created for an advertising job caught the eye of author Bill Martin, Jr., who solicited Carle's work for a series of books he had written.

Eric Carle's many picture books are immediately recognizable because of his unique painted tissue-paper collages. Perhaps his best-known book is *The Very Hungry Caterpillar,* in which a little egg hatches and the hungry caterpillar eats its way through various foods, spins a cocoon, and becomes a butterfly. This lesson on metamorphosis is accompanied by an introduction to numbers and the days of the week. Carle's many toy books, described earlier in this chapter, employ partial pages, holes, cutouts, pop-ups, electronic sound chips, lights, and more. Carle tries to create books that combine heartfelt stories with opportunities for learning and play, and without a doubt, he has succeeded frequently. Among his well-known titles are *The Grouchy Ladybug, The Very Busy Spider,* and *The Very Quiet Cricket.*

Carle has a mission to honor and preserve the creation of picture books and has established a museum in his name as a place to examine and celebrate picture books. In addition, his website offers viewers an explanation of how he creates his art, and his book *The Art of Eric Carle* offers readers an opportunity to study his works. For his "substantial and lasting contribution to literature for children," Carle was awarded the Laura Ingalls Wilder Award by the American Library Association in 2003, and named the U.S. nominee for the IBBY Hans Christian Anderson Award in 2010.

Leo and Diane Dillon

The artwork created by Leo and Diane Dillon is unique in that each piece is truly a work of collaboration, so much so that neither artist can identify who contributed which part to a finished product. They speak of a "third artist" who is a combination of both of them, yet different from each as individuals. The Dillons attribute their collaborative ability to their control of artistic techniques: They maintain that one of them could begin a line and the other could continue it without detectable interruption.

The first and second children's books the Dillons illustrated earned them the distinction of being the first (and only, so far) to receive the Caldecott Medal in two consecutive years. Verna Aardema's *Why Mosquitoes Buzz in People's Ears: A West African Tale,* told in cumulative verse format, has various animals passing along different versions of a rumor. For this book, the Dillons interpreted the text with stylized watercolor paintings that were influenced by batik art. Margaret Musgrove's *Ashanti to Zulu: African Traditions,* uses an alphabet book format to describe aspects of daily life among the diverse cultures of Africa. For this book, the Dillons created art that was factually accurate as well as elegant and that captured both the commonality and diversity of human experiences.

The Dillons have collaborated on some books with their son, Lee Dillon, a painter and sculptor. Lee and his parents created the artwork for *Pish, Posh, Said Hieronymus Bosch,* a poem by Nancy Willard that describes the influence of the famous painter's imaginative creatures on his housekeeper. Lee carved a frame, incorporating some of these unusual creatures. Leo and Diane's paintings are centered in this frame, giving it the look of a "window" through which readers view the story. *Aida,* by Leontyne Price, is another book on which the three

Dillons collaborated. Lee created a metal frame that was used as the border of each page. Leo and Diane's attention to detail is reflected in the design of this book. Of particular interest is their incorporation of marbleized paper and their creation of highly decorative endpapers.

In addition to illustrating picture books, the Dillons have created the art for many book jackets and for longer works of fiction. For the body of their work and the lasting contribution they have made to children's books, the U.S. Board of Books for Young People (USBBY) selected Leo and Diane Dillon as the 1996 U.S. nominees for the Hans Christian Andersen Award.

Lois Ehlert

Lois Ehlert was encouraged by her parents to engage in creative constructions; her mother gave her scraps of colored cloth from her sewing, and her father gave her woodworking materials from his projects. They set up a card table for her, and she spent much time creating various projects while growing up. Later, a wooden cutting board and a tin can converted the same table into a drawing board in art school, and she continues to use it today, with its drilled holes, razor cuts, and ink spills.

Her books such as *Color Zoo* and *Color Farm* employ basic concepts of color and shape that use cutouts that combine and intrigue children with images of animals and natural things in their world. Books like *Planting a Rainbow* and *Eating the Alphabet* show flowers and food through brilliantly colored illustrations. And books such as *Feathers for Lunch* and *Waiting for Wings* have story lines that delight readers while introducing names of birds or the concept of metamorphosis. Her books based on folklore include *Moon Rope: A Peruvian Folktale* and *Cuckoo: A Mexican Folktale,* both offered bilingually in English and Spanish.

Ehlert's dazzling colors and graphic illustrations have been appreciated by children and adults for their ability to entertain and to notice what she values about the world. Her books are addressed to the young child, but invite participation from adults and children together. Ehlert researches and shares facts in her books, but her intent is not to didactically teach; rather, she compares herself to a grandmother who shares what she values in everyday life with young children.

Kevin Henkes

Best known for his books portraying mice in real-life, childlike situations, Kevin Henkes enjoys wide popularity as a picture book author and illustrator. His cartoon-style drawings of mice, done in pen and ink with watercolors, take on personalities of typical children (and adults). Henkes depicts the personalities through facial expressions, the movements of the mice, and the poses they take. The predicaments the mice face—arrival of a new sibling, being teased by classmates, having an imaginary friend—are situations that are familiar to almost everyone. His ability to pace his stories creates just the right emotional tension throughout his books.

Henkes's mice characters are memorable: Chrysanthemum, with whom we empathize over the agonies of being teased for her name; Sheila Rae, the bravest girl imaginable, who discovers that she needs her quiet little sister, who has an inner strength that shines in times of distress; Chester and Wilson, who live predictable lives filled with routines and precautions until they encounter Lilly, the self-proclaimed queen, who lives for thrilling moments of adventure. Henkes has both written and illustrated most of his books. Among his many popular titles are *Chrysanthemum*; *Julius, the Baby of the World*; *Sheila Rae, the Brave*; *A Weekend with Wendell*; and *Lilly's Purple Plastic Purse.* In 1994, Henkes's *Owen* was named a Caldecott Honor Book. This book shows how one mouse family deals with a soon-to-be-kindergartener who refuses to give up a security blanket. In *Wemberly Worried,* Henkes portrays the emotions of a child who worries about absolutely everything, real and imagined. More recently, he has created board books for babies and toddlers that match the emotions they face.

Kevin Henkes was born in Wisconsin and still lives there today with his wife, Laura Dronzek, also an accomplished author/illustrator of picture books. Although they typically create separate books, the two collaborated on the creation of *Birds*, which Kevin wrote and Laura illustrated. Henkes's book, *Kitten's First Full Moon,* was awarded the 2005 Caldecott Medal. Henkes is also the author of a number of award-winning realistic novels that sensitively deal with serious issues faced by preteens and teens. These titles are discussed in Chapter 9, "Contemporary Realistic Fiction."

Ask the Author/Ask the Illustrator Jon Scieszka and Lane Smith

Favorite Books as a Child

(Scieszka) (Smith)

Green Eggs and Ham **The Carrot Seed**
by Dr. Seuss by Crockett
  Johnson

Grimms' Fairy Tales **Treehorn ∞∞ 3**
  by Florence

The Carrot Seed
by
Crockett Johnson

Parry Heide,
illustrated by
E. Gorey
**How the Grinch
Stole Christmas**
by Dr. Seuss

*How do you come up with
such imaginative and unique
books?*

I would love to describe how I get up
before dawn every day, light my special candle of inspiration, and sit
down to write for twelve hours. But I
never do that. Then I could say I sit in a
little shed and write on an old board I put
across my lap, but Roald Dahl already
said that. Maybe I used to work at an ad
agency and someone challenged me to
write a book for kids using only 100 different words. Nah. That was Dr. Seuss.

I don't know. Lane, how do we come
up with such imaginative and unique
books?

"I get up before dawn every day, light
my special candle of inspiration, and sit
down to paint and draw for twelve hours."
You do not.
"I go out to my little shed and draw on
an old board I put across my lap?"
No.
"I used to work in an ad agency . . ."
Thanks for your help, Dr. Seuss.
I've never really given much thought
to how we put our books together. I do
the writing thing just like most other
authors—writing, rewriting, reading the
stuff to kids and teachers, then rewriting
some more. And Lane does the sketching,
painting, and repainting thing like most
other illustrators.
But, now that I think of it, we do have
two secret ingredients that set us apart
from those other Brand X books.

Jerry Pinkney

Encouraged by support for his early interest in drawing, Jerry Pinkney began his art career with
a greeting card company; he later established his own studio to do advertising and textbook
illustrating. His wide array of creations includes calendars and postage stamps. Pinkney has
been illustrating since the 1960s. Jerry Pinkney's watercolor illustrations are widely recognized
for their natural reflection of people, animals, and the world in which they live. As he paints,
he relies on models for inspiration and reference, often using family members. Along with other
family members, he even dressed up and posed as an animal when illustrating Julius Lester's
book *The Tales of Uncle Remus.* He takes particular pride in his devotion to illustrating
African Americans, which has been recognized through his three Coretta Scott King Awards:
in 1986 for Valerie Flournoy's *The Patchwork Quilt,* in 1987 for Crescent Dragonwagon's *Half
a Moon and One Whole Star,* and again in 1988 for Patricia McKissack's *Mirandy and
Brother Wind.* He also has four Caldecott Honor Books: *The Talking Eggs: A Folktale from
the American South* by Robert San Souci, *Mirandy and Brother Wind* by Patricia McKissack,
John Henry by Julius Lester, and *The Ugly Duckling.* He won the Caldecott Award for *The
Lion and the Mouse.*

Pinkney's goal of serving as an inspiration to his own family and to other African
Americans has clearly been realized. Jerry's wife, Gloria Jean Pinkney, has authored picture books such as *The Sunday Outing;* Jerry's son Brian Pinkney is a highly acclaimed
illustrator, who has worked in collaboration with his wife, Andrea Davis Pinkney, on such
works as *Duke Ellington: The Piano Prince;* and Jerry's son Myles has used his talent in
photography to illustrate books of poetry such as Nikki Grimes's *It's Raining Laughter* and
wife Sandra Pinkney's *Shades of Black.*

Maurice Sendak

Maurice Sendak spent many of his childhood years sick in bed, reading comics, drawing,
writing stories, and imagining the lives of the people in the houses in his neighborhood. From

Go to the Extension Activities
section of Chapter 3 in the
MyEducationKit for your book
and complete activity #2 to
compare print and film versions
of a picture book.

One, Lane and I are friends and work together. After I get a story to where I like it, I give it to Lane. He thinks about it, fools around with different ways to illustrate it; then we talk and goof around with changes in both the writing and the illustration to fit the new ideas. A lot of authors and illustrators never get this chance to work together.

Two, we have a secret weapon—our designer Molly Leach (who also happens to be Lane's wife and my wife's best friend and part of the reason Lane and I met and started working together and . . . that's a whole other story). As the designer, Molly is the one who takes the text and the illustrations and decides how to weave them together and present them on the page so everything works together.

So, in *The Stinky Cheese Man*, it was Molly who came up with the idea to have the type grow and shrink to fit the page.

And when Jack was telling his story endlessly over and over and over, I thought it would be funny if the text just ran off the page. Molly showed us how it would look better if the type got smaller and smaller.

For a book like *Math Curse*, the story stayed pretty close to the early finished draft. Lane came up with the idea to show the narrator under the spell of the curse. And we left it up to Molly to figure out how to cram all of the words, problems, and paintings into a picture book that looked kind of like a math book but not so ugly or so much like a math book that it would scare all of our readers away.

Our books look unique because we get to work in a unique way. Three people collaborate on getting the text, the illustration, and the design working to tell one story.

So, in conclusion, Lane and I make our imaginative and unique books by get-

ting up before dawn every day, sitting in a little shed, working for an ad agency, and thanking our lucky stars that we get to work together and with Ace Designer, Molly Leach.

Jon Scieszka is the author of *The True Story of the 3 Little Pigs!; The Frog Prince, Continued; The Stinky Cheese Man and Other Fairly Stupid Tales; The Book That Jack Wrote; Math Curse;* and the *Time Warp Trio* series. He's a lumberjack in his spare time. He once climbed Mount Everest in his bare feet. And he enjoys potato chips and making up lies. Lane Smith's bio is exactly the same as Jon's, except a couple of the book titles are different.

---

this beginning came a career devoted to the arts. Sendak is known for creating characters who are imaginative, strong-willed, and clever. In 1962, Sendak created *The Nutshell Library,* a set of four two-by-four-inch books: *Chicken Soup with Rice: A Book of Months, One Was Johnny: A Counting Book, Alligators All Around: An Alphabet,* and *Pierre: A Cautionary Tale.* These stories remain popular today.

The publication of *Where the Wild Things Are* in 1963 brought much attention. Many adults feared that the Wild Things were too frightening for young children, but others applauded the central character's ability to deal with the strong emotions children face. The book was honored with the 1964 Caldecott Medal and remains one of the most popular and best-known picture books for children.

Other Sendak books have also been the subject of controversy. When *In the Night Kitchen* was published in 1970, it was criticized for the nudity of the central character and for the use of cartoon-style illustration. Some found the portrayal of babies' experiences in *Outside Over There* disturbing. Both books arose out of Sendak's own experiences, and he believes that they are personally significant. More recently, *We Are All in the Dumps with Jack and Guy* has disturbed some readers with its portrayal of homelessness.

In 1966, Maurice Sendak was the first American to be a recipient of the International Board on Books for Young People's Hans Christian Andersen Award. Since then, Sendak has stretched his artistic contributions beyond picture books. In addition to illustrating books, Sendak creates sets and costumes for children's theater, often based on his own books.

William Steig

William Steig is an illustrator and author whose accomplishments in both areas are laudable. Steig began his first career as a freelance artist, most notably as a cartoonist for *The New Yorker*. Steig's entry into the children's book field came at the age of sixty, at the instigation of a colleague at *The New Yorker,* children's book author Robert Kraus. His first book was *C D B!,* a book of word games. Only a year later, *Sylvester and the Magic Pebble* brought him recognition as a highly talented creator of children's books, as it won numerous awards, including the 1970 Caldecott Medal. It is the story of a donkey whose parents miss him after he is turned into a rock. *The Amazing Bone* was a 1977 Caldecott Honor Book. The magical powers of the amazing bone save Pearl the Pig from being gobbled up by the wolf. Steig's Newbery Honor Books are *Abel's Island,* in 1977, and a picture book, *Doctor De Soto,* in 1983. In *Doctor De Soto,* a mouse dentist is asked to remove a bothersome tooth from a fox patient, leading readers to ponder who the clever one is in this story. Steig's signature cartoon style uses anthropomorphized animals to tell humorous tales of moral behavior. Magical happenings are taken in stride as wondrous, but believable events in daily life. *Pete's a Pizza* features a human child who is saddened to see the rain alter his outdoor plans; his parents good-naturedly play with him indoors, pretending to make him into a pizza.

Steig's illustrations have a doodling quality to them; they show movement and spontaneity in their lines. For the totality of his contribution to children's literature worldwide, William Steig was designated a U.S. nominee for the Hans Christian Andersen Award in both the illustration category and the writing category. Steig died in 2003.

Chris Van Allsburg

Chris Van Allsburg's first book, *The Garden of Abdul Gasazi,* was published in 1979 and was a 1980 Caldecott Honor Book. Within a few years, he had achieved notoriety as a remarkable creator of picture books and won two Caldecott Medals. The first was in 1982 for his second book, *Jumanji.* This jungle adventure story is about two children playing a board game in which landing on particular squares has real consequences: Lions roar, monkeys create havoc, rhinos stampede, and a volcano erupts. The second Caldecott Medal was awarded in 1986 for *The Polar Express,* in which children board a late-night "polar express" train and visit Santa at the North Pole. The book quickly became established as a Christmas classic, especially popular among adult readers reminiscing on their childhoods.

Van Allsburg's early work was done in black pencil, but his later works are full-color paintings. Stories like *The Wreck of the Zephyr* cross between reality and fantasy in ways that make fantasy believable and reality questionable; the illustrations have similar effects. One of his books that requires readers to let their imaginations fill in the unknown is *The Mysteries of Harris Burdick.* It takes the form of a portfolio of paintings, each with only a title and a caption. Readers are supposed to imagine the story behind each painting. Perhaps the appeal of Van Allsburg's books for children and adults alike lies in this lack of distinction between reality and fantasy—and in the subtlety of the interpretations allowed by his highly imaginative work.

More recently, Van Allsburg has created picture books with a social message. *Just a Dream* raises the issue of what happens when people don't take care of their environment. Walter abuses the environment until a nightmare reveals what his future will be like. Walter's attitude and behavior toward the environment make a complete turnaround when he awakens. Readers find a cautionary tale in *The Sweetest Fig,* in which Monsieur Bibot is given two figs in payment for extracting a tooth—figs that can make his dream come true. An unexpected turn of events leaves readers pondering after they close the book, "How will Monsieur Bibot's treatment of his dog and of others repay him in the future?"

Rosemary Wells

Rosemary Wells creates humorous stories about animals who are caught in situations and relationships much like those in which children find themselves with their friends and siblings. She cites events in her own and her children's lives as the models for many of her situations. Wells believes that her animal characters are able to convey deeply felt emotions that are familiar to children and adults alike. In many of her books, the succinct dialogue is supplemented by a narrator's voice that offers humorous explanations of what thoughts are going through the characters' heads and what the characters are doing.

Perhaps the best known of Wells's works are her stories about Max and Ruby, rabbit siblings. The interactions between little brother Max and big sister Ruby reflect ways in which human siblings often interact. In a board book series about this brother-sister pair, readers find Ruby giving instructions that Max pretends not to understand; the humor comes from Ruby's

...ight, Officer Buckle watched himself
...o'clock news.

...rtoon illustrations and ...e of Boys Have the Best ...are seen enjoying a week of ...various explorations at ...from *A Couple of Boys Have the* ...t © 2008 by Marla Frazee, ...n of publisher Houghton Mifflin ...pany.)

21 The flying frogs in *Tuesday* are an example of surrealism, showing what could never happen in our world as we know it. (From *Tuesday* by David Wiesner. Copyright © 1991 by David Wiesner. Reprinted by permission of Clarion Books, an imprint of Houghton Mifflin Company. All rights reserved.)

22 Illustrator Margaret Chodos-Irvine uses various print-making techniques to depict this story of a little girl asserting her independence as she gets dressed. (Illustrations from *Ella Sarah Gets Dressed*, © 2003 by Margaret Chodos-Irvine, reprinted by permission of Harcourt, Inc.)

23 A combination of hand-created and computer-manipulated art comes together to form the digitized version of these illustrations. (Illustration from *Cook-A-Doodle-Doo!* by Janet Stevens and Susan Stevens Crummel. Illustrations copyright © 1999 by Janet Stevens, reprinted by permission of Harcourt, Inc.)

It was Grandma's birthday.
Max made her an earthworm birthday cake.
"No, Max," said Max's sister, Ruby. "We are going to make Grandma an angel surprise cake with raspberry-fluff icing."

26 In an effort to decorate his earthworm cake for Grandma's birthday, Max repeatedly attempts to write "Red-Hot Marshmallow Squirters" on the grocery list. (Cover from *Bunny Cakes* by Rosemary Wells, copyright © 1997 by Rosemary Wells. Used by permission of Dial Books for Young Readers, A Division of Penguin Young Readers Group, A Member of Penguin Group (USA) Inc., 345 Hudson Street, New York, NY 10014. All rights reserved.)

27 Suzy Lee's visually captivating book *Wave* simply portrays a little girl on a beach playing with a wave as if it were a playmate. (From *Wave* © 2008 by Suzy Lee. Used by permission of Chronicle Books LLC, San Francisco. Visit ChronicleBooks.com.)

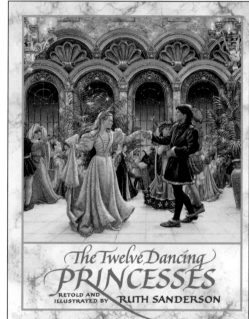

29 Glimmering bejeweled princesses in an opulent setting offer an example of romanticism in illustrations. (Book cover illustration, *The Twelve Dancing Princesses* retold and illustrated by Ruth Sanderson, 1990. Reprinted by permission of Little, Brown and Company, Inc.)

24 *The House in the Night*, a Caldecott-winning book, has illustrations done in black and white scratchboard with touches of golden yellow to give golden glowing highlights throughout the book. (Cover from *The House in the Night* by Susan Marie Swanson, pictures by Beth Krommes. Jacket art copyright © 2008 by Beth Krommes. Reprinted by permission of Houghton Mifflin Harcourt Publishing Company. All rights reserved.)

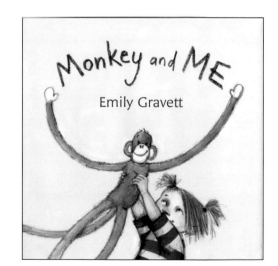

25 In Emily Gravett's *Monkey and Me*, a little girl and her stuffed monkey playfully describe having been to see the penguins, elephants, kangaroos, and monkeys and how they came home to tea. (Reprinted with permission of Simon & Schuster Books for Young Readers, an imprint of Simon & Schuster Children's Publishing Division from *Monkey and Me* by Emily Gravett. Copyright © 2008 Emily Gravett.)

28 Trina Schart Hyman's borders in *St. George and the Dragon* remind viewers of stained glass images on church windows. (From *Saint George and the Dragon* by Margaret Hodges. Copyright © 1984 by Margaret Hodges (Text); Copyright © 1984 by Trina Schart Hyman (Illustrations). Reprinted by permission of Little, Brown and Company, Inc.)

30 In Jeremy Tankard's *Grumpy Bird*, a bird is followed around by various animal friends who imitate his antics, and before long, his mood changes as he has fun with an impromptu game of "follow the leader." (From *Grumpy Bird* by Jeremy Tankard. Scholastic Inc./Scholastic Press. Copyright © 2007 by Jeremy Tankard. Reprinted by permission.)

1 Good stories, simple text, well-matched illustrations, and the effective use of line breaks and white space all combine to give beginning readers successful reading experiences. Arnold Lobel's *Frog and Toad Are Friends* is a good example of an inviting book for beginning readers. (*Frog and Toad Are Friends* by Arnold Lobel. Text copyright © 1970 Arnold Lobel. Used by permission of HarperCollins Publishers.)

4 When Sophie is made to share a toy with her sister, the changes in Sophie's feelings are reflected in the changes in the colors used in the story's illustrations. (From *When Sophie Gets Angry—Really, Really Angry . . .* by Molly Bang. Scholastic Inc./ Blue Sky Press Copyright © 1999 by Molly Bang. Reprinted by permission of Scholastic Inc.)

9 The illustrations for this delightful West African story are painted on ceramic tiles. (From *The Hatseller and the Monkeys* by Baba Wagué Diakité. Scholastic Inc./Scholastic Press. Copyright © 1999 by Baba Wagué Diakité. Reprinted by permission of Scholastic Inc.)

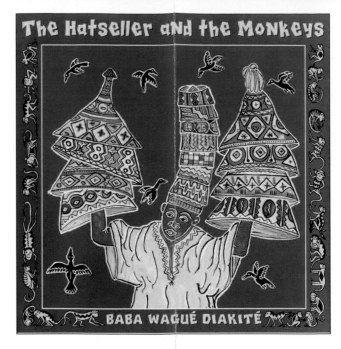

2 Leo and Diane Dillon used stylized watercolor paintings patterned after batik art to illustrate this winner of the Caldecott Medal. (From *Why Mosquitoes Buzz in People's Ears* by Verna Aardema, pictures by Leo and Diane Dillon, copyright © 1975 by Leo and Diane Dillon, pictures. Used by permission of Dial Books for Young Readers, A Division of Penguin Young Readers Group, A Member of Penguin Group (USA) Inc., 345 Hudson Street, New York, NY 10014. All rights reserved.)

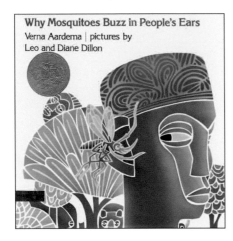

5 Eric Carle uses painted tissue-paper collages to tell the story of a hungry caterpillar that eats its way through a host of foods before spinning a cocoon and finally becoming a butterfly. (From *The Very Hungry Caterpillar* by Eric Carle, copyright © 1969 and 1987 by Eric Carle. Used by permission of Philomel Books, A Division of Penguin Young Readers Group, A Member of Penguin Group (USA) Inc., 345 Hudson Street, New York, NY 10014. All rights reserved.)

6 Lithography was commonly used to create illustrations for children's picture books of the past. (From *Puss in Boots* by Charles Perrault, illustrated by Hans Fischer. Copyright © 1996 by Nord-Sud Verlag AG Gossau Zurich, Switzerland. Used by permission of North-South Books, Inc., New York.)

10 The pastel hues of Stephen Gammell's colored pencils add to the sense of family intimacy as a grandfather recreates for his grandchildren his days in vaudeville. (From *Song and Dance Man* by Karen Ackerman, copyright © 1988 by Karen Ackerman. Illustrations copyright © 1988 by Stephen Gammell. Used by permission of Alfred A. Knopf, an imprint of Random House Children's Books, a division of Random House, Inc.)

3 Artist Jeannie Baker uses many natural materials like leaves, dirt, and wool to assemble the collage art for her books that have an environmental focus. (*Home* by Jeannie Baker. Copyright © 2003 by Jeannie Baker. Used by permission of HarperCollins Publishers.)

7 Using three-dimensional art for the illustrations in *Look-Alikes*, Joan Steiner creates a world of miniature scale from real objects. (From *Look-Alikes* by Joan Steiner. Copyright © 1999 by Joan Steiner. By permission of Little, Brown and Company, Inc.)

8 In illustrating *Scary Stories to Tell in the Dark*, Stephen Gammell used black-and-white pencil drawings to create a mood of impending peril. (*Scary Stories to Tell in the Dark* by Alvin Schwartz, illustrated by Stephen Gammell, 1987. Used by permission of HarperCollins Publishers.)

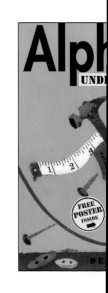

exasperation as Max revels in his responses to her edicts. In ***Max's Breakfast,*** Ruby tries repeatedly to convince Max to eat his egg. The joke is on Ruby when Max announces, "All Gone," as Ruby finishes the egg in her attempt to show Max how yummy it is. In ***Bunny Cakes,*** Max is making Grandma an earthworm birthday cake, but Ruby thinks that an angel surprise cake with raspberry-fluff icing is more appropriate. As Ruby sends Max to the store for flour and eggs, he repeatedly attempts to write on the grocery list the Red-Hot Marshmallow Squirters he needs for his earthworm cake. Wells perceptively captures Max's initial, but determined attempts at written communication, while all throughout the production of the cakes, the big sister Ruby/little brother Max relationship continues as expected.

David Wiesner

David Wiesner is the youngest of five children, and was fortunate to have parents who supplied him with art materials to nurture his imagination and creative expression. He experimented with ink, paint, and pastels throughout his childhood and was influenced by an artistic older brother and sister. After graduating from the Rhode Island School of Design, he launched his illustrating career with *Cricket* magazine.

At first, he illustrated the work of others, and then collaborated on a book with his wife, surgeon Kim Kahng. It was his first solo book, the wordless book ***Free Fall,*** that won him national recognition when it was named a Caldecott Honor Book. Since then, his books have been wordless or nearly wordless, with the illustrations carrying the story. He was awarded the Caldecott Medal for his illustration of ***Tuesday,*** in which frogs fly on lily pads through the night. In many of his other books, he also has various flying figures and objects: various vegetables in ***June 29, 1999,*** pigs in his Caldecott-winning ***The Three Pigs,*** a boy who boards a cloud on a field trip to the Empire State Building in ***Sector 7,*** and gargoyles in Eve Bunting's ***The Night of the Gargoyles.*** With the publication of ***Flotsam***, Wiesner was awarded his third Caldecott Medal. As with many of his earlier books, he relies on minimal to virtually no text, but invites viewers to look carefully and critically as they "read" the illustrations for the story within. He was the U.S. nominee for the prestigious international Hans Christian Andersen Award, and a 2008 illustrator finalist.

Ed Young

Born and raised in China, Ed Young immigrated to the United States when he was twenty years old. His childhood years in China influence much of his work as an artist. Early in his career,

PEARSON
myeducation**kit**™

Read the interview where David Wiesner discusses his retold version of *The Three Pigs* by going to the Conversations section of Chapter 3 in the MyEducationKit for your book.

Issue to Consider

Are Picture Books Being Designed More for Adult Buyers Than for Child Readers?

Picture books are the biggest selling type of children's book. In the past, picture books were designed for preschoolers and young children. Decades ago, books such as those produced by Marie Hall Ets and Virginia Lee Burton were created for that audience. Today, picture books such as those by Eric Hill, Denise Fleming, and Mem Fox are still appropriate for young children. However, many picture books have reached a level of sophistication in both art and text that raises a question as to whom the books were created for.

Certainly, there are picture books today that appeal to all ages. Sally Lodge (1992) calls these sophisticated books "crossovers," books that are successful in both juvenile and adult markets. She believes that publishers cannot always predict which books will become crossover books. Celebrities such as Julie Andrews Edwards, Madonna, and Sarah Ferguson have recently published picture books that publishers hope will appeal to adult buyers who recognize such names. There are also picture books that have reprints of fine art from museums around the world or illustrations that reflect an adult sensibility in art appreciation. The text of some books seems to address issues that many children are not yet prepared to understand.

What do you think? Are picture books purchased for their appeal to the adult buyers or for their appeal to child readers? Are the exquisite art and sophisticated humor of many picture books more appealing to parents than to children? Who, then, is the audience for these picture books?

he primarily illustrated the writing of others. The most noted among his early illustrated books is Jane Yolen's ***The Emperor and the Kite,*** which was a 1969 Caldecott Honor Book. Young illustrated several other texts with Chinese origins, including ***Chinese Mother Goose Rhymes*** by Robert Wyndham, ***Yeh-Shen: A Cinderella Story from China*** by Ai-Ling Louie, ***White Wave: A Chinese Tale*** by Diane Wolkstein, and ***The Hunter: A Chinese Folktale*** by Mary Casanova.

Ed Young has both written and illustrated a number of books. For his 1989 book, ***Lon Po Po: A Red Riding Hood Story from China,*** Young was awarded the Caldecott Medal. In this version, the children make good decisions and outwit the wolf. A 1994 Caldecott Honor Book, ***Seven Blind Mice,*** is the story of six blind mice who separately explore a mysterious "thing" and report different interpretations to the others. The seventh mouse examines the whole "thing" more thoroughly and combines the other six interpretations to reveal what the "thing" is. The origin of the Chinese zodiac, a twelve-year cycle of years named for animals, is explained in ***Cat and Rat.*** One of the most interesting aspects of Young's work is the diverse range of media he works with, from chalk, watercolor, and collage to mixed media.

Experiences for Further Learning

1. Study some illustrations and practice using the vocabulary that describes what you see. Try seeing if you can identify the artistic media and the style. Then see if you can talk with others about the influence of the media and the style on your overall impression of the book. Remember that what matters is not so much whether you can classify a book correctly, but whether you can articulate how the art influences your understanding of the story as the reader. This is particularly true when considering that artists sometimes use mixed media and some illustrators' work can be interpreted as being influenced by more than one artistic style.

2. Study some picture books that you would be most likely to select for your own pleasure. What qualities appeal to you as an adult? What qualities do you think appeal to children? Are the same qualities likely to appeal to both adults and children? What features make picture books appeal to a wide age range of readers?

3. Select a book from an earlier era, such as the ones discussed in the section of this chapter entitled "Authors and Illustrators Who Have Defined the Field." What qualities still appeal to readers today? What qualities appear dated? What qualities in recently published books are likely to remain popular in future years? What qualities are likely to be time sensitive?

4. Select some alphabet books for different audiences, such as preschoolers who don't yet know the alphabet, elementary school children who are learning the alphabet and its function in literacy, some that appeal to all ages, and others that appeal more to those who already know the alphabet. What makes each alphabet book appropriate for its intended audience? What purpose do alphabet books serve for those who already know the alphabet?

Book Plate Illustrations

The following covers and interior illustrations appear on the color book plate insert:

1 *Frog and Toad Are Friends* by Arnold Lobel, 1970
2 *Why Mosquitoes Buzz in People's Ears* by Verna Aardema, pictures by Leo and Diane Dillon, 1975
3 *Home* by Jeannie Baker, 2003
4 *When Sophie Gets Angry—Really, Really Angry . . .* by Molly Bang, 1999
5 *The Very Hungry Caterpillar* by Eric Carle, 1969/1987
6 *Puss in Boots* by Charles Perrault, illustrated by Hans Fischer, 1996
7 *Look-Alikes* by Joan Steiner, 1999
8 *Scary Stories to Tell in the Dark* by Alvin Schwartz, illustrated by Stephen Gammell, 1987
9 *The Hatseller and the Monkeys* by Baba Wagué Diakité, 1999
10 *Song and Dance Man* by Karen Ackerman, illustrated by Stephen Gammell, 1988
11 *The Paperboy* by Dav Pilkey, 1996
12 *The Paperboy* by Dav Pilkey, 1996
13 *The Paperboy* by Dav Pilkey, 1996
14 *Alphabet Under Construction* by Denise Fleming, 2002
15 *Lilly's Purple Plastic Purse* by Kevin Henkes, 1996
16 *Officer Buckle and Gloria* by Peggy Rathmann, 1995
17 *Officer Buckle and Gloria* by Peggy Rathmann, 1995
18 *Seven Blind Mice* by Ed Young, 1992
19 *Duck! Rabbit!* by Amy Krouse Rosenthal, illustrated by Tom Lichtenheld, 2009
20 *A Couple of Boys Have the Best Week Ever* by Maria Frazee, 2008
21 *Tuesday* by David Wiesner, 1991
22 *Ella Sarah Gets Dressed* by Margaret Chodos-Irvine, 2003
23 *Cook-A-Doodle-Doo!* by Janet Stevens and Susan Stevens Crummel, illustrated by Janet Stevens, 1999
24 *The House in the Night* by Susan Marie Swanson, pictures by Beth Krommes, 2008
25 *Monkey and Me* by Emily Gravett, 2008
26 *Bunny Cakes* by Rosemary Wells, 1997
27 *Wave* by Suzy Lee, 2008
28 *St. George and the Dragon* by Margaret Hodges, illustrated by Trina Schart Hyman, 1984
29 *The Twelve Dancing Princesses* retold and illustrated by Ruth Sanderson, 1990
30 *Grumpy Bird* by Jeremy Tankard, 2007

 ## *Recommended Books*

I indicates interest level by age (P = preschool, YA = young adult)
The picture books in this chapter are not marked with an asterisk since all are picture books. The picture books that are listed within the genre chapters that follow are marked with an asterisk.

Toy Books

Ahlberg, Janet, and Allan Ahlberg. *The Jolly Postman or Other People's Letters.* Little, Brown, 1986. A postman delivers letters to and from various fairy tale characters. Miniature letters, cards, and postcards are included. (**I:** P–8)

Cousins, Lucy. *Maisy's Pop-Up Playhouse.* Candlewick, 1995. Pages of this book fold down to create rooms in a playhouse. (**I:** P)

Ehlert, Lois. *Color Zoo.* HarperCollins, 1989. As they turn the pages, children see various shapes that unlayer to reveal different animal faces. Shape names and animal names are included. A related title is *Color Farm* (1990). (**I:** P)

Gravett, Emily. *Meerkat Mail.* Simon, 2007. Postcards are used as a toy component to both offer information and to advance the story of a meerkat who leaves home and travels the world. (**I:** K–7)

Hill, Eric. *Where's Spot?* Putnam, 1980. Sally looks for Spot, who has not eaten his dinner. Children lift flaps to help search for the missing puppy. Over twenty other books about Spot (with Spanish versions of some titles) are available. (**I:** P)

Hoban, Tana. *Black on White.* Greenwillow, 1993. This board book shows black shapes of familiar objects such as an elephant, a butterfly, and a leaf on a white background. Its companion book is *White on Black* (1993). *Black and White* (2007). (**I:** P)

Inkpen, Mick. *Where, Oh Where, Is Kipper's Bear?* Red Wagon Books/Harcourt, 1995. Kipper, the dog's teddy bear, is missing; flaps, pop-ups, and pull tabs help readers search for the missing bear. (**I:** P)

Park, Linda Sue. *Mung-Mung: A Fold-Out Book of Animal Sounds*. Clarion, 2006. This guessing-game format book features animal sounds from around the world. (**I:** P–7)

Pelham, David. *Sam's Sandwich*. Illustrated by David Pelham and Harry Willock. Dutton, 1990. Sam sneaks in creatures from the garden as his sister Samantha assembles her sandwich. The covers of the book are the bread, and readers unfold pages that serve as the sandwich fillings. A related title is *Sam's Pizza* (1996). (**I:** P–7)

Sabuda, Robert. *Cookie Count: A Tasty Pop-up*. Little Simon, 1997. This book presents delicious-looking and intricately crafted pop-up cookies from one to ten. (**I:** P–8)

Seeger, Laura Vaccaro. *Black? White! Day? Night! A Book of Opposites*. Roaring Brook, 2006. This book incorporates clever use of cutouts and lift-the-flap features to explore the concept of opposites, including a question/answer format that engages readers. (**I:** P–6)

Sendak, Maurice. *The Nutshell Library*. Harper & Row, 1962. A set of four miniature books: *Alligators All Around, Chicken Soup with Rice: A Book of Months, One Was Johnny: A Counting Book*, and *Pierre: A Cautionary Tale*. The first is an alphabet book; the second is a series of poems about enjoying chicken soup all the months of the year; the third is a counting book; and the fourth is a cautionary tale. (**I:** P–7)

Wells, Rosemary. *Max's First Word*. Dial/Viking, 1979/1998. Ruby works hard to expand Max's vocabulary from his one word—"bang." Other humorous stories in board book format about Max and Ruby are *Max's Bedtime* (1985/2003), *Max's Birthday* (1985/2004), and *Max's Breakfast* (1985/2004). (**I:** P)

Zelinsky, Paul O. *Knick-Knack Paddywhack!* Dutton, 2002. The familiar children's song is set to a visual narrative with detailed paper engineering. (**I:** P–8)

———. *The Wheels on the Bus*. Dutton, 1990. This pop-up rendition of a popular action song shows movements for each verse as readers push, pull, or lift tabs on the pages. (**I:** P–6)

Alphabet Books

Base, Graeme. *Animalia*. Abrams, 1987. For each letter of the alphabet, an alliterative phrase describes what various animals are doing. Illustrations are filled with items beginning with the featured letter. (**I:** all ages)

Bayer, Jane. *A, My Name Is Alice*. Illustrated by Steven Kellogg. Dial, 1984. This familiar jump-rope and ball-bouncing chant has a verse for every letter of the alphabet. The animals and their names, the places they come from, and the things they sell all begin with the featured letter. (**I:** P–7)

Dragonwagon, Crescent. *Alligator Arrived with Apples: A Potluck Alphabet Feast*. Illustrated by José Aruego and Ariane Dewey. Atheneum, 1987. Alliterative text describes various animals bringing food for a Thanksgiving feast. (**I:** P–7)

Ehlert, Lois. *Eating the Alphabet: Fruits and Vegetables from A to Z*. Harcourt, 1989. Fruits and vegetables are displayed in alphabetical order. (**I:** P–7)

Feelings, Muriel. *Jambo Means Hello: A Swahili Alphabet Book*. Dial, 1974. Readers are introduced, via the alphabet, to the Swahili culture. (**I:** P–9)

Fleming, Denise. *Alphabet Under Construction*. Holt, 2002. A mouse playfully constructs an alphabet—"airbrushing the A, buttoning the B," etc. in this brilliantly colored alphabet book. (**I:** P–7)

Floca, Brian. *The Racecar Alphabet*. Atheneum, 2003. Through alliterative text and energetic watercolors, cars race through the alphabet from a 1901 Ford 999 to a 2001 Ferrari F1. (**I:** 6–10)

Kitchen, Bert. *Animal Alphabet*. Dial, 1984/1992. Each letter of the alphabet is shown with an unusual animal whose name begins with the letter. (**I:** P–6)

Lessac, Frané. *Caribbean Alphabet*. Tambourine, 1989. The alphabet is used to organize images of the Caribbean islands, from food and animals to popular culture. (**I:** P–8)

Lobel, Anita. *Alison's Zinnia*. Greenwillow, 1990. This alphabet book has a game-like format, using girls' names and flower names. (**I:** 6–8)

Lobel, Arnold. *On Market Street*. Illustrated by Anita Lobel. Greenwillow, 1981. Alphabet letters are depicted as people whose bodies are made up of objects beginning with that letter. (**I:** P–7)

MacDonald, Suse. *Alphabatics*. Bradbury, 1986. Each letter spins and changes into an object whose name begins with that letter. (**I:** P–7)

McMullan, Kate. *I Stink!* Illustrated by Jim McMullan. HarperCollins, 2002. A garbage truck goes out on the night route, picking up trash from A to Z. (**I:** P–7)

Martin, Bill, Jr., and John Archambault. *Chicka Chicka Boom Boom*. Illustrated by Lois Ehlert. Simon & Schuster, 1989. The alphabet letters race up a coconut tree in this rhythmic, rhyming verse. (**I:** P–7)

Musgrove, Margaret. *Ashanti to Zulu: African Traditions*. Illustrated by Leo and Diane Dillon. Dial, 1976. Twenty-six African tribes are shown in alphabetical order, and their cultural traditions are described. (**I:** 7–11)

Provensen, Alice, and Martin Provensen. *A Peaceable Kingdom: The Shaker Abecedarius*. Viking, 1978. The alphabet animal rhymes first published in the Shaker manifesto of July 1882 are newly illustrated in this edition. (**I:** P–7)

Rankin, Laura. *The Handmade Alphabet*. Dial, 1991. The American Sign Language hand sign for each letter of the alphabet is shown, along with an item whose name begins with the letter. (**I:** P–9)

Seeger, Laura Vaccaro. *The Hidden Alphabet*. Porter/Roaring Brook, 2003. This lift-the-flap book cleverly shows a portion of the picture first so readers can engage in guessing what the entire picture representing the letter of the alphabet is. (**I:** K–7)

Shannon, George. *Tomorrow's Alphabet*. Illustrated by Donald Crews. Greenwillow, 1996. The concept of things changing over time is explored in this alphabet book—for example, "A is for seed—tomorrow's apple." (**I:** P–6)

Van Allsburg, Chris. *The Z Was Zapped*. Houghton Mifflin, 1987. Twenty-six one-act plays show what happens to each letter of the alphabet. (**I:** 8–10)

Counting Books

Anno, Mitsumasa. *Anno's Counting Book*. Crowell, 1977. Illustrations of landscapes include objects that can be counted. (**I:** P)

———. *Anno's Counting House*. Philomel, 1982. Cut-out windows of two houses show ten people who move from one house to the other. Readers can try to figure out who has moved and what items they have taken with them, adding to one house and subtracting from the other to count the ten people. (**I:** P–7)

Bang, Molly. *Ten, Nine, Eight*. Greenwillow, 1983. Objects are counted backwards in this bedtime story. (**I:** P)

Carle, Eric. *1, 2, 3 to the Zoo*. Putnam, 1968. Beginning with one elephant and ending with ten birds, each car in the train has one more zoo animal than the one before it. At the end, readers unfold a page to see all the animals at their destination and an empty train along the bottom of the page. (**I:** P)

Christelow, Eileen. *Five Little Monkeys Jumping on the Bed*. Clarion, 1989. Humorous illustrations accompany this familiar chant of what happens when, one by one, the monkeys fall off and hit their heads. (**I:** P–7)

Crews, Donald. *Ten Black Dots*. Greenwillow, 1986. Big black dots are counted from one to ten and shown as parts of familiar objects. For example, "Three dots can make a snowman's face." (**I:** P–5)

Ehlert, Lois. *Fish Eyes: A Book You Can Count On*. Harcourt, 1990. The text is narrated in the voice of a young child who imagines touring the underwater world and seeing brightly colored fish. This counting book includes the concept of "one more" as the guide fish is added to the count on each page. (**I:** P–6)

Feelings, Muriel. *Moja Means One: A Swahili Counting Book*. Illustrated by Tom Feelings. Dial, 1971. Scenes of Africa are shown in this counting book. (**I:** P and up)

Fleming, Denise. *Count!* Holt, 1992. This vibrantly colored counting book shows one through ten animals to be counted. There are also small creatures to be counted by tens. (**I:** P)

Giganti, Paul, Jr. *Each Orange Had 8 Slices: A Counting Book*. Illustrated by Donald Crews. Greenwillow, 1992. Mathematical concepts are shown in the illustrations. (**I:** P–8)

Nikola-Lisa, W. *One Hole in the Road*. Illustrated by Dan Yaccarino. Holt, 1996. The numbers 1 through 10 are introduced while workers fix a hole in the road. (**I:** P–6)

Pomeroy, Diana. *One Potato: A Counting Book of Potato Prints*. Harcourt, 1996. Potato print illustrations are used to count fruits and vegetables from one to ten, then by tens to fifty; the book ends with an illustration of 100 sunflower seeds. (**I:** P–7)

Sayre, April Pulley, and Jeff Sayre. *One Is a Snail, Ten Is a Crab: A Counting by Feet Book*. Illustrated by Randy Cecil. Candlewick, 2003. Various creatures bicycle, limbo, and play volleyball on the beach as readers count, add, and multiply their feet. (**I:** P–7)

Walsh, Ellen Stoll. *Mouse Count*. Harcourt, 1991. A hungry snake counts mice. After they trick the snake into looking for more mice to fill up his jar, the mice tumble out as they "uncount" themselves. (**I:** P–7)

Concept Books

Crews, Donald. *Freight Train*. Greenwillow, 1978. As a freight train passes by, readers are introduced to colors, names of train cars, and the concepts of darkness and light. (**I:** P–7)

Cumpiano, Ina. *Quinito, Day and Night/Quinito, día y noche*. Illustrated by José Ramírez. Children's Book Press, 2008. Bilingually told in Spanish and in English, Quinito's day is portrayed through opposites. (**I:** P–6)

Ehlert, Lois. *Planting a Rainbow*. Harcourt, 1988. As the colored strips—in rainbow order—are flipped, flowers in the featured color appear. (**I:** P–5)

———. *Shapes, Shapes, Shapes*. Greenwillow, 1986. Shapes in the environment are shown in photographs. (**I:** P)

———. *26 Letters and 99 Cents*. Greenwillow, 1987. Open the book one way, and find letters of the alphabet matched with objects whose names begin with each letter. Turn the book over and open it from the opposite end, and count money up to 99 cents. (**I:** P–8)

Hall, Michael. *My Heart is Like a Zoo*. Greenwillow, 2009. Similes compare the emotions of a heart to 20 animals, and illustrations depict those animals, created with varying sizes and colors of heart shapes. (**I:** K–8)

Jonas, Ann. *Color Dance*. Greenwillow, 1989. Dancers with colored scarves introduce the primary colors. When their scarves overlap, the secondary colors are visible. (**I:** P–5)

McMillan, Bruce. *Counting Wildflowers*. Lothrop, Lee & Shepard, 1986. Colored photographs of wildflowers provide children with opportunities to count. (**I:** P)

———. *One, Two, One Pair*. Scholastic, 1991. Illustration shows objects that come in pairs. (**I:** P)

Seeger, Laura Vaccaro. *First the Egg*. Roaring Brook, 2007. This concept book explores the relationship between what comes first and what follows, making a full circle to end with, "First the chicken, then the egg." (**I:** P–7)

Walsh, Ellen Stoll. *Mouse Paint*. Harcourt, 1989. Three white mice splash around in primary colored paint. When they dance in each other's colors, they make new colors. But when the cat comes around, they must find a way to keep from being seen. (**I:** P–5)

Wordless and Nearly Wordless Books

Anno, Mitsumasa. *Anno's Journey*. Philomel, 1978. The small towns and cities of Europe are shown, with cultural and historic details hidden throughout each page. Also by this author/illustrator are *Anno's Britain* (1982), *Anno's Italy* (1980), and *Anno's U.S.A.* (Putnam, 1983/1992). (**I:** 7 and up)

Baker, Jeannie. *Window*. Greenwillow, 1991. Collage illustrations show environmental changes as seen through a window of a house, as the boy who lives there grows from babyhood to adulthood. See also *Where the Forest Meets the Sea* (1988) and *Home* (2004). (**I:** 6–9)

Bang, Molly. *The Grey Lady and the Strawberry Snatcher*. Simon, 1980. The strawberry snatcher follows the Grey Lady through town and forest in hopes of snatching her strawberries, but instead comes across blackberries along the way. (**I:** P–6)

Banyai, Istvan. *Zoom*. Viking, 1995. Like a camera's zoom lens, each page backs up to show more and more of the big picture so that readers are challenged to think about what they see as part of a larger scene. See also *Rezoom* (1995). (**I:** 7 and up)

Briggs, Raymond. *The Snowman*. Random House, 1978. A boy enjoys an adventurous night with a snowman that comes to life. (**I:** P–9)

dePaola, Tomie. *Pancakes for Breakfast*. Harcourt, 1978. This wordless book tells a story of how pancakes are made. (**I:** P–6)

Hutchins, Pat. *Changes, Changes*. Simon, 1971. A story unfolds as two wooden dolls continuously change the things they create out of wooden blocks. (**I:** P–7)

Hyewon, Yum. *Last Night*. Foster/Farrar, 2008. Linocut illustrations expressively tell the story of a girl who is sent to bed when she does not like her dinner, and embarks on a dream adventure. (**I:** P–6)

Jenkins, Steve. *Looking Down*. Houghton Mifflin, 1995. The book begins by looking down onto earth from space, and gradually focuses closer and closer until it ends on a ladybug. (**I:** P–8)

Lee, Suzy. *Wave*. Chronicle, 2008. A little girl plays with a wave as if it were a playmate on the beach in this simply yet evocatively illustrated story. (**I:** P–6)

McCully, Emily Arnold. *Picnic*. Harper & Row, 1984. When the family goes on a picnic, one mouse is bumped out of the car and left behind. The mice are also featured in *School* (1987). (**I:** P–8)

Pinkney, Jerry. *The Lion and the Mouse*. Dial, 2009. Across the landscape of Africa, the folktale of the lion and the mouse is told nearly wordlessly with only the onomatopoeic sounds made by the animals. (**I:** P–8)

Spier, Peter. *Peter Spier's Rain*. Doubleday, 1982. A brother and sister don their rain gear and enjoy playing outside during a rainstorm. (**I:** P–8)

Van Allsburg, Chris. *The Mysteries of Harris Burdick*. Houghton Mifflin, 1984. The book begins with an explanation of how Harris Burdick delivered a stack of pictures with titles and captions, but mysteriously disappeared without delivering the accompanying stories. (**I:** 8–12)

Wiesner, David. *Flotsam*. Clarion, 2006. A magnifying glass, binoculars, microscope, camera—all add up to encourage viewers to consider the various ways in which we view this particular story that is set on the seaside, but also look at how we view our world in which we live. (**I:** K–9)

———. *Sector 7*. Clarion, 1999. A boy is whisked into the clouds while on a school field trip and discovers a use for his artistic talent and imagination when he goes to Sector 7, where clouds are given assignments. (**I:** P–9)

———. *Tuesday*. Clarion, 1991. On a mysterious Tuesday night, frogs float through the air on their lily pads. The mystery of this strange occurrence is complicated when the book closes with shadows of flying pigs. (**I:** P–9)

Wietzman, Jacqueline Preiss, and Robin Preiss Glasser. *You Can't Take a Balloon into The Metropolitan Museum*. Dial, 1998. When a little girl's balloon that she has left for safekeeping with a museum guard flies out over the city, viewers are treated to city scenes that parallel the art seen in the museum by the little girl and her grandmother. See also *You Can't Take a Balloon into The National Gallery* (2000). (**I:** P–8)

Books with Minimal Text

Bang, Molly. *When Sophie Gets Angry—Really, Really Angry*. Scholastic, 1999. The power of a young child's emotional outpouring when required to share a toy is realistically presented. (**I:** P–7)

Dunrea, Olivier. *Gossie*. Houghton Mifflin, 2002. An endearing gosling discovers one red boot missing one day—only to find it on the foot of another gosling—Gertie. See also *Gossie and Gertie* (2002) and others. (**I:** P–7)

Gravett, Emily. *Monkey and Me*. Simon & Schuster, 2007. A little girl and her stuffed monkey tell about having been to see the penguins, elephants, kangaroos, and monkeys and then coming home to tea. (**I:** P–6)

———. *Orange Pear Apple Bear*. Simon & Schuster, 2007. A bear juggles, balances, and ultimately, eats, an apple, an orange, and a pear. (**I:** P–K)

Portis, Antoionette. *Not a Box*. HarperCollins, 2006. Through spare design and minimal text, this book portrays a rabbit playing with a simple cardboard box with a consistent message of using one's imagination when playing. See also: *Not a Stick* (2007). (**I:** P–7)

Raschka, Chris. *Yo! Yes?* Orchard, 1993. Two boys use expressive body language and one- and two-word utterances to communicate. One is lonely; the other offers to be his friend. (**I:** P–7)

Rathmann, Peggy. *Good Night, Gorilla*. Putnam, 1994. In this nearly wordless story, as a zookeeper says good night to the animals in the zoo, the gorilla follows, unlocking their cages so that the animals can follow the zookeeper home. (**I:** P)

Rosenthal, Amy Krouse. *Duck! Rabbit!* Illustrated by Tom Lichtenheld. Chronicle, 2009. Arguing back and forth, two voices claim that the one figure they see is a duck—or a rabbit—and each side's viewpoint is reinforced by how one looks at the pictures. (**I:** P–6)

Shannon, David. *No, David!* Blue Sky/Scholastic, 1998. Mother must repeatedly tell her preschool son "No" in an attempt to stop his inappropriate behavior. See also *David Goes to School* (1999) and *David Gets in Trouble* (2002) (**I:** P–6)

Tafuri, Nancy. *Have You Seen My Duckling?* Greenwillow, 1984. A mother duck leads her ducklings around the lake as they search for a missing duckling. (**I:** P)

Tankard, Jeremy. *Grumpy Bird*. Scholastic, 2007. Wonderfully visually descriptive story about a grumpy bird that is greeted by various animals who play "follow the leader" until their bird leader snaps out of his grumpiness and they all fly off with him. (**I:** P–2)

Easy Readers

Bang-Campbell, Monika. *Little Rat Sets Sail*. Illustrated by Molly Bang. Harcourt, 2002. Little Rat learns to overcome her fear of water as she learns to sail. See also: *Little Rat Rides* (2006), *Little Rat Makes Music* (2007). (**I:** 6–9)

Byars, Betsy. *My Brother, Ant*. Illustrated by Marc Simont. Viking, 1996. Ant's big brother narrates a series of stories that depict a delightfully realistic sibling relationship. The sequel is *Ant Plays Bear* (1997). (**I:** P–7)

Cazet, Denys. *Minnie and Moo Go Dancing*. DK Ink, 1998. Humorous short stories describe the antics of two cows; they wonder with horror if the hamburgers being served as refreshments at the dance are former friends. There are many titles in this series. (**I:** P–7)

dePaola, Tomie. *26 Fairmount Avenue*. Putnam, 1999. Short chapters relay the incidents of Tomie's own childhood as his family built and moved to their new home. The sequels are *Here We All Are* (2000), *On My Way* (2001), *What a Year!* (2002), and *Things Will Never Be the Same* (2003). (**I:** P–7)

Grant, Judyann Ackerman. *Chicken Said, "Cluck!"* Illustrated by Sue Truesdell. HarperCollins, 2008. A "Turnabout" story in which the chicken who is shooed away from a pumpkin patch ends up saving the day. (**I:** K–7)

Howe, James. *"Pinky and Rex"* series. Illustrated by Melissa Sweet. Athanaeum. Pinky and Rex are best friends who experience everyday adventures. (**I:** K–8)

Kvasnosky, Laura McGee. *"Zelda and Ivy"* series. Candlewick, 1998–2006. Three short stories focus on the day-to-day events that show the bond as well as sibling rivalry between two fox sisters, Zelda and Ivy. (**I:** P–7)

Lin, Grace. *Ling & Ting: Not Exactly the Same!* Little Brown, 2009. Ling and Ting are twins whose stories are told in short vignettes. Some are culturally grounded, such as making Chinese dumplings and eating with chopsticks, while most are culturally generic experiences such as haircuts, library visits, etc. (**I:** P–6)

Lobel, Arnold. *Frog and Toad Are Friends.* HarperCollins, 1970/1979. Five short stories tell of the friendship between Frog and Toad. Sequels are *Frog and Toad Together* (1972) and *Frog and Toad All Year* (1976). (**I:** P–8)

Marshall, (James) Edward. *Fox and His Friends.* Illustrated by James Marshall. Dial, 1982. In this humorous story, Fox wishes his tag-along sister would not be with him when he plays with his friends. There are numerous other books about Fox. (**I:** 6–8)

———. *Three by the Sea.* Illustrated by James Marshall. Dial, 1981. Lolly, Spider, and Sam go to the seashore and try to outdo each other in telling the most interesting story. See also *Four on the Shore* (1985). (**I:** 6–8)

Rylant, Cynthia. *Henry and Mudge: The First Book of Their Adventures.* Illustrated by Sucie Stevenson. Simon & Schuster/Aladdin, 1987–2008. A lonely boy named Henry finds companionship with a big dog named Mudge in this popular series. (**I:** 6–8)

———. *"Mr. Putter and Tabby"* has over 15 titles in this popular series. (**I:** 6–8)

Seeger, Laura Vaccaro. *Dog and Bear: Two Friends, Three Stories.* Roaring Brook, 2007. A toy patchwork bear and a real dachshund humorously interact in stories that model how good friends interact. (**I:** P–2)

———. *One Boy.* Roaring Brook, 2008. Using cutout windows to mask and unveil word parts, Seeger offers opportunities for beginning readers to examine words and word parts. (**I:** K–7)

Seuss, Dr. *The Cat in the Hat.* Random House, 1957. One rainy day, when two children are home alone, an entertaining cat comes and creates chaos and wild fun. The sequel is *The Cat in the Hat Comes Back* (1958). (**I:** P–8)

———. *Green Eggs and Ham.* Random House, 1960. Sam-I-Am insists on a favorable response from the dog to his offering of green eggs and ham, but the dog remains persistent in refusing. (**I:** P–8)

———. *Hop on Pop.* Random House, 1963. Words with short "o" sounds tell a humorous story of creatures hopping on Pop. Other Seuss titles are *One Fish, Two Fish, Red Fish, Blue Fish* (1960) and *Fox in Socks* (1965). (**I:** P–7)

Van Leeuwen, Jean. *Tales of Oliver Pig.* Illustrated by Arnold Lobel. Dial, 1979–2008. The "Oliver and Amanda" series has numerous popular titles. (**I:** P–8)

Willems, Mo. *Are You Ready to Play Outside?* and other titles in the "Elephant and Piggie" books. Hyperion, 2007–8. These stories of friendship appeal on every level—with readable, humorous, and emotionally satisfying episodes. (**I:** P–7)

Predictable Books

Fox, Mem. *Hattie and the Fox.* Illustrated by Patricia Mullins. Bradbury, 1987. As Hattie the hen tries to warn the barnyard animals of danger, more and more of a fox is revealed in the bushes. (**I:** P–7)

———. *I Went Walking.* Illustrated by Julie Vivas. Harcourt, 1990. A child goes walking and encounters a series of ani-mals, with their tails showing on the previous page to offer clues of what animal is next. (**I:** P–7)

Langstaff, John. *Oh, A-Hunting We Will Go.* Illustrated by Nancy Winslow Parker. Simon, 1974. Rhyming couplets in this folk song tell of a group of children who go hunting and find vari-ous animals they place somewhere temporarily—for example, "We'll catch a goat, and put him in a boat, and then we'll let him go." (**I:** P–8)

Martin, Bill, Jr. *Brown Bear, Brown Bear, What Do You See?* Illustrated by Eric Carle. Holt, 1967/1983. Patterned, repeti-tive language is used to introduce colors and animal names. See also *Polar Bear, Polar Bear, What Do You Hear?* (1991) and *Panda Bear, Panda Bear, What Do You See?* (2003). (**I:** P–7)

Numeroff, Laura Joffe. *If You Give a Mouse a Cookie.* Illustrated by Felicia Bond. Harper, 1985. A circular story of cause and effect, beginning and ending with a mouse and a cookie. There are several related titles. (**I:** P–8)

Shaw, Charles G. *It Looked Like Spilt Milk.* Harper, 1947. Patterned language describes various objects that can be seen in clouds. (**I:** P–7)

Shulevitz, Uri. *One Monday Morning.* Macmillan, 1967. Repetitive text depicts visitors on one Monday morning. (**I:** P–6)

Wood, Audrey. *The Napping House.* Illustrated by Don Wood. Harcourt, 1984. It is naptime, and the little boy, his granny, and various animals are piled on the bed. One wakeful flea causes everyone to spring up from naptime. (**I:** P–7)

Picture Storybooks

Aardema, Verna. *Who's in Rabbit's House?* Illustrated by Leo and Diane Dillon. Dial, 1969/1977. Someone is inside Rabbit's house and won't let her in. (**I:** P–9)

———. *Why Mosquitoes Buzz in People's Ears: A West African Tale.* Illustrated by Leo and Diane Dillon. Dial, 1987. A mos-quito tells a lie to an iguana and sets off a chain of events. (**I:** 6–9)

Ackerman, Karen. *Song and Dance Man.* Illustrated by Stephen Gammell. Knopf, 1992. Grandpa reminisces about the bygone days when he danced in vaudeville. (**I:** 6–8)

Agee, Jon. *Milo's Hat Trick.* Hyperion, 2001. Milo the Magnificent is about to lose his job when a bear helps him by offering to pop out of a hat for him. Tired after performing 762 times, he teaches Milo a very important lesson. (**I:** P–7)

Aliki. *A Medieval Feast.* Harper & Row, 1983. Preparations for a medieval feast at an English manor house are described with accompanying lavish illustrations. (**I:** 7–10)

Allard, Harry. *Miss Nelson Is Missing!* Illustrated by James Marshall. Houghton Mifflin, 1977. The children behave badly, and their sweet teacher, Miss Nelson, disappears. She is replaced by Miss Viola Swamp, who is out to set the children straight. Sequels are *Miss Nelson Is Back* (1982) and *Miss Nelson Has a Field Day* (1985). (**I:** 6–9)

Avi. *Silent Movie.* Illustrated by C. D. Mordan. Atheneum, 2003. In 1909, when a boy and his mother fail to find the boy's father upon immigrating to the United States, it is the boy's role in a silent movie that enables the father to find them. The story is depicted in the style of black-and-white silent movies of that era. (**I:** 8–11)

Baer, Gene. *Thump, Thump, Rat-a-Tat-Tat.* Illustrated by Lois Ehlert. Harper & Row, 1989. Bold illustrations show a march-ing band getting louder and larger as it approaches and then becoming softer and smaller as it continues down the street. Also in board book format. (**I:** P–7)

Baker, Jeannie. *Where the Forest Meets the Sea*. Greenwillow, 1988. Exquisitely detailed and textured collage illustrations show an Australian forest. (**I:** 6–9)

Bang, Molly. *Goose*. Blue Sky/Scholastic, 1996. A goose egg rolls out of its nest, and the baby goose is adopted by a woodchuck family. (**I:** P–7)

Best, Cari. *Three Cheers for Catherine the Great!* Illustrated by Giselle Potter. DK Ink, 1999. When Grandma Catherine announces No Presents for her birthday, Sara must creatively think of a way to celebrate her grandmother's birthday (**I:** 6–9)

Birdseye, Tom. *Airmail to the Moon*. Illustrated by Stephen Gammell. Holiday House, 1992. Ora Mae Cotton dreams of what she'll do with the money from the tooth fairy, but before the tooth fairy can come, Ora Mae discovers that her tooth is missing. She vows to send the thief "airmail" to the moon— when she shoves her hand into her pants pocket and feels something hard. (**I:** 6–9)

Blos, Joan W. *Old Henry*. Illustrated by Stephen Gammell. Morrow/Mulberry, 1987. Henry is misunderstood by his neighbors and sent away. (**I:** 6–9)

Brett, Jan. *The Mitten*. Putnam, 1989. Nicki's lost mitten provides snug shelter for various animals until a bear sneezes. See also *The Hat* (1997). (**I:** P–8)

Brown, Marcia. *Once a Mouse*. Scribner's, 1961. This fable from India, where a mouse that keeps changing into other animals learns a lesson about vanity, is illustrated with woodcuts. (**I:** 6–9)

———. translator and illustrator. *Shadow*. Macmillan, 1982. Brown's translation of a poem by French poet Blaise Cendrars is about a dancing image, Shadow, that rises from ashes, brought to life by African storytellers. (**I:** 7–9)

Brown, Margaret Wise. *Goodnight Moon*. Illustrated by Clement Hurd. Harper, 1947. A young rabbit says good night to various objects in the room and outside the window. (**I:** P)

Browne, Anthony. *Voices in the Park*. Knopf, 1998. A mother and her daughter take their dog to the park, and a father and his son take their dog to the park. This book depicts four points of view on this singular event. (**I:** 6–9)

Bunting, Eve. *Smoky Night*. Illustrated by David Diaz. Harcourt, 1994. The Los Angeles riots provided the impetus for the creation of this book. Families learn about acceptance and being good neighbors in order to survive difficult times. (**I:** 9–11)

Burleigh, Robert. *Flight*. Illustrated by Mike Wimmer. Philomel, 1991. Charles Lindbergh's 1927 nonstop solo flight from New York to Paris is described in this book. (**I:** 6–9)

Burningham, John. *Come Away from the Water, Shirley*. Crowell, 1977. There are two stories in this family's trip to the beach. One is Shirley's daydreaming about pirate ships and gangplanks; the other is about the actual events and the parental warnings about how to behave at the beach. See also *Time to Get Out of the Bath, Shirley* (1978) (**I:** P–8)

———. *Mr. Gumpy's Outing*. Harper, 1976. Mr. Gumpy meets many animals that ask to go along on his boat outing. A related title is *Mr. Gumpy's Motor Car* (1976). (**I:** P–6)

Burton, Virginia Lee. *The Little House*. Houghton Mifflin, 1942/1978. A house that was built in the countryside finds that, as the years go by, it is becoming run-down and is being surrounded by a city. (**I:** P–7)

———. *Mike Mulligan and His Steam Shovel*. Houghton Mifflin, 1939. Mike Mulligan and his steam shovel, Mary Anne, prove that they can dig more in one day than one hundred men can dig in a week. (**I:** P–7)

Carle, Eric. *The Grouchy Ladybug*. Scholastic, 1977. Each hour of the day, a grouchy ladybug asks increasingly larger creatures if they want to fight. Ultimately, the ladybug learns a lesson. (**I:** P–7)

———. *A House for Hermit Crab*. Picture Book Studio, 1987. A hermit crab outgrows its shell and seeks a larger home. (**I:** P–7)

———. *Mister Seahorse*. Philomel, 2004. A seahorse meets other underwater creatures where the father is in charge of caring for the eggs. (**I:** P–7)

———. *Rooster's Off to See the World*. Picture Book Studio, 1972. A rooster sets off to see the world. In this book featuring mathematical concepts of addition and subtraction, Rooster is joined by others who return home when it gets dark. (**I:** P–7)

———. *The Secret Birthday Message*. Harper & Row, 1986. A little boy receives a letter with a coded set of directions on how to find his birthday present. (**I:** P–7)

———. *The Tiny Seed*. Picture Book Studio, 1991. In autumn, many seeds blow high in the wind and encounter various perils, but a surviving tiny seed grows into a flower. (**I:** P–7)

———. *The Very Hungry Caterpillar*. Philomel, 1984. A little caterpillar eats "holes" through the food on the pages, and the cycle of metamorphosis is explained when the caterpillar emerges from a cocoon as a butterfly. See also *The Very Busy Spider* (1985), *The Very Quiet Cricket* (1990), *The Very Lonely Firefly* (1995), and *The Very Clumsy Click Beetle* (1999). (**I:** P–7)

Cherry, Lynne. *The Great Kapok Tree: A Tale of the Amazon Rain Forest*. Harcourt, 1990. When a man takes a nap before cutting down the great kapok tree in the rain forest, the animals that depend on the tree for their survival appear in a dream and convince him not to chop it down. (**I:** 6–9)

———. *A River Ran Wild: An Environmental History*. Harcourt Brace, 1992. This book traces the history of the Nashua River from 7,000 years ago until recent times, with double-spread pages featuring significant influences to the river. (**I:** 9–12)

Child, Lauren. *Who's Afraid of the Big, Bad Book?* Hyperion, 2003. A boy falls asleep and enters into the world of his fairy tale book; he wakes up resolved to fix all of his mischievous markings and cutouts that changed the lives of the characters. See also *Beware of the Storybook Wolves* (2001). (**I:** 7–10)

Chodos-Irvine, Margaret. *Ella Sarah Gets Dressed*. Harcourt. 2003. Chodos-Irvine employs a variety of printmaking techniques to show Ella Sarah's confidence in cheerfully selecting her own attire for the day. (**I:** P–7)

Cole, Joanna. *The Magic School Bus on the Ocean Floor*. Illustrated by Bruce Degen. Scholastic, 1992. In the *Magic School Bus* series, Ms. Frizzle takes her class on many field trips on the magic school bus. This time, they go to the ocean floor and explore life there. (**I:** 6–8)

Cooney, Barbara. *Miss Rumphius*. Viking, 1982. Miss Rumphius travels the world, making it more beautiful as she plants lupines. (**I:** 6–9)

Crews, Nina. *You Are Here*. Greenwillow, 1998. Two sisters shrink and embark on a magical journey. (**I:** P–8)

Cronin, Doreen. *Click, Clack, Moo: Cows That Type*. Illustrated by Betsy Lewin. Simon, 2000. Farmer Brown's cows have gotten a hold of a typewriter that they use to negotiate in getting their needs met. (**I:** 6–9)

Cuyler, Margery. *That's Good! That's Bad!* Illustrated by David Catrow. Holt, 1991. In alternating courses of good luck and bad luck, a little boy's balloon starts him on an adventure. (**I:** P–7)

dePaola, Tomie. *The Art Lesson.* Putnam, 1997. In this autobiographical story, Tomie recalls his childhood passion for drawing and how it was met by adults with frustration as well as support. (**I:** P–7)

———. *Nana Upstairs and Nana Downstairs.* Autobiographical stories of Tomie's relationship with his grandmothers. Putnam, 1973. See also *Now One Foot, Now the Other* (1981), *Tom* (1993), and *Watch Out for the Chicken Feet in Your Soup* (1974). (**I:** 6–8)

———. *Strega Nona.* Simon & Schuster, 1979. "Grandma Witch" hires a helper, Big Anthony, who thinks that he has found the secret of how to make the magic pot cook pasta. What he doesn't know is how to make it stop. Several sequels were published between 1996–2006. (**I:** P–7)

Diakité, Baba Wagué. *The Magic Gourd.* Scholastic, 2003. Traditional motifs are used to paint ceramic bowls, plates, tiles, and mud cloths that decorate this trickster tale from Mali about gaining peace through generosity and friendship. (**I:** 7–10)

Dupasquier, Philippe. *Dear Daddy.* Puffin, 1988. A little girl's daily activities are depicted alongside the daily activities of her father, who is away at sea. (**I:** 6–8)

Duvoisin, Roger. *Petunia.* Knopf, 1950. Petunia is a silly goose who thinks that all she has to do to gain wisdom is carry a book. (**I:** P–7)

Ehlert, Lois. *Feathers for Lunch.* Harcourt, 1990. A housecat hopes to catch one of the birds in the backyard for lunch, but all get away safely, and the cat ends up with only feathers. Bird descriptions are included. (**I:** P–7)

———. *Growing Vegetable Soup.* Harcourt, 1987. Father and child plant seeds and sprouts and grow the vegetables that make a soup. (**I:** P–5)

———. *Market Day.* Harcourt, 2000. Collages of folk art show the trip to town square and the events of market day. (**I:** P–7)

———. *Red Leaf, Yellow Leaf.* Harcourt, 1991. The life cycle of a maple tree is shown through collage illustrations. (**I:** P–7)

———. *Snowballs.* Harcourt, 1995. Children create a snow family, using a large variety of items they had saved: a luggage tag, a toy fish, popcorn, etc. (**I:** P–6)

———. *Waiting for Wings.* Harcourt, 2001. The process of metamorphosis from caterpillar to butterfly is told through lyrical text and breathtaking illustrations. (**I:** P–7)

Emberley, Barbara. *Drummer Hoff.* Illustrated by Ed Emberley. Simon & Schuster, 1967. The story of how a cannon is fired is told through rhyming couplets in cumulative text. (**I:** 5–8)

Ernst, Lisa Campbell. *Zinnia and Dot.* Viking Penguin, 1992. Zinnia and Dot are two hens that are full of pride. When a weasel steals their eggs, they must learn to cooperate to save the one egg that is left behind. (**I:** 6–9)

Falconer, Ian. *Olivia.* Atheneum, 2000. Through text and illustration, readers see Olivia as a little pig whose daily life is lived fully and expressively. (**I:** P–8)

Fleming, Denise. *Barnyard Banter.* Holt, 1994. Barnyard animals noisily occupy their places on the farm, but the goose is missing. See also: *In the Tall, Tall Grass* (1991), *In the Small, Small Pond* (1993). (**I:** P–6)

———. *Where Once There Was a Wood.* Holt, 1996. Many kinds of wildlife lose their homes when housing developments are constructed. Endnotes invite readers to take action in creating wildlife habitats in their backyards and communities. (**I:** P–8)

Flournoy, Valerie. *The Patchwork Quilt.* Illustrated by Jerry Pinkney. Dial, 1985. Creating a quilt leads to collecting many family memories. (**I:** 6–9)

Fox, Mem. *Koala Lou.* Illustrated by Pamela Lofts. Harcourt, 1988. Koala Lou longs for the days before the other children came along, when her mother used to tell Koala Lou how much she loved her. Koala Lou enters a race in her attempt to win her mother's affections again. (**I:** P–7)

———. *Night Noises.* Illustrated by Terry Denton. Harcourt, 1989. Lily Laceby, rumored to be ninety, dozes in her chair and dreams of years gone by. Her dog, Butch Aggie, hears strange noises outside—lots of relatives arriving for a surprise party! (**I:** P–7)

———. *Possum Magic.* Illustrated by Julie Vivas. Harcourt, 1990. Grandma Poss turns Hush invisible and Hush enjoys many adventures because she can't be seen. But later, Grandma Poss and Hush must travel throughout Australian cities, eating Australian foods, in an attempt to remember the magic to make Hush visible again. (**I:** P–7)

———. *Wilfrid Gordon McDonald Partridge.* Illustrated by Julie Vivas. Kane/Miller, 1985. Wilfrid Gordon McDonald Partridge is worried because everyone is talking about Miss Nancy's lost memory. In his attempt to find out what "memory" is, he restores Miss Nancy's memory in an unusual way. (**I:** 6–9)

Frazee, Marla. *A Couple of Boys Have the Best Week Ever.* Harcourt, 2008. Cartoon illustrations and upbeat text portray two boys enjoying a week of bonding through their various explorations at "nature camp." (**I:** K–7)

Gág, Wanda. *Millions of Cats.* Coward, McCann, 1929. When a lonely old man cannot choose among hundreds of cats, thousands of cats, millions and billions and trillions of cats, the cats fight it out as each claims to be the prettiest. (**I:** P–7)

Gerstein, Mordicai. *The Man Who Walked Between the Towers.* Roaring Brook Press, 2003. This true story shows the courage of a young Frenchman who walked on a tightrope between the World Trade Center Towers in 1974. (**I:** 7–10)

Goble, Paul. *The Girl Who Loved Wild Horses.* Macmillan, 1978. A girl finds that she communes with horses more easily than she does with her people and goes to join the wild horses. (**I:** P–7)

Graham, Bob. *"Let's Get a Pup!" Said Kate.* Candlewick, 2001. Even though Kate and her parents find the perfect pup at The Rescue Center, they cannot forget the old, gray dog they passed up. (**I:** P–8)

Gravett, Emily. *Wolves.* Simon & Schuster, 2007. A rabbit goes to the library and discovers information about wolves that is distressing. (**I:** P–7)

Haley, Gail E. *A Story, a Story.* Atheneum, 1970. This is an African tale in which Anansi the Spider makes a bargain with the Sky God. (**I:** P–8)

Hall, Donald. *The Ox-Cart Man.* Illustrated by Barbara Cooney. Viking, 1979. In nineteenth-century New England, a family fills an ox cart with the extra things they have grown or made during the previous year. After everything in the cart is sold, the family purchases supplies and goes through another year of growing things and making things to sell. (**I:** 6–8)

Heide, Florence Parry, and Judith Heide Gilliland. *The Day of Ahmed's Secret.* Illustrated by Ted Lewin. Lothrop, 1990. Young Ahmed works in his city of Cairo, anticipating the end of his day when he can share his proud secret with his family. (**I:** P–8)

Henkes, Kevin. *Chester's Way.* Greenwillow, 1988. Chester and Wilson, two inseparable friends, find room in their friendship for another when Lilly moves into the neighborhood and proves herself a true friend. (**I:** P–7)

———. *Chrysanthemum.* Greenwillow, 1991. Chrysanthemum is pleased with her name until classmates tease her about it. With the help of the music teacher's affirmation, Chrysanthemum "blooms" as she regains pride in her name. (**I:** P–6)

———. *Julius, the Baby of the World.* Greenwillow, 1990. Lilly cannot stand the attention showered on her new baby brother, Julius. She suddenly develops pride in him when a cousin makes unpleasant remarks about him. (**I:** P–8)

———. *Kitten's First Full Moon.* Greenwillow, 2004. Kitten mistakes a full moon for a bowl of milk and sets off on a quest to reach it. (**I:** P–8)

———. *Lilly's Purple Plastic Purse.* Greenwillow, 1996. Lilly disrupts class to show off her new purple plastic purse and is devastated when Mr. Slinger, the teacher whom she idolizes, confiscates the purse until the end of the day. (**I:** P–8)

———. *Old Bear.* Greenwillow, 2008. A bear in hibernation dreams of the passing of seasons. (**I:** P–6)

———. *Owen.* Greenwillow, 1993. Owen is about to start school, and his nosy next-door neighbor is sure that there must be a way to get Owen to give up his security blanket. (**I:** P–7)

———. *Sheila Rae, the Brave.* Greenwillow, 1987. Sheila Rae isn't afraid of anything, or so it seems, until she takes a wrong turn on the way home one day. It is little sister Louise—whom Sheila Rae refers to as the "scaredy cat"—who comes to the rescue. (**I:** P–6)

———. *A Weekend with Wendell.* Greenwillow, 1987. Wendell is a weekend guest at Sophie's house, and he makes all the rules and demands they play by them. Sophie decides to stand up to Wendell's tyranny and makes him be the burning building while she plays the role of fire chief. (**I:** P–6)

———. *Wemberly Worried.* Greenwillow, 2000. Wemberly worries obsessively about everything, from big things to little things, and needs much assurance. (**I:** P–7)

Hesse, Karen. *Come On, Rain.* Illustrated by Jon Muth. Scholastic, 1999. The arrival of rain at last cools off the heat of summer as mothers join their daughters outside. (**I:** P–8)

Hest, Amy. *Baby Duck and the Bad Eyeglasses.* Illustrated by Jill Barton. Candlewick, 1996. Baby Duck is unhappy about her new eyeglasses until her Grandpa helps her overcome her feelings. (**I:** P–7)

Ho, Minfong. *Hush!* Illustrated by Holly Meade. Orchard, 1996. In this lullaby set in Thailand, a mother tries to quiet the animals so that her baby can sleep. (**I:** P–8)

Hoban, Russell. *A Baby Sister for Frances.* Illustrated by Lillian Hoban. Harper & Row, 1964. Frances the badger tries to adjust to having a new baby sister around. A few of the other stories about Frances are *Bread and Jam for Frances* (1964), *Best Friends for Frances* (1969), and *A Bargain for Frances* (1970). (**I:** 6–8)

Hodges, Margaret. *St. George and the Dragon.* Illustrated by Trina Schart Hyman. Little, Brown, 1984. This adaptation of Edmund Spenser's *Faerie Queene* tells how the Red Cross Knight slays the dragon and ends its terrorizing of the English countryside. (**I:** 8–12)

Hogrogian, Nonny. *One Fine Day.* Macmillan, 1971. A thirsty fox drinks milk from an old woman's pail, and she cuts off its tail. The woman will not return the tail until the fox returns her milk. Thus begins the circular tale in which the fox must ask for the help of many to retrieve its tail. Based on an Armenian folktale. (**I:** P–8)

Houston, Gloria. *My Great-Aunt Arizona.* Illustrated by Susan Condie Lamb. HarperCollins, 1992. A girl reflects on her great-aunt's teaching career in the Appalachian mountains. (**I:** 6–8)

Hughes, Shirley. *Dogger.* 1977. Lothrop, 1988. A favorite stuffed dog is missing, and the loss creates agony for the owner. (**I:** P–8)

Hutchins, Pat. *The Doorbell Rang.* Greenwillow, 1986. Ma has baked cookies for Victoria and Sam, but every time the door-bell rings, more friends join them and there are fewer cookies to go around. (**I:** P–7)

Hyman, Trina Schart. *Little Red Riding Hood.* Holiday House, 1983. Beautiful paintings illustrate this Caldecott-winning version of the familiar tale of a little girl who is sent to visit her sick grandmother. (**I:** 6–9)

Isaacs, Anne. *Swamp Angel.* Dutton, 1994. Illustrated by Paul O. Zelinsky. A tall tale about a bear-wrestling heroine who helps settlers in Tennessee. (**I:** 6–9)

Isadora, Rachel. *Ben's Trumpet.* Greenwillow, 1979. Ben wants to learn to play a trumpet, and a nightclub owner helps him realize his dream. (**I:** 6–9)

Jenkins, Steve and Robin Page. *Move!* Cut paper collage illustrations and text design effectively portray the motion of how animals move. This husband and wife team have created numerous books that exemplify this style. (**I:** P–8)

Johnson, Crockett. *Harold and the Purple Crayon.* Harper & Row, 1958. Harold goes on a walk, using his purple crayon to draw pictures that create an adventure. Three sequels are *Harold's Trip to the Sky* (1957), *Harold's Circus* (1959), and *A Picture for Harold's Room* (1960). (**I:** P–7)

Johnston, Tony. *The Wagon.* Illustrated by James E. Ransome. Tambourine/Morrow, 1996. A boy born into slavery builds a wagon for his master, imagining that it is the glorious chariot of freedom in the song "Swing Low, Sweet Chariot." (**I:** 6–9)

Jonas, Ann. *Round Trip.* Greenwillow, 1983. The journey begins at dawn in a quiet neighborhood and passes through the countryside on the way to the city. Then readers turn the book upside down and see what the illustrations depict when viewed from the opposite direction, completing a round trip back to the neighborhood. (**I:** P–9)

Joyce, William. *George Shrinks.* HarperCollins, 1991. George is suddenly a "Tom Thumb" in his normal-sized world, and he encounters the delights and fears of being small. (**I:** 6–9)

Kasza, Keiko. *A Mother for Choco.* Putnam, 1992. Choco goes in search of mother, only to find that nobody looks like him. Instead, he meets a mother who asks what a mother would do. (**I:** P–7)

———. *The Rat and the Tiger.* Putnam, 1993. Tiger always bullies his small friend Rat, until one day Rat decides to turn the tables. (**I:** P–7)

———. *Wolf's Chicken Stew.* Putnam, 1987. Wolf is very hungry for chicken stew and finds the perfect chicken. His attempts to fatten her up backfire. (**I:** P–7)

Keats, Ezra Jack. *Goggles!* Macmillan, 1969. Archie and Willie are met by bullies and must think quickly to return home safely. (**I:** P–7)

———. *Peter's Chair*. Harper, 1967. Peter is jealous of his new baby sister and refuses to give her his chair until he discovers that he has outgrown it. (**I:** P–7)

———. *The Snowy Day*. Viking, 1962. Peter plays outside following a big snowfall. (**I:** P–7)

Kellogg, Steven. *A Rose for Pinkerton*. Dial, 1981. A family's Great Dane and a kitten are intended to be friends. See also *Pinkerton, Behave!* (1979) and *Prehistoric Pinkerton* (1987). (**I:** 6–9)

Kraus, Robert. *Leo the Late Bloomer*. Illustrated by José Aruego. Windmill, 1971/2000. Father tiger is anxious as his young son, Leo, seems unable to do anything yet. But in time, Leo finds that he has developed at his own rate. (**I:** P–6)

Landowne, Youme. *Selavi, That Is Life: A Haitian Story of Hope*. Illustrated by Youme Landowne. Cinco Puntos, 2004. This story of homeless children in Haiti depicts children who work together and care for each other. (**I:** K–8)

Leaf, Munro. *The Story of Ferdinand*. Illustrated by Robert Lawson. Viking, 1936. Ferdinand grows to be a big strong bull, but he is interested only in sitting and smelling flowers. When he accidentally sits on a bumblebee, his resulting behavior causes him to be chosen for the bullfights in Madrid. (**I:** P–9)

Lionni, Leo. *Frederick*. Knopf, 1967. The field mice work hard to prepare for winter, and it appears that Frederick is shirking his responsibilities. However, when winter comes, he is able to entertain the other mice with his poems describing the warmth of the sun and the colors of the flowers. A sequel is *Frederick and His Friends* (1981). (**I:** P–7)

———. *Inch by Inch*. Astor-Honor, 1962. To avoid being eaten by the birds who hold him captive, an inchworm cleverly sets off to measure the length of a nightingale's song. (**I:** P–7)

———. *Little Blue and Little Yellow*. Astor-Honor, 1959. Abstract shapes depict members of the blue family and the yellow family. When their children play and hug, they turn green. (**I:** P–6)

———. *Swimmy*. Pantheon, 1963. A little fish comes up with a clever plan to protect the small fish in the school from being eaten by larger fish: They swim together in the formation of a giant fish. (**I:** P–7)

Lobel, Arnold. *Fables*. Harper & Row, 1980. This collection has many fables told in the style of Aesop. (**I:** 7–9)

———. *The Rose in My Garden*. Greenwillow, 1984. Illustrated by Anita Lobel. Cumulative text tells the story of a bee asleep on a rose in the garden—until a cat chases a mouse through the garden. (**I:** P–8)

Macaulay, David. *Black and White*. Houghton Mifflin, 1990. This Caldecott winner presents four separate stories—or one intertwined story—about children, parents, trains, and cows. (**I:** 8–12)

———. *Why the Chicken Crossed the Road*. Houghton Mifflin, 1987. This is a cause-and-effect story that starts and ends with a chicken crossing the road. (**I:** P–9)

Marshall, James. *George and Martha*. Houghton Mifflin, 1972. George and Martha are two hippos who share a fun-filled day. Other titles are *George and Martha Encore* (1973), *George and Martha Rise and Shine* (1976), *George and Martha One Fine Day* (1978), *George and Martha Back in Town* (1984), and *George and Martha 'Round and 'Round* (1988). (**I:** P–8)

Martin, Bill, Jr., and John Archambault. *The Ghost-Eye Tree*. Illustrated by Ted Rand. Holt, 1985. When a brother and sister are sent to fetch a pail of milk one dark and spooky night, their imaginations run wild as they hurry past the Ghost-Eye Tree. (**I:** P–8)

Martin, Rafe. *Will's Mammoth*. Illustrated by Stephen Gammell. Putnam, 1989. While playing in the snow one day, a little boy lets his imagination take off. (**I:** P–8)

Maruki, Toshi. *Hiroshima No Pika*. Lothrop, 1982. Expressionistic illustrations accompany the story, which describes what happens to a family after the atomic bombing of Hiroshima in August 1945. (**I:** 10 and up)

Mayer, Mercer. *There's a Nightmare in My Closet*. Dial, 1969. A boy is sure there is a nightmare living in his closet, but decides that he must confront the monster. (**I:** P–7)

McCloskey, Robert. *Blueberries for Sal*. Viking, 1948. A little girl goes blueberry picking with her mother and a little bear follows its mother, but the two children get their mothers mixed up! (**I:** P–7)

———. *Make Way for Ducklings*. Viking, 1941. Mr. and Mrs. Mallard set off in search of a perfect place to raise their family. They find that Boston Public Garden provides just the right home. (**I:** P–8)

McCully, Emily Arnold. *Mirette on the High Wire*. Putnam, 1992. When a formerly great tightrope artist becomes fearful of walking the rope, it is a little girl, Mirette, who must help him overcome his fears. (**I:** 6–9)

McKissack, Patricia. *Mirandy and Brother Wind*. Knopf, 1988. Illustrated by Jerry Pinkney. Mirandy seeks Brother Wind as a partner to win the cake walk. (**I:** 6–9)

McLerran, Alice. *Roxaboxen*. Illustrated by Barbara Cooney. Lothrop, 1991. Marian and her sisters enjoy imaginary play with their friends as they create a community out of rocks on a hill. (**I:** 6–9)

McPhail, David. *Fix-It*. Dutton, 1984. Emma Bear is distressed to find that the television won't turn on, until Mother Bear reads her a good book. (**I:** P–6)

———. *Pigs Aplenty, Pigs Galore!* Dutton, 1993. Late one night, a man is reading when he discovers "pigs aplenty, pigs galore" in his house. More and more pigs arrive, wearing outrageous costumes and creating havoc. (**I:** P–8)

Meddaugh, Susan. *Hog-Eye*. Houghton Mifflin, 1995. When the family demands an explanation for why a little pig missed school one day, she launches into a wild story of how she got on the wrong bus, took a shortcut through the forest, and met a wolf who tied her up and made her teach him how to make soup. The pig tells how she outwitted the wolf through the magic of "Hog-Eye." (**I:** 6–9)

———. *Martha Speaks*. Houghton Mifflin, 1992. Martha the dog is able to speak after eating alphabet soup. Her family is thrilled to be able to communicate with her verbally and hear her thoughts on various subjects. Sequels are *Martha Calling* (1994), *Martha Blah Blah* (1996), *Martha Walks the Dog* (1998), and *Martha and Skits* (2000). (**I:** 6–9)

Moser, Madeline. *Ever Heard of an Aardwolf? A Miscellany of Uncommon Animals*. Illustrated by Barry Moser. Harcourt, 1996. Twenty unusual animals such as the aardwolf, the loris, the pangolin, the viscacha, and the solenodon are introduced with a brief paragraph about each animal; an appendix gives more detailed information. Illustrations are synthetic wood engravings. (**I:** 6–9)

Moss, Lloyd. *Zin! Zin! Zin! a Violin*. Illustrated by Marjorie Priceman. Simon & Schuster, 1995. A trombone begins playing solo and is joined by the trumpet, French horn, cello, violin, flute, clarinet, oboe, bassoon, and harp. (**I:** P–8)

Myers, Christopher. *Wings*. Scholastic, 2000. Ikarus Jackson is mocked for being different from others: He has wings. When the narrator learns to stand up for Ikarus, they both understand the power of embracing differences and celebrating individuality. (**I:** 6–10)

Narahashi, Keiko. *I Have a Friend*. Macmillan, 1987. A little boy talks about his friend who goes everywhere with him: his shadow. (**I:** P–7)

Ness, Evaline. *Sam, Bangs and Moonshine*. Holt, 1966. Sam always tells stories that her father calls "moonshine." One day, Sam's moonshine almost takes her friend Thomas's life. (**I:** 6–9)

Nivola, Claire A. *Planting the Trees of Kenya*. FSG, 2008. This story shows Wangari Maathai's influence on the preservation of the Kenyan land and its effect on the daily lives of her people led to her winning the Nobel Peace Prize. (**I:** 7–10)

Noble, Trinka Hakes. *The Day Jimmy's Boa Ate the Wash*. Illustrated by Steven Kellogg. Dial, 1980. A little girl tells her mother an outrageous story of her class field trip to the farm in reverse cause-and-effect order. A sequel is *Jimmy's Boa Bounces Back* (1984). (**I:** 6–9)

Pattison, Darcy. *The Journey of Oliver K. Woodman*. Illustrated by Joe Cepeda. Harcourt, 2003. Uncle Ray sends a wooden man to his niece via various travelers who are driving from coast to coast, sending postcards along the way. (**I:** 6–9)

Peet, Bill. *Big Bad Bruce*. Houghton Mifflin, 1977. Bruce has fun rolling boulders down the hill and scaring the small creatures of Forevergreen Forest. When he almost hits Roxy, a little fox who is a witch, Bruce is in for a surprise. (**I:** P–8)

Perkins, Lynne Rae. *Pictures from Our Vacation*. Greenwillow, 2007. Mother gives the children cameras and notebooks to document memories of their family trip, but it isn't until they connect with family members that the true experiences get captured in their memories. (**I:** K–8)

Pilkey, Dav. *The Paperboy*. Orchard, 1996. Readers get a sense of ritual as a boy gets out of bed and goes about his daily routine of delivering the newspaper. (**I:** P–8)

Polacco, Patricia. *Appelemando's Dreams*. Philomel, 1991. Appelemando's dreams are vivid and entertaining, but only the children appreciate them at first. (**I:** 6–9)

———. *Thunder Cake*. Philomel, 1993. Grandmother helps her granddaughter overcome her fear of thunder. (**I:** 6–9)

Pomerantz, Charlotte. *The Chalk Doll*. Illustrated by Frané Lessac. Lippincott, 1989. Rose asks her mother to talk about her childhood in Jamaica. (**I:** 6–8)

Potter, Beatrix. *The Tale of Peter Rabbit*. Warne, 1902/1986. This is the story of Peter, a naughty rabbit who disobeys his mother and ends up caught in Mr. McGregor's garden. (**I:** P–8)

Ransome, Arthur. *The Fool of the World and the Flying Ship*. Illustrated by Uri Shulevitz. Farrar, 1968. A Russian boy of poor background marries the czar's daughter. (**I:** 7–10)

Rathmann, Peggy. *Officer Buckle and Gloria*. Putnam, 1995. Officer Buckle makes school rounds, giving safety tips to children. His dog, Gloria, pantomimes the safety tips and is the one who actually keeps the children amused. (**I:** 6–9)

Recorvits, Helen. *My Name is Yoon*. Illustrated by Gabi Swiatkowska. Farrar, 2003. A young Korean immigrant's adjustment to a new culture is depicted through surreal illustrations showing her daydreaming thoughts. (**I:** 6–9)

Rey, H. A. *Curious George*. Houghton Mifflin, 1941. George is a monkey who leaves the jungle with the man with a yellow hat. His mischievousness and curiosity get him into trouble. Other books about George—*Curious George Takes a Job* (1947), *Curious George Rides a Bike* (1952), *Curious George Gets a Medal* (1957), *Curious George Flies a Kite* (1973), and *Curious George Goes to the Hospital* (1973)—were written by H. A. Rey's wife, Margaret Rey. (**I:** P–8)

Rosen, Michael. *We're Going on a Bear Hunt*. Illustrated by Helen Oxenbury. Macmillan, 1989. A father takes his children on an imaginary bear hunt. They bravely go through various obstacles until they encounter the bear and make a mad dash home. Alternating full-color and black-and-white illustrations depict what part of the story actually happens and what part is imagination. (**I:** P–6)

Rylant, Cynthia. *When I Was Young in the Mountains*. Illustrated by Diane Goode. Dutton, 1982. Through poetic text that repeatedly begins "When I was young in the mountains," the narrator reminisces about her childhood in the Appalachian Mountains. (**I:** 6–9)

Sakai, Komako. *The Snow Day*. Levine/Scholastic, 2009. A little rabbit wakes to find a wondrous world filled with snow, and kindergarten canceled. (**I:** P–6)

San Souci, Robert D. *The Faithful Friend*. Illustrated by Brian Pinkney. Simon & Schuster, 1995. This is a retelling of a folktale from the Caribbean island of Martinique. The close bonds of friendship between Clement and Hippolyte break the spell cast by Monsieur Zabocat, a wizard, who opposes the marriage of his niece, Pauline, to Clement. (**I:** 7–10)

———. *Sukey and the Mermaid*. Illustrated by Brian Pinkney. Four Winds, 1992. Sukey lives on an island off the coast of South Carolina. When she runs to her secret hiding place by the sea to escape from the hard work imposed by her new stepfather, she meets a black mermaid named Mama Jo, who changes her life forever. (**I:** 6–9)

Say, Allen. *Emma's Rug*. Houghton Mifflin, 1996. Emma learns that inspiration for art is in the world all around her and that she does not have to rely on the images she "sees" in her special rug. (**I:** 6–9)

———. *Grandfather's Journey*. Houghton Mifflin, 1993. Say tells his own grandfather's story and expresses their mutual sense of belonging to both Japan and America. (**I:** 8–10)

———. *Tree of Cranes*. Houghton Mifflin, 1991. A Japanese woman brings a small pine tree indoors, folds origami cranes to decorate it, and shares memories with her son of spending her childhood Christmases in America. (**I:** P–8)

Schaefer, Carole Lexa. *The Squiggle*. Illustrated by Pierr Morgan. Crown, 1996. On an outing with her class, a little girl finds a rope that she imagines to be part of a dragon, the Great Wall of China, and various other things. See also *Someone Says* (2003). (**I:** P–7)

Schroeder, Alan. *Minty: A Story of Young Harriet Tubman*. Illustrated by Jerry Pinkney. Dial, 1996. Throughout Harriet Tubman's childhood, she dreamed and planned of escaping from slavery. (**I:** 6–9)

Schwartz, Amy. *Annabelle Swift, Kindergartner*. Orchard, 1988. Before the beginning of kindergarten, Annabelle's older sister gives tips on what to do at school. (**I:** P–6)

Scieszka, Jon. *Baloney (Henry P.)* Illustrated by Lane Smith. Viking, 2001. When Henry P. Baloney is late for class again,

Miss Bugscuffle demands an excuse good and believable enough to keep him out of permanent lifelong detention. His explanation includes words from many different languages. (**I:** 7–10)

Sendak, Maurice. *Where the Wild Things Are*. Harper & Row, 1963/1989. When he is punished and sent to bed without supper, Max sails off to an imaginary world where he is the king of the Wild Things. (**I:** P–8)

Seuss, Dr. *And to Think That I Saw It on Mulberry Street*. Vanguard, 1937. A little boy imagines what would happen if the horse and cart he sees on his street were transformed into a circus bandwagon. (**I:** P–8)

———. *The Five Hundred Hats of Bartholomew Cubbins*. Random House, 1938. When Bartholomew tries to remove his hat to show respect to the king, another hat appears in its place. (**I:** P–8)

———. *Horton Hatches the Egg*. 1940/1968. Random House. Mayzie the bird leaves for a vacation and leaves Horton the elephant to sit on her nest and tend her egg. (**I:** P–8)

Sheth, Kathmira. *My Dadima Wears a Sari*. Illustrated by Yoshiko Jaeggi. Peachtree, 2007. Rupa's admiration for her grandmother's (Dadima's) saris grows as she learns the many uses of the sari, and the stories behind each one. (**I:** P–7)

Shulevitz, Uri. *Snow*. Farrar, Straus, & Giroux, 1998. A little boy discovers a snowflake falling, but the adults do not pay attention. Soon, the boy is delightedly playing in snow with Mother Goose characters from a sign that come and join him. (**I:** P–7)

Simmons, Jane. *Come Along, Daisy!* Little, Brown, 1997. Mama Duck calls out, "Come along, Daisy!" But her duckling is too busy playing; suddenly she discovers that she is all alone. (**I:** P)

Soto, Gary. *Chato and the Party Animals*. Illustrated by Susan Guevara. Putnam, 2000. Chato, the coolest cat in el barrio, throws a surprise party for his friend, Novio Boy. See also *Chato's Kitchen* (1995). (**I:** 6–10)

Steen, Sandra, and Susan Steen. *Car Wash*. Illustrated by G. Brian Karas. Putnam, 2001. When children take a trip through a car wash, their imaginations fly as they compare each stage to an underwater excursion. Bits of towels, shells, and pearls are collaged onto a background of textured paper. (**I:** P–7)

Steig, William. *The Amazing Bone*. Farrar, 1983. Pearl, a pig, finds a talking bone in the forest and picks it up to take home. When she encounters danger in the forest, the bone does amazing things to keep them safe. (**I:** 6–9)

———. *Doctor De Soto*. Farrar, 1982. A fox with a toothache tries to get a mouse dentist to work on the tooth—but the fox also has other plans for the mouse. A related title is *Doctor De Soto Goes to Africa* (1992). (**I:** 6–9)

———. *Pete's a Pizza*. HarperCollins, 1998. Pete is upset that rain has ruined his outdoor plans, but his parents cheer him up by pretending to make him into a pizza. (**I:** P–8)

———. *Spinky Sulks*. Farrar, 1988. Spinky sulks about everything, but circumstances change his attitude and behavior. (**I:** 6–9)

———. *Sylvester and the Magic Pebble*. Simon & Schuster, 1969. When Sylvester, a donkey, makes a wish while holding an extraordinary rock and turns himself into a rock, he finds that he is unable to turn himself back into a donkey. (**I:** 6–9)

Steiner, Joan. *Look-Alikes*. Little, Brown, 1998. A closer look at what appears to be a hotel lobby, an amusement park, or a general store reveals that everyday objects were used to create a miniature world. See also *Look-Alikes, Jr.* (1999). (**I:** P–10)

Steptoe, John. *Stevie*. Harper, 1969. A small boy resents having to share his mother with a little boy who is temporarily staying with them, until he realizes that the little boy is "kinda like a brother." (**I:** P–7)

———. *The Story of Jumping Mouse: A Native American Legend*. Lothrop, 1984. An unselfish mouse gives away what other animals need. Ultimately, the mouse is transformed into an eagle as a reward for its generosity. (**I:** 6–9)

Stevens, Janet. *And the Dish Ran Away With the Spoon*. Harcourt, 2001. When dish and spoon run away at the end of the traditional rhyme, they do not return, so dog, cat, and cow set off in search of them and encounter various other nursery rhyme characters along the way. (**I:** 6–9)

———. *Tops & Bottoms*. Harcourt, 1995. Clever and hard-working Hare outsmarts the land-rich but lazy Bear in order to "cash in" on the crops he grows. (**I:** 6–9)

———. and Susan Stevens Crummel. *Cook-a-Doodle-Doo!* Illustrated by Janet Stevens. Harcourt Brace, 1999. A hungry rooster seeks help in cooking up Great Granny's recipe for strawberry shortcake in this twist on the story of "The Little Red Hen." (**I:** 6–9)

Stevenson, James. *Could Be Worse!* Greenwillow, 1977. Grandpa tells his grandchildren a wild story. (**I:** 6–8)

Stewart, Sarah. *The Gardener*. Illustrated by David Small. Farrar, 1997. When Lydia is sent to live in an unfamiliar city and work for her uncle, she brightens her life and her surroundings with her garden. (**I:** 6–9)

Stuve-Bodeen, Stephanie. *Elizabeti's Doll*. Illustrated by Christy Hale. Lee & Low, 1998. In this story set in Tanzania, Mother has a new baby and Elizabeti adopts a rock to serve as her doll. See also *Mama Elizabeti* (2000) and *Elizabeti's School* (2001). (**I:** P–7)

Swanson, Susan Marie. *The House in the Night*. Illustrated by Beth Krommes. Houghton Mifflin, 2008. Lyrical and poetic text describe a fantastic journey through the night in a world created through black and white scratchboard with golden glows and highlights. (**I:** K–8)

Taback, Simms. *Joseph Had a Little Overcoat*. Viking, 1999. In this traditional tale, an old overcoat is recycled into a jacket, vest, scarf, necktie, handkerchief, button, and finally story. (**I:** P–8)

Teague, Mark. *Dear Mrs. LaRue: Letters from Obedience School*. Scholastic, 2002. A dog writes letters from obedience school to his owner, depicting a jail-like place instead of the spa-like reality. (**I:** 6–10)

Tejima, Keizaburo. *Swan Sky*. Putnam, 1988. A young swan is unable to fly with the family when it is the season for migration. (**I:** P–8)

Thomas, Joyce Carol. *I Have Heard of a Land*. Illustrated by Floyd Cooper. HarperCollins, 1998. In the 1880s, an African American woman stakes a claim for free land in Oklahoma. (**I:** 6–10)

Tunnell, Michael O. *Mailing May*. Illustrated by Ted Rand. Tambourine/Greenwillow, 1997. Based on a true story, this book tells of a little girl sent on a train by parcel post mail in 1914 so that she can visit her grandmother. (**I:** 6–9)

Vail, Rachel. *Sometimes I'm Bombaloo*. Illustrated by Yumi Heo. Scholastic, 2002. Dealing with strong emotions can be hard for a young child to learn, and sometimes it becomes "bombaloo" before things calm down again. (**I:** P–7)

Van Allsburg, Chris. *The Garden of Abdul Gasazi*. Houghton Mifflin, 1979. Alan chases Fritz the dog through the magician's garden and imagines that Fritz has been turned into a duck. (**I:** P–8)

———. *Jumanji*. Houghton Mifflin, 1981. Peter and Judy find an unusual board game that comes alive and turns the house into a jungle. (**I:** 7–10)

———. *Just a Dream*. Houghton Mifflin, 1990. Walter is careless about how he treats his environment. In a dream one night, he sees what the future will be like if everyone abuses the earth. He wakes up with a new determination. (**I:** P–8)

———. *The Polar Express*. Houghton Mifflin, 1985. Children board a night train headed for the North Pole. Santa grants the first wish of Christmas to a boy who asks for a bell from Santa's sleigh. (**I:** 6–9)

———. *The Sweetest Fig*. Houghton Mifflin, 1993. A woman leaves two figs as payment for work on her teeth, telling Monsieur Bibot that the figs make dreams come true. (**I:** 7–10)

———. *Two Bad Ants*. Houghton Mifflin, 1988. Two ants in search of sugar crystals for their queen divert from the path to seek adventure in the house. Their experiences prove terrifying. (**I:** 7–10)

Waber, Bernard. *Ira Sleeps Over*. Houghton Mifflin, 1972. Two boys have a sleepover and each is relieved to find that the other still sleeps with a stuffed animal. (**I:** P–7)

Waddell, Martin. *Can't You Sleep, Little Bear?* Illustrated by Barbara Firth. Candlewick, 1992. Little Bear's fear of the dark keeps him from falling asleep until Big Bear takes him outside to see the moon and the stars. (**I:** P–6)

———. *Farmer Duck*. Illustrated by Helen Oxenbury. Candlewick, 1992. A duck is overworked by a lazy farmer, and the barnyard animals rescue the duck and keep his family intact. (**I:** P–7)

Ward, Lynd. *The Biggest Bear*. Houghton Mifflin, 1952. When Johnny decides that he would like a bearskin on his wall, he goes out seeking the biggest bear. (**I:** 6–8).

Watt, Mélanie. *Scaredy Squirrel*. Kids Can, 2006. Engaging illustrations capture the emotions of a squirrel who overcomes the fear of going beyond the security of his own oak tree. See also: *Scaredy Squirrel Makes a Friend* (2007), *Scaredy Squirrel at the Beach* (2008), *Scaredy Squirrel at Night* (2009). (**I:** P–7)

Wattenberg, Jane. *Henny-Penny*. Scholastic, 2000. Henny-Penny outfoxes the fox in this retelling of the familiar tale, illustrated with digitized photo compositions. (**I:** 6–9)

Wells, Rosemary. *Bunny Cakes*. Dial, 1997. In an effort to decorate his earthworm cake for Grandma's birthday, Max repeatedly attempts to write "Red-Hot Marshmallow Squirters" on the grocery list. See also *Bunny Money* (1997). (**I:** P–8)

———. *Bunny Party*. Viking, 2001. As Ruby directs the preparations for Grandma's birthday party, Max underhandedly gets his own toys in attendance. See also: *Bunny Money* and *Ruby's Beauty Shop* (2004). (**I:** P–7)

Wiesner, David. *June 29, 1999*. Clarion, 1992. Holly sends her science experiment vegetable seedlings high into the air. On June 29, 1999, a little over a month later, enormous vegetables appear all over earth, but when vegetables Holly did not send up begin to appear, everyone wonders where they came from. (**I:** 6–9)

———. *The Three Pigs*. Clarion, 2001. The traditional story of the three pigs takes a twist when the pigs fly out of the story and into others. (**I:** 6–9)

———. *Tuesday*. Clarion, 1991. One Tuesday, a surreal scene of frogs flying on lily pads startle those they encounter. (**I:** 6–9)

Williams, Sherley Anne. *Working Cotton*. Illustrated by Carole Byard. Harcourt, 1992. A migrant family works in the cotton fields. (**I:** P–8)

Williams, Vera B. *A Chair for My Mother*. Greenwillow, 1982. When a fire destroys everything they own, a little girl saves money to buy Mother a comfortable chair in which to sit when she returns home from work. A sequel is *Something Special for Me* (1983). (**I:** P–8)

———. *"More More More," Said the Baby: Three Love Stories*. Greenwillow, 1990. Three love stories show the loving relationships between each child and his or her parent. (**I:** P)

Willems, Mo. *Don't Let the Pigeon Drive the Bus!* Hyperion, 2003. A very persistent pigeon uses a full range of tactics to get to drive the bus. (**I:** P–8)

———. *Knuffle Bunny: A Cautionary Tale*. Trixie's beloved "knuffle bunny" gets left behind at a laundromat, causing emotional distress that her babbling cannot communicate to her father. See also: *Knuffle Bunny, Too: A Case of Mistaken Identity* (2007). (**I:** P–7)

Wisniewski, David. *The Golem*. Clarion, 1996. A rabbi creates a clay giant, the golem, and brings it to life to help protect the Jews in Prague during the sixteenth century. (**I:** 9–12)

Wolkstein, Diane. *White Wave: A Chinese Tale*. Illustrated by Ed Young. Philomel, 1979. A Chinese farmer who finds a snail and cares for it discovers that the snail is nurturing him by providing him with food. The snail turns into White Wave, a moon goddess, and returns to the sky. (**I:** 6–9)

Wood, Audrey. *King Bidgood's in the Bathtub*. Illustrated by Don Wood. Harcourt, 1985. Throughout the day and into the night, King Bidgood won't leave his tub, to the great distress of his court. (**I:** P–8)

Yagawa, Sumiko. *The Crane Wife*. Illustrated by Suekichi Akaba. Translated by Katherine Paterson. Morrow, 1981. This traditional Japanese tale tells of a lonely man whose curiosity over the identity of his lovely wife leads to her departure. (**I:** 6–10)

Yolen, Jane. *The Emperor and the Kite*. Illustrated by Ed Young. Putnam, 1967/1988. The diligence and loyalty of the emperor's smallest daughter allow him to rule the land again after being overthrown by evil plotters. The watercolor paintings are reminiscent of Chinese cut-paper art. (**I:** 6–9)

———. *Encounter*. Illustrated by David Shannon. Harcourt, 1992. The arrival of Columbus in San Salvador in 1492 is seen through the eyes of a young Taino boy. (**I:** 9–12)

———. *Owl Moon*. Illustrated by John Schoenherr. Philomel, 1987. A young boy goes "owling" with his father. (**I:** 7–9)

Yorinks, Arthur. *Hey, Al!* Illustrated by Richard Egielski. Farrar, 1986. Al is a janitor who lives in an apartment with his dog, Eddie. A large bird, calling "Hey, Al," offers them a new life in a place where they can be free of worries and cares. But Eddie and Al find their paradise back home. (**I:** 7–10)

Young, Ed. *Cat and Rat: The Legend of the Chinese Zodiac*. Holt, 1995. The Jade Emperor invites all the animals to participate in a race. This story tells how the twelve animals became part of the zodiac and why cat and rat will always remain enemies. (**I:** 6–9)

———. *Lon Po Po: A Red Riding Hood Story from China*. Philomel, 1989. This Chinese variation of the Red Riding Hood story depicts three children left home alone when their mother goes to visit their grandmother. When the wolf enters the house, the children outsmart the wolf and get rid of it. (**I:** 6–10)

———. *Seven Blind Mice*. Philomel, 1992. One by one, the blind mice feel the "thing" and describe various body parts they each feel. (**I:** P–9)

———. *What About Me?* Putnam, 2002. In this Sufi tale, a young boy in search of wisdom is sent off to embark on a circular story by a Grand Master. (**I:** 7–10)

Zelinsky, Paul. *Rumpelstiltskin*. Dutton, 1986. Zelinsky's oil paintings richly depict this familiar tale of a young woman who must either discover the name of the little man or give him her first-born child in exchange for assistance in weaving straw into gold. (**I:** 7–9)

Ziefert, Harriet. *A New Coat for Anna*. Illustrated by Anita Lobel. Knopf, 1986. In Europe at the end of World War II, there is no money for a new coat. Anna's mother gives away her precious belongings to have a coat made for Anna. (**I:** P–8)

Zolotow, Charlotte. *Do You Know What I'll Do?* Illustrated by Javaka Steptoe. HarperCollins, 2000. This 1958 text of a loving brother and sister relationship has been reillustrated with collage images of African American siblings. (**I:** P–7)

Resources

Aliki. *How a Book Is Made*. Harper & Row, 1986.

Bader, Barbara. *American Picturebooks from Noah's Ark to the Beast Within*. Macmillan, 1976.

Bang, Molly. *Picture This: Perception and Composition*. Sea Star Books, 1991/2000.

Carle, Eric. *The Art of Eric Carle*. Philomel, 1996.

Christelow, Eileen. *What Do Authors Do?* Clarion, 1995.

———. *What Do Illustrators Do?* Clarion, 1999.

Cianciolo, Patricia J. *The Illustrations in Children's Books*. William C. Brown, 1976.

———. *Picture Books for Children*. 4th ed. American Library Association, 1997.

Cummings, Pat, comp. and ed. *Talking with Artists* (3 vols.). Bradbury, 1992, 1995, 1999.

Cummins, Julie. *Children's Book Illustration and Design* (2 vols.). PBC International, 1998.

Elleman, Barbara. *Tomie dePaola: His Art & His Stories*. Putnam, 1999.

———. *Virginia Lee Burton: A Life in Art*. Houghton Mifflin, 2002.

Evans, Dilys. *Show & Tell: Exploring the Fine Art of Children's Book Illustration*. Chronicle Books, 2008.

Lacy, Lynn. *Art and Design in Children's Picture Books*. American Library Association, 1986.

Lewis, David. *Reading Contemporary Picturebooks: Picturing Text*. Routledge, 2003.

Marcus, Leonard S. *Author Talk: Conversations with Judy Blume, Bruce Brooks, Karen Cushman, Russell Freedman, Lee Bennett Hopkins, James Howe, Johanna Hurwitz, E. L. Konigsburg, Lois Lowry, Ann M. Martin, Nicholasa Mohr, Gary Paulsen, Jon Scieszka, Seymour Simon, and Laurence Yep*. Simon & Schuster, 2000.

———. *A Caldecott Celebration: Six Artists Share Their Paths to the Caldecott Medal*. Walker, 1998.

———. *Side by Side: Favorite Picture Book Teams Go to Work*. Walker, 2001.

———. *Ways of Telling: Conversations on the Art of the Picture Book*. Dutton, 2002.

Nikolajeva, Maria and Scott, Carole. *How Picturebooks Work*. Routledge, 2001.

Nodleman, Perry. *Words about Pictures: The Narrative Art of Children's Picture Books*. Univ. of Georgia Press, 1988.

Pitz, Henry C. *Illustrating Children's Books*. Watson-Guptill, 1963.

Schwarcz, Joseph H., and Chava Schwarcz. *The Picture Book Comes of Age*. American Library Association, 1991.

Sipe, Lawrence and Sylvia Pantaleo (eds.). *Postmodern Picturebooks: Play, Parody, and Self-Referentiality*. Routledge, 2008.

Shulevitz, Uri. *Writing with Pictures: How to Write and Illustrate Children's Books*. Watson-Guptill, 1985/1997.

Silvey, Anita. *Children's Books and Their Creators*. Houghton Mifflin, 1995.

Spitz, Ellen Handler. *Inside Picture Books*. Yale Univ. Press, 1999.

Stevens, Janet. *From Pictures to Words: A Book about Making a Book*. Holiday House, 1995.

Styles, Morag and Bearne, Eve (eds.). *Art, Narrative and Childhood*. Trentham Books, 2003.

Stewig, John Warren. *Looking at Picture Books*. Highsmith, 1995.

Weiner, Stephen. *The 101 best graphic novels*. Nantier, Beall, Minoustchine Publishing, 2001.

References

Adoff, Arnold. *Love Letters*. Illustrated by Lisa Desimini. Blue Sky Press/Scholastic, 1997.

Ancona, George. *Carnaval*. Harcourt, 1999.

Andersen, Hans Christian. *The Ugly Duckling*. Adapted and illustrated by Jerry Pinkney. Morrow, 1999.

Anno, Mitsumasa. *Upside-Downers: More Pictures to Stretch the Imagination*. Weatherhill, 1971.

Blake, William. *Songs of Innocence and Songs of Experience*. Dover, 1789/1992.

Brown, Marcia. *Stone Soup: An Old Tale*. Aladdin, 1947/1987.

Carroll, Lewis. *Alice's Adventures in Wonderland*. Illustrated by John Tenniel. Macmillan, 1865.

Casanova, Mary. *The Hunter: A Chinese Folktale*. Illustrated by Ed Young. Atheneum/Simon & Schuster, 2000.

Craft, K. Y. (Illustrator). *Cinderella*. New York: Sea Star, 2000.

Crane, Walter. *Absurd ABC*. George Routledge & Sons, c. 1865.

———. *The House That Jack Built*. George Routledge & Sons, c. 1865.

———. *Sing a Song of Sixpence*. George Routledge & Sons, c. 1865.

Davol, Marguerite W. *The Paper Dragon*. Illustrated by Robert Sabuda. Atheneum, 1997.

Del Negro, Janice. *Lucy Dove*. Illustrated by Leonid Gore. DK Ink, 1998.

de Paola, Tomie. *Charlie Needs a Cloak*. Prentice-Hall, 1973.

———. *The Cloud Book*. Holiday House, 1975.

———. *The Popcorn Book*. Holiday House, 1988.

Diakité, Baba Wagué. *The Hatseller and the Monkeys*. Scholastic, 1999.

———. *The Hunterman and the Crocodile*. Scholastic, 1997.

Dragonwagon, Crescent. *Half a Moon and One Whole Star*. Illustrated by Jerry Pinkney. Aladdin, 1990.

Ehlert, Lois. *Moon Rope/Un lazo a la luna*. Translated into Spanish by Amy Prince. Harcourt, 1992.

Eibl-Eibesfeldt, Iraneus. *Ethology: The Biology of Behavior*, 2nd ed. Holt, 1975.

Flack, Marjorie. *Ask Mr. Bear*. Macmillan, 1960.

Gilman, Phoebe. *Something from Nothing*. Scholastic, 1993.

Greenaway, Kate. *A—Apple Pie*. Warne, 1886.

Grimes, Nikki. *It's Raining Laughter*. Photographs by Myles C. Pinkney. Dial, 1997.

Heo, Yumi. *The Green Frogs: A Korean Folktale*. Houghton Mifflin, 1996.

Holdaway, Don. *The Foundations of Literacy*. Ashton Scholastic, 1979.

Keats, Ezra Jack. *Apt. 3*. Viking, 1974/1999.

Kiefer, Barbara Z. *The Potential of Picturebooks: From Visual Literacy to Aesthetic Understanding*. Merrill/Prentice-Hall, 1995.

Kunhardt, Dorothy. *Pat the Bunny*. Golden Books, 1940/2001.

Lester, Julius. *John Henry*. Illustrated by Jerry Pinkney. Dial, 1994.

———. *The Tales of Uncle Remus: The Adventures of Brer Rabbit*. Illustrated by Jerry Pinkney. Dutton, 1987.

Lodge, Sally. "The Making of a Crossover: One Book, Two Markets." *Publisher's Weekly 239* (23 Nov. 1992): 39–42.

Louie, Ai-Ling. *Yeh-Shen: A Cinderella Story from China*. Illustrated by Ed Young. Putnam, 1982.

Martin, Jr., Bill. *The Maestro Plays*. Illustrated by Vladimir Radunsky. Holt, 1994.

McCallum, Robyn. "Metafiction and Experimental Work." 397–409. In *International Companion Encyclopedia of Children's Literature*. Edited by Peter Hunt. London and New York: Routledge, 1996.

McCloskey, Robert. *Time of Wonder*. Viking, 1957.

Moebius, William. "Introduction to Picturebook Codes." *Word & Image 2.2* (1986): 141–152.

Myers, Walter Dean. *Brown Angels: An Album of Pictures and Verse*. HarperCollins, 1993.

———. *Glorious Angels: A Celebration of Children*. HarperCollins, 1996.

Perrault, Charles. *Cinderella*. Illustrated by Marcia Brown. Scribner's, 1954.

———. *Puss in Boots*. Illustrated by Hans Fischer. Translated by Anthea Bell. North-South Books, 1958/1996.

———. *Puss in Boots*. Illustrated by Fred Marcellino. Translated by Malcolm Arthur. Farrar, 1990.

Pinkney, Andrea Davis. *Duke Ellington: The Piano Prince and His Orchestra*. Illustrated by Brian Pinkney. Hyperion, 1998.

Pinkney, Gloria. *The Sunday Outing*. Illustrated by Jerry Pinkney. Dial, 1994.

Pinkney, Sandra. *Shades of Black: A Celebration of Our Children*. Illustrated by Myles C. Pinkney. Scholastic, 2000.

Powers, Alan. *Children's Book Covers: Great Book Jacket and Cover Design*. London: Mitchell Beazley, 2003.

Price, Leontyne. *Aida*. Illustrated by Leo Dillon and Diane Dillon. Harcourt, 1990.

Roser, N. L., M. Martinez, K. McDonnold, & C. Fuhrken. "Beginning Chapter Books: Their Features and Their Support of Children's Reading." In C. M. Fairbanks, J. Worthy, B. Malock, J. V. Hoffman, & D. L. Schallert (Eds.), *53rd Yearbook of the National Reading Conference*. Oak Creek, WI: National Reading Conference. 2004.

Sabuda, Robert. *Saint Valentine*. Aladdin, 1992.

Sanfield, Steve. *Bit by Bit*. Philomel, 1995.

San Souci, Robert D. *The Talking Eggs: A Folktale from the American South*. Illustrated by Jerry Pinkney. Dial, 1989.

Schwartz, Alvin. *Scary Stories to Tell in the Dark*. Illustrated by Stephen Gammell. HarperCollins, 1985.

Schwartz, Joseph H. *Ways of the Illustrator: Visual Communication in Children's Literature*. American Library Association, 1982.

Sendak, Maurice. *Caldecott and Co.* Farrar, Straus, & Giroux, 1990.

———. *In the Night Kitchen*. Harper, 1970.

———. *Outside Over There*. HarperCollins, 1981.

———. *We Are All in the Dumps with Jack and Guy: Two Nursery Rhymes with Pictures*. HarperCollins, 1993.

Siebold, J. Otto. *Mr. Lunch* series. Viking.

Spirin, Gennady. *The Tale of the Firebird*. Philomel, 2002.

Steig, William. *Abel's Island*. Farrar, 1976.

———. *C D B!* 2nd ed. Simon & Schuster, 2000.

Steiner, Joan. *Look Alikes*. Little, Brown, 1998.

———. *Look Alikes, Jr.: Find More Than 700 Hidden Everyday Objects*. Little, Brown, 1998.

Steptoe, John. *Baby Says*. HarperCollins, 1988.

Toy Hong, Lily. *Two of Everything*. Whitman, 1993.

Van Allsburg, Chris. *The Wreck of the Zephyr*. Houghton Mifflin, 1983.

Vail, Rachel. *Sometimes I'm Bombaloo*. Illustrated by Yumi Heo. Scholastic, 2002.

Willard, Nancy. *Pish, Posh, Said Hieronymus Bosch*. Illustrated by Lee Dillon. Harcourt, 1991.

Winter, Jonah. *Frida*. Illustrated by Ana Juan. Levine/Scholastic, 2002.

Wyndham, Robert. *Chinese Mother Goose Rhymes*. Illustrated by Ed Young. PaperStar, 1968/1998.

4

Literature Representing Diverse Perspectives

> **"I'm a sophomore,"** Sheila said. "Three more years in this place."
>
>   "And you just got here, Maizon," Charli said, bouncing down next to me. She had more energy than Li'l Jay.
>
>   "Buckle your seat belt, girlfriend, 'cause you in for one heck of a ride."
>
>   "Charli. You're slipping," Marie said, frowning.
>
>   "Oh, chill out, Marie." Charli waved her hand and lay back on the bed. "We're among our own."
>
> —*from* Maizon at Blue Hill
> *by Jacqueline Woodson*

In *Maizon at Blue Hill,* a girl enters a private academy and discovers that she is one of only five African American students there. Incidents throughout the book reveal how she feels in this situation, how she sees her place in this setting, and how she interacts with others. The passage above implies that people feel and act differently when they are able to say, "We're among our own." How does being among people whose perspectives are different from your own make you feel? Reading and discussing books such as *Maizon at Blue Hill* allows children to reflect on what it means to live in a diverse world and to consider how issues of diversity affect them.

Why should we have multicultural literature, really? That is a fair question. Some critics worry that the rise of multicultural education in the United States may fragment our loyalties and loosen our civic ties to each other. For example, a noted historian wrote a book entitled *The Disuniting of America* (Schlesinger, 1991) that offers this premise. But James Banks (2000), an energetic proponent of multicultural education, argues that multicultural education is fully American because the United States is a society that was founded on the premise of providing justice and the pursuit of happiness for its citizens; therefore, recognizing the culture and potential of different groups is necessary to their pursuit of happiness and justice.

Multicultural children's books can make a contribution here. Beverlee Tatum, a psychologist who has studied racism, explains why. Most of us live in racially segregated neighborhoods (Tatum, 1999). Tatum suggests that our earliest experiences take place among people of the same race as ourselves. We count on secondhand sources—books, movies, and television—for our impressions about people from other races, ethnic groups, or religious backgrounds. If those sources give caricatured representations of other races or leave them out altogether, we are likely as children to form deep-seated notions that people of other races are silly, unimportant, or, at the very least, much different than we are. If we belong to a race that is caricatured or excluded, we might internalize the idea that we are unimportant in the eyes of the world.

The best defense against allowing racist views to take hold of our children is to surround them with rich, realistic information about children from many other races. If they have that information, then the concepts or preconceptions they form will more genuinely reflect people from other races as they are, with their differences, similarities, and individuality. This is the role that multicultural literature needs to fill.

PEARSON
myeducationkit

Go to the Assignments and Activities section of Chapter 4 in the MyEducationKit and complete the activities. As you work through the activities and answer the accompanying questions, consider the importance of evaluating multicultural literature for children.

Diverse Perspectives in the United States

Schools in the United States are experiencing a tremendous increase in the cultural and ethnic diversity of the children they serve. According to the 2000 census, "people of color" make up 25 percent of the U.S. population. It is believed that by 2020, nearly half of the students in U.S. schools will be "of color" (Pallas, Natriello, & McDill, 1989). That reality, along with our expanding relationships with countries around the world, increases the need for children to perceive themselves as members of a multicultural global community. Because good literature reaches the minds and hearts of its readers, reading and discussing multicultural literature will broaden children's perspectives and increase their understanding in a way that affects—for the better, we hope—how people live in this pluralistic society. Yet the books being published do not reflect the depth and breadth of our diversity. The Cooperative Children's Book Council in Wisconsin maintains annual statistics on the publication of multicultural books because of its commitment to raising awareness for the continuing need for representations of multicultural experiences.

Multicultural education theorists define *pluralism* as diversity in "ethnic, racial, linguistic, religious, economic, and gender [characteristics], among others" (Nieto, 1996). Nieto argues "that all students of all backgrounds, languages, and experiences need to be acknowledged, valued, and used as important sources of their education" (p. 8). This inclusive definition of pluralism correlates with beliefs about the need for diverse perspectives in education. Banks (1999) asks that multicultural education include voices that have been marginalized in the past, but urges that it not ignore the achievements of Western civilization in doing so. The goal of multicultural education is freedom—helping students develop the knowledge, attitudes, and skills that will allow them to participate in a democratic and free society. Banks acknowledges that students should know their own culture before they can successfully participate in other cultures.

The United States is a diverse society, and this diversity has many sources. The obvious ways in which both the general and school populations are diverse are gender, culture, ethnic and racial background, language, and physical and mental abilities. Less often acknowledged are differences in social class. All of these differences can affect the ways people see themselves and others. And all must be taken into account in forging a working democracy or maintaining a harmonious classroom.

The Role of Schools in Presenting Multiple Perspectives

Schools face many demands in shaping the curriculum. Some of these demands are made by people who want the curriculum to be presented from one perspective—their own. Multiple viewpoints serve students best. If students are shown only male, white, able-bodied characters, then female students, children of ethnic diversity, students with disabilities, and children with learning exceptionalities are likely to feel that the school day is not planned with them in mind. They may even feel that their place in society in general is questionable. Although strides have been made in creating an anti-bias curriculum that promotes social justice, more work is needed. Schools can be instrumental in providing opportunities for students to read and discuss material from multiple viewpoints. Such discussions are important in developing attitudes of open-mindedness about diversity. This chapter (and this book) recommends books that offer multiple perspectives.

Literature's Potential for Influencing the Reader's Perspective

What role does literature have in influencing children's understanding of diverse perspectives? Depending on their experiences, some children feel uncomfortable when presented with an opportunity to interact with someone who is different from them. How can children resolve their misunderstanding, lack of understanding, or fear? Developing a hypersensitivity that leads to avoidance is a serious mistake. "Many people have an inhibition about talking with someone in a wheelchair. They don't know quite what to say, so they don't say anything at all and ignore both the person and the chair" (Haldane, 1991, n. pag.). People may respond to any kind of diversity in this way. Although it is a vicarious experience, interacting with diverse people through literature can help. Literature that portrays diversity in natural ways can provide realistic images as well as inspire discussion.

Fiction and informational books are powerful vehicles for helping students understand other cultures because they offer cultural insights in natural ways. Such books should not be narrowly viewed as replacements for social studies textbooks; too often, students miss the richness of the writing if they read merely to locate cultural information. However, fiction and informational books can enhance children's understanding of cultures by involving them emotionally. The narrower focus of such books allows for deeper exploration of the thoughts, feelings, and experiences of people from diverse groups. Thus, through story, readers take an emotional stake in understanding how and why people live as they do. Julius Lester (2004) sees the power of story in helping us "to reach out to others and forge relationships." He describes how the intimacy of storytelling binds us to others: "We need to share our stories because in so doing, we hope to be understood, and being understood we are no longer so alone."

Milton Meltzer (1989) believes that the writer has a social responsibility and that "writing about social issues need not depress and dispirit readers; it should provide them with courage. If they learn to confront life as it is, it may give them the heart to strive to make it better" (p. 157). Meltzer is saying that literature is a powerful vehicle when it treats issues honestly. But, as Jean Little (1990) points out, literature that is designed to present object lessons, in which teachers point out the "good messages," appears self-righteous and rarely changes people's opinions. Well-written books that speak from the writer's vision pull readers into the characters' experiences and emotions and build compassion, thereby having a lasting effect on readers' understandings of the world in which they live.

Books depicting diverse perspectives are found in all genres of children's literature. In this chapter, we will examine the criteria for viewing multicultural and international issues in children's books. These criteria form a foundation for evaluating the literature you encounter in all the genre chapters that follow.

What Is Multicultural Literature?

Although there is general agreement that multicultural literature is about people who are not in the mainstream, there is no consensus as to what constitutes nonmainstream populations (Cai & Sims Bishop, 1994). Some contend that multicultural literature is written by or about people of color in the United States. Many include literature about religious minorities (such as the Amish and Jews) or about people who live in specific regions of the United States (such as Appalachia). Some include literature about diverse lifestyles (such as families headed by same-sex parents or people with disabilities). Some include books about people in countries outside the United States. There is value in having an inclusive definition when considering issues of diversity; however, too broad a definition dilutes the focus.

We define multicultural literature as works that reflect the multitude of cultural groups within the United States. To address the issues of multiculturalism that are most salient to our study of children's literature, we will focus on literature that reflects ethnic and regional groups whose cultures historically have been less represented than European cultures. A related body of literature is international literature—literature that was originally written and published in countries outside the United States. This type of literature will be discussed in the next chapter.

One reason we focus on books about ethnic groups within the United States is that these books reflect experiences of the children in U.S. schools today, since most were either born or raised in this coun-

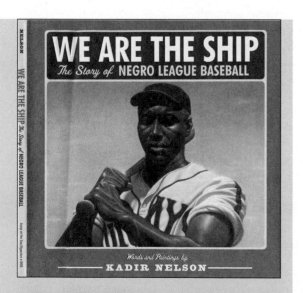

ILLUSTRATION 4.1 In *We Are the Ship*, readers learn of the talent, determination, and dedication of the players in the Negro League Baseball despite the discrimination, circumstances and obstacles they faced. (From Kadir Nelson's *We Are the Ship: The Story of Negro League Baseball* © 2008 by Kadir Nelson. Reprinted by Permission of Disney•Hyperion, an imprint of Disney Book Group LLC. All Rights Reserved.)

try. Often, books of this type are classified as African American, Asian American, Latino/a, or Native American. We use the term "multicultural" rather than "minority," with its implied reference to groups that have been historically "minor" in number compared to the "majority." Some groups that historically have been considered "minorities" are no longer numerically in the minority. Unfortunately, however, underrepresentation and misrepresentation of these groups continue. Virginia Hamilton's (1993) term "parallel cultures" has gained wide acceptance because it defines various cultures as parallel to the mainstream, rather than in a minority status. However, we have not yet reached Hamilton's ideal for parallel status of the various cultural groups. In addition, the ideal is not simply existence on parallel planes, but an interaction between cultures that leads to interdependence.

The Value of Multicultural Literature

Why should children's books deliberately include the perspectives of people from many backgrounds? This is a legitimate question. Some still believe that the old analogy to a "melting pot" is the target that literature should strive for; it shouldn't accentuate ethnic and cultural differences, because these differences emphasize the stresses that are tearing apart the fabric of society.

We believe that there are two compelling reasons for making sure children's literature includes the perspectives of people from many groups. First, students feel welcome in school to the extent to which they find themselves and their experiences represented in the books and materials they find there. Second, students need to understand and empathize with people who are different from them. If books do not portray differences, students cannot learn to transcend them.

Rudine Sims Bishop (1990) uses the metaphor of mirrors and windows to emphasize these two values of multicultural literature. *Mirrors* let readers see reflections of their own lives; windows let them see others' lives. Multicultural literature provides both types of experience. What value is there in seeing oneself represented in literature? Quite simply, it engenders a sense of pride. When readers encounter images of people they consider like themselves in a book, they take more interest in the book and feel a sense of involvement in the literary discussion that follows their reading. What value is there in seeing others represented in literature? Books that act as *windows* into experiences that are different from our own stretch the range of experiences we have had. Lee Galda (2000) makes an interesting analogy connecting windows with mirrors: In certain types of light, windows show reflections of self in varying degrees of clarity. Likewise, books that are windows to outside experiences should offer the possibility that readers will see some type of reflection of themselves.

Seeing ourselves and others portrayed authentically is only one of the values of multicultural literature. The greatest value of multicultural literature lies in the opportunities for extension that these books offer. In what ways can quality multicultural books elicit insights about our world and ourselves? What kinds of discussion are elicited by reading these books? Many multicultural books have the potential to serve as springboards for considering issues of social justice. Perhaps most important, many works of multicultural literature can nudge readers to take action when social justice issues are explored in thought-provoking ways.

Technology in Practice 4.1
Web Sites Related to Multicultural Literature: www.oyate.org

Oyate is an organization committed to portraying the lives and histories of Native people in honest ways. They review and evaluate books, texts, and other teaching materials to check for authentic portrayals. They disseminate information through their resource center, examination library, and publications. This Web site serves as a way to reach a wider audience than would be reached through teacher workshops. Teachers can use this site to learn how to critique books about Native Americans. First, read a book from the "books to avoid" list without reading the critique and jot down your impressions. Then click on the book title and read the critique that is written from a Native perspective. Compare it with your own earlier opinion and consider what the similarities and differences in the opinions mean. Reread the book with the Oyate critique in mind. How does the interaction with the Oyate Web site influence your critique of books about Native Americans?

Teaching Idea 4.1
Connect Books with Similar Themes, across Differing Cultures

Present a set of books that have similar themes, but represent different cultures. Examples of themes are the search for freedom, immigration, coming of age, friendships/peer relationships, and intergenerational relationships. Have children realize the universality of many themes, but also how the details of the stories differ if they are culturally bound. For example, collect immigrant stories. Be sure to include stories of immigrants who came through Ellis Island generations ago, immigrants who came more recently under dangerous circumstances, and recent immigrants who are fortunate enough to freely travel back and forth to their homelands. Consider the variety of reasons and ways in which people have immigrated to the United States. Find similarities in their experiences as well as differences. Share books like *Grandfather's Journey* by Allen Say that speak to nearly every first-generation immigrant's feelings when it closes, "As soon as I am in one place, I'm homesick for the other."

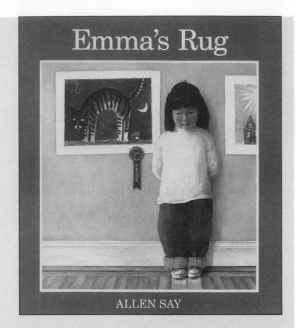

Emma's Rug

ALLEN SAY

ILLUSTRATION 4.2   Emma learns that inspiration for art is in the world all around her and that she does not have to rely on the images she "sees" in her special rug. (Cover from *Emma's Rug* by Allen Say. Copyright © 1996 by Allen Say. Reprinted by permission of Houghton Mifflin Company. All rights reserved.)

If multicultural literature is to make a difference in our world, then the value of such books must go beyond the artifact of the book and extend to the way these books make a difference in the lives of the people who read them.

Identifying Multicultural Books

All multicultural books depict people of diverse cultures, but the degree to which such books focus on cultural or social issues varies significantly. It is not enough to count the diverse faces in a book; the important thing is how the members of various cultures are portrayed. There is a range of degrees of cultural specificity in books, from merely visual inclusion that shows diverse faces to books that are entirely based on specific cultural aspects. The full range of depicting diversity is needed, but books differ in the degree and the specificity of their emphasis and, accordingly, in the cultural understandings that they offer to the reader. In some books, people of different cultures are deliberately included so that the illustrations appear visually diverse, but the text does not require that characters be of a particular culture. Diversity is incidentally depicted. In others, the culture is more than highlighted; it is central to the book. All details in the book focus on the culture. At the two ends of the continuum of specificity in depicting diversity are "culturally generic books" and "culturally specific books."

Culturally Generic Books

Culturally generic books are "generically American" in theme and plot (Sims Bishop, 1992). Sometimes, the inclusion appears to be merely incidental, and at other times, it purposefully and prominently features multicultural characters, but in all cases the theme remains generic to any culture. An example of a culturally generic book is ***Emma's Rug*** by Allen Say. In the story, Emma is an artistic child who finds inspiration by gazing at the shadows in a small white rug she has always had in her room. One day, her mother washes the rug, and Emma is sure that her inspiration can no longer be found in the very clean rug. Visually, Emma is portrayed as an Asian American child, but no details in the text identify Emma by a particular ethnicity. Emma's struggle is universal—one that children could experience regardless of their culture. Still, books that depict multicultural inclusiveness—even when the focus is not on any aspect of diversity—are important because they increase readers' exposure and awareness. In addition, books that show the universality of experiences allow students to find connections across cultures.

Culturally Specific Books

Culturally specific books illuminate the experience of members of a particular cultural group (Sims Bishop, 1992). The nuances of daily life are captured accurately, reflecting language use, attitudes, values, and beliefs of members of the group portrayed. Such details add texture to the writing, making the stories more real and more believable and therefore making it more likely that readers will see the stories as authentic. An example of a culturally specific book is Mildred Taylor's ***Roll of Thunder, Hear My Cry.*** Not only are the descriptions of situations and events historically accurate, but the character names, the forms of address, the dialogue, and the interactions are true to the culture of the people whose lives are reflected.

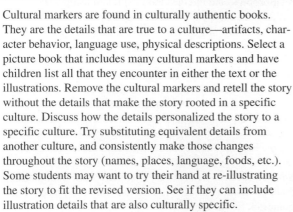

Teaching Idea 4.2
Identify Cultural Markers

Cultural markers are found in culturally authentic books. They are the details that are true to a culture—artifacts, character behavior, language use, physical descriptions. Select a picture book that includes many cultural markers and have children list all that they encounter in either the text or the illustrations. Remove the cultural markers and retell the story without the details that make the story rooted in a specific culture. Discuss how the details personalized the story to a specific culture. Try substituting equivalent details from another culture, and consistently make those changes throughout the story (names, places, language, foods, etc.). Some students may want to try their hand at re-illustrating the story to fit the revised version. See if they can include illustration details that are also culturally specific.

Although they differ in the depth of the cultural experiences they provide to readers, the full range of inclusiveness in multicultural books contributes to readers' understandings of their own and others' cultures. Sometimes, readers see themselves and others as sharing universal experiences, and therefore cultural group membership need not be explicitly discussed. But it is culturally specific books that offer the insights necessary to truly further readers' understanding of different cultures.

Evolution of Multicultural Literature

Go to the Extension Activities section of Chapter 4 in the MyEducationKit for your book and complete activity #1 to consider which books might be considered offensive due to racist language.

From the time children's books were first published in this country until well after World War II, most reflected mainstream characters, settings, values, and lifestyles. Children usually learned to read from books that presented primarily European American lifestyles and values. People who did not resemble the so-called American ideal—people of African, Asian, Latino/a, and Southern European origins, as well as Native Americans—were regularly singled out for discrimination. Likewise, early portrayals of nonmainstream characters tended to be highly stereotypical. Such characters were portrayed as cute, savage, primitive, uncouth, untrustworthy, or underdeveloped. Since the late 1960s, increasing efforts have been made to include honest depictions of people from all cultural groups in children's books—not simply to talk about them, but to narrate their perspectives and experiences through their eyes and in their voices.

Although several individuals (for example, Augusta Baker, Virginia Lacy, and Charlamae Rollins) campaigned for inclusion of people of diversity in children's books before 1965, the wake-up call that made the U.S. public aware of the situation is usually considered to be Nancy Larrick's 1965 article in the *Saturday Review,* "The All-White World of Children's Books." In her study, Larrick found that only 6.7 percent of children's books published between 1962 and 1964 included any African Americans in illustrations or text, and just 0.9 percent depicted them in contemporary settings. Other cultural groups were represented even less. The decade that followed saw an increase in the number of books that included people of diversity. The Council on Interracial Books for Children was founded in 1966 to heighten public awareness of diversity issues related to children's books. The Coretta Scott King Award was established in 1969 to give annual recognition to an African American author and an African American illustrator who contributed the most distinguished work during the previous year.

Larrick's study was replicated a decade later in order to examine how things had changed (Chall, Radwin, French, & Hall, 1985). The percentages had more than doubled: 14.4 percent of all children's books published from 1973 to 1975 included African Americans in text or illustrations, and 4 percent showed them in contemporary settings. This increase was attributed in part to the civil rights movement, along with long overdue recognition of the inequities highlighted by Larrick and others. However, Rollock (1984) found that these increases were only temporary and that in the five years after the Chall study, between 1979 and 1984, only 1.5 percent of newly published children's books included African Americans. The politically conservative 1980s fostered a decline in the publication of multicultural literature.

Limited data are available on representation in children's books of groups other than African Americans. But sources such as the Council on Interracial Books for Children (1975), Nieto (1983), Schon (1988), and Sims (1985) indicate that there has been even less representation of groups such as Asian Americans, Native Americans, and Latino/as. Quiroa (2004) notes that the numbers of Latino-themed books published in the United States comprised .02 percent of children's literature published between 1990 and 2000, and these numbers have not kept pace with the increases in this population. The Cooperative Children's Book Center of the University of Wisconsin has maintained annual statistics about the publication of African American literature since 1985, and statistics about the publication of literature by and about Asian Pacific Americans, American Indians, and Latinos since 1994. This information can be accessed on the center's website at *http://www.soemadison.wisc.edu/ccbc/pcstats.htm.*

The beginning of the 1990s saw the largest surge to date in multicultural publishing in the children's book field. Sims Bishop's (1991) note of optimism reflected a general increase in the level of awareness and understanding of the importance of multicultural literature. But despite the increase in numbers of multicultural publications, a study by Reimer (1992) revealed a lack of multicultural representation in popular booklists such as the International Reading Association's annual "Children's Choices" (the 1989 list was used in her study), Jim Trelease's *The New Read-Aloud Handbook* (1989), and former U.S. Secretary of Education William Bennett's list of recommended reading for elementary students (Bennett, 1988).

Other problems were highlighted in the early 1990s. Because of the predominance of European American writers and illustrators, multicultural literature was presented primarily from an "outside" perspective. Related to this problem was the fact that some Native Americans believed that mainstream authors had "stolen" stories without considering the cultural rules regarding who had access to those stories. Another problem was the grouping of related, but distinctly separate cultures under one label (for example, labeling Mexican Americans, Puerto Rican Americans, and Cuban Americans as "Hispanic"). In addition, there was a lack of teacher awareness of the importance of including multiple cultural perspectives in the classroom (Harris, 1997; Reimer, 1992; Sims Bishop, 1992). Unfortunately, inaccuracies, stereotypes, tokenism, bias, language flaws, and narrowness of representation continued to plague some books (Barrera, Thompson, & Dressman, 1997).

Although the total number of multicultural books published in recent years has declined since the mid-1990s, authors, illustrators, publishers, and educators are paying more attention to the issues of "authenticity" that were raised in the early 1990s and before. And authors and illustrators from diverse cultures are accepting the call to create culturally authentic work. (Ironically, many had tried unsuccessfully to have their work published in earlier years. In numerous cases, it was the annual contest sponsored by the Council on Interracial Books for Children that led to the publication of books written by people from diverse cultures.) Today, publishers are seeking ways both to encourage new multicultural authors and to ensure authenticity in the books they produce. For example, Lee and Low Publishers sponsors a New Voices award and the winners receive a cash award and a contract for publishing their book. Librarians and reviewers are recognizing authenticity as a critical criterion in evaluating multicultural books. And teachers are working to include authentic multicultural books as featured reading materials in their classrooms. However, librarians and teachers should also look critically at the books from years past that are still found on the shelves of many school libraries and in classrooms. Although such books have value in specialized collections that allow people to see historic trends in the publication of multicultural books, teachers should make sure that young readers are not exposed to these books without some discussion of the damaging racist or stereotypical images they contain. In an interview by K. T. Horning (2008), Rudine Sims Bishop talks about African American literature being purposeful. "Sewn throughout the fiction are threads of African American history, mentions of African American heroes, and references to African American music, so that there's a whole idea of making sure that Black children have a sense of the culture in which they live. It's that notion again of being teachy but not preachy, of giving information and trying to empower them without preaching at them." (p. 256) Despite the rise in African American literature from that of decades past, Sims Bishop still precautions reviewers to be sensitive to the historical context of African American Literature and to take the context into consideration. She expresses hope for more quantity, availability, marketing because they continue to be "perennially . . . underrepresented in the field."

Many of the authors and illustrators who were among those who defined the field are profiled in the section on major authors and illustrators. However, some who were notable for their early contributions are not included here for a number of reasons; for example, John Steptoe was a major contributor, but his untimely death at the age of 38 has ceased his contributions. As early as his high school years, Steptoe recognized a need for children's books containing authentic dialogue that black children could relate to and the 1969 publication of *Stevie* received much attention. To tell this story of a little boy who initially resents having to share his mother and his possessions with a younger boy who eventually becomes like a little brother, the nineteen-year-old author and illustrator used black dialect and depicted an urban setting. The numerous awards bestowed on this book were just precursors to the many others Steptoe would earn in his short life. His final book, **Baby Says,** was one of the first board books for babies that depicted an African American baby.

Issues Related to Multicultural Literature

To evaluate the influence of multicultural literature on children's understanding of the world around them and to establish criteria for good multicultural literature, we need to consider several issues: (1) whether a work presents cultural details authentically, (2) whether the author writes from an inside or an outside perspective, (3) whether a work promotes stereotypes, and (4) which cultural group is being described in the work. Consideration of these issues can guide teachers in selecting multicultural literature and facilitating discussions of such literature among their students.

Cultural Authenticity

When a book presents a theme that is true to a culture and is filled with specific details that are authentic, members of that culture who read it feel that their experiences have been genuinely reflected and illuminated for others to share. Culturally authentic books are written by authors who have developed a "culturally conscious" way to "provide exceptional aesthetic experiences: [to] entertain, educate, and inform; and . . . engender racial pride" (Harris, 1990, p. 551). However, when a book distorts or misrepresents information about a culture, such misinformation leads to misunderstandings about that culture by those from other cultures and makes members of the misrepresented culture feel betrayed.

Examples of culturally authentic books are Carmen Lomas Garza's *In My Family/En mi familia* and her earlier book *Family Pictures/Cuadros de familia.* Based on the author's life in South Texas, these books include various paintings that illustrate events in her childhood, accompanied by bilingual text. In *Family Pictures/Cuadros de familia,* the page entitled "Birthday Party/Cumpleaños" begins with "That's me hitting the piñata at my sixth birthday party." Following the English text is the Spanish translation: "Ésa soy yo, pegándole a la piñata en la fiesta que me dieron cuando cumplí seis años." Readers can identify specific details, such as the framed picture of the Last Supper, the flamenco dancers on the calendar, and the assembling of the tamales, all of which are culturally authentic. Through illustrations and text, *In My Family/En mi familia* tells about the making of empañadas, birthday barbecue parties, and summer dance time. Mexican American readers can feel a sense of kinship with the creator of such books—a sense of shared experiences and understandings. Readers outside the culture can gain new insights from these authentic depictions of the culture.

Birthday Party

That's me hitting the piñata at my sixth birthday party. It was also my brother's fourth birthday. My mother made a big birthday party for us and invited all kinds of friends, cousins and neighborhood kids.

You can't see the piñata when you're trying to hit it, because your eyes are covered with a handkerchief. My father is pulling the rope that makes the piñata go up and down. He will make sure that everybody has a chance to hit it at least once. Somebody will end up breaking it, and that's when all the candies will fall out and all the kids will run and try to grab them.

Cumpleaños

Ésa soy yo, pegándole a la piñata en la fiesta que me dieron cuando cumplí seis años. Era también el cumpleaños de mi hermano, que cumplía cuatro años. Mi madre nos dio una gran fiesta e invitó a muchos primos, vecinos y amigos.

No puedes ver la piñata cuando le estás dando con el palo, porque tienes los ojos cubiertos por un pañuelo. Mi padre está tirando de la cuerda que sube y baja la piñata. Él se encargará de que todos tengan por lo menos una oportunidad de pegarle a la piñata. Luego alguien acabará rompiéndola, y entonces todos los caramelos que tiene dentro caerán y todos los niños correrán a cogerlos.

10

ILLUSTRATION 4.3 Many Mexican Americans feel that both the text and the illustrations in *Family Pictures* authentically reflect their own family's stories. (From *Family Pictures, Cuadros de familia* by Carmen Lomas Garza. Reprinted with the permission of the publisher, Children's Book Press, San Francisco, CA, www.childrensbookpress.org. Copyright © 1990 by Carmen Lomas Garza.)

When a book lacks authenticity, it is likely to convey misleading images of a culture. Sometimes, the text gives readers a stereotyped or dated image of a culture; other times, confused illustrations depict a culture in inappropriate ways. Readers outside the portrayed culture might not be able to discern what is authentic and what is not. In such cases, misinformed and inauthentic images continue to perpetuate and negatively influence readers' beliefs and understandings about that culture.

Perspective: Insider or Outsider

The perspective of the writer has become a major issue in multicultural literature: Does the author have an "inside" or an "outside" perspective on the culture being portrayed? An author with an inside perspective writes as a member of the culture and therefore is more likely to portray the cultural group authentically. An author with an outside perspective writes from a point of view of a nonmember of the group being portrayed. But even among those inside a culture, the range of cultural experiences and opinions regarding the depictions of the culture may vary, revealing the multidimensionality of any culture (Noll, 1995).

Members of the dominant culture have had multiple opportunities to see their world interpreted through eyes like their own. But they may not have had the experience of being wrongly portrayed, and therefore they may not know the feeling of betrayal at having their culture misrepresented. An outsider might miss the rhythm, accent, and flavor that enliven the ethnic experience for the insider audience. An outsider's interpretation of an ethnic experience may be filled with details that are factually accurate, but the presentation may be bland and dry, lacking the cultural nuances that would make it come alive. A simple missed or misrepresented detail may be enough to negate authenticity for members of the culture being portrayed (Kaplan, 1995).

In his article "Can We Fly across Cultural Gaps on the Wings of Imagination? Ethnicity, Experience, and Cultural Authenticity," Cai (1995) compares a novel by Laurence Yep, an insider of the Chinese culture, to one by Vanya Oakes, an outsider. Through detailed comparisons, Cai clearly outlines the differences between the inside and outside perspectives. Can those born outside a culture produce authentic material about that culture? Some say no. Others, such as scholar Henry Louis Gates, Jr., W. E. B. Du Bois Professor of Literature at Harvard, believe that an inside perspective can be gained by cultural outsiders. Gates believes that "no human culture is inaccessible to someone who makes the effort to understand, to learn, to inhabit another world" (cited in Sims Bishop, 1992, p. 42). Certainly, stereotypes do not exist in all books by mainstream writers and illustrators that depict diversity. Good depictions can be found in the works of Ezra Jack Keats and Demi. Some, through their own life experiences and extensive research, have been able to create culturally authentic portrayals of a group different from the one into which they were born. Many African Americans view Arnold Adoff's writing as having an inside perspective, yet he is not African American. Many of his books, such as *black is brown is tan,* speak from his biracial family's experiences. Similarly, Demi's picture books, such as *The Empty Pot* and *Chingis Khan,* are set in China. Although Demi was not born Chinese, her thoroughness of research is evident, and readers who are Chinese find that her work reflects the perspective of insiders. Author Laura Krauss Melmed (1999) documents the thoroughness of research that she and illustrator Jim LaMarche completed in creating a picture book set in Japan, *Little Oh.*

Clearly, the issue of insider versus outsider authorship is complex. However, books that present authentic voices and images—no matter who created them—offer a uniquely valuable contribution to literature about a culture. They allow readers within the culture to enjoy the sense of kinship and pride that come from having one's own experience accurately portrayed. They also broaden the perspective of readers from other cultures and offer them fresh insights about the cultural group depicted.

Stereotyping and Other Unacceptable Depictions of Cultural Groups

When a single set of attributes is assigned to an entire cultural group, diversity and individuality are overlooked, and stereotyping results. A stereotyped impression of a cultural group

Go to the Extension Activities section of Chapter 4 in the MyEducationKit for your book and complete activity #2 to investigate the controversy surrounding *The Story of Little Black Sambo*.

may be created by how characters are portrayed, how characters interact with one another, how a book's setting is described, how a theme is treated, or simply how information is conveyed. It is important to remember, though, that stereotypes often originate in some kernel of behavior that is true to a culture. How do we distinguish between details that make up cultural specificity and globalized stereotypes? Usually, negative (but sometimes positive) attributes that are assumed always to be true simply because of their association with a cultural group are stereotypes. It is sometimes very difficult to distinguish between cultural details and stereotypes. One way to make this distinction is by finding out whether members of the cultural group embrace that attribute as defining themselves.

In the past, literature often depicted nonmainstream cultures in patronizing and condescending ways. Stereotypes abounded in images created by mainstream writers and illustrators. Books such as the 1899 book by Bannerman, *The Story of Little Black Sambo,* and Bishop's 1938 *The Five Chinese Brothers* presented negative and stereotyped images of blacks and Asians, respectively. Although *The Story of Little Black Sambo* is set in India, the illustrations in the original edition depict negative caricatures of African Americans. The story line of *The Five Chinese Brothers* requires that the brothers look alike; however, the book depicts all the Chinese people of the village as identical and with yellow skin. Some more recent books are also controversial because of their stereotyped images. Despite the explanations at the end of the book that document distinctions among ten of the tribes, Native Americans believe that Virginia Grossman and Sylvia Long's 1991 book, *Ten Little Rabbits,* is problematic. Too often, Native American characters are portrayed as animals or depicted as something to be "counted," perpetuating the myth that all Native American people are alike— in this case, "they just wear different blankets" (McCarty, 1995). Stereotyped images of Latinos include "Mexican men wearing wide-brimmed hats snoozing under a giant cactus" and images of "sarapes, piñatas, burros, bare feet, and broken English" (Council on Interracial Books for Children, 1974).

Many books that present stereotypical images of a cultural group are still in print and may be on the shelf of your local bookstore, school library, or public library. Sometimes, these books are purchased by adults who remember them from their childhood and want to share them with young children. However, having loved a book as a child is not in itself an adequate selection criterion, unless you are prepared to take advantage of this teachable moment to discuss stereotypes in older books that represent dominant cultural mores of those times. Ginny Moore Kruse, Director of the Cooperative Children's Book Center at the University of Wisconsin, Madison, cautions against the use of materials that contain "hurtful images" or perpetuate erroneous information about cultures (1991).

In recent years, efforts have been made to remedy stereotyped images in old stories by publishing new versions of the stories. Sometimes, the original author/illustrator team creates the revised version, as in the case of a story set in Alaska and titled *On Mother's Lap,* written by Ann Herbert Scott and illustrated by Glo Coalson. Margaret Mahy provided new text for *The Seven Chinese Brothers,* which was illustrated by Jean and Mou-sien Tseng. Julius Lester and Jerry Pinkney collaborated in the creation of *Sam and the Tigers,* a retelling of the Sambo story in the African American tradition. In *The Story of Little Babaji,* Fred Marcellino re-illustrated Helen Bannerman's original text for the Sambo story, renaming the characters with Indian names and depicting the setting in India, as the text indicates. Khorana (1996) objects that the stereotype now has moved from caricatures of African Americans to reflect British colonialism in illustrations that depict the boy (Little Babaji) as a royal maharajah instead of a village boy as the story indicates. Khorana reports that "cultural details are used for their exotic appeal and are inconsistent with the professional and socioeconomic status of the family in the story."

Identification of Cultural Groups

For some time, there has been ongoing discussion as to which groups should be included under the "multicultural literature" umbrella. African Americans, Asian Americans, Latino/as, and Native Americans are always included. An extensive bibliography at the end of this chapter lists recommended books that represent these cultural groups. As our population shifts to include less represented groups, their stories are also needed. For example,

Top Shelf 4.1

Multiracial Characters

Aneesa Lee and the Weaver's Gift by Nikki Grimes. Illustrated by Ashley Bryan.

black is brown is tan by Arnold Adoff. Illustrated by Emily Arnold McCulley.

Habibi by Naomi Shihab Nye.

I Love Saturdays y domingos by Alma Flor Ada. Illustrated by Elivia Savadier.

Molly Bannaky by Alice McGill. Illustrated by Chris Soentpiet.

ILLUSTRATION 4.4   A new child from Somalia finds a way to communicate with his classmates through his drawing of his homeland. (Cover from *Color of Home* by Mary Hoffman, illustrated by Karin Littlewood, copyright © 2002 by Karin Littlewood. Used by permission of Phyllis Fogelman Books, A Division of Penguin Young Readers Group, A Member of Penguin Group (USA) Inc., 345 Hudson Street, New York, NY 10014. All rights reserved.)

Muslim Americans are seldom found in ethnic American literature. There are other groups outside the mainstream that have also been underrepresented and misrepresented in children's literature and therefore deserve attention as teachers and librarians evaluate and select multicultural literature. Reading and discussing books that are culturally and historically distinct helps readers gain insights that "mainstream" literature alone cannot provide.

Jewish Americans

Because of the years of oppression and misrepresentation they have experienced, attention needs to be given to books that authentically reflect the history, religion, and culture of Jewish people. Books such as Lois Lowry's **Number the Stars** share an important part of Jewish history with readers who may or may not be familiar with the Holocaust. The story is about both a strong friendship and people who help others who are facing unjust treatment. The specific circumstances focus on the Danish resistance to the Holocaust, but the themes are universal.

Some contemporary works are important in that they offer possibilities for understanding the lives of Jewish Americans today. Patricia Polacco tells of her own Jewish Russian family's heritage and traditions in most of her books, including **The Keeping Quilt.** Passing on the traditions of her heritage is the important theme of this book, which is filled with such cultural markers as a babushka and a wedding huppa.

Other religious groups, such as the Amish and Mennonites, are also misunderstood and need better representation. In Sarah Stewart's **The Journey,** a young Amish girl makes a trip to the city of Chicago. Although it is improbable that two Amish women would take a trip to a city merely for sightseeing, the comparisons and contrasts of the city to the girl's home serve to show readers how differently we view a world outside our own experiences. Raymond Bial's informational books such as **Amish Home** and **Visit to Amish Country** also help readers to understand the Amish world through nonfiction descriptions.

Appalachian Americans

Another group that has historically been underrepresented in children's literature is the people of the Appalachian region of the United States, who have a distinct culture and way of life. Cynthia Rylant, George Ella Lyon, and Gloria Houston have written books that authentically reflect this group's experiences. In Gloria Houston's **My Great-Aunt Arizona,** for example, details of the schoolhouse are accurately depicted. Also, the fact that five generations of the family in the book attended the same school and had Aunt Arizona as their teacher is typical of real-life Appalachian families of the era. **The Relatives Came** by Cynthia Rylant reflects the universal experience of family members coming together for a reunion. However, that experience takes on a special meaning from the fact that Appalachian people are separated from their neighbors by mountains and therefore often live in relative isolation. Both text and illustrations support the sense of distance traveled along small mountain roads. But it is the activities of the family—"hugging and eating and breathing together"— that give readers vivid insight into the experience.

Two books that offer authentic historic fiction are **Spitting Image** and **Ghost Girl.** In Shutta Crum's **Spitting Image,** twelve-year-old Jessie's concern for the well-being of her family and that of her neighbors leads her to be a helpful informant for a government program intended to offer assistance to those in poverty. But her plan to help others backfires and national publicity portrays the people she loves in a negative light that brings them embarrassment and shame. Likewise, **Ghost Girl** by Delia Ray is set in the Blue Ridge Mountains, and the extreme poverty of the region results in a lack of resources for the community. When President and Mrs. Hoover build a school and April hopes for her first real chance to attend one, she must face opposing forces in her mother, who does not approve her enrolling in a school, and her grandmother, who wants April to get her education. Issues such as this are always complicated by other matters, and in this case, it is the death (and the untold secret about the death) of a sibling that must be dealt with.

European Americans

European American cultures have been excluded from the multicultural umbrella because they generally have been well represented in the literature. Because such literature most frequently depicted a generic American experience, not much separate attention was given to European American cultures. Therefore, although literature about European American cultural groups does not need the corrective attention that misrepresented or underrepresented groups might call for, teachers and librarians should not overlook books that give insight into the experiences of specific European American cultures. More recent stories from Europe have culturally and historically specific details that distinguish them from culturally generic stories of mainstream life. *Girl of Kosovo* by Alice Mead is an example of a book that is about the ethnic cleansing war that took place in Kosovo in 1999, seen from the point of view of eleven-year-old Zana, who wonders why the world sends reporters to record the devastation and death, but not give help to her people. Books like this one depict a culturally distinct experience and should be considered as meeting the goals for multicultural literature.

Muslim Americans and the Middle East

The Muslims in America and in the Middle East have long been underrepresented. In Naomi Shihab Nye's **Habibi,** biracial Liyana explores what it means to move to Jerusalem as a teenager when she has been raised in St. Louis, and recounts how she struggles to understand cultural differences and the way they affect her identity. Books like Mary Hoffman's **The Color of Home** show readers that despite language barriers, the basic human need to communicate about things that are important to each of us—home, family, community—can be done through illustration and interpreters. In her **Breadwinner** trilogy, Deborah Ellis explores what it means to be a female child, living in modern-day Afghanistan under the Taliban regime. In **The Breadwinner,** eleven-year-old Parvana hides her gender identity in order to obtain a job to feed her family when her father is suddenly taken away. In **Parvana's Journey,** after her father's death, she sets out to find her missing family. **Mud City** switches to the story of Parvana's friend, Shauzia, and describes how she survives the streets as she longs to escape to France.

Criteria for Evaluating and Selecting Multicultural Literature

With the growth in the number of multicultural books, it is important to select those of high quality. Naturally, when judging the quality of multicultural books, a teacher should apply the criteria for evaluating the various genres of children's literature that are discussed throughout this text. In addition, there are specific questions to consider regarding multicultural books:

- Do the author and illustrator present authentic perspectives?
- Is the culture portrayed multidimensionally?
- Are cultural details naturally integrated?
- Are details accurate and is the interpretation current?
- Is language used authentically?
- Is the collection balanced?

Teaching Idea 4.3
Research Family History and Stories

Begin by reading examples of books that are based on personal stories and family stories. For example, you might read aloud any of the many books that are based on family stories by Tomie dePaola or Patricia Polacco and geared to younger children. To older students, you may want to read excerpts from first-generation immigrant literature. Explain to students that many such stories began with a personal or family story and that sometimes authors tell them in as straightforward a manner as possible to maintain the original history. In other cases, some authors have clarified or embellished the stories to fictionalize what began as a personal or family story. Have children ask their families about their heritage and what stories the adults remember from their childhood. Families could tell the stories into a tape recorder or videocamera or write them down to be shared with the class. This might serve as the beginning of a book, created by the child.

Top Shelf 4.2

Growing Up in a World of Political or Social Unrest

Before We Were Free by Julia Alvarez

Girl of Kosovo by Alice Mead

Grab Hands and Run by Frances Temple

The Other Side of Truth by Beverley Naidoo

Red Scarf Girl by Ji Li Jiang

Zlata's Diary: A Child's Life in Sarajevo by Zalata Filipovec

Do the Author and Illustrator Present Authentic Perspectives?

The author should maintain an insider's mindset and point of view when writing about a cultural group in order to portray it authentically. Voices such as Patricia Polacco's and Pat Mora's convey an insider's perspective because these authors write of experiences based on their own heritage. Polacco's *The Keeping Quilt* and Mora's *A Birthday Basket for Tía* both tell of the authors' personal lives. However, as we discussed earlier in this chapter, the crucial issue is not heritage by fact of birth, but whether the author thinks as a member of the group or as an outsider looking in. Careful research and experience living within the culture contribute to Demi's insider voice in a book such as *Liang and the Magic Paintbrush.* Outsider perspective that offers authentic portrayals include contemporary photo essays such as those by Diana Hoyt-Goldsmith, in which she depicts the daily lives of children who have particularly strong ethnic heritage. Her subjects vary from Vietnamese American to different Native American tribes, but in each case, she offers as true a portrayal as possible, highlighting things that would be interesting to both those within and outside the culture.

Illustrations should be accurate, true to the time period portrayed, and culturally authentic. They must not stereotype, homogenize, or ridicule any cultural group. Racial groups should be depicted with a variety of physical features that are not overemphasized. Illustrations play a major role in transmitting cultural images, especially in picture books. Often, a book's cover illustration sends an immediate message about the book's perspective.

Is the Culture Portrayed Multidimensionally?

Cultural groups should be presented multidimensionally to help readers realize the depth and breadth of experiences within cultures. For example, *El Chino,* a biography of Billy Wong by Allen Say, tells the story of a son of Chinese immigrants who became a bullfighter despite what was expected of him by others. To pursue his dream, he had to clash with those expectations. Others said, "Who's ever heard of a Chinese athlete?" and "Only the Spaniards can become true matadors." But he remembered what his father had said: "In America, you can be anything you want to be." Presenting a culture's multidimensionality means portraying the members of that culture in a range of ways. A book should especially be free of any tokenism, in which cultures might be represented only in order to give a head count for politically correct inclusion.

Cultural groups should not be presented through images that could lead to stereotyping. There is no particular experience that is so universal that it can be defined as "The _____ Experience." Rather, multiple dimensions of all cultures should be presented objectively, without bias. Roles of cultural members should also be varied, as in Mildred Pitts Walter's *Justin and the Best Biscuits in the World,* in which the African American grandfather serves as an important role model for his ten-year-old grandson. During a visit to his grandfather's ranch, Justin learns that cowboys must become self-sufficient by learning to do the jobs that Justin had earlier deemed were "women's work."

Are Cultural Details Naturally Integrated?

The cultural details necessary to make a story come alive should not impede the flow of the story. These details should be presented in context so that cumbersome explanations are not necessary. If longer explanations are needed, footnotes or endnotes can serve to clarify. Laurence Yep's *Dragon's Gate* is filled with cultural details. The hardships endured, the power relationships and the actions they lead to, the dialogues among the Chinese workers, and the dialogues between the Chinese workers and their white bosses are all described with a completeness that gives readers insight into the lives of the men who left their families behind in hopes of getting rich in a foreign land. These details are necessary for readers to deepen their understanding and empathy.

Are Details Accurate and Is the Interpretation Current?

Details must be accurate and true to the situation in which they are presented. Factual errors, omissions, and changes may indicate sloppy research and presentation. Sometimes, these

How Much Artistic License Should Be Given to Illustrators as They Create Images of a Culture?

Some illustrators argue that demands for absolute accuracy of every detail rob the illustrator of the right to use imagination and individual style in portraying an image. They contend that unless the illustrations are photographs, the style of illustration will influence the degree of attention to detail.

Others argue that accurate details in illustrations create the overall sense of cultural authenticity. They point out that misconceptions may develop from incorrect images. In some cases, highly regarded illustrators whose work is exceptional from an artistic viewpoint have been criticized for creating images that "mix" cultures. Critics say that this mixing of cultures robs each culture of its distinction. Yet the illustrators express their desire to create unified images of cultures that sometimes share a common voice. One example is *Brother Eagle, Sister Sky: A Message from Chief Seattle* (1991) by Susan Jeffers. Controversy arose over the text because the words were based on a script for a 1971 television commercial decrying pollution. Controversy arose over the illustrations because of mixed images of Native American cultures that contained inaccuracies of both history and culture. Jeffers defended her position by stating that the important point is that the book reflects a Native American philosophy (Noll, 1995).

How do you view this issue of authenticity versus artistic license in children's book illustrations? How will the type of illustrations affect child readers who do not intimately know the culture portrayed? How will the illustrations affect child readers whose own cultures are portrayed?

What do you think?

problems may actually reflect an attempt on the author's part to meet the expectations of a mainstream readership that has preconceived notions of cultures. Series books that focus on children in various countries are sometimes guilty of such intentional errors. One book featuring a child in the Netherlands included all the preconceived images that mainstream readers might expect to find: A blonde girl wakes up, puts on her wooden shoes, and passes a windmill and a field of tulips on her way to school!

There are also series books that are written according to a formula, such as books about other countries in which authors fill in the blanks of standardized formats. In many cases, these authors have no firsthand experience with the country they are discussing. Currency of interpretation can sometimes be evaluated by considering recency of copyright and thoroughness of revision. Books that claim to cite "current" statistics should be carefully analyzed to determine whether the statistic reported is still appropriate, years after the book is published. Sometimes, the interpretation of factual information is more influential than the facts themselves. The author's understanding of the culture determines his or her choice of words, which in turn influences the readers' perceptions. For example, reference to a Japanese father as "honorable father" is a literal translation of the word *otoosan*. The "o" at the beginning of the word for father denotes the honoring of the person addressed. However, constantly referring to each adult as "honorable" may lead readers to an exaggerated, stereotypical view that is not in keeping with the actual personal interactions described in the story.

Is Language Used Authentically?

The language and dialect spoken by characters should authentically portray the kinds of interactions that are typical of those characters, and terminology that refers to aspects of culture should be acceptable by contemporary standards. For example, Gary Soto writes from the perspective of a Mexican American who grew up in California. Readers who have a background similar to his sense a true voice of their experiences. In his book **Pacific Crossing,** Soto portrays two teenage Mexican American boys as foreign exchange students in Japan. Soto uses terminology and phrases that Mexican Americans might use to communicate with each other. He also follows the Japanese language's very strict rules of verbal exchange, which take into consideration the gender, the age, and the familiarity of the speakers. Katherine Paterson's translations of Japanese folktales such as Momoko Ishii's **The Tongue-Cut Sparrow** and Sumiko Yagawa's **The Crane Wife** retain onomatopoeic words that echo the sounds of the Japanese language within the storytelling format.

Is the Collection Balanced?

It is important to present children with a balanced collection of multicultural books. The term "collection" refers to the books that are available in a school, classroom, or public library as well as the books selected to serve as teaching units within a classroom. Budget constraints, space limitations, and the need to present readers with the best possible choices make careful decisions regarding book collections a necessity. Readers need to be able to find recommended books readily, not buried under an avalanche of mediocre books. It is generally accepted that purchasing multiple copies of excellent books is better than including mediocre books simply to increase the size of the collection. Because a great number of high-quality multicultural books are available today, there is no need to include books simply to fulfill a quota.

To compile a balanced multicultural collection, a teacher or librarian should assess needs and match available quality books with those identified needs. In assessing needs, consideration should be given to (1) readers' preferences, (2) existing multicultural books in the collection, (3) curricular needs, (4) the availability of quality multicultural books, and (5) provision of a strong selection across genres. In addition, the compiler should ensure that adequate numbers of books are available for recreational reading, for teacher read-alouds, and for placement in the classroom library.

Consider Readers' Preferences

Both teachers and librarians need to acquire an understanding of the general background knowledge and the preferences of the readers for whom the particular collection is being developed, including the range of materials they enjoy and the types of books they choose. Often, children will be interested in reading books about their own cultural group, but that is not always the case. Some readers will voluntarily read books about other cultural groups; others might need to be introduced to and encouraged to select such books.

Survey Multicultural Books Already in the Collection

Multicultural books that are already in the collection form the core of the collection and help to determine what is needed. Overselecting or underselecting certain types of books can be avoided by conducting a careful inventory of existing books in the collection. Is there an overabundance of folktales from various cultures? Are there enough contemporary stories about people of diversity? Are there books that show multiple perspectives? Familiarity with the existing collection also enables a teacher or librarian to weed out and discard books that are not culturally appropriate.

Assess Curricular Needs

It is important to assess curricular needs to determine what is needed to supplement units of study. Literature-based curriculum calls for high-quality books to be used in all curricular areas. As teachers and librarians work together to obtain books that fit the needs of the curriculum, they should attempt to include books that extend beyond the basic information and enhance multicultural understanding.

Determine the Availability of High-Quality Multicultural Books

Determine the availability of quality multicultural books because no matter what the needs are, only high-quality books should be considered. Obtaining lower-quality books simply to fill a shelf is not recommended.

Provide a Strong Selection across Genres

Another goal in establishing a balanced collection of multicultural books is to provide a variety of different genres. For example, when creating a collection of books about Mexico, the teacher or librarian should make a point to include folklore, history, informational books, picture books, historical fiction, biography, poetry, and modern realistic fiction. There should be books set in Mexico as well as books about Mexican Americans. The books must represent a broad range of experiences and voices if readers are to understand the diverse nature of Mexico and its people.

Awards for Multicultural Literature

Multicultural books qualify for all of the general awards that are given to children's literature, such as the Caldecott, Newbery, or Sibert Medals. Several multicultural books have been recipients of such awards. For example, Ed Young was presented the Caldecott Medal for ***Lon Po Po: A Red-Riding Hood Story from China.*** Linda Sue Park was presented the Newbery Medal for ***A Single Shard.*** The same year, An Na was presented the Sibert Medal for ***A Step from Heaven***. Such recognitions have caused some to question the continuation of ethnicity-based awards (Aronson, 2001). However, the need for awards that are designated specifically for the purpose of examining and awarding books and their creators for the criteria of cultural depiction continues. Awards are sometimes given to previously unpublished authors and illustrators to encourage the writing and illustrating of books on multicultural subjects, and have played an important role in launching the careers of authors and illustrators. Awards provide public recognition for a book, author, or illustrator and serve as selection and evaluation tools.

The Coretta Scott King Award

At an American Library Association conference in 1969, after lamenting the fact that a "minority" author or illustrator had never been awarded the Newbery or Caldecott Medal, school librarians Mabel McKissick and Glyndon Greer were encouraged by publisher John Carroll to launch a new award highlighting the accomplishments of African American authors and illustrators. The award was named in honor of Coretta Scott King to "commemorate the life and work of Martin Luther King, Jr." as well as to honor his wife for "courage and determination in continuing to work for peace and brotherhood" (Smith, 2004). The Coretta Scott King Award has been presented at the annual meeting of the American Library Association since 1972 and has been recognized as an official ALA award since 1982. Selection criteria for the award have evolved with the increase in the number of books from which to choose. In the beginning, any book that reflected some aspect of the black experience or embraced concepts of brotherhood was considered. In recent years, however, the criteria have become more stringent and now specify that "recipients are African American authors and illustrators whose distinguished books promote an understanding and appreciation of the culture and contribution of all people to the realization of the 'American dream.'" Refer to Appendix A for a list of past winners and honor books.

Since 1993, the Genesis Award certificate of recognition has been given to African American authors and illustrators who show significant promise in their work. Basic criteria for this award are the same as for the Coretta Scott King Award, but winners can have no more than three published works.

The Pura Belpré Award

The Pura Belpré Award, established in 1996, is sponsored jointly by Reforma (a national association to promote library services to Spanish speakers) and the American Library Association's Association of Library Services to Children. It is awarded biannually to a Latino/a

ILLUSTRATION 4.5   Children can share in other countries' heritages by reading folktales from those cultures, such as *Lon Po Po*, the Chinese "Little Red Riding Hood." (Cover from *Lon Po Po* by Ed Young, copyright © 1989 by Ed Young. Used by permission of Philomel Books, A Division of Penguin Young Readers Group, A Member of Penguin Group (USA) Inc., 345 Hudson Street, New York, NY 10014. All rights reserved.)

ILLUSTRATION 4.6   The story of *Tar Beach* (both a winner of the Coretta Scott King Award and a Caldecott Honor Book in 1992) originally appeared in the form of a "story quilt," with the text surrounding a central picture on a quilt. [*Tar Beach (Woman on a Beach Series #1)* by Faith Ringgold. Faith Ringgold © 1988. Reproduced with permission of Faith Ringgold Studio. Photograph by David Heald © The Solomon R. Guggenheim Foundation, New York. Book published by Random House, Inc.]

ILLUSTRATION 4.7   Readers learn about aviator Bessie Coleman as her family, friends, and others share their memories of her from various perspectives. (Jacket illustration copyright © 2002 by Earl Lewis from *Talkin' About Bessie* by Nikki Grimes. Scholastic Inc./Orchard Books. Reprinted by permission of Scholastic Inc.)

writer and illustrator whose work best depicts and celebrates Latino heritage. A complete list of past winners can be found in the Appendix.

Tomás Rivera Mexican American Children's Book Award

This award was established in 1995 at Texas State University—San Marcos, in honor of a distinguished alumnus who published widely on topics relevant to the lives of Mexican Americans. It is awarded annually to the author/illustrator of the book selected as the most distinguished book of the previous publication year that authentically reflects the lives of Mexican American children and young adults in the southwestern United States. A complete list of past winners can be found in the Appendix.

The Américas Book Award for Children's and Young Adult Literature

This award was established in 1993 and is sponsored by the National Consortium of Latin American Studies Programs, a United States Department of Education National Resource Center housed at the University of Wisconsin. Winners and commended titles are announced annually to recognize works that were published in either English or Spanish in the previous publication year and that portray Latin America, the Caribbean, or Latinos in the United States authentically and engagingly. The intent is to focus on cultural heritage and to acknowledge the link of the Americas. In addition to recognizing literary merit, exceptional design, and cultural context, the potential for classroom use is considered. A complete list of past winners can be found in the Appendix.

The Asian Pacific American Literary Award

The Asian Pacific American Award for Literature was presented for the first time in 2001 by the National Conference on Asian Pacific American Librarians. It is given every three years to Asian Pacific American writers in three categories, one of which is literature for children and young adults. Authors of fiction and nonfiction books are eligible, and both the author and the illustrator of picture books are jointly eligible.

Go to the Extension Activities section of Chapter 4 in the MyEducationKit for your book and complete activity #3 to examine books that should be avoided about Native Americans.

The American Indian Youth Literature Award

This award was created to identify and honor the best books written and illustrated by and about American Indians. Books are to depict American Indians in the "fullness of their humanity, in either past or present contexts." Every two years, up to three books can be recognized for the award in the following categories: Best Picture Book, Best Middle School Book, and Best Young Adult Book. The first awards were named in 2006.

The Jane Addams Children's Book Award

Since 1953, the Jane Addams Children's Book Award has been presented annually by the Women's International League for Peace and Freedom (WILPF) and the Jane Addams Peace Association to the children's book published during the preceding year that most effectively promotes the cause of peace, social justice, and world community. A picture book category was added in 1993. The award honors Jane Addams, who in 1931 became the first woman to win the Nobel Peace Prize. The Jane Addams Peace Association was founded for the purpose of promoting understanding among the people of the world, with the goal of avoiding wars and living in peace. A complete list of past winners can be found in the Appendix.

ILLUSTRATION 4.8 Pablo goes about his town near Oaxaca, Mexico, gathering special food and preparing for the big festivities of The Day of The Dead. (*Pablo Remembers* by George Ancona, 1993. Used by permission of HarperCollins Publishers.)

Although the numbers have decreased in the last few years, more multicultural books have been published in the last decade than in any previous decade. Thus, teachers and parents have both the opportunity and the responsibility to select high-quality multicultural books. In her book *Against Borders,* Hazel Rochman (1993) suggests that teachers and parents look for books that fight against the idea of borders that separate people and seek out books that help readers tear down those borders by enabling them to understand people around the world.

Major Authors and Illustrators of Multicultural Literature

Because multicultural book publishing has a relatively short history, most of the authors and illustrators profiled here are among the early ones who defined the field and continue to write today. Only a few authors and illustrators whose work cuts across multiple genres are profiled in this section. Most are ones who were early contributors to multicultural literature. Others are included in the genre sections throughout Part Two of this book.

Alma Flor Ada

Alma Flor Ada was born in Cuba, educated in Spain and Peru, and now lives in San Francisco, where she was formerly a professor at the University of San Francisco. She is active in the promotion of bilingualism, writing books in both Spanish and English as well as translating books written by others. As a child, Alma Flor Ada was fortunate to have been surrounded by storytellers. Her grandmother and her uncle told many stories, and her father passed on his knowledge of the world by making up stories. Ada worked with Isabel Campoy to publish

ILLUSTRATION 4.9 In *Harvesting Hope*, readers learn about the concept of nonviolent protest through respect and determination, exemplified in the life and leadership of Cesar Chavez. (Cover from *Harvesting Hope: The Story of Cesar Chavez,* copyright © 2003 by Kathleen Krull, illustrations copyright © 2003 by Yuyi Morales, reproduced by permission of Houghton Mifflin Harcourt Publishing Company.)

Tales Our Abuelitas Told: A Hispanic Folktale Collection. Ada's books include retellings of traditional tales and a contemporary story set in a Latin American country, as well as a story about the cultural conflict experienced by a child who grows up in an ethnic community in the United States.

The Gold Coin tells the story of how a thief is transformed. A young thief follows Doña Josefa, with the intent of taking her gold coin, but changes his mind as he meets the people whom Doña Josefa has helped. *My Name Is María Isabel/Me llamo María Isabel* is about a little girl who must find a way to express pride in her heritage while interacting with people who misunderstand her culture. Ada's autobiographical book, *Under the Royal Palms: A Childhood in Cuba,* was awarded the Pura Belpré Award in 2000.

Joseph Bruchac

Listen to Joseph Bruchac discuss mentoring a love of reading in children by going to the Conversations section of Chapter 4 in the MyEducationKit for your book.

Joseph Bruchac's rich cultural heritage includes Abenaki ancestry, and his writing is lauded for its authentic images of Native Americans. He has written novels, compiled anthologies of poetry and folktales, and coauthored volumes of stories and activities. *Keepers of the Earth: Native American Stories and Environmental Activities for Children* is part of a series of books coauthored with Michael J. Caduto that present stories about animals and other aspects of nature, followed by various activities for children, with guidance for teachers or other adults.

Bruchac has written poems and retold folktales that have been published as picture books. He and Jonathan London coauthored *Thirteen Moons on Turtle's Back: A Native American Year of Moons.* The thirteen poems are based on the belief of many Native American groups that each of the thirteen moons in a year holds a story; each poem reflects a different Native American group. *The First Strawberries: A Cherokee Story* is a retelling of the legend of a couple whose quarrel was resolved when the sun sent gifts of raspberries, blueberries, blackberries, and finally strawberries. In *A Boy Called Slow,* Bruchac offers a portrayal of the

Ask the Author

Alma Flor Ada

Favorite Books as a Child

I learned to read at a very young age, and read voraciously. Since there never were enough new books, I read them over and over again, until I almost knew them by heart. Poetry was always a delight, and I memorized very many poems, which I still remember today. My very first book was *Heidi* by Johanna Spyri, in a copy inherited from my mother, and it continued being a favorite throughout childhood, because I also was blessed with the opportunity to spend long hours alone in nature. *Little Women* by Louisa May Alcott came next and perhaps gave me the secret aspiration to write. I also loved long, well-told adventure stories like Dumas's *The Three Musketeers*, Emilio Salgari's *Sandokan*, and all of Dickens.

How do you feel about the argument that one has to be a member of a culture to write about it?

The more intimately connected an author is with the reality she explores, the greater the possibility to portray it authentically and to make a positive impression on the reader. Does this require that the author be a member of a specific culture? Not necessarily. If an author possesses ample knowledge about a culture and can develop the understanding of its intricacies, she will be able to write with a responsible degree of authenticity.

Otherwise, authors would be tremendously restricted about what they can write: Men could not write about women, nor women about men, and historical novels would not be possible.

It is not only a matter of cultural background, but of the responsibility one takes in learning, observing, reflecting, experiencing, suffering, struggling to understand that makes the vision of an author sincere.

But let's be aware that authors frequently write about another culture opportunistically, because there is an interest or a demand, because the culture seems colorful or appealing.

It is very difficult to become intimately familiar with another culture, even after living many years in its midst. Therefore, there is a great risk that, in spite of the best intentions, the author who writes from outside a culture may not do justice to its essence. Even while knowing many things factually about a culture, an author can miss the intrinsic expression of the cultural values that make all the difference.

What must not be forgotten is that children always deserve the truth at its best.

Children who belong to minority cultures and see themselves and their people constantly stereotyped, ignored, or misrepresented deserve to hear authentic voices showing the complexity and richness of their experience. Children who may have limited or dubious understanding of other cultures deserve to get to know them from those who can best represent them.

In the multicultural society of the United States, many times the books we have are visions from specific cultures, but we still are short on books that portray the cultures interacting with each other: the friendships, rivalry, love, sharing, losses, experienced by characters of diverse backgrounds as they come together. Perhaps better than reclaiming the right to write about the other, we would do well in writing about us in relationship to the other, or about us as someone else's other, until such glorious day in which there will be no other, but us, each in our radiant uniqueness, enriched by our past and our culture, but equally central, equally respected, equally valued and embraced in brotherly, in sisterly, love.

Alma Flor Ada is the author of many award-winning books for children and adolescents including childhood memories *Under the Royal Palms* and *Where the Flame Trees Bloom*; whimsical letter collections *Dear Peter Rabbit* and *Yours Truly, Goldilocks*; and beloved stories such as *The Gold Coin* and *My Name Is Maria Isabel*. Alma Flor, a retired professor at the University of San Francisco, attributes her productivity to the support of her four children and now rejoices in sharing her books with her eight grandchildren.

childhood life of Sitting Bull, a Lakota hero. Books such as *Eagle Song* and *In the Heart of a Chief* offer rare glimpses into contemporary lives of Native Americans who balance their identity and pride in their heritage with their struggle with their image and role in the world outside their reservations. *Bowman's Store* is Bruchac's autobiography.

Ashley Bryan

Ashley Bryan says that he cannot remember a time when he wasn't a creator of books. Even as early as kindergarten, he created hundreds of handmade books with the encouragement of his family, immigrants from Antigua. Bryan later pursued the formal study of art and has taught art to both children and adults. He developed his own style based on the influences of the art of his African ancestors. Bryan has done block printing, painting that is reminiscent of woodcuts, and painting in other styles.

Bryan is known for both writing and illustrating. *Beat the Story-Drum, Pum-Pum*; *What a Morning! The Christmas Story in Black Spirituals*; and *Ashley Bryan's ABC of African American Poetry* were honored with the Coretta Scott King Award for illustration. *Lion and the Ostrich Chicks and Other African Folk Tales* was awarded the Coretta Scott King Award for writing. Another of the books for which he is well known is *The Dancing Granny,* which was inspired by Bryan's grandmother's visit from the West Indies when she was in her seventies. She learned the latest dance steps and outdanced her great-grandchildren.

Bryan's passion for text, music, and art is evident in his books, as he combines these elements to create an overall effect. Bryan's text is influenced by his study of African American poets and his belief that poetry and stories are meant to be shared aloud. His dramatic storytelling style can be "heard" in his texts, which make readers feel as though they were listening to a storyteller. To research folktales, Bryan begins with the scholarly collections made in the nineteenth century by missionaries and anthropologists. He then relies on his own background knowledge and his storytelling ability to create an original version. *Beautiful Blackbird* is an example of this combination. Distinct rhythm resonates in the text as well as in the illustrations in the telling of the African tale about how blackbird "blackens" and beautifies other birds. In addition, Bryan has published several collections of African American spirituals. His desire in sharing them is to bring the musical genius of these works to a wider audience.

Today, Bryan lives on a small island off the coast of Maine, where he has spent summers painting for over sixty years. He continues to produce books for children; entertain others with his storytelling; and collect beach glass, shells, and driftwood for creating puppets. In 2006, Ashley Bryan was named the U.S. nominee for the international Hans Christian Andersen Award, and in 2009, he was honored with the American Library Association's Laura Ingalls Wilder Award for lifetime achievement. His autobiography, *Ashley Bryan: Words to My Life's Song* is a celebration of his love of art, nature, and community.

Virginia Hamilton

For nearly forty years, Virginia Hamilton published a wide variety of work that included folktales, biographies, and stories about families. All are tied together in their focus on African American experiences. Hamilton said that she regarded herself as a storyteller and believed that people tell stories to "keep their cultural heritage safe, to save the very language in which heritage is made symbolic through story" (Hamilton, 1995):

> I see my books and the language I use in them as empowering me to give utterance to my dreams and wishes and those of other African Americans like myself. I see the imaginative use of language and ideas as a way to illuminate a human condition, lest we forget where we came from. All of us came from somewhere else.
>
> My work, as a novelist, a biographer, and a creator and compiler of stories, has been to portray the essence of a people who are a parallel culture community in America. (p. 440)

Among Hamilton's many awards are the 1975 Newbery Medal for *M. C. Higgins, the Great*; the Newbery Honor Book awards for *The Planet of Junior Brown* in 1972, *Sweet Whispers, Brother Rush* in 1983, and *In the Beginning: Creation Stories from around the*

Ask the Author

Julius Lester

Favorite Books as a Child

I didn't have any favorite books as a child. I read mostly comic books. I also read books, but can't recall even one.

You must know how grateful readers are to you for rescuing the Uncle Remus stories from the patronizing white traditions through which they came down to us. How did you find the original stories and the voice to tell them in? What was most challenging about it?

Retelling the Uncle Remus stories was relatively easy. It is a project that came naturally to me because I grew up in the southern black storytelling tradition and I had previously done retellings of stories in *Black Folktales* (1969) and *The Knee High Man* (1972). So, I don't know that there was anything especially challenging involved. It was a fun project and relatively easy to do.

As for how I did it, it has been quite a few years since I did those books, but as I recall they were the first books I did using a computer. This was back in 1986 or so.

The how of doing any book is essentially the same. Sit in the chair and work, work, work.

Born in St. Louis, Missouri, the son of a Methodist minister, Lester later converted to Judaism. Lester spent much of his childhood in the South of the 1940s and 1950s, where he dealt firsthand with Southern attitudes about race and segregation. In 1960, Lester graduated from Fisk University with a degree in English. He became politically active in the civil rights movement. In the mid-1960s, he joined SNCC, the Student Non-Violent Coordinating Committee, where he served as head of their photo department. Lester originally was a musician who recorded two albums, performed with Pete Seeger, Phil Ochs, and Judy Collins, and worked as a radio announcer in New York City. His first book, *The 12-String Guitar as Played by Leadbelly: An Instructional Manual*, dealt with black folk music. Most of Lester's earlier works were written for adults. In 1969, he published two works which established his success as a children's author. These two works were *To Be a Slave*, a Newbery Honor Book, and *Black Folktales*. His subsequent works continued to show his interest in African American history, folklore, and politics. Since the early 1970s, Lester has served as a professor at the University of Massachusetts at Amherst.

World in 1989; Coretta Scott King awards for *The People Could Fly: American Black Folktales* in 1986, *Anthony Burns: The Defeat and Triumph of a Fugitive Slave* in 1989, and *Her Stories* in 1996. The 1992 Hans Christian Andersen Award was presented by the International Board on Books for Young People for the body of her work and the influence it has had on young readers around the world. Her books are widely translated. In 1995, Virginia Hamilton became the first children's book author to be awarded the MacArthur Foundation "Genius" Grant. She died in 2002, but her legacy lives on through the wealth of books she wrote.

Walter Dean Myers

Walter Dean Myers's writing career was launched in 1968 when he won the Council on Interracial Books for Children's picture book competition. A multitalented writer, Myers began his writing career with picture books and informational books. However, he is best known for his notable contribution to young adult literature reflecting the lives of contemporary African Americans. Many of his novels draw on his childhood experiences growing up in New York City's Harlem. *Fast Sam, Cool Clyde, and Stuff* and *Scorpions* are both stories of gang rivalry in an urban setting. *The Mouse Rap* tells the story of an urban youth called Mouse, who opens each chapter with rap verse.

Myers's publications since the 1990s reveal a shift in his creative focus. He won the 1991 Coretta Scott King Award for the informational book *Now Is Your Time! The African American Struggle for Freedom,* and the biography *Malcolm X: By Any Means Necessary* was a 1994 Honor Book. He paired with his artist son, Christopher, to create *Harlem,* which won both the 1998 Caldecott Honor Award and a Coretta Scott King Honor Award. For two volumes of poetry, *Brown Angels: An Album of Pictures and Verse* and *Glorious Angels,* he collected old photographs and imagined the lives behind them. *Glory Field* is a historical novel that traces 250 years of a family's history. *Shadow of the Red Moon* is a futuristic fantasy. He turns to writing biography in *At Her Majesty's Request: An African Princess in Victorian England.* His books *Patrol* and *Blues Journey* are both picture books.

Myers's awards are numerous and varied. He has won the Coretta Scott King Award five times and two of his books have been named Newbery Honor Books. In 1992, Walter Dean Myers was named the winner of the Margaret A. Edwards Award for Outstanding Contribution to Literature for Young Adults. *Monster* was named the first winner of the Michael Printz Award for excellence in young adult literature in 2000. In 2010, Myers was named the first recipient of the Virginia Hamilton Lifetime Achievement Award, given to an African American for "significant and lasting literary contribution." The same year, Myers was nominated by the USBBY for the international Hans Christian Andersen Award.

Allen Say

Read the interview where Allen Say discusses his creation process by going to the Conversations section of Chapter 4 in the MyEducation-Kit for your book.

Born and raised in Japan, Allen Say immigrated to the United States when he was sixteen and is now a U.S. citizen. Say's books often have themes showing his love of both countries. His talent and interest in drawing led him to be apprenticed to a renowned cartoonist by age twelve. In his 1979 autobiography, *The Ink-Keeper's Apprentice,* Say recounts his early life and the start of his career as an artist. Some of his picture books, including *Grandfather's Journey* and *Tea with Milk,* are autobiographical.

Say's illustrations are extremely effective in capturing the overall ambience of his settings and are painstakingly accurate in detail. For example, whereas the scissors used by the woman sewing in *The Boy of the Three-Year Nap* are Japanese sewing scissors, the scissors used by the mother in *Tree of Cranes* are the kind used in Japan for flower arranging and gardening. Although such details might not be noticeable to all, his attention to them confirms the overall impression of authenticity in Say's work.

Allen Say has received wide recognition for his work. *The Boy of the Three-Year Nap* was a 1989 Caldecott Honor Book. Say won the 1994 Caldecott Medal for *Grandfather's Journey.*

Gary Soto

It was not until 1990 that Gary Soto, author of books and poetry for adults, published his first juvenile work, *Baseball in April and Other Stories.* Since then, he has published other widely acclaimed collections of short stories and poetry, novels, and picture books. The details of Soto's writing reflect his Mexican American ancestry, as he recounts various experiences growing up in the industrial part of Fresno, California. Soto's childhood memories are revealed in his poems in *Neighborhood Odes.* In "Ode to a Sprinkler," Soto reminisces about the sprinkler that provided many hours of water play in the summer. He recalls his love of competition and playground games, as well as hours of play with the discarded things in his neighborhood.

In *Taking Sides,* Lincoln Mendoza moves from the barrio of his childhood to a suburban neighborhood where being Latino sets him apart from his basketball teammates. Readers can follow Lincoln's continuing search for his cultural identity as he goes abroad as a foreign exchange student in *Pacific Crossing.* Soto has published a number of picture books, including *Too Many Tamales* and *Chato's Kitchen. Too Many Tamales* tells the story of a little girl who secretly tries on her mother's ring while making tamales, then must talk her cousins into eating a mound of tamales to try and find the lost ring. In *Chato's Kitchen,* Chato the cat's plan to "welcome" the mice family into the barrio humorously ends differently than he anticipated. In addition to receiving other awards, Soto's *Baseball in April* was recognized as an honor book in the first year of the Pura Belpré Children's Book Award.

Laurence Yep

Laurence Yep grew up in a black neighborhood, felt like an outsider at his school in Chinatown because he didn't speak Chinese, and attended a high school with mostly white students. He identifies writing as the activity that helped him clarify his own cultural identity. Six years of researching Chinese American history led to the writing of *Dragonwings,* one of his most highly acclaimed books. Yep found extensive factual documentation of the work experiences of the Chinese men who immigrated to the United States during the nineteenth century, yet it required much imagination to portray the human emotions arising from the daily life experiences and the hardships these men suffered. *Dragonwings* was named a 1976 Newbery Honor Book, in addition to receiving numerous other prestigious awards. The inspiration for this story began when Yep read about a Chinese American, Fung Joe Guey, who built and flew "dragonwings" at about the same time the Wright brothers made their first flights. Another work of historical fiction reflecting the experiences of early Chinese immigrants is Yep's 1994 Newbery Honor Book *Dragon's Gate.* This book recounts the involvement of the Chinese in building the transcontinental railroad.

Yep has written science fiction, fantasy, historical fiction, realistic fiction, a biography, and an autobiography; he has also retold folktales. He has edited Asian American short stories and poetry and published picture books and a number of shorter, realistic stories that reflect the contemporary experiences of young Chinese Americans. In *Later, Gator,* two brothers who usually do not get along at all collaborate on a scheme to hide a pet alligator. The story continues in *Cockroach Cooties.*

Top Shelf 4.3

Immigrant Stories

Grandfather's Journey by Allen Say

In the Year of the Boar and Jackie Robinson by Bette Bao Lord

Journey of the Sparrows by Fran Leeper Buss

Literature Portraying Other Diverse Perspectives

Literature plays a vital role in providing vicarious experience in interacting with others, whether those others are like ourselves or very different. In some cases, literature confirms a reader's firsthand experiences in interacting with people of differing perspectives; in other cases, literature substitutes for experiences the reader might not have had firsthand.

Literature Portraying Gender Equity and Gender Roles

Father leaves for the office carrying a briefcase and wearing a topcoat and hat. Mother stays home and does housework, wearing a dress. Boys have adventures and are brave. Girls need protection and are passive. Images such as these abounded in children's books of the past and can still be found in some books today. The danger is that children who experience only books with these messages will come away with the idea that these images represent the norm of gender roles. Well-written gender-sensitive literature fights stereotypes by depicting the diversity and multidimensionality of men and women, girls and boys.

The following criteria (Rudman, 1995) should be used to evaluate the content of messages that are sent to readers regarding gender issues:

- Occupations should be gender-free.
- Achievements should be judged without gender bias.
- Both parents should share family responsibilities.
- Gender stereotyping based on physical description and behaviors should be avoided.

Teaching Idea 4.4

Assess Gender Roles in Books Published in the Past

Begin the discussion by having children list gender characteristics they believe to be true. Find some books (for example, *Dear Garbage Man*) that show outdated images of gender roles. Challenge the children to identify ways the books no longer reflect society. Read aloud some books that intentionally challenge traditional gender roles (for example, *The King's Equal*). Lead a discussion that focuses on issues of gender equality. Consider how these issues play out in the classroom. (Read professional literature such as Roxanne Henkin's [1998] book, *Who's Invited to Share?*) Compare comments made during the discussion with the gender characteristics identified earlier. Then share a range of books that show a variety of gender roles, ranging from some traditional roles to nontraditional roles.

It is important to evaluate character portrayal, interactions among characters, and societal expectations of character roles. Sexist language is a sign of the writer's perspective on gender roles and therefore should be avoided at all times.

Gender Equity

Gender equity has different facets. A book reflecting gender equity shows equal opportunities for both genders in the workplace and depicts multiple and diverse personal roles for individuals of both genders. Children begin receiving messages about their gender's role in society from the time they are infants. These messages come from family, friends, books, media, and society in general. What are the messages found in books?

Let's examine a message from a book published in 1957. Gene Zion's **Dear Garbage Man** is still in print and available to children through book club order forms distributed in schools. In it, Stan the garbage man tries to "recycle" people's unwanted trash by redistributing it to others. The accompanying text reads, "After everyone had helped themselves, fathers went to work and mothers went back to the dishes." The next day, the new owners realize that these items are indeed trash and return them to the garbage man. At first, he is disappointed, but then a "big smile brighten[s] his face" as he says, "All this stuff will fill in lots and lots of swamps!" The driver responds, "Stan, you're a real garbage man now!" This book presents several gender stereotypes: Jobs involving physical labor are reserved for men; all garbage collectors are men; men go to work and women do dishes. And, of course, the environmental message of this book is troubling. Because books often reflect societal values and prejudices that prevail at the time of writing, some older books contain themes and messages that are not considered appropriate for children today.

Some books do a good job of portraying nontraditional gender roles in believable ways that are natural to the story. For example, Katherine Paterson's **The King's Equal** depicts a prince who is searching for a princess who is "his equal," only to find that he must prove to be "her equal." Rachel Isadora's **Max** is about a boy who finds that taking dance class with his sister is a great way to warm up for his baseball games on Saturdays. Betsy Hearne's **Seven Brave Women** describes the strength and contributions of women from her own life. These women's lives are not marked by the wars they fought in history, but each tells "her-story" of courage and leadership nevertheless. In Ms. Frizzle, a teacher who takes her class on field trips on the **Magic School Bus** in the series by Joanna Cole, readers find a female who is not just having an adventure but leading many outrageous adventures.

It is a problem, though, when books try too hard—when they depict the opposites of the stereotyped gender roles in hard-to-believe ways or are didactic in presentation. Anthony Browne's **Piggybook** addresses the problem of women who are enslaved to their families. The front cover shows the mother carrying her husband and two sons "piggyback." As the story unfolds, the illustrations show the males of the family (and their surroundings) turning more and more pig-like until finally the mother leaves them, with a note stating, "You are pigs." When they plead for her return, this mother—who has previously been depicted washing dishes, vacuuming carpets, making beds, ironing, cooking, and washing clothes in shadowy pictures without her face showing—now fixes the car! The story is humorous in many ways. But such a dramatic change in roles, while possible, is not likely, especially one that requires the sudden acquisition of specific knowledge, is hardly believable, and perhaps trivializes the importance of representing equal gender opportunities and roles.

Same-Sex Partners and Families with Same-Sex Parents

The school curriculum at the primary level is most often developed around the concept of a nuclear family composed of a mother, father, and their children. However, over the past several decades, schools have become increasingly populated with children whose home life does not fit that model. In the past, people typically thought of a nontraditional family as a single-parent family or one in which grandparents raise the children, but in fact, increasing numbers of families are headed by lesbian or gay parents. When the New York State Board of Education required that first-grade curricula include the reading of Michael Willhoite's **Daddy's Roommate,** much controversy surrounded the issue of alternative lifestyles. This picture book depicts a divorced father who lives with his homosexual partner. In **Mom and**

Mum are Getting Married, Ken Setterington portrays a joyous celebration of marriage between Rosie's two mothers. In a book for older children, Jacqueline Woodson's *From the Notebooks of Melanin Sun,* the central character is a boy whose mother is in love with a woman. More recently, Patricia Polacco's picture book, *In Our Mothers' House*, is a very intentional and idealized look at a racially mixed family of adopted children with two mothers. In Pat Austin's article on "Opening the Door to Tolerance," she recommends books including gay and lesbian characters with themes of inclusion. Books such as these portray what it means for the children when their parents have a partner of the same gender. Books such as *And Tango Makes Three* have been celebrated (as well as considered by some as controversial) for its portrayal of same-sex parenting. The fact that this is a penguin family highlights the need for more realistic portrayals of humans in same-sex partnerships to be naturally included in literature for children.

Surprisingly, at the beginning of the twenty-first century, there is still a dearth of high-quality literary publications in which both parents are of the same gender; most are still didactic in nature. On the other hand, there has been an increase in both the number and the quality of books for young adults that honestly explore the complex issues surrounding sexual identity and what it means in the range of relationships including family and peers.

Literature Portraying Social Diversity

Society also shows its diversity in many ways besides the cultural identities of ethnicity, race, physical/mental ability, and gender. Poverty, low social class, homelessness, illiteracy, and a migrant lifestyle, among other factors, just as significantly create an identifying culture. Living and working under those circumstances affect both the way people experience the world and the way the world views them. It is important to note that poverty, the most common of social diversities, is often found in conjunction with other types of social diversity, so children's books dealing with any form of social diversity may touch on poverty as well.

In choosing children's books that depict social diversity, it is of utmost importance to find authentic, nonstereotyped portrayals that are believable. Readers of Frances Temple's *Grab Hands and Run* find themselves drawn into the story of a family escaping a threat on their lives in El Salvador. Through the eyes of the young narrator, Felipe, the story of the dangerous journey north to Canada is told. In Fran Leeper Buss's *Journey of the Sparrows,* three siblings are smuggled into the United States nailed into crates. Once in the United States, they must hide from immigration officials, find work so that they can get food and shelter, and save enough money to send for the rest of the family they have left behind. The rich details throughout both books fill in gaps in the experiences of most readers. Most of us can't imagine a life filled with constant hunger and fear of being found and returned to a land of certain death. Because of the array of human emotions that ring true, readers come to believe in the reality of the situations portrayed in these books.

Literature about People with Exceptionalities

Literature about people with exceptionalities or special needs portrays those with physical, mental, emotional, or learning disabilities, as well as individuals who are gifted and talented. Sometimes, an exceptionality is a life-threatening or debilitating illness that alters a person's ability to lead life in the same way a healthy person can. At other times, the individual leads a fairly mainstream life, but needs support in order to participate fully.

There are many stereotyped views that distort children's understanding of exceptional learners and give rise to fear, pity, and misunderstandings of intellectual and social abilities. Exceptional children should be portrayed in books as individuals with many facets to their lives. They should not be considered heroic for learning to live with disabilities and differing abilities. Also important is how people with exceptionalities are treated by others. When a book portrays exceptional learners in unconventional ways, readers might feel betrayed or may be led to accept an inaccurate representation.

A number of informational books use photographs and narration to provide contemporary images of people with disabilities. *Helping Hands: How Monkeys Assist People Who Are Disabled* by Suzanne Haldane is the story of a teenager with quadriplegia and his helper monkey, a capuchin named Willie. The text and accompanying photographs show how Willie is trained to assist: He can fetch a sandwich from the refrigerator, warm it in the microwave, and serve it on a tray. Such information can help children to get a sense of one aspect of daily life for someone who is quadriplegic. In **Handtalk School** by Mary Beth Mather, readers follow a day at a residential school for the deaf and see children communicating through American Sign Language (ASL) as well as with a telephone device for the deaf (TDD). The book shows signed messages with accompanying text so that readers can follow along.

Biographies of both famous and ordinary people provide glimpses into the lives of exceptional learners. The life of Wilma Rudolph is depicted in Kathleen Krull's **Wilma Unlimited.** The book explores her childhood battle with polio and the ensuing physical disabilities, and shows how her determination to walk again and eventually run led her to become one of the fastest female runners in the world. Fantasy books can provide an interesting vehicle by which to consider the perspective of people with disabilities. In Franny Billingsley's **Well Wished,** Nura wishes at the magic well that her friend Catty, who is wheelchair bound, could have a body like hers. What happens instead is that the two girls exchange bodies. The notion of "don't judge until you've experienced someone else's life" is illustrated in a way that is not possible in real life. Nevertheless, this fantasy offers readers an opportunity to take another point of view.

Fictional books can depict exceptional children in ways that provide insight for readers. In Alfred Slote's **Hang Tough, Paul Mather,** the protagonist is twelve-year-old Paul, who has leukemia. Paul's enthusiasm for baseball and his relationship with his teammates give readers a realistic glimpse of what it means to live with the illness and the accompanying treatments. In Terry Trueman's **Stuck in Neutral,** fourteen-year-old Shawn is believed to have the mental age of three or four months. But Shawn narrates the story, showing that he has an amazing memory and perceptive thinking; it's just that his total inability to control his muscles, because of cerebral palsy, makes him unable to communicate. This is speculative fiction; we do not truly know what goes on in the minds of those who appear to be incapable of communicating. But reading a book such as this will certainly cause readers to pause and reflect on our reactions and responses to people with disabilities.

In **A Corner of the Universe,** Ann Martin reveals many complex interpersonal relations of people with extraordinary mental and emotional disabilities. Twelve-year-old Hattie learns that she has a twenty-one-year-old Uncle Adam who had been sent to a school many years ago, but is returning upon its closing. In many ways, he acts as though he is close to her in age, but not always. He embraces new experiences with great enthusiasm, but not always. Life gets out of control from time to time, and Hattie must juggle her great affection for him along with responsibility in understanding why her grandparents are so protective of him.

Educators' Roles in Presenting Multiple and Diverse Perspectives

It is important for educators to read a wide variety of books. Personal reading of high-quality adult books depicting diverse perspectives enhances our understanding of the world. In addition, professional reading offers teachers theories on why reading a broad range of books is helpful and often offers suggestions for how to expand the canon. Reading children's books allows teachers to identify texts appropriate in content and level for the children with whom they will be shared. All in all, educators who are committed to sharing diverse perspectives have many opportunities for reading at the personal and professional levels. To read more about international books, see Chapter 5.

Understanding Diverse Perspectives through Adult Literature

Reading is important both to enhance current understandings and to add new perspectives on the world. Teachers frequently seek out books that provide such reading experiences for their students. But it is also important for teachers to read adult books so that they also can better understand diverse perspectives. A children's book offers a certain level of insight into diversity. A young adult book allows more space and time to reflect on issues. But an adult book allows readers to think about these issues in even greater depth.

Research indicates that students frequently relate best to a teacher's messages when the students' cultural background is similar to that of the teacher (Au, 1993; Delpit, 1988). Teachers understand the world from their own cultural perspectives, and it is impossible to share the background of each of their students. One way in which teachers can try to build their understanding is by joining a discussion group that examines adult books depicting diverse viewpoints; such discussions take the understandings gained from reading to a deeper level. By building their own understanding, teachers can enhance their ability to facilitate discussions of literature with their students.

Understanding Diverse Perspectives through Professional Literature

Teachers can choose from a variety of professional materials dealing with literature that reflects diversity. Such professional materials discuss the importance of reading multicultural literature; recommend criteria for evaluation and selection; and present methods for discussing and eliciting responses to the literature. Often, there are annotated bibliographies to help teachers identify books that may interest students. Professional materials promote an understanding of the critical role teachers play in making multicultural literature accessible to children.

ILLUSTRATION 4.10 Over 40 children's book authors and illustrators offer stories and images that define their ideas on human rights. (From *Tikvah: Children's Book Creators Reflect on Human Rights* by Leo and Diane Dillon. © 2001 by Leo and Diane Dillon. Used with permission from Chronicle Books LLC. Visit www.ChronicleBooks.com.)

Helping Children Gain Diverse Perspectives

It is generally accepted that children's reading choices are often based on recommendations of peers and influential adults. Therefore, teachers, library media specialists, and other influential adults have a responsibility to be knowledgeable about books that offer a wide variety of perspectives.

Teachers can help to ensure that their students gain a variety of perspectives by keeping diversity in mind when they are selecting reading material for the whole class and when they are deciding what choices to offer to students in literature circles and for individual free choice reading. The importance of the school librarian or media specialist in acting as a consultant to both the teacher and individual students in choosing reading materials cannot be overlooked.

Here are some steps that lead to a richer sense of the role reading about diversity plays in children's developing understanding of the world in which they live:

1. Begin by being inclusive when collecting books for the classroom library. This makes multicultural books accessible to all students.
2. Read multicultural books aloud to the class and/or choose them as book selections for literature circles. Then facilitate a discussion in which students have opportunities to consider their own ideas about diversity and to learn by engaging in talk with each other.
3. Connect various multicultural books to each other in order to deepen thematic understanding.
4. Make an action plan for putting into practice a commitment to making a difference in the world by becoming advocates and activists.

Even more important than the role teachers and librarians play in the selection of reading materials is their role in facilitating discussions and in providing opportunities for responding to literature. Chapter 13 details the critical role of the teacher in leading discussion. Chapter 14 describes the many ways in which teachers can provide opportunities for students to respond to literature.

To check your comprehension on the content covered in this chapter, go to the MyEducation-Kit for your book and complete the Study Plan for Chapter 4. Here you will be able to take a chapter quiz and receive feedback on your answers.

Experiences for Further Learning

1. Divide children into separate groups by gender, and have each of them create a list of books that they find especially meaningful. What similarities do you find in their preferences? What differences are there? What might this mean for you, in terms of the kinds of books you read and recommend to children? Does your own reading reflect a gender or cultural bias? How can you, as a teacher or librarian, address gender-based preferences in children's reading material?

2. Select an issue such as homelessness, abuse, poverty, or illiteracy that calls for social justice, and find several children's books about it. Compare and contrast the treatments of the issue. Do the books present the issue in a believable way? Do they deal with the issue honestly? What messages are communicated to children? How can you, as a teacher or librarian, scaffold a discussion on these difficult and sensitive topics in ways that help children broaden their understanding and sensitize their feelings?

3. Storytelling is popular throughout the world, and many cultures have unique ways of telling stories. Select a story to tell, study the culture's storytelling style, and practice presenting the story to others. Resources that may be of help include Anne Pellowski's *Hidden Stories in Plants* (1990), *Family Story-Telling Handbook* (1987), and *The Story Vine* (1984). Be sure to visit the resources at the Web site: *http://www.ala.org/ala/alsc/alscresources/forlibrarians/StorytellingResources.htm* and Web sites of storytelling publishers such as August House.

Now go to Chapter 4 in the MyEducationKit (www.myeducationkit.com) for your book, where you can:

- Find learning outcomes for Chapter 4.
- Access the Children's Literature Database for your own exploration.
- Complete Assignments and Activities that can help you more deeply understand the chapter content.
- Extend knowledge with content-specific Web Links.
- Deepen and apply content understanding with Extension Activities.
- Learn first hand about how authors and illustrators utilize their craft with podcasts and written interviews in the Conversations section for the chapter.
- Check your comprehension on the content covered in the chapter by going to the Study Plan. Here you will be able to take a chapter quiz and receive feedback on your answers.
- Find the following updated appendices: Major Children's Book Awards, Children's Magazines, Professional Organizations, Children's Book Publishers' Addresses, Book Selection Aids, and Children's Literature Web Sites.

Recommended Books

* indicates a picture book; **I** indicates interest level (P = preschool, YA = young adult)

Multicultural literature and literature portraying various types of diversity can be found throughout this textbook. These lists represent a sampling of recommended books. In particular, Chapter 9, "Contemporary Realistic Fiction," includes titles that depict realistic portrayals of people of diversity. A list of recommended books can be found at the end of that chapter.

African and African American

*Aardema, Verna. *Who's in Rabbit's House? A Masai Tale.* Illustrated by Leo Dillon and Diane Dillon. Dial, 1977. Rabbit's friends try to get rid of a mysterious Long One that is occupying Rabbit's House—and the solution is a surprising one. The illustrations portray this story as a play, acted out by Masai wearing masks. (**I:** P–8)

*Adoff, Arnold, ed. *My Black Me: A Beginning Book of Black Poetry.* Dutton, 1974/1994. This anthology opens with Adoff's words "This book of Black is for you." Poets such as Langston Hughes, Lucille Clifton, Nikki Giovanni, and Imamu Amiri Baraka contributed to the anthology. (**I:** 9–YA)

Alexander, Elizabeth and Marilyn Nelson. *Miss Crandall's School for Young Ladies and Little Misses of Color.* Illustrated by Floyd Cooper. Wordsong/Boyds Mills, 2007. In highly prejudiced 1830s Connecticut, Miss Crandall accepts African American women into her school, believing in their right to education. (**I:** 10–YA)

Brimmer, Larry Dane. *We Are One: The Story of Bayard Rustin.* Calkins Creek, 2007. Bayard Rustin's commitment to nonviolent activism and his perseverance are portrayed in this informational book. (**I:** 9–13)

*Bryan, Ashley. *Ashley Bryan: Words to My Life's Song.* Atheneum, 2009. Bryan's autobiography is a celebration of his love of art, nature and community, told in scrapbook album style. (**I:** All Ages)

———. *Ashley Bryan's ABC of African American Poetry.* Atheneum, 1998. Poetry of African American poets (arranged in alphabetical order) is accompanied by Bryan's colorful illustrations. (**I:** 6–9)

———. *Beat the Story-Drum, Pum-Pum.* Atheneum, 1980. This collection of retellings includes five Nigerian folktales. (**I:** 7–10)

*———. *Beautiful Blackbird.* Atheneum, 2003. Based on an Ila tale from Zambia, beautiful blackbird shares the beauty of being black with other birds who ask to be beautified. (**I:** 6–9)

Cameron, Ann. *Gloria's Way.* Illustrated by Lil Toft. Foster/Farrar, 2000. Six warm-hearted short stories are about Gloria and her parents and friends Julian, Huey, and Latisha from Cameron's earlier books. See also *The Stories Julian Tells* (1981), *The Stories Huey Tells* (1995), etc. (**I:** 6–8)

*Clifton, Lucille. *Some of the Days of Everett Anderson.* Illustrated by Evaline Ness. Holt, 1970/1987. Everett Anderson, a black six-year-old who lives in Apt. 14A, tells how he spends his time. Related titles are *Everett Anderson's Friend* (1976), *Everett Anderson's Christmas Coming* (1971/1991), and *Everett Anderson's Goodbye* (1983/1988). (**I:** P–7)

*Cooper, Floyd. *Coming Home: From the Life of Langston Hughes.* Philomel, 1994. This picture book biography of the African American poet describes his childhood and his search for "home." (**I:** 7–10)

*Crews, Donald. *Bigmama's.* Greenwillow, 1991. This is an autobiographical story about going to "Bigmama's" house and visiting with relatives in the summertime during Donald Crews's youth. Also by Crews is *Shortcut* (1992). (**I:** P–8)

Curtis, Christopher Paul. *Bud, Not Buddy.* Delacorte, 1999. In 1930s Michigan, Bud leaves the orphanage to seek the jazz musician he believes is his father. (**I:** 10–YA)

———. *The Watsons Go to Birmingham–1963.* Delacorte, 1995. The Watsons are an African American family from Flint, Michigan. Their 1963 summer visit to Grandmother in Alabama changes their lives dramatically. (**I:** 10–YA)

*Diakité, Penda. *I Lost My Tooth in Africa.* Illustrated by Baba Wagué Diakité. Scholastic, 2006. When Amina loses her tooth on vacation in Mali, she hides it under a calabash and the tooth fairy brings her a chicken. (**I:** P–7)

*Elliott, Zetta. *Bird.* Illustrated by Shadra Strickland. Bird, nickname for a young African American boy, relies on his love of drawing as he deals with trying to make sense of his older brother's drug addiction and the death of his grandfather. (**I:** 8–11)

Feelings, Tom. *The Middle Passage: White Ships Black Cargo.* Dial, 1995. This wordless book dramatically depicts the hardships of the journey across the Atlantic Ocean made by Africans bound for slavery in America. (**I:** 10–YA)

*———. *Soul Looks Back in Wonder.* Dial, 1993. Feelings created the stunning art, which is accompanied by the voices of noted poets, including Maya Angelou, Langston Hughes, and Lucille Clifton, who write of their African American heritage. (**I:** 9–YA)

*Flournoy, Valerie. *The Patchwork Quilt.* Illustrated by Jerry Pinkney. Dial, 1985. As Tanya helps her mother and grandmother create a quilt from the scraps of their family's clothes, she comes to realize the stories and memories the quilt holds. A sequel is *Tanya's Reunion* (1995). (**I:** 6–9)

*Giovanni, Nikki. *Spin a Soft Black Song.* Illustrated by George Martins. HarperCollins, 1971/1985. This is a collection of poems reflecting African American children's everyday thoughts in their own voices. (**I:** 6–10)

Govenar, Alan (collector and editor). *Osceola: Memories of a Sharecropper's Daughter.* Illustrated by Shane W. Evans. Jump at the Sun/Hyperion, 2000. In her straightforward and personal voice, Osceola Mays recalls a childhood in the early 1900s as a sharecropper's daughter. (**I:** 8–12)

*Greenfield, Eloise. *Honey, I Love and Other Love Poems.* Illustrated by Diane Dillon and Leo Dillon. Harper, 1978. These poems, narrated by a young African American girl, tell of love and friendship. (**I:** 7–9)

*———. *Nathaniel Talking.* Illustrated by Jan Spivey Gilchrist. Black Butterfly, 1988. Through various forms of poetry, Nathaniel talks about the happenings in his neighborhood from his eight-year-old perspective. A related title is *Night on Neighborhood Street* (Dial, 1991). (**I:** 7–9)

*Grimes, Nikki. *My Man Blue: Poems.* Illustrated by Jerome Lagarrigue. Dial, 1999. Damon, a boy without a father, and

Blue, a man who lost his son to the streets, form a unique friendship and bond with each other. (**I:** 6–9)

*———. *Talkin' About Bessie: The Story of Aviator Elizabeth Coleman*. Illustrated by E. B. Lewis. Orchard/Scholastic, 2002. Following her funeral, various people reflect on their memories of who Bessie Coleman was through monologues that reveal many sides of her. (**I:** 7 and up)

Hamilton, Virginia. *Her Stories: African American Folktales, Fairy Tales, and True Tales*. Illustrated by Leo and Diane Dillon. Scholastic, 1995. This collection of stories is about women in African American folktales, fairy tales, animal stories, supernatural tales, legends, and biographical accounts. (**I:** 9–YA)

———. *The House of Dies Drear*. Illustrated by Eros Keith. Simon & Schuster, 1968. When a history professor and his son move into a rented house, they find the spirits of the past—those who passed through the house when it was a station on the Underground Railroad. The sequel is *The Mystery of Drear House* (1987). (**I:** 10–YA)

———. *M. C. Higgins, the Great*. Macmillan, 1974. M.C. has to reconcile his love for his mountain home with its pending destruction by a slag heap. (**I:** 10–12)

———. *The People Could Fly: American Black Folktales*. Illustrated by Leo Dillon and Diane Dillon. Knopf, 1985/1999. This collection of 24 American black folktales includes a range from familiar to lesser known. (**I:** 9–13) *(Picture book version, 2004).

*Harrington, Janice. *The Chicken-Chasing Queen of Lamar County*. Illustrated by Shelley Jackson. FSG, 2007. Initially determined to catch the only chicken this self-proclaimed queen of chicken chasing cannot get, she instantly rethinks her goal when she discovers that Miss Hen has a family of baby chicks. Intriguing, multi-textured collages illustrate the book. (**I:** 6–9)

Hill, Laban Carrick. *Harlem Stomp: A Cultural History of the Harlem Renaissance*. Foreword by Nikki Giovanni. Little Brown, 2003. The important period of history during which the artistic, political, and cultural community of African Americans convening and creating in Harlem is documented in this book. (**I:** 12–YA)

*hooks, bell. *Be Boy Buzz*. Illustrated by Chris Raschka. Jump at the Sun/Hyperion, 2002. Simple yet powerful words describe a boy's sense of self. (**I:** P–8).

*Hopkinson, Deborah. *Sweet Clara and the Freedom Quilt*. Illustrated by James Ransome. Knopf, 1993. Clara is determined to be reunited with her mother and to find their way north to freedom. She uses her skills as a seamstress, listens to the conversations around her, and creates a quilt that maps the way to freedom. (**I:** 7–10)

*Howard, Elizabeth Fitzgerald. *Aunt Flossie's Hats (and Crab Cakes Later)*. Illustrated by James Ransome. Clarion, 1991. For Sarah and Susan, visiting their great-great-aunt Flossie means sipping tea and eating cookies while trying on her many hats and listening to the stories associated with them. (**I:** 6–9)

*Hudson, Wade, comp. *Pass It On: African-American Poetry for Children*. Illustrated by Floyd Cooper. Scholastic, 1993. This book of poetry about African American experiences has contributions by poets such as Langston Hughes, Nikki Giovanni, Eloise Greenfield, and Lucille Clifton. See also *How Sweet the Sound: African-American Songs for Children*, 1995. (**I:** 8–10)

Hurmence, Belinda. *Slavery Time When I Was Chillun*. Putnam, 1997. This is a selection of twelve oral histories from former slaves, taken from the over 2,000 that were collected by the Library of Congress in 1936. (**I:** 10 and up)

*Johnson, Angela. *Do Like Kyla*. Illustrated by James E. Ransome. Orchard, 1990. All day long, a little girl follows her big sister Kyla around, "doing like Kyla," but at the end of the day, "Kyla does just like me." See also: *One of Three*. Illustrated by David Soman. Orchard, 1991. (**I:** P–7)

———. *Heaven*. Simon & Schuster, 1998. Twelve-year-old Marley's understanding of her life turns upside down when she discovers that the people she believed were her parents are actually her aunt and uncle. (**I:** 12–YA)

*———. *Tell Me a Story, Mama*. Illustrated by David Soman. Scholastic, 1989. At bedtime, a little girl asks, "Tell me a story, Mama, about when you were little." But then, she tells a story herself, with Mama only adding comments. (**I:** P–8)

Jurmain, Suzanne. *The Forbidden Schoolhouse: The True and Dramatic Story of Prudence Crandall and Her Students*. Houghton Mifflin, 2005. The story of a Miss Crandall and her belief in offering education to African American girls during the racist 1830s is dramatically portrayed in this book. (**I:** 12–YA)

*Lawrence, Jacob. *Harriet and the Promised Land*. Simon & Schuster, 1968. The life of Harriet Tubman is described in verse, and the story of her commitment to helping fellow slaves to freedom is told. (**I:** 9–11)

Lester, Julius. *The Blues Singers: Ten Who Rocked the World*. Illustrated by Lisa Cohen. Jump at the Sun/Hyperion, 2001. This book features ten blues singers who became "legends" and explores the blues as an art form. (**I:** All ages)

———. *Long Journey Home: Stories from Black History*. Dial, 1972/1993. Six stories, based on the lives of real people, tell about the impact of escaping from slavery on the lives of individuals and families. (**I:** 11–YA)

*———. *Sam and the Tigers*. Illustrated by Jerry Pinkney. Dial, 1996. Based on the story "Little Black Sambo," this new version is told in Lester's "Southern black storytelling voice," with Pinkney's illustrations setting the story in the mythical land of Sam-sam-sa-mara. (**I:** 6–9)

———. *The Old African*. Illustrated by Jerry Pinkney. Dial, 2005. Based on legend, this tale of magical realism recounts the horrific treatment of slaves that results in the emergence of a silent, spiritual "old African" to lead his people into water as they walk toward freedom. (**I:** 12–YA)

*Levine, Ellen. *Henry's Freedom Box: A True Story from the Underground Railroad*. Illustrated by Kadir Nelson. Scholastic, 2007. Henry decides to have himself put in a box and mailed along a dangerous path to freedom. (**I:** 7–9)

Mathis, Sharon Bell. *The Hundred Penny Box*. Illustrated by Leo and Diane Dillon. Puffin, 1975. Great-great-aunt Dew is a hundred years old and has a box with a penny in it for each of her birthdays. Michael loves to listen to the stories each penny holds and intercedes on her behalf when his mother wants to throw out the old "hundred penny box" and buy a new one. (**I:** 8–10)

Mattox, Cheryl Warren. *Shake It to the One That You Love the Best: Play Songs and Lullabies from Black Musical Traditions*. Illustrated by Varnette P. Honeywood and Brenda Joysmith. Sobrante, CA: Warren-Mattox, 1989. African American songs that accompany jump rope, hopscotch, and other games are featured in this collection. (**I:** P–9)

*McCully, Emily Arnold. *The Escape of Oney Judge: Martha Washington's Slave Finds Freedom*. FSG, 2007. Raised to be the personal slave of the nation's First Lady, Oney faces a difficult decision when Martha Washington's death leads to being her resold rather than receiving freedom. (**I:** 7–10)

*McKissack, Patricia. *Flossie and the Fox*. Illustrated by Rachel Isadora. Dial, 1986. A little girl meets a creature in the woods and insists on his proof of identity as a fox before she will give up her eggs. (**I:** 7–9)

*———. *Someplace Special*. Illustrated by Jerry Pinkney. Atheneum, 2001. During the 1950s amidst Jim Crow segregation laws in the South, "Tricia Ann sets off on her first solo trip by bus to go someplace special—the 'Public Library: All Are Welcome.' " (**I:** 7–9)

*Mollel, Tololwa M. *My Rows and Piles of Coins*. Illustrated by E. B. Lewis. Clarion, 1999. Saruni saves his piles of coins, arranged in rows, in hopes of buying a bicycle to help his mother carry heavy goods to market in Tanzania. (**I:** 6–9)

Myers, Walter Dean. *At Her Majesty's Request: An African Princess in Victorian England*. Scholastic, 1999. In the 1840s, an orphaned African princess is rescued from becoming a live sacrifice and taken to England, where her upbringing is overseen by Queen Victoria. (**I:** 10–YA)

*———. *Brown Angels*. HarperCollins, 1993. Photographs of African American children from the turn of the century provide inspiration for the poems written by Myers. A related title is *Glorious Angels* (1995). (**I:** 7–9)

———. *Darnell Rock, Reporting*. Delacorte, 1994. Joining the school newspaper staff changes Darnell's attitudes about and engagement in school. (**I:** 10–13)

*———. *Harlem*. Illustrated by Christopher Myers. Scholastic, 1997. Poetic text and vibrant collage illustrations offer vivid images of everyday life, as well as the art, music, and literature that define Harlem. (**I:** 12 and up)

*———. *Jazz*. Illustrated by Christopher Myers. Holiday House, 2006. Through musical poetry and accompanying illustration, the father-son team introduce jazz, its history, background and features. (**I:** 10–YA)

———. *Malcolm X: By Any Means Necessary*. Scholastic, 1993. This is the story of the famous civil rights leader Malcolm X. (**I:** 9–11)

Naidoo, Beverley. *Journey to Jo'burg: A South African Story*. Harper, 1986. Naledi travels from her South African village to Johannesburg to deliver news of her baby sister's near-death from an illness to her mother, who works and lives in the home of some white people. (**I:** 9–11)

Nelson, Kadir. *We Are the Ship: The Story of Negro League Baseball*. Jump at the Sun/Hyperion, 2008. The talent, determination and dedication of the players in the Negro League Baseball allowed them to rise above the discrimination, circumstances, and obstacles they faced. (**I:** 9–YA)

Nelson, Marilyn. *Carver: A Life in Poems*. Front Street, 2001. 44 poems from different voices paint a picture of George Washington Carver, son of slaves who became a famous scientist, inventor, botanist, painter, musician and educator. (**I:** 13–YA)

*Nelson, Vaunda Micheaux. *Almost to Freedom*. Illustrated by Colin Bootman. Carolrhoda, 2003. Sally is a beloved rag doll who is accidentally left behind when her owner escapes North to freedom, but becomes a companion for another child who stops at the Underground Railroad stop and needs to find comfort. (**I:** 6–9)

*Nivola, Claire A. *Planting the Trees of Kenya: The Story of Wangari Maathai*. Farrar, Straus, & Giroux, 2008. The extraordinary work of a Nobel Peace Prize winner, a Kenyan woman who mobilized the people in her country to plant trees to save the land from environmental damage. (**I:** 7–10)

*Pinkney, Andrea Davis. *Dear Benjamin Banneker*. Illustrated by Brian Pinkney. Harcourt, 1994. Benjamin Banneker was an accomplished mathematician and astronomer and was the first black creator of an almanac. When he realized the injustice of the words in the Declaration of Independence proclaiming that "all men are created equal," he wrote to Secretary of State Thomas Jefferson. (**I:** 7–9)

———. *Let It Shine: Stories of Black Women Freedom Fighters*. Illustrated by Stephen Alcorn. Harcourt, 2000. This collection of brief biographies describes how black women like Sojourner Truth, Harriet Tubman, Rosa Parks, and Shirley Chisholm have fought for freedom. (**I:** 10–13)

*———. *Seven Candles for Kwanzaa*. Illustrated by Brian Pinkney. Dial, 1993. This book describes the seven-day festival of Kwanzaa, a holiday during which Americans of African descent celebrate their ancestral values. (**I:** 6–9)

*Pinkney, Brian. *JoJo's Flying Side Kick*. Simon & Schuster, 1995. When JoJo is to be tested to earn her yellow belt in tae kwon do class, she gets a lot of advice from others. At the moment of the test, though, she realizes for herself how to perform the flying side kick and break the board. (**I:** P–8)

*Pinkney, Gloria. *Back Home*. Illustrated by Jerry Pinkney. Dial, 1992. Eight-year-old Ernestine takes a train trip to visit relatives at the North Carolina farm where she was born. The prequel is *The Sunday Outing* (1994). (**I:** 6–9)

*Rappaport, Doreen. *Martin's Big Words: The Life of Martin Luther King, Jr.* Illustrated by Bryan Collier. Hyperion, 2001. Text pulled from King's speeches, paired with illustrations, offers an image of a man who used "big words" to powerfully make his views known. (**I:** 6 and up)

*Raschka, Chris. *Charlie Parker Played Be Bop*. Orchard, 1992. Lively words in rhythmic text seem like the bebop music of the famous jazz saxophonist. (**I:** P–8)

*Ringgold, Faith. *Tar Beach*. Crown, 1991. A young girl remembers spending summer evenings on the "tar beach" on the roof of their apartment building, imagining that she could fly over Manhattan and claim all she saw for herself and her family. (**I:** 6–9)

*Schroeder, Alan. *Minty: A Story of Young Harriet Tubman*. Illustrated by Jerry Pinkney. Dial, 1996. Harriet Tubman's "cradle" name was Araminta, and therefore she was nicknamed Minty. She was a slave on the Brodas plantation in the 1820s, and not only did she always long to escape, she prepared for it. (**I:** 7–9)

Schwartz, Virginia Frances. *Send One Angel Down*. Holiday House, 2000. Raised in the hardship of slavery, Eliza, fathered by her master, finds unexpected freedom when a northern abolitionist buys her. (**I:** 12–YA)

*Sisulu, Elinor Batezat. *The Day Gogo Went to Vote: South Africa*. Illustrated by Sharon Wilson. Little, Brown, 1996. Thembi and her great-grandmother participate in the election on the historic day on which black South Africans were allowed to vote for the first time. (**I:** 7–10)

*Steptoe, Javaka, illustrator. *In Daddy's Arms I Am Tall: African Americans Celebrating Fathers*. Lee & Low, 1997. A collection of poetry focusing on the important role of fathers in the lives of their children. (**I:** P–10)

*Steptoe, John. *Baby Says*. Lothrop, Lee & Shepard, 1988. In this nearly wordless book, a baby and his big brother learn to play together. (**I:** P)

Taylor, Mildred. *The Friendship*. Illustrated by Max Ginsburg. Dial, 1987. In 1930s rural Mississippi, the four Logan children witness a confrontation when Mr. Tom Bee, an elderly black man, calls a white storekeeper by his first name. Other titles about the Logans include *Road to Memphis* (1990) and *The Well* (1995). (**I:** 8–11)

———. *The Gold Cadillac*. Illustrated by Michael Hays. Dial, 1987. Father brings home a new gold Cadillac, and 'Lois and Wilmato are proud to be riding in it. But driving south from Ohio to Mississippi to visit relatives, the family faces prejudice and racism and must temporarily trade the Cadillac for a less conspicuous car. (**I:** 8–11)

———. *Mississippi Bridge*. Illustrated by Max Ginsburg. Dial, 1990. In the 1930s, amidst racial tension, black passengers are ordered off a bus to accommodate white passengers. Crossing the flooded river on a weak bridge, the bus is swept off and the passengers die. (**I:** 10–12)

———. *Roll of Thunder, Hear My Cry*. Illustrated by Jerry Pinkney. Dial, 1976. The Logan family faces many problems associated with being black in the rural South during the Depression. The sequel is *Let the Circle Be Unbroken* (1981). See also the prequel, *The Land* (2005) and *Song of the Trees* (1975). (**I:** 11–13)

Walter, Mildred Pitts. *Justin and the Best Biscuits in the World*. Illustrated by Catherine Stock. Lothrop, Lee & Shepard, 1986. Justin lives in a house full of women and considers cooking and cleaning to be "women's work." Spending time on his grandfather's ranch shows Justin a different view of work. (**I:** 9–11)

*Weatherford, Carole Boston. *Moses: When Harriet Tubman Led Her People to Freedom*. Illustrated by Kadir Nelson. Hyperion/Jump at the Sun, 2006. Harriet Tubman's spiritual strength is depicted as she follows God's call for her to be the "Moses" of her people and to lead them to freedom. (**I:** 7–10)

*Winter, Jonah. *Dizzy*. Illustrated by Sean Qualls. Scholastic/Arthur A. Levine, 2006. This picture book biography depicts the life of jazz musician Dizzy Gillespie, from his abusive childhood to his brilliant creation of bebop through musically portrayed text and illustration. (**I:** 8–11)

Woodson, Jacqueline. *Last Summer with Maizon*. Delacorte, 1992/2002. Margaret knows that after the summer ends, her best friend, Maizon, will be leaving their neighborhood in Brooklyn to attend a boarding school to which she has won a scholarship. See also *Maizon at Blue Hill* (1992/2002) and *Between Madison and Palmetto* (1995/2002). (**I:** 11–YA)

*———. *The Other Side*. Illustrated by E. B. Lewis. Putnam, 2001. In the days of segregation, two girls are told not to cross the fence, so they find a way to befriend one another without going to the other side. (**I:** 7–9)

Asian and Asian American

*Chinn, Karen. *Sam and the Lucky Money*. Illustrated by Cornelius Van Wright and Ying-Hwa Hu. Lee & Low, 1995. Chinese New Year means gifts of money in red envelopes for children. When he sees a homeless man, Sam struggles with the knowledge that he is free to spend his "lucky money" in any way he wishes. (**I:** 6–9)

*Choi, Sook Nyul. *Halmoni and the Picnic*. Illustrated by Karen M. Dugan. Houghton Mifflin, 1993. When the class plans a field trip, a classmate invites Yunmi's halmoni (grandmother) to serve as a chaperone. Yunmi worries about what her class-

mates will think of her grandmother's Korean ways and foods. (**I:** 6–9)

*Coerr, Eleanor. *Sadako*. Illustrated by Ed Young. Putnam, 1993. Believing in the Japanese tradition that folding a thousand origami cranes will restore her health, a little girl named Sadako tries to survive the leukemia that resulted from the bombing of Hiroshima. See also the novel *Sadako and the Thousand Paper Cranes*. (**I:** 9–12)

Compestine, Ying Chang. *Revolution Is Not a Dinner Party*. Holt, 2007. Set in China during the days of the Cultural Revolution, Ling describes her daily life and the persecution her family and neighbors endure. (**I:** 12–YA)

*Demi. *Chingis Kahn*. Holt, 1991. This picture book presents a biography of the famous king of the Mongols. (**I:** 9–11)

———. *The Dragon's Tale and Other Animal Fables of the Chinese Zodiac*. Holt, 1996. Twelve fables tell the stories of the animals of the Chinese zodiac. (**I:** 7–11)

*———. *The Empty Pot*. Holt, 1990. The Emperor distributes seeds to children across China, and the one who grows the best flower will inherit the kingdom. Ping finds that he must face the emperor honestly with his empty pot when springtime comes, as nothing has grown from the seed he was given. (**I:** 6–9)

*———. *Liang and the Magic Paintbrush*. Holt, 1980. A small boy in China is given a paintbrush, and everything he paints magically comes to life. (**I:** 6–9)

*Hamanaka, Sheila. *The Journey*. Orchard, 1990. A historical look at Japanese Americans is provided through close-up details of an actual mural, accompanied by text explaining the significance of each section. (**I:** 10–YA)

*Heo, Yumi, reteller. *The Green Frogs: A Korean Folktale*. Houghton Mifflin, 1996. In this pourquoi tale, two frog sons always do the opposite of what their mother requests, so disobedient children in Korea today are called "green frogs." (**I:** 6–10)

*Hong, Lily Toy. *Two of Everything*. Whitman, 1993. While digging in his field, Mr. Haktak finds a big pot, and everything he puts in it comes out doubled. He faces a dilemma when his wife falls into the pot! (**I:** 6–9)

Kadohata, Cynthia. *Weedflower*. Atheneum, 2006. Sumiko and her family are sent to live in a Japanese internment camp, where she develops an unexpected friendship with a Native American boy who is curious about the people he has been hired to fence in. (**I:** 10–13)

Lin, Grace. *The Year of the Dog*. Little Brown, 2005. Grace is an American girl of Taiwanese heritage, and throughout the "year of the dog" in the Chinese calendar, she navigates the differences of her two cultures. Sequel: *The Year of the Rat* (2008). (**I:** 8–10)

*Look, Lenore. *Uncle Peter's Amazing Chinese Wedding*. Illustrated by Yumi Heo. Simon & Schuster/Anne Schwartz, 2006. The marriage of Uncle Peter brings uncertain feelings to Jenny when the celebration takes place in traditional Chinese style. (**I:** K–8)

Lord, Betty Bao. *In the Year of the Boar and Jackie Robinson*. HarperCollins, 1984. In 1947, ten-year-old Chinese immigrant Shirley Temple Wong finds inspiration in Jackie Robinson, a grandson of a slave who has become an American hero, and she vows to view America as a land of opportunity. (**I:** 9–11)

*Mahy, Margaret. *The Seven Chinese Brothers*. Illustrated by Jean and Mou-sien Tseng. Scholastic, 1990. When one brother is ordered to be executed, the seven brothers take turns escaping death by virtue of their extraordinary abilities. (**I:** 6–9)

*Melmed, Laura Krauss. *Little Oh*. Illustrated by Jim LaMarche. Lothrop, 1997. An origami doll is separated from the woman who made her, but the ensuing adventure and reunion turn her into a live daughter. (**I:** 7–9)

*Mochizuki, Ken. *Baseball Saved Us*. Illustrated by Dom Lee. Lee & Low, 1993. While forced to live in an internment camp for Japanese Americans during World War II, a young boy learns to play baseball. (**I:** 6–9)

*Morimoto, Junko. *My Hiroshima*. Viking, 1987. The author recalls her childhood in Hiroshima and what happened on the day the atomic bomb was dropped. (**I:** 9–12)

*Say, Allen. *El Chino*. Houghton Mifflin, 1990. This picture book biography of Bong Way "Bill" Wong tells how he became a famous Chinese American bullfighter in Spain. (**I:** 6–9)

*———. *Emma's Rug*. Houghton Mifflin, 1996. Emma finds artistic inspiration in her small white rug, but when her mother washes it clean, Emma is sure that she can no longer draw or paint. (**I:** 6–9)

*———. *Grandfather's Journey*. Houghton Mifflin, 1993. A Japanese man immigrates to the United States and learns to love his new home, but still misses his homeland. When visiting Japan, he finds that the war will keep him from returning to the United States. A related title is *Tree of Cranes* (1991). (**I:** 6–9)

*———. *Tea with Milk*. Houghton Mifflin, 1999. A Japanese American woman returns with her parents to Japan in the 1950s and resolves conflicts between her American ways and the customs of women in Japan. (**I:** 9–12)

*Shea, Pegi Deitz. *The Whispering Cloth: A Refugee's Story*. Illustrated by Anita Riggio. Stitched by You Yang. Boyds Mills, 1995. Mai practices stitching borders in embroidered story cloths while in a Thai refugee camp with her grandmother. She finds a story within herself so that she, too, can stitch her own pa'ndau. (**I:** 7–10)

*Uchida, Yoshiko. *The Bracelet*. Illustrated by Joanna Yardley. Philomel, 1976/1993. Emi and her family are sent to an internment camp during World War II. Emi loses the bracelet that was a gift from her best friend, but she comes to realize that she does not need the physical reminder of her friendship in order to remember. (**I:** 6–9)

———. *A Jar of Dreams*. Macmillan, 1981. Faced with the prejudice against Japanese in the 1930s in California, Rinko wants to be as American as possible. When Aunt Waka visits from Japan, Rinko begins to understand the strength of her family and the Japanese American community. Related titles are *The Best Bad Thing* (1983) and *The Happiest Ending* (1985). (**I:** 9–11)

*Wong, Janet. *Apple Pie, Fourth of July*. Illustrated by Margaret Chodos-Irvine. Harcourt, 2002. A young girl thinks that nobody will want to come to their Chinese restaurant on the Fourth of July but is pleasantly surprised. (**I:** 6–9)

*———. *The Trip Back Home*. Illustrated by Bo Jia. Harcourt, 2000. A Korean American child visits her mother's homeland with her. (**I:** 6–9)

*———. *This Next New Year*. Illustrated by Yangsook Choi. Farrar, Straus, & Giroux, 2000. Celebrating Chinese New Year in America is a multicultural experience enjoyed by this Chinese Korean boy and his many other non-Chinese friends. (**I:** 6–9)

*Xiong, Blia. *Nine-in-One, Grr! Grr! A Folktale from the Hmong People of Laos*. Adapted by Cathy Spagnoli. Illustrated by Nancy Hom. Children's Book Press, 1989. Tiger is promised nine cubs a year by the god, Shao. Bird fears that tigers will overtake the land and tries to think of a way to prevent that from happening. (**I:** 6–10)

*Yee, Paul. *Ghost Train*. Illustrated by Harvey Chan. Groundwood, 1996. Choon-Yi finally arrives in North America to join her father, but he has been killed while building the railroad. Summoned to put her talent in painting to create a "fire-train," she dreams a fantasy that brings all who have died on board her painted train so that their souls may return home to China with her. (**I:** 9–12)

Yep, Laurence. *Angelfish*. Putnam, 2001. In this continued story of a biracial Chinese American girl, her ballet dancing brings about new understandings for herself and her neighbor who had been "reeducated" during the Cultural Revolution in China. See earlier books: *Ribbons* (1996) and *The Cook's Family* (1998). (**I:** 10–13)

———. *Dragon's Gate*. HarperCollins, 1993. In 1867, Chinese men came to the United States and found work digging and dynamiting tunnels through the rocks of the Sierra Mountains so that the railroad could cross the nation. (**I:** 11–YA)

———. *Dragonwings*. Harper, 1975/1987. Moon Shadow leaves his remote Chinese village in 1903 to join his father, Windrider, in California. Together, they survive the 1906 earthquake and the hardships of life in the "Golden Mountain" as they work to realize their dream of building a dragon-like flying machine. (**I:** 10–12)

———. *Later, Gator*. HarperCollins, 1995. Two brothers who usually do not get along find that they must cooperate with each other when they wind up with a pet alligator they know their parents will not approve of. See also *Cockroach Cooties* (2000). (**I:** 8–10)

———. *The Star Fisher*. Morrow, 1991. This fictionalized biography of Laurence Yep's grandmother tells of fifteen-year-old Joan Lee and her family's move from Ohio to West Virginia in the 1920s. Being the only Asians in the community, they face the problem of being "different" from their neighbors. (**I:** 11–YA)

*Young, Ed. *Cat and Rat: The Legend of the Chinese Zodiac*. Holt, 1995. This is the story of how the twelve animals became part of the Chinese zodiac. (**I:** 7–10)

*———. *Lon Po Po: A Red-Riding Hood Story from China*. Philomel, 1989. When mother leaves the children at home, a wolf enters their house. The children must think quickly and come up with a plan to outsmart the wolf. (**I:** 7–10)

*———. *Monkey King*. HarperCollins, 2001. This picture book version of the Chinese epic, *Journey to the West*, tells the beginning of the monkey king's pursuit of an enlightened state.

Latino/Latina

*Ada, Alma Flor. *The Gold Coin*. Atheneum, 1991. When a thief follows a healer woman in an attempt to steal her gold coin, he finds himself transformed by witnessing her acts of kindness. (**I:** 7–10)

———. *My Name Is María Isabel/Me llamo María Isabel*. Atheneum, 1993. When María Isabel Salazar Lopez enters a new classroom, the teacher decides to call her "Mary Lopez" because there are already two girls named Maria in the class. (**I:** 7–10)

———. *Under the Royal Palms: A Childhood in Cuba*. Atheneum, 1998. Author Ada offers a memoir of her childhood, with vivid descriptions of island life with her family. This is a companion book to *Where the Flame Trees Bloom* (1994). (**I:** 9–12)

Alvarez, Julia. *Before We Were Free.* Knopf, 2002. Twelve-year-old Anita lives in the Dominican Republic in the 1960s when freedom was controlled by the government (**I:** 12–YA)

———. *How Tía Lola Came to ~~Visit~~ Stay.* Knopf, 2001. When his parents divorce, Tía Lola comes from the Dominican Republic to Vermont to help out with the boys, who try to keep their flamboyant aunt out of their friends' sight. (**I:** 9–12).

*Ancona, George. *Pablo Remembers: The Fiesta of the Day of the Dead.* Lothrop, Lee & Shepard, 1993. Pablo and his family prepare for the three-day fiesta of El Día de Los Muertos, a festival to honor the spirits of the dead. (**I:** 6–9)

*———. *The Piñata Maker/El piñatero.* Harcourt, 1994. Don Ricardo is a craftsman in Ejutla de Crespo in southern Mexico. He makes piñatas for birthday parties and other fiestas. Bilingual text. (**I:** 6–9)

Andrews-Goebel, Nancy. *The Pot That Juan Built.* Illustrated by David Diaz. Lee & Low, 2002. Two parallel texts exist throughout the book; one is a cumulative story about the creating of a pot in the style of "The House that Jack Built" and the other a biography of the potter, Juan Quezada. (**I:** 6–9)

*Cowley, Joy. *Gracias, the Thanksgiving Turkey.* Illustrated by Joe Cepeda. Scholastic, 1996. Papa sends Miguel a turkey with instructions to fatten the bird for Thanksgiving dinner, but Miguel becomes attached to his new pet. (**I:** 6–9)

*Delacre, Lulu. *Arroz con leche: Popular Songs and Rhymes from Latin America.* Scholastic, 1989. The songs and rhymes in this bilingual collection are known throughout the Spanish-speaking countries. A related title is *Las Navidades: Popular Christmas Songs from Latin America* (1990). (**I:** P–8)

———. *Golden Tales: Myths, Legends and Folktales from Latin America.* Scholastic, 1996. The twelve classic tales in this collection come from four cultures of Latin America—Taino, Zapotec, Muisca, and Inca—and from many different countries. (**I:** 9–12)

*Emberley, Rebecca. *My House/Mi casa: A Book in Two Languages.* Little, Brown, 1990. Things commonly found in a house are labeled throughout the illustrations in both English and Spanish. A related title is *Taking a Walk/Caminando: A Book in Two Languages* (1990). (**I:** P–7)

Engle, Margarita. *The Poet Slave of Cuba: A Biography of Juan Francisco Manzano.* Illustrated by Sean Qualls. Holt, 2006. Told through multiple-voiced poetry, the horrors and pain of slavery are powerfully reflected on. (**I:** 12–YA)

———. *The Surrender Tree.* Poetic telling of the hardships of life in Cuba during the War for Independence in the latter 1800s. Holt, 2008.

*Garza, Carmen Lomas. *Family Pictures/Cuadros de familia.* Spanish language text by Rosalma Zubizaretta. Children's Book Press, 1990. Bilingual text accompanies folk art illustrations depicting the author's experiences of growing up Mexican American in South Texas. Another book by Garza is *In My Family/En mi familia* (1996). (**I:** 6–10)

González, Lucía M. *Señor Cat's Romance and Other Favorite Stories from Latin America.* Illustrated by Lulu Delacre. Scholastic, 1997. Each of the six tales about outrageous Señor Cat, silly Juan Bobo, and others is followed by a note about the culture it comes from. (**I:** 6–9)

Jimenez, Francisco. *The Circuit: Stories from the Life of a Migrant Child.* Houghton Mifflin, 1999. An autobiographical account of

a childhood journey from Mexico to California in a migrant farm family in the 1940s. See also *Breaking Through* (2001).

Johnston, Tony. *Any Small Goodness: A Novel of the Barrio.* Scholastic, 2001. Set in East Los Angeles, eleven-year-old "Turo" navigates his way through daily experiences with his family, his friends, and his community. (**I:** 8–11)

*Krull, Kathleen. *Harvesting Hope.* Illustrated by Yuyi Morales. Harcourt, 2003. This biography focuses on the role that Cesar Chavez played in the 1965 nonviolent protest against poor working conditions for migrant farm workers. (**I:** 7–10)

*Madrigal, Antonio Hernández. *Erandi's Braids.* Illustrated by Tomie dePaola. Putnam, 1999. Set in 1940s Mexico, this story tells how Erandi sells her braids so that her mother can get a new fishing net. (**I:** 6–9)

*Martinez, Alejandro Cruz. *The Woman Who Outshone the Sun/La mujer que brillaba aún más que el sol.* Illustrated by Fernando Olivera. Story by Rosalma Zubizarreta, Harriet Rohmer, and David Schecter from a poem by Alejandro Cruz Martinez. Children's Book Press, 1991. This retelling of a Zapotec Indian legend from Mexico is the story of Llucia Zenteno, a beautiful woman who possesses magical powers. When she is sent away from a mountain village, she takes its water away in punishment. (**I:** 7–10)

Mohr, Nicholasa. *Felita.* 1979. Bantam, 1990. Moving is always hard, but when Felita's family moves to an area where there aren't other Puerto Rican families speaking Spanish, the adjustment feels even more lonely. Also by Mohr is *Going Home* (1986). (**I:** 9–12)

*Mora, Pat. *A Birthday Basket for Tía.* Illustrated by Cecily Lan. Macmillan, 1992. Cecila wants to find the perfect present for her great-aunt's ninetieth birthday. (**I:** P–6)

*———. *Tómas and the Library Lady.* Illustrated by Raúl Colón. Knopf, 1997. A librarian helps Tómas connect his life with books while living in Iowa as a migrant farm worker. (**I:** 6–9)

Ryan, Pam Muñoz. *Becoming Naomi Leon.* Scholastic, 2004. When Naomi Leon's mother reappears after a seven-year absence and threatens to change the peaceful life Naomi Leon has had with her younger brother and her Gram, a journey to Mexico in search of an estranged father helps her define who she is and where she belongs. (**I:** 10–13).

———. *Esperanza Rising.* Scholastic, 2000. Esperanza lives a privileged and wealthy life in Mexico; then, circumstances force her to flee to California with her mother, and work in a farm labor camp. (**I:** 12–YA)

Soto, Gary. *Baseball in April and Other Stories.* Harcourt, 1990. The eleven short stories in this collection tell of the author's experiences growing up Mexican American in Fresno, California. (**I:** 9–12)

*———. *Chato's Kitchen.* Putnam, 1995. Illustrated by Susan Guevara. Cool cat Chato is thrilled to see who has moved into the barrio—a family of tasty-looking mice. When they accept a dinner invitation, Chato is filled with anticipation as he prepares the frijoles, guacamole, arroz, tortillas, and more, but things go differently than he expects when the mice's friend shows up. See also *Chato and the Party Animals* (2000). (**I:** 7–9)

———. *Neighborhood Odes.* Illustrated by David Diaz. Harcourt, 1992. These twenty-one poems describe various everyday joys of growing up in a Mexican American neighborhood. (**I:** 9–YA)

*———. *The Old Man and His Door.* Illustrated by Joe Cepeda. Putnam, 1996. The story is based on a Mexican song that goes

"La puerta. El puerco. There's no difference to el viejo." Misunderstanding his wife's instructions on what to take to a party, an old man takes a door instead of a pig. But the door proves useful along the way, and the old man has many surprises for his wife. (**I:** P–8)

———. *Taking Sides*. Harcourt, 1991. Lincoln Mendoza moves from his familiar neighborhood to the suburbs when his mother gets a better-paying job. When the basketball team of his new school plays against his former team, he realizes he needs to sort out his self-identity. (**I:** 10–12)

*———. *Too Many Tamales*. Illustrated by Ed Martinez. Putnam, 1993. While helping to make tamales, Maria slips her mother's diamond ring on her hand to admire it. When she realizes that the ring is missing, she enlists the help of her cousins in eating the tamales until the ring is found. (**I:** 6–9)

*Torres, Leyla. *Saturday Sancocho*. Mirasol/Farrar, 1995. María Líli's mother decides to make sancocho but needs a chicken; the two go to the marketplace to trade eggs for a series of items. (**I:** 6–9)

Native American

Alexie, Sherman. *The Absolutely True Diary of a Part-Time Indian*. Illustrated by Ellen Forney. Little Brown, 2007. This is a work of fiction, but with elements autobiographical to the author's growing up on a reservation and going to school outside, feeling bullied and trying to figure out where he belonged and what his identity was. (**I:** 12–YA)

*Begay, Shonto. *Navajo: Visions and Voices across the Mesa*. Scholastic, 1995. Twenty paintings and original poems are paired to present a personal voice of what it means to live as a Navajo in today's world. (**I:** 10 and up)

Bierhorst, John. *The Deetkatoo: Native American Stories about Little People*. Illustrated by Ron Hilbert Coy. Morrow, 1998. This book compiles twenty-two stories of little people from fourteen different native cultures and is well documented with notes, a guide to cultures, and a bibliography. (**I:** 10 and up)

Bruchac, James, and Joseph Bruchac. *The Girl Who Helped Thunder and Other Native American Folktales*. This is a collection of retold Native American folktales across many tribal groups. Illustrated by Stefano Vitale. Sterling, 2008.

*Bruchac, Joseph. *A Boy Called Slow*. Illustrated by Rocco Baviera. Philomel, 1994. A Lakota boy's childhood name "Slow" is changed to "Sitting Bull" as he matures through his deeds. (**I:** 9–12)

———. *Eagle Song*. Dial, 1997. Fourth-grade Danny Bigtree leaves the Mohawk Reservation and moves to Brooklyn and must learn to balance pride in his heritage with life in a new, urban environment. (**I:** 9–13)

*———. *The First Strawberries: A Cherokee Story*. Illustrated by Anna Vojtech. Dial, 1993. This folktale tells how the first man's arrogance causes the first woman to leave when he becomes angry at her for spending time on flowers rather than on preparing dinner. (**I:** P–8)

———. *In the Heart of a Chief*. Dial, 1998. This story of a contemporary eleven-year-old boy explores what it means to be a Penacook Indian who lives on a reservation, but encounters conflicts with schoolmates outside the reservation. (**I:** 10–13).

*———, and Jonathan London. *Thirteen Moons on Turtle's Back: A Native American Year of Moons*. Illustrated by Thomas Locker. Philomel, 1992. Many Native American tribes relate the thirteen moons of the year to the pattern of thirteen large scales on the turtle's back. Poems—each based on a story from a different Native American nation, such as the Cherokee, Cree, or Sioux—make up the text for this book. (**I:** 8–10)

Caduto, Michael J., and Joseph Bruchac. *Keepers of the Earth: Native American Stories and Environmental Activities for Children*. Illustrated by John Kahionhes Fadden and Carol Wood. Golden, CO: Fulcrum, 1988. This book's purpose is to teach children about Native American cultures and the link between humans and nature through an interdisciplinary approach. Twenty-three sets of lessons each feature a story followed by suggested activities to enhance learning. See also *Keepers of the Animals: Native American Stories and Wildlife Activities for Children* (1991); *Keepers of Life: Discovering Plants through Native American Stories and Earth Activities for Children* (1994). (**I:** 6–12)

*Cohen, Caron Lee. *The Mud Pony*. Illustrated by Shonto Begay. Scholastic, 1988. A poor boy creates a mud pony and cares for it as if it were real. He dreams that the pony comes alive, and he awakens to find that it will guide him through many ordeals. (**I:** 6–9)

Dorris, Michael. *Morning Girl*. Hyperion, 1992. Morning Girl and her younger brother Star Boy describe their island life in alternating chapters. The story closes with the arrival of the first Europeans to her world. (**I:** 9–12)

*Ekoomiak, Normee. *Arctic Memories*. Holt, 1988. Appliqued, stitched, and painted illustrations show everyday and special events in the lives of Inuits of the past. Through bilingual Inuktitut and English text, the author/illustrator describes his memories of childhood in an Inuit community in northern Quebec. (**I:** 7–10)

Erdrich, Louise. *The Birchbark House*. Hyperion, 1999. Seven-year-old Omakayas is an Ojibwa girl whose daily life on an island in Lake Superior is depicted during the U.S. westward movement. Sequels: *The Game of Silence* (2005), *The Porcupine Year* (2008). (**I:** 7–10)

*Goble, Paul. *Death of the Iron Horse*. Bradbury, 1987. Fearful of what will happen as the white men approach their territory, a group of Cheyenne braves derail a freight train in 1867, believing it to be an Iron Horse whose rails are binding Mother Earth. (**I:** 8–10)

*———. *The Girl Who Loved Wild Horses*. Macmillan, 1978. A girl's love of horses leads her to be among them, where her family finds her. She finds that she feels a sense of belonging when she is with the horses. (**I:** 6–8)

*Littlechild, George. *This Land Is My Land*. Children's Book Press, 1993. Through striking illustrations and accompanying essays, Littlechild recounts historical events and their implications on his people. (**I:** 9–12)

*Ortiz, Simon. *The People Shall Continue*. Children's Book Press, 1988. This book briefly presents an overview of the history of the North American Indians from Creation to the present. (**I:** 9–12)

*Ross, Gayle. *How Rabbit Tricked Otter*. Illustrated by Murv Jacob. Parabola, 2003. Fifteen tales about Rabbit from the Cherokee storytelling tradition. (**I:** 6–9)

*Scott, Ann Herbert. *On Mother's Lap*. Illustrated by Glo Coalson. Clarion, 1972/1992. Michael enjoys rocking in Mother's lap—along with Dolly, Boat, reindeer blanket, and puppy—until Mother hears the baby crying. The illustrator created the original sketches while living in an Inuit village. (**I:** P–6)

*Steptoe, John. *The Story of Jumping Mouse: A Native American Legend*. Lothrop, Lee & Shepard, 1984. Jumping Mouse sets out to find the "far-off land." He finds that his generosity pays off as each of the animals he encounters bestows a gift to ensure his safe passage to his "far-off land." (**I:** 9–13)

*Yolen, Jane. *Encounter*. Illustrated by David Shannon. Harcourt, 1992. This story is narrated by a young Taino boy, who tells of the arrival of Columbus and his ships in 1492. (**I:** 7–11)

Other Cultural Groups

Appalachian and Other Specific Regional and Religious Cultural Groups

Bial, Raymond. *Amish Home*. Houghton Mifflin, 1993.

———. *Visit to Amish Country*. Phoenix Publishing, 1995.

Crum, Shutta. *Spitting Image*. Clarion, 2003. Twelve-year-old Jessie is mortified when her intended plan to help her neighbors in the poverty-ridden Appalachians backfires and brings them shame and embarrassment during the days of President Johnson's War on Poverty. (**I:** 10–13)

*Houston, Gloria. *My Great-Aunt Arizona*. Illustrated by Susan Condie Lamb. Harper, 1992. Arizona Houston Hughes was born in a log cabin in the Blue Ridge Mountains, and she grew up to become a teacher in the one-room school she had attended as a child. Arizona inspires generations of children to imagine the faraway places they will someday visit. (**I:** 6–9)

Ray, Delia. *Ghost Girl*. Clarion, 2003. When President and Mrs. Hoover build a school in the Blue Ridge Mountains, April realizes her first opportunity to attend school. She faces the opposition of her mother, but has the support of her grandmother. (**I:** 10–13)

*Rylant, Cynthia. *The Relatives Came*. Illustrated by Stephen Gammell. Bradbury, 1985. This book celebrates a family reunion in the Appalachian Mountains, where relatives must travel over winding mountain roads for a visit. (**I:** P–8)

*Stewart, Sarah. *The Journey*. Illustrated by David Small. FSG, 2001. An Amish girl takes her first trip to the city—Chicago—and connects the new things she sees with her life at home. (**I:** 7–9)

Caribbean

*San Souci, Robert D. *The Faithful Friend*. Illustrated by Brian Pinkney. Simon & Schuster, 1995. In this traditional tale from the French West Indies island of Martinique, Clemente and Hippolyte are friends who find love, strange zombies, and danger. (**I:** 7–10)

*Youme. Sélavi. *That is Life: A Haitian Story of Hope*. Cinco Puntos Press, 2005. The street children in Haiti tolerate inhumane treatment and brutality, but the loving support of some help them ban together for hope and survival. (**I:** K–7)

European Americans

*Best, Cari. *Three Cheers for Catherine the Great!* Illustrated by Giselle Potter. Kroupa/DK Ink, 1999. Sara's beloved Russian grandmother asks for "no presents," but Sara finds a special present: She and her grandmother exchange language lessons. (**I:** 6–9)

*Polacco, Patricia. *The Keeping Quilt*. Simon & Schuster, 1988. A quilt made of scraps from clothes of family members left behind in Russia is passed down through the generations. The quilt serves a multitude of purposes: to welcome babies into the world, as a tent during play time, as a picnic cloth for a romantic date, and as a wedding huppa. (**I:** 7–10)

*Sís, Peter. *The Wall: Growing Up Behind the Iron Curtain*. Farrar, 2007. Through images and text, Sís describes the experiences of his childhood in Prague during the communist era, and his search for artistic expression.

Jewish and Jewish Americans

Lowry, Lois. *Number the Stars*. Houghton Mifflin, 1989. When the Nazis come to find the Jews, ten-year-old Annemarie's family shelters a Jewish girl and participates as part of the Danish resistance in helping Jews escape to Sweden. (**I:** 10–13)

*Polacco, Patricia. *Mrs. Katz and Tush*. Bantam, 1992. A lonely Jewish widow gains companionship when an African American boy gives her a kitten. (**I:** 6–9)

The Middle East

*Alalou, Elizabeth, and Ali Alalou. *The Butter Man*. Illustrated by Julie Klear Essakalli. Charlesbridge, 2008. While Nora anxiously waits for her baba to finish making the couscous and vegetables dinner, her father tells the story of his childhood in Morocco and waiting hungrily for the butter man to come by. (**I:** P–8)

Barakat, Ibtisam. *Tasting the Sky: A Palestinian Childhood*. FSG, 2007. Set during the horror of war and occupation during the Arab-Israeli Six-Day War, this memoir recounts various episodes that define what the experience meant to her personally. (**I:** 12–YA)

Budhos, Marina. *Ask Me No Questions*. Simon & Schuster/Ginee Seo, 2006. Following 9/11, Muslim men were required to register with the U.S. government. As an illegal immigrant from Bangladesh, their father is detained for attempting to leave the country and 14-year-old Nadira and her older sister must make a case for his release. (**I:** 12–YA)

Ellis, Deborah. *The Breadwinner*. Groundwood, 2001. Trapped inside the one-room family home after the Taliban takeover of Afghanistan, Parvana must bravely make a dangerous decision when her breadwinner father is taken away. See also: *Parvana's Journey* (2003) and *Mud City* (2004) (**I:** 10–12)

*Hoffman, Mary. *The Color of Home*. Illustrated by Karin Littlewood. Fogelman/Penguin, 2002. Hassan, a recent immigrant from Somalia, has an interpreter to help him communicate about his illustrations to his new classmates. (**I:** P–8)

Nye, Naomi Shihab. *Habibi*. Simon & Schuster, 1998. Liyana and her family move from St. Louis to Jerusalem because her father wants his children to know the other half of their heritage. (**I:** 12–YA)

*———. *Sitti's Secrets*. Illustrated by Nancy Carpenter. Four Winds, 1994. An American girl can't speak Arabic, the language of her grandmother—her sitti—but she remembers that they learned to communicate during time they spent together in Palestine. (**I:** 6–9)

*Rumford, James. *Silent Music*. Roaring Brook, 2008. In a contemporary story set in Baghdad, Ali loves soccer, dancing, and especially calligraphy. The story reflects on Iraq's long history of valuing literacy as a powerful means of communication. (**I:** 7–10)

Multiple Cultures

*Ada, Alma Flor. *I Love Saturdays y domingos*. Illustrated by Elivia Savadier. Atheneum, 2002. A biracial girl visits her European American grandparents on Saturdays and her Mexican American abuelo and abuela on domingos (Sundays). (**I:** P–8)

*Adoff, Arnold. *black is brown is tan*. Illustrated by Emily Arnold McCully. Harper, 1973. Two children with a "chocolate momma," a "white" daddy, and "granny white and grandma black" share the joys of being a family. (**I:** 6–9)

*Dooley, Norah. *Everybody Cooks Rice*. Illustrated by Peter J. Thornton. Carolrhoda, 1991. It is dinner time and Carrie sets out to find her little brother. At each home, she finds that rice is part of the family's evening meal, but that it is prepared differently because of the various cultural backgrounds of the families. A related title is *Everybody Bakes Bread* (1996). (**I:** 6–9)

*Grimes, Nikki. *Aneesa Lee and the Weaver's Gift*. Illustrated by Ashley Bryan. HarperCollins, 1999. A multiethnic girl—black, white, Asian—is a talented weaver, and her beautiful tapestries form a metaphor for the range of experiences and emotions she expresses. (**I:** 6–9)

Hamilton, Virginia. *Plain City*. Scholastic, 1993. Buhlaire, a child of mixed racial heritage, is ostracized by peers for her family's unusual habits. Her mother sings in clubs, and she thinks her father is Missing in Action—until one day, a homeless man appears. (**I:** 11–YA)

Kuklin, Susan. *Families*. Hyperion, 2006. Double-paged spreads with photographs introduce fifteen families of varying composition, including divorced parents, stepfamilies, gay parents, adopted children, immigrants, and special needs children. (**I:** K–9)

Kurtz, Jane. *The Storyteller's Beads*. Gulliver/Harcourt, 1998. Sahay realizes that she must flee to Sudan for her survival when her family is violently killed during a time of famine in Ethiopia. Rahel, who is blind and Jewish, is fleeing also, but with hopes of getting to Israel to escape prejudice as well as hunger. The story is set in the 1980s during the Israeli airlifts. (**I:** 12 and up)

*McGill, Alice. *Molly Bannaky*. Illustrated by Chris K. Soentpiet. Houghton Mifflin, 1999. Molly is banished from England for the punishable crime of a cow upsetting the milk pail. As an indentured servant in America, she buys and (illegally) marries a slave, and a Benjamin Bannker eventually is born as her grandson. (**I:** 8–10)

Nelson, Vaunda Micheaux. *Mayfield Crossing*. Illustrated by Leonard Jenkins. Putnam, 1993. When the school in Mayfield Crossing closes and its black students are sent to another school, they face racial and socioeconomic prejudices for the first time. See also *Beyond Mayfield* (1999). (**I:** 8–12)

*Nikola-Lisa, W. *Bein' with You This Way*. Illustrated by Michael Bryant. Lee & Low, 1994. Through upbeat rhythm, the text points out and celebrates people's physical similarities and differences. (**I:** P–8)

*Tingle, Tim. *Crossing Bok Chitto: A Choctaw Tale of Friendship and Freedom*. Illustrated by Jeanne Rorex Bridges. Cinco Puntos, 2006. When a Choctaw girl hears that a slave boy's mother is to be sold, she leads the family across the Bok Chitto River that forms the divide between freedom and slavery. (**I:** 8–11)

Woodson, Jacqueline. *Maizon at Blue Hill*. Delacorte, 1992/2002. Maizon enters a private boarding school and learns to deal with being one of only five African American students. She spends much time reflecting on what it feels like to be different from most. (**I:** 11–YA)

World Cultures Compared/Contrasted

*Anno, Mitsumasa. *All in a Day*. Philomel, 1986. The narrator, on a deserted island near the international date line, describes how children in eight countries celebrate New Year's Day. (**I:** 6–9)

*Lankford, Mary. *Mazes around the World*. Illustrated by Karen Dugan. HarperCollins, 2008. This series makes comparisons of practices around the world, and includes notes on geography, history, and cultural traditions for each topic in the series. See also: *Hopscotch Around the World* (1992); *Dominoes Around the World* (1998) among others. (**I:** 6–10)

*Lewin, Ted. *Visiting Markets Around the World!* HarperCollins, 2006. A look at marketplaces around the world, showing the various things people bring to sell or trade. Companion book to *Market!* (**I:** 6–9)

*Morris, Ann. *Houses and Homes*. Photography by Ken Heyman. Lothrop, Lee & Shepard, 1992. Through photographs and simple text, readers are introduced to the varieties of homes in which people around the world live, ranging from Buckingham Palace to houses on stilts, houses on boats, and straw huts. Morris and Heyman have created several other books in the same format. (**I:** 5–9)

Nye, Naomi Shihab, ed. *This Same Sky: A Collection of Poems from Around the World*. Four Winds, 1992. The many forms of life under "this same sky"—human, animal, and nature—are reflected in poems written by 129 poets from 68 different countries. (**I:** 10–YA)

Smith, David J. *If the World Were a Village: A Book About the World's People*. Illustrated by Shelagh Armstrong. Kids Can Press, 2002. Translating the various statistics of our world's population into a village of 100 people, this book presents facts about language, economics, and how people live on this planet in numbers that are easier for children to understand. (**I:** 6–10)

Growing Up in a World of Political or Social Unrest

Alvarez, Julia. *Before We Were Free*. Knopf, 2002. In 1960 in the Dominican Republic, twelve-year-old Anita wonders what it would be like to be "free" of a terrifying dictator and the secret police. (**I:** 11–YA)

*Bunting, Eve. *Smoky Night*. Illustrated by David Diaz. Harcourt, 1994. The Los Angeles race riots are seen from the perspective of a little boy and his mother as they seek shelter from danger. (**I:** 9–11)

Buss, Fran Leeper. *Journey of the Sparrows*. Penguin/Lodestar, 1991. Three siblings escape the war in El Salvador and head for the hope of new life, nailed into a crate on the back of a truck. They end up in Chicago, where they live a new life as illegal immigrants. (**I:** 12–YA)

Filipovec, Zalata. *Zlata's Diary: A Child's Life in Sarajevo*. Viking, 1994. A ten-year-old Croatian girl begins her diary in during prewar times and continues writing for three years until her family flees the former Yugoslavia and goes to Paris. (**I:** 11–YA)

Ho, Minfong. *The Clay Marble*. Farrar, 1991. Rebuilding homes and lives in a camp near the Thai border, families struggle to survive the destruction of war. A marble made from clay serves as a toy and a gesture of friendship between children in this camp. (**I:** 12–YA)

Jiang, Ji Li. *Red Scarf Girl: A Memoir of the Cultural Revolution*. HarperCollins, 1997. Ji Li wore her red scarf as the emblem of her devoted membership in the Young Pioneers, committed to the future of Communist China, when the course of her entire world changed with the beginning of the Chinese Cultural Revolution in 1966. (**I:** 10–YA)

Mead, Alice. *Girl of Kosovo*. Farrar, Straus, & Giroux, 2001. Eleven-year-old Zana struggles to survive and make sense of a world that seems to stand by as family members are killed and ethnic Albanians are nearly wiped out. (**I:** 11–YA)

Naidoo, Beverly. *The Other Side of Truth*. HarperCollins, 2001. Twelve-year-old Sade's father criticizes the government in their homeland of Nigeria and a bullet intended for him hits and kills her mother. The children are sent to London for safe-keeping, but are placed in foster care. (**I:** 12 and up)

Temple, Frances. *Grab Hands and Run*. Orchard, 1993. Felipe and his family face threats to their lives at their home in El Salvador. He tells the story of their escape and the dangerous journey to Canada. (**I:** 12–YA)

———. *Tonight, by Sea*. Orchard, 1995. Poverty and government brutality make life in Haiti unbearable, so Paulie and other villagers help her uncle build a boat so that they can secretly attempt to escape to the United States. (**I:** 12–YA)

Social and Economic Diversity

*Dugan, Barbara. *Loop the Loop*. Illustrated by James Stevenson. Greenwillow, 1992. While playing outside, Anne encounters Mrs. Simpson, a woman who rides in a wheelchair, claims to be 969 years old, and performs fabulous tricks with a yo-yo. When Mrs. Simpson breaks her hip, Anne takes Mrs. Simpson's cat and a yo-yo to the hospital. (**I:** 6–9)

*Hausherr, Rosemarie. *Celebrating Families*. Scholastic, 1997. Color photos and accompanying text introduce children from single-parent families, adoptive families, extended families, and other types of families. (**I:** 6–9)

Holt, Kimberly Willis. *When Zachary Beaver Came to Town*. Holt, 1999. In west Texas in 1971, Toby deals with his mother's departure and befriends 600-pound Zachary Beaver. (**I:** 9–12)

Paterson, Katherine. *The Flip Flop Girl*. Viking, 1994. Father's death is hard enough to cope with, but moving to a new place, living with grandmother, and dealing with poverty make life even more difficult. (**I:** 9–12)

———. *The Great Gilly Hopkins*. Crowell, 1978. Gilly's attempts to be difficult and unlikable lead to her being moved from one foster home to another. Trotter, a foster mother, helps Gilly accept the love and security she craves. (**I:** 9–12)

*Pearson, Susan. *Happy Birthday, Grampie*. Illustrated by Ronald Himler. Dial, 1987. Age has taken away Grampie's vision, and he has forgotten English and reverted to his mother tongue, Swedish. Martha makes Grampie a card he can feel and hopes that it will communicate her birthday wishes. (**I:** 6–9)

Gender Issues and Portrayals of Same-Sex Parents

*Hearne, Betsy. *Seven Brave Women*. Illustrated by Bethanne Andersen. Greenwillow, 1997. This book tells of seven women whose lives are not marked by their contributions to

wars in history, but who showed courage and strength in "her-story." (**I:** 7–10)

*Hoffman, Mary. *Amazing Grace*. Illustrated by Caroline Binch. Dial, 1991. When Grace is told by classmates that she can't be Peter Pan in the class play because she's black and a girl, she proves otherwise. See also *Boundless Grace* (1995); and *Starring Grace* (2000). (**I:** 6–8)

*Isadora, Rachel. *Max*. Macmillan, 1976. Max finds that taking dance lessons with his sister is a nice warm-up to his after-noon baseball games. (**I:** 5–8)

Krull, Kathleen. *Marie Curie*. Illustrated by Boris Kulikov. Viking, 2007. This biography in the "Giants of Science" series portrays the life of the woman who discovered radiation, defy-ing all stereotypes of women's roles in her time. (**I:** 9–12).

*Martin, Rafe. *Storytelling Princess*. Illustrated by Kimberly Bulcken Root. Putnam, 2001. A strong-willed princess refuses to accept her parents' choice in a negotiated arranged mar-riage, and circumstances allow her to make her own choice in a groom who values her intellect and personality. (**I:** 6–9)

*Paterson, Katherine. *The King's Equal*. Illustrated by Vladimir Vagin. HarperCollins, 1992. A prince in search of a princess to be his equal finds that he must prove to be her equal as well. (**I:** 7–10)

———. *Lyddie*. Penguin/Lodestar, 1991. In the mid-1800s, Lyddie becomes a factory girl in the mill town of Lowell, Massachusetts, to earn wages in an attempt to save the family farm. (**I:** 11–YA)

*Polacco, Patricia. *In Our Mothers' House*. Philomel, 2009. Two mothers lovingly raise a mixed-race family of adopted chil-dren in an idealized world. (**I:** K–7)

*Richardson, Justin and Peter Parnell. *And Tango Makes Three*. Illustrated by Henry Cole. Simon & Schuster, 2005. Two male penguins in NYC Central Zoo are given an egg to hatch and raise when it becomes obvious that they want to raise a young one together. (**I:** K–8)

*Setterington, Ken. *Mom and Mum are Getting Married*. Illustrated by Alice Priestley. Rosie celebrates the marriage of her Mum and Mom in a joyful celebration. (**I:** P–2)

*Willhoite, Michael. *Daddy's Roommate*. Alyson Wonderland, 1990. Following a divorce, Daddy lives with another man. (**I:** P–8)

Woodson, Jacqueline. *From the Notebooks of Melanin Sun*. Scholastic/Blue Sky, 1995. Melanin Sun faces the everyday challenges of a thirteen-year-old growing up, but life is com-plicated when he hears rumors about his mother's love for a woman of a different race. (**I:** 12–YA)

Exceptional Learners

Billingsley, Franny. *Well Wished*. Atheneum, 1997. When Nuria wishes at a magical well that wheelchair-bound Catty could have a body like hers, the two girls surprisingly end up in each other's body. (**I:** 9–12)

*Booth, B. D. *Mandy*. Illustrated by Jim Lamarche. Lothrop, Lee & Shepard, 1991. Mandy's musings about why she fears the dark and her wonderings about the sounds of the world allow readers to get inside the thinking of a child with hearing loss. (**I:** 6–8)

*Brown, Tricia. *Someone Special Just Like You*. Photographs by Fran Ortiz. Holt, 1982. Photographs and simple text addressed to the reader show children with various disabilities engaged in activities in which all children participate. (**I:** P–6)

Byars, Betsy. *Summer of the Swans*. Illustrated by Ted CoConis. Viking, 1970. Sara learns to cope with her feelings of resentment toward her younger brother, who is developmentally delayed. (**I:** 10–13)

*Cohen, Miriam. *See You Tomorrow, Charles*. Illustrated by Lillian Hoban. Greenwillow, 1983. In this book (part of a series), Charles is a child with vision loss in a class of first-graders who learn with and from each other. (**I:** 5–7)

Fleischman, Paul. *Mind's Eye*. Holt, 1999. Courtney is paralyzed at sixteen, and her eighty-eight-year-old roommate teaches her to rely on her mind in order to survive. (**I:** YA)

*Fleming, Virginia. *Be Good to Eddie Lee*. Illustrated by Floyd Cooper. Philomel, 1993. Christy learns to appreciate the sensitive heart of Eddie Lee, a child with Down syndrome, when he noisily tags along on a visit to the woods in search of frog eggs. (**I:** 7–9)

*Fraustino, Lisa Rowe. *The Hickory Chair*. Illustrated by Benny Andrews. Levine/Scholastic, 2001. An African American boy who is blind shares a loving relationship with his grandmother, and a special way of communication that his grandmother calls "blind sight." (**I:** 7–9)

*Haldane, Suzanne. *Helping Hands: How Monkeys Assist People Who Are Disabled*. Dutton, 1991. A teen boy with quadriplegia performs daily routines with the aid of a monkey. (**I:** 6–12)

*Krull, Kathleen. *Wilma Unlimited*. Illustrated by David Diaz. Harcourt Brace, 1997. Wilma overcomes wearing braces on her legs to become a winning Olympic runner. (**I:** 6–10)

Martin, Ann. *A Corner of the Universe*. Scholastic, 2002. In the summer of 1960, twelve-year-old Hattie meets her twenty-one-year-old Uncle Adam, whose mental and emotional disabilities result in behaviors that are both endearing and frightening. (**I:** 10 and up)

McMahon, Patricia. *Dancing Wheels*. Illustrated with photographs by John Godt. Houghton Mifflin, 2000. The Dancing Wheels dance company includes both "standing" dancers and "sitting" dancers, who travel across the country, performing with energy and commitment. (**I:** 8–12)

*Miller, Mary Beth, and George Ancona. *Handtalk School*. Four Winds, 1991. A guide to a day in a boarding school for children with hearing loss shows, through color photographs, the use of American Sign Language to communicate. (**I:** all ages)

Miller, Sarah. *Miss Spitfire: Reaching Helen Keller*. Atheneum, 2007. This biography describes how Annie Sullivan, a half-blind orphan, taught a deaf, blind, and completely incorrigible child to communicate. (**I:** 9–12)

*Millman, Isaac. *Moses Goes to School*. Foster/Farrar, 2000. Moses and other deaf children in his school are shown communicating in ASL and learning to read and write in standard English. American Sign Language accompanies the text and illustrations. See also *Moses Goes to a Concert* (1998) and *Moses Goes to the Circus* (2003). (**I:** P–8)

Philbrick, Rodman. *Freak the Mighty*. Blue Sky Press/Scholastic, 1993. A boy with physical size and might and a boy with intellectual brilliance are the book's main characters. Separately, each lacks what the other has, but together they become "Freak the Mighty." (**I:** 10–14)

Slote, Alfred. *Hang Tough, Paul Mather*. HarperCollins, 1973/1985. Twelve-year-old Paul's enthusiasm for baseball helps him through the difficulty of living with treatments for leukemia. (**I:** 9–11)

Trueman, Terry. *Stuck in Neutral*. HarperCollins, 2000. Narrator fourteen-year-old Shawn describes his exceptional ability to remember all he hears, but the world believes that he is retarded because cerebral palsy has left him with a total inability to control his muscles in any communicable way. (**I:** 12–YA)

*Willis, Jeanne and Tony Ross. *Susan Laughs*. Andersen Press, 1999. (UK) Brief text describes all the things that Susan does, and the closing illustration depicts Susan in a wheelchair, "like me and you." (I: P–7)

Resources

Austin, Patricia. (2010). Opening the Door to Tolerance. *Book Links, 19*(2), 42–45.

Cai, Mingshui. *Multicultural Literature for Children and Young Adults: Reflections on Critical Issues*. Greenwood, 2002.

Day, Frances Ann. *Latina and Latino Voices in Literature: Lives and Works. (updated and expanded edition)*. Greenwood, 2003.

Fox, Dana L., and Kathy G. Short. *Stories Matter: The Complexities of Cultural Authenticity in Children's Literature*. National Council of Teachers of English, 2003.

Friedberg, Joan Brest, June B. Mullins, and Adelaide Weir Sukiennik. *Portraying Persons with Disabilities: An Annotated Bibliography of Nonfiction for Children and Teenagers*. Bowker, 1992.

Henkin, Roxanne, and Junko Yokota. "Inclusive Reading: Literature Portraying Families with Gay and Lesbian Parents." *Democracy & Education, 13* (3) (1999): 60–61.

Jones, Guy W., and Sally Moomaw. *Lessons from Turtle Island: Native Curriculum in Early Childhood Classrooms*. Red Leaf Press, 2002.

Kruse, Ginny Moore, Kathleen T. Horning, and Megan Schliesman, with Tana Elias. *Multicultural Literature for Children and Young Adults: A Selected Listing of Books by and about People of Color, Volume 2*. Cooperative Children's Book Center, 1997.

Pellowski, Anne. *The Family Story-Telling Handbook: How to Use Stories, Anecdotes, Rhymes, Handkerchiefs, Paper, and Other Objects to Enrich Your Family Traditions*. Illustrated by Lynn Sweat. Macmillan, 1987.

———. *Hidden Stories in Plants: Unusual and Easy-to-Tell Stories from around the World Together with Creative Things to Do While Telling Them*. Macmillan, 1990.

Robertson, Debra. *Portraying Persons with Disabilities: An Annotated Bibliography of Fiction for Children and Teenagers*. Bowker, 1992.

Rochman, Hazel. *Against Borders: Promoting Books for a Multicultural World*. American Library Association, 1993.

Rudman, Masha Kabakow. *Children's Literature: An Issues Approach*. 3rd ed. Longman, 1995.

Schon, Isabel. *The Best of the Latino Heritage 1996–2002: A Guide to the Best Juvenile Books about Latino People and Cultures.* Scarecrow Press, 2003.

———. *Recommended Books in Spanish for Children and Young Adults: 2000–2004.* Scarecrow Press, 2004.

Seale, Doris, and Beverly Slapin. *A Broken Flute: The Native Experience in Books for Children.* Alta Mira Press, 2004.

Sims Bishop, Rudine. *Free Within Ourselves: The Development of African American Children's Literature.* Greenwood, 2007.

Sims Bishop, Rudine, and the Multicultural Booklist Committee, eds. *Kaleidoscope.* National Council of Teachers of English, 1995.

Slapin, Beverly, and Doris Seale. *Through Indian Eyes: The Native Experience in Books for Children.* American Indian Studies Center, University of California, 1998.

Smith, Henrietta M., ed. *The Coretta Scott King Awards: 1970–2004.* (4th ed.). American Library Association, 2009.

Tikvah: Children's Book Creators Reflect on Human Rights. Introduction by Elie Wiesel. Jacket Art by Leo and Diane Dillon. SeaStar/North-South Books, 2001.

Yokota, Junko. "Issues in Selecting Multicultural Children's Literature." *Language Arts 70* (1993): 156–67.

———, ed. *Kaleidoscope: A Multicultural Booklist for Grades K–8.* 3rd ed. National Council of Teachers of English, 2000.

———, and Bates, Ann. *Asian American Literature: Voices and Images of Authenticity.* In Darwin L. Henderson & Jill P. May (Eds.), *Exploring Culturally Diverse Literature for Children and Adolescents: Learning to Listen in New Ways.* Allyn & Bacon, 2005, pp. 323–335.

———, and Cai, Mingshui. (2002). "Social Justice in Children's Books." *Language Arts, 79* (5), 72–78.

———, and Frost, Shari. (2003). "Multiracial Characters in Children's Literature." *Book Links, 12* (3), 51–57.

———, and Martinez, Miriam. (2004). "Multicultural Audio Books: How Does the Reader Affect the Listeners' Sense of Culture?" *Book Links, 13* (3), 30–34.

References

Aronson, Marc. "Slippery Slopes and Proliferating Prizes." *Horn Book,* 2001.

Au, Kathryn H. *Literacy Instruction in Multicultural Settings.* Harcourt, 1993.

Banks, James. *Cultural Diversity and Education: Foundations, Curriculum, and Teaching.* Allyn & Bacon, 2000.

———. *An Introduction to Multicultural Education.* 2nd ed. Allyn & Bacon, 1999.

Bannerman, Helen. *The Story of Little Babaji.* Illustrated by Fred Marcellino. HarperCollins, 1996.

———. *The Story of Little Black Sambo.* HarperCollins, 1899.

Barrera, Rosalinda B., Verlinda D. Thompson, and Mark Dressman, eds. *Kaleidoscope: A Multicultural Booklist for Grades K–8.* 2nd ed. National Council of Teachers of English, 1997.

Bennett, William. "Education Secretary Bennett's Suggested List for Elementary-School Pupils." *Chronicle of Higher Education* (1988, September 14): B3.

Bishop, Claire Huchet. *The Five Chinese Brothers.* Illustrated by Kurt Wiese. Coward, 1938.

Brenner, Barbara, and Julia Takaya. *Chibi: A True Story from Japan.* Illustrated by June Otani. Clarion, 1999.

Browne, Anthony. *Piggybook.* Knopf, 1986.

Bruchac, Joseph. *Bowman's Store: A Journey to Myself.* Lee & Low, 1997/2001.

Bryan, Ashley. *The Dancing Granny.* Aladdin, 1987.

———. *Lion and the Ostrich Chicks and Other African Folk Tales.* Aladdin, 1986/1996.

———. *What a Morning! The Christmas Story in Black Spirituals.* Little Simon, 1987/1996.

Cai, Mingshui. "Can We Fly across Cultural Gaps on the Wings of Imagination? Ethnicity, Experience, and Cultural Authenticity." *The New Advocate* 8.1 (1995): 1–16.

———. "Multiple Definitions of Multicultural Literacy: Is the Debate Really Just 'Ivory Tower' Bickering?" *The New Advocate 11* (1998): 311–324.

———, and Rudine Sims Bishop. "Multicultural Literature for Children: Towards a Clarification of the Concept." *The Need for Story: Cultural Diversity in Classroom and Community.* Ed. Anne Haas Dyson and Celia Genishi. National Council of Teachers of English, 1994.

Chall, Jeanne S., Eugene Radwin, V. W. French, and C. R. Hall. "Blacks in the World of Children's Books." *The Black American in Books for Children.* 2nd ed. Ed. Donnarae MacCann and G. Woodard. Scarecrow, 1985, pp. 211–221.

Council on Interracial Books for Children. Special Issue on Chicano Materials. *Bulletin of the Council on Interracial Books for Children 5* (1975).

———. Special Issue on Puerto Rican materials. *Bulletin of the Council on Interracial Books for Children 4* (1974).

Delpit, Lisa D. "The Silenced Dialogue: Power and Pedagogy in Educating Other People's Children." *Harvard Educational Review 58* (1988): 280–298.

Galda, Lee. Personal communication, November 2000.

Gollub, Matthew. *Cool Melons Turn to Frogs! The Life and Poems of Issa.* Illustrated by Kazuko G. Stone. Lee & Low, 1998.

Grossman, Virginia, and Sylvia Long. *Ten Little Rabbits.* New York: Chronicle, 1991.

Hamilton, Virginia. *Anthony Burns: The Defeat and Triumph of a Fugitive Slave.* Laureleaf, 1988/1993.

———. "Everything of Value: Moral Realism in Literature for Children" (May Hill Arbuthnot Lecture). *Journal of Youth Services in Libraries 6* (Summer 1993): 363–377.

———. *In the Beginning: Creation Stories from Around the World.* Illustrated by Barry Moser. Harcourt, 1988.

———. "Laura Ingalls Wilder Medal Acceptance." *Horn Book* 71.4 (July/August 1995): 436–441.

———. *The Planet of Junior Brown.* Macmillan, 1971.

———. *Sweet Whispers, Brother Rush.* Putnam, 1982.

Harris, Violet J. "African American Children's Literature: The First One Hundred Years." *Journal of Negro Education 59* (1990): 540–555.

———. *Using Multicultural Literature in the K–8 Classroom.* Christopher-Gordon Publishers, 1997.

Henkin, Roxanne. "Who's Invited to Share?": Using Literacy to Teach for Equity and Social Justice. Heinemann, 1998.

———, ed. *Using Multiethnic Literature in the K–8 Classroom.* Christopher-Gordon Publishers, 1997.

Horning, K. T. (2008). An interview with Rudine Sims Bishop. *Hornbook, 84*(3), 247–259.

Jeffers, Susan. *Brother Eagle, Sister Sky: A Message from Chief Seattle.* Dial, 1991.

Kaplan, Esther. Personal communication, December 1995.

Khorana, Meena G. Editorial. *Bookbird* 34.4 (1996): 2–3.

Kruse, Ginny M., and Kathleen T. Horning, with Megan Schliesman. *Multicultural Literature for Children and Young Adults Vol. 2 1991–1996.* Cooperative Children's Book Center, 1997.

Larrick, Nancy. "The All-White World of Children's Books." *Saturday Review* (1965, September 11): 63–65.

Lester, Julius. *On Writing for Children & Other People.* Dial, 2004.

Little, Jean. *Little by Little: A Writer's Education.* Penguin, 1987.

———. "A Writer's Social Responsibility." *The New Advocate* 3.2 (1990): 79–88.

McCarty, Teresa L. "What's Wrong with Ten Little Rabbits?" *The New Advocate* 8.2 (1995): 97–98.

McCloskey, Robert. *Make Way for Ducklings.* Viking, 1941.

Melmed, Laura Krauss. "Little Oh: A Story Unfolds." *Book Links* (1999): 4–44.

Meltzer, Milton. "The Social Responsibility of the Writer." *The New Advocate* 2.3 (1989): 155–157.

Myers, Walter Dean. *Blues Journey.* Illustrated by Christopher Myers. Holiday House, 2003.

———. *Fast Sam, Cool Clyde, and Stuff.* Viking, 1975/1988.

———. *Glory Field.* Scholastic, 1994; Point, 1996.

———. *Monster.* HarperCollins, 2000.

———. *The Mouse Rap.* HarperTrophy, 1990/1992.

———. *Now Is Your Time! The African American Struggle for Freedom.* HarperCollins, 1991.

———. *Patrol: An American Soldier in Vietnam.* Illustrated by Ann Grifalconi. HarperCollins, 2002.

———. *Shadow of the Red Moon.* Point, 1997.

Nieto, Sonia. *Affirming Diversity.* 2nd ed. Longman, 1996.

———. "Puerto Ricans in Children's Literature and History Texts: A Ten-Year Update." *Bulletin of the Council on Interracial Books for Children 14* (1983).

Noll, Elizabeth. "Accuracy and Authenticity in American Indian Children's Literature: The Social Responsibility of Authors and Illustrators." *The New Advocate* 8.1 (1995): 29–43.

Pallas, A. M., G. Natriello, and E. L. McDill. "The Changing Nature of the Disadvantaged Population: Current Dimensions and Future Trends." *Educational Researcher* 18.5 (1989): 16–22.

Quiroa, Ruth. "Painting a Picture of Mexican American-themed Children's Literature: Trends, Issues and a Historical Overview." National-Louis University, Wheaton, IL. May 10, 2004.

Reimer, K. M. "Multiethnic Literature: Holding Fast to Dreams." *Language Arts* 69 (1992): 14–21.

Rochman, Hazel. *Against Borders: Promoting Books for a Multicultural World.* American Library Association, 1993.

Rollock, Barbara. *The Black Experience in Children's Books.* 2nd ed. New York Public Library, 1984.

Rudman, Masha Kabakow. *Children's Literature: An Issues Approach.* 3rd ed. Longman, 1995.

Say, Allen. *The Boy of the Three-Year Nap.* Houghton Mifflin, 1988.

———. *The Ink-Keeper's Apprentice.* Houghton Mifflin, 1979.

Schlesinger, Arthur M. *The Disuniting of America.* The Larger Agenda Publishers, 1991.

Schon, Isabel. *A Hispanic Heritage: A Guide to Juvenile Books about Hispanic People and Culture.* 3rd ed. Scarecrow, 1988.

Sims, Rudine. "Children's Books about Blacks: A Mid-Eighties Status Report." *Children's Literature Review 8* (1985): 9–13.

———. *Shadow and Substance: Afro-American Experience in Contemporary Children's Fiction.* 2nd ed. National Council of Teachers of English/American Library Association, 1982.

Sims Bishop, Rudine. "African American Literature for Children: Anchor, Compass, and Sail." *Perspectives 7* (1991): ix–xii.

———. "Mirrors, Windows, and Sliding Glass Doors." *Perspectives 6* (1990): ix–xi.

———. "Multicultural Literature for Children: Making Informed Choices." *Teaching Multicultural Literature in Grades K–8.* Ed. Violet Harris. Christopher-Gordon, 1992, pp. 37–54.

Smith, Henrietta M., ed. *The Coretta Scott King Awards: 1970–2004.* (3rd ed.). American Library Association, 2004.

Steptoe, John. *Stevie.* HarperTrophy, 1969/1986.

Tatum, Beverlee. *Why Are All the Black Kids Sitting Together in the Cafeteria?* St. Martins, 1999.

Trelease, Jim. *The New Read-Aloud Handbook.* 5th ed. Viking Penguin, 2001.

Tsutsui, Yoriko. *Anna's Secret Friend.* Illustrated by Akiko Hayashi. Viking, 1987.

Zion, Gene. *Dear Garbage Man.* Illustrations by Margaret Bloy Graham. Harper & Row, 1957.

5

International Literature

What Is International Literature?

J. K. Rowling, Margaret Mahy, Mitsumasa Anno, Polly Horvath, and Garth Nix are just a few
of the well-known authors who reside in countries outside North America. Their works form
a category of literature that can provide readers a different way of looking at the world, through
the eyes of observers who live or have lived in different corners of it. Traditionally, the term
"international literature" has meant books written and originally published outside the United
States or Canada (Tomlinson, 1998). Swiss author Johanna Spyri's **Heidi**, A.A. Milne's **Winnie
the Pooh**, and Juan Ramón Jiménez' **Platero and I** are examples of what were traditionally
considered international books. Some international books, such as **Heidi** and **Platero and I**,
were initially written in a language other than English and were translated for the U.S. audience. But in recent years, many books set entirely in other countries have been written by U.S.
or Canadian authors and published in North America (Freeman & Lehman, 2001). From a
United States perspective, these books, too, are considered international literature. Natalie
Savage Carlson's **The Family Under the Bridge** (set in Paris), Ann Cameron's **The Most
Beautiful Place in the World** (set in Guatemala), Frances Temple's **Taste of Salt** (set in

Haiti), and Deborah Ellis's ***The Breadwinner*** (set in Afghanistan) are examples of this other type of international book. Carlson, Cameron, and Temple are from the United States, and Ellis is Canadian.

Literature That Originates Outside of the United States

The first category of international literature is books written and published in countries outside the United States and translated into English (if originally written in another language). Christina Bjork's series about Linnea is an example of quality international literature that has been translated. ***Linnea in Monet's Garden*** was originally written in Swedish and then was translated into English and made available to the U.S. audience. German author Cornelia Funke's books ***The Thief Lord*** and ***Inkheart*** have recently sold well in North America in English translation. Mem Fox's ***Possum Magic*** is an English-language book originally published in Australia. In this fantasy about a possum made invisible by magic, the possum's grandmother tries to remember how to make him visible once again. Along the way, readers hear the names of the Australian cities to which Hush and Grandmother journey and the various Australian foods they eat at each stop. Importing books from abroad makes the works of the best authors and illustrators in the world available to children in the United States.

Literature about Other Countries, Written and Published in the United States

The second category of international literature is books set in a country other than the United States, but written and published in English by North American authors. These books are set in a "root country"— that is, a country from which some American children's ancestors originally came. Although most children will not have lived long, if ever, in the country of their family's origin, they still may feel a connection to it.

Although earlier editions of our textbook included this second category of books, we realize now that the climate for international interest has sufficiently improved to the point where defining the field more precisely and focusing within this chapter only on books that originate from outside of the United States is more meaningful for our current needs. Therefore, we will now only discuss books that *originated from outside the United States, and were later or simultaneously published in the United States (and translated into English if they were originally written in another language).*

The primary purpose for all international books is the same: to tell a compelling story. A benefit of international literature is that children have opportunities to read books published around the world. Many times, international literature opens the eyes of readers in the United States to circumstances in countries of which they have very limited knowledge. In Naidoo's book, ***The Other Side of Truth,*** a man speaks out against his government in Nigeria, and the bullet intended for him strikes his wife and kills her. The daughters are sent to London, but the mysterious disappearance of their uncle results in the girls being placed in foster care. When their father arrives in England through illegal means, twelve-year-old Sade must fight to keep him from being

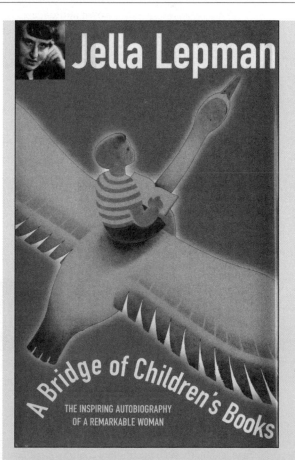

ILLUSTRATION 5.1   The Story of Nils is alluded to on the cover of *A Bridge of Children's Books,* the autobiography of Jella Lepman. It represents an international story well known around the world. (*A Bridge of Children's Books* by Jella Lepman. Cover courtesy of The O'Brien Press Ltd.)

Top Shelf 5.1

Depictions of War in Picture Books

Rose Blanche by Christophe Gallaz. Illustrated by Roberto Innocenti

Hiroshima no Pika written and illustrated by Toshi Maruki

The Donkey of Gallipoli: A True Story of Courage in World War I by Mark Greenwood Illustrated by Frané Lessac

deported. Circumstances such as these are not often the direct experience of readers in the United States. But through international literature, all readers can hear a first-hand telling and expand their understanding of the world around them.

Evolution of International Literature

The world continues to read the "cornerstone" stories from various countries: ***Pippi Longstocking*** from Sweden, ***Finn Family Moomintroll*** from Finland, ***The Wonderful World of Nils*** from Sweden, ***Pinocchio*** from Italy, ***A Bell for Ursli*** from Switzerland, ***Emil and the Detectives*** from Germany, and many others. Stories that have their roots in folklore, but were later written down and published as books, include the Anansi stories from various parts of Africa and Monkey King stories from China. Although these books have been translated into English, they are less known by children in North America as part of their literary heritage. However, countries that are more openly embracing of books that are in translation provide their readers with numerous editions that are readily available.

In many English-speaking countries, there is a wealth of literature for children and adolescents available, and the publishing industry has developed sufficiently to offer a rich legacy of quality books to young readers. This lack of need for new materials has precipitated the abundance of what is already at hand. This abundance—coupled with a seeming lack of urgency to learn about the world or to engage in international conversations—has led to an insular sensibility of focusing on literature that was exclusively written and created for our own audiences. Ultimately, it means that in the United States, there was very little literature available for our readers that originated from outside the country. In fact, less than 1 percent of books published in the United States have their roots outside the country (Tomlinson, 1998). Differences in sensibility of story structure, literary language, and thematic importance led to many books being rejected by publishers. Artistic sensibility and difference in interpretation of visual narrative also impacted what appealed to acquisition editors. And even at the level of details, there was rejection of word use and illustration that was viewed as "inappropriate." The United States is noted for its protective attitude toward the content of reading and viewing materials for children; this attitude is regarded as startling to individuals in other countries where showing the reality of life is viewed as natural. Details such as alcohol consumption (i.e., a can of beer in an urban street scene, the drinking of wine with a meal) or nudity (i.e., a bathing scene, breastfeeding an infant) were rejected and either removed or re-illustrated to adapt a book for U.S. audiences. Even vocabulary differences between British English and American English were changed (i.e., *lift – elevator, lorrie – truck*).

Various efforts have been made over the years for international literature to have its place in the United States. Committed editors have been making their way to the Bologna Book Fair, Frankfurt Book Fair, and other places where they seek books that are likely to appeal to readers in the United States or that the editors hope to introduce to new readers. Often, this has been done in the face of possible financial risk. In earlier eras, publishers were able to "balance the books" for the company when they knew that some books would make enough money to enable them to publish others that would fulfill the company's editorial vision and goals even though it was unlikely they would regain the revenue from the new books. A complicating factor is that few editors were able to read multiple languages well enough to make independent assessments of books from non-English language countries. The search for people who had language expertise, an understanding of the children's literature field, and the ability to make recommendations regarding the viability of a book's acceptance in a new country was easier for some languages than for others. Initial assessments were often made based on "rough translations" in which editors had to determine whether thorough translations would lead to better

Teaching Idea 5.2

Point It Out!

Sometimes, readers are not aware that a book originates outside their own country. One way to highlight the origin of a book is to note the information on the back flap of a book that states where the author and illustrator live and work. Other information, such as the details on the Library of Congress Cataloging in Publication information on the copyright page, explicitly state the original country of publication. Teachers who note such details and explain it to students are able to quickly note that the book is one that children in other countries are also reading. Using a map at this point to simply point to the country may visually help readers see the relative location of a country outside their own.

text. In those early post-war years, the profession as a whole sought to appreciate and reward such efforts; the American Library Association established the Margaret Batchelder Award to applaud publishers who provided the best translated book for readers in the United States.

The 1990s saw the conglomeration of publishing companies in which smaller, independent children's book publishers became entities within larger corporations. This move meant that the responsibility of overseeing financial decisions was no longer solely within the children's divisions; rather, it was viewed through the lens of financial viability from a different perspective. Each book was examined for its likelihood of sales, and editorial vision had to be fiscally responsible at the "individual" book level rather than at the "group of books published within each season" level. Publishers sought books they knew would sell and sales popularity became an increasingly dominant factor in acquisition decisions.

In more recent times, we have become progressively more aware of our need and desire for access to the wealth of good literature available around the world, a more international perspective for our young people to see and read about, and a commitment to making extra efforts to maintaining the purity of the artistic conceptualization of the original book.

Issues Related to International Literature

The primary areas of concern related to international literature are predominantly about *access*: that there are so few books that are translated into English, and that when they are, relatively few are published in the United States and only a rare few make it into children's hands. This is also the consequence of those who serve as gatekeepers, who make decisions about which books to review, purchase, and promote to readers. Just as in multicultural literature, the more different the experience, the more scaffolding and recommendation is required to successfully connect the material to new audiences.

A related issue regarding access has to do with *balance*. Regarding genre balance, most of the international books available in English are in the categories of folklore, historical fiction, and fantasy. Just as in multicultural literature, they lend an air of "long ago and far away," forgoing the idea that there are contemporary stories of realistic fiction that would allow us to take a peek into the lives of people in various parts of the world today. But even beyond genre balance, when considering what is available in terms of topics, there are certain topics that are more frequently made available from outside the United States. For example, many books about World War II have been imported, creating a wealth of perspectives, but skewing the numbers of books from outside the United States in terms of representing varying time periods and topics. And finally, the need for "balance" also implies the importance of understanding that no one book can fairly represent a country, and the more books of wide range that are made available, the better off the readers are in terms of trying to see the complexity of how books represent countries and their literature.

Another area of concern is in creating *relevance* of international books for a new audience. Some are concerned that references to details that are "foreign" to young children may make a book incomprehensible. For example, in Jackie French's ***Josephine Wants to Dance***, Josephine is a kangaroo who loves to dance, despite her younger brother Joey saying that "kangaroos don't wear tutus and they never wear silk ballet shoes." She remains determined, and ends up stepping in to fill the lead role when the prima ballerina twists her ankle. She

---

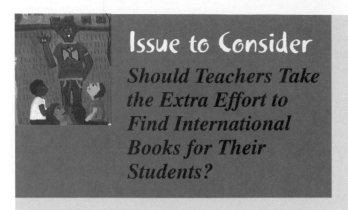

Go to the Extension Activities section of Chapter 5 in the MyEducationKit for your book and complete activity #1 to create a text set that includes international literature.

had learned to dance from and with the brolgas, lyrebirds, and emus, and practiced and practiced. This reference to animals unknown to young children in countries outside of Australia may feel like too much new information at one time, but the introduction to new concepts through a quality picture book can be a welcome introduction to things newly encountered. Thematically, this book works well when compared to Mary Hoffman's *Amazing Grace*, illustrated by Caroline Binch. In this realistic story, a young girl wants to be Peter Pan in the school play, but is told by some that she can't get the role; her belief that she can is rewarded when she wins the part through her hard work and determination. Both of these books originate outside the United States; the realistic fiction picture book is from the United Kingdom and requires less new background knowledge for readers in the United States. Introducing these two books together allows readers to make thematic connections of perseverance, hard work, and believing in yourself.

ILLUSTRATION 5.2   *Samir and Yonatan* by Daniella Carmi is a story of an Israeli boy and a Palestinian boy who end up side-by-side in a Jewish hospital in Israel. (Jacket art copyright © 2000 by Rafal Oblinski from *Samir and Yonatan* by Daniella Carmi. Scholastic Inc./Arthur A. Levine Books. Reprinted by permission.)

Criteria for Evaluating International Literature

With the exception of authenticity, the evaluation and selection issues previously discussed in connection with multicultural literature are also important for international literature originating outside the United States. Although many countries publish material that is about cultures other than their own, the books that are exported to other countries tend to be about native experiences. When one's own country is the setting, cultural authenticity is expected, as both author and illustrator have an insider perspective. Two crucial issues specific to international literature are the intended audience and the quality of the translation.

Intended Audience

An international book is originally written from the perspective of an author within the country, with readers in that country as the intended audience. Only later is the book taken abroad to other countries. When a book travels away from its intended audience, sometimes readers in the new audience need support to help them understand it. Teachers should consider these questions: Is the book geared specifically toward readers in the book's country of origin, or does it make the transition to a broader audience outside of that country? Who will be able to empathize and identify with the story? Books written in the United States and intended for

American children tend to include explanations of things that readers native to the country portrayed take for granted. Similarly, books originally written for readers in another country often assume understandings that only the original intended audience would have. Sometimes, misinterpretations may occur when details are not understood; at other times, an inability to pick up details doesn't detract from the reader's understanding of the story as a whole.

As an example, let's examine Akiko Hayashi's illustrations of the series of books about Anna. The pictures are laden with cultural details—mailboxes attached on the inside of the front door, slippers in the entryway, artificial flowers on the street light, a place where children wash their hands at the park. Even the way Anna steps on the back of her shoes shows she is rushing as she tries to discover the identity of her new friend in *Anna's Secret Friend.* Japanese children would pick up these details because they are very natural to their understanding of home and community. American children might not take particular note of these details or might find them interesting, but not different enough to interfere with their understanding of the story.

Sometimes, certain details in the original edition of a book that would be innately understood by the original audience are explained when the book is prepared in an international edition. Uri Orlev's Batchelder Award book *The Lady with the Hat* has two characters stopping for a meal while on a trip in a remote area of Palestine. Foods such as hummus, tahini, shashlik, kebab, baklava, and Turkish coffee are described for readers who are unfamiliar with them—for example, "small cakes filled with pistachio nuts and honey that were called baklava."

ILLUSTRATION 5.3 Details of daily life in Japan are depicted throughout the books of modern realistic fiction stories illustrated by Akiko Hayashi, a nominee for the Hans Christian Andersen Award. (*Anna's Secret Friend* by Yoriko Tsutsui, illustrated by Akiko Hayashi, 1987. Used by permission of Viking Juvenile, A Division of Penguin Young Readers Group, A Member of Penguin Group (USA) Inc., 345 Hudson Street, New York, NY 10014. All rights reserved.)

Translation

An issue of critical concern with international books is translation. When a book was originally published in a language other than English, the translator who makes it available to English-language readers plays an important role in the way the material is received by the new audience. The translator is as important as the author and illustrator in presenting the story. A skilled translator does not merely present the author's words in another language, but instead interprets the words, selecting ways to evoke images and emotions that reflect the author's original intent. The translator must consider several things:

- Creating a flow in the translated language, despite differences in the sentence structures of the two languages

- Balancing the amount of "foreign" information to maintain readability and reader attention while retaining the unique details that make the work authentic

- Explaining foreign situations that are unknown to readers while maintaining the pace of the original text

Even when a book is from another English-language country, some differences in language use are noticeable to U.S. readers. Should these differences be changed? When comprehension may suffer significantly, the answer is yes. But maintaining as much of the original language as possible is part of maintaining the authenticity of the book. In Mem Fox's book, *Shoes from Grandpa*, originally published in Australia, the family was enjoying a "barbie." A U.S. audience, unexposed to this name for a barbecue, might imagine the doll known as Barbie. The word was changed in this case. Yet in another of Mem Fox's books, *Possum Magic,* references to Australian foods such as "mornay, vegemite and pavlova" were maintained in the U.S. version. Although these words are unfamiliar to most American children, they do not interfere with an understanding of the story. With the words left in, the story remains true to the original context of the Australian culture. A benefit of this approach is that U.S. children are introduced to vocabulary that expands their knowledge of another country.

Teaching Idea 5.3
International Pen Pals

There are different ways to find opportunities to have international pen pals, including a personal connection to someone in a different country or a connection made through an Internet-based teacher/classroom exchange program such as ePals. Find a teacher and classroom in another country that would like to exchange a favorite picture book and send each other the book and a set of class responses to that book, done through some sort of artwork. For example, students may want to draw a favorite scene from a book, or create bookmarks that depict a character from that book. It does not matter whether the exchange is in the same language, as long as the teachers can communicate with one another. It may be an opportunity to add some books in languages other than in English to the class or school library!

Teacher/Librarian Partnership
Making International Books Accessible

Because some international books are difficult to obtain, your own school or public library may not have them on the shelves. Librarians are prepared to request interlibrary loans from outside their libraries, and serve a critical role in making hard-to-obtain books more accessible to readers. Depending on the policy of the inter-library loan, books can be sent from another library in the system, even across city, state, and country borders! Teachers and librarians working together can support one another in making international books more readily available by promoting them to their students.

It does require extra effort to make international books accessible to U.S. audiences, but the benefits gained from including international books in children's repertoire make the extra effort worthwhile. One notable example of an international book is Mitsumasa Anno's *All in a Day*. A young child is on a deserted island, somewhere near the International Date Line. Each double-page spread shows this child in the center section, with text to one side. Across the top and the bottom of the spread are depictions of what New Year's Day might be like for children in eight different countries; each picture is by an illustrator from that country. Each time the reader turns a page, three hours have passed. In the preface to the book, Anno asks readers to consider the fact that while some children sleep, others play, and while some swim, others build snowmen. He points out that differences exist around the world in homes, clothes, languages, and other aspects of life, but he also notes that there are some things that remain the same around the world, such as facial expressions, the sounds of laughing or crying, and the moon and the sun in the sky. Anno and his team of illustrators offer a note of optimism. Their hope—and ours as well—is that by the time the children of today grow up, the world will have become a better place. This book exemplifies a sense of world community from a child's point of view. Although the book was originally published in Japanese, the composition of the illustration team and the theme make this book truly international.

ILLUSTRATION 5.4 Mitsumasa Anno created *All in a Day* because he believes that world understanding begins with children imagining the lives of other children around the world. (Cover from *All In a Day* by Mitsumasa Anno, copyright © 1985 by Kuso-Kobo, Raymond Briggs, Ron Brooks, Gian Calvi, Eric Carle, Leo & Diane Dillon, Akiko Hayashi, Nicolai Ye. Popov, and Zhu Chengliang. Used by permission of Philomel Books, A Division of Penguin Young Readers Group, A Member of Penguin Group (USA) Inc., 345 Hudson Street, New York, NY 10014. All rights reserved.)

Major Authors and Illustrators of International Literature

Mitsumasa Anno

Mitsumasa Anno, a Japanese author and illustrator, is a world-renowned contributor to the picture book field. He is best known for his wordless "journey" books, mathematical game books, and books with playful twists of visual perceptions. Anno's highly detailed and imaginative work appeals to all ages because his books offer multiple levels of humor and intrigue. His books combine technical sophistication with creative text, illustrations, and design. Many of his books also include detailed historic, scientific, or mathematical information for adult readers who share them with children.

Anno delights in including mathematical and scientific details to make learning these ways of thinking enjoyable and interesting. In *Anno's Counting House,* the reader first sees all ten children living in the house on the left side of the double-page spread, and then watches them move into the house on the right one by one. Children can see who has moved and what belongings the child has taken, but they can also note that the total number of children shown in both houses is always ten.

Anno also manipulates visual perception in a way that makes the physically impossible seem probable. For example, ***Upside-Downers: More Pictures to Stretch the Imagination*** is a book that bends the "rules" for enjoying books. A pair of jokers and the four kings leave a deck of cards, but nobody can tell what's up and what's down. In the author's postscript, Anno suggests that a child can sit opposite a parent and they can read the book to each other at the same time—or a child can read alone, turn the book around, and then read it from the other direction, upside down.

Anno's Journey begins a series of books that are filled with images of the countries he visits. Historical events, literary figures, and cultural markers fill the pages of the wordless books simply titled ***Anno's U.S.A., Anno's Italy,*** and ***Anno's Britain.*** On the double-page spread depicting New York City in ***Anno's U.S.A.,*** readers will delight in discovering the surprises embedded in the art: the Macy's Thanksgiving Day Parade with floats representing characters from *Where the Wild Things Are,* Tarzan, and the New York Public Library lions; Marilyn Monroe standing on a street corner with the wind sweeping her skirt up; and Native Americans selling Manhattan island.

Anno was born and raised in a small town in western Japan. He taught art at an elementary school in Tokyo for ten years before becoming a full-time artist. In addition to his numerous picture books, Anno creates many other works of art such as paintings, calendars, and stationery. In 1985, he was awarded the Hans Christian Andersen Award for Illustration, given by the International Board on Books for Young People to honor an illustrator who has made a significant contribution to children's literature worldwide.

Ana Maria Machado

Born in 1941 in Rio de Janeiro, Ana Maria Machado is widely recognized as one of the most influential writers not only in her native Brazil and in South America, but around the world. She began her career as a painter and later as a journalist, but by 1969, she began to focus on writing for children. "I belong to that generation of writers who began to write during the military dictatorship, as children's literature, alongside poetry and song texts, were amongst the few literary forms with which, through the poetic and symbolic use of language, you could make the ideas of a joie de vivre, individual freedom and respect for human rights

Top Shelf 5.2

Stories of Friendships

Manolita Four Eyes by Elvira Lindo

Secret Letters, 0-10 by Susie Morgenstern

The Friends by Kazumi Yumoto

ILLUSTRATION 5.5   Knowledge of history and popular culture will enable readers to find many interesting details in this double-page picture of New York City by Anno. (Cover from *Anno's USA* by Mitsumasa Anno, copyright © 1983 by Kuso-kobo. Translation copyright © 1983 by Philomel Books. Used by permission of Philomel Books, A Division of Penguin Young Readers Group, A Member of Penguin Group (USA) Inc., 345 Hudson Street, New York, NY 10014. All rights reserved.)

known" (10th International Literature Festival, Berlin <http://www.literaturfestival.com/
bios1_3_6_456.html>). Clearly, her writing has political themes and social implications that
prompt readers to think about their world; but Machado focuses on telling a story, and trusts
her young readers to be able to think for themselves.

Perhaps her best known picture book abroad is *Nina Bonita*, in which a white rabbit
falls in love with a dark-skinned girl, asking her to reveal her beauty secrets. The rabbit goes
on to marry a black rabbit, and they produce children of various mixes of their colors.

In *From Another World,* Machado explores Brazil's history through the device of a
contemporary setting with the ghost story revealing historic experiences. When Mariano's
mother and friend purchase a historic homestead and convert it into an inn, the ghost of
a nineteenth century slave girl appears and relays the story of her family's demise, appealing for help to Mariano and his friends. Similarly, *Me in the Middle* relies on elements
of fantasy to connect the past, present and future. Bel is nearly 13, and finds that she hears
the voice of her grandmother, as well as that of her future great granddaughter, and both
offer advice as they compete for Bel's attention while Bel learns to live in the present.

Ana Maria Machado's books for children and adults number over a hundred, and have
been translated and published in seventeen countries. The Hans Christian Andersen Award
was bestowed on her in 2000, in worldwide recognition of her contribution to children's
literature.

Beverley Naidoo

Beverley Naidoo was born in 1943 and raised in South Africa, and grew up with the privileges of being a white person in an apartheid country. Looking back as an adult, she realized that she had been raised to accept that white people were "superior" because of the rights
they had—that there was "no justice, no equality and no democracy" for the black people
of the country, despite the legacy of their ancestry in the land. Exposed to new ways of seeing the laws of her land while in college, she became part of the resistance movement, and
ended up spending eight weeks in jail at the age of twenty-one. Shortly thereafter, she went
into exile and moved to England, marrying another exile with whom she could not have lived
and raised children had they stayed in South Africa because it forbade marriage between
black and white people.

Naidoo exemplifies how stories are often best told by a person who has experienced the
situation first hand, and has developed a deep sensitivity on a topic through having lived that
experience. Her book, *Journey to Jo'burg: A South African Story,* tells of how Naledi travels to Jo'burg to deliver the news of her baby sister's near-death from an illness to her mother,
who works and lives in the home of white people. The circumstances described in the story
accurately reflect a relatively recent period in South African history. For political reasons,
this book could not have been published in South Africa initially; in fact, when the author
sent copies of the book to nieces still living in South Africa, they were "seized and banned"
by the government that was still operating under apartheid. *Chain of Fire* is the sequel to
Journey to Jo'burg. In this story, Naledi and Tori discover that the painted number on their
door identifies that they are being moved from their neighborhood to "home lands," a move
of displacing Black people at the will of the government.

Naidoo's novels explore themes of family, identity, conflict, and survival, mostly within
the context of political racism and challenges for freedom, and set in South Africa. In the
Carnegie Medal winning book, *The Other Side of Truth*, she explores the plight of two
Nigerian children seeking asylum from political oppression as refugees in London. Yet life
as a refugee in London is not at all what was anticipated when their tragically widowed father
sent Sade and her brother Femi because he feared for their lives. *Web of Lies* is the sequel,
exploring the impact of gang influence on Femi.

Beverley Naidoo is also the author of a number of picture books that explore similar
themes of identity, relationships, and equity in ways that are appropriate for very young children; however, most are not published in the U.S. She teamed up with her daughter, Maya,
to write *Baba's Gift,* set in South Africa, and explored the present-day lives of family relationships through the story of two sisters who play with (and lose) their boat, a gift their
grandfather has made for them.

Authors from Past Decades

Many authors and illustrators from decades past have made a mark on children's literature around the world. Those who have defined the field in this way include: Astrid Lindgren, Johanna Spyri, Erik Kästner, and many others. Some we may know better because their work was originally written in English and perhaps was more accessible: A. A. Milne, P. L. Travers, James Barrie.

In contemporary times, authors and illustrators of international recognition can often be identified through awards such as the IBBY (International Board on Books for Young People) Hans Christian Andersen Award, given by an international jury to an author and an illustrator nominated by their national section biannually. In addition to one winner in each category, honor winners are also named, and each nominee is considered a "winner" from each of their countries, an indication of their high regard by their own country. A complete list can be found in the Appendix and on the IBBY website at www.ibby.org.

We have chosen to list authors and illustrators by their countries of origin; some are well known and are sometimes featured within the genre chapters (i.e., Philip Pullman, Cornelia Funke, Roald Dahl, Eva Ibbotson, Diana Wynne Jones, Brian Jacques, J. K. Rowling—all of whom happen to be fantasy writers!)

Countries from Which There Are Books in English Available in the United States

Australia: Jeannie Baker, Graeme Base, Mem Fox, Jackie French, Bob Graham, Robert Ingpen, Shaun Tan, Patricia Wrightson, Markus Zusak

Canada: Brian Doyle, Deborah Ellis, Sarah Ellis, Polly Horvath, Jean Little, Tim Wynne-Jones, Paul Yee

Ireland: Eoin Colfer, P. J. Lynch, Kate Thompson, Martin Waddell

New Zealand: Joy Cowley, Margaret Mahy

United Kingdom: David Almond, Quentin Blake, Anthony Browne, Aidan Chambers, Lauren Child, Roald Dahl, Michael Foreman, Shirley Hughes, Hilary McKay, David McKee, Philip Pullman, J. K. Rowling

---

Countries from Which There Are Books Translated into English

Austria: Linda Wolfsgruber, Lisbeth Zwerger

Belgium: Kitty Crowther

Brazil: Ana Maria Machado, Lygia Bojunga Nunes

Czech Republic: Kveta Pacovská

Denmark: Svend Otto S., Bjarne Reuter

Finland: Tove Jansson

France: Tomi Ungerer

Germany: Michael Ende, Wolf Erlbruch, Peter Härtling, Erich Kästner

Greece: Eugene Trivizas

Israel: Uri Orlev

Italy: Roberto Innocenti

Japan: Suekichi Akaba, Mitsumasa Anno, Akiko Hayashi, Michio Mado, Keizaburo Tejima, Kazuo Yumoto

Netherlands: Guus Kuijer, Max Velthuijs

Russia: Nicolai Popov

Slovenia: Lila Prap

South Africa: Niki Daly, Piet Grobler, Beverley Naidoo

Sweden: Astrid Lindgren, Barbro Lindgren, Eva Eriksson

Switzerland: Alois Corigiet, Etienne Delessert, Jürg Schubiger

Ask the Author
Beverley Naidoo

Favorite Books as a Child

The big book of my childhood was *The Diary of Anne Frank*. It told me that literature was real and could be powerfully

connected to life. I knew that if I had been born in Europe, I too would probably have been killed because my mother was Jewish. But there was a terrible irony in my admiration for Anne. I was a white child in a racist society where white South Africans committed their own crimes against humanity. I cried over Anne without seeing the crimes all around me. It was only years later that I began to understand that Anne was not just writing about racism against Jews. She condemned racism itself—against anyone. I still love the freshness and brave outspokenness of her voice, her despising of hypocrisy and passion for justice—for everyone.

You were born in South Africa during the apartheid, and raised in a world where "white privilege" was the norm. What compels you to write the stories you do about South Africa, racism, and politics?

As a child, I believe I was schooled, not educated. I grew up very blinkered to the world around me. I cried over *The Diary of Anne Frank* without realizing that there were atrocities all around me. When I came to the age of reason and began to be challenged to see the world around me for what it was, I felt angry that the adult society, including teachers, had not encouraged me to question. Then, finding myself in exile in England, how could I tell my own children and the children of South Africa the stories of what was really going on? I have always loved story and thought of it as the way to opening up the world.

The issues I write about (the breaking up of families, war, and so forth) are very fundamental issues, not just to do with South Africa. My first novel was set in South Africa, but its meaning carries across time and place. It resonates with witness literature from other places; for example, Mildred Taylor's work, set in

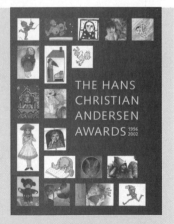

ILLUSTRATION 5.6

(Book cover, *Hans Christian Andersen Awards* 1956–2002, copyright 2002 IBBY (www.ibby.org). Reprinted by permission.)

PEARSON
myeducationkit

Go to the Extension Activities section of Chapter 5 in the MyEducationKit for your book and complete activity #2 to learn about an international literature award winner.

Awards for International Literature
The Hans Christian Andersen Award

The International Board on Books for Young People (IBBY) established the Hans Christian Andersen Award in 1956. The purpose of this international award is to honor an author who has made a significant contribution to children's literature; an award for illustrators has been offered since 1966. The entire body of work by an author or an illustrator is considered, and national IBBY chapters nominate an author and an illustrator from their country. This award is given every two years at the IBBY World Congress, which is held in various locations throughout the world. Past U.S. winners include author Meindert DeJong in 1962, illustrator Maurice Sendak in 1970, author Scott O'Dell in 1972, author Paula Fox in 1978, author Virginia Hamilton in 1992, and author Katherine Paterson in 1998. Some winners from other countries have had books published in the United States, including Astrid Lindgren from Sweden, Svend Otto S. from Denmark, Suekichi Akaba and Mitsumasa Anno from Japan, Lygia Bojunga Nunes from Brazil, Patricia Wrightson and Robert Ingpen from Australia, Lisbeth Zwerger from Austria, and Anthony Browne from England. A complete list of past winners can be found in the Appendix.

the United States but fundamentally about the same issues, spoke to me.

Books are like a window onto the world, and writers can invite us in. The important thing to me is to say that not only is this person's pain important but also to begin to connect us. Some of my books, such as *The Other Side* and *Web of Lies*, are largely set in London. But the fundamental themes of families and dislocation carry across time and place. The universal story of building walls by the "haves" who think they can ignore the "have nots" on the other side is what I care about. The building of these walls is not going to be the solution.

Witness literature is a genre of circumstance, of time and place. It is literature that connects umbilically with the society; in other words, it is not just literature about characters (stories about self) but about how characters connect to wider society (stories that examine an individual person's consciousness as it relates to the larger society). My writing especially is about experiences that fracture society. Although individuals have the experiences, what they go through reflects issues and movements in that wider society. Much more African literature is written from a witness literature perspective than that which emanates from Western industrialized countries. Witness literature is about seeing things, observing and noting what is happening in this human condition so that you can't say, "I didn't know." It is a dramatic story and a personal story that is contextualized to relate to larger perspectives.

I always consider the questions, "Who is telling the story, and whose story is it?" It takes a tremendous amount of sensitivity, awareness, and research to know what you don't know.

I agree that white writers do not have that sense of firsthand detail and can't write it in that way that a person from the culture can, but a white writer can enter a story in a different way. We have to consider to what extent we can get into each other's lives; can we imagine each other's lives—whether it is a difference of class, culture, geography or some other factor. The key is authenticity.

Beverley Naidoo grew up in South Africa under the apartheid system. An active resister to apartheid, she lived in her home country until departing to study at the University of York in England. There she began writing in exile and in 1985 published her first children's book, the award-winning *Journey to Jo'burg*, which was dedicated to her nanny's two daughters who died from diphtheria because only white people were inoculated at the time. *Journey to Jo'burg* was banned in South Africa until 1991. Beverley Naidoo has taught primary and secondary school in London and worked as an Advisor for English and Cultural Diversity in Dorset. She has a Ph.D. in exploring issues of racism with young people through literature and works tirelessly to promote children's entitlement to grow up free from racism and injustice. Her novel *The Other Side of Truth* won the prestigious Carnegie Medal.

The Astrid Lindgren Memorial Award

Astrid Lindgren, author of such famous books as ***Pippi Longstocking*** and ***Ronia, the Robber's Daughter,*** is Sweden's best known author for children. This award was established to honor her memory and as a gift from the people of Sweden to the world of international children's literature as an encouragement for reading. It carries a significant monetary award of five million Swedish crowns and is the largest monetary award for children's literature in the world; it is the second largest literary prize in general. Because of its broad goals, not only are authors eligible, but also illustrators, storytellers, and individuals or organizations that promote reading. In fact, in its first several years, among the winners have been noted U.S. illustrator/author Maurice Sendak, U.S. author Katherine Paterson, Austrian author Christine Nöstlinger, U.K. author Philip Pullman, Japanese illustrator Ryoji Arai, the Venezuelan reading promotion organization Banco del libro and Australian author Sonya Hartnett.

The Mildred Batchelder Award

The Mildred Batchelder Award was established in 1966 by the American Library Association's Association of Library Services to Children (ALSC) to promote international exchange of books for young people; it has been given to a U.S. publisher annually since

ILLUSTRATION 5.7 Astrid Lindgren Memorial Award is a major international award in children's literature named in honor of the famous Swedish author of many books, including *Pippi Longstocking*. (Cover from *Pippi Longstocking* by Astrid Lindgren, illustrated by Lauren Child, 2007. Used by permission of Viking Juvenile, A Division of Penguin Young Readers Group, A Member of Penguin Group (USA) Inc., 345 Hudson Street, New York, NY 10014. All rights reserved.)

ILLUSTRATION 5.8 Roberto Innocenti, world-renowned and winner of the Hans Christian Andersen Award for Illustration, teams with Christophe Gallaz to tell a story not usually found in picture books in the English language, depicting war, Holocaust victims, and death. (Cover, *Rose Blanche* by Christophe Gallaz, illustrated by Roberto Innocenti. © Creative Education, an imprint of the Creative Company, Mankato, MN. Reprinted by permission.)

To check your comprehension on the content covered in this chapter, go to the MyEducation-Kit for your book and complete the Study Plan for Chapter 5. Here you will be able to take a chapter quiz and receive feedback on your answers.

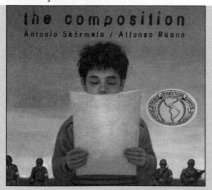

ILLUSTRATION 5.9 In *The Composition* by Antonio Skarmeta, illustrated by Alfonso Ruano, students read about military dictatorship and what it means to the lives of children in such countries. (From *The Composition*. Text copyright 1998 by Antonio Skarmeta. Illustrations copyright 2000 by Alfonso Ruano. With permission from Groundwood Books. www.groundwoodbooks.com.)

1968, unless no book is deemed worthy in a particular year. The award is named in honor of a former executive director of the ALSC. Books originally published in a foreign language in a foreign country and translated and published in the United States in the year preceding the award are considered. The citation is given to publishers to recognize their commitment to bringing books from abroad and making them available to young people in this country. With the exception of a few picture books, including the 1983 winner *Hiroshima No Pika* by Toshi Maruki and the 1987 winner *Rose Blanche* by Roberto Innocenti, most books are novels for older children. A complete list of past winners can be found in Appendix A.

The White Ravens Award

The International Youth Library in Munich, Germany, annually names books from around the world that have a universal theme and exceptional or innovative artistic and literary style and design. The books are noted in the following ways:

- *Special Mention:* Books to which the language specialists at the International Youth Library wish to draw special attention.

- *International Understanding:* Books that have content that is likely to contribute to understanding among cultures and people; such books are most likely to fit the mission under which Jella Lepman founded the library.

- *Easily Understandable:* Books for which the text is easy to understand but the content appeals to older readers, making such books particularly important for foreign language collections in libraries around the world.

These books are notable in that they are considered with one set of criteria, but across languages and cultures in their original version. The list is announced annually at the Bologna Children's Book Festival and is on exhibit at the library in Munich afterward. The complete list of past winners can be linked, with annotation, through the website of the International Children's Digital Library. The online catalogue includes nearly 4000 annotations for books from over 80 countries in 60 languages, published since 1993 and can be accessed at: *<http://www.icdlbooks.org/servlet/WhiteRavens>*

Other International Book Awards

Many countries have book awards equivalent to the Caldecott and Newbery Medals. Great Britain has the Kate Greenaway Medal and the Carnegie Medal. Canada has the Amelia Frances Howard-Gibbon Medal and the Canadian Children's Book of the Year award. Australia has the Picture Book of the Year award and the Australian Children's Book of the Year for Young Readers award. The major book awards given by other English-language countries are included in Appendix A.

Outstanding International Books for Children

Each year, a committee of USBBY (United States Board on Books for Young People) members selects approximately 25 outstanding books that they want to feature and recommend to children and young people and that are published in the United States. Many of these books come from countries in which they were published in English originally—the United Kingdom, Ireland, Canada, Australia, and so on. Others were originally published in various languages, but have been translated and are made available in English in the United States now. These titles are announced at the USBBY meeting at the American Library Association's Midwinter Conference each year, and annotated and recommended in *School Library Journal*'s February issue. The annual lists are also available in bookmark format at *www.usbby.org*.

Experiences for Further Learning

1. Select a theme for which you will select books across country origins. Try to pick a broad theme that can be interpreted in many ways, such as "effects of war," or "immigration," or "international boundary crossing." Or you can pick a theme that is universal enough to comprise books that are not necessarily about being from a specific country, such as "intergenerational relationship," or "bedtime stories," or "coming of age." Your selection of books should include several different countries, and show different ways of looking at your theme. When possible, include books across genre lines as well so that informational books and poetry are included along with works of fiction.

2. Read a variety of international books. Select one for which you can find a "partner book(s)" that you already know. Think of ways in which you can make connections between your known book and your new book, taking into consideration the differences and similarities that exist in the two books. Are any of the differences due to differences of country origin, or to other factors? Plan ways in which you might be able to support children who are reading the "partnered" books.

3. Read a variety of international books that have won international awards. You may want to begin with winners of the Batchelder Award and those on the Outstanding International Books for Children list, as those books are readily available in English in the United States. Consider ways in which you can incorporate the reading aloud of these books, or passages from longer works, to introduce them to students. Keep in mind that the more a book is different from their past reading materials, the more they will need an adult to scaffold the new book experience for them.

ILLUSTRATION 5.10
(USBBY Logo. Reprinted by permission of the United States Board on Books for Young People, Inc.)

Now go to Chapter 5 in the MyEducationKit (www.myeducationkit.com) for your book, where you can:

■ Find learning outcomes for Chapter 5.

■ Access the Children's Literature Database for your own exploration.

■ Complete Assignments and Activities that can help you more deeply understand the chapter content.

■ Extend knowledge with content-specific Web Links.

■ Deepen and apply content understanding with Extension Activities.

■ Check your comprehension on the content covered in the chapter by going to the Study Plan. Here you will be able to take a chapter quiz and receive feedback on your answers.

■ Find the following updated appendices: Major Children's Book Awards, Children's Magazines, Professional Organizations, Children's Book Publishers' Addresses, Book Selection Aids, and Children's Literature Web Sites.

Recommended Books

* indicates a picture book; **I** indicates interest level (P = preschool, YA = young adult)

International literature can also be found at the end of other chapters. All titles included here are available in English. (Many international books have also been recommended within the various genre chapters.)

*Aldana, Patsy (ed.). *Under the Spell of the Moon: Art for Children from the World's Great Illustrators.* Groundwood, 2004. (Canada) This collection includes illustrators representing more than 25 countries, accompanied by poetry or brief text bilingually presented in the illustrator's own language and in English. Katherine Paterson's introduction describes the vision of Jella Lepman in founding IBBY (International Board on Books for Young People). (**I:** all ages)

*Anno, Mitsumasa. *Anno's Journey.* Philomel, 1977. (Japan). This wordless book depicts a rider crossing Europe, encountering various scenes from famous paintings, children's games and stories, and historical events. The detail-filled double spreads offer glimpses that add up to an overall sense of a traveler, looking into various parts of Europe. (**I:** all ages)

———. *Math Games, I – III.* Philomel, 1987, 1989, 1991. (Japan). Various mathematical concepts are explored playfully and imaginatively, and the focus is on intuitive understanding of mathematics rather than on accuracy of answers. (**I:** P–9)

*Bae, Hyun-Joo. *New Clothes for New Year's Day.* Kane/Miller, 2007. (Korea) A young girl in Korea enthusiastically prepares for Lunar New Year and dons her new "traditional" clothes. (**I:** P–7)

*Beake, Lesley. *Home Now.* Illustrated by Karin Littlewood. Charlesbridge, 2007. (UK) An AIDS orphaned child in a South African township relates to an orphaned baby elephant and comes to realize that her aunt is providing "home now." Author's Note helps provide additional support information on the AIDS crisis. (**I:** K–7)

*Berner, Rotraut Susanne. *In the Town All Year 'Round.* Translated by Neeltje Konings & Nick Elliott. Chronicle, 2008. (Germany) Wordless book of illustrations invites viewers to follow characters in vignettes within larger scenes, with various activities that change by seasons. (**I:** P–6)

*Bjork, Christina. *Linnea in Monet's Garden.* Illustrated by Lena Anderson. Farrar, Straus, & Giroux, 1987. (Sweden) Linnea visits impressionist painter Claude Monet's home and garden in Giverny, France, and readers learn about his art. (**I:** 9–12)

*Baasansuren, Bolormaa. *My Little Round House.* Adapted by Helen Mixter. Groundwood, 2009. (Japan) Set in Mongolia, this book portrays the nomadic lifestyle of Jilu's first year from his point of view. (**I:** P–6)

*Brenner, Barbara, and Julia Takaya. *Chibi: A True Story from Japan.* Illustrated by June Otani. Clarion, 1996. (Japan) In a story reminiscent of McCloskey's *Make Way for Ducklings,* a wild duck family seeks a safe home in the Imperial Palace moat in downtown Tokyo. (**I:** P–8)

*Burningham, John. *It's a Secret.* Candlewick, 2009. (UK) Marie Elaine wonders, "Where do cats go at night?" Seeing Malcolm, her cat, all dressed up in fancy clothes, she asks where he is going. He replies that "It's a secret" but she gets herself invited to go along and join in the festivities. Mixed media illustrations of paints, pencils and collage create a visual treat. (**I:** P–7)

*Campbell, Nicola I. *Shin-chi's Canoe.* Illustrated by Kim LaFave. Groundwood, 2008. (Canada) Shi-shi-etko prepares her six-year-old brother for the strength he will need to retain his spirit as they are put on a cattle truck to go to a mandatory residential school for Native children in Canada (as was also done in the United States). A purposeful story, it describes the injustice done to Native people, the separation of family members, and the loss of culture and language they were forced to endure. (**I:** 1–3)

Carroll, Lewis. *Alice in Wonderland.* Illustrated by Lisbeth Zwerger. Penguin, 2007. (Switzerland) The classic tale of fantasy in which Alice embarks on a magical adventure has been illustrated by world famous artist, Lisbeth Zwerger in her signature style and palette. (**I:** 9–12)

Carter, Anne Laurel. *The Shepherd's Granddaughter.* Groundwood, 2008. (Canada) Amani is a Muslim teen in Palestine, following the family tradition of tending sheep with her grandfather. When Israeli settlers threaten their lifestyle, her father takes a militant response while she struggles to make sense of her changing world. (**I:** 10–13)

*Daly, Niki. *Jamela's Dress.* Farrar, Straus, & Giroux, 1999. (South Africa) Jamela can't resist playing with her mother's new fabric, intended for a wedding. See also: *Happy Birthday, Jamela* (2006) (**I:** P–8)

*De Déu Prats, Joan. *Sebastian's Roller Skates.* Illustrated by Francesc Rovira. Kane/Miller, 2005. (Spain) Sebastian is a shy boy who gains confidence when he finds a pair of abandoned roller skates and learns how to use them. (**I:** K–8)

Ellis, Deborah. *Three Wishes: Palestinian and Israeli Children Speak.* Frances Lincoln, 2007. (Canada) Ellis shares the viewpoints of Palestinian and Israeli youth, age 8 to 18, who describe three wishes for their lives amidst the tension and war they live in. (**I:** 11–YA)

*Foreman, Michael. *Mia's Story: A Sketchbook of Hopes and Dreams.* Candlewick, 2006. (UK) Set in the Andes, Mia and her family live near the city dump and each day, they gather usable items that they then take into the city to sell. (**I:** 8–10)

*Fox, Mem. *Possum Magic.* Illustrated by Julie Vivas. Harcourt, 1991. (Australia) Hush is an invisible possum whose request to Grandma Poss to make her visible again leads them on a quest, searching Australian cities for Australian foods for the solution. (**I:** P–8)

*French, Jackie. *Diary of a Wombat.* Illustrated by Bruce Whatley. Clarion, 2003. (Australia) Diary entries describe a wombat day: slept, slept, ate grass, scratched, ate grass, slept. When humans move in, the wombat discovers that they make good pets and are easily trainable to provide carrots or rolled oats upon demand. (**I:** P–7)

*———. *Joesephine Wants to Dance.* Illustrated by Bruce Whatley. HarperCollins, 2006. (Australia) Josephine the kangaroo loves to dance, and is able to take what she has learned from the brolgas, lyrebirds, and emus to fill the lead role when the prima ballerina twists her ankle. (**I:** P–7)

Funke, Cornelia. *The Thief Lord.* Translated from German by Oliver Latsch. Chicken House/Scholastic, 2002. (Germany) A thirteen-year-old "Thief Lord" serves as a leader for a group of runaway and homeless children in Venice. (**I:** 10 and up)

*Gallaz, Christophe, and Roberto Innocenti. *Rose Blanche.* Illustrated by Roberto Innocenti. Creative Education, 1985. (Italy) In a story set in World War II Germany, Rose's curiosity leads her to follow a truck and discover a concentration camp, where she is compelled to try to help by sharing her food. (**I:** 10 and up)

Goscinny, René. *Nicholas.* Translated by Anthea Bell. Illustrated by Jean-Jacques Sempé. Phaidon, 2005. (France) For almost half a century, this book, set in an all boys' school, has been a favorite among French school children. This translation introduces American readers to a boy and his classmates at an all-boys' school. A 2006 Batchelder Honor Book. (**I:** 9–11)

*Graham, Bob. *Greetings from Sandy Beach.* Kane/Miller, 1992. (Australia) A family takes a vacation at the beach, and meets unlikely heroes—a motorbike group who turn out to be friendly and helpful. (**I:** 6–9)

*———. *How to Heal a Broken Wing.* Candlewick, 2008. (Australia). Will finds a bird with a broken wing and takes it home to nurse it back to health. (**I:** P–7)

*Gravett, Emily. *Meerkat Mail.* Simon, 2007. (UK). A meerkat who lives with his family in the Kalahari Desert decides to venture out on his own. He sends home a series of postcards that show the various places he travels. Gravett incorporates information throughout the book, alongside the story of Sunny the meerkat. Observant viewers will notice that there is a jackal that is lurking dangerously throughout the book. Sunny returns home with deepened appreciation for his family.

*———. *Monkey and Me.* Simon, 2008. (UK). A little girl plays with her stuffed monkey, imitating various animals in a series of enchantingly rhythmic text and playful illustrations. (**I:** P–6)

*Greenwood, Mark. *The Donkey of Gallipoli: A True Story of Courage in World War I.* Illustrated by Frané Lessac. Candlewick, 2008. (Australia) The story of two boyhood friends who grow up in England, selling donkey rides across the beach, and ends with the two young men during wartime, with one leading a donkey carrying the other on his back in Turkey. Front endpapers and back endpapers reflect the opening and closing of the story setting. (**I:** 8–11).

*Grimm, Jakob and Wilhelm. *Little Red Riding Hood.* Retold and Illustrated by Bernadette Watts. NorthSouth, 2009. (Switzerland) This familiar folk tale is retold and drawn with oil pastel illustrations that have a charming appeal. (**I:** P–8)

*Heydlauff, Lisa. *Going to School in India.* Illustrated by Nitin Upadhye. Charlesbridge, 2005. (India) This informational book weaves together photographs, first-person narrative, and information about the culture studied. (**I:** 8–11)

*Hole, Stian. *Garmann's Summer.* Illustrated by the author. Translated by Don Barlett. Eerdmans, 2008. (Norway) Garmann considers his fear of starting school as the familiar routines of summer end. Collage illustrations effectively contrast the soothing and predictable patterns with slightly off-proportioned figures to contrast the familiar with the unexpected. (**I:** K–7).

*Ichikawa, Satomi. *My Father's Shop.* Kane/Miller, 2008. (France) Mustafa goes through the market, draped with a Moroccan rug from his father's shop. A rooster follows him, and tourists along the way share the different ways in which a rooster crow is depicted in their own countries. (**I:** K–7)

*Kwon, Yoon-duck. *My Cat Copies Me.* Kane/Miller, 2008. (South Korea) A girl begins a game in which her cat plays with her, but then, the roles reverse and the girl takes the cat's perspective as she copies her cat. (**I:** K–7)

*Lee, Suzy. *The Zoo.* Kane/Miller, 2007. (Korea) While visiting the zoo with her parents, a little girl runs off for a surreal adventure with the animals before collapsing into a dream world on a bench, where her worried parents find her. (**I:** K–8)

Lindgren, Astrid. *Pippi Longstocking.* Translated by Florence Lamborn. Illustrated by Louis S. Glanzman. Viking, 1950/1997. (Sweden) Pippi has extraordinary physical strength and engages in unpredictable antics that living alone permits her to do. (**I:** 8–12)

Lindo, Elvira. *Manolito Four-Eyes.* Translated by Joanne Moriarty. Illustrated by Elimio Urberuaga. Marshall Cavendish, 2008. (Spain) Humorous episodes tell of the everyday life of 10-year-old Manolito, who lives in Madrid with his family. (**I:** 8–10)

*Louis, Catherine. *Liu and the Bird: A Journey in Chinese Calligraphy.* Calligraphy by Feng Xiao Min. Translated by Sibylle Kazeroid. (France) The origin and evolution of Chinese writing is engagingly told through the story of a child who visits her grandfather. The picture transformation into calligraphic characters is symbolic and understandable. (**I:** 6–10)

Machado, Ana Maria. *From Another World.* Illustrated by Lucía Brandâo. Translated from Portuguese by Luisa Baeta. Groundwood, 2005. (Brazil) When Mariano and friends stay overnight in a building designated to be turned into an inn by Mariano's mother, they are confronted by the ghost of a nineteenth century slave girl who tells her tragic story and seeks their help. (**I:** 9–13)

———. *Me in the Middle.* Illustrated by Caroline Merola. Translated from Portuguese by David Unger. Groundwood, 2003. (Brazil) In this fantasy story, an almost-13-year-old Bel comes to realize who she is in this present day while her grandmother relays wisdom and life from the last century and her great granddaughter offers words of the future. (**I:** 9–12)

———. *Nina Bonita.* Illustrated by Rosana Faría. Kane Miller, 1996. (Brazil) A white rabbit falls in love with a dark-skinned girl and learns that the root of her physical beauty lies in her heritage. (**I:** K–7)

*Mahy, Margaret. *Bubble Trouble.* Illustrated by Polly Dunbar. Clarion, 2009. (UK) When Mabel blows a bubble that envelops her baby brother, mayhem ensues as the baby's bubble goes bouncing around and is chased by neighbors and family fearing for the baby's safety. (**I:** P–6)

*Maruki, Toshi. *Hiroshima No Pika.* Illustrated by Toshi Maruki. Lothrop/Morrow, 1982. (Japan) The effect of the atomic bombing of Hiroshima is described, including what happens to seven-year-old Mii and her parents. (**I:** 10 and up)

*Milway, Katie Smith. *One Hen: How One Small Loan Made a Big Difference.* Illustrated by Eugenie Fernandes. Kids Can, 2008. (Canada). Kojo is a small boy in Ghana, and he and his mother sell firewood for their livelihood. A small loan allows him to buy one hen, and selling the eggs allows him to buy more hens. The profits build and this example of microfinance shows the impact a small loan makes on a large future. In addition to the narrative that explains the concept of microfinance, the cumulative text format of building on one line of text is appropriate for paralleling this story's theme. (**I:** K–8).

Morgenstern, Susie. *A Book of Coupons*. Illustrated by Serge Bloch. Translated from French by Gill Rosner. Penguin Putnam, 2001. (France) An unconventional teacher gives each student a gift-wrapped book of coupons that excuse them from various behaviors like being late, forgetting homework, etc. (**I:** 9–12)

————. *Secret Letters from 0 to 10*. Translated from French by Gill Rosner. Penguin Putnam, 2000. (France) Ten-year-old Ernest leads a mundane life when vivacious Victoria enters his life and helps him to see the joy of living. (**I:** 10–13)

Naidoo, Beverley. *Journey to Jo'burg*. HarperCollins, 1988. When their baby sister is gravely ill, and grandmother has no money for medicine or doctors, Naledi and Dineo walk more than 300 km to seek the help of their mother, who lives with the white family she works for. The sequel is *Chain of Fire* (1990). (**I:** 9–11)

————. *The Other Side of Truth*. HarperCollins, 2001. (UK). When terrorists miss their intended target, their journalist father, Sade and Femi lose their mother instead. The children are sent to London, but when they arrive, the uncle who is to care for them has mysteriously disappeared. *Web of Lies* is the sequel. (**I:** 12–YA)

Naidoo, Beverley and Maya. *Baba's Gift.* Illustrated by Karin Littlewood. Viking, 2004. (South Africa) Lindi and Themba receive a handmade gift from their grandfather, but inadvertently lose it while playing with a new friend. (**I:** P–6)

Orlev, Uri. *The Lady with the Hat*. Translated by Hillel Halkin. Houghton Mifflin, 1995. (Israel) Seventeen-year-old Yulek is a concentration camp survivor who resolves to begin a new life in a Palestinian kibbutz, despite the British blockade. See also *The Man from the Other Side* (1991). (**I:** 12 and up)

*Pacovská, Kveta. *The Little Flower King*. Minedition, 2007. (Czech Republic) A king who fills his world with flowers realizes he needs something else for true happiness. He sets out in search of a princess, and finds his true love among his tulips. (**I:** P–8)

*Rao, Sandhya. *My Mother's Sari*. Illustrated by Nina Sabnani. North-South, 2006. (India) Children use their mothers' saris as they play in various imaginary ways—train, stage backdrop, a place to hide, etc. (**I:** P–7)

*Ravishankar, Anushka. *Elephants Never Forget!* Illustrated by Christiane Pieper. Houghton Mifflin, 2008. (India) A lonely elephant feels at home with a herd of buffaloes he joins, but when encountering a herd of elephants, he must make a choice. (**I:** P–7)

*Rinck, Maranke. *I Feel a Foot!* Illustrated by Martijn van der Linden. Boyds Mills/Lemniscaat. (The Netherlands) Five animal friends meet up with a huge something in the dark, and each "feels" that it is a giant version of themselves. (**I:** P–7)

Rivera, Raquel. *Arctic Adventures: Tales from the Lives of Inuit Artists*. Illustrated by Jirina Marton. Groundwood, 2008. (Canada) Four modern artists from the Canadian Arctic portray themselves, their work, and stories from their culture. (**I:** 8–11)

*Rosen, Michael. *Michael Rosen's Sad Book*. Illustrated by Quentin Blake. Candlewick, 2005. (UK) Author Michael Rosen presents the emotions of love, anger, and grief as he reflects on the death of his teenaged son. (**I:** 9–12)

*Sellier, Marie. *Legend of the Chinese Dragon*. Translated by Sibylle Kazeroid. Illustrated by Catherine Louis. Calligraphy and chop marks by Wang Fei. North South, 2008. (France) The legend of the Chinese dragon describes how warring factions of the past united under one spirit. The illustrator uses stunning lino-block prints to accompany the bilingually presented text with Chinese calligraphy. (**I:** 8–10)

*Sellier, Marie, Louis, Catherine, & Fei, Wang. *What the Rat Told Me: A Legend of the Chinese Zodiac*. NorthSouth, 2009. (France) This pour quoi tale adaptation from the Chinese Buddhist legend tells of twelve animals who responded to an invitation from the Great Emperor of Heaven to become the symbols of the Chinese zodiac. Beautiful black and red linoleum prints on cream paper ground the story in its Chinese roots. (**I:** 6–10)

Tan, Shaun. *Tales from Outer Suburbia*. Arthur A. Levine/Scholastic. (Australia) Fifteen illustrated short stories take place in a surreal suburban world where inexplicable events occur regularly. (**I:** 9–12)

Thompson, Kate. *The New Policeman*. Greenwillow/HarperCollins, 2008. (Ireland) Descendant in a family of musicians, 15-year-old Liddy sets off to fulfill his mother's birthday wish for "more time." Unknowingly, he set off on a quest that reveals family secrets and unrealized identities. Elements of Irish mythology and culture are important to the story. See Also: *The Last of the High Kings* (2009). (**I:** 13–YA)

*Tjong-Khing, Thé. *Where is the Cake?* Abrams, 2007. (Netherlands) This wordless book begins by asking the reader to find out what happened to the cake and where it is. But as viewers follow the visual maze, many other stories are revealed, and the puzzle becomes increasingly curious and entertaining. See also: *Where is the Cake Now?* (2009). (**I:** P–8)

Uehashi, Nahoko. *Moribito: Guardian of the Spirit*. Translated from Japanese by Cathy Hirano. Arthur Levine/Scholastic, 2008. (Japan) Balsa is a warrior who is compelled to save others in atonement for past lives lost. She saves a prince and serves as his bodyguard to protect him from the emperor, his father, who wants him dead. The first in the ten-volume *Guardian* fantasy series, it is popular also as radio, manga and anime adaptations. See Also: *Moribito II: Guardian of the Darkness*. (**I:** 7–YA)

Varmer, Hjørdis. *Hans Christian Andersen: His Fairy Tale Life*. Translated from Danish by Tiina Nunnally. Illustrated by Lilian Brøgger. Groundwood, 2005. (Denmark) Hans Christian Andersen's own true-life fairy tale biography is told in this engaging book, complete with illustrations both reminiscent of Andersen's cut paper style, as well as some original ones by Andersen. (**I:** 10–13)

*Velthuijs, Max. *Frog in Love*. Holt, 2004. (Netherlands) Frog does not understand why his insides are "thump thumping" and he is turning hot and cold when Piglet diagnoses the symptoms as "being in love" with Duck. See also many other books about Frog. (**I:** P–6)

*Wild, Margaret. *Bobbie Dazzler*. Illustrated by Janine Dawson. Kane Miller, 2007. (Australia) Bobbie the kangaroo wants to be able to do the splits. Despite her efforts, she cannot do the splits. Finally, when her persistence pays off, koala, wombat, and possum follow her example. (**I:** P–7)

Wilson, Jacqueline. *Candyfloss*. Illustrated by Nick Sharratt. Deborah Brodie/Roaring Brook, 2008. (UK). Flossie's mother, stepdad, and half-brother are moving to Australia for six months and Flossie stays in London with her father because of her allegiance and adoration of her best friend. When her father's inability to care for them means that Flossie is snubbed by her former social circle, her new friend helps Flossie to realize what friendship can and should be. (**I:** 9–11)

Resources

Gebel, Doris, ed. *Crossing Boundaries with Children's Books.* Scarecrow, 2006.

Pellowski, Anne. *The Story Vine: A Source Book of Unusual and Easy-to-Tell Stories from around the World.* Illustrated by Lynn Sweat. Macmillan, 1984.

Stan, Susan, ed. *The World Through Children's Books.* Scarecrow, 2002.

Tomlinson, Carl M., ed. *Children's Books from Other Countries.* Scarecrow Press, 1998.

Yokota, Junko. "Ten International Books for Children." *Journal of Children's Literature, 25*(1) (1999): 48–54.

———. International literature: Inviting students into the global community. pp. 242–253. In S. Lehr (Ed.), *Shattering the looking glass: Challenges, risk and controversy in children's literature.* Christopher-Gordon, 2008.

References

Freeman, Evelyn, and Barbara Lehman. *Global Perspectives in Children's Literature.* Allyn & Bacon, 2001.

Freeman, Evelyn, Barbara Lehman, and Pat Scharer. Panel Presentation at the IBBY (International Board on Books for Young People) Congress, Cape Town, South Africa, 2001.

Tsutsui, Yoriko. *Anna's Secret Friend.* Illustrated by Akiko Hayashi. Viking, 1987.

Part Two

Exploring the Genres of Children's Literature

6

Poetry for Children

What Is Poetry?

Categories of Poetry for Children

Mother Goose Rhymes and Other Rhymes of the Nursery • Jump-Rope and Counting-Out Rhymes • Folk Songs Popular among Children • Lyric or Expressive Poems • Narrative Poems • Nonsense Verse • **ASK THE POET:** Naomi Shihab Nye • **ISSUE TO CONSIDER:** Should We Distinguish between "Poems" and "Rhymes"? • Form Poems: Limericks • Form Poems: Haiku • Dialogue Poems • Free Verse • Poetry Collections • Novels in Verse

The Evolution of Children's Poetry

Early Poetry for Children • More Sympathetic Voices • Contemporary Poetry for Children • The Many Voices of Children's Poetry

Elements of Poetry

Sounds • Images • Comparisons • Forms • Insight

Children's Preferences in Poetry

Criteria for Evaluating Poetry

How Can We Expand Children's Taste in Poetry? • **ISSUE TO CONSIDER:** How Can We Keep Children's Liking for Poetry Alive?

Major Children's Poets and Their Works

Nikki Grimes • **ASK THE POET:** Nikki Grimes • Naomi Shihab Nye • Paul Janeczko • Janet Wong • Douglas Florian • Jack Prelutsky • Shel Silverstein • Lee Bennett Hopkins • The National Council of Teachers of English Award for Poetry for Children

What Is Poetry?

It is impossible to coin a definition of poetry that some poem or other won't slither around. We might say that poems are made of rhymed language—but poems like this one are not:

Snowboots snuggled over fat wool socks
Closed mouth muffled by a scratchy scarf
Arms pulled back by a bulging bookbag
Fingers slotted into gloves' thin sleeves
Hat scrunched low
Ready, set, go
Straight out the door
To the grumbling bus.

We might say that poems are words arranged in a visually striking fashion that is different from the arrangement of prose—but some poems aren't. One example is "Football" by Walt Mason:

Football

The game was ended, and the noise at last had died away, and now they gathered up the boys where they in pieces lay. And one was hammered in the ground by many a jolt and jar; some fragments never have been found, they flew away so far. They found a stack of tawny hair, some fourteen cubits high; it was the halfback, lying there, where he had crawled to die. They placed the pieces on a door, and from the crimson field, that hero then they gently bore, like soldier on his shield. The surgeon toiled the livelong night above the gory wreck; he got the ribs adjusted right, the wishbone, and the neck. He soldered on the ears and toes, and got the spine in place, and fixed a gutta-percha nose upon the mangled face. And then he washed his hands and said: "I'm glad that task is done!" The halfback raised his fractured head, and cried: "I call this fun!"

We might say poems wed image and sound in especially pleasing ways—but good prose often does this, too. For example, consider this excerpt from *Charlotte's Web*, by E. B. White:

The barn was very large. It was very old. It smelled of hay and it smelled of manure. It smelled of perspiration of tired horses and the wonderful sweet breath of patient cows. It often had a sort of peaceful smell—as though nothing bad could happen ever again in the world. (p. 13)

Still, we know poetry when we see it. Poetry is a precise form of language, with intense feeling, imagery, and qualities of sound that bounce pleasingly off the tongue, tickle the ear, and leave the mind something to ponder. Poetry is a memorable structure for language: Things we want to remember and want our children to remember have always been put in poetic form and passed on. Poetry is the pinnacle of language use: From the communication tool we billions of humans use unthinkingly throughout the day, a few choice items are elegantly constructed, to be admired for their beauty, artistry, and power. Poetry is a celebration of awareness: Poets regularly name things people have felt but could not name, and thus they expand our consciousness and our discerning. Often with bouncing rhythms and sparkling words, poetry has a special appeal to children—yet it also inspired the great American poet Emily Dickinson to exclaim, "If I read a book and it makes my whole body so cold no fire can ever warm me, I know that it is poetry."

Poetry has a special place in education. Through the daily barrage of language to which people young and old are subjected—the purring lies of advertisements, the droning tone-deaf bloodless facts of textbooks, the obtuse obscenities shouted down the street—it would be easy to lose our reverence for language, to leave mostly untouched the half million (and counting) English words—each one an invitation to pay attention, to notice a nuance that might go undetected. We really need poetry to help children celebrate what is clear, precise, beautiful, artful, and true in our language.

Categories of Poetry for Children

Children enjoy several widely acknowledged kinds of poetry: nursery rhymes, jump-rope rhymes, folk poems, lyric poems, narrative poems, and nonsense verse. Poems can also be classified by their forms: sonnets, limericks, haiku, concrete poems, and others. Some poems, of course, resist easy categorization.

Mother Goose Rhymes and Other Rhymes of the Nursery

Babies love to be bounced on grownups' knees, and the bouncers need rhythms and poems to sustain that rhythmic motion. Perhaps that is how nursery rhymes were born. Nursery rhymes are verses by anonymous poets that are highly rhythmic, tightly rhymed, and popular with small children. Although nursery rhymes have been recited to and by children since medieval times in English, they were associated with the name "Mother Goose" when the publisher John Newbery borrowed the name from quite a different publication [see the box].

Why Do We Call Them "Mother Goose" Rhymes?

The Frenchman Charles Perrault first used the name "Mother Goose" in the title of a collection of eight tales (not rhymes) that included "Cinderella," "The Sleeping Beauty in the Woods," and "Little Red Riding Hood." Perrault called his collection *Histoires ou Contes du Temps Passé, Avec des Moralités: Contes de Ma Mère l'Oye* (*Stories or Tales of Times Past, With Moral: Tales of My Mother Goose*). This collection was published in France in 1697, and was translated and published in England by Robert Samber as *Histories, or Stories of Times Past*, in 1729. Still, they were popularly called "Mother Goose Stories." Publisher John Newbery had found it profitable to publish books for the children of England's growing middle class, and when he brought out a collection of nursery rhymes for children, he appropriated Perrault's popular title and named it *Mother Goose's Melody, or Sonnets for the Cradle*. This was a collection of rhymes and jingles, which began the association of the name "Mother Goose" with highly rhythmic nursery rhymes.

Indeed, the associations in many nursery rhymes can be traced back several centuries.

Baa, baa, black sheep, have you any wool?
Yes, sir, yes, sir—three bags full.
One for my master and one for my dame,
And one for the little boy who lives down the lane.

This traditional rhyme dates from feudal times, when vassals paid shares of their produce to the powerful lords and ladies (masters and dames) who owned the lands of England.

Ring around the roses,
Pocket full of posies,
Ashes, ashes,
We all fall down.

This rhyme is said to refer to the Black Death, the bubonic plague, which killed a fourth of the population of England in the fourteenth century. The ring around the roses was a telltale rash of an infected person; the pocket full of posies was for protection against the "bad airs" that were believed to spread the sickness; and the ashes and falling down refer to the people who were stricken and died with dramatic suddenness (the disease ran its course in four days) and whose bodies were piled up and burned. Maybe so, but centuries of children have kept it alive out of fascination with its rhythms and their accompanying movements.

Nursery rhymes have pleasing sounds. This one sends the tongue tapping around all parts of the mouth—perhaps that is why small children love to recite it:

Polly put the kettle on,
Polly put the kettle on,
Polly put the kettle on,
We'll all have tea.
Sukey take it off again,
Sukey take it off again,
Sukey take it off again,
They've all gone away.

Many traditional rhymes also have accompanying motions. This one is a favorite when bouncing small children on one's knees:

This is the way the ladies ride,
Tri, tre, tre, tree!
Tri, tre, tre, tree!
This is the way the ladies ride,
Tri, tre, tre, tree!

And small children delight in having their toes wiggled to "This Little Piggie":

This little piggy went to market.
This little piggy stayed home.
This little piggy ate roast beef.
This little piggy ate none.
This little piggy cried "Wee! wee! wee!"
All the way home.

ILLUSTRATION 6.1   The illustrations of works for children by Joseph Kronheim (1810–1869) were popular for a hundred years. This little piggy is having roast beef.

Mother Goose Rhymes Through the Years

Over the past two centuries, many of the greatest illustrators of children's books have published editions of these familiar rhymes. Randolph Caldecott's picture book *Hey Diddle Diddle* was published in the 1882. In the same year, Kate Greenaway produced a beautiful version of *Mother Goose or the Old Nursery Rhymes*. Arthur Rackham's *Mother Goose: The Old Nursery Rhymes* was originally published around the end of the nineteenth century. Other classic versions were created by Tasha Tudor, Blanche Fisher Wright, and Feodor Rojankovsky.

Mother Goose equivalents and nursery rhymes are found in cultures around the world, and they developed separately from the ones known in the Western world. Among books of Mother Goose and nursery rhymes from other cultures that have been published for English-speaking children are Robert Wyndham's *Chinese Mother Goose Rhymes,* illustrated by Ed Young, and Lulu Delacre's *Arroz con Leche: Popular Songs and Rhymes from Latin America.* A popular bilingual Spanish/English collection of rhymes in the Mother Tradition is *Tortillitas Para Mama and Other Spanish Nursery Rhymes,* selected and translated by Margot C. Griego, Betsy L. Bucks, Sharon S. Gilbert, and Laurel H. Kimball and illustrated by Barbara Cooney. A more recent choice is Nelly Palacio Jaramillo's *Grandmother's Nursery Rhymes/ Las Nanas de Abuelita: Lullabies, Tongue Twisters, and Riddles from South America,* illustrated by Elivia Savadler. Patricia Polacco's *Babushka's Mother Goose* includes Russian names and alludes to experiences from the Russian heritage.

Jump-Rope and Counting-Out Rhymes

Unlike nursery rhymes, which are usually introduced to children by their parents or sitters, children's folk rhymes are anonymous verses passed on from child to child. Thus, they constitute—as *The Lore and Language of School Children* (2001), the title of the well-known book by British experts Iona and Peter Opie, suggests—an actual folklore that is the province of children themselves.

Hand-clapping rhymes such as this one often accompany children's play:

My boyfriend's name is Davy
He's in the U.S. Navy
With a pickle for his nose, cherries on his toes
That's the way my story goes.

Counting-out rhymes are perennially popular, too:

Bubble gum, bubble gum in a dish
How many pieces do you wish?
1, 2, 3 . . .

Children also enjoy rhythmic alphabet games such as this one:

A, my name is Annie,
And my husband's name is Al.
We come from Arkansas,
And we sell apples.
B, my name is Barbara,
And my husband's name is Bill . . .

And here's a popular jump-rope rhyme:

Cinderella
Dressed in yellow
Went upstairs
And kissed a fellow
Made a mistake and kissed a snake.
Came back down with a belly ache.
How many doctors does it take?
One . . . Two . . . Three . . . Four . . .

Francelia Butler's *Skipping around the World* has 350 skipping rhymes collected over forty years from seventy countries, and many of them turn out to have reworked adult themes, including historic military campaigns, politics, death, love, and sex.

Several collections of children's folk rhymes are currently in print (see the Recommended Books list at the end of this chapter). That these rhymes have to be written down at all shows adults' recognition that children's oral traditions need some bolstering against the inroads of canned commercial media.

Folk Songs Popular among Children

Another source of folk rhymes is folk songs that are popular with children. Some children's folk songs go back hundreds of years. "Oats, Peas, Beans, and Barley Grow" was sung in medieval times in England. Perhaps it's no coincidence that the plants in the song are mentioned in just the order of proper crop rotation practiced by farmers for centuries.

Other folk songs that are popular with children are from more recent times. The song about the legendary John Henry, a mythical turn-of-the-century African American railroad worker, was made into a picture book by Julius Lester. Here is a verse:

When John Henry was a little baby
Sittin' on his mama's knee,
He picked up a hammer and a little piece of steel
And said, "Hammerin's gonna be the death of me, Lord, Lord,
Hammerin's gonna be the death of me."

John Langstaff made a number of excellent picture books of English folk songs over the years. His *Oh, A-Hunting We Will Go*, first published in 1974, is still a favorite. Ashley Bryan and John Langstaff collaborated on books of African American spirituals, such as *What a Morning!* An interesting collection of Appalachian riddles, rhymes, and folk songs for children is *Granny Will Your Dog Bite? and Other Mountain Rhymes,* collected by Gerald Milnes and illustrated by Kimberly Bulcken Root (the book is available with a recorded sound track). The delightfully absurd folk song "There Was an Old Lady Who Swallowed a Fly" was developed into a picture book with hilarious illustrations by Caldecott Award-winning illustrator Simms Taback. *Gonna Sing My Head Off!* (Kathleen Krull, illustrated by Allen Garns, 1992) is a collection of sturdy American folk songs that have been staples of campfire singers for generations. They are fine fare for singing in class, too. Annie

ILLUSTRATION 6.2   Jakobsen's folk art style appropriately bring to life this folk anthem by an American original, Woody Guthrie. (From This *Land Is Your Land* by Woody Guthrie. Reprinted by permission of Little, Brown and Company, Inc.)

Patterson and Peter Blood's *Rise Up Singing!* (1988), which was compiled for the publishers of *Sing Out! Magazine,* is currently the most popular song collection among folk musicians. And the value of folk music is as compelling today as it ever was, if you believe children should have the right to do their own singing and even playing of music, and not have to purchase *all* of their music on CDs and MP3s.

Woody Guthrie was the most famous American folk singer, and his "This Land Is Your Land" comes close to being an alternative national anthem. In 1998, folk artist Kathy Jakobsen brought out a picture book version of the song, with a tribute to Guthrie by Pete Seeger and illustrations of the places Guthrie traveled. The book includes verses, not usually sung, that show Guthrie's commitment to poor people:

In the shadow of the steeple, I saw my
   people
By the relief office I seen my people;
As they stood there hungry, I stood
   there asking,
Is this land made for you and me?*
      (Guthrie, 1944; Jakobsen, 2008).

*This *Land Is Your Land* Words and Music by Woody Guthrie. TRO-©-Copyright 1956 (Renewed) 1958 (Renewed) 1970 (Renewed) 1972 (Renewed) Ludlow Music., Inc., New York, NY. Used by permission.

Guthrie's song and the illustrations in this provocative book might inspire a class inquiry into the social history of the United States during the Depression and the Dust Bowl era.

Teaching Idea 6.1

Using Folk Music in the Classroom

Folk songs connect students to both the emotions and the esthetic tone of historical periods. Learning and singing folk songs makes an excellent enhancement to reading books on historical periods or different parts of the world.

For a study of the Civil War, for example, novels like Irene Hunt's *Across Five Aprils*, Mary Pope Osborne's *After the Rain*, and Paul Fleischman's *Bull Run* can make history come alive for the reader through individual narratives. And students can sing folk songs as they read novels to make the stories feel even more alive. Fitting songs for the Civil War period include "Tenting Tonight on the Old Campground," which was sung by exhausted soldiers on both sides of the conflict. "Eating Goober Peas" was popular with Confederate troops, and "The Battle Hymn of the Republic" inspired the Northern troops. A good source of these songs and other folk songs is Peter Blood's *Rise Up Singing.*

Lyric or Expressive Poems

The original lyrics were Greek poems that were accompanied on the lyre, a small harp. Today's lyric or expressive poems are works of emotion, observation, or insight. The category includes a huge number of poems—just about any poem that is not narrative, or nonsense, or does not follow a recognized form is likely to be a lyric poem if it conveys the poet's thoughts on a topic.

A good example of the genre is found in Kam Mak's *My Chinatown: One Year in Poems* (2002). Kam Mak is an illustrator and poet who grew up in New York City's Chinatown.

In the fish tank,
The carp are crowded
Nose to tail, scale to scale.
In plastic tanks on the sidewalk,
Eels slither, frogs scramble.

My mother points out the fish she wants.
He waves his tail gently
And looks straight at me.

That night I say I'm sick
So I won't have to eat him.
      (Unpaged, 2002)

Naomi Shihab Nye, a poet and anthologist frequently seen in the schools, collected this lyric poem from an elementary-aged poet named Peter Acosta who participated in one of her writing workshops; it was published in **Salting the Ocean: 100 Poems by Young Poets**:

Ode to My Size
I sing to the size I am,
small and black-haired person.
There are two boys and two girls
that are taller than me.
And when they pass by I wish,
I wish I was tall myself.
I sing the size of me and my
companion that sits beside me. We
are both small but he is a little bigger
than me but I don't care about that.
I am just glad that I am a person.

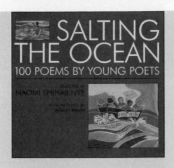

ILLUSTRATION 6.3 Like their art, children's poetry can show off pleasing and startling images and insights that compare well with the more self-conscious craft of adult poets writing for children. (*Salting the Ocean* by Naomi Shihab Nye, illustrated by Ashley Bryan. Cover art copyright © 2000 by Ashley Bryan. Used by permission of HarperCollins Publishers.)

Narrative Poems

Poems that tell stories are among the oldest of all poems, for at one time all stories that had wide currency were told in verse form. **The Odyssey, The Iliad, Beowulf,** and the **Poema de Mio Cid** were all originally told in verse. In the Middle Ages, ballads—long narrative poems—told the stories of Robin Hood, Lord Randall, and other heroes.

Narrative poetry written expressly for children began in the nineteenth century. Clement Clarke Moore's "A Visit from St. Nicholas, or 'Twas the Night before Christmas," published in 1822, not only helped to establish the genre of narrative poetry for children but also contributed to the Santa Claus lore that is still widely circulated in North America. Robert Service's poems have long been popular for their exciting plots involving tough men in wilderness settings: the Yukon and the old West. The most famous of his poems, **The Cremation of Sam McGee**, was brought out in 1986 as a picture book with inspired illustrations by Ted Harrison. Here is a sample of the poem:

There are strange things done
in the midnight sun
By the men who moil for gold;
The arctic trails have their secret tales
    That would make your blood run cold;
The Northern Lights
        have seen queer sights,
    But the queerest they ever did see
Was that night on the marge of Lake Lebarge
I cremated Sam McGee.

One of the great American narrative poems is Ernest Lawrence Thayer's "Casey at the Bat," a favorite of generations of young people:

The outlook wasn't brilliant for the Mudville nine that day;
The score stood four to two with but one inning left to play . . .

Ludwig Bemelmans popularized rhyming narratives for modern children with his many books about Madeline, the feisty young resident of the convent school in Paris. And Roy Gerrard turned out imaginative contributions to the narrative poem genre: **Rosy and the Rustlers, Sir Frances Drake,** and others, until his death in 1997.

Nonsense Verse

In the middle of the last century, the English poet Edward Lear was the first to publish nonsense verse. Lear's "The Jumblies" is also known as "They Went to Sea in a Sieve":

Ask the Poet . . .   Naomi Shihab Nye

Naomi Shihab Nye

Favorite Books as a Child

Favorite Poems Old & New
edited by Helen Ferris

The Important Book
by Margaret Wise Brown

Mister Dog
by Margaret Wise Brown

What advice do you have for teachers who want to help children appreciate poetry that isn't necessarily playful?

Poems have as many moods as people do. Often, when we're little, we learn nursery rhymes and funny, bouncy poems. We like repeating rhythms, even nonsense words—poems that make us laugh and stretch the boundaries of language. Some of us continue to like these poems no matter what age we are.

But there is much more to poetry. As we grow, hopefully we have a chance to read poems of many styles which echo all the varieties of human experience. Poems may help us understand universal human moods such as sadness, loneliness, alienation, anger, confusion better and more quickly than any other kind of writing, since poetry is such an intimate, immediate kind of writing. Surprisingly, poems about silence and emptiness can be some of the most moving poems! Many teenagers say they write best when they are depressed because a "negative emotion" often causes them to focus intensely. After writing, people often feel better, too, because that "serious emotion" found a shape for itself, a simple, comforting outlet, in words.

As readers, we bring our own experiences to every poem that we read. Quickly we understand that not all people will respond to every poem or understand every poem in the same way. Some poems may not "touch us" at all. A lot depends on what we have experienced ourselves, our individuality, our personal taste. Sometimes a single image will invite us into a poem. A metaphor or simile may awaken a fresh understanding of something we thought we knew. Reading poems makes us larger people—It extends our empathy, helping us understand how others feel and giving us insight into the many worlds within and around all of us, whether the subjects and moods are things we too have experienced or things we learn about mostly through reading.

Naomi Shihab Nye has written poems since she was six years old. Her most recent collections of poems are *Fuel* and *Red Suitcase*. She has also edited anthologies of poetry for young readers, including *This Same Sky, The Tree Is Older Than You Are*, and *What Have You Lost?* She also writes children's books, essays, and novels for teens. She lives in San Antonio with her husband and son. ∎

They went to sea in a sieve, they did;
 In a sieve they went to sea;
In spite of all their friends would say,
On a winter's morn, on a stormy day,
 In a sieve they went to sea.

Nonsense poetry is alive and well among modern writers. Here is North Carolina poet Bucksnort Trout's tongue-in-cheek protest against too much television ("telly") watching:

Nelly watched the telly
'Til her brains turned to jelly
'Til they flowed through her nose
And ran down her belly.
Mama said, "Hey, Nelly!"
Nelly said, "Huh? What?"
Then she sat there a-staring
Like some kind of a nut.

Issue to Consider
Should We Distinguish between "Poems" and "Rhymes"?

When Emily Dickinson spoke of poetry as writing that made her so cold no fire could ever warm her, presumably she didn't mean the likes of "Jack Sprat could eat no fat/His wife could eat no lean." Some authorities would say that this is not real poetry but rather should be called "verse" or "rhyme" (Lukens, 1992). According to that way of thinking, "poetry" is written expression that strikes readers in many ways at once—with sound, image, and meaning—and that repays careful rereading to savor the artistry and ponder the associations.

Works that fall short—although perhaps very enjoyable—should be called "verse" or "rhymes."

The "Emily Dickinson test" might work with most nursery rhymes, but how would the Belle of Amherst's body temperature have responded to the poems of Shel Silverstein or Jack Prelutsky or David McCord or Eve Merriam? And if it could be proved—as some claim to have done—that many nursery rhymes contain cleverly encoded social and political messages, would we still be content to call these works mere rhymes?

The poem-versus-rhyme distinction is useful if it keeps us from expecting too much from every bit of verse we read. But the distinction is bound to lead to some unhappiness, as someone sniffs that one of your favorite poems is not a poem at all, but only a rhyme.

What do you think? Should we make a distinction between poems and rhymes?

Elizabeth Swados evoked a poetry slam (see Teaching Idea 6.2) in her *Hey, You! C'Mere! A Poetry Slam* (2002). Here's a sample poem:

> Uh-Oh
>
> *Chomp chomp,*
> I'm naht suwposed to tawlk
> Wid moy moudth fulled.
> *Chomp chomp,*
> Itds bayad mahnners.
> *Chomp chomp*
> (2002, page 21)

Nonsense verse and other humorous poetry have always been popular with children.

Form Poems: Limericks

Up until the beginning of this century, most poems in English had identifiable rhyme schemes and rhythmic patterns. Today, poetry is more varied in its structure and use of sounds. A few common forms of poetry persist, however. The limerick is one of the most popular current forms. Why? X. J. and Dorothy Kennedy (1999) offer a poem by way of explanation:

> Well, it's partly the shape of the thing
> That makes the old limerick swing—
>   Its accordion pleats
>   Full of light, airy beats
> Take it up like a kite on the wing!

Limericks came into being in the early nineteenth century and found an early champion at midcentury in the nonsense poet Edward Lear. Lear so popularized the form that it is closely identified with him. Here is one of his limericks:

> There was an Old Man who said, "Hush!
> I perceive a young bird in this bush!"
>   When they said, "Is it small?"
>   He replied, "Not at all;
> It is four times as big as the bush!"

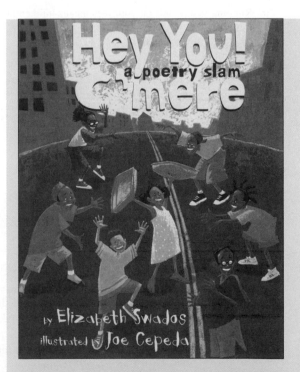

ILLUSTRATION 6.4 Poetry slams are popular with young urban adults. Here Swados, with the help of Cepeda's lively art, promotes the practice of slamming among a school-aged audience. (From the cover of *Hey You! C'Mere* by Elizabeth Swados. Cover illustration by Joe Cepeda. Copyright © 2002 by Joe Cepeda. Reprinted by permission of Scholastic Inc.)

Teaching Idea 6.2
A Poetry Slam

For the past 20 years or so, urban poets from all across the country have been engaging in a highly energetic competition based on performance poetry. Called Poetry Slams, the events give several poets limited amounts of time to hurl their poems into eager crowds, who then serve as juries and render scores for each performance. As the sponsoring group, Poetry Slam, Inc., defines it, "Simply put, a poetry slam is the competitive art of performance poetry. It puts dual emphasis on writing and performance, encouraging poets to focus on what they're saying and how they're saying it. A poetry slam is an event in which poets perform their work and are judged by members of the audience. . . ."

To host a Poetry Slam in a classroom, prepare students to present their poems—either individually or in teams—during a competition in which they are given fixed amounts of time, such as two minutes. (Points may be subtracted if they go over the time limit.)

The performances can be scored by a panel of judges, usually students—although a teacher or two may participate. They are given rubrics on which to score each poet. The criteria should deal with both presentation and content (assuming the student wrote the poem). If a panel of judges gives the scores, then the audience may be instructed to respond as follows:

a. Rubbing your hands on your legs means mild enthusiasm.
b. Snapping your fingers means more enthusiasm.
c. Slapping your hands on your thighs means still more enthusiasm.
d. Stomping your feet means the most enthusiasm.

More information on Poetry Slams is available from Poetry Slam, Inc., at **http://www.poetryslam.com.**

Form Poems: Haiku

Another common form of poetry is the haiku, a three-line non-rhyming poem developed in Japan. Haiku poems traditionally contain seventeen syllables, five in the first line, seven in the middle, and five in the last (although English-language haiku don't always follow that requirement). Most haiku make an observation about nature in a particular moment and a particular place:

Now at the black pond
twilight slowly abandons
the lone blue heron.

Dialogue Poems

Poems for two or more voices are enjoyable to read aloud. Dialogue poems are as old as Mother Goose rhymes:

"Old woman, old woman,
Shall we go a'shearing?"
"Speak a little louder sir,
I'm very hard of hearing."
"Old woman, old woman,
Shall I kiss you dearly?"
"Yes, sir, yes, sir,
I hear you very clearly."

Dialogue poems are sometimes used to highlight social justice issues. For example, here is a dialogue poem showing a conversation between two children.

My mother is nice
    My mother is my mother
My mother drives me to school
    I don't go to school
My mother commutes to work on a train
    My mother walks four miles to fetch water
My mother cooks dinner in a microwave
    My mother gathers sticks and makes a fire to boil our rice
My mother is trying to lose weight
    My mother sweats and trembles with malaria
My mother reads to me at night
    My mother sings to me in the dark
Good night
    Goodnight

Free Verse

Poetry that has no discernible form at all is free verse. Free verse has no rhyme or particular rhythm, but makes its impressions with an intensity of insight or feeling, a clarity of vision, and sounds and rhythms that ebb and flow with the intensity of the poet's feelings about the subject matter. Here is an example of free verse by Valerie Worth from ***All the Small Poems:***

Dog
Under a maple tree
The dog lies down,
Lolls his limp
Tongue, yawns,
Rests his long chin carefully between

Front paws:
Looks up, alert;
Chops, with heavy
Jaws, at a slow fly,
Blinks, rolls
On his side,
Sighs, closes
His eyes: sleeps
All afternoon
In his loose skin.

Here, with no meter or rhyme scheme to worry about, the poet can let the poem take its own shape. She sets out a series of images. She makes cadences in patterns and then suddenly breaks them, reflecting the erratic behavior of the poem's subject. She uses a series of sounds that echo each other (the dog lies down . . . Lolls his limp . . .), and then she shifts to other sounds.

Poetry Collections

If you are a teacher or are becoming one, you may not care so much about whether a poem is a lyric or a narrative. You want to know what its topic is or its theme. There is nothing wrong with you! A good and natural way to share poetry with children is to find poems that suit an occasion, or comment on what the class happens to be thinking about.

Editors of some (but not all) of the larger anthologies have thoughtfully included topical indexes. ***The Random House Book of Poetry for Children*** (selected by Jack Prelutsky and illustrated by Arnold Lobel) has 572 poems, along with an index that locates poems on such finely tuned topics as "Death, Dinosaurs, Dogs, Dreams, Fall, Family, Fantasy, Fathers, February, Fire, Fish . . ."

Another good bet is to seek out thematically chosen anthologies. Poetry anthologies are available on a host of topics. ***In Daddy's Arms I Am Tall*** (Steptoe, 2001) is subtitled ***African Americans Celebrating Fathers.*** Here is a selection:

Promises
Dear Daddy,
I'm sorry I did not do what you told me to do.
If I do better
Can I still be your little boy?

Dear Son,
You will be
My little boy
For all of your little-boy days.
And when
You are no longer a little boy
I will still be your daddy.

(David A. Anderson)

In ***Insectlopedia***, Douglas Florian makes humorous comments on insects from black widow spiders to ticks in 21 rhyming poems with his own watercolor and ink illustrations. His ***Mammalabilia*** does the same in 21 poems about mammals, from aardvarks to otters.

Barbara Juster Esbensen wrote 25 poems to highlight patterns in nature—circles, spirals, and polygons and published them in ***Echoes for the Eye*** (illustrated by Helen K. Davie). Paul Janeczko, a poet and former teacher, collected haiku about urban scenes in ***Stone Bench in an Empty Park*** (illustrated with black and white photographs by Henry Silburman, 2000) and songs in voices of animals or other objects in ***Dirty Laundry Pile*** (illustrated by Melissa Sweet, 2001). Jack Prelutsky has assembled some longer anthologies that include ***Imagine That***, a celebration of purely imaginative topics from the land of "never-was"

Teaching Idea 6.3
Writing Dialogue Poems

Children can write dialogue poems between any two characters: a hunter and a deer, or a plate of food and a diner. They will write more powerful poems if they are given powerful subjects. After reading Robert Coles's *The Story of Ruby Bridges* (illustrated by George Ford), the students can write a dialogue between Ruby and one of the white parents who are heckling this young African American girl each day as she is escorted by federal marshals to a previously all-white New Orleans school. The dialogue poems can each be written by a single student, or by having each student write one speaker's lines.

Further suggestions for using dialogue poems for teaching social justice are found on the websites of Rethinking Schools (**http://www.rethinkingschools.org/archive/19_01/dial191.shtml**) and of Concern America (**http://www.concernamerica.org/WETS/ednews-Mexico.pdf**).

(illustrated by Kevin Hawkes, 1998), and *The Beauty of the Beast* (illustrated by Meilo So, 1997), a thick book of 200 poems by 100 poets that chronicle the animal kingdom from the whale to the earthworm. Note, too, the amazing range of topics covered by the dozens of poetry collections by Lee Bennett Hokpins. (See pages 197–198.)

Novels in Verse

Some of the oldest stories in the world were told in poetry. The oldest written story, *Gilgamesh*, was recorded in verse nearly 5,000 years ago. Of course, the longer epics such as *The Odyssey* and *The Iliad*, and the ballads of King Arthur and Robin Hood, were told in verse. Longer narrative poems were popular in the nineteenth and earlier twentieth centuries: we have already mentioned Clement Clarke Moore's *The Night Before Christmas* from 1822 and Ernest L. Thayer's *Casey at the Bat*, from 1888. There was also Henry Wadsworth Longfellow's long poem *Evangeline*, about the resettlement of the French-speaking families and two star-crossed lovers from Nova Scotia to Southern Louisiana, published in 1847. In recent years novels in verse have occasionally appeared in the adult fiction market, notably the poet Derek Wolcott's *Omeros* (Walcott, 1992), a retelling of *The Odyssey* with a cast of Caribbean fishermen.

Happily, several novels in verse have been written in the past decade for middle grade children. Three of these are by authors who have achieved acclaim with their more conventional novels for young people.

Karen Hesse had written a dozen successful novels for young people before she won the Newbery Medal for 1998 for *Out of the Dust*. Through the first person voice by fourteen-year-old Billy Jo, the reader experiences firsthand the calamity of the Dust Bowl on the hard-bitten farmers who tried to survive it. Hesse followed with *Aleutian Sparrow* (2003), another novel in a difficult historical setting: this one about the Aleuts, the native people of the Aleutian Islands, who were forcibly removed from their homes during World War II by the U.S. government and put in settlement camps, where many died.

Love That Dog (2001), by Newbery Award Winner Sharon Creech (*Walk Two Moons*) is a celebration of poetry itself that appeals to fourth through sixth grade readers. And *Locomotion* (2003), by Coretta Scott King Award winner Jacqueline Woodson, uses several forms of poetry—like Creech, with the sensitive agency of an insightful teacher who encourages her students to write it—for eleven-year-old Lonnie Collins Motion (AKA "Locomotion") to unburden himself of a story of tragedy and loss. Additionally, poet Nikki Grimes (see pages 193–194), in *Bronx Masquerade,* has highlighted both the appeal of the poetic form, and the lives of the urban high school students who have found their voices through poetry.

Teaching Idea 6.4

Using Poetry Anthologies

Choose one topic you will be teaching. It doesn't have to be a literary one, or even a touchy-feely social one. It might be a geometric pattern, or an insect. Find three poems that relate to that topic. Try to find at least one that is fairly literal, and one that is metaphorical. Have the students compare what they learn about the same concept from the two different poems.

If the topic is circles, for instance, you might use Barbara Juster Esbensen's "Think of a Circle" (from *Dance With Me* by B. J. Esbensen, illustrated by M. Lloyd (1995) and "Circles" by Myra Cohn Livingston, from M.C. Livingston, *There Was a Place and Other Poems* (1988).

The Evolution of Children's Poetry

Early Poetry for Children

A historical review of poems written in the English language for children does not begin well. Up until William Blake published *Songs of Innocence,* in 1789, children's poems from Great Britain were often cheerless, moralistic, didactic, and often downright mean-spirited. Here, for instance, is the beginning of an alphabet poem from around 1700:

A was an Archer, and shot at a frog,
B was a Blindman, and led by a dog,
C was a Cutpurse, and lived in disgrace,
D was a Drunkard, and had a red face.
E was an Eater, a glutton was he,
F was a Fighter, and fought with a flea,
G was a Giant, and pulled down a house . . .

Early American poems for children were every bit as dour. Some poems exalted early death as the greatest aspiration of a young child; for by dying young, children reduced their chances of falling into sin. Other poems impressed on children the horrors of eternal damnation for their "original sin."

More Sympathetic Voices

The poems of the English poet William Blake (1757–1827) were something new. They addressed topics that appealed to children and approached childhood with sympathy.

> *The Lamb*
> Little Lamb who made thee?
> Dost thou know who made thee?
> Gave thee life and bid thee feed
> By the stream and o'er the mead;
> Gave thee clothing of delight,
> Softest clothing woolly bright;
> Gave thee such a tender voice,
> Making all the vales rejoice.
> Little Lamb who made thee?
> Dost thou know who made thee?
> . . .

Blake's sympathy for children led him to become a voice for social justice. His poem, "The Chimney Sweeper," helped begin the long struggle in England to ban the worst forms of child labor:

> *The Chimney Sweeper*
> When my mother died I was very young,
> And my father sold me while yet my tongue
> Could scarcely cry "'weep!'weep!'weep!'weep!"
> So your chimneys I sweep, and in soot I sleep.
> . . .

The better poets from Blake's time on left off the moralizing and wrote for children's enjoyment. The long narrative poems of Robert Browning (1812–1889) are imaginative and entertaining. Here is the beginning of ***The Pied Piper of Hamelin***:

> Hamelin Town's in Brunswick,
>   By famous Hanover city;
> The river Weser, deep and wide,
> Washes its wall by the southern side;
> A pleasanter spot you never spied;
>   But, when begins my ditty,
> Almost five hundred years ago,
> To see the townsfolk suffer so
>   From vermin, was a pity.
>   Rats!
> They fought the dogs and killed the cats,
>   And bit the babies in their cradles,
> And ate the cheeses out of vats,
>   And licked the soup from cooks' own ladles,
> Split open kegs of salted sprats,
> Made nests inside men's Sunday hats,
> And even spoiled the women's chats
>   By drowning their speaking
>   With shrieking and squeaking
> In fifty different sharps and flats . . .

From the mid-nineteenth century on, the poetry gets more and more delightful. We've already mentioned Edward Lear's nonsense verse, which plays with language and enlivens

Top Shelf 6.1

Books About Poetry

These books will inform and guide you as you help children appreciate poetry, perform it, and write it.

Cullinan, Bernice, and David Harrison. Easy Poetry Lessons That Dazzle and Delight (Grades 3–6). Teaching Resources, 1999. Bea Cullinan is one of our most passionate and resourceful advocates of children's poetry. Here she and David Harrison show how to lead children from warm-ups to finished poems.

Fletcher, Ralph. ***Poetry Matters: Writing a Poem from the Inside Out***. Harper Trophy, 2002. Fletcher, an accomplished writing teacher, assembles the insights of many published poets to show how to get in touch with an idea and express it on paper.

Janeczko, Paul. ***The Place My Words Are Looking For: What Poets Say About and Through Their Work***. Simon and Schuster, 1990. A treasury of good poems and comments by the poets that wrote them, such as Jack Prelutsky, Eve Mirriam, Myra Cohn Livingston, Karla Kuskin, Naomi Shihab Nye, and others.

Koch, Kenneth. ***Wishes, Lies, and Dreams: Teaching Children to Write Poetry***. Perennial, 2000. First published twenty years ago, poet Kenneth Koch's unconventional ideas for exercising different aspects of a poet's art are illustrated with the New York City children's poems they inspired.

McClure, Amy. ***Sunrises and Songs: Reading and Writing Poetry in an Elementary Classroom***. Heinemann, 1990. By sharing evocative poetry with children, Amy McClure inspires children to get their own feelings and observations out in verse form.

Wolf, Alan. ***It's Show Time! Poetry From Page to Stage***. Poetry Alive Publications, 1993. Poetry Alive! is a theater company that brings poetry to life through lively performances. Alan Wolf, one of the troupe's arrangers, shows teachers how to direct students in sharing poems through voice choirs and dramatizations.

the imagination. In *Alice's Adventures in Wonderland* (1865), Lewis Carroll (1832–1898) confidently spoofed the moralistic doggerel that was so prominent in poetry for children just a short time before:

> Speak roughly to your little boy,
> And beat him when he sneezes:
> He only does it to annoy,
> Because he knows it teases.

Here is an excerpt from the poem that Carroll was spoofing.

> *Speak Gently*
> Speak gently to the little child!
> Its love be sure to gain;
> Teach it in accents soft and mild: —
> It may not long remain.
>
> Speak gently to the young, for they
> Will have enough to bear —
> Pass through this life as best they may,
> 'T is full of anxious care!
>   David Bates (1809–1870)

Christina Rossetti (1830–1894) could be thoughtful and accessible at the same time, as in "The Wind" (from *Complete Poems of Christina Rossetti*):

> Who has seen the wind?
>   Neither you nor I;
> But when the leaves hang trembling
>   The wind is passing through.
> Who has seen the wind?
>   Neither you nor I;
> But when the trees bow down their heads
>   The wind is passing by.

Robert Louis Stevenson (1850–1894) gave us the great adventure novels *Treasure Island* and *Kidnapped*. His *A Child's Garden of Verses*, written at the end of the nineteenth century, is still much admired; through the middle of the twentieth century, it was among the most widely read of poetry collections. Stevenson could be gentle, yet savvy to a child's point of view:

> *Looking Forward*
> When I am grown to man's estate
> I shall be very proud and great,
> And tell the other girls and boys
> Not to meddle with my toys.

At the turn of the century and after, Rudyard Kipling, A. A. Milne, T. S. Eliot, and others appealed to children with exciting and delightful poems, with words and rhythms well suited to their themes.

Kipling's poems reflected the high adventure of a life lived in exotic places, as this fragment of "The Smuggler's Song" (from *Puck of Pook's Hill*) shows:

> If you wake at midnight and hear horses' feet,
> Don't go drawing back the blind, or looking in the street,
> Them that asks no questions isn't told a lie.
> Watch the wall, my darling, while the Gentlemen go by!
> Five and twenty ponies,
> Trotting through the dark—
> Brandy for the parson,
> 'Baccy for the Clerk
> Laces for a lady; letters for a spy;
> And watch the wall, my darling, while the Gentlemen go by!

Contemporary Poetry for Children

During the twentieth century, poetry for children continued to evolve. One noticeable change was freedom from formality: Non-rhyming poems became more common, and the language of poetry more folksy. Beginning with the poetry of Langston Hughes in the 1920s, published children's poems began representing the experiences of children who were not white and were not middle class. Yet another change was a more honest and direct voice in the poetry. As we saw, in earlier centuries, the attitude of the poet could be aloof and punishing. Later, it became sentimental and reassuring. In the contemporary era, the voice of the poet has become more honest and confiding—both poet and child live in a troubled world, and even adults sometimes feel powerless. Modern poets may try to be hopeful, but they do not offer a naive reassurance they do not feel.

The voice of Langston Hughes's narrator in "Mother to Son" (from ***The Dream Keeper and Other Poems***) reflects the shift. The narrator is teaching a message of optimism, but the optimism is based on perseverance in grim circumstances. This world is a far cry from the cozy, sheltered world of the imagination constructed by poets in the nineteenth century. Note how Hughes uses a staircase in a slum dwelling as a metaphor for a hard life:

Mother to Son
Well, son, I'll tell you:
Life for me ain't been no crystal stair.
It's had tacks in it,
And splinters,
And boards torn up,
And places with no carpet on the floor—
Bare.
But all the time
I'se been a-climbin' on,
And reachin' landin's,
And turnin' corners,
And sometimes goin' in the dark
Where there ain't been no light.
So, boy, don't you turn back.
Don't you set down on the steps
'Cause you finds it kinder hard.
Don't you fall now—
For I'se still goin', honey,
I'se still climbin',
And life for me ain't been no crystal stair.

The honest and not superior voice is evident in the work of many modern poets who write for children, such as Eve Merriam, Myra Cohn Livingston, Nikki Giovanni, and Gary Soto. It is evident in Nikki Giovanni's "dance poem" (from ***Spin a Soft Black Song***), in which the mother sounds almost desperate as she tries to cheer her children—or have them cheer her:

come nataki dance with me
bring your pablum dance with me
pull your plait and whirl around
come nataki dance with me
won't you tony dance with me
stop your crying dance with me
feel the rhythm of my arms
don't let's cry now dance with me
tommy stop your tearing up
don't you hear the music
don't you feel the happy beat
don't bite tony dance with me
mommy needs a partner . . .

Contemporary children's poets still write with insight and humor about the joys and scrapes of childhood. The humor is more biting than in previous generations, and sometimes more irreverent—see for example the poems of Shel Silverstein and Jack Prelutsky on pages 190, 196, and 197 in this chapter. And much of it is very funny, such as Nikki Grimes's poem "True Love Blues" (from *Hopscotch Blues*):

True Love Blues
Love means putting others first—
That's what love's about.

Lord says you gotta put me first
'Cause that's what love's about.
But the way you hog that apple pie
Proves you still ain't figured that out.

But modern poets also write about urban issues, about poverty and racism, about the dangers of environmental pollution, about the over-mechanization of our lives, with the attendant erosion of human values—as in this poem by Eve Merriam (from *Chortles*):

Sing a Song of Subways
Sing a song of subways
Never see the sun;
Four-and-twenty people
In room for one.
When the doors are opened—
Everybody run.

The Many Voices of Children's Poetry

Many contemporary poets write to foster racial pride, as oppression has made pride hard to come by. Lucille Clifton writes eloquently to this end in "listen children" (in Arnold Adoff's *My Black Me*):

listen children
keep this in the place
you have for keeping
always
keep it all ways

we have never hated black

listen
we have been ashamed
hopeless   tired   mad
but always
all ways
we loved us

we have always loved each other
children   all ways

pass it on

A breakthrough in contemporary literature for children was the publication of poetry from all quarters of American culture and from around the world as well. Poetry from the Caribbean is earthy and colorful, as this poem by Monica Gunning (from *Not a Copper Penny in Me House*) demonstrates:

The Corner Shop
"Chil', me stone broke," Grandma sighs.
"Not a copper penny in me house.

Go tell Maas Charles at the corner shop
I want to trust a pound of codfish
and two pounds of rice.
I'll pay him when the produce dealer
buys me dried pimento crop in season."
Maas Charles never says no.
He knows everyone in the village
by their first names.
He scoops from his bin, weighs and wraps,
adds to his credit sheet on the wall
a new amount under Grandma's name.
Grandma always says,
"Thank God for Maas Charles."

Poetry from Latin American communities can be worldly and upbeat or wise and deep. Many collections are available in Spanish and English translations, such as ***The Tree Is Older Than You Are***, edited by Naomi Shihab Nye.

A clear and lively new voice in poetry for children is Janet Wong, an American poet of Korean and Chinese descent. Wong writes for young people of many ages. She writes about racism. She writes about driving automobiles. For young children, she writes about sounds around the house, in ***Buzz,*** illustrated by Margaret Chodos-Irvine:

Mommy grinds coffee
BUZZZZZZZZZZ

While I fly my airplane
BUZZZZZZZZZZ

over the oatmeal
BUZZZZZZZZZZ

and past the apple juice
BUZZZZZZZZZZ—

OH NO!
Splash
    Landing!

Though poetry for children continues to evolve, evolution in poetry for children is not the same thing as evolution, say, in the design of automobiles. A hybrid SUV is obviously a more sophisticated car than a Model T Ford, but a poem by Jack Prelutsky is not more sophisticated than a poem by A. A. Milne or one by Langston Hughes. As new poems are written, they add to the body of poetry available to children, without necessarily replacing it. Children today have access to exciting new poems that speak to contemporary realities; they can also enjoy the best poems of the past.

Elements of Poetry

Ask yourself this question: What do you like about a favorite poem? If you can't quite put your finger on it, consider the main features that critics agree make up a good poem: sounds, images, and forms.

Sounds

Most poetry for children is crafted with a keen ear for sound. That's why it is usually best read aloud. Sounds are the musical aspect of poetry. Just as music is said to speak the language of the emotions, so the sounds of poetry—rhythm, rhyme, alliteration, and onomatopoeia—choreograph much of the listener's emotional experience.

Rhythm

Rhythm is the beat of a poem. Rhythm can be a direct route to the emotions. The rhythm of a slow heartbeat has a calming effect even on a newborn baby, whereas the sound of a fast heartbeat causes anxiety. The pulse of a graduation march sweeps us along with dignity and pride; the pounding of a military drum keeps soldiers advancing in step with one another. The rhythm of a marching band makes us want to run to get a better look. Wallace Stevens captured the martial rhythm of a marching band in his poem "John Smith and His Son, John Smith" (from *The Collected Poems of Wallace Stevens*):

> John Smith and his son, John Smith,
>   And his son's son John, and-a-one
>   And-a-two and-a-three
> And a rum-tum-tum, and-a
> Lean John, and his son, lean John,
>   And his lean son's John, and-a-one
>   And-a-two and-a-three
> And a drum-rum-rum, and-a
> Rich John, and his son, rich John,
>   And his rich son's John, and-a-one
>   And-a-two and-a-three . . .

The rhythm of this poem implicitly compares a proud parade of marchers to the passing of generations within a family.

Rhythm is prominent in many children's poems—and perhaps nowhere more so than in the work of NCTE award-winner David McCord. In his poem "The Pickety Fence" (from *One at a Time*), you can hear the rhythm of a stick dragging staccato across the pickets:

> The pickety fence
> The pickety fence
> Give it a lick it's
> The pickety fence
> Give it a lick it's
> A clickety fence
> Give it a lick it's
> A lickety fence
> Give it a lick
> Give it a lick
> Give it a lick
> With a rickety stick
> Pickety
> Pickety
> Pickety
> Pick

Children delight in clapping along to the rhythm of such poetry.

Rhyme

Along with rhythm, rhyme lends a musical quality to poetry by building patterns of repetition. Rhymes delight us—but they do more. Rhymes function in a poem to link words, to play them against each other, and to build on their emotional content, as we see in this poem by Walter de la Mare (1923):

The Horseman
I heard a horseman
    Ride over the hill;
The moon shone clear,
The night was still;
His helm was silver,
    And pale was he;
And the horse he rode
    Was of ivory.

Rhymes are most pleasing when they surprise us. And poets can build up suspense by delaying rhymes when they are expected, as in this excerpt from Charles Temple's **Train**:

The train stands trembling on the C&O track,
As the whistle puffs a warning, long and low.
Now the smoke starts chuffing from the short smokestack
And the lights go sweeping
And the engine goes rumbling
And the wheels go squeaking kind of slow . . .

Of course, the rhyming words should suit the meaning of the poem, and not be included merely for the sake of sound. The rhymes in Christina Rossetti's "Caterpillar" (from **Complete Poems of Christina Rossetti**) are skillfully done:

Brown and furry
Caterpillar in a hurry,
Take your walk
To the shady leaf, or stalk,
Or what not,
Which may be the chosen spot.
No toad spy you,
Hovering bird of prey pass by you;
Spin and die,
To live again a butterfly.

Alliteration

Poems also may have repeated sounds that are more subtle than rhymes. These repeated sounds come in two common forms: *consonance,* the stringing together of similar consonant sounds, and *assonance,* the making of a series of similar vowel sounds. Together, consonance and assonance are known as *alliteration.*

Listen to this line from a poem by Rowena Bennett: "There once was a witch of Willowby Wood. . . ." A series of similar consonant sounds ties her words together; this is an example of consonance. No matter that "once" begins with *o;* the initial *w* sounds knit Bennett's words into a sonorous fabric.

Consonance doesn't have to be smooth, though. A succession of percussive consonants can sound like feet walking on dry sticks, as in this anonymous Welsh poem translated by Gwyn Williams (in **The Rattle Bag**, edited by Heaney and Hughes):

Dinogad's speckled petticoat
was made of skins and speckled stoat:
whip whip whipalong
eight times we'll sing the song.

The succession of consonant clusters in Alfred, Lord Tennyson's "The Eagle" (1851) helps us to see and feel the bird's harsh, desolate

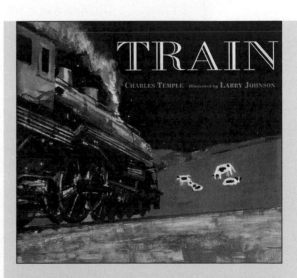

ILLUSTRATION 6.5 A banjo picker and storyteller, Temple stresses rhyme, rhythm, and sound in his poems—many of which were begun as a relief from long church sermons or graduation speeches. (Cover from *Train* by Charles Temple, illustrated by Larry Johnson. Jacket illustration copyright © 1996 by Larry Johnson. Reprinted by permission of Houghton Mifflin Harcourt Publishing Company. All rights reserved.)

perch; when the consonants give way to smoother sounds, they suggest the expansive beauty of the landscape below:

> He clasps the crag with crooked hands;
> Close to the sun in lonely lands,
> Ringed with the azure world, he stands . . .

Assonance, the use of a series of similar vowel sounds, also ties the words in a line together. Note the repeated short vowel sounds in "clasps," "crag," and "hands" in Tennyson's poem. Carl Sandburg also used assonance skillfully in "Splinter" (from *The Complete Poems of Carl Sandburg*):

> The voice of the last cricket
> across the first frost
> is one kind of goodbye.
> It is so thin a splinter of singing.

Note the high thin "ih" sounds in the last line, holding out against the more ponderous "ah" sounds in the second.

Onomatopoeia

When words in a poem imitate actual sounds of things (such as "moo," "oink," "bam"), the poet is using onomatopoeia. Hilaire Belloc gave us some fine examples of onomatopoeia as he described Spanish dancers in these lines from "Tarantella" (in *The Rattle Bag*):

> . . . And the Hip! Hop! Hap!
> Of the clap
> Of the hands . . .
> . . . And the Ting, Tong, Tang of the Guitar . . .

In sum, poets use sounds deliberately to approximate the emotional qualities of their subjects and to weave words together into tight compositions. Good poets blend sounds so skillfully that we feel the effects without being aware of the devices they have used. Note how Rodney Bennet employs rhythm, rhyme, alliteration, and onomatopoeia in this poem (in *Knock at a Star,* edited by Kennedy and Kennedy):

> *Windy Nights*
> Rumbling in the chimneys,
>   Rattling at the doors,
> Round the roofs and round the roads
>   The rude wind roars;
> Raging through the darkness,
>   Raving through the trees
> Racing off again across
>   The great grey seas.

Images

When a poem seems to "put us in the picture," chances are the poet has used imagery, an appeal to the senses, employing details that enable us to imagine how things look, sound, feel, smell, or taste.

In "The Child on Top of a Greenhouse," Theodore Roethke first anchors our impressions in the narrator's point of view by reporting what the narrator sees, hears, and feels:

> The wind billowing out the seat of my britches,
> My feet crackling splinters of glass and dried putty,
> The half-grown chrysanthemums staring up like accusers,
> Up through the streaked glass, flashing with sunlight,
> A few white clouds all rushing eastward,

A line of elms plunging and tossing like horses,
And everyone, everyone pointing up and shouting!

By the end of the poem, the danger of the narrator's situation sinks in. We realize that the child's absorption in sensory details, in which we have shared, has made him oblivious to the perils of climbing on top of a greenhouse.

Mary O'Neill's poem "My Fingers" about the sense of touch is full of tactile imagery:

My fingers are antennae.
Whatever they touch:
Bud, rose, apple,
Cellophane, crutch—
They race the feel
Into my brain,
Plant it there and
Begin again.
This is how I knew
Hot from cold
Before I was even
Two years old.

Teaching Idea 6.5
Creating Metaphors

Mary O'Neill's poem "My Fingers" (shown left) is really a list of tactile sensations. Ask your students to imitate her poem by writing list poems. For example, they may list everything that is cold, or empty, or warm, or prickly, or too much, or slow. Demonstrate how to begin with a class poem. Encourage them to mix literal things with figurative ones. For "things that are cold," they might list:

A winter's dawn
A snow shovel
A car that won't start
An enemy's heart

Using her poem as a model, ask a group of children to write a list of tastes, or sounds, or shapes, or colors. Remind them to think metaphorically; for example, "round" can refer to a wheel or to the consequences of a bad deed ("Whatever goes around comes around.").

Comparisons

Imagery is one of poetry's great contributions to human awareness. With imagery, poems name sensations and expand people's consciousness of their minute-to-minute experiences. Toddlers have the wonderful power to put words together in new ways: A naked child spread his arms and proclaimed, "I'm barefoot all over!" Making words do new work is one of the poet's greatest talents, too. Poets often use language in fresh ways by making comparisons: similes and metaphors and personifications.

The definitions of these terms never do justice to their power. A *simile* is defined as an explicit comparison, using the word "like" or "as." A *metaphor* lacks those two words and is a direct comparison in which one thing is described as if it were another. *Personification* is a sort of metaphor in which an inanimate thing is described as if it were human (or, at least, had sensations and will). But look what writers do with these literary devices. Practically all mythology is built on personification. The ancient Norse myths, for example, personified the reckless forces of nature in the character of Thor. Most religious writing is built around metaphor and simile: Having no direct experience of any world but this one, religious writers use familiar terms to speak of things beyond.

The Mexican poet Alberto Forcada compares a belly button to the knot in a balloon in this translated poem (in *The Tree Is Older Than You Are*, edited by Naomi Shihab Nye), making a simile:

Ombligo	Belly Button
Como los globos	Like the balloons
que flotan en las fiestas,	that float at parties,
tengo, para no desinflarme,	I have a knot on my belly
un nudo en el estómago.	so I won't go flat.

In "Mirrorment" (in *Sing a Song of Popcorn*, edited by de Regniers et al.), A. R. Ammons equates flowers and birds, making a metaphor:

Birds are flowers flying
and flowers perched birds.

Roethke's young narrator in "The Child on Top of a Greenhouse" said that the half-grown chrysanthemums were "staring up at him like accusers." This comparison gave the

Teaching Idea 6.6
Creating a Poem Collage

One way to interrupt children's expectations that a poem will have a literal meaning is to have them play with parts of poems out of order. Invite the students to make a poem collage. Pass out copies of a lyric or expressive poem. Have the children read it aloud, with each child taking a line. Then go around the room, having each child chant out a line or phrase he or she found especially striking. Finally, invite them to cut the poems apart and reassemble the lines or phrases as they see fit. If they want, they may repeat a line or phrase, for special emphasis.

flowers human senses and motives—it personified them. Langston Hughes personified rain in his "April Rain Song" (from *The Dream Keeper and Other Poems*):

Let the rain kiss you.
Let the rain beat upon your head with silver liquid drops.
Let the rain sing you a lullaby.
The rain makes running pools in the gutter.
The rain plays a little sleep-song on our roof at night.
And I love the rain.

In summary, all of these ways of making likenesses—similes, metaphors, and personification—expand the power of language. In so doing, they expand our perceptions, too: They make us, the readers and hearers, experience the world in new ways.

Forms

The arrangement of words on the page affects their look, readers' progress through them, and the emphasis given to some of the words.

Sometimes poets arrange their words to look like their topic. Shel Silverstein makes his poem "Valentine" (from *Where the Sidewalk Ends*) look like a list maintained by a child who is keeping score:

I got a valentine from Timmy
    Jimmy
    Tillie
    Billy
    Nicky
    Micky
    Ricky
    Dicky
    Laura
    Nora
    Cora
    Flora
    Donnie
    Ronnie
    Lonnie
    Connie
    Eva even sent me two
    But I didn't get none from you.

This poem's arrangement invites reading one name at a time, as if a child were keeping track of who her friends are. When the poem looks like the thing it describes, it is called a *concrete poem*.

Insight

Above and beyond the effects of particular literary devices, poems often startle us with insight—a noticing of things that makes us say, "Yes—that's it! But I never found a way of saying it before." Some insights are simple but still surprising, like this one in Philip Whalen's poem "Early Spring" (in Paul Janeczko's *This Delicious Day*):

The dog writes on the window with his nose.

Some insights are more complicated, such as those in this poem by Naomi Shihab Nye (from *Words under the Words*):

Famous

The river is famous to the fish.
The loud voice is famous to silence,
which knew it would inherit the earth
before anybody said so.
The cat sleeping on the fence is famous to the birds
watching him from the birdhouse.
The tear is famous, briefly, to the cheek.
The idea you carry close to your bosom
is famous to your bosom.
The boot is famous to the earth,
more famous than the dress shoe,
which is famous only to floors.
The bent photograph is famous to the one who carries it
and not at all famous to the one who is pictured.
I want to be famous to shuffling men
who smile while crossing streets,
sticky children in grocery lines,
famous as the one who smiled back.
I want to be famous the way a pulley is famous,
or a buttonhole, not because it did anything spectacular,
but because it never forgot what it could do.

Imagery is one of poetry's great values, but insight is even greater. Good poems are often noteworthy for their concentrated clarity of understanding. The insight expressed in Naomi Shihab Nye's poem might well have been elaborated by another writer into a book-length manuscript.

Children's Preferences in Poetry

Young children have an affinity for poetry. Unfortunately, children's pleasure in poetry does not always survive middle childhood, when poetry for the young moves beyond the merely playful, to more ambitious uses of language.

What sorts of poetry do elementary school children like? Studies of children's poetry preferences over the past quarter-century have yielded fairly consistent answers. A study by Kutiper and Wilson (1993) reached findings very similar to those of a landmark study done by Terry (1974) twenty years earlier. Kutiper and Wilson summarized their findings as follows (pp. 28–35):

1. The narrative form of poetry is popular with readers of all ages, while free verse and haiku are the most disliked forms.
2. Students prefer poems that contain rhyme, rhythm, and sound.
3. Children most enjoy poetry that contains humor, familiar experiences—and animals.
4. Younger students (elementary and middle school and junior high age) prefer contemporary poems.
5. Students dislike poems that contain (extensive) visual imagery or figurative language.

In terms of particular poets, according to the same study, elementary-grade students prefer the light and funny poetry of Jack Prelutsky and Shel Silverstein far above any other. Poetry that critics deem to have greater literary merit has nowhere near the circulation of the works of these two poets.

Teaching Idea 6.7
Making Concrete Poems

In *Love That Dog*, Sharon Creech's novel in verse, Jack creates a concrete poem of his dog:

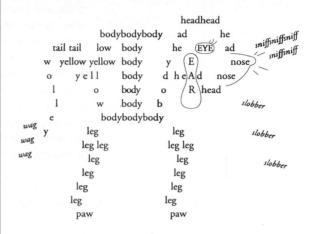

MY YELLOW DOG
by Jack

Share Jack's creation with your students, and challenge them to come up with a concrete poem of their own. They should use words to depict an object that is important to them, such as a baseball bat, a boat, a bicycle, a computer, or a cat.

Consider making a whole class anthology of their concrete poems.

Technology in Practice 6.1
Form Poems on the Web

It can be interesting to sample ideas for teaching children to write poetry from different parts of the country and even different parts of the world. Two interesting websites on writing form poems are found at:

http://www.poetspath.com/exhibits/magnificentrainbow.html

http://www.standards.dfes.gov.uk/primary/teaching resources/literacy/nls_teaching_writing/404257/nls _npp_poem_y4t3forms.pdf

Criteria for Evaluating Poetry

1. **Sounds.** Poems don't have to rhyme. The better ones among those that do, though, have *exact* rhymes (they don't try to pass off near misses, like "alone" as a rhyme for "home"). Better poems also have *fresh* rhymes: Readers cannot predict with boring certainty what the words at the ends of the lines will be. Above all, the rhymes don't get in the way of the poem's images and meanings. Poems do not have to have fixed rhythms. But if they do, the rhythms should be consistent enough for children to discern them, yet not so consistent as to become monotonous. It is a very tall order to mix rhymes with exact word choices and to use clear rhythms that aren't cloying. No wonder so many modern poets avoid rhymes and fixed rhythms altogether. If a poet opts for blank verse, though, we still expect a careful handling of sound and meter. If their poems don't rhyme, poets must match the sounds of their words to the emotional tone of their topics. If their poems don't have a fixed rhythm throughout, poets must write in syllables that match the pace of the reading to the meaning of the poem.

2. **Images.** Good poems bring clear images to the mind's eye. Whether they use language denotatively with precise word choices or connotatively with metaphors, similes, and symbols—good poems serve as models of the ways in which language can name experiences and even as vehicles that take readers beyond experience.

3. **Insight.** Good poems surprise us with fresh or wise observations. In so doing, they expand our awareness and raise our spirits.

4. **A positive stretch.** There are many poems that appeal mainly to children's mischievous side; the better ones feature creative word play or illuminating observations or both.

5. **Appropriateness for occasions.** Poems can deepen our awareness of any celebration, whether it be a holiday, a birthday, the loss of a pet, or the occasion of getting to know a new friend. Acquaint yourself in advance with poems for different occasions, so you will be ready with the right one at the right time.

How Can We Expand Children's Taste in Poetry?

Of course, findings about children's poetry tastes like those above don't settle anything. If worth were reducible to popularity, all children's fiction would come from the Junie B. Jones series, and all their food would be chosen from the McDonald's menu. Since what children enjoy is largely synonymous with whatever is most familiar to them, our task as advocates of literature is to expand the range of poetry children know and, eventually, the range that they consider enjoyable.

There are three main ways to enhance children's appreciation of poetry. One way is to share poetry informally with children every chance you get. Children will appreciate poems if you offer them for their content—for the insights and feelings they communicate—rather than as complex objects to be analyzed. A second way to promote poetry is to have children practice choral speaking and performance. Most poetry is best read aloud, and the variations possible with a voice choir can make poems sound magnificent. A third way to encourage appreciation of poetry is to encourage children to write it. Writing poetry gives children a connection to what poets are trying to do. Ways of engaging children in poetry are described at length in Chapter 13, "Inviting Children into Literature."

Major Children's Poets and Their Works

Hundreds of poets have written for children, but we will look closely at only a handful who are especially noteworthy, both for their insight and literary skill and for their acceptance by children over the years.

Issue to Consider

How Can We Keep Children's Liking for Poetry Alive?

Jack Prelutsky, a very popular poet among North American children, explains the problem this way (1983, p. 18):

> For very young children, poetry is as natural as breathing. . . . But then something happens to this early love affair with poetry. At some point during their school careers, many children seem to lose their interest and enthusiasm for poetry and their easygoing pleasure in its sounds and images.

What is to be done? What kinds of poems will keep children's interest alive? Here is Prelutsky's answer (1983, p. 18):

> . . . poems that evoke laughter and delight, poems that cause a palpable ripple of surprise by the unexpected comparisons they make, poems that paint pictures with words that are as vivid as brushstrokes, poems that reawaken pleasure in the sounds and meanings of language.

A contrasting opinion was expressed by Myra Cohn Livingston (1992, p. 9):

> [Poetry] is now pouring from the publishers, but much of it is little more than prose arranged as poetry, overblown metaphors, tired clichés, and light verse that caters to many of the baser emotions, calculated to give children a quick laugh. It has, in many instances, no sign of helping children evolve, but on the contrary [allows them to] remain in the same old place.

Prelutsky and Livingston have written very different poetry. Prelutsky creates rhymed and rhythmic poems that are noted for their humor and surprising twists. Livingston's poems take more varied forms, including blank verse, and most of them explore serious themes. One has the feeling, reading their comments, that each might consider the other's poetry part of the problem.

What do you think? In order to keep children's interest in poetry alive, should we offer them mostly poems that are enjoyable? Or should we offer them mostly poems that take their inner complexities seriously? Should the poems be immediately rewarding? Or should they challenge children to ponder their meanings and associations? Or is there some middle ground?

Nikki Grimes

Nikki Grimes describes herself as a poet who thrives on challenges. She has written poems to match the happy moods of photographs (***It's Raining Laughter***, with photographs by Myles Pinkney), poems about family relationships (***A Dime a Dozen***, illustrated by Angelo), and poems that say new things about love (***Hopscotch Love: A Family Treasury of Love Poems,*** illustrated by Melodye Benson Rosales). A collection of her poems that explore a friendship between two girls (***Meet Danitra Brown***, illustrated by Floyd Cooper) won the Coretta Scott King Award.

Grimes can touch important and difficult themes with a sense of hope and confidence that opens the way for children to talk about the same themes. Consider "Sister Love," for instance:

My sister and I dream of adoption—someday.
In the dream, we're never apart.
Then this nice lady comes to the group home
With a girl-shaped hole in her heart.
The nice lady seemed to like Kari and me
But she only had spare room for one.
Her home was fairly small, she said,
And she already had a son.
My age was closest to her boy's
So she asked if I wanted to go.
I squeezed my sister's trembling hand
And whispered, "Thanks, but no."

Ask the Poet . . .   Nikki Grimes

Favorite Books as a Child

I grew up in and out of foster homes, and did not have books of my own until I was in high school. Dependent on school and public libraries for all my reading materials, I read whatever I could get my hands on, and never remember reading any book more than once, so I never developed favorites.

Some material is drawn from my own life ("Sister Love," Jazmin's Notebook, A Dime a Dozen—the only truly autobiographical work I've written to date). Most of my material, though, derives from a lifelong discipline of observing people around me, both young and old.

When I was in my early teens, my father encouraged me to develop a writer's eye and a writer's ear, to always be attentive, watchful, listening. It's second nature to me, now. I'm forever picking up snatches of dialogue, of dialect, forever noticing certain gestures, mannerisms, and so on. I file them all away in my memory for later use. When I sit down to write a new poem, a new story, these observances come forth, unbidden. The voices I've heard suddenly ring in my ear, the swagger I've seen passes before my eyes yet again. The encyclopedia of my memory provides everything I need.

Having my senses "on" at all times may sound like a lot of work, but it's automatic, at this point. I'm hardly aware that I'm doing it, anymore!

Great advice, Dad. Thanks!

Nikki Grimes does not consider herself a bona fide storyteller, but, as she told an audience at the Library of Congress, she is happy to own the title Poet. Born and raised in New York City, Nikki began composing verse at the age of six and has been writing ever since. She has received extraordinary acclaim for her poetry and novels for children and young adults. She won the 2006 NCTE Award for Excellence in Poetry for Children. Her works have been designated as ALA Notable books and have won the Coretta Scott King Award. Her most recent honored works are *What Is Goodbye?* (an ALA Notable book), *Jazmin's Notebook, Dark Sons,* and *The Road to Paris* (Coretta Scott King Author Honor Books). Other honored works are the novels *Bronx Masquerade* (Dial), winner of the 2003 Coretta Scott King Author Award, and *Jazmin's Notebook* (Dial), a Coretta Scott King honor book and Bank Street College Book of the Year; the popular poetry collections *Danitra Brown Leaves Town* (HarperCollins) and *Meet Danitra Brown* (Lothrop), an ALA Notable and Coretta Scott King honor book, *Hopscotch Love* (Lothrop); *Under the Christmas Tree* (Harper); *Talkin' About Bessie*, the 2003 Coretta Scott King Illustrator Award winner and Author Award honor book, and Horn Book Fanfare book (Orchard); *Aneesa Lee & the Weaver's Gift*, an American Bookseller Pick of the List (Lothrop); *From a Child's Heart* (Just Us Books); *A Dime A Dozen, My Man Blue* (Dial); *Come Sunday* (Eerdman's), an ALA Notable book; *At Break of Day and When Daddy Prays* (Eerdman's). An accomplished and widely anthologized poet of both children's and adult verse, Grimes has conducted poetry readings and lectures at international schools in Russia, China, Sweden and Tanzania, while short-term mission projects have taken her to such trouble spots as Haiti. Ms. Grimes lives in Corona, California. ■

Naomi Shihab Nye

Naomi Shihab Nye began writing poetry when she was six years old and published her first poem the next year. The daughter of a Palestinian father and an American mother, Nye has traveled back to the Middle East to explore her roots. Her own poems, collected in *Fuel, The Red Suitcase, Words under the Words,* and *A Maze Me: Poems for Girls,* are simply worded works of insight and wisdom, and they hold a special appeal to middle-grade and older students. She has edited a collection of poems from many countries (*This Same Sky*), a book of bilingual (English and Spanish) poems (*The Tree Is Older Than You Are*), and a collection of poems written by young poets in the many workshops she has conducted in the schools (*Salting the Ocean*).

Nye's commitment to the human race, one person at a time, comes through in "Shoulders":

Shoulders
A man crosses the street in rain,
stepping gently, looking two times north and south,
because his son is asleep on his shoulder.
No car must splash him.
No car drive too near to his shadow.
This man carries the world's most sensitive cargo
but he's not marked.
Nowhere does his jacket say FRAGILE,
HANDLE WITH CARE.
His ear fills up with breathing.
He hears the hum of a boy's dream
deep inside him.
We're not going to be able
to live in this world
if we're not willing to do what he's doing
with one another.
The road will only be wide.
The rain will never stop falling.

ILLUSTRATION 6.6 Here the Palestinian-American poet Naomi Shihab Nye gives us poems to remind us that Arab culture is generous and humble, poetic and clever. (*19 Varieties of Gazelle: Poems of the Middle East* by Naomi Shihab Nye, illustrated by Michael Nye. Cover art copyright © Michael Nye. Used by permission of HarperCollins Publishers.)

Paul Janeczko

Anyone wishing to infect students from upper elementary grades through high school with a love for poetry wants to be familiar with poet and anthologist Paul Janeczko's work. Janeczko was a high school teacher before the poet's life took over, and since then he has crisscrossed the United States doing readings and giving workshops on poetry for young people and their teachers. At the same time, he has published more than two dozen collections of poems for young people, including *A Poke in the I: Concrete Poems, Stone Bench in an Empty Park, Don't Forget to Fly: A Cycle of Modern Poems, This Delicious Day: 65 Poems, A Kick in the Head, A Foot in the Mouth,* and *The Music of What Happens: Poems That Tell Stories.* Many of Janeczko's collections and other books teach readers about poetry, with commentaries by Janeczko the editor and by the poets themselves, as in *The Place My Words Are Looking For: What Poets Say about and through Their Work, Poetspeak: In Their Work, About Their Work,* and *Poetry from A to Z: A Guide for Young Writers.* His own poems have been collected in *Brickyard Summer* (illustrated, by K. Rush) and *That Sweet Diamond: Baseball Poems.*

Here is one of Janeczko's haiku:

Screeching and clawing
A trash truck drowns out the protests
from the alley cat

Janet Wong

Janet Wong left a career as a lawyer for Hollywood film producers to try her luck at writing for children. As a Californian with Chinese and Korean ancestry, she writes with real feeling from the point of view of non-white children, with a solid commitment to the open and egalitarian society the United States aspires to be. But she also has written really funny poems about driving that have been featured on National Public Radio's *Car Talk* program; a book of somewhat slobbery poems about buzzing sounds for preschoolers; and one insightful poem that rode around in 5,000 buses and subways through a New York City arts-in-transportation program. She has read her poetry at the Easter Egg Roll at the White House. She also has won the International Reading Association's "Celebrate Literacy" Award.

Her books include **The Dumpster Diver, A Suitcase of Seaweed, Good Luck Gold, Buzz, The Rainbow Hand—Poems About Mothers and Children, A Suitcase of Seaweed,** and **Knock on Wood,** from which comes this poem about salt:

> It is said
> salt is magic.
> The pure kind, sea crystals.
> Spilled salt is magic flung wild.

Douglas Florian

With 30 books of poetry for children to his credit, Douglas Florian is a New York City-based poet and illustrator whose poems explore the natural world with a keen eye and a quick wit. Many of Florian's poems take their subjects from nature, but even when they do, the poet doesn't let verisimilitude—or even standard spelling and grammar get in the way of a funny line.

Florian's **Mammalabilia** and **Insectlopedia** were instant favorites. His **Comets, Stars, the Moon, and Mars: Space Poems and Paintings,** short poems about astronomy with accompanying illustrations, is also popular. His **Beast Feast** won the Lee Bennett Hopkins Poetry Award from the Pennsylvania Center for the Book. Other animal-themed books are **Zoo's Who: Poems and Paintings, Lizards, Frogs, and Polliwogs,** and **On the Wing.**

Jack Prelutsky

America's first Children's Poet Laureate (Really! He was so named by the Poetry Foundation in 2006), Jack Prelutsky has produced a prodigious amount of poetry for the young over the past three decades. His poems are funny, ironic, often irreverent, and always lively as they address the challenges and joys of modern childhood. An example is "No Girls Allowed":

> . . . We play hide-and-go-seek
> and the girls wander near.
> They say, "Please let us hide."
> We pretend not to hear.
> We don't care for girls
> so we don't let them in,
> we think that they're dumb—
> and besides, they might win.

Prelutsky has produced many books of poems, including **My Dog May Be a Genius** (with an audio version available of the poet singing his poems), **It's Raining Pigs and Noodles, A Pizza the Size of the Sun, The Baby Uggs Are Hatching,** and **The New Kid on the Block** that were all illustrated by James Stevenson. **Beneath a Blue Umbrella** was illustrated by Garth Williams and **The Dragons Are Singing Tonight** was illustrated by Peter Sis. He has also edited many popular anthologies, including **For Laughing Out Loud** and the **Random House Book of Poetry for Children**, illustrated by the late Arnold Lobel. Recently published is a collection of some of his own best poems, **Be Glad Your Nose Is on Your Face and Other Poems: Some of the Best of Jack Prelutsky**, illustrated by Brandon Dorman. He has written guides to help children write poetry, including **Pizza, Pigs, and Poetry: How to Write a Poem** and **Read a Rhyme, Write a Rhyme.**

The Gorilla

A gentle giant
Blessed with grace . . .
It's still a
Gorilla—
Don't get in its face.

ILLUSTRATION 6.7   Don't look to this book for zoological facts, but rather for a perfect blend of poetic and visual evocation of its animal subjects. ("The Gorilla" from *Mammalabilia,* copyright © 2000 by Douglas Florian, reprinted by permission of Houghton Mifflin Harcourt Publishing Company.)

Shel Silverstein

In the 1970s, Shel Silverstein was to children's poetry what Judy Blume was to children's novels—a fresh and irreverent voice that projected a mischievous take on life and utterly resisted the sentimentality that had long been associated with children's poetry. He had many other sides to his professional life besides writing for children. He was long a cartoonist for *Playboy* and other magazines. As a songwriter, he had numerous hits for other singers, including "A Boy Named Sue" for Johnny Cash, and "Sylvia's Mother" for Dr. Hook. Silverstein's books of poetry, which include *Where the Sidewalk Ends* and *A Light in the Attic*, are eminently popular with children and were huge commercial successes. Silverstein died in 1999.

> *Oh Have You Heard?*
> Oh have you heard it's time for vaccinations?
> I think someone put salt into your tea.
> They're giving us eleven-month vacations.
> And Florida has sunk into the sea.
> Oh have you heard the President has measles?
> The principal has just burned down the school.
> Your hair is full of ants and purple weasels—
>   April Fool!

Lee Bennett Hopkins

Lee Bennett Hopkins deserves special mention for his tireless efforts to promote poetry among young people. Hopkins has been a classroom teacher, a curriculum specialist, a poetry anthologist, a poet, a consultant to publishers, a television show host, and a patron of two prestigious awards for poets and poems in his long career. He has published over 80 books for children, most of them poetry collections. His guide to using poetry in the classroom, *Pass the Poetry, Please*, is still a favorite with teachers after 25 years. A recent book of his own autobiographical poems, *Been to Yesterdays*, related the story of a childhood in the housing projects of Newark, New Jersey. Hopkins is a passionate advocate of the power of poetry to help every child—from the reluctant reader to the verbally gifted—and to help everyone expand awareness and experience the power of words. His *City I Love*, illustrated by Marcellus Hall, is a series of poetic observations of cities.

Read the interview where Lee Bennett Hopkins discusses the importance of teaching poetry and the difference between light verse and true poetry by going to the Conversations section of Chapter 6 in the MyEducationKit for your book.

Hopkins's recently published collections of other people's poems are prolific and valuable. As was said above (see "Poetry Collections"), one of the very best ways to approach poetry with children is to link just the right poem with a topic they are interested in. Look, then, at the focus of some of Hopkins's recent collections. He calls attention to language itself with poems by Eve Mirriam, Carl Sandburg, Pat Mora, and others in ***Wonderful Words: Poems About Reading, Writing, Speaking, and Listening*** (2004), illustrated by Karen Barbour. He celebrates books and reading in ***Good Books, Good Times*** (2000, illustrated by Harvey Stevenson, 2000), the regions of the United States in ***My America*** (illustrated by Stephen Alcorn 2000), science topics in ***Spectacular Science*** (illustrated by Virginia Halstead, 1999), mathematics in ***Marvelous Math*** (illustrated by Karen Barbour, 2001), weather conditions in ***Weather*** (1995), athletics in ***Sports! Sports! Sports!*** (illustrated by Brian Floca, 1999), famous Americans in ***Lives*** (1999), and remarkable members of the animal kingdom in ***Hoofbeats, Claws, and Rippled Fins*** (illustrated by Stephen Alcorn, 2002). In 2009, Lee Bennett Hopkins won The National Council of Teachers of English Award for Poetry for Children.

The National Council of Teachers of English Award for Poetry for Children

Several of the poets mentioned above have been recipients of an award for poetry for children that is given by the National Council of Teachers of English.

In 1977 the NCTE began recognizing excellence in poets who write for children ages 3–13. The award is given for the body of a poet's work and not for individual poems. The NCTE Award for Poetry for Children was given annually until 1982, and since then it has been awarded every three years. The award is based on four criteria:

1. Literary merit (art and craft of aggregate work).
2. The poet's contributions (meaning the poet's potential for further achievement in the field of poetry).
3. The evolution of the poet's work (meaning that the poet is expected to explore new dimensions of poetry rather than staying with one style).
4. Appeal to children. (Note that this is not the first criterion; and indeed many children's poets with the biggest sales have not won the award.)

The following poets have been winners of the award:

2009 — Lee Bennett Hopkins	1985 — Lilian Moore
2006 — Nikki Grimes	1982 — John Ciardi
2003 — Mary Ann Hoberman	1981 — Eve Merriam
2000 — X. J. Kennedy	1980 — Myra Cohn Livingston
1997 — Eloise Greenfield	1979 — Karla Kuskin
1994 — Barbara Juster Esbensen	1978 — Aileen Fisher
1991 — Valerie Worth	1977 — David McCord
1988 — Arnold Adoff	

For more information on the award you may visit the organization's website at http://www.ncte.org/about/awards/sect/elem/106857.htm.

Go to the Extension Activities section of Chapter 6 in the MyEducationKit for your book and complete activity #3 to learn about an NCTE Poetry Award winner.

To check your comprehension on the content covered in this chapter, go to the MyEducation-Kit for your book and complete the Study Plan for Chapter 6. Here you will be able to take a chapter quiz and receive feedback on your answers.

Experiences for Further Learning

1. Compile your own anthology of poems for children. Organize it around a theme or an issue—for example, poems for choral reading, poems from many cultures, or poems to celebrate holidays. So that you can become acquainted with contemporary poetry, use ten different sources, choose no more than two poems per source, and make sure they were published within the last fifteen years. (Thanks to Linnea Henderson for this suggestion.)

2. A good poem may sound natural, but on examination it is likely to turn out to have been very carefully crafted. Take a poem such as A. A. Milne's "Happiness" (from ***When We Were Very Young***). Try substituting other words for any of Milne's. Does the poem sound as good?

3. Put together a collection of rhymes that accompany activities—jump-rope rhymes, work poems, poems to accompany explorations, poems that accompany science study. Ask for examples from friends and fellow students. Be especially attuned to rhymes from different cultures: Mexican American, Asian American, African American, and Appalachian.

4. Since singing folk songs is an excellent way to participate in poetry and rhyme, learn to play a musical instrument—one that lets you play and sing at the same time. The easiest is the autoharp; all you do is press the button marked with the letter of the chord (most song books include guitar chords). A guitar is not too hard, once your fingers get adjusted, and there are four-string versions, to make the chording simpler to learn.

Now go to Chapter 6 in the MyEducationKit (www.myeducationkit.com) for your book, where you can:

- Find learning outcomes for Chapter 6.

- Access the Children's Literature Database for your own exploration.

- Complete Assignments and Activities that can help you more deeply understand the chapter content.

- Extend knowledge with content-specific Web Links.

- Deepen and apply content understanding with Extension Activities.

- Learn first hand about how authors and illustrators utilize their craft with written interviews in the Conversations section for the chapter.

- Check your comprehension on the content covered in the chapter by going to the Study Plan. Here you will be able to take a chapter quiz and receive feedback on your answers.

- Find the following updated appendices: Major Children's Book Awards, Children's Magazines, Professional Organizations, Children's Book Publishers' Addresses, Book Selection Aids, and Children's Literature Web Sites.

Recommended Books

* indicates a picture book; **I** indicates interest level (P = preschool; YA = young adult).

Comprehensive Anthologies

Berry, James, ed. *Classic Poems to Read Aloud.* Larousse Kingfisher, 1995. An excellent collection of poems from many cultures. (**I:** 10–YA)

Cullinan, Bernice, ed. *A Jar of Tiny Stars: Poems from NCTE Award-Winning Poets.* Wordsong/Boyds Mills Press, 1996. Thirty-five hundred children chose their five favorite poems from the works of each of the poets who won the NCTE poetry award through 1994. (**I:** 6–13)

dePaola, Tomie. *Tomie dePaola's Book of Poems.* Putnam, 1988. These eighty-six poems, many well known, range from works by contemporary poets such as Aileen Fisher, Valerie Worth, and Jack Prelutsky to poems by Emily Dickinson, Robert Louis Stevenson, and William Blake. (**I:** 5–12)

de Regniers, Beatrice Schenk, Eva Moore, Mary Michaels White, and Jan Carr, eds. *Sing a Song of Popcorn: Every Child's Book of Poems.* Scholastic, 1988. A beautifully illustrated large-format collection (all of the illustrators are Caldecott winners). (**I:** 7–12)

Farrell, Kate, and Kenneth Koch, eds. *Talking to the Sun: An Illustrated Anthology of Poems for Young People.* Holt, 1985. A beautifully illustrated collection of poems old and new from international sources. Many won't strike you as "children's poems" on a first reading, but there is much to ponder in them. (**I:** 11–YA)

Harrison, Michael, and Christopher Stuart-Clark, eds. *The Oxford Treasury of Children's Poems.* Oxford Univ. Press, 1988. A lively collection, mostly by English poets, with classics from such authors as Robert Louis Stevenson and Edward Lear. (**I:** 6–11)

Kennedy, Caroline. *A Family of Poems: My Favorite Poetry for Children.* Illustrated by Jon J. Muth. Hyperion, 2005. This collection of over 100 classic and new poems is arranged into seven sections—About Me, That's So Silly!, Animals, The Seasons, The Seashore, Adventure, and Bedtime. (**I:** 5–12)

Kennedy, X. J., and Dorothy Kennedy, eds. *Knock at a Star,* 2nd edition. Little, Brown, 1999. This welcome second edition is a fine collection of poems organized by categories, with helpful commentary by the authors, themselves established poets. Nearly half of the poems have been changed from the first edition, which appeared in 1982, and the editors have included several more accessible poems. (**I:** 9–YA)

———, eds. *Talking Like the Rain.* Illustrated by Jane Dyer. Little, Brown, 1992. A large-format, illustrated collection of poems for children, drawn from many sources by these noted poets. (**I:** 7–12)

Larrick, Nancy, ed. *Piping Down the Valleys Wild.* Illustrated by Ellen Raskin. Dell, 1968. A most useful collection of pleasing poems suitable for children, drawn from a range of contemporary and classic poets. (**I:** 9–YA)

Prelutsky, Jack, ed. *The Random House Book of Poetry for Children.* Illustrated by Arnold Lobel. Random House, 1983. An extensive anthology collected by one of America's favorite children's poets. (**I:** 7–12)

Sandburg, Carl. *Good Morning, America.* Harcourt, 1928. Poems for young and old by one of America's outstanding poets. (**I:** 10–YA)

Themed Collections

*Adoff, Arnold. *All the Colors of the Race.* Illustrated by John Steptoe. Lothrop, Lee, & Shepard, 1982. Drawing on the experience of the poet's own family, these poems are about the experiences of mixed-race children. (**I:** 5–9)

———, ed. *My Black Me: A Beginning Book of Black Poetry.* Rev. ed. Dutton, 1994. Adoff includes poems by Imamu Amiri Baraka, Lucille Clifton, Nikki Giovanni, Langston Hughes, and a dozen others who are better known to adults than to children, but who all celebrate the black experience. (**I:** 9–12)

Baylor, Byrd. *Desert Voices.* Scribner's, 1981. Unrhymed poems on desert topics by the author of "I'm in Charge of Celebrations." (**I:** 8–11)

Brooks, Gwendolyn. *Bronzeville Boys and Girls.* HarperCollins, 1967. Poems for children by the first African American woman to win a Pulitzer Prize. (**I:** 8–11)

*Bruchac, Joseph. *The Earth under Sky Bear's Feet: Native American Poems of the Land.* Illustrated by Thomas Locker. Putnam, 1995. Most of these poems are reflections on the Sky Bear constellation, also known as the Big Dipper. Some of Locker's rich oil paintings are magnificent. (**I:** 7–11)

*Bryan, Ashley. *Sing to the Sun.* HarperCollins, 1992. Bryan's Caribbean background comes through in his lively poems—some with choruses—and his bright palette. (**I:** 7–10)

*Cole, Joanna. *A Zooful of Animals.* Illustrated by Lynn Munsinger. Houghton Mifflin, 1992. Forty-five poems about animals by John Ciardi, Theodore Roethke, Jack Prelutsky, and others. (**I:** 5–7)

*Esbensen, Barbara Juster. *Dance with Me.* Illustrated by Megan Lloyd. HarperCollins, 1995. Fifteen poems by an award-winning poet celebrate the dance-like movements of everyday people and objects, from grandparents remembering, to a person weeding the garden, to bubbles to dust flecks in a ray of sunlight. (**I:** 5–12)

———. *Echoes for the Eyes: Poems to Celebrate Patterns in Nature.* Illustrated by Helen K. Davie. HarperCollins, 1996. These poems celebrate visual patterns in nature: spirals, branches, polygons, meanders, and circles. (**I:** 7–11)

———. *Words with Wrinkled Knees: Animal Poems.* Illustrated by John Stadler. Boyds Mills Press, 1998. Poems the celebrate animals, by the NCTE award-winning poet. (**I:** 6–12)

*Grimes, Nikki. *Come Sunday.* Illustrated by Michael Bryant. Eerdman, 1996. A colorful series of poems brings to life Latasha's Sunday in an African American church. (**I:** 7–10)

*———. *A Dime a Dozen.* Illustrated by Angelo. Dial, 1998. A series of poems about family relationships, told with honesty and insight. (**I:** 7–10)

———. *Hopscotch Love: A Family Treasury of Love Poems.* Illustrated by Melodye Benson Rosales. Lothrop, Lee, & Shepard, 1999. Sometimes funny, sometimes touching, always insightful, this is a surprisingly fresh series of poetic comments on our most written-about emotion. (**I:** 9–12)

*———. *It's Raining Laughter*. Photographs by Myles Pinkney. Dial, 1997. Exuberant poems about the many dimensions of happiness. (**I:** 8–10)

*———. *Meet Danitra Brown*. Illustrated by Floyd Cooper. Mulberry, 1997. Danitra Brown is described in a series of poems in the voice of Danitra's best friend, with details that reveal much about what character means in a young person. (**I:** 7–9)

Florian, Douglas. *Comets, Stars, the Moon, and Mars*. Harcourt, 2007. Florian's rich descriptions of heavenly bodies will enhance the study of space in any classroom. (**I:** 6–10)

———.*Insectlopedia*. Harcourt, 1998. The illustrations are striking in this whimsical commentary on the members of the insect world. Not all of the poems will help children pass a science quiz, but they are cleverly written and imaginatively illustrated. (**I:** 8–11)

*———. *Mammalabilia*. Harcourt, 2000. These poems are also whimsical, funny, and wonderfully illustrated. (**I:** 8–11)

———. *Zoo's Who*. Harcourt, 2005. An animal or insect—from lizards and pigs to ants and slugs—is the subject of each of these short (and often humorous) poems. (**I:** 8–11)

George, Kristine O'Connell. *Hummingbird Nest: A Journal of Poems*. Illustrated by Barry Moser. Harcourt, 2004. This poetic journal chronicles the drama of hummingbirds building a nest, hatching their eggs, watching the babies grow, learn to fly, and finally, leave their safe and secure nest. (**I:** 8–12)

*Greenfield, Eloise. *Honey, I Love and Other Poems*. Illustrated by Leo and Diane Dillon. Harper Trophy, 1978. Poems celebrating favorite things in a child's life by a highly esteemed African American poet. (**I:** 6–10)

———. *In the Land of Words*. Illustrated by Jan Spivey Gilchrist. HarperCollins, 2004. This collection, which includes new poems as well as familiar favorites, celebrates the power of language and literacy. The poet explains the inspiration of each poem in Part 1. Part 2 is arranged by poetic form. (**I:** 5–8)

*———. *Night on Neighborhood Street*. Illustrated by Jan Spivey Gilchrist. Puffin, 1991. Seventeen poems depicting evening time in an urban neighborhood. (**I:** 6–10)

*Gunning, Monica. *Not a Copper Penny in Me House*. Illustrated by Frane Lessac. Wordsong/Boyds Mills, 1993. A dozen poems and naïve illustrations celebrate rural life in Jamaica. (**I:** 6–10)

Hoban, Russell. *Egg Thoughts and Other Frances Songs*. Harper, 1972. Children who like Hoban's *Frances* books will love these poems, which are Frances's musings on everything from fickle friends to Lorna Doone cookies ("You are plain and you are square/And your flavor's only fair"). (**I:** 6–9)

Hopkins, Lee Bennett, ed. *Best Friends*. Illustrated by James Watts. Harper, 1986. Poems about friends by Gwendolyn Brooks, Judith Viorst, Langston Hughes, and others. (**I:** 10–12)

———. *Good Books, Good Times*. Trumpet Club, 1990. Poems about books by a favorite children's poet and anthologist. (**I:** 8–10)

*———. *Hoofbeats, Claws, and Rippled Fins: Creature Poems*. Illustrated by Stephen Alcorn. HarperCollins, 2002. Thirteen poets were commissioned to match poems about animals to Alcorn's etchings. There are poems here about buffaloes, anteaters, camels, and frogs.

———. *Through Our Eyes: Poems and Pictures about Growing Up*. Photographs by Jeffrey Dunn. Little Brown, 1992. Poems about finding one's identity and growing up are accompanied by exquisite photographs of children. (**I:** 5–10)

Hovey, Kate. *Voices of the Trojan War*. Illustrated by Leonid Gore. Simon and Schuster, 2004. Participants in the saga of ancient Troy each tell their story in a variety of forms—free verse, rhymed, metered, shaped, and other forms. (**I:** 10 and up)

Hudson, Wade, ed. *Pass It On: African American Poetry for Children*. Illustrated by Floyd Cooper. Scholastic, 1993. Poems by Eloise Greenfield, Lucille Clifton, Gwendolyn Brooks, Langston Hughes, and others. (**I:** 8–12)

Hughes, Langston. *The Book of Rhythms*. Introduction by Wynton Marsalis. Oxford University Press, 1995. Hughes wrote this lively illustrated text to make children aware of rhythm in all things—not just in poetry, but in music, art, and life. (**I:** 7–11)

Janeczko, Paul B. *That Sweet Diamond: Baseball Poems*. Illustrated by Carole Katchen. Atheneum, 1998. Janeczko catches the tension and the grace and the joys of the sport, from the players to the plays to the fans. (**I:** 9–12)

———. *This Delicious Day: 65 Poems*. Orchard, 1987. Sixty-five thoughtful poems, presented with a minimum of editorial comment to invite meditation. (**I:** 12–YA)

Livingston, Myra Cohn. *There Was a Place and Other Poems*. Simon & Schuster/McElderry, 1988. Poems about sadnesses children bear, particularly as families have been broken apart. (**I:** 10–YA)

———. *Valentine Poems*. Holiday House, 1987. This well-known poet manages to do fresh things with a well-worn topic in this collection of poems for Valentine's Day. (**I:** 8–12)

Lewis, J. Patrick. *Monumental Verses*. National Geographic, 2005. Monuments from the modern and ancient worlds are celebrated in this collection including Stonehenge, the Great Pyramid of Cheops, the Golden Gate Bridge, the Eiffel Tower, and others. Photographs accompany each poem. (**I:** 9–12)

*Mora, Pat. *Confetti: Poems for Children*. Illustrated by Enrique O. Sanchez. Lee and Low, 1996. A baker's dozen short poems celebrate life in English, with Spanish words and a glossary. (**I:** 5–8)

Myers, Walter Dean. *Blues Journey*. Illustrated by Christopher Myers. Holiday House, 2003. This collection of 20 poems, penned in the traditional blues call-and-response style, celebrates and commemorates the range of African American history and experience. (**I:** 10 and up)

Noda, Takayo. *Dear World*. Dial, 2003. Illustrator Takayo Noda uses a young child's voice to address celebrations to the tulips, the birds, and the earth itself. This book will easily inspire writing exercises, as children craft their own "Dear _____" poems. (**I:** 5–8)

Nye, Naomi Shihab. *Red Suitcase: Poems*. Boa Editions, 1994. Nye is a Palestinian American, married to a New Englander, living in Texas. These poems shed light on her many landscapes, one at a time, with her characteristic plain-spoken wisdom and humility. (**I:** 8–adult)

———, and Paul Janeczko, eds. *I Feel a Little Jumpy around You: A Book of Her Poems & His Poems Collected in Pairs*. Simon & Schuster, 1996. A fascinating collection of ninety-six paired poems, one from a young woman's perspective and the other from a young man's, on a range of topics, including relationships. (**I:** 12–YA)

Phillip, Neil. *Singing America: Poems That Define a Nation*. Illustrated by Michael McCurdy. Viking, 1995. Containing famous and should-be-famous poems from every period of

U.S. history, the book is a wonderful source book of basic American poetry. (**I:** 8–YA)

*Prelutsky, Jack. *The New Kid on the Block*. Illustrated by James Stevenson. Greenwillow, 1984. The new kid in this collection who is intimidating the boys in the neighborhood is a girl, of course. (**I:** 5–12)

———. *Something Big Has Been Here*. Illustrated by James Stevenson. Greenwillow, 1990. These lively poems range from the hilarious to the serious. (**I:** 5–12)

*———, ed. *The Beauty of the Beast Poems from the Animal Kingdom*. Illustrated by Meilo So. Knopf, 1997. 200 poems about worms, birds, bats, and baboons, selected by a popular poet and anthologist. (**I:** 5–9)

Rosenthal, Betsy R. *My House Is Singing*. Illustrated by Margaret Chodos-Irvine. Harcourt, 2004. This collection is a tribute to the ordinary places, spaces, and objects that define home—the laundry room, the smoke detector, the vacuum cleaner, a hide-away, the hallway chair. (**I:** 5–9)

Rylant, Cynthia. *But I'll Be Back Again: An Album*. Orchard, 1989. Poems describing the difficult Appalachian childhood of a Newbery award-winning author and poet. (**I:** 12–YA)

Sisman, Joyce. *Song of the Water Boatman & Other Pond Poems*. Illustrated by Beckie Prange. Houghton Mifflin, 2005. This collection of poems chronicles plant and animal life in the pond throughout the seasons. Each double-page spread focuses on one plant or animal and includes a poem as well as a paragraph containing related scientific information. (**I:** 7–12)

*Sneve, Virginia Driving Hawk. *Dancing Teepee*. Illustrated by Stephen Gammell. Holiday House, 1989. Traditional poems still popular among Native American young people, these are mostly brief, lyrical observations on various topics. (**I:** 8–12)

Strickland, Dorothy, and Michael Strickland. *Families: Poems Celebrating the African American Experience*. Wordsong/Boyds Mills, 1994. An upbeat collection by out-standing African American poets, including Gwendolyn Brooks, Nikki Giovanni, Lucille Clifton, Langston Hughes—and also Arnold Adoff. (**I:** 7–12)

*Wong, Janet S. *Buzz*. Illustrated by Margaret Chodos-Irvine. Harcourt, 2000. A celebration of household sounds, most sounding like "buzzzz." A popular poet's first offering for young children. (**I:** 4–7)

———. *Good Luck Gold and Other Poems*. Margaret McElderry, 1994. Strong personalized poems from an Asian American point of view. (**I:** 9–YA)

*———. *The Rainbow Hand*. Illustrated by Jennifer Hewitson. McElderry, 1999. These poems are simple and unrhymed, but they shed light on many of the meanings mothers hold for us, from early childhood and through life. (**I:** 8–11)

*———. *A Suitcase of Seaweed and Other Poems*. Simon & Schuster, 1996. Wong offers poems that comment on all three of her heritages: Korean, Chinese, and American, with an autobiographical sketch introducing each section. (**I:** 8–11)

———. *Twist*. Illustrated by Julie Paschkis. Margaret K. McElderry, 2007. Each poem in this collection presents a picture and a story focused on a yoga pose. Vibrant illustrations accompany each poem. (**I:** 6 and up)

*Worth, Valerie. *All the Small Poems*. Illustrated by Natalie Babbitt. Farrar, 1987. Worth is a master at finding wonder in small and everyday things: a magnet, a cricket, a sleeping dog. (**I:** 8 and up)

Yolen, Jane. *Best Witches: Poems for Halloween*. Putnam, 1983. Yolen's assemblage of witches has a contemporary flair. (**I:** 6–10)

*———. *Dinosaur Dances*. Illustrated by Bruce Degen. Putnam, 1990. Yolen's poems invoke the unlikely spectacle of dinosaurs dancing the whole gamut of dances. (**I:** 7–9)

A Poet's Collected Works

Farjeon, Eleanor. *Eleanor Farjeon's Poems for Children*. Lippincott, 1951. Farjeon won the first Hans Christian Andersen Award for her contribution to children's literature of the world. The poems are touching, funny, and insightful. (**I:** 7–11)

———. *The Dream Keeper and Other Poems*. Illustrated by Jerry Pinkney. Knopf, 1996. Poems suitable for young people by one of America's greatest poets, who was a leader of the Harlem Renaissance. (**I:** 8–YA)

*Giovanni, Nikki. *Ego-Tripping and Other Poems for the Young*. Illustrated by George Ford. Lawrence Hill, 1993. Thirty-three poems in the lively and direct voice of a gifted urban poet. (**I:** 10–YA)

*———. *Spin a Soft Black Song*. Illustrated by George Martins. Farrar, 1985. Fine poems for children by a noted African American poet. (**I:** 8–12)

Roethke, Theodore. *The Collected Poems of Theodore Roethke*. Doubleday, 1946. Not all of these poems were written for children; nonetheless, they are full of rich imagery and some-times startling insights. (**I:** 10–YA)

Sandburg, Carl. *Rainbows Are Made: Poems*. Selected by Lee Bennett Hopkins. Harcourt, 1982. A good source of poems for children by one of America's great poets. Includes poems not often anthologized. (**I:** 9–12)

*Stevenson, Robert Louis. *A Child's Garden of Verses*. Illustrated by Tasha Tudor. Simon & Schuster, 1999. Probably the most enduringly popular collection of poems for children in the English language, charmingly illustrated by Tasha Tudor. Though over a hundred years old, most of the poems are still enjoyable. (**I:** 4–adult)

Songs and Song Collections

Axelrod, Alan, and Dan Fox, eds. *Songs of the Wild West*. Metropolitan Museum of Art/Simon & Schuster, 1991. Some favorite songs from the Old West, illustrated with fine Western art. (**I:** all ages)

*dePaola, Tomie. *The Friendly Beasts*. Putnam, 1981. This lovely old English carol of the Christmas story is a favorite of many children. With music for piano. (**I:** 5–6)

*Guthrie, Woody. *This Land Is Your Land*. Illustrated by Kathy Jakobsen. Little, Brown, 1998. A fascinating tribute to America's most prolific folk singer and the times that shaped him: the Depression Era and the Dust Bowl. (**I:** all ages)

Krull, Kathleen. *Gonna Sing My Head Off! American Folk Songs for Children*. Illustrated by Allen Garns. Knopf, 1992. With piano arrangements and guitar chords, these sixty-three songs are the best of the old and not-so-old songs that "folkies" in the United States have been singing for years. (**I:** P–12)

*Langstaff, John. *Oh, A'Hunting We Will Go*. Illustrated by Nancy Winslow Parker. Alladin, 1974/1991. An English folk song in picture book form. The couplets are spread across page turns, inviting the children to guess the endings. (**I:** 4–9)

*———. *What a Morning! The Christmas Story in Black Spirituals*. Illustrated by Ashley Bryan. Simon & Schuster/McElderry, 1987. Five spirituals with glorious illustrations, background notes, and stirring musical arrangements. (**I:** all ages)

Milnes, Gerald. *Granny Will Your Dog Bite? and Other Mountain Rhymes*. Illustrated by Kimberly Bulcken Root. Knopf, 1990. Milnes learned these songs from his West Virginia neighbors. Root's illustrations evoke the mountain setting from which the songs came. (**I:** 6–12)

Patterson, Annie, and Peter Blood. *Rise Up Singing*. Sing Out!, 1990. Hundreds of folk songs, some with music and all with guitar chords. Recordings of the songs are available. (**I:** all ages)

Seeger, Ruth Crawford. *American Folksongs for Children*. Doubleday, 1976. A fine collection of folk songs with accompanying games. Music and guitar chords are included. (**I:** all ages)

Narrative Poems

*Browning, Robert. *The Pied Piper of Hamelin*. Illustrated by Kate Greenaway. Dover Publications, 1997. This is a reprint of a version first published in England in 1887. (**I:** 4–8)

*Gerrard, Roy. *Rosie and the Rustlers*. Sunburst, 1991. A narrative poem about cowboys and girls, drawn with short bodies and tall hats. (**I:** 5–9)

*———. *Sir Francis Drake: His Daring Deeds*. Farrar, Straus, & Giroux, 1988. A narrative poem about the English privateer. (**I:** 6–10)

*Johnson, James Weldon. *The Creation*. Illustrated by James E. Ransome. Holiday House, 1994. Johnson composed "Lift Every Voice and Sing," considered by many to be the African American national anthem. His long poem "The Creation" recalls the oratory of Southern black preachers of the last century. (**I:** 7–13)

*Service, Robert W. *The Cremation of Sam McGee*. Illustrated by Ted Harrison. Greenwillow, 1986. Originally published in 1907, this narrative poem turns out to be a tall tale with a surprise ending. The illustrations are abstract but colorful. (**I:** all ages)

Sidman, Joyce. *Meow Ruff: A Story in Concrete Poetry*. Illustrated by Michelle Berg. Houghton Mifflin, 2006. Through concrete poetry, Sidman tells the story of an unlikely friendship between a puppy and an abandoned kitten. (**I:** 6–9)

*Temple, Charles. *Train*. Illustrated by Larry Johnson. Houghton Mifflin, 1996. A rhymed picture book evokes a train ride that lasts from early morning to late at night. (**I:** 6–9)

*Thayer, Ernest L. *Casey at the Bat*. 1888. Illustrated by Patricia Polacco. Putnam, 1992. A classic American baseball story set to verse. (**I:** 8–YA)

———. *Casey at the Bat*. Illustrated by Joe Morse. Kids Can Press, 2006. Morse's illustrations set this retelling of the classic narrative poem apart from earlier versions. The illustrations depict multiracial inner-city kids playing ball in an urban setting. (**I:** 8–12)

Form Poems

Burg, Brad. *Outside the Lines: Poetry at Play*. Illustrated by Rebecca Gibbon. Putnams, 2002. These are poems about play, but they also play with the arrangement of the words on the page. (**I:** 7–11)

Grandits, John. *Technically, It's Not My Fault: Concrete Poems*. Clarion Books, 2004. Each of these 27 concrete poems—with very idiosyncratic content—is written from the viewpoint of an eleven-year-old. (**I:** 10–12)

*Janeczko, Paul, ed. *Stone Bench in an Empty Park*. Illustrated by Henri Silberman. Orchard, 2000. Janeczko has directed the insight-bearing light of the haiku form to urban scenes and matched poems from Nikki Grimes, Issa, and others to black-and-white photographs by Henri Silberman. (**I:** 12–YA)

Nelson, Marilyn. *A Wreath for Emmett Till*. Illustrated by Philippe Lardy. Houghton Mifflin, 2005. This deeply moving tribute to Emmett Till, whose murder galvanized the Civil Rights movement, is written in a highly structured and unusual poetic form called a heroic crown of sonnets. (**I:** 12 and up)

Prelutsky, Jack. *If Not for the Cat*. Illustrated by Ted Rand. HarperCollins, 2004. Each of the haiku in this collection poses a simple riddle about an animal. Individual haiku appear on double-page spreads accompanied by an illustration of the creature. (**I:** 5–12)

Humorous Poems

*Ciardi, John. *Doodle Soup*. Illustrated by Merle Nacht. Houghton Mifflin, 1985. Funny poems by a master of the genre. (**I:** 6–8)

Dahl, Roald. *Revolting Rhymes*. Bantam, 1983. If you like Roald Dahl, you'll like this hilarious collection of poems—some of which are in dubious taste. (**I:** 9–12)

Langsty, Bruce. *If Pigs Could Fly . . . And Other Deep Thoughts*. Illustrated by Stephen Carpenter. Maedowbrook: 2000. These really are funny poems, and they're fine for reading aloud. This collection, says the author, was nominated for inclusion by 1,000 children. (**I:** 5–9)

Lear, Edward. *The Complete Book of Nonsense*. Dodd, Mead, 1846/1946. A complete collection of poems by the world's most influential nonsense poet. Includes "The Jumblies," or "They Went to Sea in a Sieve," and "The Owl and the Pussycat." (**I:** 5–9)

Lee, Dennis. *Alligator Pie*. Illustrated by Frank Newfield. Houghton Mifflin, 1974. These memorable poems on nonsensical subjects are as tightly rhymed and rhythmical as jump-rope rhymes. (**I:** 7–10)

*———. *Garbage Delight*. Illustrated by Frank Newfield. Houghton Mifflin, 1977. A good source for the nonsense poems of this award-winning Canadian poet. (**I:** 7–10)

Lester, Julius. *John Henry*. Illustrated by Jerry Pinkney. Dial, 1994. An African American folk song that pits the "steel-driving man" against a steam drill. (**I:** 8–10)

McCord, David. *One at a Time*. Illustrated by Henry B. Kane. Little, Brown, 1986. McCord's poems include "The Pickety Fence," a percussive and rhythmic poem. (**I:** 8–12)

Merriam, Eve. *Chortles: New and Selected Wordplay Poems*. Morrow, 1989. The late Eve Merriam was a master experimenter with words. (**I:** 9–YA)

Scieszka, Jon. *Science Verse*. Illustrated by Lane Smith. Penguin Putnam, 2004. Parody is the name of the game in this collection of songs, rhymes, and poems based on Mother Goose, Ernest Lawrence Thayer, and Edgar Allan Poe—to name but a few of the original inspirations. (**I:** 5 and up)

Silverstein, Shel. *Where the Sidewalk Ends*. HarperCollins, 1974. Funny and irreverent poems by one of the most popular of children's poets. (**I:** 5–12)

*Viorst, Judith. *If I Were in Charge of the World and Other Worries*. Illustrated by Lynn Cherry. Atheneum, 1981. Viorst penetrates to the heart of the foibles of children and their parents. (**I:** 12–YA)

Street Rhymes and Nursery Rhymes

*Cole, Joanna, and Stephanie Calmenson. *Miss Mary Mack and Other Children's Street Rhymes*. Illustrated by Alan Tiegreen. Morrow/Beech Tree, 1990. Jump-rope rhymes and more from city streets. (**I:** 4–8)

———. *The Inner City Mother Goose*. Simon & Schuster, 1969. Poems on urban themes patterned on older forms and with an ironic flavor. (**I:** 9–YA)

*Crews, Nina. *The Neighborhood Mother Goose*. New York: Amistad, 2003. Computer-enhanced photographs create a fanciful urban backdrop—photographs from the artist's neighborhood in Brooklyn—for the rollicking rhymes. (**I:** P–7)

Milne, A. A. *Now We Are Six*. Illustrated by Ernest H. Shepard. E. P. Dutton, 1988. Short rhythmic poems from a child's point of view, from the author of *The House at Pooh Corner*. (**I:** 4–7)

———. *When We Were Very Young*. Illustrated by Ernest H. Shepard. E. P. Dutton, 1988. Lively poems about lively children, these poems were originally published in 1924 and constitute some of the best-selling children's poem collections of all time. (**I:** 4–7)

Schwartz, Alvin. *And the Green Grass Grew All Around: Folk Poetry for Children*. Illustrated by Sue Truesdell. HarperCollins, 1992. You'll probably remember many of these poems from your childhood. All are suitable for children and make lively choral reading. Nice illustrations, too. (**I:** 6–YA)

*Watson, Clyde. *Father Fox's Pennyrhymes*. Illustrated by Wendy Watson. HarperCollins, 1987. Watson has an uncanny ability to create poems that sound fresh off the playground. His sister's illustrations are full of fascinating details and conversations in balloons. (**I:** P–9)

Poems Arranged for Reading Aloud

Ciardi, John. *You Read to Me, I'll Read to You*. Harper Trophy, 1987. Favorite poems for children by a much-loved poet. (**I:** 7–11)

*Fleischman, Paul. *Big Talk: Poems for Four Voices*. Illustrated by Beppe Giaccobe. Boston: Candlewick, 2000. Fleischman expands the size of the performance troupe with this set of poems for four (or more, or fewer) voices. (**I:** 9–12)

*———. *I Am Phoenix: Poems for Two Voices*. Illustrated by Ken Nutt. Harper Trophy, 1989. Poems about birds, set for two voices. (**I:** 9–12)

*———. *Joyful Noise: Poems for Two Voices*. Harper, 1988. This book of poems about insects won a Newbery Medal. (**I:** 9–12)

———. *Side by Side: Poems to Read Together*. Simon & Schuster, 1988. Another fine collection by a noted children's poet and anthologist. (**I:** 7–10)

Giovanni, Nikki. *Hip Hop Speaks to Children: A Celebration of Poetry With a Beat*. Sourcebooks Jabberwocky, 2008. With an accompanying CD, this collection features poets of the African American experience from Langston Hughes to Queen Latifah. It's Giovanni's answer to *Poetry Speaks to Children*, to which she was a contributor. (**I:** All ages)

Paschen, Elise, and Dominique Raccah. *Poetry Speaks to Children: A Celebration of Poetry With a Beat*. Illustrated by Wendy Rasmussen, Judy Love, and Paula Wendgrand. Sourcebooks Media Fusion, 2005. With an accompanying CD, this collection features a cross-cultural range of poets living and dead, from James Berry with his Caribbean poem, to Nikki Giovanni, to J.R.R. Tolkien. (**I:** All ages)

Novels in Verse

Creech, Sharon. *Love That Dog*. Joanna Cotler, 2001. A boy finds his voice through poetry in this spare rhymed novel, expresses grief over his dog, and utter delight when the writer Walter Dean Myers visits his school. (**I:** 9–12)

Grimes, Nikki. *Bronx Masquerade*. The lives of 18 urban teenagers are portrayed through verse and essay. (**I:** 12–YA)

*———. *Jazmin's Notebook*. Dial, 1998. Fourteen-year-old Jazmin, a resident of Harlem in the 1960s, puts down sketches of the people and events in her neighborhood in verse and musings. A Coretta Scott King Honor Book. (**I:** 1–14)

Hesse, Karen. *Aleutian Sparrow*. Margaret McElderry, 2003. During World War II, the inhabitants of the Aleutian Islands of Alaska were evacuated by the U.S. Government "in order to save them." This novel in verse chronicles their dislocation. (**I:** 9–12)

———. *Out of the Dust*. Scholastic, 1997. A novel in verse set in the Dust Bowl of the 1930's, Billy Jo, a fourteen-year-old piano player, endures grief and guilt over the loss of her mother. Winner of the 1998 Newbery Medal. (**I:** 9–12)

Smith, Hope Anita. *The Way a Door Closes*. Illustrated by Shane W. Evans. Henry Holt, 2003. This novel, a collection of 34 poems told from the perspective of a thirteen-year-old boy's point of view, chronicles the joys and struggle of an African American family. (**I:** 10 and up)

Williams, Vera. *Amber Was Brave, Essie Was Smart*. Greenwillow, 2001. The lives of two latchkey children are chronicled in this novel in verse. (**I:** 9–12)

Woodson, Jacqueline. *Locomotion*. Putnam, 2003. A fifth grader in a New York City school is helped by his teacher to write poetry in order to come to grips with his grief over his parents' death in a fire.

About Poetry

Janeczko, Paul. *A Kick in the Head: An Everyday Guide to Poetic Forms*. Illustrated by Chris Raschka. Candlewick, 2005. This guide to poetic forms, which features 29 forms, includes familiar forms such as the couplet and limerick, as well as less familiar forms such as the tercet and triolet. For each form, Janeczko includes an example of the form, an illustration (often humorous), and a footnote that offers a definition. (**I:** 10 and up)

———. *The Place My Words Are Looking For: What Poets Say about and through Their Work*. Bradbury, 1990. Poems by Cynthia Rylant, Gary Soto, Gwendolyn Brooks, Myra Cohn Livingston, Naomi Shihab Nye, and others, with comments by the poets. (**I:** 12–YA).

———. *Poetry from A to Z: A Guide for Young Writers*. Bradbury, 1994. Poems by Naomi Shihab Nye, Lilian Moore, Patricia Hubbell, and Myra Cohn Livingston are given, along with comments by the poets and suggestions for writing poems. (**I:** 11–YA)

Poems by Children

*The Children of Terezin Concentration Camp. *I Never Saw Another Butterfly*, 2nd Edition. Schocken, 1993. 15,000 Jewish children passed through the Nazi concentration camp of Terezin, outside of Prague. With the help of a remarkable teacher, children learned to express themselves through art and poetry, and some of their works are reproduced here. For most of the children, these poems were all that survived. (**I:** 9–YA)

Lyne, Sanford. *Ten Second Rainshowers: Poems by Young People*. Illustrated by Virginia Halstead. Simon & Schuster, 1996. Lyne has worked for many years as a poet in the schools, and here he collects poems from 130 young poets aged 8 to 18. Full-color illustrations set off each section. (**I:** 6–11)

Nye, Naomi Shihab, ed. *Salting the Ocean: 100 Poems by Young Poets*. Illustrated by Ashley Bryan. Greenwillow, 2000. Nye presents poems collected from her extensive work as a poet in the schools. The poems are lively celebrations of insight into sound, and hearing them is an invitation to other young people to take leaps with language. (**I:** 6–10)

International and Multicultural

Alarcón, Francisco X. *Poems to Dream Together: Poemas Para Soñar Juntos*. Illustrated by Paula Barragán. Lee & Low, 2005. This is a wide-ranging, thought provoking collection of bilingual poems that explores the everyday world of family and community as well as broader social issues. (**I:** 8–12)

*Burgie, Irving. *Caribbean Carnival: Songs of the West Indies*. Illustrated by Franné Lessac. Morrow/Tambourine, 1992. Thirteen songs include the familiar "Day-O," "Yellow Bird," "Michael Row the Boat Ashore," and "Jamaica Farewell." Also includes one song in Spanish, "Que Bonita Bandera!" from Puerto Rico. (**I:** 6–12)

Delacre, Lulu. *Arroz con leche: Popular Songs and Rhythms from Latin America*. Scholastic, 1989. Twelve poems from Puerto Rico, Mexico, and Argentina are first presented as verses in English and Spanish; the musical scores, with simple guitar chords, are provided in the back. (**I:** 6–11)

Demi. *In the Eyes of the Cat: Japanese Poetry for All Seasons*. Illustrated by Tze-Si Huang. Holt, 1992. Some of these short poems are four hundred years old, and some are recent. All crackle with keen observation and insight. (**I:** 7–12)

Griego, Margot, Betsy Bucks, Sharon Gilbert, and Laurel Kimball. *Tortillitas Para Mamá*. Illustrated by Barbara Cooney. Holt, 1988. Traditional Latin American nursery rhymes in two languages, with instructions for finger plays. (**I:** 5–9)

*Jaramillo, Nelly Palacio, ed. *Grandmother's Nursery Rhymes/Las Nanas de Abuelita: Lullabies, Tongue Twisters, and Riddles from South America*. Illustrated by Elivia Savadler. Holt, 1996. A bilingual book of poems from Latin America with lively illustrations. (**I:** 4–8)

Nye, Naomi Shihab, ed. *This Same Sky: A Collection of Poems from around the World*. Macmillan, 1992. English translations of more than one hundred poems from all of the continents except North America. (**I:** 8–YA)

———, ed. *The Tree Is Older than You Are: Bilingual Poems from Mexico*. Simon & Schuster, 1995. A wonderfully illustrated collection of poems from Mexico, in Spanish with side-by-side translation. (**I:** 8–YA)

Soto, Gary. *A Fire in My Hands*. Harcourt, 2006. In this revised and expanded edition of his 1999 volume of poetry, Soto brings to life everyday experiences of Mexican American youth. (**I:** 12 and up)

Tadjo, Véronique (ed.). *Talking Drums: A Selection of Poems from Africa South of the Sahara*. Bloomsbury, 2004. The poems in this multinational anthology range from praise songs to children's games to love poems to laments. They reflect the complexities of a complex land. (**I:** 8 and up)

 ## *Resources*

Copeland, Jeffrey S., ed. *Speaking of Poets: Interviews with Poets Who Write for Children and Young Adults*. National Council of Teachers of English, 1993.

Esbensen, Barbara. *A Celebration of Bees*. HarperCollins, 1987.

Hopkins, Lee Bennett. *Pass the Poetry, Please!* HarperCollins, 1987.

Janeczko, Paul B., ed. *The Place My Words Are Looking For: What Poets Say about and through Their Work*. Bradbury, 1990.

———. *Poetspeak: In Their Work, about Their Work: A Special Kind of Poetry Anthology*. Simon & Schuster, 1991.

Larrick, Nancy. *Let's Do a Poem*. Delacorte, 1991.

Livingston, Myra Cohn. *Poem-Making: Ways to Begin Writing Poetry*. HarperCollins, 1991.

———. "Poetry and the Self." *Fanfare: The Christopher-Gordon Children's Literature Annual*. Ed. Joel Taxel. Christopher-Gordon, 1992.

Lukens, Rebecca J. A *Critical Handbook of Children's Literature*, 4th edition. HarperCollins, 1992.

McClure, Amy, et al. *Sunrises and Songs: Reading and Writing Poetry in an Elementary Classroom*. Heinemann, 1990.

Wolf, Alan. *It's Show Time! Poetry from Page to Stage*. Poetry Alive!, 1993.

References

Blake, William. *Songs of Innocence and Songs of Experience.* Dover, 1789/1992.

Browning, Robert. *The Pied Piper of Hamelin.* Routledge, 1888.

Butler, Francelia. *Skipping around the World: The Ritual Nature of Folk Rhymes.* Ballantine, 1989.

Carroll, Lewis. *Alice's Adventures in Wonderland.* Illustrated by Sir John Tenniel. Dover, 1865/1993.

Ciardi, John. *The Monster Den; or, Look What Happened at My House—and to It.* Illustrated by Edward Gorey. Lippincott, 1966.

———. *The Reason for the Pelican.* Illustrated by Dominic Catalano. Wordsong/Boyds Mills, 1994.

de la Mare, Walter. Peacock Pie. Holt, 1923.

Esbensen, Barbara Juster. *Who Shrank My Grandmother's House?: Poems of Discovery.* Illustrated by Eric Beddows. HarperCollins, 1992.

Fisher, Aileen. *Always Wondering: Some Favorite Poems of Aileen Fisher.* Harper, 1991.

———. *Out in the Dark and Daylight.* Harper, 1980.

Florian, Douglas. *Beast Feast.* Voyager, 1998.

———. *On the Wing.* Voyager, 2000.

Grimes, Nikki. *Hopscotch Love: A Family Treasury of Love Songs.* Illustrated by Melodye Benson Rosales. Scholastic, 2000.

Guthrie, Woody. (1944). This land is your land. Song lyrics recorded in 1944, and republished in Elizabeth Partridge, *This Land Was Made for You and Me: The Life & Songs of Woody Guthrie* (New York: Viking, 2002), p. 85.

———, and Kathy Jakobsen (2008). *This land is your land, 10th Anniversary Edition.* Little, Brown.

Hall, Donald, ed. *The Oxford Book of Children's Verse in America.* Oxford Univ. Press, 1985.

Heaney, Seamus, and Ted Hughes. *The Rattle Bag.* Faber and Faber, 2005.

Hopkins, Lee Bennett. *Been to Yesterdays: Poems of a Life.* Illustrated by Charlotte Rendeiro. Boyds Mills, 1999.

———. *City I Love.* Illustrated by Marcellus Hall. Abrams, 2009.

———. *Marvelous Math.* Illustrated by Karen Barbour. Simon and Schuster, 2002.

———. *My America: A Poetry Atlas of the United States.* Illustrated by Stephen Alcorn. Simon and Schuster, 2000.

———. *Spectacular Science.* Illustrated by Virginia Halstead. Simon and Schuster, 2002.

———. *Sports! Sports! Sports!* Illustrated by Brian Floca. Harper Troph, 2000.

———. *Weather: Poems for All Seasons.* Illustrated by Melanie Hall. HarperCollins, 1995.

———. *Wonderful Words: Poems About Reading, Writing, Speaking, Listening.* Illustrated by Karen Barbour. Simon and Schuster, 2004.

Janeczko, Paul. *Brickyard Summer.* Illustrated by Ken Rush. Orchard Books, 1989.

———. *Dirty Laundry Pile: Poems in Different Voices.* Illustrated by Melissa Sweet. HarperCollins, 2001.

———. *Don't Forget to Fly: A Cycle of Modern Poems.* Bradbury, 1981.

———. *A Foot in the Mouth: Poems to Speak, Sing, and Shout.* Illustrated by Chris Raschka. Candlewick, 2009.

———. *The Music of What Happens: Poems That Tell Stories.* Orchard Books, 1988.

———. *A Poke in the I.* Illustrated by Chris Raschka. Walker, 2005.

Kipling, Rudyard. *Puck of Pook's Hill.* Doubleday, 1906.

Kuskin, Karla. *Any Me I Want to Be: Poems.* Harper, 1972.

———. *Dogs & Dragons, Trees & Dreams: A Collection of Poems.* Harper, 1980.

Kutiper, Karen, and Patricia Wilson. "Updating Poetry Preferences: A Look at the Poetry Children Like." *The Reading Teacher 47*.1 (September, 1993): 28–35.

Livingston, Myra Cohn. *Birthday Poems.* Illustrated by Margot Tomes. Holiday House, 1989.

———. *Earth Songs.* Illustrated by Leonard Everett Fisher. Holiday House, 1986.

Mak, Kam. *My Chinatown: One Year in Poems.* New York: HarperCollins, 2002.

Mason, Walt. "Football." *The Random House Book of Poetry for Children.* Ed. Jack Prelutsky. Illustrated by Arnold Lobel. Random House, 1983.

McCord, David. *All Small: Poems by David McCord.* Illustrated by Madelaine Gill Linden. Little, Brown, 1986.

———. *Away and Ago: Rhymes of the Never Was and Always Is.* Illustrated by Leslie Morrill. Little, Brown, 1975.

———. *Every Time I Climb a Tree.* Illustrated by Marc Simont. Little, Brown, 1967.

———. *The Star in the Pail.* Illustrated by Marc Simont. Little, Brown, 1975.

Merriam, Eve. *Blackberry Ink.* Illustrated by Hans Wilhelm. Morrow, 1985.

———. "The World outside My Skin." *Fanfare: The Christopher-Gordon Children's Literature Annual.* Ed. Joel Taxel. Christopher-Gordon, 1992.

———. *You Be Good and I'll Be Night: Jump on the Bed Poems.* Illustrated by Karen Lee Schmidt. Morrow, 1988.

Moore, Clement Clarke. "A Visit from St. Nicholas, or 'Twas the Night before Christmas." *The Oxford Book of Children's Verse in America.* Ed. Donald Hall. Oxford Univ. Press, 1985.

Moore, Lilian. *I Feel the Same Way.* Illustrated by Robert Quackenbush. Atheneum, 1967.

———. *I Thought I Heard the City.* Macmillan, 1967.

———. *Something New Begins.* Illustrated by Mary J. Dunton. Atheneum, 1982.

———. *Think of Shadows.* Illustrated by Deborah Robison. Atheneum, 1980.

Nye, Naomi Shihab. *A Maze Me: Poems for Girls.* Illustrated by Terre Maher. Greenwillow, 2005.

———. *Words under the Words.* Eighth Mountain Press, 1994.

Opie, Peter, and Iona Opie. *The Lore and Language of Schoolchildren.* New York Review of Books, 2001.

Prelutsky, Jack. *The Baby Uggs Are Hatching.* Illustrated by James Stevenson. Greenwillow, 1982.

———. *Be Glad Your Nose Is On Your Face.* Illustrated by Brandon Dorman. Greenwillow, 2008.

———. *Beneath a Blue Umbrella.* Illustrated by Garth Williams. Greenwillow, 1990.

———. *The Dragons Are Singing Tonight.* Illustrated by Peter Sis. Greenwillow, 1993.

———. *Imagine That! Poems of Never Was*. Illustrated by Kevin Hawkes. Knopf, 1998.

———. *It's Raining Pigs and Noodles*. Illustrated by James Stevenson. Greenwillow, 2005.

———, ed. *For Laughing Out Loud*. Illustrated by Marjorie Priceman. Knopf, 1991.

———. *My Dog May Be A Genius*. Illustrated by James Stevenson. Greenwillow, 2008.

———. *A Pizza the Size of the Sun*. Illustrated by James Stevenson. Greenwillow, 1996.

———. *Pizza, Pigs, and Poetry: How to Write a Poem*. Greenwillow, 2008.

———. *Read a Rhyme, Write a Rhyme*. Illustrated by Meilo So. Dragonfly, 2009.

Rosetti, Christina. *Complete Poems of Christina Rossetti*. Edited by R. W. Crump. Louisiana State Univ. Press, 1979.

Sandburg, Carl. *The Complete Poems of Carl Sandburg*. Harcourt Brace Jovanovich, 1970.

Silverstein, Shel. *A Light in the Attic*. Harper, 1981.

Steptoe, Javaka. *In Daddy's Arms I am Tall*. Lee and Low, 2001.

Stevens, Wallace. *The Collected Poems of Wallace Stevens*. Vintage, 1990.

Swados, Elizabeth. *Hey, You! C'Mere! A Poetry Slam*. Levine, 2002.

Tennyson, Alfred. "The Eagle." 1851. *Poems of Tennyson: 1830–1870*. Ed. T. Herbert Warren. Oxford Univ. Press, 1912.

Terry, Ann. *Children's Poetry Preferences: A National Survey of the Upper Elementary Grades*. National Council of Teachers of English, 1974.

White, E. B. *Charlotte's Web*. Harper Trophy, 1952.

Wolcott, Derek. *Omeros*. Farrar, Straus, & Giroux, 1992.

Wong, Janet. *Dumpster Diver*. Illustrated by David Roberts. Candlewick, 2007.

———. *Knock on Wood: Poems About Superstitions*. Illustrated by Julie Paschkis. Margaret K. McElderry. 2003.

Worth, Valerie. *Small Poems Again*. Illustrated by Natalie Babbitt. Farrar, Straus, & Giroux,1985.

7

Traditional Literature

"Once upon a time . . ."
"There was, and there was not . . ."
"In olden times when wishing still helped one . . ."
"Había una vez . . ."

These words command children's attention like no others. They announce that a traditional tale is about to be told. Fanciful events, choreographed by the storyteller, are about to dance through children's imaginations. How is it that a short patter of words can summon children's focus, ready them to step out of the present world into an imaginary one, and line up their expectations with an intricate pattern of characters, setting, plot, and theme that are about to unfold?

This chapter explores that question through the study of traditional literature. It is about folktales, fairy tales, and legends. Also myths and epics and ballads. It would be about folk songs and poems, too—but those were already discussed in Chapter 6, the chapter on poetry.

What Is Traditional Literature?

Traditional literature is the body of stories and poems that have come to us from teller to hearer, and from hearer to teller, and whose authors are unknown. "Literature" is a misnomer, though, since these works were told and heard long before they were written and read. Thus, the works that make up the body of traditional literature have met a standard that most other works for children have not: Traditional stories, rhymes, riddles, and games are so appealing and so memorable that they have been passed from generation to generation without the aid of writing. Even now that they have been written down, traditional works—because they are not considered the property of any one author—continue to inspire storytellers, writers, and artists (as well as choreographers, filmmakers, and musicians) to produce new versions.

Traditional literature consists of **folktales**, which are relatively simple stories with sparsely drawn characters and strong plots. The term **folktale** in English roughly corresponds to the term *märchen* in German and *compte* in French, both meaning "popular tales" or "household tales." One type of folktale is **fairy tales**, which rarely contain fairies or elves, as Joseph Jacobs pointed out many years ago:

> The words "Fairy Tales" must . . . be taken to include tales in which occurs something "fairy," something extraordinary—fairies, giants, dwarfs, speaking animals. (Jacobs, 1892, from the preface)

Folktales exist in every culture in the world. They are as universal as language, and, like language, the instinct to make stories is one of our defining features as human beings. Thus folklore attracts the attention not only of storytellers, teachers, and children's literature advocates, but also of scholars who study human nature: anthropologists, psychologists, and theologians. Folklore is also a branch of scholarship unto itself.

Folk traditions are both unique and universal. We can readily identify British folktales, with their sensible talking animals and their giants; and we can distinguish them from Norwegian tales, with their trolls and hags; or Russian tales, with their witch Baba Yaga, who lives in a hut that stands on chicken feet. But tales from different cultures also share similarities, and they sometimes show uncanny resemblance to each other. Thus, getting to know traditional literature is a way of getting to know other cultures, but at the same time it is a way of approaching themes that engage all of humanity.

The Value of Traditional Literature

Besides having demonstrated a timeless popularity, traditional tales and poems make up a very important part of children's literature for several reasons.

"Little pig, little pig,
Let me in!"
"Not by the hair
of my chinny, chin, chin!"

Go to the Assignments and Activities section of Chapter 7 in the MyEducationKit and complete the activities. As you work through the activities and answer the accompanying questions, consider the importance of evaluating traditional literature for children.

Go to the Extension Activities section of Chapter 7 in the MyEducationKit for your book and complete activity #1 to consider film versions of traditional stories.

Go to the Extension Activities section of Chapter 7 in the MyEducationKit for your book and complete activity #2 to compare different versions of a classic story.

Traditional stories and poems are engaging, or they would have long since died out. They invite participation by having plots that are easy to follow, characters who are clearly good or bad, chants that are repeated, rhymes or rhythms that are simple to remember, and succinct packaging. Folktales are a wonderful way to draw even the most reluctant child into the world of story and imagination.

Traditional literature is a rich source of multicultural and international literature, too. That is because in many cultures, oral traditions are far stronger than written ones, especially when it comes to children's fare. From Africa we have Ananse the Spider and Rabbit (who became Br'er Rabbit in African American folklore). From Latin America we have Juan Bobo the simpleton, and Ratoncito Perez and Cucarachita Martinez, the gluttonous mouse and the amorous roach. And from Native American stories we have the spirit-man Glooscap and the trickster Coyote. But we have far fewer realistic stories from those sources. Certainly it would be desirable to have more books about the lives of contemporary children in Africa, Latin America, and Native American communities, but for now, the folk stories are some of our few connections to peoples in many parts of the world.

Another strength of traditional literature is that folk materials are automatically considered part of "the public domain." Since they are not attributed to any particular authors, anyone is welcome to retell them for publication. Folktales and folk poems have thus been favorite fare for illustrators such as Simms Taback, Trina Schart Hyman, Paul Galdone, Stephen Kellogg, Paul Goble, and Paul Zalinsky, who have made award-winning books from them. They have also been beautifully retold by storytellers such as Jane Yolen, Joseph Bruchac, Virginia Hamilton, Julius Lester, Alma Flor Ada, Rafe Martin, Judith Sierra, and others.

Beyond all that, however, the folk tradition offers other benefits that are harder to summarize. Folk materials often take historical material and reshape its characters with psychological drives and fears to produce literature that fuses together cultural memory and entertainment. For example, the myth of George Washington cutting down the cherry tree, in the view of one historian (Vecsey, 1986), is an allegory that could symbolize the Founding Fathers' committing an act of rebellion against the colony's political father, King George. The act of rebellion made many people feel guilty, and in order to assuage the guilt, the myth has George Washington bravely and honestly owning up to his own deed, just as the founding fathers boldly affixed their names to the Declaration of Independence.

The legend of *La Llorona,* the "Weeping Woman," is told in the American Southwest and in Mexico, and the figure of La Llorona herself frightens Latino children just as the Boogie Man frightens Anglo children. Some say the legend of La Llorona is a symbolic retelling of the story of *La Malinche*—the beautiful Indian interpreter and mistress to Hernan Cortés who helped the Conquistador subdue her own people.

On a psychological level, folktales give children symbolic ways of thinking and talking about fears and urges that may be difficult to deal with directly. For example, a child who is powerless and aspires to have recognition will find solace in stories like "Jack and the Beanstalk" and "Juan Bobo." A child who feels hemmed in by siblings may quietly bask in the success of "Cinderella"—just as someone who feels her true worth has gone unrecognized because of her meager social status will identify with Jennifer Lopez's cinematic version of "Cinderella," *Maid in Manhattan.*

As the example of Ms. Lopez's movie suggests, one last value of folk literature is that it acquaints readers with plots that will be used over and over in other works of literature, including film. Some years ago, the literary critic Northrop Frye (1971) observed that literature is cumulative—that virtually everything written now draws on and builds on what was written before. Myths and folktales are our oldest stories, and they form the foundation for everything that has been written since, as contemporary works recycle plots and situations that have been used in the past. Frye maintains that we need to know those old

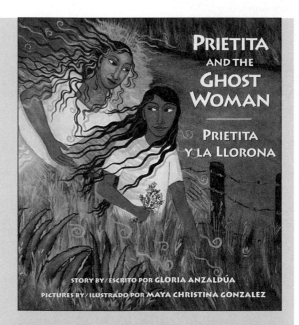

ILLUSTRATION 7.1 Widely known in oral culture, the harsh and tragic story of *La Llorona* has been softened and retold in this bilingual account, one of few print versions of this Latino story. (*Prietita and the Ghost Woman, prietita y la llorona* by Gloria Anzaldua. Reprinted with the permission of the publisher, Children's Book Press, San Francisco, CA. Pictures copyright © 1995 by Maya Christina Conzalez.)

stories so we can better understand and appreciate the new ones. Acquainting children with folktales, then, will prepare them to be better readers of more complex literature later.

How Traditional Literature Works

When you read a story in a collection such as Jane Yolen's ***Favorite Folktales from Around the World*** you are experiencing just the skeleton of the story. Written folktales often take less than a page to write down—yet in the hands of a storyteller the words take on life— they are whispered or shrieked or eerily stretched out, expanded and elaborated, adapted to this or that audience, and turned into a drama, a ritual, a play, a chant, a prayer. In the hands of an illustrator, a story is stretched onto the canvas of a 32-page picture book, and brought to life through "the drama of the turning page" and the many other devices drawn from the grammar of visual language that we met in our chapter on picture books. Indeed, storytellers keep telling the same story, and illustrators keep illustrating it, because the story is never exhausted.

Let us look now at the elements of folk stories: at their settings, characters, plots, and themes, and also at the ways readers respond to them.

Settings in Traditional Literature

In most folktales, the settings are described rather sketchily. "Once upon a time . . ." "Había una vez . . ." "There was and there was not . . ." and similar words begin many folk stories, although some get started with more enthusiasm. Here is the traditional beginning of "The Three Little Pigs":

> Once upon a time when pigs spoke rhyme
> And monkeys chewed tobacco,
> And hens took snuff to make them tough,
> And ducks went quack, quack, quack, O . . .

Either way, such beginnings serve as a signal that the reader should suspend disbelief just a little harder because something is coming that is fictional, maybe fanciful, but certainly worth listening to.

After the opening, we are told that a character may live in a hovel or in a castle. (Characters in folktales rarely live in cities, and never in suburbs or apartment buildings!) Basic as they are, these settings have associations. In European tales, the **cottage or the hovel** is where common people like us live. In the Grimms' tale, Snow White and Rose Red live simply in a cottage with their honest widowed mother. Those who live in cottages have nowhere to go but up: Maybe they have ambitions to live in more glamorous places—if they do, they may succeed—or, like the old couple in "The Fisherman and His Wife," their ambitions may get the best of them and they may have to settle for the cottage after all.

The **castle** is the place of our dreams. It is not where ordinary folk belong, but by cunning and perseverance or blind luck they may wind up there. In Charles Perrault's tale, the third son with the poorest inheritance makes his way from nowhere into a castle, thanks to the trickery of his helper, Puss in Boots. In the Russian tale, "Ivan, the Grey Wolf, and the Firebird," the youngest son of a czar wins the hand of a princess and inherits his father's castle.

The **forest** is the place where wild and dangerous things are encountered, and also where the imagination runs free. It is in the forest that Hansel and Gretel have their adventures in the Grimms' tale, and where Little Red Riding Hood meets the wolf in Charles Perrault's tale. It is in the forest where the little girl in the African American tale meets the Gunny Wolf and barely escapes with her life. And it is in the forest that the charcoal burner frees the ensnared bird who all-too-briefly becomes "The Crane Wife" in the Japanese tale.

Characters in Traditional Literature

Characters in folktales are often described sparely. Note, for instance, how the characters in "Jack and the Beanstalk" are introduced: "There was once upon a time a poor widow who

Teaching Idea 7.1

Finding the Roles Characters Play

Review the roles of *hero, rival, helper,* and *goal* with the children. Then retell the story of "Jack and the Beanstalk." Ask the children to name the hero. They will probably say that Jack is the hero. Then ask what his *goal* is. Be prepared for different answers. You may ask if he wants different things at different points in the story—if so, what do the changes in his goals say about how he may be changing? Ask who the *rival* is. Then ask who the *helper* is. Be prepared for different answers. Some may name the man with the beans, and some the giant's wife.

Later, ask the children to retell the story in a new way. This time, the giant's wife is the hero. What is her goal? Who is her rival? Who is her helper? Does she achieve what she wants? Retelling the story this way can be a shocking demonstration of the way narrative directs our attention. Once we cast Jack as the hero, we are willing to forgive his misdeeds; and since the giant's wife is only a helper, we stop thinking about her once the story follows Jack and the giant down the beanstalk.

Teaching Idea 7.2

Roles in Stories

Have the students in a class brainstorm and choose a setting for a folktale. It might be a cottage in the woods, an enchanted castle, or a remote village. Then have them name some characters that might appear in a folktale in that setting. Next, ask them to think of a goal that a character might have: It might be companionship, recognition, riches, or something to eat. Write names of possible characters on one set of cards, and words for possible goals on another set of cards. Turn the cards face down, and invite a student to draw a character card for **the hero**. Then have someone draw a card for the hero's **goal**. Next, have someone draw one of the character cards for **the rival**. Finally, have someone draw a card for **the hero's helper**. Now, either as a class or in pairs, the students can make up stories around those roles. They can compose them orally or in writing.

---

had an only son named Jack, and a cow named Milky-white." That is all we are told about them to get the story going. Now we meet the curious man who traded the beans for the cow: "He hadn't gone far when he met a funny-looking old man, who said to him: 'Good morning, Jack.'" And here the Giant's wife is introduced: ". . . . and on the doorstep there was a great big tall woman." Finally, we meet the Giant: ". . . . [T]he ogre came in. He was a big one, to be sure."

Characters in fairy tales are sometimes described at greater length, especially in the tales written at the court by Charles Perrault (see page 221). They are typically presented as very good or very bad. Here, for instance, is the way the characters in "Cinderella" are described:

> Once there was a gentleman who married, for his second wife, the proudest and most haughty woman that was ever seen. She had, by a former husband, two daughters of her own humor, who were, indeed, exactly like her in all things. He had likewise, by another wife, a young daughter, but of unparalleled goodness and sweetness of temper, which she took from her mother, who was the best creature in the world.

Perrault uses more describing words to present these characters, but the descriptions are summaries of their characteristics, with no room left for judgment by the reader. And they are contrasted in the extreme: very good or very bad.

Characters in traditional literature take on attributes almost by default according to the **roles** they play in the plot. The story assigns a character to a particular role, and the listener then instinctively ascribes qualities to that character. Whether watching a sports event or hearing a story, it is normal for us to cheer the hero, boo the rival, and keep a warm place in our hearts for the trusty helper. And as we saw in Chapter 2, all stories wittingly or unwittingly use these propensities to shape our reactions to characters: assigning this person the role of protagonist or main character, that person the role of the protagonist's helper, and that other person the role of rival or enemy. There are three common roles that characters play in folk and fairy tales: *the hero, the rival,* and *the helper*; along with one other common element, *the goal* (Souriau, 1955).

The Hero is the person whose desires and needs drive the story forward. In "Jack and the Beanstalk," the hero is Jack.

The Goal is the hero's main need or desire. In "Jack and the Beanstalk," Jack's goal changes throughout the story. At first his goal may be to satisfy curiosity, but later it is to get money, and still later, to find lasting security and enjoyment.

The Rival is the person who stands between the hero and her or his goal. The rival in "Jack and the Beanstalk" is certainly the giant.

The Helper is the person or force who helps the hero toward his or her goal. In "Jack and the Beanstalk" the helper is the curious old man who trades the magical beans for the cow.

It is no wonder then, that the characters in "Jack and the Beanstalk" are introduced with minimal description. Once they are cast in their roles, the listeners "fill in the blanks" with good or bad qualities.

Contrasts in Folktales

Hero versus villain, home sweet home versus land of adventure—folk literature is known for its stark contrasts. The French anthropologist Claude Lévi-Strauss (1957) asserted that these contrasts are not accidental. People learn about the truths of this world by paying attention first to those things that are most starkly opposite to each other: hot and cold, up and down, light and dark, male and female, very good and very bad. Only after they establish the basic contrasts in experience do they look at the middle ground—the lukewarm, the shades of gray, the moderate.

In folk literature, stark contrasts are common. Characters are young or old, sympathetic or despicable, very modest or very vain. Lévi-Strauss noted that a set of contrasts in a story can stand for another set of contrasts in the real world, and often those contrasts deal with an issue that people find too painful or controversial to talk about directly. Thus, stories become a safe way of exploring and resolving issues that people can't or won't confront.

For example, what are the contrasts in "Jack and the Beanstalk"? There are many: Jack/the giant, the earth/the sky realm, Jack's mother/the giant's wife, Jack at the beginning/Jack at the end, Jack as he seems to be/Jack as he really is.

When you contrast Jack and the giant, differences come tumbling out. Jack is young; the giant is old. Jack is small; the giant is huge. Jack has nothing but ambition; the giant has wealth and the fear of losing it. Jack seems insignificant, but is really a hero; the giant is fierce, but his brutishness makes him vulnerable. Jack is on the way up; the giant is on the way down (pun intended!).

When Lévi-Strauss looks at opposing characters such as these, he treats them as interchangeable elements in fixed relation to each other—like subjects and objects in a sentence—and sees what other items would fit in their slots. For example, for the opposing characters in the story of "Jack and the Beanstalk," we have the following:

Jack	The Giant
young	old
small	huge
clever	stupid
seems weak	seems strong
needy	greedy
poor, questing	privileged

What other characters share those sets of features? Pairs that come to mind are David and Goliath, Juan Bobo and the devil, Taran and the Horned King, Gretel and the Witch, Hamlet and Claudius, and Harry Potter and Voldemort.

What do the stories about such pairs have in common? We might say that these stories stand for, among other things, the competition between young people on their way up, trying to win the freedom and recognition that come with maturity, and the older generation, struggling to hold onto those privileges.

Plots in Traditional Literature

Plots are more prominent in folk and fairy tales than in other forms of literature. Because the tales are short, the characters flat, and the dialogue sparse, most of what we are given are the patterns of events. Plots are all the more pronounced in folktales because variations of the same plots may occur in tale after tale, even when those tales come from different parts of the world. The similarities arise according to American folklore scholar Stith Thompson (1946), because

> [t]he limitations of human life and the similarity of its basic situations necessarily produce tales everywhere which are much alike in all important structural aspects. They have as definite form and

Go to the Extension Activities section of Chapter 7 in the MyEducationKit for your book and complete activity #3 to compare several folk tales.

Teaching Idea 7.3
Finding Contrasts in Stories

Read the children the story of "Jack and the Beanstalk." On the chalkboard, draw a T-Chart, and label one side "Jack at Home" and label the other side "Jack in the Sky." Ask the students to help you list words that describe Jack's behavior at home and in the sky.

Ask them to think of other stories in which the hero seems different when he or she is away from home. If they need prompting, read them "Hansel and Gretel" and "The Orphan Boy and the Elk Dogs" (from Jane Yolen's *Favorite Folktales from Around the World*). How are the heroes in these stories different at home from the places they go on their adventures? Ask them to think of other stories in which the hero's demeanor and behavior is different at home than in the place where adventures happen.

Teaching Idea 7.4
Finding Motifs

Create a chart like the one pictured here. Label the column with these or other motifs. As the children hear or read stories during the year, add each story title to the appropriate column.

Adventures take place in a magical land	Youngest of three brothers or sisters	Beast is changed into a person by being loved	A "helper" tests the hero before giving help	A magical animal solves the hero's problems
"Jack and the Beanstalk"	"Puss in Boots"	"Beauty and the Beast"	"The Talking Eggs"	"Puss in Boots"
"East of the Sun, West of the Moon"	"Beauty and the Beast"	"The Frog Prince"	"Ivan, the Grey Wolf, and the Firebird"	"Ivan, the Grey Wolf, and the Firebird"

substance in human culture as the pot, the hoe, or the bow and arrow, and several of these narrative forms are quite as generally employed. (p. 7)

Folklore scholars for the past century have been working out ways to describe the common patterns in the plots of folktales. Antti Aarne and Stith Thompson described the commonalities of folktales in terms of **motifs** and **tale types**.

Motifs

Any reader of folktales is not surprised when a witch threatens the hero, or when the adventure happens to the youngest of three children, or when a piece of clothing such as a glass slipper serves to identify the real heroine. Elements like these that are repeated in many folktales are called *motifs*. According to Stith Thompson (1960), motifs may be

- **certain actors** (fairy godmothers, wicked stepmothers, or youngest sons or daughters);
- **certain objects** (pieces of clothing prove someone's identity, structures that connect this world to the next, or crumbs that are thrown behind to mark a trail);
- **certain actions** (spinning straw into gold, falsely boasting about one's powers).

Tale Types

A folk narrative that forms a recognizable pattern is called a *tale type* (Briggs, 1970). A tale type is a cluster of motifs, or strands of motifs woven together. For example, in a certain tale-type numbered 510 in Aarne-Thompson's (1961) scheme, the following motifs occur: *(1) A girl's mother dies and her father marries a wicked stepmother and the girl moves in with two vain and hard-hearted step-sisters (2). The girl has a fairy godmother (3). The girl is forced to do menial work (4), but finds animal helpers in birds (5), who sort peas from ashes. She wants to go to a ball to meet a prince (7), and is given the support of household items that transform themselves into a coach (8) and horses (9). The prince sees her and falls in love at first sight (10). She forgets to follow a warning to leave the ball at midnight (11), but happens to leave behind a glass slipper (12), which is later used to identify her (13). Her sisters mutilate their feet in a vain attempt to fit the glass slipper (14). The girl is recognized by the prince and (15) a royal wedding takes place (16) while (17) the stepsisters and stepmother are punished.* That pattern, with some variations, describes the German tale "Aschenputtle," the English tale "Ash Pitel," the Native American tale "The Rough Faced Girl," the Russian tale "Vasilisa the Beautiful," and, of course, the French tale "Cinderella." There are more than 400 known variations of that tale type in all.

Aarne and Thompson's index allows for some 2,500 tale types and nearly 40,000 motifs. Fortunately for teachers and librarians, the gifted storyteller and folklore scholar Margaret Read MacDonald produced a one-volume simplification of the Aarne-Thompson index,

Top Shelf 7.1

Books That Share Motifs

Motifs are devices, situations, objects, or characters that appear in several stories. Here are some motifs and some stories that share them.

The Youngest Daughter Is the Fairest

"Beauty and the Beast," a French tale about the youngest and truest daughter who transforms a beast into a husband and saves her father's life in the process. Marianna Mayer's version, illustrated by Mercer Mayer (SeaStar Books, 2002), is recommended.

"Vasilisa the Beautiful," a Russian story about a beautiful girl whose selfish step-sisters force her into the woods to borrow a light from the witch Baba Yaga. Marianna Mayer's version, called *Baba Yaga and Vasilisa the Brave*, illustrated by K.Y. Kraft (HarperCollins, 1994) is recommended. The story is also found in Jane Yolen's *Favorite Folktales from Around the World* (1988).

(continues)

called *The Storyteller's Sourcebook: A Subject, Title, and Motif-Index to Folklore Collections for Children* (1982). The work was recently updated with the assistance of Brian Sturm (2003). After a few minutes' orientation, you can easily find your way around both these works. Because MacDonald and Sturm cite children's books among other materials, you can pull together books from your own library that are variations of the same tale or that use the same motifs.

For those who want to see several variants of the same tale type, there are single-volume collections available. They are featured in Top Shelf 7.2.

The Hero Cycle

One very common kind of plot that is seen in Western folklore and mythology is the hero story: the tale of an unnoticed person who is called to a great adventure and endures many hardships before bringing some good and necessary gift back to his or her community. This kind of plot was brilliantly described by the noted scholar of mythology Joseph Campbell. After studying hundreds of myths, legends, and folktales, Campbell concluded that the traditional literature of the world often tells the **same** story. Campbell called the single story told by all hero tales **the monomyth**, or single myth, and the pattern of events that compose the monomyth **the Hero Cycle**. The **Hero Cycle** unfolds in several steps (see Figure 7.1). Here we will look at each step of the cycle, and illustrate it with reference to "Jack and the Beanstalk."

- **The hero at home.** In the beginning of the story, the hero is often the lowest of the low, unrecognized but perhaps having a questioning nature or a quiet ambition to find out who he or she really is. *Jack is poor, and is often described as lazy and foolish.*

- **The call to adventure.** Soon some problem arises that causes the hero to go on a quest. In traditional literature, the hero often has to compete for the chance to go, as he or she is naturally overlooked in favor of an older or more glamorous sibling. *Jack's mother announces they are starving, and sends Jack to market to sell the cow.*

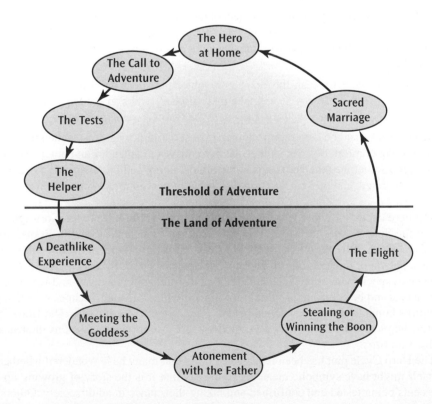

FIGURE 7.1 Campbell's hero cycle seems to tell many stories at once—a child's journey to adulthood, a rediscovery of meaning in midlife, a summary of a whole life's journey.

Top Shelf 7.1

East of the Sun, West of the Moon is a beautiful and complicated tale that begins with a bear asking for the youngest daughter and ends with her impossible journey in pursuit of her lost love. Nancy Willard has written the story as a play, with illustrations by Barry Moser (Harcourt, 1989).

The True Companion Is Recognized by a Tell-Tale Sign

Cinderella, the ultimate rags to riches story, is available in versions from around the world. Perrault's tale, the one that is most familiar to Western readers, has recently been illustrated by Susan Jeffers (Dutton, 2004).

The Golden Sandal: A Middle Eastern Cinderella Story (Hickox, 1999) is a retelling of an Iraqui tale, "The Little Red Fish and the Clog of Gold." With the tell-tale slipper and the magical aid of an enchanted fish, this tale stands midway between the Chinese "Yeh Shin" and the European tale "Cinderella."

Dogs Keep Away a Threatening Creature

"The Tailypo," an African American story about a man who lives alone and is set upon by a strange creature when he foolishly cuts off its tail. A picture book version was retold by Joanna Galdone and illustrated by Paul Galdone (1984).

"Wiley and the Hairy Man," an African American tale about a boy and his mother who seek to outwit a devilish beast who makes repeated attempts to kidnap the boy. An older picture book version by Molly Bang is recommended, although it is out of print. A satisfying version retold by Judith Sierra and illustrated by Brian Pinckney (1996) is still available. The text can be found in Jane Yolen's *Favorite Folktales from Around the World* (1988).

(continues)

Top Shelf 7.1

Kind Sister and Selfish Sisters

Mufaro's Beautiful Daughters, a Kaffir tale from Zimbabwe about the kindest and most virtuous daughter who wins the favor of the king, over her selfish sisters. A Caldecott Medal-winning version of the story was retold and illustrated by John Steptoe (1987).

The Talking Eggs, a Cajun tale strikingly similar to Vasilisa, about a young girl Blanche whose kindness and diligence is rewarded, while her sister Rose's selfishness leads to a bad end. A retelling by Robert San Souci, illustrated by Jerry Pinkney (1989), was a Caldecott Honor Book in 1990.

The Last and the Smallest One Tips the Balance

The Gigantic Turnip, a Russian literary tale about a farm family and all of their animals who strain to pull a giant turnip out of the ground, has been retold and illustrated by Niamh Sharkey (2000).

The Gecko, an East African tale about a contest among animals to dig a hole to find water in a dry stream bed, is found in Margaret Read MacDonald's *StoryTeller's Start-Up Book* (1993).

Shape Shifters

"The Crane Wife," a Japanese tale about a cloth-maker who befriends a wounded crane, and is rewarded by the companionship of a beautiful and mysterious weaver. A version retold by storyteller Odds Bodkin was given enchanting illustrations by Gennady Spirin (1998).

(continues)

- **The tests.** Before proceeding very far on the adventure, the hero is faced with challenges or tests. If these are met with cleverness, courage, or kindness, the hero often receives some magical help that enables him or her to proceed on the quest. *On his way to the market, Jack meets an old man who asks him questions. Jack answers to the man's satisfaction.*

- **The helper.** The helper is a person or peculiar creature that provides the magical aid the hero needs to cross the threshold into the place where the object of the quest is usually found. Sometimes the helper provides other miraculous equipment that enables the hero to succeed. *The old man trades a handful of magical beans for Jack's cow.*

- **The land of adventure.** The quest leads the hero into what Campbell calls "the Land of Adventure." Like Never-Never Land, Narnia, Hogwarts School, or the land beyond the "Wrinkle in Time," this is often a magical place, impossible to reach without the aid the hero received from the helper. Once the hero is there, the adventures begin in earnest, but the hero's true powers come into play, enabling the hero to rise to the challenges. *The magical beans grow a miraculous beanstalk that enables Jack to climb up to a land in the clouds.*

- **A deathlike experience.** Once the hero arrives in the Land of Adventure, he or she may have a death and rebirth experience: The hero's childish nature must die off, and his or her more mature, heroic nature must be born. Tomb imagery is very often used at this point. *Jack finds a castle in the clouds, and persuades the Giant's wife to take him to the kitchen to eat. But when she hears the Giant coming, she forces Jack to hide in the oven.*

- **Meeting the goddess.** If the hero is male, he may encounter a beautiful but formidable female figure who may challenge or love him, but in any case, confirms him as a worthy contender. *Considering the Giant's wife as a beautiful but formidable female figure may be a stretch, but it is true that Jack somehow beguiles her into acknowledging his prowess, and that she becomes his ally.*

- **Atonement with the father.** The hero often comes up against a stern father figure who challenges him or her severely. Sometimes the hero overthrows the father figure. At the least, the hero forces the father figure to recognize his or her status as a hero. *Jack shows great courage and cool-headedness in the presence of the Giant.*

- **Stealing or winning the boon.** The object of the quest is often some magical gift or some boon, elixir, or remedy that is needed back at home. The hero wins this object or steals it. *Jack steals the bag of gold coins, the hen that lays golden eggs, and the harp that plays music by itself.*

- **The flight.** If the hero steals the elixir or the object, the hero will run for his or her life, pursued by powerful forces. It will take more trickery and bravery to get away. *On the last trip, Jack flees down the bean stalk with the Giant close in pursuit.*

- **The return.** When the hero returns home, he or she brings what was needed to keep life going along comfortably. Sometimes the hero arrives in splendor and enters into royal marriage. Sometimes the hero slips home almost unnoticed but changed: more whole, more integrated, and proven. *Jack and his mother live well after that.*

The hero cycle fits a host of stories—from the story of Hercules to the Norwegian tale "East of the Sun, West of the Moon" to the Italian and French tale "Puss in Boots," to the Iroquois tale "The Boy Who Lived with the Bears." In story after story, from culture after culture, a person of humble origins who is somehow special receives a challenge, is tested and receives special aid, crosses into a land of adventure, suffers a death-and-rebirth experience, meets and bests an authority figure, wins something of value, escapes with that gift, and returns home as a fully developed person—and often a married one. The Hero Cycle captures the plot of the *Lord of the Rings* trilogy. It was consciously used as the basis for the film *Star Wars*.

The Hero Cycle plot has been repeated so often that many have wondered whether the plot itself might have symbolic meaning. Some say that it is the story of growing up—of adolescents being tested and confirmed and taking their place in adult society. Others say it applies to the psychic journey of middle-aged people seeking what the Swiss psychologist Carl Jung called *individuation*—a discovery and integration of the true powers they had unknowingly thrust aside in the strivings of adolescence and early adulthood (Jung, 1961). Indeed, it is part of the magic of stories that they can have powerful meanings for people in different stages of life, all at the same time.

The Role of the Reader in Traditional Literature

Why do people the world around keep coming back to the old stories that are told and retold in traditional literature? It may be, as Stith Thompson said earlier in this chapter, for the same reasons we keep using pots and hoes: There are just a few basic situations in life that all our stories are about. However, there is another tradition in the interpretation of folktales that suggests a deeper answer.

Sigmund Freud (1923), the first great explorer of the human unconscious, made two large claims about human nature that might shed light on the way we respond to folk and fairy tales. The first is that the most important preoccupations of people's lives—the most basic fears, secret desires, and strongest ambitions—follow patterns that were laid down in early childhood, in the drama of the relationships with parents and siblings. The second is that humans have an amazing capacity to *make symbols*, and we call on this capacity whenever we need a substitute for what we really want—especially if what we want is not readily attainable, or is not appropriate.

The first claim, about the power of the early drama of the family, suggests that since the preschool and early school years, every adult has craved affection, recognition for his or her competence, and power. The second claim, about the human capacity for symbolizing, suggests that humans produce dreams, art, and literature as symbolic (and therefore "safe") ways to explore those basic urges and to reduce some of the tensions they generate.

In 1975, the child therapist Bruno Bettelheim published the most ambitious application of psychoanalytic theory to children's reading of fairy tales. Entitled *The Uses of Enchantment* (1975), Bettelheim's book is an extensive exploration of the deeper meanings that the most familiar fairy tales might have for people's lives.

Many of Bettelheim's interpretations seem plausible. For example, he finds that "Hansel and Gretel" explores children's fears of having to separate from the family and needing to get along in the world by cultivating their own talents and relying on their own wits.

Visual Depictions of Traditional Literature

Randolph Caldecott is considered the father of picture books, and *his* first picture book was *The House That Jack Built*, an illustrated work of folklore, published in 1878. Artists since that time have enthusiastically illustrated traditional fare. Folktales and fairy tales are short enough to lend themselves very well to the 32-page picture book format. And because traditional material is by definition in "the public domain" (a legal term that means anyone is free to publish it), any artist can illustrate a traditional story or poem. Besides, there is a perennial market for books of folktales and poems. Any bookstore with more than a minimal offering of children's books usually sets aside a section for folktales and other traditional literature.

Many illustrated versions of the same tale are in circulation at any one time. Comparing versions of the same tale provides a fascinating exercise in visual literacy: a study of the ways an artist brings a text to life through illustration. For example, "Snow White and the Seven Dwarves" is available in many children's libraries in more than one version. The Disney Corporation's entry by Liza Baker (1999) uses illustrations from the well-known movie. That mega-corporation may deserve credit for bringing traditional lore to modern viewers and readers, but this book is a bland and predictable rendering (maybe it is predictable because we have seen the movie) that makes other works stand out for their originality. The version written by Paul Heins and illustrated by Trina Schart Hyman (1974) explores the drama and mystery of the story with engaging illustrations. Hyman's illustrations create almost a parallel story with

Top Shelf 7.1

Dawn, Molly Bang's retold and illustrated version of "The Crane Wife," uses the coast of New England as her setting (reissued by SeaStar Books in 2002).

Greyling is Jane Yolen's story of a selchie, a mythical creature that alternates between the form of a seal and a human being (1992). There are other folk stories about selchies in Yolen's *Favorite Folktales Around the World* (1988).

Wishes

"The Stone Cutter," a tale about a man whose wishes for power lead him back to the place from which he started. A picture book version by Demi set in China (1995) is available. Gerald McDermott illustrated a version that he called a Japanese folktale in 1978.

"The Old Woman in the Vinegar Bottle," an English tale about a woman whose series of wishes escalate to the point where she is returned to her former estate. A picture book version with suggestions for storytelling is available from Margaret Read MacDonald with illustrations by Nancy Dunaway (1995).

One Potato, Two Potato, a Chinese tale reborn as an Irish folktale in this picture book by Cynthia DeFelice, about a magic pot that makes two of everything. With illustrations by Andrea U'Ren.

Top Shelf 7.2

Story Collections by Tale Type

Several collections have been published recently that assemble variations of the same tale type. Children's author and storyteller George Shannon assembled a multicultural collection of tales that follow the victim-hero pattern (see below), called *A Knock at the Door*. The victim-hero pattern extends to stories like "The Three Little Pigs" and "Lon Po Po." Judith Sierra found twenty-four versions of the Cinderella tale for her collection, *Cinderella* (Oryx, 1992). Shirley Climo has rewritten several single-volume picture book versions of the Cinderella story (*The Korean Cinderella, The Egyptian Cinderella, The Persian Cinderella*, and *The Irish Cinderlad*). Betsy Hearne's *Beauties and Beasts* brings together stories of that tale type in one volume. Hearne has also analyzed several different versions of the story in her *Beauty and the Beast: Visions and Revisions of an Old Tale*. Judith Sierra's *Can You Guess My Name?* (2002) is a collection of tales that are examples of five tale types in one volume. They are: "I'll Blow Your House In" (victim-hero tales); "Just the Right Friends" (tales in the form of "The Brementown Musicians"); "Can You Guess My Name?" (tales like "Rumplestiltskin"); "I Married a Frog" (tales like "The Frog Prince"); and "Scary House in the Big Woods" (tales like "Hansel and Gretel").

their focus on the once-beautiful stepmother who is losing her place to the fresh and wholesome charm of the step-daughter. Nancy Eckholm Burkert (1987) illustrated a Caldecott Honor-winning book with a text translated from the German by the poet Randall Jarrell. Her illustrations are placed sparingly through the book, and, rather than showing events that have already been revealed in the narration, they offer emphasis and visual commentary. For example, the last frame, at the point when the story tells us the stepmother was made to dance to her death down to the dungeon in red-hot shoes, shows a startled dog staring down a black tunnel, too frightened to bark.

Because folktales are usually told with so few details, illustrators are free to create different settings for the same story. The storyteller controls the words, but the illustrator provides the costumes and the scenery. Simms Taback won a Caldecott Medal for his hilarious post-modern version of the Jewish folktale, *Joseph Had a Little Overcoat*. His rendering of the American folksong, *There Was an Old Lady Who Swallowed a Fly*, with die-cut holes that reveal the outrageous contents of the gluttonous woman's belly, was a Caldecott Honor Book. Paul O. Zelinsky set his Caldecott medal-winning version of *Rapunzel* (1997) in Renaissance Italy, and used an oil painting technique with a rather flat perspective that dates from that place and time. This was no accident: although "Rapunzel" first reached English speakers through the Grimms' collection, the earliest known version of the story was published by the Italian, Giambattista Basile, in 1637 under the name "Petrosinella." Thus Zelinsky's version takes the Rapunzel story back to its roots. Christine San Jose and Debrah Santini fast forwarded "Cinderella" to nineteenth century New York City in their version of the story (1994). They certainly have license to do this. Although most English speakers know the story from Frenchman Charles Perrault's late seventeenth century version, "Cinderella" has hundreds of known versions from many parts of the world. The Cinderella story transcends time and geography.

Besides finding original ways to depict the events in familiar tales, or new settings for them, several writers and artists have taken to spoofing folk and fairy tales. The troubling gender stereotypes in the Cinderella story have been humorously exploded in Frances Minters' *Cinder-Elly*, Ellen Jackson's *Cinder Edna* (with illustrations by Kevin O'Malley), and Babbette Cole's *Prince Cinders*. Phillip Pullman followed one of Cinderella's coachmen past the end of the story in his provocative short novel, *I Was a Rat!*

Jon Scieszka and his illustrators delighted readers with *The True Story of the Three Little Pigs* (Lane Smith) and *The Frog Prince, Continued* (illustrated by Steve Johnson). *The Stinky Cheese Man* (illustrated by Lane Smith) and *The Book That Jack Wrote* (illustrated by Daniel Adel) go a step further and have manic fun with the conventions of picture book layout. *The Book That Jack Wrote* weaves in characters and language from other familiar folktales and poems. Like David Weisner's Caldecott Medal-winning *The Three Pigs*, the book takes for granted that the reader is familiar with other folktales and rhymes. These books are a source of hilarity for children who are quite familiar with both the picture book medium and the folk materials they point to. But such books may be a little puzzling to children with less exposure to the original tales and poems.

Criteria for Evaluating Traditional Literature

1. Is the story well written according to literary standards outlined in Chapter 2?

2. Is the story reasonably authentic—that is, does it stay true to its source or sources? Responsible retellers usually identify the sources of their story and if they change them significantly, they indicate that they have done so.

3. Does the story reveal important insights into the culture of the people who told it? Many stories are enjoyable in their own right, but since folk stories are grounded in culture, it is an added bonus if the tale gives us a glimpse of how other people think and what they value.

The Evolution of Traditional Literature

> Beloved friend, my boon companion . . .
> start now to sing with me, begin to recite together . . .
> Let us clasp hand in hand, fingers in fingers,
> so that we may sing fine things, give voice to the best things
> for those dear ones to hear, for those desiring to know them
> among the rising younger generation . . .
> (from *The Kalevala*, Compiled by Elias Lonnrot)

These words introduce the long collection of ancient Finnish verses called ***The Kalevala,*** twenty thousand lines of wisdom and magic that recount the exploits of heroes and common folk from Viking times. For well over a thousand years before they were written down, the verses that make up ***The Kalevala*** were committed to memory by storytellers, who, huddled with their listeners around peat fires, could recite them for a whole week of evenings.

Where did the literature in the oral tradition come from? And how did it develop into written material? Of course, we cannot know what the first stories were, but those opening words of ***The Kalevala*** offer a clue about their nature:

> Let us . . . give voice to the best things
> for those dear ones to hear, for those desiring to know them
> among the rising younger generation . . .

Stories surely arose because people wanted to remember the best things (and sometimes the worst) and pass them on. For young Iron Age Finns, the stories that make up ***The Kalevala*** answered certain questions: "Who are we?" "What should we believe?" "How should we behave?" Most of the oldest stories offered answers to the important questions about the human experience and passed on a people's accumulated wisdom as to what the young should know, aspire to, and believe, forging a cultural identity in the process.

The Oral Tradition

Whether we are speaking of ***The Kalevala, The Odyssey*** (the epic of the ancient Greek hero Odysseus), or ***The Popol Vuh*** (the legend of the Toltec emperor Quetzalcoatl), traditional works relied on strong plots, legendary characters, fantastic events, and the clear polarization of qualities such as good and evil. They employed chants, refrains, and poetic language, for these devices aid memory. They also relied on the economy of symbolism; though often short, the old stories could be understood on many levels and invited pondering for their truths and their applications to real life, long after the telling was done.

As writing and formal education advanced, however, the oral tradition was pushed to the periphery. In Europe, formal schools such as those inspired by the German theologian Martin Luther (1483–1546) were established to teach people to read the Bible, and then other works. Science slowly matured, with theories to rival mythical accounts of the world's origins. With the spread of education, culture slowly divided between knowledge that was written down and folk beliefs. Among the educated, the terms "myth" and "old wives' tale" took on the connotations they still have in popular parlance: the unreliable lore of unsophisticated people.

But traditional lore still flourished, especially outside church and school. Folktales and legends drew their truths from the old myths and religious stories and continued to mix these with the people's own fantasies and fears. Folktales and legends came to constitute the unofficial lore of a culture. In church, the priest said, "Thou shalt not steal" and urged the congregation to practice mercy and forgiveness; in the words of the storyteller, however, Jack

Teaching Idea 7.5

Discovering the Hero Cycle in Stories

After explaining the steps of the hero cycle, read "Hansel and Gretel" to children (in third grade or higher) and ask them to see how many matches they can find between that story and the hero cycle. Read them the stories of Hercules and of Orpheus (from the d'Aulaires' *Book of Greek Myths*), and ask them to read them again on their own. Later, see whether they can find parallels to the hero cycle in folktales such as "The Orphan Boy and the Elk Dogs" (From Jane Yolen's *Favorite Folktales from Around the World*), "East of the Sun, West of the Moon," *The Firebird* (single volume versions have been retold and illustrated by Gennady Spirin and by Demi, and the tale also appears in Aleksandr Afanasyev's collection of Russian folktales), and Anthony Manna's *Mr. Semolina-Simolinus* (illustrated by Giselle Potter).

still robbed fabulous riches from the giant, and Snow White still honeymooned while her wicked stepmother danced to hell in hot iron shoes. Teachers stressed book learning and the virtues of hard work, but in folktales, a simpleton such as Juan Bobo was often more likely to succeed than someone more diligent.

The oral tradition retreated before industrialization and the schooling that came with it. But this happened at different times in different places. Speaking of his native England, Kevin Crossley-Holland notes:

> During the second half of the [eighteenth] century, the Industrial Revolution rapidly eroded rural life and continuities. The sons and daughters of people who never had occasion to stray more than a mile or two from their own villages, and for whom a trek to the county town— perhaps for a fair—was an annual event, gravitated to new mill and mining towns, or emigrated. This process, and the further advance of literacy that followed Sir Robert Peel's Education Act of 1834, naturally accelerated the demise of folk beliefs and the tales in which they were dressed. (1988)

But through the nineteenth centuries and into the twentieth century, the storytelling tradition persisted in rural Romania and Russia, in Haiti and Puerto Rico, in the coves of Appalachia, and on the islands of Scotland. And the stories were for everyone, old and young alike. Here is an account of a storytelling event in the Scottish Hebrides, some time in the late 1800s.

> The house is roomy and clean, if homely, with its bright peat fire in the middle of the floor. There are many present—men and women, boys and girls. All the women are seated, and most of the men. Girls are crouched between the knees of fathers or brothers or friends, while boys are perched wherever—boy-like—they can climb . . . The houseman is twisting twigs of heather into ropes to hold down thatch, a neighbor crofter is twining quicken roots into chords to tie cows, while another is plating bent grass into baskets to hold meal. The housewife is spinning, a daughter is carding, another daughter is teasing, while a third daughter, supposed to be working, is away in the background conversing in low whispers with the son of a neighboring crofter. Neighbor wives or neighbor daughters are knitting, sewing, or embroidering. The conversation is general . . . [The houseman is asked to tell a story, and after a while he complies]
>
> The tale is full of incident, action, and pathos. It is told simply yet graphically, and at time dramatically—compelling the undivided attention of the listener. At the pathetic scenes and distressful events the bosoms of the women may be seen to heave and their silent tears to fall. Truth overcomes craft, skill conquers strength, and bravery is rewarded . . . When the story is ended it is discussed and commented upon, and the different characters praised or blamed according to their merits and the views of the critics.
>
> (From Alexander Carmichael, quoted in Briggs, 1970, p. 10)

Stories and Culture: Mythos and Logos

Some scholars claim that the stories told in a society constitute the people's way of understanding themselves. Anthropologist Roy Rapaport (1986), for example, argues that the stories told and read in a society are "loosely joined into a more or less coherent *mythos*, which, in its entirety, expresses or represents that society's *logos* (its conception of the world's moral and natural order) and how it came to be" (p. 319).

For example, from reading folktales from England ("Jack and the Beanstalk," "The Three Little Pigs," "The Old Woman and the Pig," "The Old Woman and the Vinegar Bottle"), the ballads about Robin Hood, and even contemporary books like Roald Dahl's **Danny the Champion of the World**, we can discern a *mythos*, a collective impression left by the stories, that might go something like this:

> *We British are simple, ordinary folk. Occasionally we can improve our lot by taking something from the rich people, who are wealthy and aloof and don't care about us anyway. On the other hand, if we get too ambitious, and try to be like the rich people, we turn our back on our own kind—and then we might lose everything.*

There are facts in English history that might constitute the *logos* that these impressions point to, such as memories of the feudal structure, the fence laws that pushed the peasants off lands that were once held in common, and property laws that gave wealthy landowners dominion over even the wild animals that passed through their woods and the fish that swam in their streams.

Reading the French fairy tales that came to us through Charles Perrault, a *mythos* more like this arises:

> *We French used to be noble people. But our true identity has been unjustly denied us by conniving competitors—stepsisters, and such. We need to find some way to get the attention of the ruler, so he will restore us to our proper place among the nobility. Then we will have the ornate clothes we deserve, and attend the sumptuous balls to which people of our class are entitled. No more scrubbing out pots for us!*

The *logos* to which this impression points is easy to find. Charles Perrault was allied to Louis XIV of France, "the Sun King," who built the enormous palace at Versailles. He created apartments at Versailles for the nobles from all over France, and he inspired each one to try to be more stylish and popular at courtly matters than the other, and thus kept them from causing him any real trouble. The stories collected by Perrault were first told by the wives of these nobles (they learned them from their chambermaids, and embellished them to their own tastes)—women whose standing in the courtly pecking order was presumably of great importance to them.

African American folktales tend to form a different sort of *mythos* altogether. Consider, for example, the tales collected from African American tellers in the southeastern United States during the Depression and reprinted in B. A. Botkin's ***Treasury of American Folklore***. "Wiley and the Hairy Man," "The Tailypo," "Barney McCabe," and "Little Eight John" have protagonists that start out poor, and then are intruded on or encounter some malevolent force. If they act with savvy and self-discipline, they may escape harm. If they don't, they will die. In no case do they end up any better off than they started. The *mythos* shared by these stories celebrates knowing how to get by. But, unlike European stories, the *logos* to which it points holds no promise of greater rewards.

Retellers of National Folktales

The first collection of written stories expressly for children was published by Giovanni Francisco Straporola around 1550, and contained the earliest written version of "Puss in Boots." His countryman Giambattista Basile published ***The Tale of Tales, or Entertainments for Little Ones*** fifty years later. This collection contained the first written versions of "Rapunzel" and "The Sleeping Beauty." But the preponderance of adult themes ties this work more closely to collections such as Boccaccio's ***The Decameron*** (published in 1353) or ***The Thousand and One Nights*** (compiled between the ninth and fifteenth centuries). The problem is that in Europe, children's interests were not fully separated from those of adults until well into the sixteenth century; both enjoyed roughly the same entertainments.

Charles Perrault

In France, Charles Perrault (1628–1703), a minor poet, a lawyer for the court of Louis IV, and the Director of the Academie Francaise, published a popular collection of French fairytales called ***Histoires ou Contes du Temps Passé, Avec des Moralités: Contes de Ma Mère l'Oye (Stories or Tales of Times Past, With Morals: Tales of My Mother Goose)***. The collection appeared in 1697 and included "Cinderella," "The Sleeping Beauty in the Woods," "Little Red Riding Hood," "Puss in Boots," "The Foolish Wishes," and "Blue Beard." The title gave the world the title "Mother Goose," which Englishman John Newbery later popularized with a collection of rhymes rather than tales. Perrault's story collection was translated into English in 1729.

Ask the Librarian . . .   Margaret Read MacDonald

Margaret Read MacDonald

Favorite Books as a Child

All of the Oz books by L. Frank Baum

All of the Dr. Doolittle Books

Twenty-One Balloons by William Penn DuBois

I think the thing I loved most about all of these books was the exciting travel to exotic places.

Now that I am grown I can do that myself!

You've worked brilliantly to keep alive the tradition of storytelling. Why? What is the difference between reading a story to children and telling them a story? Should teachers bother to learn to tell stories?

Much of my work has been in discovering and retelling folktales from world cultures. These wonderful tales will be lost in time if we don't breathe life back into them. I have taken on a responsibility to share these tales.

Throughout the ages, stories have been used to teach children morals, to advise them on proper and safe behavior, to help them understand the thinking of their group. We need to keep using stories for those important reasons. Tales also open a window to the world's many cultures. And selecting tales from our students' own cultures can honor their traditions. But there is an even more important reason to share tales. In the moment of a story, a bonding of listeners takes place. Pleasure is felt as listeners join with teller in creation of story images, each in his own mind, but all bonded together by the movement of the tale. When the audience is well led by the teller, there is delight in this group creation of story. The joy of that moment is all the reason you need to make time for story.

Reading to children is basic to their literary and spiritual growth. But make time too for the moment when the book is put aside and the story just flows from your heart to theirs. This magical moment can only occur when you share freely a story that you love. This is a gift that you give. The children recognize its special gifted quality.

It really isn't such a bother as you might think. Just find a story you love. Read it over a few times. Put the book away and start retelling it in your own words. Keep telling it over and over in your head for a few days. Then open your mouth and let it come out! Children are such eager audiences that the story will literally *leap* from your mouth.

There is nothing like the moment when the teller's tale connects with the listener's heart. This is an art form which comes directly from one soul to another. Anyone can tell a story. It takes only a well-loved tale, a moment taken to internalize the tale, and an eagerness to take time to share.

Margaret Read MacDonald, who has a Ph.D. in Folklore from Indiana University, has taken her tales to Kota Kinabalu, Surabaya, Shanghai, Buenos Aires, and many other spots. She loves finding new tales and putting these into books for children and their teachers to enjoy. It is her hope that teachers and children will tell some of these tales and pass them on. She is the author of *The Storyteller's Start-Up Book: Finding, Learning, Performing, and Using Folktales: Including Twelve Tellable Tales* and *Three-Minute Tales: Stories from Around the World to Tell When Time Is Short.* ■

The Brothers Grimm

In the early nineteenth century, Jacob and Wilhelm Grimm built a sturdy bridge between the oral tradition and the written one. The brothers, born in 1785 and 1786 in Hanau, Germany, were well known in their time as scholars of language. While studying law at Marburg, the Grimm brothers became fired with the conviction that the spirit and culture of the German people resided in the old tales and legends. Soon after, the Grimms began their quest for German folktales. The two hundred tales they gathered have been translated into seventy languages and have made a contribution to world literature that has been likened to that of the Bible.

Germany in the early nineteenth century was a loose federation of principalities, where landowners held most of the wealth and the peasants' lives were kept primitive. Roads were bad, communication was limited, and education was largely unavailable to the poor—conditions that made for hard lives but created fertile ground for storytelling. These conditions would soon change—so it appears that the Grimms started their collecting at just the right moment. They collected stories from many people, but their most fruitful source was a peasant woman named Frau Viehmannin who lived near Kassell.

As linguists, the Grimms proposed to keep their tales faithful to the original telling, and Frau Viehmannin, or "Gammer Grethel," as she was later called, learned to tell her tales slowly enough that the brothers could write them down almost verbatim. Still, some editing was inevitable as they heard competing versions of the same tales from different sources. For example, some tellers had a wolf, not a witch, occupying the house of sweets where Hansel and Gretel's misadventures took place. The Grimms did considerable rewriting, as can be seen over the several editions of their works as they became less bawdy and more Christian in their themes.

The Grimms published the first volume of their *Kinder und Hausmärchen (Nursery and Household Tales)* in 1812 and the second in 1815. The books received a cool critical reception, but they sold briskly and were soon translated and read throughout Europe and the United States. The Grimms introduced "Hansel and Gretel," "Snow White," "Little Red Riding Hood," and a host of other stories to a wide audience. The commercial success of their books aroused new interest in the few existing collections of oral tales and inspired other people to collect tales in their own countries.

Joseph Jacobs

Although he was born in Australia and died in New York, Joseph Jacobs (1854–1916) is considered the father of English folklore. Jacobs spent most of his professional life in England, where he edited a journal devoted to folklore. Sensing that traditional English tales had been pushed aside by the invasion of Perrault's tales from France, and later the Grimms' tales from Germany, Jacobs set out to show that England, too, had its own folk stories. He found 140 tales he considered uniquely English, and published several dozen of them. Most of his tales came from secondary sources, including contributions sent in to his own journal from around England—but he also included several tales that were told among British immigrants to America, others he had heard as a child in Australia, and still others from Scotland. Jacobs published *English Fairy Tales* in 1890 and *Celtic Fairy Tales* in 1892, and put many well-known tales into wide circulation, including "Jack and the Beanstalk," "The Three Little Pigs," "The Three Bears," "Henny Penny," "Molly Whoopie," and "Tom Tit Tot." After Jacobs became the editor of *The Jewish Encyclopedia*, he immigrated to America, where he died in 1916.

Hans Christian Andersen

The Dane Hans Christian Andersen (1805–1875) ranks with the Grimms as a giant of world literature for children. His tales have been published in 100 languages and have been reprinted more than any work except the Bible and Shakespeare's plays. Born poor in the slums of Odense, Denmark's third largest city, Andersen had a difficult childhood. His father was a shoemaker, a literate man who claimed to have fallen from nobility. He read to his son, and took him to the theater. His mother was a washerwoman. She introduced him to folktales that were told by rural people in their neighborhood. His mother died of alcoholism, and his sister may have been a prostitute. At the age of fourteen, Andersen moved to Copenhagen, entered school at a late age, and was embarrassed by being so much taller and older than other children. After finishing high school he tried his hand at acting and singing before becoming a writer. Andersen lived his life as something of an outsider: Although he was recognized as a popular and successful writer, because of his lowly origins he was shunned by the polite society of Copenhagen.

Like the Frenchman Charles Perrault, Andersen retold traditional tales with his own particular twist. His story "The Emperor's New Clothes" (retold from an old Spanish tale with

Moorish origins) has become a worldwide metaphor for the dangers of believing in other people's pretensions. But most of his tales were original. His stories "The Ugly Duckling," "The Little Mermaid," and "The Steadfast Tin Soldier" are crystalline tales, laced with sadness, but affirming values of honesty and loyalty.

Every two years since 1955, the International Board on Books for Young People (IBBY) has presented the Hans Christian Andersen Award to "a living author and illustrator whose complete works have made a lasting contribution to children's literature." The patron of the award is Her Majesty Queen Margrethe II of Denmark, and it is considered the "Nobel Prize of International Children's literature." A list of recipients is found in Appendix A.

Folklore and Folktales in America

In the United States, Joel Chandler Harris (1848–1908) collected stories he had learned as a boy from slaves in Georgia and later narrated them in the voice of a fictional character named Uncle Remus. The tales of "The Tar Baby" and "Brer Rabbit and Brer Fox," among many others, were first written down by Harris, who took pains to transcribe the African American dialect as he heard it (although versions better suited to the contemporary ear have become available since—especially those retold by Julius Lester).

Native American stories were collected early in the twentieth century by anthropologists and linguists (although many stories that have never been "collected" are still being told by Native Americans today).

Many tall tales—especially of lumberjacks, cowboys, riverboat characters, and canal boat drivers—arose from the American experience and became famous all over the world (creating interesting stereotypes of what American life was like).

The 1930s saw a great harvest of American folktales. During the Great Depression a New Deal program sent writers and anthropologists into the cabins of the rural South, ahead of power lines and telephones, collecting tales such as "Wiley and the Hairy Man," "The Taily Po," and "Little Eight John." Richard Chase visited storytellers in Appalachia in the 1940s to collect the *Jack Tales,* American variants of European folktales reworked in a mountain setting.

Farther west, stories of ranch life and cattle drives were collected from men and women who experienced them and were written up in many fine books by the Texan, J. Frank Dobie (1888–1964), and others. In New York state, stories of the Erie Canal were collected by Walter D. Edmonds, and they inspired his original works, including *The Matchlock Gun*, which won the Newbery Award in 1942.

Throughout the first decades of the twentieth century, folksong collector John Lomax gathered cowboy songs throughout the Southwest. Later, his son Alan Lomax, with the support of the Smithsonian Institute, continued collecting songs among African American workers and prisoners in the Southeast and from people in the mountain cabins of the Appalachians. The result of their work, *The Folksongs of North America*, complements the collections by poet Carl Sandburg and balladeer John Jacob Nyles and offers an amazing variety of songs from the common folk of this country.

Types of Folk Literature

As Stith Thompson (1960) reminds us, the anonymous storytellers and singers who kept the folk tradition alive never heard of the categories we have imposed on folklore. Still, teachers and librarians find it useful to recognize types of traditional literature, because those types highlight the features that groups of stories have in common, and can guide children's responses to them. The types we will recognize here are *cumulative tales, animal tales and trickster tales, humorous tales, tall tales, ghost stories, fairy tales, realistic tales, legends, epics and ballads, fables, myths* (including pour quoi *tales*), and *religious stories*. Finally, there is another form closely related to these other forms: *Literary tales* can be shaped like any of these other genres, but are distinct because they were created by authors whose identities are known.

Cumulative Tales

Cumulative tales are created by repeating phrases and adding to them. "The House That Jack Built" is a fine example. A version with lively post-modern illustrations by Simms Taback was published in 2002.

The House That Jack Built
This is the house that Jack built.

This is the malt
That lay in the house that Jack built.

This is the rat
That ate the malt
That lay in the house that Jack built.

This is the cat,
That killed the rat,
That ate the malt
That lay in the house that Jack built . . .

The Cuban folktale called ***The Bossy Gallito*** is another cumulative tale. A rooster is dressed up and is making his way to his uncle's wedding when he spies a kernel of corn lying in a mud puddle. Pecking it, he muddies his beak, so he commands the grass to clean his beak. The grass refuses, so he commands a lamb to frighten the grass; but the lamb refuses, so he commands a dog to frighten the lamb; and so on. Finally, some creature agrees and sets a whole sequence of coercion in motion until the rooster's beak is cleaned and he can proceed to the wedding. The story is available in a version retold by Lucia M. Gonzalez and illustrated by Lulu Delacre.

The structure of ***The Bossy Gallito*** closely parallels the English story of "The Old Lady and the Pig," collected by Joseph Jacobs, in which an old woman calls on a series of helpers to goad a pig who is stuck in a stile (a passageway through a fence).

The Vietnamese story ***Toad Is the Uncle of Heaven***, retold and illustrated by Jeanne M. Lee, tells of an honorable toad who recruits other thirsty helpers as he makes his way to the palace of the King of Heaven to plead for rain. Each helper adds just the needed touch to achieve a solution, exactly as they do in the German tale "The Brementown Musicians." Songs such as "The Twelve Days of Christmas," "There Was an Old Woman Who Swallowed a Fly," and the Spanish folksong "Estaba la Rana Sentada Cantando Debajo del Agua" follow cumulative patterns. The form of the cumulative tale was well suited to the oral tradition, since the repetition of lines gave the listeners plenty of chances to learn them. These tales are agreeable to children for the same reason.

Animal Tales and Trickster Tales

Animal tales have been popular for thousands of years. Native American peoples liked to accommodate to themselves the spirits of animals, and told stories about their qualities. The Greek slave Aesop wrote his fables (see below) almost exclusively about animal characters, perhaps in the belief that his messages about human foibles would be less offensive if portrayed by animals.

European folktales are rife with animal characters. "The Three Little Pigs," "The Three Bears," "Henny Penny," and "Chicken Little" come from England. "The Brementown Musicians," and "Little Red Riding Hood" come from France; "The Three Billy Goats Gruff" comes from Norway.

A particular group of animal tales are **trickster tales**. Tricksters are characters who try to get the better of others through cunning and guile. Brer Rabbit, from the ***Tales of Uncle Remus***, is a trickster. Many trickster stories that were told among African American slaves used animals as codes for power relationships: Brer Bear has far more power than Brer Rabbit, but sometimes Brer Rabbit outsmarts the bear with his cunning—just as slaves could sometimes outwit their more powerful masters. A trickster tale from Africa that features Rabbit is ***The Magic Gourd***, by Baba Wagué Diakité, from Mali, West Africa.

THE POT OF WISDOM
ANANSE STORIES

ADWOA BADOE ✳ BABA WAGUÉ DIAKITÉ

ILLUSTRATION 7.2 This author and writer team from West Africa take the Ananse stories back to their roots. These are stories about the world's most popular trickster figure. (Cover illustration from *Pot of Wisdom*, text copyright © 2001 by Adwoa Badoe, illustrations copyright © Baba Wagué Diakité. First published in Canada by Groundwood Books Ltd. Reproduced by permission of the publisher.)

Another trickster of African origin is Spider, the hero of many tales told in West Africa and in the English-speaking islands of the Caribbean. A wealth of children's books about the best-known spider, Ananse (or Anansi) are available, including **The Pot of Wisdom**, by Adoa Badoe and illustrated by Baba Wagué Diakité (2001); **Ananse's Feast: A Tale from the Ashanti,** retold by Tololwa Mollel and illustrated by Andrew Glass, and many others.

In Native American tales, Coyote is a trickster, and he is featured in many books available for children, including **Coyote: A Trickster Tale From the American Southwest**, by Gerald McDermott (1999) and **The Tale of Rabbit and Coyote** by Tony Johnston (illustrated by Tomie dePaola [1998]).

Trickster tales are popular with children, who like the idea of weak characters using their wits to get the better of more powerful characters.

Humorous Tales

Children's sense of humor is notoriously slow to develop. Even second graders have difficulty coordinating the joke with the punch line. Thus humorous tales appeal to children somewhat later than other forms of folktales. A common form of humorous tales is the numbskull tale. Numbskull tales are stories of fools and idiots who succeed in spite of themselves.

Numbskull tales are popular around the world, from China to the Appalachian Mountains. Hans Christian Andersen's "Hans Clodhopper" tells of the numbskull brother who wins the hand of the princess when he speaks up stupidly but confidently in her presence. From England, by way of Appalachia, comes the story of "The Three Sillies," a Jack tale in which a spouse goes in search of a sillier person than the other spouse. Martha Hamilton of the Beauty and the Beast storytelling duo has a collection of numbskull tales called **Noodlehead Stories**. The success of movies like *Forrest Gump* and many films starring Jim Carrey shows that we still like to believe that a numbskull might just win the day.

Tall Tales

Tall tales are greatly exaggerated accounts of the exploits of local heroes. Often these heroes are members of a vocational group. For example, New England sailors told the tale of Stormalong, a sailor who was larger than life. Cowboys in the Old West told the exaggerated adventures of Pecos Bill. Loggers on the American frontier had the story of Paul Bunyan and Babe the Blue Ox. African American laborers had the story of John Henry, the steel-driving man. Even Japanese women had the wonderful tale of the "Three Strong Women." After all, bragging is a way for members of a group to express who they are; when the bragging takes the form of a story, we have a tall tale. While tall tales more often feature men than women, recently, to add some balance to the gender ratio of these exaggerated heroes, Anne Isaacs has given us an original tall tale, **Swamp Angel**. From the American Southwest comes the kind-hearted giant woman who made tortillas big enough for children to raft down the river, in **Doña Flor** by Pat Mora, illustrated by Raúl Colon. Another Western supergirl figure is the African American **Thunder Rose**, who played with lightning and lifted up a cow to get a drink, in Jerdine Nolen's story illustrated by Kadir Nelson. Not to be forgotten among larger-than-life female characters is Astrid Lindgren's **Pippi Longstocking**.

Ghost Stories

The literary critic Northrop Frye wrote that literature shows us the heaven we seek and the hell we wish to avoid, and ghost stories come from the second end of that spectrum. Even young children love ghost stories, if they are chosen carefully so as not to be too gruesome.

Alvin Schwartz's *Scary Stories to Tell in the Dark* has been so popular with children that he published three volumes of them, with spooky illustrations by Stephen Gammell. Cynthia DeFelice, who was a children's librarian and storyteller before she became an author, has a good ear for scary but not-too-scary stories for children. She has paired up with illustrator Robert Andrew Parker to produce *The Dancing Skeleton*, a Southern ghost story, and *Cold Feet*, from Scotland.

Ghost stories have their greatest effect if they are told, rather than read. Margaret Read MacDonald's *When the Lights Go Out* is one of the best ghost story collections for learning and retelling, and these stories also work when read aloud. Storyteller Martha Hamilton's *Scared Witless: Thirteen Eerie Tales to Tell* are good fare for those who want to learn the stories and tell them, since each story is followed by tips for retelling.

Fairy Tales

Fairy tales are folk stories that involve the intervention of magic in the plot. The best known fairy tales have royal settings. Tales retold by Charles Perrault from France such as "Cinderella" and "The Sleeping Beauty in the Woods" have magical elements to them. So do the fairy tales of the Grimm Brothers, "Snow White and the Seven Dwarves," "The Frog Prince," and "Hansel and Gretel." And so do many of the Russian fairy tales collected by Aleksandr Afanasyev, such as "Vasilisa the Beautiful." An African version of the Cinderella tale from Zimbabwe, "Mufaro's Beautiful Daughters," and the Louisiana Creole tale "The Talking Eggs" also have fairy tale elements.

Many fairy tales take the form of **apprenticeship tales, or hero tales**. The stories explain how a character rises from a lowly estate to a high one or from being ignored or threatened to being recognized and rewarded for her or his qualities. Apprenticeship tales such as the English tale "Jack and the Beanstalk," the Iroquois "Bending Willow," and the French "Beauty and the Beast" are exciting, but they are also partly didactic: All teach lessons about qualities of character such as pluck and bravery or steadfastness that are likely to be rewarded in the end.

Realistic Tales

There are many folk stories in circulation that *could have* happened. The Greek folktale retold by Aliki as *The Eggs*, for example, tells of a sea captain who is suddenly called away from a restaurant before he can pay for a meal of eggs. Years later, the restaurant owner confronts the captain with an inflated bill for the meal, based on the profits the restaurateur might have made if the eggs had hatched chickens, and chickens had proliferated. The captain's lawyer presents a wonderfully apt defense to exonerate him. The events in the story could have happened—everything stays within the realm of possibility.

A type of realistic tale that is still actively being produced is called an **urban legend.** Jan de Brunvand has made something of a career out of publishing volumes of "friend of a friend" stories—so named because they are often prefaced by the claim that they actually happened to a friend of a friend— like *The Disappearing Hitchhiker, The Choking Doberman,* and *Curses, Broiled Again!* Many of these tales are supernatural, like the tale of the person who picks up a mysterious young girl who is begging for a ride by the side of the road, only to find that she died years before.

Legends

Legends are stories about saints or other heroes who might actually have lived. The most famous legends in English are the stories of King Arthur and Robin Hood. Both of these characters may have been based on historical people, but their exploits have been embellished by generations of storytellers. The legend of St. George and the Dragon is also a popular one with children's authors and illustrators. Closer to the present day is the legend of Johnny Appleseed, a historical figure who went across the American frontier in advance of the settlers, planting apple trees to greet them when they arrived. Rip Van Winkle was the creation of Washington Irving in *The Legend of Sleepy Hollow*. Thus his story should be considered a literary tale (see below).

Technology in Practice 7.1

Resources on the Web

There are several excellent web sites devoted to folktales and folklore. Kay E. Vandergrift maintains a site useful for its access to variations of common tales at **http://www.scils.rutgers.edu/~kvander/swlinks.html.**

Professor D. L. Ashliman's web site contains links to a host of folk stories and other resources, including instruction in storytelling at **http://www.pitt.edu/~dash/ashliman.html.** Once you are there, you can explore the web sites from the main page.

The de Grummond Children's Literature Collection of the University of Southern Mississippi has a site at **http://www.lib.usm.edu/~degrum/html/aboutus-welcome.shtml,** especially biographies of children's authors. There are three domains devoted to collections of scores of versions of "Jack and the Beanstalk," "Cinderella," and "Little Red Riding Hood." Many of the texts and illustrations can be viewed online.

Heidi Anne Heiner's *Sur la Lune* has annotated fairy tales—forty-nine of them as of this writing—and there are links to the versions of the tales that are still in print and available from Amazon.com. The address of her site is **http://www.surlalunefairytales.com.**

Epics and Ballads

Epics are extended accounts of the exploits of national heroes, often intended to provide the young with models to emulate and ideals to embrace. In former times, their telling could carry over several days; in written form, they fill whole books. The ancient story of the voyage of Odysseus was composed by the blind poet Homer in the eighth century B.C. The English epic **Beowulf** about a Scandinavian hero living in the sixth century was written before the tenth century A.D. The exploits of the Spanish Christian adventurer Rodrigo Diaz de Bivar against the Moors in Spain were recorded in the twelfth century as the **Poema de mio Cid**.

Ballads, which are narratives in song, were especially popular in England from the fourteenth century on. English and Scottish ballads are mostly built of four-line stanzas and can run from a half-dozen stanzas (the length of a modern popular song) to more than four hundred (a whole evening's entertainment, and then some).

Francis James Child (1825–1896) collected five volumes of **English and Scottish Popular Ballads** and published them between 1884 and 1898. Thirty-seven of them tell about the exploits of Robin Hood. Here is a sample.

125A.1   WHEN Robin Hood was about twenty years old,
With a hey down down and a down
He happend to meet Little John,
A jolly brisk blade, right fit for the trade,
For he was a lusty young man.

125A.2   Tho he was calld Little, his limbs they were large,
And his stature was seven foot high;
Where-ever he came, they quak'd at his name,
For soon he would make them to fly.

125A.3   How they came acquainted, I'll tell you in brief,
If you will but listen a while;
For this very jest, amongst all the rest,
I think it may cause you to smile.

125A.4   Bold Robin Hood said to his jolly bowmen,
Pray tarry you here in this grove;
And see that you all observe well my call,
While thorough the forest I rove.

125A.5   We have had no sport for these fourteen long days,
Therefore now abroad will I go;
Now should I be beat, and cannot retreat,
My horn I will presently blow.

The ballad form was carried from the British Isles to North America, where, in the nineteenth and early twentieth centuries, it had an even more robust following than in Europe. The Appalachian Mountains have a strong tradition of narrative songs, such as "Tom Dooley" and "Little Omie Wise." In the western United States, many cowboy ballads, such as "The Streets of Laredo" and "The Colorado Trail," followed the ballad tradition.

Fables

Fables are brief dramatic tales, often with animal characters, that illustrate a clear lesson. The lesson is often stated explicitly at the end, where it takes the form of a proverb: a short memorable statement of advice or an observation about human nature. For example, the fable

"The Dog and His Shadow" tells of a greedy dog, carrying a piece of meat over a bridge across a brook, who sees its reflection in the water and snaps at the illusory meat, only to lose the meat it already had. "A bird in the hand is worth two in the bush" is the moral we are given at the end. "He who tries to please everybody pleases nobody" concludes the fable of "The Farmer, His Son, and the Ass," about a pair who try, ridiculously, to follow strangers' advice as they take their donkey to market.

The fables attributed to the Greek storyteller Aesop, who was said to have been a slave living around 600, have instructed children and their parents for thousands of years, although different generations have changed the morals to suit the mores of the day. Aesop's fables include such well-known tales as "The Town Mouse and the Country Mouse," "The Fox and the Grapes," and "The Lion and the Mouse." The seventeenth-century French poet Jean de La Fontaine published several of Aesop's fables in verse form. A modern collection of fables written and illustrated by Arnold Lobel is fittingly entitled *Fables*.

Myths

Myths and religious stories are texts that try to explain the mysteries of the universe in terms that are understandable to the average person. As Carl Jung observed, because people's certainty stops with the world they have at hand, myths use familiar images as symbols to point beyond what people can know directly (Jung, 1961).

Myths offer answers to questions such as "How did the world come to be?" "Why are we here?" "What is a good person, and why does it matter if I am a good person?" and "What happens to us after we die?"

Sometimes mythical answers clash with scientific explanations. For example, both the account of the creation offered by the Biblical story of Adam and Eve and the Native American tales of the world forming on Turtle's back clash with the scientific explanations of the Big Bang theory and the origins of life on earth as arising from certain amino acids. Just as often, though, myths offer a different kind of truth from scientific explanations. The Greek myth of Dionysus, for example, warns us with gruesome examples that great unhappiness may result when men and women are too far polarized, with one gender supposed to be unfeeling, rigid, and punishing and the other limited to qualities of physical beauty, sensuality, and intuition. In a similar way, the Zuñi myth that Kristina Rodanas retold and illustrated as *Dragonfly's Tale* warned that famine and unhappiness would surely come if the people took nature's bounty for granted. The truths of both these myths are arguably still relevant today.

Occupying an important category of myths are **creation stories**. Where we come from is a question that has fascinated people everywhere for all time, and the oldest explanations come to us in the form of myths. The Bible contains two different accounts of the origin of human beings in the Book of Genesis, and widely different versions are found in different cultures. Virginia Hamilton and illustrator Barry Moser assembled a popular collection from many cultures in their *In the Beginning: Creation Stories from Around the World.* James Weldon Johnson's African American poem of the Book of Genesis, *The Creation*, was powerfully illustrated by James Ransome and won the Coretta Scott King Award.

Pour quoi Tales

Pour quoi tales—stories that explain why—came about to feed, in often delightful ways, children's insatiable thirst for explanations. (*Pour quoi?* means "Why?" in French.) *Pour quoi* tales range from the serious to the playful: from the seven days of creation in the book of Genesis to the Greek explanation for the seasons in the story of Demeter; to the beautiful (East African) Masai story *The Orphan Boy*, retold by Tololwa Mollel and illustrated by Paul Morin, which gives an account of why the planet Venus appears as the morning star in the east but as the evening star in the west; to the Cuban story of *Medio Pollito/Half-Chicken*, a tongue-in-cheek account of the origin of the ornamental rooster that sits atop many a weathervane, retold in Spanish and English by Alma Flor Ada with illustrations by Kim Howard.

Religious Stories

Most of the oldest stories known to us are religious. They have a special status, of course, because all of them are sacred to one group of people or another. Religious stories thus present something of a dilemma for teachers in public schools because of the constitutional separation between church and state. Public schools cannot promote any particular religion, but that doesn't mean they should avoid teaching children about religions. Religion is an important part of the human experience, and students cannot make sense of history or current events without some knowledge of the world's religions.

There are many publishers that specialize in religious literature, and they market their wares to families and to religious institutions. Their books are not discussed here. Mainstream publishing houses also publish books of religious stories, not to convert children to a particular religious faith but rather to retell important stories and acquaint young readers with religious traditions. Those books are discussed here.

Besides the many stories of creation (see the discussion under "Myths," above), compelling children's books have been written around the lives of the founders of the world's great religions, as well as the lives of the saints.

From the Christian tradition are several picture book versions of the life of Jesus, including *The Life of Jesus* by Newbery Award-winner Katherine Paterson; and *Jesus*, retold and illustrated by Demi. Brian Wildsmith has also retold and illustrated the story of Jesus' life, synthesized from the four gospels in a work also entitled *Jesus.* Wildsmith published other stories based on the Christian Bible, including *The Easter Story, Joseph,* and *Exodus*.

Many picture books tell stories from the lives of Christian saints. Trina Schart Hyman's *St. George and the Dragon* won a Caldecott Medal for her illustrated version of this medieval tale. Tomie dePaola has retold and illustrated several popular stories about Christian saints, including *Mary: The Mother of Jesus, Christopher: The Holy Giant,* and *Patrick, Patron Saint of Ireland*. Robert Sabuda has retold and illustrated the original story of *Saint Valentine*.

The life of the eighth century Saint Francis of Assisi has had several retellings, including *Francis* by Tomie dePaola that appeared in 1982; *Brother Francis and the Friendly Beasts*, retold by Margaret Hodge and illustrated by Ted Lewin; and *Saint Francis*, by illustrator Brian Wildsmith. Demi, the noted illustrator, has recently retold and illustrated the story of *Mary,* and also *The Legend of Saint Nicholas.* To learn about the life of a caring and selfless person from our own time who is in the process of being canonized (recognized as a saint), readers have the beautiful and informative book, *Mother Teresa*, written and illustrated by Demi.

Jewish holidays have powerful stories behind them. Many children's books from the Jewish faith explain Jewish holidays to Jewish and non-Jewish children alike. Maida Silverman wrote and illustrated *My Jewish Holidays*. Peter Catalanatto illustrated Melvin Berger's *Celebrate! Stories of the Jewish Holiday.*

Jewish Bible stories from the Old Testament can appeal to all children. Collected volumes include *A First Book of Jewish Bible Stories* from DK Publishers and Adele Geras' *A Treasury of Jewish Stories* from Kingfisher. A particularly noteworthy collection of twenty Biblical legends is Eric Kimmell's *Be Not Far from Me: Legends from the Bible*, illustrated by David Diaz.

Stories from other religious traditions that are written for children are fewer and farther between. The respected illustrator Demi has written and illustrated a number of picture books to expand children's awareness of religions beyond Christianity and Judaism. Her accounts of Eastern religions include *Buddha* and *Buddha Stories*, as well as *The Dalai Lama*. Her *The Legend of the Lao Tzu and the Tao Te Ching* tells the story of the possibly mythical Chinese prophet who was considered the founder of Taoism.

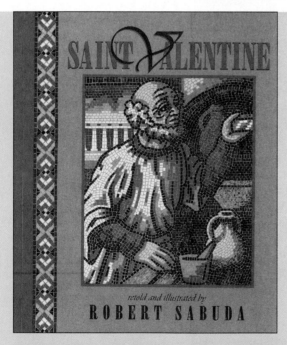

ILLUSTRATION 7.3   Robert Sabuda, well known for his pop-up books, wrote and illustrated a moving story of Valentine, a Roman physician who was martyred in 214 A.D. for his Christian beliefs. A letter he wrote from prison was said to have restored the sight of his jailor's daughter. (Reprinted with permission of Atheneum Books for Young Readers, an imprint of Simon & Schuster Children's Publishing Division from *Saint Valentine* by Robert Sabuda. Copyright © 1992 Robert Sabuda.)

Demi created a picture book presentation *Muhammed*, which recounts, in somewhat reverential terms, the life of the founder of Islam and of one of the most powerful political movements of all time. Reteller Susan Douglass and illustrator Jeni Reeves' *Ramadan,* from the series "On My Own Holidays," explains this Muslim celebration to non-Muslim readers. National Geographic Press published Deborah Heligman's book on Muslim religious observances with photographic illustrations, called *Holidays Around the World: Celebrate Ramadan and Eid Al-Fitr.*

The religious books available do not end with those, of course. Anyone wanting more expressly religious books can look up "religious books for children" or "Islamic books for children," etc., on any search engine.

Literary Tales

The final category of traditional literature doesn't quite belong. Literary tales have known authors and are written with the same jewel-like wisdom and succinctness as the stories from the oral tradition. Indeed, many of them are retold by storytellers, as if they had been found in the oral tradition. Many people wouldn't guess that these stories hadn't passed from story-teller to storyteller for centuries: "The Emperor's New Clothes," "The Princess and the Pea," "The Steadfast Tin Soldier," and "Pinocchio." In fact, all but the last were penned by Hans Christian Andersen. "Pinocchio" was written by Carlo Lorinzini, otherwise known as Collodi.

Hans Christian Andersen (see pages 223–224) was the most prolific author of literary tales. His tales, such as "The Matchbox Girl," "The Little Mermaid," and "The Steadfast Tin Soldier," are so compelling that many have been retold by storytellers for generations. They are favorites with children's book illustrators, too.

Traditional Literature from Many Cultures

There is an abundance of outstanding examples of literature from traditional sources. A good number of the illustrated books that have won the Caldecott Medal have been traditional tales. When it comes to traditional tales from parallel cultures, the offerings are rich indeed.

Classical Myths from Greece and Rome

Greek and Roman myths gave us the names of the planets: Mercury, Venus, Mars, Jupiter, Saturn, Uranus, Neptune, and Pluto. They gave us the names of many of the months and one day of the week: January (named for the Roman god Janus, the god who looks forward and backward), March (named for the Roman god Mars, the god of war), June (named for Juno, in Roman mythology, the queen of the gods), and Saturday (for the Roman god Saturn, the god of agriculture). Norse mythology gave us the names for other days of the week: Tuesday (for Tiw, the Norse god of war), Wednesday (for Woden, also called Oden, the chief god of Norse mythology), Thursday (for Thor, the god of thunder and oldest son of Woden), and Friday (for Friga, Woden's wife, the goddess of love and the hearth).

The myths we most often hear mentioned are the Greek and Roman myths. (The gods who figure in the Roman myths were essentially Greek gods by other names.) These gods are described in Figure 7.2 with both their Greek and Latin names.

The gods of Greek and Roman mythology had their raunchy sides, and children who do research on them—with the wealth of uncensored information available on the Internet— will soon be asking their teachers about the behavior of deities who would now be eligible for long jail terms if they treated their sisters and their rivals that way.

Irish author Padraic Colum (1881–1972) retold *The Odyssey* and *The Iliad* in his *The Children's Homer*. The lively narrative style and illustrations by Willy Pogany will appeal to upper elementary grade children. From England comes Adrian Mitchell's version of *The Odyssey*, illustrated by Stuart Robertson, which combines a well-written narrative line with illustrations of the characters, drawings of ships, maps of the Mediterranean, and photographs of ancient Greek armor and other artifacts.

Greek and Roman Gods			
Greek Name	**God of—**	**Known for—**	**Roman Name**
Zeus	ruler of the universe	Son of Chronos, and first among the twelve gods of the Pantheon. He lived on Mount Olympus; from there, he could observe the goings-on of humans and sometimes meddle in them.	Jupiter
Hera	goddess of marriage	Zeus's wife, and also his older sister. She is jealous of his dalliance with earthly women.	Juno
Poseidon	the god of the sea	Brother of Zeus; storms at sea were considered his making. He is often depicted holding a trident.	Neptune
Hestia	goddess of the hearth	Sister of Zeus, Hestia was the goddess of family order. In her honor, home fires in ancient Greece were kept burning perpetually.	Vesta
Hades	lord of death and governor of the underworld	Brother of Zeus, who governed the land, and Poseidon, who governed the sea; together the three brothers governed creation.	Pluto
Ares	god of war	Son of Zeus, associated with reckless violence rather than strategy.	Mars
Apollo	god of light	Son of Zeus. Drove the sun chariot across the sky. Favorite god of the poets, since he was the maker of music.	Apollo
Artemis	goddess of the forest and the hills, and of the hunt	Daughter of Zeus and twin sister of Apollo. When Actaeon spied on her bathing, she turned him into a stag, and he was killed by his own hounds.	Diana
Athena	goddess of wisdom	Zeus's favorite daughter, born from his forehead. She was also the goddess of weaving and of crafts, and of the more strategic side of war.	Minerva
Aphrodite	goddess of love, lust, and beauty	Born of the sea foam, she is often depicted standing on a seashell.	Venus
Hermes	messenger of the gods	The Son of Zeus and the nymph Maia, Hermes was a busy god—the god of boundaries and those who crossed them, of travelers, and of thieves and robbers. He was also the god of athletics, invention, and of literature. He was known for his cunning.	Mercury
Hephaestus	god of fire	Son of Zeus, forged the armor of the gods and became the favorite of blacksmiths and crafts persons. Hephaestus was born crippled.	Vulcan

FIGURE 7.2 Greek and Roman Gods

Traditional Tales from the British Isles

England, Scotland, Wales, and Ireland are different nations within the British Isles. England is home to peoples who are descendants of the Angles and Saxons—Germanic stock—as well as of Vikings from Denmark and French from Normandy. Scotland, Ireland, and Wales are peopled by Celts, an ancient race from Central Europe, whose shaping influence on language and culture continues—especially with the various Celtic revival movements—to this day.

In Ireland and Wales, the oral tradition was highly organized, owing to the institution of the bards, professional poet/historians who were commissioned by the kings to learn and recite epic poems and genealogies. Bards were expected to know as many as four hundred epic poems, and they often studied for twenty years to learn them. Indeed, a bardic college was established in Tara, the ancient capital of Ireland, to pass on the old stories. In England, literacy was more widespread. Because literacy and the oral tradition are somewhat incompatible, the oral tradition was much more scattered in England than in Ireland.

Irish Folklore

In Ireland, everyone knows everyone, or so it seems, and even the folktales are likely to mention people with real names. Irish folklore tells of legendary Irish heroes: CuCulhain, Finn McCool, Cormac MacArt, and Saint Patrick. There are stories of courageous and honorable acts, and there are stories of the struggle of Christianity to assert itself over the older Celtic religion of the Druid priests—stories that may go back sixteen hundred years. There is often magic in the tales, usually centering on giants or the little people called fairies or leprechauns. The little people keep to themselves, though once in a lifetime some human might happen on a group of them. Then there is a chance of hearing "the fulparenee and the folparnee and the rap-lay hoota, and the roolya-boolya" (Jacobs, 1958) as the little people make merry. Fairies and leprechauns possess magical powers that humans can sometimes use, but the fairies and leprechauns rarely cooperate willingly. From time to time, fairies are said to steal a human baby and take it below ground to strengthen their stock; such a baby is called a strayaway child. If fairies steal a human child, they replace her or him with one of their own. These fairy babies—called changelings—look like the children they replace, but they have awful tempers and can never be taught good manners. So if your baby is especially difficult, the tradition advises, chances are it's a changeling.

The Moorchild, a Newbery Honor Book by Eloise McGraw, evokes Irish village life while it explores the "what if?" question: What if a child were a changeling—an elf-child forced to grow up in a human family? Robert San Souci's Irish tale, ***Brave Margaret***, illustrated by Sally Wern Comport, is a welcome addition to the small collection of hero tales featuring female protagonists. Tomie dePaola has retold the Irish tall tale ***Finn M'Coul: The Giant of Knockmany Hill***, whose wife Oonagh helps him get the best of the giant, Cucullin. DePaola has also given us ***Jamie O'Rourke and the Big Potato: An Irish Folktale***, about a lazy Irish farmer who is the beneficiary of a leprechaun's magic.

Scottish Folklore

Scottish folklore has tales of Rob Roy, Robert Bruce, and other Scottish chiefs. These and many others were compiled in an extensive collection called ***The Scottish Tradition: A Collection of Scottish Folk Literature*** by David Buchan. The storytelling tradition has been kept alive to this day, especially by the tinkers, itinerant traders who live on the fringes of society, much as gypsies do. Duncan Williamson, author of a fine collection of Scottish folktales (***Tales of the Seal People: Scottish Folk Tales***), was a tinker in his younger days. His tales of the selchies, or seal people, tap an especially interesting vein of Scottish folklore.

Welsh Folklore

In Wales, much of the folklore recalls exploits of real or fictional heroes, just as it does in Ireland. A fourteenth-century epic called ***The Mabinogion*** compiled the most cherished hero stories of Wales. The prolific children's author Lloyd Alexander traces his ancestry from Wales and credits the Welsh epics with the romantic adventurism of his own tales.

Teaching Idea 7.6

Tales of Transformation

For children in grade three and up, read them either "The Selchie" from Jane Yolen's *Favorite Folktales From Around the World*, or any of Duncan Williamson's stories from *Tales of the Seal People*. Later, have them read either Molly Bang's *Dawn* or *The Crane Wife*, retold by Odds Bodkin. Discuss each story, and enter the students' responses to the questions on a chart like the one below.

	Who changed?	What made the person change?	What made the person change back?	How do we feel about what happened?
Selchie Story				
The Crane Wife				

English Folklore

In England, the oral tradition included the epic of Beowulf, a stirring tale of the hero's struggle against Grendel, the water monster. Probably composed in the eighth century, Beowulf was drawn from both the old Viking tradition and early Christian beliefs.

At the heart of the English oral tradition is the story of King Arthur and the Knights of the Round Table. The story has been traced back to the seventh century and seems to have derived from old Celtic hero tales. Arthur, illegitimate son of Uther Pendragon, shows his heroic qualities by pulling the sword, Excalibur, from the stone. Merlin, the court magician, reveals Arthur's royal lineage. Arthur marries Guinevere, arms himself with the great sword Excalibur, and is joined at the Round Table by the famous knights Sir Lancelot, Sir Gawain, Sir Galahad, and others.

Just as central to the English oral tradition is the ballad of Robin Hood and his Merry Men. Robin Hood has an uncertain historical basis, but the background to the ballad of the poacher-hero was real enough: the landowners' excluding people from hunting or fishing in vast expanses of countryside. (To this day in England, landowners own the fish in their streams and the deer in their woods.)

Other shaping events of the later Middle Ages were the Crusades, idealistic campaigns by English and other European Christians to drive the Moslems out of the Holy Land, which was considered to be the eastern Mediterranean city of Jerusalem and its surroundings. At the same time, Christian heroes sought the Holy Grail, the chalice with which Jesus Christ was said to have celebrated the Last Supper. Even after centuries of striving, neither effort was successful, but both provided the grist for many tales.

English folklore, as its chronicler Katherine Briggs notes, is short on fairy tales; English folk characters are more likely to succeed on cunning and pluck than by magical aid. On the other hand, there may be other-worldly villains—giants, particularly, as in stories like "Jack the Giant-Killer" and "Jack and the Beanstalk." There are stories that make fun of both pretensions and silliness—especially the tale "The Three Sillies," in which a groom, on a bet, goes in search of three people sillier than his fiancée's family. "The Little Red Hen" and "The Three Little Pigs" (both available in picture books by Paul Galdone) stress the virtue of industry. "The Old Woman Who Lived in a Vinegar Bottle" (available in a picture book, retold by Margaret Read MacDonald and illustrated by Nancy Fowlkes) is a variation of "The Fisherman and His Wife"; both show the folly of wishing for more than you have. On the other hand, the hero of "The Pedlar of Swaffham" (retold and illustrated as *The Treasure* by Uri Shulevitz) succeeds by following a dream.

The legends of King Arthur have inspired many fine books for children. In Kevin Crossley-Holland's ***The Arthur Trilogy***, readers may experience life in Medieval England and also enjoy the Arthurian legend on a human scale, as a coming of age adventure. The first volume, *The Seeing Stone*, was published in 2001. The second, *At the Crossing Places,* appeared in 2002, and the third, *The King of the Middle March*, was published in 2004.

German Traditional Tales

German traditional literature was ably collected and distributed by Jacob and Wilhelm Grimm. "Hansel and Gretel," "Rapunzel," "Rumplestiltskin," "The Brementown Musicians," and "Snow White and the Seven Dwarfs" are a few of the great number of favorite tales that came from German sources. Paul O. Zelinsky has executed breathtaking oil painted versions of both *Rumpletstiltskin* (Caldecott Honor) and *Rapunzel* (Caldecott Medal). One German tale, "Iron John," was not often told to children until it became the basis for a men's movement led by the prominent American poet Robert Bly (1992). Now Eric Kimmel has a retelling of the story illustrated by Trina Schart Hyman (1996). The story tells of an ancient man who has lain for centuries beneath the moss at the bottom of a pond. The boy in the story drains the pond, resurrects Iron John, and learns the lessons of manhood from him. Bly believes that the story stands for the importance of having manly things communicated from man to man; without this, he claims, the male spirit sickens.

Jewish Folktales

The influence of the Jews has long been felt in nearly every field of creativity, from the sciences to medicine to politics to scholarship to the arts. Jews have made major contributions to the culture of the world, but Jews also have their own culture and their own folklore. Jews are sometimes called "the people of the book," because their religious documents and their stories have played such a defining role in Jewish identity. Even before the time of Christ, Jews were leaving their homeland and living as minorities in foreign lands in a movement called the Jewish Diaspora. Jewish culture today is a mix of the places they have lived: principally Spain, North Africa, the South Caucasus, Germany, Russia, and the United States. In Germany, perhaps a thousand years ago, the Hebrew language coalesced with German to yield a creole language called **Yiddish**. Yiddish spread through Eastern Europe and into the United States, giving us words like *shlep,* "to drag"; *mentch,* "a nice gentleman"; and *kakameyme,* "helter-skelter." Yiddish stories became something of their own genre in Jewish folklore, and a great many that originated in Eastern Europe in the nineteenth and early twentieth centuries are still told.

The legend of the Golem tells of a powerful ogre formed from clay and given life by Rabbi Loew in sixteenth century Prague. The Rabbi wished to save the Jewish people from oppression, at the time of "the Blood Lie," when non-Jews were seized by the belief that Jews were killing Christian children and mixing their blood with flour to make matzo. A version of the book illustrated by David Wisniewski won the Caldecott Medal in 1998.

Later Jewish folktales have absorbed their trappings from the places Jews have lived in the Diaspora. Some of the most beloved Jewish folktales are Eastern European stories from the nineteenth and early twentieth centuries. Many were told in Yiddish, and still contain Yiddish words. For example, they tell of life in the *shetl,* the poor village. Many were set in Chelm (pronounced "Helm"), a fictional village where extremely foolish people lived.

The Adventures of Hershel of Ostropol (1998) are ten stories of a penniless but indomitable ne'er do well in a poor nineteenth century Ukrainian town. So clever was this man that his exploits have passed from mouth to mouth for nearly two hundred years. All of the stories feature humor and wisdom, and an underlying ethical sense. Eric Kimmel assembled these stories, and he has written many other picture books and collections of Jewish folktales, such as *Hayyim's Ghost, The Jar of Fools: Eight Hanukkah Stories from Chelm* (2000), *Hershel and the Hanukkah Goblins* (1994), and *The Chanukkah Guest* (1992).

Jewish stories found one of their most charming voices in the literary tales of Isaac Bashevis Singer (1985). Singer's stories come from the oral tradition, tweaked by his Nobel Prize-winning artistry. There are stories of goodness and kindness and wisdom. The stories are moral: There is the expectation that one will do the right thing. Yet it is also acknowledged that the reader has a mind, and most often will use his or her ingenuity to discern the right course of action.

Scandinavian Traditional Tales

The northernmost countries of Europe were home to seafaring folk who for centuries passed the time during the long, dark winters by telling stories. Those stories are so forceful and eloquent that they are known around the world. The Norse mythology told tales of Balder, the god of light; of Tiw, the god of war; of Woden, the giver of order and creator of man and woman; of Thor, the god of thunder and might; and of Friga, Woden's wife and the goddess of love and domesticity—deities who gave us the names of days of the week.

The best-known collection of Scandinavian folktales is *Norwegian Folk Tales*, published in 1845 by Peter Christen Asbjorsen (1812–1885) and Jorgen Moe (1813–1882) and translated by the Englishman Sir George Webbe Dasent (1817–1896). The most famous of these tales is "The Three Billy Goats Gruff," which is a perennial favorite with young children and a great text for dramatizing. Paul Galdone's version, originally published in 1981, is still available and still recommended. Glen Rounds' pen and ink version from 1993 is understated, but fun.

A more serious tale from this collection is "East of the Sun and West of the Moon," a lively story that begins much like the French story "Beauty and the Beast," but goes on to become a quest story that includes the mix of trolls, giants, witches, and hags that is typical of Norwegian folktales. Mercer Mayer retold and illustrated a version of this book more than twenty years ago that is still available and recommended. *The Man Who Kept House* is a hilarious tale about a farmer who thought his wife had it easy.

French Traditional Tales

A startling number of the best-known fairytales came to us from French versions, including "Little Red Riding Hood," "Cinderella," "Beauty and the Beast," "Puss in Boots," and "Sleeping Beauty." That is not to say they originated in France; variations of most of them were told in other parts of the world, too. As we noted earlier in this chapter, the basic story in "Cinderella" was told from China to Persia to England to the sweat lodges of the Algonquin people. The British could have chosen the German tale "Aschenputtel" or one in which the heroine had a black sheep for a fairy godmother. But the tale happened to be popularized in England when it came over in Charles Perrault's *Histoires ou Comtes de Temps Passé*, and the French version is what was passed on to North Americans.

These stories have been published many, many times. It can be interesting to compare the way different artists have brought them to life. Trina Schart Hyman's *Sleeping Beauty* was recently released in a twenty-fifth anniversary edition. Hyman's more subtle treatment might be contrasted with Kathyn Hapka's Read Aloud storybook of the same tale, illustrated by Disney in 1959 and reissued in 2003. K. Y. Craft illustrated a particularly ornate version of *Cinderella* (2000), which is in keeping with its origins with Charles Perrault and the Court of Louis XIV. *Beauty and the Beast*, like the other tales just mentioned, has a Disney film version that took considerable liberties with Madame de Beaumont's story. Marianna Mayer's retelling (2002), with illustrations by Mercer Mayer, is much closer to the original and, although originally published in 1978, is still very much recommended.

Russian Folktales

Russian folktales are a treasure trove of adventure stories, wonder tales, and anecdotes. Often playful, the tales abound in impossible quests, mysterious helpers, magical transformations, and dazzling rewards. Many of the structural features of other European tales are there: The old Tsar is dying, and he needs something. Three brothers are called on a quest, but the youngest and least significant—he may be a peasant or of noble birth—is the one who triumphs.

But Russian folktales are played out on a wider canvas than most. Heroes on their quests are propelled "through the thrice-ninth land to the thrice-ninth kingdom"—images that reflect the vastness of the Russian motherland. Russian folktales also have one of the great fixtures of world folklore: Baba Yaga ("Baba" means "Granny"). Baba Yaga lives in a hut perched on chicken feet that spins around three times and stops with the door facing you—provided you say the right words. Her nose grows down to her chin, and she flies around in a mortar, spurring it with a pestle, sweeping the way in front of her with a broom, and crying "Foo! foo! foo! foo!" She is too weird to be really frightening—and besides, although the young heroes are sometimes sorely tested by her, they always triumph.

The champion of Russian fairytales was Aleksandr Afanasyev (1826–1871), an ethnographer who collected and published six hundred tales between 1855 and 1864. Unlike the Grimms, whom he sought to emulate, Afanasyev got all but a dozen of his tales from other collectors.

Gennady Spirin, an illustrator from Russia, has done a sumptuous job of illustrating "Ivan, the Grey Wolf, and the Firebird," which he simply calls *The Firebird* (2002). Marianna Mayer has retold Afanasyev's *Baba Yaga and Vasilisa the Brave*, with a rather terrifying version of Baba Yaga in the illustrations by K. Y. Kraft (1994). Patricia Polacco gives us a kinder, gentler Baba Yaga in her *Babushka Baba Yaga* (2002). Critic Alison Lurie has retold *Black Geese: A Baba Yaga Story from Russia* with collage illustrations by Jessica Souhami (1998). Also not to be missed is Aleksei Tolstoy's tale, "The Great Big Enormous Turnip." Everyone tries to pull up the turnip: husband, wife, cow, dog, cat, chickens, geese, but it is finally the little mouse who adds the needed heft and pulls the thing from the ground. This cumulative tale is a favorite of young children, and is great for dramatizing. Many picture book versions are available, but Niamh Sharkey's post modern illustrations (1999) seem well suited to the absurdity of the tale.

Folklore from North America

Although folklore exists wherever people have established traditions, a few strands of North American folklore are especially well known: the Native American, African American, Appalachian, pioneer, Western, and Hispanic. There are also the tall tales and historical legends. The oldest—by twenty thousand years—and perhaps the only American folklore that can truly claim to be original—is the Native American tradition.

Native American Tales

Of course, Native American tales are as diverse as the hundreds of tribes in North America. Nonetheless, there are themes that are common to most Native American tribes as egalitarian tribal societies, just as there are themes that are common to most European nations as hierarchically arranged, power-and-ownership societies.

For example, many Native American tales speak of animals. But unlike European animal tales, in which animals are so often stand-ins for human characters, Native American tales more often have as their point helping listeners better understand the animals' characteristics. Curiosity about the real powers of animals stems from the totemic tradition, in which traditional peoples identify with an animal in order to share its wisdom and prowess. Identifying with, rather than having control over, is a powerful dynamic in Native American folklore, and it has led to this folklore's being tied naturally to environmental education, as the warm reception of Joseph Bruchac's *Keepers of the Earth* and *Keepers of the Animals* has demonstrated.

Native American folklore also has many trickster stories, often featuring Coyote. There are creation stories, too, which are important because stories about beginnings explain a people's understanding of how things are ordered.

Gerald McDermott has retold and illustrated a series of Native American tales, including *Arrow to the Sun* (a Pueblo tale, and a Caldecott Medal winner) and two trickster tales: *Raven: A Trickster Tale from the Pacific Northwest* (also a Caldecott Honor book) and *Coyote, A Trickster Tale from the American Southwest*.

Paul Goble has retold and illustrated several anthropologically careful books from the Plains Indians: *The Girl Who Loved Wild Horses* [recipient of a Caldecott Medal in 1979], *The Gift of the Sacred Dog* (1984), *Buffalo Woman* (1987), *Dream Wolf* (1997), *Mystic Horse* (2003), and a series of books about Iktomi, a Plains Indian trickster figure.

Ask the Author . . .   Joseph Bruchac

Favorite Books as a Child

It is hard to remember a time when I wasn't reading. I read everything from poetry to novels to non-fiction books about nature. My grandmother loves books and there were bookshelves in every room in the house. My grandparents had a little gas station and general store and I saved tips I got from pumping gas and washing windshields to buy more books of my own.

Alcott, Baum, Cooper, Haggard, Kipling, Lewis, Milne, Poe, Stevenson, Tolkien, Wells. Their books were trusted friends and guides to magic and adventure. I still have many of those volumes that were my childhood friends, from *A Child's Garden of Verses* and *The Hardy Boys* series, *Treasure Island* and *Just So Stories*, *Rabbit Hill* and *Lad, A Dog* and anything, anything by Dr. Seuss.

Scary stories were also a big favorite, including Bram Stoker's *Dracula* (the granddaddy of all vampire novels) and the creepy tales of H. P. Lovecraft. My own series of scary novels such as *Skeleton Man* owe a debt of gratitude to those masters of suspense and to traditional American Indian monster stories that I've heard more often than read.

But one of my very favorite books from my childhood is a gentle one that is still popular today. It brings smiles to a lot of kids when I mention it during my school visits—*Mr. Popper's Penguins*.

You are a scholar of comparative literature as well as an accomplished collector and re-teller of traditional Native American tales. When we read your "The Boy Who Lived with the Bears," we are struck by the parallel to the European tale "Hansel and Gretel." Are you struck by the similarities of some of their tales to tales told among other cultures far removed from them?

As a storyteller and student of comparative mythology, I am struck by the parallels that are often found in stories from very different cultures and different continents. That may be because there are so many things that all humans have in common—family, the importance of caring for our children, and so on.

In this case, however, I think there are more differences than similarities. Unlike Hansel and Gretel, the boy who is abandoned in the Iroquois tale is not threatened by some exterior malevolent force, but endangered by the bad action of his own uncle. The natural world, in the form of a Mother Bear, rescues the boy and also provides a lesson for the Uncle (who is reformed at the tale's end) in the proper way that adults and relatives should care for children. Further, it establishes and deepens the familial connection between animals and humans—not as separate, with humans dominating the natural world, but as co-equal beings. In fact, the animals serve as teachers to the humans. This exemplifies the Iroquois world view of humans being part of the natural world, of animals being not mindless creatures, but "animal people."

Joseph Bruchac is a writer and storyteller whose work often reflects his Abenaki Indian ancestry. He and his wife Carol live in the same house he was raised in by his grandparents in the Adirondack Mountains foothills town of Greenfield Center, New York. His books and those co-authored with his older son Jim (who, like his dad, is a martial arts teacher) have won many awards. ∎

African American Folklore

The experiences of slavery, faith, resistance, and solidarity have given a unique character to African American folklore. African Americans have a rich oral tradition that encompasses folk and gospel music as well as verbal games and stories.

Africans brought stories and proverbs to the New World (indeed, most West African languages are riddled with stories and proverbs). Many stories told of tricksters—usually a spider (sometimes called Anansi, a name given this character by the Ashanti people of Ghana), a turtle, or a hare.

Slaves were taught the Christian religion, and their religious songs, known as spirituals, such as "Twelve Gates to the City," "Rock My Soul in the Bosom of Abraham," "Michael,

Row the Boat Ashore," and "I Am a Poor Wayfaring Stranger," are some of the most stirring folk music we have. To the chagrin of the whites, slaves seized on the liberation message of Christianity—the story of the Hebrew children in bondage and their miraculous flight out of Egypt, led by Moses. Themes of liberation were reflected in many black spirituals, including "Go Down, Moses."

Some songs also contained coded encouragements for slaves to escape along the Underground Railroad. The best known is "Follow the Drinking Gourd," referring to the Big Dipper, a beacon in the northern sky for slaves escaping from Southern plantations.

Book versions of African American tales flourished throughout the first half of the twentieth century with retellings of Joel Chandler Harris's *Uncle Remus Tales*, which spawned a popular animated Disney movie in the 1950s, complete with the cheerful song, "Zipady-Doo-Dah." The film, of course, played in segregated movie theaters, and by the time the civil rights movement had captured the American landscape less than a decade later, reading stories about happy black slaves in the South was decidedly out of fashion.

It took Julius Lester, an African American scholar of black history and Jewish studies, to rescue what are still very good stories from the complicated history through which they came down to us. His *Tales of Uncle Remus* (1987), *More Tales of Uncle Remus*, (1988), *Further Tales of Uncle Remus* (1990), and *The Last Tales of Uncle Remus* (1994), all illustrated by Jerry Pinkney, are lively mixes of excellent storytelling in the Gullah dialect with occasional references to shopping malls and running shoes. They make a good read, and provide a valuable reconnection to stories that are an important part of not just African American, but American culture.

Virginia Hamilton, winner of the Newbery Medal and the Hans Christian Andersen Award, has written several African American folk tales of note. Her *The People Could Fly: African American Folktales* (1985) are sometimes chilling, often painful, and always rousing stories of the black experience in America.

Appalachian Folklore

Settlers of Scottish, Irish, and English descent moved to the mountains of the southeastern United States. Proudly self-reliant and somewhat isolated from the outside by the terrain,

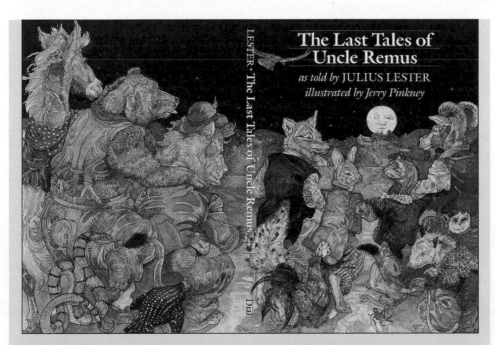

ILLUSTRATION 7.4 Julius Lester, a specialist in African American studies, has recently created lively retellings of the stories of Uncle Remus. (From *The Last Tales of Uncle Remus* by Julius Lester, illustrated by Jerry Pinkney, copyright © 1994 by Jerry Pinkney, illustrations. Used by permission of Dial Books for Young Readers, A Division of Penguin Young Readers Group, A Member of Penguin Group (USA) Inc., 345 Hudson Street, New York, NY 10014. All rights reserved.)

Ask the Author . . .

Patricia C. McKissack

Patricia C. McKissack (signature)

Favorite Books as a Child

Worldwide fairy tales, myths, and legends are the kinds of reading materials I'd want with me on a desert island, but Hans Christian Andersen's "The Ugly Duckling" was my childhood favorite. The story helped me cope with the day-to-day humiliation I encountered growing up in the segregated South.

A Complete Collection of Poems by Paul Laurence Dunbar was one of my favorite books, because I enjoyed Dunbar's ability to write using several language patterns.

I loved scary stories, especially Edgar Allan Poe's "The Fall of the House of Usher."

Are you struck more by the universal qualities of African American folktales or by the particular insights they provide about the experiences of African Americans?

"Children growing up without stories are adrift without an anchor," said Joseph Campbell. From fairy tales, myths, and legends, children learn about their world and how to live with others in it. When I was growing up, however, my classroom literature anthologies didn't contain any folktales from the African American culture. I wasn't encouraged to read them either. And sadly, "plantation stories" recorded from our oral tradition were written in such an unfamiliar dialect that I felt ashamed and embarrassed when they were presented. Had it not been for my family, all of whom were master storytellers, I would have, indeed, been "adrift without an anchor."

Now, as a writer and storyteller, I am particularly proud of the way my slave ancestors salvaged West African story remnants, reshaped old folk heroes, and cast them in new tales. These stories were sometimes humorous, sometimes sad, and sometimes very scary, but each one recorded the unique experiences of African Americans—who used their lore to teach, to entertain, and to cope in a cruel and hostile environment. African American folktales have survived the horrors of slavery and have even transcended the adverse effects of racism and discrimination. I am pleased that today they are rightfully placed among the larger body of respected American folktales with universal appeal.

I guess that's why I am an advocate of multicultural literacy, because I believe it is important to expose children to a variety of story experiences. It broadens the pool of ideas from which to expand their problem-solving and decision-making skills. Actually, it takes nothing from one culture to appreciate another culture's stories. The results might be as exciting as a meeting between Br'er Rabbit and Peter Rabbit or between my Flossie and Little Red Riding Hood.

Patricia C. McKissack and her husband, Fredrick L. McKissack, have co-authored many award-winning nonfiction titles. However, Pat's solo picture books—*Mirandy and Brother Wind, Flossie and the Fox, A Million Fish . . . More or Less,* and *Nettie Jo's Friends*—have won the hearts of young readers all over the world. When Pat isn't writing, she enjoys traveling in search of new stories. ■

people of the Appalachian mountains nurtured a culture rich in stories, riddles, and folk songs. Much of the folklore is traceable to the British Isles; in fact, entire ballads from the seventeenth and eighteenth centuries were sung in the mountains well into the twentieth century. Stories of Jack abound, as do various stories of the wiles of the devil and the ways in which clever people can trick him.

Some of the favorite stories of the Appalachians were recorded by Richard Chase in the *Jack Tales: Tales from the Southern Appalachian Mountains*, first published in the 1940s, and *Grandfather Tales*, published thirty years later. These stories tell the story of a sometimes bumbling trickster figure who originally came from rural England, but took root in the Southern mountain soil. Jack tales have modern champions in Donald Davis, author of *Southern Jack Tales* (1997), and Gail E. Haley, who wrote *Mountain Jack Tales* (1992). Davis is an accomplished storyteller, who performs throughout the United States, and Haley is a Caldecott Medal-winning author. A book that captures the Appalachian penchant for exaggerated similes is James Still's *Jack and the Wonder Beans* (illustrated by Margot Tomes, 1977, reissued 1996).

Tall Tales and Labor Stories

Wherever people worked hard and formed close-knit communities, folklore abounded. Lumberjacks lived long weeks and months in the woods, cutting trees to make lumber and harvesting logs to fire the steel mills that supported the early Industrial Revolution in North America. Felling the huge trees with axes and cutting them to length with handsaws were jobs so hard and thankless that they are almost unimaginable now. When dark crept through the silent woods, lumberjacks retired to rude and drafty shanties, where they took turns sitting in the "deacon's chair" and telling whoppers. The greatest whoppers of them all were those told about Paul Bunyan, with his two-headed axe that could cut trees "coming and going."

Cowboys lived almost the whole year out in the open, in every kind of weather. They told a number of tall tales—the best-known of which tells of the larger-than-life cowboy, Pecos Bill. Other folk stories have preserved the life and times of Mississippi riverboat people, of pioneers and settlers, of people along the Erie Canal, of railroad workers, and of farmers from all regions.

Legends and tales abound from every period of U.S. history. Revolutionary times, the Civil War, World War I, the Great Depression, the migration from the farm to the cities, the labor movement, World War II, the civil rights struggle, the women's movement—all of these and more have evoked tales that run the gamut from true accounts to far-fetched legends.

Stephen Kellogg has done a brilliant job of retelling and illustrating *Pecos Bill, Paul Bunyan*, and *Johnny Appleseed*, all with delightful changes of perspective and animated faces. Muriel Hodges's *The True Tale of Johnny Appleseed* sticks closely to the historical Johnny Chapman, who slept under logs, wore a cooking pot on his head, and went about leaving chapters of books for the far-flung settlers to read.

Julius Lester's retelling of *John Henry* is full of surprising anachronisms and wise phrases, and the scratchboard illustrations by Jerry Pinkney explore every nuance of the story. Pat McKissick's *The Dark Thirty*, winner of the Newbery Medal for 1993, with illustrations by Brian Pinckney, contains ten stories from the Black experience in the South. Some are ghost stories—some are probably true—but all help illuminate a painful and horrifying aspect of American history.

Hispanic Folklore

Americans with Hispanic backgrounds share a culture that was brought from Spain but mixed with the cultures of the peoples the Spaniards encountered in the New World or imported as slaves: Indians from North, Central, and South America, as well as Africans. (A word or two on terms is in order. "Hispanic" refers to people of partly Spanish descent living in North or South America. "Latin American" refers to people of partly Spanish, Portuguese, or French descent from Central or South America or the Caribbean. People of partly Spanish descent who are living in the United States often refer to themselves as "Latinos" or "Latinas.")

Mexican and Mexican American folklore mixes stories of Christian saints with traditional beliefs that go back to the Aztecs and the Mayans. The folk medical practice known as *curanderismo*, still practiced among Hispanic peoples of Mexico and the Southwest, exemplifies this same mix. Spanish priests brought the belief that prayers to specific saints, as well as the use of plants and herbs, were effective against troubles of the body and spirit. Indigenous peoples grafted these beliefs onto local practices and expanded on them by applying their greater knowledge of local medicinal herbs. Spiritual medicine hasn't been taught by the Catholic Church in Spain for centuries, but the practice of *curanderismo* continues in the New World to this day.

Among Mexican Americans in the Southwest, stories are still told of people's attempts to outwit the devil; many of these feature Pedro de Ordinales, a rough-and-ready lucky bumbler who was apparently imported from Spain. A character who plays a similar role in Mexican and Mexican American folklore is Juan Bobo.

Cuban, Puerto Rican, and Dominican folklore reflects influences from Africa as well as Spain; it also preserves some stories from the original peoples of those islands, who were driven to extinction within fifty years of the arrival of the Europeans in 1492. This folklore includes many animal stories. One of the oddest involves Ratoncito ("Mousy") Perez (also a Spanish import) and Cucarachita ("Little Cockroach") Martina. Cucarachita Martina is serious about marriage, but Ratoncito Perez is apparently in it only for the wedding feast. In any case, his gluttony brings him to a bad end. Curiously, in Spain, Ratoncito Perez is the tooth fairy.

The Bossy Gallito/El Gallo de Bodas, by Lulu Delacre, is a cumulative Cuban folktale in two languages. Julia Alvarez recently published a tale about a Dominican folk belief, the Ciguapas (reclusive beings who have their feet on backwards, to help escape detection) in *The Secret Footprints* (illustrated by Fabian Negrin). A popular Nicaraguan tale, *El Sombrero de Tío Nacho/Tío Nacho's Hat*, retold in a bilingual book by Harriet Rohmer, with illustrations by Mira Reisberg, tells a gentle lesson about change. Verna Aardema, of *Why Mosquitoes Buzz in People's Ears* fame, retold and illustrated a delightful Mexican trickster tale, *Borreguita [Little Lamb] and the Coyote*. *Rabbit Wishes* is an Afro-Cuban *pour quoi* tale retold by Linda Schute. The work is sprinkled with Spanish phrases, which are explained in a glossary. *The Woman Who Outshone The Sun / La Mujer Que Brillaba Aún Más Que El Sol* is a Mexican legend with a strong theme of the importance of accepting people different from you. It is retold by Alejandro Cruz Martinez and illustrated by Fernando Olivera.

Middle Eastern Folklore

The Middle East has an old and rich storytelling tradition. Flying carpets, magic lanterns and genies, these and more fixtures of children's imaginary lore came from *The Arabian Nights*, 1001 tales composed over hundreds of years with contributions from Persia, Egypt, and Arabia. Although many of the tales in the collection are not for children, collections for children have been made. "Aladdin and his Magic Lamp," "Ali Baba and the Forty Thieves," and "Sinbad the Sailor," can be found in *Sinbad the Sailor and Other Tales from the Arabian Nights* and *Aladdin and Other Tales from the Arabian Nights* by NJ Dawood, a noted Iraqi-born scholar. Frequent evocations of Allah will be found, and women are often treated as rewards for valiant warriors.

A pleasing tradition in Middle Eastern literature is the many stories about wise men. *Hosni the Dreamer*, an Arabic tale retold by Ehud Ben Ezer and illustrated by Uri Shulevitz, tells the story of a seeming simpleton who spends his money on the saying of a wise man, and though he is at first derided by his companions, he is rewarded many times over by his choice.

A famous wise man from Turkey, Nasreddin Hoca (1208–1284), composed tales exalting human qualities such as piety, simplicity, and charity. The often-witty tales have been told throughout the Muslim world for seven hundred years; many of the stories now attributed to him actually were written by others. Demi retold and illustrated *The Hungry Coat*, a Turkish tale attributed to Nasreddin Hoca.

A rich source of tales of wisdom are the Sufis, a group of Muslim mystics, who have for centuries spun tales of that are allegories of how we should live. The tales are for adults more than for children, but many appeal to readers of all ages. The best available collection is the Iranian Idries Shah's ***Tales of the Dervishes: Teaching Stories of the Sufi Masters Over the Past Thousand Years.***

African Folklore

In the thousand years before Europeans colonized Africa, the continent saw several great empires: Zimbabwe in the east and Mali, Ghana, and Songhai in the west. Moslem traders and missionaries linked much of Africa to Arabia and to Islamic culture. In the fifteenth century, when the Portuguese came to Benin (now in Nigeria), they were so impressed with the level of civilization that they opened diplomatic relations with that country.

Africa's long history was kept alive in poem and song. In West Africa, the *griots*, like the bards of Ireland, kept official histories. Some of their recitations could take twelve days. Poets, too, composed lays (ballads or verses) to praise kings or mourn them.

Africans who were not converted to Islam or Christianity (and these conversions began over a thousand years ago) shared beliefs that are collectively called *animism.* Many objects in nature are thought by ani-

ILLUSTRATION 7.5 Like the American media in general, American children's books give us woefully little to help us understand Muslim culture. This book makes a rare contribution. (Reprinted with the permission of Margaret K. McElderry Books, an imprint of Simon & Schuster Children's Publishing Division from *The Hungry Coat* by Demi. Jacket illustrations copyright © 2004 Demi.)

mists to be endowed with spirits—so many that there is no real separation between religion and secular life. The tasks of daily living are carried out with the spirits in mind.

Storytelling was always popular in many parts of Africa, and stories deal with many themes. There are creation myths, stories of the gods, animal stories (especially the trickster tales featuring a turtle, hare, or spider), stories of arguments between neighbors or between men and women, and many proverbs that point out the proper way to live.

Tanzanian-born Tololwa Mollel has retold several East and West African folktales to critical acclaim. ***The Orphan Boy*** (illustrated by Paul Morin) and ***Rhinos for Lunch and Elephants for Supper*** (illustrated by Barbara Spurll) are two of the few books in English from the Maasai people, an itinerant East African tribe that has largely resisted modern ways.

Ananse tales from West Africa and the Caribbean are now plentiful. Although first made popular for U.S. children's audiences by Gerald McDermott's Caldecott-winning version ***Anansi the Spider***, Adwoa Badoe's ***The Pot of Wisdom: Ananse Stories*** (illustrated by Baba Wagué Diakité) represents a version from a West African author and illustrator team. Badoe trained as a physician in her native Ghana, and is now a storyteller and dance instructor living in Ontario, Canada. Baba Wagué Diakité is from Mali, and he is now an artist living in Oregon. Diakite's own books are popular with children, too. His ***The Hatseller and the Monkeys*** won the IRA Children's Choice Award, and his ***The Hunterman and the Crocodile*** was a Coretta Scott King honor book.

Margaret Musgrove, author of the Caldecott-winning ***Ashante to Zulu,*** has written ***The Spider Weaver: A Legend of Kente Cloth***, illustrated by Julia Cairns, a fascinating account of where Kente cloth, a highly prized handwoven fabric from Ghana, comes from.

Ashley Bryan recently won the Coretta Scott King Award for his retelling of a folktale from the Ila-speaking people of Zambia. ***Beautiful Blackbird*** shares a "Black is beautiful!" message in ebullient text and verse and colorful collage art.

Asian Folklore

Asia is a big and diverse place. One fifth of humanity lives in China alone, so it is hard to make generalizations about Asian folklore that would not also seem true for many other parts of the world. Nonetheless, China and Japan—to speak of two countries—had ancient cultures and written literature before the Europeans did. Japan has a highly developed contemporary literature for children.

Many Asian folktales seem almost parable-like. There is the Burmese story of the man who was so impatient that he pulled his rice plants up a little every day to make them as tall as those of his neighbors. Of course, the plants withered and died. There is the Chinese story of a woman who is threatened by a monster and who receives offers of help from a number of different strangers; together, they defeat the monster for good. "Cultivate virtues, especially those of prudence, modesty, and a collaborative spirit" seems to be the message of many of these tales.

A story from India, Demi's *One Grain of Rice: A Mathematical Folktale* tells of a young woman who is offered a reward for a good deed done to the raja. She asks for only one grain of rice—on the first day, twice that much on the second day, twice again the third day, and so on for thirty days. Guess how much rice she has at the end of the month? (A table is enclosed for those who don't want to work it out in their heads.)

"The Stone Cutter" tells of a working man who magically is allowed to trade his station for a series of more important ones, until at last he ends up where he started. It is a cumulative tale of sorts, that closely parallels the English tale of "The Old Woman in a Vinegar Bottle," but with a kinder spirit, and it is a perennial favorite among story retellers and illustrators. Demi did a version in a Chinese setting in 1995.

Robert San Souci's retelling of *The Silver Charm*, illustrated by Yoriko Ito, is a rare story from the Ainu people, a linguistic and cultural minority group who live on Hokkaido and Sakhalin islands. It is a tender story, in which a puppy and a fox cub save their young master's life.

Folklore across Cultures

We have endeavored to show what distinguishes the folklore of many different cultural groups. Nonetheless, if you read widely in the folklore of the world, you are far more likely to be struck by the similarities than by the differences.

In the earliest written story known to humankind, the Mesopotamian hero Gilgamesh is bereft when a close friend dies. Gilgamesh tries to the limits of his being to understand where his friend has gone and maybe even to bring him back. Many of us have been there. Gilgamesh is our brother.

A father in a folktale from Burma—a place about as far from the United States as you can get—sends his son into the world. He wishes more than anything for his son to have a good life, but his son thinks that having a good life means enjoying many material things. Will the son learn real values in time? Do you know any parents who haven't fretted over that question as their child approached maturity?

Parents must sometimes be away from home, and they warn their children not to let strangers in. A malicious stranger comes. The children are on their own to face the danger. Have you ever seen a child not shiver with anticipation at such a prospect?

As storytellers the world over know, the most important things are the most basic. The Greeks even made gods out of those basic qualities and concerns: power, wisdom, insight, reverie, love, mirth, skill, art, science, the earth, the sea, home, marriage, fate, war, and death. For many of the same basic qualities and concerns, the Celts had runes—symbols carved on bones and carried in a pouch—to be read at crucial points in people's lives. The Chinese considered roughly the same factors in the *I Ching: The Book of Changes*. As Vladimir Propp concluded many decades ago, all folktales have a common source: the human spirit.

To check your comprehension on the content covered in this chapter, go to the MyEducation-Kit for your book and complete the Study Plan for Chapter 7. Here you will be able to take a chapter quiz and receive feedback on your answers.

Derivative Folk Literature

A host of books have been written in the form of, as embellishment on, or as a direct spoof of some traditional story. Jane Yolen's *Greyling* is an original version of a selchie story; this noted U.S. author lives much of the time in Scotland, where such tales are part of the folklore. Her novel-length retelling of *Briar Rose* has also won praise.

Two retellings of the "Cinderella" story have recently delighted readers. Gail Carson Levine's *Ella Enchanted* gives us a feisty Cinderella, and was a Newbery Honor Book in 1999. In Margaret Peterson Haddix's *Just Ella*, published in 1999, the life of a princess married for her looks alone turns out to be worse than boring.

Robin McKinley has rewritten the story "Beauty and the Beast" as a fantasy novel, called *Beauty*. Her *Outlaws of Sherwood* brings the Robin Hood legend to life for a contemporary audience.

The Irish superstition of "the changeling" (see page 233) is beautifully developed into a novel entitled *The Moorchild,* a Newbery Honor Book in 1996 by Eloise McGraw. A generation earlier, Mollie Hunter's novel *A Stranger Came Ashore* explored the legend of the selchie at novel length.

Jon Scieszka is a master at spoofs on folktales, and his hilarious books delight children who know the originals. *The True Story of the Three Little Pigs!*, illustrated by Lane Smith, tells the other side of the story, as narrated by A. Wolf from behind bars. (As Jerome Bruner has written, narrative was born with the first excuse!) Scieszka's *The Frog Prince, Continued* takes up the question "What happens after the 'happily ever after'?" And his *The Stinky Cheese Man and Other Fairly Stupid Tales* violates every imaginable convention of fairy-tale books.

Robert Munsch's *The Paper Bag Princess* is a popular modernist rejoinder to the active prince/passive princess syndrome. Jane Yolen's *Sleeping Ugly*, another spoof on the traditional formula of "handsome prince wins beautiful heroine," explores what really counts in a relationship.

All of these books are interesting in their own right, and especially for the comparisons to traditional literature that they invite.

Experiences for Further Learning

1. Find as many variations as you can of a familiar European fairy tale. If you choose "Cinderella," you might also read *The Rough Faced Girl* by Rafe Martin, as well as these books by Shirley Climo: *The Irish Cinderlad, The Korean Cinderella, The Persian Cinderella,* and *The Egyptian Cinderella.* If you choose *Hansel and Gretel*, a parallel story is Joseph Bruchac's *The Boy Who Lived With the Bears*. If you read *The Three Little Pigs*, you might also read Ed Young's *Lon Po Po* and William Steig's *The Amazing Bone*. Construct a chart to illustrate what your tales have in common. Do they strike you as the "same" story? What makes each one unique to its cultural setting?

2. Read four tales from Charles Perrault's fairy tale collection and four from either Mexico, Japan, or Africa. For each tale, describe the characteristics of the heroes, the situations they find themselves in, the kinds of solutions they try, and the message the story suggests. On the basis of these tales, try to make statements about the sorts of issues that are important to each culture.

3. Analyze a familiar fairy tale, such as "Sleeping Beauty," "Snow White and the Seven Dwarfs," or "Cinderella." Describe as explicitly as you can what the story seems to be saying to readers about their lives. What are the story's symbols, and what do they mean? Compare your analysis with the ones offered by Bruno Bettelheim in *The Uses of Enchantment* (1975).

Top Shelf 7.3

Novels from Folk and Fairy Tales

As we wrote earlier in this chapter, written folktales are skeletons, waiting for a storyteller or an illustrator to flesh them out with details and nuances. We would add one more group to those who bring folktales to life, and they are the novelists who explore their themes in protracted narratives. One of the most brilliant is Donna Jo Napoli, who has written a number of novels that explore the nuances of well-known fairy tales. Her *Beast* lets the reader imagine what it would be like to be a young man whose consciousness is suddenly thrust into the body of a lion, who must survive as an animal, and who must somehow win the affection of a human female. *Breath* tells of an asthmatic narrator who meets a charismatic flute player in the woods. *Zel* makes it almost possible to see why a childless woman would entrap a young girl in a tower without stairs, and how the young girl would only gradually shift her loyalties to a male suitor she barely knows. *The Prince of the Pond* takes our imaginations into a frog's body, and even reproduces the speech we would utter if we had the vocal apparatus of frogs. (If anyone should know, Napoli, who is a professor of linguistics, might.) *Crazy Jack* involves a giant and a beanstalk. The stories are so intricately and plausibly told that if you didn't read the jacket you might not know until the very end that you were reading retellings of "Beauty and the Beast," "The Pied Piper of Hamelin," "Rapunzel," and "The Frog Prince."

Now go to Chapter 7 in the MyEducationKit (www.myeducationkit.com) for your book, where you can:

- Find learning outcomes for Chapter 7.

- Access the Children's Literature Database for your own exploration.

- Complete Assignments and Activities that can help you more deeply understand the chapter content.

- Extend knowledge with content-specific Web Links.

- Deepen and apply content understanding with Extension Activities.

- Check your comprehension on the content covered in the chapter by going to the Study Plan. Here you will be able to take a chapter quiz and receive feedback on your answers.

- Find the following updated appendices: Major Children's Book Awards, Children's Magazines, Professional Organizations, Children's Book Publishers' Addresses, Book Selection Aids, and Children's Literature Web Sites.

Recommended Books

* indicates a picture book; **I** indicates interest level (P = preschool, YA = young adult).

Greek and Roman Myths

*Aliki. *The Gods and Goddesses of Olympus*. HarperCollins, 1994. This book tells the story of how the gods and goddesses came to live at Olympus and provides a sketch of each of the twelve major gods and goddesses. (**I:** 6–10)

D'Aulaire, Ingri, and Edgar Parin D'Aulaire. *Book of Greek Myths*. Doubleday, 1962. The stories of the major Greek gods and goddesses are intelligently told and beautifully illustrated. (**I:** 8–12)

*Wells, Rosemary. *Max and Ruby in Pandora's Box*. Puffin, 1998. The characters of Max and Ruby tell the story of Pandora's box as an object lesson. You probably won't find mythology made any more accessible to younger children than it is here. (**I:** 5–7)

North American Tales

Chase, Richard. *Grandfather Tales*. Houghton Mifflin, 1948. Twenty-five tales from the Appalachians are interspersed with the banter of the teller and his family. (**I:** 8–YA)

———. *The Jack Tales: Folk Tales from the Southern Appalachians*. Houghton Mifflin, 1943. Recently reissued in paperback, this is a collection of hair-raising stories featuring the plucky folk hero. (**I:** 8–YA)

———. *Mountain Jack Tales*. Dutton, 1992. More tales of the Appalachian tricksters Jack and Mutsmag (Jack's female counterpart) by a storyteller and folklorist who is also a consummate illustrator. (**I:** 8–12)

*Hooks, William. *Moss Gown*. Illustrated by Donald Carrick. Clarion, 1987. A Cinderella story from the author's native eastern North Carolina. (**I:** 7–10)

*Isaacs, Anne. *Swamp Angel*. Illustrated by Paul Zelinsky. Dutton, 1994. An original tall tale with a female character. Zelinsky painted the illustrations for the book on wood veneers for an antique look. (**I:** 6–9)

*Kellogg, Steven. *Johnny Appleseed*. Morrow, 1988. Active and expressive drawings illustrate this entry in Kellogg's tall tales series. (**I:** 6–10)

*———. *Mike Fink: A Tall Tale*. Morrow, 1992. Another colorful entry in Kellogg's American tall tales series. (**I:** 6–10)

*———. *Paul Bunyan*. Morrow, 1988. Kellogg's art brings this tall tale of a lumberjack to life. (**I:** 6–10)

*———. *Pecos Bill*. Mulberry, 1986. Lively and expressive drawings and clever details highlight this retelling of the Western tall tale of Pecos Bill and Slewfoot Sue. (**I:** 6–10)

*Mora, Pat. *Doña Flor: A Tall Tale About a Giant Woman with a Great Big Heart*. Illustrated by Raúl Colon. Knopf, 2005. A tall tale about a Latina heroine from the Southwest, by the same duo who created *Tomás and the Library Lady*. (**I:** 6–10)

*Nolen, Jerdine. *Thunder Rose*. Illustrated by Kadir Nelson. Voyager, 2007. A tall tale from the Wild West featuring an African American heroine. (**I:** 6–10)

Folktales from Great Britain

*Aylesworth, Jim. *The Gingerbread Man*. Illustrated by Barbara McClintock. Scholastic, 1998. This is a lively retelling of the tale of the runaway Gingerbread Man. (**I:** P–8)

Briggs, Katherine, ed. *British Folktales*. Pantheon, 1977. A collection of traditional tales as they were heard from folk storytellers, in interesting dialects. (**I:** YA)

Buchan, David. *Scottish Tradition: A Collection of Scottish Folk Literature*. Routledge, 1984. An adult collection, but suitable for read-alouds. (**I:** YA)

*Chaucer, Geoffrey. *The Canterbury Tales*. Adapted by Barbara Cohen. Illustrated by Trina Schart Hyman. Lothrop, Lee, & Shepard, 1988. Four beautifully illustrated tales from Chaucer's story of a medieval English pilgrimage to Canterbury. (**I:** 11–YA)

Crossley-Holland, K. *The Seeing Stone* (The Arthur Trilogy, Book One). Scholastic, 2001. 2002 ALA Notable Book. Readers can get a flavor of life in the Middle Ages through this Arthurian tale set in 1199 England. Arthur struggles with day-to-day issues while pursuing his life purpose in this coming of age story. (**I:** Middle School)

*DeFelice, Cynthia. *Cold Feet.* Illustrated by Robert Andrew Parker. DK, 2000. A clever tale of a man who takes boots from a frozen stranger and gets his feet in the bargain. Winner of the Horn Book Award. (**I:** Middle School)

*Galdone, Paul. *The Little Red Hen.* Seabury, 1973. An old tale of industry and rewards that is good for acting out. (**I:** 5–7)

Green, Roger Lancelyn. *The Adventures of Robin Hood.* Puffin, 1995. A novel-length version of Robin Hood and his Merrie Men, drawn from many sources. (**I:** 8–10)

*Hodges, Margaret. *St. George and the Dragon.* Illustrated by Trina Schart Hyman. Little, Brown, 1984. A Caldecott Honor Book with stunning illustrations. (**I:** 8–10)

*———. *Merlin and the Making of the King.* Illustrated by Trina Schart Hyman. Holiday House, 2004. The legend of the sword in the stone. (**I:** 8–10)

Jacobs, Joseph. *Celtic Fairy Tales.* 1st World Library, 2006. Originally published in 1890, these tales from Scotland, Ireland, and Wales are full of intricate heroism and magic. (**I:** 9–12)

———. *English Fairy Tales.* Illustrated by John D. Batten. Dover, 1967. (Originally published in 1898.) Well-told versions of stories familiar to Anglo-Saxon children. (**I:** 9–12)

*Kellogg, Steven. *The Three Sillies.* Candlewick, 1999. Convinced that the girl he is courting and her family are outrageously silly, the gentleman declares that he will marry the girl only if he can find three sillier people on his travels. (**I:** P–8)

*Marshall, James. *Goldilocks and the Three Bears.* Dial, 1988. A humorous adaptation by the creator of George and Martha. (**I:** 5–8)

Williams, Marcia. *The Adventures of Robin Hood.* Walker Books, 2007. Eleven adventures of the man who robbed the rich and gave to the poor are retold in lively comic strip format. (**I:** 8–10)

Yolen, Jane. *Sword of the Rightful King.* Magic Carpet Books, 2004. A master storyteller gives us a novel-length weaving of many stories from the Arthurian legend, including "the loathly lady," and "the sword in the stone." (**I:** 8–12)

German Folktales

*Galdone, Paul. *Hansel and Gretel.* Illustrated by Paul Galdone. McGraw-Hill, 1982. A version that will not horrify young children. (**I:** 7–9)

*Hyman, Trina Schart. *Little Red Riding Hood.* Illustrated by Trina Schart Hyman. Holiday House, 1983. A beautiful adaptation by an award-winning artist. (**I:** 7–9)

*Kimmel, Eric. *Iron John.* Illustrated by Trina Schart Hyman. Holiday House, 1994. The story of a prince who is trained in manly things by the wild man who lives in the woods. (**I:** 8–12)

*Zelinsky, Paul O. *Rapunzel.* Dutton, 1997. Zelinsky's elaborate retelling of this tale from the Grimms draws on elements from early French and Italian sources, and the illustrations are oil paintings from the Italian Renaissance tradition. The book won the Caldecott Medal for 1997. (**I:** 6–11)

*———. *Rumplestiltskin.* Dutton, 1986. Paul O. Zelinsky won a Caldecott Medal for this version of the world's best known guess-my-name story. (**I:** 7–9)

French Folktales

*Brown, Marcia. *Cinderella.* Alladin, 1997. This version is a reprint of Brown's Caldecott Medal winner from 1955. (**I:** 5–9)

*Hyman, Trina Schart. *Little Red Riding Hood.* Holiday House, 1987. Hyman won a Caldecott Honor for this fascinating retelling, with pictures within pictures on every page. (**I:** 5-9)

*———. *The Sleeping Beauty.* Little, Brown, 1977. Hyman won the Caldecott Medal for this retelling of Charles Perrault's tale. (**I:** 5–9)

*Marshall, James. *Read Riding Hood.* Picture Puffins, 1993. Marshall's cartoony rendering brings energy and wit to this cautionary tale from Charles Perrault. (**I:** 5–9)

*Mayer, Marianna. *Beauty and the Beast.* Illustrated by Mercer Mayer. Macmillan, 2002. The ink and watercolor drawings are very expressive in this tale of love's redeeming powers. The Mayers originally produced their version before the Disney movie appeared, and it is closer to Madame de Beaumont's original. (**I:** 8–11)

Perrault, Charles. *The Complete Fairy Tales of Charles Perrault.* Translated by Neil Phillip and illustrated by Sally Holmes. Clarion, 1993. Thirteen tales, including "Cinderella," "The Sleeping Beauty," "Little Red Riding Hood," and "Bluebeard," plus a biography of Perrault, with translator's notes. (**I:** 6–10)

*Pinkney, Jerry. *Little Red Riding Hood.* Little, Brown, 2007. Pinkney's watercolors make Riding Hood a sympathetic character and the wolf a real threat, in this traditional retelling of Perrault's tale. (**I:** 5–9)

*Pullman, Phillip. *Puss in Boots: The Adventures of that Most Enterprising Feline.* Illustrated by Ian Beck. Knopf, 2001. Pullman, author of many distinguished children's books in many genres, including *The Golden Compass,* and *I Was a Rat!,* gives an energetic and humorous retelling of this classic from Charles Perrault. (**I:** 6–9)

Greek Folktales

*Manna, Anthony, and Christoudula Mitakidou. *Mr. Semolina Semolinus: A Greek Folktale.* Illustrated by Giselle Potter. Alladin, 2003. In a quest tale with a feminist twist, Areti, a young princess, fashions a perfect suitor for herself out of cookie ingredients, but has to retrieve him when an evil queen snatches him away. (**I:** 6–9)

Mitakidou, Soula, Anthony Manna, and Melpomeni Kanatsouli. *Folktales from Greece: A Treasury of Delights.* Libraries Unlimited, 2002. Twenty Greek folktales are made accessible for reading aloud, or for oral retelling. (**I:** 6–12)

Jewish Folktales

*Jaffe, Nina. *The Way Meat Loves Salt: A Cinderella Tale from the Jewish Tradition.* Illustrated by Louise August. Henry Holt, 1998. This Yiddish tale from Eastern Europe is part Cinderella and part King Lear. When a father asks his children how much they love him, Mireleh, the youngest and most honest, replies, "The way meat loves salt." The father takes offense and banishes her until one day she is able to teach him the true meaning of her words. (**I:** 7–11)

*Kimmel, Eric. *The Adventures of Hershel of Ostropol.* Illustrated by Trina Schart Hyman. Holiday House, 1995.

Yiddish trickster tales from a Jewish community in Ukraine. (**I:** 7–11)

*———. *Asher and the Capmakers: A Hanukkah Story*. Illustrated by Will Hillenbrand. Holiday House, 1993. Not exactly a folktale, Kimmel's offering for Hanukkah shows off the wonders of Jerusalem through the eyes of a young boy who is taken there by fairies. (**I:** 6–9)

*Singer, Isaac Bashevis. *Mazel and Shlimazel: Or the Milk of a Lioness*. Translated by Elizabeth Shub, with photographs by Margot Zemach. Farrar, Straus, & Giroux, 1995. Mazel is the spirit of good luck, and Shlimazel is the spirit of bad luck. Guess which one wins out and helps the hapless young man marry the princess? Isaac Bashevis Singer won the Nobel Prize for Literature in 1978. (**I:** 6–9)

*———. *The Fools of Chelm and Their History*. Translated by Elizabeth Shub and illustrated by Uri Shulevitz. Farrar, Straus, & Giroux, 1988. Accounts of the foolish citizens of a legendary Yiddish town, by a master storyteller. Out of print, but widely available. (**I:** 8–11)

*Taback, Simms. *Joseph Had a Little Overcoat*. Viking, 2000. Taback won a Caldecott Medal for this lively retelling in story form of a Yiddish folk song. The die-cut illustrations add to the amusement. Song lyrics and music are included. (**I:** all ages)

*Wisniewski, David. *Golem*. Houghton Mifflin, 1996. Wisniewski won the Caldecott Medal for this retelling of a Jewish legend from the ghetto of Prague, in which a giant is brought to life out of clay for the protection of a community of Jews in danger of persecution. (**I:** 7–10)

Scandinavian Folktales

Andersen, Hans Christian. *The Complete Hans Christian Andersen Fairy Tales*. Edited by Lily Owens. Grammercy, 1993. Hans Christian Andersen, from Denmark, is a special case in folklore. He was more a creator than a collector, but his tales shine with the brilliance and insight of the best folktales, and stories like "The Emperor's New Clothes," "The Ugly Duckling," "The Little Mermaid," and "The Princess and the Pea" are well known the world over. (**I:** all ages)

*———. *The Little Mermaid*. Illustrated by Lisbeth Zwerger. Minedition, 2004. Zwerger, who won the Hans Christian Andersen Award in 1990, stays close to Andersen's beautiful and sad original tale about a mermaid who seeks independence and love. (**I:** 6–10)

*———. *The Princess and the Pea*. Illustrated by Lauren Child. Hyperion, 2006. Child recreates Andersen's classic tale about a lumpy bed and a real princess with photographs of doll furniture. (**I:** 5–10)

*———. *The Ugly Duckling*. Illustrated by Jerry Pinkney. Morrow, 1999. Pinkney has won the Coretta Scott King Award and the Caldecott Medal, and here he does a fine job of illustrating a tale about a little waterfowl who was different. (**I:** 4–9)

*Asbjornsen, Peter Christen. *The Man Who Kept House*. Illustrated by Svend Otto Sorensen. Margaret McElderry, 1992. In this traditional Norse tale, a man finds that keeping house is not as easy as he had claimed. (**I:** 6–9)

*———. *The Three Billy Goats Gruff*. Illustrated by Glen Rounds. Holiday House, 1993. Glen Rounds's pen-and-ink and watercolor illustrations add character to the popular story of goats, a bridge, and a troll. (**I:** 5–9)

*d'Aulaire, Ingri, and Parin d'Aulaire. *D'Aulaires' Trolls*. Dell, 1972/1993. The d'Aulaires provide a wealth of lore about trolls as they recount a few of the Norse legends from which they came. (**I:** 6–10)

*Lynch, P. J. *East O' the Sun and West O' the Moon*. Candlewick Press, 1991. Lynch's illustrations capture the wonder and mystery of this Norwegian quest tale—with a female hero who does the questing. (**I:** 6–10)

Russian Folktales

Afanasyev, Aleksandr. *Russian Folk Tales*. Translated by Robert Chandler. Illustrated by Ivan Bilibin. Random House, 1984. These seven tales are perfectly illustrated by Bilibin. Children will want to hear them again and again. (**I:** 7–12)

*Gilchrist, Cherry. *Prince Ivan and the Firebird*. Illustrated by Andrei Troshkov. Barefoot, 1994. One of the most exciting of Afanasyev's tales, richly illustrated. (**I:** 6–10)

MacAughrean, Geraldine. *Grandma Chickenlegs*. Carolrhoda Picture Books, 1999. A retelling of a Baba Yaga story in lively contemporary language: A young girl survives a trip to the witch's house. (**I:** 5–9)

*Mayer, Marianna. *Baba Yaga and Vasilisa the Brave*. Illustrated by K. Y. Craft. Morrow, 1994. Two of children's favorite Russian characters in one story. Vasilisa succeeds with the help of the doll her dead mother gave her. (**I:** 6–10)

*Spirin, Gennady. *The Tale of the Firebird*. Philomel, 2002. Russian-born Sirin uses a rich palette to bring this Russian hero tale to life. (**I:** 5–10)

African American Stories

*Bang, Molly Garrett. *Wiley and the Hairy Man*. Macmillan, 1976. A spooky African American tale from Alabama, taken from Botkin's *Treasury of American Folklore*. (**I:** 6–9)

*DeFelice, Cynthia. *Willy's Silly Grandma*. Illustrated by Shelley Jackson. Orchard, 1997. DeFelice reworks the story "Little Eight John," a traditional African American story, into a new story that is a larger exploration of superstition. (**I:** 6–9)

Hamilton, Virginia. *Her Stories: African American Folktales, Fairy Tales, and True Tales*. Illustrated by Leo and Diane Dillon. Scholastic, 1995. Sixteen folktales and three true accounts from American black women. (**I:** 9–YA)

———. *The People Could Fly: American Black Folktales*. Illustrated by Leo and Diane Dillon. Knopf, 1985. Twenty-four tales plus a bibliography; includes "Wiley, His Mother, and the Hairy Man" and "Little Eight John." Some of the stories are full of emotional power. (**I:** 9–YA)

———. *Bruh Rabbit and the Tar Baby Girl*. Illustrated by James E. Ransome. Bluesky Press/ Scholastic, 2003. Bruh Rabbit fools the luckless Bruh Wolf in Hamilton's retelling of the Tar Baby story. (**I:** 5–8)

Harris, Joel Chandler. *The Tales of Uncle Remus*. Adapted by Julius Lester and illustrated by Jerry Pinkney. Dial, 1987. Lester's voice makes these tales a joy to read aloud, and Pinkney's illustrations bring the characters to life. A Coretta Scott King Award Honor Book. (**I:** all ages)

———. *More Tales of Uncle Remus*. Adapted by Julius Lester and illustrated by Jerry Pinkney. Dial, 1988. More tales in this series, retold in a more accessible voice by a scholar of African American literature and Hebrew studies and illustrated in scratchboard by a talented artist. A Coretta Scott

King Award Honor Book. (**I:** all ages)

————. *Further Tales of Uncle Remus*. Adapted by Julius Lester and illustrated by Jerry Pinkney. Dial, 1989. Further tales in the same series. (**I:** all ages)

————. *The Last Tales of Uncle Remus*. Adapted by Julius Lester and illustrated by Jerry Pinkney. Dial, 1994. Lester and Pinkney have given us a fine gift by rescuing these stories from the aura of an earlier generation of white people's romanticizing of slavery. (**I:** all ages)

*Lester, Julius. *John Henry*. Illustrated by Jerry Pinkney. Dial, 1994. A lively and careful retelling of this tall tale that pits human against machine. (**I:** 8–10)

*San Souci, Robert D. *The Talking Eggs*. Illustrated by Jerry Pinkney. Dial, 1989. An African American variant of the Cinderella story. (**I:** 5–10)

*Wahl, Jan. *Tailypo!* Illustrated by Will Clay. Holt, 1996. A man cuts off the tail of a night visitor, and it comes back to haunt him. (**I:** P–8)

*Winter, Jeanette. *Follow the Drinking Gourd*. Knopf, 1992. The song was said to have been a sort of oral roadmap for the Underground Railroad during slave times. The somber illustrations bring some of the drama to life. (**I:** 5–8)

Native American Stories

*Bruchac, Joseph. *The First Strawberries: A Cherokee Story*. Illustrated by Anna Vojtech. Dial, 1993. A touching and lyrical story about the first man and the first woman, the overcoming of anger, and the origin of strawberries. (**I:** 7–10)

*————. *The Great Ball Game: A Muskogee Story*. Illustrated by Susan L. Roth. Dial, 1994. In this *pour quoi* tale, the birds and the animals square off in a game of stickball to decide who will have dominion over the land; the bat sides with the animals and wins the game. (**I:** 7–10)

*————, and Gayle Ross. *The Girl Who Married the Moon*. Troll/BridgeWater, 1994. Tales with girl protagonists from sixteen Indian nations, with commentary. (**I:** 10–13)

*Cohen, Caron Lee. *The Mud Pony*. Illustrated by Shonto Begay. Scholastic, 1988. A boy rises from his lowly origin to the position of chief with the aid of a magical pony in this Pawnee tale. The first children's book illustrated by Begay, a Navajo. (**I:** 7–10)

*Goble, Paul. *Dream Wolf*. Bradbury, 1990. A brother and sister wander off from their family and spend the night on the mountainside. A wolf rescues them and leads them to safety. With illustrations inspired by traditional paintings of Plains tribes. (**I:** 7–10)

*————. *Her Seven Brothers*. Bradbury, 1988. In this Cheyenne *pour quoi* tale about the origin of the Big Dipper, an only child goes in search of brothers after making beautiful clothing for them in the certainty that she will one day find them. (**I:** 8–11)

*————. *Iktomi and the Buzzard: A Plains Indian Story*. Orchard, 1994. Another in a series about Iktomi, the trickster of the Plains Indians. (**I:** 7–10)

*McDermott, Gerald. *Coyote: A Trickster Tale from the American Southwest*. Harcourt, 1994. A Native American trickster tale from the Zuni people, presented by a master illustrator. (**I:** 6–9)

*Pollock, Penny. *The Turkey Girl: A Zuni Cinderella Story*. Illustrated by Ed Young. Little, Brown, 1996. This rich *pour quoi* tale with a moral about keeping one's word is also a

valuable take on the Cinderella story, with breathtaking illustrations. (**I:** 7–9)

*Rodanas, Kristina. *Dragonfly's Tale*. Clarion Books, 1992. This Zuni tale with young protagonists promotes conservation and generosity and has a *pour quoi* twist, too. (**I:** 6–9)

*Ross, Gayle. *How Rabbit Tricked Otter and Other Cherokee Stories*. Illustrated by Murv Jacob. HarperCollins, 1994. Fifteen tales about the trickster Rabbit, by a master storyteller of Cherokee descent. (**I:** 8–12)

*San Souci, Robert. *Sootface: An Ojibwa Cinderella Story*. Illustrated by Daniel San Souci. Bantam, 1997. In a story that closely parallels the Algonquin tale "The Rough Faced Girl," an invisible warrior chooses as his bride the young woman with the truest qualities, and this turns out to be the Sootface, she who cooks and washes for her more outwardly beautiful and vainer sisters. (**I:** 6–9)

Hispanic and Latin America Stories

*Ada, Alma Flor. *The Gold Coin*. Illustrated by Neil Waldman. Aladdin, 1991. In this original folktale, a thief is made into an honest man in spite of himself, as he pursues a woman whose wealth turns out to be her generous spirit. (**I:** 5–11)

*————. *The Great-Great-Granddaughter of Cucarachita Martina*. Illustrated by Ana Lopez Escriva. Scholastic, 1993. A modern retelling of a Caribbean folktale. (**I:** 6–10)

*————. *Medio pollito/Half-Chicken*. Illustrated by Kim Howard. Doubleday, 1995. In Spanish and in English, this tongue-in-cheek *pour quoi* tale from Cuba explains the origin of the weather vane. (**I:** 6–10)

*————. *The Rooster Who Went to His Uncle's Wedding*. Illustrated by Kathleen Kuchera. Putnam, 1993. A cumulative tale from Cuba (same as the bilingual story *The Bossy Gallito/El gallo de bodas*). (**I:** 6–10)

Aldana, Patricia, ed. *Jade and Iron: Latin American Tales from Two Cultures*. Translated by Hugh Hazleton. Illustrated by Luis Garay. Douglas & McIntyre, 1996. The first group of seven stories comes from indigenous peoples of Central and South America; the second group of seven came to Central and South America from Spain. (**I:** 8–13)

*Arnold, Sandra. *Child of the Sun*. Illustrated by Dave Albers. Troll Associates, 1995. A Cuban creation story from the Ciboney people, a pre-Columbian tribe, which tells of the first man and woman and explains the origin of solar eclipses. (**I:** 7–11)

Campos, Anthony John. *Mexican Folktales*. Univ. of Arizona Press, 1977. The author learned these twenty-seven short tales from his family, who came to California from Jalisco, Mexico. (**I:** 8–12)

Campoy, I., and A. F. Ada. *Tales Our Abuelitas Told: A Hispanic Folktale Collection*. Illustrated by Felipe Dávalos Viví Escrivá, Susan Guevara, and Leyla Torres. Atheneum, 2006. Twelve tales retold by two noted Latina storytellers, with copious notes on the stories' origins and styles for telling. A Spanish-language version, *Cuentos Que Contaban Nuestras Abuelas,* is also available.

*dePaola, Tomie. *The Legend of the Poinsettia*. Putnam, 1994. A Mexican legend of Christmas. (**I:** 7–10)

*Ehlert, Lois. *Moon Rope: A Peruvian Folktale/Un lazo a la luna: Una leyenda Peruana*. Harcourt, 1992. A *pour quoi* tale in English and Spanish that explains why Mole lives in the ground and why we see Fox's likeness in the moon. (**I:** 6–8)

*Gonzalez, Lucia M. *The Bossy Gallito/El gallo de bodas.* Illustrated by Lulu Delacre. Harcourt, 1994. A Spanish/English version of the cumulative tale of a rooster who wanted his beak cleaned (the same story as *The Rooster Who Went to His Uncle's Wedding*). (**I:** 7–10)

*Johnston, Tony. *The Tale of Rabbit and Coyote.* Illustrated by Tomie dePaola. Putnam, 1994. A Zapotec *pour quoi* tale from the Oaxaca region of Mexico, told with some Spanish terms, explaining why Coyote howls at the moon. (**I:** 6–9)

*Martinez, Alejandro Cruz. *The Woman Who Outshone the Sun/La mujer que brillaba aún más que el sol.* Illustrated by Fernando Olivera. Children's Book Press, 1991. With a touch of magical realism, this ancient Zapotec myth from Southern Mexico shares a message of the importance of accepting differences. (**I:** 6–10)

Montes, Maria. *Juan Bobo Goes to Work.* Illustrated by Joe Cepeda. HarperCollins, 2000. The simpleton, Juan Bobo, does everything just wrong, with humorous results. (**I:** 8–11)

*Ober, Hal. *How Music Came to the World: An Ancient Mexican Myth.* Illustrated by Carol Ober. Houghton Mifflin, 1994. The sky god and the wind god cooperate to bring music to the earth in this ancient story. (**I:** 8–11)

Philip, Neil. *Horse Hooves and Chicken Feet: Mexican Folktales.* Illustrated by Jacqueline Mair. Clarion Books, 2003. These Mexican tales have some familiar forms: There is a "Cinderella" variant here, as well as a numbskull tale. There is also a mix of Catholicism, too. With an informative introduction by the anthologist. (**I:** 9–11)

*Reasoner, Charles. *Night Owl and the Rooster: A Haitian Legend.* Troll Associates, 1995. A touching tale of an owl who is helped to accept his odd looks by his true love. (**I:** 7–10)

*Rohmer, Harriet. *Uncle Nacho's Hat/El sombrero de Tio Nacho.* Illustrated by Mira Reisberg. Children's Book Press, 1989. Originally a play performed by the Puppet Workshop of Nicaraguan National Television, the story explores the difficulty of getting rid of an old hat (or an old habit) when given a new one. (**I:** 7–11)

*Salinas, Bobbi. *Los Tres Cerdos: Nacho, Tito, y Miguel.* Piñata Books, 1998. In this rich, original offering, the author not only gives us a hip Tex Mex version of the "Three Little Pigs," but also throws in a recipe for green chilly stew and ideas for enacting the story in class. The occasional Spanish words will delight students—but may require a little practice in advance if the book is read aloud, as it should be. (**I:** 8–11)

Sánchez, Enrique O. *The Golden Flower: A Taino Myth from Puerto Rico.* Illustrated by Enrique O. Sanchez. Simon & Schuster, 1996. (**I:** 8–11)

Tales from Africa

*Aardema, Verna. *Bringing the Rain to Kapiti Plain: A Nandi Tale.* Illustrated by Beatrice Vidal. Dial, 1981. Can there be more rhythmic language than in this tale from Kenya? This poem is written in a cumulative format. (**I:** 6–10)

*———. *Rabbit Makes a Monkey of Lion: A Swahili Tale.* Illustrated by Jerry Pinkney. Dial, 1989. To "make a monkey" of someone is to make the person appear to be a fool, and this Swahili tale is about a little rabbit that outwits the big lion. (**I:** P–7)

*———. *Why Mosquitoes Buzz in People's Ears.* Illustrated by Leo and Diane Dillon. Dial, 1978. A cumulative *pour quoi* tale. (**I:** 5–10)

*Bryan, Ashley. *Beat the Story-Drum, Pum-Pum.* Atheneum, 1987. A collection of African tales to be read aloud—or, if you've ever heard Bryan read, you might say roared aloud. (**I:** 6–10)

*———. *Beautiful Blackbird.* Atheneum, 2003. Long ago, when blackbird was voted the most beautiful bird, all the other birds asked that he decorate them with black paint. This *pour quoi* tale explains the markings of the birds. The "songs" of birds are interwoven throughout the text. (**I:** 4–8)

*Diakité, Baba Wagué. *The Magic Gourd.* Scholastic, 2003. This folktale from Mali tells the story of rabbit who is rewarded with a magic gourd by Chameleon for his generosity. Malian phrases are incorporated throughout this beautifully designed picture book. (**I:** 6–10)

*Gerson, Mary-Joan. *Why the Sky Is Far Away: A Nigerian Folktale.* Illustrated by Carla Golembe. Little, Brown, 1992. A lively *pour quoi* tale whose theme is the importance of preventing waste. This pairs nicely with *The Dragonfly's Tale*, a Native American story. (**I:** 6–10)

*Haley, Gail E. *A Story, a Story.* Atheneum, 1970. A traditional African tale about how Anansi won stories from the Sky God; a Caldecott winner. (**I:** 5–10)

*Kimmel, Eric. *Anansi and the Moss-Covered Rock.* Illustrated by Janet Stevens. Holiday House, 1988. Kimmel and Stevens teamed up to produce lively renditions of the Anansi tales, which are popular in West Africa and the Caribbean. In this tale, Anansi tricks the animals in the forest with a moss-covered rock until little deer gives him his come-uppance. The repetition makes this story good for reading aloud and for storytelling. (**I:** 6–9)

*———. *Anansi Goes Fishing.* Illustrated by Janet Stevens. Holiday House, 1993. The tables are turned when Anansi sets out to trick his friend into doing all the work. (**I:** P–8)

*———. *Anansi and the Talking Melon.* Illustrated by Janet Stevens. Holiday House, 1995. Anansi the trickster bores his way into one of elephant's melons and insults the animals one by one in this very funny tale. (**I:** 6–9)

*Knutson, Barbara. *Why the Crab Has No Head.* Carolrhoda, 1987. A *pour quoi* tale from Zaire. (**I:** 5–9)

*Lester, Julius. *How Many Spots Does a Leopard Have?* Illustrated by David Shannon. Scholastic, 1989. Folktales from Africa and from the Jewish tradition. (**I:** 9–12)

*McDermott, Gerald. *Anansi the Spider.* Holt, 1972. A Caldecott-winning tale of the trickster from West Africa. (**I:** 7–10)

*Mollel, Tololwa. *The Orphan Boy.* Illustrated by Paul Morin. Clarion, 1990. A touching *pour quoi* tale from the Maasai people of East Africa, about the tragic power of overweening curiosity and the reason for the transit of Venus. (**I:** 6–10)

*Steptoe, John. *Mufaro's Beautiful Daughters.* Lothrop, Lee & Shepard, 1987. The humblest and kindest daughter gets the reward in this Caldecott winner. (**I:** 6–10)

Asian Folktales

*Bodkin, Odds. *The Crane Wife.* Illustrated by Gennady Spirin. Voyager, 2002. In repayment for a kind deed, a crane turns into a beautiful woman who becomes a peasant's wife and weaves exquisite cloth to support him. Molly Bang's *Dawn* is a resetting of the same story. (**I:** 8–10)

*Casanova, Mary. *The Hunter.* Illustrated by Ed Young. Atheneum, 2000. A retelling of a Chinese tale in which a generous hunter is given a magical gift that allows him to provide for his village in a time of drought—but only if he does not reveal the source of the magic. (**I:** 7–11)

*Climo, Shirley. *The Korean Cinderella*. Illustrated by Ruth Heller. HarperTrophy, 1996. Pear Blossom plays the Cinderella role in this Asian story, and the magical aid comes to her by means of tokgabis, magical creatures in the forms of frogs, sparrows, and an ox. (**I:** 4–8)

*Demi. *The Donkey and the Rock*. Holt, 1999. When the townspeople attend a trial between a donkey and a rock, they discover the folly of yielding to idle curiosity. (**I:** 5–8)

*Lee, Jeanne M. *Toad Is the Uncle of Heaven*. Holt, 1985. Something of a cumulative tale, about a toad that asks the king of heaven to end a drought. The many helpers whom he recruits lend their aid at propitious moments, just as they do in the Grimms' "The Brementown Musicians" or in the Chinese tale "The Terrible Nung Gwama." (**I:** 7–10)

*McDermott, Gerald. *The Stonecutter*. Puffin, 1975. Tasaku, a lowly stonecutter, wishes for increasing power. (**I:** 7–12)

Sakade, Florence, ed. *Japanese Children's Favorite Stories*. Illustrated by Yoshisuke Kurosaki. Tuttle, 1958. Here are twenty classic folktales of Japan, with authentic illustrations. (**I:** 10–12)

———. *Kintaro's Adventures and Other Japanese Children's Stories*. Illustrated by Yoshio Hayashi. Tuttle, 1958. These are stories well known among Japanese children, retold in traditional settings. (**I:** 10–12)

*San Souci, Robert. *Fa Mulan: The Story of Woman Warrior*. Illustrated by Jean Tseng and Mou-sien Tseng. Hyperion, 1998. The story of Fa Mulan dates back to the fifth or sixth century A.D. and tells of a girl who cuts her hair and joins the Chinese army to battle against the Tartars because her aged father has been conscripted. (**I:** 7–11)

*So, Meilo. *Gobble, Gobble, Slip, Slop: A Tale of a Very Greedy Cat*. Knopf, 2004. This is a retelling of the folktale about the fat cat that eats every creature it encounters until two little crabs figure out how to save all the creatures that have been consumed. (**I:** 4–7)

*Uchida, Yoshiko. *The Wise Old Woman*. Illustrated by Martin Springett. McElderry, 1994. A Japanese tale about a village that discriminates against old people. An old woman's wisdom saves the village from a marauding conqueror. (**I:** 6–10)

*Xiong, Blia. *Nine-in-One, Grr! Grr!* Adapted by Cathy Spagnoli. Illustrated by Nancy Hom. Children's Book Press, 1989. When the great god Shao tells First Tiger how many cubs she will have, Bird confuses her into believing she will have fewer—and so she does. A story from the Hmong people of Laos. (**I:** 6–10)

*Young, Ed. *Lon Po Po*. Philomel, 1989. Sisters outwit the evil wolf in this Chinese variant of "Little Red Riding Hood." (**I:** 5–9)

Middle Eastern Folktales

*Climo, Shirley. *The Persian Cinderella*. Illustrated by Robert Florczak. HarperCollins, 1999. Climo has retold other Cinderella tales. In this one, from ancient Persia by way of *The Arabian Nights*, Settareh, whose name means "star," is helped by a magical blue jar to rise above her rags and attract the favor of the prince at the New Year's celebration. (**I:** 7–11)

*Hickox, Rebecca. *The Golden Sandal: A Middle Eastern Cinderella Story*. Illustrated by Will Hillenbrand. Holiday House, 1999. In this retelling of an Iraqi folktale "The Little Red Fish and the Clog of Gold," the Cinderella figure is named Maha, her magical helper is a fish, and the glass slipper is—can you guess? (**I:** 4–8)

*Kimmel, Eric. *The Three Princes: A Tale from the East*. Illustrated by Leonard Everett Fisher. Holiday House, 1994. An unnamed princess has three princes for suitors, and although she loves the youngest, he has nothing to give her, so she sends the three of them on a quest to find the most wonderful things. The rivals end up saving her life, and the story becomes a model of cooperation as well as competition. (**I:** 7–11)

Derivative Folktales and Spoofs

*Ada, Alma Flor. *With Love, Little Red Hen*. Illustrated by Leslie Tryon. Atheneum, 2001. When Little Red Hen moves into Hidden Forest and starts to grow corn for her chicks, she finds some of her neighbors unwilling to help out. However, others—including Goldilocks and Little Red Riding Hood—generously lend a helping hand. Readers will enjoy this exchange of letters among familiar folklore characters. (**I:** 5–8)

Buehner, Carolyn. *Fanny's Dream*. Illustrated by Mark Buehner. Dial, 1996. A great modern look at the notion of why women don't need to wait for a fairy godmother. (**I:** 8–11)

*Hartman, Bob. *The Wolf Who Cried Boy*. Illustrated by Tim Raglin. Putnam, 2002. Little Wolf longs for his favorite dish—Boy, but Boys are hard to come by. So Little Wolf entertains himself by yelling "Boy" and sending his parents on wild goose chases in search of the elusive Boy. Little Wolf has great fun—until he see the real thing. (**I:** 5–8)

*Minters, Frances. *Cinder-Elly*. Illustrated by G. Brian Karas. Viking, 1994. In this story, told in a fast moving rhyme, an urban Cinderella longs to go to the basketball game, gets there with the magical aid of a bag lady, and wins the attention of Prince Charming, the star shooter. (**I:** 7–11)

*Munsch, Robert. *The Paper Bag Princess*. Illustrated by Michael Martchenko. Annick Press, 1988. Canadian author Munsch created a popular tale in which a female hero, Princess Elizabeth, rescues Prince Ronald from captivity by a dragon who has burned all Elizabeth's clothes and left her draped in a paper bag. Vain Prince Ronald doesn't approve of women who dress in paper bags, even if they do save his life. Read on. (**I:** 7–9)

*Scieszka, Jon. *The Frog Prince, Continued*. Illustrated by Steve Johnson. Puffin, 1994. Jon Scieszka has carved out a niche for himself with his clever retellings of classic fairy tales. This one explores what might have happened if the prince really had tried to give up his froggy ways and live happily ever after with a human beauty. (**I:** 6–11)

*———. *Squids Will Be Squids*. Illustrated by Lane Smith. Puffin, 1998. Starting with the premise "If you can't say something nice about someone, change the guy's name to Donkey or Squid," Scieszka goes on to coin a host of fables about the moral challenges of modern life, such as believing what you see on TV or taking pride in having a lot of possessions. (**I:** 6–11)

*———. *The Stinky Cheese Man and Other Fairly Stupid Tales*. Illustrated by Lane Smith. Viking, 1992. This book not only turns half a dozen classic fairy tales on their ears, but trashes the conventions of book layout too. Scieszka is aided in this inspired assault on tradition by the artist Lane Smith and an ingenious book designer. (**I:** 6–11)

*———. *The True Story of the Three Little Pigs*. Illustrated by Lane Smith. Puffin, 1996. Everyone has a story to tell, it seems; this one, narrated from behind bars, is an attempt by A. Wolf to put a positive spin on those unfortunate events concerning three pigs. (**I:** 6–11)

*Wiesner, David. *The Three Pigs*. Clarion, 2001. In this variant of the familiar folktale, the wolf blows the three little pigs right out of the story and into a series of other familiar stories. (**I:** P–8)

*Williams, Jay. *Petronella*. Illustrated by Margaret Organ-Kean. Moon Mountain Publishing, 2000. The original of this reworking of the stereotyped active-male/passive-female hero story was published in 1973 and is out of print, but the story is well worth having and this new version is welcome. *Petronella*, about a nontraditional hero by that name, makes an interesting story to look at through the lens of Joseph Campbell's hero cycle. (**I:** 7–11)

*Yolen, Jane. *Sleeping Ugly*. Illustrated by Diane Stanley. Paper Star, 1997. Jane Yolen's nearly classic spoof on the beautiful princess paradigm has depth. The handsome prince bypasses Princess Miserella and takes up with Plain Jane, a nicer, lower-maintenance companion. (**I:** 7–11)

Multicultural Collections

Hamilton, Martha, and Mitch Weiss. *Noodlehead Stories: World Tales Kids Can Read and Tell*. August House, 2000. Twenty-three tales from all parts of the world that can be read or told. Each story has notes on its origin, and tips for telling by the professional storytelling duo who go under the professional name of Beauty and the Beast. Beauty and the Beast promote storytelling by children. Their guide, *Children Tell Stories: Teaching and Using Storytelling in the Classroom* 2nd Edition (Richard C. Owen, 2002), comes with a DVD showing young storytellers. Highly recommended! (**I:** 7–11)

———. *Scared Witless: Thirteen Eerie Tales to Tell*. House, 2006. Ghost stories with notes and telling tips. (**I:** 7–11)

Hearne, Betsy, ed. *Beauties and Beasts*. Illustrated by Joanne Caroselli. Oryx Press, 1993. Hearne has researched the Beauty and the Beast tale type and has here reproduced two dozen versions of it from nearly every part of the world. (**I:** 7–11)

———. *Through the Grapevine: World Tales Kids Can Read and Tell*. August House, 2001. Here are thirty-two more tales for reading or telling with notes by the authors. Many of the tales echo themes children will know from other stories. (**I:** 6–10).

Sierra, Judith, ed. *Cinderella*. Illustrated by Joanne Caroselli. Oryx Press, 1992. Cinderella tales from many parts of the world are written out here for reading aloud or storytelling, with scholarly notes on sources added as an appendix. (**I:** 5–10)

———, and Robert Kaminski, eds. *Multicultural Folktales: Stories to Tell to Young Children*. Oryx Press, 1991. Dozens of tales from most parts of the world, prefaced by instructions on telling stories and using the flannel board and accompanied by flannel board cutouts. (**I:** 4–7)

Walker, Richard. *The Barefoot Book of Trickster Tales*. Illustrated by Claudio Muñoz. Barefoot Books, 1998. Nine trickster tales from around the world, including a tale about Jack, one about Ananse, and one about the Mullah Nasruddin. (**I:** 7–11)

Resources

Baker, Liza. *Snow White and the Seven Dwarfs: A Read-Aloud Storybook*. RH/Disney, 1999.

Bettelheim, Bruno. *The Uses of Enchantment*. Vintage, 1975.

Bronner, Simon, ed. *American Children's Folklore*. August House, 1988.

Heins, Paul. *Snow White*. Illustrated by Trina Schart Hyman. Little, Brown, 1974/1999.

Jarrell, Randall, *Snow White and the Seven Dwarves*. Illustrated by Nancy Eckholm Burkert. Farrar, Straus, & Giroux, 1987.

Luthi, Max. *The European Folktale: Form and Future*. ISHI, 1981.

McCarthy, William Bernard, ed. *Jack in Two Worlds*. University of North Carolina Press, 1994.

McGlathery, James, ed. *The Brothers Grimm and Folktale*. University of Illinois Press, 1991.

Miller, Jay. Introduction. *Coyote Stories, by Mourning Dove*. University of Nebraska Press, 1990.

Ong, Walter. *Orality and Literacy: The Technologizing of the Word*. Methuen, 1985.

Perrault, Charles. *The Complete Stories of Charles Perrault*, illustrated by Sally Holmes. Clarion, 1993.

Von Franz, Marie Louise. *Interpretation of Fairy Tales*. Spring Publications, 1970.

References

Aardema, Verna. *Borreguita and the Coyote*. Illustrated by Petra Mathers. Dragonfly, 1988.

Aarne, Antti. *The Types of the Folktale*. Translated and revised by Stith Thompson. Folklore Fellows Communication No. 184. Academia Scientiarum Fennica, 1961.

Aliki. *The Eggs*. HarperCollins, 1994.

Alvarez, Julia. *The Secret Footprints*. Illustrated by Fabin Negrin. Dragonfly, 2002.

Badoe, Adwoa. *The Pot of Wisdom: Ananse Stories*. Illustrated by Baba Waqué Diakité. Groundwood, 2008.

Bang, Molly. *Dawn*. SeaStar Books, 2002.

Beatty, Judith S. (Ed.). *La Llorona: Encounters With the Weeping Woman*. Santa Fe: Sunstone Press, 2004.

Berger, Melvin. *Celebrate! Stories of the Jewish Holiday*. Illustrated by Peter Catalanatto. Scholastic, 2002.

Bettelheim, Bruno. *The Uses of Enchantment*. Vintage, 1975.

Bly, Robert. *Iron John: A Book about Men.* Vintage, 1992.

Bodkin, Odds. *The Crane Wife.* Illustrated by Gennady Spirin. Gulliver Books, 1998.

Botkin, B. A. *A Treasury of American Folklore.* Random House, 1993.

Briggs, Katherine. *British Folktales.* Marboro Books, 1979.

Bronner, Simon, ed. *American Children's Folklore.* August House, 1988.

Bruchac, Joseph. *Keepers of the Animals.* Fulcrum, 1991.

———. *Keepers of the Earth.* Fulcrum, 1988.

Bryan, Ashley. *Beautiful Blackbird.* New York: Atheneum, 2003.

Campbell, Joseph. *The Hero with a Thousand Faces.* Bollingen, 1968.

Cole, Babette. *Prince Cinders.* Putnam, 1997.

Colum, Padraic. *The Children's Homer.* Illustrated by Willy Pagany. Aladdin, 2004.

Crossley-Holland, Kevin. *Folktales of the British Isles.* New York: Pantheon, 1988.

Cypress, Sandra Messinger. *La Malinche in Mexican Literature: From History to Myth.* Austin: University of Texas Press, 1991.

Dahl, Roald. *Danny the Champion of the World.* Puffin, 2007.

Davis, Donald. *Southern Jack Tales.* August House, 1993.

Dawood, N.J. *Aladdin and Other Tales from the Arabian Nights.* Penguin, 1997.

Deen, Rosemary, and Ann Marie Ponsot. *Beat Not the Poor Desk.* Boynton-Cook, 1980.

DeFelice, Cynthia. *The Dancing Skeleton.* Illustrated by Robert Andrew Parker. Aladdin, 1996.

Delacre, Lulu. *Arroz con leche: Popular Songs and Rhymes from Latin America.* Scholastic, 1989.

Demi. *The Hungry Coat: A Tale from Turkey.* Margaret K. McElderry, 2004.

———. *Jesus.* Margaret K. McElderry, 2005.

———. *The Legend of St. Nicholas.* Margaret K. McElderry, 2003.

———. *Mary.* Margaret K. McElderry, 2006.

———. *Mother Teresa.* Margaret K. McElderry, 2005.

———. *One Grain of Rice: A Mathematical Folktale.* Scholastic, 1997.

dePaola, Tomie. *Fin M'Coul: The Giant of Knockmany Hill.* Holiday House, 1981.

———. *Jamie O'Rourke and the Big Potato: An Irish Folktale.* Putnam, 1992.

Diakité, Baba Waqué, *Hatseller and the Monkeys.* Scholastic, 1999.

———. *The Hunterman and the Crocodile.* Scholastic, 1997.

Douglass, Sisan L. *Ramadan.* Illustrated by Jeni Reeves. CarolRhoda, 2003.

Edmonds, Walter D. *The Matchlock Gun.* Dodd Mead, 1941.

Ezer, Ehud Ben. *Hosni the Dreamer.* Illustrated by Uri Shulevitz. Farrar, Straus, & Giroux, 1997.

Freud, Sigmund. *New Introductory Lectures on Psychoanalysis.* Norton, 1923.

Frye, Northrop. *Anatomy of Criticism.* Princeton University Press, 1971.

Galdone, Joanna. *The Tailypo: a Ghost Story.* Illustrated by Paul Galdone. Clarion, 1984.

Goble, Paul. *The Girl Who Loved Wild Horses.* Atheneum/Richard Jackson, 2001.

Griego, Margot C., Betsy L. Bucks, Sharon S. Gilbert, and Laurel H. Kimball. *Tortillitas para Mama and Other Spanish Nursery Rhymes.* Illustrated by Barbara Cooney. Holt, 1981.

Haddix, Margaret Peterson. *Just Ella.* Aladdin, 2001.

Hamilton, Virginia. *In the Beginning: Creation Stories from Around the World* Illustrated by Barry Moser. Sandpiper, 1991.

Heligman, Deborah. *Holidays Around the World: Celebrate Ramadan and Eid Al-Fitr.* National Geographic, 2009.

Hickox, Rebecca. *The Golden Sandal: A Middle Eastern Cinderella Story.* Illustrated by Will Hillenbrand. Holiday House, 1999.

Hitz, Demi. *The Stonecutter.* Knopf, 1991.

Hodge, Margaret. *Brother Francis and the Friendly Beasts.* Illustrated by Ted Lewin. Atheneum, 1991.

Holland, Norman. *Five Readers Reading.* Yale University Press, 1975.

Hunter, Mollie. *A Stranger Came Ashore.* HarperCollins, 1977.

Hyman, Trina Schart. *The Sleeping Beauty.* Little, Brown, 1977.

Irving, Washington. *The Legend of Sleepy Hollow.* Book Jungle, 2007.

Jackson, Ellen. *Cinder Edna.* Illustrated by Kevin O'Malley. HarperCollins, 1998.

Jacobs, Joseph. *Celtic Fairy Tales.* Frederick Muller, 1958.

Jaramillo, Nelly Palacio. *Grandmother's Nursery Rhymes/Las Nanas de Abuelita: Lullabies, Tongue Twisters, and Riddles from South America.* Illustrated by Elivia Savadler. Holt, 1996.

Johnson, James Weldon. *The Creation.* Illustrated by James E. Ransome. Holiday House, 1991.

Jung, Carl, ed. *Man and His Symbols.* Dell, 1961.

———. *Memories, Dream, and Reflections.* Vintage, 1989.

Kimmel, Eric. *Be Not Far From Me: Legends from the Bible.* Illustrated by David Diaz. Simon and Schuster, 1998.

———. *The Chanukkah Guest.* Illustrated by Gloria Karmi. Holiday House, 1992.

———. *Hayyim's Ghost.* Simcha Media Group, 2004.

———. *Hershel and the Hanukkah Goblins.* Illustrated by Trina Schart Hyman. Holiday House, 1994.

———. *The Jar of Fools: Eight Hanukkah Stories from Chelm.* Illustrated by Mordecai Gerstein. Holiday House, 2000.

Levine, Gail Carson. *Ella Enchanted.* HarperCollins, 1997.

Lévi-Strauss, Claude. "The Structural Study of Myth." *Structural Anthropology.* Basic Books, 1957.

Lobel, Arnold. *Fables.* HarperCollins, 1980.

Lomax, Alan. *The Folksongs of North America.* Dolphin, 1975.

Lonnrot, Elias, comp. *The Kalevala.* Translated by Francis Peabody Magoun, Jr. Harvard University Press, 1963.

Lurie, Alsion. *Black Geese: A Baba Yaga Story from Russia.* Illustrated by Jessika Souhami. DK Publishers, 1999.

MacDonald, Margaret Read. *When the Lights Go Out.* H.W. Wilson, 1988.

———. *The StoryTeller's Sourcebook: A Subject, Title, and Motif-Index to Folklore Collections for Children.* Neal-Schuman/Gale Research, 1982.

———. *The StoryTeller's Start-Up Book Finding, Learning, Performing, and Using Folktales: Including Twelve Tellable Tales.* August House, 1993.

———. *The Old Woman Who Lived in a Vinegar Bottle: A British Folktale.* Illustrated by Nancy Dunaway. August House, 1995.

———, and Brian Sturm. *The Storyteller's Sourcebook: A Subject, Title, and Motif-Index to Folklore Collections for Children, 2nd Edition.* Gacl. Sturm, 2001.

Martinez, Alejandro Cruz. *La mujer que brillaba aún más que el sol / The Woman Who Outshone the Sun.* Illustrated by Fernando Olivera. Children's Book Press, 1997.

McDermott, Gerald. Arrow to the Sun: A Pueblo Indian Folktale. Puffin, 1977.

———. Raven: A Trickster Tale from the Pacific Northwest. Sandpiper, 2001.

———.The Stonecutter: A Japanese Folktale. Puffin, 1978.

McGraw, Eloise. The Moorchild. Aladdin, 2006.

McKinley, Robin. Beauty. 1978.

McKissick, Patricia. The Dark Thirty: Southern Tales of the Supernatural. Illustrated by Brian Pinckney. Perfection Learning, 2000.

Mitchell, Adrian. The Odyssey. Illustrated by Stuart Robertson. DK Publishers, 2002.

Mollel, Tololwa. Ananse's Feast. Illustrated by Andrew Glass. Sandpiper, 2002.

———. Rhinos for Lunch and Elephants for Supper! Illustrated by Barbara Spurll. Sandpiper, 2007.

Paterson, Katherine. The Life of Jesus for Children. Scholastic, 2008.

Phelps, Ethel Johnston. The Maid of the North: Feminist Folktales from around the World. Holt, 1981.

———. Tatterhood and Other Tales. Illustrated by Pamela Baldwin-Ford. Feminist Press at the City University of New York, 1978.

Polacco, Patricia. Babushka Baba Yaga. Putnam, 1999.

———. Babushka's Mother Goose. Putnam, 1995.

Propp, Vladimir. The Morphology of the Folktale. 1928. Univ. of Texas Press, 1968.

Rapaport, Roy. "Desecrating the Holy Woman: Derek Freeman's Attack on Margaret Mead." American Scholar 55(3) (Summer 1986): 313–347.

Sabuda, Robert. St. Valentine. Aladdin, 1999.

San Jose, Christine. Cinderella. Illustrated by Debra Santini. Boyds Mills Press, 1994.

———. The True Story of the Three Little Pigs. Illustrated by Lane Smith. Puffin, 1996.

San Souci, Robert. Brave Margaret. Illustrated by Sally Wern Comport. Aladdin, 2002.

———. The Silver Charm. Illustrated by Yoriko Ito. Doubleday, 2002.

———.The Talking Eggs. Illustrated by Jerry Pinkney. Dial, 1989.

Schute, Linda. Rabbit Wishes. HarperCollins, 1995.

Schwartz, Alvin. Scary Stories to Tell in the Dark. HarperCollins, 1985.

Scieszka, Jon. The Book That Jack Wrote. Illustrated by Dan Adel. Puffin, 1997.

———. The Frog Prince, Continued. Illustrated by Steve Johnson. Puffin, 1994.

———.The Stinky Cheese Man and Other Fairly Stupid Tales. Illustrated by Lane Smith. Viking, 1992.

Shah, Idries. Tales of the Dervishes: Teaching Stories of the Sufi Masters Over the Past Thousand Years. Octagon Press, 1967.

Shulevitz, Uri. The Treasure. Farrar, Straus, & Giroux, 1979.

Sierra, Judith. Wiley and the Hairy Man. Illustrated by Brian Pinckney. Dutton, 1996.

Silverman, Maida. My First Book of Jewish Holidays. Dial, 1994.

Singer, Isaac Bashevis. Stories for Children. Farrar, Straus, & Giroux, 1985.

Souriau, Etienne. Les Deux Cent Milles Situations Dramatiques. Flamarion, 1955.

Steptoe, John. Mufaro's Beautiful Daughters. Amistad, 1987.

Still, James. Jack and the Wonder Beans. Illustrated by Margot Tomes. University Press of Kentucky, 1977/1996.

Taback, Simms. There Was an Old Lady Who Swallowed a Fly. Viking, 1997.

Thompson, Stith. The Folktale. Holt, Rinehart, and Winston, 1960 (originally published in 1946).

Tolkien, J.R.R. "On Fairy-Stories." In Essays Presented to Charles Williams, Ed. C.S. Lewis. Grand Rapids: Eerdmans, 1966. 38–89.

Tolstoy, Alexis. The Enormous Turnip. Illustrated by Niamh Sharkey. Barefoot Books, 2009.

Weisner, David. The Three Pigs. Clarion, 2001.

White, T. H. The Once and Future King. Putnam, 1939.

Wildsmith, Brian. Saint Francis. Wm. B. Eerdmans Publishing Company, 1996.

Williamson, Duncan. Tales of the Seal People: Scottish Folk Tales. Interlink, 1992.

Winner, Ellen. Invented Worlds: A Psychology of the Arts. Harvard University Press, 1982.

Wyndham, Robert. Chinese Mother Goose Rhymes. Illustrated by Ed Young. Putnam, 1968.

Yolen, Jane. Favorite Folktales from Around the World. Pantheon, 1988.

———.Greyling. Illustrated by David Ray. Philomel, 1991.

Zipes, Jack. Beauty and the Beast, and Other Classic French Fairy Tales. Signet, 1997.

8

Modern Fantasy and Science Fiction

> *She [Kate] said,* "Watch," and she dipped the funnel into the dish and blew through it, and out of the funnel grew the most magnificent bubble I have ever seen, iridescent, gleaming.
>
> "Look at it from here," said Kate, intent. "Just look at the light!" And in the sunlight, all the colors in the world were swimming over that glimmering sphere—swirling, glowing, achingly beautiful. Like a dancing rainbow the bubble hung there for a long moment; then it was gone.
>
> I thought: That's fantasy.
>
> I said: "I wish they didn't have to vanish so soon."
>
> "But you can always blow another," Kate said.
>
> —*from* Dreams and Wishes: Essays on Writing for Children
> *by Susan Cooper*

This bubble metaphor comes from fantasy writer Susan Cooper, who was sitting in her study, contemplating a description of "fantasy," when her daughter Kate entered the room. It provides a visual image that shows how fantasy takes shape when a believer makes a new creation possible. Writers of fantasy do just that—they create magnificent bubbles so achingly beautiful that readers can only marvel and enjoy.

Go to the Assignments and Activities section of Chapter 8 in the MyEducationKit and complete the activities. As you work through the activities and answer the accompanying questions, consider the importance of evaluating modern fantasy for children.

What Is Modern Fantasy? What Is Science Fiction?

Definition of Modern Fantasy

Fantasy literature has unexplainable magic, and it is this element that captures the minds and hearts of children. According to Lynn (2005),

> Fantasy has been variously described as imaginative, fanciful, visionary, strange, otherworldly, supernatural, mysterious, frightening, magical, inexplicable, wondrous, dreamlike, and, paradoxically, realistic. It has been termed an awareness of the inexplicable existence of "magic" in the everyday world, a yearning for a sudden glimpse of something strange and wonderful, and a different and perhaps truer version of reality. (p. xxi)

Jean Greenlaw (1995a) adds that fantasy literature goes beyond the known world and imaginatively creates a new or transformed world. "Nonrational phenomena" have a significant role in fantasy, as do events, settings, and creatures that don't exist in the real world. The imaginative creation must be so well crafted that readers accept the fantasy through a "willing suspension of disbelief," although this happens only when story details are totally consistent with the fantastic elements.

Fantasy extends reality into the unknown. It gives readers a way of understanding the world they live in by going beyond it to a wider, imaginative vision. Sometimes, people mistakenly think that fantasy is merely an escape from the complexity of reality to a simplistic world. On the contrary, the world created by fantasy can "refresh . . . delight . . . give a new vision," as it artfully presents rich characters and engaging and complex plots that are woven with fantastic elements (Alexander, 1971). For some readers, the strength and depth of emotion they experience as they triumph and despair along with fantasy characters go beyond what they could experience in a realistic world.

Modern fantasy falls into two major classifications: low fantasy and high fantasy. All authors who write fantasy draw on the here and now, what Lloyd Alexander calls the "primary world"—people's knowledge and experience of real life—for "raw material" (Alexander, 1971, p. 164). Low fantasy is actually set in the primary world, but the magical elements of fantasy make the story impossible. In contrast, writers of high fantasy take information and experiences from the primary world and project this information to create images and situations of a "secondary world." Authors of high fantasy create a secondary world whose concrete elements are impossible according to the logic of the primary world, but consistent with its own laws. Some high fantasy stories remain totally in the created world, and some travel between that world and the primary world. Others involve a world within the primary world, marked by boundaries that keep the magic inside the created world (Tymn, Zahorski, & Boyer, 1979).

Definition of Science Fiction

Go to the Extension Activities section of Chapter 8 in the MyEducationKit for your book and complete activity #1 to propose a science fiction novel.

Science fiction is a variety of fantasy in which an author, inspired by real developments in science, has conceived a version of reality different from the one we inhabit. Science fiction writers weave scientific concepts that are extrapolations of current scientific understandings into stories and make them plausible (Greenlaw, 1995b). In short, they make readers believe the unbelievable because they convince them that it is possible.

Because works of science fiction make readers entertain possibilities that go well beyond everyday occurrences, they have a useful role to play in educating the imagination, to borrow a phrase from the literary critic Northrop Frye (1957). The imagination, as Frye points out, is the source of all human invention. For example, people told stories about human flight for thousands of years before the Wright brothers' plane flew off a sand dune at Kitty Hawk. Humans would never have gotten off the ground if they hadn't long imagined the wonders of flight. Such imagining can be nourished by stories.

Distinction between Fantasy and Science Fiction

Greenlaw (1982) differentiates modern fantasy and science fiction this way: "Fantasy never could be. Science fiction has the possibility of being—maybe not in our time or on our planet, but the possibility of happening within some time and in some place" (p. 64). In other words, a story that is clearly impossible is called *fantasy;* a story with aspects of the improbable is called *science fiction*. The possibility that someday an invention or new knowledge could make feasible something that is seemingly improbable is what distinguishes science fiction from other forms of fantasy. In 1869, Jules Verne wrote **Twenty Thousand Leagues under the Sea.** The idea of a submarine obviously existed in Verne's imagination, but no real submarine had yet been built. A submarine might have seemed improbable at the time, but as it turned out, it was very possible.

At times, it is difficult to make a clear distinction between science fiction and fantasy because certain books have characteristics of both genres. These hybrid books may present details purported to have a scientific basis, yet they also include elements that make the story clearly impossible. The result is a type of science fiction called "science fantasy." Science fantasy includes elements that were previously considered traditional in high fantasy (such as dragons, wizards, and fairies) as well as elements that are traditional in science fiction (space travel or interplanetary exploration). Science fantasy begins with an extrapolation based on scientific understanding, but the story is predominantly a fantasy.

We will discuss modern fantasy in the first half of this chapter and science fiction in the second half. This parallel structure will allow a more focused look at each genre.

Twenty Thousand Leagues Under the Sea
Jules Verne

ILLUSTRATION 8.1 In *Twenty Thousand Leagues Under the Sea*, Jules Verne created the captivating, visionary tale of Captain Nemo and his majestic *Nautilus*, an elaborate submarine—an undersea vehicle that had yet to be invented. Aboard the *Nautilus*, three captive castaways experience harrowing yet marvelous undersea adventures that test the limits of their imagination, courage, and mental resilience. (Cover taken from the 1873 English edition published by Geo. M Smith & Co., Boston.)

Go to the Extension Activities section of Chapter 8 in the MyEducationKit for your book and complete activity #2 to examine *The Wind in the Willows*.

The Evolution of Modern Fantasy

Myths, legends, and folktales are predecessors of the modern genres of fantasy and science fiction. For centuries, the oral tradition of storytelling passed along many tales of magical beings, fantastic occurrences, and otherworldly places. The beginning of modern fantasy as a genre can be traced to the nineteenth century, when stories that later became known as literary fairy tales were created in the style of stories from the oral tradition. These literary fairy tales included features of works from traditional folklore: generic settings in kingdoms far away in a distant time "long, long ago," one-dimensional stock characters, magical elements, and, quite often, happy endings. Unlike stories from the oral tradition, however, literary fairy tales have known authors. A notable example is the work created by Hans Christian Andersen in the mid-nineteenth century. In Andersen's "The Princess and the Pea," the elements of folklore are present: the setting in a time period described simply as "there once was . . . ," the stock characters of a prince and a princess, the magical way in which the princess felt the pea through layers and layers of mattresses, and the "lived happily ever after" ending.

Several nineteenth-century British writers turned their attention to creating fantasy for children. Many of these early works are now considered classics and are still enjoyed by today's children. *Alice's Adventures in Wonderland,* written by Charles Lutwidge Dodgson and published in 1865 under the pseudonym Lewis Carroll, was regarded as representing a turning point in literature for children because it was written with humor and imagination rather than with a didactic purpose. In the story, Alice falls into a rabbit hole and enters a fantastic world—a world that demands a sense of humor and an imaginative mind. Another early work of fantasy is George MacDonald's *At the Back of the North Wind,* published in 1871, about a boy who was swept off to an imaginary land where he has adventures with a cab-horse. Published in 1894, Rudyard Kipling's *The Jungle Book* is the story of Mowgli, a human child left in the jungle, raised by wolves, and nurtured by the wisdom of a bear, a python, and a panther.

J. M. Barrie's play *Peter and Wendy* had a large impact on fantasy literature for children when it was published in 1904; it was re-published in 1911 as *Peter Pan.* The story of how Peter teaches three children how to fly to Never Never Land so that they will never have to grow up is still well known and loved among children. Beatrix Potter is another early genius of the fantasy genre. Her childhood study of animals led to a thorough understanding of them and enabled her to draw and write imaginative stories that somehow seemed true to the animals' natures. Beginning in 1902 with the publication of *The Tale of Peter Rabbit,* Potter created a series of "little books," each featuring a different animal character. Another milestone book about personified animals, *The Wind in the Willows,* was created in 1908 by British writer Kenneth Grahame. In this series of stories depicting day-to-day events, woodland animals bond in complex friendships that reflect the trials and rewards that human beings experience. A. A. Milne published *Winnie-the-Pooh,* with illustrations by Ernest Shepard, in 1926, and the book became a classic story of personified toy animals. Milne gave each character a distinct personality—Pooh, Eeyore, Tigger, Piglet, Owl, Kanga, and Roo— and young readers find the predictability of their words and actions in various circumstances reassuring.

Other lighthearted fantasies written in the first half of the twentieth century include Hugh Lofting's *The Story of Doctor Dolittle* in 1920 and P. L. Travers's *Mary Poppins* in 1934. Doctor Dolittle is an animal doctor who sets off for Africa with his dog, duck, pig, parrot, and owl to cure monkeys of a disease. In Travers's book, a seemingly prim and proper nanny named Mary Poppins enters the Banks household, and her arrival "on the East Wind" foreshadows the magical adventures ahead for the two children.

Fantasy literature was also published in other European countries. Carlo Collodi's personified toy story *The Adventures of Pinocchio* was published in Italy in 1881. Children are still intrigued by this story of a lonely man who carves a marionette that comes to life and becomes his little boy. Young readers can relate to the choices that Pinocchio must learn to make: to do what is expected by parents, not to be enticed by strangers who offer tempting alternatives, and to tell the truth. The two-volume edition of *The Wonderful Adventures of*

Nils (1906–1907), by Selma Lagerlöf, was originally published as a geography primer for Swedish children. The story became a classic when it was translated into other languages; children around the world were enchanted by the story of how Nils Holgersson became elf-sized and traveled all over Sweden on the back of a goose. In 1937, with *Babar,* France's Jean de Brunhoff began a series of stories recounting the adventures of an elephant named Babar and his family. Tove Jansson's *Finn Family Moomintroll* was the first in a series of humorous books published during the 1940s and 1950s in Finland about the Moomins, imaginary troll-like creatures who held magical powers. In Sweden in 1945, Astrid Lindgren published *Pippi Longstocking,* a fantasy featuring an eccentric protagonist: a little girl who lives her life in such an uncharacteristic way that children who read of her adventures are fascinated by the possibility that a child like that might exist. Pippi is a nine-year-old who does as she pleases whenever she wants to because she lives alone with no adults to supervise her activities. Mary Norton's *The Borrowers,* a story of a family of "little people" who live by "borrowing" everyday objects from humans, was published in England in 1953. This popular book was the start of a series about the Borrowers.

The first modern fantasy for children published in the United States was *The Wonderful Wizard of Oz,* created by Frank Baum in 1900. Baum created thirteen more volumes about Oz. They were so immensely popular that after his death in 1919, his publisher hired Ruth Plumly Thompson to write nineteen more stories to satisfy the literary appetite of readers who loved the world of Oz.

Robert Lawson won the 1945 Newbery Medal for his personified animal story *Rabbit Hill.* The story takes place in the Connecticut countryside, where Father and Mother Rabbit and Little Georgie live. Rumor has it that new folks are coming to live in the big house, and all the animals who live in the surrounding area wonder what this will mean to them—how will they be treated?

A few years later, in 1952, E. B. White published a book that was to become a favorite of children around the world. *Charlotte's Web* tells the story of Wilbur, a runt pig who is rescued from slaughter and then catapulted into fame by Charlotte, a kind spider who spins words of praise for Wilbur in her web. Despite its lighthearted tone, the themes of friendships, death, and legacy are serious and enduring.

Low fantasy stories are particularly prevalent in picture book format. Currently, authors such as Kevin Henkes, Rosemary Wells, Susan Meddaugh, and Lisa Campbell Ernst are producing high-quality picture book fantasies. Their work is discussed in more detail later in this chapter.

The mid-twentieth century marked the beginning of the publication of high fantasy series for children. J.R. R. Tolkien published *The Hobbit* in 1937. This book has been read by millions of children and adults, and translated into over twenty-five languages. Tolkien's thorough understanding of mythology was the basis of a trilogy entitled *The Lord of the Rings,* in which the protagonist, Frodo Baggins, goes on a quest.

The Chronicles of Narnia, a seven-volume series, was published between 1950 and 1956 by C. S. Lewis, who wove Christian allegories throughout his stories set in the fantasy world of Narnia. *The Chronicles of Prydain,* a high fantasy series by Lloyd Alexander, began in 1964 with the publication of *The Book of Three.* Robin McKinley's quest fantasy *The Hero and the Crown* was published in 1984 and won the Newbery Medal in 1985. It was unusual among high fantasy books because it featured a female protagonist. A high fantasy series featuring characters portrayed as animals is Brian Jacques's *Redwall* series, whose first volume was published in England in 1987. Philip Pullman's *Dark Materials* trilogy started with *The Golden Compass,* published in 1996, and ended with *The Amber Spyglass,* published in 2000.

Fantasy reading at the beginning of the twenty-first century is marked by extraordinary levels of readership and fervor. The most popular series of the 1990s was R. L. Stine's *Goosebumps*. Although the literary quality of most of these books does not match that of others listed in this section, the series created an addiction to fantasy reading in a large sector of the elementary school population—and the merit of this cannot be overlooked. Terry Pratchett's books set in Discworld have been popular since the early 1980s. The publication of J. K. Rowling's *Harry Potter* books marks a phenomenon perhaps unequaled by any previously published books for children. With the first book, *Harry Potter and the Sorcerer's*

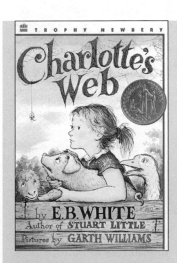

ILLUSTRATION 8.2 The life of a shy runt pig is saved through the efforts of a clever, articulate spider named Charlotte in this extraordinarily popular animal fantasy by E. B. White. (*Charlotte's Web* by E. B. White, illustrated by Garth Williams. Copyright © 1999. Used by permission of HarperCollins Publishers.)

Stone, readers—both children and adults—were hooked, and the seven books led to record-high levels of excitement, sales, and movies. All of this means that more people are reading and discussing fantasy than ever before, and more fantasies are being published in the twenty-first century than ever before.

Categories of Modern Fantasy

This section examines several categories of fantasy. However, as Egoff (1988) has pointed out, good literature "can never be fitted into one sterile slot." Some books fit into multiple genres. For example, Jane Yolen's *The Devil's Arithmetic* can be considered historical fiction because it is set mainly during the Holocaust; yet it might also be considered modern fantasy because the book's protagonist experiences a slip in time. Gail Carson Levine's *Ella Enchanted* is based on the fairy tale of Cinderella, yet it is a fully developed fantasy that goes far beyond the traditional tale. Even within the genre of fantasy, books can be placed in more than one category. In Jon Scieszka's *Time Warp Trio* series, each story concerns a time slip, yet each begins with an object of magical power: a book. In addition, authors are increasingly including elements of science fiction with fantasy. T. A. Barron uses elements of science fiction, mythology, and fantasy in his works. Although it is hard to put books into neat categories, trying to do so allows for interesting comparisons.

Low fantasy features nonrational events that occur without explanation in the real world. Low fantasy is also known as light fantasy, for the tone is usually rather lighthearted, often humorous. Children typically read such fantasy at a younger age and tend to read it more than high fantasy overall. The forms of low fantasy include stories about personified animals, personified toys, outlandish characters and situations, magical powers, embellished fairy tales, extraordinary worlds, supernatural elements, and time slips. These forms are discussed here in the order in which children are likely to be introduced to them, which corresponds roughly to young readers' increasingly higher levels of engagement in the fantasy elements.

Personified Animals

Stories with animals talking and behaving as humans do are often called personified animal fantasies. Typically, this is the first type of fantasy book that young children encounter. Animal characters who behave like humans are said to be anthropomorphic. In fact, many picture books for young children contain personified animals as characters, yet the situations they face and how they deal with them are quite realistic to the children who read such books.

Beatrix Potter's many personified animals may be among the first fantasy characters children are introduced to. In *The Tale of Peter Rabbit,* Potter mixes behaviors typical of rabbits with behaviors of humans. Peter and his family live in a sand bank underneath the roots of a tree, play in the fields, eat garden vegetables, and hop away from danger—all rabbit-like behaviors. But Mrs. Rabbit talks to her children using words, and the rabbits wear clothing and drink chamomile tea—all human behaviors.

Kevin Henkes has written and illustrated many stories about personified mice. Sheila Rae, the brave older sister who suddenly panics and relies on the wits of her younger sister in *Sheila Rae, the Brave,* and Chester and Wilson, whose particular ways of doing things are disrupted by Lilly's move into the neighborhood in *Chester's Way,* are all mice. However, they not only behave like people but think like them, too. As children get older, they may encounter William Steig's personified animals. In *Doctor De Soto,* a fox gets a toothache and seeks the help of a dentist who is a mouse. This dilemma has both an animal and a human dimension: As a dentist, Dr. De Soto feels a moral obligation to help someone with a toothache, but as a mouse, he fears that the fox could have ulterior motives.

Lois Lowry's *Stay! Keeper's Story* begins, "I needed a child." Keeper, a dog, continues with an explanation of behaviors adults impose on their dogs (like insisting that dogs like to sleep in a cage or on a flea-retardant bed with cedar shavings) and how a child would bet-

Go to the Extension Activities section of Chapter 8 in the MyEducationKit for your book and complete activity #3 to consider how a story with personified animals would change if the characters were human.

Top Shelf 8.1

Personified Animal Characters in Picture Books

Lilly and friends books by Kevin Henkes

Martha the talking dog books by Susan Meddaugh

Max and Ruby books by Rosemary Wells

Peter Rabbit and friends books by Beatrix Potter

ter understand what a dog wants: "Dogs prefer to sleep snuggled right up beside a human, their heads on a feather pillow, with ears nicely spread out and the rest of the body curled on an innerspring mattress covered by percale sheets smelling of human breath and sweat." In stories like this, the dog's behavior is doglike, but his ability to have and to express thoughts in human language makes this book a fantasy.

In Avi's "Tales of Dimwood Forest" stories, *Poppy,* a deer mouse tries to convince her family to move close to a large cornfield because it could provide food for them forever. This move is thwarted when the tyrannical great horned owl, Mr. Ocax, refuses to give his consent. An unlikely group of personified animals interacts in Cynthia Rylant's *Gooseberry Park.* A Labrador retriever named Kona befriends Stumpy, a squirrel in Gooseberry Park. When Stumpy is separated from her babies during an ice storm, a bat named Murray and a hermit crab named Gwendolyn team up with Kona to reunite the newborns with their mother.

Several popular stories about personified animals center around a community of animals. *Charlotte's Web* by E. B. White is an immensely popular example. When Wilbur is about to be slaughtered as the runt of the litter, he is rescued by a little girl, Fern. However, it is Charlotte, a spider, who calls the entire cast of barnyard animals into action to truly save Wilbur's life. As in E. B. White's books, the barnyard animals in British writer Dick King-Smith's stories such as *Babe: The Gallant Pig* become the community within which the story takes place. *The Wind in the Willows,* by Kenneth Grahame, also features a community of animals. The four good friends—Ratty, Mole, Badger, and Toad—are animals with strong personal characteristics that define their roles. George Selden's *The Cricket in Times Square* is about a community of city-dwelling animals; other books in the series center on the same animals' visits to the country.

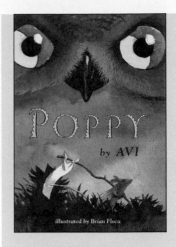

ILLUSTRATION 8.3   The situations in which the characters in *Poppy* find themselves are set in the animal world, but the solutions arise out of thoughts and behaviors that are quite human. (Jacket illustration copyright © 1995 by Brian Floca from *Poppy* by Avi. Scholastic Inc./Orchard Books. Reprinted by permission of Scholastic Inc.)

Personified Toys

Another type of fantasy that children enjoy features personified toys (as well as other inanimate objects) that come to life. In these books, toys are able to talk and behave like humans. The toys that come to life are typically stuffed animals or dolls. The reason may be that when children play, they frequently pretend that stuffed animals and dolls have human attributes.

Perhaps the best-known personified toy story is A. A. Milne's classic work *Winnie-the-Pooh.* The story was inspired by Milne's son, Christopher Robin, and his collection of stuffed animals.

The Castle in the Attic, by Elizabeth Winthrop, is a personified toy story in which a finger-high knight in a model castle comes alive when William, the young protagonist, picks him up. But when William's desire to keep his nanny from leaving shrinks her to the doll size, he, too, must enter the toy-sized life and seek to undo the magic. Lynne Reid Banks's *The Indian in the Cupboard* and its sequels are also popular among children. A toy Indian and other toys come alive when Omri puts them in a magical cupboard. Having toys come alive, seeing the unfolding adventure as the toys engage in lifelike situations, and realizing what responsibility means are all part of the drama Omri and his friend Patrick experience. Although these popular books address the question "What if toys came alive?" the toy people in them do not rise above stereotypes of Indians and cowboys, and the portrayal of the Indian is particularly problematic.

Ann Martin and Laura Godwin teamed up to create *The Doll People,* in which a hundred-year-old doll family is brought from England to America and passed down through the generations to the current owner, Kate. Eight-year-old Anabelle is a doll who reads her Aunt Sarah's journal and becomes obsessed with the need to solve the mystery of her aunt's disappearance in 1955. Humorous clashes of the ages come about with the arrival of a plastic family next door, with modern amenities such as a microwave oven. Illustrations by Brian Selznick throughout the book keep readers engagingly immersed in the doll world.

Kate DiCamillo's *The Miraculous Journey of Edward Tulane* describes a china rabbit doll who is vain, selfish, and heartless. He belongs to ten-year-old Abilene, until a disastrous series of events takes him on a long and distant journey, through which he encounters physical damage to his toy body but a building of his emotional self through his various owners and his relationships with them.

Outlandish Characters and Situations

Stories that appear to be realistic fiction but have characters who behave in outrageous, highly exaggerated ways that are utterly impossible are classified as fantasy with outlandish characters. When these characters merely possess abilities that are outside the range of normal human behavior or act in eccentric ways, but everything in the story is still humanly possible, they are classified as "magical realism," a type of realistic fiction. As with other types of categorization, there are seeming overlaps that make it difficult to determine whether the story is more realistic or more fantasy. For the purpose of our textbook, we have chosen to differentiate what is physically possible in our known world as "magical realism" in realistic fiction, and what is utterly impossible in our known world as "outlandish characters and situations" in fantasy.

P. L. Travers created a series of stories about a character with magical abilities. The first of these was *Mary Poppins,* in which the unusual nanny arrives at the home of Jane and Michael Banks by way of an umbrella that carries her airborne on a gust of wind.

Swedish writer Astrid Lindgren is known around the world as the creator of *Pippi Longstocking* and two sequels, as well as more than a hundred other books. Pippi lives alone, without any adult supervision, and displays outrageous and eccentric behavior that keeps the neighborhood children constantly amused. What makes Pippi's story a fantasy is that she is given physical abilities that are beyond human; for example, as a young girl, she can lift a horse.

Polly Horvath writes many books that seem to fit into both categories of magical realism and outlandish characters and situations. While all of her books are filled with exaggeration and dry humor, some, like *The Pepins and Their Problems,* have elements that are not possible, such as a cow that dispenses lemonade. Horvath uses the device of presenting the Pepins' problems to readers and eliciting their suggestions for dealing with the family's hilariously absurd problems, prompting the sharing of the equally nonsensical responses supposedly sent in from across the United States.

Popular series books have created quite a following of readers. Both Lemony Snicket's *A Series of Unfortunate Events* and Philip Ardagh's Eddie Dickens trilogy rely on exaggeration and humor to tell stories that are outlandish and preposterous. Both are also plays on Victorian novels and offer multiple levels of humor through the use of language play on figures of speech and vocabulary.

Magical Powers

The notion that magic might exist is an intriguing thought to children: Could there be sayings that make magical things happen, objects that hold magical powers, or other ways of bringing about magical events?

What could be more enticing than the dream that a better life than the one we live is owed to us and that we have magical powers? In J. K. Rowling's *Harry Potter and the Sorcerer's Stone,* Harry's existence is so lowly that readers are sure to recognize it as an unfair life. On the eve of his eleventh birthday, he receives an invitation to Hogwarts School of Witchcraft and Wizardry—and the news that he is the most famous wizard alive! Magical events abound throughout the Harry Potter books, and somehow all seem believable to the reader.

Teaching Idea 8.1

Magical Abilities

Select a book that features a character with magical abilities. Would you like to possess such abilities? Why or why not? Explain what your life would be like if you had those magical abilities. Carefully consider the pros and cons of having such abilities. How would this change your relationship with your friends, your family, and society as a whole?

In Cornelia Funke's book, *Inkheart,* Meggie's father has magical power and inadvertently reads characters right out of a book and into real life, where they create havoc by engaging in the kind of criminal behavior and adventurous lifestyles they lived in the book. Meggie's burning question is: What happened to her mother, and how can they find her? What kind of magical ability will be needed to solve this mystery?

Natalie Babbitt's *Tuck Everlasting* has the ultimate magic in it: a spring that gives eternal life to those who drink from it. The source of this water is not explained, nor does the story offer an explanation of how it gives eternal life. All readers know is the magical consequences of drinking from the spring. The moral question is: Is it better to drink the water and live eternally or to live the continuous flow of the known life cycle?

Picture books also have stories with magical powers. In Chris Van Allsburg's *Jumanji*, the children play a board game and as they land on the squares that describe their journey through the game, the jungle comes to life with lions, monsoon rains, and destructive monkeys that will not go away until the game is played out to the end. In William Steig's picture book *Sylvester and the Magic Pebble*, Sylvester is portrayed as a donkey who comes across a special pebble for his pebble collection—one that grants wishes. The problem arises when Sylvester wishes to turn into a rock temporarily to escape trouble, but cannot revert back to being a donkey. This story of personified animals includes elements of magic.

Embellished Fairy Tales

In recent years, many fairy tales have been embellished with rich character development, detailed descriptions of setting, and finely developed plot, presenting a fuller story than the original traditional tales offered. In many cases, they answer questions provoked by the original tale: Why was Rumpelstiltskin interested in the miller's daughter's child? Why was Rapunzel's mother so loving, yet so cruel in locking up her daughter? Why did Jack trade a cow for a handful of magic beans? In almost all cases, the expanded versions remain true to the essential components of the original tales as we know them, but put a new twist on or offer a different perspective to readers.

In Gail Carson Levine's *Ella Enchanted*, a gift of "obedience" is bestowed on Ella by the fairy Lucinda, and it turns out to be a curse rather than a blessing. The story explores what happens when a child must be obedient, even against her own will. Robin McKinley offers readers two books based on Beauty and the Beast: *Beauty* and *Rose Daughter*. Published twenty years apart, the books have certain details that remain consistent, yet they offer two different stories based on the same essential framework.

The most prolific author in this category is Donna Jo Napoli. In *Zel*, she considers three perspectives on the Rapunzel story: those of the thirteen-year-old peasant daughter Zel, the nobleman who falls in love with her and wants to marry her, and the mother—who turns out to be a witch with a motive for locking up her daughter. Napoli continued her frog-turned-prince story, *Prince of the Pond*, in *Jimmy, the Pickpocket of the Palace*. When Jimmy, the frog son of a frog prince, shows up at the palace with a hurt leg, a princess kisses it. In keeping with the fairy tale story of the frog prince, Jimmy turns into a human. Searching for a magic ring that will convert him back into a frog so that he can save his pond from an evil hag, he leaves himself open to accusations of theft. Books like these offer readers opportunities to ponder what other known stories offer possibilities for embellishment.

Extraordinary Worlds

The first task of an author who creates a world that is very different from the one in which we live is to make it believable to readers. Sometimes a story begins with convincing characters in the known world who then move into an extraordinary world through various devices. For example, when Milo enters the mysterious tollbooth in Norton Juster's popular novel *The Phantom Tollbooth*, he finds an extraordinary world. In Roald Dahl's *Charlie and the Chocolate Factory*, the search for gold tickets hidden in chocolate bars takes place in the real world, but an invitation to

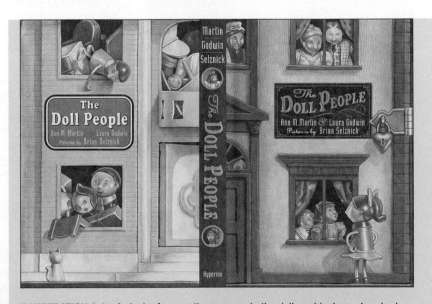

ILLUSTRATION 8.4 A clash of generations occurs in the doll world when a hundred-year-old doll family meets a modern plastic doll family. (From Laura Godwin's *The Doll People* © Laura Godwin, illustrated by Brian Selznick. Reprinted by permission of Disney•Hyperion Books For Children.)

Teaching Idea 8.2
Embellish a Fairy Tale

Select a fairy tale, and write down the essential points of the fairy tale after reading several versions in picture books and collected volumes. What are the unanswered questions? What events make you curious? What do you wish would happen? Using the essential major points as the basis, write an expanded version of your own. Be sure to add rich details that still connect to the major points. Also check to be sure that it makes sense as to why those details were added. Illustrate to add the visual component of your story.

enter a mysterious chocolate factory leads a selected few into an extraordinary world. In *Alice's Adventures in Wonderland,* Alice, a seemingly ordinary child, falls into a rabbit hole and finds an extraordinary world at the other end. In Eloise McGraw's *The Moorchild,* the human world and the "folk world" coexist side by side; the folk world is accessible only to folk, but folk can move in and out of the human world. In Eoin Colfer's *Artemis Fowl,* the twelve-year-old genius criminal mastermind must steal a fairy handbook and crack its code in an attempt to steal their gold and restock his family's fortune. The subterranean world of fairies is complex and highly guarded by the LEPrecon (Lower Elements Police reconnaissance group). Other stories are set entirely in an extraordinary world. What makes the extraordinary world believable in Mary Norton's *The Borrowers* is the author's careful attention to minute details when describing how the tiny Borrowers adapt various everyday human-size objects to their own uses.

In Roderick Townley's *The Great Good Thing,* the last existing copy of an extraordinary fairy tale is discovered by the daughter of the original owner. When she opens the book and begins reading, the characters in the story must act it out as though they were actors and actresses, reciting the lines of text that are in the book, but on a stage that is the setting of the story. Whenever the reader puts the book down, though, the characters are free to lead their own lives as long as they are ready to instantly move to their spots whenever a reader opens the book. In the sequel, *Into the Labyrinth,* the story is now posted to a Web site and many readers can access it simultaneously. But how will the characters who have long had their lines and parts memorized, deal with sudden shifts in added phrases, deleted passages, and uneven scroll-throughs of lines? These characters live in an extraordinary world within the book, unbeknownst to readers.

In Cornelia Funke's *Dragon Rider,* a young boy realizes his destiny of becoming a dragon rider. Set in an extraordinary world of dragons, brownies, and other creatures not in our world today, readers are treated to a fantastic world of magical happenings.

Two picture book illustrators who create some of the most extraordinary of worlds are Shaun Tan and David Wiesner. Interestingly, Wiesner does so almost exclusively through illustration, with minimal text, if any. Tan uses both illustration and text to depict the extraordinary worlds he creates, although the illustrations could carry the stories, even without the text. Wiesner has won the Caldecott for *Tuesday*, in which flying frogs on lily pads leave the townspeople in wonder; *The Three Pigs,* in which various folk stories with pigs and wolves weave through the book in unexpected mixings; and *Flotsam*, in which an underwater world is suggested and introduced. In Shaun Tan's *The Arrival,* the utterly confusing and at times lonely experience of being an immigrant is compared to being an alien in an unknown world.

Supernatural Elements

Scary stories with supernatural elements—ghosts, haunted houses, and the like—intrigue children. Margaret Mahy tells the story of a family with psychic powers in *The Haunting.* The family members struggle with what these powers do to their relationships with one another. Pam Conrad's *Stonewords* tells about Zoe, who is visited by the ghost of Zoe Louise. Zoe realizes that she must prevent Zoe Louise's untimely death, and to do so she must go back in time and change the course of events. In Mary Downing Hahn's *Wait till Helen Comes,* the ghost of Helen, who died years ago, waits by the pond to drown other

ILLUSTRATION 8.5 Shaun Tan imagines the immigrant experience by comparing it to experiencing the foreignness of the unknown fantasy world in which aliens of all kinds exist alongside humans. (From *The Arrival* by Shaun Tan. Scholastic Inc./Arthur A. Levine Books. Copyright © 2006 by Shaun Tan. Reprinted by permission.)

children her age in hopes of getting a playmate. Molly must save her new stepsister from joining Helen.

Books with supernatural elements are not necessarily scary. Supernatural elements are taken in stride in stories such as Franny Billingsley's **The Folk Keeper.** Corinna knows that her unusual qualities would frighten some people, so she keeps them to herself and takes her "different abilities" in stride as she explains them to the reader with a matter-of-fact voice. Neil Gaiman's **The Graveyard Book** depicts the growing up of "Nobody" in a graveyard, with ghosts as parents and caretakers. But as Nobody grows up, he faces life in a world outside the protection of his cemetery home and relationships with people who are living, and not ghosts.

Among the most popular books with children today are stories that can be classified as fantasies with supernatural elements. Many children eagerly seek out these "horror stories" and "scary stories." The most popular series of the 1990s was R. L. Stine's **Goosebumps,** with over fifty titles. Although as mentioned earlier they vary in literary quality, typically such books are of enormous mass appeal among children.

Time Slips

In time-slip stories, characters move from one time period to another. This element of time travel allows the author to explore themes in ways not possible in stories that take place in a single time period. Typically, the time slips allow the characters to develop an understanding that enhances their development. Barbara Elleman (1985, p. 1407) notes that "time-slip plots often center on a particular historical period, a mystery that needs to be solved, or a common problem shared across generations." Going back in time allows characters to gain firsthand experience that deepens their understanding of how historical events influence the present. Time slips in mysteries allow characters to find the clues to solve the mysteries. Sometimes, issues span generations, and in some time-slip stories, the protagonist finds ways to cope with issues by meeting others who have faced them in an earlier time. In **Tom's Midnight Garden,** Philippa Pearce tells the story of a boy who is bored with his summer until he discovers that when the grandfather clock strikes thirteen, he can enter the garden and play with a child from the past.

Jon Scieszka has written a series of books about three boys who make up the Time Warp Trio: **Knights of the Kitchen Table; The Not-So-Jolly Roger; The Good, the Bad, and the Goofy; Your Mother Was a Neanderthal; 2095; Tut, Tut;** and **Summer Reading Will Kill You.** The device that allows the boys to travel in time is a magical object, "The Book," which Joe receives as a birthday present from his uncle, a magician. When Joe and his two friends, Fred and Sam, open the book, they are whisked off to a different place and time—the medieval days of King Arthur, the days of pirates and buried treasure, the nineteenth century in the Old West, the Stone Age, the twenty-first century, or ancient Egypt.

Mary Pope Osborne's **Magic Tree House** books are a very popular series of beginning chapter books. Siblings Jack and Annie read books in their tree house and are magically transported to various times and places, where they learn historical, scientific, and cultural information. The books include time destinations as varied as the days of dinosaurs, the Revolutionary War, and Shakespeare's era.

Belinda Hurmence's **A Girl Called Boy** and Jane Yolen's **The Devil's Arithmetic** are time-slip stories as well as works of historical fiction. In both, the protagonists question what they believe to be excessive pride in heritage and an almost obsessive need to remember the past. In **A Girl Called Boy,** Blanche ("Boy") is transported back to the days of African American slavery. In **The Devil's Arithmetic,** Hannah is transported to the time of the Holocaust. Both return to the present with a deeper understanding of themselves as descendants of a particular heritage and a commitment not to forget the past. In another work of historical fiction and time slip, **King of Shadows,** Susan Cooper explores the days of Shakespeare. As Nat Fields acts out his role as Puck in "The Midsummer Night's Dream," both in the present day and with Will Shakespeare himself, Nat's present-day character

Teaching Idea 8.3
Time Slip

Select a character in a time-slip book, and imagine what it would be like if that person slipped into your present-day life. What would surprise that person about the world you live in? What might seem familiar? What might that person learn? Take notes on these questions, and then pretend to be that person while your classmates ask you questions and you answer in character.

Teaching Idea 8.4

If You Traveled in Time. . . .

If you could slip through time, which time period would you select? Explain why you made the choice and what you would hope to learn by slipping into a different time period. Describe how your life would be different in that time period, and how it would be similar.

comes to terms with his father's death through the relationship he has with Will Shakespeare in the past time period. The device of the time slip also allows readers to see the past through a present-day character's eyes, with explanations that clarify the differences. In a reverse pattern, Linda Sue Park's *Archer's Quest* incorporates elements of Korean history and legend as a way for twelve-year-old Kevin to help a king from ancient Korea return to the past when he suddenly appears in contemporary times.

Dan Gutman uses the device of a baseball card to allow the holder to travel back in time to the era of the person whose card he is holding. What baseball card-collecting kid wouldn't be enthralled at imagining such a thing? In *Shoeless Joe and Me,* Stosh travels back to 1919 when Shoeless Joe and others were caught "throwing" the World Series and expelled from baseball for life. Stosh hopes that if he can prevent this from happening, Shoeless Joe Jackson can be inducted into the Baseball Hall of Fame. Other ball players about whom the time travel series has been written include Jackie Robinson, Honus Wagner, Babe Ruth, Mickey Mantle.

Two other books have protagonists whose travel back in time allows them to explore their relationships with their parents. In Cynthia Voigt's ***Building Blocks,*** Brann is frustrated with his father and cannot understand him. When Brann creates a fortress with his father's childhood building blocks and enters it, he finds himself transported to the time of his father's childhood. In Canadian author Kit Pearson's *A Handful of Time,* a twelve-year-old girl finds an old watch under the floor while visiting her cousins. The watch takes her back to the time when her mother was the same age.

In Mary Hoffman's ***Stravaganza*** trilogy, a "Stravaganti" is someone who can traverse time periods. In the first book, *City of Masks,* Lucien lives in twenty-first century London and is undergoing chemotherapy for cancer when his father brings him a beautiful Italian notebook in which he can write and communicate when his throat hurts too much to talk. The notebook turns out to be a talisman that transports him to the time period of the stravaganti who brought it into the twenty-first century. Lucien quickly adapts to his life in the Italian Bellezza as Luciano, apprentice to a "magical" scientist Rodolfo, himself a stravaganti. Through the device of the time slip, Lucien/Luciano is able to lead a more complete life. Rebecca Stead's Newbery-winning book, ***When You Arrive,*** has allusions to Madeline L'Engle's *A Wrinkle in Time*. The book seems more like realistic fiction for much of the story, but then, things happen that remind readers that not everything is explainable in the world as we know it. Ultimately, the mystery that forms at the beginning of the story is resolved through an answer in which the device of time travel explains why certain things had to happen.

Go to the Extension Activities section of Chapter 8 in the MyEducationKit for your book and complete activity #4 to develop your movie of a fantasy series.

High Fantasy

As we mentioned earlier, high fantasy takes place in a created secondary world. Although much high fantasy is enjoyed by young adults, many middle school students and some elementary school readers are attracted to works of high fantasy. There are various categories of high fantasy: myth fantasy, gothic fantasy, epic/heroic fantasy, and sword and sorcery fantasy. Myth fantasy can be retellings of old myths, modern adaptations of old myths, or new inventions. Gothic fantasy includes elements such as fear of the unknown and the unnatural. Epic/heroic fantasy tries to recreate the world of the medieval epic and romance. Such fantasies are grand in their design and often have a strong emotional impact on readers. Heroic actions stem from the protagonist's commitment to serve "the common good." In many ways closely related to legends from the oral tradition, epic/hero fantasies often contain components of Arthurian, Welsh, Scandinavian, or other myths and legends. Sword and sorcery fantasy is similar to heroic fantasy. However, sword and sorcery fantasy is not to be confused with the "sword and sinew subgenre," which violates many of the characteristics of high fantasy. That subgenre includes a barbarian superhero, has much action, lacks thematic substance, uses a colloquial style of language, and sensationalizes violence (Egoff, 1988; Tymn, Zahorski, & Boyer, 1979).

Heroic romance is a form of high fantasy that draws from mythology and includes stories of heroes and worlds of great power. Alexander (1971) has called heroic romance a "cauldron of story" in which is found a "mythological minestrone" that combines real history with imaginary history. Included is an array of characters, events, and situations—quests, tasks, swords, dragons, and other elements of heroic romance. Because fantasy is written on many levels, Alexander suggests that readers may "ladle up whatever suits (their) taste" and "digest it, assimilate it" as thoroughly as possible.

Tymn, Zahorski, and Boyer (1979) characterize high fantasy as having "noble characters, archetypes, and elevated style." The focus on morality in high fantasy requires a hero who is compassionate, courageous, and humane and who accomplishes many good deeds. The hero is often a representative human being, "Everyman," who may be a commoner-hero or a morally ambivalent hero. The commoner-hero is at first reluctant to become involved in the events that are unfolding, but proves courageous, loyal, and generous. The morally ambivalent hero is basically good, but is more concerned with maintaining independence and individuality. The imagery for the created world is often supported by the elevated speaking style of noble characters. The themes that are explored in high fantasies usually appear unrelated to personal concerns. They are generally universal and focus on an all-out struggle between good and evil in which entire worlds are at stake. These other worlds tend to be reminiscent of medieval worlds; Tolkien's Middle-Earth, Alexander's Prydain, and Lewis's Narnia are just a few. Authors of high fantasy often provide readers with a detailed map of the lands in the secondary world.

Lloyd Alexander (1978, p. 442) classifies the plots in high fantasy into five categories:

- Tests of identity, endurance, and character
- Tasks, imposed or undertaken voluntarily
- Quests for marvelous objects or animals
- Escapes from death, through disguise or substitution or with help
- Journeys to other lands or worlds

Sometimes authors combine two or more of the five plot categories, either in one book or in a series of books. Although a work of high fantasy presents an impossible world, the "undercurrent of rationality" makes the story believable. The universal vitality of fantasy is timeless and eternal (Alexander, 1971).

How Fantasy Works

Asked why anyone reads or writes fantasy, author Susan Cooper (1981) explained that fantasy goes one stage beyond realism in requiring complete intellectual surrender. Fantasy asks more of readers, and the best works of fantasy may offer readers more. She argues that the escape so often attributed to fantasy is indeed offered, but it is an inward rather than an outward escape, as readers learn to discover themselves. Cooper suggests that by going beyond the time and space of the known world, readers allow themselves to enter a dreamlike world that contains accumulated images and emotions of the human race.

Although different authors have their own thoughts on what makes a work fantasy, a number of generalizations can be made. First, fantasy includes literary elements that are characteristic of good literature, but one or more of these elements is transformed by the author into something magical or not possible in the known world. Fantasy is made believable by the consistent use of logic or laws of the created world and descriptive detail. The fantasy element cannot be brought out suddenly to magically solve problems. Whatever element makes the story a fantasy must be an integral part of the story, and all details must be consistent with that element. Fantasy is not an escape from reality, but a mirror in which reality is reflected and extended in the imagination. Finally, fantasy occurs in a secondary world created by the author, in the real world (the primary world) but with changed rules of logic, or in both worlds.

When reading fantasy, we accept the impossible by suspending disbelief. We know that donkeys cannot turn into rocks, little people do not live under the floor, and inquisitive girls do not go down rabbit holes. Those things simply don't happen. But if the author has done a good job, the power of the story is such that we suspend disbelief to find out what happens next. If at any time the author misses a detail and leaves the reader wondering about the inconsistency, the reader is apt to drop out, losing interest in what happens because he or she hasn't been convinced that the story could happen. Authors engage readers in fantasy by anchoring stories in plausibility. Authors also use a combination of devices to make the fantasy elements of a story believable to readers. These devices are described within the context of the literary elements in the section that follows, applying the understanding of those elements to *Tuck Everlasting,* by Natalie Babbitt.

Setting

Many authors firmly ground a story in reality before gradually moving into fantasy. In other words, they begin the story in the primary world and move into the secondary world. Details of setting are an integral part of the story. Good authors make details so vivid that readers can see, hear, and feel the setting as they read the description. Babbitt's masterful description of the summer heat in August that opens the story is often read aloud as an exemplary passage describing the setting.

Character

Authors have one of the characters mirror the disbelief of the reader. The narrator or protagonist reassures readers that the fantastic events are normal or real. When a believable character who initially doubted the fantasy is convinced, readers are likewise convinced. Authors use consistent and distinct language for each character or group. Winnie must be kidnapped before she can have the truth revealed to her so her reaction can be monitored.

Plot

The plot must have internal consistency and logic. The idea of eternal life and never aging is a fascinating thought, but not logically consistent with our world as we know it. In order for readers to suspend disbelief in this concept and embrace the idea that in a fantasy world eternal life without aging might be a possibility, all elements of plot must be consistent with what it would be like to never age. How do people who have eternal life live among those who do not? What must be kept "secret" from the world, and why?

Theme

The theme must be one that matters to people in our known world. Whether we should desire eternal life or live the life cycle as we now know it is a question that people today care about. We ponder with Winnie as to what to do with that magical potion that promises eternal life and wonder what decision we might make ourselves, if we were the ones holding that bottle of "water."

In *Tuck Everlasting,* Natalie Babbitt grounds the story in reality by first introducing a setting, a character, and a mood that are perfectly normal in the real world. Winnie Foster, the protagonist, has lost patience with the rules of all the adults in her life and considers running away from home. She is frustrated and wants more adventure. When the plot steps into the realm of the fantastic, Winnie tries to understand how people who drink special water could possibly live forever. As Winnie struggles with the decision she must make, readers are also convinced of the power of the water. They become intrigued with Winnie's dilemma and suspend disbelief in what they rationally know is not possible; they follow Winnie into the fantasy. The author has created a story with internal consistency, and the intertwining of details about characters and plot development leaves no loose threads or contradictions.

Issue to Consider

Can Reading Fantasy Be Inappropriate for Children?

Fantasy literature has often been the subject of controversy. Some adults do not consider children capable of distinguishing between reality and fantasy, even though school curricula often state (and psychological studies hold) that children in the primary grades should be able to make that distinction. Others worry that fantasy is a genre that allows an escape from reality and that reading works of fantasy takes time away from more important kinds of reading that children need to be doing. Still others complain that fantasy literature is inappropriate for children because it refers to the supernatural.

In recent years, parents and others in some communities have opposed the reading of fantasy literature in schools and have called for censorship of certain types of books. In his experiences with such groups, school administrator Rick Traw (1996) found that the presence of magic, witchcraft, and animism caused the most concern. Traw found that even the slightest hint of the supernatural made a book appear on the list of censored materials. For example, a reference to Halloween or a story about a city witch and a country witch might get the work into trouble.

Michael Tunnell (1994) writes about fantasy and censorship as the "double-edged sword." He believes that "fantasy is fundamentally the most important kind of story to share with [children]." He also believes that "children vicariously vent frustrations in healthy ways by subconsciously identifying with . . . heroes." In addition, Tunnell believes that fantasy gives children "a sense of hope about their ultimate abilities to succeed in the world."

What do you think?

Criteria for Evaluating Modern Fantasy

- Is the story well written according to literary standards outlined in Chapter 2?
- Is the theme compelling to readers in a "real world" as well as in the fantasy world?
- Are the elements that make the story a fantasy convincing, consistent, and well-developed? Does the story allow readers to suspend disbelief?
- Does the author maintain a sense of logic and order within the created world?

Major Writers of Fantasy and Their Works

Many writers of fantasy and their works have already been mentioned in this chapter and numerous others are listed in the section on recommended books. Here, we highlight a few authors who have made significant contributions to the genre.

Lloyd Alexander

Lloyd Alexander knew that he wanted to be a writer from a young age. He claims that the seeds of his stories were planted by the extensive reading he did as a child, as well as the military assignments that allowed him to travel and live in Wales, Germany, and France. Alexander began his career as a writer for adults, but his fantasy stories for children have been his major literary contribution. *The Chronicles of Prydain* is among the most widely read fantasy series for children and young adults. *The Book of Three* sets the story in the created world of Prydain, in which readers meet Taran, the Assistant Pig-Keeper, who is in search of an oracular pig named Hen Wen. The evil Arawn uses inhumane tactics to fight the nobility in Prydain, and Taran leads the expedition to fight against the evil. The series continues with *The Black Cauldron, The Castle of Llyr, Taran Wanderer,* and *The High King. The Black Cauldron* was named a Newbery Honor Book in 1966, and *The High King* was awarded the Newbery Medal in 1969. Alexander died in 2008, shortly after he was named the U.S. nominee for the Hans Christian Andersen award.

Susan Cooper

Susan Cooper is the author of the acclaimed high fantasy series *The Dark Is Rising.* She was an established writer when she began this series, inspired by a contest. The first book in the series is *Over Sea, Under Stone.* In the second book, *The Dark Is Rising,* a 1974 Newbery Honor Book, eleven-year-old Will Stanton discovers that he is the last of the "Old Ones" and a servant of the Light. In this story, which draws on the legend of King Arthur and other British legends and myths, it is his destiny to fight Evil and to protect the Light. The series continues with *Greenwitch, The Grey King,* for which Cooper received the Newbery Medal in 1976, and *Silver on the Tree,* as Will searches for the remaining Things of Power needed to fight the final rising of the Dark. Her more recent book, *King of Shadows,* is a time travel between the present day and the time of Shakespeare, four hundred years earlier. Born and educated in England, Cooper was first married to an American, who brought her to the United States, where she began her writing career. She believes that her imagination was as lonely and homesick as she was and therefore turned to fantasy as a home.

Bruce Coville

Bruce Coville is a prolific writer of fantasy, whose work is enjoyed by many children. He was born in Syracuse, New York, and has lived in central New York most of his life. He was an earnest reader who read fantasies like *Mary Poppins* and *Dr. Doolittle* as well as devouring series books and comic books. His only regret is having wasted time watching television. He realized he liked writing when a teacher gave him time to write a long story, and by seventeen, he was working seriously toward becoming a writer. Before he began selling enough stories to be a full-time writer, he had numerous jobs, including being a gravedigger, a toymaker, and an elementary teacher of grades two and four. Married to artist Katherine Dietz since age nineteen, they have created some books together.

Among his most popular books are ones that include dragons. In *Jeremy Thatcher, Dragon Hatcher,* a beautiful ball turns out to be a dragon egg and the hatching of the egg brings about many interesting times with a dragon. In Coville's series about aliens, beginning with *My Teacher Is An Alien,* a group of sixth-graders try to keep aliens from taking control of Earth. Nowadays, Coville continues to write, but also spends a great deal of time in his business of producing full-cast audio books.

Roald Dahl

Roald Dahl's work is tremendously popular among children. Children who discover his work find themselves compelled to read one book after the other. They are delighted by his stories' irreverent voice and zany events. His portrayals of truly detestable characters—usually adults but sometimes children—powerfully engage children's emotions. For example, Dahl sometimes sets up a character, such as the grandmother in *George's Marvelous Medicine,* or a whole class of characters, such as the witches in *The Witches,* and invites readers to hate them without remorse. Not all teachers and critics are convinced that this is a healthy practice, however.

Some say that Roald Dahl's childhood influenced his writings. Born to Norwegian parents in South Wales, Dahl moved to England with his mother upon the death of his father. He entered boarding school at age eight and was subjected to disciplinary measures bordering on torture. Dahl's early life is recounted in his book *Boy.* Perhaps his best-known book is *Charlie and the Chocolate Factory,* in which a poor boy finds a lucky golden ticket that allows him to visit Willy Wonka's Chocolate Factory and earn a chance to be Willy Wonka's successor. The story has enormous appeal for its "underdog rising to glory" journey of the protagonist; however, it is unfortunate that his portrayals of the chocolate factory workers is objectionable as stereotype.

Cornelia Funke

Long regarded as one of the most prominent and widely read authors in Germany, where she is author of over forty books, it wasn't until *The Thief Lord* was translated in 2002 that readers in the English-speaking world were introduced to her work. The highly successful

Ask the Author . . . Bruce Coville

Favorite Books As a Child

The Dr. Dolittle Books
by Hugh Lofting

The Mushroom Planet Books
by Eleanor Cameron

Tom Swift in the City of Gold
(my first "big book," and the only book I
can remember my father reading to me)
tales of the gods and heroes—numerous
different collections

*You have produced many
audiobooks based on fantasy
stories. What challenges and
rewards do you find in focusing on fantasy?*

When I began producing audio-books, it seemed natural to focus on fantasy, since that was what I wrote, and also the bulk of what I read. But as it turns out, there are numerous reasons why fantasy works particularly well on audio—especially in the full cast form that I produce in, where we use a separate actor for each major character.

To begin with, fantasy grows out of the oral tradition. The roots of most fantasy novels can be found in myth, legend, and folklore—all things that were origi-nally meant to be heard. Whether con-sciously or not, I think this has an effect on the writing of fantasy. Good fantasy, especially good children's fantasy, is just plain fun to listen to. It's also fun to read aloud, since the characters tend to be large (sometimes larger than life), vividly realized, and vocally interesting. So we usually have a great time in the studio!

Of course, this also represents a chal-lenge. What, for example, does a dragon sound like? The recording is made or lost in the casting process, and over the years I have had to find actors to play every-thing from bunnies to dragons, with stops along the way for an effete Phoenix, a cranky toad, numerous wicked witches, a pair of talking rats, a gang of mice, and several gods from the Greek and Norse pantheons. The actors love this—it gives them a chance to go places more realistic fiction doesn't allow for. But it does mean we spend a lot of time trying to work out how each of these creatures should sound!

One of the real joys of this form is that it allows us to bring a book to life for the child listener in a way that still leaves room for imaginative participation. Unlike film and television, where the images are set and finished, with audio the child has to engage, and create the images in his or her head. Film and televi-sion do all the work for you, and can dull the imagination. Audiobooks engage and stimulate it.

After all, no matter how good special effects become, nothing will ever beat the dragon you create in your own imagination!

Bruce Coville is the author of 90 books for children and young adults, including the inter-national bestseller *My Teacher Is an Alien*, and the wildly popular *Unicorn Chronicles* series. He has been, at various times, a teacher, a toy-maker, a magazine editor, a gravedigger, and a cookware salesman. He is also the founder of *Full Cast Audio*, an audiobook publishing company devoted to producing full cast, unabridged recordings of material for family listening. Mr. Coville lives in Syracuse, New York, with his wife, illustrator Katherine Coville. ■

reception of the Batchelder award-winning first English language translation of her books led to the publication of ***Inkheart,*** a page-turning adventure in which book characters come to life, and was followed by additional novels such as ***Dragon Rider*** and picture books as well. Later, the publication of ***Inkspell*** and ***Inkdeath*** completed the trilogy. Her books are widely translated and she has won numerous prestigious international awards. Born in 1958, she now lives in California, with her husband, daughter, and son. She began her career with a degree in education theory from the University of Hamburg, followed by a degree in book illustration. Funke became a designer of board games and a book illustrator before embark-ing on her own writing career. Now Funke focuses almost exclusively on writing and only creates pen and ink illustrations for chapter openers in her own books; when creating pic-ture books, she works with another illustrator. Funke believes that it's only a small step from imagination to reality, and her books carry readers easily in that transition. Magical carousel

ILLUSTRATION 8.6 Animals engage in action-packed quests and battles in the *Redwall* high fantasy series. (Cover from *Redwall* by Brian Jacques, illustrated by Troy Howell, copyright © 1997 by Troy Howell, illustrations. Used by permission of Philomel Books, A Division of Penguin Young Readers Group, A Member of Penguin Group (USA) Inc., 345 Hudson Street, New York, NY 10014. All rights reserved.)

rides that transform people in age, storybook characters that come to life, dragons that seek a peaceful place to live—all become believable to readers caught up in her powerful story-telling. A film version of *The Thief Lord* was produced in 2006.

Brian Jacques

Born in Liverpool, England, Brian Jacques became a sailor at age fifteen. After working as a radio broadcaster, comedian, and truck driver, Jacques wrote his first book to entertain students at a school for the blind. *Redwall,* published in 1987, was the first book in a series of fan-tasies about the animals living at Redwall Abbey. Since then, many other books in the Redwall series have been published, and they have a following of readers who are anxious to hear more about the mice, rats, and other field animals engaged in classic fantasy quests and struggles between those who are good and those who are evil. The series includes *Mossflower, Mattimeo, Mariel of Redwall, Salamandastron, Martin the Warrior, The Bellmaker, Outcast of Redwall, The Long Patrol, Marlfox,* and *The Legend of Luke.* Jacques has used his considerable talent in storytelling to create an audiotaped version of *Redwall.* In it, he is the narrator, and a full cast of characters engagingly tell the story (including his son, who takes on the lead voice of Martin).

Diana Wynne Jones

While studying at Oxford, Diana Wynne Jones attended lectures given by C. S. Lewis and J. R. R. Tolkien, and her classmates included Penelope Lively and Jill Paton Walsh, who also went on to become writers of fantasy literature for children. About her creation of fantasy for children, Diana Wynne Jones observes, "What I am after is an exciting and exacting wis-dom, in which contemporary life and potent myth are intricately involved and superimposed" (Olendorf & Telgen, 1993, p. 116). Jones has succeeded in producing not only exciting, diverse, and wise stories but humorous ones as well. She says that as a child, she "suffered from perpetual book starvation" and began to write. It was not until she had her own chil-dren, however, that Jones began writing for children.

Three of Jones's books won Carnegie commendations. *Dogsbody* is about Sirius the Dog Star, who is reborn on Earth as a puppy and fulfills a mission to find the murder weapon of the stars. *Power of Three* is about a curse threatening the English moors and how three children and some strange creatures work together to save them. *A Charmed Life* is based on Jones's own unusual childhood and is the first volume in the Chrestomanci cycle of linked novels. The protagonist is a young boy magician who is manipulated by his sister. The other titles in the series are *The Magicians of Caprona,* in which the children of two feuding families make magical peace; *Witch Week,* which takes place in a school where the teacher suspects someone in the class is a witch; and *The Lives of Christopher Chant,* which recounts the training of the next Chrestomanci, or controller of magic.

Some of Jones's more recent books include *Dark Lord of Derkholm,* which tells of a popular tourist destination where lords and wizards role play the parts of the dark lord and a wizard while tourists follow their fate as members of Pilgrim Parties. In the sequel, *Year of the Griffin,* problems at Wizard's University are destined to be straightened out in response to the havoc created by its students. In *Howl's Moving Castle,* Sophie Halter is turned into an old woman by a jealous competitor in the hat business, so she takes refuge in the wizard Howl's strangely moving castle. This popular fantasy has been adapted into a Japanese anime film.

Philip Pullman

Philip Pullman was born in Norwich, England, but lived in Australia and other parts of the world during his childhood. He had a childhood love of comics, particularly Superman and Batman. He attended Exeter College in Oxford, England, and taught middle school students in Oxford for twelve years. Later, he became a lecturer at Westminster College, Oxford. Although he is now a full-time writer, he still chooses to live in Oxford, where he writes in a shed at the bottom of his garden. Pullman finds the air at Oxford to be inspirational for a writer of fantasy and believes that the ambience of the city has contributed to the fantasy-writing careers of Tolkien, Lewis, and himself. As Silvey (1995) says, "Pullman's greatest strength is his ability to weave complex and riveting plots that wrap the reader in suspense" (p. 544).

His extraordinary fantasy, the *Dark Materials* trilogy, begins with ***The Golden Compass,*** in which Lyra seeks to save children from scientific experiments that threaten their lives. In the second book, ***The Subtle Knife,*** Lyra's world extends into the Oxford of a different time; there, she meets Will, who must accept the responsibility for crossing worlds with the aid of the subtle knife. ***The Amber Spyglass*** closes the story of Lyra and Will, leaving them in the garden. This popular trilogy has been produced as a full-cast audio book narrated by Pullman himself, and as a stage production as well. ***The Golden Compass*** was released as a film in 2007.

On his Web site, Pullman humorously describes two essentials to his writing: Blu-Tack and Post-it Notes™. He uses Blu-Tack to stick various pictures, notes, reminders, and whatever else to the wall; and he uses sixty or more of the smallest Post-it™ Notes to write different scenes and move them around on large sheets of paper until he is satisfied with the order.

J. K. Rowling

Joanne Rowling was born near Bristol, England. She had an inclination toward storytelling from a young age, as she shared stories with a younger sister and created serial stories for her school friends at lunch time. While living in Portugal and working as an English teacher, she began writing a story about a boy named Harry Potter who is sent to wizard school. She moved to Edinburgh and lived on welfare there, an unemployed single mother. She was offered a job as a teacher of French and vowed to finish her book before the job began, with much of it being written in a coffee shop while her toddler daughter napped. With the publication of that first book, ***Harry Potter and the Sorcerer's Stone*** (the original title in England is ***Harry Potter and the Philosopher's Stone***), Rowling was propelled into fame and fortune.

Harry is an orphan who is being raised by an aunt and uncle, and leads a miserable existence under the ridicule and abuse of their son, Dudley. On his eleventh birthday, he discovers that he is a famous wizard who survived an attack by the evil Voldemort the night his wizard parents were killed. Harry goes off to Hogwarts School of Witchcraft and Wizardry, and the adventures begin. The books have been characterized as engaging, funny, suspenseful, and brilliantly written. From the beginning of her writing, Rowling had planned out all seven books in the series in great detail. The Harry Potter books have been translated into sixty-two languages, and have stayed on best-seller lists for adults as well as for children.

Jane Yolen

Jane Yolen is highly regarded as a writer of many genres. Although she is a former president of the Science Fiction Writers of America, she is best known for her work in the world of fantasy. She has written numerous books in the genre and has served as editor of her own imprint of fantasy books, Jane Yolen Books/Harcourt Brace. Her books have won numerous awards and are frequently on lists of best books. Her professional book ***Touch Magic: Fantasy, Faerie and Folklore in the Literature of Childhood*** (Yolen, 2000) is now in its second edition and is considered a classic reference. Books in her *Commander Toad* series, such as ***Commander Toad and the Voyage Home,*** are notable as easy reader science fiction stories. The time-slip book ***The Devil's Arithmetic*** has been recognized with numerous awards, including finalist for the Nebula Award. Jane Yolen's interests and hobbies span a wide range, from kite flying to folk singing and dancing.

Other Notable Writers of Modern Fantasy

There is no way to include every noteworthy author in a section on major authors and illustrators of modern fantasy. Some noted writers of fantasy are discussed in other chapters. For example, picture book creators Maurice Sendak, William Steig, and Chris Van Allsburg are featured in Chapter 3, and Laurence Yep and Virginia Hamilton are included in Chapter 4.

PHILIP PULLMAN

ILLUSTRATION 8.7 Lyra is an orphan who embarks on a dangerous journey to save her friends and other children from some kind of terrible experimentation. (From *The Golden Compass* by Philip Pullman, copyright © 1995 by Philip Pullman. Cover art copyright © 1996 by Eric Rohmann. Cover art copyright © 2002 by Alfred A. Knopf. Art imaging by Ericka Meltzer O'Rourke and title lettering by Lilly Lee. Used by permission of Alfred A. Knopf, an imprint of Random House Children's Books, a division of Random House, Inc.)

Technology in Practice 8.1

The making of fantasy epics into feature-length movies has been a popular move in recent years. We have seen the Tolkien "Lord of the Rings" cycle made on a grand scale and to much fanfare. The Harry Potter books have been turned into films of enormous popularity. Even single titles like Diana Wynne Jones' *Howls' Moving Castle* is being made into a Japanese "anime" by Ghibli Studio. But what does all of this mean for the books from which these movies originate? Some argue that the movies inspire viewers to seek out the original book. They go so far as to say that movies give a context to better understand the books, many of which are several hundred pages long and quite complex. Some say movies give people the incentive to read books and they are never disappointed, unlike people who read the book first and then compare what was cut out or changed in the film.

Yet in an interview found on the Internet <http://slate.msn.com/id/2111107/> (last accessed August 2009), award-winning author Ursula LeGuin describes what happened to her books when they were translated into a television miniseries. The article is titled, "A Whitewashed Earthsea: How the Sci Fi Channel Wrecked My Books." In it, she describes how she had a contract that gave her the role of "consultant" but that, in fact, she had no say in the studio's interpretation of the books and creation of the production. In particular, she takes issue with the fact that she creates her characters as people of color in a "conscious and deliberate" decision, and that race is essential to her desire to be inclusive of people who are underrepresented in fantasy literature. Over the years, she has protested when publishers claimed that book covers featuring non-white characters "won't sell." With increasing clout, she has been able to make her statement. Yet in the film version of the book, the characters are cast as white.

This is but one difference between films and books. What are the many ways that teachers and librarians need to consider when scaffolding the discussion of students making a comparison between original books of fantasy and science fiction and their film counterparts? Written text and audio books?

Other writers of fantasy who are very popular include Lois Duncan, Ursula Le Guin, Anne McCaffrey, Tom McGowen, Garth Nix, Tamora Pierce, Meredith Ann Pierce, and Scott Westerfield, but much of their work is intended for and read predominantly by young adults.

The Evolution of Science Fiction

The first work of science fiction may have been English author Mary Wollstonecraft Shelley's best seller *Frankenstein,* published in 1811. This novel used medical science as the point of departure from reality and anticipated by over a century and a half the possibility of inventing new life forms and of transplanting organs.

In the mid-nineteenth century, the Frenchman Jules Verne was inspired by rapidly advancing technology to publish works of science fiction. Some of his stories anticipated later inventions. The submarine was featured in the 1869 novel *Twenty Thousand Leagues under the Sea,* and rocket travel was part of the 1865 book *From the Earth to the Moon.*

At the turn of the century, a biology teacher named H. G. Wells wrote *War of the Worlds,* the first book about an invasion from outer space. Later, on Halloween of 1938, Orson Welles's broadcast of the story as a radio play caused thousands of people to panic. Although the announcer indicated throughout the broadcast that it was a work of science fiction, the genre was so new to American audiences that many believed the Earth was under attack from aliens in spaceships.

At about the same time, pulp magazines started publishing stories with science fiction themes. The term "science fiction" was coined by Hugo Gernsback, who created the magazine *Amazing Stories* in 1926; Gernsback later published Science Wonder Stories. Many notable science fiction writers got their start in those pages, including Edgar Rice Burroughs, Isaac Asimov, and Robert A. Heinlein.

Both Heinlein and Asimov owe the early nurturing of their careers to *Amazing Stories* editor John W. Campbell, who later began the magazine *Astounding Science Fiction.* Campbell helped to launch the careers of many science fiction writers of the time. Robert Heinlein is credited with transforming the way science fiction stories are told. Rather than relying on pure fantasy, he researched contemporary scientific discoveries and made careful extrapolations on which he based the plots of his novels and short stories. Heinlein's 1947 book *Rocket Ship Galileo* and the twelve junior novels that were published in the succeeding years are considered to be the first children's science fiction published in the United States. Asimov's carefully researched writing allows readers—children and adults alike—to gain clear understandings of scientific and technical concepts.

Isaac Asimov coined the term "robotics" in his prolific writings about robots. He formally outlined the "Three Laws of Robotics" that have guided the way in which robots have been portrayed in science fiction ever since. With his wife, he coauthored a series about Norby, a robot.

Women often had to overcome gender bias in being accepted as writers of science fiction. Andre Norton, a pseudonym used by Alice Mary Norton, is actually a combination of two others that she also used: Andrew North and Allen Weston. Her use of pseudonyms arose from her conviction that masculine names would give her works credibility with male read-

Ask the Author . . .

Jane Yolen

Jane Yolen [signature]

Favorite Books as a Child

The Andrew Lang Color Fairy Books

The Sword in the Stone
by T. H. White

The Jungle Book
by Rudyard Kipling

What do you say to those who criticize your choice to write and publish fantasy books for children?

I think that fantasy books speak to reality heart to heart. They are metaphoric shorthand. No one reading them—children or adults—is fooled into believing them word for word; that is, the reader does not believe in the actuality of dragons, unicorns, flying horses. But these stories are like points on a map, acting as a guide to life as we actually live it by showing us life as it could be lived.

For those folks who are afraid of fantasy books, seeing Satan where none exists, I tell them that they do not understand the role of metaphor in literature. But if they persist in seeing devils and the hand of hell in these stories, I cannot change their minds. And I do not try to.

What I look for in fantasy books is a strong story line, a character who changes and grows, and wonderful chewy prose. I am not interested in generic sword and sorcery, but in invention, imagination, and a prose style that sings. I have read a lot of fantasy novels in my life. So I want to be surprised, delighted, and have the little hairs on the back of my neck stand up with recognition, just as I do when I read a poem by Emily Dickinson. A fantasy book should force me to confront my real world with the imagined world.

Jane Yolen, who has been referred to as "America's Hans Christian Andersen" and the "Twentieth-Century Aesop" because of her many fairy tales and fantasy stories, is the author of over 170 books for children and adults. Her fantasy and science fiction imprint, Jane Yolen Books, part of Harcourt Brace & Company, published books by such authors as Bruce Coville (*Jeremy Thatcher, Dragon Hatcher*, 1991), Patricia C. Wrede (*Dealing with Dragons*, 1990), Vivian Vande Velde (*Companions of the Night*, 1995) and Caroline Stevermer (*River Rats*, 1992). ■

---

ers. At the start of her writing career in the 1930s, Norton had to convince publishers—who believed that girls would not read science fiction and that boys would not read about female protagonists in a science fiction story—to accept her work. Author of over a hundred books, often about interplanetary adventures, Norton was first published at the age of twenty and was eventually awarded the Nebula Grand Master Award for lifetime achievement in science fiction.

In 1957, the Soviet Union launched Sputnik, the first satellite, and spurred not only the U.S. space initiative but also a competition among authors to provide children with imaginative stories set in outer space. Several authors wrote "space fantasies" in the 1950s. Ellen MacGregor wrote the *Miss Pickerell* series. Jay Williams wrote a series of space fantasy stories such as ***Danny Dunn and the Anti-Gravity Paint.*** Louis Slobodkin's ***The Space Ship under the Apple Tree,*** published in 1952, was followed ten years later by ***The Three-Seated Space Ship: The Latest Model of the Space Ship under the Apple Tree.*** Although the limited amount of scientific information in these books is accurate, the premises of the stories are based on imagination.

In the 1960s, the movie *2001: A Space Odyssey* and the television series "Star Trek" enlarged the audience of young devotees of space fiction. In 1969 came the actual landing

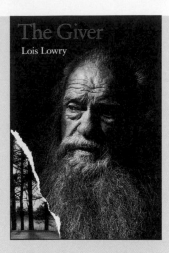

ILLUSTRATION 8.8   Readers of Lois Lowry's *The Giver* will ponder whether a utopian society can truly exist and whether a controlled society is a desirable goal. (Cover from *The Giver* by Lois Lowry. Copyright © 1999 by Lois Lowry. Reprinted by permission of Clarion Books, an imprint of Houghton Mifflin Harcourt Publishing Company. All rights reserved.)

on the moon by manned spacecraft—a true space adventure; and in the following decade, a few well-made movies, especially *Star Wars* and *E.T.,* continued to enhance the popularity of science fiction.

In 1963, Madeleine L'Engle's *A Wrinkle in Time* was the first science fiction book to be named a winner of the Newbery Medal. Along with the prestige of the award came the recognition that science fiction had a wider readership among children than in years past.

Today, serious themes abound in science fiction for young people. Many authors of science fiction say that they choose to write in this genre because other-world settings help readers to explore serious questions about their own world from a more distant perspective and thus with clearer vision. Madeleine L'Engle, for example, explores ethical and theological questions in her books. When Monica Hughes creates a futuristic society in which educated and talented young people find no employment and are instead invited to play a game that turns out to be a fight for survival in a new world in *Invitation to the Game,* she is asking her readers to question whether society today is guilty of similarly wasting the talents of young people. In *The Ear, the Eye and the Arm,* Nancy Farmer creates a horrendous community living under the garbage heaps of a city. With a little imagination, a reader can visualize the local landfill producing characters like the vlei people. In the same book, readers enter a controlled, militaristic society in which buildings are hundreds of stories high and no one is safe. Readers are forced to ask themselves how they can prevent this future from becoming reality. Readers of *The Giver,* by Lois Lowry, find a society in which memory of the past is erased and all matters of family, work, and pleasure are determined by an unknown few who control the society. When one child is chosen to receive the memory for the whole society from the Giver of memories, he questions what is important in order to remain human. Good science fiction is entertaining, addictive, and inevitably thought-provoking.

Categories of Science Fiction

Some would prefer the plural term "science fictions" for this genre of literature, for the many works labeled science fiction provide very different reading experiences. It is also interesting to note that this is one of the genres in which there is much crossover reading: adults read young adult science fiction, and older children and teens read adult science fiction. This has resulted in cross marketing in which the covers signify the difference in who is likely to pick the book up.

Projecting Scientific Principles

One kind of science fiction takes one or more principles known to science, extrapolates what the principles might lead to, and plays the possibilities out in a narrative, often in an everyday setting not unlike the real world. Peter Dickinson's *Eva* is an example of a book in which a scientific principle is explored in a story about a possible future. After an accident, a young girl's body is destroyed but her brain survives and is transplanted into a chimpanzee's body. The story probes who Eva will be: the human Eva in a chimpanzee's body or the chimpanzee Kelly with a human mind? How will she live: as a human or as a chimpanzee? *Eva* is a gripping work that questions human feelings of superiority to animals.

In *Anna to the Infinite Power* by Mildred Ames, twelve-year-old Anna discovers that she is a clone. In 1981, when the book was published, cloning seemed like a true science fiction idea; today, it is close to reality. The idea of creating a clone has fascinated people for years and is also explored in other books for young readers. William Sleator addresses the idea of multiple clones in *The Duplicate.* At first, sixteen-year-old David thinks that it would be convenient to have a clone, but by the time he realizes the difficulties involved in living with Duplicate A, the experiment has gotten out of hand and Duplicate B arrives.

Utopian and Dystopian Societies

Societies different from the one we live in have been explored in adult literature for thousands of years. The Biblical Eden was one of several detailed versions of an ideal society, or utopia; others were Plato's **Republic** (in the fourth century B.C.) and St. Augustine's **The City of God** (in the fourth century A.D.). Dante's **Inferno** (written between 1307 and 1321), a detailed account of what hell is like, provided an early example of a dystopia, a terrible place to live.

In John Christopher's **Tripod** trilogy, the Earth is conquered by alien Tripods who cap humans' heads, thereby controlling and enslaving them by making them docile. Henry, Beanpole, and Will embark on a perilous journey to free the humans and rescue the Earth from destruction and later intercede in the interplanetary war between the Tripods and the Masters. **When the Tripods Came,** about aliens landing on Earth, is the prequel to the Tripod trilogy. In H. M. Hoover's **The Delikon,** an alien race has conquered Earth, and Varina, a Delikon, has been assigned to teach two youngsters who revolt against the aliens. A theme in many of Hoover's books is the negative aspects of colonization of one society by another.

The Ear, the Eye and the Arm, by Nancy Farmer explores a futuristic society in Zimbabwe. What might appear initially to be utopian—a highly efficient, technologically managed society—soon shows its dystopian side as readers are introduced to the vlei people, who live in what was a city dump. Likewise, what appears to be a utopia at the beginning of Lois Lowry's **The Giver** is a supposedly ideal society where people are free from all hardship, but also lack freedom of choice. The revealed dystopia highlights the negative implications of social planning. Lowry's book makes readers stop to consider whether an ideal society is possible—or desirable. In **Gathering Blue,** a related book, Lowry explores a world that has regressed from technology to primitiveness. Kira, a lame girl who worries about her place in this society, is given the task of preserving memories by weaving the history of the world on the Singer's robe. In the third related book, **Messenger,** a utopian world suddenly changes and closes its boundaries to outsiders as other negative decisions are also being made. Matty discovers he has the power of healing, but because it takes such a toll on him, he must decide how and when to use this special gift.

Monica Hughes's **Invitation to the Game** introduces a group of teenagers who are told, on the day they graduate from high school, "Congratulations on graduating with honors! Enjoy your leisure years!" Ironically, the educated, eager-to-work protagonists are sent to a community for the unemployed to play "the game"—not a game at all, but a master plan to dispose of excess population. Hughes reports that the situation for the book was suggested by a friend from Liverpool, England, where unemployment has been so entrenched for so long that many teachers see their greatest challenge to be preparing young people for a life without work. Reading about this situation in the genre of science fiction frees readers from making associations with particular social classes and historical moments and helps them to see the larger point of the work: that individual opportunities for a meaningful life may depend on the sort of social and economic system in which a person lives.

Rodman Philbrick's **The Last Book in the Universe** has what appear to be utopian and dystopian societies; it is an action-packed story where gangs rule a futuristic society after Earth has been nearly ruined by "The Big Shake." While people are ruining their minds by injecting themselves with probes that allow them to imagine a better world, there is a secret place called Eden where only humans who have been genetically perfected are allowed to live. Spaz ventures into dangerous territory to see a dying foster sister and is joined by Ryter, an old man who owns the last book in the universe, an orphan called Little

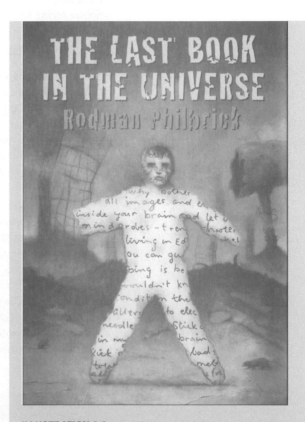

ILLUSTRATION 8.9 In a fast-paced, futuristic world after the ruin of Earth as we know it, survivors seek to build and hold on to relationships. (Jacket illustration copyright © 2000 by David Shannon from *The Last Book in the Universe* by Rodman Philbrick. Scholastic Inc./Blue Sky Press. Reprinted by permission Scholastic Inc.)

Face who seeks a family, and a genetically perfected "proov" named Lanaya. This fast-paced story carefully balances chilling moments with heartwarming ones of hope.

Surviving Environmental Catastrophes

Some science fiction deals with survival in the future, following some kind of environmental catastrophe. This catastrophe could be a nuclear holocaust, pollution, overcrowding, or destruction of other aspects of the Earth's environment.

Louise Lawrence's *Children of the Dust* tells of three generations of an English family following a nuclear holocaust. The lives of those who live in a sheltered but restricted bunker are compared with the lives of those who live outside and suffer from mutations.

Phoenix Rising, by Karen Hesse, seems to be a work of science fiction that deals with the issue of survival following an accident at a nuclear power plant. Nyle's life on a Vermont sheep farm changes as she and others in her family and community attempt to survive the effects of the fallout. She must learn to deal with contamination, illnesses, and death. However, even though something as extreme as what is described in *Phoenix Rising* has not occurred, it is possible—and, in fact, was based on the author's response to the Chernobyl incident. This book represents a fine line between realistic fiction and science fiction, but because the theme and issues are more relevant to those found in other books about surviving environmental catastrophes, *Phoenix Rising* is best discussed here.

In *Floodland,* Marcus Sedgewick writes about a future in which global warming melts the polar regions and causes most of the land masses to disappear under water. When ten-year-old Zoe is accidentally separated from her parents as they board the last boat headed to the safety of the mainland, she must figure out a way to be reunited with them. She discovers and fixes a small boat and sets out across the water, but must resist a gang of kids who are trying to survive on a small island.

Science Fantasies

Books that include extrapolations of scientific understandings but are based predominantly on imagination are classified as science fantasy. What some have previously called space fantasy—books about space travel, interplanetary exploration, alien visitors—are also included in this category. In *Company's Coming,* Arthur Yorinks writes about a spaceship whose alien passengers are invited for dinner. (James) Edward Marshall's extraterrestrial creature in *Space Case* is mistaken for a Halloween trick-or-treater. Pamela Service's *Stinker from Space* and *Stinker's Return* are about an agent from outer space, Tsynq Yr, who, not knowing the nature of the beast, enters the body of an earthly skunk for camouflage.

Paula Danziger's *This Place Has No Atmosphere* is a humorous story about a family's move from the Earth to the Moon in the twenty-first century. Daniel Pinkwater's science fantasies are based on the foibles of people on Earth. In *Fat Men from Space,* invaders attempt to steal all the junk food on Earth.

William Sleator's *Interstellar Pig* is another example of science fantasy. Barney, the hero of Sleator's book, gradually discovers that his new neighbors in an isolated Cape Cod beach setting are shape-shifting aliens, involved in a deadly game of keep-away that has been going on for over a century. As the tale of the aliens' game unfolds, readers are led to imagine the many possible consequences of contact between humans and creatures who have a far greater variety of body forms, a larger territorial range, and more complex relationships to time.

How Science Fiction Works

One of the questions readers ask themselves when they encounter a new book is what genre it belongs to. Some works of science fiction identify their genre right away. For example, because Monica Hughes's *The Keeper of the Isis Light* occurs on a remote planet, readers know from the beginning that they are reading science fiction. Other works plant ambiguous clues. William Sleator's *The Boy Who Reversed Himself* raises readers' curiosity when the protagonist creates mirror writing, but they don't discover until further into the book that, through some scientific process, the boy has reversed himself and can go into the fourth dimension. Like other works from Sleator, this book gives readers an extra taste of suspense before the genre is made clear, making them wonder not only about the explanations behind events but also about the kind of reality those explanations belong to: Is it the logic of daily life or the more imaginative realm of fantasy or science fiction?

It is easy for an author of science fiction to get caught up in the adventure of the plot or the setting and give insufficient thought to developing the characters. The best works of science fiction, then, are those that draw believable characters—with complex but understandable feelings and perceptions—even when those characters are members of some invented species. Good science fiction makes its premises plausible: There is a logic to the setting, the characters, and the situation that is accessible to young readers so that they can "think their way around" in the work just as they could in any other sort of fiction. Finally, good science fiction does not merely dazzle the reader with bizarre details, but instead plants clues and invites the reader to guess and predict what is happening or what will happen.

Once a work has opened up the possibility of the fantastic—scientific or otherwise—readers interpret events in the work within that realm of possibility and even reconstruct the parts of the work they read earlier in light of fantastic explanations. But even fantasy or science fiction is based on reality. Readers must have some points of identification with a work—something they find familiar and understandable—or they are not likely to be able to comprehend what they read.

Understanding the remote and strange in terms of the familiar is a challenge that readers face not only in science fiction, but also to some degree in all literature. Authors often begin with familiar details and lead readers gradually into the unfamiliar. Pamela Sargent begins *Alien Child* this way:

> Nita's earliest memory was of the day she had nearly drowned in the pool. She was toddling down the wide, lighted hall of her home; but her short legs could not keep pace with her guardian's long strides. Llipel suddenly retracted her claws, picked Nita up as the door to the garden slid open, and carried her outside. (p. 1)

Is Llipel Nita's dog or cat? If so, who is the guardian? Or is Llipel a guardian with claws? The questioning begins after the reader steps into what appears to be a human child's memory. Science fiction plays on the wonderful human capacity to project from real experiences to other-worldly ones. At its best, it allows us to touch the stars from our own living rooms.

Criteria for Evaluating Science Fiction

- Is the story well written according to literary standards outlined in Chapter 2?
- Has the author made clear how the characters feel about their world and their dilemmas?
- Are there clear plot threads for the reader to follow in the invented world?
- Are there familiar guideposts that serve as jumping-off places from reality to imagination for the reader?
- Does the author allow the reader to feel a sense of delight (even if it is tinged with fear and suspense) that encourages him or her to continue reading about an imaginary place?

Awards for Fantasy and Science Fiction

There are few awards specifically for children's books of fantasy or science fiction, although fantasy and science fiction books qualify for general awards such as the Newbery Medal. There are, however, some general science fiction awards that have categories for juvenile literature. The Hugo Award is named after Hugo Gernsback, the founding editor of *Amazing Stories* magazine and the person who coined the term "science fiction." This award, known officially as the Science Fiction Achievement Award, is given annually for outstanding achievement in the writing of science fiction. Several winners of this award have written science fiction for both adults and children. The Nebula Award is awarded by members of Science Fiction and Fantasy Writers of America. Nebula Awards are given in several categories, one of which is juvenile fiction.

Major Writers of Science Fiction and Their Works

Some authors of science fiction and their major works were mentioned earlier in this chapter because they also write a lot of fantasy. Also, many writers such as Douglas Adams (who wrote *The Hitchhiker's Guide to the Galaxy*) or M. T. Anderson (who wrote *Feed*) who are major contributors to the genre are not listed in this section because their books are read predominantly by young adults rather than by children. Some prominent authors, such as Isaac Asimov, John Christopher, Robert Heinlein, H. M. Hoover, Monica Hughes, Louise Lawrence, and Andre Norton, are not included below because they are people who contributed to the defining of the field of science fiction rather than authors who are currently being read as widely now by children.

Peter Dickinson

Peter Dickinson was born in Zambia and spent his early years there; he eventually moved to England and attended Eton College. After serving in the army and then graduating from Oxford University, he worked as a crime novel reviewer for a British humor magazine. It was not until he was in his forties that Dickinson turned to writing as a career. He writes for both children and adults.

Dickinson's first book for children, *The Weathermonger,* was published in 1968. It later became part of *The Changes* trilogy, in which Geoffrey and his sister Sally are among those in England who fear the impact of technology and machines that destroy nature; they seek to recreate the culture of the Dark Age. The trilogy was written and published in reverse chronological order. The first book of the trilogy is *The Devil's Children,* in which the siblings are abandoned and homeless; the second book is *Heartsease.* In *The Weathermonger,* Geoffrey controls the weather, but when his power is gone, technology again invades their world.

Madeleine L'Engle

In the 1980s, Madeleine L'Engle was among the top six best-selling authors of children's books (*Dictionary of Literary Biography,* 1986), and her popularity continues today. She won the Newbery Medal in 1963 for *A Wrinkle in Time,* in which three children go to the planet of Camazotz to find Meg and Charles Wallace's father. Ironically, the story was rejected by twenty-six publishers before being accepted, yet it continues to be L'Engle's most popular novel. In this first book of a trilogy, L'Engle clearly defines the good and evil forces that help and impede the children's search. *A Wind in the Door* expands the story: Meg must save Charles Wallace from the evil in the cosmos as well as from the evil within himself. *A Swiftly Tilting Planet* continues the plot in a fast-moving story involving time shifts and moral dilemmas facing the characters.

In 1981, L'Engle's *A Ring of Endless Light* was a Newbery Honor Book. It explores issues of death, a common theme in L'Engle's books. It also features members of the Austin family, who were first introduced in *Meet the Austins.* Often, characters from one of L'Engle's books appear in others written later.

Madeleine L'Engle says that you can't write science fiction out of your own experience, so you have to search for something deeper. She states that her books are about the clash between good and evil on a cosmic level. L'Engle was the U.S. nominee for the 1964 Hans

Christian Andersen Award for the body of her work, and she received the 1984 Catholic Library Association's Regina Award for consistent, sustained quality of work.

William Sleator

William Sleator comes from a family of scientists, which likely led to his own early interest in science. He believes that his hobbies of playing the piano, reading, and writing allow him to explore his interest in expressing his feelings about the supernatural. After spending many years as an accompanist for ballet companies, he turned to full-time writing. Sleator now lives in Thailand and the United States. He likens his life in an exotic foreign country to being on another planet because he has had to learn a new language and a new lifestyle. *Interstellar Pig* begins with characters playing an unusual board game and then reveals that some of the players are aliens. In *Strange Attractors,* Max finds himself having to protect a time travel device from its inventor and his alter ego from another time warp.

To check your comprehension on the content covered in this chapter, go to the MyEducation-Kit for your book and complete the Study Plan for Chapter 8. Here you will be able to take a chapter quiz and receive feedback on your answers.

Experiences for Further Learning

1. Fantasy books have often been censored as dangerous and inappropriate reading material for children. Others regard fantasy books as frivolous when there is so much for children to learn through their reading. As the popularity of books such as those in the *Harry Potter* series grows, the objections also increase. Consider these objections, and try to identify through popular media the reasoning behind the objections. If you encountered parents who objected to their children's reading fantasy in school, how might you respond? If you can, research the plan that your local school district has for parents and local citizens to file complaints on books. Discuss how you would go about finding out the information you would need to respond to such complaints.

2. Select a book with personified animals. Think about the author's choice of particular animals to represent certain personality traits. What animal traits do you find that are carried over to a particular animal character in personified animal stories? Now find a picture book that has human characters in it. If you were to select an animal to represent each character, what would you select, and why?

3. A recurring statement made by female authors of fantasy and science fiction is that their publishers have asked them to adopt a male pseudonym to mask their gender. The belief that "boys won't want to read fantasy/science fiction by female writers" prevails even today, as the extraordinarily popular author of the *Harry Potter* series was asked to use the initials "J. K." instead of the name under which she submitted her manuscript, Joanne Rowling. How does this belief in the male gender appeal of this genre play out in classrooms filled predominantly with female teachers and school librarians?

Recommended Books: Fantasy

* indicates a picture book; **I** indicates interest level (P = preschool, YA = young adult)

Personified Animals

Avi. *Poppy*. Illustrated by Brian Floca. Orchard, 1995. Poppy the deer mouse tries to convince her family to move closer to a large cornfield that could provide plentiful food forever. The frightening king of the forest, a great horned owl named Mr. Ocax, denies them permission to make the move. The story continues in *Poppy and Rye* (1998), *Ragweed* (1999), and *Ereth's Birthday* (2000). (**I:** 9–12)

Bond, Michael. *A Bear Called Paddington*. Illustrated by Peggy Fortnum. Houghton Mifflin, 1960. This is the first of a series of more than twenty books about the adventures of a bear found at Paddington train station and adopted by the Brown family.

Cleary, Beverly. *The Mouse and the Motorcycle*. Illustrated by Louis Darling. Morrow, 1965. A boy named Keith shows Ralph, a mouse, how to ride a toy motorcycle. Other books in the series include *Runaway Ralph* (1970) and *Ralph S. Mouse* (1982). (**I:** 7–9)

DiCamillo, Kate. *The Tale of Despereaux: Being the Story of a Mouse, a Princess, Some Soup, and a Spool of Thread*. Illustrated by Timothy B. Ering. Candlewick Press, 2003. A mouse named Despereaux falls in love with the human Princess Pea and is sent to the dungeon by the other mice for his unmouse-like behavior. Good overcomes evil while hope and forgiveness persevere in this story. (**I:** 9–12)

Grahame, Kenneth. *The Wind in the Willows*. Illustrated by E. H. Shepard. Scribner's, 1908/1933. Rat, Mole, Badger, and Toad of Toad Hall, a group of loyal friends with very distinct personalities, enjoy various adventures in the outdoors. (**I:** 7–11)

*Henkes, Kevin. *Chester's Way*. Greenwillow, 1988. Chester and Wilson are very particular about how things are done, and they never vary from their routines. One day, Lilly moves into the neighborhood, and she is full of surprises. (**I:** P–8)

*———. *Sheila Rae, the Brave*. Greenwillow, 1987. Sheila Rae is very brave and quite proud of how brave she is. One day, she gets lost and finds that she is not as brave and fearless as she thought. (**I:** P–8)

Howe, James, and Deborah Howe. *Bunnicula*. Illustrated by Leslie Morrill. Atheneum, 1979. This humorous fantasy is about the belief of two family pets that the newest arrival, a rabbit, is actually a vampire bunny. Other books in the series include *Howliday Inn* (1982), *The Celery Stalks at Midnight* (1983), and *Nighty-Nightmare* (1987). (**I:** 8–10)

King-Smith, Dick. *Babe: The Gallant Pig*. Illustrated by Mary Rayner. Crown, 1985. This story is about a barnyard community and how Babe, a pig, learns to be a champion sheepherder. (**I:** 8–11)

———. *Martin's Mice*. Illustrated by Jez Alborough. Crown, 1989. Martin the cat keeps Drusilla the mouse as his pet. He helps with her babies and protects them from mice-eating cats. (**I:** 8–11)

Lawson, Robert. *Rabbit Hill*. Viking, 1944. The animals on Rabbit Hill anxiously await the arrival of the new folks. Will they bring traps and guns? (**I:** 9–11)

Lowry, Lois. *Stay! Keeper's Story*. Illustrated by True Kelley. Houghton Mifflin, 1997. Narrated by a dog named Keeper, this humorous account explains a dog's interpretation of life. (**I:** 8–12)

*Meddaugh, Susan. *Martha Speaks*. Houghton Mifflin, 1992. When Martha, the family dog, eats alphabet soup, she is suddenly able to speak and express her thoughts to her family. Among the many about Martha are *Martha Calling* (1994) and *Martha Blah, Blah* (1996). (**I:** 7–9)

Oppel, Kenneth. *Silverwing*. Simon & Schuster, 1997. The runt of the Silverwing bat colony, Shade, is separated from the others during a storm and must rejoin them on their dangerous migration South. The sequels are *Sunwing* (2000) and *Firewing* (2003). (**I:** 10 and up)

*Potter, Beatrix. *The Tale of Peter Rabbit*. Warne, 1902. This is the classic story of a rabbit who finds himself in trouble when he gets caught sneaking into Mr. McGregor's garden. It is the first of a number of stories about animals. (**I:** P–7)

Rylant, Cynthia. *Gooseberry Park*. Illustrated by Arthur Howard. Harcourt, 1995. A Labrador retriever, a hermit crab, and a bat must work together to come to the aid of their friend, a squirrel, who has become separated from her babies during an ice storm. (**I:** 7–10)

Selden, George. *The Cricket in Times Square*. Illustrated by Garth Williams. Farrar, 1960. Chester the cricket finds himself transported from the country to the city in a picnic basket. With new friends, he finds a home in a newspaper stand in a subway station below Times Square. Other books in the series include *Tucker's Countryside* (1969), *Chester Cricket's Pigeon Ride* (1981), and *The Old Meadow* (1987). (**I:** 7–11)

Sharp, Margery. *The Rescuers*. Illustrated by Garth Williams. Little, Brown, 1959. Miss Bianca and friends go on a dangerous journey to save a poet from imprisonment. Other books in the series include *Miss Bianca* (1962) and *Bernard the Brave* (1977). (**I:** 8–11)

Steig, William. *Abel's Island*. Farrar, 1976. A gentrified town mouse named Abel is swept away from his bride, Amanda, in a storm and learns to survive the elements for a year on a deserted island. (**I:** 8–10)

*———. *The Amazing Bone*. Farrar, 1976. The amazing bone can talk, and this magical ability saves a piglet from being eaten by a fox. (**I:** P–7)

*———. *Doctor De Soto*. Farrar, 1982. A fox visits a mouse dentist with the hope of having the dentist for dinner after his tooth has been fixed. (**I:** P–8)

*———. *Sylvester and the Magic Pebble*. Simon & Schuster, 1969. Sylvester, a donkey, comes across a special pebble for his pebble collection—one that grants wishes. The problem arises when Sylvester wishes to turn into a rock temporarily to escape trouble but cannot revert back to being a donkey. (**I:** P–8)

White, E. B. *Charlotte's Web*. Illustrated by Garth Williams. Harper & Row, 1952. A runt pig named Wilbur is saved by Fern, who wants to show him at the fair. Meanwhile, Charlotte the spider enlists the barnyard animals in a campaign to keep Wilbur alive. (**I:** 7–11)

Personified Toys

Collodi, Carlo. *The Adventures of Pinocchio*. Translated by M. L. Rosenthal. Illustrated by Troy Howell. Lothrop, Lee & Shepard, 1881/1983. This classic story, available in many editions, is about a wooden puppet named Pinocchio whose creator is lonely and longs for company. When Pinocchio comes alive, his naiveté lands him in an adventure that forces him to learn about truthfulness. (**I:** 9–12)

DiCamillo, Kate. *The Miraculous Journey of Edward Tulane*. Illustrated by Bagram Ibatoulline. Candlewick, 2006. A vain and heartless china rabbit doll ends up on a journey that tears at his physical beauty but builds his emotional heart. (**I:** 8–12)

Godden, Rumer. *The Doll's House*. Illustrated by Tasha Tudor. Penguin, 1947/1976. The arrival of a new doll upsets the resident dolls of a Victorian dollhouse. (**I:** 7–10)

———. *Four Dolls*. Illustrated by Pauline Baynes. Greenwillow, 1984. These four stories about four spirited dolls and their owners were originally published as separate books: *Impunity Jane* (1954), *The Fairy Doll* (1956), *The Story of Holly and Ivy* (1958), and *Candy Floss* (1960). (**I:** 8–10)

Hoffmann, E. T. A. *The Nutcracker*. Illustrated by Maurice Sendak. Crown, 1816/1984. Clara dreams on Christmas Eve that her toy nutcracker comes to life and takes her to a magical world filled with music and dancing flowers and candy. The story has been published in other editions with various illustrators. (**I:** 8–11)

Martin, Ann M., and Laura Godwin. *The Doll People*. Hyperion, 2000. Anabelle is a doll who is determined to solve the mystery of her Aunt Sarah, who has been missing for nearly fifty years. The arrival of the plastic family next door provides a friend and fellow sleuth, Tiffany. The story continues in *The Meanest Doll in the World* (2003). (**I:** 8–12)

Milne, A. A. *Winnie-the-Pooh*. Illustrated by Ernest H. Shepard. Dutton, 1926. Christopher Robin and his friends Winnie-the-Pooh, Eeyore, Piglet, Owl, Tigger, Kanga, and Roo share many adventures in the Hundred Acre Wood. The sequel is *The House at Pooh Corner* (1928). (**I:** P–10)

Waugh, Sylvia. *The Mennyms*. Greenwillow, 1994. In England, a family of life-sized rag dolls have continued to live in the house of their deceased creator for forty years, but now the new homeowner intends to come for a visit. See also *Mennyms in the Wilderness* (1996), *Mennyms Alive* (1997), *Mennyms Under Siege* (1997), and *Mennyms Alone* (1998). (**I:** 10 and up)

*Williams, Margery. *The Velveteen Rabbit*. Illustrated by Michael Hague. Holt, 1922/1983. A well-loved toy rabbit is discarded and then transformed into a real rabbit. Several other editions have been published with various illustrators. (**I:** 6–9)

Winthrop, Elizabeth. *The Castle in the Attic*. Illustrated by Donna Green. Holiday House, 1985. William receives a wooden model of a castle and discovers that the silver knight comes alive in his hands. Sir Simon leads William on an adventure in which they battle a fiery dragon and an evil wizard. The sequel is *The Battle for the Castle* (1993). (**I:** 9–11)

Outlandish Characters and Situations

Ardagh, Philip. *A House Called Awful End*. Holt, 2002. When his parents suddenly take ill and mysteriously turn yellow, Eddie Dickens is sent with Mad Uncle Jack to journey to a house called Awful End, only to find himself in a totally nonsensical series of events. First in a trilogy. (**I:** 8–11)

Babbitt, Natalie. *The Devil's Storybook*. Farrar, 1974. This is a collection of short stories about the devil's attempts to recruit more members to his world. The sequel is *The Devil's Other Storybook* (1987). (**I:** 9–12)

———. *The Search for Delicious*. Farrar, 1969. Twelve-year-old Gaylen is sent out to seek the true meaning of the word "delicious" when there is disagreement among members of the court. What he discovers is a secret plot for the queen's brother to take over the kingdom. (**I:** 8–11)

Dahl, Roald. *Matilda*. Illustrated by Quentin Blake. Viking, 1988. Matilda uses her intellectual genius and psychic abilities to bestow a childlike interpretation of justice on the good and the bad. (**I:** 9–11)

Horvath, Polly. *The Pepins and Their Problems*. The Pepins are unable to solve their various unusual problems, so readers are asked to submit their suggestions in this humorous set of stories. (**I:** 8–11)

Le Guin, Ursula K. *Catwings*. Illustrated by S. D. Schindler. Franklin Watts, 1988. Mrs. Jane Tabby is pleased that her kittens have wings, for they can escape the dangers of the city—only to meet with the dangers of the woods. Sequels are *Catwings Return* (1989) and *Wonderful Alexander and the Catwings* (1994). (**I:** 7–10)

Lindgren, Astrid. *Pippi Longstocking*. Illustrated by Louis S. Glanzman. Viking, 1945/1950. Pippi Longstocking lives without adult supervision in a town in Sweden. She leads an outrageous lifestyle and keeps the neighborhood children entertained. The sequel is *Pippi in the South Seas* (1959). (**I:** 7–11)

Snicket, Lemony. *The Bad Beginning*. HarperCollins, 1999. This first volume in a series of books about the Baudelaire children begins with the worst news: their parents and everything in their home have been lost in a fire. The dead-pan humor of absurdly impossible events continues in a total of 13 books in this "Series of Unfortunate Events." (**I:** 9–12)

Travers, Pamela L. *Mary Poppins*. Illustrated by Mary Shepard. Harcourt, 1934/1962. Mary Poppins arrives with the East Wind to care for the Banks children. The nanny's unusual ways surprise and delight the children. Other books in the series include *Mary Poppins Comes Back* (1935) and *Mary Poppins in Cherry Tree Lane* (1982). (**I:** 7–11)

Magical Powers

Babbitt, Natalie. *Tuck Everlasting*. Farrar, 1975. Winnie discovers that the Tuck family drank from a spring that has given them eternal life. When the Tucks reveal their feelings about having eternal life, an enterprising man overhears the secret and attempts to capitalize on it by selling the water. (**I:** 8–12)

Barrie, Sir James Matthew. *Peter Pan*. Random House, 1911/1957. Peter Pan teaches three children how to fly to Never Never Land, where they will never have to grow up, but a jealous fairy intervenes and leads them astray into danger on Captain Hook's pirate ship. The story has been published in many editions. (**I:** 8–12)

Brittain, Bill. *The Wish Giver: Three Tales of Coventry*. Illustrated by Andrew Glass. Harper & Row, 1983. A stranger appears, granting the wishes of a few children who are surprised at the result. Related titles are *The Devil's Donkey* (1981) and *Dr. Dredd's Wagon of Wonders* (1987). (**I:** 9–12)

Coville, Bruce. *Jeremy Thatcher, Dragon Hatcher*. Harcourt, 1991. Jeremy stumbles on Mr. Eilve's Magic Shop, which mysteriously appears. A beautiful ball from the store turns out to be a dragon's egg, and many adventures follow as the dragon grows larger and larger. (**I:** 9–12)

Funke, Cornelia. *Inkheart*. Translated from German by Anthea Bell. Chicken House/Scholastic, 2003. When Meggie's father Mo reads aloud, some characters magically come to life. When these villains enter their real world, Meggie and Mo find themselves in the middle of the fast-paced adventure. The trilogy continues in *Inkspell* (2005) and *Inkdeath* (2008). (**I:** 10 and up)

———. *The Thief Lord*. Translated from German by Oliver Latsch. Chicken House/Scholastic, 2002. A thirteen-year-old "Thief Lord" serves as a leader for a group of runaway and homeless children in Venice. (**I:** 10 and up)

Jones, Diana Wynne. *A Charmed Life*. Greenwillow, 1977. Witchcraft enables Gwen to trade places with a twentieth-century girl in this time travel story. This is the first volume in a series about a young boy magician who is manipulated by his sister. The prequel is *The Lives of Christopher Chant* (1988), about a Chrestomanci-in-training who will become the next controller of magic. The other titles in the Chrestomanci series are *The Magicians of Caprona* (1980), in which the children of two feuding families make magical peace, and *Witch Week* (1982), which takes place in a school where the teacher suspects that someone in class is a witch. Short stories about Chrestomanci are found in *Warlock at the Wheel* (1985) and *Dragons and Dreams* (Harper, 1986). (**I:** 11–YA)

———. *Dark Lord of Derkholm*. Greenwillow, 1998. The story tells of a popular tourist destination, where lords and wizards role-play the parts of the dark lord and a wizard while tourists follow their fate as members of Pilgrim Parties. The sequel is *Year of the Griffin* (2000). (**I:** 12 and up)

———. *Power of Three*. Greenwillow, 1978. A curse threatens the English moors, and three children and some strange creatures work together to save them. (**I:** 11 and up)

———. *Stopping for a Spell: Three Fantasies*. Illustrated by Joseph A. Smith. Greenwillow, 1993. "Unusual visitors" is the theme of three humorous short stories. In one, an Auntie turns up with a conjurer's kit; in another, a little girl gets turned into a teddy bear when four Grannies come to babysit; in the third, pieces of furniture work together to get rid of an unwelcome visitor who has offended them. (**I:** 8–11)

*Mendez, Phil. *The Black Snowman*. Illustrated by Carole Byard. Scholastic, 1989. Jacob must overcome his anger about being poor and black. A black snowman uses the magical power of an old Ashanti kente cloth to show Jacob why he should be proud of his heritage. (**I:** 6–9)

Nimmo, Jennie. *Midnight for Charlie Bone*. Scholastic, 2003. When ten-year-old Charlie realizes that he can hear people talking in pictures as though he were present when the picture was taken, this is recognized as a sign that he has been bestowed with a "gift" as a half-descendent of the Red King family line. His enrollment in a school for the education of "bestowed" children leads to many adventures. See other titles in *The Children of the Red King* quintet: *Charlie Bone and the Time Twister* (2003), *Charlie Bone and the Invisible Boy* (2004), and *Charlie Bone and the Castle of Mirrors* (2005). (**I:** 9–12)

O'Shea, Pat. *The Hounds of the Morrigan*. Holiday House, 1985. The forces of good and evil gather to fight over a book of magic that ten-year-old Pidge discovers in an Irish bookstore. (**I:** 10–YA)

Pierce, Tamora. *Magic Steps*. Scholastic, 2000. In this first book in the *The Circle Opens* quartet, Sandry, a young mage, discovers a boy dancing a spell and becomes his new teacher. The two team up to rid the power of invisible killers. (**I:** 11–YA)

———. *Sandry's Book*. Scholastic,1997. In the *Circle of Magic* quartet, four mages-in-training practice the art of magic. The others are *Tris's Book* (1998), *Daja's Book* (1998), and *Briar's Book* (1999). (**I:** 11–YA)

Pratchett, Terry. *The Wee Free Men*. Harper, 2003. Nine-year-old witch-to-be Tiffany Aching defeats the Queen of Fairyland and rescues her kidnapped brother, bravely making her way through the constantly changing landscape of Fairyland, armed with a frying pan and with the aid of six-inch high Nac Mac Feegle. Further titles in the Tiffany Aching Adventures include: *A Hat Full of Sky* (2004) and *Wintersmith* (2006), one of the many set in Pratchett's Discworld. (**I:** 10–13)

*Ringgold, Faith. *Aunt Harriet's Underground Railroad in the Sky*. Crown, 1992. When flying around one day, Cassie and her brother Be Be find a train in the sky. The woman conductor is Harriet Tubman, and she leads Cassie on the Underground Railroad so that Cassie will never forget the experiences of her ancestors. (**I:** 6–9)

*———. *Dinner at Aunt Connie's House*. Hyperion, 1993. While playing hide-and-go-seek at Aunt Connie's house, Melody and Lonnie find a dozen portraits of African American women. The paintings speak, telling the women's historically significant stories. (**I:** 7–10)

Rowling, J. K. *Harry Potter and the Sorcerer's Stone*. Scholastic, 1998. An orphaned boy discovers that he is the most famous wizard alive and begins his education at Hogwarts School of Witchcraft and Wizardry. The story continues in *Harry Potter and the Chamber of Secrets* (1999), *Harry Potter and the Prisoner of Azkaban* (1999), and *Harry Potter and the Goblet of Fire* (2000), *Harry Potter and the Order of the Phoenix* (2003), *Harry Potter and the Half Blood Prince* (2005), and concluding with *Harry Potter and the Deathly Hallows* (2007). (**I:** 9–14)

Sage, Angie. *Septimus Heap: Magyk*. HarperCollins, 2005. An auspicious birth of the seventh son of a seventh son changes course as he is presumed to be born dead. This fast-paced story of magical creatures and much adventure marks the beginning of the fantasy series, Septimus Heap. Sequels: *Flyte* (2006), *Physik* (2007), *Queste* (2008). (**I:** 9–12)

*Van Allsburg, Chris. *Jumanji*. Houghton Mifflin, 1981. Peter and Judy begin the jungle adventure board game of Jumanji, only to find that with each play, real parts of the jungle appear: Monkeys tear up the kitchen, rhinos stampede through the house, and a monsoon begins in the living room. (**I:** 6–10)

Vande Velde, Vivian. *Magic Can Be Murder*. Harcourt, 2000. Nola, a witch, tries to hide her magical abilities from authorities, but a crying spell and a murder threaten to reveal her. (**I:** 12–YA)

Wrede, Patricia C. *Dealing with Dragons*. Scholastic, 1990. Princess Cimorene, bored with palace life, voluntarily becomes a dragon's princess and fights wizards to keep them from interfering with the dragons as they choose their new king. Other books in the *Enchanted Forest Chronicles* series are *Searching for Dragons* (1991), *Calling on Dragons* (1992), and *Talking to Dragons* (1993). (**I:** 12–YA)

Yep, Laurence. *Dragon of the Lost Sea.* HarperCollins, 1982. Shimmer is a dragon princess on a quest to find the lost sea that is her home. Although she dismisses the human Thorn as unable to help, she realizes that being homeless, they have common bonds. Related titles are *Dragon Steel* (1985) and *Dragon Cauldron* (1991). (**I:** 12–YA)

Embellished Fairy Tales

Hale, Shannon. *The Goose Girl.* Bloomsbury, 2003. When the crown princess is sent to be a bride in another kingdom, her entourage betrays her and she must rely on her gift of communicating with animals as she takes on the identity of "Goose Girl" before she can claim her rightful place. (**I:** 9–12)

Levine, Gail Carson. *Ella Enchanted.* HarperCollins, 1997. Ella is given the gift of obedience at the celebration of her birth, and this gift turns out to be more of a curse, as Ella cannot control her obedience. This story has an underlying Cinderella tale, but offers readers more depth and richness in this embellished book version. (**I:** 10 and up)

McKinley, Robin. *Rose Daughter.* Greenwillow, 1997. The author of *Beauty* (1978) once again takes up the story of Beauty and the Beast, expanding it into a full novel of her own creation. (**I:** 11 and up)

———. *Spindle's End.* Putnam, 2000. In this lengthy expansion of the Sleeping Beauty story, "Rosie" is rescued from the palace and raised by an apprentice fairy who gives her the gift of talking to animals. (**I:** 12 and up)

Napoli, Donna Jo. *Beast.* Atheneum, 2000. In this story set in ancient Persia, a curse changes Prince Orasmyn into a lion. He struggles to remain true to his human belief in Islamic principles as he travels from India to France, seeking redemption and love. (**I:** YA)

———. *Crazy Jack.* Delacorte, 1999. In this expansion of the Jack and the Beanstalk story, Jack is tormented by nightmares about his father's absence and called crazy for his behavior, including his sale of a cow for magic beans. (**I:** 10 and up)

———. *Jimmy, the Pickpocket of the Palace.* Illustrated by Judith Byron Schachner. Dutton, 1995. When a princess kisses a frog with a hurt leg, he turns into a human boy. To revert back into a frog, he must somehow obtain a ring that does not belong to him. A related title is *Prince of the Pond* (1992). (**I:** 9–12)

———. *Zel.* Dutton, 1996. The story of Rapunzel is explored from three perspectives: the thirteen-year-old peasant girl Zel, the nobleman who falls in love with her, and the mother who loves her daughter too much to let her go. (**I:** 12–YA)

Pullman, Philip. *I Was a Rat.* Knopf, 2000. Illustrated by Kevin Hawkes. A rat who had been turned into a human boy to serve as Cinderella's coachman missed his midnight curfew and must now make his way in the world of people. (**I:** 8–12)

Vande Velde, Vivian. *The Rumpelstiltskin Problem.* Houghton Mifflin, 2000. Six alternative versions explore the "holes" in the traditional Rumpelstiltskin tale: Why did the miller tell the king his daughter could spin straw into gold? Why did Rumpelstiltskin want a baby anyway? (**I:** 10–YA)

Extraordinary Worlds

Baum, L. Frank. *The Wonderful Wizard of Oz.* Oxford Univ. Press, 1900/1997. Dorothy is transported from her home in Kansas to the Land of Oz by way of a tornado. In her search for a way home, she meets a scarecrow who wants a brain, a tin man who wants a heart, and a lion who wants courage. To get their wishes, they must kill the Wicked Witch of the West. There are forty "officially recognized" sequels, of which Baum wrote the first fourteen. (**I:** 9–12)

Carroll, Lewis. *Alice's Adventures in Wonderland.* Castle Books, 1865/1978. Alice follows a rabbit down a rabbit hole and finds herself in an extraordinary world. (**I:** 10–YA)

———. *Through the Looking Glass and What Alice Found There.* Macmillan, 1872. When Alice steps through a mirror, she finds herself in a backwards world. (**I:** 11–YA)

Colfer, Eoin. *Artemis Fowl.* Hyperion, 2001. Twelve-year-old Artemis Fowl is a genius son in a family of criminals. In this high-action adventure story, he manages the impossible feat of obtaining a fairy handbook and decoding it in order to reach his goal of stealing fairy gold. Sequels include: *The Arctic Incident* (2002), *The Eternity Code* (2003), *The Opal Deception* (2005), *The Lost Colony* (2006), *The Time Paradox* (2008). (**I:** 10 and up)

Collins, Suzanne. *Gregor the Overlander.* Scholastic, 2003. Eleven-year-old Gregor and his two-year-old sister fall through the laundry grate in their apartment building into "Underland," an underground world of overgrown rodents and cockroaches and discover that his long-missing father is being held captive. The story continues in *Gregor and the Prophecy of Bane* (2004). (**I:** 9–12)

Dahl, Roald. *Charlie and the Chocolate Factory.* Illustrated by John Schindelman. Knopf, 1964. Charlie is one of five lucky winners who find a golden ticket that allows them to tour Willy Wonka's mysterious chocolate factory. Inside the factory are imaginative processes for creating Wonka chocolate. (**I:** 8–10)

———. *James and the Giant Peach.* Knopf, 1961/1996. James's unhappy life takes a turn when the magical contents of a bag make a peach grow large enough to enter and garden insects grow large enough to be his friends. (**I:** 7–11)

DiTerlizzi, Tony, and Holly Black. *The Field Guide.* Simon, 2003. The five-book series of the *Spiderwick Chronicles* begins when thirteen-year-old Mallory and twin nine-year-olds Jared and Simon move into the Spiderwick Estate and enter the world of faeries and fantastic creatures. (**I:** 7–11)

Funke, Cornelia. *Dragon Rider.* Translated by Anthea Bell. Chicken House/Scholastic, 2004. Set in a world of dragons, brownies, and other fantastic creatures, a boy becomes the Dragon Rider of a silver dragon who derives energy from moonlight. (**I:** 8–12)

Gaiman, Neil. *Coraline.* HarperCollins, 2002. One day, the fourteenth door in Coraline's house leads her into an eerily "mirror" apartment—and her alternate mother and father want to keep her on *their* side of the door. (**I:** 11–YA)

Ibbotson, Eva. *The Secret of Platform 13.* Dutton, 1998. A doorway at a railway station in London serves as the entrance to a magical island kingdom where fantastical creatures like mermaids and ogres live. This doorway is open for only nine days every nine years, and the infant heir to the kingdom is kidnapped. (**I:** 10 and up)

———. *Island of the Aunts.* Illustrated by Kevin Hawkes. Dutton, 2000. Sisters who find they need help caring for an island full of magical and unusual creatures decide they must kidnap three children who can help them out. (**I:** 8–11)

Juster, Norton. *The Phantom Tollbooth*. Illustrated by Jules Feiffer. Random House, 1961. Milo thinks that learning is a waste of time and there's never anything to do. Entering a tollbooth, he finds himself in the Kingdom of Wisdom, where he learns to seek Rhyme and Reason and not to jump to Conclusions; Tock teaches Milo not to waste time. (**I:** 9–11)

McGraw, Eloise. *The Moorchild*. Simon & Schuster, 1996. Saaski is a child of the "folk," who live in a secret world along the moor, but travel invisibly within the human world. When she is traded by the folk for a human child, she grows up realizing that she is not human like her "parents," yet not fully folk either. (**I:** 10–14)

Naylor, Phyllis Reynolds. *Sang Spell*. Simon, 2000. Joshua's hitchhiking trip to his new home, following the death of his mother, leads unexpectedly to a primitive world where the Mulungeon people have retreated to the Appalachian backwoods and created a world where the landscape changes and all roads and rivers are circular. (**I:** 12–YA)

Norton, Mary. *The Borrowers*. Illustrated by Beth and Joe Krush. Harcourt, 1953. Pod, Homily, and Arietty Clock are a family of little people who "borrow" everyday items from a human family and use them in ways that suit people their size. When Arietty befriends a human boy, the family fears for their safety. There are several more books in the series: *The Borrowers Afield* (1955), *The Borrowers Afloat* (1959), *The Borrowers Aloft* (1961), *Poor Stainless* (1971), and *The Borrowers Avenged* (1982). (**I:** 8–11)

Pratchett, Terry. *Nation*. HarperCollins, 2008. Two young teens of vastly different backgrounds must figure out how to live in a world that has been completely changed by a destructive tsunami. When other survivors start arriving and looking up to them for answers, they must put aside what they knew about how the world should work and create new ways of understanding how to live. (**I:** 13–YA)

*Tan, Shaun. *The Arrival*. Scholastic, 2008. (Australia). This beautifully designed book wordlessly explores what it means to be an immigrant in a new land, at times, depicting the setting as if it is an alien world. (**I:** 9–12).

Townley, Roderick. *The Great Good Thing*. Atheneum, 2001. Characters in an out-of-print and rarely read fairy tale enjoy life as they want until a reader begins to read their book. All must scramble to take their places and act out each part whenever a reader opens the book. (**I:** 9–11)

———. *Into the Labyrinth*. Atheneum, 2002. In a related book to *The Great Good Thing,* the story has now been uploaded onto a Web site and the already-stressed characters are introduced to a whole new set of problems: lines scrolling quickly by, entire passages disappearing, etc. (**I:** 10–13)

*Wiesner, David. *Flotsam*. Clarion, 2006. When a camera washes up on a beach, a young boy develops the film inside and discovers mysterious and surprising images suggesting a world unlike what we know exists. What will he make of these images, and who will be the next in imagining the stories? (**I:** 6–12)

Supernatural Elements

Almond, David. *Skellig*. Delacorte, 1999. Michael's life is uncertain: His parents are occupied with his baby sister's fight for life, and his family has just moved to a new home. He discovers a "Skellig" in the rundown garage and, with the help of a new friend, must decide how to help the Skellig stay alive. (**I:** 10–14)

Bellairs, John. *The House with a Clock in Its Walls*. Illustrated by Edward Gorey. Dial, 1973. Lewis's uncle has magical abilities that Lewis tries to imitate, but when he does, he unexpectedly creates a wicked ghost. There are numerous sequels written by Brad Strickland. (**I:** 10–12)

Billingsley, Franny. *The Folk Keeper*. Simon & Schuster, 1989. Based on Selkie lore, this is the story of Corinna, who hides her identity to take the job of the Folk Keeper—risking her own safety and well-being to keep the Folk that live underground from doing harm to the world. Her truest identity is revealed through unexpected events, described in journal entry format. (**I:** 10–14)

Cameron, Eleanor. *The Court of the Stone Children*. Dutton, 1973. The ghost of a French girl from the nineteenth century appears to a contemporary girl. The ghost's father was executed for treason, and now she wants Nina to help prove his innocence. (**I:** 10–12)

Conrad, Pam. *Stonewords: A Ghost Story*. HarperCollins, 1990. Zoe is visited by the ghost of Zoe Louise, a person from the past. When Zoe realizes that she must prevent Zoe Louise's untimely death, she goes back in time to the 1850s. (**I:** 10–12)

Gaiman, Neil. *The Graveyard Book*. HarperCollins, 2008. An orphan named "Nobody" is raised by the ghosts who inhabit a cemetery when his own family is killed in a triple murder at the start of the story. (**I:** 9–12)

Hahn, Mary Downing. *Wait till Helen Comes*. Clarion, 1986. Helen is a ghost from the nineteenth century who is trying to convince another child to drown in the same lake that she did so they can be playmates. (**I:** 8–12)

Hunter, Mollie. *The Kelpie's Pearls*. Blackie & Son, 1964. An aging loner becomes friendly with a kelpie, whose gift of pearls sets off a series of troublesome events. (**I:** 9–12)

———. *A Stranger Came Ashore: A Story of Suspense*. HarperTrophy, 1975/1994. In a suspenseful story based on Selkie lore, twelve-year-old Robbie suspects that the stranger who came ashore during a terrible storm and was befriended by his family is an evil Selkie. (**I:** 9–12)

Kindl, Patrice. *Owl in Love*. Houghton, 1993. Fourteen-year-old Owl is a "were-owl"—a girl by day, facing the challenges of schoolgirl crush on a teacher and being an owl by night. (**I:** 10–13)

Lively, Penelope. *The Ghost of Thomas Kempe*. Illustrated by Antony Maitland. Dutton, 1973. James and his family move into an old house in an English village. When the resident ghost begins to act out, James gets blamed. (**I:** 10–12)

Mahy, Margaret. *The Changeover*. Atheneum, 1984. A girl's supernatural abilities save her brother. (**I:** 10–13)

———. *The Haunting*. Macmillan, 1982. Barry, an eight-year-old, begins receiving mental messages from an uncle who was presumed dead. (**I:** 10–12)

Peck, Richard. *The Ghost Belonged to Me*. Viking, 1975. Richard tries to solve the mystery of a missing girl and ends up unwillingly receiving the assistance of Blossom Culp, his nemesis. Sequels are *Ghosts I Have Been* (1977) and *The Dreadful Future of Blossom Culp* (1983). (**I:** 10–YA)

Yep, Laurence. *The Ghost Fox*. Illustrated by Jean and Mou-sien Tseng. Scholastic, 1994. While Little Lee's father is away at sea, Little Lee is responsible for taking care of his mother, including getting rid of the ghost that is trying to take over her soul. This is an adaptation of a story taken from the ancient Chinese tradition of ghost storytelling. (**I:** 7–10)

Time Slips

Boston, L. M. *The Children of Green Knowe*. Illustrated by Peter Boston. Harcourt, 1989. A lonely boy moves to his grandmother's old English house, only to find that various children who played in the house over the years reappear to be his playmates. There are several sequels: *The Treasure of Green Knowe* (1989), *A Stranger at Green Knowe* (1989), *An Enemy at Green Knowe* (1989), and *The River at Green Knowe* (1989). (**I:** 9–11)

Cooper, Susan. *King of Shadows*. McElderry, 1999. Nat Fielding plays the role of *The Midsummer Night's Dream*'s Puck in the newly reconstructed Globe Theatre, but finds himself transported four hundred years back to play the same role with Will Shakespeare as Oberon. (**I:** 12–YA)

Fleischman, Sid. *The 13th Floor: A Ghost Story*. Illustrated by Peter Sís. Greenwillow, 1995. Buddy Stebbins steps off an elevator on the thirteenth floor of an old building and follows his sister three hundred years back in time. They end up on a pirate ship captained by one of their own ancestors. (**I:** 9–12)

Gutman, Dan. *Shoeless Joe and Me*. HarperCollins, 2002. In another of the *Baseball Card Adventure* series, Stosh travels back to 1919 and attempts to stop Shoeless Joe from throwing the World Series and being expelled from baseball for life. (**I:** 8–11)

Hoffman, Mary. *Stravaganza: The City of Masks*. Bloomsbury, 2002. In this time-slip story in modern-day England/sixteenth-century Venice, a boy undergoing cancer treatment finds that he can travel every night to Venice and lead an exciting, cancer-free life of adventure there. The sequel is *The City of Stars*. (**I:** 10–YA)

Hurmence, Belinda. *A Girl Called Boy*. Houghton Mifflin, 1982. Blanche goes back in time to 1853 in North Carolina and experiences slavery when she becomes one of her ancestors. (**I:** 10–12)

McKay, Hillary. *The Amber Cat*. Simon & Schuster, 1997. In this time-slip and ghost story, as Robin recovers from chickenpox, he and his friends are fascinated by his mother's stories of a mysterious girl who used to appear in her childhood. *Dog Friday* (1995), *Dolphin Luck* (1999). (**I:** 8–11)

Osborne, Mary Pope. *Magic Tree House* series. In this beginning chapter book series, siblings Jack and Annie are magically transported from their tree house where they are reading to various times and places where they learn historical, scientific, and cultural information. (**I:** 7–9)

Park, Linda Sue. *Archer's Quest*. Clarion, 2006. When a king of ancient Korea suddenly appears in twelve-year-old Kevin's room, he must figure out a way to help return the king to his own time and place. (**I:** 10–12)

Park, Ruth. *Playing Beatie Bow*. Atheneum, 1982. A contemporary Australian girl finds that she has traveled back in time to the nineteenth century. (**I:** 10–12)

Pearce, Philippa. *Tom's Midnight Garden*. Illustrated by Susan Einzig. Harper, 1984. Tom is bored with his summer until he finds that he can visit a garden that appears only when the grandfather clock strikes thirteen every night. There he develops a special friendship with a mysterious girl named Hatty. (**I:** 10–12)

Pearson, Kit. *A Handful of Time*. Viking, 1988. A twelve-year-old finds a watch under the floor while visiting her cousins one unhappy summer. The watch takes her back to the time her mother was the same age and allows her to gain insights about her mother. (**I:** 11–13)

Scieszka, Jon. *Knights of the Kitchen Table*. Illustrated by Lane Smith. Viking, 1991. Joe, Fred, and Sam, the Time Warp Trio, travel back to the days of King Arthur when they open "The Book" that a magician uncle sent Joe for a birthday present. Other *Time Warp Trio* stories include *The Not-So-Jolly Roger* (1991), *The Good, the Bad, and the Goofy* (1992), *Your Mother Was a Neanderthal* (1993), *2095* (1995), *Tut, Tut* (1996), *Summer Reading Will Kill You* (1998), with new ones being published every year or two. (**I:** 8–11)

Voigt, Cynthia. *Building Blocks*. Atheneum, 1984. A boy's journey back into the time of his father's childhood helps him to understand his father better. (**I:** 9–11)

Wiseman, David. *Jeremy Visick*. Houghton Mifflin, 1981. A contemporary Cornish boy goes back in time to try to discover the location of a boy named Jeremy, who was lost in a mine accident in 1852. (**I:** 10–12)

Yolen, Jane. *The Devil's Arithmetic*. Viking, 1988. Hannah finds herself transported as Chaya back to the days of the Holocaust. Through the device of time travel, she grows in her understanding of her Jewish heritage. (**I:** 9–12)

High Fantasy

Alexander, Lloyd. *The Arkadians*. Dutton, 1995. An unlikely cast of unusual characters each tell a story filled with elements of magic and Greek mythology. Their companionship is based on bravery, loyalty, compassion, and love. (**I:** 11–13)

———. *The Book of Three*. Holt, 1964/1999. *The Chronicles of Prydain* tells of the struggle between the people of Prydain and the Lord of the Land of Death. Other books in the series are *The Black Cauldron* (1965/1999), *The Castle of Llyr* (1966/1999), *Taran Wanderer* (1967/1999), and *The High King* (1968/1999). (**I:** 10–13)

———. *The Remarkable Journey of Prince Jen*. Dutton, 1991. In this coming-of-age story set in China during the Tang Dynasty, the brave Prince Jen embarks on a dangerous journey, bearing six unusual gifts. (**I:** 10–13)

Barron, T. A. *The Lost Years of Merlin*. Philomel, 1996. Merlin as a young boy searches for his identity. He has lost his memory and doesn't trust that the woman he is with is really his mother. His journey to discover his past introduces the reader to how Merlin gained magical sight and became a wizard. The story continues in *The Seven Songs of Merlin* (1997), *The Fires of Merlin* (1998), *The Mirror of Merlin* (1999) and concludes with *The Wings of Merlin* (2000). (**I:** 11–YA)

Chetwin, Grace. *Gom on Windy Mountain*. Lothrop, Lee & Shepard, 1986. When Gom's father, Stig, sends his strange wife away, Gom's mother leaves him a rune with magical powers. Chetwin's saga *Tales of Gom in the Legends of Ulm* includes *The Riddle and the Rune* (1987), *The Crystal Stair* (Bradbury, 1988), and *The Starstone* (1989). (**I:** 10–YA)

Cooper, Susan. *Over Sea, Under Stone*. Illustrated by Alan E. Cover. Atheneum, 1965. A search for King Arthur's grail begins this story of fighting evil and protecting Light. The series continues in *The Dark Is Rising* (1973), *Greenwitch*

(1974), *The Grey King* (1975), and *Silver on the Tree* (1977). (**I:** 10–13)

Divakaruni, Chitra Banerjee. *The Conch Bearer*. Roaring Brook, 2003. Twelve-year-old Anan's quest begins in modern day Calcutta and takes him on a dangerous journey through the Himalayas with his companion, Nisha, to return a magical conch to its rightful place. Book II of the Brotherhood of the Conch: *The Mirror of Fire and Dreaming* (2005). (**I:** 10–13)

Farmer, Nancy. *The Sea of Trolls*. Atheneum/Richard Jackson, 2004. In this epic adventure with roots based in Norse mythology, a bard's apprentice, Jack, and his little sister are kidnapped by Viking "berserkers" and he is sent on a quest across the dangerous Sea of Trolls to try and reverse a spell gone awry (**I:** 11–YA)

Jacques, Brian. *Redwall*. Philomel, 1987. Matthias leads the mice in protecting Redwall Abbey from Cluny the Scourge and the rats. The series includes *Mossflower* (1988), *Mattimeo* (1990), *Mariel of Redwall* (1991), *Salamandastron* (1993), *Martin the Warrior* (1994), *The Bellmaker* (1994), *Outcast of Redwall* (1996), *The Long Patrol* (1998), *Marlfox* (1999), *Legend of Luke* (2000). Additional titles appear at a rate of a new title a year. (**I:** 11–13)

Jones, Diana Wynne. *The Crown of Dalemark*. Greenwillow, 1993. This final book in a quartet about the mythical kingdom of Dalemark continues the story of Mitt, who is joined by Moril and Maewen in the quest to reunite Dalemark with Adon's gifts: the ring, the sword, and the cup. Earlier books in the quartet are *Cart and Cwidder* (1977), *Drowned Ammet* (1978), and *The Spellcoats* (1979). (**I:** 12–YA)

———. *Dogsbody*. Morrow, 1988. Sirius, the Dog Star, is reborn on Earth as a puppy and fulfills a mission to find the murder weapon of the stars. (**I:** YA)

———. *Howl's Moving Castle*. Greenwillow, 1986. When Sophie Halter is turned into an old woman by a jealous competitor, she finds refuge in the wizard Howl's mysterious moving castle. Related title: *Castle in the Air* (1990). (**I:** 9–12)

Le Guin, Ursula K. *A Wizard of Earthsea*. Illustrated by Ruth Robbins. Parnassus, 1968. This first book in a series describes how Ged studies wizardry, becomes a wizard, and confronts evil. Other books in the series are *Tombs of Atuan* (Atheneum, 1971/1985), *The Farthest Shore* (Atheneum, 1972/1985), *Tehanu* (Atheneum, 1990), *Tales from Earthsea* (Harcourt, 2001), and *The Other Wind* (Harcourt, 2001). (**I:** 13–YA)

Lewis, C. S. *The Lion, the Witch and the Wardrobe*. Illustrated by Pauline Baynes. Macmillan, 1950. Four children discover that they can go through the back of a wardrobe to enter the magical world of Narnia. There, they meet the lion Aslan, who is trying to free Narnia from the evil spell cast by the White Witch. The Narnia stories continue in *Prince Caspian* (1951), *The Voyage of the Dawn Treader* (1952), *The Silver Chair* (1953), *The Horse and His Boy* (1954), *The Magician's Nephew* (1955), and *The Last Battle* (1956). (**I:** 9–YA)

McKinley, Robin. *The Blue Sword*. Greenwillow, 1982. Princess Aerin's mysterious powers help her to slay dragons as she fights to save her kingdom. The prequel is *The Hero and the Crown* (1984). (**I:** 12–YA)

Pierce, Meredith Ann. *The Darkangel*. Little, Brown, 1982. This is the first book in Pierce's *Darkangel* trilogy. Other titles are *A Gathering of Gargoyles* (1984) and *The Pearl of the Soul of the World* (1990). (**I:** 13–YA)

———. *Dark Moon*. Joy Street, 1992. In Book 2 of the *Firebringer* trilogy, the protagonist, Jan, is prince of the unicorns, and he journeys to obtain fire from two-footed creatures to save the unicorns from enemies. Book 1 is *Birth of the Firebringer* (1985); Book 3 is *The Son of Summer Stars* (Little, Brown, 1996). (**I:** 13–YA)

Pierce, Tamora. *Wild Magic*. Atheneum, 1992. In this first book in a series called *The Immortals,* thirteen-year-old Daine faces battle with dreadful immortal creatures. (**I:** 12–YA)

Pullman, Philip. *The Golden Compass*. Knopf, 1998. In this first book of *His Dark Materials,* Lyra realizes that she must find a way to prevent kidnapped children from being victimized as scientific experiments. The second book is *The Subtle Knife* (1997); the trilogy ends with *The Amber Spyglass* (2000). (**I:** 11–YA)

Sutcliff, Rosemary. *The Sword and the Circle: King Arthur and the Knights of the Round Table*. Dutton, 1981. These stories about King Arthur, Merlin, and Sir Lancelot are mostly drawn from *Le Morte d'Arthur* by Sir Thomas Malory (1485). Sutcliff's rendition of the Arthurian trilogy continues with *The Light beyond the Forest: The Quest for the Holy Grail* (1980) and *The Road to Camlann* (1982). (**I:** 11–YA)

Tolkien, J. R. R. *The Fellowship of the Ring*. Houghton Mifflin, 1955/1967. This is the first part of the *Lord of the Rings* trilogy, in which Frodo Baggins inherits a magic ring from his Uncle Bilbo (hero of *The Hobbit*) and must eventually take the ring to Mount Doom, where it will be destroyed to help the good forces win against the Dark Lord. Other volumes in the trilogy are *The Two Towers* (1967) and *The Return of the King* (1967). (**I:** 12–YA)

———. *The Hobbit*. Houghton Mifflin, 1937. Bilbo Baggins, a peaceful Hobbit, is tricked by a wizard into going on a dangerous quest to retrieve stolen dwarf treasure from a dragon. The story of Middle Earth continues in the *Lord of the Rings* trilogy. (**I:** 11–YA)

Yolen, Jane. *Merlin and the Dragons*. Illustrated by Li Ming. Cobblehill/Dutton, 1995. Young King Arthur has troublesome dreams and visits Merlin, from whom he hears stories of Merlin's childhood. On hearing tales of dragons, King Vortigern, and Uther Pendragon, Arthur is reassured of his right to the crown. See also the Merlin trilogy: *Passager, Hobby* and *Merlin*. (**I:** 8–11)

Recommended Books: Science Fiction

Projecting Scientific Principles

Ames, Mildred. *Anna to the Infinite Power*. Macmillan, 1981. A twelve-year-old discovers that she is a clone. (**I:** 11–13)

Dickinson, Peter. *Eva*. Delacorte, 1989. Following an accident, a young girl's body is destroyed, but her brain survives and is transplanted into a chimpanzee's body. As she struggles to establish her identity, will she choose to live with her human family or with the chimps? (**I:** 12–YA)

Etchemendy, Nancy. *The Power of UN*. Front Street/Cricket, 2000. A mysterious old man presents Gib with an "unner"—a device that allows Gib to undo mistakes by going back in time. (**I:** 10–12)

Heinlein, Robert. *Farmer in the Sky*. Ballantine, 1950/1990. Bill and his father leave the overpopulated Earth and settle on Ganymede, the third moon of Jupiter, seeking better resources for living. (**I:** 12 and up)

———. *Rocket Ship Galileo*. Macmillan, 1948. Mystery surrounds efforts to build the first rocket ship. (**I:** 12–YA)

———. *Space Cadet*. Scribner, 1948/1987. The bravest and strongest become Space Cadets, the elite group who work to keep peace in the Solar System, and Matt must prove his worth before being accepted into the ranks. (**I:** 12 and up)

*Pinkney, Brian. *Cosmo and the Robot*. Greenwillow, 2000. In this story set on Mars, Cosmo uses his new "Super Solar System Utility Belt" to locate and repair his damaged robot, Rex. (**I:** 7–10)

Sleator, William. *The Duplicate*. Dutton, 1988. At first, sixteen-year-old David delights in having a clone, Duplicate A. Just when he realizes the complications it causes, Duplicate B arrives. (**I:** 11 and up)

Verne, Jules. *Twenty Thousand Leagues under the Sea*. Washington Square Press, 1976. An eccentric captain successfully makes an electric submarine. (**I:** YA)

Utopian and Dystopian Societies

Butler, Susan. *The Hermit Thrush Sings*. DK Ink, 1999. Leora lives the life of an outcast in her village because her webbed hand marks her as one of the "defectives." When she frees a baby birmba, Leora's life takes a sudden change of course, leading her past the locked gates of her village and into the "outside" forbidden world. (**I:** 12 and up)

Christopher, John. *When the Tripods Came*. Dutton, 1988. The Tripods arrive on Earth and brainwash Earthlings with hypnotic caps. *The White Mountains* series continues in *The White Mountains* (Macmillan, 1967), *The City of Gold and Lead* (1967), and *The Pool of Fire* (1968). (**I:** 10–13)

Farmer, Nancy. *The Ear, the Eye and the Arm*. Orchard, 1994. In Zimbabwe in the year 2194, three mutants—the Ear, the Eye, and the Arm—form a detective agency and are hired to find the kidnapped children of General Matsika. (**I:** 11–YA)

Haddix, Margaret Peterson. *Among the Hidden*. Simon, 1998. Set in a futuristic society that enforces a "two-child only" policy, additional children are kept hidden from the community until they begin to rebel against the repression and fight for their existence. *The Shadow Children* series continues in *Among the Imposters* (2001), *Among the Betrayed* (2002), *Among the*

Barons (2003), *Among the Brave* (2004), and *Among the Enemy* (2005). (**I:** 8–12)

Heinlein, Robert. *Citizen of the Galaxy*. Macmillan, 1957. A young boy is able to leave slavery to fulfill a mission and learns that there is more to the galaxy than he realized. (**I:** 11–13)

Hoover, H. M. *The Delikon*. Penguin, 1977. The Delikon is an alien race whose control of the Earth is destroyed by two children and their teacher. (**I:** 12–YA)

Hughes, Monica. *Invitation to the Game*. Simon & Schuster, 1990. Recent high school graduates, unemployed in an overpopulated world, find themselves playing a mysterious game of survival in a different world. (**I:** 11–YA)

———. *The Keeper of the Isis Light*. Macmillan, 1981. Olwen lives with a robot on a barren planet until another human lands. (**I:** 12–YA)

Lowry, Lois. *The Giver*. Houghton Mifflin, 1999. Knowledge is controlled in a futuristic society, and Jonah must grapple with the right to make choices when he begins to receive memories. Related books include *Gathering Blue* (2000) and *Messenger* (2003). (**I:** 11–YA)

Norton, Andre. *The Beast Master*. Ballantine, 1987. A Navajo, Hosteem Storm, survives the destruction of her planet and is able to settle on the planet of Arzor. (**I:** 12–YA)

Philbrick, Rodman. *The Last Book in the Universe*. Blue Sky Press/Scholastic, 2000. A mission takes four unlikely companions into dangerous territory where gangs rule a post-apocalyptic future that is nearly demolished by "The Big Shake." Meanwhile, genetically perfected humans live in the utopian world of Eden. (**I:** 12–YA)

Surviving Environmental Catastrophes

Lawrence, Louise. *Children of the Dust*. Harper, 1985. Earth is devastated by a nuclear war, and a small group of people in England struggle to survive through three generations in a new world where children are born with mutations. (**I:** 12–YA)

O'Brien, Robert. *Z for Zachariah*. Atheneum, 1975. Ann Burden believes that she is the only person left after a nuclear holocaust, until Mr. Loomis arrives. (**I:** 12–YA)

Sedgwick, Marcus. *Floodland*. Delacorte, 2001. Most of the world is underwater due to global warming and the polar regions melting. Ten-year-old Zoe is separated from her parents and must come up with a plan for rejoining them on the remaining mainland. (**I:** 10–13)

Walsh, Jill Paton. *The Green Book*. Illustrated by Lloyd Bloom. Farrar, 1982. A group of colonists try to grow food on a hostile new planet called Shine, when the dying planet of Earth can no longer sustain life. (**I:** 9–12)

Science Fantasies

Alcock, Vivien. *The Monster Garden*. Delacorte, 1988. Frankie plays with her father's genetic experiments and creates a monster. (**I:** 9–12)

Asimov, Janet, and Isaac Asimov. *Norby and the Invaders*. Walker, 1985. Norby is a robot who helps to solve a mystery on Earth. See also *Norby and the Oldest Dragon* (1990), in which Jeff faces a mysterious phenomenon on planet Jamyn, and *Norby and the Court Jester* (1991), in which Jeff and robot Norby travel to planet Izz. (**I:** 10–13)

Coville, Bruce. *My Teacher Is an Alien*. Pocket Books, 1991. A teacher comes from outer space to study the human brain, which is believed to be defective, since humans kill one another. This theme is carried on in a series of other titles, such as *Aliens Ate My Homework* (1993). (**I:** 8–11)

Danziger, Paula. *This Place Has No Atmosphere*. Dell, 1987. Humorous story of a move to the moon by reluctant Aurora and her family. (**I:** 11–YA)

Dickinson, Peter. *The Devil's Children*. Delacorte, 1986. Abandoned and homeless, Geoffrey and his sister Sally are among those in England who fear the impact of technology and instead recreate the culture of the Dark Age. *The Changes* trilogy continues in *Heartsease* (1969) and *The Weathermonger* (1968). (**I:** 12–YA)

Etra, Jonathan, and Stephanie Spinner. *Aliens for Lunch*. Illustrated by Steve Bjorkman. Random House, 1991. In this early chapter book, aliens appear out of the microwave, and desserts are at risk in the universe. See also *Aliens for Breakfast* (1988) and *Aliens for Dinner* (1994). (**I:** 7–9)

Gilmore, Kate. *The Exchange Student*. Houghton Mifflin, 1999. Fen is a seven-foot alien exchange student from a planet that is suffering from ecological disasters, including the death of animal life that would have kept the insect life under control. This loss leads to Fen's extraordinary interest in Earth's animals. (**I:** 12 and up)

Heinlein, Robert A. *Podkayne of Mars: Her Life and Times*. Baen, 1963/1995. Podkayne "Paddy" Fries, a Martian who aspires to be the first female starship captain, jumps at the chance to accompany her uncle on a trip to Earth by way of Venus, although she believes that Earth isn't fit for habitation. (**I:** 12 and up)

Howarth, Lesley. *Maphead*. Candlewick, 1994. In this coming-of-age story, a twelve-year-old who has the ability to flash on his head a map of any location returns to Earth with his alien father to meet his human mother. The sequel is *Maphead: The Return* (1997). (**I:** 11 and up)

Klause, Annette. *Alien Secrets*. Delacorte, 1993. Puck befriends a troubled alien while traveling to another planet. (**I:** 10–YA)

Lawrence, Louise. *Star Lord*. Harper & Row, 1978. Erlich crashes on the mountain Mawrrhyn, not unlike the mountains of Wales, and explains that he comes from eleven light years across space. A brother and sister protect him from the military on Earth until he escapes. (**I:** 12–YA)

L'Engle, Madeleine. *A Wrinkle in Time*. Farrar, 1962. Meg and Charles Wallace go to the planet Camazotz to search for their scientist father. The sequels are *A Wind in the Door* (1973) and *A Swiftly Tilting Planet* (1978). (**I:** 10–YA)

Lively, Penelope. *Uninvited Ghosts and Other Stories*. Dutton, 1985. This book of short stories features both science fiction and fantasy, including "A Martian Comes to Stay," "Uninvited Ghosts," and "A Flock of Gryphons." (**I:** 9–11)

Mahy, Margaret. *Raging Robots and Unruly Uncles*. Overlook, 1993. Two fathers find that robots behave worse than children. (**I:** 9–11)

*Marshall, (James) Edward. *Space Case*. Dial, 1980. An extraterrestrial creature is mistaken for a Halloween trick-or-treater. (**I:** P–8)

Norton, Andre. *The Time Traders*. Baen, 1958/2000. In this book in the *Time Travel* series, the protagonist, Ross Murdock, is saved from going to jail. Instead, he is sent across several periods of time and finds alien spaceships in the Bronze Age. (**I:** 12 and up)

O'Brien, Robert C. *Mrs. Frisby and the Rats of NIMH*. Illustrated by Zena Bernstein. Atheneum, 1971. Laboratory rats who have been made superintelligent escape and help a field mouse, Mrs. Frisby, who in turn helps them get away. O'Brien's daughter, Jane Leslie Conly, has written two sequels, illustrated by Leonard Lubin: *Racso and the Rats of NIMH* (Harper, 1986) and *R-T, Margaret, and the Rats of NIMH* (Harper, 1990). (**I:** 10–12)

Peck, Richard. *Lost in Cyberspace*. Dial, 1995. While working on a research paper, two sixth-grade boys discover time travel through a laptop computer. The sequel is *The Great Interactive Dream Machine* (1996). (**I:** 10–12)

Pinkwater, Daniel. *Fat Men from Space*. Dodd, Mead, 1977. The men from space are most interested in the Earth's junk food. (**I:** 8–11)

Sargent, Pamela. *Alien Child*. HarperCollins, 1988. Nita and Sven are raised by guardians in an alien society. They discover that they were left as embryos by their parents until a time when Earth's inhabitants could overcome the violent and destructive side of their nature. (**I:** YA)

Service, Pamela. *Stinker from Space*. Scribner's, 1988. Tsynq Yr, a secret agent from space, enters the body of a skunk. The story continues in *Stinker's Return* (1993). (**I:** 9–12)

Sleator, William. *The Boy Who Reversed Himself*. Puffin, 1998. Laura discovers that Omar has created mirror writing, and that he has reversed himself and can go into the fourth dimension. When Laura, a novice in four-space, tries to go there alone, she realizes that she doesn't know how to get back. (**I:** 11 and up)

———. *Interstellar Pig*. Dutton, 1984. As Barney plays a strange board game, it becomes real. (**I:** 11–YA)

———. *Strange Attractors*. Puffin, 1991. In this fictional depiction of chaos theory, "strange attractors" are beings from a parallel universe. Max finds himself having to protect a time travel device from its inventor and his alter ego from another time warp. (**I:** 11 and up)

Yolen, Jane. *Commander Toad and the Voyage Home*. Illustrated by Bruce Degen. Putnam, 1998. Commander Toad and his homesick crew aboard the Star Warts craft are heading home, but instead land on an uncharted planet. This is another volume in the easy reader series of humorous space travel stories. (**I:** 7–10)

*Yorinks, Arthur. *Company's Coming*. Crown, 1988. When a space ship lands, Shirley invites two visitors from outer space to dinner, to Moe's chagrin. (**I:** 6–8)

 *Resources*

Asimov, Isaac. *Asimov on Science Fiction*. Doubleday, 1981.

Barron, Neil, ed. *Anatomy of Wonder 4: A Critical Guide to Science Fiction*. R. R. Bowker, 1995.

———. *What Fantastic Fiction Do I Read Next? A Reader's Guide to Recent Fantasy, Horror, and Science Fiction*. Gale Research, 1997.

Cameron, Eleanor. *The Green and Burning Tree: On the Writing and Enjoyment of Children's Books*. Little, Brown, 1969.

Collier, Laurie, and Joyce Nakamura. *Major Authors and Illustrators for Children and Young Adults: A Selection of Sketches from Something about the Author*. Gale Research, 1993.

Cook, Elizabeth. *The Ordinary and the Fabulous: An Introduction to Myths, Legends, and Fairy Tales*. Cambridge Univ. Press, 1976.

Cooper, Susan. *Dreams and Wishes: Essays on Writing for Children*. McElderry, 1996.

Egoff, Sheila A. *Thursday's Child: Trends and Patterns in Contemporary Children's Literature*. American Library Association, 1981.

Greenlaw, M. Jean. "Fantasy." *Children's Books and Their Creators*. Ed. Anita Silvey. Houghton Mifflin, 1995.

Knight, Damon Francis. *In Search of Wonder: Essays on Modern Science Fiction*. Advent, 1967.

Le Guin, Ursula K. *The Language of the Night: Essays on Fantasy and Science Fiction*, rev. ed. HarperCollins, 1992.

Lynn, Ruth Nadelman. *Fantasy Literature for Children and Young Adults: A Comprehensive Guide*, 5th ed. Libraries Unlimited, 2005.

Sullivan, C. W. III, ed. *Science Fiction for Young Readers*. Greenwood, 1993.

Tymn, Marshall B., Kenneth J. Zahorski, and Robert H. Boyer. *Fantasy Literature: A Core Collection and Reference Guide*. R. R. Bowker, 1979.

 References

Adams, Douglas. *The Hitchhiker's Guide to The Galaxy*. Harmony, 1979.

Alexander, Lloyd. "High Fantasy and Heroic Romance." *The Horn Book 47* (December 1971): 577–594.

———. "Fantasy as Images: A Literary View." *Language Arts 55* (1978): 440–446.

———. "Future Conditional." *Children's Literature Quarterly 10.4* (Winter 1986): 164.

Andersen, Hans Christian. *The Princess and the Pea*. Houghton Mifflin, 1840/1979.

Anderson, M. T. *Feed*. Candlewick, 2002.

Asimov, Isaac, David C. Yeager, and Martin H. Greenberg (eds.). *Fantastic Reading: Stories and Activities for Grades 5–8*. Scott, Foresman, 1984.

Banks, Lynne Reid. *The Indian in the Cupboard*. Doubleday, 1985.

Cooper, Susan. "Escaping into Ourselves." *Celebrating Children's Books: Essays on Children's Literature in Honor of Zena Sutherland*. Ed. Betsy Hearne and Marily Kaye. Lothrop, Lee & Shepard, 1981, pp. 14–23.

Dahl, Roald. *Boy: Tales of a Childhood*. Farrar, 1984.

———. *George's Marvelous Medicine*. Illustrated by Quentin Blake. Knopf, 1982.

———. *The Witches*. Illustrated by Quentin Blake. Farrar, 1983.

de Brunhoff, Jean. *Babar*. Random House, 1937.

Dictionary of Literary Biography, vol. 52. Gale Research, 1986, p. 249.

Egoff, Sheila A. *Worlds Within: Children's Fantasy from the Middle Ages to Today*. American Library Association, 1988.

Elleman, Barbara. "Popular Reading-Time Fantasy Update." *Booklist* 81.19 (1985): 1407–1408.

Frye, Northrop. *The Educated Imagination*. Indiana Univ. Press, 1957.

Greenlaw, M. Jean. "Fantasy." *Children's Books and Their Creators*. Ed. Anita Silvey. Houghton Mifflin, 1995a.

———. "Science Fiction." *Children's Books and Their Creators*. Ed. Anita Silvey. Houghton Mifflin, 1995b.

———. "Science Fiction: Images of the Future, Shadows of the Past." *Top of the News 39* (1982): 64–71.

Heinlein, Robert A. *Starship Troopers*. Putnam, 1959.

Hesse, Karen. *Phoenix Rising*. Holt, 1994.

Hunter, Mollie. *Talent Is Not Enough: Mollie Hunter on Writing for Children*. Harper, 1976.

Jansson, Tove. *Finn Family Moomintroll*. Benn, 1950.

Kipling, Rudyard. *The Jungle Book*. Macmillan, 1894.

Lagerlöf, Selma. *The Wonderful Adventures of Nils*. Dover, 1906–07/1995.

L'Engle, Madeleine. *Meet the Austins*. Vanguard, 1960.

———. *A Ring of Endless Light*. Farrar, Straus, & Giroux, 1980.

Lofting, Hugh. *The Story of Doctor Dolittle*. Stokes, 1920.

Olendorf, D., and D. Telgen, eds. "Diana Wynne Jones." *Something about the Author,* vol. 70. Gale Research, 1993, pp. 116–117.

MacDonald, George. *At the Back of the North Wind*. Illustrated by Charles Mozley. Penguin, 1871/1985.

Major Authors and Illustrators for Children and Young Adults: A Selection of Sketches from Something About the Author. 2nd ed. Gale, 2002.

Shelley, Mary Wollstonecraft. *Frankenstein*. Dutton, 1818/1963.

Silvey, Anita. *Children's Books and Their Creators*. Houghton Mifflin, 1995.

Slobodkin, Louis. *The Space Ship under the Apple Tree*. Macmillan, 1952.

———. *The Three-Seated Space Ship: The Latest Model of the Space Ship under the Apple Tree*. Macmillan, 1962.

Traw, Rick. "Beware! Here There Be Beasties: Responding to Fundamentalist Censors." *The New Advocate 9.1* (1996): 35–56.

Tunnell, Michael O. "The Double-Edged Sword: Fantasy and Censorship." *Language Arts 71* (1994): 606–612.

Tymn, Marshall B., Kenneth J. Zahorski, and Robert H. Boyer. *Fantasy Literature: A Core Collection and Reference Guide.* R. R. Bowker, 1979.

Verne, Jules. *From the Earth to the Moon.* Hertzel, 1865.

Wells, H. G. *War of the Worlds.* Random House, 1898/1960.

Wiesner, David. *The Three Pigs.* Clarion, 2001.

————. *Tuesday.* Clarion, 1991.

Williams, Jay. *Danny Dunn and the Anti-Gravity Paint.* McGraw, 1956.

Yolen, Jane. *Touch Magic: Fantasy, Faerie and Folklore in the Literature of Childhood,* 2nd ed. August House, 2000.

9

Contemporary Realistic Fiction

What Is Contemporary Realistic Fiction?

The Value of Contemporary Realistic Fiction

The Evolution of Realistic Fiction

The Nineteenth Century • The Twentieth Century • From New Realism to Diverse Perspectives

Categories of Contemporary Realistic Fiction

ISSUE TO CONSIDER: Are Contemporary Books Too Realistic? • Books about Self-Discovery and Growing Up • Books about Families and Family Diversity • Books about Interpersonal Relations • Books about School • Books about Sports • Books about Nature and Animals • Books about Adventure and Survival • Books about Romance and Sexuality • Books about Mental, Physical, Emotional, and Other Challenges • Books about Moral Dilemmas and Moral Responsibility • Books about Social Diversity and Society

• Books about Aging, Death, and Dying • Mystery and Suspense Books • Humorous Books • Series Books • Books with Multicultural and International Themes • Books That Are Magical Realism

How Contemporary Realistic Fiction Works

Setting • Plot • Theme • Character • Point of View

Criteria for Evaluating Contemporary Realistic Fiction

Major Writers of Contemporary Realistic Fiction and Their Works

Avi • Judy Blume • Beverly Cleary • E. L. Konigsburg • Phyllis Reynolds Naylor • Katherine Paterson • **ASK THE AUTHOR:** Sharon Creech • Gary Paulsen • Cynthia Rylant • Cynthia Voigt • Vera Williams • Jacqueline Woodson • Charlotte Zolotow

---

"Your room's a firetrap. It will be as neat as a pin when we're done. You'll like it. You'll see." The tone of Henry's voice seemed to say, I know everything there is to know about anything that matters.

But Fanny did not like it. Her room looked empty, less comfortable, sad even.

—*from* Protecting Marie
by Kevin Henkes

Go to the Assignments and Activities section of Chapter 9 in the MyEducationKit and complete the activities. As you work through the activities and answer the accompanying questions, consider the importance of evaluating contemporary realistic fiction for children.

What Is Contemporary Realistic Fiction?

All fiction bears some relation to life as we know it. Kenneth Grahame's fanciful animal story *The Wind in the Willows* tells us much about friendship. C. S. Lewis's allegorical fantasy *The Lion, the Witch and the Wardrobe* warns that youthful selfishness can lead to corruption. Nonetheless, the trappings of such books are fanciful: We wouldn't think of learning about the driving habits of toads from reading *The Wind in the Willows*, nor would we expect to find a trapdoor in the back of our closet after reading *The Lion, the Witch and the Wardrobe* (although some of us might check, just to be sure!). Realistic fiction, however, is a different story. Although the particular characters and plots are made up, the trappings of realistic novels are drawn from the world as it is.

In the above passage from *Protecting Marie*, the father tries to help clean Fanny's room, imposing his standards of neatness on his daughter; meanwhile, she struggles with her feelings on the matter. What is amazing about this passage, and many others like it, is that Henkes masterfully depicts emotions, thoughts, and behaviors that ring true to many preteen girls. This story raises many issues: a father trying to deal with his own aging and career direction, a daughter dealing with her own adolescence, relationships among family members. But the multifaceted, complex nature of this book allows it to rise above those "problem novels" that feel didactic or have a bibliotherapeutic intent. This is a book about relationships and self-identity, in which issues are explored within the context of the family.

Contemporary realistic fiction, then, brings the same moral challenges as other types of fiction. But it presents these challenges in a here-and-now setting and in a way that says "Hey—this is happening. You or somebody near you could be going through these very experiences."

Contemporary realistic fiction is derived from actual circumstances, with realistic settings and characters who face problems and opportunities that are within the range of what is possible in real life. It differs from historical fiction in that it is set in contemporary times; the stories could take place in the world as we know it today. In addition, the events portrayed in realistic fiction raise moral questions that a reader might face in real life. Characters in realistic fiction for children usually have certain characteristics:

- They resemble real people.
- They live in a place that is or could be real.
- They participate in a plausible, if not probable, series of events.
- They are presented with a dilemma that is of interest to children.
- They discover a realistic solution.

Realistic fiction is not fantasy. There are no animals that talk; no anthropomorphized machines; no ghosts, giants, or supernatural happenings. Of course, works of realistic fiction do not literally recount real life, either. Those types of works are considered biographies or informational books. Some realistic fiction may seem improbable—but there are no details included that are impossible. A work may be so far-fetched as to be entirely unlikely, but the lack of totally impossible happenings makes it remain a type of realistic fiction called magical realism.

Go to the Extension Activities section of Chapter 9 in the MyEducationKit for your book and complete activity #1 to select a contemporary realistic fiction book and explain your choice to parents.

The Value of Contemporary Realistic Fiction

Of all the genres of children's literature, realistic fiction is the one that most closely approaches the reality of children's own lives. Reading realistic fiction can benefit children in several ways:

- They may come to feel that they are not alone.
- They may learn to reflect on the choices in their own lives.

- They may develop empathy for other people.
- They may see life experiences beyond their own.
- They may take a humorous, enjoyable look at life.

When child readers recognize something in a story that is similar to their own feelings or thoughts, they realize they are not alone. Realistic fiction helps readers to empathize with other people.

Realistic fiction enables readers to see beyond the limitations of their own experience. In Frances Temple's ***Tonight, by Sea***, Paulie and her family are so harassed by government-backed thugs that they take their chances and escape in a small boat in an attempt to cross the ocean. That boat eventually brings Paulie to the United States. Although most young readers are unlikely to get to know any of the many thousands of real "boat people" whom they may have heard about on the news, they get to know Paulie's story. They know what happened to her and how she felt about it. They know why she sailed in that boat. They believe that in her place, they might have made the same choice. This book extends readers' knowledge of life experiences beyond their own.

Realistic fiction, then, offers readers the opportunity to see themselves reflected in the literature, as well as the opportunity to see the lives of people with very different lifestyles. It offers readers realistic views of the world in which they live.

Teaching Idea 9.1
Real Life versus Fiction

Ask students in grades 3 through 6 to record in a diary all the events that happen to them in a single day—just the facts, without embellishment. Then have them exchange diaries with a friend and write up the friend's account as if it were a chapter in a work of realistic fiction. Encourage students to embellish the story with dialogue, details about setting, and clearly described characters. Afterward, ask the students to compare the two versions. What was added to make the fictionalized version? What was left out? How did the dramatic contour (that is, the pattern of building suspense and its resolution) of the diary version compare with that of the fictionalized version? What was made clearer about the events of the day when they were fictionalized? What was distorted?

The Evolution of Realistic Fiction

Realistic fiction has been available for children for a long time. The first title read by children that might be called realistic fiction was Daniel Defoe's ***Robinson Crusoe***, published in 1719. Although written for the general reader, it became associated with children in the mid-eighteenth century, when the philosopher Jean Jacques Rousseau recommended it for children. Rousseau's recommendation coincided with a transition publishers had already begun to make—away from merely producing books for children focused on dying and repentance and toward publishing new forms of writing, including realistic fiction.

The Nineteenth Century

The first significant works of realistic fiction written expressly for children appeared in the mid-nineteenth century in England. Hannah More began writing fictionalized religious lessons that appealed to children more than the common didactic tracts. Anna Laetitia Barbauld wrote realistic nature stories at the same time.

Meanwhile, in the United States, there was a movement away from instructional and sectarian books and toward books that could be called entertaining realistic fiction. The adventure story came into being with the works of James Fenimore Cooper. His ***The Last of the Mohicans***, set on the frontier of New York State and published in 1826, is considered the first American novel. Louisa May Alcott's ***Little Women*** appeared in 1868. Alcott's work was the first to present the dilemma facing young women: how to balance interests inside and outside of the home.

For boys, Horatio Alger published over one hundred books beginning in 1867 with ***Ragged Dick***. These books provided strong fictional images of the American dream of lowly urban heroes getting rich through determination, cleverness, and impressing powerful people.

Mark Twain's ***The Adventures of Tom Sawyer*** and ***The Adventures of Huckleberry Finn***, published in the late nineteenth century, are considered by some to be two of the best American novels of any period (but current views point to the books as representative of the negative race portrayals of the time). Both are quintessentially American novels, complete with a strong sense of place—the Mississippi River towns, issues of race, and the conflict between over-pious religion and the boisterous spirits of real people. Like other fiction books of the period, Twain's works exalted "boys will be boys" naughtiness, but restricted girls to straitlaced behavior.

The first of the great realistic fiction horse stories for children, Anna Sewell's **Black Beauty**, was published in 1877 and paved the way for the continuing popularity of realistic animal stories. Although **Black Beauty** is still read today, new editions have expurgated the elements of racism found in the original.

Toward the end of the nineteenth century, shortly after the Indian Wars drew to a close and the great cattle drives ended, many adventurers from the West, such as Buffalo Bill Cody, went East to glamorize the cowboy's and cowgirl's life in "Wild West Shows." The mass-produced dime novel appeared at the same time, and scores of these were written about the wild West.

The end of the nineteenth century saw a resurgence of sentimentalism toward the child. Frances Hodgson Burnett published **Little Lord Fauntleroy** in 1886; its somewhat saccharine plot involving a good and gentle boy who loves everyone and solves everyone's problems was a runaway success. After she moved to the United States, Burnett wrote **The Secret Garden**, a book with a more believable theme of children's redemptive effects on each other. This book is still popular with children.

The Twentieth Century

At the dawn of the twentieth century, writers continued to romanticize the innocence and beauty of children. The domestic novel flourished and was epitomized by Eleanor Potter's **Pollyanna**, who gains power over difficulties by following her father's advice to face each hardship by finding something to be glad about. "Glad" clubs formed all over the United States—their members emulating Pollyanna's unquenchably optimistic view of the world.

Perhaps the most influential development in realistic fiction for children in all of the twentieth century came when Edward Stratemeyer began a "fiction factory" in 1905. Stratemeyer generated brief plot summaries and handed them to hack writers, who completed the books under fictitious names. Hundreds of series books about the Rover Boys, the Hardy Boys, Tom Swift, the Bobbsey Twins, and others were products of Stratemeyer's fertile imagination, if not his typewriter.

Stratemeyer produced thirteen hundred of his plot summaries by the time he died in 1930, and at that point, his daughter Harriet Stratemeyer Adams began churning out the Nancy Drew series under the pen name Carolyn Keene. She is said to have written three hundred titles in the series, and two hundred million copies of them had been sold by the time she died in 1982, at age 89.

The Hardy Boys and Nancy Drew books are still updated and marketed to new generations. But today, series realistic fiction books come from the Babysitters Club, Encyclopedia Brown, Marvin Redpost, Sammy Keyes, and others, which crowd the shelves of bookstores and worry some teachers, parents, and librarians because of their predictability and scant literary quality.

Between the two world wars, a host of now-classic writers and illustrators began their work. Robert McCloskey wrote and illustrated nature stories for younger children and humorous ones for older children, the most famous of which are **Make Way for Ducklings** and **Homer Price**. A large crop of still-popular realistic fiction was published for the mid-elementary school reader, such as **The Boxcar Children** by Gertrude Warner and **The Moffats** by Eleanor Estes, both of which were followed by more books about the same characters.

From New Realism to Diverse Perspectives

Until the eve of World War II, most of the protagonists in children's realistic fiction were white and middle class. Then Florence Crannell Means, herself white, wrote some books about children of color: **Shuttered Windows**, about an African American girl in an all-white school, and **The Moved Outers**, about the World War II internment of Japanese Americans.

In 1945, Jesse Jasper Jackson published *Call Me Charley*, the first children's book by an African American to openly introduce the subject of racism. The character Charley was the only person of color in an all-white school.

Sexuality appeared in books for girls before the subject was addressed for boys. *Seventeenth Summer* by Maureen Daly introduced awakening sexuality and the teenage romance novel. The book was enormously popular through the 1960s. In the 1970s, Judy Blume's *Are You There, God? It's Me, Margaret* and *Forever* brought loud protests from censors because of their open discussion of sexuality. John Donovan's *I'll Get There, It Better Be Worth the Trip* tells of two thirteen-year-old boys, Davy and Altschuler, who suddenly find themselves facing the question of homosexuality when they exchange a kiss.

In the 1970s, the unvarnished picture of children's life that was emerging in realistic fiction was described as "New Realism" (Root, 1977) New Realism looked at the downside of life: children suffering from poverty, racism, sexism, war, economic upheavals, and parental irresponsibility. Characters often faced unsolvable problems or moral dilemmas. New Realism focused to a large degree on adolescents as a distinct social group. Writing about problems in what became known as "problem novels" became a way of describing life.

Since then, more writers of different races, nationalities, income groups, and sexual preferences have appeared on the children's book scene, writing about life as they know it. Their themes go beyond New Realism, in that differences and hardships may be background factors in works that focus on the development of character or the pursuit of a worthwhile life. Contemporary authors of the young adult novel such as Laurie Halse Anderson, M. T. Anderson, Sonya Sones, Ellen Wittlinger, and Jacqueline Woodson, sympathetically depict the culture of children and adolescents and their social and personal problems, as well as the new possibilities they face. Yet as Lambert (2008) comments, there is a continued need to expand the definition and representation of diverse representation of family compositions.

The broader range of topics in contemporary realistic fiction certainly expands young readers' awareness of the varieties of possible experience. But it also gives rise to disagreements between those who would shelter children from such material and those who believe that it is healthy for young people to explore difficult real-life issues in books. In this chapter, we introduce literature that portrays perspectives that reflect diversity of all kinds—not only ethnic diversity, but also diversity based on gender, religion, socioeconomic background, political affiliation, or differing abilities, to name a few. If we are to work toward a world that believes in social justice, then all types of diversity must be considered and addressed.

Categories of Contemporary Realistic Fiction

Over the generations, when children have been asked what topics they enjoy in realistic fiction, their preferences have remained fairly constant. Barbara Elleman's (1986) retrospective bibliographies in *Booklist*, a publication of the American Library Association, are arranged by genres most requested by children. The most popular categories of realistic fiction are humor, mystery, and stories about survival. Hurley (1970) found in a summary of research that "there is an amazing consistency in patterns of reading interest, beginning in preschool" (p. 96).

It is surprising how many of these topics writers can get into one book. *Yolonda's Genius* by Carol Fenner, a 1996 Newbery Honor Book, works in the topics of school and friendship—as well as physical size and body image, music, drugs, single-parent families, and life in the city versus life in the suburbs. In *Dancing Carl*, author Gary Paulsen includes sports (ice skating), school, and the meaning of love. Betsy Byars has humor, school, romance, writing, and moving away in *The Burning Questions of Bingo Brown*.

It's clear that good books are not easily put into tidy categories. Rather, they transcend multiple categories as they address the complexities of realistic portrayals of life. Some books sit on the fence between realistic fiction and fantasy. What separates them is the level to which "possibility" is present, despite unlikeliness, and the level to which a story is entirely

Issue to Consider

Are Contemporary Books Too Realistic?

"**N**ew" or not, realism is still a dominant element in fiction for children. Truly disturbing social problems are depicted even in books that win critical acclaim. For example, of the four 1996 Newbery Honor Books, three are works of realistic fiction. Of these, one, **What Jamie Saw** (1995) by Carolyn Coman, is about child abuse; another, **Yolonda's Genius** (1995) by Carol Fenner, portrays drug abuse, racism, and obesity. The winner of the Newbery Medal, Karen Cushman's **The Midwife's Apprentice** (1995), is a work of historical fiction, but its protagonist is a homeless girl who sleeps in dung heaps and never experiences home or family. The winning books in the previous few years aren't much different. You might wonder whether such books are robbing children of the joy of reading about happy childhood. And is the continuing popularity of "gentler" books, such as Laura Ingalls Wilder's **Little House** series, or **The Boxcar Children,** or the many titles by E. Nesbit, an indication that many children, parents, and teachers do not appreciate the stronger contemporary fare?

On the other hand, Katherine Paterson was probably correct when she wrote, "Children who have never felt the sting of prejudice, who laugh freely and bring their parents joy are a tiny minority of all the children in the world" (1993, p. 67). Surely, as teachers and parents, we have some obligation to expose children to the realities of life as other people live it.

What do you think? Would you advocate choosing works of contemporary realism that includes tough issues for reading in school?

---

improbable, despite the fact that there is nothing impossible. We refer to these books as "magical realism."

The following categories are broad ones, but they are the topics of the books that children, teachers, and parents regularly seek out.

Read the interview where Lois Lowry discusses realistic fiction and her Anastasia series by going to the Conversations section of Chapter 9 in the MyEducationKit for your book.

Books about Self-Discovery and Growing Up

Many works of realistic fiction enable children to explore their own thoughts, feelings, and predispositions and to compare their inner experiences with those of others. Good books about self-discovery are even available for preschoolers. *"More More More" Said the Baby*, a Caldecott Honor Book by Vera Williams, promotes self-discovery with three stories in which a baby is the center of play and is given loving attention by a father, a grandmother, and a mother. Bernard Waber created the now-classic *Ira Sleeps Over*, in which he answered unasked questions of young children, such as "Am I the only person who sleeps with a teddy?" (Ira, of course, discovers that he is not.)

Another way to discover one's self is to find one's own talents and passions. There are scores of titles about becoming good at sports (these will be treated in a later section), but *The Facts and Fictions of Minna Pratt*, by Patricia MacLachlan, is one of a few books that feature a child developing abilities in another area—in this case, playing the cello. Zilpha Keatley Snyder's main character in *Libby on Wednesday* wins a writing contest and ends up belonging to a writers' club, despite her aversion to being social. Libby learns to develop her writing—and her socialization and interpersonal relationships as well. In Beverly Cleary's *Dear Mr. Henshaw*, Leigh Botts is assigned by teachers to write to an author, and soon he is writing for writing's sake. Nonetheless, given the importance of children's developing a sense of industry and competence during their early school years (an issue discussed in Chapter 1), it is lamentable that there are not more books celebrating children's development of their various talents.

Having navigated the sometimes arduous path to maturity, many adults have an impulse to share what they have learned with young people. So they write. For their part, children often say that they "can't wait" to grow up. So they enjoy reading about the processes of maturing and learning. No wonder growing up is a popular theme in children's literature. *Baseball in April and Other Stories*, by Gary Soto, depicts Mexican American young people on both sides of the mysterious threshold of adolescence, who are striving to get by in a California neighborhood where people make do with high hopes and limited means.

Overcoming self-doubt is one of the aspects of growing up. Written almost seventy years ago, but still read today, *The Hundred Dresses*, by Eleanor Estes, is a now-classic story about overcoming the cruelty of peer prejudice. Wanda Petronski is belittled by Peggy and Maddie for wearing the same dress every day, even though she claims to have one hundred dresses at home. When Wanda's family moves away because of the prejudices they face, Wanda mails Peggy and Maddie drawings of themselves, each pictured in one of the hundred dresses she has designed. Maddie's and Peggy's consciences are pricked by Wanda's responding to malevolence with kindness. In Gina Willner-Pardo's *Daphne Eloise Slater, Who's Tall for Her Age*, Daphne Eloise bears the name-calling of classmate Leonard, who insists on calling her a giraffe. In the end, Daphne Eloise comes to the realization that she can't change Leonard, but she can control her reaction to his behavior and what she says to him. All in all, she realizes that she is a "pretty nice kid."

In Gennifer Choldenko's *Notes from a Liar and Her Dog*, Antonia lies so frequently that she has to make sure that she keeps her stories straight. Certain that she is adopted, she writes to her "real parents" in a notebook that contains all the things she wants to tell them someday when she is reunited with them. Antonia values only her dog, Pistachio, and her best friend Harrison as "real" in her life. Gradually, she comes to the realization and acceptance that more is true in her life than her dog and best friend, and she begins to understand what her own identity really is.

Sometimes, when life seems to be going "your way," a change in circumstances forces you to grow up. In Katherine Hannigan's first novel, *Ida B*, fourth-grader Ida B is an indulged only child; in addition, home schooling has allowed her to march to her own drummer at her own pace for her elementary years. When her mother's cancer changes their family circumstances, she must adjust to public schooling and the sale of part of their family property, resulting in sharing the land and trees she considered her own. Ida B must learn to deal with her anger and feelings of betrayal as she has lessons on growing up imposed on her.

ILLUSTRATION 9.1 The third in the Breadwinner cycle of books by Deborah Ellis, Shauzia longs to leave the Afghan refugee camp and seek a new home. (Cover illustration from *Mud City*, text copyright © 2003 by Deborah Ellis. Cover illustration by Pascal Milelli. First published in Canada by Groundwood Books Ltd. Reproduced by permission of the publisher.)

There are many series books about self-discovery and growing up. Perhaps this is because once an author has created a strong, memorable character, readers want to know how that character handles other issues of growing up. Characters such as Betsy Byars's Bingo Brown, Beverly Cleary's Ramona Quimby, Paula Danziger's Amber Brown, Lois Lowry's Anastasia Krupnik, Phyllis Reynolds Naylor's Alice, and Sara Pennypacker's Clementine also allow readers to enjoy growing up along with their "friends" in books. These books usually offer humorous yet serious looks at daily aspects of growing up.

Books about Families and Family Diversity

Family stories are important in realistic fiction because families form a child's first identity and first set of relationships, helping define who the child is in relation to the world. These stories take as many twists and turns as do families in the real world. In addition to nuclear families, extended families, alternative family structures, and new ways of considering what constitutes "family" are commonplace in today's literature. In *Shiloh*, Phyllis Reynolds Naylor has created a stable nuclear family in which each member cares about the others. Marty expresses that sense of belonging when he says, "You ask me the best place to live, I'd say right where we are, a little four-room house with hills on three sides." Yet contemporary stories like twelve-year-old Annabel's in *The Steps* show that having multiple families filled with a variety of step-siblings and half-siblings can offer a different, yet very real sense of "family."

Humorous accounts of growing up and dealing with family relationships are often found in books offered in series, such as *Ramona Quimby, Age 8*, one of the books in the long-running series of Ramona, Beezus, and Henry books created by Beverly Cleary. Sibling relations are at the center of *Tales of a Fourth Grade Nothing*, by Judy Blume, which features Peter Hatcher and his exasperating but endearing little brother Fudge. Phyllis Reynolds Naylor's series chronicles Alice's experiences as she grows up from a young child into her teen years; in *Alice in April*, Alice demands more appreciation from her father and brother.

In a different kind of family, a single mom and her daughter lose everything in a fire in Vera Williams's picture book *A Chair for My Mother*. The family works together to save enough money to buy a soft, comfortable chair—one in which mom and daughter can snuggle together. Getting acquainted with past generations of her African American family is important to Emily in *Toning the Sweep*, by Angela Johnson. Emily videotapes the storytelling that goes on while she helps her grandmother prepare for chemotherapy and eventual death. In Hillary McKay's *Saffy's Angel*, thirteen-year-old Saffron realizes that she is adopted and tries to make sense of her personal history by putting together the pieces of her background that she and her delightfully eccentric siblings remember.

Parents who are incapable of taking care of their children force us to reconsider the definition of family. In Janet Taylor Lisle's *Afternoon of the Elves*, Hillary is enchanted by Sara-Kate's imagination and talent for creating a tiny world for "elves" in her junky backyard. What Hillary begins to realize is that Sara-Kate does not have adults who take care of her. Is her father really in jail? What's wrong with the mother who is hidden from the public by Sara-Kate? In Barbara O'Connor's *Moonpie and Ivy*, twelve-year-old Pearl feels rejected as her mother abandons her at the house of an aunt she hardly knew she had in the backwoods of Georgia; this is contrasted by the loving parental relationship that her Aunt Ivy has with the neighbor boy, Moonpie. Although Pearl spends her summer staring down the road and waiting for her mother's car to reappear, she learns some family history and some reasons for her mother's erratic behavior. Difficult situations like this one have no easy resolution, but readers find hope for a future despite the circumstances.

Loss of family and seeking a place in the world are themes in Jacqueline Woodson's *Locomotion*. Lonnie is placed in a foster home while his little sister is adopted, so in *Peace, Locomotion*, he writes a series of letters to her that he plans to give to her some day so she will know what he had been thinking about during their years of separation.

Divorce, alcoholism, child abuse, and same-sex relationships—all nearly absent from books written in previous generations—are now widely treated in children's realistic fiction. The stress between family members of different generations in their extended family disturbs the youngest child in Sharon Bell Mathis's novel *The Hundred Penny Box*. In *From the Notebooks of Melanin Sun*, Jacqueline Woodson treats very sensitively the issue of a young teenage boy's discovery that his mother is a lesbian. And in the picture book *Mini Mia and Her Darling Uncle*, Mini Mia acts out to try to keep the attention of her beloved Uncle Tommy when his friend Fergus appears on the scene.

Books about Interpersonal Relations

Some useful works of realistic fiction revolve around the problems of getting along with others. In this area, a work of fiction can do what real life cannot: It allows us to experience the perspectives of more than one character. Charlotte Zolotow is a master at authoring picture books about relationships. *The Hating Book*, *The Quarreling Book*, and others of her works are about learning to get along with others. In Patricia McKissack's picture book, *The Honest-to-Goodness Truth*, Libby vows to tell only the truth after she is punished by her mother for telling a lie. When she tells truths about holes in socks, a classmate not doing homework, or someone forgetting a line in a play, Libby learns that some truths do not have to be told and that there is an art to successful communication in relationships.

The protagonist of *Harriet the Spy*, by Louise Fitzhugh, believes that she can become a writer by spying on her friends and neighbors and writing up her unflattering observations. However, after her friends see what she has written about them, she discovers that she needs friends more than she needs the aloofness she had associated with being a writer who exposed the private sides of people's lives.

In *Crazy Lady!*, a Newbery Honor Book by Jane Leslie Conly, Vernon's mother has died, and his kindly but barely literate father is unable to assist Vernon in his troubled efforts to read. Vernon meets Maxine, the neighborhood alcoholic (commonly called the "Crazy Lady"), and her mentally challenged, mute son. As Vernon reaches out to help Maxine and her son Ronald, the relationship helps Vernon to come to terms with his learning disability as well as the loss of his mother.

In Chris Crutcher's ***Ironman***, Beau's training for the triathlon is interrupted when he is mandated to attend anger management class in his high school. Beau had been using his sports training to take his mind off emotional and relationship issues; he must now take time from his training to deal with these serious issues. His relationship with his father has long been a troubled one, but upon hearing that his coach might be gay, Beau suddenly turns his back on the man who has always been a staunch supporter and confidant.

Martha is the protagonist in Kevin Henkes's ***Olive's Ocean***. When her classmate, Olive, is killed in a car accident, Martha becomes aware of the paths they had unknowingly shared: Olive, like Martha, wanted to be a writer, she wanted to see the ocean (where Martha would spend her summer), and she wanted to be Martha's friend. Martha thinks of Olive throughout the summer, finds out more about who she was, and finally says goodbye to her at the end of summer. Martha's relationship with her grandmother offers her security and love through these difficulties. She worries about "copying" her father's attempt to be a writer. Martha also encounters a "first love"—or her belief that it is—only to be humiliated. These many complex and varied relationships all help reveal the character of Martha.

Books about School

The school day is a source of constant drama for young people. School is their stage, their proving ground, their source of social contacts. There are many good works of realistic fiction that explore the pushes and tugs of schooling.

Young children just entering school worry about what the experience will be like. Amy Schwartz's ***Annabelle Swift, Kindergartner*** helps to answer that question for children. Annabelle's sister informs her about what she needs to know to begin kindergarten. Annabelle, however, prefers to make her own way. Schwartz creates a believable kindergarten setting in this reassuring book. Sometimes it is the parent who worries about what the school experience will be like—as is the case in David Shannon's ***David Goes to School***. The noncompliant but endearing David is now at school, engaging in antics for which the teacher must constantly reprimand him. Some children will find a kindred spirit in David and feel reassured when David wins praise for a job well done. A playground bully is cause for fearfulness in Alexis O'Neill's ***The Recess Queen***. But when new girl Katie Sue arrives and doesn't know the "playground rules" imposed on everyone by Jean, she exuberantly invites Mean Jean to join her in jumping rope.

No one has succeeded better at helping children see the teacher's point of view than Harry Allard in ***Miss Nelson Is Missing!*** and ***Miss Nelson Is Back*** (both illustrated by James Marshall). In the first, the children's bad behavior comes abruptly to an end when kind and gentle Miss Nelson appears to go on leave, and is replaced by a terrible disciplinarian, Miss Viola Swamp.

There are many books in series about school. Most are lighthearted and humorous looks at daily events and dilemmas faced at various grade levels. Among those just beginning to read chapter books, Suzy Kline's Horrible Harry series is popular. For example, in ***Horrible Harry and the Dungeon***, students in Room 2B wonder whether Harry will be new teacher Mr. Skooghammer's first "victim" of the dungeon—the suspension room in the basement. Likewise, Patricia Reilly Giff's Polk Street School kids provide book after book of school stories. In ***Look Out, Washington, D.C.!***, they take a field trip to Washington, D.C. In the series on eight-year-old Jake Drake, he must learn to deal with a bully in his fourth grade classroom in ***Jake Drake, Bully Buster***. The pitfalls of life as a middle schooler is at the core of experiences described in Jeff Kinney's ***Diary of a Wimpy Kid*** and its sequels. Begun as a Web cartoon, the series humorously depicts Greg Heffley's diary entries through narrative text as well as cartoon images.

Andrew Clements has written numerous school stories that are humorously told while dealing with important issues. In ***The Landry News***, fifth-grader Clara Landry decides to exercise freedom of speech and writes an editorial about a formerly creative teacher who

has burned out to the point of merely passing out worksheets to students. Similarly, Avi's *Nothing but the Truth* explores issues of freedom of speech in the classroom.

Johanna Hurwitz addresses a common peer group problem in *Class Clown*, in which third-grader Lucas Cott decides to turn over a new leaf, only to discover that changing one's role in a group turns out to be more difficult than he thought. Among the other books by Hurwitz is *Class President*, in which Julio hides his own ambitions in order to campaign for a classmate to win the nomination for class president. This book also deals with a culturally specific issue—how to pronounce a name. The book opens with a chapter entitled, "Who is who-lio?" Julio's Latino teacher asks him whether he would like his name pronounced the Spanish way with a /h/ sound for the beginning of his name, or the /j/ sound like his previous teachers have pronounced it. Julio thinks about how his family pronounces his name, and how all his classmates have pronounced his name over the years. He decides on the Spanish origin of his name. At first, the classmates take humor at lunchtime by pronouncing everything that begins with a "j" as an "h"—for example, jello is called *hello*. Julio takes the teasing good-naturedly, and soon everyone settles down to using the Spanish pronunciation of his name. Because this happens at the very beginning of the book, readers who may not be aware of the difference in pronunciation are also tuned in to how to pronounce his name.

School experience is problematic and even traumatic for some. In Susan Shreve's *The Flunking of Joshua T. Bates*, Joshua is devastated to learn that he must repeat the third grade. He faces taunting from former classmates, but a sympathetic teacher helps him find his strengths. In Elizabeth Levy's *Keep Ms. Sugarman in the Fourth Grade*, Jackie chains herself to a desk in protest when Ms. Sugarman is promoted to principal, because Ms. Sugarman was the first teacher to help her overcome self-doubt and reduce her visits to the principal's office. The teacher compares Jackie's efforts to great social protests in history, and Jackie learns to value her independence of thought rather than condemn herself for it.

At other times, school or a school assignment is merely the impetus for sounding an alarm that makes people aware of problems stemming from self and family. A school assignment to keep a journal becomes a mechanism through which characters reveal some harsh truths about their home lives. In Margaret Peterson Haddix's *Don't You Dare Read This, Mrs. Dunphrey*, Tish finds her journal to be a safe place in which to spill her concerns about how to care for herself and her younger brother since her mother abandoned them.

Books about Sports

Sports enthusiasts enjoy reading play-by-play accounts of athletic contests. *Shoot for the Hoop*, by Matt Christopher, satisfies this craving. Beyond merely describing basketball action, however, the author creates a hero who not only is a good basketball player but also struggles with diabetes. In *Penalty Shot*, Jeff's skill on the ice is secondary to his struggles off the ice. Who is sabotaging his effort to improve his grades? And who is sending (in his name) threatening notes to his best friend? Matt Christopher writes voluminously—he has published over fifty sports titles—and is the focus of a fan club. Good-quality sports books such as Christopher's go beyond simply describing games and offer imaginative twists, well-developed characters, and a wide range of settings. Alfred Slote is another author who has written numerous popular sports stories for elementary school-age students. In *Hang Tough, Paul Mather*, Paul deals with his incurable blood disease by involving himself in baseball. In *Finding Buck McHenry*, a boy tries to enlist the school janitor as the Little League team coach, because he believes the janitor is a former famous baseball player from the Negro League.

There's a Girl in My Hammerlock, by Jerry Spinelli, describes a wrestling team that comes unglued when a girl joins the team. When Maisie doesn't make the cheerleading team, she decides to join the wrestling team to have an excuse to be closer to Eric, but eventually she develops a real interest in the sport itself and realizes that she truly enjoys wrestling. Avi's *S.O.R. Losers*, in which an unlikely soccer team strives for a winless season, is a hilarious antidote to the "winning is everything" ethos of too many school sports teams.

Robert Lipsyte has written over a dozen excellent sports books for older readers. *The Contender* tells of Alfred's desire to be a boxer; his coach teaches him the difference between being a contender (one who feels the effort is its own reward) and being a champion (one who stands by truth and principles). Alfred becomes both. Chris Lynch has written excellent sports stories about teenage boys, in which sports serve as a metaphor for the development of the characters. Like his earlier book *Iceman*, which is about hockey, *Slot Machine* has plenty of play-by-play narrative to please the enthusiast, as well as an excellent thematic thread on friendship and wrestling with one's own identity—or finding one's "slot," as the story has it. Bruce Brooks's *The Moves Make the Man*, a story in which basketball provides metaphors for living in the world, was named a Newbery Honor Book.

Books about Nature and Animals

Authors who write animal and nature stories for children provide information about the natural world; they also help children build a commitment to the living things with which they share the world. Often, animals and nature serve to teach children important lessons about their own lives.

Many realistic fiction picture books for younger children explore the multifaceted wonders of nature. In Denise Fleming's *In the Small, Small Pond*, a child watches the variety of pond life in amazement. Lois Ehlert's *Red Leaf, Yellow Leaf* has a child planting and caring for a sugar maple tree. The informational aspect of the text adds much to the story. In the Caldecott-winning book *The Snowy Day*, by Ezra Jack Keats, Peter enjoys a snowy day in a variety of ways: making tracks, smacking snow off branches, making snow angels, throwing snowballs, and even taking one home. In *Owl Moon*, another story that takes place in the snow, John Schoenherr illustrates a night on which a father and a child go owling. Jane Yolen's text describes the setting vividly so that readers can vicariously experience the cold night and the awe of seeing the great owl. *Come a Tide*, written by George Ella Lyon and illustrated by Stephen Gammell, shows an Appalachian community undergoing a storm and flooding.

Beginning chapter books about animals make this topic accessible to those who are just starting to read independently. In Jessie Haas' *Runaway Radish*, a young girl learns from her pony—just the right size for her to ride—named Radish. In Star Livingstone's *Harley*, a llama turns out to be better at herding sheep than training to be a pack animal.

Many children, especially girls, go through a horse story phase. Why? Perhaps the association with horses gives girls a sense of freedom and power, as Poll (1961) suggests. Horse stories by Marguerite Henry and Walter Farley are perennial favorites. Both wrote about horses and other animals for over thirty years. Henry's *Misty of Chincoteague* and Farley's series of books about *The Black Stallion* remain justifiably popular. Jessie Haas continues to write horse stories for readers; her stories, such as *Beware the Mare*, are set in rural Vermont.

A good number of Gary Paulsen's books celebrate animal life and the wilderness, especially in the cold northern lands. His *Dogsong* takes readers on a dogsled ride with Inuit boy Russell Susskit, introducing them to the interactions of dogs and humans. Another book in which Paulsen explores sled dogs is *Woodsong*, which describes the Iditarod race.

That animals provide companionship for humans is well accepted. But beyond that, animals offer life lessons for humans. That point is illuminated in a series of short stories found in *Every Living Thing* by Cynthia Rylant. In Kate DiCamillo's *Because of Winn-Dixie*, Opal adopts a stray dog from the local grocery store and names him after the store, Winn-Dixie. The friendly dog helps Opal adjust to her new community and also aids her in facing the reality of who she is and understanding that the mother who abandoned her seven years ago isn't likely to ever return.

Books about Adventure and Survival

Adventure stories are marked by fast-paced, exciting—even thrilling—action in which the main character perseveres through many struggles and overcomes the odds. Often, the adventure goes so far as to be considered a survival story. There are numerous

Top Shelf 9.2

School Stories with an International Perspective

*The Color of Home by Mary Hoffman, Illustrated by Karin Littlewood

*Elizabeti's School by Stephanie Stuve-Bodeen, Illustrated by Christy Hale

*My Name is Yoon by Helen Recorvits, Illustrated by Gabi Swiatkowska

*Someone Says by Carole Lexa Schaefer, Illustrated by Pierr Morgan

*The Upside Down Boy by Juan Felipe Herrera, Illustrated by Elizabeth Gómez

Teaching Idea 9.2

Anthropomorphic Animal Fantasies or Realistic Fiction?

Provide students with a range of picture books in which animal characters take on human characteristics. Have students study them to find out why books that are characterized as fantasy have qualities that make them seem like realistic fiction. For example, what qualities in Kevin Henkes's picture books about anthropomorphic mice make the mice appear to resonate with human characteristics? What qualities in *Charlotte's Web* make the situations and solutions appear to be like those that humans face? In what ways do they continue to behave as farm animals?

ways of considering what constitutes survival. It could be surviving tough experiences such as peer taunting and tormenting because a child does not fit in for some reason. It could also be surviving life circumstances. But most often when we think of survival, we think of surviving life-threatening situations.

In some books for children, nature is presented as a harsh adversary; in others, nature helps characters to survive. In many books, nature is portrayed as both harsh and helpful. In Gary Paulsen's Newbery Honor Book *Hatchet*, Brian finds himself alone in the wilderness after an airplane crash, and he must come to understand nature in order to find food and shelter to stay alive. In *Brian's Winter*, a companion book offering an alternative ending, the "what if" is explored: What if Brian had not been rescued and had been forced to try to survive through winter in the Canadian wilderness? In Will Hobbs's *Far North*, Gabe and his Dene Indian roommate, Raymond, find themselves survivors of a plane crash. They make it through the winter in the Canadian wilderness with the guidance of a Dene elder who also survived the crash.

In *Julie of the Wolves*, a Newbery Medal winner by Jean Craighead George, Julie escapes from an arranged marriage in her Inuit village, surviving in the desolate Alaskan tundra by living with wolves. To be accepted by the wolves, she observes and mimics the intricacies of their behavior.

The sibling protagonists in *Toughboy and Sister*, by Kirkpatrick Hill, are eleven- and eight-year-old Athabascans who are stranded in a Yukon River camp after their father dies of alcoholism. The children struggle to find food and shelter until they are rescued by a neighbor, Natasha. In the sequel, *Winter Camp*, Natasha takes the children camping "like in the old days." A sled driver is injured, Natasha has to leave to get help, and the children must run the camp, all the time wishing for modern conveniences as nature threatens them with cruel cold, unsafe ice, and potentially dangerous fire.

Books about Romance and Sexuality

Works of realistic fiction that focus on romance cover topics that run the gamut from girl-boy friendships to explicit aspects of sexuality to the true meaning of love. It is often said that the experience of falling in love is indescribable, but several authors of realistic fiction have succeeded in finding apt words for intense feelings. Going to a movie with a boy and receiving a first kiss are explored in Sharon Creech's *Absolutely Normal Chaos*. *Anastasia at This Address*, one of a series of books by Lois Lowry about Anastasia's growing up, lets the reader share the heroine's experience of falling in love as she answers a personals ad.

In *The Exiles in Love*, the Conroy sisters all succumb to what their Grandmother calls the "family failing": That is, they fall in love easily. In humorously written text, Hilary McKay explores how four teenaged sisters deal with their emotions as well as the practicalities of relationships.

In addition to discussing teens' growing interest in romance and their emerging sexuality, Young Adult novels, which are beyond the scope of this book, deal more directly with issues of sexuality. These issues range from dealing with sexual behavior and its consequences, such as pregnancy, to the identity of sexual orientation.

Listen to Jack Gantos discuss writing authentic, honest fiction by going to the Conversations section of Chapter 9 in the MyEducationKit for your book.

Books about Mental, Physical, Emotional, and Other Challenges

People in real life can flourish in spite of challenging mental, physical, and emotional conditions. The limiting factors they face are not just the challenging conditions, but also their own sense of the possible or reduced expectations of those around them. The trick for authors is to create characters who can achieve success without having the disability seem to give them special powers. Books that depict this diverse perspective are also discussed in Chapter 4.

In 1971, author Betsy Byars won a Newbery Medal for *The Summer of the Swans*, in which the protagonist Sara has a brother who is mentally retarded. Sara feels awkward and self-conscious about both her brother's condition and just about everything else in her life. When her brother is lost, Sara struggles to determine what really counts about herself and her relationships with others.

For younger children, *Be Good to Eddie Lee* by Violet Fleming is a picture book that has a character with Down syndrome. Eddie Lee is able to see flowers and frog's eggs better than other children.

Emotional trauma can result in challenges that significantly alter life. In E. L. Konigsburg's *Silent to the Bone*, the story opens with thirteen-year-old Branwell dialing 911 to report that his baby sister is having difficulty breathing, but he is so traumatized that he cannot speak. He is sent to live in a juvenile behavioral center, and it is through his best friend's efforts that communication is restored. At first, it is merely blinking an eye in response to a question, then pointing a finger at cards when cued. Branwell must work through his emotional trauma before he can reestablish communication with the world.

In Jack Gantos's *Joey Pigza Swallowed the Key*, the world is seen from the perspective of a third-grade boy who is "out of control"—he has attention deficit/hyperactivity disorder. As adults, we may know what it's like to be around a child with ADHD, but how does it feel to be the child with ADHD or the classmates of the child? In one sequel, *Joey Pigza Out of Control*, Joey comes to know his previously absent father as he finds out the effects of being on and off his "meds," not just for school, but generally in day-to-day living. In *I Am Not Joey Pigza*, he comes to value his own identity despite his parents' hope that a new name will lead to a new identity.

In Cynthia Lord's *Rules*, twelve-year-old Catherine has many rules to live by, and she finds them necessary for living with an autistic younger brother. But a friendship with a nonverbal paraplegic helps her to realize that "normal" is not easily definable nor attainable, and perhaps living by rules is not as important as she had believed.

Books about Moral Dilemmas and Moral Responsibility

Many works of realistic fiction for young people pose moral dilemmas like those confronting people in the real world. Some are personal dilemmas that characters cannot avoid; others have to do with social issues in which characters can choose to become involved. The word "dilemma" refers to the difficulty of making choices; often, there is no clear right or wrong—just a decision with consequences.

A good example of an unavoidable personal dilemma is found in Sharon Bell Mathis's Newbery Honor Book *The Hundred Penny Box*, in which Michael, the young protagonist, is caught in the middle of a conflict between his mother and a one-hundred-year-old aunt: Does he obey his mother's rules, or does he protect Aunt Dew's memories and dignity?

A story about a character caught up in a moral dilemma of his own making is Avi's *Nothing but the Truth: A Documentary Novel*, in which high school student Phillip Malloy falsely reports that his English teacher refused to let him sing the national anthem. The book has no narrator but rather uses diaries, newspaper clippings, memos, letters, dialogues, and radio talk-show scripts to recount the disastrous consequences of a distortion of the truth.

In *Shiloh*, Marty's desire for a dog begins the cycle of moral decision making. The dog he finds, Shiloh, belongs to someone who abuses him. Which is morally worse: Marty's "stealing" a dog that he knows has an owner (by hiding it and lying to his parents) or returning the dog to Judd Travers, who will continue to physically abuse it? Moral questions are posed throughout the book, and readers have opportunities to discuss them as they explore their own beliefs.

In Jacqueline Woodson's *Hush*, thirteen-year-old Toswiah's father is the one with the moral dilemma, and his family lives with his decision: Knowing he is receiving death threats for speaking up, is he willing to testify that a fellow police officer did not shoot and kill a boy in self-defense? This issue is complicated by race: Both Toswiah's father and the boy who was killed are African American and the officer on trial for the shooting is not. The family

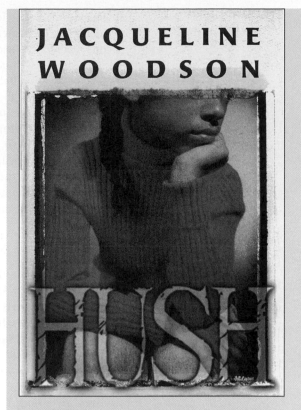

ILLUSTRATION 9.2 Standing up to tell the truth means that a police officer and his family must leave their lives behind as they enter the Witness Protection Program. (Cover from *Hush* by Jacqueline Woodson, copyright © 2001 by Barry David Marcus, jacket art. Used by permission of G.P. Putnam's Sons, A Division of Penguin Young Readers Group, A Member of Penguin Group (USA) Inc., 345 Hudson Street, New York, NY 10014. All rights reserved.)

ILLUSTRATION 9.3 Yolanda plans various schemes to get her younger brother Andrew recognized for his musical genius. (Book cover illustration, *Yolonda's Genius* by Carol Fenner, illustrations by Stephen Marchesi, 1995. Reprinted by permission of Stephen Marchesi.)

Top Shelf 9.3

Books About Aging and Intergenerational Relationships

The Hundred Penny Box by Sharon Bell Mathis

Loop the Loop by Barbara Dugan, Illustrated by James Stevenson

Singing with Momma Lou by Linda Jacobs Altman, Illustrated by Larry Johnson

Toning the Sweep by Angela Johnson

The Wednesday Surprise by Eve Bunting, Illustrated by Donald Carrick

Wilfrid Gordon McDonald Partridge by Mem Fox, Illustrated by Julie Vivas

must immediately leave town under the Witness Protection Plan, and take on entirely new identities. The father can never be a police officer again, and each family member deals with this incredible sense of identity loss in different ways.

Carl Hiassen takes on the tension between monetary greed at the cost of environmental conservation in both *Hoot!* and *Flush*. In *Hoot!*, an unlikely alliance forms between a new kid in town, the tough girl who faces up to the bully attacking the new kid, and a mysterious homeless runaway boy. They work together to save the endangered baby owls when the prospective ground breaking of a franchise restaurant threatens to tear up the home of the owls. In *Flush*, a father's arrest for sinking a casino boat suspected of dumping raw sewage into the ocean leads to his two children working to find a way to prove the casino's responsibility in order to vindicate their father, but also to stop the polluting of the waters of the Florida Keys. In both books, the characters walk the fine line of moral decision making in the face of the law and making moral choices about what to do.

Books about Social Diversity and Society

Getting along in different types of communities is the subject of many books written for young people. In *Amber Was Brave, Essie Was Smart*, written and illustrated by Vera B. Williams, two girls deal with their lives in poverty and their feelings of loneliness as their mother works late hours and their father is in jail for forging checks. A very different look at communities, *Smoky Night* by Eve Bunting, is based on the Los Angeles riots of 1993. The neighborhood conflicts raise questions of race and class, as the people consider basic human relations within their community. In Michael J. Rosen's *ChaseR*, fourteen-year-old Chase moves from the mid-sized city of Columbus, Ohio to a rural area about an hour away. He contrasts his life in the city and the interactions with people there to his new life in a rural area. Chase tells the story entirely through a series of e-mails (complete with emoticons and pictures he creates with computer symbols), and he begins by describing the lack of quick and easy access to Internet service. His surprise at the number of cicadas turns to annoyance. His uneasiness escalates and turns into hostility about guns and the hunting that people around him engage in. His teen perceptions of the differences in the two communities he has lived in are shared through the e-mails he sends to his friends back in the city and to his brother.

In *Junebug*, Alice Mead depicts the life of a boy who dreams of a big future but fears, as his tenth birthday approaches, that the local gangs and drug dealers will be pressuring him to join them. It is just this situation that worries Yolonda's mother in Carol Fenner's *Yolonda's Genius*. She moves from the inner city to the suburbs, looking for safety. However, Yolonda soon realizes that there are different types of danger to fear in different communities.

Homelessness is a subject in increasing numbers of children's books. Eve Bunting's picture book *Fly Away Home*, illustrated by Ronald Himler, depicts a boy and his father living at an airport, constantly moving around and trying to avoid being noticed by officials there. Although with current security measures, it would be difficult, yet not impossible, to live at an airport, the story could very well have taken place in other public places. Paula Fox's *Monkey Island* is a haunting story of an eleven-year-old boy, Clay, who lives in a hotel room with his mother until she leaves and never comes back. He is befriended by two homeless men, who help him survive on the streets. Frances Temple's *Grab Hands and Run* was fictionalized from a true account of the flight of the surviving members of a Salvadoran family from their homeland and their search for a permanent home in the North after the father has been assassinated.

Books about Aging, Death, and Dying

Realistic fiction examines many aspects of death and dying: the natural process of aging, caring for the sick, grieving for lost loved ones, and the stages that lead from grief to acceptance. The death of an animal or pet is often a child's first experience with death, although books for children also describe the deaths of peers, siblings, parents, and grandparents. The books in this section focus on relationships between the living and those who are dying or have died and are not merely about death.

Perhaps the death of a pet is a child's first introduction to such a loss. In Judith Viorst's *The Tenth Good Thing about Barney*, the protagonist's mother suggests that he think of ten good things about the cat Barney, for the family to recite at its funeral.

A Taste of Blackberries is Doris Buchanan Smith's sensitive contribution to understanding the stages of grief over the loss of a friend. When Jamie dies of an allergic reaction to a bee sting, his best friend must face the fact that Jamie will never return. The Newbery winner *Bridge to Terabithia*, by Katherine Paterson, gives the reader a rich character in Leslie, who will be remembered long after her accidental death.

The aging and death of a grandparent is a theme that allows authors to write of death as a natural phenomenon associated with age. *Blackberries in the Dark*, by Mavis Jukes, shows a child and her grandmother going through rituals as a way of remembering the grandfather. In *Sun & Spoon* by Kevin Henkes, ten-year-old Spoon searches for a tangible object by which to remember his grandmother—perhaps one of the sun-themed objects she collected. Likewise, in *The Hundred Penny Box*, Michael intervenes when his mother tries to discard his great-great aunt's box of pennies she had collected, because he values the stories each penny tells.

The death of parents is most difficult for children to endure. In Cynthia Rylant's *Missing May*, the aunt who has raised Summer dies, but the loss is doubly hard because Summer has already lost her mother and father. For younger children, Lucille Clifton's *Everett Anderson's Goodbye* is a poetic account of the grief felt on the death of a father. In *The Eagle Kite*, Paula Fox describes Liam's anger, which arises not only because his father died of AIDS but also because he had not known of his father's homosexuality. Nikki Grimes shows two siblings dealing with the death of their brother in *What is Goodbye?* Jesse and Jerilyn have opposite ways of reacting to the loss, and after a year, the family realizes that despite their missing family member who can never be replaced, they can still be a whole family.

The treatment of death and dying varies across cultures, but there are obvious similarities. Three sixth-grade boys in Japan become curious about death in *The Friends*, by Kazumi Yumoto, and stake out an old man's house so that they may better understand what dying and death are about. However, it is their eventual friendship with the older man and their engagement in his life that enables the boys to understand death more fully.

Aging leads to death eventually. However, aging occurs years prior to death in many cases, and in other cases, age is not a factor in death. Many books include healthy portrayals of aging people. In Barbara Dugan's *Loop the Loop*, elderly Mrs. Simpson is wheelchair bound, and she knows the coolest yo-yo tricks. When she has to move into a nursing home after breaking her hip, her young friend Anne shares the yo-yo tricks she has managed to learn. This delightful story of intergenerational friendship shows a physically aging person with a sharp mind, sharing a wonderful relationship with an elementary school-aged girl. In *Wilfrid Gordon McDonald Partridge*, author Mem Fox tells about a little boy who goes in search of Miss Nancy's memory because he overhears his parents saying she's lost it. He asks the residents of the "old people's home" and gets many answers, all metaphors he interprets in his own way. His obvious affinity for Miss Nancy and his empathy for her dilemma shows another example of a good intergenerational friendship.

Mystery and Suspense Books

Mysteries have long been favorite recreational reading for adults, ever since Edgar Allan Poe published "The Murders in the Rue Morgue" in 1841. Mysteries enjoy wide appeal, especially among readers who enjoy the challenge of following the author's hints and diversions as they seek a solution. In an article entitled "The

Technology in Practice 9.1

The International Children's Digital Library

The International Children's Digital Library's Web site, launched in November 2002, offers digitized children's picture books from around the world. Their goal is to house approximately 10,000 books from 100 cultures. The University of Maryland's Human-Computer Interaction Lab and the Internet Archive, a non-profit organization based in San Francisco, are responsible for the conception, design, data entry, and management. Children contributed ideas and feedback during the early stages of development by indicating the types of books they wanted, how they wanted to search for them, and how they wanted to read them. One nine-year-old commented that "the book is never checked out" and others remarked that there is access to books beyond what your local library has physically available.

The books available span quite a range: from classics with expired copyrights and now in public domain to newer books still under copyright but donated to the project by various publishers. Books from various countries have been donated by international libraries and organizations. Despite some questions that are still being addressed regarding focus, design, use, and accessibility, the site is ready for those who have cable modem or DSL connections.

Links: International Children's Digital Library

<http://en.childrenslibrary.org>

Scene of the Crime," Jeanette Larson (2008) cites the value of mysteries in that they "encourage readers to define problems, sequence events, look for clues, assess evidence, and reach conclusions—all valuable skills for research and learning."

Mystery books for young readers have as much variety as adult mysteries. In ***The Westing Game***, a Newbery Honor Book by Ellen Raskin, the characters are involved in a battle of wits to inherit a million dollars. In her Newbery-winning adventure/mystery ***From the Mixed-up Files of Mrs. Basil E. Frankweiler***, E. L. Konigsburg writes about a set of young protagonists in New York City who run away from home. Because of their familiarity with the Metropolitan Museum of Art, they figure out how to spend nights there without being detected. In a mystery set across the Atlantic Ocean, two siblings search for their missing cousin who goes up the famous ferris wheel but does not come down in Siobhan Dowd's ***The London Eye Mystery***.

In ***The Secret of Gumbo Grove***, author Eleanora Tate incorporates African American community history, which the protagonist delves into to solve a mystery. Virginia Hamilton does much the same thing in ***The House of Dies Drear***, which uses the history of the Underground Railroad and a huge old house with secret passages as background for a mystery plot.

Many mysteries can be found in series. David Adler has penned a series of mysteries, one of which is ***Cam Jansen and Ghostly Mystery***. Cam uses her intellect and her photographic memory to solve the mystery of a robbery at the ticket booth while they are waiting in line to buy tickets for a rock concert. A "Young Cam Jansen" series introduces younger readers to mystery stories that are easy to read. The books in the Encyclopedia Brown series by Donald Sobol call for readers to get involved in solving cases along with the son of a police chief. Each book contains several short mysteries, and the solutions are in the back of the book.

Humorous Books

In much realistic fiction, humorous incidents serve as a release from the more serious topical themes explored by the author. Many of the books previously discussed in this chapter fit into this category.

Authors who write humorous books for children are careful not to poke fun at the natural surprises children experience—and, often, their ineptness—as they learn about life. The challenge for authors of realistic fiction is to help children empathize with others and see the humor in the plight of characters whose first stabs at life's opportunities fail. Leigh Botts's letters in ***Dear Mr. Henshaw***, by Beverly Cleary, are a good example. The letters begin when Leigh is in the second grade, so his growth up to sixth grade is clear, and it is okay to laugh about what he didn't know earlier.

The first book in which author Megan McDonald introduces readers to Judy is in ***Judy Moody (Was in a Mood. Not a Good Mood. A Bad Mood.)***. In this book, we see Judy in quite a range of moods in many different situations—all of which will feel familiar to readers. As a third grader, she deals with school situations such as not wanting to cooperate with the teacher and being asked to return in a better mood the next day. At home, she deals with her little brother named Stink, who overfeeds her "favorite pet" Venus flytrap. And with her peers, she deals with a toad that pees by creating a Toad Pee Club.

Judy Blume's stories about sibling rivalry and parental approval are favorites among children—***Tales of a Fourth Grade Nothing*** and ***Superfudge***, in particular. In the former, Peter Hatcher is annoyed at his little brother's antics, but they are funny to the reader. Peter's unnecessary concern about his own status in the family will ring true to many young readers. When Fudge swallows Peter's pet turtle, readers can feel Peter's pain and laugh at the same time.

Jamie Gilson is a popular writer of humorous stories. In ***Hello, My Name Is Scrambled Eggs***, Tuan Nguyen's family moves in with the Trumbles. Harvey Trumble's attempt to teach Tuan the English language and American ways provides laughs for American readers. Gilson pokes enlightening fun at vegetarian cooking, the captivating influence of television, and horoscopes in ***Can't Catch Me, I'm the Gingerbread Man***. Endangered Animal Month sets

Richard and Ben in competition with Dawn Marie and troublesome Patrick over the real story about bats in *It Goes Eeeeeeeeeeeee!*

Adults often either function as the butt of the humor or buffer the pain of characters who are being laughed at. In Paula Danziger's *Make Like a Tree and Leave*, the humor includes puns, such as the title, and bathroom humor. For several pages, the characters argue about who is responsible for putting on a new toilet paper roll. Mrs. Martin tells her children about "making out" when she was young, and the children are horrified at the thought—and at the thought that Mr. and Mrs. Martin still make out—giving expression to the exact thoughts of many a child. Danziger has published a long list of amusing books for young and older children.

Beverly Cleary's characters, including Ramona and Henry Huggins, are strong, admirable children who can carry on in spite of embarrassing mistakes and goofs. Readers laugh at their misunderstandings. Throughout *Ramona the Brave*, Ramona assumes that her teacher thinks she is a nuisance. The misconception motivates her to compensate and try to win approval, and all the time the reader is enjoying her mistake.

Annie Barrows and Sophie Blackall have created the series of stories about two seemingly opposite people who become friends: Ivy, who seems to always be reading, and Bean, who loves to play tricks and is lively. Together, they humorously turn everyday routines into fun adventures, and seal their friendship with acts of loyalty.

Sheila Greenwald's heroine, Rosy Cole, provides amusing adventures for younger readers. In *Rosy Cole: She Walks in Beauty*, Rosy tries to become a model, giving the author the opportunity to point out some of the absurdities of the modeling profession. Many series books about growing up include much humor.

Series Books

Series books are popular with children because they take the guesswork out of choosing something to read. Their very sameness, however, means that these books do less to expand a child's awareness of and appreciation for literature than one-of-a-kind books. Nonetheless, parents and teachers, eager to foster the reading habit, often forgive the shortcomings of series books in the hope that once children are "hooked on books," they may move beyond series books to more substantial reading. Teachers are also aware that reading series books may be something of a status symbol in elementary school.

Series books have been available to children for over one hundred years, at least since the time of the fiction-writing syndicate of Edward Stratemeyer, the prolific producer of the books about Tom Swift, the Bobbsey Twins, the Hardy Boys, and Nancy Drew. Nowadays, series books are more popular than ever, and virtually all publishers welcome authors who can and will write engaging books in series.

Just as with any other books, the quality of series books varies. The worst are plagued by thin description, flat characters, and plots that pull readers from one suspenseful moment to another. The best—those by authors who have established themselves for their individual books—can be funny, upbeat, and full of delightful language play. Fourth-grader Amber Brown appears in a series of funny stories by Paula Danziger. Phyllis Reynolds Naylor writes a series about Alice, a thirteen-year-old whose mother's death means that she must become the "woman of the house" for her father and much older brother. Johanna Hurwitz's Aldo finds just about everything "interesting." In *Aldo Applesauce*, his becoming a vegetarian earns him various nicknames. In *Aldo Peanut Butter*, his puppies are named Peanut and Butter. All of these series books use good language, engaging themes, and well-rounded characters to give substance to the plots.

Books with Multicultural and International Themes

Books that portray the real-life experiences of people growing up in parallel cultures, outside the mainstream cultures of North America, have become more plentiful in the last few decades. In Cynthia Leitich-Smith's *Jingle Dancer*, Jenna lives in a contemporary suburban world, yet cherishes her heritage. When she finds that she needs jingles in order to participate

ILLUSTRATION 9.4 A Chinese American girl is delighted to find that some families today enjoy Chinese food for this traditionally "American" holiday. ("Book Cover" from *Apple Pie Fourth of July* by Janet S. Wong, illustrations copyright © 2002 by Margaret Chodos-Irvine, reprinted by permission of Houghton Mifflin Harcourt Publishing Company.)

as a dancer in the next Pow Wow, she figures out a way to get a few from each relative so nobody's dress will lose its voice. In the picture book, *Apple Pie, 4th of July*, Janet Wong tells the story of a young girl who wishes her parents would understand that nobody will come to their Chinese restaurant today because it is the Fourth of July—the day for apple pie. To her surprise, when the parade ends, people come in—and they do want Chinese food! This book expands the definition of what constitutes the way people celebrate "American" celebrations. In *Child of the Owl* and later in *Thief of Hearts*, Laurence Yep explores how Chinese American girls struggle to come to terms with their own identities. The title character in *Julie*, by Jean Craighead George, is an Alaskan Inuit who is faced with a difficult choice as she straddles two cultures; she learns to accommodate both old and new cultures.

Books set outside North America cover the range of themes we have been discussing. Many highlight foreign settings, however, with the clear intention of expanding readers' awareness of life in other places. A moving book written by Pegi Deitz Shea (with illustrations by Anita Riggio and stitched in traditional Hmong pa'ndau by You Yang), *The Whispering Cloth* shows in pictures and text the pathos of leaving one's native land.

Frances Temple published her first book in 1992 and died in 1995, but in her brief career she broke new ground with her realistic works on political themes, set in other countries. Two of her books, set in Haiti, explore young people's struggles against political oppression: *Taste of Salt: A Story of Modern Haiti* won the Jane Addams Peace Award, and *Tonight, by Sea* won the Américas Award.

Overcoming prejudice is a major theme in multicultural books. The eight children in *Mayfield Crossing*, by Vaunda Micheaux Nelson, are excited about two things: baseball and going to a new, integrated school in the fall. The children at the new school, however, are unwilling to accept African American children on their ball team. The possibility of changing racist traditions opens up when blond and friendly Ivy accepts Meg's invitation to become the ninth player on the Mayfield Crossing team.

For many more authors and titles of multicultural books and international books and a discussion of issues related to books from parallel cultures, see Chapters 4 and 5.

Go to the Extension Activities section of Chapter 9 in the MyEducationKit for your book and complete activity #2 to show how a contemporary realistic fiction book can function as a mirror to students' lives.

Books That Are Magical Realism

Many books use the device of exaggeration or an enchanted realism. In these books, there is nothing impossible that takes place in the physical world, but many aspects of the situation make it highly improbable. Perhaps one of the most pervasive characteristics is the lack of "real world" emphasis given to the gravity of some situations and the dry humor of taking such enormity into stride. Polly Horvath is a master of this style of writing. In *Everything on a Waffle*, eleven-year-old Primrose Squarp's father disappears at sea during a storm, and her mother sets off in a small skiff to search for him; when neither returns, the townspeople assume that Primrose must now be an orphan. In this humorous story, quirky yet endearing characters engage in illogical situations with matter-of-fact explanations.

In Louis Sachar's *Holes*, Stanley Yelnats is sent to a juvenile detention camp in the desert of Texas for a crime he did not commit. Each day, the boys are commanded to dig holes that are five feet wide and five feet deep in order to "build character." From the wildly unlikely circumstances to the acceptance of the family curse of bad luck, readers root for Stanley's luck to change.

The concept of magical realism is being debated by many critics: Is it a type of fantasy? Is it a type of reality? Most agree that magical realism blurs the lines between the two, and how much a book leans toward fantasy or reality defines where it belongs. Many of these books are characterized by nonsense and absurdity. What makes a magical realism book move toward fantasy in our definition is the inclusion of things that could NEVER happen.

For example, in Polly Horvath's ***The Pepins and Their Problems***, a cow produces lemonade. However, we acknowledge that in the art world and in adult literature from various countries, magical elements in predominantly realistic stories are recognized and accepted as magical realism.

How Contemporary Realistic Fiction Works

The term "realistic fiction" is something of a paradox. A work of fiction is contrived, yet readers are meant to believe that a work of realistic fiction is real, at least while they are engrossed in reading it. But this paradox contains some other seeming contradictions as well. Exploring two of them will clarify how realistic fiction "works."

Setting

In Kate DiCamillo's ***Because of Winn-Dixie***, the story is set in the South. Details about the setting help readers to get a clear picture of how the setting influences the way the story moves along. Even the title's reference to Winn-Dixie may prove to be confusing for children who do not realize it is the name of a southern supermarket chain.

Plot

An effective work of realistic fiction makes us believe that what it describes might really have happened. Yet because it is fiction, the work is organized into a plot—and that makes it quite different from real life, in which the lion's share of our days is full of meaningless details: minutes spent waiting for traffic lights to change, minutes spent searching for lost papers or misplaced keys, minutes spent half-listening to uninteresting conversations. In contrast, just about every detail in a work of fiction is meaningful. Why aren't we aware of the difference right off?

Although realistic fiction does not resemble day-to-day reality, it does convey the ways in which we represent that reality to ourselves and others. Fiction is not like life—but it is like our stories of our lives. By taking events from life and giving them meaning, fiction shows us how we find significance and purpose in our lives.

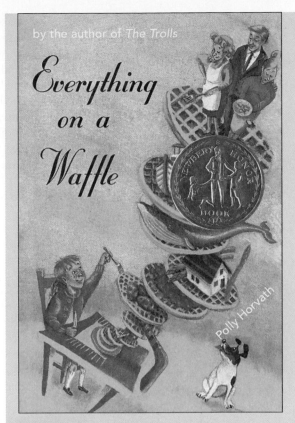

ILLUSTRATION 9.5   Despite the lack of physically impossible magic, the extraordinary use of exaggeration in this book makes the story so unlikely that it is an example of magical realism. (Jacket design by Gina Freschet from *Everything on a Waffle* by Polly Horvath. Jacket art copyright © 2001 by Gina Freschet. Reprinted by permission of Farrar, Straus, & Giroux, LLC.)

Theme

Theme refers to the underlying meaning that is either suggested or explicitly stated within a story in a way that brings an important idea to the reader's consciousness. In realistic fiction, the theme is an issue of contemporary relevance; some are timeless and others are grounded in the current time. Many people attribute "death" as the central theme in Katherine Paterson's book, ***Bridge to Terabithia***. And, indeed, the death in the story is explored in depth. However, this book is more about the theme of friendship, self-identity, and ultimately, the emotions surrounding death.

Character

Characters are created through physical descriptions, through their actions, through their thoughts and speech, and through their relationship with others. In realistic fiction, characters are developed in ways that are conceivable for people in contemporary times to live and behave. In Phyllis Reynolds Naylor's ***Shiloh***, Judd Travers, a man without awareness who acts violently in the world, unthinkingly recreates the violence with which he was raised.

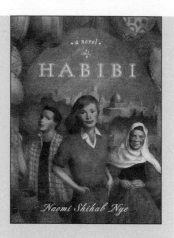

ILLUSTRATION 9.6 Liyana negotiates adolescent and cultural identity when she moves from St. Louis to Jerusalem after her parents decide the children should get to know the "other half" of their heritage. (*Habibi* by Naomi Shihab Nye, illustrated by Raul Colon, 1987. Cover illustration reprinted by permission of Raul Colon/Morgan Gaynin, Inc.)

The boy Marty makes a commitment to protect the dog Shiloh and, in so doing, goes beyond blind obedience to his father and also beyond his mother's unexamined code of ethics. Marty is aware of what he is doing. He gradually comes to understand the reasons behind his father's demands, his mother's pure but insufficient morality, and Judd Travers's brutish nature—after which he reaches his own conclusions about what he should do.

Thanks to Naylor's narrative, the reader is privileged to see these several ways of thinking through the moral issues in **Shiloh** and is allowed to make a personal judgment about them. It is not too great a step for readers to think of the issues in their lives in the complex ways Naylor reveals to them as they read **Shiloh**. It is no wonder scholars who have studied the effects of literacy have claimed that reading expands awareness (Luria, 1976; Postman, 1994; Stanovich, 1992). Over time, the habit of reading allows children to see patterns in their lives, to look into their own motives and those of others, and to see possibilities for independent action.

Point of View

A story might seem to tell "what happened," but it almost invariably makes a point that causes readers to see the events in a certain way—with a slant. Realistic fiction explores contemporary issues of significance in the characters' lives, and the point of view from which those issues are explored is particularly important in determining the ways in which reader empathy is elicited. The slant of **Shiloh** vindicates Marty's opposition to the adults around him as he chooses to care for the dog. But the story might have been told differently: If Judd Travers had narrated the story, he might have stressed Marty's theft, disobedience of his parents, and violation of community norms. Because stories tend to emphasize one way of seeing events, it can be revealing to ask, in discussions about literature, "How would the events in this story have looked from a different character's point of view?"

Adults often provide a view of the world and pass on some of the wisdom they have gained over the course of their lives. It is not surprising that even the best of writers succumb once in a while to "teaching and preaching" in realistic fiction, especially when they feel that child readers might need a little help in getting at an important idea, but it doesn't contribute to the telling of a good story. A little nudging toward an insight isn't objectionable, but if it's overdone, the writing may seem didactic. So even if the story is told from the adult point of view, we should remain wary of statements and attitudes that seem to condescend, implying that children wouldn't be capable of making their own moral judgments or of understanding the consequences of a character's actions.

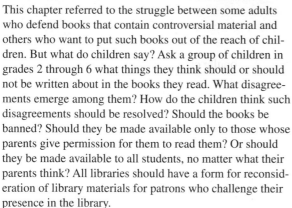

Teaching Idea 9.3
Censorship and Propriety

This chapter referred to the struggle between some adults who defend books that contain controversial material and others who want to put such books out of the reach of children. But what do children say? Ask a group of children in grades 2 through 6 what things they think should or should not be written about in the books they read. What disagreements emerge among them? How do the children think such disagreements should be resolved? Should the books be banned? Should they be made available only to those whose parents give permission for them to read them? Or should they be made available to all students, no matter what their parents think? All libraries should have a form for reconsideration of library materials for patrons who challenge their presence in the library.

Criteria for Evaluating Realistic Fiction

- Is the story well written according to literary standards outlined in Chapter 2?
- Do the characters resemble real people in our world?
- Are the events plausible? Will children believe that they could happen?
- Is the plot resolution believable—not contrived to end in a certain way?

Beyond entertainment, worthwhile realistic fiction leaves children with something to reflect on about their own lives or the lives of others.

Major Writers of Contemporary Realistic Fiction and Their Works

The writers discussed in the following sections are all from the United States. Of course, there are stellar writers who come from other English-speaking countries and others whose books have been translated into English. Some of those writers are discussed earlier in this chapter and in Chapter 4.

Avi

After a publisher accepted his first book, Avi Wortis was asked how he wanted his name to appear on the book. He answered "Avi," and his books have appeared without his last name ever since. As a child, Avi had problems with both reading and writing; now he likes to show his manuscripts covered with red pencil marks to special students in schools he visits. His book *The Man from the Sky* features a child who has difficulty reading books, but has other abilities that initially are ignored by others. His desire to write novels followed attempts at playwriting and many years of working as a librarian and, he claims, grew out of a stubborn wish to prove something to those who had criticized his writing.

Avi writes historical fiction as well as realistic fiction. In 1991, he won the *Boston Globe-Horn Book* Award for a historical novel, *The True Confessions of Charlotte Doyle*, which was also a Newbery Honor Book. The next year, he won the same awards for a work of realistic fiction, *Nothing But the Truth*. In 2003, Avi was awarded the Newbery Medal for *Crispin*, a work of historical fiction. Among Avi's other popular and award-winning novels are *Romeo and Juliet, Together (and Alive) at Last* and *Who Was That Masked Man Anyway?* His strength as a writer lies mainly in his respect for children, but his books are also notable for gripping first chapters, terse, action-filled writing, thematic richness, and imaginative variety in format. He has created "serials"—stories that are published bit by bit in a daily newspaper, and he has written graphic novels as well.

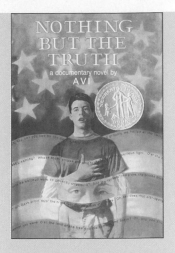

ILLUSTRATION 9.7 Ninth-grader Philip hums along to the national anthem and ends up suspended from school for two days. The story includes news clips, diary entries, school memos, and dialogue transcriptions. (Jacket illustration copyright © 1991 by Peter Catalanotto from *Nothing But The Truth* by Avi. Scholastic Inc./Orchard Books. Reprinted by permission of Scholastic Inc.)

Judy Blume

In 1996, Judy Blume received the Margaret Edwards Award for her lifetime contribution to literature for young adults. With millions of books sold, she is one of the most popular children's authors of all time—and also one of the most controversial. Blume took the world of children's books by storm during the 1970s with stories on subjects—such as the viciousness of peer groups, sexuality, and hypocrisy—that were of intense concern to children, but difficult for many adults to explore with them. That her works have struck a chord with children is obvious from their popularity, but their frankness—and perhaps the absence of any helpful or caring adult figures in many of them—has made them the most consistently controversial children's books ever. Judy Blume has stood up to her critics forthrightly and has long been active in the fight against those who would limit children's access to either her books or those by other authors.

Blume's first book, *The One in the Middle Is the Green Kangaroo*, was published in 1969, and it remains a favorite for younger children. *Tales of a Fourth Grade Nothing* and its sequels are enormously popular with children in the middle elementary grades. Designed for young adolescents, *Are You There God? It's Me, Margaret* openly discusses menstruation and emerging female sexuality. Blume has said that she considers *Blubber*, a book about a group of children victimizing an overweight peer, her most important work because children must be told about their own cruelty if they are to raise their level of moral behavior. *Forever* is the target of the most censorship because it describes a sexual encounter explicitly, and *Starring Sally J. Freedman as Herself* is the most autobiographical, according to Blume.

Beverly Cleary

Beverly Cleary was a school librarian for a brief period, and she says in her autobiographies, *A Girl from Yamhill: A Memoir* and *My Own Two Feet: A Memoir*, that she wrote books she sensed schoolchildren wanted and needed—books about other children who were like them, in ordinary settings and with ordinary lives. She certainly succeeded; the characters in Beverly Cleary's books—Henry Huggins, Beezus, the dog Ribsy, Otis Spofford, and, above all, Ramona—are as familiar to most middle elementary school children as their classmates. The eight books about Ramona span a forty-four-year writing period. Ramona starts as a four-year-old and progresses through the eight books to third grade. *Ramona Quimby, Age 8* and *Ramona and Her Father* were Newbery Honor Books. Cleary's books are marked by their strong character delineation, humor, and joyfulness.

Cleary won the Newbery Medal for *Dear Mr. Henshaw*, a story related through the correspondence between an elementary school boy and a children's author. In 1975, Cleary won the Laura Ingalls Wilder Medal for lifetime achievement in children's literature.

E. L. Konigsburg

E. L. Konigsburg studied chemistry in college and began her adult life as a chemistry teacher. As a mother of three young children, she began writing in secret during the hours she spent waiting for children, doctors, and shoe salesmen. Her stories emerged out of these very experiences. Many of her books feature middle-class characters, inspired by her experiences with her own students and with her children. Often, her books feature children whose exceptional intelligence makes them outsiders to the mainstream of childhood experiences and who imaginatively create paths for themselves. Likewise, her own writing is imaginative, with intricate plot structures and character development.

Konigsburg published two books in 1967: *From the Mixed-up Files of Mrs. Basil E. Frankweiler* and *Jennifer, Hecate, Macbeth, William McKinley, and Me, Elizabeth*. The first won the Newbery Medal, and the second was a Newbery Honor Book. Thirty years later, in 1997, Konigsburg won the Newbery Medal again for *The View from Saturday*, a book about precocious sixth-graders. In *The Outcasts of 19 Schuyler Place*, a group of socially conscious campers fight for the cause of rescuing three towers of "art" from demolition.

Phyllis Reynolds Naylor

Phyllis Naylor studied to be a clinical psychologist, but her interest in writing began in childhood. The author of over seventy books, Naylor is tuned in to the experiences of children and teens, and she writes on a wide range of topics. Her plots are designed to reveal interpersonal relationships, but are laced with humor rather than didacticism. Her 1992 Newbery Medal winner, *Shiloh*, demonstrates her ability to suggest to young readers the larger moral issues that emerge from everyday, ordinary personal problems.

Naylor's series of books about Alice is set in the household of this upbeat, assertive middle-school girl. Alice's mother is dead, and she lives with her father and her much older brother. The stories are at once funny, wise, and convincing. *Alice in Rapture, Sort Of* tells of Alice's first boyfriend. In *Reluctantly Alice*, Alice tries to advise her father and brother about their love lives.

Katherine Paterson

As the daughter of missionaries, Katherine Paterson grew up in China; she later lived in Japan as a missionary herself. Today, even when she is writing about an American setting, Paterson is able to show insight into the lives of an unusually broad range of characters. The *Great Gilly Hopkins* lets readers get to know a foster child who is learning about love; *Come Sing, Jimmy Jo* explores the music and the aspirations of Appalachian people; and Newbery Medal winner *Bridge to Terabithia* brings together children of different social classes.

Katherine Paterson's stories are notable for the richness of their philosophical and religious underpinnings. Her Newbery Medal-winning historical fiction *Jacob Have I Loved* is notable for its sense of place and the depth with which Paterson explores the rivalry between twin sisters. Paterson uses an afterword as a device to help the reader reflect on the themes. Paterson's writing weaves together multiple plot strands, each maintained through symbols and strong imagery. Her stories often reflect happenings or emotions in her own life. For example, her son's loss of a close friend is a tragedy that is portrayed in *Bridge to Terabithia*.

Ask the Author . . .

Sharon Creech

Sharon Creech (signature)

Favorite Books as a Child

Unfortunately, I have a terrible memory for what books I read as a child. There is only one I clearly remember:

The Timbertoes
by Edna Aldredge and Jessie McKee,
illustrated by John Gee

How do you create and weave together the strands of your intricate plots?

Most of my stories begin with the image of a person and a place, and I write to discover the story. Very early on, the main character will mention other people, and I know that these people will have their own stories to tell. It is these stories that evolve into other strands of the plot.

Weaving them together is not as difficult as it might sound, because each day I merely pick up the previous strands and go wherever it feels right to go. If I feel the need to spend some time with the main character's grandparents, for example, I will do that, and then return to the central story. That central story will be affected by what I've learned from the grandparents, and so the different strands begin to intertwine.

Often I use the image of clearing a trail to describe the writing process. Like Zinny Taylor, who clears a long trail in *Chasing Redbird*, I am only clearing a little bit of the story trail at a time. Sometimes there are side paths that look interesting, and I'll follow those and then return to the main trail.

It is wonderful when you begin to see the patterns emerge—when you can see enough of the story to sense how one part relates to another. If I tried to predict the pattern—or the course of the story trail—in advance, I don't think I'd be so willing to allow it to change and evolve, and it is this changing and evolving that becomes most interesting to me. At the end, I can see how all the parts of the trail are connected, and then I revise, clearing patches that aren't yet smooth enough.

Sometimes students worry when they're writing their own stories that they have to know the whole story before they begin. I find it more exciting to know very little at the beginning, and to run down that trail wondering what I will find along the way.

Sharon Creech is the author of *Walk Two Moons*, which received the Newbery Medal; *The Wanderer; Absolutely Normal Chaos; Bloomability; Pleasing the Ghost;* and *Chasing Redbird*. After spending eighteen years teaching and writing in Europe, Sharon Creech recently returned with her husband and grown children to the United States to live. ■

It is Paterson's ability to place her own feelings into her writing and characters that gives her books their power. Katherine Paterson has been awarded the Hans Christian Andersen Award in recognition of her contribution to the world's children's literature, as well as the Astrid Lindgren Memorial Award.

Gary Paulsen

Gary Paulsen had a rough childhood and an equally rough and varied adulthood before finding success as a children's author. He has more than fifty books to his credit, and many have won awards. His works are informed by his range of experiences—working as a truck driver, construction worker, and lumberjack and in other physically demanding jobs—and are permeated by the theme of survival. Paulsen has a passionate tie to nature and the wilderness, evident in his poetic, vivid writing about protagonists learning from nature as they set out on their own life journeys.

The brighter side of Paulsen's own childhood is reflected in the hilarious episodes of **Harris and Me: A Summer Remembered**; some of the less happy moments are recounted in **Eastern Sun, Western Moon: An Autobiographical Odyssey**. **Hatchet**, a Newbery Honor Book, is the story of a boy's survival in the Canadian wilderness. Paulsen wrote two sequels in response to popular demand: **The River**, in which his protagonist returns to collect data on survival for scientists, and ***Brian's Winter***, in which the original story is extended. ***The Winter Room***, another Newbery Honor Book, is a descriptive piece about a Minnesota logging cabin and the people in it. The Iditarod, a cross-Alaska dogsled race in which Paulsen has participated, plays a central role in two of his books, ***Winterdance*** and ***Woodsong***. Paulsen's realistic fiction is intense and emotion-packed.

Cynthia Rylant

The works of versatile and prolific Appalachian writer Cynthia Rylant range from poetry to easy readers to young adult novels to picture books. Her books have been enhanced by a variety of illustrators; she has illustrated some herself. Rylant's topics range from aging to rural life, animal life, and nature. She won the Newbery Medal for ***Missing May***, mentioned earlier. ***A Fine White Dust***, about religious choice, was a Newbery Honor Book. Other memorable books for older readers include ***Soda Jerk***, poetic reflections on small-town life from the perspective of a teenage boy, and ***A Kindness***, which chronicles a young boy's adjustment to his mother's romantic involvement. Among Rylant's Appalachian stories is ***A Blue-Eyed Daisy***, set in the coal mining country of West Virginia. Her own childhood experiences in West Virginia, living with her grandparents, led to such picture books as ***The Relatives Came***, ***When I Was Young in the Mountains***, and ***Appalachia: The Voices of Sleeping Birds***.

Rylant also produced over twenty Henry and Mudge stories, all easy readers for younger children. First- and second-graders go from one emotional trauma to another with Henry and his dog Mudge in books such as ***Henry and Mudge and the Careful Cousin***. Her easy reader books about Mr. Putter and Tabby are enjoyed by those who read beyond the Henry and Mudge books.

Cynthia Voigt

Although Cynthia Voigt knew since the ninth grade that she wanted to be a writer, it wasn't until she was a fifth-grade teacher that she began to seriously explore a writing career. She won a Newbery Medal for her first book, ***Homecoming***, about a teenage girl who takes her brothers and sisters on a difficult journey to make a home with their estranged grandmother when their mother proves too incompetent to keep them. Voigt wrote five other books about the Tillerman family. ***Dicey's Song*** relates Dicey's hard work in making a family with her emotionally aloof grandmother on the eastern shore of Maryland.

Voigt provides rich and complex plots about siblings making their way in the world against great odds, often without strong adult guidance, but with courage and family loyalty. Making a life after a car accident and an amputation is the subject of ***Izzy, Willy-Nilly***. Voigt wrote about divorce in ***A Solitary Blue***, a Newbery Honor Book. ***When She Hollers*** is a story about child abuse. Rich in imagery and undercurrents of emotion, and with a strong sense of place, Voigt's stories are unforgettable.

Vera Williams

The artist in Vera Williams preceded the writer, but since she began writing, Williams has written and illustrated lasting realistic fiction picture books for young readers. Williams's stories are typically about strong, ethnically diverse girls and women. Her personal commitment to peace creates books with tranquil plots and characters who hold affectionate bonds with one another. Caldecott Honor book ***A Chair for My Mother*** and ***Music, Music for Everyone*** and ***Something Special for Me*** all revolve around one member of a family wanting to do something nice for another; the dilemmas usually involve financing the favor. Her characters often have a sincere enjoyment of the simpler sides of life. ***Cherries and Cherry Pits*** is a dreamy story about a child who draws

ILLUSTRATION 9.8 When a fire destroys their belongings, a little girl saves coins to help buy a chair for the mother to rest on after working all day as a waitress. (*A Chair for My Mother* by Vera B. Williams. Copyright © 1982 by Vera B. Williams. Used by permission of HarperCollins Publishers.)

pictures and tells tales to go with them. Her Caldecott Honor book *"More, More, More," Said the Baby: Three Love Stories* has three adults enjoying simple playtime activities with babies.

Adjusting to a move and her parents' divorce is the task facing *Scooter*, who accomplishes it with the help of her no-nonsense mother. In *Amber Was Brave, Essie Was Smart*, Williams explores the effect of poverty, latch-key childhood, and having a jailed father on the daily lives of two young sisters. Books that celebrate the power of ordinary people to help each other—a theme that is all too rare in American children's literature—are Williams's considerable contribution to children's literature.

Jacqueline Woodson

Jacqueline Woodson was born in Columbus, Ohio, and grew up in South Carolina and New York City. From her childhood, she wrote constantly. She admits to writing on anything and everything—shoes, sidewalk, and even her name in graffiti on a building. She told stories (lies, she admits) and wrote stories. By fifth grade, she was the literary editor of her school magazine.

Her commitment in her writing is clear: She writes about the people she calls the "invisible" people—people who are outside mainstream America and she finds to "exist on the margins." But Woodson's characters are not intended to fight for social justice; rather, they focus on the individual and the individual's relationship with others. She gives voice to a wide variety of individuals and their experiences. Woodson is particularly concerned with preteens and teens, as they suffer from low self-esteem during this vulnerable period in their lives. While several of her young adult books include "sensitive" topics that are often avoided (teen pregnancy, alcoholism, homosexual parents, molestation, etc.), Woodson maintains the focus on dealing with issues from the perspective of the individual child/teen. Both *Miracle's Boys* and *Locomotion* begin with the death of parents, necessitating that the children become wards of an older sibling or foster homes. The situations are sad—heartbreaking, even— but always portrayed honestly and with hope.

Jacqueline Woodson has also written a number of picture books. The stories range from celebrating family experiences to looking at issues of race relations from a child's perspective. In *The Other Side*, two girls—one African American and the other white—are told not to climb over the fence that divides their back yards. After observing each from their own sides, the girls find a resolution in sitting together on the fence to get to know each other without going against their mothers' directives. Throughout Woodson's books, readers can count on strong female characters, the power of friendship, and the dignity of each person.

Charlotte Zolotow

Charlotte Zolotow has said, "We are not different from the children we were, only more experienced, better able to disguise our feelings from others, if not from ourselves." From her books we know that Zolotow did not lose touch with childhood. Her books show unusual sensitivity in exploring children's relationships with family and other children. Several of her books are concerned with children's views of parents and grandparents. *A Father Like That* is a boy's description of what he would like in a father. *My Grandson Lew* is a tender book about remembering a grandfather's words after his death. *May I Visit?* expresses a child's fear that she won't be able to return home when she grows up. *Say It!* is a loving conversation between a mother and daughter as they take a walk. In *William's Doll*, a father becomes convinced that dolls help boys learn how to be better fathers.

Other stories develop an understanding of communication among children. *The Unfriendly Book* is about jealousy; *The Hating Book* and *The Quarreling Book* are about other emotions. *The Old Dog* is about grief. Zolotow's poetic prose and hopeful tone reveal the possibilities of the real world for young children. In recognition of Zolotow's wonderful way with words, The Charlotte Zolotow Award was established to recognize exemplary writing in picture books.

PEARSON
myeducationkit

To check your comprehension on the content covered in this chapter, go to the MyEducation-Kit for your book and complete the Study Plan for Chapter 9. Here you will be able to take a chapter quiz and receive feedback on your answers.

Experiences for Further Learning

1. Within the genre of contemporary realistic fiction, select a controversial issue (child abuse, abandonment by parents, parents/partners of the same gender, reference to sexuality, etc.). Gather a sampling of books related to that issue. Consider how that issue is treated in each book, and in what ways it is or is not believable. Consider what makes the issue more controversial and likely for censorship in some books and why it may be less controversial in the way it is presented in other books. Then gather some books of the same or related theme from other genres (poetry, informational books, etc.). Discuss how thinking about potentially controversial issues by reading widely across genres influences the reader.

2. Read a work of contemporary realistic fiction that is set in an area of which you have intimate knowledge. In what ways does the author establish authenticity of the locale through the theme, plot, or characters? Find details in both illustrations and in text that let you know that the author also knows this setting well and confirms for you the reality of the setting. How do these details influence the believability of the setting?

3. With one or more partners, go to the library and locate a sampling of picture books that are works of contemporary realistic fiction. Take turns reading them aloud without showing the pictures first, and write a quick response about the pictures painted in your mind as you listen. Then explore the pictures and discuss how the pictures contribute to the overall impression of the story. Look carefully at details that give you information about the characters' emotions and responses, in addition to a sense of the overall setting and actions.

PEARSON

Now go to Chapter 9 in the MyEducationKit (www.myeducationkit.com) for your book, where you can:

- Find learning outcomes for Chapter 9.

- Access the Children's Literature Database for your own exploration.

- Complete Assignments and Activities that can help you more deeply understand the chapter content.

- Extend knowledge with content-specific Web Links.

- Deepen and apply content understanding with Extension Activities.

- Learn first hand about how authors and illustrators utilize their craft with podcasts and written interviews in the Conversations section for the chapter.

- Check your comprehension on the content covered in the chapter by going to the Study Plan. Here you will be able to take a chapter quiz and receive feedback on your answers.

- Find the following updated appendices: Major Children's Book Awards, Children's Magazines, Professional Organizations, Children's Book Publishers' Addresses, Book Selection Aids, and Children's Literature Web Sites.

Recommended Books

* indicates a picture book; **I** indicates interest level (P = preschool, 6–10 = age 6 through 10, YA = young adult)

Books about Self-Discovery and Growing Up

Blume, Judy. *Are You There, God? It's Me, Margaret*. Richard Jackson/Atheneum, 1970. A preteen girl goes through puberty angst and openly discusses menstruation and emerging female sexuality. (**I:** 9–11)

Choldenko, Gennifer. *Notes from a Liar and Her Dog*. Putnam, 2001. Antonia lies constantly and writes to her "real parents" in a notebook because she is sure she must be adopted. Only her dog, Pistachio, and best friend Harrison are real to her as she seeks to understand her identity and searches for a sense of belonging. (**I:** 10–12)

Cleary, Beverly. *Beezus and Ramona*. Morrow, 1955. The first of a series about the indomitable and spirited Ramona and her older sister; here Ramona is a preschooler. (**I:** 8–10)

———. *Dear Mr. Henshaw*. Illustrated by Paul Zelinsky. Morrow, 1983. Lee first writes to an author as part of a school assignment. In the continued correspondence, Lee increasingly confides in Mr. Henshaw about various issues that concern him—his parents' divorce, relationships with peers, and so on. (**I:** 9–11)

*Cuyler, Margery. *Stop, Drop, and Roll*. Illustrated by Arthur Howard. Simon & Schuster, 2001. Jessica worries constantly—and over everything. But when it comes to understanding fire safety, she realizes that she must first overcome her fears and worries. (**I:** P–7)

Danziger, Paula. *Amber Brown Is Not a Crayon*. Illustrated by Tony Ross. Putnam, 1994. In this popular series about a spunky girl's dilemmas as she grows up, Amber's best friend Justin is moving away. Selected sequels are *Amber Brown Goes Fourth* (1995), *Amber Brown Sees Red* (1997), and *I, Amber Brown* (2000). (**I:** 8–11)

———. *Get Ready for Second Grade, Amber Brown*. Illustrated by Tony Ross. Putnam, 2002. In a series intended for younger grades, Amber is just starting second grade. (**I:** 6–8)

Estes, Eleanor. *The Hundred Dresses*. Harcourt, 1944. Wanda acts with kindness toward those who ridiculed her for wearing the same dress every day. (**I:** 7–10)

Gantos, Jack. *Joey Pigza Swallowed the Key*. Farrar, Straus, & Giroux, 1998. Joey knows that he is "wired," and his behavior is out of control unless he is on his medication for ADHD. The sequels are *Joey Pigza Out of Control* (2000), *What Would Joey Do?* (2002), and *I Am Not Joey Pigza* (2007). *Jack Adrift* (2003) is a prequel. (**I:** 9–12)

Haddix, Margaret Peterson. *Don't You Dare Read This, Mrs. Dunphrey*. Simon & Schuster, 1996. Tish confides in her school-assigned journal her fears about her mother's whereabouts and how she will cope with caring for herself and her younger brother in their mother's absence. (**I:** 12–YA)

Hannigan, Katherine. *Ida B*. Greenwillow/HarperCollins, 2004. Home-schooled, only-child Ida B faces major life change when her mother's cancer means she must go to public schools and share the trees and land she considered to be her own with the family that buys their property. (**I:** 8–12)

*Hoffman, Mary. *Amazing Grace*. Dial, 1991. Illustrated by Caroline Binch. Grace has an amazing ability to act, but she is told by classmates that she cannot be Peter Pan in the class play because she is a girl and she is black. The sequel is *Boundless Grace* (1995), and a related chapter book is *Starring Grace* (2000). (**I:** P–7)

Lowry, Lois. *Anastasia Krupnik*. Houghton Mifflin, 1979. In this first book in the series of many titles about Anastasia, the ten-year-old girl faces her first love and the news that she will soon have a baby brother. (**I:** 9–12)

MacLachlan, Patricia. *The Facts and Fictions of Minna Pratt*. HarperCollins, 1988. Minna plays the cello and learns about life and passions from her family, friends, and Mozart. (**I:** 10–YA)

———. *Journey*. Delacorte, 1991. When two children are left by their mother, the grandparents make a home for them. (**I:** 9–12)

Mori, Kyoko. *Shizuko's Daughter*. Holt, 1993. Following her mother's suicide, twelve-year-old Yuki must face her adolescent years amidst difficult relationships with her father and stepmother, as her creative spirit rebels against a culture that restricts her individuality. (**I:** 12 and up)

Myers, Walter Dean. *Darnell Rock Reporting*. Delacorte, 1994. A thirteen-year-old's family and friends doubt that Darnell will make it as a writer for the school newspaper. (**I:** 11–YA)

Paulsen, Gary. *Harris and Me: A Summer Remembered*. Harcourt, 1993. A city boy goes to live with his distant cousin on a farm, where he finds love and hilarious adventures. (**I:** 9–12)

Snyder, Zilpha Keatley. *Libby on Wednesday*. Delacorte, 1990. Libby wins a writing contest and finds herself in a writing club where her writing flourishes but peer relationships are difficult. (**I:** 9–12)

Soto, Gary. *Baseball in April and Other Stories*. Harcourt, 1990. Tender stories of children fitting into families and of the Latino culture of California. (**I:** 10–YA)

*Waber, Bernard. *Ira Says Goodbye*. Houghton Mifflin, 1988. The story deals with the recognition of sadness that a child feels when a friend moves. The sequel is *Ira Sleeps Over* (1972). (**I:** P–7)

*Williams, Vera. *"More, More, More" Said the Baby: 3 Love Stories*. Greenwillow, 1990. A father, mother, and grandmother follow playful rituals with their babies. (**I:** P–K)

Willner-Pardo, Gina. *Daphne Eloise Slater, Who's Tall for Her Age*. Illustrated by Glo Coalson. Clarion, 1997. Daphne Eloise resolves her reaction and attitude about being called a giraffe by a mean-spirited classmate. (**I:** 6–8)

*Zolotow, Charlotte. *The Old Dog*. HarperCollins, 1995. A boy remembers the fun he had with his dog. (**I:** P–K)

*———. *William's Doll*. Illustrated by William Pene du Bois. Harper & Row, 1972. A boy and his father disagree about playing with dolls. (**I:** P–7)

Books about Families

*Altman, Linda Jacobs. *Singing with Momma Lou*. Illustrated by Larry Johnson. Lee & Low, 2002. When Tamika's grandmother gets Alzheimer's, Tamika must figure out alternate ways of communicating with her and helping her to remember who she is. (**I:** 6–9)

Blume, Judy. *The One in the Middle Is the Green Kangaroo.* Simon & Schuster, 1969/1981. A middle child gains self-confidence by being in a school play. (**I:** 7–9)

————. *Tales of a Fourth Grade Nothing.* Dutton, 1972. Readers will laugh and sympathize with Peter Hatcher's embarrassment over and envy of his pesky two-year-old brother, Fudge. Sequels are *Superfudge* (1980) and *Fudge-a-Mania* (1990). (**I:** 7–9)

Cleary, Beverly. *Ramona Quimby, Age 8.* Morrow, 1981. As a third-grader, Ramona finds that her life changes drastically when her father goes back to school. See also *Ramona and Her Father* (1977), in which Ramona campaigns to get her father to quit smoking, and *Ramona's World* (HarperCollins, 2001). (**I:** 7–9)

Cohn, Rachel. *The Steps.* Simon & Schuster, 2003. Twelve-year-old Annabel learns to balance a life filled with step-brothers, step-sisters, half siblings in her complex family network. (**I:** 10–12)

Creech, Sharon. *Walk Two Moons.* HarperCollins, 1994. A thirteen-year-old girl and her grandparents follow the journey of her mother after she leaves them. (**I:** 10–YA)

*Gauch, Patricia Lee. *Christina Katerina and the Time She Quit the Family.* Illustrated by Elise Primavera. Putnam, 1987. Christina Katerina decides to "quit" her family so that she can do things her own way, but discovers that being part of a family isn't so bad after all. A sequel is *Christina Katerina and the Great Bear Train* (1990). (**I:** 6–9)

Henkes, Kevin. *Protecting Marie.* Greenwillow, 1995. Twelve-year-old Fanny, who is dealing with adolescence, and her temperamental artist father, who is trying to handle turning 60, have a tenuous relationship; a pet dog helps to establish trust. (**I:** 10–YA)

Johnson, Angela. *Toning the Sweep.* Orchard, 1993. Three generations of women come together and share memories of the past as the dying grandmother prepares to move in with her daughter and granddaughter. (**I:** 11–YA)

*Jukes, Mavis. *Like Jake and Me.* Illustrated by Lloyd Bloom. Knopf, 1984. A spider brings Alex and his stepfather closer together. (**I:** 8–10)

*Lindenbaum, Pija. *Mini Mia and Her Darling Uncle.* Illustrated by Elisabeth Kallick Dyssegaard. R & S Books, 2007. Mini Mia adores her Uncle Tommy, so when he turns his attention to Fergus, Mini Mia acts out in an attempt to be noticed. (**I:** 5–8)

Lisle, Janet Taylor. *Afternoon of the Elves.* Orchard, 1989. Fascinated by her friend Sara-Kate's imagination and careful caring for her creation, a playground for "elves," Kate worries about who takes care of Sara-Kate. (**I:** 9–12)

Mathis, Sharon Bell. *The Hundred Penny Box.* Viking Press, 1975. Michael intercedes when his mother tries to toss out his beloved great-great Aunt Dew's memorabilia. (**I:** 8–10)

McKay, Hillary. *Saffy's Angel.* McElderry/Simon & Schuster, 2002. Saffy realizes that she is adopted, and with the help of her loving and eccentric siblings, she tries to make sense of the mystery of her past. (**I:** 9–12)

Myers, Walter Dean. *Me, Mop, and the Moondance Kid.* Delacorte, 1988. Two adopted boys remain friends with an orphan girl who seeks to be adopted, too. (**I:** 9–12)

Naylor, Phyllis Reynolds. *Alice in April.* Atheneum, 1993. Thirteen-year-old Alice demands more appreciation from her father and older brother. Other books about Alice include

Alice in Rapture, Sort Of (1989), *Reluctantly Alice* (1991), and *All But Alice* (1992). (**I:** 10–13)

O'Connor, Barbara. *Moonpie and Ivy.* Farrar, Straus, & Giroux, 2001. When twelve-year-old Pearl's mother abandons her at the home of an aunt she didn't even know she had, Pearl struggles to define what family means as she observes the relationship between the neighbor boy, Moonpie, and her Aunt Ivy. (**I:** 11–13)

*Okimoto, Jean Davies, and Elaine Aoki. *The White Swan Express: A Story About Adoption.* Illustrated by Meilo So. Clarion, 2002. Four families travel to China to meet the babies they have adopted. (**I:** 6–8)

Paterson, Katherine. *Flip-Flop Girl.* Dutton, 1994. A young girl finds it difficult to accept that her father has died, her mother is distraught and they move in with a grandmother she hardly knows, and her younger brother becomes mute. (**I:** 10–YA)

————. *The Same Stuff as Stars.* Clarion, 2002. Neglected by her mother and with a father in prison, eleven-year-old Angel has long been the stable feature in her brother Bernie's life. But when their mother abandons them at the home of their great-grandmother, Angel's responsibilities seem staggering until a mysterious star man and a kind librarian reach out to help. (**I:** 10–14)

Voigt, Cynthia. *Dicey's Song.* Atheneum, 1982. Dicey and her siblings, abandoned by their mother, try to adjust to life with their grandmother. The preceding book in the series is *Homecoming* (1981); the following book is *A Solitary Blue* (1983). (**I:** 12–YA)

*Williams, Vera. *A Chair for My Mother.* Greenwillow, 1983. After all their furniture is lost in a fire, the family saves their spare change to buy a chair for mother. See also *Cherries and Cherry Pits* (1986), *Music, Music, for Everyone* (1984), and *Something Special for Me* (1983). (**I:** P–8)

Williams-Garcia, Rita. *Like Sisters on the Homefront.* Lodestar, 1995. A troubled teenager is sent South to live with relatives and experiences the healing power of family roots. (**I:** 12–YA)

Woodson, Jacqueline. *From the Notebooks of Melanin Sun.* Blue Sky/Scholastic, 1995. A teenage boy copes with the news that his mother is in love with another woman. (**I:** YA)

————. *Locomotion.* Putnam, 2003. Lonnie C. Motion has a good family life when he is suddenly orphaned and sent to live in a foster home while his younger sister is adopted and her new family resists her seeing him. Sequel: *Peace, Locomotion* (2009).

Books about Interpersonal Relationships

Conly, Jane Leslie. *Crazy Lady!* HarperCollins, 1993. Vernon Dibbs is finding junior high a tough time in life, especially since the death of his mother. After he befriends an alcoholic neighbor, Maxine, and her special needs son, Ronald, Vernon learns many life lessons as he takes up the cause of raising enough money to send Ronald to the Special Olympics. (**I:** 10–12)

Crutcher, Chris. *Ironman.* Greenwillow, 1995. Beauregard Brewster, "Ironman," aspires to do well in the upcoming triathlon, but his training is interrupted when he is required to attend an anger management class in his high school to deal with personal relationships. (**I:** YA)

Danziger, Paula, and Ann M. Martin. *Snail Mail No More.* Harcourt, 1998. Tara and Elizabeth continue their correspondence begun in an earlier book, *P.S. Longer Letter Later*

(1998), and consult each other via e-mail on various issues related to family and peer relationships. (**I:** 9–12)

Fitzhugh, Louise. *Harriet the Spy.* Harper & Row, 1964. Harriet learns that writing down everything you think can get you in trouble with your friends. The sequel is *The Long Secret* (1965). (**I:** 9–11)

Henkes, Kevin. *Olive's Ocean.* Greenwillow, 2003. Martha grows in her understanding of herself as she deals with different relationships—her father, grandmother, a potential boyfriend, a good friend, and a deceased classmate. (**I:** 11 and up)

*McKissack, Patricia C. *The Honest-to-Goodness Truth.* Illustrated by Giselle Potter. Anne Schwartz/Atheneum, 2000. Libby's vow to only tell the truth backfires when her honesty reveals embarrassing situations for her friends. (**I:** 6–9)

Mead, Alice. *Junebug and the Reverend.* Farrar, Straus, & Giroux, 1998. When "Junebug" moves to a new school and becomes the target of the school bully, an intergenerational friendship with the Reverend helps him gain perspective and strength. (**I:** 9–12).

Mohr, Nicholasa. *Felita.* Dial, 1979. Felita is an eight-year-old Puerto Rican girl growing up in a close-knit urban community; she is confronted with racism when her family moves to a new neighborhood. (**I:** 7–9)

———. *Going Home.* Puffin, 1986. When eleven-year-old Felita goes to Puerto Rico for the summer, she at first feels like an outsider but later learns to embrace her heritage. (**I:** 10–12)

Namioka, Lensey. *April and the Dragon Lady.* Browndeer, 1994. April is a Chinese American teenager, torn between her Americanized adolescence and caring for her grandmother, who adheres to Chinese customs and expectations about relationships. (**I:** 10–YA)

Rylant, Cynthia. *Henry and Mudge and the Careful Cousin.* Simon & Schuster, 1994. Annie visits her cousin Henry and his constantly drooling big dog, Mudge. Annie must adjust to Mudge's gregariousness and Henry must adjust to her timidity. (**I:** P–7)

Woodson, Jacqueline. *I Hadn't Meant to Tell You This.* Delacorte, 1994. Racial and class barriers are overcome as two girls who have both lost their mothers bond in a friendship that allows them to confront the sexual abuse by one girl's father. (**I:** 12–YA)

———. *Maizon at Blue Hill.* Delacorte, 1992/2004. Winning a scholarship at a boarding school does not ensure Maizon's acceptance by the almost all-white student body. Companion books are *Last Summer with Maizon* (1992/2004) and *Between Madison and Palmetto* (1995/2004). (**I:** 12–YA)

Yep, Laurence. *Cockroach Cooties.* Hyperion, 2000. Two brothers figure out how a cockroach can be handy when dealing with the class bully. (**I:** 9–11)

*Zolotow, Charlotte. *The Hating Book.* Illustrated by Ben Schechter. HarperTrophy, 1969/1989. Two little girls think they hate each other until they talk about it. See also *The Quarreling Book* (illustrated by Arnold Lobel, 1963/1982). (**I:** P–7)

Books about School

*Allard, Harry. *Miss Nelson Is Missing!* Illustrated by James Marshall. Houghton Mifflin, 1985. Their beloved and kind teacher, Miss Nelson, is missing, and the strange substitute teacher, Viola Swamp, has the class worried. Sequels are *Miss Nelson Is Back* (1985) and *Miss Nelson Has a Field Day* (1985). (**I:** 7–10)

Borden, Louise. *The Day Eddie Met the Author.* Illustrated by Adam Gustavson. McElderry/Simon & Schuster, 2001. An author is coming to Eddie's school and all the students are reading and preparing to meet her. (**I:** 6–8)

Clements, Andrew. *Frindle.* Simon & Schuster, 1996. Ten-year-old Nick likes to create distractions in school. As a challenge to his vocabulary-loving teacher, he attempts to introduce a new word into the English language. Among the many school stories Clements has written are *The Janitor's Boy* (2000), *The School Story* (2001) and *A Week in the Woods* (2002). (**I:** 8–11)

———. *Jake Drake, Bully Buster.* Simon & Schuster, 2001. When SuperBully Link Baxter moves to the neighborhood, Jake Drake must learn how to stand up for himself. See also other Jake Drake books in the series. (**I:** 8–10)

———. *The Landry News.* Simon & Schuster, 1999. Clara Landry, aspiring journalist, publishes an editorial exposing the lack of teaching in her fifth-grade classroom, motivating Mr. Larson back into action as an inspired teacher. (**I:** 9–12)

*Cohen, Miriam. *Will I Have a Friend?* Illustrated by Lillian Hoban. Macmillan, 1967. Jim is entering kindergarten, and he worries about whether he will have a friend. This series includes *Starring First Grade* (Bantam, 1985) and *See You in Second Grade* (1990). (**I:** P–7)

Danziger, Paula. *The Cat Ate My Gymsuit.* Delacorte, 1974. Marcy, a junior high student who always tries to get out of gym class, leads the campaign to reinstate an unconventional teacher who was fired. The sequel is *There's a Bat in Bunk Five* (1980). (**I:** 11–YA)

DeClements, Barthe. *Sixth Grade Can Really Kill You.* Puffin, 1995. Acting up to compensate for reading problems is the way Helen handles her learning disabilities. See also *Nothing's Fair in Fifth Grade* (1981). (**I:** 9–12)

*Frasier, Debra. *Miss Alaineus: A Vocabulary Disaster.* Harcourt, 2000. When Sage mistakes the vocabulary word "miscellaneous" and is embarrassed at her classmates' reaction, she learns to make the best of the situation by participating as "Miss Alaineus" in the vocabulary parade. (**I:** 7–10)

Giff, Patricia Reilly. *Look Out, Washington, D.C.!* Dell, 1995. In this book from the Polk Street School series, the Polk Street School kids take a field trip to Washington, D.C. (**I:** 7–9)

Greene, Stephanie. *Owen Foote, Second Grade Strongman.* Illustrated by Dee De Rosa. Clarion, 1996. Owen does not like being called a "pipsqueak" by the school nurse on height-and-weight measuring day and becomes a class hero by defending his friend when the nurse calls him "too fat." Among the many sequels is *Owen Foote, Frontiersman* (1999). (**I:** 6–9)

Gutman, Dan. *The Homework Machine.* Simon & Schuster, 2006. In a series of first-person entries, fifth-grade students, teacher, and even a police chief consider the ethics and the draw of a "homework machine" in contemporary days of computer use, updating the idea popularized by *Danny Dunn and the Homework Machine* back in 1958. (**I:** 9–12)

*Herrera, Juan Felipe. *The Upside Down Boy/El niño de cabeza.* Illustrated by Elizabeth Gómez. A Spanish-speaking boy fears starting a new school where he must learn a new language, thinking he might feel "upside down." (**I:** 6–9)

*Hoffman, Mary. *The Color of Home.* Illustrated by Karin Littlewood. Fogelman/Penguin Putnam, 2002. Hassan is a new child from Somalia and draws a picture of his homeland.

An interpreter comes and helps him to communicate his picture verbally to his classmates. (**I:** P–7)

Hurwitz, Johanna. *Class President*. Illustrated by Sheila Hamanaka. Scholastic, 1990. Julio hides his ambitions in order to campaign for a classmate to win the nomination for class president, but discovers that he has leadership qualities as well as aspirations. The sequel is *School Spirit* (1994). See also *Class Clown* (1987) and *Teacher's Pet* (1988). (**I:** 10–12)

Kinney, Jeff. *Diary of a Wimpy Kid*. Abrams, 2007. Begun as a Web book on www.funbrain.com, this humorous story tells of a middle schooler's trials and triumphs through this "novel in cartoons." Sequels: *Roderick Rules* (2008), *Do-It-Yourself-Book* (2008) *The Last Straw* (2009), *Dog Days* (2009). (**I:** 9–12)

Kline, Suzy. *Herbie Jones*. Putnam, 1985. In this book in the Herbie Jones series, third-grader Herbie and his friend Raymond work to be moved up from the lowest reading group. There are many other books in this popular early chapter book series. (**I:** 7–9)

———. *Horrible Harry and the Dungeon*. Illustrated by Frank Remkiewicz. Viking, 1966. Students in Room 2B wonder whether Harry will be the new teacher Mr. Skooghammer's first "victim" of the dungeon—the suspension room in the basement. There are many other books in this popular early chapter book series. (**I:** 6–9)

Konigsburg, E. L. *The View from Saturday*. Atheneum, 1996. Four "gifted" and eccentric sixth-graders form the school's winning Academic Bowl Team. Their lives and stories intersect in interesting ways. (**I:** 10–13)

*O'Neill, Alexis. *The Recess Queen*. Illustrated by Laura Huliska-Beith. Scholastic, 2002. "Mean Jean" is the recess queen—the bully of the playground—until a new girl comes and exuberantly invites Jean to play. (**I:** P–8)

Park, Barbara. *Junie B. Jones and Her Big Fat Mouth*. Illustrated by Denise Brunkus. Random House, 1993. Junie B. Jones is a kindergartner whose challenges with daily tasks have humorous results. There are numerous other sequels, including ones in which she has moved on to first grade, where her language development has more consistently improved. (**I:** P–7)

*Recorvits, Helen. *My Name is Yoon*. Illustrated by Gabi Swiatkowska. Farrar, Straus, & Giroux, 2003. At first, Yoon is a shy newcomer to America from her homeland of Korea, but the challenge of choosing her "American name" allows her to assert and claim her identity. (**I:** P–7)

Sachar, Louis. *There's a Boy in the Girls' Bathroom*. Knopf, 1987. An inept, troublesome fifth-grader, Bradley Chalkers, finds a friend in the school counselor. (**I:** 10–12)

*Schaefer, Carole Lexa. *Someone Says*. Illustrated by Pierr Morgan. Viking, 2003. Young Chinese children engage their imaginations as they participate in pretend play throughout the school day. (**I:** P–7)

*Schwartz, Amy. *Annabelle Swift, Kindergartner*. Orchard, 1988. Annabelle's older sister Lucy teaches her what to expect in kindergarten, but when Annabelle gets there, her knowledge sparks laughter among the children. Ultimately, Annabelle wins the classmates' approval. (**I:** P–7)

*Shannon, David. *David Goes to School*. Blue Sky/Scholastic, 1999. David's misbehaviors that were at home in *No, David* (1998) now humorously but maddeningly continue in school as he breaks rules and must stay after school. (**I:** P–7)

Shreve, Susan. *The Flunking of Joshua T. Bates*. Illustrated by Diane DeGroat. Knopf, 1984. When Joshua finds out that he must repeat the third grade, he is devastated. He faces taunting from former classmates, but a sympathetic teacher helps him find his strengths. Sequels are *Joshua T. Bates Takes Charge* (1993) and *Joshua T. Bates in Trouble Again* (1997). (**I:** 7–10)

Smith, Greg Leitich. *Ninjas, Piranhas, and Galileo*. Little Brown, 2003. This humorously told story is about three seventh-graders who fret over their school science fair experiment gone awry, a budding romantic triangle, and a strong friendship that endures through it all. (**I:** 9–12)

*Stuve-Bodeen, Stephanie. *Elizabeti's School*. Illustrated by Christy Hale. Lee & Low, 2002. Set in modern-day Tanzania, Elizabeti misses being at home, but enjoys her first day of school. (**I:** 6–9)

Books about Sports

Avi. *S.O.R. Losers*. Bradbury, 1984. The South Orange River soccer team is composed of unlikely seventh-grade athletes, who strive for an all-losing season. (**I:** 12–YA)

Bloor, Edward. *Tangerine*. Harcourt Brace, 1997. Despite the fact that Paul is legally blind, he convinces his parents to hide his disability so that he can use his amazing skill as a master soccer goalie. His ability to "see" life in ways of which others seem oblivious allows him to realize what's really wrong with his football hero older brother. (**I:** 12–YA)

Brooks, Bruce. *The Moves Make the Man*. HarperTrophy, 1995. An African American boy and a Caucasian boy, at first distrustful of each other, become friends through basketball. (**I:** 12–YA)

Christopher, Matt. *Penalty Shot*. Little, Brown, 1997. Jeff is a talented soccer player who gets suspended from the team for bad grades. His attempts to rejoin the team are sabotaged, and he must figure out a way to rectify the situation. There are many books in the series of sports stories by this author, including *Shoot for the Hoop* (1995). (**I:** 9–12)

Cohen, Barbara. *Thank You, Jackie Robinson*. Lothrop, 1974. The love of baseball helps a fatherless boy, Sam, cross boundaries of race, age, and religion to become close friends with a hotel cook named Davy. As Davy lies in a hospital bed dying, Sam brings him an autographed ball from Jackie Robinson. (**I:** 9–11)

Crutcher, Chris. *Staying Fat for Sarah Byrnes*. Greenwillow, 1993. Overweight Eric and burn-scarred Sarah are fast friends, bonded by their physical problems. When Eric trains for the swim team, their friendship is threatened, and Sarah must face the horrible truth of the accident that left her scarred. (**I:** YA)

Lynch, Chris. *Iceman*. HarperCollins, 1994. Eric is a fourteen-year-old ice hockey player who transfers his anger and emotional vulnerability to violent behavior on the ice. See also *Slot Machine* (1995). (**I:** YA)

Slote, Alfred. *Finding Buck McHenry*. HarperCollins, 1991. A boy tries to enlist the school janitor he believes is a former famous baseball player from the Negro League to be the Little League team coach. (**I:** 9–12)

———. *Hang Tough, Paul Mather*. HarperTrophy, 1973/1993. Paul deals with his incurable blood disease by involving himself in baseball. (**I:** 9–12)

Soto, Gary. *Taking Sides*. Harcourt, 1991. Lincoln Mendoza moves to a white neighborhood and has to take sides on the basketball court. The sequel is *Pacific Crossing* (1992). (**I:** 9–12)

Spinelli, Jerry. *Crash*. Knopf, 1996. Crash earned his name by being a star athlete from babyhood to middle school, but he earned friendship through different behaviors. (**I:** 10–YA)

———. *There's a Girl in My Hammerlock*. Simon & Schuster, 1991. Maisie Potter doesn't make the cheerleading team, so she decides to be a wrestler in order to be close to Eric. Despite opposition from the coach, teammates, and girlfriends, Maisie discovers that she loves the sport. (**I:** 10–12)

Books about Nature and Animals

Byars, Betsy. *The Midnight Fox*. Viking, 1968. Ten-year-old Tom resents being sent to his uncle and aunt's farm while his parents travel, but becomes interested in a black fox he follows to her den. (**I:** 9–12)

DiCamillo, Kate. *Because of Winn-Dixie*. Candlewick, 2000. Ten-year-old Opal encounters a friendly stray dog at the grocery store and, through him, learns to adapt to her new community in small-town Florida and comes to peace with her mother's leaving. (**I:** 9–12)

Dickinson, Peter. *Chuck and Danielle*. Delacorte, 1996. This is a set of humorous episodic stories about Danielle and her high-strung and paranoid whippet, Chuck. Danielle is sure that her dog will one day save the world. (**I:** 9–12)

*Ehlert, Lois. *Red Leaf, Yellow Leaf*. Harcourt, 1991. A child describes how a sugar maple tree was planted and cared for, with informational text adding details. (**I:** P–8)

Farley, Walter. *The Black Stallion*. Random House, 1941/1991. When Alec is shipwrecked on a deserted island, he and a black stallion form a bond as he works to tame and then train him. This is the first of a series. (**I:** 9–12)

*Fleming, Denise. *In the Small, Small Pond*. Holt, 1993. A child observes pond life and activity with awe. (**I:** P–8)

Haas, Jessie. *Beware the Mare*. Greenwillow, 1993. Illustrated by Martha Haas. In a story set in rural Vermont, Lily and her horse-trading Gramp wonder why her new mare is named "Beware." Sequels are *A Blue for Beware* (1995), *Be Well, Beware* (1996), and *Beware and Stoogie* (1998). (**I:** 7–10)

———. *Runaway Radish*. Illustrated by Margot Apple. Greenwillow, 2001. This easy chapter book features a young girl and how she learns from her pony named Radish. (**I:** 6–8)

Henry, Marguerite. *Misty of Chincoteague*. Illustrated by Wesley Dennis. Simon & Schuster, 1990. Paul and Maureen obtain a wild horse and her colt on the island of Chincoteague, off the eastern shore of Virginia. Sequels are *Sea Star* (1949/1991) and *Stormy, Misty's Foal* (1963/1991). (**I:** 9–11)

Hesse, Karen. *Sable*. Illustrated by Marcia Sewall. Holt, 1994. Sable, ten-year-old Tate's dog, is constantly stealing things and must be given away to a friend. Tate is determined to show responsibility and earn the right to keep her dog. (**I:** 7–9)

*Keats, Ezra Jack. *The Snowy Day*. Viking, 1962. Peter enjoys the variety of ways he can play in the snow. (**I:** P–7)

Livingstone, Star. *Harley*. Illustrated by Molly Bang. SeaStar, 2001. In this easy reader, a llama turns out to be better at herding sheep than training to be a pack animal. (**I:** 6–8)

*Lyon, George Ella. *Come a Tide*. Illustrated by Stephen Gammell. Orchard, 1990. A girl provides an account of the spring floods at her rural homeplace. (**I:** P–8)

Mikaelsen, Ben. *Stranded*. Hyperion, 1995. Twelve-year-old Koby saves the lives of two injured pilot whales in the Florida Keys. In doing so, she confronts her feelings about her own injury that resulted in an artificial foot and the resulting tensions between her parents. (**I:** 10–YA)

Paulsen, Gary. *Dogsong*. Bradbury, 1985. The cold and mysteries of the wilderness are made real to readers of this story of a fourteen-year-old Eskimo boy who journeys 1400 miles on a dog sled. (**I:** 10–YA)

———. *Woodsong*. Bradbury, 1990. A family in the wilds of northern Minnesota recount their first dealings with sled dogs and the Iditarod race. (**I:** 12–YA)

Rylant, Cynthia. *Every Living Thing*. Macmillan, 1985. In a series of short stories, animals play an important role in helping people come to a better understanding of themselves and others. (**I:** 9–12)

*Yolen, Jane. *Owl Moon*. Illustrated by John Schoenherr. Putnam, 1987. A father and child go owling on a winter night. (**I:** P–8)

Books about Adventure and Survival

Farmer, Nancy. *A Girl Named Disaster*. Orchard, 1996. Eleven-year-old Nhamo flees from her village in Mozambique to escape an arranged marriage to a cruel man. She travels alone to Zimbabwe in search of a father she does not know. (**I:** 10–YA)

George, Jean Craighead. *Julie of the Wolves*. Harper & Row, 1972. Running away from marriage at age thirteen means learning to live with wolves to survive. Sequels are *Julie* (1996) and *Julie's Wolf Pack* (1997). (**I:** 9–12)

———. *My Side of the Mountain*. Penguin, 1959/1988. When Sam runs away to the Catskill Mountains, an old hollow tree becomes his home and a falcon and weasel his companions in the struggle for survival in the wilderness. The trilogy continues with *On the Far Side of the Mountain* (1990) and *Frightful's Mountain* (Dutton, 1999). (**I:** 10–12)

Hill, Kirkpatrick. *Toughboy and Sister*. McElderry, 1990. Siblings lose their parents and are stranded in a Yukon River camp. The sequel is *Winter Camp* (1993). (**I:** 9–11).

Hobbs, Will. *Far North*. Morrow, 1996. Fifteen-year-old Gabe, his Dene Indian roommate Raymond, and Dene elder Johnny Raven are stranded in the Canadian wilderness after a plane crash. The boys learn the skills they need to survive the harsh winter weather, the animals, and other dangers. See also *The Maze* (1998). (**I:** 12–YA)

Kehret, Peg. *Earthquake Terror*. Cobblehill, 1996. Following an earthquake, twelve-year-old Jonathon and his six-year-old sister Abby, whose walker is damaged, must figure out a way to survive on an island where they are camping. (**I:** 9–12)

Naylor, Phyllis Reynolds. *The Fear Place*. Atheneum, 1994. Twelve-year-old Doug must overcome his fear of heights and hatred for his older brother in order to rescue him from the dangerous ridge of a cliff. (**I:** 9–12)

Paulsen, Gary. *Hatchet*. Viking, 1987. Surviving fifty-three days in the wilderness helps Brian learn to cope with his parents' divorce. Companion books are *The River* (1991), *Brian's Winter* (1996), and *Brian's Return* (1996). (**I:** 9–12)

Books about Romance and Sexuality

Avi. *Romeo and Juliet, Together (and Alive) at Last*. Orchard, 1987. This funny story tells of Ed's intent to play matchmaker when two shy students are cast as the leads in the class production of Shakespeare's "Romeo and Juliet." (**I:** 10–12)

Bauer, Marion Dane, ed. *Am I Blue? Coming Out from the Silence*. HarperCollins, 1994. Sixteen short stories about homosexuality by such authors as Jane Yolen and M. E. Kerr deal with growing up gay or lesbian or having parents or friends who are gay or lesbian. (**I:** YA)

Creech, Sharon. *Absolutely Normal Chaos*. HarperCollins, 1995. Thirteen-year-old Mary Lou Finney is wrapped up in adolescence, as she chaotically deals with family, friends, and her feelings for Alex, with whom she exchanges her first kiss. (**I:** 10–12)

Greene, Bette. *Philip Hall Likes Me, I Reckon Maybe*. Dial, 1974. Eleven-year-old Beth thinks that Philip is the smartest of all, until she realizes that she is letting him beat her at everything. (**I:** 10–12)

Lowry, Lois. *Anastasia at This Address*. Houghton Mifflin, 1991. Thirteen-year-old Anastasia thinks that she is ready for romance and answers an ad in a singles column of the newspaper. (**I:** 9–12)

McKay, Hilary. *The Exiles in Love*. McElderry/Simon & Schuster, 1999. The four Conroy sisters have what Grandma calls their "family failing". . . they fall in love easily. The numerous stories about the sisters ends with *Forever Rose* (2008). (**I:** 11–13)

Naylor, Phyllis. *Alice in Rapture, Sort of*. Atheneum, 1989. The summer before entering seventh grade becomes one of turmoil, as Alice discovers that falling in love is not what she thought it would be. This is the first in a series of books about Alice growing up. (**I:** 10–12)

Books about Mental, Physical, Emotional and Other Challenges

See also other titles in the Chapter 4 bibliography.

Byars, Betsy. *The Summer of the Swans*. Viking, 1970. Sara is self-conscious about her brother, who is mentally disabled, but reconsiders her feelings when he gets lost searching for the wild swans that return each year. (**I:** 10–YA)

*Fleming, Violet. *Be Good to Eddie Lee*. Illustrated by Floyd Cooper. Philomel, 1993. Eddie Lee is able to see flowers and frog's eggs better than other children. (**I:** 7–9)

Konigsburg, E. L. *Silent to the Bone*. Jean Karl/Atheneum, 2000. Baby Nikki is in a coma, and thirteen-year-old Branwell is traumatized and has become mute. When the British au pair says that Branwell dropped the baby and shook her, best friend Connor must figure a way to communicate with Branwell.

Lord, Cynthia. *Rules*. Scholastic, 2006. Twelve-year-old Catherine reconsiders the importance of rules in living with an autistic younger brother when a friendship with a nonverbal paraplegic helps her to question what it means to be "normal." (**I:** 9–12)

*Millman, Isaac. *Moses Goes to School*. Farrar, Straus, & Giroux, 2000. Moses and his friends attend a special school for children who are deaf, where adaptations include typing a letter into a computer that translates into standard spoken English. All of the Moses books are accompanied by American Sign Language. (**I:** P–8)

Pennypacker, Sara. *Clementine*. Illustrated by Marla Frazee. Hyperion, 2006. Third grader Clementine has good intentions, but her inability to pay attention means that things often go awry. Other books include: *The Talented Clementine* (2007), *Clementine's Letter* (2008).

Books about Moral Dilemmas and Moral Responsibility

Avi. *Nothing but the Truth: A Documentary Novel*. Orchard, 1991. A ninth-grader's suspension for humming "The Star Spangled Banner" becomes the center of media attention as misinformation and misinterpretation create havoc. (**I:** 12–YA)

Bauer, Marion Dane. *On My Honor*. Clarion, 1986. After promising "on his honor" to his father that he will not go swimming, Joel feels responsible for Tony's drowning when the two friends break the promise. (**I:** 10–YA)

Hiaasen, Carl. *Flush*. Knopf, 2005. When Dad is arrested for sinking a casino boat he suspects is responsible for dumping raw sewage directly into the ocean, a brother and sister team up to solve the mystery and help put a stop to the polluting of the water surrounding the Florida Keys. (**I:** 10–YA)

———. *Hoot!* Knopf, 2002. A cast of three unlikely friends—a boy who has just moved to the town, a homeless runaway, and a bully-confronting tough girl—work together to save an endangered species of owls from having their home destroyed by the construction of a franchise pancake restaurant. (**I:** 10–YA)

Konigsburg, E. L. *The Outcasts of 19 Schulyer Place*. Atheneum, 2004. A group of socially conscious campers fight for the cause of rescuing three towers of "art" from demolition. (**I:** 11–13)

Naylor, Phyllis Reynolds. *Shiloh*. Atheneum, 1991. Marty's desire to keep a mistreated beagle that he found in the hills surrounding his West Virginia home causes him to make many moral decisions about what's right and what's wrong. Sequels are *Shiloh Season* (1996) and *Saving Shiloh* (1997). (**I:** 9–12)

Rylant, Cynthia. *A Fine White Dust*. Bradbury, 1986. Thirteen-year-old Peter is captured in a hypnotic spell by a charismatic preacher and struggles to reconcile his own religious beliefs with those of family and community. (**I:** 10–YA)

Woodson, Jacqueline. *Hush*. Putnam, 2002. When a police officer testifies that a fellow officer was not acting in self-defense when he shot and killed a boy, his family must enter the Witness Protection Program and their lives are forever changed. (**I:** 12–YA)

———. *Miracle's Boys*. Putnam, 2000. When their father's drowning and their mother's death from diabetes leave three brothers orphans, Ty'ree gives up his college plans and focuses on trying to keep Charlie from a life of crime and Lafayette from inward withdrawal. (**I:** 12–YA)

Books about Social Diversity and Society

See also other titles in the Chapter 4 bibliography.

*Bunting, Eve. *Fly Away Home*. Illustrated by Ronald Himler. Clarion, 1991. A homeless boy and his father who live in an airport find hope in the freedom of a bird. (**I:** 7–9)

*———. *Smoky Night*. Illustrated by David Diaz. Harcourt Brace, 1994. The story depicts people of different ethnic backgrounds coming together during the Los Angeles riots of 1993. (**I:** 9 and up)

Fenner, Carol. *Yolonda's Genius*. McElderry, 1995. When Yolonda's mother moves her children from the dangers of city life to a rural area, Yolonda's genius lies in discovering not only her own but also her brother's talent. (**I:** 10–YA)

Fleischman, Paul. *Seedfolks*. Illustrated by Judy Pedersen. Harper, 1997. Suspicious neighbors become inspired by one another to transform a trash-filled city lot into a beautiful garden. (**I:** 12–YA)

Fox, Paula. *Monkey Island*. Orchard, 1991. Two men help a homeless boy after his mother abandons him. (**I:** 10–12)

Mead, Alice. *Junebug*. Farrar, 1995. Junebug has dreams of a better life and of becoming a boat captain someday, but worries that his tenth birthday will bring pressures to join the gang of older boys in his housing project. The sequel is *Junebug and the Reverend* (1998). (**I:** 9–12)

Rosen, Michael J. *ChaseR*. Candlewick, 2002. A move from a city to a rural community exposes fourteen-year-old Chase to differences in lifestyle and life attitudes. (**I:** 10–YA)

*Tamar, Erika. *The Garden of Happiness*. Illustrated by Barbara Lambase. Harcourt, 1996. Marisol plants a seed in a crack in the sidewalk near her neglected neighborhood block. The sunflower that grows delights the neighborhood. (**I:** P–7)

Temple, Frances. *Grab Hands and Run*. Orchard, 1993. A Salvadoran family struggles to escape oppression and move to Canada. (**I:** 10–YA)

Williams, Vera B. *Amber Was Brave, Essie Was Smart*. Greenwillow, 2001. Two sisters share a loving relationship while trying to deal with poverty, latchkey loneliness, mother's long hours at work, and father away at jail for forging checks. (**I:** 7–10)

Wolff, Virginia Euwer. *Make Lemonade*. Holt, 1993. Fourteen-year-old LaVaughn is determined to escape poverty, but ends up babysitting for a single teen mom who has many problems to face. (**I:** 11–YA)

Books about Aging, Death, and Dying

Bohlmeijer, Arno. *Something Very Sorry*. Translated by the author. Houghton Mifflin, 1996. (Originally published in the Netherlands as *Ik moetje iets heel jammers vertellen* by Vangorr Publishers, 1994.) Nine-year-old Rosemyn is in the hospital following a car accident in which all of her family members were seriously injured. What makes this book remarkable is the honesty of the narrator's voice as she anguishes over her mother's death. (**I:** 9–12)

*Clifton, Lucille. *Everett Anderson's Goodbye*. Illustrated by Ann Grifalconi. Holt, 1983. A story of Everett's grief at losing his father, told in rhyme. (**I:** P–7)

*Dugan, Barbara. *Loop the Loop*. Illustrated by James Stevenson. Elderly Mrs. Simpson and little Anne form a friendship and share yo-yo tricks with each other. (**I:** P–8)

*Fox, Mem. *Sophie*. Illustrated by Aminah Brenda Lynn Robinson. Harcourt Brace, 1989. Sophie holds onto her grandfather's hand as she grows up. He holds onto hers as he gets smaller and older. (**I:** P–6)

*———. *Wilfrid Gordon McDonald Partridge*. Illustrated by Julie Vivas. Kane Miller, 1985. A little boy is concerned when he hears that his elderly friend, Miss Nancy, has lost her memory. (**I:** P–9)

Fox, Paula. *The Eagle Kite*. Orchard, 1995. Liam's father is dying of AIDS. His mother says that he got it from a blood transfusion, but Liam remembers the day he broke and buried his eagle kite—the day he saw his father embracing another man on the beach. (**I:** 10–YA)

Grimes, Nikki. *What is Goodbye?* Illustrated by Raúl Colon. Hyperion, 2004. Two siblings deal in very different ways with the death of their brother. (**I:** 8–12)

Henkes, Kevin. *Sun & Spoon*. Greenwillow, 1997. When Spoon Gilmore's Gram dies, family members all search for ways to deal with their grief. Spoon searches for a concrete object by which he can remember her. (**I:** 10–YA)

Jukes, Mavis. *Blackberries in the Dark*. Knopf, 1985/1993. Following his grandfather's death, Austin goes to visit his grandmother, and they share their sadness as they work through their grief. (**I:** 8–11)

Lowry, Lois. *A Summer to Die*. Houghton Mifflin, 1977. Thirteen-year-old Meg gives up feelings of envy when she learns that her beautiful sister is fatally ill. (**I:** 10–YA)

Park, Barbara. *Mick Harte Was Here*. Knopf, 1995. Thirteen-year-old Phoebe Hart narrates the story of losing her younger brother to a bike accident. (**I:** 9–12)

Paterson, Katherine. *Bridge to Terabithia*. Crowell, 1977. Despite their different backgrounds, Jess and Leslie forge an unexpected and special friendship when tragedy strikes. (**I:** 9–12)

Rylant, Cynthia. *Missing May*. Dell, 1992. Orphaned, Summer feels fortunate to have an aunt and uncle who share their deep love for each other with her. But when Aunt May dies, Summer and Uncle Ob search for ways to overcome grief. (**I:** 10–YA)

Smith, Doris Buchanan. *A Taste of Blackberries*. Crowell, 1973. Jamie dies of an allergic reaction to a bee sting suffered while out picking blackberries, and his best friend grieves. (**I:** 8–10)

*Viorst, Judith. *The Tenth Good Thing about Barney*. Illustrated by Erik Blegvad. Macmillan, 1971. At a funeral in his backyard, a little boy tries to think of ten good things to remember about his cat, Barney. (**I:** P–8)

Yumoto, Kazumi. *The Friends*. Translated by Cathy Hirano. Farrar, Straus, & Giroux, 1996. (Originally published in Japan as *Natsu no niwa*, Fukutake Publishing, 1992.) Three boys are curious about death and spend their summer keeping surveillance on a man they are sure is old enough to die soon. Through the ensuing intergenerational friendship, the boys learn about life, living, and aging before they encounter death. (**I:** 10–YA)

Mystery and Suspense Books

Adler, David. *Cam Jansen and the Ghostly Mystery*. Viking, 2008. A photographic memory helps Cam solve mysteries, and in this case, a ticket booth is robbed while selling rock concert tickets. There are many other Cam Jansen mysteries in this series. (**I:** 8–11)

———. *Young Cam Jansen and the Lost Tooth*. Illustrated by Susanna Natti. Viking, 2008. Cam Jansen helps Annie discover the mystery of her missing tooth in this title from the mystery series written as easy-to-read stories. (**I:** 6–8)

Byars, Betsy. *The Dark Stairs: A Herculeah Jones Mystery*. Viking, 1994. Thirteen-year-old Herculeah Jones, daughter of a police officer and a private investigator, and her partner Meat investigate the disappearance of the owner of Dead Oaks, an old house surrounded by stories of murder and insanity. Others in the Herculeah Jones Mystery series include *Tarot Says Beware* (1995), *Dead Letter* (1996), *Disappearing Acts* (1998), and *King of Murder* (2006). (**I:** 9–12)

Clifford, Eth. *Help! I'm a Prisoner in the Library*. Houghton Mifflin, 1979. In this title in the series of mysteries about two sisters, Jo-Beth and Mary Rose, they get trapped in a public library all night during a blizzard, and their fascination with the displays turns into fear as they hear strange noises in the dark. (**I:** 8–11)

Dowd, Siobhan. *The London Eye Mystery*. Fickling, 2008. Twelve-year-old Ted has Asperger's syndrome, and his obsessions play into his search to make sense of the world when he and his sister join together to solve the mystery of the disappearance of his visiting cousin who goes up in a capsule of the London Eye ferris wheel, but is not in it when it comes back down. (**I:** 10–13)

Hamilton, Virginia. *The House of Dies Drear*. Silver Burdett Ginn, 1968. Members of an African American family find themselves dealing with a number of "ghosts" when they move into an old house where slaves used to be harbored in an Underground Railroad station. The sequel is *The Mystery of Drear House* (1987). (**I:** 10–YA)

Kline, Suzy. *Horrible Harry Cracks the Code*. Illustrated by Frank Remkiewicz. Viking, 2007. Horrible Harry sets out to solve a mystery of a mathematical code to prove to his classmates that he is second only to Sherlock Holmes. (**I:** 7–9)

Konigsburg, E. L. *From the Mixed-up Files of Mrs. Basil E. Frankweiler*. Atheneum, 1967. Siblings determine to remain hidden in the Metropolitan Museum of Art until they discover who created a mysterious sculpture. (**I:** 9–11)

Nixon, Joan Lowery. *The Other Side of Dark*. Delacorte, 1986. Lisa was thirteen when a gunshot put her into a four-year coma. When she wakes up, she realizes that she is the only witness to the identity of her mother's murderer. This book won the Edgar Allan Poe Mystery Writer's Award. (**I:** 12–YA)

Raskin, Ellen. *The Westing Game*. Dutton, 1978. When millionaire Sam Westing dies, he leaves words to the song "America the Beautiful" as clues for sixteen heirs to work out an intricate riddle and identify his murderer. (**I:** 9–12)

Sobol, Donald. *Encyclopedia Brown and the Case of the Slippery Salamander*. Delacorte, 1999. This is one in a series of detective stories starring ten-year-old Encyclopedia Brown and his partner Sally. Ten short cases are presented, challenging readers to figure out how they were solved, with answers at the back of the book. (**I:** 9–12)

Tate, Eleanora E. *The Secret of Gumbo Grove*. Watts, 1987. Raisin loves hearing stories of African Americans in the "old days," but while helping to clean up the church cemetery, she stumbles onto a mystery. (**I:** 9–12)

Humorous Books

Barrows, Annie. *Ivy and Bean*. Illustrated by Sophie Blackall. Chronicle, 2007. Bean loves to play tricks, and when the seemingly quiet new neighbor, Ivy, saves her from a trick gone wrong, the two seal the beginning of a wonderful friendship. Sequels: *Ivy and Bean and the Ghost that Had to Go* (2006), *Break the Fossil Record* (2007), *Take Care of the Babysitter* (2008).

Bauer, Joan. *Squashed*. Delacorte, 1992. In a humorous story, sixteen-year-old Lisa competes in a pumpkin-growing contest, trying to get her pumpkin, Max, to put on 200 pounds while she herself loses 20 pounds. (**I:** 12–YA)

Cameron, Ann. *The Stories Julian Tells*. Illustrated by Ann Strugnell. Knopf, 1981. Six short stories humorously describe events in Julian's life as he grows up. Other titles are *More Stories Julian Tells* (1986), *The Stories Huey Tells* (1995), and *More Stories Huey Tells* (1997). (**I:** 6–8)

Cleary, Beverly. *Ramona the Brave*. Morrow, 1975. This Ramona story has some of the funniest episodes in the series, including Ramona's breaking a raw egg on her head. (**I:** 9–12)

Danziger, Paula. *Make Like a Tree and Leave*. Delacorte, 1990. Martin has a knack for getting himself in trouble. For one, he wants to do a super job on his Egypt unit project, so he wraps a classmate in a plaster cast and then encounters trouble removing it. (**I:** 9–12)

Gilson, Jamie. *It Goes Eeeeeeeeeeeee!* Illustrated by Diane DeGroat. Houghton Mifflin, 1994. Patrick, a new boy in school, is put in his place when Dawn Marie corrects his misinformation about bats. See also *Can't Catch Me, I'm the Gingerbread Man* (1981) and *Hello, My Name Is Scrambled Eggs* (1985). (**I:** 8–11)

Greenwald, Sheila. *Rosy Cole: She Grows and Graduates*. Orchard, 1997. Rosy is now an eighth-grader, and she and her friends are in the midst of making a decision about where to attend high school. Earlier titles include *Give Us a Great Big Smile, Rosy Cole* (1981), *Write on, Rosy!* (1988), and *Rosy Cole: She Walks in Beauty* (1994). (**I:** 10–12)

McDonald, Megan. *Judy Moody (Was in a Mood. Not a Good Mood. A Bad Mood.)*. Illustrated by Peter Reynolds. Candlewick, 2000. Judy starts third grade in a bad mood, and her teacher asks her to return with a better mood the next day. Among the many sequels are *Judy Moody Saves the World* (2002), *Judy Moody Gets Famous* (2003), *Judy Moody, M.D.: The Doctor Is In* (2004). (**I:** 6–9)

———. *Judy Moody Predicts the Future*. Illustrated by Peter H. Reynolds. Candlewick, 2003. Judy Moody adopts the name "Madame M," and with the help of a mood ring and a Magic 8 ball, she makes outrageous predictions about the future. (**I:** 6–9)

Robinson, Barbara. *The Best Christmas Pageant Ever*. Tyndale House, 1972. The six rowdy Herdman siblings find themselves in the community Christmas pageant. The sequel is *The Best School Year Ever* (1994). (**I:** 8–12)

Rockwell, Thomas. *How to Eat Fried Worms*. Franklin Watts, 1973. Ten-year-old Billy decides on a bet to eat fifteen worms in fifteen days to earn $50 toward buying a new minibike. Luckily, his friends help by creating new concoctions each day. (**I:** 9–12)

Soto, Gary. *Summer on Wheels*. Scholastic, 1995. Hector and Mando go on a biking adventure in California, encountering a range of personalities along the way. This is the sequel to *Crazy Weekend* (1994). (**I:** 11–YA)

Books with Multicultural and International Themes

See also the extensive list of titles in the Chapter 4 bibliography.

Cameron, Ann. *Colibrí*. Farrar, Straus, & Giroux, 2003. Rosa barely remembers her first family—the family from whom she got "lost," before she ended up living with Uncle, traveling from place to place throughout Guatemala and living a life of scams and hiding. (**I:** 10–YA)

*English, Karen. *Nadia's Hands*. Illustrated by Jonathan Weiner. Boyds Mills, 1999. Nadia has henna applied decoratively to her hands when participating in her Aunt's traditional Pakistani wedding. (**I:** 7–10)

Joseph, Lynn. *The Color of My Words*. HarperCollins, 2000. Twelve-year-old Ana Rosa writes on any scrap of paper she can find—but she is told that only the President in her native Dominican Republic is allowed to write books. Her beloved brother tries to use words to fight injustice, but faces dangerous political oppression. (**I:** 10–YA)

Nelson, Vaunda Micheaux. *Mayfield Crossing*. Putnam, 1993. The children in an all-white school gradually learn to accept their African American counterparts. See also *Beyond Mayfield* (1999). (**I:** 9–12)

Nye, Naomi Shihab. *Habibi*. Simon & Schuster, 1987. Liyana faces adjustment to a new culture when her parents move the family from St. Louis, Missouri, to Jerusalem so that she can become familiar with the "other half" of her heritage. (**I:** 10–13)

*Rylant, Cynthia. *The Relatives Came*. Bradbury, 1985. Family members come from various places to gather for a family reunion in this Appalachian setting (**I:** P–8). Other books that offer images of Appalachia include *When I Was Young in the Mountains* (illustrated by Diane Goode, Dutton, 1982), quiet reflections on a childhood of simple pleasures in the Appalachians (**I:** P–8); *A Blue-Eyed Daisy* (Dell, 1987), in which eleven-year-old Ellie's life in a coal mining town in West Virginia is portrayed (**I:** 9–12); and *Appalachia: The Voices of Sleeping Birds* (illustrated by Barry Moser, Harcourt, 1991), in which text and illustrations offer poetic images that establish a strong sense of the place and the people of the Appalachians. (**I:** P–8)

*Shea, Pegi Deitz. *The Whispering Cloth: A Refugee's Story*. Illustrated by Anita Riggio. Stitched by You Yang. Boyds Mill, 1994. Mai practices stitching borders in embroidered story cloths while in a Thai refugee camp with her grandmother. She finds a story within herself so that she, too, can stitch her own pa'ndau. (**I:** 6–9)

*Smith, Cynthia Leitich. *Jingle Dancer*. Illustrated by Cornelius Van Wright and Ying-Hwa Hu. Jenna borrows a few jingles from several relatives in order to participate as a dancer in the next Pow Wow. (**I:** P–8)

Temple, Frances. *Taste of Salt: A Story of Modern Haiti*. Orchard, 1992. Djo tells his story of suffering under the Haitian military dictatorship and the countermovement led by Aristide. (**I:** 12–YA)

———. *Tonight, by Sea*. Orchard, 1995. A Haitian family and friends finally complete the construction of a boat, which helps them escape the tyranny of the government before Aristide returns. (**I:** 11–YA)

*Wong, Janet. *Apple Pie, 4th of July*. Illustrated by Margaret Chodos-Irvine. Harcourt, 2002. A little girl is pleasantly surprised when people come in to buy Chinese food at her family's restaurant as part of their Fourth of July celebration. (**I:** P–8)

Yep, Laurence. *Child of the Owl*. HarperTrophy, 1990. A twelve-year-old girl living with her grandmother in San Francisco learns about her Chinese heritage. (**I:** 10–12)

———. *Thief of Hearts*. HarperCollins, 1995. Stacey has to decide whether to report a theft or to be loyal to another Chinese American girl. (**I:** 11–YA)

Books with Magical Realism

Horvath, Polly. *Everything on a Waffle*. Farrar, Straus, & Giroux, 2001. When Primrose is "orphaned" after her mother leaves to search for her father who has been lost at sea, she goes to live with an uncle. (**I:** 9–12)

Sachar, Louis. *Holes*. FSG, 1998. Stanley Yelnats is sent to a correctional camp for a crime he did not commit, and must dig holes every day to "build character." (**I:** 9–12)

Resources

Asher, Sandy, ed. *But That's Another Story*. Walker, 1996.

Baskin, Barbara H., and Karen H. Harris. *More Notes from a Different Drummer: A Guide to Juvenile Fiction Portraying the Disabled*. R. R. Bowker, 1984.

Blume, Judy. *Letters to Judy: What Your Kids Wish They Could Tell You*. Putnam, 1986.

Dreyer, Sharon Spredemann. *The Bookfinder: A Guide to Children's Literature about Interests and Concerns of Youth Aged 2–18*, volumes 1–5. American Guidance Service, 1994.

Henkin, Roxanne, and Junko Yokota. "Inclusive Reading: Literature Portraying Families with Gay and Lesbian Parents." *Democracy & Education, 13* (3) (1999): 60–61.

Lambert, Megan. (May/June 2008). "Reading about families in my family." *Hornbook, 84*(4), 261–263.

Larson, Jeanette. "The Scene of the Crime: Investigating New Mysteries." *Book Links, 17* (3) (2008): 24–28.

Rudman, Masha K., Kathleen Dunne Gagne, and Joanne E. Bernstein. *Books to Help Children Cope with Separation and Loss*, 4th ed. Bowker, 1994.

Silvey, Anita. *Children's Books and Their Creators*. Houghton Mifflin, 1995.

References

Alcott, Louisa May. *Little Women*. Macmillan, 1868/1962.

Alger, Horatio. *Ragged Dick, and Mark, the Match Boy*. Collier, 1897/1962.

Avi. *Crispin: The Cross of Lead*. Hyperion, 2002.

———. *The True Confessions of Charlotte Doyle*. Orchard, 1990.

———. *Who Was That Masked Man Anyway?* Orchard, 1992.

Blume, Judy. *Blubber*. Bradbury, 1974.

————. *Forever.* Bradbury, 1975.

————. *Starring Sally J. Freedman as Herself.* Bradbury, 1977.

Burnett, Frances Hodgson. *Little Lord Fauntleroy.* Scribner, 1886.

————. *The Secret Garden.* Lippincott, 1910/1962.

Cleary, Beverly. *A Girl from Yamhill: A Memoir.* Morrow, 1988.

————. *My Own Two Feet: A Memoir.* Morrow, 1995.

Collier, Laurie, and Joyce Nakamura. *Major Authors and Illustrators for Children and Young Adults: A Selection of Sketches from Something about the Author.* Gale Research, 1993.

Cooper, James Fenimore. *The Last of the Mohicans.* Scott, Foresman, 1826/1950.

Cushman, Karen. *The Midwife's Apprentice.* Clarion, 1995.

Daly, Maureen. *Seventeenth Summer.* Dodd, 1942.

Defoe, Daniel. *Robinson Crusoe.* Running Press, 1719/1991.

Dodge, Mary Mapes. *Hans Brinker, or the Silver Skates.* Doubleday, 1865/1932.

Donovan, John. *I'll Get There, It Better Be Worth the Trip.* Harper, 1969.

Elleman, Barbara. "Introduction." *Popular Reading for Children, II.* American Library Association, 1986, pp. v–vi.

Estes, Eleanor. *The Moffats.* Harcourt, 1941.

Grahame, Kenneth. *Wind in the Willows.* Scribner's, 1933.

Horvath, Polly. *The Pepins and Their Problems.* Farrar, Straus, & Giroux, 2004.

Hurley, Richard J. "Reading Patterns of Children: What and Why They Read." *Reading Interests of Children and Young Adults.* Ed. Jean Kujoth. Scarecrow, 1970, pp. 96–97.

Jackson, Jesse Jasper. *Call Me Charley.* Harper, 1945.

Konigsburg, E. L. *Jennifer, Hecate, Macbeth, William McKinley, and Me, Elizabeth.* Atheneum, 1968.

Lambert, Megan. (May/June 2008). "Reading about families in my family." *Hornbook, 84* (4), 261–263.

Lewis, C. S. *The Lion, the Witch and the Wardrobe: A Story for Children.* Macmillan, 1950.

Lowry, Lois. *The Giver.* Houghton Mifflin, 1993.

————. *Number the Stars.* Houghton Mifflin, 1989.

Luria, A. R. *Cognitive Development: Its Cultural and Social Foundations.* Harvard Univ. Press, 1976.

McCloskey, Robert. *Homer Price.* Viking, 1943.

————. *Make Way for Ducklings.* Viking, 1941.

Means, Florence. *The Moved Outers.* Houghton Mifflin, 1945.

————. *Shuttered Windows.* Houghton Mifflin, 1938.

Naylor, Alice Phoebe, and Carol Wintercorn. "Judy Blume." *Dictionary of Literary Biography: American Writers for Children Since 1960: Fiction*, Vol. 52. Gale Research, 1986, pp. 30–38x.

Paterson, Katherine. *Jacob Have I Loved.* Crowell, 1980.

————. *The Zena Sutherland Lectures: 1983–1992.* Edited by Betsy Hearne. Clarion, 1993.

Paulsen, Gary. *Dancing Carl.* Bradbury, 1983.

————. *Eastern Sun, Western Moon: An Autobiographical Odyssey.* Harcourt, 1993.

————. *The Winter Room.* Orchard, 1989.

————. *Winterdance: The Fine Madness of Running the Iditarod.* Harcourt, 1994.

Poll, Bernard. "Why Children Like Horse Stories." *Elementary Education* 38 (November, 1961): 473–474.

Porter, Eleanor. *Pollyanna.* L. C. Page, 1913.

Postman, Neil. *The Disappearance of Childhood.* Delacorte, 1994.

Root, Shelton. "The New Realism: Some Personal Reflections." *Language Arts* 54.1 (1977): 19–24.

Rosen, Michael. *ChaseR: A Novel in E-Mails.* Candlewick, 2002.

Rylant, Cynthia. *Soda Jerk.* Orchard Books, 1990.

Sewell, Anna. *Black Beauty: The Autobiography of a Horse.* Dodd, Mead, 1877/1941.

Spyri, Joanna. *Heidi.* Scribner's, 1884/1946.

Stanovich, Keith. "Are We Overselling Literacy?" *Stories and Readers: New Perspectives on Literature in the Elementary Classroom.* Ed. Charles Temple and Patrick Collins. Christopher-Gordon, 1992, p. 217.

Twain, Mark. *The Adventures of Huckleberry Finn.* Chanticleer, 1885/1950.

————. *The Adventures of Tom Sawyer.* Scott, Foresman, 1876/1949.

Usrey, Malcolm. *Betsy Byars.* Twayne, 1995.

Voigt, Cynthia. *Izzy, Willy-Nilly.* Atheneum, 1986.

————. *When She Hollers.* Scholastic, 1994.

Warner, Gertrude Chandler. *The Boxcar Children.* Scott, Foresman, 1950.

Zolotow, Charlotte. *A Father Like That.* Illustrated by Joanne Scribner. HarperCollins, 1971/2001.

————. *May I Visit?* Illustrated by Erik Blegvad. HarperCollins, 1976.

————. *My Grandson Lew.* Illustrated by William Pene du Bois. HarperCollins, 1974/1986.

————. *Say It!* Greenwillow, 1980.

————. *The Unfriendly Book.* Illustrated by William Pene du Bois. HarperCollins, 1975.

10

Historical Fiction

"White folks don't want colored folks in their pool."
"You're wrong, John Henry," I say,
but I know he's right.
"Let's go back to Fiddler's Creek," I say.
"I didn't want to swim in this old pool anyway."
John Henry's eyes fill up with angry tears.
"I did," he says. "I wanted to swim in this pool.
I want to do everything you can do."
I don't know what to say,
but as we walk back to town,
my head starts to pop with new ideas.

I want to go to the Dairy Dip with John Henry,
sit down and share root beer floats.
I want us to go to the picture show, buy popcorn,
and watch the movie together.
I want to see this town with John Henry's eyes.

ILLUSTRATION 10.1 Set in the South during the Civil Rights Movement, *Freedom Summer* has the potential to evoke rich conversations. (Reprinted with the permission of Atheneum Books for Young Readers, an imprint of Simon & Schuster Children's Publishing Division from *Freedom Summer* by Deborah Wiles, illustrated by Jerome Lagarrigue. Jacket illustrations copyright © 2001 Jerome Lagarrigue.)

Set in the South during the Civil Rights era, *Freedom Summer* by Deborah Wiles features the friendship of two boys—Joe, who is white, and John Henry, who is black. When the town fills the local swimming pool with asphalt rather than integrating it, Joe begins to understand what segregation means for his best friend. Quality historical fiction has the potential to broaden the way we see the world and to influence our beliefs about others' experiences, just as Joe's views were transformed in *Freedom Summer*. That is why it is so important to ensure that today's children read widely in this genre.

What Is Historical Fiction?

Historical fiction is widely defined as a work of fiction set in a time prior to when it was written. How far in the past must a story be set to qualify as historical fiction? Some say twenty-five years; others say fifty. For our purposes, the precise number of years doesn't matter. What matters most is the child's perspective. To a child, a story set forty years ago qualifies as being about olden times. So, a book such as Gary Schmidt's *The Wednesday Wars* falls in the realm of historical fiction, even though many adults view the Vietnam War era of the 1970s as something that happened "just yesterday."

Even the general definition given here may sometimes be too limiting. Some books feature events that were contemporary at the time they were written, but with the passing of time, the situations have gained historical significance. One such book is Beverly Naidoo's *Journey to Jo'burg,* which details the journey of two black South African children who experience the harsh realities of apartheid as they travel from their homeland to Johannesburg. At the time of its publication, the book described contemporary conditions in South Africa. However, the apartheid system has since been dismantled, so the events in Naidoo's book are significant from an historical perspective. Books like this one can be considered historical fiction rather than contemporary realistic fiction.

Time Periods Emphasized in Historical Fiction

Authors in the United States who write historical fiction have typically chosen to write about the United States. This means that comparatively little historical fiction set in other parts of the world is readily available to American audiences. There is also an imbalance in the subjects and time periods about which American authors have chosen to write. Some topics and periods in American history that have been written about most extensively include the American Revolutionary War, slavery and the Civil War, the westward movement, immigration, and World War II. (The Recommended Books at the end of this chapter are organized by major historical periods.) One way to broaden historical perspectives for American students is to include international literature in the array of historical fiction made available in the classroom. Outstanding authors of international historical fiction include Uri Orlev, Rosemary Sutcliff, Beverly Naidoo, Christophe Gallaz, and Toshi Maruki.

Value of Historical Fiction

Why should teachers introduce children to historical fiction? First, many works of historical fiction present wonderful stories that children can "step into" for a rich aesthetic experience.

Go to the Assignments and Activities section of Chapter 10 in the MyEducationKit and complete the activities. As you work through the activities and answer the accompanying questions, consider the importance of evaluating historical fiction for children.

Go to the Extension Activities section of Chapter 10 in the MyEducationKit for your book and complete activity #1 to think about definitions of historical fiction.

After all, who can read Helen Frost's beautifully crafted verse in *The Braid* and not be touched by the plight of twins separated through immigration? Readers of Richard Peck's *The River Between Us* will be moved by Tilly Pruitt's determination to find her soldier brother and bring him home from the ravages of the Civil War. Who won't chuckle over Michael Tunnell's *Mailing May,* a picture book in which a young girl is mailed (by train) to see her grandmother because the family cannot afford a train ticket?

Teachers also want children to read historical fiction because children are naturally curious about the past, and historical fiction offers answers to some of their questions. Historical fiction has another special value: The genre may help readers develop consciousness of how time and place influence who they are. That is, by having a better understanding of the past, children can gain a greater awareness of themselves, their community, their culture, and the world. In fact, the problems of today can often be understood only in light of times past.

Why are we recommending turning to historical fiction to help children learn about the past? Why not turn exclusively to textbooks and informational books written for children? Textbooks and informational books are important as sources of background information for readers. In fact, Chapter 11 of this textbook features many informational books and biographies that serve as outstanding companion pieces to works of historical fiction. However, historical fiction offers something special to readers. Through historical fiction, children "encounter the complexities of historical events, where facts from the past become living, breathing drama, significant beyond their own time" (Levstik, 1989, p. 136). Although this dramatic element is also found in informational books by fine writers such as Susan Bartoletti and Russell Freedman, it is too often missing from textbooks. According to Carl M. Tomlinson, Michael O. Tunnell, and Donald J. Richgels (1993), readers need "historical empathy" to develop historical understanding. That is, readers "must be able to perceive past events and issues as they were experienced by the people at the time" (p. 54). Helping readers to develop historical empathy is what historical fiction does best, by emphasizing human motives and ordinary people.

It is also important to note that historical coverage in textbooks differs dramatically from what is presented in works of historical fiction. Writers of textbooks aim for broad coverage, whereas writers of historical fiction focus on a single subject and examine it in depth. Certainly, readers need the broad view to place a story situation in proper perspective, but historical background is not sufficient by itself.

Top Shelf 10.1

International Books Set in the World War II Era

Rose Blanche by Christophe Gallaz

Hiroshima no pika by Toshi Maruki

The Island on Bird Street by Uri Orlev

The Man from the Other Side by Uri Orlev

The Lady with the Hat by Uri Orlev

Run, Boy, Run by Uri Orlev

The Book Thief by Marcus Zusak

Issue to Consider

Does Historical Fiction Have a Place in the Study of History?

Those who argue that historical fiction is an important tool in history instruction maintain that students must develop historical or social empathy to develop social studies understandings (Tomlinson, Tunnell, & Richgels, 1993). These advocates believe that children's literature is a tool that can help students develop such empathy. For example, in discussing history instruction, Levstik (1989) has observed that through literature students "encounter the complexities of historical events, where facts from the past become living, breathing drama, signifi-cant beyond their own time" (p. 136). Further, advocates argue that because writers of historical fiction do extensive research on the eras about which they write, literature is often a rich source of information.

On the opposing side are those who argue that literature must not be expected to bear the burden of social studies instruction. Literature is a fragile medium, they remind us, and it can readily be crushed if it is forced to bear too heavy an efferent load. When students are asked to read literature for the purpose of learning about the past, they may fail to enter the story world on aesthetic terms.

What do you think?   Should historical fiction serve as a springboard for learning about the past? Or should readers primarily be encouraged to read historical fiction for an aesthetic experience? If you have read *The Midwife's Apprentice*, would you want students to read the book primarily as a means of learning about medieval times, or would you choose to have students explore the theme of living a fulfilling life through this book?

Teaching Idea 10.1

Head, Heart, Hands: Nurturing Character Empathy

Since one of the benefits of reading historical fiction involves being able to empathize with a character experiencing a particular time in history, make a Head, Heart and Hands chart about a character from historical fiction. Divide a piece of paper into thirds from top to bottom. In the top section, or the "head," write about what the character knows as the story unfolds. In the middle "heart" section, write about what the character feels. And in the bottom "hand" section, write about what the character does.

In Patricia Polacco's *The Butterfly*, Monique finds out (knows/head) about the secret room in her own home and has conflicting feelings (heart) about the purpose of the room until she joins (what she does/hands) her mother in helping a Jewish family escape from Nazi-occupied France.

The Evolution of Historical Fiction

It is not possible to identify a single creator for most literary genres, but this is not the case with historical fiction. Sir Walter Scott is generally believed to be the first person to write a work of what we now call historical fiction (Blos, 1993). *Waverly,* Scott's first piece of historical fiction, was published in 1810 and was followed by others, including *Ivanhoe.* Although Scott didn't write specifically for children, his books were read by young and old alike.

Early historical fiction consisted primarily of adventure stories and contained lengthy descriptive passages and many historical inaccuracies. The early writers who wrote historical fiction specifically for children had their own agenda—teaching students historical information. By the 1930s, many of these works had become romantic, highly idealized views of the past that contained an overwhelming amount of information (Tomlinson, Tunnell, & Richgels, 1993).

Fortunately, historical fiction has changed considerably. The genre is no longer viewed primarily as a vehicle for conveying historical information. Rather, writers strive to tell stories—stories that show how living in a particular time and place in the past shaped the lives of people, especially ordinary people. And although ordinary people sometimes become caught up in major historical events, historical fiction, in large part, is not about those events. Laura Ingalls Wilder was perhaps the first writer of historical fiction for children who gained renown as a storyteller. Her books, inspired by her own childhood experiences, were among the early works of historical fiction for children that had stories to tell rather than information to convey. *The Little House in the Big Woods,* published in 1932, was the first of the Little House books. Like the others in the series, it is a warm story full of the everyday experiences of a close-knit frontier family. By the 1940s and 1950s, serious works of historical fiction were being written for children, including Newbery Medal winners *Johnny Tremain* by Esther Forbes, *The Door in the Wall* by Marguerite de Angeli, and *The Witch of Blackbird Pond* by Elizabeth George Speare. And historical fiction writer Scott O'Dell, writing in the 1960s and 1970s, is one of the few Americans to have won the prestigious Hans Christian Andersen Award.

Style

The style of writing used in historical fiction has also changed. The ornate descriptions, the sometimes archaic language, and the lengthy factual passages are gone. The language of today's historical fiction is likely to be accessible to children. Consider the opening passage from Patricia MacLachlan's *Sarah, Plain and Tall:*

> "Did Mama sing every day?" asked Caleb. "Every-single-day?" He sat close to the fire, his chin in his hand. It was dusk, and the dogs lay beside him on the warm hearthstones.
>
> "Every-single-day," I told him for the second time this week. For the twentieth time this month. The hundredth time this year? And the past few years? (p. 1)

It is the simplicity and immediacy of MacLachlan's language that pulls the reader into this story.

Historical Perspective

One of the most striking changes in historical fiction for children is in the perspective from which stories are told. Today's writers are less likely to assume idealized views of the past. Joel Taxel (1983) analyzed thirty-two pieces of historical fiction about the American Revolution written between 1899 and 1976, and discussed two of these books at length. The first, Esther Forbes's *Johnny Tremain,* which was published in 1943, encapsulates an idealized view of the American Revolution: The American patriots are viewed as a united people involved in a divinely inspired struggle for freedom and equality. The perspective in James and Christopher Collier's *My Brother Sam Is Dead,* written in 1974, stands in marked contrast: The colonists are a divided people, with many remaining loyal to the king of England. Tim Meeker, the book's protagonist, questions the values of the revolutionaries, eventually choosing not to become part of the revolutionary fervor. Differing perspectives can be explained in large part by the times in which authors live and write. *Johnny Tremain* was written in the midst of the patriotic fervor of World War II, whereas *My Brother Sam Is Dead* was published in 1974, when the United States was waging an unpopular war in Vietnam.

In recent historical fiction for children, many new perspectives have emerged. For example, in *Encounter,* Jane Yolen used a picture book format to show Columbus through the eyes of a Taino child who tries to warn his people of the coming destruction he has seen in a dream. *Morning Girl* is a chapter book that also explores the Columbus story from the Taino point of view. This book is told in alternating voices between two siblings, one enthusiastic about the coming of the white men and the other more cautious. Perspectives on pioneer times have also changed in historical fiction for children. In earlier years, the common perspective on pioneer life was of the sort seen in the *Little House* books: Although times were hard, a warm, united family was an ever-present, sustaining force. More recent books, such as Pam Conrad's *Prairie Songs* and Eve Bunting's *Dandelions,* explore the loneliness and isolation of pioneer life from a woman's perspective.

Subject Matter

The subject matter of historical fiction for children has also changed. Authors of historical fiction set in the United States are writing about less well-known historical events, periods, and places. Karen Cushman's *Rodzina* focuses on the orphan trains that transported children to the West for adoption from the 1850s to the 1920s. Gail Carson Levine's *Dave at Night* features a young boy in a Jewish orphanage situated in Harlem in the midst of the Harlem Renaissance. Christopher Paul Curtis sets *Elijah of Buxton* in Buxton Settlement, a haven for freed slaves established in 1849 in Canada. In *The Surrender Tree,* author Margarita Engle explores Cuba's wars for independence through the lives of Rosa, a nurse who tended those injured in the bitter struggles, and her husband José. Linda Sue Park's *The Kite Fighters,* set in 1473, centers around the tradition of kite competitions in ancient Korea.

Writers of earlier times adhered to an unspoken code that children needed to be protected from the less savory aspects of the past (Tunnell, 1993). This is no longer true. Mildred Taylor and other writers have written about the senseless prejudice and violence that African Americans have faced. In *Journey to Topaz,* Yoshiko Uchida wrote movingly about the experiences of Japanese Americans in internment camps during World War II. In *Malka,* Mirjam Pressler tells the story of seven-year-old Malka trying to survive the horrors of Nazi-occupied Poland on her own. Julius Lester's *Day of Tears* tells the story of the largest

Technology in Practice 10.1

Many teachers are finding multiple uses for software programs such as *Inspiration* that allow teachers and students to easily create graphic organizers that can be applied in any number of subject areas. Ready-made templates can be used, or designs can be customized.

Using *Inspiration,* or a program like it, create a Venn diagram of overlapping circles to compare a period of history with today. On one circle, write the things that were unique to the historical time period (e.g., traveling by wagon). In the other circle, write descriptors for the way things are today (e.g., traveling by car). In the center section created by the overlapping circles, write down things that both times have in common (e.g., going to school). Topics such as transportation, clothing, occupations, and men's and women's roles can be addressed. Comparisons between cultures can be made. Any time there are two topics, events, or characters to be compared or contrasted, the Venn diagram is a useful graphic organizer to use.

Creating their own Venn diagrams engages students in the subject matter in more complex ways.

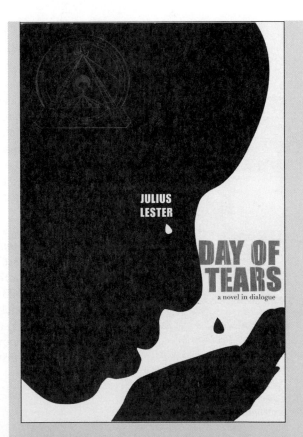

ILLUSTRATION 10.2 In *Day of Tears,* Julius Lester explores the human impact of the largest slave auction in American history. (From Julius Lester's *A Day of Tears* © 2007 by Julius Lester. Reprinted by Permission of Disney•Hyperion, an imprint of Disney Book Group LLC. All Rights Reserved.)

Top Shelf 10.2

Historical Fiction Picture Books

Kindle Me a Riddle: A Pioneer Story by Roberta Karim

Sweet Clara and the Freedom Quilt by Deborah Hopkinson

Mailing May by Michael Tunnell

Sweet Potato Pie by Kathleen Lindsey

What Zeesie Saw on Delancey Street by Elsa Okon Rael

Silent Movie by Avi

The Bracelet by Yoshiko Uchida

ILLUSTRATION 10.3   In Karen Cushman's *The Midwife's Apprentice*, a homeless waif seeks to do more than survive in the harsh world of medieval England; she seeks to become someone. (Cover from *The Midwife's Apprentice* by Karen Cushman. Jacket illustrations copyright © 1995 by Trina Schart Hyman. Reprinted by permission of Clarion Books, an imprint of Houghton Mifflin Harcourt Publishing Company. All rights reserved.)

slave auction in the United States and the way it impacted the lives of those touched by the sale. The increasing availability of historical fiction of this type makes it an important tool for launching classroom discussions about issues of social justice.

Historical fiction about other parts of the world, especially Third World countries, is increasingly available to American audiences. For example, in Minfong Ho's **Rice without Rain,** Jinda and her family are caught up in the turbulence of the 1945 student movement in Thailand as they struggle to survive the drought that has hit their homeland. Margarita Engle's **The Surrender Tree: Poems of Cuba's Struggle for Freedom** centers around Cuba's wars for independence. There is still too little historical fiction about other countries and cultures available to young American readers, but this situation is beginning to change.

Picture Books

The emergence in recent years of many works of historical fiction in picture book format is a noteworthy change. Some of these stories, such as Michael Tunnell's **Mailing May**, are appropriate for children as young as ages 5 to 8, whereas stories such as Yin's **Coolies,** about the bigotry and harsh treatment faced by two Chinese boys who are helping to build the transcontinental railroad in the United States, are better suited for older elementary children. Still other picture books, such as Margaree Mitchell's **Uncle Jed's Barbershop,** a story about the segregated South during the Depression era and Toshi Maruki's **Hiroshima no pika,** which focuses on the day Hiroshima was bombed and the after-effects of that event, are even appropriate for students in middle school and beyond. Many readers especially enjoy the picture book format because illustrations can bring hard-to-imagine settings to life and can help readers to develop a feeling for bygone eras that words alone cannot evoke.

Historical Fiction Series

Historical fiction series emerged as a strong trend in the 1990s. These series included **Dear America, Orphan Train Children, American Diaries,** and **Children of America.** Although the quality of series books varies, major children's authors have contributed to the literary quality of some of these series. For example, Kathryn Lasky, Jim Murphy, Patricia McKissack, and Karen Hesse are among the authors who have written books in the **Dear America** series. Many historical fiction series books have been pitched toward a younger audience and have featured female protagonists more often than male protagonists. Many educators have welcomed the arrival of these series, claiming that they have awakened a new interest in history and cultivated a devoted following, especially among young girls.

All the changes in the genre in recent decades make for a bright future for children's historical fiction. Certainly, books in this genre have been awarded an impressive number of Newbery Medals in recent years: Patricia MacLachlan's **Sarah, Plain and Tall** (1985), Lois Lowry's **Number the Stars** (1989), Karen Cushman's **The Midwife's Apprentice** (1995), Karen Hesse's **Out of the Dust** (1997), Christopher Curtis's **Bud, Not Buddy** (1999), Richard Peck's **A Year Down Yonder** (2001), Linda Sue Park's **A Single Shard** (2002), Avi's **Crispin** (2003), and Laura Amy Schlitz's **Good Masters! Sweet Ladies!** (2007). In 2008, Brian Selznick was awarded the Caldecott Medal for **The Invention of Hugo Cabret**. Set in a Paris train station at the turn of the twentieth century, this story about an orphan is told through an innovative blending of illustration, text, and cinematic technique. Given the special values of historical fiction, many teachers look forward to even more books of this caliber.

Categories of Historical Fiction

Joan Blos (1993) identifies three types of historical fiction: (1) fictionalized memoirs, (2) fictionalized family history, and (3) fiction based on research. She notes that the author's relationship to the material is different for each type.

Ask the Author . . .   Richard Peck

Favorite Books as a Child

The Adventures of Huckleberry Finn by Mark Twain

The Red Badge of Courage by Stephen Crane

Gone with the Wind by Margaret Mitchell

Your works of historical fiction run the gamut from the humor of A Year Down Yonder *to the gravity that infuses* The River Between. *What inspires such diverse stories?*

In the months and now the years after the 9/11 attack upon the city where I live and work, I've gone forth on my school visits with new purpose. How is the signal event of modern history being expressed to the young?

Are schools bringing back maps to the classrooms, now that we know geography is no defense against history? Are we requiring foreign language at every age level of every student, now that we know we don't have enough language to decode our adversaries? Are we bringing back twelve years of non-elective, sequential history—and how it repeats?

Not as far as I can see. The schools I visit seem eerily trapped in the twentieth century. But then any real curricular change might well require the kind of authority parents withdrew from schools a generation ago.

What can I do about that? I can devote the rest of my career to writing historical fiction for young readers. After all, I fell in love with the Civil War not in history class but in the pages in *Gone with the Wind* and *The Red Badge of Courage.*

These were two radically different views of a mythic war, a reminder that many roads lead to the past. The great need is to bring as many young readers as possible along on the travel through time in the knowledge that no single book wins them all. I look high and low for new ways to lure the young into the past. Humor works. It certainly did for Mark Twain. His *The Adventures of Huckleberry Finn* has been called the first real American novel. But it was an historical novel too, written after the Civil War about a vanished ante-bellum world. In fact, it was nostalgia with a sting in its tail—my favorite thing. Mark Twain

reminds us of the uses of humor, and how humor is anger that was sent to finishing school.

And so in a good many of my novels, *The Teacher's Funeral, Fair Weather, The Ghost Belonged to Me, A Long Way from Chicago,* the historical content is dramatized in a series of comic scenes.

Not all of history can be lightly told, as 9/11 proves. But the past has a glamour that eludes the history textbook. In a book of mine about the Civil War, *The River Between Us,* there's limited scope for lightness and less for laughter. I turn, instead, to suspense and a secret. But the story takes place on Twain's own river, flowing like history itself, and it turns out to be about a family secret.

All of our stories are family stories, written to invite the young to look back at the traditions of their own families. And all of our stories are about how history repeats, written for readers too young to have seen that for themselves.

Richard Peck has written thirty novels, and is the only children's book author ever to have received a National Humanities Medal. In addition, he has won a number of other major awards for the body of his work, including the Margaret A. Edwards Award, the ALAN Award, and the Medallion from the University of Southern Mississippi. Virtually every publication and association in the field of children's literature has recommended his books, including Mystery Writers of America, which twice gave him their Edgar Allan Poe Award. His *A Year Down Under* won the 2001 Newbery Medal. Its prequel, *A Long Way from Chicago,* was a National Book Award finalist and Newbery Honor Book. He lives in New York City, and spends a great deal of time traveling around the country to speaking engagements at conferences, schools, and libraries. ■

Fictionalized Memoirs

Because writers of fictionalized memoirs have lived through the era about which they write, they are able to draw on their own experiences in crafting their narratives. The result is often a story that is full of extraordinarily rich details about daily life and that holds a special sense of immediacy for the reader. For example, it is easy to imagine how, in writing *Little House on the Prairie,* Laura Ingalls Wilder drew on personal memories to describe the family's first Christmas on the prairie:

> For Christmas dinner there was the tender, juicy, roasted turkey. There were the sweet pota-toes, baked in the ashes and carefully wiped so that you could eat the good skins, too. There was a loaf of salt-rising bread made from the last of the white flour.
>
> And after all that there were stewed dried blackberries and little cakes. But these little cakes were made with brown sugar and they did not have white sugar sprinkled over their tops.
>
> Then Pa and Ma and Mr. Edwards sat by the fire and talked about Christmas times back in Tennessee and up north in the Big Woods. But Mary and Laura looked at their beautiful cakes and played with their pennies and drank their water out of their new cups. And little by little they licked and sucked their sticks of candy, till each stick was sharp-pointed on one end.
>
> That was a happy Christmas. (pp. 251–252)

Writers of fictionalized memoirs may draw on personal memories, but these memoirs are seen from an historical perspective, because the time about which the authors write may be vastly different from the time in which they are writing. You may wonder why fictional-ized memoirs are not considered biography if personal experiences serve as the inspiration for them. The reason is, quite simply, that the writers fictionalize their personal experiences. For example, in the first paragraph of *Little House on the Prairie,* Wilder says that Baby Carrie made the trip from the Big Woods, but her real sister Carrie had not yet been born when the family left their home in Wisconsin (Frey & Griffith, 1987).

Fictionalized Family History

Many families treasure a tradition of passing family stories from one generation to the next, and family stories have fed the historical fiction of many writers. Sometimes historical fic-tion develops from only the barest snippet of a family story. Such was the case for writer Ann Turner. As Turner and her aunt looked at an old trunk, her aunt remembered another old trunk (Turner, 1993):

> "You know, there used to be a very old trunk in Grandpa's house, in the basement. . . . It was an eighteenth-century trunk . . . a big, black domed thing covered with leather. . . . And there were two stories about it. One was that during the early period of settlement some of our ancestors escaped from an Indian attack in that trunk. The other story is that when the rebels came, some children were hidden in that trunk and escaped the rebels."
>
> "You mean we were Tories?" . . .
>
> "Oh, yes, some were . . . Anyway, I wonder what happened to that trunk." (p. 11)

From this fleeting exchange grew *Katie's Trunk,* a story set during the American Revolution in which a Tory child hides in the family trunk when a band of patriots comes to her house.

In other instances, relatively well developed stories are passed down, stories that writ-ers can use with only a little fleshing out. According to Patricia Polacco, *Pink and Say,* her story of the friendship between a black Union soldier and a white Union soldier, was passed down through her family from her great-great-grandfather, who happened to be the white soldier in the story. In writing *Our Only May Amelia,* Jennifer Holm drew on the actual diary written by her great aunt to fashion this story about a young Finnish-American girl born on the Nasel River in Washington during the late nineteenth century.

Fiction Based on Research

Probably the bulk of historical fiction for children fits into the third category: fiction based on research. Writers who set their stories in eras about which they have no firsthand knowledge must perform research to ensure authenticity. The amount of information available to writers can vary extensively. Writers who feature cultures with no writing systems frequently have only scant anthropological evidence from which to draw. Michael Dorris faced this situation when writing **Morning Girl.** Set on a Bahamian island in 1492, the book centers on a sister and brother of the Taino tribe. The story ends as Morning Girl greets the white visitors who paddle to shore—men from Columbus's ship. Dorris (1992) noted that the Tainos had no writing system, and within a generation or two of Columbus's coming, the tribe was wiped out by disease. The only written reference to these people was one entry Columbus included in his journal. By contrast, writers who focus on literate societies often have a wealth of original sources as well as extensive reference material from which to draw their information. Frances Temple (1994) described the research she did in writing **The Ramsay Scallop,** a story about a couple's religious pilgrimage, set in Europe in 1300:

> More than seventy books turn up cited in my notes for **The Ramsay Scallop**, some in English, some in French or Spanish, some in medieval French. . . . One source led to another: art books; religious meditations; playscripts; a guidebook written in 1190 by a priest, with tips on where to find clean water and what to use to discourage fleas; histories, where I found a picture of Nana Sybille in her wheelbarrow; and song books. (p. 18)

Research can take other forms as well. In writing **The Apprenticeship of Lucas Whitaker,** a book about the devastation caused by consumption 150 years ago, author Cynthia DeFelice interviewed a pathologist and an archaeologist, examined old burial grounds using radar technology, and spent a day in an anthropologist's lab learning about folk medical practices (DeFelice, 1998).

How Historical Fiction Works

Historical fiction differs—at least in some ways—from other genres. In particular, a work of historical fiction contains "time markers" that clearly situate it in a particular time period. Let's consider some of the critical aspects of historical fiction, which affect both how it is written and how it should be read.

Setting

Because historical fiction takes place in a time removed from the reader, setting is an especially important element. The writer's obligation is to bring place and time to life for the reader by providing details that are neither romanticized nor distorted, but are as authentic as possible, given what is known about the era in which the story is set. Research is the most likely means by which the writer obtains these details.

The importance of rich details of setting is evident in Gary Blackwood's **The Shakespeare Stealer.** As the young apprentice Widge views a new neighborhood of London, the first city he has ever visited, he is struck by all he sees:

> Here there were no gold-plated buildings or great cathedrals, only shabby rows of houses, cheek by jowl. With no space to spread sidewise, they had arched over the street, like the trees on that desolate stretch of road where we had met the outlaws, nearly meeting above our heads, shutting out the sun.
>
> There were no street vendors here, nor prosperous merchants, only sullen wives emptying their slop jars into the street, sometimes missing the scrawny, shoeless children playing there, sometimes not. Falconer strode heedlessly along, as if daring anyone to empty a chamber pot on his head. No one did. One house had been boarded up, and a crude wooden cross nailed to its front door. Beneath the cross were scrawled the words LORD HAVE MERCY UPON US.
>
> "Is that a church?" I said.
>
> Falconer gave a derisive laugh. "That's a plague house, boy." (p. 42)

The details that Blackwood includes make it easy for the reader to envision how dramatically different the London of Shakespeare's day must have been from our own times. Details about

Top Shelf 10.4

Pairing Related Picture Books and Lengthier Works of Historical Fiction

American Revolution

Katie's Trunk by Ann Turner

My Brother Sam Is Dead by James Collier and Christopher Collier

Slavery and the Civil War

Pink and Say by Patricia Polacco

Silent Thunder by Andrea Pinkney

The Secret to Freedom by Marcia Vaughan

Elijah of Buxton by Christopher Paul Curtis

Westward Movement in the United States

Dandelions by Eve Bunting

Prairie Songs by Pam Conrad

Train to Somewhere by Eve Bunting

Rodzina by Karen Cushman

Coolies by Yin

Dragon's Gate by Laurence Yep

World War II

Sadako by Eleanor Coerr

Sadako and the Thousand Paper Cranes by Eleanor Coerr

The Butterfly by Patricia Polacco

Number the Stars by Lois Lowry

Hirohima no pika by Toshi Maruki

Hiroshima by Laurence Yep

The Bracelet by Yoshiko Uchida

Journey to Topaz by Yohiko Uchida

setting are crucial, although it is equally important not to include so many as to overwhelm the story. Further, setting details must advance the story, as they do in *The Shakespeare Stealer*. Widge's attention to his new surroundings helps the reader to see just how inexperienced with city ways the young apprentice is.

The time and place in which a writer situates a story must be integral to the story. How can a reader judge whether this is the case? If the story could just as easily have been set in another era, then the setting is not essential to the story. The setting of *The Midwife's Apprentice* is clearly pivotal to the story. Cushman's story is set in medieval England, at a time when daily life was harsh and even cruel for those who were not members of the privileged classes. At the beginning of the book, the daily realities of survival so completely dominate the reality of the protagonist that, as she burrowed in a dung heap for warmth, "she dreamed of nothing, for she hoped for nothing and expected nothing. It was as cold and dark inside her as out in the frosty night" (p. 2).

Plot

According to Jean Fritz (1986), the original sense of the word *history* is "to ask questions," and writers of historical fiction must do just that. It is easy to imagine some of the questions Karen Hesse, author of *Letters from Rifka,* might have asked as she researched and wrote her novel. The book is about a young Jewish girl who sets out from Russia with her family, but is not allowed by officials to cross the Atlantic because she has contracted ringworm. Left behind in the care of strangers, Rifka eventually makes the journey alone. In creating this dramatic immigration story, Hesse may well have posed questions like these: What was it like to cross the ocean in search of a new life in a new land? Who were the people who made those journeys? Why did they do it? What uncertainties did they face? Such questions suggest possibilities for story conflict and the events that culminate in an eventual resolution of the conflict. Still other kinds of questions are posed in an attempt to ensure historical authenticity. In writing *Nowhere to Call Home,* a story about children who become hobos during the Great Depression, Cynthia DeFelice (1998) sought answers to a multitude of questions about train travel in 1930:

> How long would it have taken to ride from Pittsburgh to Cincinnati in a boxcar? What was the price of a passenger ticket from Philadelphia to Chicago? Did freight and passenger trains load and unload in different places? What did Broad Street station in Philadelphia look like then? Did trains have bathrooms and running water? Had refrigerator cars been invented yet? (p. 33)

Jean Fritz expressed the hope that readers of historical fiction would also ask questions as they read a book—questions that might be quite similar to those asked by the writer. However, Violet Harris (1995) warns that young readers might not have sufficient historical knowledge of a period about which they are reading to ask questions, and she suggests that they be given opportunities to read informational books to gain the necessary background information. Reading informational books may be especially important when the historical time periods or events featured in the historical fiction are less well known to the reader, particularly when those events are outside the cultural group of the reader.

Yet another way of preparing students to read longer works of historical fiction is by pairing them with historical fiction picture books set in the same era. The carefully selected picture book can provide the reader with a preview that helps set the stage for the longer work. For example, *Baseball Saved Us*, a picture book about life in a Japanese American concentration camp during World War II, can be paired with *Journey to Topaz,* a longer and more complex work with a similar focus.

In historical fiction, the writer creates a conflict that grows out of the time in which the story is set. Events must unfold plausibly, and the conflict must be resolved in a manner that is consistent with the historical context in which the story is situated. Gary Blackwood achieves all this in *The Shakespeare Stealer.* Widge, the book's protagonist, is an apprentice in the England of Shakespeare's day, a period in which England was a "paradise for women, a prison for servants, and a hell for horses. Prentices were too lowly to even deserve mention"

(p. 7). Caught up in the often abusive apprenticeship system, Widge struggles to hide from the cruel master who has purchased him for the sole purpose of having him steal the script of *Hamlet* from the Globe's theatrical company. Widge is also an "apprentice to friendship." When the Globe's troupe offers him the chance to become an apprentice, Widge, who has spent most of his life serving uncaring masters, must struggle to accept the caring friendship extended by troupe members.

Jacqueline Kelly's ***The Evolution of Calpurnia Tate*** offers yet another example of a story in which the conflict clearly grows out of the time period in which the story is set. Young Calpurnia Tate discovers that her growing interest in nature and science is not deemed an acceptable interest for a young girl in a rural Texas community in 1899. Her mother's pressure to make Calpurnia into a proper lady is counterbalanced only by the support of her grandfather, an amateur naturalist.

Characters

More often than not, the characters in historical fiction are ordinary people rather than figures of historical importance. Sometimes, they are swept up in great historical events of their time, as happens in Richard Peck's ***On the Wings of Heroes,*** a World War II story in which a young boy and his family are caught up in the war effort, making sacrifices that include sending a son off to war. As often as not though, the characters in historical fiction are living what can be best described as commonplace lives. For example, ***Good Masters! Sweet Ladies!*** features monologues by ordinary young people living in a Medieval village—the plowboy, the blacksmith's daughter, the glassblower's apprentice, and the village beggar, among others.

ILLUSTRATION 10.4   In *The Evolution of Calpurnia Tate,* a young girl seeks to follow an unconventional dream in rural Texas in 1899. (Cover of *The Evolution of Calpurnia Tate* written by Jacqueline Kelly. Cover courtesy of Henry Holt and Company, 2009. Reprinted by arrangement with Henry Holt and Company, LLC.)

At times, though, major historical figures do enter into works of historical fiction. Sometimes, they play only a minor role; for example, Frederick Douglass figures briefly in Christopher Paul Curtis's ***Elijah of Buxton***. In other books, historical figures play more prominent roles. In Ann Rinaldi's ***Finishing Becca,*** the protagonist is employed in the home of General Benedict Arnold and is able to observe the general's treason firsthand.

Whether their characters are ordinary people or important historical figures, writers of historical fiction strive to create authentic characters who behave in ways that are consistent with the period. For example, Puritan New England, the setting of ***The Witch of Blackbird Pond,*** was an era in which women did not often assert themselves. Yet Kit, Elizabeth George Speare's protagonist, is a strong-willed young woman who leaves her grandfather's home in Barbados after he dies to live with her aunt and uncle in New England. Speare legitimizes Kit's behavior and makes her a believable character by allowing readers to discover, as the story unfolds, that the culture of Barbados was one in which young women were allowed far more independence than they were in Puritan New England.

The need to create characters who behave in believable ways for the time period can create a quandary for the author, who must also develop a character with whom today's readers can identify. Some critics argue that in creating her character Birdy for the book ***Catherine, Called Birdy***, Karen Cushman paid more attention to the present-day reader than to the ways in which young girls behaved in medieval times. Yet Birdy is an immensely popular character with young readers. If Cushman had opted for total historical accuracy about a period in which girls did very

Teaching Idea 10.2
Exploring Important Historical Events

To help students pick out the important historical events from a work of historical fiction, have them create a storyboard using a large piece of newsprint or legal-sized paper. (The larger sized paper allows more to be written and accommodates larger size print.) Divide the paper into five columns and two rows. (This will result in a total of 10 sections on the storyboard.) Help the students identify five important events that occurred over the course of the book. They should record a different event in each column of the top row. Students can either write about the event or draw a picture of the event with an appropriate caption. Then, in the second row beneath each event, have the students summarize how the protagonist was changed or affected by the event.

When students are first learning how to identify important events, this type of activity can be done with the whole class. Once students become proficient, they can work alone or with a partner.

Technology in Practice 10.2

Publishing software, such as *Word Publisher*, allows teachers and students to create professional-looking publications in the form of pamphlets and newsletters. Have students create headlines about an historical event that was the focal point in a work of historical fiction. They can then summarize the event through the characters' eyes by using reporters' questions (*who, what, when, where, how,* and *why*) to cover the salient facts about the event as it is reported in the book.

Imagine the interview between a student reporter and Asia from Jeanette Ingold's *Pictures, 1918*. Asia, as a girl in 1918, wants to learn photography. She is encouraged by some and discouraged by others. Meanwhile she is getting to know Nick better and better. The interviewer could capture the different angles on this human interest story through Asia's eyes, her grandmother's, the camera store owner's, and possibly Nick's. Read all about it.

little, the story would not have offered much to hold modern readers' interest—with the result that many readers might never have gotten a taste of medieval life.

Theme

We can discern a great deal about life by learning about our past, and writers of historical fiction frequently explore themes that are significant not only for the historical period of the story but also for the present. In a listing of the themes that she explored in her Newbery Medal winner *A Gathering of Days: A New England Girl's Journal, 1830–1832,* Joan Blos (1993) includes "parent loss, death, remarriage, teacher accountability, community control, civil rights, moral responsibility versus personal loyalty" (p. 14). All are still relevant today.

The themes found in historical fiction are diverse and significant: the senselessness of prejudice and violence, the importance of family and community, the destructiveness of oppression, the need for freedom and independence, the importance of loyalty, faith and honor, the need to reach out to others. Kathy Broderick (1994) observed that "we learn about the present from studying the past. Though some of the problems of the past have been solved, there are questions that the characters in . . . [books] ask that we are still asking today" (p. 19). For this reason, historical fiction can be used to launch rich and relevant discussions focused on issues of social justice.

Criteria for Evaluating Historical Fiction

Teaching Idea 10.3

Interviewing Characters from History

When studying a particular period of history, have one group of students read informational books about the targeted period while a second group reads a work of historical fiction set in the same period. Students who read the informational books will become interviewers. They will prepare for this role by using information from the books to develop a list of questions about the historical period being studied. Students who read the historical fiction will "become" a character in the story and will be interviewed. The interviewee must answer the interview questions from the perspective of the character in their story.

For example, while studying the westward movement in the United States, the interviewer could use various books to create questions about what the westward experience was like. Meanwhile, two other students read Jane Kurtz's *I'm Sorry, Almira Ann*. One student can play the part of Almira Ann and the other can play the part of her friend Sarah. The interviewer can ask them questions about their experience moving westward with their families. The students would answer as if they were the girls, inferring answers to the interview questions based on the information from the story.

- Is the story well written according to literary standards outlined in Chapter 2?

- Does the writer bring the setting to life through the inclusion of authentic details that do not overwhelm the story?

- Do the characters behave in ways that are believable, given the time period in which they live?

- Are the conflicts in the story plausible in light of the time period in which the story is set?

- Although the story is set in the past, is the theme still relevant for today's readers?

Major Writers of Historical Fiction and Their Works

This section introduces a handful of authors who have written extensively in the genre of historical fiction. In addition to the writers featured in this section, many other authors contributed to defining the genre. For example, Laura Ingalls Wilder introduced readers to the days of the westward movement and life on the prairie and Yoshiko Uchida helped readers understand the tragedy of Japanese Americans being imprisoned in their own country during World War II. Many other major writers of

Ask the Author . . .

Katherine Paterson

Katherine Paterson

Favorite Books as a Child

Winnie-the-Pooh by A. A. Milne

The Secret Garden by Frances Hodgson Burnett

The Yearling by Marjorie Kinnan Rawlings

What draws you to writing historical fiction?

I think the short answer to this question is I write about the past because I want to understand the present. Jill Paton Walsh once said, "If you want to understand a period in history, don't read the contemporary literature of that time, read the historical fiction." We're using the past, we who write historical fiction, to shed light on our own time.

I am blessed, as many of my contemporaries are, with a condition known as presbyopia. I always thought it very appropriate for a Presbyterian elder to have presbyopia, which coming from the Greek means "elderly eyes" and refers to the condition of not being able to focus on nearby objects, a condition that tends to afflict those of us who are aging. It is treated by prescribing spectacles. Now it seems to me as the torrent of events of the recent past has engulfed me, how difficult it has been to focus properly. Like everyone of you, I suspect, I am asking for some coherent explanation of Kosovo, of Columbine. Even the newspapers are asking: What in the past has led us to this tragic day? So history becomes a pair of spectacles through which we try to focus our vision of the chaotic present.

We're not good at this. Since the 1960s, we've discounted history. We haven't thought it important for our young people to know the past. More recently, we have decided that the Internet will answer all their questions far better than any dusty book.

But history is story, and story doesn't fare well on the web. The web presupposes that one will wish to jump about and grab bits and pieces of information from a wide variety of sources. History is narrative in form; it deals with causes and effects, with acts and the consequences of those actions. History cares about space and linear time. The web eschews narrative, ignores cause and effect, honors neither space nor time. It is everywhere anytime, and thus no particular time or particular place is of real importance. I am not advocating closing down the Internet, but I am pleading that we pay attention to what we are doing when we allow it to reign unquestioned and supreme.

Still the history found in history books is the telling of events (usually wars) and the lives of the powerful. I love to embellish that record with the lives of ordinary people—young persons whose hopes and feelings and dreams a twenty-first-century young person might understand and care about. To me, the Industrial Revolution is only gears and machinery and statistics until I find in the midst of it a homesick farm girl working four looms in the lint-filled, ear-shattering weaving room of a nineteenth-century cotton mill.

Katherine Paterson is the author of thirteen novels for children and young people, including *Bridge to Terabithia* and *Jacob Have I Loved*, Newbery winners in 1978 and 1981, and *The Great Gilly Hopkins*, a Newbery Honor Book. *The Great Gilly Hopkins* and *The Master Puppeteer* were National Book Award winners in 1979 and 1977. Other works of historical fiction that have won awards are *Of Nightingales That Weep* (Phoenix Award, 1994), *Lyddie* (IBBY Honor Book, 1996), *Jip, His Story* (Scott O'Dell Award, 1997), and *Preacher's Boy* (Jefferson Cup, 2000). In 1998, she was awarded the highest international prize for children's literature, the Hans Christian Andersen medal; and in 2000, the Library of Congress named her a Living Legend.

Katherine Paterson was born in China. She is a graduate of King College, Bristol, Tennessee, and holds master's degrees from both the Presbyterian School of Christian Education, Richmond, Virginia, and Union Theological Seminary, New York City. She lived and worked for four years in Japan before her marriage. The Patersons live in Vermont and have four grown children and six grandchildren. ∎

historical fiction were mentioned earlier in this chapter. And some writers who have created truly notable works of historical fiction are not included as major writers of the genre because they do not write primarily historical fiction. This would include writers such as Katherine Paterson and Lois Lowry, who are featured in other chapters in this book.

Christopher Paul Curtis

Christopher Paul Curtis has published a number of works of contemporary realistic fiction, but it is his historical fiction that has garnered numerous accolades. To date he has published three works of historical fiction—*The Watsons Go to Birmingham—1963, Bud, Not Buddy*, and *Elijah of Buxton*. *The Watsons Go to Birmingham—1963*, Curtis's first book, was named a Newbery Honor book and also received the Coretta Scott King Award. *Bud, Not Buddy* became the first book ever to receive both the Newbery Medal and the Coretta Scott King Award. His third work of historical fiction, *Elijah of Buxton*, was also named a Newbery Honor book and was awarded the Coretta Scott King Award.

Curtis explores the African American experience in his three works of historical fiction, but the books are set in distinctly different time periods and places. *The Watsons Go to Birmingham—1963* takes place in both Michigan and Alabama during the Civil Rights Movement. *Bud, Not Buddy* is set in Flint, Michigan during the Great Depression, and *Elijah of Buxton* is set in the Buxton Settlement, a haven for freed slaves in Canada. Despite the diversity in locales and time periods, there is a commonality among these award-winning books—the remarkable blend of emotion, drama, and humor that have become hallmarks of Christopher Paul Curtis's writing.

Karen Cushman

To date, Karen Cushman has published six books, all historical fiction, and she has established a remarkable record. Her first book, *Catherine, Called Birdy,* was named a 1995 Newbery Honor Book, and the second, *The Midwife's Apprentice,* was awarded the 1996 Newbery Medal. These two books are set in the Middle Ages, as is *Matilda Bone. The Ballad of Lucy Whipple* is set in the California gold rush of 1848, and *Rodzina* explores the experiences of an Orphan Train rider. Her most recent book, *The Loud Silence of Francine Green,* is set in Hollywood in the midst of the McCarthy era.

Cushman says that she long ago turned away from a fascination with queens and kings and princesses and princes, and moved toward an interest in ordinary people. That interest led her to do extensive research on the lives of ordinary people in medieval England, the setting of three of her six books. The protagonist of *Catherine, Called Birdy* is a strong-willed young lady who is determined not to marry the man her father has selected for her. In her journal, Birdy records, with frequent humor, her ongoing battle with her father, her changing perspectives on life, and many everyday occurrences. In *The Midwife's Apprentice,* a homeless and nameless girl is literally pulled from the dung heap where she is sleeping and given the opportunity to become a midwife's apprentice. Cushman chronicles the girl's transformation from a nameless waif to a person with a name, a place in the world, and a vision of who she can become. In *Matilda Bone,* a young girl who has been raised and educated in the manor house is sent by the priest to live on Blood and Bone Alley. Matilda is at first dismayed by what she perceives to be the coarseness of life on Blood and Bone Alley, and only slowly does she come to appreciate the dependable, hardworking people she meets in her new life.

Teaching Idea 10.4

Jackdaws for Introducing Historical Fiction

In order to introduce a story and the period of history in which it is set, assemble a collection of artifacts that represent important facets of the story. One by one, pull the artifacts from a bag or box and encourage the students to ask questions and make guesses about the role of the object in the story. As each object is revealed, encourage students to consider how the artifacts might be related. Students will likely be motivated to make some predictions about the setting or context for the artifacts—who uses them and how they might be used.

For example, before one teacher introduced *Sarah, Plain and Tall*, she filled a brown paper bag with a map, a bonnet, a toy seal, and seashells. She pulled one item out at a time, inviting her students to make predictions about the story. All their predictions were accepted. In doing so the teacher not only motivated the students' interest in the story, but she was able to informally assess what kind of background knowledge they had about the story setting and establish a purpose for reading—to find out if their predictions were accurate or not.

Karen Hesse

Karen Hesse writes in various genres, but her works of historical fiction are of particular note. Her books explore wide-ranging
topics and are set in a variety of different historical periods. They
are notable for their distinctive crafting. The young Jewish immigrant in Hesse's first work of historical fiction, **Letters from
Rifka,** documents her experiences in a series of letters written in
the margins of a beloved book of poetry. Hesse's second work
of historical fiction, **Out of the Dust,** won the 1998 Newbery
Medal. Written in sparse free verse, she documents the suffering and grim realities of life
in Oklahoma during the Great Depression. Hesse has written two additional historical works
as free verse poetry. **Aleutian Sparrow,** told in the voice of a girl of Aleut and Caucasian
heritage, explores the prejudice and sorrow the Aleutian people faced when forced by the
United States to relocate to Alaska during World War II. **Witness,** also written in free verse,
is crafted as a drama in five acts. This work of historical fiction, set in 1924, relies on the
voices of eleven townspeople to tell the story of what happened in their small Vermont town
when the Ku Klux Klan moved in and attempted to recruit members. Hesse's other historical novels include **Stowaway** and **A Light in the Storm: The Civil War Diary of Amelia
Martin, Fenwick Island, Delaware, 1861**. The latter is part of the **Dear America** series.
Hesse has also written historical fiction in picture book format in **The Cats in Krasinski
Square,** a story of Jewish resistance in Warsaw during World War II.

Technology in Practice 10.3

Visit the teachingbooks.net website to hear
Christopher Paul Curtis talk about some of
the questions he asked when doing
research for **Elijah of Buxton**, a work of
historical fiction set in Buxton Settlement,
a haven for freed slaves in Canada.

Uri Orlev

Uri Orlev, now an Israeli citizen, was born in Warsaw, Poland, in 1931. World War II broke
out when he was six and lasted until he was fourteen. Orlev has said that the Holocaust was
his childhood, and he has written about that tragic time for children. **The Island on Bird
Street** tells the story of a Jewish boy who hides in a bombed-out building in the ghetto. In
this "island," he struggles with terror, loneliness, and near starvation as he waits for his father
to return. The story ends on a hopeful note as the boy and his father join the partisans who
are resisting the Nazis. In **The Man from the Other Side,** a Polish boy and his father risk their
lives to help the Jews who are confined to the Warsaw ghetto. The protagonist of **Run, Boy,
Run** is a ghetto survivor who escapes into the Polish countryside and adopts a Catholic identity in order to survive.

All of Orlev's books have been translated into English. He has been recognized inter-
nationally for his writing for children, and a number of his books have won the Mildred L.
Batchelder Award, given annually by the American Library Association for the most outstanding book in translation published originally in a foreign language. In recognition of his
body of work, Orlev received the Hans Christian Andersen Award in 1996.

Linda Sue Park

The daughter of Korean immigrants, Linda Sue Park has a growing body of historical fiction, all of which is set in Korea. Her works give young American readers a glimpse into worlds
about which most will know little—until reading these engaging books. Having visited Korea
only once as a child, Park relies on meticulous research to gather the materials needed to
bring to life the social orders of a variety of eras of historic Korea.

A relative newcomer to the world of children's literature, Park published her first children's book, **Seesaw Girl,** in 1999. Set in seventeenth century Korea, Jade Blossom, a girl from
a well-to-do family, is restricted to her family's compound until her marriage. Longing to see
the world, Jade Blossom devises a clever escape that places her in danger. **The Kite Fighters**
centers around the sport of competitive kite flying in the fifteenth century as well as the
rivalry between two brothers who bring vastly different talents to the sport. For her third book,
A Single Shard, Park won the Newbery Medal. The main character of this moving tale, set
in twelfth century Korea, is Tree-ear, an orphan who becomes captivated by the art of pottery

making and dreams of becoming a potter. However, the restrictive traditions of twelfth century Korea threaten to preclude Tree-ear from following in the footsteps of his mentor.

While much of Park's work is set in ancient Korea, *When My Name Was Keoko* is set in mid-twentieth century Korea, a period in which the country was occupied by Japan prior to and during World War II. Two siblings struggle to maintain their dignity in the face of the harsh conditions of Japanese occupation that ban all Korean traditions and even force Koreans to adopt Japanese names. *When My Name Was Keoko* has given attention to a historical time period about which far too little is known or acknowledged.

Richard Peck

Richard Peck's fiction has a wide range: from horror and mystery to realism and historical fiction. It is his historical works that have been the most widely recognized. *A Long Way from Chicago* was named a Newbery Honor book in 1999, and in 2001 the sequel, *A Year Down Yonder,* won the Newbery Medal. Both books feature Grandma Dowdel, a larger than life trickster living in a small town in Illinois. In *A Long Way from Chicago,* Joey and his sister, Mary Alice, visit Grandma Dowdel summer after summer. Early on, they are taken aback by the outrageous antics of their grandmother, but soon, they join in the fun themselves. In *A Year Down Yonder,* set in the midst of the Depression, Joey is working in the Civilian Conservation Corps, and Mary Alice goes to live with her grandmother for a year. The humor that permeates these novels has been compared to that of Mark Twain. *Fair Weather* and *The Teacher's Funeral: A Comedy in Three Parts* are equally hilarious. In *Fair Weather,* three siblings leave their small town to visit a wealthy aunt in Chicago and attend the 1893 Columbian Exposition. The children are accompanied by their unconventional grandfather, whose antics soon turn their aunt's social life upside down. Set in rural Indiana in the early twentieth century, *The Teacher's Funeral: A Comedy in Three Parts* is equally amusing. When the only teacher of the town's one-room schoolhouse dies in August, Russell Culver thinks he's been given an opportunity to escape farm life and head for adventure in the Dakotas. But when his sister Tansy steps into the role of teacher, Russell's dreams die and he fears his worst nightmares might be realized.

Much of Peck's historical fiction is distinct because of its humor, strong story lines, and richly drawn characters. Peck demonstrated his versatility as a writer of historical fiction in *The River Between Us,* a Civil War story that is equally rich in characterization, but filled with mystery and pain. When a fair-skinned young lady accompanied by a dark-skinned young woman disembark from a steamboat that has traveled up the Mississippi from New Orleans, the Pruitt family takes in the mysterious strangers. As the Civil War breaks out, the lives of the Pruitts and the young women who have joined their household are intricately entwined in this dramatic and richly layered story.

Mildred Taylor

Mildred Taylor has given a special gift to children's literature: the gift of the Logan family, an African American family living in rural Mississippi during the Depression. Readers met the Logan family in Taylor's first book, *Song of the Trees*. For *Roll of Thunder, Hear My Cry,* her second novel about the Logans, Taylor was awarded the Newbery Medal. The family's determination to keep their land and their efforts to survive the racism directed at African Americans in rural Mississippi of the 1930s create the central tensions in *Roll of Thunder, Hear My Cry*. Taylor continued to write about the themes and characters of her earlier books in later works, including *Let the Circle Be Unbroken, The Friendship, The Gold Cadillac, Mississippi Bridge, The Well,* and *The Land*.

Taylor's historical fiction is fictionalized family history. Reviewers and critics have long marveled that someone who did not live through the Depression could write about that era of American history with such authenticity. The answer lies, at least in part, in the family stories that Taylor listened to as a child. She was born in Mississippi, but her family moved to Toledo, Ohio, while she was still a baby. Although Taylor grew up in the North, she was connected to the South through the stories her father told about his own childhood in rural

Mississippi. Also, each summer, the Taylors traveled to Mississippi to visit their extended family. Family stories were woven into the fabric of those summer visits with the Taylor clan, and many of the events narrated in those stories became events in the stories Taylor wrote.

Awards for Historical Fiction

To check your comprehension on the content covered in this chapter, go to the MyEducation-Kit for your book and complete the Study Plan for Chapter 10. Here you will be able to take a chapter quiz and receive feed-back on your answers.

There is a lot of historical fiction for children available today, and teachers and librarians will want to choose the best to offer young readers. Looking for award-winning books is one way to be assured of selecting high-quality books. As you've seen from earlier sections of this chapter, historical fiction is well represented among Newbery Medal winners and Honor Books. In addition, the Scott O'Dell Award for Historical Fiction was established in 1981 to encourage the writing and reading of historical fiction. The National Council for Social Studies annually identifies Notable Children's Trade Books in the Field of Social Studies, and historical fiction is frequently included among these books.

These award-winning works of historical fiction, as well as other historical fiction titles, are important windows onto the past for young readers. In the following chapter we explore informational books and biography. Teachers can create rich contexts for learning by using historical fiction in conjunction with these genres.

Experiences for Further Learning

1. Published authors of historical fiction draw from a variety of sources when gathering the historical information they need to write their stories. Family stories are often a valuable source of information. Mildred Taylor is one author of historical fiction who has drawn heavily from family stories. Many stories about racial discrimination and the economic struggles during the Great Depression were passed directly down through her family, and Taylor has incorporated many of them into her fiction.

   Typically, writers of historical fiction—even those who draw on family stories—also engage in additional research. Published authors often include notes at the end of their books that explain how they did the research for their stories. For example, Michael Tunnell notes in an afterword that he was inspired to write *Mailing May* after reading a story while researching another book. He explains that in order to write *Mailing May,* he researched railroad museum archives to verify the exact dates in his story as well as other details such as time schedules and the cost of mailing packages. There actually was a little girl, who was under the care of a relative who worked on the train, who was mailed to her grand-mother. The rate that her parents were charged was based on the cost of shipping baby chicks. The research that an author must do to write a work of historical fiction can be extensive, requiring months or even years of investigation. Gather several picture books and novels of historical fiction that contain afterwords to see how different authors of his-torical fiction did their research.

   Now try gathering information that you might use to write a work of historical fic-tion. You might interview family members to learn about stories passed down across gen-erations or use some of the research techniques described in the afterwords of published books. Students can also be guided to use these same techniques.

2. Have you ever read a work of historical fiction and, after completing it, been convinced that you really understood the historical period featured in the story? In fact, after reading the book, you may have felt like an expert on life during the Middle Ages or on the challenges of crossing the continent in a covered wagon. Writers of historical fiction sweep us back in time into the lives of the famous, the infamous, and the common people and convince us we were there with them.

   How well does a fictional work reflect history? Read a book such as *Crispin* or *Fever 1793.* Then create a T-chart. On the left side of the chart, list information included in the story that you believe accurately reflects history. To try and verify what you have included on your chart, read informational texts about the period. Then, on the right side of the chart opposite each of your original statements, indicate if your original statement was verified through your research or, if any statements were not verified, write a corrected statement opposite the original statement. To what extent does it appear that the author grounded the story in careful research?

3. More and more historical fiction is being published in picture book format, and some of these picture books explore potentially disturbing subject matter. Teachers must make judgments about whether these books are appropriate for their students. Read a sampling of historical fiction picture books, and discuss with your classmates the most appropriate audience for these books. You might want to read Toshi Maruki's ***Hiroshima no pika***, ***The Whispering Cloth*** by Pegi Shea, and ***Baseball Saved Us*** by Ken Mochizuki. Then discuss how reading aloud a picture book and engaging the class in a discussion can build background knowledge and set the stage for reading a related novel.

Now go to Chapter 10 in the MyEducationKit (www.myeducationkit.com) for your book, where you can:

- ■ Find learning outcomes for Chapter 10.
- ■ Access the Children's Literature Database for your own exploration.
- ■ Complete Assignments and Activities that can help you more deeply understand the chapter content.
- ■ Extend knowledge with content-specific Web Links.
- ■ Deepen and apply content understanding with Extension Activities.
- ■ Check your comprehension on the content covered in the chapter by going to the Study Plan. Here you will be able to take a chapter quiz and receive feedback on your answers.
- ■ Find the following updated appendices: Major Children's Book Awards, Children's Magazines, Professional Organizations, Children's Book Publishers' Addresses, Book Selection Aids, and Children's Literature Web Sites.

Recommended Books

* indicates a picture book; **I** indicates interest level (P = preschool, YA = young adult)

Ancient Times through the Medieval Period

Avi. *Crispin: The Cross of Lead*. Hyperion, 2002. Accused of a crime he did not commit and having lost his mother—his only living relative—Crispin must flee his village. Pursued by unknown enemies, Crispin joins up with a juggler named Bear and finds himself swept up in the political intrigues of medieval England. Sequel: *Crispin: At the Edge of the World*. (**I:** 10 and up)

Barrett, Tracy. *Anna of Byzantium*. Delacorte, 1999. Anna, a princess and her father's successor to rule the Byzantine Empire, is confident of her place in the world until her will collides with that of her powerful and manipulative grandmother. (**I:** YA)

Cadnum, Michael. *The Book of the Lion*. Viking, 2000. Edmund avoids punishment as a counterfeiter by joining Crusaders in the Holy Land, where he discovers compassion, friendship, and the brutality of war. (**I:** YA)

Cushman, Karen. *Catherine, Called Birdy*. Clarion, 1994. Through her journal, a young girl chronicles her daily life in medieval England. (**I:** 11–YA)

———. *Matilda Bone*. Clarion, 2000. Having grown up in a manor under the care of the local priest, Matilda is appalled at life on Blood and Bone Alley, where she has been sent to serve Peg the Bonesetter. (**I:** 10–14)

———. *The Midwife's Apprentice*. Clarion, 1995. A homeless waif in medieval England is given the opportunity to become a midwife's apprentice. (**I:** 10–14)

de Angeli, Marguerite. *The Door in the Wall*. Doubleday, 1949/1989. A young boy loses the use of his legs and is still able to save the town and serve the king. (**I:** 8–12)

Ellis, Deborah. *A Company of Fools*. Fitzhenry & Whiteside, 2002. Henre's quiet life behind the abbey walls changes when street urchin Micah arrives at the abbey. Together, the boys face unfathomable despair when the plague sweeps through Paris and their abbey. (**I:** 10 and up)

Love, D. Anne. *The Puppeteer's Apprentice*. McElderry/Simon & Schuster, 2003. After running away from the drudgery of manor life, Mouse sees a puppet show and determines to become a puppeteer. (**I:** 9–12)

Park, Linda Sue. *The Kite Fighters*. Houghton Mifflin, 2000. Two brothers in fifteenth-century Korea share a passion for kite flying, but bring vastly different talents to the sport. (**I:** 8–12)

———. *Seesaw Girl*. Illustrated by Jean and Mou-Sien Tseng. Clarion, 1999. Confined to her parents' compound until marriage, a young girl longs to see the outside world and uses the Korean method of jumping on seesaws to catch a glimpse or two. (**I:** 8–12)

———. *A Single Shard*. Clarion, 2001. Though a homeless orphan, Tree-ear's life with his friend Crane-man had always felt satisfying—until he discovers the pottery made by the master Min. This story of a boy's pursuit of his dream is set in twelfth-century Korea. (**I:** 10 and up)

Paterson, Katherine. *The Master Puppeteer*. Harper, 1976. A youth describes life as a puppeteer in eighteenth-century Japan. (**I:** YA)

*Porter, Barbara Ann. *Ma Jiang and the Orange Ants*. Illustrated by Annie Cannon. Orchard, 2000. When the men in her family are forced to leave home to serve the emperor, Ma Jiang must figure out a way to safely capture the fierce orange ants to sell in order to provide for her family. (**I:** 7–11)

Schlitz, Laura Amy. *Good Masters! Sweet Ladies!: Voices from a Medieval Village*. Candlewick, 2007. In this series of monologues set in the Middle Ages, children and young adults from various stations in life step forward to tell their tales. (**I:** 10 and up)

Spradlin, Michael P. *The Youngest Templar: Keeper of the Grail*. Putnam, 2008. An orphan raised by monks, Tristan's world changes forever when he becomes a squire to Sir Thomas, a respected knight of the Templars, and is caught up in political intrigue of the period. (**I:** 10 and up)

Sutcliff, Rosemary. *The Eagle of the Ninth*. Illustrated by C. Walter Hodges. Farrar, 1954/1993. The story of a young Roman centurion in second-century England. Other books in the trilogy include *The Lantern Bearers* (1959) and *The Silver Branch* (1957). (**I:** YA)

Temple, Frances. *The Ramsay Scallop*. Orchard, 1994. A young couple's pilgrimage from England to Spain transforms their views of the world and each other. (**I:** 11–YA)

The European Renaissance

Blackwood, Gary. *The Shakespeare Stealer*. Dutton, 1998. Ordered by a cruel master to steal the script of *Hamlet* from the Globe Theatre, Widge confronts a new world when he is taken in and befriended by the Globe company members. Sequels are *Shakespeare's Scribe* (2000) and *Shakespeare's Spy* (2003). (**I:** 10 and up)

Gilson, Jamie. *Stink Alley*. HarperCollins, 2002. Orphaned in Holland where her family had moved with William Brewster and his English followers, strong-willed Lizzy is unable to fit in with her Pilgrim community and becomes friends with a precocious young Dutch artist who has an even greater mischievous streak than Lizzy's. (**I:** 8–11)

Hesse, Karen. *Stowaway*. Margaret K. McElderry, 2000. This fictionalized diary documents the actual journey of an eleven-year-old stowaway on Captain Cook's ship, the *Endeavour*. (**I:** 8–11)

Hooper, Mary. *At the Sign of the Sugared Plum*. Bloomsbury, 2003. It is 1665, and Hannah is thrilled to be moving to London to help her sister run her sweetmeats shop, but Hannah's excitement soon turns to terror as the plague sweeps London. (**I:** 11–14)

Meyer, Carolyn. *Beware, Princess Elizabeth*. Harcourt, 2001. When Henry VIII dies, Princess Elizabeth's brother and sister—both of whom assume power before her—take steps to keep Elizabeth from ever inheriting the throne. This work of historical fiction is based on the early life of Elizabeth. (**I:** 11 and up)

Richardson, V. A. *The House of Windjammer*. Bloomsbury, 2003. When his father dies and debtors threaten to take over the family shipping business, Adam struggles to maintain the family honor and hold the House of Windjammer together. The story is set in 1636 in Amsterdam. (**I:** 12 and up)

Sturtevant, Katherine. *A True and Faithful Narrative*. Farrar, Straus, & Giroux, 2006. Meg longs to be a writer—something women do not become in 1681. Yet it is only when her friend's brother is sold into slavery in North Africa that she comes to understand the real power of words. (**I:** 12 and up)

The Americas before 1600

Dorris, Michael. *Guests*. Hyperion, 1994/1999. This story of a young Native American boy's coming of age is entwined with the story of the first Thanksgiving. (**I:** 8–12)

———. *Morning Girl*. Hyperion, 1992. Life on an island is described by two Taino children prior to and on the day that Columbus lands. (**I:** 8–12)

O'Dell, Scott. *The Captive*. Houghton Mifflin, 1979. In the New World, a Jesuit priest journeys with a Spanish expedition and witnesses the enslavement and exploitation of the Mayans. Other titles in the trilogy include *The Amethyst Ring* (1983) and *The Feathered Serpent* (1981). (**I:** 11–YA)

———. *The King's Fifth*. Houghton Mifflin, 1966. Esteban de Sandoval is waiting to be tried for not turning over to the King of Spain a fifth of the treasure he found on his expedition through Mexico. (**I:** 11–YA)

*Yolen, Jane. *Encounter*. Illustrated by David Shannon. Harcourt, 1992. A Taino boy tries to warn his people of coming destruction when Columbus arrives on their island. (**I:** 8–12)

The American Colonies, 1600–1774

*Bowen, Gary. *Stranded at Plimoth Plantation 1626*. HarperCollins, 1994. An orphan stranded at Plimoth Plantation documents his life in the village. (**I:** 10–12)

*Bruchac, Joseph. *Squanto's Journey*. Illustrated by Greg Shed. Harcourt, 2000. This is the story of the Native American who befriended the settlers of Plymouth, despite his own suffering at the hands of the Europeans. (**I:** 8–11)

Fleischman, Paul. *Saturnalia*. HarperCollins, 1992. A Narragansett boy, captured by whites at age 8, works as a printer's apprentice until he begins his search for his roots. (**I:** 9–12)

Koller, Jackie French. *The Primrose Way*. Harcourt, 1992. A young girl in the New World becomes an interpreter between the Puritans and the Pawtuckets. (**I:** 9–12)

Rees, Celia. *Witch Child*. Candlewick, 2000. When the grandmother who raised her is executed for witchcraft, a mysterious woman sends Mary to join a group of Puritans who are journeying to America. Mary is soon marked as "different" from the others in their remote American settlement and faces the dangers that emerge from prejudice. (**I:** 10–14)

Rinaldi, Ann. *A Break with Charity: A Story about the Salem Witch Trials*. Harcourt, 1992. A young girl struggles to find the courage to tell the truth about the Salem witch hunt. (**I:** YA)

Speare, Elizabeth George. *The Witch of Blackbird Pond*. Houghton Mifflin, 1958. A girl is accused of witchcraft in colonial New England. (**I:** 10–YA)

The American Revolution

Anderson, Laurie Halse. *Fever 1793*. Simon & Schuster, 2000. The future looks bright to Mattie, who helps her mother run a coffeehouse in the bustling capital of the newly formed United States. Then, yellow fever strikes Philadelphia, and Mattie's life turns into a living nightmare. (**I:** 10–14)

Bruchac, Joseph. *The Arrow Over the Door*. Dial, 1998. Samuel and his Quaker community fear the approaching British and Indian raiders, while Stands Straight views all Americans as enemies. An encounter at a Quaker meeting brings new understandings to both boys and their communities. (**I:** 9–12)

Collier, James Lincoln, and Christopher Collier. *My Brother Sam Is Dead*. Simon & Schuster, 1974/1984. A family is torn apart as members take different sides during the American Revolution. (**I:** 10–YA)

Forbes, Esther. *Johnny Tremain*. Houghton Mifflin, 1943. A silversmith's apprentice becomes part of the Sons of Liberty. (**I:** 10–YA)

Rinaldi, Ann. *Finishing Becca*. Harcourt, 1994. Becca, sent to work for a wealthy family in Philadelphia, finds herself caught up in the intrigues of the American Revolution. (**I:** YA)

———. *Or Give Me Death*. Harcourt, 2003. When the wife of Patrick Henry, who is slowly losing her mind, becomes a danger to the family, her husband confines her to the basement of their home. Rinaldi explores the tragic impact of this state of affairs on the family of Patrick Henry. (**I:** YA)

*Turner, Ann. *Katie's Trunk*. Illustrated by Ron Himler. Macmillan, 1992. A Tory child hides in a trunk when Patriots come to her home. (**I:** 5–9)

Life in the Early to Mid-Nineteenth Century

DeFelice, Cynthia. *The Apprenticeship of Lucas Whitaker*. Farrar, 1996. Having lost his family to consumption, Lucas becomes a physician's apprentice and hopes to save his new community from consumption with a macabre folk remedy. (**I:** 10–13)

Giff, Patricia Reilly. *Nory Ryan's Song*. Delacorte, 2000. Faced with uncompromising English landlords and a blight that destroys the potato crop throughout Ireland, Nory must find a way to save herself and her family from starvation. The sequel is *Maggie's Door* (2003). (**I:** 10–13)

Hudson, Jan. *Sweetgrass*. Putnam, 1989/1999. Sweetgrass must help her people survive smallpox in the winter of 1838. (**I:** 9–12)

Wait, Lea. *Stopping to Home*. Margaret K. McElderry, 2001. When their mother dies of smallpox in Wiscasset, Maine, Abbie is afraid of what the future holds for her and her little brother Seth. Determined to stay with Seth, Abbie finds a way of making their temporary home with Widow Chase into a real home. (**I:** 9–11)

———. *Wintering Well*. McElderry, 2004. When Will loses his leg in a farm accident, he and his sister Cassie leave the family's Maine farm and move to town where both Will and Cassie have the opportunity to find new lives. (I: 9–12)

Slavery, the Civil War, and Reconstruction

Curtis, Christopher Paul. *Elijah of Buxton*. Scholastic, 2007. The first free child born in the Buxton Settlement, a Canadian haven established in 1849 for freed slaves, Elijah comes to understand the horrors of slavery when he journeys to America to help a friend. (**I:** 9–12)

Fleischman, Paul. *Bull Run.* HarperCollins, 1993. The first battle of the Civil War is described from the perspectives of sixteen different characters. (**I:** 10–YA)

Hesse, Karen. *A Light in the Storm: The Civil War Diary of Amelia Martin, Fenwick Island, Delaware, 1861.* Hyperion, 1999. In this book set during the Civil War, the daughter of a lighthouse keeper in the divided state of Delaware sees both her country and her family being torn apart. Part of the *Dear America* series. (**I:** 8–12)

*Hopkinson, Deborah. *Sweet Clara and the Freedom Quilt.* Illustrated by James Ransome. Knopf, 1993. Determined to escape from slavery, Clara sews a quilt that maps the way to freedom. (**I:** 8–12)

Lester, Julius. *Day of Tears.* Hyperion, 2005. This dramatic story of the biggest slave auction in American history can easily be adapted for readers' theater. (**I:** 12 and up)

Matas, Carol. *The War Within: A Novel of the Civil War.* Simon & Schuster, 2001. Because Hannah has always viewed herself first as a Southerner and then as a Jew, she can't understand how her sister could fall in love with one of the Yankees occupying their town, even if he was Jewish. Then, when General Grant orders the evacuation of all Israelites, Hannah begins to question what she has always held to be the truth. (**I:** 10–14)

McMullan, Margaret. *How I Found the Strong.* Houghton Mifflin, 2004. At the age of 10, "Shanks" sees his daddy and older brother leave to fight for the Confederacy. He dreams of joining them, but soon the reality of war becomes too clear—even for those left behind. (**I:** 9–12)

Paterson, Katherine. *Jip, His Story.* Puffin, 1998. Jip, an orphan who has grown up on a poor farm in Vermont, is caught up in the struggles between slave owners and abolitionists. (**I:** 10–13)

Peck, Richard. *The River Between Us.* Dial, 2003. With the Civil War rapidly approaching, Tilly and her family do not know what to expect when a steamboat docks in their small Illinois town bringing a glamorous young lady and her black servant from the South. The upheavals in their lives come from both the war and the newcomers. (**I:** 11 and up)

Pinkney, Andrea Davis. *Silent Thunder.* Hyperion, 1999. Both Summer and her brother Rosco have their own "silent thunder"—deep-seated longings that roar within them. Summer dreams of learning to read, while Rosco longs to join the Union army. But these are dangerous dreams for children born into slavery. (**I:** 9–12)

*Polacco, Patricia. *Pink and Say.* Philomel, 1994. During the Civil War, an African American Union soldier befriends a white one. (**I:** 8–12)

Rosen, Michael J. *A School for Pompey Walker.* Illustrated by Aminah Brenda Lynn Robinson. Harcourt, 1995. A former slave remembers how he raised money to build a school for all children. (**I:** 9–12)

*Vaughan, Marcia. *The Secret to Freedom.* Illustrated by Larry Johnson. Lee & Low, 2001. Using quilts as part of a secret code, a young slave girl and her brother help their fellow slaves escape on the Underground Railroad. (**I:** 8–10)

*Winnick, Karen B. *Cassie's Sweet Berry Pie.* Boyds Mill, 2005. While making a berry pie, Cassie gets news that the Yankees will arrive within the hour. A clever bit of trickery saves her family's home from the enemy. (**I:** 7–10)

Westward Movement in the United States

Avi. *The Barn.* Orchard, 1994. Set in the Oregon territory, this story tells of three children who build a barn in a vain attempt to keep a promise to their dying father. (**I:** 10–12)

Bruchac, Joseph. *Sacajawea.* Harcourt, 2000. This fictional account of the Lewis and Clark expedition is told alternately from the viewpoints of William Clark and Sacajawea, the Indian translator and guide who accompanied the explorers. (**I:** 10–14)

*Bunting, Eve. *Dandelions.* Illustrated by Greg Shed. Harcourt, 1995. A family experiences mixed emotions as they travel across the prairie to settle in the Nebraska territory. (**I:** 8–12)

*———. *Train to Somewhere.* Illustrated by Ronald Himler. Clarion, 1996. The story of New York orphans taken out West to be placed with families. (**I:** 8–11)

Conrad, Pam. *Prairie Songs.* Harper, 1985. Louisa sees her neighbor driven mad by the loneliness she endures on the prairie. (**I:** 9–12)

Cushman, Karen. *The Ballad of Lucy Whipple.* Clarion, 1996. When Lucy, her mother, and her siblings arrive in California in the midst of the gold rush, Lucy directs every waking thought to figuring out how she will get back home to Massachusetts. (**I:** 10–12)

———. *Rodzina.* Clarion, 2003. After her parents die, Rodzina begins a lonely journey west on an orphan train, sure that she will be one of the orphans no one will want. (**I:** 9–12)

Erdrich, Louise. *The Birchbark House.* Hyperion, 2002. Readers follow an Ojibwa girl and her family through the cycle of four seasons including a devastating outbreak of smallpox. Sequels: *The Game of Silence* and *The Porcupine Year.* (**I:** 9–12)

Fleischman, Paul. *The Borning Room.* Scholastic, 1991/1998. Georgina Lott, her life nearly over, reminisces about all that has happened to her. (**I:** 11–YA)

*Hall, Donald. *Ox Cart Man.* Illustrated by Barbara Cooney. Viking, 1979. Life on a New England farm throughout a year. (**I:** P–9)

*Helldorfer, M. C. *Hog Music.* Illustrated by S. D. Schindler. Viking, 2000. When Aunt Liza sends her niece Lucy a birthday present from Baltimore, the box takes a delightfully circuitous route to Lucy's new home in Illinois. (**I:** 5–8)

Holm, Jennifer. *Boston Jane: An Adventure.* HarperCollins, 2001. Schooled to become a lady, Jane Peck leaves her native Philadelphia and travels to the Washington Territory to wed her childhood idol. When she learns her fiancé has moved on, Jane has no choice but to move in with a group of scruffy men and make her own way in an alien world. The sequel is *Boston Jane: Wilderness Days* (2002). (**I:** 9–12)

*Karim, Roberta. *Kindle Me a Riddle: A Pioneer Story.* Illustrated by Bethanne Andersen. Greenwillow, 1999. As a pioneer family shares riddles throughout the day, young readers gain insights into the pioneer way of life. (**I:** 7–10)

Kurtz, Jane. *I'm Sorry, Almira Ann.* Illustrated by Susan Havice. Holt, 1999. Sometimes unable to contain her "hasty spirit" as her family crosses the country by covered wagon, young Sarah must find a way to make amends when her exuberance accidentally results in harm to her best friend. (**I:** 7–10)

O'Dell, Scott. *Island of the Blue Dolphins.* Houghton Mifflin, 1960/1990. When her people leave their island home, Karana is left to survive on her own. (**I:** 10–YA)

———. *Sing Down the Moon*. Houghton Mifflin, 1970. A Navajo girl recounts her journey to Fort Sumner as an Army prisoner. (**I:** 10–YA)

*Wilder, Laura Ingalls. *The Little House in the Big Woods*. Illustrated by Garth Williams. Harper, 1932. This first book about the Ingalls family details their life in the Big Woods of Wisconsin. Other books in the series include *Little House on the Prairie* (1935), *The Long Winter* (1940). (**I:** 7–11)

Yep, Laurence. *Dragon's Gate*. HarperCollins, 1993. A Chinese boy joins his father in America, where he works under dire conditions to build the transcontinental railroad. (**I:** 10–YA)

———. *The Traitor*. HarperCollins, 2003. Michael Purdy is an outcast in his small Wyoming mining town, as is Joseph Young, the son of a Chinese miner. Their friendship leads Michael and his mother to save the lives of Joseph and his father when prejudice against the Chinese boils over into a vicious race riot. The story unfolds in alternating chapters narrated by Michael and Joseph. (**I:** 12 and up)

Industrialization

*McCully, Emily Arnold. *The Bobbin Girl*. Dial, 1996. This story about the injustices suffered by the women who worked in the cotton mills in Lowell, Massachusetts, is told from the perspective of a ten-year-old mill worker. (**I:** 8–12)

Paterson, Katherine. *Bread and Roses, Too*. Clarion, 2006. Two children—one whose family is caught up in a 1912 labor strike in Lawrence, Massachusetts, and the other the victim of extreme poverty—find compassion when they go to live with a family in Barre, Vermont. (**I:** 9–12)

———. *Lyddie*. Dutton, 1991. After losing her parents and being separated from her brother and sister, Lyddie works in the textile mills to earn money to reunite her siblings. (**I:** 10–YA)

Immigration (See Recommended Books in Chapter 15 for a more extensive list of immigration titles.)

*Avi. *Silent Movie*. Atheneum, 2003. An immigrant boy and his mother are unable to find his father on their arrival to America. Eventually the silent movies lead to their reunion. (**I:** 7–10)

Frost, Helen. *The Braid*. Farrar, Straus, & Giroux, 2006. Written in verse, this is the story of twins separated when most of the family, evicted from the Western Isles of Scotland, chooses to immigrate to America. (**I:** 10 and up)

Giff, Patricia Reilly. *Maggie's Door*. Wendy Lamb Books/Random House, 2003. In this sequel to *Nory Ryan's Song,* Nory and Sean leave Ireland and survive a harrowing trip across the Atlantic to finally be reunited with surviving members of their families. (**I:** 9–12)

Hesse, Karen. *Letters from Rifka*. Puffin, 1993. Rifka writes about fleeing Russia and having to stay behind in Belgium when her family goes on to the United States. (**I:** 9–12)

*Hest, Amy. *When Jessie Came Across the Sea*. Illustrated by P. J. Lynch. Candlewick, 1997. A thirteen-year-old Jewish orphan reluctantly leaves her grandmother and immigrates to New York City, where she works for three years sewing lace and earning money to bring her grandmother to the United States. (**I:** 8–12)

*Rael, Elsa Okon. *What Zeesie Saw on Delancey Street*. Illustrated by Marjorie Priceman. Simon & Schuster, 1996. A young Jewish girl living in Manhattan attends her first "package party" and learns a lesson about generosity in her immigrant community. (**I:** 6–10)

*Yin. *Brothers*. Illustrated by Chris Soentpiet. Philomel, 2006. Ming is lonely after his arrival from China until he is befriended by an Irish boy. (**I:** 9–12)

*———.*Coolies*. Illustrated by Chris Soentpiet. Philomel, 2001. Shek and Little Wong have come to America to help build the railroad across the West. Only the love and loyalty between the two brothers enables them to endure the bigotry and harsh treatment they find on the railroad. (**I:** 9–12)

Life in the Late Nineteenth Century and Early Twentieth Century

Avi. *The Secret School*. Harcourt, 2001. When the teacher of her one-room school leaves her position before the end of the school year, Ida fears how the situation will impact her future. If she can't attend high school, Ida will be unable to prepare for the teaching profession. Determined to realize her dream, Ida commits to secretly keeping the school open and serving as the children's teacher. (**I:** 10–12)

Choldenko, Gennifer. *Al Capone Does My Shirts*. Putnam, 2004. Moose moves with his family to Alcatraz where his father will be a guard so his disabled sister can attend a special school. He soon discovers that all kinds of complications come with life on Alcatraz. (I: 9–14)

*Christiansen, Candace. *The Ice Horse*. Illustrated by Thomas Locker. Dial, 1993. Before refrigerators, men harvested blocks of ice from the rivers to be used all year round. (**I:** 5–10)

Curtis, Christopher Paul. *Bud, Not Buddy*. Delacorte, 1999. Bud's mother has died, and the placements the orphanage finds for him never work out. So Bud sets out to find the man he is convinced must be his father. (**I:** 8–12)

DeFelice, Cynthia. *Nowhere to Call Home*. Farrar, 1999. Instead of going to live with her aunt in Chicago after her father commits suicide, Frankie decides to join the throngs of other children who have chosen the hobo life. (**I:** 9–12)

Hahn, Mary Downing. *Anna on the Farm*. Clarion, 2001. Anna is delighted to escape the summer heat of the city when her aunt and uncle invite her for a vacation on their farm. However, Anna never dreamed that her uncle's teasing and tricky nephew would also be at the farm. (**I:** 8–10)

*Hall, Donald. *When Willard Met Babe Ruth*. Illustrated by Barry Moser. Harcourt, 1996. Babe Ruth touches the lives of three generations of the Babson family. (**I:** 6–10)

Hesse, Karen. *Out of the Dust*. Scholastic, 1997. In free-verse poetry, Billie Jo chronicles the seeming hopelessness of her Depression-era life during the dust storms in the Oklahoma panhandle. (**I:** YA)

———. *Witness*. Hyperion, 2001. Told in free verse, this story documents the Ku Klux Klan's attempt to recruit members in a small Vermont town in 1924. (**I:** 10 and up)

Holm, Jennifer. *Our Only May Amelia*. HarperCollins, 1999. May Amelia, the only girl ever born on the Nasel River in Washington, finds adventure, joy, and tragedy in her Finnish-American frontier community. (**I:** 8–12)

*Houston, Gloria. *The Year of the Perfect Christmas Tree*. Illustrated by Barbara Cooney. Dial, 1988. Because her father is away at war, Ruthie and her mom deliver the Christmas tree to the church. (**I:** 5–9)

Ingold, Jeanette. *Pictures, 1918*. Harcourt, 1998. In the midst of World War I, Asia becomes intrigued with exploring the possibilities of photography and with nurturing her relationship with Nick. (**I:** YA)

*Johnston, Tony. *Amber on the Mountain*. Illustrated by Robert Duncan. Dial, 1994. A mountain girl learns to read and write with the help of a friend. (**I:** 5–10)

Kelly, Jacqueline. *The Evolution of Calpurnia Tate*. Henry Holt, 2009. As she strives to follow in the footsteps of her beloved grandfather, an amateur naturalist, Calpurnia Tate discovers that society holds very different expectations for young women in rural Texas in 1899. (**I:** 10 and up)

Larson, Kirby. *Hattie Big Sky*. Delacorte, 2007. Sixteen-year-old Hattie travels alone to Montana where she faces incredible odds as she struggles to keep the homestead she has inherited. (**I:** 10 and up)

Levine, Gail Carson. *Dave at Night*. HarperCollins, 1999. When Dave is placed in the Hebrew Home for Boys, an orphanage known also as the Hell Hole for Brats, he encounters cruelty, friendship, and (beyond the orphanage) the joys of the Harlem Renaissance. (**I:** 9–12)

*Lindsey, Kathleen D. *Sweet Potato Pie*. Illustrated by Charlotte Riley-Webb. Lee & Low, 2003. When the drought comes, Sadie's family can only save the sweet potato crop, so they have no idea how to repay the loan at the bank to save the farm. Then, Mama comes up with an idea that the entire family turns into a reality. (**I:** 6–9)

MacLachlan, Patricia. *Sarah, Plain and Tall*. Harper, 1985. A brother and sister hope that Sarah will choose to stay on the prairie and become their mother. Sequels: *Skylark, Caleb's Story, More Perfect than the Moon*. (**I:** 9–12)

*Miller, William. *The Piano*. Illustrated by Susan Keeter. Lee & Low, 2000. Tia loves music so much that she accepts a job as a maid in the home of a white woman so that she can hear more music. This is the story of how music bridges a racial divide in the deep South of the early 1900s. (**I:** 7–11)

*———. *Rent Party Jazz*. Illustrated by Charlotte Riley-Webb. Lee & Low, 2001. When his mother loses her job, Sonny knows the rent man will evict them. Then, in Jackson Square, Sonny meets Smilin' Jack, a jazz musician who volunteers to go to Sonny's neighborhood and throw a rent party to help raise money for Sonny and his mother. (**I:** 8–11)

*Mitchell, Margaree. *Uncle Jed's Barbershop*. Illustrated by James Ransome. Simon & Schuster, 1993. Even in the face of racial prejudice and economic hardship caused by the Depression, Uncle Jed pursues his dream of owning his own barbershop. (**I:** 9 and up)

Paterson, Katherine. *Preacher's Boy*. Clarion, 1999. Robbie's high-spirited ways often land him in the doghouse with his preacher father, but when one of his schemes endangers the life of someone else, Robbie finds the courage to face up to the consequences of his actions. (**I:** 9–12)

Peck, Richard. *A Long Way from Chicago*. Dial, 1998. Joey and his sister spend summers with their outrageous trickster grandmother. (**I:** 9–12)

———. *A Year Down Under*. Dial, 2000. Mary Alice is spending a full year with Grandma Dowdel and is soon learning to conduct outrageous schemes from the master. (**I:** 9–12)

———. *Fair Weather*. Dial, 2001. It is 1893, the year of the World's Columbian Exposition, and Rosie Beckett's aunt has invited Rosie and her siblings to Chicago to see all the wonders of the fair. A world of wonder and adventure await the Beckett family. (**I:** 9–12)

———. *Here Lies the Librarian*. Dial, 2006. Set at the time when cars are replacing horses, a tomboy named PeeWee wants nothing other than running the gas station with her older brother—until three sophisticated and independent librarians move into town. (**I:** 9–12)

———. *The Teacher's Funeral: A Comedy in Three Parts*. Dial, 2004. Convinced the school board won't be able to replace the teacher who dies in August, Russell looks forward to running away to the Dakotas—until his own sister takes over their one-room schoolhouse. (**I:** 9–12)

*Pinkney, Andrea Davis. *Mim's Christmas Jam*. Illustrated by Brian Pinkney. Harcourt, 2001. Mim and the kids are sad; Pap is away building the New York subway and can't get home for Christmas. But the jar of Mim's special belly-hum jam that the family sends to Pap results in the unexpected. (**I:** 5–8)

Ray, Delia. *Ghost Girl*. Clarion, 2003. April's world begins to open up when President Hoover builds a school deep in the Blue Ridge Mountains and she is able to attend school for the first time. Yet when her dark secret is revealed, April's newfound hope is threatened. (**I:** 10 and up)

Ritter, John H. *Choosing Up Sides*. Philomel, 1998. Luke is torn between becoming the baseball pitcher he longs to be and accepting the beliefs of his preacher father, who condemns all sports as evil. (**I:** 10–14)

Ryan, Pam Muñoz. *Esperanza Rising*. Scholastic, 2000. When tragedy strikes her well-to-do Mexican family, Esperanza and her mother must flee to California in the midst of the Great Depression. In a Mexican farm labor camp, Esperanza learns to relinquish her past and embrace the future in her new community. (**I:** 11 and up)

*Rylant, Cynthia. *When I Was Young in the Mountains*. Illustrated by Diane Goode. Dutton, 1982. The memories of a young girl growing up in the Appalachian Mountains. (**I:** 5–9)

Schmidt, Gary D. *Lizzie Bright and the Buckminster Boy*. Clarion, 2004. Turner hates being the new boy in town—and the minister's son. But life take a positive turn for Turner when he is befriended by Lizzie, a descendent of slaves who lives in an island off the Maine coast—until the town elders determine to force Lizzie and her people off their island home. (**I:** 9–12)

Selznick, Brian. *The Invention of Hugo Cabret*. Scholastic, 2007. Set in a Paris train station at the turn of the twentieth century, this is the story of an orphan that is told through an innovative blending of illustration, text, and cinematic technique. (**I:** 10 and up)

*Stewart, Sarah. *The Gardener*. Illustrated by David Small. Farrar, 1997. The story is told in a series of letters. After Lydia Grace's father loses his job, she goes to live with her Uncle Jim in the city, but takes her love for gardening with her. (**I:** 7–11)

Taylor, Mildred D. *Roll of Thunder, Hear My Cry*. Dial, 1976. An African American family faces prejudice and discrimination in the South. Other books about the Logan family: *Let the Circle Be Unbroken, The Friendship, Mississippi Bridge, The Well, The Land, Song of the Trees*. (**I:** 10–12)

*Tunnell, Michael O. *Mailing May*. Illustrated by Ted Rand. Greenwillow, 1997. In 1914, a young girl is mailed (by train) to see her grandmother because her family cannot afford a train ticket. (**I:** 5–9)

Williams, Marcia. *Archie's War*. Candlewick, 2007. Ten-year-old Archie maintains a scrapbook in which he documents the impact of World War I on his own life as well as on the lives of those who write him from the front. (**I:** 9–12)

Yep, Laurence. *Dragonwings*. Harper, 1975. The story of a Chinese boy immigrating to San Francisco to join his father. (**I:** YA)

World War II

* Borden, Louise. *The Greatest Skating Race*. Illustrated by Niki Daly. Margaret K. McElderry, 2004. A Dutch boy dreams of becoming a great skater racing along the frozen canals of the Netherlands. He gets an unexpected chance to become a hero when his neighbors are threatened by the Germans and he must skate with them to safety in Brussels. (**I:** 8–12)

Coerr, Eleanor. *Sadako and the Thousand Paper Cranes*. Putnam, 1977. The story of a survivor of the Hiroshima bombing who tries to make a thousand paper cranes to make her wish for health come true. The picture book version, *Sadako*, was illustrated by Ed Young: *Sadako* (1993). (**I:** 10–12)

Gallaz, Christophe. *Rose Blanche*. Illustrated by Robert Innocenti. Translated by Martha Coventry and Richard Craglia. Creative Education, 1985. A young German girl stumbles upon a concentration camp outside her town and discovers its horrors. (**I:** 10 and up)

Giff, Patricia Reilly. *Lily's Crossing*. Delacorte, 1997. Feeling alone when her father enlists in the army, Lily befriends a refugee from the Nazis. Sequel: *Willow Run* (2005). (**I:** 9–12)

Hahn, Mary Downing. *Stepping on the Cracks*. Clarion, 1991. While her brother is away at war, Elizabeth befriends an army deserter. The sequel is *As Ever, Gordy* (1998). (**I:** 10–12)

Hesse, Karen. *Aleutian Sparrow*. McElderry, 2003. A young Aleutian girl relates the suffering of her people who are forced to evacuate their island during World War II as the Japanese advance. The text is written in free verse. (**I:** 10 and up)

*————. *The Cats in Krasinski Square*. Scholastic, 2004. When a young Jewish girl and her sister learn of a Gestapo plan to arrest people smuggling food into the Warsaw Ghetto, they devise their own plan to foil the Gestapo. (**I:** 9–12)

*Johnston, Tony. *The Harmonica*. Illustrated by Ron Mazellan. Charlesbridge, 2004. Inspired by a Holocaust survivor, this is the story of a boy sent to a concentration camp who found hope for himself and for others by playing the harmonica his father gave him. (**I:** 10 and up)

Lowry, Lois. *Number the Stars*. Houghton Mifflin, 1989. A story of how the Danes aided Jews in their flight to freedom. (**I:** 10–12)

*Maruki, Toshi. *Hiroshima no pika*. Lothrop, 1980. The poignant story of one family's experiences on the day Hiroshima was bombed and the after-effects for atomic bomb survivors. (**I:** 10 and up)

*Mochizuki, Ken. *Baseball Saved Us*. Illustrated by Dom Lee. Lee & Low, 1993. A Japanese American boy's memories of life in an internment camp. (**I:** 8–12)

Morpurgo, Michael. *The Amazing Story of Adolphus Tips*. Scholastic, 2005. Lily and her family's lives are turned upside down when their entire English village is ordered to evacuate so the Allies can practice for a D Day landing. (**I:** 9–12)

Napoli, Donna Jo. *Stones in Water*. Dutton, 1997. Taken from their native Venice, transported to the Ukraine, and forced to provide labor for the Nazis, Roberto and his friend Samuele sustain one another as they unite to keep the secret of Samuele's Jewish identity. When Samuele dies, Roberto's only hope lies in escape. (**I:** 12 and up)

Orlev, Uri. *The Island on Bird Street*. Translated by Hillel Halkin. Houghton Mifflin, 1984. A boy struggles to survive in the Warsaw ghetto as he waits for his father to return. (**I:** 11–YA)

————. *The Lady with the Hat*. Translated by Hillel Halkin. Houghton Mifflin, 1995. The sole survivor of his family, a seventeen-year-old boy seeks his future in Palestine, not knowing an aunt disowned by the family is trying to find him. (**I:** 12 and up)

————. *The Man from the Other Side*. Translated by Hillel Halkin. Houghton Mifflin, 1991. A man and his son risk their own lives to help the Jews in the Warsaw ghetto. (**I:** YA)

————. *Run, Boy, Run*. Translated by Hillel Halkin. Houghton Mifflin, 2007. This is the story of a ghetto survivor who escapes into the Polish countryside and adopts a Catholic identity in order to survive. (**I:** 10 and up)

Park, Linda Sue. *When My Name Was Keoko*. Clarion, 2002. Two siblings struggle to maintain their dignity during the Japanese occupation of Korea prior to and during World War II. (**I:** 10 and up)

Peck, Richard. *On the Wings of Heroes*. Dial, 2007. Davy seems to find time for fun and adventure, even though World War II is beginning to impact his everyday life in myriad ways. Then, when his beloved brother ships out, the war begins to creep too close for comfort. (**I:** 10–14)

*Polacco, Patricia. *The Butterfly*. Philomel, 2000. When Monique discovers the Jewish family her mother has hidden in their basement, she joins her mother in finding the courage to defy the Nazis who occupy their French village. (**I:** 10 and up)

Pressler, Mirjam. *Malka*. Philomel, 2003. Seeking to escape the Nazi persecution of Jews in Poland, Malka's family is split apart, and seven-year-old Malka finds herself trying to survive the horrors of Nazi-occupied Poland on her own. (**I:** 12 and up)

*Rappaport, Doreen. *The Secret Seder*. Illustrated by Emily Arnold McCully. Hyperion, 2005. Living with his family in France where they pretend to be Catholics, Jacques and his father risk their lives to celebrate a secret seder. (**I:** 10–12)

Spinelli, Jerry. *Milkweed*. Knopf, 2003. Set in the Warsaw ghetto, this is the story of an orphan who doesn't even know his name, yet is determined to be part of a family and community while living in the midst of the horror and devastation of the Nazi regime. (**I:** YA)

*Uchida, Yoshiko. *The Bracelet*. Illustrated by Joanna Yardley. Philomel, 1993. Sent away to an internment camp during World War II, a young Japanese American girl discovers the power of memory. (**I:** 7–11)

————. *Journey to Topaz*. Creative Arts, 1988. A Japanese American family is sent away to an internment camp when World War II breaks out. The sequel is *Journey Home* (1978). (**I:** 10–12)

Wolff, Virginia Euwer. *Bat 6*. Scholastic, 1998. For 49 years, the sixth-grade girls from Barlow and Bear Creek Ridge have met for an annual softball game—a game played to bring the two communities together. But the prejudices that linger in the aftermath of World War II have set this year's teams on a collision course. (**I:** 11 and up)

Yep, Laurence. *Hiroshima*. Scholastic, 1995. The story of Sachi and the day the atomic bomb was dropped on her city of Hiroshima. (**I:** 10–12)

*Zee, Ruth Vander. *Erika's Story*. Illustrated by Roberto Innocenti. Creative Editions, 2003. This is the story of an infant thrown from a train bound for a concentration camp that was rescued by a German woman who raised the baby as her own. (**I:** 9 and up)

Zusak, Markus. *The Book Thief*. Knopf, 2006. Through the love and support of her beloved foster father, Liesel finds the courage to take her own stand against injustice in Nazi Germany. (**I:** YA)

The Mid-Twentieth Century

Almond, David. *The Fire-Eaters*. Delacorte, 2003. Bobby Burns sees many faces of suffering in his small English town—McNulty the fire-eater whose life was misshapen by World War II, the cruelty inflicted on children by school masters, and the fear sparked by the Cuban missile crisis. Yet in the midst of suffering, Bobby and his family find hope. (**I:** 10 and up)

Curtis, Christopher Paul. *The Watsons Go to Birmingham—1963*. Delacorte, 1995. An African American family from Detroit visits Birmingham in 1963, the summer of the fateful church bombing that set the civil rights movement in motion. (**I:** 10–12)

Cushman, Karen. *The Loud Silence of Francine Green*. Clarion, 2006. Francine has always been happy to follow her father's advice and stay out of trouble, but this pathway becomes unacceptable to her as she witnesses McCarthy's attacks on innocent people she knows. (**I:** 12 and up)

English, Karen. *Francie*. Farrar, 1999. Francie longs for the time when she and her family can leave behind their life in Noble, Alabama, and all the prejudices and hardships it holds for African Americans. (**I:** 10 and up)

Ho, Minfong. *Rice without Rain*. Lothrop, 1990. As Jinda and her family struggle to survive the drought that has hit Thailand, strangers from the city seem to offer a way to survive, but soon Jinda and her family are caught up in the turbulence of the 1945 student movement. (**I:** YA)

Holm, Jennifer. *Penny from Heaven*. Random House, 2006. Penny doesn't understand the divide that exists between her widowed mother and her father's Italian American family. This story is filled with everyday details of life in the 1950s as well as the bigotries that were a reality for Italian Americans of the time. (**I:** 9–12)

Holt, Kimberly Willis. *My Louisiana Sky*. Holt, 1998. After her Granny dies, Tiger Ann Parker wants to live with her aunt in Baton Rouge, leaving behind her mentally deficient parents in Saitter, Louisiana. Only when a hurricane strikes Saitter does Tiger Ann recognize the importance of family and home. (**I:** 10–14)

———. *When Zachary Beaver Came to Town*. Holt, 1999. Toby is having a hard summer, with his mother having left for Nashville and his best friend's brother in Vietnam. Then, when the "fattest boy in the world" comes to his small Texas town, Toby's summer becomes like no other he has ever known. (**I:** 10–13)

*Johnson, Angela. *Just Like Josh Gibson*. Illustrated by Beth Peck. Simon & Schuster, 2004. In an era when little girls couldn't join baseball teams, an African American girl dreams of being just like Josh Gibson, the hero of the Negro Leagues. (**I:** 6–9)

Laird, Elizabeth. *Kiss the Dust*. Penguin Putnam, 1991/1994. A Kurd family is driven from their home in Iraq to a harsh life in a refugee camp in Iran. (**I:** 10–YA)

*Littlesugar, Amy. *Freedom School, Yes!* Illustrated by Floyd Cooper. Philomel, 2001. With the arrival of the new Freedom School teacher, Jolie's Mississippi community comes under attack. Yet the besieged community unites to ensure that the young people can learn about their rich African American heritage. (**I:** 7–11)

Martin, Ann M. *Belle Teal*. Scholastic, 2001. Unexpected events seem to shape Belle Teal's year in fifth grade with Miss Casey. Her grandmother's mind is slipping, the new girl in school won't give Belle Teal any peace, and African American students enroll in the school for the first time ever. (**I:** 9–12)

Naidoo, Beverley. *Journey to Jo'burg: A South African Story*. HarperCollins, 1987. A brother and sister are caught up in the cruelty of apartheid when they journey to Johannesburg to find their mother. (**I:** 10–12)

Nelson, Vaunda Micheaux. *Mayfield Crossing*. Putnam, 1993. When the school at Mayfield Crossing closes, Meg and her friends must learn to deal with the prejudice they encounter at their new school. The sequel is *Beyond Mayfield* (1999). (**I:** 8–12)

Robinet, Harriette Gillem. *Walking to the Bus-Rider Blues*. Atheneum, 2000. It is 1956, and Alfa finds that his life as an African American boy living in Montgomery, Alabama, is shaped both by forces of prejudice and by the philosophy of the bus boycott in which his people are caught up. (**I:** 9–12)

Schmidt, Gary. *The Wednesday Wars*. Clarion, 2007. When his classmates attend Wednesday religious school, Holling is left alone with his seventh grade teacher who he is convinced hates him. However, the year holds surprises for Holling. (**I:** 11 and up)

Shea, Pegi Deitz. *The Whispering Cloth: A Refugee's Story*. Illustrated by Anita Riggio. Stitched by You Yang. Boyds Mill Press, 1994. A young Hmong refugee stitches her own story on her first "story cloth." (**I:** 7–11).

Taylor, Mildred. *The Gold Cadillac*. Illustrated by Michael Hays. Dial, 1987. An African American family from the North experiences prejudice when they visit the South. (**I:** 9–12)

White, Ruth. *Tadpole*. Farrar, Straus, & Giroux, 2003. The Collins family always seems to face monetary obstacles, but they quickly put their own struggles in perspective when their beloved cousin Tadpole appears on their doorstep hoping to escape his abusive uncle. (**I:** 9–12)

*Wiles, Deborah. *Freedom Summer*. Illustrated by Jerome Lagarrigue. Atheneum, 2001. Joe and John Henry are best friends. They play marbles together and swim together in the creek, and both boys want to be firefighters. But Joe is white and John Henry is African American, and in the 1960s in the deep South, that means there are some things Joe and John Henry cannot do together. (**I:** 6–9)

Woods, Brenda. *The Red Rose Box*. Putnam, 2002. When Leah visits her aunt in California, she discovers a world of affluence and freedom where there are no Jim Crow laws. Leah dreams of this new world becoming her own; yet when the dream becomes a reality, Leah recognizes what the loss of her family and rural Louisiana community means. (**I:** 9–12)

*Woodson, Jacqueline. *The Other Side*. Illustrated by E. B. Lewis. Putnam, 2001. Clover wonders why a fence separates the black side of town from the white side. Then summer comes, and when a white girl begins to sit on the fence each day, Clover discovers a new friend from the other side of that fence. (**I:** 6–10)

Other Books

Engle, Margarita. *The Surrender Tree: Poems of Cuba's Struggle for Freedom*. Henry Holt, 2008. Written in verse, this novel focuses on the sacrifices of Rosa and her husband who care for those fighting for Cuba's independence during three nineteenth century wars. (**I:** 12 and up)

 ## Resources

Albright, Lettie K., and Sylvia M. Vardell. "1950 to 2000 in Picture Books." *Book Links 13.1* (2003): 21–25.

Bachrach, Susan. *Tell Them We Remember: The Story of the Holocaust*. Little, Brown, 1994.

Beck, Cathy, Shari Nelson-Faulkner, and Kathryn Mitchell Pierce. "Talking about Books: Historical Fiction: Teaching Tool or Literary Experience?" *Language Arts 77* (2000): 546–555.

Bial, Raymond. *One-Room School*. Houghton Mifflin, 1999.

Chatton, Barbara. "The Civil War, Part I: Update." *Book Links 5.1* (1995): 42–50.

———, and Judy Parks. "The Colonial Period." *Book Links 4.3* (1995): 44–53.

———, and Shirley Tastad. "The Depression Years." *Book Links 2.3* (1993): 31–37.

———. "1900–1919." *Book Links 3.4* (1994): 50–56.

Cooper, Michael L. *Dust to Eat: Drought and Depression in the 1930s*. Clarion, 2004.

Elleman, Barbara. "The Columbus Encounter—Update." *Book Links 2.1* (1992): 31–34.

Freedman, Russell. *Immigrant Kids*. Puffin, 1995.

Freedman, Russell. *Kids at Work: Hine Lewis and the Crusade Against Child Labor*. Clarion, 1998.

Hopkins, Lee Bennett, ed. *More Books by More People*. Citation, 1974.

Murphy, Jim. *An American Plague: The True and Terrifying Story of the Yellow Fever Epidemic of 1793*. Clarion, 2003.

Murphy, Jim. *The Boys' War: Confederate and Union Soldiers Talk about the Civil War*. Clarion, 1993.

Scales, Pat. "Racism and the Civil Rights Movement." *Book Links 9.1* (September, 1999): 59–62.

Steiner, Stanley, and Linda Marie Zaerr. "The Middle Ages." *Book Links 4.2* (November, 1994): 11–15.

Tunnell, Michael O., and Richard Ammon, eds. *The Story of Ourselves: Teaching History through Children's Literature*. Heinemann, 1993.

 ## References

Blos, Joan W. "Perspectives on Historical Fiction." *The Story of Ourselves: Teaching History through Children's Literature*. Eds. Michael O. Tunnell and Richard Ammon. Heinemann, 1993, pp. 11–17.

Broderick, Kathy. "*The Ramsay Scallop* by Frances Temple." *Book Links 4.2* (November 1994): 19.

Conrad, Pam. "Finding Ourselves in History." *The Story of Ourselves: Teaching History through Children's Literature*. Eds. Michael O. Tunnell and Richard Ammon. Heinemann, 1993, pp. 33–38.

Cooper, Michael L. *Dust to Eat: Drought and Depression in the 1930s*. Clarion, 2004.

DeFelice, Cynthia. "The Bones beneath the Flesh of Historical Fiction." *Book Links 8.2* (November 1998): 30–34.

Dorris, Michael. "On Writing *Morning Girl*." *Book Links 4.1* (September 1992): 32–33.

Frey, Charles, and John Griffith. *The Literary Heritage of Childhood: An Appraisal of Children's Classics in the Western Tradition*. Greenwood, 1987.

Fritz, Jean. "There Once Was." *The Horn Book Magazine* (July/August 1986): 432–435.

Harris, Violet. "Historical Fact and Fiction: Using Informational Books to Provide Background for Using Multicultural Literature." *Teaching for Lifelong Learning*, 85th Annual Convention of the National Council of Teachers of English, San Diego, November 1995.

Levstik, Linda. "A Gift of Time: Children's Historical Fiction." *Children's Literature in the Classroom: Weaving Charlotte's*

Web. Eds. Janet Hickman and Bernice E. Cullinan. Christopher-Gordon, 1989, pp. 135–145.

Paterson, Katherine. *Bridge to Terabithia*. HarperCollins, 1978.

———. *The Great Gilly Hopkins*. HarperTrophy, 1987.

———. *Jacob Have I Loved*. Ty Crowell, 1980.

———. *Of Nightingales That Weep*. HarperTrophy, 1989.

Rinaldi, Ann. *My Heart Is on the Ground*. Scholastic, 1999.

Scott, Sir Walter. *Ivanhoe*. Edited by Graham Tulloch. Penguin, 2000.

———. *Waverly*. Edited by Andrew Hook. Viking, 1981.

Taxel, Joel. "The American Revolution in Children's Fiction." *Research in the Teaching of English 17* (1983): 61–83.

Temple, Frances. "Researching *The Ramsay Scallop*." *Book Links 4.2* (November 1994): 18.

Tomlinson, Carl M., Michael O. Tunnell, and Donald J. Richgels. "The Content and Writing of History in Textbooks and Trade Books." *The Story of Ourselves: Teaching History through Children's Literature*. Eds. Michael O. Tunnell and Richard Ammon. Heinemann, 1993, pp. 51–62.

Tunnell, Michael O. "Unmasking the Fiction of History: Children's Historical Literature Begins to Come of Age." *The Story of Ourselves: Teaching History through Children's Literature*. Eds. Michael O. Tunnell and Richard Ammon. Heinemann, 1993, pp. 79–90.

Turner, Ann. "On Writing Katie's Trunk." *Book Links 2.5* (May 1993): 11.

11

Informational Books and Biography

> *Saturday, August 3, 1793.* The sun came up, as it had every day since the end of May, bright, hot, and unrelenting. The swamps and marshes south of Philadelphia had already lost a great deal of water to the intense heat, while the Delaware and Schuylkill Rivers had receded to reveal long stretches of their muddy, root-choked banks. Dead fish and gooey vegetable matter were exposed and rotted, while swarms of insects droned in the heavy, humid air.
>
> —*from* An American Plague: The True and Terrifying Story of the Yellow Fever Epidemic of 1793 *by Jim Murphy*

This passage from an award-winning informational book piques readers' curiosity and prompts several questions. Why are the fish dead? Why were the insects swarming? Informational books and biographies allow children to delve more deeply into a subject or learn more about their favorite person. They also spark a child's interest and curiosity to find out about a new topic or concept. Informational books and biographies offer endless possibilities for use in the classroom. Children may select them for independent reading and teachers may choose them to read aloud to the class. These books provide material for readers' theatre, process drama, and a variety of response activities. They support content area learning and foster a spirit of inquiry. They establish a foundation for children's own investigations and projects. Informational books and biographies also serve as strong models and mentor texts for children's writing.

Go to the Assignments and Activities section of Chapter 11 in the MyEducationKit and complete the activities. As you work through the activities and answer the accompanying questions, consider the importance of evaluating informational books and biographies for children.

What Are Informational Books?

An American Plague: The True and Terrifying Story of the Yellow Fever Epidemic of 1793, by Jim Murphy, is an example of an informational book, one of a genre of books whose main purpose is to inform readers about a particular subject, issue, or idea. *Informational books,* sometimes referred to as the *literature of fact,* convey factual information about the world. A good informational book, however, not only informs—it also excites. Russell Freedman has written many wonderful informational books and biographies for children, including the Newbery Medal winner *Lincoln: A Photobiography.* Here is how he describes his mission: "Certainly the basic purpose of nonfiction is to inform, to instruct, hopefully to enlighten. But that's not enough. An effective nonfiction book must animate its subject, infuse it with life. It must create a vivid and believable world that the reader will enter willingly and leave only with reluctance" (Freedman, 1992, p. 3).

Although biographies and informational books are generally classified as nonfiction, many writers of informational books prefer not to refer to their work as "nonfiction." They take exception to the term because it identifies their genre by what it *isn't* rather than what it *is.*

Why should informational books be included in a literature program? First, children are naturally curious about their world, and informational books satisfy their desire to know. Books such as *The Top of the World: Climbing Mount Everest* by Steve Jenkins enable children to travel to distant places. Books such as *Days of Jubilee: The End of Slavery in the United States* by Patricia C. and Fredrick L. McKissack allow children to experience the past; they also reward children's curiosity about their ancestors as well as their nation's history. Informational books help children to understand the natural world, explore science topics, learn how things work, play a game, or do a craft.

Even when children are not seeking the answer to a question, a good informational book may capture their attention with a colorful cover or catchy title, draw them in, and deepen their curiosity about a topic, while also informing them about science, social studies, mathematics, the arts, or sports. Some children prefer nonfiction, and teachers have documented success with reluctant readers when they share informational books of interest to students (Caswell &Duke, 1998; Jobe & Dayton-Sakari, 2002).

Both of these reasons lead to a third reason for making informational books readily available: As psychologists since Jean Piaget have pointed out, knowing a little bit about a topic gives a child a basis for learning more about it. When children read an informational book, they establish a framework, or schema, to assist them in reading more complex material about the topic in the future. Therefore, providing interesting informational books has the promise of making children more engaged learners.

It is no small achievement to write a book that nurtures young readers' curiosity at the same time that it informs them. Although people tend to reserve the word "creative" to describe writing that creates fictional worlds, a considerable amount of creativity also goes into producing a successful informational book. Works of fiction can count on plots—narrative structures—to engage their readers' curiosity and pull them into and through a work. Writers of informational books rely on expository structures to do the same thing. The writer of an informational book does not create a fictional world; rather, he or she must use words (and often illustrations) carefully to create a unique vision of a portion of the actual world and draw readers into wondering about it, observing it, and understanding it. Three expository text structures that are used to do this are (1) asking a question about an effect and then answering it by tracing a cause, (2) following a chronological sequence of events, and (3) comparing and contrasting the members of a group. In addition to these text structures, authors use other techniques as well to create engaging informational books for children. They may organize and share information in many types of formats. For instance, they may craft a true story and use narrative structures; pose questions and answer them; integrate original source material such as diaries; or create an ABC book on their topic.

Readers benefit in several ways from becoming accustomed to the structure of informational books. In the same way that coming to know story structure enables students to read various stories more successfully, learning to follow expository text enables readers to comprehend informational books more successfully. Wise teachers say, "Children learn to read by reading." It is particularly true that children learn to read informational books by reading informational books. Duke and Bennett-Armistead (2003; Duke, 2004) have advocated for the importance of informational text in primary classrooms, and they describe how teachers can foster children's comprehension of informational text.

Another advantage of reading informational books is that they draw children into the patterns of inquiry used by specialists in the fields in which the books are written. Susan Campbell Bartoletti's ***Black Potatoes: The Story of the Great Irish Famine, 1845–1850*** not only informs readers but also allows them to think along with a gifted writer conducting an historical inquiry. By reading ***The Chimpanzees I Love: Saving Their World and Ours*** by Jane Goodall, young readers see how a famous scientist makes discoveries about the animal world. Studying Walter Wick's magnified stop-action color photographs in ***A Drop of Water*** enables young readers to see the many states of water, such as ice, steam, and dew.

The Evolution of Informational Books

Orbis Sensualium Pictus ("The Visible World in Pictures," usually referred to as *Orbis Pictus*), written by Moravian bishop Johannes Amos Comenius, was published in 1657. Considered the first informational book for children, it was a picture dictionary illustrated with woodcuts; the content was in Latin and focused mainly on natural history. It was used as a textbook throughout Europe until the late eighteenth century. In the nineteenth century,

Teaching Idea 11.1

Writing in a Comparison/ Contrast Format

Introduce children to books whose purpose is to compare and contrast two animals or concepts—for example, ***Toad or Frog, Swamp or Bog?*** by Lynda Graham-Barber, and ***A Wasp Is Not a Bee*** by Marilyn Singer. After discussing the techniques the author used to make the comparisons, ask children to write their own comparison of two animals, plants, or items.

travel books emerged as the dominant type of informational books for children. Evelyn L. Wenzel (1982) describes the format of these books: "A family or an adult escorting a group of children takes a series of trips to a foreign land (usually several countries of Europe); the children are instructed by the adult, who, of course, attends to morals as well as to mind" (p. 18).

In 1922, the first Newbery Medal was awarded to an informational book, *The Story of Mankind,* by Hendrik Willem Van Loon. Twenty years later, a book that broke new ground by informing through lavish illustrations was named a Caldecott Honor Book. The author and illustrator was Holling C. Holling. The book, *Paddle-to-the-Sea,* was a fictionalized but geographically accurate account of an expedition through the Great Lakes to the Atlantic Ocean.

Edwin Tunis was a pioneering author/illustrator of informational books whose passion for American history is evident in his books. Tunis's finely detailed black-and-white line drawings present a visual representation of the social history of the United States. *Frontier Living,* one of his many books on colonial life and early American history, was a Newbery Honor Book in 1962.

Informational science books for children have been strongly influenced by the work of Millicent Selsam and Herbert Zim. With a strong background in biology and botany, Selsam published her first book, *Egg to Chick,* in 1946. Herbert Zim, an elementary science teacher, initiated the single-species title, writing focused accounts of individual species in *Snakes, Sharks,* and *Golden Hamsters.*

The photo-essay format made its debut in the world of children's informational books in the 1970s and remains very popular today. In 1976, photographer Jill Krementz published *A Very Young Dancer,* which became the first in a series of photo-essays about individual children engaged in various activities. Also during the 1970s, David Macaulay began crafting informational picture books in which text and illustrations formed a unified whole. Macaulay's specialty is oversized books about architecture that are illustrated with intricate pen-and-ink drawings. Two books following this format were named Caldecott Honor Books: *Cathedral* in 1974 and *Castle* in 1978.

Even though informational books have been around a long time, the genre has had the reputation of being boring, best used mainly for report work, and unpleasantly difficult for children to read. In other words, applying the term "nonfiction" to a book was like adding "unsweetened" to chocolate—likely as not, synonymous with "disappointment."

Since the 1980s, however, informational books have gained momentum, establishing a position as a popular and important genre in children's literature. During the 1980s, several nonfiction titles were named Newbery Honor Books: *Sugaring Time* by Kathryn Lasky, *Volcano: The Eruption and Healing of Mount St. Helens* by Patricia Lauber, and *Commodore Perry in the Land of Shogun* by Rhoda Blumberg. *The Glorious Flight: Across the Channel with Louis Blériot, July 25, 1909* by Alice and Martin Provensen received the Caldecott Medal in 1984. This book's carefully researched paintings recreate France in the early twentieth century, the flying machines developed by Blériot, and his dramatic flight across the English Channel in 1909. Informational books did not fare as well in the 1990s in the Newbery and Caldecott categories, with only two honorees. *The Great Fire,* Jim Murphy's carefully researched story of the Chicago fire of 1871, was named a Newbery Honor Book in 1996. *Tibet Through the Red Box* by Peter Sís was named a Caldecott Honor Book in 1999.

In 2004, Jim Murphy was again an author of a Newbery Honor Book, *An American Plague*. And in 2006, **Hitler Youth: Growing Up in Hitler's Shadow** by Susan Campbell Bartoletti was named a Newbery Honor Book. In the Caldecott category, informational books have achieved prominence since 2000, further reflecting the trend for the increased importance of visual elements in conveying information. The Caldecott Medal was awarded to *So You Want to Be President* by Judith St. George in 2001 and to *The Man Who Walked Between Two Towers* by Mordicai Gerstein in 2004. Caldecott Honor Book designations were given to *What Do You Do With a Tail Like This?* by Steve Jenkins and Robin Page in 2004 and *Gone Wild: An Endangered Animal Alphabet* by David McLimans in 2007.

Several recent trends in children's informational books reflect the lives of today's visually oriented children in this digital age. Desang and McClelland (1999) discuss how children's

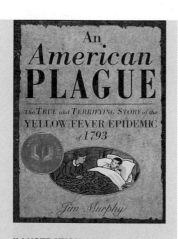

ILLUSTRATION 11.1 Jim Murphy recounts the story of the yellow fever epidemic that occurred in Pennsylvania in this award winning book. (Cover from An *American Plague: The True and Terrifying Story of the Yellow Fever Epidemic of 1793* by Jim Murphy. Jacket Illustration copyright © 2003 by Leslie Evans. Reprinted by permission of Clarion Books, an imprint of Houghton Mifflin Harcourt Publishing Company. All rights reserved.)

books reflect "interactivity, connectivity, and access that permeate our emerging digital society" (p. 160). Kerper (2001) describes the changes in nonfiction book design that include a nonlinear format, varied arrangements of text on the page, unusual fonts, and the nonsequential exploration of information through sidebars, boxed information, and marginal material. An example of these new approaches to design in children's informational books can be found in ***Team Moon: How 400,000 People Landed Apollo 11 on the Moon*** by Catherine Thimmesh. This oversized, coffee table-like book features black pages with white text that transport readers into space and its unknowns. The placement of text and photographs varies on each page and boxed captions supply detailed information about the photographs provided by NASA.

The increase in informational picture books, for both primary and older children, is another trend. The visual elements in these books may include more traditional illustrations, photographs, or a mixed media approach. In ***Secrets of the Sphinx*** by James Cross Giblin, detailed, realistic paintings by Bagram Ibatoulline portray ancient Egypt. The illustrations fill the pages in varied placements, including several wordless double-page spreads.

Today informational books abound—they cover a myriad of topics and display exciting, aesthetically appealing designs and strong, expressive writing. The establishment of prestigious awards specifically dedicated to nonfiction titles, such as the Orbis Pictus Award for Outstanding Nonfiction for Children and the Robert F. Sibert Informational Book Award, are further testament to the important place of informational books as a literary genre.

Categories of Informational Books

Informational books examine all kinds of topics and appear in many types of formats. Some informational books present a comprehensive view of their subject; others discuss one facet in depth. Let's look at a variety of informational books that are currently available.

Go to the Extension Activities section of Chapter 11 in the MyEducationKit for your book and complete activity #1 to create a text set on a nonfiction topic.

Issue to Consider

Is It Acceptable to Fictionalize Informational Books?

A relatively new issue with regard to informational books is the value of a hybrid type often referred to as an *informational storybook*. Although the primary purpose of these books is to inform, they also contain fictionalized elements. The popular *Magic School Bus* books written by Joanna Cole and illustrated by Bruce Degen fit in this category. In these books, Ms. Frizzle and her class experience a fantasy adventure while they learn about the subject of the book, such as the waterworks, dinosaurs, or hurricanes. Because accuracy and authenticity are critical criteria in selecting informational books, this mixing of genres has become a controversial issue. Sayers (1982) stated, "The outstanding tenet of writing for children . . . is the insistence on first-hand authenticity in science, the arts, history, biography, and travel" (p. 97).

The blurring of the lines between fact and fiction is not a new issue. Margery Fisher (1982) has written that "the distinction between fiction and nonfiction is blurred and constantly shifting, but we still use it and need it" (p. 13). Mixed-genre or blended books are the focus of debate because of their popularity with children on the one hand and their potential to mislead and confuse children on the other.

On the positive side, Leal (1993) points out some benefits of informational storybooks. They enable readers to "become involved in an engaging story" (pp. 63–64), identify with a main character, activate prior knowledge about the topic, generate interest for further content study, participate in discussion, and experience a model of process writing. Leal's research has confirmed children's positive responses to informational storybooks. On the other hand, Zarnowski (1995) believes that informational storybooks "introduce irrelevant, distracting, and potentially confusing 'information'" (p. 185). According to this view, students may have difficulty distinguishing fact from fiction in the story and thus may come away confused or with inaccurate information on the subject.

What do you think? Supporters and detractors of informational storybooks present compelling arguments.

Concept Books

Concept books help the youngest readers to know about their physical, natural, and social world. In concept books, information is conveyed through illustrations and text so that concepts are visually represented to young readers. Books about the alphabet, counting, colors, and shapes are popular kinds of concept books; a wide variety of topics are also presented to young readers in concept books. Different feelings and emotions are explained through innovative color photographs of fruit and vegetable sculptures in **How Are You Peeling? Foods with Moods** by Saxton Freymann and Joost Elffers. Young readers learn about colors and their significance in kente cloth from Ghana and Togo in **Kente Colors** by Debbi Chocolate. John Ward's vivid paintings illustrate the symbolic colors and patterns of the cloth. Frank Asch shares information about the sun in simple text and colorful watercolor illustrations in **The Sun Is My Favorite Star.** Color photographs guide young children in understanding puppies in **Puppies, Puppies Everywhere!** by Cat Urbigkit. (See Chapter 3: Picture Books for further discussion of concept books.)

Listen to Robert Burleigh discuss the poetry of writing picture books for children by going to the Conversations section of Chapter 11 in the MyEducation-Kit for your book.

History

Some informational books help readers travel back in time to find out about people, places, and events of long ago. Through such books, children can catch a glimpse of the past.

Flight by Robert Burleigh takes readers across the Atlantic Ocean with Charles Lindbergh on the *Spirit of St. Louis*. Magnificent, vibrant paintings by Mike Wimmer contribute to the excitement and tension. Every detail of this transatlantic flight is described, including strategies Lindbergh used to stay awake, the critical importance of staying on course, and the means Lindbergh used to lighten the plane. Lindbergh's diary is quoted as a primary source throughout the book.

Two books, **Shipwreck at the Bottom of the World: The Extraordinary True Story of Shackleton and the Endurance** by Jennifer Armstrong and **Ice Story: Shackleton's Lost Expedition** by Elizabeth Cody Kimmel, recount the adventure of Sir Ernest Henry Shackleton, who, in 1914, led an expedition to the Antarctic in the ship *Endurance*. When the ship is crushed, Shackleton must lead his crew across ice and stormy seas to reach inhabited land. Both books are illustrated with maps and archival black-and-white photographs.

Informational books provide a more in-depth look into aspects of U.S. history and highlight the role of underrepresented groups and their contributions to our country. In Jerry Stanley's **Hurry Freedom: African Americans in Gold Rush California,** readers gain a perspective on the Gold Rush from the perspective of Mifflin Wistar Gibbs, an African American from Philadelphia who headed west in search of gold in 1850. Michael Cooper's **Remembering Manzanar: Life in a Japanese Relocation Camp** incorporates primary source material to depict the lives of Japanese Americans interned during World War II. Penny Colman also uses primary sources and archival photos in **Girls: A History of Growing Up Female in America**. She explains, "The story about growing up female in America is not one girl's story but many girls—Native American; colonial; slave; immigrant; pioneer; rich, middle-class, poor" (p. 15).

Understanding Peoples and Cultures

Some informational books introduce young readers to children like themselves who live in other parts of the world or in other areas of the United States. These books help children to understand the concept of culture and to appreciate similarities and differences among peoples around the world.

Author Ann Morris takes primary-aged children on a photographic journey around the globe to share how people celebrate in **Weddings,** work together in **Teamwork,** or live together in **Families.** In her books, Morris communicates the similarities among people of the world while also creating an awareness and appreciation of cultural differences. The United Nations Children's Fund has collaborated with DK Publishing to produce **A Life Like Mine: How Children Live Around the World**. Illustrated with color photographs, this compendium guides readers on a trip to visit children in all corners of the world and learn about their daily lives.

In *One Child, One Seed: A South African Counting Book* by Kathryn Cave, readers meet Nothando from South Africa. Color photographs and a counting format provide children a glimpse into Nothando's life.

Children from various cultures within the United States are the subjects of books by Diane Hoyt-Goldsmith, who has teamed with photographer Lawrence Migdale to present portraits of cultures through a child's eyes. Ibraheem introduces Islam as he and his family observe Ramadan, the Islamic month of daylight fasting in *Ramadan*. Rosie, who lives in Hercules, California, celebrates Mexican history and traditions in *Cinco de Mayo: Celebrating the Traditions of Mexico*. Author and photographer George Ancona shares the life of José Luís, who lives in the Mission District of San Francisco, in *Barrio: José's Neighborhood*.

Nature

Many informational books explore the natural world and lead children to discoveries about animals, plants, geology, geography, and the human body. Readers can travel to a wildlife refuge in Kenya to meet the orphaned baby hippo Owen, who befriends the 130-year-old tortoise Mzee in *Owen & Mzee: The True Story of a Remarkable Friendship* by Isabella Hatkoff, Craig Hatkoff, and Dr. Paula Kahumbu. Color photographs by Peter Greste visually portray this friendship for young readers. Children may be surprised to learn that one of their favorite foods comes from a plant. In *Chocolate: Riches from the Rainforest*, author Robert Burleigh takes an in-depth look at the cacao tree of the rainforest and the popular treat that is produced from it.

For an exciting adventure, children can read *Quest for the Tree Kangaroo: An Expedition to the Cloud Forest of New Guinea* by Sy Montgomery with amazing photographs by Nic Bishop. Readers join the author, photographer, scientist Lisa Dabek, and an international crew as they journey to New Guinea to learn more about the Matschie's tree kangaroo. Informational books even offer adventures inside the human body. In *Lungs: Your Respiratory System*, Seymour Simon guides readers inside their bodies to explore the various parts of their lungs and what they do. Published with the Smithsonian Institution, the book includes full-page color photographs and diagrams, a glossary and an index.

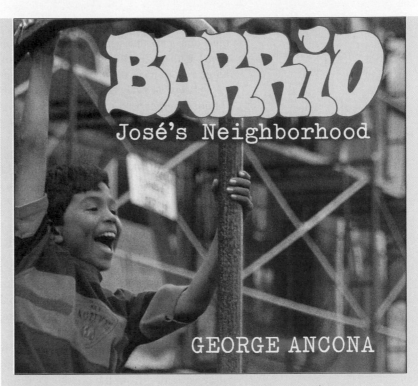

ILLUSTRATION 11.2   Photographer George Ancona travels to San Francisco to follow the daily life of José, an eight-year-old Mexican American who lives in the Mission District. (Cover illustration from *Barrio: José's Neighborhood*. Photo Essay and Text, © George Ancona. Mural © 1995 Juana Alicia, Margo Bors, Susan K. Cervantes, Gabriela Lujan, Olivia Quevedo, Elba Rivera. Reprinted by permission of Brooke Oliver Law Group P.C. on behalf of the artists & photographer.)

The Arts

Art, music, drama, and dance enrich people's lives; through the arts, children creatively express thoughts and feelings, tell stories, and celebrate life. Children are introduced to the art world through books such as *Baby Animals: Little Ones at Play in 20 Works of Art* by William Lach and *Look Closer: Art Masterpieces through the Ages* by Caroline Desnoëttes. In *Baby Animals*, young readers learn about the babies of 20 different animals, each illustrated by a work of art. Readers have an interactive experience in *Look Closer* as they lift flaps to gain information about

Teaching Idea 11.2

Informational Books as Models for Writing

Share informational books with children that present text in varied formats, including ABC books, counting books, diaries or journals, question and answer, letters, and postcards. These books can then be used as models for children's own writing in these formats.

famous paintings. More than twenty paintings by Rod Brown that have been exhibited in museums and other venues chronicle the history of slavery in *From Slave Ship to Freedom Road,* with text by Julius Lester. In the book's introduction, Lester comments that his "challenge was to meet the paintings at the depth of being from which they had been painted."

In *Dancing Wheels* by Patricia McMahon, readers learn about a special dance company founded by Mary Verdi-Fletcher, who was born with spina bifida. This dance company includes both "stand up dancers" as well as "sit down dancers" who express themselves with their arms, legs, and faces, and also their wheelchairs.

The world of theater is brought to children by author and illustrator Aliki in *William Shakespeare & the Globe.* Aliki tells the history of the famous Globe Theatre, describes Shakespeare's life and work, and discusses recent efforts to reconstruct the Globe Theatre in London.

Discovering How Things Work

Children are naturally curious about how things work. David Macaulay's *The New Way Things Work* provides a comprehensive introduction to the mechanics of movement, the elements, waves, electricity, the digital domain, and the invention of machines. The book is heavily illustrated with Macaulay's intricate, detailed drawings, which both convey and clarify information.

In *Construction Zone*, Cheryl Willis Hudson takes young readers to the actual construction site of MIT's Stata Center. Color photographs by Richard Sobol document the process of construction from the architect's drawings to the building's completion. Stephen M. Tomecek invites readers to learn about forty-five technological milestones throughout history in *What a Great Idea! Inventions That Changed the World*. From the hand ax to the laser, Tomecek gives an introduction to each invention, describes how it works, discusses its impact, and lists what he calls "children of the invention," other inventions that the original one spawned.

Sports, Recreation, and How-to Books

Informational books can help children to develop and pursue hobbies. Children who want to improve their culinary talents might consult *Emeril's There's a Chef in My World! Recipes that Take You Places* by Emeril Lagasse, which instructs children about a wide range of foods from around the world and provides recipes for each one.

To find out how to work with clay and use a potter's wheel, children can consult *The Kids 'N' Clay Ceramics Book* created by Kevin Nierman and written by Elaine Arima. In this book, children will find basic ceramic techniques and detailed instructions for specific projects such as decorating in leather and working with hard or soft clay. Curtis H. Arima's illustrations help to clarify each step in the directions.

Sports is a high-interest topic for many children. Two books about baseball will certainly please young fans. Baseball Hall of Famer Cal Ripkin, Jr. discusses the Baltimore Orioles' losing 1988 season in *The Longest Season*. In *We Are the Ship: The Story of Negro League Baseball*, Kadir Nelson provides a history of the league that provided opportunity for African American players before baseball was integrated. In *Lacrosse: The National Game of the Iroquois*, Diane Hoyt-Goldsmith's text instructs children about the game, and Lawrence Migdale's color photographs illustrate specific lacrosse skills such as cradling the ball and checking with the stick.

Information books themselves can engage children in play and recreation. Walter Wick's *Can You See What I See? Once Upon a Time* is an interactive book that invites children to carefully observe and find objects embedded in scenes from twelve fairytales.

Series Books

Series books are developed by publishers to provide works about related topics. The books have a specified format, which means that every book in the series is organized in the same way. For example, the *Count Your Way* series of Lerner Publishing for grades 2 to 5 highlights cultures around the world, using a counting format to convey information about the culture. One book in the series is **Count Your Way through Egypt**, written by Jim Haskins and Kathleen Benson. The *Eyewitness Books,* a popular series published by Dorling Kindersley, present information on many different topics and are extensively illustrated with color photographs.

In recent years, there has been increasing attention given to the importance of younger children independently reading informational books. Many publishers have series books specifically geared to children in the primary grades. The *Let's Read-and-Find-Out Science* series from HarperCollins was initiated by Dr. Franklyn M. Branley, an astronomer and former chairperson of the American Museum-Hayden Planetarium. Well-known children's authors have contributed to the series, including Patricia Lauber with **Be a Friend to Trees** and Wendy Pfeffer and Steve Jenkins with **Wiggling Worms at Work.** The Scholastic *Question and Answer Series* by Melvin and Gilda Berger models a stance of inquiry as questions are posed and answered on a variety of science topics, such as **Where Have All the Pandas Gone? Questions and Answers about Endangered Species.**

How Informational Books Work

What distinguishes informational books from other literary genres? Writers of informational books face the challenging task of compiling all their research on a topic and then selecting facts, concepts, and ideas to include in the book. Further, they must decide how to organize this information in a way that is appealing and accessible to their readers. Authors of informational books employ an expository style of writing to explain, inform, and describe. Expository writing uses various organizational patterns to present information, such as description, chronological sequencing, explanation, comparison/contrast, defining with examples, and problem-solution. For example, Jim Murphy organizes **Across America on an Emigrant Train** sequentially; readers follow Robert Louis Stevenson's travels from Scotland to San Francisco in search of his true love. Vicki Cobb explains and defines terms with examples in **The Secret Life of Cosmetics:** "There has been an almost endless list of *dentifrices,* substances used for cleaning the teeth. These included, at one time or another: ground chalk, ground charcoal, powdered pumice stone, soap, lemon juice, ashes, tobacco mixed with honey, a mixture of cinnamon and cream of tartar (ugh!) to name a few" (p. 25).

Authors of informational books must also generate and maintain readers' interest. The beginning chapters of James Cross Giblin's books pique readers' interest. Note, for example, this first paragraph from **Chimney Sweeps:**

> On a sunny October morning, a van pulls up in front of a ranch-style house in an American suburb. Out jump a young man and woman dressed in black tailcoats and top hats. They are both professional chimney sweeps, and are wearing the costume that has been the trademark of chimney sweeps for almost four hundred years. (p. 1)

An author's enthusiasm for the topic is usually evident in a good informational book. Writers use various literary techniques to engage the reader: posing a question, addressing the reader directly as "you," and using highly descriptive language and imagery. Informational books need not be serious, and many writers incorporate humor to sustain readers' involvement. A good example is Judith St. George's **So You Want to Be President?**, a compilation of interesting facts about the presidency presented in an amusing way. Award-winning, cartoon-style illustrations by David Small contribute to the lighthearted tone of the book. For example, one humorous page shows an obese President Taft lying in a large sling and being lowered into his oversize bathtub by pulleys suspended from the ceiling.

Many authors of informational books consider themselves storytellers—they are telling a story, but one that is true rather than fictional. As Rhoda Blumberg, author of many award-winning informational books, states: "Stories are enchanting, and for me true stories—from history—are the most enchanting" (Sibert, 1995). In these books, which are often referred to as "narrative nonfiction," authors employ literary techniques from fiction as well as nonfiction in telling their true story to readers. For example, authors are now using the first person

ILLUSTRATION 11.3 This Caldecott Medal Book gives readers a humorous perspective on forty-one U.S. presidents. (Cover from *So You Want to Be President?* by Judith St. George, "Illustrations" by David Small, copyright © 2000 by David Small, illustrations. Used by permission of Philomel Books, A Division of Penguin Young Readers Group, A Member of Penguin Group (USA) Inc., 345 Hudson Street, New York, NY 10014. All rights reserved.)

Top Shelf 11.1

Works of Narrative Nonfiction

Rosie the Riveter: Women Working on the Home Front in World War II by Penny Colman

The Race to Save the Lord God Bird by Phillip Hoose

Shutting Out the Sky: Life in the Tenements of New York 1880–1924 by Deborah Hopkinson

The Great Fire by Jim Murphy

Dog of Discovery: A Newfoundland's Adventures with Lewis & Clark by Laurence Pringle

Surviving Hitler: A Boy in the Nazi Death Camps by Andrea Warren

---

PEARSON
myeducationkit™

Go to the Extension Activities section of Chapter 11 in the MyEducationKit for your book and complete activity #2 to think of various primary sources you could use in the classroom.

Technology in Practice 11.1

Many books naturally connect to technology. Jean Fritz's *Leonardo's Horse* intertwines two true stories: one of long ago about Leonardo da Vinci's drawings and model for a horse that never was cast into bronze; and the other of present day about Charles Dent's dream to recreate Leonardo's horse as a gift to the city of Milan. The book encourages curiosity, inquiry, and problem solving. There is reference to a website: **www.leonardoshorse.org** that includes extensive information about all aspects of Leonardo da Vinci's horse. Students may also want to check a search engine and type in "Leonardo's Horse." Many other websites can then be visited with an article from the *Smithsonian Magazine*, reference to a 1977 *National Geographic* article, and other interesting material. Through these other references, students can engage in greater depth to learn about Leonardo da Vinci, Charles Dent, the famous horse, and the city of Milan.

narrative, a literary technique generally associated with fiction, as seen in *To the Top of the World: Adventures with Arctic Wolves,* by Jim Brandenburg, a *National Geographic* photographer who writes a firsthand account of his experiences on Ellesmere Island in Canada's Northwest Territories. Top Shelf 11.1, "Works of Narrative Nonfiction," lists several books that represent this storytelling approach.

Graphics play an important role in informational books. They can help to clarify abstract concepts that may be unknown to readers or difficult to understand. They can convey specific facts and specialized vocabulary or present a realistic visual rendering of a concept. They can help to provide the background knowledge necessary for readers' understanding. Graphics take many forms, including photographs, paintings, drawings, charts, diagrams, maps, and copies of documents.

There has been a trend toward an increased emphasis on visual elements in informational books, rendering them more colorful, aesthetically pleasing in appearance, and varied in format. Today's children are more visually oriented and are accustomed to television, animation, and other visual media. The design of informational books reflects children's preferences for visually appealing materials. The layout of many books presents text and illustrations in more interactive ways, encouraging children's engagement with the book. Illustrations may extend information in the text or convey additional information. Teachers can take advantage of these visual elements to support children's skills in observing and viewing, as they guide children to "read" the illustrations as well as the text. In this way, children's visual literacy is being developed and their comprehension of the material is enhanced.

Authors of informational books may provide readers with other aids for locating and understanding material, such as an index, glossary, table of contents, or list of additional facts. Print features, such as headings, captions, and bold or italicized print, assist readers in accessing information. A reference list or an acknowledgment regarding the sources or experts consulted is usually included.

Informational books invite readers to engage in critical thinking, as they are called on to distinguish fact from opinion and theory. Readers should consider the author's spirit of inquiry and what kind of research and investigation went into the book. Authors of informational books have "inquiring minds" and carefully research their material. This research may take many forms—authors may experience firsthand the topic they are writing about; they may consult primary source material such as original letters, diary entries, or newspaper accounts; they may travel to libraries, museums, or historical sites in other cities to secure the information they need; they may interview experts in the field; and they may consult secondary sources such as books and contemporary articles about the topic. In a "Note from the Author," Sally M. Walker discusses her research process in order to write *Secrets of a Civil War Submarine: Solving the Mysteries of the H. L. Hunley*. She traveled to Washington, D.C. and Charleston, interviewed people by phone and in person, toured the *Hunley,* and observed a conservator at work. Authors have their own points of view and perspectives, and readers must decide whether the author has presented a balanced discussion or biased it in some way. After gleaning all the information in the book, readers draw inferences and reach their own conclusions.

Major Writers of Informational Books and Their Works

Many authors write informational books for children. Several who have received recognition for their significant contributions to the genre are discussed in this section.

George Ancona

George Ancona, photographer and writer of children's books for over thirty-five years, began his career as an art director in New York City. When he entered the world of children's publishing, he took the photographs for books written by others. He often collaborated with authors Joan Anderson (e.g., *The First Thanksgiving Feast*) and Maxine B. Rosenberg (e.g., *Making a New Home in America*). He also collaborated with Remy Charlip and Mary Beth Miller for the Handtalk series, four books that introduce children to finger spelling and sign language. The first book he wrote and photographed, *Monsters on Wheels*, published in 1974, is an informational book about machines. Several of his recent books, such as *Mayeros, Pablo Remembers: The Fiesta of the Day of the Dead*, and *The Pinata Maker/El Pinatero*, focus on his Yucatan and Mexican heritage.

Ancona has written and/or photographed more than 75 books for children. Garcia-Johnson (1996) pointed out that Ancona "is renowned for his vivid photo essays that allow children to immerse themselves in new ideas and cultures, to appreciate labor that so often goes unnoticed behind the scenes of daily life, and to accept themselves as well as others" (p. 7). His work has received many honors and consistently appears on the list of *Notable Children's Trade Books in the Field of Social Studies*. One of his recent books, *Carnaval*, transports readers to Olinda, Brazil, to participate in the five-day Carnaval in February and see the famous giant puppets. In 2002, Ancona received the *Washington Post*-Children's Book Guild Nonfiction Award for his body of work.

Teaching Idea 11.3

Critically Reviewing Books on the Same Topic

Ask children to select a topic and read at least two books about it. For example, students can compare *Shipwreck at the Bottom of the World* by Jennifer Armstrong with *Ice Story: Shackleton's Lost Expedition* by Elizabeth Cody Kimmel. Have children develop categories for comparison and chart the similarities and differences in the books. This idea can also be applied to biographies. Ask children to read two or more biographies about an individual and chart their similarities and differences.

Joanna Cole

Joanna Cole has been writing informational science books for children since the 1971 publication of *Cockroaches.* For more than twenty years, she has been teaming with Bruce Degen to create the popular *Magic Schoolbus* series, which emphasizes the joy of science and shows that complex information can be conveyed with humor and enthusiasm. *The Magic School Bus at the Waterworks*, their first collaboration in 1986, was named a *Boston Globe-Horn Book* Honor Book. In 2006, they produced *The Magic School Bus and the Science Fair Expedition*, a humorous introduction to famous scientists.

Cole collaborated with photographer Jerome Wexler on several books introducing young children to the anatomy of animals and amphibians: *A Cat's Body, A Frog's Body*, and *A Horse's Body.* In clear, lucid prose, Cole explains technical vocabulary and presents the animal's anatomy to primary-grade children. Cole's books have been selected as American Library Association *Notable Books* and as *Outstanding Science Trade Books for Children* by the National Science Teachers Association. Her contribution to nonfiction literature for children was recognized in 1991 by the *Washington Post*-Children's Book Guild Nonfiction Award.

Gail Gibbons

As an author and illustrator of more than one hundred informational picture books, Gail Gibbons has introduced primary-grade children to a range of topics. After receiving an undergraduate degree in fine arts, she pursued a career as a staff artist for a New York television station. Gibbons has the special ability to explain complicated information lucidly and concisely for young children. Her illustrations help to introduce concepts and show children a visual representation of them.

Through watercolor illustrations and text, *Ice Cream: The Full Scoop* gives the history of this favorite food and guides young readers through a tour of an ice cream factory. The book contains many helpful aids for readers, such as labeled illustrations, definitions of vocabulary, and a concluding page of additional information. If young children wish to satisfy their curiosity about spiders, Gibbons's *Spiders* will answer their questions. Gibbons explains that spiders are not insects and shows young readers the differences between the two in detailed, labeled diagrams of a spider's body and an insect's body.

Gail Gibbons's work has been widely recognized. Two of her books, *The Milk Makers* and *Sunken Treasure,* were selected for "Reading Rainbow." Gibbons received the *Washington Post*-Children's Book Guild Award for her contribution to children's nonfiction.

James Cross Giblin

James Cross Giblin had a successful career as a children's book editor before he began writing nonfiction for children. After majoring in English and dramatic arts at Case Western Reserve University, he earned a master's degree in playwriting from Columbia University. As a writer of children's informational books, he is known for his imaginative and engaging treatment of unusual topics. For example, *From Hand to Mouth or, How We Invented Knives, Forks, Spoons, and Chopsticks and the Table Manners to Go with Them* traces the history of eating utensils in great detail.

Giblin does careful research, not only for the text of his books but also for the illustrations, which are carefully selected photographs, prints, and drawings. In *The Riddle of the Rosetta Stone: Key to Ancient Egypt,* Giblin uses illustrations from the British Museum and the Metropolitan Museum of Art. His books have received many honors: *Chimney Sweeps: Yesterday and Today* was awarded the 1983 American Book Award for Children's Nonfiction, and *The Truth about Santa Claus* was named a *Boston Globe-Horn Book* Nonfiction Honor Book in 1986. Giblin's *The Life and Death of Adolf Hitler* was named the 2003 Robert F. Sibert Medal winner. Giblin's contribution as a writer of nonfiction for children was honored in 1996 when he received the *Washington Post*-Children's Book Guild Award.

Steve Jenkins

Steve Jenkins has written and illustrated more than thirty books for children. Most of these are informational science picture books for young children that feature his signature and stunning cut paper collage illustrations. On his website, Jenkins writes: "The world is an extraordinary place, full of amazing and unexpected things. In the books I write and illustrate for children, I want to share my own fascination with the natural world." (*http://www.stevejenkins.com* accessed June 21, 2008) With a degree in graphic design, Jenkins worked in advertising and design before starting his own graphic design firm with his wife Robin Page.

His books have received many awards and honors. *The Top of the World: Climbing Mount Everest* received the 1999 *Boston Globe/Horn Book* Award. *What Do You Do With a Tail Like This?*, co-authored with his wife, was named a Caldecott Honor Book in 2003. This book presents different animal body parts and invites young readers to "guess which animal each belongs to and how it is used." Two of his books were Orbis Pictus Honor Books: *Hottest Coldest Highest Deepest*, a geographic excursion around the globe, in 1999; and *Actual Size*, with illustrations of animals and their parts shown in their actual size, in 2005. Jenkins was the recipient of the 2003 *Washington Post*–Children's Book Guild Nonfiction Award.

ILLUSTRATION 11.4 Using torn-and-cut-paper collages, Steve Jenkins shows animals or their body parts in actual size. (Cover from *Actual Size* by Steve Jenkins. Copyright © 2004 by Steve Jenkins. Reprinted by permission of Houghton Mifflin Harcourt Publishing Company. All rights reserved.)

Kathryn Lasky

A versatile writer who skillfully writes both fiction and nonfiction for children, Kathryn Lasky commented, "People often ask me how and why I do both fiction and nonfiction. I am equally attracted to both kinds of writing because for me the most important thing is if a story is real. Real stories can be either fiction or nonfiction" (Scribner's, 1985). In 1981, Kathryn Lasky received the *Boston Globe-Horn Book* Award for Nonfiction for *The Weaver's Gift,* a collaboration with her husband, photographer Christopher Knight. Another collaboration, *Sugaring Time,* was named a Newbery Honor Book in 1983. Lasky

Ask the Author . . .   James Cross Giblin

James Cross Giblin

Favorite Books as a Child

When I was a child, I loved picture books set in long ago times and far off places. I'd pore over them for hours, virtually memorizing the illustrations. Three of my special favorites were *The Painted Pig*, a story of Mexico by Elizabeth Morrow; *Skippack School*, by Marguerite DeAngeli, about a Mennonite boy in colonial Pennsylvania; and *The Story of Ferdinand*, by Munro Leaf. I identified completely with Ferdinand, the young bull who would rather smell the flowers than fight in the bullring.

How do you take complex informational material and make it both understandable and appealing to a child audience?

The first thing I do when I begin to research a new nonfiction book is to look for the story line in the material. For every subject—whether it's a biography, or a history of plagues, or the life cycle of the woolly mammoth—has an implicit story line within it, just as every novel has a plot. It's what keeps readers turning the pages, eager to find out what comes next.

A good example of a nonfiction story line can be found in my biography of Charles A. Lindbergh. It embraces the entire sweep of Lindbergh's life, from his historic nonstop flight across the Atlantic in 1927, to the kidnapping and death of his firstborn son, to his determined efforts to keep the United States out of World War II. The story line reaches its climax when Lindbergh became involved late in life with the conservation movement, saying, "I would rather have birds than airplanes."

Young people today are exposed to every facet of a public figure's personality via television and the Internet. In light of this, I believe writers for children have an obligation to present a full and rounded picture of the people and events they explore in their books. That's why I decided to discuss Lindbergh's controversial views in the years before World War

II and why I subtitled the biography "A Human Hero." I hoped the phrase would suggest that even a hero like Charles Lindbergh may not always act in a heroic fashion.

When I research a book, I always keep my eye out for details that will flesh out the subject and bring it to life for young readers. Examples of such details are the lavatory facilities (or lack of them) aboard Lindbergh's plane, *The Spirit of St. Louis*, and the way that rats, and the fleas they hosted, spread the deadly Black Death in the Middle Ages. I described the latter in *When Plague Strikes: The Black Death, Smallpox, AIDS*.

Every informational book I research and write is first of all a voyage of discovery for me, the author. And if I shape the material in a lively and dramatic way, I hope it will be just as entertaining and informative a voyage for my readers.

James Cross Giblin is the author of many well-received books for children and young adults. Among his recent titles are *The Amazing Life of Benjamin Franklin, The Mystery of the Mammoth Bones,* and *The Life and Death of Adolf Hitler*. When Jim isn't writing, he enjoys reading; going to plays, art exhibits, and movies; and exploring New York City, where he lives. ■

received the 1986 *Washington Post*-Children's Book Guild Award for her body of work in children's nonfiction.

Lasky and Knight experience firsthand the subjects that they write about and photograph. They traveled to an island south of Iceland to research ***Surtsey: The Newest Place on Earth,*** about the creation of an island by a 1963 volcanic eruption in the Atlantic Ocean. Each chapter of the book begins with a selection from the Icelandic creation myth, the *Edda,* as Lasky intertwines Icelandic folklore with a description of the island's creation. Her descriptive language, rich in imagery, engages readers in this amazing event of the natural world.

Patricia Lauber

Patricia Lauber has written more than eighty informational books on science topics for children. She writes, "Overall, my aims are to help children understand how the earth (or its parts) works and to try to imbue them with some of my own sense of wonderment, in the hope that they will grow up to be good stewards, who will take care of the earth, not just use (or abuse) it" (1992, pp. 14–15).

Lauber's books have received much critical acclaim: *Volcano: The Eruption and Healing of Mt. St. Helens* was named a 1987 Newbery Honor Book, and *Seeing Earth from Space* was a 1991 Orbis Pictus Honor Book. Patricia Lauber was recognized for her contribution to children's nonfiction with the 1983 *Washington Post*-Children's Book Guild Award.

In *The News about Dinosaurs,* Lauber promotes the spirit of inquiry as she points out that what were previously considered "facts" about dinosaurs are being altered by new discoveries. She juxtaposes what scientists used to think with "The News Is," which presents the most current scientific knowledge. For example, although "scientists used to think dinosaurs did not take care of their young. . . . The News Is: At least some dinosaurs do seem to have cared for their young" (p. 26).

Milton Meltzer

Milton Meltzer has been writing outstanding informational books and biographies for children for more than forty-five years. His books focus on history, social issues, and underrepresented groups in society. Meltzer's books feature the authentic voices of people about whom he writes and information from primary source materials. On writing history for children, Meltzer (1981) says, "The writing of history is as much an art as the writing of poetry or fiction. The writer tries to express his vision of history and to communicate it to the reader. As historian he does not invent that past, but he must give it artistic shape if he is to connect with the reader" (p. 96).

Meltzer's books have received wide recognition and have appeared on various notable book lists. *All Times, All Peoples: A World History of Slavery* was awarded the 1980 Christopher Award; *Never to Forget: The Jews of the Holocaust* was designated a 1976 *Boston Globe-Horn Book* Nonfiction Honor Book; and *The Jewish Americans: A History in Their Own Words, 1650–1950* was named a 1983 *Boston Globe-Horn Book* Honor Book.

In *The Amazing Potato: A Story in Which the Incas, Conquistadors, Marie Antoinette, Thomas Jefferson, Wars, Famines, Immigrants and French Fries All Play a Part,* Meltzer provides a fascinating, thoroughly researched social history of the potato. In the foreword, Meltzer points out that he wanted young readers to see "how such an everyday object, one we scarcely notice except perhaps when we have a hankering for french fries, can be of such vast significance in the history of humankind" (n. pag.).

Jim Murphy

Award-winning author Jim Murphy was born in Newark, New Jersey. After graduating from Rutgers University with a degree in English, he worked for Seabury Press (which became Clarion Books), beginning as an editorial secretary, where he worked for James Cross Giblin, and eventually becoming a managing editor. Murphy's first book, *Weird and Wacky Inventions*, was named a Children's Choice Book by the International Reading Association. Since then, he has penned more than thirty books, many of which focus on topics related to American history. Many of his books feature children; Murphy comments on the reason why: "Because kids—even very young kids—weren't just observers of the events that shaped our nation's history. They often participated in an active, heroic way and then wrote eloquently about their experiences. Unfortunately, many historians focus exclusively on the important adults involved—a president, general, scientist or other powerful individual—and never let us see who else was there." (*www.jimmurphybooks.com*, retrieved August 8, 2004)

His books usually are illustrated with carefully researched archival photographs and have received many prestigious awards. *The Great Fire* was named a Newbery Honor Book and received the Orbis Pictus Award. In 2004, *An American Plague* was a "Triple Crown" winner, awarded the Robert F. Sibert Informational Books Medal, the *Boston Globe-Horn Book* Award for Nonfiction, and the Orbis Pictus Award. It was also named a Newbery Honor Book. In 2001, Murphy received the *Washington Post*-Children's Book Guild Nonfiction Award for his body of work.

Laurence Pringle

Former editor of *Nature and Society,* published by the American Museum of Natural History, Laurence Pringle has contributed significantly to informational science books for children. Drawing on his degrees in wildlife biology, Pringle has written more than one hundred books that focus primarily on nature, wildlife, and ecology and environmental issues. In discussing what it means to "do science," Pringle (1981) wrote, "Doing science means being curious, asking questions. It means having a healthy skepticism toward authority and announced truths. It is both a way of looking at the world and a way of thinking. It values both fantasy and reality, and provides a framework for telling the difference" (p. 110).

Pringle's one-hundredth book, *Whales! Strange and Wonderful,* describes the various kinds of whales, the sounds they produce, and other interesting information about this strange and wonderful mammal. The 1998 Orbis Pictus Award-winning *An Extraordinary Life: The Story of a Monarch Butterfly* traces the migratory flight of one monarch butterfly from Massachusetts to its winter home in Mexico and back again. Detailed paintings by Bob Marstell enhance the text, which gives readers information about the life cycle and migration patterns of these beautiful butterflies. Pringle received the 1999 *Washington Post*-Children's Book Guild Award for Nonfiction.

Seymour Simon

Seymour Simon, a prolific writer of more than two hundred informational science books for children, attended the Bronx High School of Science. After receiving a bachelor's degree, he began teaching science in New York City schools. His first children's book, *Animals in Field and Laboratory: Projects in Animal Behavior,* was published in 1968. In 1979, after more than twenty years of teaching, Simon decided to pursue writing full time. He received the Eva L. Gordon Award from the American Nature Society and the *Washington Post*-Children's Book Guild Award for Nonfiction. Many of his books have been named Outstanding Science Trade Books by the National Science Teachers Association.

Simon's conversational, clear, and direct writing style enables children to understand a host of science topics. He immediately creates interest among his readers, as in the beginning of *Sharks* (1995, n. pag.): "It never fails. You're at the ocean, swimming in the surf, and someone pretends to be a shark. They sing ominous music and then lunge at you." Full-page color photographs support the text, which attempts to convey "the truth about sharks" so that readers will "see them as the fascinating creatures they are, instead of the monsters of myth."

 ## Criteria for Evaluating Informational Books

- Is the book accurate and authentic in conveying factual, documented material?
- Is the information presented in an organized way?
- Is the format and design of the book appealing and accessible to children?
- Is the author's writing style clear and does it generate enthusiasm for the topic?

Technology in Practice 11.2

An invaluable resource for teachers is the website developed by nonfiction author Penny Colman, **www.pennycolman.com**. Her essays and articles give teachers further understanding about nonfiction literature. Teachers and their students also can learn more about this award-winning author whose books focus on women and American history. Instructional ideas for several of her books are also included.

What Is Biography?

Some of the oldest books for children are biographies—works that describe and discuss the lives of real individuals. In earlier periods, it was common to expose children to the (sometimes idealized) lives of national and cultural heroes. The practice still exists, but in a somewhat altered form. For one thing, in the United States, there is growing recognition that the society is made up of more than one culture, so the goal of many writers of biography has become to promote a more inclusive view of noteworthy Americans. For another thing, the trend toward exposure-oriented journalism—journalism that delves below the surface—has become steadily stronger since the Vietnam War era. Thus, today's children are less likely than their counterparts in previous generations to believe larger-than-life accounts of heroes. Third, the study of history has become less preoccupied with great people and great events and more focused on the common people and the ambience of earlier times. Thus, even though a biography might have a well-known person as its subject, the author is likely to explain that person in the context of his or her time, along with the concerns, available choices, and social movements of the day.

How does biography differ from historical fiction? Biographies that focus on famous individuals from the past offer insight into historical times just as historical fiction does. However, the information presented in a biography is based on known facts about the individual and her or his time period. Incidents, dialogue, and people are not invented or imagined, as they are in historical fiction. Autobiographies and memoirs differ from biographies in that their authors are writing about themselves.

Biographies have some unique features that justify their inclusion in a literature program. First, they help children learn from the lives of others. In a biography, children can see how choices a person makes early in life can bear fruit later on or how inauspicious beginnings can lead to a good outcome. Reading biographies can also encourage children to recognize links between people's lives and the social and historical times in which they lived. For instance, in her biography *You Want Women to Vote, Lizzie Stanton?* Jean Fritz writes, "Yes, Elizabeth Cady Stanton did want women to vote. It was an outlandish idea, but that's what she wanted. Not at first. As a child, she knew that girls didn't count for much, but she didn't expect to change that. First she had to grow up" (p. 1). This biography of Stanton, who dedicated her life to women's suffrage in the United States, describes gender roles during the nineteenth century and reasons for people's beliefs about women's suffrage. Through biographies, children come to understand the people who have shaped history, created inventions, discovered scientific principles, composed music, crafted works of art, and contributed to their local communities. Children realize that they, too, can make a difference in the world.

Teaching Idea 11.5

Inquiry Project

Involve children in an inquiry project in which they assume the role of an author writing an informational book or biography. Children can work individually, with a partner, or in small groups as they research a topic of interest or a famous person. Guide children in generating sources of information that include both primary and secondary sources. After their research is completed, the children can organize their information and write their own informational book or biography.

The Evolution of Biography

In the past, biographies for children were criticized for poor writing, invented details, and exaggeration of the positive side of their subjects. Moreover, in the first half of this century, the subjects of biographies were mostly limited to white males who were political leaders or who had made some other historical contribution to society. The prevailing thought—alive and well since ancient times—was that children should hear or read biographies of individuals who displayed admirable virtues and thus could serve as role models to emulate. These individuals were idealized—presented as being morally perfect. Because societal norms dictated that children should not be exposed to the less savory realities of life, such as discrimination, violence, or abuse, early biographies were bland and unrealistic.

Fictionalization was also an accepted practice in earlier children's biographies. For instance, authors routinely invented conversations and scenes for which there was no historic basis. True, authors had good motives for these distortions. In explaining why he fictionalized biography for children, F. M. Monjo (1982) pointed out that he used a child associated with the "great figure" as narrator because it "makes possible a casual intimacy which, I believe, young readers find congenial" (p. 99). Author Robert Lawson included fantastic elements in his fictionalized biographies. His study of Christopher Columbus, *I Discover Columbus,* was narrated by Aurelio, a parrot; Lawson's biography of Benjamin Franklin, *Ben & Me,* was told by a mouse named Amos. Although these books were very popular with children, they raised the question of whether it was necessary to fictionalize biographies to such an extent in order to make them palatable to young readers. The answer was decades away.

As with informational books in general, critical recognition of biographies for children was slow in coming. The first Newbery Medal for a work of biography was awarded in 1934 to *Invincible Louisa,* a biography of Louisa May Alcott, written by Cornelia Meigs. In 1940, James Daugherty received the Newbery Medal for *Daniel Boone.* (Contemporary readers, however, may be appalled at the book's portrayal of Native Americans.) In the same year, the Caldecott Medal for the best illustrated book of the year went to a biography, *Abraham Lincoln*, by Ingri D'Aulaire and Edgar Parin D'Aulaire. This book is said to have "established the picture-book biography for younger children as a valued staple of library-book collections" (Hoke, 1995, p. 188). Still, biographies for children had a long way to go.

The 1970s were a turning point for children's biographies. With the publication of *And Then What Happened, Paul Revere?* in 1973, author Jean Fritz set a new standard. Fritz created an authentic biography for children without any invented dialogue; she also included "Notes from the Author," containing additional facts keyed to various pages of the book. Fritz did not rely on the fictionalizing of earlier days to make her books congenial to young readers. Her conversational, humorous, and easily accessible writing style—as well as her focus on one or two interesting events—is what drew and still draws readers to her works.

Since the early 1970s, biographies have advanced further, to give children wider representation of noteworthy people. Biographies written in the past four decades have featured men, women, and children of many ethnic and racial backgrounds engaging in a variety of occupations and contributing in many different ways to society. For example, *Harvesting Hope: The Story of Cesar Chavez* by Kathleen Krull, describes the Mexican American leader who organized the National Farm Workers Association; *When Marian Sang* by Pam Muñoz Ryan, highlights the life of Marian Anderson, the talented singer who was the first African American to perform with the Metropolitan Opera. During the 1980s, the picture book biography became more recognized as a format to chronicle an individual's life. For instance, Alice and Martin Provensen skillfully combined illustrations and text in a unique pop-up book about the life of Leonardo da Vinci, *Leonardo da Vinci: The Artist, Inventor, Scientist in Three-Dimensional Movable Pictures.* In the 1990s, more authors chose to write partial biographies about the childhoods of famous individuals. Cheryl Harness presents a picture book biography about the childhood of John Quincy Adams, who would become the sixth president of the United States, in *Young John Quincy.*

ILLUSTRATION 11.5 Beautiful illustrations combine with the text in this biography of Marian Anderson, the first African American to sing with the Metropolitan Opera. (Jacket illustration copyright © 2002 by Brian Selznick from *When Marian Sang* by Pam Muñoz Ryan. Scholastic Inc./Scholastic Press. Reprinted by permission of Scholastic Inc.)

In 1988, Russell Freedman received the Newbery Medal for *Lincoln: A Photobiography,* establishing a new era for the prestige and recognition of authentic biography for children. James Cross Giblin, himself a distinguished author of informational books as well as an editor, explains that the significance of *Lincoln* in the evolution of children's biography is that it offers a "fresh approach to familiar material, demythologizing Lincoln without debunking him," telling "a dramatic true story," emphasizing the visual with its photo-essay format, and providing an "accessible yet literate text" (1992, p. 25).

In 1999, the Caldecott Medal was awarded to *Snowflake Bentley,* written by Jacqueline Briggs Martin and illustrated by Mary Azarian. This picture book biography describes the life of Wilson Bentley, whose fascination with snowflakes led to his dedicated work photographing snowflakes, documenting the unique features of each one, and becoming an authority on them. Azarian's woodcut illustrations, hand-tinted with watercolors, document Bentley's life and the beauty of snowflakes. In 2002, two Caldecott Honor Books were biographies: *The Dinosaurs of Waterhouse Hawkins* by Barbara Kerley, with carefully researched illustrations by Brian Selznick; and *Martin's Big Words: The Life of Martin Luther King, Jr.* by Doreen Rappaport, with watercolor and cut paper illustrations by Bryan Collier. In recent years, biographies have continued to garner Caldecott Honor designation: *Rosa* by Nikki Giovanni with watercolor and collage illustrations by Bryan Collier in 2006; *Moses: When Harriet Tubman Led Her People to Freedom* by Carole Boston Weatherford with paintings by Kadir Nelson in 2007; and *The Wall: Growing Up Behind the Iron Curtain* written and illustrated by Peter Sís in 2008.

Categories of Biography

Biographies for children feature contemporary people, historical figures, athletes, and entertainers—as well as young people who are similar to those reading the biographies. A current trend in children's biographies is the publication of series biographies. These biographies follow a specified format and include the same types of information for each individual. The Lerner Publishing Group has several biography series: *Creative Minds* and *Gateway* are two series targeted for children in grades 4 to 8. They include biographies of Susan B. Anthony, Booker T. Washington, Jonas Salk, and Sandra Day O'Connor. For primary grades, Holiday House has its *Picture Book Biographies* by David Adler, who has written *A Picture Book of Amelia Earhart* and *A Picture Book of Thurgood Marshall.* Scholastic's *Science Super Giants* provides biographies of such greats as Thomas Edison and Albert Einstein that children in the primary grades can read independently.

Partial Biographies

Instead of presenting an entire life, a writer may create a more interesting work by selecting one segment from the person's life and exploring it in depth and detail. Jean Fritz's biographies of famous early Americans are good examples of partial biographies. For example, in *Why Don't You Get a Horse, Sam Adams?* Fritz recounts how patriot Samuel Adams walked the streets of pre-Revolutionary Boston promoting independence from England. (Was he earthbound out of fear of horses or because he wanted to stay closer to the people?) Another example of a partial biography is *Coming Home: From the Life of Langston Hughes* by Floyd Cooper, which limits its coverage to the groundbreaking poet's childhood.

Complete Biographies

In a complete biography, the author recounts a person's life from birth to the present or to the person's death if he or she is no longer living. Candace Fleming chronicles the life of beloved first lady Eleanor Roosevelt in *Our Eleanor: A Scrapbook Look at Eleanor Roosevelt's Remarkable Life*. Archival photographs, diary entries, and letters combine with the text in documenting the life of Eleanor Roosevelt. For older readers, Albert Marrin has written about the life of U.S. President Andrew Jackson in *Old Hickory: Andrew Jackson and the American People.* This detailed biography explores the complexity of the first popularly elected president as well as the controversies, such as the Trail of Tears, surrounding his presidency.

Collective Biographies

A collective biography is a book describing the lives of several people who have something in common. In *Uncommon Champions: Fifteen Athletes Who Battled Back,* Marty Kaminsky tells the story of fifteen athletes who overcame serious illnesses, physical disabilities, and other adversity to achieve in various sports. Kaminsky, a fourth-grade teacher, points out in the introduction that these athletes "are remarkable not just for their achievements on the playing fields, courts, and tracks, but for the tremendous courage they demonstrated while overcoming major obstacles in their lives" (p. 9).

Another approach to collective biography is seen in the collaborative work of author Kathleen Krull and illustrator Kathryn Hewitt. They have produced many collective biographies, including *Lives of the Musicians: Good Times, Bad Times (and What the Neighbors Thought), Lives of the Artists: Masterpieces, Messes (and What the Neighbors Thought),* and *Lives of Extraordinary Women: Rulers, Rebels (and What the Neighbors Thought).* The format of these appealing and humorous books includes biographical sketches of the individuals accompanied by watercolor illustrations. Krull has carefully researched each individual, discovering little-known information that will fascinate readers.

Autobiographies and Memoirs

In an autobiography, a person writes about his or her own life. Many children's authors have written their autobiographies. Children who delight in these authors' books will enjoy reading about their childhoods and how they became writers. Lois Lowry incorporates family photographs and quotes from her books to recount her life in *Looking Back.* The "Meet the Author" collection, published by Richard C. Owen, includes autobiographies of children's authors and illustrators such as Joseph Bruchac's *Seeing the Circle* and Denise Fleming's *Maker of Things.*

A memoir differs from an autobiography in that it shares events from the author's life based on his or her recollection. Often, a memoir focuses on one particular event or time period in the person's life and reflects on the meaning of that event for the author. Memoirs are becoming increasingly popular in children's literature. Award-winning children's book illustrator Anita Lobel shares recollections of her childhood as a Polish Jew during the Holocaust in *No Pretty Pictures: A Child of War.* Another Holocaust memoir, *The Cat with the Yellow Star: Coming of Age in Terezin*, is the story of Ela Weissberger as told to author Susan Goldman Rubin. Ela was born in Czechoslavkia and was sent to the Terezin Concentration Camp in 1942 when she was eleven. Siena Cherson Siegel shares her childhood learning to dance in *To Dance: A Ballerina's Graphic Novel,* illustrated by Mark Siegel. This memoir, with its graphic novel format, seamlessly combines text and illustrations as the author describes her early life and training at the School of American Ballet.

Ordinary individuals often experience extraordinary events or inspire others with their courage and determination. Ruby Bridges gives readers a glimpse into her childhood in *Through My Eyes.* Ruby was six years old in 1960 when federal marshals escorted her to school. Ruby's historic childhood as the young girl who integrated the New Orleans public school system is shared in this award-winning book. Ibtisam Barakat recounts her early years living under Israeli occupation in *Tasting the Sky: A Palestinian Childhood*.

Picture Book Biographies

The number of picture book biographies written for children continues to increase. In the picture book biography, the illustrations and the text join together in portraying a person's life. There are picture book biographies that appeal to younger readers, as well as ones for older children. For instance, in *Rachel: The Story of Rachel Carson*, Amy Ehrlich's text is enriched by the beautiful watercolor and gouache paintings of Wendell Minor. Rachel's love of nature is depicted in two double page spreads that are wordless.

The life of 2004 Nobel Peace Prize recipient Wangari Maathai is portrayed in text and illustrations in *Planting the Trees of Kenya: The Story of Wangari Maathai* by Claire A. Nivola. Nivola's watercolor illustrations complement the text about the life of the woman who began the Green Belt Movement. In *Freedom River,* author Doreen Rappaport recounts an incident in the life of John Parker, an ex-slave who became a successful businessman in Ohio and a conductor on the Underground Railroad. Bryan Collier's illustrations are rendered in collage and watercolors. A picture book for older children is *The Tree of Life* written and illustrated by Peter Sís. The life of Charles Darwin is recreated through intricate and detailed illustrations along with text from Darwin's own diaries, letters, and writings.

Biographies: The Lives of All Kinds of People

Who are the subjects of biographies for children? Biographies have been written about people from both the past and the present day. They have featured people in all kinds of occupations, from aviators to zookeepers. They have also described the lives of everyday individuals, often children, whose experiences have touched us in some way.

Discovery and exploration enable civilizations to move forward, as people continue taking risks to tackle the unknown. Biographies have told the story of these scientists and inventors. Madam Curie was the first woman to receive a Nobel Prize for her scientific discoveries; Carla Killough McClafferty describes her life in *Something Out of Nothing: Marie Curie and Radium*. Wilbur and Orville Wright invented and built the first airplane; their life is described in *To Fly: The Story of the Wright Brothers* by Wendie Old. Bessie Coleman was eleven years old in 1903 when Wilbur and Orville embarked on their historic flight. Her inspirational story about becoming the first African American pilot is told in *Fly High! The Story of Bessie Coleman* by Louise Borden.

Political leaders have always been a popular subject for biographies. Numerous political biographies of the U.S. presidents, and of many of their wives, have been written for children over the years. Authors have also focused on courageous individuals in other parts of the world who have led their people to freedom. For example, Floyd Cooper's *Mandela: From the Life of the South African Statesman* chronicles the life of the beloved South African leader. Social reformers are dedicated to the betterment of people's lives. In *Jeannette Rankin: Political Pioneer,* Getchen Woelfel provides an insightful look at the Montana woman who became the first female in Congress even before women had the right to vote.

Many biographies feature individuals who have contributed to the arts through music, art, dance, drama, entertainment, and writing. *Footwork: The Story of Fred and Adele Astaire* by Roxane Orgill with illustrations by Stéphane Jorisch tells the story of the siblings who became great dancers. Duke Ellington, the great jazz musician and composer, is described in Andrea Davis Pinkney's *Duke Ellington,* a picture book biography with illustrations by Brian Pinkney. The life of artist Jacob Lawrence is recounted in *Story Painter: The Life of Jacob Lawrence* by John Duggleby. This acclaimed African American artist grew up during the Harlem Renaissance, and his paintings depict the history of the African American experience.

Throughout history, people in cultures and nations throughout the world have faced persecution because of religion, race, or ethnicity. Others have endured terrible economic or political conditions. The stories of how people have persevered against seemingly insurmountable obstacles provide inspiration and teach valuable lessons.

Religious and ethnic persecution have provided the backdrop for many biographies. In *The Road from Home: The Story of an Armenian Girl,* David Kherdian describes the life of his mother, who, as a child in Turkey, survived the Turkish persecution of Armenians during the early years of the twentieth century. Not all children survived the Holocaust of World War II. Probably the best-known child of the Holocaust, Anne Frank, is remembered in *Anne Frank: A Hidden Life* by Mirjam Pressler.

African Americans' quest for freedom began during slavery; their quest for equal treatment progressed through the civil rights movement and continues today. Those who have been part of this struggle have been featured in many biographies: Martin Luther King, Jr., Harriet Tubman, Frederick Douglass, Sojourner Truth. Rosa Parks became famous for refusing to sit in the back of a Montgomery, Alabama, bus in 1955. Jim Haskins collaborated with

Parks to tell her life story in **Rosa Parks: My Story.** A picture book biography, **Rosa,** by Nikki Giovanni and illustrated by Bryan Collier, is a partial biography focusing on Rosa's refusal to give up her seat on the bus. The man who broke the racial barrier in baseball, Jackie Robinson, is lovingly remembered by his daughter Sharon Robinson in **Promises to Keep: How Jackie Robinson Changed America.** In **Playing to Win: The Story of Althea Gibson**, Karen Deans describes how Althea Gibson overcame discrimination to become a champion tennis player. An Author's Note indicates that Althea was also the first African American to play for the Ladies Professional Golf Association. Biographies also feature ordinary people, whose lives, due to unexpected circumstances, inspire us by their example of courage and dedication. One such person is Peter J. Ganci Jr., Chief of the Fire Department of New York City, who lost his life on September 11, 2001. **Chief: The Life of Peter J. Ganci, A New York City Firefighter,** is written in the first person by his son Chris Ganci as a tribute to his father and to the brave firefighters everywhere.

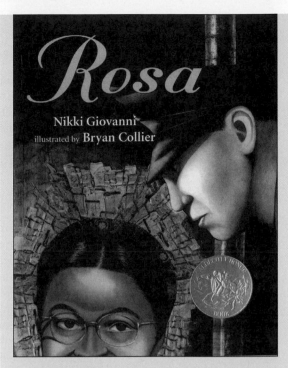

ILLUSTRATION 11.6 In this award-winning biography, author Nikki Giovanni and illustrator Bryan Collier share the story of Rosa Parks and the Montgomery bus boycott. (Cover of *Rosa* written by Nikki Giovanni. Illustrated by Bryan Collier. Illustrations copyright © 2005 by Bryan Collier. Reprinted by arrangement with Henry Holt and Company, LLC.)

How Biographies Work

Biographies are stories about real people. Like the writer of any good story, the biographer must create a main character about whom children care and want to learn more. Biographers develop their subjects' personalities and recreate their lives by describing their actions and interactions with others, what they say, and the ways in which others talk about them. Descriptive language creates visual pictures in readers' minds, which helps readers to put themselves in the time and place of the biography's subject. Although biographers present lives of real people based on careful research, they must also interpret facts and events. As Zarnowski (1990) points out:

> While biographers do gather all the information they can, they also filter that information through their minds. Biographers are active decision makers, deciding what to include and what to omit, what to highlight, and what to place in the background, and what to claim as truth and what to suggest as informed speculation. Biographers are interpreters of the information they collect. (p. 9)

Just as biographers interpret information, readers must interpret critically what they are reading. They must decide whether the portrait of the person is balanced, whether any aspects of the person's life have been fictionalized, whether dialogue is authentic, and whether the person is presented in a believable way.

As a biographer recounts an individual's life story, he or she needs to attend to the literary elements of narrative that comprise a compelling story such as plot, theme, character development, and setting. Biographies work well when readers can identify with these life stories. Christine Duthie (1996) discusses the important role biographies play in the literacy program in her first-grade classroom. She indicates that "primary-age children are easily engaged by the life stories of people" (p. 90) and further points out how reading biography fosters empathy in young children. "Biography encourages children to see that other people also have needs much like theirs and how others perceive, address, and resolve problems" (p. 95). By reading biographies, children can relate a person's life to the setting—the historical and cultural time and place in which he/she lived. They can see how people made important decisions that impacted their own lives and the lives of others.

Teaching Idea 11.6

Readers' Theater

Have groups of three or four children read the same biography (for example, *Kate Shelley: Bound for Legend* by Robert D. San Souci) and create a readers' theater script of the biography. After writing the script, the group can present it to the entire class.

Major Writers of Biographies and Their Works

A number of authors have established themselves as writers of biographies for children. The husband and wife team of Ingri D'Aulaire and Edgar Parin D'Aulaire were pioneers in the field of children's biography; they were both artists known for their oversized picture-book biographies of famous Americans, such as *Abraham Lincoln, Benjamin Franklin,* and *George Washington.* Four contemporary authors who have influenced the nature and evolution of children's biographies are discussed in this section.

David Adler

David Adler, a former math teacher, has written books for children since 1976. A prolific writer of almost two hundred children's books, he pens novels and informational books as well as biographies. Adler is known for his picture-book biographies that primary school children can read independently. He notes, "The picture book biographies must be short, but that makes them very difficult to write" (Olendorf & Telgen, 1993, p. 4). Many of his biographies and informational books focus on Jewish persons or topics, including the Holocaust.

His first biography, *Our Golda: The Story of Golda Meir,* named a Carter G. Woodson Award Honor Book by the National Council for the Social Studies, traces Golda Meir's life from her childhood in Russia through her immigration to Milwaukee in 1906, her marriage and move to Palestine, her participation in the shaping of Israel, and her election in 1969 as Israel's Prime Minister.

A Hero and the Holocaust: The Story of Janusz Korcazk and His Children tells the story of Janusz Korcazk, the Polish Jewish doctor who was director of the Jewish orphans' home in Warsaw. Although he could not save the orphans who were sent to Treblinka death camp, he never left them and "died there with his children." Oil paintings by Bill Farnsworth enhance the story.

Adler's first comprehensive biography for middle-grade students is *B. Franklin, Printer,* the detailed life of Benjamin Franklin. This carefully researched biography includes a table of contents, chronologies, source notes, recommended websites, and an index.

His books have been translated into many languages and also published in Braille.

Russell Freedman

Russell Freedman graduated from the University of California at Berkeley and worked for the Associated Press and on several television shows before becoming a writer of books for children in 1961. He has distinguished himself as an authentic biographer, conducting meticulous research to craft insightful portraits of real people. His biographies are illustrated with carefully selected photographs and include indexes, references, and lists of places to visit if one wants to learn more about the subjects. Freedman's biographies have received many awards: *Franklin Delano Roosevelt* received the 1991 Orbis Pictus Award; *The Wright Brothers: How They Invented the Airplane* was named a Newbery Honor Book in 1992; and *Eleanor Roosevelt: A Life of Discovery* was a 1994 Newbery Honor Book. In 2005, *The Voice that Challenged a Nation: Marian Anderson and the Struggle for Equal Rights* received the Sibert Award and was named both a Newbery Honor Book and an Orbis Pictus Honor Book.

Lincoln: A Photobiography, which received the Newbery Medal in 1988, includes carefully researched illustrations to support and complement the text. In reflecting about this book, Freedman (1992) said, "The more I studied Lincoln, the more I came to appreciate his

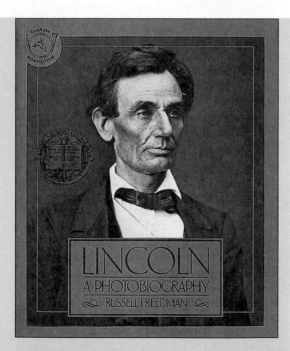

ILLUSTRATION 11.7 Winner of the Newbery Medal, Russell Freedman's photobiography provides a sympathetic, yet realistic picture of one of the most compelling of the U.S. presidents. (Cover from *Lincoln: A Photobiography* by Russell Freedman. Jacket copyright © 1987 by Houghton Mifflin Company. Reprinted by permission of Clarion Books, an imprint of Houghton Mifflin Harcourt Publishing Company. All rights reserved.)

subtleties and complexities. The man himself turned out to be vastly more interesting than the myth" (p. 9).

In 1992, Freedman received the *Washington Post*-Children's Book Guild Nonfiction award for his contribution to nonfiction for children.

Read the interview where Russell Freedman discusses writing history and biography by going to the Conversations section of Chapter 11 in the MyEducationKit for your book.

Jean Fritz

Jean Fritz has shaped and directed the genre of children's biography for more than thirty-five years. In addition to writing biography, Fritz also writes historical fiction and informational books. Attention to detail, the use of humor, and the ability to present historical figures in an interesting, appealing way are characteristics of her work. Fritz (1995) commented, "I like to think of a historian or a biographer as an artist who has made a compact with the past to be true to it. As an artist, the historian has to use his or her imagination to penetrate the record, to dig deep into the past to the place where life emerges" (p. 257).

Several of Fritz's biographies have received prestigious awards: *Stonewall* and *Will You Sign Here, John Hancock?* were *Boston Globe-Horn Book* Honor Books; *The Great Little Madison* was named both the Orbis Pictus Award winner and the *Boston Globe-Horn Book* Nonfiction Award recipient in 1990; and *Where Do You Think You're Going, Christopher Columbus?* was an American Book Award Honor Book. Her memoir of her childhood in China, *Homesick: My Own Story*, was a Newbery Honor Book in 1983. For her significant contributions to children's literature, Fritz received the Laura Ingalls Wilder Award of the American Library Association in 1986. She was one of the first recipients of the *Washington Post*-Children's Book Guild Award in 1979.

Diane Stanley

Diane Stanley has achieved prominence for her picture book biographies for children in the upper elementary grades. She was born in Texas, grew up in New York City, and began her artistic career as a medical illustrator. She transferred her talent for detailed, realistic drawing and painting to children's books, and her first biography, *Peter the Great,* was published in 1986. Since then, she has collaborated with her husband, Peter Vennema, and her mother, Fay Stanley, to produce more than ten picture book biographies. Stanley also has self-illustrated several picture books, illustrated books written by others, and written novels. Stanley's work is described in *Something about the Author* (2000):

> Acknowledged for clearly identifying what is known and what is speculative about the lives she is outlining, Stanley writes her works in concise prose and illustrates them with elegant, detailed watercolor and gouache illustrations that are done in the artistic style of the periods in which subjects lived. (p. 193)

Her books have been named to the list of *Notable Children's Trade Books in the Field of Social Studies* by the National Council for the Social Studies and have received many awards. She illustrated *The Last Princess: The Story of Princess Ka'iulani of Hawai'i* by Fay Stanley, which received the Carter G. Woodson Award; *Leonardo da Vinci* received the Orbis Pictus Award and the *Boston Globe-Horn Book* Award for Nonfiction. Stanley was named recipient of the 2000 *Washington Post*-Children's Book Guild Award for Nonfiction.

Criteria for Evaluating Biographies

- Is the person someone whose life will be of interest to young readers?
- Has the author presented the person in such a way that readers can identify with him or her as an authentic, believable human being?
- Is the information about the person accurate and authentic?
- Has the author written in an engaging style that maintains readers' attention?

Teaching Idea 11.7
Archival Photographs

Organize children into small groups, and give each group a book illustrated with archival photographs. Ask children to "read" these photographs and to compile a list of the facts and concepts that they learned from carefully viewing the photographs.

PEARSON
myeducationkit™

To check your comprehension on the content covered in this chapter, go to the MyEducation-Kit for your book and complete the Study Plan for Chapter 11. Here you will be able to take a chapter quiz and receive feedback on your answers.

Awards for Informational Books and Biographies

Although many awards, such as the Newbery Medal and the Caldecott Medal, may be given to a children's book of any genre, certain awards focus exclusively on nonfiction for children. Many of these awards are indicated on the book in some way—for example, by a seal that appears on the book jacket. The National Council of Teachers of English annually bestows the Orbis Pictus Award for Outstanding Nonfiction for Children, with one book receiving the award and several others being cited as Honor Books. The *Boston Globe-Horn Book* Award, which has a separate category for nonfiction, is given annually to one book, with up to three books being designated as Honor Books. The National Council for the Social Studies sponsors the Carter G. Woodson Book Award to honor children's books that sensitively and accurately deal with ethnic minorities and race relations. The Washington, D.C., Children's Book Guild, in conjunction with the *Washington Post,* annually presents the *Washington Post*-Children's Book Guild Nonfiction Award to an author in recognition of his or her contribution to children's nonfiction. The American Nature Society honors an author for his or her contribution to science writing for children with the Eva L. Gordon Award for Children's Science Literature. The Golden Kite Award of the Society for Children's Book Writers has a nonfiction category, which includes one winner and one Honor Book annually. The Jefferson Cup Award, sponsored by the Virginia Library Association, is presented to a book of fiction and a book of nonfiction dealing with U.S. history or biography. In addition, the Children's Book Council, in cooperation with both the National Council for the Social Studies and the National Science Teachers Association, develops annual lists of outstanding books from all genres: *Notable Children's Trade Books in the Field of Social Studies* and *Outstanding Science Trade Books for Children.*

Bestowed for the first time in 2001, the Robert F. Sibert Informational Book Award is presented annually to the author of the most distinguished informational book published during the preceding year. The award honors the long-time president of Bound to Stay Bound Books, Inc. and is sponsored by the company. The American Library Association's Association for Library Services to Children (ALSC) administers the award. In 2001, the first Sibert Award went to Marc Aronson for **Sir Walter Ralegh and the Quest for El Dorado.** For the purpose of this award, informational books are defined as "those written and illustrated to present, organize and interpret documentable factual material for children." Poetry and traditional literature are not eligible. Honor books may be named if they are truly distinguished.

Experiences for Further Learning

1. Review an award-winning informational book such as *The Great Fire* by Jim Murphy and an award-winning biography such as *The Life and Death of Adolf Hitler* by James Cross Giblin. Critique each book according to the criteria presented in this chapter. Would you agree that the books are worthy of the awards they received? What do you see as their strengths and weaknesses?

2. Select a topic that interests you—say, wolves. Compare the treatment of the topic in an informational book (such as *To the Top of the World: Adventures with Arctic Wolves* by Jim Brandenburg) to its treatment in other genres such as novels (for example, *Julie of the Wolves* by Jean Craighead George), picture books (*Wolf's Favor* by Fulvio Testa), and folktales (*Peter and the Wolf* retold by Selina Hastings). How do different genres contribute to your understanding of the topic?

3. Select two informational books on the same topic. For example, for the civil rights movement, you could use *Freedom Walkers: The Story of the Montgomery Bus Boycott* by Russell Freedman, and *Freedom Riders: John Lewis and Jim Zwerg on the Front Lines of the Civil Rights Movement* by Ann Bausum. Review the archival photographs in each book. How do the photographs convey information? What kind of information is presented? What design features do you notice in each book? Compare the photographs and design features on a chart, with a column for each book. Share your findings with classmates.

4. Compare the scope, content, and presentation of material about a science topic in an informational book and a textbook. How are the books alike? How are they different? Which type of book do you think is more effective in conveying information? Why? Discuss these issues with your classmates.

Now go to Chapter 11 in the MyEducationKit (www.myeducationkit.com) for your book, where you can:

- Find learning outcomes for Chapter 11.
- Access the Children's Literature Database for your own exploration.
- Complete Assignments and Activities that can help you more deeply understand the chapter content.
- Extend knowledge with content-specific Web Links.
- Deepen and apply content understanding with Extension Activities.
- Learn first hand about how authors and illustrators utilize their craft with podcasts and written interviews in the Conversations section for the chapter.
- Check your comprehension on the content covered in the chapter by going to the Study Plan. Here you will be able to take a chapter quiz and receive feedback on your answers.
- Find the following updated appendices: Major Children's Book Awards, Children's Magazines, Professional Organizations, Children's Book Publishers' Addresses, Book Selection Aids, and Children's Literature Web Sites.

Recommended Books

* indicates a picture book; **I** indicates interest level (P = preschool, YA = young adult)

History

Anderson, Joan. *The First Thanksgiving Feast.* Photographs by George Ancona. Clarion, 1989. Recreates the first Thanksgiving with photographs taken at Plimouth Plantation. (**I:** P–10)

Armstrong, Jennifer. *Shipwreck at the Bottom of the World: The Extraordinary True Story of Shackleton and the Endurance.* Crown, 1998. Chronicles the 1914 expedition to Antarctica led by Ernest Shackleton and the perils he and his crew experienced. (**I:** 10–YA)

Bartoletti, Susan Campbell. *Black Potatoes: The Story of the Great Irish Famine, 1845–1850.* Houghton Mifflin, 2001. Primary source material was consulted to document the potato blight in Ireland. (**I:** 9–14)

———. *Hitler Youth: Growing Up in Hitler's Shadow.* Scholastic, 2005. This book discusses the children and teenagers who participated in the Nazi Party as Hitler Youth between 1933 and 1945. (**I:** 10–YA)

Bausum, Ann. *Freedom Riders: John Lewis and Jim Zwerg on the Front Lines of the Civil Rights Movement.* National Geographic, 2006. The story of the Freedom Riders through the perspective of two participants. (**I:** 9–14)

Blumberg, Rhoda. *Commodore Perry in the Land of the Shogun.* Lothrop, Lee & Shepard, 1985. Describes Matthew Perry's important voyage to Japan to open trade and whaling ports to America. (**I:** 10–YA)

———. *Full Steam Ahead: The Race to Build a Transcontinental Railroad.* National Geographic Society, 1996. A fascinating account of the race between the Central Pacific and the Union Pacific to finish laying the tracks for the transcontinental railroad. (**I:** 10–YA)

———. *York's Adventures with Lewis and Clark: An African-American's Part in the Great Expedition.* HarperCollins, 2004. This book discusses the important role played by William Clark's slave, York, in the famous expedition. (**I:** 10–YA)

*Burleigh, Robert. *Flight.* Illustrated by Mike Wimmer. Philomel, 1991. Chronicles Charles Lindbergh's 1927 solo flight across the Atlantic from New York to Paris. (**I:** 8–12)

Colman, Penny. *Girls: A History of Growing Up Female in America.* Scholastic, 2000. Eyewitness accounts from journals, slave narratives, and letters document the history of growing up female in America. (**I:** 10–YA)

———. *Rosie the Riveter: Women Working on the Home Front during World War II.* Crown, 1995. Details the role of women in the wartime workforce. (**I:** 9–YA)

———. *Thanksgiving: The True Story.* Holt, 2008. A well-researched look at the history of this national holiday. (**I:** 9–14)

Cooper, Michael. *Remembering Manzanar: Life in a Japanese Relocation Camp.* Clarion, 2002. An account of the experiences of Japanese Americans living in Manzanar relocation camp during World War II. (**I:** 10–YA)

Freedman, Russell. *Children of the Great Depression.* Clarion, 2005. Archival photographs help to convey what life was like for children during the Depression. (**I:** 9–14)

———. *Freedom Walkers: The Story of the Montgomery Boycott.* Holiday House, 2006. Archival photographs and text convey information about the Montgomery bus boycott in the 1950s. (**I:** 9–14)

*Gibbons, Gail. *Sunken Treasure.* Crowell, 1988. Full-color illustrations help to describe the sinking of an ancient Spanish galleon and the discovery of its treasures. (**I:** 6–10)

Giblin, James Cross. *Good Brother, Bad Brother: The Story of Edwin Booth and John Wilkes Booth.* Clarion, 2005. Although they were both actors, one brother would assassinate Abraham Lincoln. (**I:** 10–YA)

———. *The Riddle of the Rosetta Stone: Key to Ancient Egypt.* Crowell, 1990. The story of the discovery of the ancient Rosetta Stone and the deciphering of its hieroglyphics. (**I:** 8–12)

———. *Secrets of the Sphinx.* Illustrated by Bagram Ibatoulline. Scholastic, 2004. Egypt's most famous sites and the theories about their origins are described. (**I:** 9–14)

Haskins, James. *Get on Board: The Story of the Underground Railroad.* Scholastic, 1993. Chronicles the Underground Railroad, which shepherded slaves to freedom in the North. (**I:** 8–12)

Hopkinson, Deborah. *Shutting Out the Sky: Life in the Tenements of New York 1880–1924.* Orchard, 2003. The lives of five immigrants living on the Lower East Side of New York are described. (**I:** 9–YA)

Kimmel, Elizabeth Cody. *Ice Story: Shackleton's Lost Expedition.* Clarion, 1999. When Shackleton's boat, the *Endurance,* is crushed, he and his crew brave a dangerous journey to land. (**I:** 10–YA)

Lawrence, Jacob. *The Great Migration: An American Story.* HarperCollins, 1993. A narrative sequence of vibrant paintings helps to tell the story of African Americans' migration from the South to the North around World War I. (**I:** 8–12)

McKissack, Patricia C., and Fredrick L. McKissack. *Christmas in the Big House—Christmas in the Quarters.* Scholastic, 1994. A fascinating and insightful comparison of life in a Virginia plantation house and in the slave quarters around Christmas time in 1859. (**I:** 8–12)

———. and Fredrick L. McKissack. *Days of Jubilee: The End of Slavery in the United States.* Scholastic, 2003. Slave narratives, letters, and diaries are used to recount the emancipation of the slaves. (**I:** 10–YA)

Murphy, Jim. *Across America on an Emigrant Train.* Clarion, 1993. The story of Robert Louis Stevenson's trip from Scotland to San Francisco in 1879 in search of his true love is combined with a history of the railroad. (**I:** 10–YA)

———. *An American Plague: The True and Terrifying Story of the Yellow Fever Epidemic.* Clarion, 2003. A detailed account of the Yellow Fever epidemic that hit Philadelphia in the eighteenth century. (**I:** 10–YA)

———. *The Great Fire.* Scholastic, 1995. Describes the Chicago fire of 1871 and its effects on individual people and the city. (**I:** 10–YA)

Myers, Walter Dean. *Amistad: A Long Road to Freedom.* Dutton, 1998. The story of the famous rebellion aboard the slave ship *Amistad* and the court cases that followed. (**I:** 10–YA)

Nelson, Scott Reynolds with Marc Aronson. *Ain't Nothing But a Man: My Quest to Find the Real John Henry.* National

Geographic, 2008. As he leads readers through historical research, the author describes how the railroad was built in the South and how he learned the truth about the legendary John Henry. (**I:** 9–14)

Pringle, Laurence. *Dog of Discovery: A Newfoundland's Adventures with Lewis and Clark*. Boyds Mills Press, 2002. With excerpts from the journals of Lewis and Clark, this carefully researched book documents the famous expedition and the participation of Seaman, a Newfoundland dog. (**I:** 8–12)

*Provensen, Alice, and Martin Provensen. *The Glorious Flight: Across the Channel with Louis Blériot*. Viking, 1983. In 1909, Blériot flies across the English Channel from France to England in thirty-seven minutes. (**I:** 7–10)

*St. George, Judith. *So You Want to be President?* Illustrated by David Small. Philomel, 2000. A humorous discussion of the U.S. presidency from George Washington to Bill Clinton. (**I:** 6–12)

Stanley, Jerry. *Children of the Dust Bowl: The True Story of the School at Weedpatch Camp*. Crown, 1992. The inspirational story of how educator Leo Hart and Okie children built their own school during the Depression in California. (**I:** 10–YA)

———. *Hurry Freedom: African Americans in Gold Rush California*. Crown, 2000. The life of African Americans during the California Gold Rush is documented through the true story of Mifflin Gibbs, who became a successful businessman and civil rights activist. (**I:** 10–14)

———. *I Am an American: A True Story of Japanese Internment*. Crown, 1994. Discusses the relocation of Japanese Americans from 1942 to 1945. (**I:** 10–YA)

Walker, Sally M. *Secrets of a Civil War Submarine: Solving the Mysteries of the H. L. Hunley*. Carolrhoda, 2005. The mysteries of the buried Civil War submarine are revealed in this book. (**I:** 8–12)

Warren, Andrea. *Orphan Train Rider: One Boy's True Story*. Houghton Mifflin, 1996. The story of Lee Nailling, who rode the orphan train in 1926, provides the framework for discussing this train, which transported orphaned and abandoned children from the East Coast to the Midwest from 1854 to 1929. (**I:** 9–12)

———. *Surviving Hitler: A Boy in the Nazi Death Camps*. HarperCollins, 2001. The story of a Holocaust survivor and his life in the concentration camps. (**I:** 10–14)

Understanding Peoples and Cultures

Ancona, George. *Barrio: José's Neighborhood*. Harcourt Brace, 1998. This photo-essay describes the daily life of an eight-year-old Mexican American boy living in the Mission District of San Francisco. (**I:** 6–10)

———. *Carnaval*. Harcourt Brace, 1999. Travel to Olinda, Brazil, to celebrate the annual Carnaval. (**I:** 6–10)

———. *Mayeros: A Yucatec Maya Family*. Lothrop, Lee & Shepard, 1997. Photo-essay presents the history and contemporary life of the Mayeros, who live in the Yucatan, Mexico. (**I:** 6–10)

———. *Pablo Remembers: The Fiesta of the Day of the Dead*. Lothrop, Lee & Shepard, 1993. Pablo remembers his grandmother in the three-day Mexican celebration. (**I:** 6–10)

———. *The Piñata Maker/El piñatero*. Harcourt Brace, 1994. This bilingual text describes how Don Ricardo crafts piñatas in southern Mexico. (**I:** 6–10)

*Cave, Kathryn. *One Child, One Seed: A South African Counting Book*. Photographs by Gisèle Wulfsohn. Holt (in Association with Oxfam), 2002. This photographic essay with a counting book format shares the life of Nothando, a young girl from South Africa. (**I:** 4–8)

Cha, Dia. *Dia's Story Cloth: The Hmong People's Journey of Freedom*. Stitched by Chue and Nhia Thao Cha. Lee & Low, 1996. A hand-embroidered story cloth recounts the story of the Hmong people of ancient China and Laos and their emigration to the United States. (**I:** 8–12)

*Chocolate, Debbi. *Kente Colors*. Illustrated by John Ward. Walker, 1996. Explains the meaning of the colors and patterns of the kente cloth worn by Ashanti and Ewe peoples. (**I:** P–8)

Giblin, James Cross. *When Plague Strikes: The Black Death, Smallpox, AIDS*. HarperCollins, 1995. Discusses epidemic diseases and their political, social, religious, and cultural consequences. (**I:** 10–YA)

Haskins, Jim, and Kathleen Benson. *Count Your Way through Egypt*. Illustrated by Sue Rama. Millbrook, 2007. A counting format conveys information about Egypt. (**I:** 7–12)

Hoyt-Goldsmith, Diane. *Cinco de Mayo: Celebrating the Traditions of Mexico*. Photographs by Lawrence Migdale. Holiday House, 2008. Rosie and her family celebrate Mexican history and traditions. (**I:** 7–12)

———. *Celebrating Ramadan*. Photographs by Lawrence Migdale. Holiday House, 2001. Ibraheem introduces readers to his Muslim heritage and the fast of Ramadan. (**I:** 7–12)

*Morris, Ann. *Families*. HarperCollins, 2000. Explains how families around the world are alike and different. (**I:** P–8)

*———. *Teamwork*. Lothrop, Lee & Shepard, 1999. Shows how teams around the world work together to get things done. (**I:** P–8)

*———. *Weddings*. Lothrop, Lee & Shepard, 1995. Presents marriage customs and rites around the world. (**I:** P–8)

Morris, Ann, and Heidi Larson. *Tsunami: Helping Each Other*. Lerner, 2005. This photographic essay describes the 2004 tsunami from the perspective of two brothers. (**I:** 8–12)

Onyefulu, I. *Ogbo: Sharing Life in an African Village*. Harcourt, 1996. Six-year-old Obioma explains the Nigerian tradition of ogbo, or age group, in this photo-essay. (**I:** 7–11)

Osborne, Mary Pope. *One World, Many Religions: The Ways We Worship*. Knopf, 1996. Photographs and text describe the world's major religions: Judaism, Christianity, Islam, Hinduism, Buddhism, Confucianism, and Taoism. (**I:** 8–YA)

Sís, Peter. *Tibet Through the Red Box*. Farrar, Straus, & Giroux, 1998. The diary of the author's father, a filmmaker who was lost in Tibet for many years, guides readers on a travel expedition to this country. (**I:** 9–14)

Tanaka, Shelley. *Mummies: The Newest, Coolest & Creepiest from Around the World*. Abrams, 2005. Readers travel the globe to learn about mummies and their civilizations. (**I:** 9–14)

United Nations Children's Fund. *A Life Like Mine: How Children Live Around the World*. Dorling Kindersley, 2002. Organized around the four themes of survival, development, protection, and participation, this photographic essay takes readers on a journey to meet children around the globe. (**I:** 6–12)

Science and Nature

*Asch, Frank. *The Sun Is My Favorite Star*. Harcourt, 2000. This informational picture book shares ways the sun helps the earth. (**I:** P–8)

*Berger, Melvin, and Gilda Berger. *Where Have the Pandas Gone?* Scholastic, 2001. Information is provided about endangered species in a question-and-answer format. (**I:** 5–10)

*Bishop, Nic. *Spiders*. Scholastic, 2007. Amazing color photographs combine with the text to present information about spiders. (**I:** 4–9)

Brandenburg, Jim. *To the Top of the World: Adventures with Arctic Wolves*. Walker, 1993. Magnificent color photographs enhance this personal account of the author's observations of a wolf pack. (**I:** 6–12)

Burleigh, Robert. *Chocolate: Riches from the Rainforest*. Harry N. Abrams, 2002. Published in association with Chicago's Field Museum, the book presents a history of chocolate. (**I:** 8–12)

Cole, Joanna. *The Magic School Bus and the Science Fair Expedition*. Illustrated by Bruce Degen. Scholastic, 2006. Ms. Frizzle and her class visit a science museum and meet famous scientists. (**I:** 5–8)

Cone, Molly. *Come Back, Salmon*. Photographs by Sidnee Wheelwright. Sierra Club, 1992. The inspiring story of the students at Jackson Elementary School in Everett, Washington, who adopted the stream by their school and brought it back to life. (**I:** 7–12)

Dewey, Jennifer Owings. *Wildlife Rescue: The Work of Dr. Kathleen Ramsay*. Photographs by Don MacCarter. Boyds Mills, 1994. Describes the wildlife center in rural New Mexico founded by veterinarian Ramsay, who takes care of injured and sick animals. (**I:** 7–12)

*Freymann, Saxton, and Joost Elffers. *How Are You Peeling? Foods with Moods*. Scholastic, 1999. Fruit and vegetable sculptures convey various moods and emotions. (**I:** P–8)

*Gibbons, Gail. *The Milk Makers*. Macmillan, 1985. Describes how dairy cows produce milk and the steps in getting it to the store. (**I:** P–8)

*———. *Spiders*. Holiday House, 1993. A picture-book examination of different kinds of spiders and their characteristics. (**I:** P–8)

Goodall, Jane. *The Chimpanzees I Love: Saving Their World and Ours*. Scholastic, 2001. The renowned scientist introduces readers to the chimpanzees of Tanzania and the importance of protecting the chimpanzee populations. Illustrated with color photographs. (**I:** 8–12)

Gore, Al. *An Inconvenient Truth: The Crisis of Global Warming*. Viking, 2007. This book is a version of the adult book and documentary designed for young readers. (**I:** 10–YA)

*Hatkoff, Isabella, Craig Hatkoff, and Dr. Paula Kahumbu. *Owen & Mzee: The True Story of a Remarkable Friendship*. Photographs by Peter Greste. Scholastic, 2006. An orphaned baby hippo befriends a giant tortoise in a Kenyan nature preserve. (**I:** P–10)

*———. *Owen & Mzee: The Language of Friendship*. Photographs by Peter Greste. Scholastic, 2006. After more than a year together, the hippo and tortoise have developed their own way to communicate. (**I:** P–10)

Hoose, Phillip. *The Race to Save the Lord God Bird*. Farrar, 2004. The attempts to save the Ivory-billed Woodpecker from extinction are described in this compelling book. (**I:** 10–YA)

*Jenkins, Steve. *Actual Size*. Houghton Mifflin, 2004. Animals and their body parts are illustrated in their actual size. (**I:** P–8)

*———. *Hottest Coldest Highest Lowest*. Houghton Mifflin, 1998. Takes readers on a geographic excursion around the globe. (**I:** P–8)

———, *The Top of the World: Climbing Mount Everest*. Houghton Mifflin, 1999. The author discusses his attempts to climb Mount Everest and provides information about mountaineering. (**I:** 8–12)

*———, and Robin Page. *What Do You Do With a Tail Like This?* Houghton Mifflin, 2003. Information about animals' sense organs is discussed in question-and-answer format. (**I:** P–8)

Lasky, Kathryn. *Sugaring Time*. Photographs by Christopher Knight. Macmillan, 1983. Describes maple sugar time on a Vermont family farm. (**I:** 8–12)

———. *Surtsey: The Newest Place on Earth*. Hyperion, 1992. Describes the creation of Surtsey, a volcanic island off the coast of Iceland. (**I:** 8–12)

Lauber, Patricia. *The News about Dinosaurs*. Bradbury, 1989. Examines new discoveries about dinosaurs that challenge what scientists previously believed. (**I:** 6–12)

———. *Seeing Earth from Space*. Orchard, 1990. NASA photographs complement the text, which provides a unique perspective on the earth. (**I:** 10–YA)

———. *Volcano: The Eruption and Healing of Mount St. Helens*. Bradbury, 1986. Illustrated with color photographs, this book describes the 1980 eruption of Mount St. Helens and its aftermath. (**I:** 8–12)

Markle, Sandra. *Science to the Rescue*. Atheneum, 1994. Describes contemporary problems and discusses ways in which science is solving them. (**I:** 8–12)

*McLimans, David. *Gone Wild: An Endangered Animal Alphabet*. Walker, 2006. Information about 26 endangered species is presented in alphabetical order. (**I:** 6–10)

Montgomery, Sy. *Quest for the Tree Kangaroo: An Expedition to the Cloud Forest of New Guinea*. Photographs by Nic Bishop. Houghton Mifflin, 2006. Chronicles the amazing journey to learn more about Matschie's tree kangaroo. (**I:** 9–14)

Patent, Dorothy Hinshaw. *When the Wolves Returned: Restoring Nature's Balance in Yellowstone*. Photographs by Dan Hartman and Cassie Hartman. Walker, 2008. Discusses the reintroduction of wolves to Yellowstone National Park in 1995 to restore the balance of nature. (**I:** 6–12)

*Peterson, Cris. *Clarabelle: Making Milk and So Much More*. Photographs by David R. Lundquist. Boyds Mill, 2007. This is the story of Clarabelle and her newborn calf who live on a Wisconsin dairy farm. (**I:** P–8)

*Pfeffer, Wendy, and Steve Jenkins. *Wiggling Worms at Work*. HarperCollins, 2004. A Let's-Read-and-Find-Out Science book that tells all about earthworms. (**I:** P–8)

Pringle, Laurence. *An Extraordinary Life: The Story of a Monarch Butterfly*. Illustrated by Bob Marstall. Orchard, 1997. Traces migration of the monarch butterfly from Massachusetts to Mexico. (**I:** 8–12)

———. *Fire in the Forest: A Cycle of Growth and Renewal*. Illustrated by Bob Marstall. Atheneum, 1995. An explanation of the fire cycle and its relationship to the forest ecology. (**I:** 6–12)

*———. *Whales! Strange and Wonderful*. Illustrated by Meryl Henderson. Boyds Mills Press, 2003. Describes the different species of whales, and current whale conservation efforts. (**I:** P–10)

Simon, Seymour. *Sharks*. HarperCollins, 1995. With full-page photographs, this book dispels many myths about these fascinating creatures. (**I:** 7–12)

————. *Wolves*. HarperCollins, 1993. Color photographs enhance the discussion of the characteristics and habits of wolves. (**I:** 5–12)

*Urbigkit, Cat. *Puppies, Puppies Everywhere!* Boyds Mills, 2006. Color photographs and rhyming text introduce young children to puppies. (**I:** P–6)

Wick, Walter. *A Drop of Water*. Scholastic, 1997. Magnificent photographs help explain properties of water and its different forms. (**I:** 8–12)

The Arts

Aliki. *William Shakespeare & the Globe*. HarperCollins, 1999. Discusses Shakespeare's life, the famous Globe Theatre of London, and recent efforts to reconstruct it. (**I:** 8–12)

Burleigh, Robert. *Toulouse-Lautrec: The Moulin Rouge and the City of Light*. Abrams, 2005. Published in conjunction with The Art Institute of Chicago, this book focuses on the art of Toulouse-Lautrec. (**I:** 8–12)

Desnoëttes, Caroline. *Look Closer: Art Masterpieces through the Ages*. Walker, 2006. Readers have an interactive experience lifting flaps to learn about famous paintings. (**I:** 8–12)

Fritz, Jean. *Leonardo's Horse*. Illustrated by Hudson Talbott. G. P. Putnam's Sons, 2001. This book is two stories in one— Leonard da Vinci's unfinished work on a bronze horse for the duke of Milan, and the dream of Charles Dent to create Leonardo's horse as a gift from the American people to Italy. (**I:** 6–12)

*Gerstein, Mordicai. *The Man Who Walked Between Two Towers*. Roaring Brook Press, 2003. French aerialist Philippe Petit tightrope walks between the World Trade Center Towers in 1974. (**I:** P–12)

Greenberg, Jan and Sandra Jordan. *Christo and Jeanne-Claude: Through the Gates and Beyond*. Roaring Brook, 2008. The story behind the 23-mile art installation in Central Park in 2005. (**I:** 9–14)

Haskins, Jim. *One Nation Under a Groove: Rap Music and Its Roots*. Hyperion, 2000. The history of rap music from its African roots to its popularity today. (**I:** 10–14)

*Lach, William. *Baby Animals: Little Ones at Play in 20 Works of Art*. Abrams, 2007. The babies of 20 animals are illustrated by famous works of art. (**I:** P–7)

Lester, Julius. *From Slave Ship to Freedom Road*. Paintings by Rod Brown. Dial, 1998. More than twenty paintings chronicle the history of slavery, with supporting text. (**I:** 9–14)

McMahon, Patricia. *Dancing Wheels*. Photographs by John Godt. Houghton Mifflin, 2000. A description of a children's dance troupe for wheelchair-bound ("sit-down") dancers as well as "stand-up" dancers. (**I:** 8–12)

How Things Work

Cobb, Vicki. *The Secret Life of Cosmetics*. Illustrated by Theo Cobb. Lippincott, 1985. Science experiments provide understanding of how shampoo, toothpaste, soap, and nail polish work. (**I:** 10–YA)

Cole, Joanna. *The Magic School Bus at the Waterworks*. Illustrated by Bruce Degen. Scholastic, 1987. Ms. Frizzle and her class visit a water treatment plant. (**I:** 5–8)

————. *The Magic School Bus inside the Human Body*. Illustrated by Bruce Degen. Scholastic, 1989. Ms. Frizzle and her class discover how the human body and its systems work. (**I:** 5–8)

*Gibbons, Gail. *Ice Cream: The Full Scoop*. Holiday House, 2006. Illustrations and text convey the history of ice cream and how it is made today. (**I:** 4–10)

*Hudson, Cheryl Willis. *Construction Zone*. Photographs by Richard Sobol. Documents how a building is constructed over a three-year period. Candlewick, 2006. (**I:** 4–8)

Macaulay, David. *Castle*. Houghton Mifflin, 1977. Detailed description of how a thirteenth-century Welsh castle was constructed. (**I:** 9–YA)

————. *Cathedral: The Story of Its Construction*. Houghton Mifflin, 1973. Explains the intricate process of building a Gothic cathedral. (**I:** 9–YA)

————. *The New Way Things Work*. Houghton Mifflin, 1998. A tribute to technology, this book explains how all kinds of machines work. (**I:** 10–YA)

*Schwartz, David M. *If You Made a Million*. Illustrated by Steven Kellogg. Lothrop, Lee & Shepard, 1989. This informational picture book introduces readers to various forms of money and personal finance. (**I:** 6–12)

Simon, Seymour. *Lungs: Your Respiratory System*. HarperCollins, 2007. Explains how the lungs and respiratory system work. (**I:** 8–12)

Thimmesh, Catherine. *Team Moon: How 400,000 People Landed Apollo 11 on the Moon*. Houghton Mifflin, 2006. The behind-the-scenes story of the successful mission of Apollo 11. (**I:** 8–14)

Tomecek, Stephen M. *What a Great Idea! Inventions That Changed the World*. Illustrated by Dan Stuckenschneider. Scholastic, 2003. Chronicles the history of inventions from the ancient world to the present. (**I:** 8–YA)

Sports, Recreation, and How-to Books

Blumenthal, Karen. *Let Me Play: The Story of Title IX, the Law that Changed the Future of Girls in America*. Atheneum, 2005. The history of the 1972 Title IX legislation and its impact. (**I:** 9–14)

Hoyt-Goldsmith, Diane. *Lacrosse: The National Game of the Iroquois*. Photographs by Lawrence Migdale. Holiday House, 1998. Information about lacrosse and instructions for playing it. (**I:** 7–12)

Lagasse, Emeril. *Emeril's There's a Chef in My World! Recipes that Take You Places*. HarperCollins, 2006. Information about foods from around the world with recipes that children can prepare. (**I:** 8–12)

Macy, Sue. *Freeze Frame: A Photographic History of the Winter Olympics*. National Geographic, 2006. This book presents a comprehensive history of the Winter Olympics. (**I:** 8–12)

Nelson, Kadir. *We Are the Ship: The Story of Negro League Baseball*. Hyperion, 2008. Beautiful paintings and text recount the story of the Negro Baseball league. (**I:** 6–12)

Nierman, Kevin, and Elaine Arima. *The Kids 'N' Clay Ceramics Book*. Illustrated by Curtis H. Arima. Tricycle Press, 2000. Illustrated step-by-step instructions to create clay ceramic items. (**I:** 8–12)

Ripkin, Cal, Jr. *The Longest Season*. Illustrated by Ron Mazellan. Philomel, 2007. The Hall of Fame baseball player describes the Orioles' 1988 losing season. (**I:** 5–10)

*Wick, Walter. *Can You See What I See? Once Upon a Time*. Scholastic, 2006. Subtitled "Picture Puzzles to Search and

Solve," this interactive book invites readers to use their imagination to search for objects from fairy tales. (**I:** P–10)

U.S. Political Leaders and Social Activists

Adler, David. *B. Franklin, Printer*. Holiday House, 2001. An
extensively researched biography of statesman Benjamin
Franklin. (**I:** 10–14)

*Cooney, Barbara. *Eleanor*. Viking, 1996. This picture book
biography focuses on the childhood of Eleanor Roosevelt.
(**I:** 6–12)

Bolden, Tonya. *M.L.K.: Journey of a King*. Abrams, 2007. A
well-researched biography of Dr. Martin Luther King.
(**I:** 9–14)

Fleming, Candace. *Our Eleanor: A Scrapbook Look at Eleanor
Roosevelt's Remarkable Life*. Atheneum, 2005. A comprehen-
sive biography of the beloved and longest-serving First Lady.
(**I:** 9–YA)

Freedman, Russell. *Eleanor Roosevelt: A Life of Discovery*.
Clarion, 1993. The life of a famous first lady, wife of
President Franklin Delano Roosevelt, who devoted herself to
public service and worked on behalf of human rights.
(**I:** 9–YA)

———. *Franklin Delano Roosevelt*. Clarion, 1990. The life of
Franklin Delano Roosevelt, who was president during the
Depression and World War II. (**I:** 10–YA)

———. *Indian Chiefs*. Holiday House, 1987. A collective biography of six famous Native American leaders. (**I:** 10–YA)

———. *Kids at Work: Lewis Hine and the Crusade against Child
Labor*. Clarion, 1994. The biography of photographer and
social reformer Lewis Hine, whose photographs helped ensure
the passage of child labor laws. (**I:** 9–YA)

———. *Lincoln: A Photobiography*. Clarion, 1987. A biography
of Abraham Lincoln, who was president during the Civil War.
(**I:** 9–YA)

Fritz, Jean. *And Then What Happened, Paul Revere?* Illustrated
by Margot Tomes. Coward McCann, 1973. A humorous biography of patriot Paul Revere. (**I:** 7–12)

———. *Bully for You, Teddy Roosevelt!* Illustrated by Mike
Wimmer. Putnam, 1991. A biography of the twenty-sixth
president, who was also a conservationist. (**I:** 9–12)

———. *The Great Little Madison*. Putnam, 1989. A biography of
James Madison, fourth President of the United States and the
father of the Constitution. (**I:** 9–12)

———. *Stonewall*. Illustrated by Stephen Gammell. Putnam,
1979. A biography of Thomas J. Jackson, the Confederate
Civil War general. (**I:** 10–YA)

———. *Where Do You Think You're Going, Christopher
Columbus?* Illustrated by Margot Tomes. Putnam, 1980. A
biography of explorer Christopher Columbus. (**I:** 7–12)

———. *Why Don't You Get a Horse, Sam Adams?* Illustrated by
Trina Schart Hyman. Coward McCann, 1974. Describes the
reluctance of Sam Adams to ride a horse while campaigning
for independence for the American colonies. (**I:** 7–12)

———. *Will You Sign Here, John Hancock?* Illustrated by Trina
Schart Hyman. Coward McCann, 1974. A biography of the
famous signer of the Declaration of Independence.
(**I:** 7–12)

———. *You Want Women to Vote, Lizzie Stanton?* Illustrated by
DyAnne DiSalvo-Ryan. Putnam, 1995. A biography of
Elizabeth Cady Stanton, a pioneer in the women's suffrage
movement. (**I:** 8–12)

*Harness, Cheryl. *Young John Quincy*. Bradbury, 1994. This picture book biography focuses on the childhood of John Quincy
Adams, the sixth president of the United States. (**I:** 5–10)

Haskins, James. *Bayard Rustin: Behind the Scenes of the Civil
Rights Movement*. Hyperion, 1997. The biography of civil
rights activist, Bayard Rustin, who worked closely with
Martin Luther King, Jr. (**I:** 10–14)

*Kerley, Barbara. *What to Do About Alice?* Illustrated by Edwin
Fortheringham. Scholastic, 2008. A biography of President
Theodore Roosevelt's daughter, subtitled "how Alice
Roosevelt broke the rules, charmed the world, and drove her
father Teddy crazy!" (**I:** 6–10)

Klausner, Janet. *Sequoyah's Gift: A Portrait of the Cherokee
Leader*. HarperCollins, 1993. A biography of the Cherokee
leader who developed the system of writing the Cherokee language. (**I:** 9–12)

*Krull, Kathleen. *Harvesting Home: The Story of Cesar Chavez*.
Illustrated by Yuyi Morales. Harcourt, 2003. A picture book
biography of the leader of the migrant farm workers. (**I:** 5–10)

Marrin, Albert. *Old Hickory: Andrew Jackson and the American
People*. Dutton, 2004. A detailed biography of Andrew
Jackson, whose controversial presidency included the Trail of
Tears. (**I:** 10–YA)

———. *Unconditional Surrender: U. S. Grant and the Civil War*.
Atheneum, 1994. This biography describes the role of Ulysses
S. Grant as a military leader during the Civil War. (**I:** 10–YA)

*Rappaport, Doreen. *Martin's Big Words: The Life of Dr. Martin
Luther King, Jr*. Illustrated by Bryan Collier. Hyperion, 2001.
A picture book biography of the Nobel Peace Prize recipient,
with quotations from his speeches and sermons. (**I:** P–12)

San Souci, Robert D. *Kate Shelley: Bound for Legend*. Illustrated
by Max Ginsburg. Dial, 1995. The courage of a fifteen-year-
old prevents a train disaster in Iowa in 1881. (**I:** 8–12)

Woelfle, Gretchen. *Jeannette Rankin: Political Pioneer*. Boyds
Mills, 2007. Jeanette Rankin from Montana became the first
woman in Congress even before women had the right to vote.
(**I:** 9–14)

World Leaders

Adler, David A. *Our Golda: The Story of Golda Meir*. Illustrated
by Donna Ruff. Puffin, 1986. Biography of the first female
prime minister of Israel. (**I:** 7–11)

Cooper, Floyd. *Mandela: From the Life of the South African
Statesman*. Philomel, 1996. Describes the life of Nelson
Mandela from his birth in a tiny South African village in 1918
to his release from prison in 1990. (**I:** 8–12)

Giblin, James Cross. *The Life and Death of Adolf Hitler*. Clarion,
2002. A carefully researched biography of the life of the
German leader, who was responsible for the deaths of millions
of people. (**I:** 10–YA)

Krull, Kathleen. *Lives of Extraordinary Women: Ruler, Rebels
(and What the Neighbors Thought)*. Illustrated by Kathryn
Hewitt. Harcourt, 2000. Biographical vignettes of twenty historic women leaders, including Indira Gandhi and Golda Meir.
(**I:** 8–12)

*McDonough, Yona Zeldis. *Peaceful Protest: The Life of Nelson
Mandela*. Illustrated by Malcah Zeldis. Walker, 2002. The
inspiring life of the South African leader and Nobel Peace
Prize recipient. (**I:** 6–10)

*Nivola, Claire A. *Planting the Trees of Kenya: The Story of
Wangari Maathai*. Farrar, 2008. The biography of the Kenyan

woman who received the 2004 Nobel Peace Prize and founded the Green Belt Movement. (**I:** 5–8)

Stanley, Diane. *Peter the Great*. Morrow, 1986. The life of Tsar Peter Alexeevich of Russia. (**I:** 10–YA)

———, and Peter Vennema. *Cleopatra*. Morrow, 1994. Full-page paintings complement the story of the famous Egyptian queen. (**I:** 10–YA)

Stanley, Fay. *The Last Princess: The Story of Princess Kaiulanai of Hawaii*. Illustrated by Diane Stanley. Four Winds, 1991. The story of the brave princess who failed to save her country from annexation and died at age 23. (**I:** 10–YA)

Tanaka, Shelley. *Amelia Earhart: The Legend of the Lost Aviator*. Illustrated by David Craig. Abrams, 2008. A biography of the famous pilot who disappeared in the South Pacific in 1937. (**I:** 8–12)

Explorers and Scientists

Aronson, Marc. *Sir Walter Ralegh and the Quest for El Dorado*. Houghton Mifflin, 2000. The life of the English explorer who led voyages to the New World and searched for the legendary city of El Dorado. (**I:** 10–YA)

*Borden, Louise, and Mary Kay Kroeger. *Fly High! The Story of Bessie Coleman*. Illustrated by Teresa Flavin. Simon and Schuster, 2001. The biography of the first African American to earn a pilot's license. (**I:** 5–10)

*Ehlrich, Amy. *Rachel: The Story of Rachel Carson*. Illustrated by Wendell Minor. Harcourt, 2003. The biography of Rachel Carson, whose book *Silent Spring* is considered the beginning of the environmental movement. (**I:** 5–10)

Freedman, Russell. *The Wright Brothers: How They Invented the Airplane*. Holiday House, 1991. The lives of Wilbur and Orville Wright. (**I:** 9–YA)

Kerley, Barbara. *The Dinosaurs of Waterhouse Hawkins*. Illustrated by Brian Selznick. Scholastic, 2001. The biography of Victorian artist, Waterhouse Hawkins, who built the first life-size models of dinosaurs. (**I:** 6–12)

*Martin, Jacqueline Briggs. *Snowflake Bentley*. Illustrated by Mary Azarian. Houghton Mifflin, 1998. The life of Wilson Bentley, a self-taught scientist who studied and photographed snowflakes. (**I:** 6–10)

McClafferty, Carla Killough. *Something Out of Nothing: Marie Curie and Radium*. Farrar, 2006. The life of Marie Curie, the Polish chemist who was the first woman to receive a Nobel Prize. (**I:** 9–14)

Old, Wendie. *To Fly: The Story of the Wright Brothers*. Illustrated by Robert Andrew Parker. Clarion, 2002. The story of the famous brothers, Orville and Wilbur Wright, and how they built and flew the first airplane. (**I:** 6–12)

Sís, Peter. *Starry Messenger*. Farrar, Straus, & Giroux, 1996. Exquisite illustrations help recount the life of astronomer Galileo Galilei. (**I:** 7–11)

———. *The Tree of Life*. Farrar, Straus, & Giroux, 2003. The life of Charles Darwin, "naturalist, geologist, and thinker." (**I:** 9–14)

Artists and Authors

Bruchac, Joseph. *Seeing the Circle*. Richard C. Owen, 1999. The autobiography of the Native American children's author. (**I:** 9–12)

*Cooper, Floyd. *Coming Home: From the Life of Langston Hughes*. Philomel, 1994. This picture-book biography focuses on the childhood of the well-known African American poet. (**I:** 6–12)

Cummings, Pat. *Talking with Artists*. Bradbury, 1992. Biographical interviews with fourteen well-known children's book illustrators. (**I:** 5–12)

Duggleby, John. *Story Painter: The Life of Jacob Lawrence*. Chronicle, 1998. The biography of the African American painter known for paintings that tell stories about the African American experience. (**I:** 10–YA)

Fleming, Denise. *Maker of Things*. Richard C. Owen, 2003. The autobiography of the children's author and illustrator. (**I:** 4–8)

Freedman, Russell. *The Voice that Challenged a Nation: Marian Anderson and the Struggle for Equal Rights*. Clarion, 2004. This photobiography tells the life of singer Marian Anderson. (**I:** 9–14)

Fritz, Jean. *Homesick: My Own Story*. Putnam, 1982. The author's memoir of her childhood in China. (**I:** 8–12)

Krull, Kathleen. *Lives of the Artists: Masterpieces, Messes (and What the Neighbors Thought)*. Illustrated by Kathryn Hewitt. Harcourt, 1995. Biographical sketches of sixteen artists, including Georgia O'Keeffe, Diego Rivera, and Frida Kahlo. (**I:** 8–12)

———. *Lives of the Musicians: Good Times, Bad Times (and What the Neighbors Thought)*. Illustrated by Kathryn Hewitt. Harcourt, 1993. Biographical sketches of twenty musicians and composers, including Bach and Scott Joplin. (**I:** 8–12)

Lobel, Anita. *No Pretty Pictures: A Child of War*. Greenwillow, 1998. The award-winning author and illustrator describes her life as a Polish Jew during World War II and its aftermath. (**I:** 10–YA)

Lowry, Lois. *Looking Back: A Book of Memories*. Houghton Mifflin, 1998. Illustrated with family photographs, this book is an autobiography of the Newbery Award-winning author. (**I:** 9–14)

Monceaux, Morgan. *Jazz: My Music, My People*. Knopf, 1994. Biographical sketches of jazz musicians from the early years to bebop and modern jazz. (**I:** 8–12)

*Orgill, Roxane. *Footwork: The Story of Fred and Adele Astaire*. Illustrated by Stéphane Jorisch. Candlewick, 2007. This picture book biography features the siblings who became famous dancers. (**I:** P–9)

*Pinkney, Andrea Davis. *Duke Ellington*. Illustrated by Brian Pinkney. Hyperion, 1998. The biography of the jazz musician and composer. (**I:** P–9)

Reich, Susanna. *Clara Schumann: Piano Virtuoso*. Clarion, 1999. The life of the German pianist who was the wife of composer Robert Schumann. (**I:** 10–YA)

Ryan, Pam Muñoz. *When Marian Sang*. Illustrated by Brian Selznick. Scholastic, 2002. The life of contralto Marian Anderson, the first African American to sing with the Metropolitan Opera. (**I:** 7–12)

Siegel, Siena Cherson. *To Dance: A Ballerina's Graphic Novel*. Illustrated by Mark Siegel. Atheneum, 2006. In a graphic novel format, the author shares her early years studying ballet at the School of American Ballet. (**I:** 8–14)

Sís, Peter. *The Wall: Growing Up Behind the Iron Curtain*. Farrar, 2007. The award-winning author recounts his childhood in Czechoslovakia. (**I:** 8–YA)

Stanley, Diane. *Leonardo da Vinci*. Morrow, 1996. A picture-book biography of the famous painter and scientist. (**I:** 10–YA)

Stanley, Diane, and Peter Vennema. *The Bard of Avon: The Story of William Shakespeare*. Morrow, 1992. A picture-book biography of the most famous British playwright. (**I**: 10–YA)

People Who Persevered

Adler, David. *A Hero and the Holocaust: The Story of Janusz Korcazk and His Children*. Illustrated by Bill Farnsworth. Holiday House, 2002. The biography of the Polish doctor and Jewish educator who founded an orphanage and died with his children during the Holocaust. (**I**: 8–12)

Barakat, Ibtisam. *Tasting the Sky: A Palestinian Childhood*. Farrar, 2007. This memoir describes the author's childhood living under Israeli occupation. (**I**: 9–14)

Bolden, Tonya. *Maritcha: A Nineteenth-Century American Girl*. Abrams, 2005. The biography of a girl who overcame adversity to become the first black to graduate from Providence Rhode Island High School in 1869. (**I**: 9–14)

Bridges, Ruby. *Through My Eyes*. Scholastic, 1999. The life and times of Ruby Bridges, who integrated the New Orleans schools in 1960 when she was six years old. (**I**: 8–12)

*Deans, Karen. *Playing to Win: The Story of Althea Gibson*. Illustrated by Elbrite Brown. Holiday House, 2007. This picture book biography describes how Althea Gibson overcame discrimination to become a champion tennis player. (**I**: 5–9)

Ganci, Chris. *Chief: The Life of Peter J. Ganci, A New York City Firefighter*. Orchard Books, 2003. A biography of the Chief of the Fire Department of New York who died on September 11, 2001, written by his son. (**I**: 8–12)

Giovanni, Nikki. *Rosa*. Illustrated by Bryan Collier. Henry Holt, 2005. This picture book biography focuses on the refusal of Rosa Parks to give up her seat on the bus. (**I**: 6–10)

Kaminsky, Marty. *Uncommon Champions: Fifteen Athletes Who Battled Back*. Boyds Mills Press, 2000. Inspirational biographies of fifteen individuals who overcame physical and emotional challenges to achieve athletically. (**I**: 8–12)

*Krull, Kathleen. *Wilma Unlimited: How Wilma Rudolph Became the World's Fastest Woman*. Illustrated by David Diaz.

Harcourt, 1996. Striking paintings help to tell the story of Wilma Rudolph, who overcame childhood polio to win three gold medals for track at the 1960 Olympics. (**I**: 6–12)

Littlefield, Bill. *Champions: Stories of Ten Remarkable Athletes*. Illustrated by Bernie Fuchs. Little, Brown, 1993. Ten athletes, including Satchel Paige and Roberto Clemente, are featured in this biographical collection of athletes who persevered to become champions in their sports. (**I**: 8–YA)

Parks, Rosa, with Jim Haskins. *Rosa Parks: My Story*. Dial, 1992. The biography of the courageous woman whose refusal to give up her seat on a Montgomery, Alabama, bus in 1955 led to a boycott. (**I**: 10–YA)

Pressler, Miriam. *Anne Frank: A Hidden Life*. Translated by Anthea Bell. Dutton, 2000. A description of the life of Anne Frank and the Nazi occupation of the Netherlands during World War II. (**I**: 10–YA)

Rappaport, Doreen. *Freedom River*. Illustrated by Bryan Collier. Hyperion, 2000. The story of John Parker, an ex-slave, who became a successful businessman and conductor on the Underground Railroad. (**I**: 6–10)

Robinson, Sharon. *Promises to Keep: How Jackie Robinson Changed America*. Scholastic, 2004. Jackie Robinson's daughter recounts the life of the first African American to play major league baseball in this biography extensively illustrated with photographs. (**I**: 8–14)

Rubin, Susan Goldman with Ela Weissberger. *The Cat with the Yellow Star: Coming of Age in Terezin*. Holiday House, 2006. Ela Weissberger shares her childhood at Terezin Concentration Camp in this memoir. (**I**: 9–14)

Sullivan, George. *Helen Keller: Her Life in Pictures*. Scholastic, 2007. This is a photobiography of the remarkable life of Helen Keller. (**I**: 8–12)

*Weatherford, Carole Boston. *Moses: When Harriet Tubman Led Her People to Freedom*. Illustrated by Kadir Nelson. Hyperion, 2006. Text and illustrations convey the life of the most famous conductor on the Underground Railroad. (**I**: 5–10)

Resources

Bamford, Rosemary A., and Janice V. Kristo. *Checking Out Nonfiction, K–8: Good Choices for Best Learning*. Christopher-Gordon, 2000.

———, and Janice V. Kristo. *Making Facts Come Alive: Choosing Quality Nonfiction Literature, K–8*. Christopher-Gordon, 1998.

Duke, Nell K., and Bennett-Armistead, V. Susan. *Reading & Writing Informational Text in the Primary Grades*. Scholastic, 2003.

Duthie, Christine. *True Stories: Nonfiction Literacy in the Primary Classroom*. Stenhouse, 1996.

Freeman, Evelyn B., and Diane Goetz Person. *Connecting Informational Children's Books with Content Area Learning*. Allyn & Bacon, 1998.

Harvey, Stephanie. *Nonfiction Matters: Reading, Writing, and Research in Grades 3–8*. Stenhouse, 1998.

Moss, Barbara. *Exploring the Literature of Fact: Children's Nonfiction Trade Books in the Elementary Classroom*. The Guildford Press, 2003.

Whitin, David J., and Sandra Wilde. *It's the Story That Counts: More Children's Books for Mathematical Learning, K–6*. Heinemann, 1995.

Zarnowski, Myra. *History Makers: A Questioning Approach to Reading and Writing Biographies*. Heinemann, 2003.

———, Richard M. Kerper, and Julie M. Jensen, eds. *The Best in Children's Nonfiction: Reading, Writing, & Teaching Orbis Pictus Award Books*. National Council of Teachers of English, 2001.

References

Adler, David. *A Picture Book of Amelia Earhart*. Holiday House, 1998.

———. *A Picture Book of Thurgood Marshall*. Holiday House, 1997.

Ancona, George. *Monsters on Wheels*. Dutton, 1974.

Caswell, Linda J., and Nell K. Duke. "Non-narrative as a Catalyst for Literacy Development." *Language Arts* 75 (1998): 108–117.

Cole, Joanna. *A Cat's Body*. Photographs by Jerome Wexler. Morrow, 1982.

———. *Cockroaches*. Morrow, 1971.

———. *A Frog's Body*. Photographs by Jerome Wexler. Morrow, 1980.

———. *A Horse's Body*. Photographs by Jerome Wexler. Morrow, 1981.

Daugherty, James. *Daniel Boone*. Viking, 1939.

D'Aulaire, Ingri, and Edgar Parin D'Aulaire. *Abraham Lincoln*. Doubleday, 1939.

———. *Benjamin Franklin*. Doubleday, 1950.

———. *George Washington*. Doubleday, 1936.

Desang, Eliza T., and McClelland, Kathryn. "Radical Change: Digital Age Literature and Learning." *Theory into Practice* 38 (1999): 160–167.

Duke, Nell K. "The Case for Informational Text." *Educational Leadership* 61 (2004): 40–44.

Duke, Nell K., and Bennett-Armistead, V. Susan. *Reading & Writing Informational Text in the Primary Grades*. Scholastic, 2003.

Duthie, Christine. *True Stories: Nonfiction Literacy in the Primary Classroom*. York, ME: Stenhouse, 1996.

Fisher, Margery. Introduction to *Matters of Fact. Beyond Fact: Nonfiction for Children and Young People*. Ed. J. Carr. American Library Association, 1982, pp. 12–16.

Freedman, Russell. "Fact or Fiction?" *Using Nonfiction Trade Books in the Elementary Classroom: From Ants to Zeppelins*. Ed. E. B. Freeman and D. G. Person. National Council of Teachers of English, 1992, pp. 2–10.

Fritz, Jean. "Voices of the Creators." *Children's Books and Their Creators*. Ed. A. Silvey. Houghton Mifflin, 1995, p. 257.

Garcia-Johnson, R. "Ancona, George." *Something about the Author*, Vol. 85. Ed. K. S. Hile. Gale Research, 1996, pp. 5–13.

George, Jean Craighead. *Julie of the Wolves*. Harper & Row, 1972.

Giblin, James Cross. *Chimney Sweeps: Yesterday and Today*. Illustrated by Margot Tomes. HarperCollins, 1982.

———. *From Hand to Mouth or, How We Invented Knives, Forks, Spoons, and Chopsticks and the Table Manners to Go with Them*. Crowell, 1987.

———. "The Rise and Fall and Rise of Juvenile Nonfiction, 1961–1988." *Using Nonfiction Trade Books in the Elementary Classroom: From Ants to Zeppelins*. Ed. E. B. Freeman and D. G. Person. National Council of Teachers of English, 1992, pp. 17–25.

———. *The Truth about Santa Claus*. Crowell, 1985.

Graham-Barber, Lynda. *Toad or Frog, Swamp or Bog? A Big Book of Nature's Confusables*. Illustrated by Alec Gillman. Simon & Schuster, 1994.

Hastings, Selina. *Peter and the Wolf*. Illustrated by Reg Cartwright. Henry Holt, 1990.

Hoke, Elizabeth C. "Edgar Parin D'Aulaire and Ingri D'Aulaire." *Children's Books and Their Creators*. Ed. A. Silvey. Houghton Mifflin, 1995, pp. 188–189.

Holling, Holling Clancy. *Paddle-to-the-Sea*. Houghton Mifflin, 1941.

Jobe, Ron, and Dayton-Sakari, Mary. *Info-Kids: How to Use Nonfiction to Turn Reluctant Readers into Enthusiastic Learners*. Pembroke, 2002.

Kerper, Richard M. "Nonfiction Book Design in a Digital Age." *The Best in Children's Nonfiction*. Eds. M. Zarnowski, R. M. Kerper, and J. M. Jensen. National Council of Teachers of English, 2001, pp. 22–31.

Kherdian, David. *The Road from Home: The Story of an Armenian Girl*. Greenwillow, 1979.

Krementz, Jill. *A Very Young Dancer*. Knopf, 1976.

Lacey, Elizabeth. *What's the Difference? A Young Naturalist's Guide to Some Familiar Animal Look-Alikes*. Clarion Books, 1993.

Lasky, Kathryn. *The Weaver's Gift*. Photographs by Christopher Knight. F. Warne, 1980.

Lauber, Patricia. *Be a Friend to Trees*. Illustrated by Holly Keller. HarperCollins, 1994.

———. "The Evolution of a Science Writer." *Using Nonfiction Trade Books in the Elementary Classroom: From Ants to Zeppelins*. Ed. E. B. Freeman and D. G. Person. National Council of Teachers of English, 1992, pp. 11–16.

Lawson, Robert. *Ben & Me*. Little, Brown, 1939.

———. *I Discover Columbus*. Little, Brown, 1941.

Leal, Dorothy. "Storybooks, Information Books and Informational Storybooks: An Explication of an Ambiguous Grey Genre." *The New Advocate* 6 (1993): 61–70.

Meigs, Cornelia. *Invincible Louisa*. Little, Brown, 1933.

Meltzer, Milton. *All Times, All Peoples: A World History of Slavery*. Illustrated by Leonard Everett Fisher. Harper and Row, 1980.

———. *The Amazing Potato: A Story in Which the Incas, Conquistadors, Marie Antoinette, Thomas Jefferson, Wars, Famines, Immigrants ad French Fries All Play a Part*. HarperCollins, 1992.

———. "Beyond the Span of a Single Life." *Celebrating Children's Books: Essays on Children's Literature in Honor of Zena Sutherland*. Ed. B. Hearne and M. Kaye. Lothrop, Lee & Shepard, 1981, pp. 87–96.

———. *The Jewish Americans: A History in Their Own Words, 1650–1950*. Crowell, 1982.

———. *Never to Forget: The Jews of the Holocaust*. HarperCollins, 1976.

Monjo, F. N. "The Ten Bad Things about History." *Beyond Fact: Nonfiction for Children and Young People*. Ed. J. Carr. American Library Association, 1982, pp. 99–103.

Murphy, Jim. *Weird and Wacky Inventions*. Crown, 1978.

Olendorf, D., and D. Telgen. "David Adler." *Something about the Author*, Vol. 70. Gale Research, 1993, pp. 1–4.

Pringle, L. "Science Done Here." *Celebrating Children's Books: Essays on Children's Literature in Honor of Zena Sutherland*.

Ed. B. Hearne and M. Kaye. Lothrop, Lee & Shepard, 1981, pp. 108–115.

Provensen, Alice, and Martin Provensen. *Leonardo da Vinci: The Artist, Inventor, Scientist in Three-Dimensional Movable Pictures*. New York: Random House, 1984.

Rosenberg, Maxine. *Making a New Home in America*. Photographs by George Ancona. Lothrop, Lee & Shepard, 1986.

Sayers, F. C. "History Books for Children." *Beyond Fact: Nonfiction for Children and Young People*. Ed. J. Carr. American Library Association, 1982, pp. 95–98.

Selsam, Millicent. *Egg to Chick*. Illustrated by Barbara Wolff. Harper and Row, 1946.

Scribner's. Promotional pamphlet about Kathryn Lasky, 1985.

Sibert, Martha F. "Blumberg, Rhoda." *Children's Books and Their Authors*. Ed. Anita Silvey. Houghton Mifflin, 1995, pp. 65–66.

Simon, Seymour. *Animals in Field and Laboratory: Projects in Animal Behavior*. McGraw, 1968.

Singer, Marilyn. *A Wasp Is Not a Bee*. Illustrated by Patrick O'Brien. Holt, 1995.

Something about the Author. "Stanley, Diane," Something about the Author (Vol. 115). Gail Group, 2000, pp. 191–198.

Testa, Fulvio. *Wolf's Favor*. Dial Books, 1986.

Tunis, Edwin. *Frontier Living*. World, 1961.

van Loon, Hendrik Willem. *The Story of Mankind*. Boni & Liveright, 1921.

Wenzel, E. L. "Historical Backgrounds." *Beyond Fact: Nonfiction for Children and Young People*. Ed. J. Carr. American Library Association, 1982, pp. 16–26.

Zarnowski, M. *Learning about Biographies: A Reading-and-Writing Approach for Children*. National Council of Teachers of English, 1990.

———. "Learning History with Informational Storybooks: A Social Studies Educator's Perspective." *The New Advocate* 8 (1995): 183–196.

Zim, Herbert. *Golden Hamsters*. Illustrated by Herschel Wartik. Morrow, 1951.

———. *Sharks*. Illustrated by Stephen Howe. Morrow, 1966.

———. *Snakes*. Illustrated by James Gordon Irving. Morrow, 1949.

Part Three
Creating the Literature-Based Classroom

12

Literary Meaning-Making and Children's Responses to Literature

Response to Literature

A Model of Literary Meaning-Making • Research on Children's Responses to Literature

Diverse Perspectives on Reader Response

Developmental Perspective on Reader Response • Social Perspective on Reader Response • Cultural Perspective on

Reader Response • Textual Perspective on Reader Response • **ASK THE AUTHOR:** Pat Mora • **ISSUE TO CONSIDER:** Should Teachers Encourage Students to Focus on Author's Craft during Literature Discussion?

> *. . . but there was another reason* why Meggie took her books whenever they went away. They were her home when she was somewhere strange. They were familiar voices, friends that never quarreled with her, clever, powerful friends—daring and knowledgeable, tried and tested adventurers who had traveled far and wide. Her books cheered her up when she was sad and kept her from being bored . . .
>
> —*from* Inkheart
> *by Cornelia Funke, pp. 15–16*

Meggie, the protagonist in Cornelia Funke's *Inkheart*, has discovered the power of books to captivate and to open new worlds to their readers. It is just this kind of engagement that teachers long to see in their own students. Reading is commonly described as a reader/text interaction, and teachers who understand both the readers (the children who will be reading and listening to literature) and the texts (children's literature) are likely to be in a good position to nurture this type of engagement. The major thrust of this book has been on learning about the literature you'll be channeling into the hands of children;

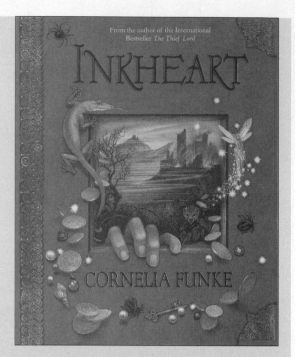

ILLUSTRATION 12.1   In *Inkheart,* a host of evil characters emerge from a book and their lives become entangled with those of Meggie and her family. (From *Inkheart* by Cornelia Funke, jacket art by Carol Lawson. Scholastic Inc./The Chicken House. Original text copyright © 2003 by Dressler Verlag, English Translation copyright © 2003 by The Chicken House, cover illustration copyright © 2003 by Carol Lawson. Reprinted by permission of Scholastic Inc. and the Chicken House Publishing Ltd.)

Develop a text set of titles that could be used to elicit various reader responses by using the Children's Literature Database in Chapter 12 of the MyEducationKit for this book.

however, this chapter ventures into different territory. Here we consider what happens when readers read literature, how reading literature may differ from other types of reading, and what research reveals about how children respond to literature.

Response to Literature

When readers read literature, their personal memories, feelings, and thought associations may be evoked by the text—regardless of whether the author anticipated those reactions (and how would you know?). When we look at readers' personal responses during an encounter with a piece of literature, we are viewing reading as a transaction. This perspective on reading is also known as **reader response theory.**

In recent years, reader response theory, which was first articulated by Louise Rosenblatt in 1938, has had a major impact in elementary and middle school classrooms. To understand reader response theory, you might find it helpful to reflect on your own reading experiences. Think of a story you have really gotten into and try to describe what that experience was like. Perhaps you became so wrapped up in the book that you flew from page to page to discover how the twists and turns of the story line would unfold, and even though it was 2:00 A.M., you simply could not stop reading. Maybe it was a different sort of book, one in which you found so much to ponder that you spent as much time reflecting and wondering as you did reading. Perhaps it was a book in which a character's plight moved you to tears. Or was it a poem whose language was so evocative that you read it aloud just to savor the words? When a person becomes immersed in reading a piece of literature, she or he is engaged in what Louise Rosenblatt (1993) calls "aesthetic reading." Rosenblatt describes the experience this way:

> In aesthetic reading . . . we draw on our reservoir of past experience with people and the world, our past inner linkage of words and things, our past encounters with spoken or written text. We listen to the sound of the words in the inner ear; we lend our sensations, our emotions, our sense of being alive, to the new experiences which, we feel, correspond to the text. We participate in the story, we identify with the characters, we share their conflicts and their feeling. (p. 9)

According to Rosenblatt, aesthetic reading lies at one end of a reading continuum, while what she has called "efferent reading" lies at the other end. When reading efferently, readers are intent on gaining information—finding out when to take their medicine, how to put the bookshelves together, or what position a candidate takes on immigration. Readers who pick up particular texts move more toward one end or the other of the reading continuum, depending on their purposes for reading. In aesthetic reading, the reader's role is of great importance, and because readers bring their own experiences, feelings, and perspectives to a text, the literary experience can be very personal. This is not to say, however, that the text is unimportant. Rosenblatt has described the text as the blueprint that guides readers as they construct literary meaning, drawing on both their own experiences and the text itself.

Children can become totally caught up in the world of a story. However, this won't happen if we ask them to read literature only to search for information—to answer comprehension questions or to find five new words in the story. So, if we are to succeed in nurturing committed, lifelong readers, it is essential that we help children discover the joys of reading literature. As you prepare to help students read literature aesthetically, you will find it helpful to understand more about the nature of literary reading and how children respond to literature.

A Model of Literary Meaning-Making

Judith Langer (1990) has proposed a model that we find useful in thinking about literary reading. She uses the term "envisionment building" to describe literary meaning-making. According to Langer, an envisionment is what a reader understands about a story, and as readers move through stories, their understanding grows and sometimes even changes dramatically. For example, one preservice teacher reported that she initially envisioned Jerry Spinelli's *Maniac Magee* as a book about homelessness, but as she read on, she began to envision it as being about racial divisiveness and conflict.

According to Langer, in creating their envisionments, readers may assume any one of four different stances (or different relationships with a text) as they read:

- *Being out and stepping in:* Readers make their initial contact with a book.

- *Being in and moving through:* Readers build a personal envisionment.

- *Being in and stepping out:* Readers reflect on the way(s) in which a book relates to their own life or the lives of others.

- *Stepping out and objectifying the experience:* Readers reflect on the story as a crafted object.

Being Out and Stepping In

Readers assume the stance of being out and stepping in as they make their initial contact with a book. They try to get enough information about the genre, setting, characters, and story line to begin to build an envisionment. They might even start this process before reading the first page as they look at the dust jacket or book cover. The process continues as they begin reading the story, make the acquaintance of characters, and discover the basic story situation. For example, a reader picking up Louis Sachar's *Holes* might first note that the dust jacket shows a scene of what appears to be a crater-pocked surface of a distant planet. In the first chapter, the reader makes a number of important discoveries: The story is set not in space, but at Camp Green Lake, a place described as a wasteland in Texas. Camp Green Lake is run not by a camp director, but by a warden, and the campers at Camp Green Lake spend their time digging holes, not playing tennis or riding horses. At this point, the reader is likely to have more questions than answers and consequently may still feel very much "outside" the

Young children begin to learn how to enage in "envisionment building" by participating in storybook reading with mature readers.

Lindfors Photography

Top Shelf 12.1

Character-Rich Chapter Books

Spitting Image by Shutta Crum

The Watsons Go to Birmingham-1963 by Christopher Paul Curtis

Because of Winn-Dixie by Kate DiCamillo

Pictures of Hollis Woods by Patricia Reilly Giff

The Same Stuff as Stars by Katherine Paterson

Swear to Howdy by Wendelin Van Draanen

Love, Ruby Lavender by Deborah Wiles

Amber Was Brave, Essie Was Smart by Vera Williams

story. In fact, at the beginning of Chapter 2, the narrator poses the very question the reader may be asking at this point:

Why would anyone go to Camp Green Lake?

The reader soon discovers the answer: Camp Green Lake isn't a summer camp at all. It is a juvenile detention center. And with that information revealed, the reader is likely to enter into the world of ***Holes***.

It may be more difficult to step into some stories than others. Young readers may find, for example, that it is difficult to step into a work of historical fiction when the story world is far removed from their everyday world. For example, at the beginning of Karen Cushman's ***The Midwife's Apprentice,*** which is set in medieval England, readers may be perplexed to discover a protagonist who sleeps in a dung heap for warmth and is happy to find a dirt-covered turnip for dinner. In a similar fashion, readers of Marcus Zusak's ***The Book Thief*** may initially be bewildered by the seemingly unrelated clues about the soon-to-unfold storyline that are offered by the narrator in the book's early pages:

It's just a small story really, about, among other things:
*A girl
*Some words
*An accordionist
*Some fanatical Germans
*A Jewish fist fighter
*And quite a lot of thievery (p. 5)

Zusak's carefully planted clues may appear even more puzzling as readers realize that the story is being narrated by none other than Death. Books like ***The Book Thief*** appear to demand more of readers, who may, in turn, need support and guidance in stepping into those story worlds.

Being In and Moving Through

When readers are "in and moving through" an envisionment, they become absorbed in the story world, using text information and their own store of experiences and knowledge to build their envisionment. This can be a complicated process, especially in more complex story worlds such as those found in chapter books, which typically require readers to follow and weave together various narrative strands. Moving through the story world also involves connecting pieces of the story—filling in the many gaps that stories naturally offer. To do this, readers must draw on textual clues as well as their personal experiences and knowledge about the world.

Teaching Idea 12.1

Helping Children Step into Stories

Sometimes it is difficult to step into a story. Share with your students things efficient readers do as they begin a new book. Consider the reading process as you think aloud and talk with your students. What do you know about the author? Have you read other books by him or her? In what way does the cover illustration assist in understanding what the book will be about? How does information on the book cover or dust jacket help you step into the story world? Are you reading it aesthetically or efferently? To give students further help with initial envisionment building, you might sometimes read the first chapter of a book aloud and then let students continue to read on their own.

Character and plot are especially important story elements to focus on as readers move through story worlds. Because these elements are "the building blocks of narratives" (Cochran-Smith, 1984), readers must be actively involved in determining the intentions of story characters and in understanding how characters shape the story line and, in turn, are shaped by it (Lukens, 1999). In recent decades, stories written for children have increasingly featured rich, complex characters (Nikolajeva, 2002), and for these stories, in particular, character becomes an especially crucial conduit for moving through story worlds. Understanding characters' desires, feelings, and beliefs is central to literary reading (Emery, 1996). In fact, it may be that by grappling with the moral and ethical dimensions of characters' problems, readers arrive at deeper (thematic) understandings of stories (Martinez & Roser, 1995).

The centrality of understanding character is apparent in reading a book such as Patricia Reilly Giff's ***Pictures of Hollis Woods***. Initially, readers are likely to be drawn into this book by Hollis Woods, a tough foster child who is a "mountain of trouble" for all the foster families with whom she is placed. However, readers soon discover that beneath a calloused exterior, there is a child who longs to be part of a family. Readers are likely to find themselves pulled through the pages of this book as they seek to understand the seeming contradictions of Hollis Woods's character and to find out if she will indeed let herself be reunited with the family she loves.

While character and plot pull readers through many story worlds, this does not mean that other literary elements are not important. In fact, some books, such as Janice Harrington's *Going North,* "beg" readers to attend to other literary elements. Harrington's rich descriptions help the reader understand just why young Jessie doesn't want to leave her Big Mama and her home in Alabama because Big Mama's house means "swapping stories, and watching Big Mama knife-scrape a sweet potato, dragging its blade across orange pulp and sharing a sweet treat." (unpaged)

Being In and Stepping Out

When readers are "in and step out" of a story world, they use the text as a basis for reflecting on their own lives, on the lives of others, or even on the human experience. For example, when *Holes* becomes the stimulus that leads to a discussion of issues related to the juvenile justice system, readers are stepping out of the story world. Even young children can step out of story worlds to reflect on how those stories relate to the world in which they live. For example, when a teacher shares picture books about homelessness with her students—books such as *December, Fly Away Home,* and *Sam and the Lucky Money*, the class can both explore the problems faced by the homeless characters in the stories and reflect on homelessness in their own community and on ways of helping the homeless.

Stepping Out and Objectifying the Experience

Langer's final stance, stepping out and objectifying the experience, is one in which readers distance themselves from the text world and talk about the work as a crafted object, about other texts the story reminds them of, or about their own responses to the story. When a reader of *Pictures of Hollis Woods* remarked on the way Patricia Reilly Giff repeatedly used flashbacks to reveal Hollis Woods's past, she was reflecting on the way in which the author structured the work. So was the second-grader who interrupted her teacher's reading of Mercer Mayer's *Liza Lou and the Yeller Belly Swamp* to observe, "This story has three stories in it!"

Children can also be invited to step out of the story world and objectify the experience by examining stories from different perspectives. For example, children can be asked to examine a folktale from a structural perspective, identifying the roles that characters typically play in a folktale: the hero, the villain, the helper, and so on. Or children can be invited to question a set of ideas about society—for example, the roles of male and female, black and white, or rich and poor. A book such as Robert Munsch's *The Paper Bag Princess* encourages readers to do just this. The author casts a princess in a liberated role that contrasts sharply with the stereotypically passive heroine usually found in traditional folktales. *The Paper Bag Princess* tends to call into question the all-too-commonplace practice of assigning females to more passive roles.

Research on Children's Responses to Literature

The preceding examples suggest that in reading literature, children engage in the envisionment building Judith Langer described. However, researchers have not directly used Langer's model as a lens through which they examine young children's literary meaning-making. It is evident from existing research, though, that

Teaching Idea 12.2
Helping Children Talk about Literary Crafting

Langer says that readers sometimes step out and objectify a literary experience. In doing so, readers think about or talk about how a story is crafted. However, we have found that children do not always choose to talk about the ways authors and illustrators craft their works. One way of encouraging children to think about issues of crafting is to share distinctly crafted stories with them. For example, in *Two Bad Ants*, Chris Van Allsburg repeatedly draws attention to perspective in his illustrations. Bill Martin, Jr., and John Archambault's spooky story *The Ghost-Eye Tree* offers the perfect opportunity to talk about a story's mood. Author/illustrator Jan Brett creates distinctive borders for the illustrations in her picture books. Illustrator Julie Vivas uses space in a dramatic fashion in her illustrations. Author Eric Carle frequently relies on repetition in his work. You are likely to find that as you share such distinctive works with children, they become more sensitive to how authors and illustrators craft their stories. In addition to sharing distinctly crafted books with children, you will also want to share your own observations about craft with your students. Is there a particular rhythm to the story? A familiar refrain? How effective is the author's lead in hooking the reader into wanting to read more? Does the author begin with dialogue that draws us straight into discovering something about the character or is there a flashback that draws us into the plot? Some authors entice us to enter by describing the setting so vividly that we feel as if we are stepping into the scene ourselves. As readers become more aware of the tools writers use, they feel as if they can use the same tools in their own writing.

Technology in Practice 12.1

Create a PowerPoint presentation of children responding to a story. Take digital pictures of them discussing or writing their responses. Write their responses as captions in the presentation. Group the pictures of the responses by Langer's stances: those that are examples of the student being out and stepping in, being in and moving through, etc. The completed presentation can be used with children to talk about the different ways that readers think about and respond to literature or it can be used instructionally with your peers.

children's responses to story worlds are both text-centered and reader-centered (Martinez & Roser, 2002).

Text-Centered Responses

Children typically choose to linger in the webs cast by stories (Martinez & Roser, 1994; Sipe, 2000a). The earliest studies of children's literary meaning-making yielded a narrow view of children's responses, suggesting that young children's text-centered responses occurred primarily at literal levels (Applebee, 1978). However, more recent research has shown that children's engagement in story worlds is active and dynamic: In reading, children (even young ones) make interpretations (Galda, 1982; McGee, 1992), analyze text and illustrations (Sipe, 2007); and generate thematic understandings of stories (Lehr, 1988).

Children also respond to the ways in which an author has crafted a work of literature, what Langer described as "stepping out of the story to objectify the experience." This is just what Marcia, a fifth-grader, did when discussing Sharon Creech's **Chasing Redbird** with her classmates: "Sharon Creech made this book interesting because it has a lot of mysteries and you want to read more to find out." Although response to craft appears to be less frequent than other types of response (Hancock, 1993; McGee, 1992), children seem especially likely to respond to the crafting of literature when teachers direct attention toward the artistry of literature (Bloem & Manna, 1999). When Ms. Sharp invited her fifth graders to talk about the crafting of Deborah Wiles's **Love, Ruby Lavender**, the students talked at length about techniques the author used to reveal character relationships:

Ms. Sharp: Deborah Wiles didn't just say that Miss Eula and Ruby Lavender are close. What did she do instead of telling us that they are close?

Henry: They are close because they do a lot of things together, risk-taking things together like when Miss Eula and Ruby kidnapped the chickens.

Pedro: And when Eula said that she was going to Hawaii but she said she'd be back, Ruby started crying because Miss Eula was like her best friend. She liked to hang out with her, and they understood each other.

Ms. Sharp: So she didn't have to say, "They were close." She has shown us. And she described them getting into the scrap with the chickens.

Pedro: Oh, like it says they were partners.

Sandy: And they write letters to each other. And Ruby said something like you're the best partner or something.

Teacher: So they expressed those feelings with each other.

Reader-Centered Responses

Children respond to literature in reader-centered ways as well as text-centered ways. That is, they build bridges between their personal experiences and the literature they read, making what Marilyn Cochran-Smith (1984) has termed "life to text connections." For example, children might talk about their own pets after listening to a story about a child and her pet. Janet Hickman (1981) described the personal associations children make when reading literature, as have numerous other researchers (e.g., Short, 1992; Sipe, 1998). Children also become personally involved with story characters as they vicariously step into character roles and make judgments about how they would feel if they were in a character's situation (Hancock, 1993; Wollman-Bonilla & Werchadlo, 1995).

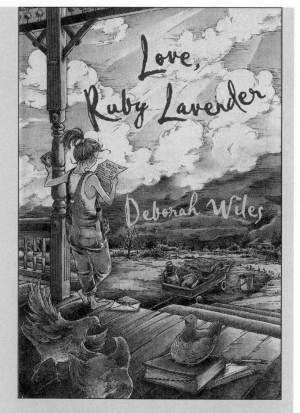

ILLUSTRATION 12.2   When her grandmother leaves for Hawaii, Ruby Lavender is sure that she will be unable to cope with the obstacles she faces in her small Mississippi town. ("Book Cover" from *Love, Ruby Lavender*, Copyright © 2001 by Deborah Wiles, reprinted by permission of Houghton Mifflin Harcourt Publishing Company. This material may not be reproduced, stored in a retrieval system, or transmitted in any form or by any means without the prior written permission of the publisher.)

The personal experiences children bring with them to literature study also include experiences with other texts, and various researchers have found that children make intertextual connections when responding to literature (Short, 1992; Sipe, 2000b). These intertextual connections appear to help children interpret language and narrative elements such as story characters and plot as well as make generalizations about genre and story structure (Sipe, 2000b).

Researchers have also found that children do what Langer termed "stepping out of stories" to reflect on how the stories relate to their own lives or the lives of others. For example, McGinley and Kamberelis (1996) found that third- and fourth-graders attempted to understand and negotiate social relationships and significant social problems through literature. In effect, the children in their investigation used literature as a lens through which they could better understand their own personal experiences and their world. Cochran-Smith (1984) even found that preschoolers engaged in text-to-life transactions in which they extended or related story situations or information to their own life experiences. Sometimes they made these text-to-life trans-

Teaching Idea 12.3

Helping Children Connect Life and Literature

Children come from families with very different literature traditions. Not all children are in a habit of making what Cochran-Smith (1984) called "text-to-life transactions." That is, not all children use stories as lenses through which to view the world. Teachers can encourage this type of response by modeling. Develop the habit of encouraging children's literature-to-life experiences. For example, you might describe bad days as "Alexander days"—a reference to Judith Viorst's *Alexander and the Terrible, Horrible, No Good, Very Bad Day*. And there is no better description for a mischievous child than David from David Shannon's *No, David!*

actions long after hearing a story, as they played or worked in situations that were well removed from storybook reading. In *Wally's Stories: Conversations in the Kindergarten* (1981), author and kindergarten teacher Vivian Paley includes many examples of such text-to-life connections. In one instance, a kindergartner told her about going to another child's house, only to find that the child would not let him in. A classmate proposed a literature-inspired solution: going down the chimney of the house. A second classmate provided a caution (also inspired by "The Three Little Pigs"): Going down the chimney just might result in getting boiled. It is evident that the story experience does not always end for young children when the reading is finished; a story can become a lens through which children attempt to understand their world.

Diverse Perspectives on Reader Response

We can gain further insight into the way children read and respond to literature by looking at their literary meaning-making from four additional perspectives: developmental, social, cultural, and textual (Beach, 1993). See Table 12.1 for a definition of each perspective.

Developmental Perspective on Reader Response

Educators who assume a developmental perspective on reader response realize that children in different stages of cognitive, moral, and social development think about the world in very different ways and that these differences are reflected in the ways they respond to stories. Arthur Applebee (1978) and Janet Hickman (1981) conducted extensive studies of how children's responses to literature change across age levels. Applebee interviewed six-year-olds and nine-year-olds about stories, and asked thirteen-year-olds and seventeen-year-olds to write about literature. Hickman obtained her data by spending a full semester observing and recording children's spontaneous responses to literature in three combined-grade classrooms: kindergarten-first, second-third, and fourth-fifth. Both researchers found distinctive differences in the ways children of different ages respond to literature.

Applebee found that when young children (the six-year-olds in his study) were invited to talk about a favorite story, they did so by retelling the plot in great detail. However, nine-year-olds responded to the same invitation ("Tell about a favorite story") by briefly summarizing the story. Applebee also included thirteen- and seventeen-year-olds in his study. None of the six- and nine-year-olds whom he interviewed analyzed or made generalizations about

Table 12.1   Four Perspectives on Reader Response

Perspective	Definition
Developmental	A perspective that recognizes that children in different stages of cognitive, moral, and social development respond to literature differently
Social	A perspective that recognizes that a reader's literary transaction can be shaped by the responses of other readers
Cultural	A perspective that recognizes that readers' cultural values, attitudes, and assumptions shape their transactions with texts
Textual	A perspective that recognizes that readers' responses are influenced by their knowledge of narrative conventions, literary elements, genre conventions, and other aspects of a text

stories; in contrast, the thirteen- and seventeen-year-olds, with their more sophisticated cognitive abilities, typically analyzed the structures of stories and made generalizations about their meanings.

Hickman found that the children she observed spontaneously expressed their ideas, feelings, and understanding about stories in many different forms, not just by talking and writing. The children responded to literature through movement—by clapping, smiling, and even kissing book covers. Their literature-based artwork, writing, and dramatic presentations were also vehicles for expressing their thinking about stories. The younger children in Hickman's study were especially likely to rely on nonverbal ways of expressing their responses. Hickman found other differences in the responses of the younger (kindergarten-first grade) and older (fourth-fifth grade) children in her study. These differences are summarized in Table 12.2. However, the responses of the second- and third-graders in her study were harder to characterize. Sometimes, they responded much as the kindergartners and first-graders did; at other times, their responses were more sophisticated, like those of the fourth- and fifth-graders. What set the second- and third-graders apart was their concern with becoming independent readers. They spent long periods of time reading and had much to say about the conventions of print.

Hickman, like Applebee, found that younger children were likely to become caught up in the action of stories. However, Hickman found that the kindergartners and first-graders could also reduce stories to "lessons" when invited to interpret the meaning of a story. For example, one first grader offered the following thematic statement for "The Little Red Hen": "When someone already baked a cake and you haven't helped, they're probably just gonna say no." This child expressed the story's lesson in the context of the story situation. By contrast, the fourth- and fifth-graders in Hickman's study expressed their understanding by using more abstract thematic statements that were not tied directly to the content of a story.

Although the work of both Applebee and Hickman helps to explain the developmental differences in children's responses, Hickman's work, which was done in a naturalistic classroom setting, also demonstrates how important it is to watch children closely if you want to understand how they interact with literature. Just asking children questions about stories doesn't give a complete picture; it might tell you about their story comprehension, but not necessarily about what they are thinking, feeling, and wondering. To learn about those things, it is important to observe students throughout the day—watching their body movements; seeing how they express their ideas about stories through art, writing, and drama; and listening to their spontaneously expressed ideas during storybook reading and literature discussion.

As the research described in this section suggests, children of different ages respond to literature in different (although equally interesting) ways. Therefore, it is important for

| Table 12.2   Characteristic Responses of Children in Hickman's Study ||
Responses of Kindergartners and First Graders	Responses of Fourth and Fifth Graders
Relied on their bodies to express responses as they imitated movements in stories, acted out story elements to explain them, and incorporated story elements in their dramatic play	Expressed strong feelings for and against particular selections
"Collected" story elements in pictures rather than trying to present a cohesive story line through their artwork	Demonstrated extensive knowledge of story conventions and story structure in their literature-based writing, artwork, and skits
Spent time browsing in their independent contacts with books—that is, picked up a book, briefly flipped through its pages, and then moved on to the next book	Sustained their attention for long periods of time in their independent contacts with books
Were concerned with sorting out what was happening in stories and frequently used a retelling strategy when answering questions about stories	Had less need to focus on literal meanings in their verbal responses
Made personal statements loosely tied to the story	Often revealed connections between their own experiences and an interpreted story meaning
Expressed a concern with the reality of stories by talking about whether stories were "true" or "possible"	Relied on literary terminology in discussing the reality of stories
Could reduce stories to "lessons" when invited to interpret their meaning	Expressed understanding of stories using disembedded thematic statements
Expressed more interest in stories than in the authors of stories	Clearly recognized the role of author as the creator of a story

teachers to become attuned to how children of different ages think about literature. Yet it is also important to realize that children of the same age may exhibit individual styles of response (Galda, 1982; Hancock, 1993). For example, Lawrence Sipe (1998) characterized one of the first-graders in his study as a child whose specialties in responding were logical reasoning and close analysis. By contrast, second-grader Charles typically expressed his response through performance, while first-grader Krissy frequently invented alternatives to the plots of stories. So age alone doesn't prepare children to get the most out of books. Factors such as exposure to and experience with literature—factors that teachers can certainly influence—are equally important.

Social Perspective on Reader Response

Social factors also affect reader response, as do the context and temporal factors that are integrally bound up with social factors in the classroom. Research in this area is especially important for educators because of the insights it yields about how to create classrooms that nurture children's thinking about literature. Just as teachers can't wait for children to become better readers or to master increasingly complex math concepts, they also shouldn't wait for children to respond more deeply to literature. Instead, teachers need to take the necessary steps to ensure that such growth occurs. To do this, they must understand the social, contextual, and temporal factors that influence children's thinking about literature.

The Literature-Rich Classroom

Janet Hickman was the first person in the United States to study children's spontaneous responses to literature in a naturalistic setting. She noticed the way in which context shaped the children's responses and she carefully described those classroom contexts. Hickman found that the teachers in her study invited responses to literature through the physical context they created, the way they used time, and the methods they used to encourage response. Based on her research, Hickman (1981) recommended that teachers do the following:

- Build extensive book collections and fill the classroom with attractive displays of books.
- Select high-quality books and present them in related sets.
- Set aside ample time for all children to interact with books daily.
- Share literature with children daily by reading aloud and by introducing new books before putting them on display in the classroom.
- Encourage students to share their thinking about literature.
- Support children's understanding of literary craft by providing them with critical terminology when they have an idea but are lacking the words to talk about it more easily.
- Encourage children to explore books through art, writing, and drama, and support their efforts by providing time, space, materials, and ideas for projects and by ensuring that they have opportunities to share their work with peers.
- Provide children with opportunities to revisit some books repeatedly.

In Chapters 13, 14, and 15, we explore more fully how teachers can create classrooms that nurture rich responses to literature.

Evolution of Response

Children's responses to stories can evolve over time, becoming deeper and more insightful. Reading stories repeatedly to children seems to be an effective vehicle for fostering such growth. Janet Hickman identified repeated readings of stories as one of the classroom fac-

Children enjoy expressing their responses to literature through their artwork.

tors that encourage rich responses. A number of investigators have looked specifically at what happens when children hear stories repeatedly. Miriam Martinez and Nancy Roser (1985) found that the story talk of preschoolers changed when parents and teachers read stories to them repeatedly. The children talked more about familiar stories than unfamiliar ones. Also, on a first reading of a story, the children tended to share fewer observations about the story and instead asked more questions as they worked to sort out characters and story events. On subsequent readings, the children chose to explore different aspects of the stories. This finding suggests that as children gained control over particular facets of the story, they became able to shift their attention to other elements. However, if they did return to discuss a portion of a story they had previously talked about, the children showed more insightful thinking than they had initially. Lesley Morrow (1988) compared the responses of four-year-olds who heard stories read repeatedly with those of other four-year-olds who listened to different stories read only one time. The children who heard repeated readings of a story made more comments than did those who listened to different books, and they also shared a wider variety of responses and more complex interpretive responses. Researcher Amy McClure (1985) investigated responses to poetry in a combined fifth- and sixth-grade classroom. The teacher in this classroom frequently reread the same poems, and these rereadings enabled her students to move beyond hearing the words of the poem to reflecting more deeply on meaning.

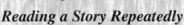

Teaching Idea 12.4
Reading a Story Repeatedly

One way of deciding which book to read repeatedly to younger students is to invite them to select a book they want to hear again. More likely than not, children will select a book they find both interesting and challenging. If you work with younger children, you want repeated readings to become routine in your classroom. One way of doing this is to designate a particular day of the week as the day on which you'll revisit an "old friend." However, it seems that as the grade level increases, teachers often lament that their students complain that they have heard a story before. The teachers lament that the stories they teach are no longer fresh; there are no surprises. When students have the attitude that their "old friends" are like their favorite foods, they won't turn them down. What child turns his head away when offered pizza or tacos, hamburgers or spaghetti? And what about macaroni and cheese!? *Charlotte's Web* is the macaroni and cheese of children's literature! Students discover new facets of a story with each repetition.

Other strategies, in addition to repeated readings of literature, also encourage the deepening of children's responses over time. Joanne Golden and her colleagues (1992) and Lynda Weston (1993) found children's responses to stories continued to grow as they engaged in drama, art, and writing activities based on literature. These types of activities are discussed in Chapter 14.

Children gain new insights into a story by listening to what their peers and teachers say about it.

Teaching Idea 12.5

Encouraging Variety in Responses

Some teachers are willing to give up their own lunch period once a week to meet with students in a Literary Lunch Bunch. Students apply by filling out a simple application stating the reason why they would like to be a member of the group. Six to eight students are selected from one teacher's classroom, or, if two teachers combine classes, as many as twelve can usually participate in the discussion without too much competition. Ideally the teacher distributes copies of the same title to each of the participants and divides the book into manageable chunks to be read over a week's time. A paper bookmark specifies the pages to be read and has a place for a question to be written. Each group member should come prepared with a question to ask or a wondering or observation to share. Fifth graders have especially enjoyed books such as *Roll of Thunder Hear My Cry*, *Number the Stars*, *Love, Ruby Lavender*, and *Chicken Boy*. Many novels can be read in four sessions without competing with homework and other demands on student time. All participants gather on the designated day to eat lunch and discuss the book. Encourage the students not to read ahead. (Inevitably, if someone has read ahead, she or he will slip up and reveal something to the rest of the group.) If any student comes unprepared for more than one session, he or she may need to be dropped from the group and replaced by another applicant. This casual setting for discussing books encourages animated responses from students. With the teacher acting only as facilitator, the discussion can become very thoughtful and support students in reading quality books that they might not have understood alone. The teacher is also able to play the role of resource person when questions spontaneously arise about World War II, the depression, or racism. The group can also pause momentarily as someone looks up information to answer someone's question.

Technology in Practice 12.2

Visit teachingbooks.net and listen to the Author Interview of Francisco Jimenez, who talks about the importance of readers seeing their own worlds reflected in books.

Literature Discussion

Although the actual reading of a text is a solitary experience, Susan Hepler and Janet Hickman (1982) observed that "the literary transaction, the one-to-one conversation between author and the audience, is frequently surrounded by other voices" (p. 279). In the classroom, these other voices belong to the teacher and classmates. Ralph Peterson and Maryann Eeds (1995) believe that when readers come together to share their varied interpretations of a piece of literature, the "meaning potential of the text is expanded" (p. 21). Literature discussion is an especially powerful instructional vehicle for fostering children's literary thinking, and Chapter 14 examines literature discussion at length, with particular emphasis on how teachers can ensure that their students have the opportunity to share their insights into literature.

Cultural Perspective on Reader Response

We are all cultural beings who belong to particular ethnic, class, and gender groups and, as members of these groups, share values, attitudes, assumptions, and knowledge with other group members. Patricia Enciso (1994) says that our cultural understandings are "everywhere and always a part of how we interpret the world and our place in it" (p. 532). So, of course, cultural understandings shape readers' transactions with texts, either supporting or constraining them. For example, a teacher's initial response to Sherley Anne Williams's *Working Cotton* reflected her cultural perspective. In this book, Williams documents a day that an African American child spends working in the cotton fields with members of her family, who are migrant workers. On first reading this book, the teacher observed how impressed she was by the beauty of the illustrations and the straightforward manner in which the story is narrated; nonetheless, she put the book aside, finding this story about a child working in the fields from sunup to sundown too painful to share with children. Her first response was constrained by cultural experiences. Only later, when she realized that *Working Cotton* is a book with which migrant students might readily connect, did it come down off her shelf.

Although we are becoming increasingly aware of the likely impact of culture on children's responses to literature, little research has been done in this area. One early study, done by Rudine Sims (1983), investigated the responses of a ten-year-old African American girl to books about African Americans. Sims interviewed the girl about the books she had read and discovered that she preferred books that related to her own African American experiences and had characters with whom she could identify. In particular, she liked strong, active, female, black characters. Elizabeth Smith (1995) also found that fifth-grade African American students in her class who were struggling and reluctant readers avidly sought out books about African Americans and responded to these books differently than they did to other books. This research underscores the importance of bringing into the classroom literature that authentically represents students' cultures. Finding the right books is likely to require an investment of time and energy, but the effort is worth making.

Coming together to talk about literature allows people with different perspectives (sometimes vastly different ones) to exchange ideas, step into the shoes of others, and thereby calibrate their own judgments. For example, Mexican American students from rural backgrounds could help their peers better understand and appreciate Carmen Lomas Garza's *Family*

Pictures. In effect, participants in literature discussion can share cultural insights that will make the literary experience a richer one for other participants. This happened in a university class when a group of preservice teachers discussed *Maniac Magee*. The students, most of whom were white middle-class females, did not believe the book was realistic—especially two scenes, one set in a house in which Maniac mistakes the roaches covering the floor for raisins and another scene in which two young boys jump through a hole in the ceiling from the second floor to the first. At this point, a student who had sat quietly on the sidelines for most of the semester spoke up, explaining that she lived in a housing project and had first-hand experience with the kinds of living conditions Spinelli described in *Maniac Magee*. Her classmates listened intently and thereafter viewed both the book and their classmate's contributions to discussion in a different light.

Cultural differences often have a positive effect when students are encouraged to help their classmates interpret a book by sharing their related cultural experiences. However, it is also important to be aware that children's conversations about a book are sometimes constrained by their cultural perspectives—just as cross-cultural conversations about social issues are too often constrained. Teachers should try to anticipate cultural roadblocks that may arise and put a damper on literature discussion, and they must attempt to help students get around those roadblocks. Constructivist theory maintains that an individual's interpretation of an event, influenced as it is by his or her unique culture-based experience, is the event. In light of this theory, it is important for teachers to encourage students to come together in literature study as diverse members of society and to consider actively the issues and experiences found in literature. The very act of considering literature will reveal how differently students think about things and will provide opportunities for understanding others' points of view.

Like students, teachers also bring cultural perspectives to texts. These perspectives can have an effect on the kinds of literature a teacher selects. More important, the way the teacher responds to and perceives the literature will influence how she or he guides the literature discussion. Teachers need to monitor their own culturally based responses to texts to ensure that they do not constrain students' responses.

Textual Perspective on Reader Response

Earlier, we said that aesthetic reading is a reader/text transaction in which the reader brings to bear on the text his or her experience, knowledge, beliefs, and feelings. Knowledge about how texts "work" is one type of knowledge readers bring to the transaction, and textual theorists place special emphasis on it. The more experience readers (or listeners) have had with literature, the greater is their store of knowledge about how literature works. This store may include knowledge of genre conventions, literary elements, literary language, and visual elements and design—the kind of information that we have explored in-depth in earlier chapters of this textbook.

Preschoolers who have been read to have already begun to build a store of literary knowledge, as evidenced by their use of "once upon a time" to begin their own stories or by the concern they express when a wolf enters the scene as they are listening to a story—they know full well that this stock character is not to be trusted. You can sometimes even anticipate how textual knowledge is likely to influence children's transactions with particular books. Children's delight in Jon Scieszka's *The Stinky Cheese Man and Other Fairly Stupid Tales* can be understood (at least in part) in light of a textual perspective on response. Scieszka's wonderfully mixed-up fantasy violates every imaginable book convention: The book begins with text, which is then followed by the title page. Readers are invited to put their own name into the dedication (which happens to be written upside down). The table of contents is shown falling onto the characters in "Chicken Licken." One of the characters (the Little Red Hen) insists on narrating her story at the most inopportune times. Children love this story—if they have already acquired an understanding of how stories work.

There are a number of ways in which teachers can help students build a rich foundation of textual knowledge. Immersion appears to be an important means of building textual knowledge. In discussing how children acquire genre knowledge, Lucy Calkins (1994) argues that such knowledge is acquired when children inhabit a given literary genre. Immersion is

Go to the Extension Activities section of Chapter 12 in the MyEducationKit for your book and complete activity #1 to examine the influences of your cultural perspective.

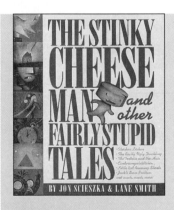

ILLUSTRATION 12.3 Both the story lines of traditional tales and the features of typical book formats are humorously manipulated in *The Stinky Cheese Man and Other Fairly Stupid Tales* (a Caldecott Honor Book). (From *The Stinky Cheese Man And Other Fairly Stupid Tales* by Jon Scieszka, illustrated by Lane Smith, copyright © 1992 by Lane Smith, illustrations. Used by permission of Viking Penguin, A Division of Penguin Young Readers Group, A Member of Penguin Group (USA) Inc., 345 Hudson Street, New York, NY 10014. All rights reserved.)

Ask the Author . . .

Pat Mora

Favorite Books As a Child

- The poetry volume of the *Childcraft* series. I remember looking at the row of orange books, pulling out this volume when I was home sick (maybe not that sick) and leisurely savoring the music.

- *Little House on the Prairie* by Laura Ingalls Wilder. What delight to discover this whole series in the El Paso Public Library long before the TV adaptations. I loved the coziness of the books, the family closeness, the triumphs over adversity.

- *Secret of the Old Clock* by Carolyn Keene. Yes, though it's not fashionable to admit it, I liked the Nancy Drew books. Part of the pleasure was sharing them with my younger sister, Cissy, and also having my aunt, whom we called Lobo, read them to us, a niece on each side.

Do you find that children from different cultural backgrounds respond differently to your work? If so, in what ways?

The question goes to the heart of the complex experience of being human. We all breathe and sleep, eat, and fear. I sometimes joke that we're all united by being post-birth and pre-death. These shared human experiences allow us at our best to be empathetic and also to savor international art, including literature. Picasso and O'Keeffe, like Tolstoy or Neruda or Dickinson, move us because of our human similarities. They too lived in skin. Neither country of origin, color, class, religion, gender, nor language changes the fact that we humans itch and dream. And yet, and yet, we do arrive into this world to particular parents in particular places. The family staple can be beans, rice, potatoes, yuca. "Aunt" and "tía" technically mean the same thing, but the words are different in the mouth. Each of us belongs to many communities—some by birth, circumstance, choice.

Children are no different, of course. They enter my books, my words bringing with them all they are—their language as well as their curiosity. Do children who are bilingual and/or Latino respond to my work in a particular way? At this time in history, yes, because they haven't seen enough families like theirs in books. I like

to think they find comfort and validation, a home in books. Though it has been years, I still feel the quiet little girl in New Jersey who rubbed up against me as she left my author presentation and whispered, "I'm Spanish, too." I knew what she meant.

But children, praise the heavens, don't always see or feel the barriers to connections that we adults do. They're not intimidated by Spanish: They want to try it. And all students know how it feels to be different the way Stella feels in *The Rainbow Tulip*. They feel with her and for their wounded selves. On a lighter note, most children like to make animal sounds. They're ready to howl like coyotes whether in English or Spanish, preferably both. Best not forget the poets of many colors. Some children enjoy the rhyming sounds in my books, the quiet spaces between the words, the smooth and prickly words, their music; the taste of the words in the mouth, some in English, some in Spanish, green and lavender flavors.

Pat Mora, *born in El Paso, Texas, has written many award-winning books for children and adults, including* Tomás and the Library Lady *and* My Own True Name. *She's the proud mother of three grown children, who are delighted that Mom now has a house in Santa Fe. Her husband Vern thinks it's not a bad idea either.* ∎

especially powerful when accompanied by opportunities to reflect on the target textual feature (e.g., how authors develop character). Instruction can also help students acquire insights into how texts work, especially when that instruction moves beyond the surface identification of text features. For example, in the following exchange, Ms. Gonzalez guided the second and third graders in her class to analyze the setting in a variety of familiar texts in order to better understand how this literary element functions in the fantasy genre:

Teacher: Today we're going to talk about setting in relation to fantasy. Who can tell me what the setting is? We've talked about that in our class before and we've looked at it in other stories.

Greg: Usually it's a place.

Teacher: A place. And so, can we add anything else to that?

Mary: It's where the book takes place. Like in **The Lion, the Witch, and the Wardrobe**, it takes place in Narnia. But like in the beginning, it's [another student says "Earth"] yeah, Earth.

Teacher: Okay, so **The Lion, the Witch, and the Wardrobe** might be one of those special cases where there's two settings. . . . Do you remember **Thunder Cake**? When we read Patricia Polacco's **Thunder Cake**? Do you remember what the setting was in this story? Where did most of this story take place? I'll give you a few little reminders with some of the illustrations.

Terry: Just at the babushka's farm.

Teacher: Yeah, the babushka's farm. So, this story took place at the farm. One place, one time, it all happened in one day. What about this story that you read last week (holds up **Zathura**)? What do you think about the setting in **Zathura**?. . .

Issue to Consider

Should Teachers Encourage Students to Focus on Author's Craft during Literature Discussion?

Reader response theorists maintain that during the reader/text interaction, readers' personal memories, feelings, and thought associations are evoked by the stories they read. So when readers—including children—get together to talk about books, they often share some of those personal stories. We also know that when reading, children are especially likely to become caught up in the story world. They are interested in the characters they meet in stories and in the events in which characters are caught up—much as they are interested in the lives of people they meet. So children very naturally explore these story worlds in their literature discussions. Given children's natural propensity to talk about story characters and events and their personal responses to the story, many educators argue that teachers should make these the topics of literature discussion groups.

Other educators take a different stance. They argue that for response to reach its richest potential, readers must move beyond the story world and personal responses to that story world to focus on issues related to the author's craft. In other words, children should be encouraged to step outside the story world and do what Langer calls objectifying their experience with the text. If they are encouraged to attend to the literary elements and the ways in which authors manipulate those elements, children will come to more fully appreciate the richness of literature and learn more about literature. Further, children who gain insights into the author's craft will be more likely to grow as writers themselves.

This position is countered by those who argue that a focus on craft is likely to result in an overanalysis of literature that is inappropriate for children. Instead, teachers should follow children's leads in discussion and build on their interests, even if this means that discussion never touches on what the author did that makes readers respond as they do.

How should teachers conduct literature discussions with children? Should they let discussions center on the topics children introduce, even if this means children only explore the story world and their personal responses to that story world? Or should the teacher at times nudge children beyond what might be their first interests to talk about the author's craft? What do you think?

Sarah: In the beginning, it's like on the ground, on Earth. And then in the middle it turns and they go into space.

Teacher: Do you know, what Sarah just said makes me think about what Mary was saying with ***The Lion, the Witch, and the Wardrobe***.

Guided discussions of this type in which children are invited to share their discoveries about particular features of books are likely to help young readers build a solid foundation of textual knowledge. In Chapters 14 and 15, we explore ways of helping children acquire understandings about text.

Intertextual Knowledge

Readers also bring knowledge of other texts to the reading of particular books, and reading a story in light of other stories can enrich readers' responses (Cairney, 1992; Short, 1992). This was true in the case of the preservice teacher who connected Florence Parry Heide and Judith Heide Gilliland's ***The Day of Ahmed's Secret*** to Eve Bunting's ***The Wednesday Surprise:*** "The story reminds me of ***The Wednesday Surprise***. In that book, it's the grandmother who learns to read, but it's the grandmother and the little girl who share the secret. And just like Ahmed, they can hardly wait to share the secret with their family."

Creating *intertextuality,* the process of using knowledge of one text to make meaning of another, is something mature readers do, and children can also be encouraged to read one story in light of another. In fact, part of the delight children find in ***The Stinky Cheese Man and Other Fairly Stupid Tales*** can be explained with reference to intertextuality. The book is a collection of folktale spin-offs; for example, the title story, "The Stinky Cheese Man," is a spin-off of "The Gingerbread Man"; "The Princess and the Bowling Ball" is a spin-off of "The Princess and the Pea"; and "Jack's Bean Problem" is clearly related to "Jack and the Beanstalk." Children who know the original tales are the ones who delight the most in Scieszka's book.

In this chapter, we have used Judith Langer's framework to examine the nature of literary meaning-making, and we have also looked at literary responses from different perspectives—developmental, social, cultural, and textual. These windows onto literary meaning-making complement one another. By understanding each perspective, you will be able to make better decisions as a teacher. In addition, by knowing that mature readers understand a text in light of others they have read, you will be more likely to encourage your students to make connections among stories; and by realizing that readers understand stories in light of their own cultural experiences, you will recognize the importance of selecting multicultural titles for your students.

PEARSON
myeducationkit

To check your comprehension on the content covered in this chapter, go to the MyEducation-Kit for your book and complete the Study Plan for Chapter 12. Here you will be able to take a chapter quiz and receive feedback on your answers.

Experiences for Further Learning

1. Langer (1990) says readers assume different stances (or different relationships to a text) as they read. Review the discussion on pages 393–395 of the four stances Langer describes: being out and stepping in, being in and moving through, being in and stepping out, and stepping out and objectifying the experience. Then select a book to read—perhaps ***Holes*** or ***Wednesday Wars***—and as you read, keep a journal in which you record your responses to the book. After completing the book, go back and identify the different stances you assumed as you responded to the book. Consider choosing several more complex picture books in order to experiment with a variety of reactions. Did you have any difficulty stepping in? In what way were you in and moving through? Were you able to personally associate with a character? Did you find yourself mesmerized by the language of the text? When were you aware of stepping out? Did you feel compelled to consider the world in which you live, any social issues, or a human condition? As you stepped out, did you recognize the literary devices used by the author? We want our students to be able to read for the sheer joy of it, but as they become aware of their stances, they marvel at the layers of meaning reading can bring to their lives.

2. Discuss a piece of multicultural literature such as Pam Muñoz Ryan's ***Esperanza Rising*** with a group of peers from different cultural backgrounds. How, if at all, do different cultural perspectives come into play in the discussion? What other perspectives were you aware of? Did you respond primarily from a cultural perspective? Were there elements in the story with which you made a personal connection? Perhaps the story stirred a social reaction in you, or it may have reminded you of another book you have read, thus eliciting an intertextual response. Take note of the various lenses through which you and your peers respond.

3. Children enjoy sharing the personal memories and feelings that stories evoke. However, some people argue that children go off on tangents when sharing personal associations. Read two stories by the same author to a group of students. For example, you might read Chris Van Allsburg's books, ***The Stranger*** and ***The Wreck of the Zephyr***, to a group of fourth- or fifth-graders. After reading one of the books, ask the students questions to check their comprehension. After reading the second story, invite them to join in an open-ended discussion by asking, "What did you notice or what were you reminded of as you listened to the story?" Share the children's responses with a group of peers and address the following question: "Are children more likely to benefit from an open-ended discussion or a discussion guided by teacher questions?"

Now go to Chapter 12 in the MyEducationKit (www.myeducationkit.com) for your book, where you can:

- Find learning outcomes for Chapter 12.
- Access the Children's Literature Database for your own exploration.
- Extend knowledge with content-specific Web Links.
- Deepen and apply content understanding with Extension Activities.
- Check your comprehension on the content covered in the chapter by going to the Study Plan. Here you will be able to take a chapter quiz and receive feedback on your answers.
- Find the following updated appendices: Major Children's Book Awards, Children's Magazines, Professional Organizations, Children's Book Publishers' Addresses, Book Selection Aids, and Children's Literature Web Sites.

Recommended Books

* indicates a picture book; **I** indicates interest level (P = preschool, YA = young adult)

*Bunting, Eve. *December*. Illustrated by David Diaz. Harcourt, 1997. A boy and his mother invited an old woman into their cardboard house one cold December evening. (**I:** 7–11)

*————. *Fly Away Home*. Illustrated by Ronald Himler. Clarion, 1991. A boy and his father, living in the airport after the mother dies, find hope when a bird trapped in the airport finds a way to freedom. (**I:** 6–10)

*————. *The Wednesday Surprise*. Illustrated by Donald Carrick. Clarion, 1989. A little girl teaches her grandmother to read. (**I:** 6–9)

*Chinn, Karen. *Sam and the Lucky Money*. Illustrated by Cornelius Van Wright and Ying-Hwa Hu. Lee & Low, 1995. When he discovers a man with no shoes in winter, Sam forgets about the excitement of the Chinese New Year celebration. (**I:** 7–11)

Creech, Sharon. *Chasing Redbird*. Joanna Cotler/HarperCollins, 1997. A young girl is determined to prove herself by clearing the long lost trail that she discovers. (**I:** 10–14)

Crum, Shutta. *Spitting Image*. Clarion, 2003. Twelve-year-old Jessie wants to find her place in the world. She wants to make the world a better place—like the Vista volunteer in her Appalachian community—and she wants to know who her father is. Readers will meet a strong and memorable protagonist in Jessie Bovey. (**I:** 12 and up)

Curtis, Christopher Paul. *The Watsons Go to Birmingham, 1963*. Delacorte, 1995. An African American family from Detroit visits in Birmingham in 1963, the summer of the fateful church bombing that set the civil rights movement into high gear. (**I:** 10–12)

Cushman, Karen. *The Midwife's Apprentice*. Clarion, 1995. A homeless waif in medieval England is given the opportunity to become a midwife's apprentice. (**I:** 10–14)

DiCamillo, Kate. *Because of Winn-Dixie*. Candlewick, 2000. Ten-year-old Opal adopts a dog that helps her make an array of friends who, in turn, help her sort out some of the issues that most perplex her. (**I:** 9–12)

Dowell, Frances O'Roark. *Chicken Boy*. Aladdin, 2007. Struggling to cope with his mother's death and the ongoing feud between his grandmother and his "no good daddy," seventh grader, Toby, finds refuge in his relationship with a new friend and in a school project involving chickens. (**I:** 10 and up)

Funke, Cornelia. *Inkheart*. Scholastic, 2003. Through a magical read-aloud, Meggie's father has brought the evil characters of a book to life, and Meggie and her family find themselves caught up in a real-world adventure centering around these book characters. (**I:** 9 and up)

*Garza, Carmen Lomas. *Family Pictures*. As told to Harriet Rohmer. Spanish version by Rosalma Zubizarreta. Children's Book Press, 1990. Artist Carmen Garza portrays scenes from her childhood in a Mexican American community in South Texas. (**I:** 6–10)

Giff, Patricia Reilly. *Pictures of Hollis Woods*. Random House, 2002. Hollis Woods longs to belong to a family, but every foster family seems to view her as a "mountain of trouble." (**I:** 9–12)

*Harrington, Janice N. *Going North*. Illustrated by Jerome Lagarrigue. Farrar, Straus, & Giroux, 2004. It is the 1960s, and a young girl resists her family's move to the North, until she has the opportunity to see firsthand the limitations imposed on her African American family as a result of living in Alabama. (**I:** 8–12)

*Heide, Florence Parry, and Judith Heide Gilliland. *The Day of Ahmed's Secret*. Illustrated by Ted Lewin. Lothrop, Lee & Shepard, 1990. As a boy moves through the streets of Cairo doing his work, he looks forward to the evening, when he can share his secret with his family: He has learned to write his name. (**I:** 6–10)

Lewis, C. S. *The Lion, the Witch, and the Wardrobe*. Macmillan, 1950. Four children enter a magical realm where they are caught up in a struggle between the forces of good and evil. (**I:** 9–YA)

*Martin, Bill, Jr., and John Archambault. *The Ghost-Eye Tree*. Illustrated by Ted Rand. Holt, 1985/1995. This story about a brother and sister's scary experience with a haunted tree can easily be adapted for readers' theater. (**I:** P–9)

*Mayer, Mercer. *Liza Lou and the Yeller Belly Swamp*. Aladdin, 1976/1997. Liza Lou proves to be too clever for the witches, haunts, and gobblygooks of the Yeller Belly Swamp. (**I:** P–8)

Mora, Pat. *My Own True Name*: New and Selected Poems for Young Adults, 1984–1999. Arte Publico, 2000. Mora's poems focus on life and family in bicultural settings. (**I:** YA)

*————. *The Rainbow Tulip*. Viking, 1999. A Mexican American immigrant girl feels caught between the Spanish- and English-speaking worlds. (**I:** P–8)

*————. *Tomás and the Library Lady*. Knopf, 1997. The true story of Tomás Rivera, a migrant worker whose interest in books, sparked by a librarian, led him to become a university chancellor. (**I:** P–8)

*Munsch, Robert. *The Paper Bag Princess*. Illustrated by Michael Martchenko. Annick Press, 1980. This modern-day fantasy turns the traditional roles of prince and princess topsy turvy. (**I:** P–8)

Paterson, Katherine. *The Same Stuff as Stars*. Clarion, 2002. Neglected by their mother, and with a father in prison, eleven-year-old Angel has long been the stable feature in her brother Bernie's life. But when their mother abandons them at the home of their great-grandmother, Angel's responsibilities seem staggering until a mysterious star man and a kind librarian reach out to help. (**I:** 10–14)

*Polacco, Patricia. *Thunder Cake*. Philomel, 1993. A grandmother helps her granddaughter overcome her fear of thunder. (**I:** 6–9).

Sachar, Louis. *Holes*. Farrar, 1998. When Stanley Yelnats is sent to a juvenile detention center for a crime he didn't commit, he is sure it is just another instance of the family curse, but his stay at Camp Green Lake presents him with the opportunity to finally break that curse. (**I:** 10 and up)

*Scieszka, Jon. The *Stinky Cheese Man and Other Fairly Stupid Tales*. Illustrated by Lane Smith. Viking, 1992. A novel format is used in presenting humorous spin-offs of familiar European folktales and fairy tales. (**I:** 6 and up)

*Shannon, David. *No, David!* Scholastic, 1998. A little boy creates mischief throughout the day as his exasperated mother tries to rein him in. (**I:** P–7)

Spinelli, Jerry. *Maniac Magee*. Little, Brown, 1990. On his way to becoming a legend, a homeless boy brings together the two sides of a racially divided town. (**I:** 9–12)

*Van Allsburg, Chris. *The Wreck of the Zephyr*. Houghton Mifflin, 1983. Behind the mystery of a wrecked sailboat high on a cliff is the story of a boy who longed to be the greatest sailor. (**I:** 9 and up)

*———. *The Stranger*. Houghton Mifflin, 1986. When Farmer Bailey takes the stranger he has accidentally hit into his home, strange occurrences begin to happen. (**I:** 9 and up)

*———. *Two Bad Ants*. Houghton Mifflin, 1988. A visit to a house spells near disaster for two ants. (**I:** P–9)

*———. *Zathura*. Houghton Mifflin, 2002. A game board becomes a portal to an outer space adventure. (**I:** 5–9)

Van Draanen, Wendelin. *Swear to Howdy*. Knopf, 2003. A summer of adventure and fun comes to a screeching halt when a tragic accident threatens to destroy the lives of Rusty and his best friend. (**I:** 10 and up)

*Viorst, Judith. *Alexander and the Terrible, Horrible, No Good, Very Bad Day*. Illustrated by Ray Cruz. Atheneum, 1972. Alexander tells about all the things that have gone wrong in a single day. (**I:** P–8)

Wiles, Deborah. *Love, Ruby Lavender*. Harcourt, 2001. When her beloved grandmother decides to spend the summer in Hawaii, Ruby Lavender is sure that she will be unable to cope with the obstacles she faces in her small Mississippi town. (**I:** 9–12)

*Williams, Sherley Anne. *Working Cotton*. Illustrated by Carole Byard. Harcourt, 1992. A young girl describes a day spent in the fields with her migrant worker family. (**I:** P–8)

Williams, Vera B. *Amber Was Brave, Essie Was Smart*. With their father away in prison and their mother working long hours, Amber and Essie turn to each other for courage and support. This memorable story is told through poems and pictures. (**I:** 7–11)

Zusak, Markus. *The Book Thief*. Knopf, 2006. Through the love and support of her beloved foster father, Liesel finds the courage to take her own stand against injustice in Nazi Germany. (**I:** YA)

Resources

Applebee, Arthur. *The Child's Concept of Story*. University of Chicago Press, 1978.

Beach, Richard. *A Teacher's Introduction to Reader-Response Theories*. National Council of Teachers of English, 1993.

Cochran-Smith, M. *The Making of a Reader*. Norwood, NJ: Ablex, 1984.

Langer, Judith A. *Literature Instruction: A Focus on Student Response*. National Council of Teachers of English, 1992.

Lehr, Susan. *The Child's Developing Sense of Theme: Responses to Literature*. Columbia University Teachers College Press, 1990.

Roser, Nancy, and Miriam Martinez, eds. *Book Talk and Beyond: Children and Teachers Respond to Literature*. International Reading Association, 1995.

Short, Kathy Gnagey, and Kathryn Mitchell, eds. *Talking about Books: Literature Discussion Groups in K–8 Classrooms*. Heinemann, 1998.

References

Applebee, Arthur. *The Child's Concept of Story*. University of Chicago Press, 1978.

Beach, Richard. *A Teacher's Introduction to Reader-Response Theories*. National Council of Teachers of English, 1993.

Bloem, Patricia L., and Anthony L. Manna. "A Chorus of Questions: Readers Respond to Patricia Polacco." *The Reading Teacher 52* (1999): 802–808.

Cairney, Trevor H. "Fostering and Building Students' Intertextual Histories." *Language Arts 69* (1992): 502–507.

Calkins, Lucy. *The Art of Teaching Writing*. Heinemann, 1994.

Cochran-Smith, Marilyn. *The Making of a Reader*. Ablex, 1984.

Emery, D. W. "Helping Readers Comprehend Stories from the Characters' Perspectives." *The Reading Teacher 49* (1996): 534–541.

Enciso, Patricia E. "Cultural Identity and Response to Literature: Running Lessons from *Maniac Magee*." *Language Arts 71* (1994): 524–533.

Galda, Lee. "Assuming the Spectator Stance: An Examination of the Responses of Three Young Readers." *Research in the Teaching of English 16* (1982): 1–20.

Golden, Joanne M., Annyce Meiners, and Stanley Lewis. "The Growth of Story Meaning." *Language Arts 69* (1992): 36–43.

Hancock, Marjorie R. "Exploring the Meaning-Making Process through the Content of Literature Response Journals: A Case Study Investigation." *Research in the Teaching of English 27* (1993): 335–368.

Hepler, Susan, and Janet Hickman. " 'The Book Was Okay. I Love You'—Social Aspects of Response to Literature." *Theory into Practice 21* (1982): 278–283.

Hickman, Janet. "A New Perspective on Response to Literature: Research in an Elementary School Setting." *Research in the Teaching of English 15* (1981): 343–354.

Langer, Judith. "Understanding Literature." *Language Arts 67* (1990): 812–816.

Lehr, Susan. "The Child's Developing Sense of Theme as a Response to Literature." *Reading Research Quarterly 23* (1988): 337–357.

Lukens, Rebecca. J. *A Critical Handbook of Children's Literature*. 6th ed. Longman, 1999.

McClure, Amy A. "Children's Responses to Poetry in a Supportive Context." Diss. The Ohio State University, 1985.

McGee, Lea M. "An Exploration of Meaning Construction in First Graders' Grand Conversations." *Literacy Research, Theory, and Practice: Views from Many Perspectives.* Eds. Charles K. Kinzer and Donald J. Leu. National Reading Conference, 1992, pp. 177–186.

McGinley, William, and George Kamberelis. "*Maniac Magee* and *Ragtime Tumpie*: Children Negotiating Self and World through Reading and Writing." *Research in the Teaching of English 30* (1996): 75–113.

Martinez, Miriam, and Nancy Roser. "Read It Again: The Value of Repeated Readings during Storytime." *The Reading Teacher 38* (1985): 782–786.

———. "Children's Responses to a Chapter Book across Grade Levels: Implications for Sustained Text." *Multidimensional Aspects of Literacy Research, Theory, and Practice.* Forty-third yearbook of the National Reading Conference. Eds. Charles K. Kinzer and Donald J. Leu. National Reading Conference, 1994, pp. 317–324.

———. "The Books Make a Difference in Story Talk." *Book Talk and Beyond: Children and Teachers Respond to Literature.* Eds. Nancy L. Roser and Miriam G. Martinez. International Reading Association, 1995, pp. 32–41.

———. "Children's Responses to Literature." *Handbook of Research on Teaching the English Language Arts.* 2nd ed. Eds. James Flood, Diane Lapp, Jim R. Squire, & Julie M. Jensen. Erlbaum, 2002, pp. 799–813.

Morrow, Lesley M. "Young Children's Responses to One-to-One Story Readings in School Settings." *Reading Research Quarterly 23* (1988): 89–107.

Nikolajeva, Maria. *The Rhetoric of Character in Children's Literature.* Scarecrow Press, 2002.

Paley, Vivian. *Wally's Stories: Conversations in the Kindergarten.* Harvard University Press, 1981.

Peterson, Ralph, and Maryann Eeds. "More Compelling Questions in Reading Education." *Reading Today* (1995, June/July): 21.

Rosenblatt, Louise M. *Literature as Exploration.* 4th ed. MLA, 1938.

———. "The Literary Transaction: Evocation and Response." *Journeying: Children Responding to Literature.* Eds. Kathleen E. Holland, Rachael A. Hungerford, and Shirley B. Ernst. Heinemann, 1993, pp. 6–23.

Short, Kathy G. "Intertextuality: Searching for Patterns That Connect." *Literacy Research, Theory, and Practice: Views from Many Perspectives: Forty-first Yearbook of the National Reading Conference.* Eds. Charles K. Kinzer and Donald J. Leu. National Reading Conference, 1992, pp. 187–197.

Sims, Rudine. "Strong Black Girls: A Ten-Year-Old Responds to Fiction about Afro-Americans." *Journal of Research and Development in Education 16* (1983): 21–28.

Sipe, Lawrence R. "Individual Literary Response Styles of First and Second Graders." *Forty-seventh Yearbook of the National Reading Conference.* Eds. Timothy Shanahan and Flora V. Rodriguez-Brown. National Reading Conference, 1998, pp. 76–89.

———. "The Construction of Literary Understanding by First and Second Graders in Oral Responses to Picture Storybook Readalouds." *Reading Research Quarterly 35* (2000a): 252–275.

———. " 'Those Two Gingerbread Boys Could Be Brothers': How Children Use Intertextual Connections during Storybook Readalouds." *Children's Literature in Education 31* (2000b): 73–90.

———. *Storytime: Young Children's Literary Understanding in the Classroom.* Teachers College Press, 2007.

Smith, Elizabeth B. "Anchored in Our Literature: Students Responding to African American Literature." *Language Arts 72* (1995): 571–574.

Weston, Lynda Hobson. "The Evolution of Response through Discussion, Drama, Writing, and Art in a Fourth Grade." *Journeying: Children Responding to Literature.* Eds. Kathleen E. Holland, Rachael A. Hungerford, and Shirley B. Ernst. Heinemann, 1993, pp. 137–150.

Wollman-Bonilla, Julie, and Barbara Werchadlo. "Literature Response Journals in a First-Grade Classroom." *Language Arts 72* (1995): 562–570.

13

Inviting Children into Literature: Classroom Libraries, Read-Alouds, and Storytelling

Grandpa took Mary Ellen inside away from the crowd. "Now, child I am going to show you what my father showed me, and his father before him," he said quietly.

He spooned the honey onto the cover of one of her books. "Taste," he said, almost in a whisper. Ellen savored the honey on her book. "There is such sweetness inside of that book too!" he said thoughtfully. "Such things . . . adventure, knowledge and wisdom. But these things do not come easily. You have to pursue them. Just like we ran after the bees to find their tree, so you must also chase these things through the pages of a book!"

—*from* The Bee Tree
by Patricia Polacco

ILLUSTRATION 13.1 A spirit of joyous adventure marks a romp through the countryside in search of a bee tree. (Cover from *The Bee Tree* by Patricia Polacco, copyright © 1993 by Patricia Polacco. Used by permission of Philomel Books, A Division of Penguin Young Readers Group, A Member of Penguin Group (USA) Inc., 345 Hudson Street, New York, NY 10014. All rights reserved.)

Develop a text set of titles that could form a classroom library by using the Children's Literature Database in Chapter 13 of the MyEducationKit for this book.

atricia Polacco's wonderful book *The Bee Tree* begins when Mary Ellen announces she is tired of reading. So, her grandfather invites her to go on an adventure—a hunt for a bee tree. In preparation, Grandpa captures several bees in a jar, and soon, Mary Ellen and Grandpa are off and running, following the first bee released from the jar. Before long, the twosome grows into a motley crew as friends and neighbors join the merry chase that ends at the bee tree. Back at Grandpa's, everyone enjoys biscuits, tea, and sweet honey. It is then that Grandpa reminds Mary Ellen that joys as sweet as honey can also be found in books.

Mary Ellen's grandfather knew the importance of motivating children to become readers. As important as it is to teach children *how* to read, that is not enough to ensure that they will *choose* to read. We know that too many children do not read. In fact, one study found that 50 percent of fifth-graders read voluntarily for four minutes a day or less, 30 percent read for two minutes a day or less, and almost 10 percent reported never reading any books during their leisure time (Fielding, Wilson, & Anderson, 1986). It's little wonder that less than half of adult Americans don't read books either (National Endowment for the Arts, 2004).

Mary Ellen's Grandpa was a wonderful teacher, and the lesson he taught Mary Ellen is one that you will want to pass on to your students: Inside the pages of a book, readers can find adventure, knowledge, and wisdom. You probably won't be able to take your students on romps through the countryside in search of bee trees. How, then, will you help them discover the joys of reading? We believe that you can best accomplish this by carefully designing your classroom, by reading aloud, by telling stories, by providing children time to read, and by demonstrating your own enthusiasm for literature.

The Classroom Library

A good classroom library is a focal area where children can go to read high-quality children's literature. Is it really necessary to have a library in the classroom, especially if your school has a well-stocked central library? We think it is essential. Estimates are that children in classrooms containing literature collections read 50 percent more than children in classrooms where literature is not available. What a difference!

Designing the Classroom Library Center

Not all library centers are equally appealing. Children beg to visit some library centers, while others stand unused. Research by Lesley Morrow (1982) has shown that there are a number of design features you can implement to create classroom libraries that children find appealing and choose to use. These features are summarized in Table 13.1.

Table 13.1   Characteristics of an Appealing Library Center

- The library center is a focal area of the classroom.
- The library center is partitioned off from the rest of the room.
- The library center is large enough to seat five or six children comfortably.
- The library center has two types of bookshelves: some that display the spines of books and others that display the covers of books.
- The library center offers comfortable seating.
- The library center offers a variety of other materials—literature-related displays, stuffed animals, and the like.
- The library center has an organizational system.
- The library center has books, books, and more books!
- The library center includes books from the school and public library.

The Center Is the Focal Area of the Classroom

Often, when you step into a classroom, your eye is drawn to one area of the room; that eye-catching part is known as "the focal area." It isn't easy to define what makes a library center a focal area; in fact, it may be all the design features taken together that do this. Whatever the explanation, it is important to create an eye-catching center that announces to students "Literature matters in this classroom." In one school, teachers created centers built around themes. One teacher built a seven-foot-high apple tree, using chicken wire covered with paper for the trunk and paper chains for the limbs. Across the tree was hung a banner that read "Don't Sit under the Apple Tree without a Good Book to Read." The apple motif was reflected throughout the center; for example, red bean-bag chairs looked just like big apples. Another teacher used a side-walk café theme and called her center "Café Escape." It was a perfect invitation to escape into a good book. To build ownership of the library center, some teachers invite their students to help them come up with the theme and the name of the library center.

The Library Is Partitioned Off

Like adults, children prefer to read in areas that are away from lots of hustle and bustle. So, it makes sense to use something—for example, bookshelves or old sofas—to partition the library off from the rest of the classroom. One teacher turned the library center into the "O.K. Corral," using mesquite posts to build a fence around it. The possibilities are limited only by your imagination.

The Seating Area Is Large Enough

To make the seating area large enough, you will have to devote a chunk of floor space to the library center. Why not just store the books in a bookcase instead and let students read at their desks? Many children don't find it comfortable to sit at their desks and read, preferring instead to lounge around in a library center. Besides, there are many times when reading becomes a social activity. Children may choose to read with a buddy or to share something they're reading. Imagine reading a riddle book without trying to stump someone! And the questions threaded throughout Steve Jenkins' and Robin Page's *What Do You Do With a Tail Like This?* simply must be posed to a friend.

The Shelving Displays Both Spines and Covers of Books

Bookshelves that display only the spines of books are necessary because they hold a lot of books. But the spines of books don't make for interesting viewing, so it's also necessary to display book covers. This is an important way of enticing children into selecting books, for many have exquisite covers (which is why most booksellers try to display as many book covers as possible).

Bookshelves that are designed to display the covers of books are expensive, and many schools can't stretch their budgets to buy them. So again, you'll need to use some ingenuity. Slightly open books can stand alone on standard shelves or on a window ledge. Chalk board trays can function as book racks. To display paperback picture books, visit a home supply center and buy a plastic chain to which clothespins are attached. Hang the chain in an accessible spot, and use the clothespins to attach the paperbacks to the chain.

The Seating Is Comfortable

It is obvious why comfortable seating is important in a library center. After all, where do you choose to read for pleasure? Sofas and upholstered chairs are far more appealing than straight-back chairs. Carpeting, beanbag chairs, pillows, and cushions are also comfortable and make the library center a cozy place for reading.

Teaching Idea 13.1
Providing Alternate Displays for Classroom Library Books

Since books should be displayed with the cover facing out in order to entice readers, and given that the cost of open-faced bookshelves is prohibitive for most classrooms, many teachers have discovered that rain gutters can serve as an alternative. Rain gutters can be purchased at home improvement centers and easily installed, allowing books to be displayed innovatively and relatively inexpensively.

Common cup hooks can be screwed into the wood under a chalk rail so that books can be clipped on with wire clothespins or various paper clips, fasteners, or clamps to hang in the empty space there. Often the space is just right for the larger "big books."

Clotheslines can be strung from one section of wall to another to hang the lighter-weight paperback books or student-published books. Either open the book midway to drape over the line or use the flat-edged, plastic-coated wire clothespins to clip the books on.

PEARSON
myeducationkit™

Go to the Extension Activities section of Chapter 13 in the MyEducationKit for your book and complete activity #1 to write a lesson helping your students learn to find book "treasures" independently.

Teacher/Librarian Partnership
Information Literacy Standards

Many states have adopted standards for students' "information literacy"—their ability to find, evaluate, use, and produce information in a variety of media. Classroom teachers are asked to make sure students meet those standards, but school librarians or media specialists are usually the prople who know the most about information literacy. Thus, they are teachers' natural allies in making sure students gain that competence. To understand what information literacy is, and what it looks like, consider the following standards that have been adopted by the school librarians and information technologists' professional associations. These standards are reflected in many states' standards for information literacy.

Standard 1: The student who is information literate accesses information efficiently and effectively

Standard 2: The student who is information literate evaluates information critically and competently

Standard 3: The student who is information literate uses information accurately and creatively

Standard 4: The student who is an independent learner is information literate and pursues information related to personal interests

Standard 5: The student who is an independent learner is information literate and appreciates literature and other creative expressions of information

Standard 6: The student who is an independent learner is information literate and strives for excellence in information seeking and knowledge generation

Standard 7: The student who is an independent learner is information literate and recognizes the importance of information to a democratic society

Standard 8: The student who contributes positively to the learning community and to society is an independent learner, is information literate, and practices ethical behavior in regard to information and information technology

Standard 9: The student who contributes positively to the learning community and to society, is an independent learner, is information literate and participates effectively in groups to pursue and generate information

To see the complete document, Information Literacy Standards for Students Learning document, visit the following Web site:

http://www.ala.org/ala/aasl/aaslproftools/information power/InformationLiteracyStandards_final.pdf

Information Literacy Standards for Student Learning, American Association of School Librarians, Association for Educational Communications and Technology. American Library Association, 1998.

Teaching Idea 13.2

Stocking the Classroom Library

Although you will probably want a set of core books to remain in your library center all year, you should rotate additional books through regularly (probably every month or so). When you rotate new books into the library center, don't just place them there without fanfare. Introduce the books one by one, helping students to make connections between the new books and ones they already know: "Here's Janet Wong's latest book; I thought you might enjoy it since we read and loved *Buzz*" or "We've been reading and writing a lot of trickster tales, so I've brought in *Tops and Bottoms* by Janet Stevens. I think you'll like the way you read this book from top to bottom—just as the title says." These brief introductions by the teacher build enthusiasm for the new selections, piquing student interest to eagerly delve into the books.

The Center Uses a Variety of Materials

Materials that highlight literature are assets in the library center. Posters showing the covers of featured books can be obtained from publishers. Displays of book jackets catch children's attention. Children's own artistic responses to literature may be an even better choice of material for decorating the library center. Younger children enjoy cuddling up with stuffed animals when they read or using flannel boards or puppets to act out stories.

The Center Uses an Organizational System

Children like organizational systems in their libraries for the same reason adults do: Organizational systems help them find books. No one particular system is best. In fact, some teachers nurture ownership of the classroom library by inviting students to create their own system. Classifying books on the basis of difficulty level can be a good approach, especially for beginning readers. Teachers can even set up systems to reinforce the literary language they want students to acquire; for example, books can be grouped by genre. In determining the best system for your classroom, consider the interests and abilities of your students as well as your instructional goals.

The Center Has Books, Books, and More Books!

Unless the library center is well stocked with a rich variety of quality books, children will not use it. The more books you have, the richer the literature context you create in your classroom; so you will want to have at least four to eight books per child (Fractor, Woodruff, Martinez, & Teale, 1993). Unfortunately, school budgets rarely stretch far enough to allow teachers to buy books for classroom libraries. However, some teachers persuade their administrators to let them order children's literature instead of reading workbooks. Even if your school provides monetary assistance for purchasing books, you'll probably still need to find creative ways of supplementing the collection. If your students have the financial means to order books from book clubs, the class can earn bonus points that can be cashed in for books. Secondhand book stores can also be a good source of inexpensive copies of worthwhile books.

Many public libraries allow teachers to check out large numbers of books for extended periods of time. In addition, you need to coordinate with your school librarian to make sure that some of the school's library collection circulates in and out of your classroom library.

Stocking the Classroom Library with Books

The *kind* of books the classroom library holds is even more important than the number of books. While in this section we offer guidelines for selecting books for the library center, the lists of Recommended Books found at the end of chapters in this text will serve as a good resource for identifying particular books.

High-Quality Literature

You owe it to your students to stock the classroom library with the highest-quality literature. Take care to choose for your center books that have distinctly crafted literary elements. Consider books such as Deborah Wiles's *Love, Ruby Lavender* for its wonderful characterization and Louise Erdrich's *The Birchbark House* for its distinctive setting. Include books with significant themes, such as Christopher Paul Curtis's *Elijah of Buxton,* and don't forget books with exquisite language, such as Cynthia Rylant's *When I Was Young in the Mountains* or Karen Hesse's *Come On, Rain!* When selecting books to motivate voluntary reading, pay special attention to the story line. A strong story line sells itself: Well-paced, action-oriented stories are a must. One such book for younger children is *How I Became a Pirate,* in which a ship full of pirates lands on the beach and the pirates invite young Jeremy Jacobs to join them on their voyage. In no time at all, Jeremy takes to the rollicking life of the pirate—a life in which no one has to mind their manners or eat vegetables or wear pajamas or do anything unless they want to! Older children will be captivated by *Inkheart,* in which young Meggie's father brings the malevolent characters of a book to life through a magical read-aloud. Soon, Meggie and her father are swept up in danger and intrigue, as they are pursued and captured by the evil henchmen who have stepped out of the book and into the real world.

Children also love books with humorous and unusual story lines. In *Click, Clack, Moo: Cows That Type,* the cows discover a typewriter, which they use to type notes making various demands on Farmer Brown. When the farmer refuses to comply, the cows go on strike. Stories with unusual formats and distinctive illustrations make good additions to the library center. For example, *Dear Mrs. LaRue: Letters from Obedience School* is written as a series of letters composed by a disgruntled dog that has been sent away to obedience school. The illustrations in which the letters of complaint are embedded tell a far different tale than do the letters! A useful resource for identifying books with "kid appeal" is the Children's Choice list that appears annually in the October issue of *The Reading Teacher,* a journal published by the International Reading Association.

A Variety of Genres and Formats

Be sure to include as many genres as possible in your library center: fantasy, folktales, contemporary realistic fiction, historical fiction, informational books, and poetry. Also find room for those odds and ends for which there is no clear genre niche: predictable

ILLUSTRATION 13.2 The barnyard is soon out of control when the cows learn to type and enter into negotiations with the farmer. (Reprinted with the permission of Simon & Schuster Books for Young Readers, an imprint of Simon & Schuster Children's Publishing Division from *Click, Clack, Moo: Cows That Type* by Doreen Cronin, pictures by Betsy Lewin. Illustrations copyright © 2000 Betsy Lewin.)

Technology in Practice 13.1

Visit **teachingbooks.net** to learn how Betsy Lewin, the illustrator of *Click, Clack, Moo: Cows That Type*, creates humor through her illustrations.

Top Shelf 13.2

Humorous Picture Books

Milo's Hat Trick by Jon Agee

Miss Nelson Is Missing! by Harry Allard

Cloudy with a Chance of Meatballs by Judi Barrett

Strega Nona by Tomie DePaola

The Two Sillies by Mary Ann Hoberman

The Wolf's Chicken Stew by Keiko Kasza

The Emperor's Old Clothes by Kathryn Lasky

Flossie and the Fox by Patricia McKissack

Mice and Beans by Pam Muñoz Ryan

Don't Let the Pigeon Drive the Bus by Mo Willems

Go to the Extension Activities section of Chapter 13 in the MyEducationKit for your book and complete activity #3 to consider the difference between reading level and interest level.

Top Shelf 13.3

Graphic Novels

City of Light, City of Dark by Avi

The Courageous Princess by Rod Espinosa

Babymouse: Puppy Love by Jennifer L. Holm and Matthew Holm

Pinky and Stinky by James Kochalka

The Legend of Hong Kil Dong: The Robin Hood of Korea by Anne Sibley O'Brien

Spiral-Bound by Aaron Renier

Owly: A Time to Be Brave by Andy Runton

Scary Godmother by Jill Thompson

books, joke and riddle books, and lift-the-flap and pop-up books. You will also want to include both picture books and chapter books, as well as books written in the increasingly popular format of the graphic novel. Top Shelf 13.3 features graphic novels that would be a good addition to your center. The more choices you provide for students, the more they'll read.

Student Interests

Just as you have particular reading preferences and reading interests, so will your students. Take the time to discover those interests. Talk to students about the books they are reading. Have them keep logs of their voluntary reading in which they record the author and title of each book they read. Monitor the logs and fill the classroom library with books related to your students' reading interests. Table 13.2 suggests some typical interests of students in different grades.

A Variety of Reading Levels

If a child believes that a book will be too challenging to read, in all likelihood she won't give it a try. To motivate children to do lots of reading, it's critical that you provide books with which they feel comfortable. Anticipate a wide range of reading levels in your classroom. A typical second-grade classroom may have some students who are beginning readers and others who are reading at a sixth-grade level. The mythical classroom of "grade-level readers" is just that—a myth. By watching students, you can discern whether they are comfortable with the books in your classroom library.

Kindergartners who have not yet learned to read conventionally also need books with which they can feel comfortable. Kindergartners are far more likely to "pretend read" predictable books, such as Michael Rosen's *We're Going on a Bear Hunt.*

Beginning readers—whether they are in first grade or higher grades— respond well to predictable books. They also need picture books with limited text and lots of illustration cues. Mo Willems' series about Elephant and Piggie is perfect for children just beginning to read. As young readers become more proficient, they will enjoy books with longer and somewhat more demanding vocabulary such as Keiko Kasza's *The Wolf's Chicken Stew* and Mary Ann Hoberman's *You Read to Me, I'll Read to You.* Beginning readers soon graduate to beginning chapter books, which are typically somewhat longer than picture books, but contain minimal text per page and offer extensive illustration support (Roser, Martinez, McDonnold, & Fuhrken, 2004). Examples of beginning chapter books include Cynthia Rylant's *Henry and Mudge* series and James Marshall's comical series about Fox.

More challenging picture books for developing readers also have a place in the classroom library, books like *The Great Fuzz Frenzy* in which a great, fuzzy, round thing lands in the middle of a prairie dog town. Children who are reading these more demanding picture books with fluency should also be invited to read what have been called "transitional chapter books." These chapter books, which range from approximately 60 to 100 pages, have a significant number of words per page, offer minimal illustration support, and generally contain a main plot line as well as secondary plot lines (Graves & Liang, 2004; Roser, Martinez, McDonnold, & Fuhrken, 2004). Books that fit this description include those in Lois Lowry's Gooney Bird series and Paula Danzinger's Amber Brown series.

Table 13.2	Children's Interests at Different Grade Levels
Grades	**Interests**
Grades 1 and 2	Animals, nature, fantasy, child characters, general and science informational materials, history
Grades 3 and 4	Nature, animals, adventure, familiar experiences
Grades 5 and 6	History, science, mystery, adventure, travel, animal stories, fairy tales
Grades 7 and 8	Science fiction, mystery, adventure, biography, history, animals, sports, romance, religion, career stories, comedy

Read-Alouds

Children are especially likely to select books that have been introduced or read to them when they are choosing books for independent reading (Hickman, 1981). They are likely to feel more confident picking up a book they have heard read aloud.

Content Units

The library center can be a tool to support and extend children's learning in other areas. For example, if you are doing a unit on the civil rights movement, stock the library with books such as Kathleen Krull's *Harvesting Hope: The Story of Cesar Chavez* and Doreen Rappaport's *Martin's Big Words: The Life of Dr. Martin Luther King, Jr.* Just as special collections within the library center support students' learning in the content areas, so also students' content studies support their voluntary reading by building background and interest. (See Chapter 15 for a detailed discussion of literature-based content units.)

Multicultural Books

Including multicultural literature in the library is important for all children, but especially for those from diverse backgrounds, who need to see themselves in the books they read. A Latino American child once said to one of us, "They don't have people like us in books." Fortunately, more and more multicultural literature is becoming available, and it is the responsibility of every teacher to ensure that students have ample opportunities to meet characters like themselves in literature.

Some teachers assume that it is not necessary to bring multicultural literature into their classrooms because none of their students are children of ethnic diversity. Nothing could be farther from the truth. It is important for children of the mainstream culture to see children from diverse backgrounds involved in situations both similar to and different from their own. Schools are preparing children to live in a diverse society, and it is important for them to understand this society. (See Chapter 4 for a complete discussion of these issues.)

Audiobooks can be a wonderful means of making multicultural literature accessible to children from other cultures. (Audiobooks and a CD player with headphones can even be part of the library center.) When multicultural literature is set in a different place, features dialects, or includes characters whose lives are very unfamiliar to children, then children may avoid these selections—unless they are mediated by an adult. In effect, a well-narrated audiobook helps to mediate the story for listeners when the narrator selects appropriate tones, brings character voices to life, and makes dialects accessible. Fortunately, there are numerous quality multicultural audiobooks on the market today that offer authentic listening experiences to children. (See Top Shelf 13.4 on p. 419.)

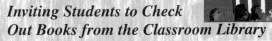

Teaching Idea 13.3
Inviting Students to Check Out Books from the Classroom Library

Many teachers make the books from their classroom library available for checkout by their students. To encourage students' accountability and responsibility, teachers stick a library pocket and its corresponding card in each of the books from the classroom library. Each student then has his or her own pocket posted on a wall or bulletin board in the room into which the card from a book is inserted in order to check it out. Commercially made number pocket charts with clear pockets also work nicely for the class checkout system. Students can return the card to the book pocket when they return the book and replace the book in the classroom library. This also helps the students find out who has a particular book when they are searching for it.

Technology in Practice 13.2
Setting Up a Student Book Referral Service

You can set up a student book referral service by inviting students to record the books they have read and their responses to those books in a database maintained on the classroom computer or in a district network folder for your classroom that is accessible to the students. The entry for each book should include title, author/illustrator, genre, summary, and response to book. A computerized database will give students great flexibility in selecting books. If they want to find a good fantasy to read, they can simply call up the category "Fantasy." If they want recommendations for books by a particular author, the computer will sort books by authors' names.

Technology in Practice 13.3

Visit **teachingbooks.net** to hear Mary Ann Hoberman read from *You Read to Me, I'll Read to You.* Listen for the way in which the author brings the text to life in her read-aloud.

Reading Aloud to Children

In its report *Becoming a Nation of Readers,* the Commission on Reading declared, "There is no substitute for a teacher who reads children good stories" (Anderson, Hiebert, Scott, & Wilkinson, 1984). That is our sentiment exactly! Research indicates that reading to children

Go to the Extension Activities section of Chapter 13 in the MyEducationKit for your book and complete activity #2 to design a lesson that introduces students to a new genre.

Technology in Practice 13.4

Many teachers currently maintain their own websites and fill them with lessons and photos from their classrooms, schedules, calendars and assignments. Consider posting your students' comments and reviews about the books they are reading in class on your school district website. Scan their illustrations to accompany their responses. Link a video recording of your students sharing their book reviews in the style of Reading Rainbow. Link your students' multimedia presentations about the books they have read over a particular unit of study. Share your students' storytelling via your district website. Posting student work (with parental permission of course) is yet another vehicle for publishing student work. The audience has just expanded.

has many positive outcomes (Teale, 2003). First, it whets their appetite for reading. Young children who are read to discover the rewards of reading and are motivated to learn to read. Second, literature nurtures children's language development and comprehension abilities. Through read-alouds, children become acquainted with the cadences of written language and discover how print functions, especially if the adult reader draws attention to print conventions. Finally, through read-alouds, children acquire the real-world knowledge that is so critical for success in school.

Read-alouds support children's literary development: Children are introduced to conventional story openers ("Once upon a time"); they discover literary devices such as the transformation motif; and they meet stock characters such as the sly fox and the tricky coyote. Read-alouds are the ideal vehicle for encouraging children to think in response to literature, and when discussion is a part of the read-aloud experience, children learn how to participate in literary conversations.

Like the Commission on Reading, we believe that read-alouds are an essential instructional activity for children of all ages. Although older children may have acquired a basic understanding of how print functions and how stories are structured, their language, reading, and literary development must continue. Also, there are many books that developing readers do not have the skill to read on their own but will delight in if the books are read aloud to them. In fact, by the time most children are able to read books such as *Winnie-the-Pooh* and *The Scarecrow and His Servant* on their own, the books are no longer age-appropriate.

Research on Read-Aloud Programs

James V. Hoffman, Nancy L. Roser, and Jennifer Battle (1993) conducted a comprehensive study on read-aloud programs in the United States. The results were disappointing. Reports

Issue to Consider

Do Computerized Reading Management Programs Have a Place in the Literacy Program?

In recent years, computerized reading management programs (CRMP) have proliferated in American schools. These systems typically consist of increased access to leveled trade books, additional time for recreational reading, computer software with tests on the books included in the program, and a database that manages students' reading records. Perhaps the best known and most widely used of these programs is Accelerated Reader, a program that awards students points for reading that can be exchanged for prizes.

Advocates of these programs see a number of advantages (Rogers, 2003). First, they argue that CRMPs foster wide reading, which in turn promotes better reading comprehension. Because the books in the system are leveled (that is the difficulty level of the book is identified), students

will be able to choose books at an appropriate level for their recreational reading. Further, advocates believe that the tests that accompany the books provide students with immediate feedback about their own comprehension. In addition, they maintain that these computerized programs provide teachers with invaluable support because teachers are able to carefully monitor their students' recreational reading. That is, teachers will know how much their students are reading and how well their students are reading.

Opponents of computerized reading management programs agree that increased access to books is important as is additional time for reading. However, they argue that these ends can easily be achieved without purchasing expensive computer programs. Further, they note that research supporting the success of CRMPs is very contradictory (Krashen, 2003). Those who argue against CRMPs observe that the tests accompanying the books focus on unimportant story details and hence encourage students to read for these details rather than important ideas. Opponents also express concern about the use of extrinsic rewards such as prizes or points for reading. They argue that we must nurture lifelong readers who are intrinsically motivated to read and that prizes and points actually work against this goal. When the rewards are no longer offered, students are likely not to choose to read.

What do you think?

from 537 classrooms revealed that 74 percent of teachers read to their students on a given day. However, there was a steady decline in the percentage of teachers reading aloud with each successive grade level. In kindergarten, 84 percent of the teachers read to their students, but in fifth grade, only 64 percent did so. There is clearly room for improvement.

Teachers at every grade level should read aloud at least once a day. All too often, teachers at upper grade levels believe that their students should be reading books on their own—which is true, of course. However, this is not an either/or situation. We hope teachers will recognize the special value of read-alouds. Another argument made by some intermediate-level teachers is that they have too much content to cover to devote time to reading aloud to students. One way of dealing with this time restriction is by "double dipping"—that is, using read-alouds to achieve both literary goals and curricular goals. If the class is studying the Civil War, then read aloud Patricia Polacco's *Pink and Say* and Barbara Kerley's *Walt Whitman: Words for America. A Company of Fools* or *Crispin* would make excellent read-alouds for a unit on medieval times.

Hoffman, Roser, and Battle (1993) also found that the nature of the typical read-aloud session was not what it should be. The teachers who responded to their survey reported read-alouds lasting only ten to twenty minutes, with minimal discussion following. In addition, the literature selections were typically unrelated to a unit of study, and generally no response activity followed the read-aloud. The researchers cautioned that this "typical read-aloud" was *not* a model, arguing that a daily read-aloud of at least twenty minutes should be scheduled in a specific time slot. Instead of selecting unrelated literature, Hoffman and his colleagues call for organizing read-aloud programs around units. After all, mature readers often read books related in some way to others that they have read, and literature units encourage students to do this. The investigators also questioned the adequacy of five minutes of literature discussion. Sustained conversation that can enrich the understanding of all participants does not occur in five minutes.

Top Shelf 13.4

Multicultural Audiobooks

Bud, Not Buddy by Christopher Paul Curtis

The Tales of Uncle Remus: The Adventures of Brer Rabbit by Julius Lester

Esperanza Rising by Pam Muñoz Ryan

Baseball in April by Gary Soto

The Skirt by Gary Soto

The Book Thief by Markus Zusak

Go to the Extension Activities section of Chapter 13 in the MyEducationKit for your book and complete activity #4 to select a book that evokes physical movement.

The Read-Aloud Experience

The read-aloud experience is one of the highlights of the school day for most children. This is especially true when the teacher carefully selects each book and spends time preparing to read it aloud.

When to Read Aloud

Read-alouds shouldn't be used merely to fill time between activities. By scheduling a read-aloud each day, you communicate to students that this is a valued activity. Besides, there is the all-too-real danger that on many days there won't be any extra time between activities.

At lower grade levels, teachers should read aloud several times a day, especially if their students have had only limited experiences with stories before entering school. Some children enter school having listened to thousands of storybook readings; others have not been read to at all. The latter children especially deserve a rich read-aloud program.

Selecting Books for Read-Alouds

Much of what was said about selecting books for the classroom library also applies to selecting read-aloud stories. First and foremost, select high-quality books with strong plots and interesting crafting. We especially encourage you to choose books that deal with significant themes, for these books have the potential to evoke insightful discussions. A picture book such as Deborah Wiles's *Freedom Summer* explores the friendship of two boys—one white and one African American—who eagerly anticipate swimming together at the town pool for the first time ever, only to witness the town's decision to close the pool rather than integrate it. This is the kind of book that offers rich fodder for conversation focused on issues of social justice.

A read-aloud becomes a special time for young children when they can gather close to the adult who is sharing the story.

Teaching Idea 13.4

Preparing a Read-Aloud

Prepare to read aloud *The Ghost-Eye Tree* by Bill Martin, Jr. In the story, a mother asks her son and daughter to walk at night to the end of the town to fetch a bucket of milk. The trip to town is uneventful, even though the children must pass the dreaded ghost-eye tree. However, on the walk home, the children, loaded down with a full bucket of milk, are certain that they see the ghost eye. This story is full of drama, tense moments, and changing emotions. Practice reading it aloud. Because there is so much dialogue between the siblings, you might want to try out different voices for the brother and sister. Vary the pace of your reading. Try reading faster as the children approach the tree. When the siblings see the ghost eye, pick up your pace even more. How might the children sound as they exchange good-natured jibes with each other? How do they feel when they spot the ghost eye? What emotions does the brother experience when his sister announces she will retrieve his lost hat? Now try reading the story to a group of children.

It is important to read books from a variety of genres, including poetry and informational books. Remember, your preferences might not be the same as those of your students. One first-grade teacher decided to let her students select the daily read-aloud books. The girls selected the same kinds of books their teacher had been selecting—picture storybooks—but much to her surprise, the boys overwhelmingly favored informational books, a genre from which she had never read aloud.

Select age-appropriate books. There are no firm and fast guidelines about which books are appropriate for particular grade levels. In fact, many books appeal to students across grade levels. Nonetheless, as a general rule, simpler, shorter books are more appropriate for both younger children and those with limited literature experience. However, this does not mean that picture books are for younger children and chapter books are for older ones. Many picture books, such as Chris Van Allsburg's *The Widow's Broom,* Anthony Browne's *Voices in the Park,* and Jean Merrill's *The Girl Who Loved Caterpillars,* are wonderful for older children. Conversely, many younger children enjoy listening to chapter books such as Ann Cameron's *The Stories Julian Tells* and E. B. White's *Charlotte's Web.*

Preparing to Read Aloud

To make read-alouds a success, remember one cardinal rule: Never read aloud a book that you have not previously read. In fact, you really should read a book out loud to yourself or to someone else before reading it to children, because sometimes a book you loved when you read it silently just doesn't flow when it is read aloud. If you plan to read a book with unfamiliar words or words from a language in which you are not fluent—Gary Soto's *Chato's Kitchen* for example—it is especially important to practice pronunciations prior to reading aloud.

In preparing for a read-aloud, thoughtfully read the book you select (see Table 13.3). Look for difficulties the story presents that might interfere with comprehension. Be alert to stopping points where you might invite predictions or discussion. Also, be sure to monitor your own responses to the story. The things you notice or wonder about are worth remembering because these spontaneous responses can become conversation starters after the reading.

If you have never read the story aloud before, it makes sense to practice pacing and expression before reading it to an audience. What feelings and moods can you convey with your voice? Is a character surprised? Does a character become angry? Is a character especially wise or silly or confused? Get to know the characters so that you can bring them to life. Don't be shy. Try out different voices and even facial expressions or gestures. And if you are reading a picture book, don't forget to practice holding the book so that the children can see the illustrations as you read. The result of all this preparation is likely to be an engaging read-aloud experience for your students.

Table 13.3   How to Prepare for a Read-Aloud

- Anticipate difficulties the story may present to students, and prepare to help them through those difficulties.
- Watch for interesting places to stop reading and invite children's predictions or discussion.
- Heed your own responses to the story as one basis for after-reading discussion.
- Practice varying your reading pace to highlight particular portions of the story.
- Become acquainted with the characters and changing moods of the story so that you can read with appropriate expression.
- Try out different voices for different characters.

Introducing the Story

Before introducing the story, gather the students together for the read-aloud. If there is room, pull chairs into a circle, and if a picture book is to be read aloud, situate all the children so that they can see the illustrations. Keep your introduction to the book in proper perspective: Time and attention should be devoted primarily to the read-aloud and to subsequent discussion. Nonetheless, an introduction offers you an opportunity to help children expand their store of literary understandings and allows you to "prime" them for the book.

In addition to introducing the story (or poem) by title, remember to mention the name of the author (and, when appropriate, the illustrator). This is an excellent way of helping students begin to develop a sense of what authors and illustrators do. Also, mention other books written by the same author, especially those with which the children are likely to be familiar. Mentioning the book's genre is a way of gently introducing children to some of the language of literature.

Before starting to read the story, you might need to build background. This may be especially important for an informational book. If some concepts necessary for understanding the book are not adequately explained within the book, pay attention to these concepts in your introduction. To set expectations for the book, you might want to invite children to make predictions based on the title or the cover illustration. Finally, if the book is being read as part of a literature unit, mention books that you have read previously.

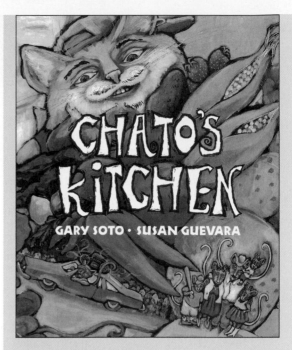

ILLUSTRATION 13.3 *Chato's Kitchen* is a humorous animal fantasy with a distinctly multicultural flavor. (Cover from *Chato's Kitchen* by Gary Soto, illustrated by Susan Guevara, copyright © 1995 by Susan Guevara, illustrations. Used by permission of G.P. Putnam's Sons, A Division of Penguin Young Readers Group, A Member of Penguin Group (USA) Inc., 345 Hudson Street, New York, NY 10014. All rights reserved.)

Reading the Story

When you finally read the story, use everything you tried out in preparing for the read-aloud. Vary your reading pace to reflect changes in mood and emotion, read expressively, and use different voices when appropriate.

Some teachers believe that stories should be read straight through without any interruptions so as not to distract from the story line. However, we encourage you to feel free to interrupt the reading of a story to talk with your students, especially younger ones. Older children are able to hold on to their responses until the read-aloud is complete, but younger children often forget their observations if required to hold on to them until the read-aloud is finished. So, if a child interrupts to ask a question or share a response, honor that interruption. Children are also likely to interrupt when you reach a point in the story that begs for predictions. Or, there might be times when you need to guide students through a tricky part of the story or briefly fill in information that is important to understanding the story. Finally, when you read predictable books, children enjoy joining in on repeated phrases.

After Reading

The read-aloud experience should not be over as soon as you've read the final page of the story. The literary transaction will continue after the reading if you provide ample opportunity for children to discuss the story. Chapter 14 focuses on literary discussion.

Pictures are an important source of the support young children need for their first story experiences.

Stories and Storytelling

Children's literature starts with the telling of stories. For thousands of years before the first story was written down, humans told stories and recited poems. The thousands of years of human experience with stories (compared to a little over a century of mass literacy) surely adapted the human mind to storytelling in a special way and nourished

Teaching Idea 13.5

Setting Up a Book Recommendation Venue

Students are happy to share their opinions about the books they read. Invite their input on what some teachers refer to as a "graffiti wall." Legitimize that desire to leave one's mark that seems to be as old as cave drawings. Simply tear off a long section of bulletin board paper and invite students to write the title of the book they wish to recommend directly on the paper. They should include their comments about the book and sign the response. The routine activity of lining up can become a learning experience when the "wall" is displayed in the hallway. Students will linger over their peers' latest reads.

an art of storytelling that still moves listeners deeply. This is why teachers must make storytelling a regular feature in the classroom.

Storytelling: The Tenacious Art

Many cultures have specific storytelling styles and rituals. In Jamaica today, a storyteller still begins a session by asking "Cric?" This means, "Do you want a story?" If the people want one, they answer "Cric," and the storyteller begins. But if they say "Crac," the storyteller passes on to find others willing to hear the tale. Japanese storytellers use *kamishibai,* a large set of pictures with text on the back; these pictures are presented in a box that looks like a traditional theater. Whatever the style, storytelling has never passed out of vogue, even with the proliferation of books. In fact, a number of recent children's books celebrate the power of storytelling, including Allen Say's **Kamishibai Man** and Jane Kurtz's **The Storyteller's Beads.**

Because storytelling is so active—from the point of view of both tellers and listeners—it is an especially appropriate activity to do with younger children. Storytelling is also appropriate with reluctant readers because it offers a bridge to literature. A wise teacher used to advocate telling stories to students. "Most children," said Edmund Henderson, "will come running when you read a story. But if one does not, tell the story instead. The told story is the older form. Hence it will have more appeal." Telling a story allows you to look your students in the eye and invite them to help you bring the story to life.

Storytelling exercises the often-neglected art of using the voice. The teller must provide the excitement, drama, and cadences that pull listeners in and play their emotions like a violin. To tell a story well, the storyteller must decide how the characters sound, where the suspenseful parts are, and what parts should be slow or fast, loud or soft.

Children enjoy telling stories, too, and there are many good reasons why they should. In this section, we will present ways to choose, practice, and tell stories, and most of our advice will apply to both the adult and the child storyteller.

Common Story Types: Personal Tales to Tall Tales

Stories differ in the amount of effort they require to learn or improvise. They also differ in the kind of attention they require of listeners and the sorts of participation they invite. These points will be made clear as we talk about different types of stories. Story types vary from personal tales, which usually evoke more inventiveness from the teller but offer less form for guidance, to already-heard stories, which offer more form but pose a challenge because they must be learned—they cannot be improvised.

Personal Stories

Personal stories are anecdotes from your own experience—about a camping trip, about being lost, about raising a pet. They can be rambling, especially if you haven't honed them down through practice. That's okay, especially when you're giving an example for children to copy when they do the telling. You can work with personal stories over time to give them more shape.

Family Stories

Family stories are true (well, maybe slightly embellished) stories about someone in your family. Because these stories may have been passed along through several generations, they are usually better formed than personal stories. Family stories often portray what people think is funniest about themselves and their relatives. They can be a lot like stories that are written down; the Ramona Quimby stories come to mind, as do many of Patricia Polacco's stories. After all, writers come from families.

Friend-of-a-Friend Stories

Friend-of-a-friend stories, or "urban legends," are accounts of bizarre events in a community, told by people who believe that they might have happened. When you try to check them out, though, it always turns out they happened to someone the teller almost knows—"a friend of a friend."

Friend-of-a-friend stories are close to the folktale tradition. In his fascinating collections, the folklorist Jan de Brunvard has compiled urban legends from newspapers, radio, and personal accounts of hundreds of people. Although the tales are generally recounted breathlessly, as if they just happened last week, de Brunvard (1981) has found variations that are hundreds of years old. For example, the story of the vanishing hitchhiker, told in contemporary Georgia, has a song version, "The Phantom 409." Some years ago in West Africa, Frances Temple heard a version of the story from a nervous nun who claimed to have been in the jeep when the hitchhiker disappeared.

Ghost Stories

Ghost stories usually lie somewhere in between friend-of-a-friend stories and folktales. Alvin Schwartz's popular collection *Scary Stories to Tell in the Dark* was collected from folktale sources. Some teachers find ghost stories good fare to tell to middle-grade children or for them to learn and tell. If the children are to do the telling, prepare to screen their choices.

Jokes and Riddles

Jokes and riddles aren't stories exactly, but they are so engaging that telling them in front of a group is good practice for children. Also, they are short enough that many children can participate in a single storytelling session.

Folktales and Fables

Folktales, the traditional stories we discussed in Chapter 7, provide excellent fare for storytelling. Because they were passed down orally, folktales have been pared down to their essentials, which makes them well formed and memorable, but this also leaves room for embellishments by the storyteller. Fables, those brief instructive tales that end with a moral, can also be fun to tell, especially when you stop and ask students to guess the moral.

Myths

Myths range from serious creation stories, such as the Iroquois tale of Da-Ga-Na-We-Da, to the lighter pour quoi tales that explain various natural phenomena, such as the African tale *Why Mosquitoes Buzz in People's Ears* retold by Verna Aardema. Teachers should have no trouble finding collections from many cultures that offer abundant fare suitable for storytelling.

Legends and Tall Tales

Legends are stories about famous cultural heroes that usually have a core of truth to them. The characters may be real; for example, George Washington is the subject of a number of legends, as is the Mexican revolutionary figure, Pancho Villa. Legends make good fare for oral telling, especially in conjunction with social studies units.

One or two steps removed from legends are tall tales, which tell about exaggerated fictitious characters. These characters usually have qualities that real people like to claim for themselves. For example, Paul Bunyan didn't exist, but lumberjacks like to be thought of as tough.

Learning Stories to Tell

As Margaret Read MacDonald (1993) says, it is certainly easiest to learn a story from another teller. A story well told is so much more than the words; it's the voices of the characters, the pauses and dramatic flourishes, the joy and sorrow and excitement and dread, all

Ask the Author . . .   Jim Aylesworth

Favorite Books as a Child

- *Rudolph the Red-Nosed Reindeer* by Robert L. May

  The first book that I remember really loving was a Christmas gift in the mid-1940s. I think my mom read it to me every day until June or July.

- *The Adventures of Jimmy Skunk* by Thornton W. Burgess

  Later, I learned to love the animal stories written by Thornton Burgess. I read them all, Jimmy Skunk being my favorite because we shared the name. I recently reread some of them and found them great still!

- Roy Rogers comic books

  I was also a big fan of comic books. They were ten cents apiece back then, and I had a large collection. Roy Rogers was my favorite hero.

What advice would you offer to novice storytellers? Know what children like!

When using stories with children, you will do well to know what children like about stories. Once you know, then simply choose to use stories based on that information. It's as simple as that. My best advice to you, the novice teacher/storyteller, is, Know what children like!

It just makes sense, don't you think?

And the best way to learn what children like is to read lots of stories, tell lots of stories, to lots and lots of children. And of course, for you teachers, this will very soon be a part of your daily lives, just as it was for me. You will read or tell stories to your children every school day. Pay attention when you are doing it. Watch their eyes. You will know when they are liking what you are doing. When things are going well, make a note of what they are responding to. Try then to find similar elements in other stories. Over time, you will create a list of things that children especially like. It will be very useful information.

At this point, I know that many of you who are reading these words have not yet had a chance to get started on your lists. You are beginners. Well, don't worry too much. It was the same for me once. No one is born with information, and it will take a while to gather it. In the meantime though, you can lean on me a little, if you want. Use my list as a starter, maybe, and add to it as you see fit. For the sake of your children, I'd be proud to help you. So get out your yellow highlighter and make some special notations.

Here is my list of things that children especially like about stories:

1. Children like sound, the louder the better. Any old noise will do. Children like onomatopoeia. Children like sound.

2. Even better, children like the more melodic sounds of our language that we call poetry and music. Children like poetry and music. They like rhythm, rhyme, repetitions of sounds. Children like alliteration, assonance.

3. Children like animals.

4. Children like other children.

5. Children like color.

6. Children like pretending, especially silly, ridiculous, absurd pretending. In other words, children like fantasy stories.

7. Children like gross stuff. If it's yucky or gooey or smelly, they will like it. Can't tell you why.

You will find other things to add, I'm sure of it, but these will get you started. Think of me maybe, and give my best to those sweet kids of yours.

Jim Aylesworth *taught first grade for twenty-five years and has been writing for children for almost as long. His recent books include* The Gingerbread Man, Through the Night, Jim Aylesworth's Book of Bedtime Stories, Aunt Pitty Patty's Piggy, *and* The Full Belly Bowl. *He says, "Writing children's books is my way of being the teacher beyond the walls of my classroom for children that I may never know." He lives in Chicago, Illinois.* ■

communicated by the storyteller. If you have a chance to listen to a storyteller who can show you all those things, you're way ahead. If you can't find a live storyteller, you can watch videotapes of live performances.

Learning the story is the first task of the storyteller. Most storytellers agree that the way to prepare a story is not to memorize it. Memorizing will make a story sound flat or set the teller up for a mental block during the telling. Besides, the beauty of a told story is that it is forever invented.

But a story is not random either. A well-told story is crisp, with the beginning, ending, and repeated parts told just so. How does a storyteller achieve this crispness without memorizing the story? Here's one way.

Get some index cards, and read through the story four times, each time with a different purpose:

1. On the first pass, read for the sense of the whole tale.
2. Next time, pay close attention to the different events in the story. Jot down each event in a few words on a separate card.
3. On the third read-through, pay close attention to the characters. On a separate card, name each character and make notes about the way she or he should sound and move. Note any gestures that you want to associate with each character.
4. Read through the story again and jot down the beginning and ending, as well as any repeated phrases. This is important. If you know exactly how a story begins, you can launch into it confidently. If you know exactly how the story ends, you can wrap it up crisply. So memorize both. In between, pay attention to repeated phrases (such as "Little pig, little pig, let me come in. Not by the hair on my chinny-chin-chin") or repeated patterns of actions.

Practice the Story

Once you have the cards prepared and arranged in the order you find most useful, tell the story repeatedly (to yourself, to a friend, to your dog) until you can tell it confidently without looking at the cards. Later, when you tell the story, keep the cards unobtrusively in your lap—but have them handy in case you begin to forget.

If children are learning stories, have them pair up and tell their stories to each other. Also have them tell the story at home a certain number of times as they learn it (say, three times a day).

Refine the Story

Once you have the gist of the story down, the fun part begins. This is when you refine the characterization, the gestures, the pauses, and other dynamics of narration.

Determine the sorts of word choices appropriate to the story you're telling. A story in a traditional setting requires the teller to say "a certain boy" or "There was an old woman who" instead of "this guy" or "this old lady." If your story is an Old English folktale, perhaps you want to sound modest and precise. If it's a Western tale from Texas, your language should be relaxed, expansive, and given to exaggeration.

You don't need to describe the characters fully to the audience, but you should have a clear idea of what they are like so that your voice and gestures will convey this information. You should decide the following for each main character in your story:

- How short or tall is she or he? How heavy? How does the character's size make her or him move?

- Is this character dignified? Sly? Lazy? Vain? How do these traits affect the way he or she talks?

- What is the character's usual mood?

If you're helping children learn storytelling, ask these questions and follow up with activities that will give the children practice in developing their characters. Have each child "get into" one of his or her characters as they all parade around the room. Call on several characters to introduce themselves in their own voices—and say what's on their minds.

Visualize the setting. When Jack steps out onto the clouds at the top of the beanstalk, how is his footing? How does he step? When he gets to the giant's castle, how big is the door? How does Jack knock on it? Having thought through such details will enable you to use voices and gestures that will help the audience to visualize—and believe—the setting.

Practice gestures. As a storyteller says the wolf's lines in "The Three Little Pigs," she or he will probably make a fist and pound on

Stories can be brought to life via classroom dramatizations.

Will Hart/PhotoEdit

Technology in Practice 13.5

Visit some of the many websites on story-telling in order to better familiarize your-self with the possibilities of storytelling and discover the professionals who want to share their craft with you and your students. You will find explanations of what storytelling really is and what it involves. These websites typically offer lesson plans for teachers as well as story libraries. Recommended books and other resources are frequently available for purchase. Articles and other links are accessible. Some websites have curriculum exchanges where teachers can post ideas they have used in their own classrooms.

Visit the following storytelling websites:

Aaron Shepherd's Storytelling Page at
   www.aaronshep.com/storytelling

www.storyarts.org by Heather Frost

www.storynet.com from the National Storytelling Network

www.storycraft.com

an imaginary door. When the storyteller says a pig's lines, she or he may pull at imaginary chin whiskers. A few gestures like these help the story, but too many will distract. Use only gestures that will give a hint of the setting, provide the signature of a character, or display a strong emotion.

Also practice facial expressions. Boston storyteller Jay O'Callahan says that storytelling is the theater of the face. Gestures are important, but facial expressions and voices convey most of the story's meaning. Storytellers must learn to make facial expressions that project the way their characters feel: innocent, cunning, frightened, and so on.

If you're working with children, have them stand in a circle. One student decides on a facial expression and, without identifying the expression, "passes" it on to the next, who duplicates it and passes it on in turn. This continues until the expression has gone completely around. Take time out to debrief: Did the students understand the expression correctly? Then another student "passes" a different expression.

The storyteller's voice must be both loud enough to carry to the back of the audience and expressive enough to portray the characters in the tale. For practice, say the line "Twinkle, twinkle, little star" in the voice of each of these characters:

- a pitiful child with a big problem who wants to make an important wish
- a mean giant who is demanding that the star twinkle
- a crafty wizard who is making a magic charm

Many stories are told in the dialect of a region or of an ethnic group, and, after watching storytellers on television, you might believe that using dialect is an important part of the storyteller's art. As a general rule, though, if a dialect is not yours, don't use it. It is very easy to insult other people if you appear to make fun of their speech.

Once children have learned stories, they should tell them before audiences that have not heard them practice, such as children in other classes or parents on Parents Night. They will make many friends and bring good cheer if they perform their stories at a Head Start Center or a senior citizens' activity center. You might even arrange a story swap: Senior citizens can tell stories of their own in exchange for the children's stories.

Other Dimensions of the Literature-Rich Classroom

If teachers wish to foster a love of literature, then they must devote ample time to reading, listening, and responding to literature. This is time above and beyond that devoted to teaching reading skills.

DEAR Time

Sometimes teachers tell students they can read "once their work is done." That works fine for strong students who consistently finish their work early, but many students never finish early. To ensure that all students get to read every day, many teachers build in a block of time when everyone in the classroom stops what they are doing and chooses a book, magazine, or newspaper to read. These blocks of reading time are known by various names such as DEAR (Drop Everything and Read) or SSR (Sustained Silent Reading).

Students need to realize that their teacher values DEAR time. Teachers can demonstrate this commitment by scheduling DEAR time daily, beginning with the first day of school, and by spending the DEAR time reading with their students. Students might need to read for shorter blocks of time at the beginning of the year (ten to fifteen minutes) and then work up to longer stretches (thirty to forty-five minutes). DEAR time is for all students; even those

Ask the Author . . .   W. Nikola-Lisa

W. Nikola-Lisa

Favorite Books as a Child

My favorite book as a child was *Nature*. My childhood days were spent in southern Texas riding horses, building forts and tree houses, and hiking to my favorite turtle pond to spend a sunny afternoon. As important as it is to read as a child, it is just as important to play and to daydream. And that is what I did a lot of as a child. Oh, I probably missed out on a lot of good stories, but what I find in my writing is that I am very attuned to rhythm and sound— and that I ascribe to my childhood days outside listening to Mother Nature and her many and varied rhythms.

What advice would you offer to novice storytellers?

I never planned to be a storyteller; rather, the ability developed within me as an act of self-defense. My first job out of college was teaching in a multi-grade alternative school. Believe me, the ability to tell a good story was essential to maintaining order within the group. But, of course, the value of storytelling far transcends this limited use. Now I tell stories for many reasons: to bring humor to a conversation, to share past personal experiences with friends, to entertain children and teachers. So, what advice might I offer a novice storyteller?

First of all, trust yourself. No matter what your story source, the story is always within you. By that I mean a person is drawn to a story because often it speaks to him or her at some deep, unconscious level. Unless I'm staying close to the text of a story, for stylistic reasons, I never worry about "getting lost" in a story. Since it is already a part of me, I have only to let the story lead me along.

Second, don't hide behind props. When I first started telling stories, I looked for all kinds of props to help me tell a story. After a while, I realized that the props just got in the way of the story; rather than an addition, they became a

distraction. Now, I look for simple, nondescript props, at most, to embellish a story.

Third, disappear within the story. I try to immerse myself in a story as I'm learning it, but especially as I'm telling it. The irony of this statement is that by losing yourself in the story (i.e., losing your ego) something magical happens: A certain objectivity arises that allows you to keep one eye on the story and one eye on the audience.

And, this leads me to my final piece of advice. When one is telling a story, it's just as important to listen as it is to speak. The "listening" I mean, of course, is to the audience's reaction as the story unfolds. Where I go in a story is often— perhaps even always—predicated upon the audience's reaction.

In the end, the best storytelling experiences are always the ones in which the story, the storyteller, and the audience become an inseparable whole.

W. Nikola-Lisa *is the author of numerous picture books including* Shake Dem Halloween Bones, The Year with Grandma Moses, *and* Bein' with You This Way. *When he's not writing, or teaching at National-Louis University in Evanston, Illinois, he can be found sharing his writing experiences with elementary school children.* ■

---

not yet reading conventionally can engage in pretend reading. There is no reason why beginning readers, for whom silent reading may not be appropriate, can't read their books out loud. (See Table 13.4.)

Author Visits

There is probably no better way to bring both existing literature and the process of creating literature to life than through a visit by a recognized children's author (or illustrator). Such a visit can usually be arranged by contacting the children's books marketing department of the author's publisher.

A visit by an author should be viewed as an opportunity to celebrate literature and literacy. Some schools do this by hosting a Young Authors' Conference in conjunction with the author's visit. Presentations by the visiting author typically get top billing at the conference. Ideally, the author will be able to present to small groups of students. Visiting authors often have wonderful stories to share with students about the inspiration for their work, and

Go to the Extension Activities section of Chapter 13 in the MyEducationKit for your book and complete activity #5 to develop a guide for hosting an author or illustrator visit.

Table 13.4   How to Make DEAR a Success
• Make DEAR time a part of students' daily routine.
• Let students choose their own reading materials for DEAR time.
• Ensure that everyone, including the teacher, reads during DEAR time.
• For students who have a difficult time reading for long stretches, begin with a few minutes of reading time (perhaps ten minutes) and build to longer blocks of time (thirty to forty-five minutes).
• For younger readers, don't require that the reading time be silent; beginning readers frequently need to hear themselves read aloud.
• Let kindergartners participate in DEAR time by "pretend reading" stories.

To check your comprehension on the content covered in this chapter, go to the MyEducation-Kit for your book and complete the Study Plan for Chapter 13. Here you will be able to take a chapter quiz and receive feedback on your answers.

illustrators frequently offer fascinating demonstrations of their art. If time permits, it is ideal to organize more informal sessions in which small groups can talk to the visitor. Some authors even choose to work with small groups of students on their writing.

The author or illustrator is the celebrity of the Young Authors' Conference, but this doesn't mean that other important things aren't happening. Students who attend the conference should be authors or illustrators themselves and should come to the conference prepared to join peer groups in which they share stories and illustrations they have created. A third type of conference event can center on children's literature selections. Students can attend sessions offered by teachers or members of the community, in which they listen to a story and participate in a response activity based on that story.

Teachers need to prepare students for an upcoming author visit. First, they must ensure that the students know the featured author's work. In the weeks preceding the visit, the teacher should read the visiting author's stories aloud. Children should have the opportunity to respond to the author's work through writing and artwork. Their responses can be displayed throughout the classroom or school. If students will have the opportunity to interview the visiting author, the teacher needs to help them generate questions about some of the author's stories as well as questions that will yield insights into how writers (or illustrators) go about their work: where they get ideas, how they budget their time to ensure that their work gets finished, the special techniques they use, and advice they might offer young writers (or artists).

Experiences for Further Learning

1. Excellent readers are not always excellent at reading aloud. Learning to read aloud is an art that must be cultivated. Many popular books are available on tape. Go to the public library and check out some of your favorites, or possibly one that you would like to learn to read aloud well. Study how the reader modulates his or her voice. At what points in the story does it slow down or speed up, grow quieter or louder? What effect does that have on the reader? Being able to read a story effectively requires practice. Read the book aloud to yourself. Does what you hear resemble what you heard on tape? Tape yourself reading. Sometimes, you must read in a way that seems exaggerated to your own ear, but the listeners only notice an interesting, exciting, and engaging tale.

   Next, prepare to read aloud a book that will challenge you. If you are not especially proficient in Spanish, then you might want to select ***Chato's Kitchen.*** For dialect, you might want to try your hand at reading a "Brer Rabbit" story. Practice reading the story until you feel confident enough to read it aloud. Then share the story with a group of peers. After reading the story aloud, discuss the challenges the book presented to you and share with your peers recommendations for preparing a challenging read-aloud.

   Because we must also read a variety of genres to our students, we may be entering areas in which we do not feel confident or comfortable. Many teachers have not had rich experiences within certain text structures. To present these to our students requires that we become familiar and comfortable with them. If reading aloud an informational text seems dry and boring to you, seek out those known to be popular. Many history books read like fictional narratives. Science topics capture young minds and encourage them to inquire.

Poetry can be humorous and clever, or moving and even informative. You will read aloud best the texts you enjoy most. In your search to find what will inspire your students, you also may find inspiration. Our students deserve no less. After all, it is up to the teacher to find the books that will turn nonreaders into readers, and good readers into better readers.

2. Visit a classroom library center. Which of the design features identified by Morrow were evident in the center? If the library is a focal area of the room, what makes it so? Is it partitioned off from the rest of the room? In what way? How many children can fit comfortably in the center at one time? How are books displayed? What kinds of books are visible? Do they seem to be age appropriate? Are a variety of genres present? Are literature-related materials, such as book posters, book jackets, or story book character puppets, evident? Can you determine by looking at the center how it is organized? How are the books arranged? Do there seem to be plenty of books for the number of children accessing the library center? Given what you saw, how would you rate the library center: basic, good, or excellent? What changes or additions would you recommend?

   Interview the teacher to find out the procedures for having students access the books in the library. When do students get to use the center? How often can they use it? Are they able to check books out to take home? How does the teacher acquire new selections to stock the library? What does the teacher consider when choosing books for the library?

   Now, develop a preliminary plan for the library you hope to have in your own classroom. How will you organize it? How will you make it an inviting area of the classroom? What kind of management system do you think you might like to have?

3. Prepare a story of your own to tell to a small group of peers. Remember, we are the best storytellers of the tales of our lives. We share our memories and the events of our lives naturally. Consider the stories you may have heard your parents or grandparents share. We often hear them repeatedly at family gatherings. What stories have you heard yourself tell so many times that you often tell them in the same way, with the same words, time after time? You are a storyteller.

   Now, honestly, have you embellished any at all? You may have hit the ball over the fence, but did you mention you were on the T-ball field with the shorter outfield? Your mother may have been pregnant when she got the flat tire out in the middle of nowhere, but she was four months pregnant, not eight, right? So, while learning to ride a bike, your brother rode it through the neighbor's wall because he hadn't learned to use the brakes yet. It seems the sheetrock cracked, but maybe the whole front tire didn't go through into the bedroom. Ah, but storytelling invites a little exaggeration. It is meant to entertain. The storyteller can take liberties with the truth. What are your stories? Consider the advice by W. Nikola-Lisa when forming your own.

   Try out your stories on your peers. Share with them what you understand about the importance of storytelling. Invite them to ask you questions if they found any parts ambiguous or needing clearer images. Their questions will help you determine if you communicated the story as effectively as you would hope. But, ultimately, you must decide whether you need to add a detail or description. It's your story. By sharing our stories, we become real, trusting humans to our students.

Now go to Chapter 13 in the MyEducationKit (www.myeducationkit.com) for your book, where you can:

- Find learning outcomes for Chapter 13.
- Access the Children's Literature Database for your own exploration.
- Extend knowledge with content-specific Web Links.
- Deepen and apply content understanding with Extension Activities.
- Check your comprehension on the content covered in the chapter by going to the Study Plan. Here you will be able to take a chapter quiz and receive feedback on your answers.
- Find the following updated appendices: Major Children's Book Awards, Children's Magazines, Professional Organizations, Children's Book Publishers' Addresses, Book Selection Aids, and Children's Literature Web Sites.

Recommended Books

* indicates a picture book; **I** indicates interest level (P = preschool, YA = young adult)

*Agee, Jon. *Milo's Hat Trick.* Hyperion, 2001. Milo the Magnificent was anything but a magnificent magician; he couldn't even pull a rabbit out of a hat. Then, Milo meets a bear—who turns his career around. (**I:** P–7)

*Allard, Harry. *Miss Nelson Is Missing!* Illustrated by James Marshall. Houghton Mifflin, 1977. When Viola Swamp becomes the sub in Room 207, the children are desperate to find their missing teacher. (**I:** P–8)

Avi. *City of Light, City of Dark.* Illustrated by Brian Floca. Orchard, 1993. In this myth-like story, a young girl and boy help to save their city. (**I:** 10–12)

———. *The Christmas Rat.* Atheneum, 2000. Christmas vacation promises to be anything but uneventful when Anje Gabrail, a vengeful exterminator, enlists Eric in his war against rats. Yet as Eric becomes caught up in Anje's crazy campaign, it becomes increasingly unclear if he is a partner or a victim. (**I:** 11 and up)

———. *Crispin: The Cross of Lead.* Hyperion, 2002. Accused of a crime he did not commit and having lost his mother—his only living relative—Crispin must flee his village, the only home he has ever known. Pursued by unknown enemies, Crispin finds himself swept up in the political intrigues of medieval England. (**I:** 10 and up)

*Barrett, Judi. *Cloudy with a Chance of Meatballs.* Illustrated by Ron Barrett. Atheneum, 1978. Storms of food fall from the sky in the town of Chew-and-Swallow. (**I:** P–8)

*Browne, Anthony. *Voices in the Park.* DK Publishing, 1998. A trip to the park is told and illustrated from four different perspectives. (**I:** 9 and up)

Cameron, Ann. *The Stories Julian Tells.* Illustrated by Ann Strugnell. Random House, 1981/1996. Julian relates humorous stories about everyday experiences. (**I:** 5–8)

*Cronin, Doreen. *Click, Clack, Moo: Cows That Type.* Illustrated by Betsy Lewin. Simon & Schuster, 2000. The cows discover an old typewriter in the barn, and Farmer Brown's farm will never be the same again. (**I:** 5–8)

Curtis, Christopher Paul. *Bud, Not Buddy.* Read by James Avery. Listening Library, 2000. A Depression Era story about an orphan who strikes out on his own in search of his father. The reading is upbeat and the recording includes jazz music of the period. (**I:** 10 and up)

———. *Elijah of Buxton.* Scholastic, 2007. Elijah, the first child born in freedom in Buxton, Canada, a settlement of runaway slaves, discovers firsthand the horrors of slavery when he travels to America in pursuit of the man who has stolen his friend's money.

*dePaola, Tomie. *Strega Nona.* Prentice-Hall, 1975. Big Anthony and the townspeople face disaster when Big Anthony can't make the magic pasta pot stop cooking. (**I:** P–8)

Downer, Ann. *Hatching Magic.* Atheneum, 2003. When a pet wyvern goes through a magic hole in search of a place to lay her egg, the medieval world of magic collides with the twentieth century in this fast-paced fantasy. (**I:** 9–12)

Ellis, Deborah. *A Company of Fools.* Fitzhenry & Whiteside, 2002. When the plague sweeps through Paris in the year 1348,

the world of the choir boys at St. Luc's is forever transformed. (**I:** 9–13)

Erdrich, Louise. *The Birchbark House.* Hyperion, 1999. An Ojibwa family experiences the joys and struggles of life on Madeline Island in Lake Superior in the mid-1800s. (**I:** 10 and up)

Espinosa, Rod. *The Courageous Princess.* Dark Horse, 2007. A princess must rescue herself from an evil dragon in order to return to her parents. The princess serves as a model of a strong female protagonist. (**I:** 8–11)

Funke, Cornelia. *Inkheart.* Chicken House/Scholastic, 2003. Through a magical read-aloud, Meggie's father has brought the evil characters of a book to life, and Meggie and her family find themselves caught up in a real-world adventure centering around these book characters. (**I:** 10 and up)

*Hesse, Karen. *Come On, Rain!* Illustrated by Jon J. Muth. Scholastic, 1999. A little girl delights in the rain that ends a long dry spell in the city. (**I:** 6–10)

*Hoberman, Mary Ann. *The Two Sillies.* Illustrated by Lynne Cravath. Harcourt, 2000. Acquiring a cat and getting rid of mice aren't simple feats for the two sillies in this easy-to-read story. (**I:** P–7)

*———. *You Read to Me, I'll Read to You.* Illustrated by Michael Emberley. Little, Brown, 2004. This collection features very short fairy tales (with a twist) that are organized for two readers to read together. (**I:** 6–9)

Holm, Jennifer L., and Matthew Holm. *Babymouse: Puppy Love.* Random, 2007. This spunky little mouse hopes to get the dog of her dreams. (**I:** 6–9)

*Jenkins, Steve, and Robin Page. *What Do You Do With a Tail Like This?* Houghton Mifflin, 2003. In this picture book with an interactive format, readers will discover some of the wonderful things animals can do. (**I:** 5–9)

*Kasza, Keiko. *The Wolf's Chicken Stew.* Putnam, 1987. A chicken outsmarts the wolf who wants her for his dinner. (**I:** P–8)

*Kerley, Barbara. *Walt Whitman: Words for America.* Illustrated by Brian Selznick. Scholastic, 2004. This biography of Walt Whitman focuses primarily on his role in the American Civil War. (**I:** 10 and up)

Kochalka, James. *Pinky and Stinky.* Top Shelf, 2002. Instead of landing on Jupiter, Pinky and Stinky land on the moon, where they are swept up in the midst of a war. (**I:** 6–9)

*Krull, Kathleen. *Harvesting Hope: The Story of Cesar Chavez.* Illustrated by Yuyi Morales. Harcourt, 2003. This biography traces Chavez's life from his boyhood to his achievements as leader of the Mexican American farm workers. (**I:** 8 and up)

Kurtz, Jane. *The Storyteller's Beads.* Illustrated by Michael Bryant. Harcourt, 1998. Fleeing their drought- and violence-stricken land, two young Ethiopian strangers overcome their prejudices and find solace in the old stories passed down by one of their grandmothers. (**I:** 9–12)

*Lasky, Kathryn. *The Emperor's Old Clothes.* Illustrated by David Catrow. Harcourt, 1999. When Farmer Henry stumbles across new finery cast off (by the emperor who wore no clothes), his new attire causes an uproar in the barnyard. (**I:** 6–10)

Lester, Julius. *The Tales of Uncle Remus: The Adventures of Brer Rabbit.* Read by the author. Recorded Books, 1999. This is a collection of stories about Brer Rabbit, the African American trickster character. The dialect is made accessible by the reader. (**I:** 8–12)

*Long, Melinda. *How I Became a Pirate*. Illustrated by David Shannon. Harcourt, 2003. When Braid Beard extends an invitation, Jeremy quickly joins the pirate crew and is in for rollicking adventures. But when Jeremy finds out what pirates don't do, home soon begins to look much better. (**I:** 4–8)

*Martin, Bill, Jr. *The Ghost-Eye Tree*. Illustrated by Ted Rand. Holt, 1985/1995. This story about a brother and sister's scary experience with a haunted tree can easily be adapted for readers' theater. (**I:** P–9)

*McKissack, Patricia. *Flossie and the Fox*. Illustrated by Rachel Isadora. Dial, 1986. Flossie turns the tables on Mr. Fox when he tries to get her basket of eggs. (**I:** 5–10)

*Merrill, Jean. *The Girl Who Loved Caterpillars*. Illustrated by Floyd Cooper. Philomel, 1992. This is a retelling of a twelfth-century Japanese story of a young girl whose passion for learning about caterpillars flies in the face of her society's values. (**I:**10 and up)

Milne, A. A. *Winnie-the-Pooh*. Illustrated by Ernest H. Shepard. Dutton/Plume, 1924/1999. Winnie-the-Pooh has marvelous adventures in the Hundred Acre Wood with his host of friends—all stuffed animals like him. (**I:** P–8)

Napoli, Donna Jo. *Three Days*. Dutton, 2001. Jackie is stranded on the side of a dark highway in Italy when her father collapses over the steering wheel of their rented car. She soon finds herself caught up in nightmarish circumstances when two men, who speak no English, pick her up and take her to an isolated house in southern Italy. (**I:** 9–12)

Naylor, Phyllis Reynolds. *The Grand Escape*. Illustrated by Alan Daniel. Atheneum, 1993. Two house cats make a grand escape to the outside world, where challenges and opportunities abound. (**I:** 6–10)

O'Brien, Anne Sibley. *The Legend of Hong Kil Dong: The Robin Hood of Korea*. Charlesbridge, 2006. This is a retelling of a Korean folktale in which a servant (who is actually the son of a nobleman) grows up to fight for the poor. (**I:** 8–12)

Paulsen, Gary. *Hatchet*. Bradbury, 1987. The sole survivor of a plane crash, a boy struggles to survive in the wilderness. (**I:** 10–YA)

*Polacco, Patricia. *The Bee Tree*. Philomel, 1993. A little girl and her grandfather are joined by friends in a merry chase through the countryside in search of a bee tree. (**I:** 5–10)

*———. *Pink and Say*. Philomel, 1994. During the Civil War, an African American Union soldier befriends a white Union soldier. (**I:** 8–YA)

Pullman, Philip. *The Scarecrow and His Servant*. Knopf, 2004. Accompanied by an orphaned boy, Scarecrow sets out in a world filled with danger to seek adventure and the place where he belongs. (**I:** 6–10)

*Rappaport, Doreen. *Martin's Big Words: The Life of Dr. Martin Luther King, Jr*. Jump Sun, 2001. Dr. King's own words are integrated throughout this biography of the great civil rights leader. (**I:** 8 and up)

Renier, Aaron. *Spiral-Bound*. Top Shelf, 2005. Three animals set out to solve the mystery of the monster in the town lake while also exploring their own creative talents. (**I:** 9 and up)

Robinson, Barbara. *The Best Christmas Pageant Ever*. Harper, 1972. Everyone anticipates disaster when the Herdmans participate in the church's Christmas pageant, but much to everyone's surprise, it's the best Christmas pageant ever. (**I:** 6–10)

*Rosen, Michael. *We're Going on a Bear Hunt*. Illustrated by Helen Oxenbury. Little Simon, 1989/1997. A surprise awaits a family who goes on a bear hunt. (**I:** P–8)

Runton, Andy. *Owly: A Time to Be Brave*. Top Shelf, 2007. This latest book in the graphic novel series tells the story of Owly and a new visitor to the forest. (**I:** 7–10)

Ryan, Pam Muñoz. *Mice and Beans*. Illustrated by Joe Cepeda. Scholastic, 2005. A band of mice help a grandmother prepare for a birthday party. (**I:** 4–7)

———. *Esperanza Rising*. Read by Trini Alvarado. Listening Library, 2001. Esperanza's privileged childhood in Mexico is suddenly lost when her father is murdered and she and her mother are forced to flee to the United States, where they become migrant workers. The reader's voice is well-matched to the lyrical style of the text. (**I:** 10 and up)

*Rylant, Cynthia. *When I Was Young in the Mountains*. Illustrated by Diane Goode. Dutton, 1982. In lyrical language, a girl tells of her life in the mountains. (**I:** 5–10)

*Say, Allen. *Kamishibai Man*, Houghton Mifflin, 2005. Missing the old days when he told stories on the streets of Japan, the kamishibai man finds a receptive audience when he decides to revive the old tradition. (**I:** 8–12)

Soto, Gary. *Baseball in April and Other Stories*. Read by Stephanie Diaz and Miguel Gongora. Audio Bookshelf, 2000. The readings of these short stories about everyday experiences of young Mexican Americans are well-paced and capture the humor that marks Soto's stories. (**I:** 11–YA)

*———. *Chato's Kitchen*. Illustrated by Susan Guevara. Penguin Putnam, 1995. Chato, the coolest cat in East L.A., can't believe his luck when a family of mice moves in next door. (**I:** P–8)

———. *The Skirt*. Read by Eileen Galindo. Recorded Books, 1993. Miata is excited and proud that she will be able to wear her mother's old folklorico skirt in an upcoming performance, but her excitement turns to anxiety when she accidentally loses the skirt. (**I:** 8–10)

*Stevens, Janet. *Tops and Bottoms*. Harcourt, 1995. Hare tricks lazy Bear by wheeling and dealing in the tops and bottoms of vegetables. (**I:** P–8)

*Stevens, Janet Crummel, Susan Stevens. *The Great Fuzz Frenzy*. Illustrated by Janet Stevens. Harcourt, 2005. A tennis ball that lands in the middle of a prairie-dog town causes quite a commotion. (**I:** 5–9)

*Teague, Mark. *Dear Mrs. LaRue: Letters from Obedience School*. Scholastic, 2002. Banished to obedience school, Ike the dog writes a series of letters to his mistress that tend to "bend" the truth. (**I:** 5–9)

Thompson, Jill. *Scary Godmother*. Sirius Entertainment, 1997. A little girl who goes trick-or-treating ends up meeting her scary godmother. (**I:** 7–10)

*Van Allsburg, Chris. *The Widow's Broom*. Houghton Mifflin, 1992. A broom with special powers brings out the prejudices of the widow's neighbors. (**I:** 8–12)

White, E. B. *Charlotte's Web*. Illustrated by Garth Williams. Harper, 1952. Charlotte the spider proves herself the truest of friends by saving the life of Wilbur the pig. (**I:** 5–10)

Wiles, Deborah. *Love, Ruby Lavender*. Harcourt, 2001. Ruby Lavender feels betrayed when she learns her best friend (and grandmother) is going to Hawaii for the summer. That means Ruby is on her own to care for the hens and contend with Melba Jane. Telling her story through a combination of narrative and letters, Wiles has created a humorous story filled with rich characterizations. (**I:** 8–12)

*———. *Freedom Summer*. Illustrated by Jerome Lagarrigue. Atheneum, 2001. Joe and John Henry are best friends. They play marbles together and swim together in the creek, and both boys want to be firefighters. But Joe is white, and John Henry is African American, and in the 1960s in the deep South, that means there are some things Joe and John Henry cannot do together. (**I:** 6–9)

Willems, Mo. *Don't Let the Pigeon Drive the Bus*. Hyperion, 2003. A determined pigeon will try any trick to realize his dream of driving the bus. (**I:** 4–8)

*Wong, Janet S. *Buzz*. Illustrated by Margaret Chodos-Irvine. Harcourt, 2000. A little boy's morning is filled with buzzes. The book can be done as a read-aloud, with young listeners joining in to produce buzzes at all the right places. (**I:** P–8)

Zusak, Markus. *The Book Thief*. Knopf, 2006. A foster girl living in Nazi Germany discovers the power of books. (**I:** YA)

Storytelling

*Aardema, Verna. *Why Mosquitoes Buzz in People's Ears*. Illustrated by Leo and Diane Dillon. Dial, 1975. In this African pourquoi tale, an unexpected chain of events explains why mosquitoes buzz in people's ears. (**I:** P–8)

Briggs, Katherine. *British Folktales*. Dorset, 1989. Some familiar tales are presented in the form in which they were traditionally told. The book also includes new tales. (**I:** YA)

Erdoes, Richard, and Alfonso Ortiz. *American Indian Myths and Legends*. Pantheon, 1985. A collection of Native American tales and lore, written for adults, but good for read-alouds. (**I:** 10–YA)

Forest, Heather. *Wonder Tales from Around the World*. August House, 1995. An international collection of fairy tales of enchantment. (**I:** 8–11)

Fujita, Hiroko. *Stories to Play With*. August House, 1999. These stories, intended for young children, come complete with directions for props to be used in telling the tales. (**I:** 5–8)

Hamilton, Martha. *Scared Witless: Thirteen Eerie Tales to Tell*. August House, 2006. This collection contains tales both funny and scary. (**I:** 9–12)

Hamilton, Martha, and Mitch Weiss. *Noodlehead Stories: World Tales Kids Can Read and Tell*. August House, 2000. This is a collection of humorous knucklehead tales from around the world. (**I:** 7–12)

Hamilton, Virginia. *Her Stories: African American Folktales, Fairy Tales, and True Tales*. Illustrated by Leo and Diane Dillon. Scholastic, 1995. These stories celebrate African American women. (**I:** 9–YA)

———. *The People Could Fly: American Black Folktales*. Illustrated by Leo and Diane Dillon. Knopf, 1985. This collection has favorites such as "Brer Rabbit and the Tar Baby" and "Wiley and the Hairy Man." (**I:** 9–YA)

Hearne, Betsy. *Beauties and Beasts*. Oryx, 1993. A fascinating collection of stories from around the world, based on the beauty-and-the-beast motif. (**I:** 9–YA)

MacDonald, Margaret Read. *Earth Care*. August House, 2005. These tales from around the world share ecological themes. (**I:** 9–12)

———. *Shake-It-Up Tales!* August House, 2000. This collection of multicultural tales invites audience participation. It contains riddle stories, singing tales, and others. (**I:** 5–8)

———. *Three-Minute Tales*. August House, 2004. This collection offers tales for all occasions. (**I:** 9–12)

———. *Twenty Tellable Tales: Audience Participation Folktales for the Beginning Story-Teller*. H. W. Wilson, 1986. These tales have been honed by repeated telling to library groups. (**I:** 9–YA)

Mourning Dove. *Coyote Stories*. Univ. of Nebraska Press, 1990. Stories of the trickster Coyote, collected in the 1930s by an Okanogan teller. (**I:** 9–YA)

Reneaux, J. J. *Cajun Folktales*. August House, 1992. Animal tales, fairy tales, funny folktales, and ghost stories from the Cajun people of the Louisiana bayou country. (**I:** 9–YA)

Schwartz, Alvin. *Scary Stories to Tell in the Dark*. HarperCollins, 1986. Stories for middle elementary grade students and up, collected by a serious folklore collector. (**I:** 8–13)

Resources

Hamilton, Martha, and Mitch Weiss. *Children Tell Stories: A Teaching Guide*. Katonah, Richard C. Owen, 1990.

Lipke, Barbara. *Figures, Facts, and Fables: Telling Tales in Science and Math*. Heinemann, 1996.

Lipson, Eden Ross. *The New York Times Parent's Guide to the Best Books for Children*. Random House, 1991.

Martinez, Miriam, and William H. Teale. "Reading in a Kindergarten Library Center." *The Reading Teacher 41* (1988): 568–572.

McClure, Amy, and Janice V. Kristo. *Adventuring with Books: A Booklist for Pre-K–Grade 6*, 13th edition. National Council of Teachers of English, 2002.

Morgan, Norah, and Juliana Saxton. *Teaching Drama: A Mind of Many Wonders*. Heinemann, 1987.

Ralston, Marion V. *An Exchange of Gifts: A Storyteller's Handbook*. Pippin Publishing, 1993.

Sawyer, Ruth. *The Way of the Storyteller*. Viking, 1942

Teale, William H., Junko Yokota, and Miriam Martinez. "The Book Matters: Evaluating and Selecting What to Read Aloud to Young Children." *Effective Early Literacy Practice*. Ed. Andrea DeBruin-Parecki. (pp. 101–122). Baltimore: High Scope.

Trelease, Jim. *The Read-Aloud Handbook*. 4th ed. Penguin, 1995.

Yokota, Junko, and Miriam Martinez. "Authentic Listening Experiences." *Book Links 13.3* (2004): 30–34.

References

Anderson, Richard C., Elfrieda H. Hiebert, Judith A. Scott, and Ian A. G. Wilkinson. *Becoming a Nation of Readers: The Report of the Commission on Reading.* National Institute of Education, 1984.

de Brunvard, Jan. *The Vanishing Hitchhiker and Other Urban Legends.* Norton, 1981.

Fielding, Linda G., Paul T. Wilson, and Richard C. Anderson. "A New Focus on Free Reading: The Role of Trade Books in Reading Instruction." *Contexts of Literacy.* Ed. Taffy Raphael and Ralph Reynolds. Longman, 1986.

Fractor, Jann Sorrell, Marjorie Ciruti Woodruff, Miriam G. Martinez, and William H. Teale. "Let's Not Miss Opportunities to Promote Voluntary Reading: Classroom Libraries in the Elementary School." *The Reading Teacher 46* (1993): 476–484.

Graves, Bonnie, and Lauren A. Liang. "Transitional Chapter Books: An Update." *Book Links 13* (2004): 12–16.

Hickman, Janet. "A New Perspective on Response to Literature: Research in an Elementary School Setting." *Research in the Teaching of English 15* (1981): 43–54.

Hoffman, James V., Nancy L. Roser, and Jennifer Battle. "Reading Aloud in Classrooms: From the Modal toward a 'Model.'" *The Reading Teacher 46* (1993): 496–503.

Krashen, Stephen D. "The (Lack of) Experimental Evidence Supporting the Use of Accelerated Reader." *Journal of Children's Literature 29* (2003): 9, 16–30.

MacDonald, Margaret Read. *The Story-Teller's Start-Up Book.* August House, 1993.

Morrow, Lesley Mandel. "Relationships between Literature Program, Library Corner Designs, and Children's Use of Literature." *Journal of Educational Research 75* (1982): 339–344.

National Endowment for the Arts. (2004). *Reading at Risk: A Survey of Literary Reading in America.* Research Division Report No. 46. Washington, DC: National Endowment for the Arts.

Rogers, Lynn. "Computerized Reading Management Software: An Effective Component of a Successful Reading Program." *Journal of Children's Literature 29* (2003): 9–15.

Roser, Nancy L., Miriam Martinez, Kathleen McDonnold, and Charles Fuhrken. "Beginning Chapter Books: Their Features and Their Support of Children's Reading." *53rd Yearbook of the National Reading Conference.* Eds. Colleen M. Fairbanks, Jo Worthy, Beth Maloch, James V. Hoffman, and Diane L. Schallert. National Reading Conference, 2004.

Teale, William H. "Reading Aloud to Young Children as a Classroom Instructional Activity: Insights from Research and Practice." *On Reading Books to Children: Parents and Teachers.* Eds. A. van Kleeck, Steven A. Stahl, & E. Bauer. (pp. 114–139). Mahwah, NJ: Lawrence Erlbaum, 2003.

14

Encouraging Response to Literature

Our two families, the Logans and the Simmses, had never much gotten along. What with the Simmses living less than a mile or so from us on that forty-acre spot of land they tenant-farmed, and we sitting on our own two hundred acres, there was always likely to be trouble, and there was. Now this was back before my papa went and bought that second two hundred acres; but still that two hundred acres we had then, that was a lot, and the Simmses didn't like it—that we had when they didn't. They didn't like it one bit. That was part of the trouble between us. Other part of the trouble was that we were colored and they were white. Fact of the matter was we ain't never had much use for the Simmses, and they ain't never had much use

> for us either; but seeing that we couldn't hardly afford trouble with them, Papa said best thing to do was try and stay out of their way much as we could. He said it was better to mind our business, let them mind theirs, and just walk away if they tried to start something.
>
> I heeded his words. My brother Hammer didn't.
>
> —*from* The Well
> *by Mildred D. Taylor*

Set in the early 1900s in the deep South, Mildred Taylor's *The Well* deals with substantive issues of racism that are not easy for readers of any age to forget once they've read about them. Yet topics of this nature are not always easy for children to understand. It is important for classroom teachers to create opportunities for their students to grapple with the issues they encounter in books such as *The Well*. In this chapter we explore a variety of instructional strategies—including discussion, writing, art, and drama—through which teachers can foster rich responses to literature. Teachers can use these strategies to guide students to "step into" story worlds, to build thoughtful personal envisionments, to reflect on the ways in which a book might relate to their own lives, and to reflect on stories as crafted objects—the stances identified by Langer (1990) in her theory of envisionment building (see Chapter 12).

Talking in Response to Literature

Reading can be an intensely satisfying solitary experience, but it can be even more meaningful when shared with others. Think of times when you've done just that. Perhaps you finished a wonderful book and discovered that a friend had also read it. No doubt you were off and talking. Or perhaps you were in the midst of a story and simply had to stop reading to tell a friend about a hilarious scene. You might have even explored books with peers in more formal settings, such as a book club at your local library. Whatever the context—informal or formal—when people come together to talk about literature, they become members of an interpretive community.

The discussions in interpretive communities are typically conversational in nature: People have compared book discussions to the kind of stimulating conversations they engage in at a memorable dinner party or around the family dinner table. You might remember many of the book conversations in which you have engaged as being lively—perhaps participants had diverse perspectives on the book that led to some informal debate. Book discussions can, of course, move in different directions. Sometimes, the participants become caught up in the story world, talking about what characters did, why they did those things, and the likely outcomes of their actions. At other times, book discussions move out of the realm of the story world and into conversations about the ways in which the story related to participants' own lives or explorations about the author's craft. Participants in book discussions often leave the group having gained deep insights from others. In short, the members of an interpretive community share impressions, wonder together, challenge each other's ideas, and explore together. Maryann Eeds and Deborah Wells (1989) have called book discussions of this nature "grand conversations."

Children in elementary and middle school classrooms can also be part of interpretive communities. Sometimes, the entire class talks about a book; at other times, smaller groups of students come together for literature discussion. These interpretive communities are known by various names: literature circles (Harste, Short, & Burke, 1988), book clubs (Raphael, Goatley, McMahon, & Woodman, 1995), literature study groups (Eeds & Wells, 1989), or

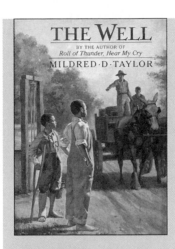

ILLUSTRATION 14.1   In *The Well*, racial conflict erupts in the midst of a drought in Mississippi in the late nineteenth century. (Cover from *The Well: David's Story* by Mildred D. Taylor, jacket cover copyright © 1995 by Max Ginsburg. Used by permission of Dial Books for Young Readers, A Division of Penguin Young Readers Group, A Member of Penguin Group (USA) Inc., 345 Hudson Street, New York, NY 10014. All rights reserved.)

Develop a text set of titles that could be used in literature circles by using the Children's Literature Database in Chapter 14 of the MyEducationKit for this book.

conversational discussion groups (Wiencek & O'Flahavan, 1994). We have chosen to use the term "literature circle" to describe the interpretive communities at work in classrooms.

Creating an Opportunity for "Grand Conversations"

To get a feel for the type of talk that can occur in literature circles, we'll look in on a literature conversation in Ms. Henry's fifth grade classroom. The students have been reading Elizabeth Kay's *The Divide* and are meeting as a small group to talk about the book. *The Divide* is a fantasy in which a young boy who is standing astride the Continental Divide in Costa Rica is transported to another world populated with brazzles (known to us as griffins), tangle children (elves), japegrins (pixies), and other mythological creatures. In this conversation, the students draw on their "store" of knowledge about the character roles frequently found in fantasy (evil characters, traitorous characters, etc.) to speculate about how the book's plot will develop:

> *Kevin:* Maybe the brazzle is trying to be a traitor to the kids.
>
> *Miguel:* I still think Ironclaw (the brazzle) is evil.
>
> *John:* I just don't think so. I just don't think he's nice.
>
> *Miguel:* He's nice, but I think he wants to be with Felix and Betony.
>
> *Kevin:* I think he is evil because overall we know that brazzles do not like to go with (inaudible).
>
> *Miguel:* Yeah, I know, and that's what's making me think he's working with Snakeweed so he can lead Felix and Betony to a different place where Snakeweed is so he can kill them.
>
> *Kevin:* Well Snakeweed doesn't want to kill Felix: he just wants to kill Betony.
>
> *John:* How would Snakeweed know that Ironclaw has Felix? How would he know all that?
>
> *Kevin:* Because, remember, Ironclaw met Felix past the griffin, and Felix was startled when he woke up.

Issue to Consider

Should the Teacher Participate in Children's Literature Circle Conversations?

Many adult readers regularly participate with friends in informal conversations about literature, and those who belong to organized book clubs engage in more formal conversations as well. In recent years, educators have become increasingly aware that they must do more than teach children how to read; they must also take steps to ensure that children become lifelong readers. One way of achieving this goal is by initiating children into the ways of book clubs. However, there is less agreement on the best way to teach children to actively come together and converse about books rather than answer a teacher's comprehension questions.

Some educators argue that children have become dependent on teachers to ask them questions about the books they read. Educators with this view maintain that the best way to break this dependency is by placing children in literature circles where there is no adult present. In this way, children will have no choice but to take responsibility for their literature conversations. It will be up to them to bring up topics for discussion, pose questions they have about the book, and exchange views on a variety of topics related to the target book.

Those on the opposing side agree that the ultimate goal is for children to learn to carry on literature conversations by themselves. However, they question whether children will learn new roles on their own. They argue that children will best learn these new roles by participating in literature circles with teachers who model new ways of talking about books and even talk with children about the ways in which literature conversations differ from the question-and-answer sessions with which children are probably more familiar.

What do you think?

John: Yeah, but how would Snakeweed know that?

Kevin: Well probably because Snakeweed remembered the brownies.

Miguel: Oooh.

Kevin: So the brownies they told it to Snakeweed. And also, japegrins are con artists. I mean Snakeweed is trying to con everybody by selling dangerous items.

John: Well, I don't think all japegrins are con artists.

Miguel: Yeah.

John: Well, some could be.

These children were engaged in the work of an interpretive community. Their lively exchange was conversational, and they did some impressive thinking as they arrived at and defended their own insights and worked together to build meaning. This discussion had all the marks of a "grand conversation."

Eeds and Wells (1989) have contrasted grand conversations with what has been described by Cazden (1988) and Mehan (1979) as "gentle inquisitions," those question-and-answer sessions in which the teacher quizzes students with comprehension questions. In gentle inquisitions, the teacher initiates a topic by asking a question, the student responds to the question, and the teacher evaluates the student's response—a pattern of interaction called I-R-E (Initiate-Respond-Evaluate). An overreliance on the I-R-E pattern means "students have little opportunity to raise topics of interest, pursue lines of thinking, or collaborate in critical problem solving" (Raphael, Goatley, McMahon, & Woodman, 1995, p. 67).

Organizing Literature Circles

How can teachers ensure that their students have the opportunity to participate in interpretive communities? We believe that five key factors impact the workings of literature circles: the books that are chosen, group size, length and frequency of sessions, who leads discussions, and whether responses are free or guided. There is no single "right" way to organize literature circles to ensure that children engage in lively and thoughtful book conversations. However, it is important to understand how each of these five factors affects the workings of a literature circle.

Selecting Books for Use in Literature Circles

Selecting the right book is one of the most important decisions you'll make. Not every book has the same potential to engage children in rich discussion. In their investigation of literature discussion groups, Eeds and Wells (1989) involved groups of fifth and sixth graders in reading and discussing one of four books: *Harriet the Spy* by Louise Fitzhugh, *After the Goat Man* by Betsy Byars, *The Darkangel* by Meredith Pierce, and *Tuck Everlasting* by Natalie Babbitt, each of which is recognized as a high-quality piece of literature. Although the adult leaders in all four groups proved to be equally skillful in facilitating discussions, the students in the *Tuck Everlasting* group shared the most insightful responses. Eeds and Wells concluded that differences in the books accounted for differences in the quality of discussion. Of the four books, only *Tuck Everlasting* had the power to launch the children into discussions of issues touching the very essence of the human experience.

To encourage diverse talk during literature circles, it makes sense to use a variety of types of literature: literature that develops significant themes, literature with strong story lines, and distinctly crafted literature. Picture books can also offer rich fodder for conversation. An example of a picture book that opens windows to rich talk is *Hooway for Wodney Wat,* a book that deals with bullying. Books likely to engender thematic-level talk include Mildred Taylor's powerful books about the Logan family, which explore racism as well as the sustaining power of family love and unity, and Lois Lowry's *The Giver,* an exploration of a utopian society that was designed to control the pain and sorrow of life as well as its joys.

Other types of books are likely to move children's talk in other directions (Martinez & Roser, 1995). When children read books with strong story lines, they tend to "step into the story" (Langer, 1992), and their talk reflects their engagement with its characters, conflicts, and events. In particular, books engender lively talk about the story world when they center on problems with which the students can easily identify and whose solutions are not readily

Go to the Extension Activities section of Chapter 14 in the MyEducationKit for your book and complete activity #1 to design an observational tool for literature circles.

Top Shelf 14.1

Picture Books with Powerful Themes

Three Cheers for Catherine the Great by Cari Best

Old Henry by Joan Blos

The Wednesday Surprise by Eve Bunting

Emily's Art by Peter Catalanotto

Miss Rumphius by Barbara Cooney

The Lotus Seed by Sherry Garland

My Great-Aunt Arizona by Gloria Houston

Yoshi's Feast by Kimiko Kajikawa

Top Shelf 14.2

Books with Strong Story Lines

The Tale of Despereaux by Kate DiCamillo

From the Mixed-up Files of Mrs. Basil E. Frankweiler by E. L. Konigsburg

Hatchet by Gary Paulsen

A Year Down Yonder by Richard Peck

Maniac Magee by Jerry Spinelli

apparent. Examples of such books are Deborah Wiles' *Love, Ruby Lavender*, Kate DiCamillo's *Because of Winn-Dixie*, Nikki Grimes' *Dark Sons*, and Wendelin Van Draanen's *Swear to Howdy*.

As teachers, we want to encourage children to sometimes step out of story worlds and consider the ways in which writers and illustrators craft their works. Students are most likely to move into this stance when they read distinctively crafted books such as David Macaulay's *Black and White,* in which four plot lines are intertwined, or Diane Stanley's *Raising Sweetness,* with its rich Texas dialect, or Brian Selznick's *The Invention of Hugo Cabret*, a 500+ page book told through a fresh blending of illustration, narrative, and cinematic techniques. Likewise, children are likely to talk about craft when they read books with distinctive patterns of organization, such as Audrey Wood's *The Napping House,* which has a cumulative structure, or Paul Fleischman's *Joyful Noise,* a collection of poems for two voices. Exquisitely illustrated books, such as Nancy Willard's *Pish, Posh, Said Hieronymus Bosch,* and books with remarkable language and imagery, such as Marilyn Nelson's *A Wreath for Emmett Till,* also encourage children to examine books as crafted objects.

You will also want to consider other factors when selecting material to use in literature circles. Perhaps the class is studying a topic in science or social studies that lends itself to further exploration in a literature circle. A teacher whose students are studying the weather might select Patricia MacLachlan's *Skylark* for use in the literature circle. This sequel to the Newbery Medal winner *Sarah, Plain and Tall* is set in the prairie in the early twentieth century and explores the impact of a devastating drought on the people who live there. Virginia Hamilton's *Drylongso* also shows the ravaging effects of drought, and the drama of Mildred Taylor's *The Well* unfolds in the context of a drought. Karen Hesse's *Out of the Dust* is set in the Dust Bowl during the Great Depression. Informational books about drought could also be used in the literature circle. Many of the books you choose to support cross-curricular studies are likely to be informational books, and discussions about informational books such as Diane McWhorter's *A Dream of Freedom*, a book about the civil rights movement, can be as lively as discussions of fiction. Literature can also be a powerful vehicle for helping students explore issues of social justice. Many contemporary works of children's literature address a range of issues that include racism, homelessness, urban upheaval, poverty, and war. For example, Eve Bunting has written about homelessness in two picture books—*Fly Away Home* and *December*. In *Breaking Through,* Francisco Jimenez tells the story of his own family's migrant experiences in California during the Great Depression. In the picture book *Working Cotton* Sherley Williams has created a poignant story about the life of migrant children. Top Shelf 14.4. features books that address racism and the struggle for racial equality in the United States. Books like these offer rich opportunities for students and teachers to look at both past and present injustices and to consider ways in which the experiences portrayed in books may relate to their own world.

Genre is yet another consideration in choosing books. Joyce Wiencek and John O'Flahavan (1994) note the importance of bringing in books from various genres so that students develop a repertoire of strategies appropriate to different genres. Although variety is important, particular genres do have the potential to offer students especially rich issues and ideas to explore. Many works of realistic and historical fiction, high fantasy, and poetry are especially likely to evoke students' best insights because of the significant themes that are often explored in these genres.

The teacher should not be the only one selecting books for use in literature circles. Louise Rosenblatt (1938) reminds us that the ultimate aim is to prepare students to select their own books wisely. Therefore, teachers must ensure that students have a voice in book selection. This can be accomplished by inviting students to suggest themes, authors, or particular titles they would like to read. Or, if a single title is to be

ILLUSTRATION 14.2 Readers will wonder if they are reading a single story or four different stories in this exquisitely designed Caldecott Medal winner. (Cover from *Black and White* by David Macaulay. Copyright © 1990 by David Macaulay. Reprinted by permission of Houghton Mifflin Harcourt Publishing Company. All rights reserved.)

used, the teacher can nominate a number of titles as possible candidates and let the students make the final selection. Yet another alternative is to have several small groups, each focusing on a different book, and give students the opportunity to decide which group to join after listening to introductions to the different books and browsing through them.

Forming the Discussion Groups

How many students should participate in a literature circle? How should students be selected for membership in a literature circle? Experienced teachers have found literature circles of widely varying sizes to be successful. Some teachers advocate having the whole class come together to talk about a book (Gonzalez, Fry, Lopez, Jordan, Sloan, & McAdams, 1995), while others believe that small groups are ideal (Short & Kauffman, 1995). There is no "best" size. It may, in fact, be a good idea to vary the size of literature circles, depending on the children's previous experience. At the beginning of the school year, if you find that most of your students have previously participated in literature discussions, they might be ready to launch immediately into small-group literature circles. However, if you work with very young children or if your students initially appear to be more at ease with traditional "gentle inquisitions," you might want to begin with whole-class literature discussion following read-aloud sessions. Then, once they feel comfortable with the format of the literature circle, students can begin working in small groups of five to seven students.

In organizing children into these smaller literature circles, be sure to consider group dynamics. Aim for a group that is balanced in terms of the students' leadership, communication, and social skills (Raphael, McMahon, Goatley, Bentley, Boyd, Pardo, & Woodman, 1992).

Length and Frequency of Literature Circles

The length of literature circles will vary. Early in the school year, sessions may be relatively short, perhaps ten or fifteen minutes (in addition to the time you may need to read the story to the students if you are presenting the literature through a read-aloud). Once children gain experience working in literature circles, they are likely to talk a lot more about engaging books—perhaps as long as thirty or forty minutes, although twenty minutes is probably a more typical length for a session.

The frequency with which literature circles meet will depend on various other decisions you make. Circles may be part of your read-aloud program, especially if your students do not yet have the reading skills needed to independently read books that have enough "meat" to engender good discussions. If this is the case, then you'll certainly be reading aloud to your students each day, and daily literature discussion will naturally go hand in hand with the read-aloud. Even if your students are able to read meaty books independently, there may still be times when you want to make literature discussion part of the daily read-aloud, especially at the beginning of the year before students are skilled in participating in book conversations. After your students have acquired experience as members of an interpretive community, you may sometimes want to make discussion an integral part of the read-aloud experience, especially when reading aloud a challenging chapter book. Some of the most interesting literature conversations occur when students are in the *midst* of a chapter book rather than at the end—and little wonder, for then students are caught up in the web of story events and very naturally have questions and predictions about how that web of events is likely to be sorted out (Martinez & Roser, 1994).

When your students do their own reading in preparation for the literature circle, you'll need to schedule reading time for them. Some teachers give students opportunities to touch base with one another while they are reading the book, even though more focused discussion is scheduled to take place when everyone has finished the book. By meeting briefly every three days or so, students can help one another to clarify any questions they might have about the book they are reading.

Some teachers set up a pacing guide for students' reading (or let students set up their own) and then gather students together for literature circle only after all of them have finished the book. When a schedule guides the literature circle, it's best to have students jot down their

Top Shelf 14.3

Picture Books with Distinctive Crafting

Uptown by Bryan Collier

In the Tall, Tall Grass by Denise Fleming

Small Green Snake by Libba Moore Gray

Snow Music by Lynne Rae Perkins

In November by Cynthia Rylant

When I Was Young in the Mountains by Cynthia Rylant

Raising Sweetness by Diane Stanley

Top Shelf 14.4

Books that Feature Racism and the Struggle for Racial Equality

Freedom Riders: John Lewis and Jim Zwerg on the Front Lines of the Civil Rights Movement by Ann Bausum

Martin's Big Words: The Life of Dr. Martin Luther King, Jr. by Bryan Collier

The Watsons Go to Birmingham-1963 by Christopher Paul Curtis

Harvesting Hope: The Story of Cesar Chavez by Kathleen Krull

Freedom's Children: Young Civil Rights Activists Tell Their Own Stories edited by Ellen Levine

A Dream of Freedom: The Civil Rights Movement from 1954 to 1968 by Diane McWhorter

Mayfield Crossing by Vaunda Micheaux Nelson

Freedom Summer by Deborah Wiles

thoughts about the book each day, either during or immediately after completing a daily reading assignment. They can then bring these notes to the literature circle.

Once students have finished reading a book, they'll be ready to get together for more focused talk. You may want to devote more than a single day to discussion. The first day could be devoted to sharing responses and even reading from their journal entries. At the end of the first session, ask students to generate a list of ideas for more intensive literature study on subsequent days. As a group, they can choose a topic (or two) from the list and prepare to talk about that topic at their next meeting. Preparation can include rereading relevant portions of the book to find support for their opinions. For example, after reading and sharing impressions about Patricia Reilly Giff's *Pictures of Hollis Woods,* Mr. Lee's class decided to spend their second literature circle exploring all of the diverse images of home found throughout the book. Such focused explorations of a book are especially likely to lead to in-depth discussion of theme and craft.

Roles of the Teacher in Literary Discussions

What roles do teachers play during literature circles? Again, there is no single answer to this question. The one thing educators agree on is that the teacher should not assume the role of sole leader, whose job it is to ask all of the questions. Beyond that, recommendations vary widely. Opinion is divided on the question of whether the teacher should be present during literature circles. Some educators argue that if teachers want students to learn to participate in literature conversations in much the same way more mature readers do, they must give students the opportunity to do so by bowing out of the picture (Raphael, et al., 1992). Others argue that students have the best opportunity to learn these skills by talking about books with experienced adult readers who model conversational roles (McGee, 1992). Adherents of both positions make valid points, so reducing the question to an either/or proposition (the teacher either is or is not present) is too simplistic. Perhaps the best question to ask is: Under what circumstances should the teacher participate in literature circles? We will address this question after taking a closer look at the roles the teacher may choose to play during literature discussions.

As participants in literature circles, teachers may, at various times, want to assume any of four different roles: (1) modeling response-based discussion, (2) helping children learn new discussion roles, (3) moving discussion forward, and (4) supporting literary learning as opportunities arise.

Teaching Idea 14.1
Responses to Books

As you engage children in literature discussions, try modeling different types of responses. For example, you might repeatedly share the things you wonder about when reading a story or talk about how the book connects to other books you have read. You can also elicit varied responses by bringing in different kinds of books. Try sharing stories that are personal narratives or memoirs (e.g., *My Man Blue* by Nikki Grimes). It's likely that the children's responses to a book like this will be personal or experiential. Share books that are also culturally distinct or books that evoke a social response (e.g., *Through My Eyes* by Ruby Bridges). How do the children's responses shift? Watch and see whether children begin to share similar responses to the ones you model during literature circle or if their responses vary with the perspective of the book.

Modeling Response-Based Discussion

Initially, on arriving in your classroom, many of your students are likely to feel comfortable only when the teacher is in charge of book talk. Students who have only participated in question-and-answer sessions will likely be reticent when first invited to share their personal thoughts about stories. Yet genuine talk about stories occurs as participants share and reflect on their own responses. The best way for students to learn how to do this is by seeing others share their thinking about stories. Thus it's important for teachers to sometimes share their own responses to stories. Students who see their teachers doing this are more likely to realize that their responses will be valued. As students gain confidence, discussion during literature circles will increasingly arise from student responses.

Teachers can also model diverse kinds of thinking about books. Ms. Gonzalez discovered that her students were not asking questions about books. So she decided to model this type of thinking when she and her students discussed Diane Stanley's *Captain Whiz-Bang,* a story in which a little girl named Annie names her new kitten Captain Whiz-Bang. At first, Annie and Captain Whiz-Bang are inseparable, but as Annie grows up, her interests turn to other things. Finally, she leaves home and

Ask the Educator . . .

Pat Scharer

Patricia L. Scharer

Favorite Books as a Child

As a child, I read constantly—under the picnic tables at the park, in a favorite tree, or under the covers quite certain that my parents didn't know I was up past my bedtime. My habit was fed by weekly trips to the public library and my personal collection of nearly every *Bobbsey Twins, Nancy Drew,* and *Hardy Boys* book published at that time. But *Charlotte's Web* was the book I loved best and returned to again and again as a child and later as an adult. I'll never forget the new insights I gained several years ago after reading an article describing Charlotte's efforts as a writer—the power of selecting just the right word but also the emotions and pain attached to the writing process. These experiences have inspired my deep appreciation for the talents and perseverance of those who write for children.

In what ways does book selection affect literary discussion?

One important way in which selection affects discussion depends on who selected the book. Was it assigned or chosen by the reader? Readers approach self-selected texts with an amazing sense of anticipation. I wonder if I'll like this book as much as Robert did? Will I think it is scary like Joanne? Will it be like other books I know by that author? This is a time when the teacher's role can shift from making assignments to sharing book talks about personal favorites and celebrating the opinions of every reader in the room to encourage others to read certain books.

The unique characteristics of each book also affect literary discussion. The sparse, tense prose of *Out of the Dust* by Karen Hesse inspires conversation not only about the relationships within the story, but also about the contribution of the format of the text on every page. Why is the story told with poetic form, a departure from narrative paragraphs, and how does this writing style affect readers' responses to the text? Some readers find the ending of Lois Lowry's *The Giver* unsettling and can't wait to discuss every possibility for what might happen next. Others devour each new *Redwall* or *Harry Potter* fantasy and rush to talk with a friend about the latest adventure or their favorite part. Picture books invite discussion not only about the text but about the illustrations as well. The elegant gold accents by Leo and Diane Dillon illustrating Virginia Hamilton's *The Girl Who Spun Gold* are important discussion points as readers make connections between the cover art, endpapers, gold-framed art in each two-page spread, and

Hamilton's tale of gold-spinning Lit'manhn and the young girl who must guess his name.

Some books, however, inspire a temporary silence. I read books like Avi's *The Barn* and Janet Hickman's *Jericho: A Novel* in one sitting, lost in the world of the book and unwilling to come out until the final page is turned. Immediately, however, I return to the text to read it one more time—not to find out what happened (I already know that!) but to experience the pleasure of the writing and gain new insights about the author's craft to share with others.

Patricia Scharer *is an associate professor at The Ohio State University, where she teaches courses in children's literature and early literacy. Her research on both topics has appeared in many journals such as* Reading Research Quarterly, The Reading Teacher, Language Arts, Reading Research and Instruction, *and* Research in the Teaching of English. *She has served as coeditor of the* Journal of Children's Literature *and the* Children's Books *column for* The Reading Teacher. *Patricia is currently coeditor of* Bookbird: A Journal of International Children's Literature. ∎

marries, leaving Captain Whiz-Bang behind with her parents. But she doesn't forget Captain Whiz-Bang and one day returns with her own child so that the little girl can meet the aged cat.

> *Ms. Gonzalez:* I wonder what kinds of things Captain Whiz-Bang will do with Annie's little girl. He can't run and jump and play as fast as he did before. So I wonder what kinds of things they did when they played together. Since he wasn't so active.

As Ms. Gonzalez continued to share wonderings of this nature, she found that it wasn't long before her students were sharing their own wonderings about the stories they read.

Helping Children Learn New Discussion Roles during Literature Circles

Unlike a traditional teacher-directed book discussion, a literature circle has no one participant who is in charge. Rather, all participants can initiate topics for discussion, and discussion proceeds as a conversation. How do you engage students in such conversations about books if they come to your classroom expecting to answer questions? Students have plenty of experience participating in conversations in other situations, and they can draw on these experiences during literature circles. Teachers can introduce students to book conversations by inviting them to think about all the times they've talked with their friends about movies or TV shows.

Since no one is "in charge" during a literature circle, you might want to establish simple guidelines for group behavior. Lea M. McGee (1995, p. 13) suggests the following:

- Sit in a circle so that everyone can see each other.
- Only one person talks at a time.
- Listen to each other.
- Stay on the topic.

One of the most important (and difficult) expectations to establish is that the literature circle is a time for conversation and it is therefore okay for students to talk directly with one another. Many of the teachers with whom we work find it helpful to remind students of this explicitly. By seating students in a circle so that they can talk to each other directly and occasionally reminding them that it makes sense to address their thoughts to peers, you will encourage them to engage in real conversations about literature.

Moving Discussion Forward

Teachers make an important contribution to literature circles when they move a flagging conversation forward. Earlier in the chapter, we pointed out that teachers do not direct literature discussion by asking question after question, but that does not mean a teacher should never pose a question. An occasional, well-placed question can jumpstart conversation. Lea McGee (1995) suggests that when preparing to meet with a literature circle, a teacher develop one or two interpretive questions that focus on "the significance of the story as a whole" and require the students to use inferential and critical thinking (p. 111). Wendy Saul (1989) calls questions of this nature "literary questions" and observes that good literary questions are connected to the story, but never have a single correct answer. A teacher might not need to ask these planned questions, depending on the direction in which the students move the conversation. However, if the students do not discuss an aspect of the story that the teacher feels is important, then the teacher may choose to pose a literary question before the literature circle concludes. The preparation of literary questions is discussed later in this chapter.

Louise Rosenblatt reminds us that not all responses are equally valid; rather, their value is determined by the extent to which readers make use of the text to defend and support their ideas (Farrell & Squire, 1990). This point suggests yet another way in which teachers can help to move conversations forward: by encouraging students to reflect on and return to the text to find support for their ideas, as Ms. Gonzalez did when her students discussed *Castle in the Attic:*

> *Chris:* I think that [the reason] Calendar didn't want to get the spells that turned the lead people into humans again is because all the guards would probably tell Alastor, and she'd be [turned] into lead.
>
> *Ms. Gonzalez:* What makes you think that?
>
> *Chris:* Remember the guards wanted to get away. It was against their will to be a guard. They didn't know that anyone was coming and they were obeying Alastor. And if Alastor found out they didn't tell him, then they would all be turned into lead.

To encourage students to address issues of social justice, teachers may also need to take steps to move literature discussion in a different direction. For example, when Ms. Silvan's students read Christopher Paul Curtis's *The Watsons Go to Birmingham-1963,* she found that her students' talk about the family car trip from Detroit to Alabama was not addressing the issues of racism that undergirded this portion of the book. So she decided to ask students why they thought the mother was planning the trip into the South so meticulously. When the students realized the planning was necessitated by the need to avoid possible encounters with racists, Ms. Silvan invited them to reflect on how they might feel if they had been traveling with the Watsons.

Supporting Literary Learning

Supporting students' literary learning is another contribution a teacher can make during literature discussions. Literary works are distinctive because of the ways in which writers structure and craft them, and Langer reminds us that readers can step outside of story worlds to reflect on the crafting of the literary work. We believe awareness of literary elements and the writer's craft can add a new dimension to students' experiences of stories. But it's important to proceed carefully in helping students learn about literary elements. Teaching about literature in a decontextualized manner—that is, without reference to actual stories—is the surest way to squelch students' love of literature. Lecturing about literature and asking students to memorize the definitions of literary terms have no place in the classroom. Yet we want children to understand how stories work, and the most appropriate way of doing this is by taking advantage of opportunities to foster awareness that arise naturally as students share their observations during literature circles. For example, the student who noticed "all the changes that keep happening in 'Cinderella'" had become aware of the transformation motif that is so prevalent in folklore. This student, who had a concept but not the literary language to name that concept, gave her teacher the perfect opening to introduce the term "transformation." The student's observation provided the teacher with an opportunity to "shoot a literary arrow" (Peterson & Eeds, 1990). Such an opportunity occurs when students, struggling to talk about the author's crafting, indicate that they have grasped a concept even though they do not have the language to talk about the element, device, or structure. Observing in elementary classrooms for extended periods of time, both Hickman (1979, 1981) and Kiefer (1983) found that children's talk about stories became more sophisticated when their teachers used the specialized language of art and literature with them during conversations about books.

We began this section with a question: What roles do teachers play during literature circles? The four roles that we have described point toward the answer to that question. At the beginning of the school year, many if not all of your students are likely to have limited experience with literature circles, and they may expect you to pose questions for them to answer. If this happens, you should initially join in as a literature circle participant. Then, as discussions become more conversational, you can let students work independently. However, we do not recommend that you pull entirely out of literature circle sessions, because opportunities to help students learn about literary crafting or explore issues of social justice can occur at any time.

Preparing to Assume Roles

Preparation is necessary if you are going to successfully assume the roles of modeling response-based discussion, moving discussion forward, and supporting literary learning. How might you best go about such preparation? On a first reading of a story, it makes sense to maintain your own response journal in which you record your initial reactions. You will then be able to draw on this record of your first spontaneous responses when modeling response-based discussion during literature circle discussions. To be in the best position to move discussions forward and support literary learning, you might want to return to the story for rereading and reflection. After reading a book that you plan to use with your class, perhaps you can join with other teachers using the same book to share insights and learn from one another. Peterson and Eeds (1990) recommend that teachers prepare to participate in literature discussions by reflecting on literary elements. They recommend that teachers reflect on questions such as the following:

- How has the author set up tension and relieved it?
- What is the central tension?
- How is it that some characters seem fully developed and others flat?

Ask the Educator . . .

Roxanne Henkin

Roxanne Henkin

How can teachers help students explore social justice issues through children's literature? Children's literature offers us an incredible venue for discussing issues of social justice. Both the lessons of history and contemporary social issues are beautifully portrayed in literature that is now available for children.

Social justice is important in all situations. Every group needs to learn about and respect others. Cross-cultural education helps us to see the universal in all peoples while at the same time affirming our roots. Those of us who teach in situations where most of our students come from one background have even more of an obligation to teach social justice.

Social justice means educating all children and inviting everyone into the classroom. We want to create classrooms where every child's voice is heard and no-one is silenced. By using read-alouds, DR-TA's, small and large group literature discussions, and writing in response to the texts, teachers can help students build on their experiences and understandings to explore social justice issues through children's literature.

I begin by using the Directed Reading-Thinking Activity (DR-TA). First, read through the text and find one or two natural stopping points. Then read the text aloud (or if the students are reading the text to themselves, have them read the story) to the first stopping point. Then close the book and ask the students the question, **What do you think will happen?** Sometimes students will give reasons with their predictions. If they don't, you can ask, **Why do you think**

so? In DR-TAs, students are trying to brainstorm as many answers as possible rather than to find just one correct answer.

After reading the book, I ask students what their questions are. For younger students, we share this in the large group. For older students, I have them write down their questions. I follow Karen Smith's (1995) ideas for discussions. After sharing our questions, I point out that each time they ask a question, they are planting the seed of an idea. Next, I demonstrate how they can make their ideas grow.

For example, fifth grade students in a Chicago Public School were reading and discussing the book *Your Move* by Eve Bunting. The book is about ten year old James. When his initiation into the gang endangers his six year old brother, Isaac, James finds the courage to walk away.

Some of the students' questions were:

- Why did he do it?
- Why did James want to be in their group?
- Why would a group of friends do that?
- Why didn't James watch out for his little brother Isaac?

- How do the events in the story bring about the growth and development of characters?
- How does place influence the characters or the mood or the movement of the story?
- Where were you moved by the story, and what did the author do to move you in this way?

Instructional Strategies to Foster Grand Conversations

It makes sense to begin discussion of a book or poem by inviting students to share and reflect on their own responses to the work. Rosenblatt (1938) has pointed out that problems may arise when teachers rely too heavily on strategies for guiding students' discussion. Once, she had become totally drawn into a poem she was reading, only to find herself rudely torn away from that web of emotion and reflection when she turned the page to find questions posed by the textbook editor asking her to identify the formal characteristics of the poem. The magic of what Rosenblatt has called the "lived through experience" was destroyed by those questions. By beginning discussions with students' ideas, teachers can avoid trivializing literary works through over-inspection (Babbitt, 1990; Cianciolo, 1982).

Although it is ideal for discussions to emerge from students' own responses to stories, this does not mean that the teacher should never guide their talk. There are many times when

Next, I demonstrate how they can make their ideas grow. I ask for volunteers to share their questions. We choose one question to use for our discussion model. For instance, we took the question:

- Why did James want to be in their group?

Students responded in the following way:

- This story makes me think about gangs and how they get people to join. It also makes me think about the fights between gangs.
- That boy that is 10 is dumb to try to do that and that he doesn't know that his friends are in a gang.
- I think that James shouldn't have gone there. It was not fun when he wrote on the sign. Why did James want to be in their group?
- It makes me think of someone trying to act tough but inside they want to cry and run but can't because they don't want their friends to think she or he's a baby. It's funny how the younger one knows best when you are alone with them. When you finally do whatever it is you think brings out the coolness in you, you really didn't want

to do it after all. You want only to take back what you've done because you joined a gang or club.

Finally, students were asked to put their thoughts in writing. The students wrote about what they were thinking after the discussion.

- The story is I think a lesson for me not to prove myself to no one or to do dangerous stuff like the boy in the story did. I learned if I were in my house with my little sister I would not do anything dangerous because my sister is six and if I would get shot or hurt, I do not know what I would do.
- Whatever James does, Isaac does even if James does something dangerous. James is ten and Isaac is six so James should watch what he does.
- James did the right thing and of course Isaac does the same. This really shows me that if you know that you have someone that wants to be exactly like you, don't make "the wrong move."

By combining DR-TAs with small and large discussion groups, we can model for students the kinds of questions and issues they might raise while reading social jus-

tice books. By debriefing with them afterward, we can highlight the great questions and ideas that they brought to the discussion, and can use in future discussions. By asking them to think about these texts through writing, we're adding another dimension to their understandings.

Using both fiction and non-fiction, we can help students to think about the complicated issues of society. Ultimately, we want students to be able to make good choices in school, the playground, and at home. But it can be difficult to talk about issues especially if they involve specific students in classrooms. By using children's literature to look at social justice issues and the ways other people deal with them, we're helping students to develop a rich array of strategies to draw on.

Good literature offers endless opportunities to think about and practice in our minds how we might act if we were to find ourselves in similar situations. By reading, writing and thinking about issues of social justice through children's literature, we offer students "the thousands of ethical conversations" needed to grow into strong and literate adults. Students also learn to problem solve, and learn that they can make a difference and change the world.

it may be necessary to move talk in a particular direction in order to reach an instructional goal. For example, assume that one of your goals in a unit entitled "Giants in Stories" is to help students explore the ways in which giants are typically characterized in literature. If students' responses do not focus on characterization, it may be necessary to use an appropriate instructional strategy to ensure that their discussion eventually moves in that direction. In this section, we present strategies designed to foster students' free responses as well as strategies for guiding responses.

Ask Open-Ended Discussion Questions

Open-ended discussion frameworks can encourage literature discussion based on students' own thinking. For example, you might begin discussion with a simple invitation: "Talk about what touched you the most" (Anzul, 1993, p. 190). Or you might choose to use a framework, based on the work of Aidan Chambers (1985) that invites students to share their (1) observations, (2) unanswered questions or wonderings, and (3) anything they were reminded of by the story (Martinez, Roser, Hoffman, & Battle, 1992). Frequently, students' observations are so insightful that lively conversations ensue. Students' wonderings are especially likely to evoke interesting discussions. Such was the case when Eric, a fourth-grader, shared one of his questions about C. S. Lewis's *The Lion, the Witch, and the Wardrobe* with his classmates:

> *Eric:* I wonder why Edmund wasn't mentioned in the last three chapters?
>
> *Ms. Fry:* Good question. Who wants to respond to that? Why hasn't the author mentioned Edmund in the last three chapters?
>
> *Carlo:* Probably because they could think that Edmund might be in the special place, like where the witch has them. Except he was a traitor, and they don't want to talk about him. They want to save him, and they talk about the other kids so that . . .
>
> *Carol:* And then like they're having the battles, and whoever wins the battle gets Edmund.
>
> *Jackie:* Cause if they kill the witch, then all the animals . . . she probably created most of her enemies. And then the witch dies; then all of her creatures die, and Edmund isn't a traitor anymore, and they can get him back.
>
> *Ms. Fry:* Boy, you got an answer to the question, I can tell! But the bottom line was that you think the author has some special purpose for holding Edmund aside for these last three chapters. Does anybody else have something to respond about Aslan, I mean keeping Edmund out of it so far?
>
> *Michelle:* Maybe the witch can turn . . . can turn one of those stone beasts into another animal, and then he could be a spy.
>
> *Ms. Fry:* That is an excellent idea. Maybe Edmund isn't what Edmund used to be anymore. That is a possibility.

An open-ended discussion framework gives students interesting alternatives for responding to a story without rigidly prescribing acceptable ways in which to respond. An added benefit of using this discussion framework is that it also works well as an invitation to journal writing, thereby integrating writing and discussion.

Pose Literary Questions for Discussion

As we noted earlier, there are times during literature discussions when teachers may want to pose questions. The best questions are real ones, that is, questions whose answers you really wonder about. In addition, if a teacher believes the students have not discussed an important aspect of a story, she or he may try to move discussion forward by asking a literary question. Carefully crafted questions can encourage students to think more insightfully about a story, explore ways in which a story may give insight into the world beyond the story, and gain insight into literary craft. According to Wendy Saul (1989), literary questions require interpretation and are the "key to literary comprehension, conversation, and enjoyment." She has identified some distinctive features of literary questions, which are listed in Table 14.1. Not every literary question will have all these features, but questions with one or more of these features have the potential to "lead children into the story and help them consider the work as a human construction where craft and effect are taken seriously" (Saul, 1989, p. 297).

Lea McGee (1995) recommends that in preparing literary questions, teachers read the story thoughtfully, staying in tune with their own responses to the story and noting conclusions they draw from it or noteworthy elements they discover. She further notes the impor-

Table 14.1   How to Ask Good Literary Questions
■ Ask questions that go beyond what is in the story but that always come back to the story.
■ Ask questions that help readers to better understand the story.
■ Ask questions that have at least two good answers, either of which can help the reader with the story.
■ Ask questions that raise issues that can be argued intelligently in different ways.
■ Ask some questions that deal with issues of craft.

tance of focusing on "the significance of the story as a whole" (p. 111). Saul (1989) describes a strategy, called "diagramming stories," that helps teachers to "focus on the structural peculiarities of a text, to comment on what in the book or story looms largest to the reader, and to describe, in something close to metaphorical terms, the essence of the book" (p. 297). Figure 14.1 shows a story diagram of Kate DiCamillo's ***Because of Winn-Dixie.*** The teacher who created the diagram explained what she was trying to do in this way:

> At the beginning of ***Because of Winn-Dixie***, Opal Buloni and the other people in her new town feel very lonely—and they are very separate. Miss Franny is in her library. Otis is in the pet store. Gloria Dump is in her yard. So that is why, on the Row 1, I have drawn Opal and all the other people by themselves. Then Opal found Winn-Dixie and he became her dog; so Opal wasn't as lonely anymore. She forms a little circle with her new dog. And you can see that happening on Row 2. But more important, Winn-Dixie helps Opal connect with other people; so I have added some circles. The first one contains Opal, Winn-Dixie, and Miss Franny. The second contains Opal, Winn-Dixie, and Otis. The last little circles contain Opal, Winn-Dixie, and Gloria Dump. But so far the townspeople are only connected to Opal, not to each other. It is only at the party given by Opal and Gloria Dump, that you see on Row 3, that everyone comes together to form a community with Winn-Dixie in the middle. And that is what the really large circle represents—a new community in which people are no longer so lonely and isolated.

Literary questions based on this story diagram might include the following:

- We see a lot of "reaching out" in this story. Opal reaches out to Miss Franny. Opal reaches out to Otis. Who is someone who reaches out to Opal? How does this "reaching out" help Opal?

- Opal's father, the Preacher, tells Opal ten things about her mother. Why is this list so important for Opal?

- At the end of the book when the Preacher says his prayer, he says, "thank you most of all for friends. We appreciate the complicated and wonderful gifts you give us in each other." Who were the "gifts" in Opal's life? How were they "complicated"? How were they "wonderful" for Opal?

- When different characters in ***Because of Winn-Dixie*** eat a litmus lozenge, they remember things that make them sad. What particular things does each character remember? What do these particular memories tell you about each character?

- Opal always describes her father as a turtle. Why do you think the author chose the turtle to represent the father?

- Why do you think the author chose to call this book ***Because of Winn-Dixie***?

FIGURE 14.1 Teachers can prepare to lead literature discussion by creating story diagrams.

Each of these questions goes beyond the text, but the answers (and there will be more than one answer to each question) naturally come back to the text. The questions should help readers to understand the story better, and the final two questions treat the story as a crafted object. Grand conversations may well be inspired when students are invited to respond to the kind of literary questions that Saul advocates.

Go to the Extension Activities section of Chapter 14 in the MyEducationKit for your book and complete activity #2 to think about ways computers can facilitate writing.

Writing in Response to Literature

Writing is another vehicle through which students can express their thinking in response to literature. The use of literature journals announces to participants the legitimacy and value of each individual's independent reaction to stories. Margaret Anzul (1993) suggests that students read with pen in hand so that they can record their immediate thoughts and feelings in their journal entries. There are a number of different kinds of journals teachers can use, including free response journals, prompted response journals, literary journals, and dialogue journals. These journals can also be used to support literature discussion.

Free Response Journals

In free response journals, students are encouraged to write about anything they choose in response to a story. The purpose of writing is to record thoughts, feelings, questions, and interpretations. If students are reading a book independently in preparation for their literature circle, they can be asked to write in their journals periodically, perhaps after completing each chapter. The primary value of free response journals is that they encourage children to "take time to think about what had been read" (Wollman-Bonilla & Werchadlo, 1995, p. 566). Children who have engaged in this type of thinking will have far more to contribute when they join their literature circles.

Free response journals can also be used effectively when the teacher reads a story aloud. Students simply spend a few minutes writing in response to the just-completed chapter or story. These few minutes of writing time give students an opportunity to record their thoughts and feelings before they are lost in the midst of discussion. The free response journal entries then serve as conversation starters. In writing in his journal about the final chapters of *Castle in the Attic,* first-grader Aidan recorded his "wonderings" (see Figures 14.2A and 14.2B) about this time travel fantasy in which William, a young boy, travels back in time on a quest with the Silver Knight:

What if the drawbridge falls off? What will William and the silver knight and Mrs. Phillips going to do? I wonder if they can swim? Who is going to give them food? When are they beginning the journey and defeat Alastor or are I wonder if they are not going to defeat Alastor? Or what if they defeat Alstor but not get the token? What if they die of hunger before they defeat Alastor and then what would they do?

When shared aloud, questions like Aidan's offer rich material for conversation.

When students first start to write in journals, especially free response journals, they might not be very comfortable recording their thoughts and feelings; instead, they might look for an easy way out by writing stock responses such as "I like this book" or "My favorite part was when the boy found the dog." Teachers can keep their own journals so that when students fall into "writing ruts," teachers can share their own entries, thereby modeling new ways of thinking about literature.

Teaching Idea 14.2
Journal Writing

When you first launch literature circles in the classroom, try engaging students in literature discussion without having them keep journals. Once they feel comfortable as members of a literature circle, encourage the students to record their responses in journals. You can then use the students' journal entries as conversation starters. How does literature discussion change with the use of journals?

As students become familiar with the open-ended nature of literature discussion, where personal connections are encouraged and all responses are valued, even reluctant students who might be hesitant to share gain confidence. When all students are invited to write a response first, and then volunteer to share, a student who has a lot to say and a student who has less to say will be on a more level playing field. The more hesitant, often less verbal student will have a response ready and be able to read right off the page rather than trail those who are quick to respond and often dominate discussions.

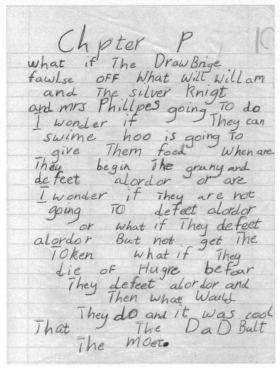

(A)   (B)

FIGURE 14.2   The ideas students record in their journals can serve as starters for literature discussion.

Prompted Response Journals

Some teachers use prompted response journals. That is, they give their students a prompt to respond to or they provide a number of prompts and encourage the students to choose one or more to use. The prompts can be generic ones that apply to almost any story:

- Select an important character and write about the kind of person she or he is.
- Choose a character you think is changing and growing in this story. Write about the ways in which the character is changing and the reasons for these changes.
- How is the setting important in this story?
- Write about some of the tensest moments in the story. How does the author make those moments tense?

Prompts can also be specific to a story. Each of the following prompts developed for ***The Giver*** was created to nudge the respondent into different stances. The first attempts to deepen the reader's engagement in the story world. The second invites students to step out of the story world and think about connections between their own world and the world created in the book. The final prompt encourages students to reflect on the crafting of the book.

- In Chapter 19 of ***The Giver,*** Jonas learns what "release" means. How do you think this knowledge will affect him?
- In what ways would our lives change if our society had a Giver who was the only person who held the memories of the past? Would you choose to live in that world or in the world as you now know it? Why?
- Why do you think Lois Lowry chose to leave the ending of her book so inconclusive?

Students who initially lack confidence in writing personal responses to a story may benefit from prompts such as these. Specific prompts also provide a means of encouraging students to respond to literature in more diverse ways.

Research supports the value of journal writing. Kelly (1990) invited her third-grade students to write in response to three open-ended prompts (What did you notice? How did you feel about the book? How is the book related to your experiences?). She found that over the school year, her students' responses grew in length and began to move from initial retellings and summaries to more analytic entries as well as those that reflected greater emotional involvement with stories. Kelly and Farnan (1991) compared the use of prompts that "emphasized and elicited readers' personal interpretations and interactions with text" (p. 278) to the use of non-reader response prompts ("Tell me about your book"). They found that the reader response prompts elicited more critical and analytic thinking from the fourth graders in their study.

Literary Journals

Pamela J. Farris (1989) has described the use of literary journals. In this type of journal, students assume the persona of one of the characters in the story and write journal entries as that character. For example, students reading **Elijah of Buxton** might become Elijah and write in their journals about their feelings when escaped slaves arrive in Buxton Settlement. Writing in a literary journal requires the reader to try to step into the shoes of the character and see story events and conflicts as that character might. Therefore, literary journals are more appropriate for older students than for younger ones, who still view the world from an egocentric perspective.

Dialogue Journals

In a dialogue journal, a student and the teacher (or another student) maintain a written dialogue about a story. The other types of journals that we have discussed can readily be shared during literature circles to spark group discussion; dialogue journals are more often used to extend discussion beyond literature circles. Researchers have found that students' responses deepen as they engage in written dialogues with adults (Farest & Miller, 1993; Nash, 1995).

Teacher/Librarian Partnership
The Nuts and Bolts

The standards for students' information literacy presented in Chapter 13 (see page 414) demonstrate several good reasons why teachers need to collaborate with librarians. Librarians understand the different forms of information, the ways it can be tested for accuracy and relevance, and the many ways it can be accessed—especially given the expanding range of electronic sources that are becoming available to schools. But teachers know what the curriculum calls for, who and what the children are reading and studying about, and what individual children's interests are. Thus each has a distinct role in their partnership.

Research has shown that children benefit from such collaboration. For one thing, librarians can help students past the "one right answer" approach to research, and put them in charge of their own inquiry as they use sources knowledgably. For another, children's search for information can be more authentic as they range further beyond the textbook, and use more resources than the teacher might have pre-arranged for them (Russell, 2000). It shouldn't be surprising that children's test scores improve the more librarians are involved with teachers in helping students

inquire and investigate. Librarians amplify the resources available to children and deepen their research skills; but they are most effective when they plan with teachers to integrate their investigative arts into the curriculum.

If you tend to think of the librarian mainly as your school's storyteller and book-checker-outer—perhaps even the person who shushes noisy children—you are not alone. Research shows that this stereotype still persists among teachers (Bishop and Larimer, 1999). The smart people who have worked closely with their librarians are the ones who are reaping the rewards for their students.

Bishop, K., & Larimer, N. (1999, October). "Literacy through collaboration." *Teacher Librarian, 27*(1), 15–20.

Manzo, K. K. "Study shows rise in test scores tied to school library resources." *Education Week on the Web*. [Online]. Available: http://www.edweek.org/ew/ewstory.cfm?slug=28libe.h19 [2000, August].

Russell, Shayne (2000). *Teachers and Librarians: Collaborative Relationships*. Syracuse: ERIC Clearinghouse on Information and Technology.

Fostering Response through Visual Sign Systems

Students can also respond to literature using the visual sign system. In fact, Short, Harste, and Burke (1996) believe that exploration of ideas in multiple sign systems is central to the learning process. Visual representations can help students to clarify and expand their initial responses and understandings; encourage multiple interpretations; and focus thoughtful discussions (Dooley & Maloch, 2005).

Art may be an especially natural outlet for literary response for younger children (Kelly, 1990; Paley, 1997). Such was the case with eight-year-old Eliseo who was listening to a read-aloud of *Miko,* a fantasy set in Lapland deep in the Arctic winter. Fearing that light would not return to the Arctic because King Winter had captured the daughter of the sun and moon, Miko journeyed to King Winter's mountain to confront the evil king. Eliseo listened intently to the description of King Winter: "His white hair streamed wildly from his skull, matted, thick, and crusted with frost. His clothes were sheer and swayed about his skeletal frame like mist on a freezing ocean. His teeth were tapered like blades of ice . . ." (p. 63). At this point Eliseo interrupted the reading to announce, "I can see him, and I'm going to draw him when we finish reading." The resulting representation reflected the child's attention to and appreciation of the text's descriptive details. (See Figure 14.3.)

FIGURE 14.3   Eliseo's artistic response to Miko.

Eliseo's artistic response was spontaneous, and teachers can actively encourage this type of response by providing space, time, a rich variety of materials, and suggestions for book-related artistic activities (Hickman, 1981). Materials can range from crayons and markers to paints, paper, cloth, and other materials. Teachers can introduce children to varied formats for responding that include paintings, drawings, collages, murals, wall hangings, and roller movies. Computer painting and drawing software, as well as scanning technology, offer still more avenues for artistic response.

Invitations to Respond through Art

In classrooms where artistic expression is valued, children will often respond to literature spontaneously through art. There may be times, however, when teachers choose to guide children's artistic responses to literature. For example, students can be invited to use art to explore a character's feelings at a critical juncture in a story or to represent what they believe to be the most important experience a character had in the story. Prompts of this nature can invite thinking about critical aspects of stories.

Visual Response Journals

Visual response journals can serve essentially the same purpose as other types of response journals. They are especially effective for use with young children, English language learners, and older students who may be reticent writers. Hubbard, Winterbourne, and Ostrow (1996) used visual response journals with primary-level children, inviting them to illustrate their favorite section of a story or to draw what was going on in their minds as they read or heard a story. They found that responding through drawing led to greater involvement in stories. Further, the children's drawings served as excellent conversation starters when they were shared during literature circles.

Sketch-to-Stretch

Sketch-to-Stretch is a strategy through which students sketch their story interpretations (Short, Harste, & Burke, 1996; Whitin, 1996). Rather than representing what happens in a story, students create symbolic sketches. This is an especially effective strategy for use with upper elementary and middle school students.

As students are introduced to Sketch-to-Stretch, teacher guidance is important. For example, for a class reading *Pictures of Hollis Woods,* a story about a foster child seeking a family of her own, the teacher might guide students to talk about Hollis's relationship to her various foster mothers. Students could be asked what symbol, sign, or shape they think might best represent Hollis and how her relationship to her various foster parents might be represented through symbols. Students could also be invited to consider how color might be used to signify Hollis's feelings toward the people in her life. As students talk about ways of representing their ideas about the story, the teacher can challenge them to consider other perspectives.

Once students understand how Sketch-to-Stretch works, they can work in small groups independent of the teacher. However, much of the strategy's value comes from opportunities for students to come together to talk about why they have represented the story in a particular way. Students expand their personal understanding of stories when they share their sketches with peers and have the opportunity to explain their interpretations and articulate their thoughts.

Exploring the Craft of Illustrators

Teachers can also use art to help students "step out" of the story world and gain insight into the craft of illustrators. As part of a literature study focused on the books of Lois Ehlert, children can try their hand at creating the same type of three-dimensional collages that Ehlert uses in many of her picture books. Or, while reading stories written by Leo Lionni, children can experiment with the torn-paper collage technique that characterizes much of this artist's work. Children can try out many of the artistic media discussed in Chapter 3 with which illustrators of children's books work. The website of the *National Center for Children's Illustrated Literature* provides directions for using the techniques of a variety of well-known children's book illustrators. To foster children's visual literacy, teachers can also encourage children to experiment with various visual elements. For example, children can be invited to carefully select colors that they believe capture the shifting moods of a story.

Promoting Response through Graphic Organizers

Teachers can also use graphic organizers to foster, guide, and capture children's responses to literature. We will highlight two different types of organizers—language charts and story webs.

Language Charts

Language charts function much as literary questions do: They focus students' thinking about literature. Language charts were originally designed for use with related sets of picture books (Roser, Hoffman, & Farest, 1990). These large charts, which are intended to be displayed on a classroom wall, are ruled into a matrix. The titles (and perhaps authors and illustrators) of the books in a set are recorded along one axis of the matrix. Questions that are devised to stimulate connections among the books are recorded along the other axis. These questions might focus attention on particular aspects of the story worlds in the featured books, on themes that emerge from the books, or on the crafting of the stories or illustrations. Students' responses to the questions are recorded on the matrix as each book is read and discussed.

A language chart devised by a kindergarten teacher for use in a Denise Fleming author/illustrator study appears in Figure 14.4. The chart, which was designed to guide

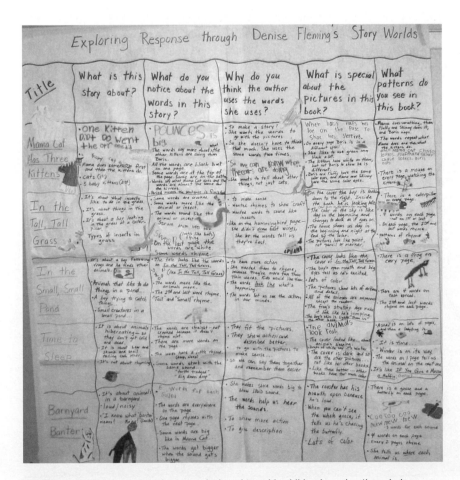

FIGURE 14.4 This language chart was designed to guide children's explorations during a Denise Fleming unit.

students to think about the distinctive ways in which Fleming uses words and the defining characteristics of her illustrations, included the following questions:

- What is the story about?
- What do you notice about the words in this story?
- Why do you think the author uses the words she uses?
- What is special about the pictures in this book?
- What patterns do you see in this book?

The kindergartners did impressive thinking in response to these prompts. For example, when asked what they noticed about the words in *In the Tall, Tall Grass*, the children observed the way in which word layout mimicked the movement of the featured animal (see Figure 14.5). In talking about patterns they saw in the book, the children noted the appearance of the caterpillar on each page, as well as Fleming's use of rhyming words throughout the book (see Figure 14.6).

A language chart designed for use with a unit entitled "Foxy Figures" appears in Figure 14.7. The questions on this chart encourage students to explore the stock character of the fox as it frequently appears in children's literature. The chart in Figure 14.8 focuses students' attention on the style of Chris Van Allsburg for a unit on that author/illustrator.

Language charts can be adapted for use with chapter books. Rather than listing titles of various books along the vertical axis of the chart, the teacher lists appropriate chunks of the chapter books. The sample chart in Figure 14.9 invites students to think about character development in *The Midwife's Apprentice,* a work of historical fiction by Karen Cushman. Students would complete a section of this particular chart after reading each chapter of the book.

Some teachers report that a language chart can become just a "worksheet on the wall" if the class begins to complete the chart too soon after reading. These charts are not meant to displace conversations about books. Rather, teachers and students should turn to the language chart only after having fully discussed a book. Teachers who have used language charts in this way report that they can be effective tools for fostering literary understandings. In fact, many teachers change the design of their language charts throughout the school year to

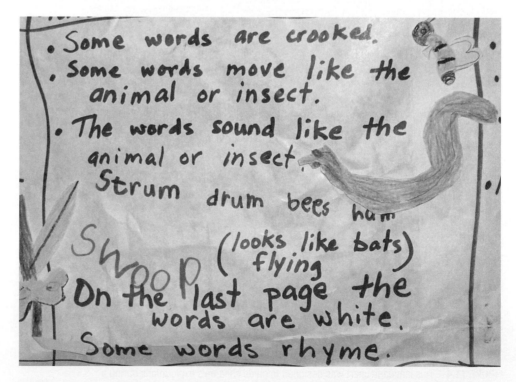

FIGURE 14.5 The teacher recorded the children's observations about Denise Fleming's distinctive use of words in *In the Tall, Tall Grass*.

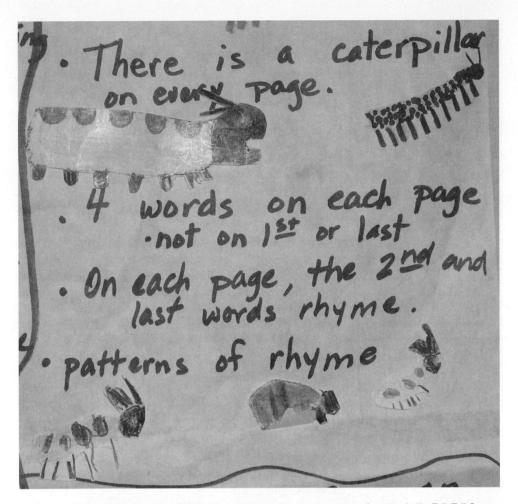

FIGURE 14.6 The teacher recorded the children's observations about patterns found in *In the Tall, Tall Grass*.

Foxy Figures					
Title	Who were the characters?	How did they meet the fox?	What was the fox's goal?	What happened to the fox in the end?	Things that made us laugh
Doctor De Soto					
Wings: A Tale of Two Chickens					
Peeping Beauty					
etc.					

FIGURE 14.7 The questions on this language chart are designed to help children explore the fox as a stock character in literature.

The Stories of Chris Van Allsburg			
Title	What strange things happened in the story?	What surprise did the ending hold?	What we noticed about Mr. Van Allsburg's illustrations
Jumanji			
The Wreck of the Zephyr			
The Sweetest Fig			
The Polar Express			

The Midwife's Apprentice			
	What do we discover about Beetle/Alyce in this chapter?	What important experience does Beetle/Alyce have in this chapter?	How does this experience impact her?
Chapter 1			
Chapter 2			
Chapter 3			
Chapter 4			
Chapter 5			
Chapter 6			
etc.			

help students continue to explore different aspects of literature. For example, the questions that Ms. Perez, a kindergarten teacher, uses on her language charts at the beginning of the year are designed to help her students learn basic literary language: Who are the characters? What is the setting? What was the problem in the story? Once students have made these concepts their own, she changes the chart questions to focus on other important literary understandings.

Story Webs

Story webs are visual displays that show how categories of information are related; the name arose because they often look like the webs spiders build. Teachers use story webs to achieve different purposes, but Karen Bromley (1991) believes that all too often, they overlook the potential of webs to foster responses to literature. Story webs, like literary questions, focus students' thinking about literature. According to Bromley (1995), webs can be used to support and extend students' literary understanding in many ways. Specifically, webs can help students:

- identify important issues in stories
- make connections between books
- understand how literary and artistic elements work
- explore characteristics of different genres
- understand the literary devices that authors use (perspective, metaphor, and so on)

Story webs can emerge from children's responses. This happened in Ms. Alducin's class when her students were discussing Barbara Nichol's **Beethoven Lives Upstairs**. This book is told almost exclusively through the correspondence between young Christoph and his Uncle Karl. To make a living after the death of Christoph's father, his mother has rented the upstairs portion of their house to Beethoven. Mistaking the famous composer's eccentric behavior for madness, Christoph is appalled. Over a period of two years, Christoph keeps his uncle updated on the happenings upstairs, and his uncle's letters gently help Christoph to develop compassion for his neighbor.

Ms. Alducin introduced the web that appears in Figure 14.10 by saying "Someone said earlier that Christoph's feelings about Beethoven changed a lot in the book, and I want us to explore that idea a little more." The web chronologically records Christoph's feelings toward Beethoven and the story details related to those feelings. Christoph's increasingly mature understanding of Beethoven reveals his own growth as a character.

Responding through Drama

Dramatization takes many forms, but in any form, it is an especially engaging way of inviting children into literature. In story dramatizations, children become story characters (at least for a little while) and look at the world through the eyes of those characters. Dramatizing even part of a story can be an engaging way for children to unpack its meaning. In this section, we'll look at three different forms of literature-based dramatizations.

Story Theater

Story theater is a form of drama in which participants mime a story as it is read aloud, in effect "moving through" the story world once again. Because no dialogue is required, story theater is probably the simplest form of drama and is especially well-suited for use with very young children. Also, because groups of participants (or all participants, for that matter) can play the same role in story theater, it is a good introduction to drama for students who feel shy about participating.

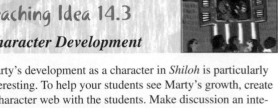

Teaching Idea 14.3
Character Development

Marty's development as a character in *Shiloh* is particularly interesting. To help your students see Marty's growth, create a character web with the students. Make discussion an integral part of the process. As a class, brainstorm different adjectives that describe Marty. Accept all of the words initially. Several can usually be combined as synonyms of others. Negotiate with the class in order to narrow the adjectives to the best four to six. (Students will need to provide rationales for their positions.) Now create a web with Marty in the middle and the descriptors at the ends of the "strands" of the web. For example, the students might say Marty was caring or compassionate. Now, on each strand write a quote or excerpt from the text that supports that descriptor. Students might say, "Marty was compassionate when he wanted to protect Shiloh from the abusive owner." Sometimes reentering the text is intimidating for students, but they are often eager to substantiate the descriptions when they have collaborated to choose the words.

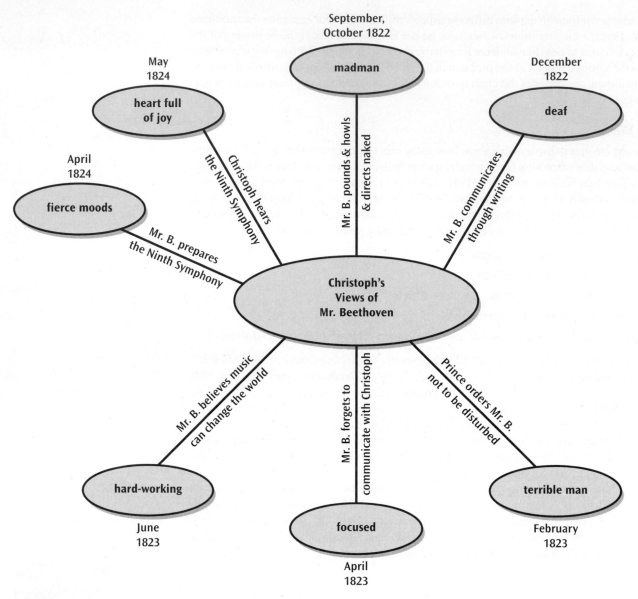

FIGURE 14.10 Character development can be explored with a web.

Typically, story theater is not performed for an audience. It is the actual acting out that is important for young children. Sometimes children won't be satisfied with playing the story only once and will ask to act the story out again immediately.

What the Player Does in Story Theater

Although the players in story theater don't have to worry about dialogue, nonetheless, they assume active parts. First, the players must listen to the narrator in order to act out the story line appropriately. Even more important, the players need to attend to characterization, and the teacher might want to encourage discussion about what the characters are like.

Selecting Stories for Story Theater

For story theater, look for stories that rely on extensive narration, have plenty of action, and use minimal dialogue. Esphyr Slobodkina's *Caps for Sale* works well. The main character is a peddler of hats who carries his wares on his head. One day the peddler goes for a walk in the country. (Imagine how carefully you would have to walk with hats piled high on your head.) When the peddler gets tired, he sits down (very carefully) and leans (very slowly) against a tree to nap; on waking, he reaches up (slowly and carefully) to make sure his hats are still in place. They're gone! (Imagine the peddler's reactions!) After a great deal of looking to the left, right, and all around, the peddler finally looks up into the tree, and on every branch of the tree, there is a monkey wearing a cap. (What a surprise!) The peddler is upset, so he shakes his fist at the monkeys, and what happens? You've heard the saying "Monkey see, monkey do." Well, that is just what happens. The monkeys shake their fists right back at the peddler, and each of the peddler's subsequent expressions of frustration is repeated precisely by the monkeys. Children love to play this story repeatedly.

Readers' Theater

In readers' theater, students don't act out stories; they read (not memorize) scripted versions of stories and rely on their voices to convey the characters' emotions. The promise of an audience can add to the success of readers' theater because students are likely to be motivated to practice and refine their readings in order to do well when they perform.

What the Player Does in Readers' Theater

Readers' theater is more formal than story theater because the aim is for the players to present as polished a reading as possible. Usually, readers need to practice reading a script repeatedly to learn to read their parts fluently and interpret them with sensitivity.

Although the players in a readers' theater presentation don't have to worry about how to act out the story, they do have to be concerned with character interpretation. What is the character like? How does he or she react to the events in the story? How (if at all) does the character change over the course of the story? What variations in speaking tone, volume, speed, or pitch might convey particular emotions? Both the teacher and fellow students can offer feedback after each practice reading, sharing what they especially liked about the interpretations and offering suggestions for improvement.

Selecting Stories and Creating Scripts for Readers' Theater

Both picture books and chapter books can be used for readers' theater. Books containing extensive dialogue are the best choices. Some picture books are perfect for readers' theater; these ready-to-use picture books are written in dialogue form without dialogue tags ("he said" or "she replied") and contain no narration. Angela Johnson's *Tell Me a Story, Mama* is a dialogue between a little girl and her mother; Chris Raschka's *Yo! Yes?* is a simple dialogue between two little boys. Picture books that contain some narration and a great deal of dialogue with dialogue tags can be made into readers' theater scripts quite easily. When searching for portions of chapter books to turn into scripts, look for the same features you would choose in picture books: minimal narration and extensive dialogue.

Older students can help to create scripts. You might want to use teacher-created scripts initially, but once students gain some experience with readers' theater, show them how you select text and turn it into scripts. Students will soon be reading stories with an eye toward whether they can be readily transformed into scripts.

Creative Dramatics

In creative dramatics, players act out the story. However, unlike staged productions of plays, creative dramatics involve no sets; few, if any, props; and usually no audience. And instead of having a script, the players improvise dialogue.

What Is Required of the Player

Creative dramatics can be challenging, especially when students first try it. Because no one reads the story (unlike story theater), the students must remember the story line. And because there is no script (unlike readers' theater), students are on their own in creating dialogue. And, of course, the players in a creative dramatics activity must be just as attuned to characterization as the players in story theater and readers' theater.

Top Shelf 14.5

Books to Use for Story Theater

Nose to Toes by Marilyn Baillie

Here Come Poppy and Max by Lindsey Gardiner

Crocodile Beat by Gail Jorgensen

We're Going on a Bear Hunt by Michael Rosen

Caps for Sale by Esphyr Slobodkina

Top Shelf 14.6

Books with Two Voices to Use for Readers' Theater

You Read to Me, I'll Read to You by Mary Ann Hoberman

Hey, Little Ant by Phillip and Hannah Hoose

Tell Me a Story, Mama by Angela Johnson

Who Took the Cookies from the Cookie Jar? by Bonnie Lass and Philemon Sturges

The Day Jimmy's Boa Ate the Wash by Trinka Hakes Noble

Yo! Yes? by Chris Raschka

Top Shelf 14.7

Books with Multiple Voices for Readers' Theater

Hattie and the Fox by Mem Fox

Brown Bear, Brown Bear, What Do You See? by Bill Martin, Jr.

There's a Dragon About by Richard and Roni Schotter

Tiger Soup by Frances Temple

Albert's Impossible Toothache by Barbara Williams

Teacher Support in Creative Dramatics

If creative dramatic activities are going to succeed, it is important for the teacher to carefully organize and support the children's efforts. In order to dramatize a story, the teacher should carry out the following steps. We will explain each one below.

- Do warm-ups to prepare the students to put on a dramatic performance.
- Choose critical moments from the story to dramatize.
- Invite students to "segment" the situation.
- Dramatize the scene.
- Coach from the side.
- Guide the students to reflect on the dramatization.

Warm the students up to do drama.   There are many warm-up activities that can be used to prepare students to act out their parts with more expression. Here are several:

1. *Stretches*. Have the students stand in a circle. Tell them to stretch their arms as high as they can as they spread their feet apart and make very wide faces. Now tell them to shrink up into tiny balls. Then stretch out big again. Have them do the same with their faces as you shout: "Lion face!" "Prune face!"

2. *Mirrors*. Have students pair up and stand opposite each other. One will be the "person" and the other will be the person's reflection in the mirror. Have one person move very slowly as the other person mirrors his or her movements. Then switch roles.

3. *Statues*. In the same pairs, have one student be the sculptor and the other be the statue. Have the sculptor arrange the statue into a pose (but not an embarrassing or a painful one). Take a moment to have the sculptors walk around the room and admire each other's work. Then switch roles.

4. *Superactions*. Explain to the students that when we do things with other people we often act on two levels: what we are doing, and what we mean by what we are doing. For example, a person in a restaurant orders a meal—that's the action. But the person may have different purposes in mind that are reflected by the way he orders the meal. He may try to engage the waiter in friendly conversation, because he is lonely. Or she may try to impress the waiter with her knowledge of fine foods because she needs approval and likes to show off. Or he may try to be as inconspicuous as possible, because he just robbed a bank and ducked into the restaurant to escape being captured. In all three cases, the actions are the same: to order a meal. But the *superactions* are variously: (1) to make friends, (2) to show off, or (3) to escape notice. Once you explain what superactions are, you can have students practice them by setting up brief situations. Tell the students that the *action* will be to greet someone. The *superactions* will be written on small pieces of paper and given privately to each actor. Superactions might be: to brush the person off (you're in a hurry), to show the person how infatuated you are with them, to enmesh the person in a long conversation, to make the person go away, to get this over with as soon as possible, or to stretch this out as long as possible—you're really in need of companionship. Have different pairs of students act out the same scene and the same actions, but with different superactions. Allow enough time for the other students to guess what they thought the superaction was and explain why they thought so.

Teaching Idea 14.4
Dramatizing with Puppets

Young children are often better able to demonstrate their story comprehension through dramatization than in writing or in verbal explanation. By studying the illustrations in the books read, they can design puppets out of construction paper and a paper lunch bag for the characters and then perform a section from a book. Classmates will be entertained and can ask questions about the selection made following the presentation. It is telling for the teacher to hear the sound of the voices the performers choose or the intonation with which the passages are read.

Choose critical moments.   It is usually best to dramatize just a few choice scenes from the story, especially the turning points—the places when the most is at stake. In the story of *Jack and the Beanstalk,* such a critical scene might be when Jack first approaches the Giant's castle, knocks on the door, and is greeted by the Giant's wife.

Segment the Situation. After you have chosen a scene for the students to dramatize, assign students to each of the roles. Note that the same scene can be acted out by more than one group; they and the audience can compare their performances. Invite each student to think about the situation from his or her character's point of view. For example, what must be on Jack's mind when he approaches the huge castle door? What do the door and the walls of the castle look like? How large are they in proportion to Jack? What does Jack hear around the place? What does he smell? How does the place make him feel? What makes him pound his fist on the door? What's at stake for him? What are his choices? What will he do if he doesn't knock on the door? Why does he decide to do it? Engage in the same thinking for the Giant's wife. How does the knocking sound to her—huge, or puny? What does she think when she sees the small but plucky boy at her door? What thoughts go through her mind, knowing what she knows about her husband? What are her feelings as she looks down at Jack? Before they begin the dramatization, ask the characters to focus their minds on a few of these considerations as they prepare to act out the scene.

Dramatize the scene. Use just a few props and minimal costumes to help students think their way into their roles. Ask the other students to watch carefully and see what the actors make them think of.

Side coach As the director, don't be passive, but take opportunities to make suggestions from the sidelines that will help children act more expressively. Sometimes it helps to offer students some choices. For example, you might ask the student playing Jack, "Do you feel scared now, or brave? How can you show us how you're feeling?"

Invite reflection. Ask the other students about what they saw. What did they think was on the characters' minds? It is a good idea to invite several groups of students to dramatize the same scene, and discuss the aspects of the situation that each performance brings to light.

Selecting Stories for Creative Dramatics

The same sorts of stories that are great for storytelling also work well for creative dramatics. In particular, stories with strong action sequences, lots of dialogue, and minimal narration work well—stories such as *Petunia* or "The Three Billy Goats Gruff." Vivian Paley (1981) found that her kindergartners enjoyed playing the longer and more complex fairy tales over and over because the stories had enough depth to challenge the players in their interpretations.

Responding to Poetry

In this section, we share ideas for engaging children in poetry. There are several ways of doing this: surrounding children with poetry, encouraging children's responses to poetry, encouraging public performances of poems, and helping children write poetry.

Making Songs and Poems a Part of the School Day

Songs and poems fit into the school day in a surprising number of ways, and the more children get used to them, the more they will enjoy them. Poems should be shared often in read-aloud

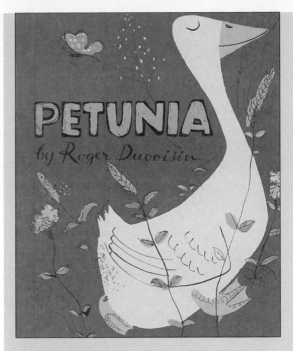

ILLUSTRATION 14.3 The story of Petunia, a silly goose who creates pandemonium in the barnyard, has become a classic. ("Book Cover," copyright 1950, 1977 by Knopf Children, from *Petunia* by Roger Duvoisin. Used by permission of Alfred A. Knopf, an imprint of Random House Children's Books, a division of Random House, Inc.)

Teaching Idea 14.5
Story Dramatizations

Dramatizing stories gives students permission to step outside of themselves and behave in different ways. Timid children can often surprise us because there is nothing timid about Amazing Grace (*Amazing Grace* by Mary Hoffman) or Despereaux (*The Tale of Despereaux* by Kate DiCamillo). However, Wemberly (*Wemberly Worried* by Kevin Henkes) worries a lot, which is a lot like being timid. Students can improvise dramatically in a mock wax museum of book characters. Very few props are necessary. Mainly the student stands frozen until a patron comes by. A "button" can be pushed or a "motion detector" can alert the character to begin the monologue. The student must be able to discuss events in the story from the point of view of the character portrayed. If the story is not told in first person or is told from another character's point of view, the portrayal can be a bit more challenging. Remind students that the character at the end of a story may have changed significantly from the beginning. Even determining which pose to hold while talking can be very interpretive of the character.

time. They should be read with an expressive voice for pure enjoyment and reflection. Topical poems can be posted around the room as comments on the seasons, on holidays, or on science or social studies units. You can find poems appropriate to nearly any occasion in anthologies such as *The Random House Book of Poetry,* edited by Jack Prelutsky, which indexes poems by topic. Children's own poems should be shared and posted along with those of published poets. Poetry can also be included along with other literary works in the readings for a thematic or literary unit (see Chapter 15).

Here are some further ideas for sharing poetry with children and young people.

Songs and Poems in the Reading Circle

Poems and songs make excellent fare for beginning reading instruction. Their catchy rhythms and rhymes give children support and alleviate some of the burden of word recognition. You might introduce kindergartners and first graders to a short poem or song lyric, with the words written on a large chart. Make smaller versions for them to keep in a growing notebook of verses.

Two reliable sources of song lyrics for children are Kathleen Krull's *Gonna Sing My Head Off!,* illustrated by Allen Garns, and the collection by Peter Blood and Annie Paterson entitled *Rise Up Singing*. Some sources of poems for children are given in the Recommended Books list at the end of Chapter 6.

Poetry and Tell

For older children, we especially like the suggestion that teachers initiate Poetry and Tell sessions (Wolf, 1993). Children are invited to choose a poem (with guidance from the teacher, as necessary) to share with the class.

With younger children, you can extend this idea by inviting them to bring in single words that intrigue them, a particularly vivid description, or a funny or interesting way of saying something—fragments of intriguing language to celebrate with the class. After all, the idea is to encourage—really, to keep alive—the fascination with language that all children were born with.

Poetry Break

Another worthwhile suggestion is having a Poetry Break every day or so (Wolf, 1993). A Poemster of the Day (the principal, a custodian, a parent, or one or more children) is elected to go from class to class reading or reciting a poem—perhaps the same poem in each class. The teacher holds up a big sign that says "Poetry Break!" and the poemster delivers!

Poetry Caravan

When the students have learned poems and interesting ways to present them, the whole class may go from room to room throughout the school, "serenading" other classes with poetry.

Encouraging Responses to Poetry

For years, teachers believed that the most reasonable way to have children respond to a poem was to have them say what it meant and analyze its parts. But poetry speaks to us on many levels beside the intellectual one, and to assume that it is possible to summarize in so many words what a poem "is really saying" is usually to miss the point. The issue often is not what the poem says or means, but what it does and how it does it.

Often the best way to respond to a poem is not analytically but expressively. Invite children to draw as you read a poem to them. Ask them to invent sound effects or movements to accompany the verses. Have them act the poem out. Tell them to shout out the phrases they like best.

Teaching Idea 14.6
Poetry Center

Children benefit from reading texts repeatedly. One way of encouraging children to reread poems, chants, and songs is by creating a poetry center constructed around the overhead projector. Type up poems you have previously read aloud to students and make them into transparencies that can be placed in a simple hanging file. Children will be enticed to read familiar poems in this new format. When the poem is placed on the projector, the light from the projector shines the words onto a wall or screen where the enlarged words beckon to be read. Many teachers supply pointers in the shape of index fingers for younger children to use in following along at the projector. Small groups of students will likely want to gather around the screen to chime in on the fun. (As the number of overhead poems increases, a ruler can be placed in the file whenever a transparency is extracted so the child can replace the sheet in the proper place to facilitate finding it again.)

Choral Reading and Reciting

Most poetry is anchored in sound and is intended to be read or recited aloud. This section shares suggestions for making an event out of oral reading and reciting. Choral reading and reciting—the reading and reciting of poems by a chorus or "voice choir"—can be great fun, as children explore the dramatic possibilities of both poems and their own voices.

Whole Chorus Presentations

The trick to having a whole chorus of children recite is to keep all the voices animated, not singsongy. Children learn to focus on their sound if they are challenged to vocalize a poem in a certain way.

Suppose you ask children to recite the traditional poem "The Grand Old Duke of York":

The Grand Old Duke of York
He had ten thousand men.
He always marched them up the hill
Then he marched them down again.
And when they were up they were up
And when they were down they were down.
And when they were only halfway up
They were neither up nor down.

To focus their attention on the sound they want to make, tell children the poem is about a group of soldiers marching along. Ask them, "Are the soldiers wounded and weary, or are they marching snappily in a parade? Which? OK, then how should they sound? Do they sound one way as they are marching proudly to battle and another way when they're dragging themselves painfully home again?"

Poems in Dialogue

Many poems can be effectively divided between two voices. When children recite A. A. Milne's poem "Happiness" in two voices—one child taking every other line—they can bring out the plodding, two-step gait of a small child in big boots and a raincoat:

John had
    Great Big
Waterproof
    Boots on;
John had a
    Great Big
Waterproof
    Hat;
John had a
    Great Big
Waterproof
    Mackintosh—
And that
    (Said John)
Is
    That.

The trick with using more than one voice is to keep the poem moving on the beat. Pairs of children can take parts and practice a poem until they can recite it smoothly. You might need to clap out the beat for them the first time through. (You might also have to tell children that in England a raincoat is called a "mackintosh.")

Inviting Children to Write Poetry

Here's a paradox: Surveys show that children prefer to listen to and read rhymed and rhythmic poetry, yet they have great difficulty writing rhymed and rhythmic poems, at least ones that make good sense. When teachers help children to write poems, they often share techniques that will lead the children to write unrhymed poems. Not only is this the most likely way of ensuring successful poetry-writing sessions, but also it broadens children's appreciation for modern poetry, since most poets these days—particularly those writing for adults—do not write rhyming poems. The following are suggestions for writing poems that are expressive but that do not rhyme.

Making Metaphors

Ask students to think of a person they believe has some particular quality—say, a lively personality. (Have them hold off writing the person's name.) They should write the answer to each of these questions on a line by itself:

- If this person were a stage of a fire, what stage (a tiny spark, roaring flames, glowing embers)?
- If this person were a season of the year, what season?
- If this person were weather, what sort of weather?
- If this person were a bird, what kind of bird?
- If this person were landscape, what landscape?
- If this person were music, what kind of music?
- If this person were footwear, what kind of footwear?
- If this person were a car, what kind of car?
- If this person were a time of day, what time of day?

On the line below their last answer, have the children write the person's name. Now they can tinker with these lines—move them around, add or take away words, letting the poem speak for itself in the best way it can.

List Poems

Throughout the ages, many fine poems have been developed around lists. Take this medieval prayer, for example:

> From Ghoulies
> And Ghosties
> And long-legged Beasties
> And Things that go bump in the night:
> Good Lord, deliver us.

You can use the idea of listing by asking students to list all of the things they know that are dark or lonely or round or scary. The effect is heightened when they include both concrete and abstract things in their lists. For example, all of these are round:

- Ripples in a pond when a pebble is thrown in
- The moon's halo
- Subway tokens
- Surprised eyes
- A ghost's mouth
- The world
- Life

It is best if children free-write the lists first, then arrange them for best effect.

Incantations

From the oldest times, the power of poetry has been used to summon energy and spirit and marshal concentration to a particular end. (Some call this magic.) In the eighth century, Saint Patrick of Ireland wrote a prayer that is part enchantment (Kennelly, 1981):

St. Patrick's Rune
I bind unto myself today
The virtues of the starlit heaven,
The glorious sun's life-giving ray,
The whiteness of the moon at even;
The flashing of the lightning free,
The howling wind's tempestuous shocks,
The stable earth, the deep salt sea
And all the old eternal rocks.

Ask students to write an incantation to make someone brave, tough, fast, lucky, or smart. Here is a format they can follow:

May the _____ of the _____ ,
The _____ of the _____ ,
The _____ of the _____ , and
The _____ of the _____
Be with me this day.

The Cinquain

A cinquain is a five-line poem tightly focused on one topic. Writing cinquains is a way for children to explore a character in a story they are reading. Here's an example, based on the hero of "Jack and the Beanstalk":

> Jack
> young, wily
> believing, climbing, winning
> brave, or just reckless?
> Giant-killer

Cinquains are written according to this formula:

1. The first line names the subject in one word.
2. The second line gives two words describing the subject.
3. The third gives three action words related to the subject and ending in *-ing*.
4. The fourth line has four words, which can be a four-word phrase related to the subject.
5. The fifth line is one word, a synonym for the subject.

In spite of the use of a formula, the results can be striking.

The Diamante

Diamantes are a variation on the cinquain form. Whereas a cinquain describes a character as she or he is now, a diamante describes how a character (or some other aspect of a story) changes over time. Let's look at the character "Jack" again:

> Boy
> young, simpleton
> loafing, goofing, grinning
> naive child/plucky hero
> "Fetch the axe!"
> proven man
> Jack

To check your comprehension on the content covered in this chapter, go to the MyEducation-Kit for your book and complete the Study Plan for Chapter 14. Here you will be able to take a chapter quiz and receive feedback on your answers.

The first half of a diamante relates to the character in the beginning of the story. Then, midway through the poem, the descriptions change and relate to the character at the end of the story. The pattern of a diamante is as follows:

1. The first line is a one-word name for the character as he or she was at the beginning of the story.
2. The second line gives two words describing the character in the beginning.
3. The third line is three action words (*-ing* words) describing the character in the beginning.

4. In the fourth line, the first two words describe the character at the beginning. Then there is a slash, followed by two words that describe the character at the end of the story.
5. The fifth line has three action words related to the character at the end of the story.
6. The sixth line has two words that describe the character at the end of the story.
7. The seventh line is a one-word name for the character at the end of the story.

Of course, there are many more ways to have children write poems, but space won't permit us to describe them here. Please consult the list of resources at the end of Chapter 6.

Experiences for Further Learning

1. Questions can be tools for "gentle inquisitions" or tools that foster "grand conversations." Select a book that offers a lot to talk about—Nikki Grimes's *My Man Blue* or Deborah Wiles's *Freedom Summer* would be good choices. Develop questions that you think are likely to promote grand conversations. Which features identified by Saul (1989) do your literary questions have? (The features appear in Table 14.1.) Share your questions with a fellow student and ask her to evaluate your questions in light of Saul's features. With the help of your partner, write final versions of your questions. Then read the story to a group of children and use the questions to launch a grand conversation. Evaluate the effectiveness of your literary questions.

2. One way in which teachers can support literary learning is by helping students to become aware of the writer's craft. Distinctively crafted books offer teachers opportunities to talk about different aspects of craft (mood, voice, tension, and so on). William Steig is noted for his use of powerful verbs in books like *Shrek!* and *The Amazing Bone.* Cynthia Rylant effectively uses repetition in *When I Was Young in the Mountains* to create a tone of fond reminiscence. Find books written by a children's author whom you especially enjoy and figure out what the author does to make these works so enjoyable. Is it a subject you find interesting? Is it free verse poetry? Is it humorous or mysterious? Are the characters just like people you know? Do the characters have conversations that sound just like those of your friends? Perhaps the author describes scenes with such vivid imagery that you can smell the freshly cut grass on a warm summer morning. Now select some well-crafted children's books, and identify in each book the aspects of craft you would like to discuss with students. Remember that students are more likely to emulate an author's craft in their own writing when attention is drawn to the books they love and keep on hand for inspiration.

3. Create a language chart designed to help children explore the use of the "enchanted journey" motif in modern fantasies. Some books that you might include on the chart are Maurice Sendak's *Where the Wild Things Are,* Chris Van Allsburg's *The Polar Express,* Melinda Long's *How I Became a Pirate* and Arthur Yorinks's *Hey, Al!* Read each book

carefully and make a list of common features you find in the books. For example, each protagonist starts out in the "real world" but then is conveyed to a fantasy world, only to return in the end to the real world. Identify other features common to the four books. Use your list of commonalities to construct four or five questions for a language chart. Be sure the questions are written in "kid friendly" language. Read the stories aloud to a group of children, and, following the read-aloud of each book, invite the children to help you complete the language chart. How did the language chart help the children gain insights into the enchanted journey motif?

4. Develop an improvisational drama based on ***The Giver.*** Often, the ending of a book suggests a situation for improvising. Present the improvisational situation you create for ***The Giver*** to a group of peers and ask them to join you in the improvisation. Experiment with alternate endings, negotiating the options to result in different endings. After several alternatives have been explored, read ***Gathering Blue*** and compare the author's treatment of the continuation of the story.

5. Experience creating a readers' theater script yourself. Begin by looking for character-rich books that are long on dialogue and short on narration. Books like Barbara Williams's ***Albert's Impossible Toothache*** and Dick Gackenbach's ***Harry and the Terrible Whatzit*** fit this bill. (However, even information books can be arranged into script formats. Learning the difference between frogs and toads is much more interesting when you hear it from the animal's own mouth.) Typically, you won't need to make many changes to the story unless narration must be shortened to keep the script moving, or a brief narration must be added to explain an important detail portrayed only in an illustration. In creating the scripts, you can turn direct quotations into a character's lines. In order to include important narration from the story, you will need to include the part of a narrator in the script.

PEARSON

Now go to Chapter 14 in the MyEducationKit (www.myeducationkit.com) for your book, where you can:

■ Find learning outcomes for Chapter 14.

■ Access the Children's Literature Database for your own exploration.

■ Extend knowledge with content-specific Web Links.

■ Deepen and apply content understanding with Extension Activities.

■ Check your comprehension on the content covered in the chapter by going to the Study Plan. Here you will be able to take a chapter quiz and receive feedback on your answers.

■ Find the following updated appendices: Major Children's Book Awards, Children's Magazines, Professional Organizations, Children's Book Publishers' Addresses, Book Selection Aids, and Children's Literature Web Sites.

Recommended Books

* indicates a picture book; **I** indicates interest level (P = preschool, YA = young adult)

Babbitt, Natalie. *Tuck Everlasting*. Farrar, 1975. A young girl is given the opportunity to drink from a spring that offers eternal life. (**I:** 10–YA)

*Baillie, Marilyn. *Nose to Toes*. Illustrated by Marisol Sarrazin. Boyds Mills, 2001. Children will delight in becoming each creature featured in this book—the hungry little lamb sniffing a treat, the robin slurping up its worm, the bear catching a slippery fish. (**I:** P–7)

Bausum, Ann. *Freedom Riders: John Lewis and Jim Zwerg on the Front Lines of the Civil Rights Movement*. National Geographic, 2005. The 1961 struggle for bus integration is told through the stories of two participants. (**I:** 12 and up)

*Best, Cari. *Three Cheers for Catherine the Great!* Illustrated by Giselle Potter. DK Ink, 1999. When Sara's Russian-speaking grandmother announces that she wants a birthday party with no presents, Sara's mother explains that there are lots of good "No Presents," as long as they come from deep inside you. The challenge for Sara is to reach deep inside and discover what she can give her grandmother. (**I:** 6–9)

*Blos, Joan. *Old Henry*. Illustrated by Stephen Gammell. Morrow, 1987. A neighborhood discovers that there is room for all kinds of people. (**I:** 6–9)

*Bunting, Eve. *December*. Illustrated by David Diaz. Harcourt, 1997. A boy and his mother invite an old woman into their cardboard house one cold December evening. (**I:** 7–11)

*———. *Fly Away Home*. Illustrated by Ronald Himler. Clarion, 1991. A boy and his father, living in the airport after the mother dies, find hope when a bird trapped in the airport finds a way to freedom. (**I:** 6–10)

*———. *The Wednesday Surprise*. Illustrated by Donald Carrick. Clarion, 1989. A little girl surprises her family by teaching her grandmother to read. (**I:** 6–10)

*Catalanotto, Peter. *Emily's Art*. Atheneum/Simon & Schuster, 2001. Emily is the class artist, but when the judge of the first grade art contest awards first place to someone else's painting, Emily begins to doubt her own talent. (**I:** 5–7)

*Collier, Bryan. *Uptown*. Holt, 2000. This tour of Harlem is made distinctive through repetitive language and eye-catching illustrations. (**I:** 8–12)

*Cooney, Barbara. *Miss Rumphius*. Puffin, 1982. A woman achieves her life's goals, including the most important one of making the world more beautiful. (**I:** 6–10)

Curtis, Christopher Paul. *Elijah of Buxton*. Scholastic, 2007. The first free child born in the Buxton Settlement, a Canadian haven established in 1849 for freed slaves, Elijah comes to understand the horrors of slavery when he journeys to America to help a friend. (**I:** 9–12)

———. *The Watsons Go to Birmingham-1963*. Delacorte, 1995. An African American family from Detroit visits in Birmingham in 1963, the summer of the fateful church bombing that set the civil rights movement into high gear. (**I:** 10–12)

Cushman, Karen. *The Midwife's Apprentice*. Clarion, 1995. A homeless waif in medieval England is given the opportunity to become a midwife's apprentice. (**I:** 10–14)

DiCamillo, Kate. *Because of Winn-Dixie*. Candlewick, 2000. Ten-year-old Opal adopts a dog that helps her to make an array of friends who, in turn, help her to sort out some of the issues that most perplex her. (**I:** 9–12)

———. *The Tale of Despereaux*. Candlewick, 2003. Despereaux, a hopelessly romantic mouse with ears far too big, has fallen in love with the Princess Pea. His story is soon intertwined with that of an evil Rat and a none-too-bright girl as Despereaux strikes out on a quest to save his beloved princess. The author pulls the reader in by having the narrator address him/her directly throughout the story. (**I:** 8–11)

Donehower, Bruce. *Miko*. Farrar, Straus, & Giroux, 1990. Miko sets out to bring light back to the Arctic north by confronting King Winter, who is holding captive the daughter of the sun and moon. (**I:** 7–10)

*Duvoisin, Roger. *Petunia*. Knopf, 1966. The barnyard will never again be the same once the silly goose Petunia finds a book and acquires "wisdom." Excellent for creative dramatics. (**I:** P–8)

Fitzhugh, Louise. *Harriet the Spy*. Harper, 1964. Harriet documents in her journal all her observations of the people around her—much to their eventual anger. (**I:** 8–11)

Fleischman, Paul. *Joyful Noise*. Illustrated by E. Beddows. HarperCollins, 1988. This distinctive collection of poems for two voices focuses on insects. (**I:** 8–YA)

*Fleming, Denise. *In the Tall, Tall Grass*. Holt, 1995. From caterpillars and ants to rabbits and bats, a boy explores the world of the animals that live in the tall grass in his backyard. (**I:** P–7)

*Fox, Mem. *Hattie and the Fox*. Illustrated by Patricia Mullins. Bradbury, 1987. Hattie spots danger on the farm. Can be easily adapted for readers' theater or creative dramatics. (**I:** P–8)

*Gardiner, Lindsey. *Here Come Poppy and Max*. Little, Brown, 2000. Poppy wants to be like all her favorite animals, and young listeners can join in the fun in a story theater activity. (**I:** P–6)

*Garland, Sherry. *The Lotus Seed*. Illustrated by Tatsuro Kiuchi. Harcourt, 1993. When the emperor in Vietnam loses his throne, a young girl sees him cry and takes a lotus seed from the pond to remember that moment. Throughout the war in her country and her relocation to the United States, the girl holds on to the lotus seed as a symbol of life and hope. (**I:** 6–12)

Giff, Patricia Reilly. *Pictures of Hollis Woods*. Wendy Lamb Books/Random House, 2002. When Hollis Woods is placed with Josie, an elderly artist, she finds a foster home that will work for her. But when Josie becomes increasingly forgetful, Hollis moves her to an isolated cabin where the system can't find them. Woven throughout this story of a young girl longing for a home is a series of flashbacks to the previous summer that Hollis spent with another family. (**I:** 11 and up)

*Gray, Libba Moore. *Small Green Snake*. Illustrated by Holly Meade. Orchard, 1994. This story of a lively little snake is told in equally lively language. (**I:** P–7)

Grimes, Nikki. *Dark Sons*. Hyperion, 2005. This free verse narrative features the parallel stories of modern day Sam and the Biblical Ishmael who must deal with very similar issues with their fathers. (**I:** 10 and up)

Hamilton, Virginia. *Drylongso*. Illustrated by Jerry Pinkney. Harcourt, 1992. An African American family, victimized by a severe drought, is helped by an unknown boy. (**I:** 8–11)

Hesse, Karen. *Out of the Dust*. Scholastic, 1997. In free-verse poetry, Billie Jo chronicles the seeming hopelessness of her Depression-era life in the Oklahoma panhandle. (**I:** YA)

*Hoberman, Mary Ann. *You Read to Me, I'll Read to You: Very Short Fairy Tales to Read Together*. Illustrated by Michael Emberly. Megan Tingley, 2004. These are short, easy-to-read dialogues based on fairy tales. Young readers can present these as two-part readers' theater scripts. (**I:** 6–8)

*Hoose, Phillip and Hannah. *Hey, Little Ant*. Illustrated by Debbie Tilley. Tricycle Press, 1998. This conversation between a boy and an ant explores whether the boy should squish the ant. Can be used, as written, as a two-part readers' theater script. (**I:** 5–9)

*Houston, Gloria. *My Great-Aunt Arizona*. Illustrated by Susan Condie Lamb. HarperCollins, 1992/1997. Arizona was born in a small community in the Blue Ridge Mountains, where she dreamed of traveling to faraway places. She never left the area but became a teacher who touched the lives of many children by teaching them about the world. (**I:** 6–10)

Jimenez, Francisco. *Breaking Through*. Houghton Mifflin, 2001. In this partial biography focused on his middle school and high school years, Jimenez tells of his migrant family's struggles to make a living in the United States and his own struggles to prepare for college. (**I:** YA)

*Johnson, Angela. *Tell Me a Story, Mama*. Illustrated by David Soman. Orchard, 1989. A little girl ends up being the storyteller when she asks her mother for a story. (**I:** P–8)

*Jorgensen, Gail. *Crocodile Beat*. Illustrated by Patricia Mullins. Macmillan, 1988. The animals' celebration is interrupted when crocodile arrives for dinner. Good for story theater. (**I:** P–7)

*Kajikawa, Kimiko. *Yoshi's Feast*. Illustrated by Yumi Heo. Dorling Kindersley, 2000. Yoshi loves broiled eel, but being a stingy man, he settles on simply smelling the ones his neighbor, the eel broiler, makes. But the eel maker—frustrated at his inability to sell eels—presents Yoshi with a bill for all the eels he has smelled. Only then does Yoshi come up with a plan to work together with his neighbor to achieve mutually beneficial ends. (**I:** 7–11)

Kay, Elizabeth. *The Divide*. Scholastic, 2003. A young boy who is standing astride the Continental Divide in Costa Rica is transported to another world populated with mythological creatures. (**I:** 9–12)

Konigsburg, E. L. *From the Mixed-up Files of Mrs. Basil E. Frankweiler*. Atheneum, 1970. Claudia and her brother run away from home and live in the Metropolitan Museum of Art. (**I:** 9–12)

*Krull, Kathleen. *Harvesting Hope: The Story of Cesar Chavez*. Illustrated by Yuyi Morales. Harcourt, 2003. This biography traces Chavez's life from his boyhood to his achievements as leader of the Mexican American farm workers. (**I:** 8 and up)

*Lass, Bonnie, and Sturges, Philemon. *Who Took the Cookies from the Cookie Jar?* Illustrated by Ashley Wolff. Little, Brown, 2000. This adaptation of the familiar folksong uses animal characters and includes visual clues to help the reader solve the mystery. The story could be used as a two-part readers' theater script. (**I:** P–7)

*Lester, Helen. *Hooway for Wodney Wat*. Illustrated by Lynn Munsinger. Houghton Mifflin, 1999. Unable to pronounce his r's, Rodney Rat is teased by his classmates—until he single-handedly saves them from the bully who makes their lives miserable. (**I:** 5–8)

Levine, Ellen. *Freedom's Children: Young Civil Rights Activists Tell Their Own Stories*. Putnam, 1993. African Americans who were children and teenagers during the 1950s and 1960s share their experiences during the civil rights movement. (**I:** 10 and up)

Lewis, C. S. *The Lion, the Witch, and the Wardrobe*. HarperCollins, 1951/1991. Four siblings enter the magical kingdom of Narnia, where they become embroiled in a struggle between good and evil. (**I:** 8–11)

*Long, Melinda. *How I Became a Pirate*. Illustrated by David Shannon. Harcourt, 2003. When Braid Beard extends an invitation, Jeremy quickly joins the pirate crew and is in for rollicking adventures—until he finds out what pirates don't do. (**I:** P–7)

Lowry, Lois. *The Giver*. Houghton Mifflin, 1993. A boy discovers the secrets behind the controlled society in which he lives. The companion book is *Gathering Blue* (2000). (**I:** YA)

*Macaulay, David. *Black and White*. Houghton Mifflin, 1990. Four stories are intertwined into one in this cleverly crafted book. (**I:** 6–10)

MacLachlan, Patricia. *Sarah, Plain and Tall*. Harper, 1985. A brother and sister hope that Sarah will choose to stay on the prairie and become their mother. (**I:** 9–12)

———. *Skylark*. HarperCollins, 1994. A sequel to *Sarah, Plain and Tall*, in which a severe drought forces Sarah and the children to journey to Maine. (**I:** 9–12)

*Martin, Bill, Jr. *Brown Bear, Brown Bear, What Do You See?* Illustrated by Eric Carle. Holt, 1967/1998. A series of rhythmical questions and answers reveals what all sorts of animals see. Can be used, as written, for readers' theater. (**I:** P–8)

McWhorter, Diane *A Dream of Freedom: The Civil Rights Movement from 1954 to 1968*. Scholastic, 2004. This is a comprehensive documentation of the various facets of the civil rights movement from 1954 to 1968. (**I:** 11 and up)

Nelson, Marilyn. *A Wreath for Emmett Till*. Illustrated by Philippe Lardy. Houghton Mifflin, 2005. This book of poetry is a memorial to the young African American boy killed in a racially motivated act of violence in the 1950s in the South. (**I:** 12 and up)

Nelson, Vaunda Micheaux. *Mayfield Crossing*. Putnam, 1993. When the school at Mayfield Crossing closes, Meg and her friends must learn to deal with the prejudice they encounter at their new school. (**I:** 8–12)

*Nichol, Barbara. *Beethoven Lives Upstairs*. Illustrated by Scott Cameron. Orchard, 1994. Through the exchange of letters with his uncle, a young boy comes to see Beethoven, his upstairs neighbor, in a new light. (**I:** 8–11)

*Noble, Trinka Hakes. *The Day Jimmy's Boa Ate the Wash*. Illustrated by Steven Kellogg. Dial, 1980. A child recounts her class's out-of-control field trip to a farm. Can be used, as written, as a two-part readers' theater script. (**I:** 5–8)

Paulsen, Gary. *Hatchet*. Bradbury, 1987. A boy stranded in the wilderness has only his hatchet and his wits to help him survive. (**I:** 10–YA)

Peck, Richard. *A Year Down Yonder*. Dial, 2000. Unable to keep the family together during the depression, Mary Alice's parents send her to live with her Grandma Dowdel—a larger than life figure in her small Illinois town. Soon Mary Alice is joining in Grandma's antics and coming up with a few of her own. This book has rich characterizations. (**I:** 9–12)

*Perkins, Lynne Rae. *Snow Music*. Greenwillow, 2003. Wild animals venture into a snowy world. A dog bolts from his house to join those animals and make snow music. Lyrical language and rich imagery capture the magic of this snowy adventure. (**I:** P–10)

Prelutsky, Jack, ed. *Random House Book of Poetry for Children.* Illustrated by Arnold Lobel. Random House, 1983. An extensive anthology of poems collected by one of America's favorite children's poets. (**I:** 7–12)

*Rappaport, Doreen. *Martin's Big Words: The Life of Dr. Martin Luther King, Jr.* Jump Sun, 2001. Dr. King's own words are integrated throughout this biography of the great civil rights leader. (**I:** 8 and up)

*Raschka, Chris. *Yo! Yes?* Orchard, 1993. A simple dialogue between two boys is the beginning of a friendship. Can be used, as written, as a two-part readers' theater script. (**I:** P–8)

*Rosen, Michael. *We're Going on a Bear Hunt.* Illustrated by Helen Oxenbury. Little Simon, 1989/1997. A surprise awaits a family that goes on a bear hunt. Perfect for use in story theater. (**I:** P–8)

*Rylant, Cynthia. *In November.* Illustrated by Jill Kastner. Harcourt, 2000. Using lyrical language, Rylant describes special joys associated with November and the coming of winter. (**I:** 5–10)

———. *When I Was Young in the Mountains.* Illustrated by Diane Goode. Dutton, 1992. The memories of a young girl growing up in the Appalachian Mountains. (**I:** 5–9)

Selznick, Brian. *The Invention of Hugo Cabret.* Scholastic, 2007. Set in a Paris train station at the turn of the twentieth century, this is the story of an orphan that is told through an innovative blending of illustration, text, and cinematic technique. (**I:** 10 and up)

*Sendak, Maurice. *Where the Wild Things Are.* HarperCollins, 1963/1998. Sent to his room, Max travels to where the Wild Things are and becomes king of all Wild Things. (**I:** P–8)

*Slobodkina, Esphyr. *Caps for Sale.* HarperCollins, 1940/1999. A peddler loses his caps to a group of monkeys. Good for story theater or creative dramatics. (**I:** P–7)

Spinelli, Jerry. *Maniac Magee.* Little, Brown, 1990. A homeless boy brings together the segregated sides of his adopted town and, in the process, becomes a legend. (**I:** 10–YA)

*Stanley, Diane. *Captain-Whiz Bang.* Morrow, 1987. A little girl grows up and, in the process, seems to forget her beloved cat. (**I:** P–8)

———. *Raising Sweetness.* Illustrated by G. Brian Karas. Putnam, 1999. After the sheriff adopts Sweetness and seven other orphans, life seems to be going well—except for the sheriff's cooking and housekeeping. This humorous story is filled with rich Texas colloquialisms. This is the sequel to *Saving Sweetness* (1996). (**I:** 5–8)

*Steig, William. *The Amazing Bone.* Farrar, Straus, & Giroux, 1983. Pearl, a pig, finds a talking bone in the forest and picks it up to take home. When she encounters danger in the forest, the bone does amazing things to keep them safe. (**I:** 6–9)

———. *Amos and Boris.* Farrar, 1999. A mouse and a whale form a deep friendship. (**I:** 6–9)

———. *Shrek!* Farrar, Straus, & Giroux, 1990. Shrek the monster sets out to find his true love in this upside-down contemporary fairy tale. (**I:** P–8)

———. *Sylvester and the Magic Pebble.* Simon & Schuster, 1989. After making a wish on a magic pebble and being transformed into a rock, Sylvester comes to realize what is important in life. (**I:** 6–9)

Taylor, Mildred. *The Well.* Dial, 1995. Racial tensions escalate between boys when the only available water comes from the well of an African American family. (**I:** 10–12)

*Temple, Frances. *Tiger Soup.* Orchard, 1994. This Jamaican Anansi tale explains why monkeys live high up in trees. A scripted version of the tale appears on the inside of the dust jacket. (**I:** P–8)

*Van Allsburg, Chris. *The Polar Express.* Houghton Mifflin, 1985. A young boy boards a train that takes him to the North Pole, where Santa offers him any gift he would like. (**I:** P–8)

*———. *The Stranger.* Houghton Mifflin, 1986. The stranger who stays on the Baileys' farm seems to be accompanied by mysterious changes in the weather. (**I:** 7–12)

*———. *The Sweetest Fig.* Houghton Mifflin, 1993. A woman leaves two figs as payment for work on her teeth, telling Monsieur Bibot that the figs make dreams come true. (**I:** 7–10)

*———. *The Widow's Broom.* Houghton Mifflin, 1992. When a widow comes into possession of a witch's broom, the broom begins to help out around the house, which raises the ire of the neighbors. (**I:** 8–YA)

*———. *The Wreck of the Zephyr.* Houghton Mifflin, 1983. The wreck of the Zephyr is on a high cliff above the sea. Did a storm with unusually high waves throw the sailboat there, or did a boy sailor use magic sails to sail it through the sky? (**I:** 8–12)

Van Draanen, Wendelin. *Swear to Howdy.* Knopf, 2003. A summer of adventure and fun comes to a screeching halt when a tragic accident threatens to destroy the lives of Rusty and his best friend. (**I:** 10 and up)

*Wiles, Deborah. *Freedom Summer.* Illustrated by Jerome Lagarrigue. Atheneum, 2001. Joe and John Henry are best friends. They play marbles together and swim together in the creek, and both boys want to be a fireman. But Joe is white, and John Henry is African American, and in the 1960s in the deep South that means there are some things Joe and John Henry cannot do together. (**I:** 6–9)

———. *Love, Ruby Lavender.* Harcourt, 2001. Ruby Lavender feels betrayed when she learns her best friend (and grandmother) is going to Hawaii for the summer. That means Ruby is on her own to care for the hens and contend with Melba Jane. Telling her story through a combination of narrative and letters, Wiles has created a humorous story filled with rich characterizations. (**I:** 8–12)

*Willard, Nancy. *Pish, Posh, Said Hieronymus Bosch.* Illustrated by Leo, Diane, and Lee Dillon. Harcourt, 1991. Strange creatures haunt Hieronymus Bosch's housekeeper. (**I:** 5–9)

*Williams, Barbara. *Albert's Impossible Toothache.* Illustrated by D. Cushman. Cambridge, MA: Candlewick. 1974/2003. His grandmother is the only one who listens when Albert (a turtle) announces he has a toothache. (I: 5–8)

*Williams, Sherley Anne. *Working Cotton.* Illustrated by Carole Byard. Harcourt, 1992. A young girl describes a day spent in the fields with her migrant worker family. (**I:** P–8)

Winthrop, Elizabeth. *Castle in the Attic.* Holiday House, 1985. A boy travels back to medieval times and confronts an evil wizard. (**I:** 7–11)

*Wood, Audrey. *The Napping House.* Illustrated by Don Wood. Harcourt, 1984. A child and her grandmother take a peaceful nap along with the family dog, cat, and a mouse—until a wakeful flea stirs things up. (**I:** P–8)

*Yorinks, Arthur. *Hey, Al!* Illustrated by Richard Egielski. Farrar, 1986. The paradise promised by a bird does not live up to the expectations of Al and his dog. (**I:** 6–12)

Resources

Blood, Peter, and Annie Paterson. *Rise Up Singing*. Sing Out! Publications, 1992.

Bromley, Karen D. *Webbing with Literature: Creating Story Maps with Children's Books*. Allyn & Bacon, 1991.

Galda, Lee. "Exploring Characters through Drama." *What a Character! Character Study as a Gateway to Literary Understanding*. Ed. Nancy L. Roser, Miriam Martinez with Junko Yokota, and Sharon O'Neal. International Reading Association, 2005.

Harste, Jerome C., and Kathy G. Short, with Carolyn Burke. *Creating Classrooms for Authors: The Reading Writing Connection*. Heinemann, 1988.

Hill, Bonnie C., Nancy J. Johnson, and Katherine L. Schlick Noe. *Literature Circles and Response*. Christopher-Gordon, 1995.

Holland, Kathleen E., Rachael A. Hungerford, and Shirley B. Ernst, Ed. *Journeying: Children Responding to Literature*. Heinemann, 1993.

Krull, Kathleen. *Gonna Sing My Head Off!* Illustrated by Allen Garns. Knopf, 1992.

Literature Study: Karen Smith's Classroom. Directed by Maryann Eeds, Carole Edelsky, Karen Smith, C. Penka, and B. Love. Center for Establishing Dialogue in Teaching and Learning, 1990.

Peterson, Ralph, and Maryann Eeds. *Grand Conversations: Literature Groups in Action*. Scholastic-TAB, 1990.

Raphael, Taffy E., Susan I. McMahon, Virginia J. Goatley, J. L. Bentley, F. B. Boyd, Laura S. Pardo, and Deborah A. Woodman. "Research Directions: Literature and Discussion in the Reading Program." *Language Arts 69* (1992): 54–61.

Roser, Nancy L., and Miriam G. Martinez, Ed. *Book Talk and Beyond: Children and Teachers Respond to Literature*. International Reading Association, 1995.

Stewig, J. W. *Exploring Language Arts in the Elementary Classroom*. New York: Holt, Rinehart, & Winston, 1983.

Wiencek, Joyce, and John F. O'Flahavan. "From Teacher-Led to Peer Discussions about Literature: Suggestions for Making the Shift." *Language Arts 71* (1994): 488–498.

 References

Almasi, Janice. "The Nature of Fourth Graders' Sociocognitive Conflicts in Peer-Led and Teacher-Led Discussions of Literature." *Reading Research Quarterly 30* (1995): 314–351.

Anzul, Margaret. "Exploring Literature with Children within a Transactional Framework." *Journeying: Children Responding to Literature*. Ed. Kathleen E. Holland, Rachael A. Hungerford, and Shirley B. Ernst. Heinemann, 1993, pp. 187–203.

Babbitt, Natalie. "Protecting Children's Literature." *Horn Book 66* (1990): 696–703.

Battle, Jennifer. "Collaborative Story Talk in a Bilingual Kindergarten." *Book Talk and Beyond: Children and Teachers Respond to Literature*. Ed. Nancy Roser and Miriam Martinez. International Reading Association, 1995, pp. 157–167.

Booth, David. "Imaginary Gardens with Real Toads: Reading and Drama in Education." *Theory into Practice 24* (1985): 193–198.

Bromley, Karen D. "Enriching Responses to Literature with Webbing." *Book Talk and Beyond: Children and Teachers Respond to Literature*. Ed. Nancy L. Roser and Miriam G. Martinez. International Reading Association, 1995, pp. 90–101.

———. *Webbing with Literature: Creating Story Maps with Children's Books*. Boston: Allyn & Bacon, 1991.

Byars, Betsy. *After the Goat Man*. Viking, 1974.

Cazden, Courtney. *Classroom Discourse: The Language of Teaching and Learning*. Heinemann, 1988.

Chambers, Aidan. *Booktalk: Occasional Writing on Literature and Children*. Harper, 1985.

Cianciolo, Patricia J. "Responding to Literature as a Work of Art—An Aesthetic Literary Experience." *Language Arts 59* (1982): 259–264.

Dooley, Caitlin, and Beth Maloch. "Children Represent and Rethink Their Understandings about Characters. *What a Character! Character Study as a Gateway to Literary Understanding*. Ed. Nancy L. Roser, Miriam Martinez, Junko, Yokota, and Sharon O'Neal. International Reading Association, 2005.

Edmiston, Brian. "Going Up the Beanstalk: Discovering Giant Possibilities for Responding to Literature through Drama." *Journeying: Children Responding to Literature*. Ed. Kathleen E. Holland, Rachael A. Hungerford, and Shirley B. Ernst. Heinemann, 1993, pp. 250–266.

Eeds, Maryann, and Deborah Wells. "Grand Conversations: An Exploration of Meaning Construction in Literature Study Groups." *Research in the Teaching of English 23* (1989): 4–29.

Farest, Cindy, and Carolyn Miller. "Children's Insights into Literature: Using Dialogue Journals to Invite Literary Response." *Examining Central Issues in Literacy Research, Theory, and Practice*. Ed. Donald J. Leu and Charles K. Kinzer. National Reading Conference, 1993, pp. 271–278.

Farrell, Edmund J., and James R. Squire. *Transactions with Literature: A Fifty-Year Perspective*. National Council of Teachers of English, 1990.

Farris, Pamela J. "Story Time and Story Journals: Linking Literature and Writing." *The New Advocate 2* (1989): 179–185.

Gonzalez, Veronica, Linda Fry, Sylvia Lopez, Julie Jordan, Cindy Sloan, and Diane McAdams. "Our Journey toward Better Conversations about Books." *Book Talk and Beyond: Children and Teachers Respond to Literature*. Ed. Nancy L. Roser and Miriam G. Martinez. International Reading Association, 1995, pp. 168–178.

Harste, Jerome C., and Kathy G. Short, with Carolyn Burke. *Creating Classrooms for Authors: The Reading Writing Connection*. Heinemann, 1988.

Hickman, Janet. "Response to Literature in a School Environment, Grades K through 5." Dissertation, Ohio State University, 1979.

———. "A New Perspective on Response to Literature: Research in an Elementary School Setting." *Research in the Teaching of English 15* (1981): 343–354.

Hoban, Lillian. Arthur's *Prize Reader*. Harper, 1978.

Hubbard, R. S., with N. Winterbourne, and J. Ostrow. "Visual Responses to Literature: Imagination through Images." *The New Advocate 9* (1996): 309–323.

Kelly, P. R. "Guiding Young Students' Response to Literature." *The Reading Teacher 43* (1990): 464–470.

Kelly, P. R., and N. Farnan. "Promoting Critical Thinking through Response Logs: A Reader-Response Approach with Fourth Graders." *Learner Factors/Teacher Factors: Issues in Literacy Research and Instruction*. Ed. Jerry Zutell and Sandra McCormick. National Reading Conference, 1991, pp. 277–284.

Kiefer, Barbara. "The Responses of Children in a Combination First/Second Grade Classroom to Picture Books in a Variety of Artistic Styles." *Journal of Research and Development in Education 16* (1983): 14–20.

Langer, Judith. "Rethinking Literature." *Literature Instruction: A Focus on Students' Response*. Ed. Judith A. Langer. National Council of Teachers of English, 1992, pp. 35–53.

———. "Understanding Literature." *Language Arts 67* (1990): 812–816.

Martinez, Miriam, and Nancy L. Roser. "Children's Responses to a Chapter Book across Grade Levels: Implications for Sustained Text." *Multidimensional Aspects of Literacy Research, Theory, and Practice*. Ed. Charles K. Kinzer and Donald J. Leu. National Reading Conference, 1994, pp. 317–324.

———. "The Books Make a Difference in Story Talk." *Book Talk and Beyond: Children and Teachers Respond to Literature*. Ed. Nancy L. Roser and Miriam G. Martinez. International Reading Association, 1995, pp. 32–41.

———, Nancy L. Roser, James V. Hoffman, and Jennifer Battle. "Fostering Better Book Discussions through Response Logs and a Response Framework: A Case Description." *Literacy Research, Theory, and Practice: Views from Many Perspectives*. Ed. Charles K. Kinzer and Donald J. Leu. National Reading Conference, 1992, pp. 303–311.

McGee, Lea M. "An Exploration of Meaning Construction in First Graders' Grand Conversations." *Literacy Research, Theory, and Practice: Views from Many Perspectives*. Ed. Charles K. Kinzer and Donald J. Leu. National Reading Conference, 1992, pp. 177–186.

———. "Talking about Books with Young Children." *Book Talk and Beyond: Children and Teachers Respond to Literature*. Ed. Nancy L. Roser and Miriam G. Martinez. International Reading Association, 1995, pp. 105–116.

Mehan, Hugh. *Learning Lessons: Social Organization in the Classroom*. Harvard University Press, 1979.

Moffett, James, and Betty Jane Wagner. *Student Centered Language Arts and Reading Handbook for Teachers,* 2nd ed. Boston: Houghton Mifflin Company, 1976.

Nash, Marcia. "Leading from Behind: Dialogue Response Journals." *Book Talk and Beyond: Children and Teachers Respond to Literature*. Ed. Nancy L. Roser and Miriam G. Martinez. International Reading Association, 1995, pp. 217–225.

Paley, Vivian G. *The Girl with the Brown Crayon*. Harvard University Press, 1997.

———. *Wally's Stories: Conversations in the Kindergarten*. Harvard University Press, 1981.

Peterson, Ralph, and Maryann Eeds. *Grand Conversations: Literature Groups in Action*. Scholastic-TAB, 1990.

Pierce, Meredith. *The Darkangel*. Atlantic Monthly, 1982.

Raphael, Taffy E., Virginia J. Goatley, Susan I. McMahon, and Deborah A. Woodman. "Teaching Literacy through Student Book Clubs: Promoting Meaningful Conversations about Books." *Book Talk and Beyond: Children and Teachers Respond to Literature*. Ed. Nancy L. Roser and Miriam G. Martinez. International Reading Association, 1995, pp. 66–79.

Raphael, Taffy E., Susan I. McMahon, Virginia J. Goatley, J. L. Bentley, F. B. Boyd, Laura S. Pardo, and Deborah A. Woodman. "Research Directions: Literature and Discussion in the Reading Program." *Language Arts 69* (1992): 54–61.

Rosenblatt, Louise M. *Literature as Exploration,* 3rd ed. Noble & Noble, 1938.

Roser, Nancy L., James V. Hoffman, and Cynthia Farest. "Language, Literature, and At-Risk Children." *The Reading Teacher 43* (1990): 554–559.

Saul, Wendy. " 'What Did Leo Feed the Turtle?' and Other Nonliterary Questions." *Language Arts 66* (1989): 295–303.

Short, Kathy G., Jerome C. Harste, and Carolyn Burke. *Creating Classrooms for Authors and Inquirers*. Heinemann, 1996.

Short, Kathy G., and Gloria Kauffman. "'So What Do I Do?' The Role of the Teacher in Literature Circles." *Book Talk and Beyond: Children and Teachers Respond to Literature*. Ed. Nancy L. Roser and Miriam G. Martinez. International Reading Association, 1995, pp. 140–149.

Smith, K. "Bringing Children and Literature Together in the Elementary Classroom." *Primary Voices, K–6 3* (1995): 22–32.

Whitin, P. *Sketching Stories, Stretching Minds*. Heinemann, 1996.

Wiencek, Joyce, and John F. O'Flahavan. "From Teacher-Led to Peer Discussions about Literature: Suggestions for Making the Shift." *Language Arts 71* (1994): 488–498.

Wolf, Alan. *It's Show Time! Poetry from Page to Stage*. Poetry Alive!, 1993.

Wollman-Bonilla, J. E., and B. Werchadlo. "Literature Response Journals in a First-Grade Classroom." *Language Arts 72* (1995): 562–570.

15

Literary and Content Units

Once upon a time, in a land far away . . . so begin many old stories and a few contemporary ones as well. Jane Yolen (1977) once said that "stories lean on stories." Certainly such "leaning" is evident in old tales handed down from past generations. It is also evident in contemporary spin-offs such as *The True Story of the 3 Little Pigs!*, which author Jon Scieszka leaned squarely on the folktale "The Three Little Pigs."

In Chapter 12, we discussed intertextuality, the process of bringing knowledge of one text to make meaning of another. This is something mature readers do, and students should also be encouraged to read one story in light of another. Literature units are especially effective vehicles for encouraging students to make literary connections. In this chapter we explore ways of devising units to achieve this goal, as well as other important literary goals and content area goals.

In the first part of the chapter we discuss the creation of literary units, which are designed to achieve literary goals. In the second part of the chapter we explore ways of using literature in content units, which are concerned primarily with achieving goals related to social studies, science, math, and other curricular areas. There are some commonalities in

ILLUSTRATION 15.1   To encourage students to make intertextual links, teachers can pair *The True Story of the 3 Little Pigs!* with the story on which it is based—"The Three Little Pigs." (Cover from *The True Story of the 3 Little Pigs!* by Jon Scieszka, illustrated by Lane Smith. Used by permission of Puffin, A Division of Penguin Young Readers Group, A Member of Penguin Group (USA) Inc., 345 Hudson Street, New York, NY 10014. All rights reserved.)

the ways that literary units and content units are organized and in some of the instructional activities used in each type of unit. What sets literary units and content units apart are their goals. In developing and implementing literary units, teachers are focused primarily on literary goals. That is, through the study of literature, teachers intend for their students to learn more about literature—about literary elements and devices, characteristics of genres, authors and illustrators, and themes explored through literature—and about how to engage in literary meaning making. In contrast, teachers organize content units to help students learn more about a particular content area. For example, a fifth-grade teacher might develop a content unit incorporating children's literature that is designed to help children understand issues related to slavery. In a unit of this type, children may learn about slavery *through* literature (as well as other resources), but the primary goal is not to learn *about* literature.

Although both types of units are important, in this chapter we emphasize literary units because we believe that for too long, the literature curriculum has been neglected in elementary schools (Walmsley, 1992). Certainly, in recent years children's books have come to play an increasingly important role in elementary classrooms in the United States (Baumann, Hoffman, Moon, & Duffy-Hester, 1998), but we believe that even today trade books are used primarily as tools to teach reading or to achieve content goals. The time has come to broaden our goals to include literary ones as well.

PEARSON
myeducationkit™

Develop a text set of titles that could form a literary unit by using the Children's Literature Database in Chapter 15 of the MyEducationKit for this book.

Literary Units

In this section, we focus on the goals of literary units and ways of organizing such units. As you read about literary units (and later as you develop your own), you will want to draw on the information you have learned throughout this textbook—information about literary elements, about the ways in which picture books work, about particular children's authors, and about the various genres that have been highlighted.

The Power of Literary Units

Teachers frequently have students read or listen to individual stories, and often times this is the best route to follow to achieve particular goals, but there are also reasons for organizing literature into units for literary study. Ralph Peterson and Maryann Eeds (1990) present evidence of the quality of responses that can be evoked when literature is presented in connected sets. They relate the story of a kindergarten teacher who read aloud three of Maurice Sendak's fantasies: *Where the Wild Things Are, In the Night Kitchen,* and *Outside Over There*. In the first book, *Where the Wild Things Are,* Max sails away from his home on a magic boat to "the land where the wild things are," where he proceeds to become the "king of all wild things." Soon, though, Max grows lonesome and chooses to sail back home. Mickey, the protagonist of *In the Night Kitchen,* wakes up one night to the clamorous noise of the night kitchen. Falling out of his bed and into the magical night kitchen, Mickey becomes a hero when he fashions an airplane out of bread dough to fly over the Milky Way to procure milk needed by the bakers in the night kitchen. Mickey's adventure concludes as he tumbles back into bed. In the final fantasy, *Outside Over There,* young Ida, having discovered that her baby sister has been stolen by goblins, determines to go "outside over there," where she outwits the goblins to bring her baby sister safely home.

After sharing these three stories with her kindergartners, the teacher invited the children to talk about the commonalities they saw in the stories. This is what they observed (Peterson & Eeds, 1990, p. 26):

- Each book is circular.
- Each book is about a child who makes a trip to an unusual place.
- Each book portrays a powerful child.
- Each book shows a brave child.
- Each book portrays magic moves.
- Each book is scary.

These children did impressive thinking in response to their teacher's invitation to compare Sendak's three stories. Would they have made such perceptive comments if they had listened to only one of the stories? We don't think so. We believe that it is the power of the literature unit that yielded such insightful commentary by kindergartners. Researchers have confirmed that children sometimes read books in light of other books they have read (Farest & Miller, 1993; Short, 1992; Sipe, 1998). Perhaps the best way of encouraging children to make such connections across books is by having them read (or listen to) and talk about books that are linked in one way or another.

Educators have recommended author study, genre study, and thematic study as approaches that encourage students to engage in higher levels of thinking in response to literature (Martinez & Roser, 2003). Anecdotal evidence suggests that a unit approach to literature study is indeed effective. For example, Joy Moss (1978) includes in her descriptions of "focus units" examples of rich student talk that reveals children's "growing store of literary ideas" (p. 485).

Nancy Roser, James Hoffman, and Cindy Farest (1990) moved beyond anecdotal evidence in documenting the effectiveness of their Language to Literacy program, which provided books organized into literature units focusing on author, theme, topic, or genre. Teachers in 78 classrooms read unit books aloud to approximately 2,500 primary-aged children whose first language was Spanish. The teachers modeled and encouraged children's responses; they then collected those responses on language charts designed to help the children discover connections among the books. Roser and her colleagues reported significant changes in language arts scores, as well as in the range of literary connections recorded on the charts (Roser, Hoffman, Farest, & Labbo, 1992).

Developing Different Types of Literary Units

Well-designed literary units provide rich contexts for children's literary learning. In this section, we will discuss four different types of literature units: genre units, author/illustrator units, literary element (or literary device) units, and thematic units. The distinctive goals of each type of unit are listed in Table 15.1.

Go to the Extension Activities section of Chapter 15 in the MyEducationKit for your book and complete activity #1 to look at literacy-related teacher tools on the Internet.

Top Shelf 15.1

Books to Include in a Unit on Trickster Tales

Borreguita and the Coyote by Verna Aardema

Rosa Raposa by F. Isabel Campoy

The Monkey and the Crocodile: A Jataka Tale from India by Paul Galdone

Iktomi and the Coyote by Paul Goble

Anansi Goes Fishing by Eric Kimmel

Coyote: A Trickster Tale from the American Southwest by Gerald McDermott

Zomo the Rabbit: a Trickster Tale from West Africa by Gerald McDermott

Flossie and the Fox by Patricia McKissack

Mrs. Chicken and the Hungry Crocodile by Won-Ldy Paye & Margaret Lippert

The Leopard's Drum: An Asante Tale From West Africa by Jessica Souhami

Tops and Bottoms by Janet Stevens

Table 15.1 Goals of Different Types of Literature Units	
Type of Unit	**Goal of Unit**
Genre unit	■ To explore the features of the focus genre that set it apart from other genres
Author/illustrator	■ To discover what is distinctive about the work of a particular author and/or illustrator
Literary element (or device)	■ To explore how authors develop and use literary elements or devices
Thematic unit	■ To explore a literary theme

Ask the Educator . . .

Nancy Roser

Nancy L. Roser

Favorite Books as a Child

Almost every time I read one of these "what were your three favorite books as a child" questions, the answers always sound to me like baby geniuses (as in "I loved *Bridge to Terabithia*, *The Chronicles of Narnia*, and *A Wrinkle in Time*"). Truth is, I met favorite books long before I could read. I loved

- *The Little Squeegy Bug* (the very first picture book by Bill Martin, Jr.—when Brown Bear wasn't yet a gleam in the author's eye)

- *Miss Sniff* (who knows who wrote it, but the beautiful black-and-white cat had textured fur, a caretaker named Polly Pinks, and a green and pink room to sleep in)

- *Pat and Penny*, two sisters with red hair who did everything together—just like Gayle and me.

- In my house, we listened to and (at last) read those books until the covers loosened, the pages gave way, and Miss Sniff went bald from touching.

What are the benefits of engaging children in literature units rather than simply presenting individual books?

Recently, I attended an exhibition in which paintings by Matisse hung next to those by Picasso. The exhibit helped me look more closely at and understand better two artists whose works occupied the same tradition and whose vibrant palettes and similar subjects formed a dialectic—each shaping and being shaped by the other. In a similar way, children understand and respond differently (and more deeply) when related pieces of literature are juxtaposed. When preschoolers or kindergartners, for example, are introduced to Rosemary Wells's *Timothy Goes to School* as well as Kevin Henkes's Wemberly (of *Wemberly Worried*), they are being given opportunity to see patterns and linkages in stories. They may recognize that if two story characters fret about school, maybe others do as well. The discovery that books share ideas or themes (and only a limited set of them!) need not be postponed until high school—or even until first grade.

Older children, too, tend to think, talk, and write differently when related books are pulled together into literature units—and when time is set aside for extended stays within a theme, a genre, or a particular author's works. Some books almost beg to be considered together. For example, children exploring the traits and antics of plucky heroes can connect with and compare Katherine Paterson's *Preacher's Boy* with the "never-say-quit" India Opal Buloni of Kate DiCamillo's *Because of Winn-Dixie*. Other units may join pieces of historical fiction with biography and relevant information text. Still others may lead to the discovery of the characteristics of genre, the exploration of story structures, or the appreciation and

tracking of tale variants. In any case, good literature units almost guarantee surprising reflections and rich talk.

Further, opportunities to think and talk about books drawn into literature units mean that all learners have entry into the curriculum: When the emphasis is on connecting literature and connecting with literature, no one need be denied access because of reading level. (I know little about art, but I made my own levels of discoveries in the Matisse and Picasso exhibit.)

Finally, when teachers and children share and study related pieces of literature, they seem more likely to give credence to literature in its own right rather than to treat it as an endless source of vocabulary and spelling words, parts of speech, answers to questions, or impetus for "activity." In a study of children and literature units, my colleagues and I found that those who were involved with literature units knew more about books, wrote and talked more insightfully, and read at higher levels than children who did not have literature study in their classrooms. So pull books together. There is strength in unity.

Nancy Roser *is not a children's book author. Rather, she teaches teachers at the University of Texas at Austin to rely on children's books in classrooms as fodder for discussion, inspiration for writing, sources of enjoyment, and for learning.* ∎

Genre Units

One way to link books for literary study is to group them by genre. Through genre units, teachers can help students discover what is distinctive about a particular genre—what sets it apart from others. For example, in a traditional literature unit centering on trickster tales, students might discover the following (among other things):

- Trickster tales have been told around the world.

- There are often clearly differentiated "good guys" and "bad guys" in trickster tales.

- In trickster tales, the character who sets out to do the tricking is all too often the one who is tricked.

- Trickster tales are typically filled with unexpected twists and humorous turns of events.

When students develop this type of knowledge about a particular genre, it affects the way they approach stories. Knowledgeable readers who are told that a story is a tall tale will have very different expectations for that story than they would for a work of contemporary realistic or historical fiction. These genre-based expectations are critically important and guide readers in the process of constructing meaning.

In developing genre units, it is first necessary to determine the *particular* focus of the unit. This is an especially important step in creating a genre unit because of the diversity of books that may fall within a genre. For example, as we discussed in Chapter 7, traditional literature includes myths, legends, and a variety of types of folktales, tall tales, and ballads. If you simply selected a story representing each of these subtypes, your unit would contain such a hodgepodge of stories that children would not be able to make any discoveries about the genre. Instead, it makes sense to develop units with a more cohesive focus. We will explore what this means by discussing some of the types of units you might build around two different genres.

Because of its diversity, traditional literature lends itself to a variety of engaging ways of organizing literature study. In Chapter 7, you learned about various categories of traditional literature, including trickster tales, pourquoi tales, tall tales, legends, cumulative tales, fairy tales, fables, hero tales, and humorous tales. Any of these subtypes can provide the underlying link for the study of traditional literature. For example, if students read and compare a variety of fairy tales, they are likely to discover that tales such as "Cinderella," "Snow White and the Seven Dwarfs," and "Rumpelstiltskin" involve magic and that the magic often functions to reward ordinary people for their goodness and steadfastness.

You also learned in Chapter 7 that many works of traditional literature share a common plot structure, which has been described by Joseph Campbell. The work of this scholar could serve as the basis for organizing traditional literature study (although you probably wouldn't want to actually talk about Joseph Campbell with children). However, you could bring together tales such as Claire Martin's **Boots and the Glass Mountain** and Vladimir Hulpach's **Ahaiyute and Cloud Eater** and guide your students to discover some of the elements of Campbell's hero cycle (see pages 215–217) in these (and other) hero tales from around the world.

Culture is yet another basis for organizing traditional literature units. As you have learned, the traditional literature from a particular culture frequently shares common features. Through literature study, students can discover some of these distinctive features. For example, in a study of Scandinavian folklore, students could discover the trolls, giants, witches, and hags that frequently appear in tales from Scandinavia. A collection such as Lunge-Larsen's **The Troll with No Heart in His Body and Other Tales of Trolls from Norway** contains a host of Scandinavian tales that can be used in such a unit. Similarly, through a unit devised around African folklore, students could discover that the trickster takes a variety of forms in African folklore; sometimes he is the spider, while in other tales he appears as the turtle or the hare.

Teaching Idea 15.1
Connecting Children's Observations

Teachers typically design language charts to help students make important connections among books that the teachers believe are important. This is done by posing particular questions on the chart. For example, in a unit featuring transformation tales, the following questions might be included on a language chart: Who or what is transformed in the tale? Into what are they transformed? How does the transformation occur? Why does the transformation occur? Questions like these will guide students to notice patterns the teacher has previously identified as important. However, students often notice things to which the teacher has paid no attention. One way of inviting children to share their own "noticings" is by adding a final column to the language chart entitled "Other Things We Noticed."

Top Shelf 15.2

Books to Include in a Unit on Cinderella Variants

The Egyptian Cinderella by Shirley Climo

Tattercoats by Margaret Greaves

Moss Gown by William Hooks

The Turkey Girl: A Zuni Cinderella Story by Penny Pollock

Cendrillon: A Caribbean Cinderella by Robert D. San Souci

Sootface: An Ojibwa Cinderella Story by Robert D. San Souci

The Talking Eggs by Robert D. San Souci

Mufaro's Beautiful Daughters by John Steptoe

Top Shelf 15.3

Books to Include in a Unit on Folktale Spin-Offs

Yours Truly, Goldilocks by Alma Flor Ada

With Love, Little Red Hen by Alma Flor Ada

The Jolly Postman or Other People's Letters by Janet and Allan Ahlberg

Goldie Locks Has Chicken Pox by Erin Dealey

Ruby by Michael Emberley

Three Cool Kids by Rebecca Emberley

The Emperor's Old Clothes by Kathryn Lasky

Cinderella's Rat by Susan Meddaugh

Once Upon a Time by John Prater

The Frog Prince Continued by Jon Scieszka

The True Story of the 3 Little Pigs! by Jon Scieszka

The House That Drac Built by Judy Sierra

Somebody and the Three Blairs by Marilyn Tolhurst

Chapter 8 offers useful information for teachers who want to build units designed to help children discover some of the distinctive features of modern fantasy. Any of the subcategories of fantasy can provide an undergirding link for a unit on this genre. For young children, you might devise a unit that features personified animals or personified toys. Older students could be invited to delve into a unit structured around Jon Scieszka's time-slip stories. Or, by grouping books that feature outlandish characters or situations—such as Linda White's *Comes a Wind* and Diane Stanley's *Saving Sweetness*—students could explore the use of exaggeration in modern fantasy. Yet another possibility is exploring how literary elements are often crafted in fantasy, such as the use of dual settings linked by a special portal or characters who set off on a quest.

Children benefit when they develop a well-defined sense of how one genre differs from another. This understanding influences their expectations for particular genres, which in turn will affect the ways in which they read and write within the genres. Organizing literature study on the basis of genres will help them develop these understandings.

Author/Illustrator Units

Mature readers commonly have favorite authors. They are always on the lookout for that writer's next book and might not even wait for the paperback version to be published before buying it. Further, readers who are about to begin a new book by a familiar writer have expectations that help them to step into the writer's story world and, when reading, to make connections across books written by the author. Understanding what sets particular writers apart from others often influences mature readers' book choices and expectations. Children can be encouraged to develop a similar sense of author (or illustrator). Those who discover the humor pervading James Marshall's *George and Martha* books might seek out other books by Marshall. Or children who are attuned to the vivid colors and lively language of Denise Fleming's books know just what to look for in new books created by this author/illustrator. Author and illustrator units are designed to help students make such discoveries. In an author unit, students study a number of works by one author in order to discover what is distinctive about that author's work. In parallel fashion, in an illustrator unit, readers read various books illustrated by the featured artist in order to discover what distinguishes that person's artwork.

Patricia Bloem and Anthony Manna (1999) engaged second and fourth graders in a study of Patricia Polacco's books to help them discover what Polacco does as a writer and illustrator that makes them think and feel the way they do. The researchers read aloud stories by Polacco, modeled questions they had about the author's work, invited the children to share their own questions, and finally had the children conduct an author interview by telephone. Bloem and Manna found that the students responded aesthetically in rich and diverse ways. Over the course of the unit, they found a shift in the children's questions from being text-based to revealing connections they were making with Polacco and with her books. The children "delighted in the nuances of the texts, and found great pleasure, at the end of the project, in learning ways that the texts reflected Polacco's history and recorded her family stories" (p. 806).

By engaging students in author or illustrator study, the teacher is helping them to build a store of knowledge about the characteristic ways in which particular authors (or illustrators) work. For example, children who have had the opportunity to explore the story worlds of Steven Kellogg through a literary unit are likely to discover that Kellogg typically writes

Technology in Practice 15.1

Learning about an Author

Listen to the interview of Denise Fleming on teachingbooks.net. What insights does this author/illustrator share about her work? How can you use this information in developing a Denise Fleming literature unit?

ILLUSTRATION 15.2   In *Pie in the Sky* a young child watches as a tree produces flow-ers, then buds and finally fruit. ("Book Cover" from *Pie In The Sky* by Lois Ehlert, copyright © 2004, reprinted by permission of Houghton Mifflin Harcourt Publishing Company.)

Books to Include in a Lois Ehlert Unit

Color Zoo by Lois Ehlert
Cuckoo: Cucú by Lois Ehlert
Feathers for Lunch by Lois Ehlert
Fish Eyes: A Book You Can Count On by Lois Ehlert
Market Day by Lois Ehlert
Moon Rope: A Peruvian Folktale/Un lazo a la luna: Una leyenda Peruana by Lois Ehlert
Nuts to You! by Lois Ehlert
Pie in the Sky by Lois Ehlert
Snowballs by Lois Ehlert
Top Cat by Lois Ehlert

fast-paced and humorous story lines, that he often fills his stories with bigger-than-life characters—be they Great Danes, the Loch Ness monster, imaginary Skogs, or legendary characters such as Paul Bunyan—and that he draws illustrations filled with details (which are often hilarious). Children engaged in a unit featuring the books of Mo Willems could be guided to discover the ways in which this author/illustrator portrays humor and charac-ter emotions through his illustrations.

To develop an author or illustrator unit, a teacher needs to first discover what is distinc-tive about the work of the artist. In addition to studying various works written or illustrated by the person, teachers can also gain insights by hearing what the author /illustrator says about his or her own work. Author websites, as well as Internet sites such as teachingbooks.net, are a wonderful vehicle for hearing what authors and illustrators have to say about their own craft.

It is relatively easy to characterize the work of some authors or illustrators because they consistently work in the same genre, repeatedly explore particular types of themes, or write in a relatively consistent style. However, others may have a large and quite diverse body of work. In organizing a literature study of a writer whose works vary widely, it may be help-ful to narrow the focus of study. For example, a writer such as Tomie dePaola has published many books in widely diverse genres including fantasy, folktales and legends, informa-tional books, realistic fiction, and wordless picture books. Although you may choose to intro-duce children to the range of this author/illustrator's work in a literature unit, it would make sense to group his works for exploration within the unit. For example, the literature study might start with an investigation of some of dePaola's realistic stories that draw heavily on his own experiences as a child: *Nana Upstairs & Nana Downstairs, Watch Out for the Chicken Feet in Your Soup, Tom, The Art Lesson, The Baby Sitter,* and *26 Fairmount Avenue*. The unit could then move on to explore dePaola's fantasies featuring Strega Nona and Big Anthony, before again moving on to feature some of the folktales and legends retold by this author/illustrator.

ILLUSTRATION 15.3   Diane Stanley's *Saving Sweetness* is full of wild exaggeration and memorable colloquialisms. (Cover from *Saving Sweetness* by Diane Stanley, illustrated by G. Brian Karas, copyright © 1996 by G. Brian Karas, illustrations. Used by permission of G.P. Putnam's Sons, A Division of Penguin Young Readers Group, A Member of Penguin Group (USA) Inc., 345 Hudson Street, New York, NY 10014. All rights reserved.)

Teaching Idea 15.2

Experimenting with Artistic Media

Children can gain a greater appreciation of an illustrator's work by trying their own hand at working in an illustrator's signature medium. Select an illustrator whose work your students especially enjoy. For example, young children typically delight in the artwork of Eric Carle, whose books are easily recognized by their unique painted tissue-paper collages. With your students, explore how Eric Carle creates his imaginative illustrations. Useful resources include the video *Eric Carle: Picture Writer* (1993) and the books *The Art of Eric Carle* (Carle, 1996) and *You Can Make a Collage* (Carle, 1998). Once children have studied Eric Carle's techniques, they can create their own painted tissue-paper collages.

Students can also try their hand at scratchboard, a medium favored by children's book illustrator Brian Pinkney. Using this technique, the artist paints a piece of paper or a board with black ink and then scratches off the ink to produce the design. A similar method often used in classrooms is to color a random, colorful, abstract design on paper. The design is then covered with ink or black paint and allowed to dry. Or the young artist can simply use a black crayon to completely cover the colorful design. When the page is completely black, students can use the edge of a pair of scissors to scratch a picture. The black comes off and reveals the colors below. This is an easy but rewarding adaptation to the kind of scratchboard that Brian Pinkney has so brilliantly mastered.

Literary Elements and Devices

Teachers can link books in such a way as to help students make discoveries about particular literary elements or literary and visual devices. For example, a teacher might create a unit featuring stories such as Arthur Yorinks's *Hey, Al!*, Chris Van Allsburg's *The Polar Express,* Melinda Long's *How I Became a Pirate,* and Maurice Sendak's *Where the Wild Things Are,* all of which feature characters who take enchanted journeys—a device that is frequently used by fantasy writers. To explore stock characterization, a teacher might link books such as William Steig's *Doctor De Soto,* James Marshall's *Wings: A Tale of Two Chickens,* and Mary Jane Auch's *Peeping Beauty;* all these books feature sly and untrustworthy foxes. To guide students in exploring how some illustrators begin their stories by including important information in the cover illustration and the endpapers, a teacher might feature books such as Janet Stevens' *The Great Fuzz Frenzy*, Anna Dewdney's *Llama Llama Mad at Mama*, Bill Martin, Jr.'s *A Beasty Story*, and Colin McNaughton's *Boo!* As students develop a conscious awareness of how writers use such devices, they are likely to want to experiment with these same devices in their own writing and illustrations. The information in Chapters 2 and 3 can be used to develop units that explore literary elements and literary and visual devices.

Thematic Units

Because literature is about life, units organized around literary themes have great potential to help students understand the human experience. As Joy Moss (1994) has observed, "literary transactions enable readers to enter into the lives of others, to live through their experiences, to see the world through their eyes. In the process, readers have opportunities to gain insights about human experience and to learn about feelings and motivation and relationships" (p. 5). Literary themes such as "Celebrations," "Memories," "Journeys," "Imagination," "Courage," "Making a Difference," and "Hopes and Dreams" offer rich potential for exploring the human experience. Such literary themes cut across literary genres and encompass many authors and illustrators.

After participating in a thematic study, students are likely to emerge with a richer understanding of the unit's central idea. For example, in a unit focused on courage, a teacher might choose to include books such as Nancy Luenn's *Nessa's Fish,* in which a girl stranded on the tundra protects her sick grandmother and safeguards their store of fish and Ann Scott's *Brave as a Mountain Lion,* in which a shy boy stands on stage during a spelling bee and faces an auditorium full of people. Because the protagonists in these books display different types of courage under very diverse circumstances, children's understanding of the full range of what it means to have courage will be enriched.

Organizing Literary Units

Once you have decided on the type of unit you wish to create, the next tasks are to select books for the unit and to organize the unit.

Selecting Unit Books

Literature units can include picture books, chapter books, or some combination of the two formats. In selecting books, it is critical that you find the right ones—that is, books that are clearly connected to the undergirding concept of the unit. The lists of recommended books in this text can serve as one source for locating unit books. Colleagues and your school librarian might be able to provide further suggestions. At times you may need to rely on various book

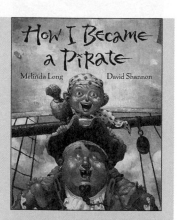

ILLUSTRATION 15.4   In *How I Became a Pirate* a young boy joins a band of pirates for a rollicking adventure. ("Book Cover" from *How I Became a Pirate* by Melinda Long, Illustrations copyright © 2003 by David Shannon, reprinted by permission of Houghton Mifflin Harcourt Publishing Company.)

selection aids to locate connected books. These aids include books such as *Children's Books in Print* (Bowker Staff, 2003) and journals such as *Book Links*. Each of these aids is organized by subject, and *Adventuring with Books,* a book selection guide published by the National Council of Teachers of English, is also organized by genre. Internet sites such as teachingbooks .net are also helpful guides for finding related titles.

Unit Structure

Although we will describe various ways of organizing units, there really is no one best way. Rather, it is important to seek the type of organization that will meet your students' needs. When you are planning your own literary units, you might use variations of the ones we describe or create an entirely new structure that will enable you to pursue the literary goals of your unit.

Nancy Roser, James Hoffman, and Cindy Farest (1990) devised an easy-to-use organizational structure for picture book units in their Language to Literacy Program. Their units revolve around ten related picture books, one of which is read aloud each day over a two-week period, although, of course, the length of units can vary. This structure works especially well with younger children who might not yet be reading or who might not yet have the skills to read more complex books on their own.

Joy Moss (1984) devised a somewhat different format for picture book units that she has termed "focus units." In a focus unit centering on picture books, a daily read-aloud by the teacher is the central activity. However, children also independently read picture books related to the focus of the unit.

In Language to Literacy chapter book units, students are engaged simultaneously with two linked books. One book is read aloud daily by the teacher on a chapter-by-chapter basis. Students read the second book independently, using a pacing guide provided by the teacher or one they negotiate themselves. At the end of the unit, activities such as discussion or the completion of a Venn diagram provide students with the opportunity to make connections between the two books.

In a focus unit centering on chapter books, students are also engaged with more than one book. At the beginning of the unit, the teacher reviews an array of books that will be available for independent reading, and each student selects two books to read independently. While the teacher reads a chapter book aloud daily on a chapter-by-chapter basis, students read their two books independently, meeting periodically in small groups to compare the stories they are reading in preparation for a culminating class discussion of all the unit books.

Technology in Practice 15.2

Selecting Unit Books

Suggestions for books to include in a literature study are found online in numerous websites dedicated to children's literature. Little time need be spent searching for book titles and connections when you use Internet resources, although it is easy to lose track of time as you surf from link to link reading the creative ideas and learning about new titles that quickly seem indispensable. Carol Hurst's website is a popular one that can be found at www.carolhurst.com. A wealth of links can be found at www.childrenslit.com . The Children's Literature Webguide by David K. Brown at www.acs.ucalgary.ca/~dkbrown/index.html includes valuable teaching guides. Another especially helpful site is teachingbooks.net, which provides links to numerous other sites. There are as many sites as you have the patience to browse.

Top Shelf 15.5

Books to Include in a Unit on Imagination

Babymouse Beach Babe by Jennifer L. Holm

The Crooked Apple Tree by Eric Houghton

Regards to the Man in the Moon by Ezra Jack Keats

A Mammoth Imagination by Philip Ross Norman

Not a Box by Antoinette Portis

The Dot by Peter H. Reynolds

The Squiggle by Carole Lexa Schaefer

Captain Bob Takes Flight by Roni Schotter

Catilda by John Stadler

Top Shelf 15.6

Books to Include in a Unit on Celebrations

Powwow by George Ancona

The World's Birthday: A Rosh Hashanah Story by Barbara Diamond Goldin

Day of the Dead by Tony Johnston

An Island Christmas by Lynn Joseph

Festivals by Myra Cohn Livingston

When Lightning Comes in a Jar by Patricia Polacco

Rivka's First Thanksgiving by Elsa Okon Rael

Moon Festival by Ching Yeung Russell

Top Shelf 15.7

Books to Include in a Unit on the Special People in Our Lives

Halmoni's Day by Edna Coe Bercaw

Full, Full, Full of Love by Trish Cooke

Granny Torrelli Makes Soup by Sharon Creech

Osa's Pride by Ann Grifalconi

My Man Blue by Nikki Grimes

Meet Danitra Brown by Nikki Grimes

My Great-Aunt Arizona by Gloria Houston

Sister Anne's Hands by Marybeth Lorbiecki

The Water Gift and the Pig of the Pig by Jacqueline Briggs Martin

Uncle Jed's Barbershop by Margaree King Mitchell

Thank You, Mr. Falker by Patricia Polacco

Elijah's Angel by Michael J. Rosen

Our Granny by Margaret Wild

Teaching Idea 15.3

Using Literature Units to Launch Writing

Literature units offer students the opportunity to take an in-depth look at some facet of literature—features associated with a particular genre, literary elements or devices, or themes that emerge from literature. Immersing students in literature in this way also prepares them to try out what they've discovered in their own writing. As a culminating activity in a literature unit, invite students to try out in their own writing what they've discovered writers doing in the just-completed literature unit. If students have been reading fantasies in which characters go on enchanted journeys, they can write their own fantasies using this literary device. Or after listening to and reading trickster tales, students can try their hand at writing a modern-day trickster tale.

Unit Activities

In Chapter 14, we described a variety of activities to support children's literary learning in the context of literature units. Children can record their personal responses to unit books in literature journals. To give children the opportunity to gather their thoughts in preparation for being active participants in literature discussion, the teacher can invite them to write in their journals immediately following a read-aloud. Journals can also be used with books the students read independently as part of the unit. Because discussion of these books is not likely to occur daily, students will want to draw on the ideas they recorded in their journals when they do meet in small groups or with the entire class.

Literature discussion is an integral part of literature units. The teacher will want to invite students to join in conversations about unit books that are read aloud, as well as those that they read independently. When teachers participate in these discussions, they can use the tools we discussed in Chapter 14: open-ended questions and literary questions. While writing and discussion are widely used as response activities, teachers should invite children to respond through art and drama as well.

Literature units are designed to help students make connections across a related set of books, and the language chart is the perfect tool to guide students in making connections. In a picture book unit in which the teacher reads a new book each day, the teacher and students can turn to the language chart, following open-ended discussion of the daily read-aloud, to record their thinking regarding how the book relates to the common elements that serve as the foundation of the unit.

Literature across the Curriculum

For too long, conventional wisdom has held that the textbook is the primary vehicle through which children learn in the content areas. Indeed, textbooks can play an important role in instruction because they typically provide a broad view of a topic. Yet textbooks should be just one of many instructional resources that innovative teachers employ. Children's literature is an alternative resource that holds great potential for nurturing children's learning across the curriculum.

Need for Children's Literature in the Content Areas

Textbooks dominate content area teaching and learning at all grade levels (Alvermann and Moore, 1991). Increasingly, educators are questioning this reliance on textbooks that critics claim have decreased in difficulty (Chall & Conard, 1991) and offer too much information with too little depth (Tyson-Bernstein & Woodward, 1989). Further, the writing in textbooks often lacks clarity and richness in vocabulary and structure (Tomlinson, Tunnell, & Richgels, 1993). Perhaps the greatest indictment of textbooks relates to the superficial manner in which topics are often treated. One way of offsetting some of these limitations is by using trade books in the classroom. Well-written trade books engage children and make them want to keep reading; and when these books open new vistas for children, they encourage young readers to keep learning as well.

Literature can be incorporated into content instruction in different ways. A single book can be used to develop a concept, initiate interest in a topic, launch a project, or generate questions about a subject. For example, a teacher can read *The Doorbell Rang* by Pat Hutchins to introduce the concept of division. The story begins as two children are getting ready to divvy up twelve cookies their mother has just baked. They are pleased to discover that each one will get six cookies—until the doorbell rings and two more children arrive. As more and more friends appear

Issue to Consider
Should Historical Fiction Have a Place in Social Studies Instruction?

Experts readily agree that well-researched and well-written biographies and informational trade books can enrich social studies instruction by providing a more in-depth and engaging look at various facets of history than textbooks typically do. Yet opinions differ regarding the place of historical fiction in social studies instruction. On one side are those concerned that children too readily believe that the fictional events portrayed in historical fiction actually occurred. In other words, children

believe that they are reading history when they read historical fiction. This may be of particular concern with historical novels such as Pam Conrad's *Pedro's Journal* or Esther Forbes's *Johnny Tremain*, in which actual historical figures play a role in the story.

On the opposing side are those who argue that it is through historical fiction that history is most likely to come to life. In historical fiction, dry facts can be infused with the drama that is history. By reading historical fiction, children can begin to understand past events and issues as they may have actually been experienced by the people of earlier times. To help ensure that children understand that historical fiction is indeed fiction and should be read with a critical eye, teachers can invite children to examine the events portrayed in works of historical fiction in light of information they have gathered through informational sources.

What do you think?

---

on the doorstep, readers will find that each child gets fewer and fewer cookies. Barbara Bash's *Urban Roosts,* which focuses on where city birds build their nests, can launch an investigation of the neighborhood surrounding the school, encouraging children to become careful observers of their own environment. *Hummingbird Nest* can be used as a model of the way in which poetry can be used as a vehicle for recording observations about nature. Trade books can also serve as valuable companions to textbooks. For example, whereas textbooks may offer only a broad overview of the topic of ecosystems, trade books can provide detailed examples of different types of ecosystems. Barbara Bash has written a series on trees that offers richly fleshed-out examples of ecosystems. Titles in this series include *Tree of Life, Ancient Ones, Desert Giant,* and *In the Heart of the Village.*

Teacher/Librarian Partnership
Partnerships for Literacy

In decades past, teachers taught students how to read, and librarians provided access to the materials for reading. Teachers set the curriculum; librarians looked up the resources. The 1980s brought about the publication of Information Power (by the AASL), and librarians became the information literacy specialist—someone who helped students locate information, evaluate information, and use that information in their research. But still, the curriculum was classroom-driven and librarians were the support personnel.

What's the future for librarian/classroom teacher partnership as both work to support student learning? Redefining past roles and looking for new ways to partner depends on the commitment and engagement of each participant. The school librarian as instructional partner with the classroom teacher indicates more of an equal partnership, with both people taking on the role of teacher. When both parties recognize that such partnerships can facilitate each person's job and potentially result in better learning opportunities for students, the necessary planning time becomes a worthwhile investment.

Top Shelf 15.8

Books to Use in a Unit on Slavery in America

A Picture Book of Frederick Douglass by David Adler

A Picture Book of Harriet Tubman by David Adler

Elijah of Buxton by Christopher Paul Curtis

Anthony Burns: The Defeat and Triumph of a Fugitive Slave by Virginia Hamilton

Sweet Clara and the Freedom Quilt by Deborah Hopkinson

Henry's Freedom Box by Ellen Levine

Jip: His Story by Katherine Paterson

Silent Thunder by Andrea Davis Pinkney

Pink and Say by Patricia Polacco

Mine Eyes Have Seen by Ann Rinaldi

A School for Pompey Walker by Michael J. Rosen

Minty: A Story of Young Harriet Tubman by Alan Schroeder

Irene Jennie and the Christmas Masquerade: The Johnkankus by Irene Smalls

A Strawbeater's Thanksgiving by Irene Smalls

The Secret to Freedom by Marcia Vaughn

Moses: When Harriet Tubman Led Her People to Freedom by Carole Boston Weatherford

Follow the Drinking Gourd by Jeanette Winter

Journey to Freedom: A Story of the Underground Railroad by Courtni C. Wright

Organizing Literature-Based Content Units

Although there are numerous ways in which children's literature can be incorporated into the curriculum, in this section we will highlight the use of trade books in literature-based units. We will illustrate the process of selecting books and structuring a literature-based content unit by describing a social studies unit focused on immigration.

Children's literature is an especially powerful tool in social studies instruction because it helps students gain the historical or social empathy needed to develop social studies understandings (Tomlinson, Tunnell, & Richgels, 1993). Linda Levstik (1989) has observed that when literature is used in history instruction, students "encounter the complexities of historical events, where facts from the past become living, breathing drama, significant beyond their own time" (p. 136).

Determining Unit Goals

The first step in planning a literature-based content unit involves outlining the facets of the topic to be explored. The web in Figure 15.1 identifies some key facets that might be explored through a unit entitled "Coming to America: Immigration across the Years." Students can discover some of the people who have immigrated to the United States across the years and some of the diverse reasons for their decisions to immigrate. They can learn about the actual journeys that immigrants have taken and hardships they have endured. In addition, they can explore what life has been (and is) like for immigrants in the United States, as well as what life has been like for those the immigrants left behind.

Selecting Unit Books

Literature-based content units frequently incorporate literature from diverse genres. In addition, it is important to try and balance different perspectives and different reading levels when selecting unit books. An immigration unit might include historical fiction, contemporary realistic fiction, biography, informational books, poetry, memoirs, and oral history. Reading in any of these genres is likely to stimulate children's questions about immigration; yet books from each diverse genre are likely to make their own special contributions to children's learning. For example, works of historical fiction and contemporary realistic fiction provide the drama of human experience. Hence, these particular genres are especially likely to help children develop historical empathy, especially when the book's protagonist is a child. Oral histories allow children to hear the voices of actual immigrants, and informational trade books will provide answers to many of the questions students raise about immigration. Shaun Tan has even written a fantasy in graphic novel format entitled ***The Arrival*** that explores the immigrant experience. Some possible titles from different genres that could be used to explore the various facets of the unit "Coming to America" are listed in Table 15.2.

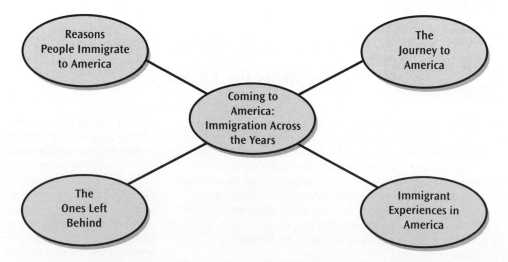

FIGURE 15.1   Students can explore various facets of the immigration experience in a literature-based content unit entitled "Coming to America."

Table 15.2 Possible Trade Books for Use in an Immigration Unit

Genre	Title	Unit Facet
Historical Fiction	*Letters from Rifka* (Hesse, 1992)	■ Journey to America ■ Reasons for Immigrating
	Goodbye, Walter Malinski (Recorvits, 1999)	■ Immigrant Experiences in America
	When Jessie Came Across the Sea (Hest, 1997)	■ Journey to America ■ Immigrant Experiences in America ■ Reasons for Immigrating
	Silent Movie (Avi, 2003)	■ Immigrant Experiences in America
	Maggie's Door (Giff, 2003)	■ Journey to America
Contemporary Realistic Fiction	*How Many Days to America?* (Bunting, 1988)	■ Journey to America
	Going Home (Bunting, 1996)	■ Immigrant Experiences in America ■ Reasons for Immigrating
	Journey of the Sparrows (Buss, 2002)	■ Immigrant Experiences in America
	Home of the Brave (Applegate, 2007)	■ Immigrant Experiences in America
Biography	*Hector Lives in the United States Now* (Hewett, 1990)	■ Immigrant Experiences in America
	Journey to Ellis Island (Bierman, 1998)	■ Journey to America
	Coming to America: A Muslim Family's Story (Wolf, 2003)	■ Immigrant Experiences in America
Informational	*Immigrants* (Sandler, 1995)	■ Journey to America ■ Immigrant Experiences in America
	Immigrant Kids (Freedman, 1980)	■ Journey to America ■ Immigrant Experiences in America
	Shutting Out the Sky (Hopkinson, 2003)	■ Immigrant Experiences in America
	Across America on an Emigrant Train (Murphy, 2004)	■ Journey to America
Poetry	*My Name Is Jorge: On Both Sides of the River* (Medina, 1999)	■ Immigrant Experiences in America
	America, My New Home (Gunning, 2004)	
Memoir	*Finding My Hat* (Son, 2003)	■ Immigrant Experiences in America
Oral History	*I Was Dreaming to Come to America* (Lawlor, 1995)	■ Multiple facets
Fantasy	*The Arrival* (Tan, 2006)	■ Journey to America ■ Immigrant Experiences in America

Top Shelf 15.9

Books to Include in a Unit on Medieval Times

A Medieval Feast by Aliki

Crispin: The Cross of Lead by Avi

Stephen Biesty's Cross-Sections Castle by Stephen Biesty

Fourteenth-Century Towns by John D. Clare

Catherine, Called Birdy by Karen Cushman

The Midwife's Apprentice by Karen Cushman

The Door in the Wall by Marguerite de Angeli

A Company of Fools by Deborah Ellis

The Puppeteer's Apprentice by Anne Love

Good Masters! Sweet Ladies!: Voices from a Medieval Village by Laura Amy Schlitz

The Ramsay Scallop by Frances Temple

The Executioner's Daughter by Laura E. Williams

In seeking selections for literature-based content units, you can use the lists of recommended books found in this text. It is likely that you will also need to turn to various book selection aids to locate unit books. *Book Links,* a publication of the American Library Association, is an especially helpful tool for identifying literature for content area units.

Unit Structure

There is no one best way to organize literature-based content units. Two organizational formats that have been recommended by educators are text sets and literature-based inquiry units.

Myra Zarnowski (1993) describes the use of text sets to engage students in the study of content area topics. She outlines three steps involved in creating and implementing this organizational plan. Step one is creating and introducing the text set. Text sets are collections of related books that focus on a particular facet of the topic under study. These collections of books are intended to "spark conversation and provide many opportunities for comparison and contrasts" (p. 36). Books in a set can be pulled from different genres and can be written at varied levels of difficulty. Table 15.3 contains possible text sets for our sample unit, "Coming to America." Over the course of the unit of study, text sets can grow as the teacher and students find new material on the topic that they want to add. Zarnowski recommends a brief introduction to each set so that students can choose a study group. These introductions can also help students to decide which books in the text set they want to read.

Study groups meet several times each week. Students prepare for their groups by reading books from their text set and writing journal entries that record ideas, responses, or information that they found interesting and might want to discuss. Then, when students gather to talk about their books, discussion can begin with students sharing from their journals.

In the final step of the investigation, students meet with people from beyond the classroom community to explore their topic in greater depth. For example, in our "Coming to America" unit, students might meet with recent immigrants to discuss their experiences. In preparation for these conversations that move beyond the classroom community, students write personal essays related to their topic of study.

Nancy Roser and Susan Keehn (2002) recommend a plan for developing literature-based inquiry units for social studies instruction. The units that they describe are organized into three phases, with each phase lasting approximately two weeks, although these times can be modified to accommodate unit goals and students' interests. In Phase 1, students are involved in a whole-class read-aloud of a chapter book. In our "Coming to America" unit, Karen Hesse's **Letters from Rifka** would be a good read-aloud choice to explore an historical immigration experience while Fran Leeper Buss's **Journey of the Sparrows** provides a window onto the contemporary experience of a young El Salvadoran immigrant (see Table 15.2).

In Phase 2 of the inquiry unit, students choose to join one of three or four small literature circles to read books that further explore the topic at hand. In the "Coming to America" unit, Phase 2 could be organized in different ways. All the literature circles might read chapter books that explore immigrants' experiences once they arrive in America. The teacher could select books of different difficulty levels to accommodate the varied reading abilities that are likely to be represented in a class. Possible choices for literature circles include Laurence Yep's **Dragon's Gate,** Helen Recorvits's **Goodbye, Walter Malinski**, and Monica Gunning's **America, My New Home**, an immigration story told through a series of poems. As an alternative, instead of having the students investigate the same topic in the second phase of the unit, the teacher could form small literature circles that explore different facets of the topic. For example, one group might choose to continue the study of the topic introduced in Phase 1, the experiences immigrants had coming to America. A second literature circle could explore experiences immigrants had on their arrival in the United States, and a third

ILLUSTRATION 15.5 In *The Trip Back Home* a little girl and her mother travel from America to Korea to see the grandparents the girl has never met. ("Book Cover" from *The Trip Back Home,* copyright © 2000 by Janet S. Wong, Illustrations copyright © 2000 by Bo Jia, reprinted by permission of Houghton Mifflin Harcourt Publishing Company.)

Table 15.3   Sample Text Sets for a Unit on Coming to America

Topic of Text Set	Titles in Text Set
Journey to America	*A Journey to the New World: The Diary of Remember Patience Whipple* (Lasky, 1996)
	Across the Wide Dark Sea (Van Leeuwen, 1995)
	An Ellis Island Christmas, (Leighton, 1992)
	Watch the Stars Come Out (Levinson, 1985)
	When Jessie Came Across the Sea (Hest, 1997)
	. . . If Your Name Was Changed at Ellis Island (Levine, 1993)
	Hannah's Journal (Moss, 2000)
	Across America on an Emigrant Train (Murphy, 2004)
Immigrant Experiences in America	*In the Year of the Boar and Jackie Robinson* (Lord, 1984)
	Grandfather's Journey (Say, 1993)
	Together in Pinecone Patch (Yezerski, 1998)
	Immigrant Kids (Freedman, 1980)
	Journey of the Sparrows (Buss, 2002)
	Home of the Brave (Applegate, 2007)
	A Day's Work (Bunting, 1994)
	Hoang Anh: A Vietnamese-American Boy (Hoyt-Goldsmith, 1992)
	Finding My Hat (Son, 2003)
	Shutting Out the Sky (Hopkinson, 2003)
	America, My New Home (Gunning, 2004)
	We Are Americans (Hoobler, 2003)
	Coming to America: A Muslim Family's Story (Wolf, 2003)
	Coolies (Yin, 2003)
	Brothers (Yin, 2006)
	The Arrival (Tan, 2006)
Those Left Behind	*Letters from Rifka* (Hesse, 1992)
	When Jessie Came Across the Sea (Hest, 1997)
	The Trip Back Home (Wong, 2000)

group might look at what it was like for the loved ones the immigrants left behind. These groups could read and discuss either a chapter book or various picture books. Literature circles could meet either daily or several times a week. Because students read Phase 2 books on their own, they can prepare to participate in their literature circle discussions by writing in journals while they are reading. The journal entries can, in turn, be used to launch and support small group discussions. In the organizational scheme created by Roser and Keehn, the purpose of Phase 3 is to give students an opportunity to explore questions about the topic of study that have emerged during the initial phases of the study. Phase 3 can be launched

Teaching Idea 15.4

Circling Up for Literature

Creating links between literature and content area instruction enriches learning in the content area. For a study of living things in science, get multiple copies of the following titles: *Stone Fox*, *The Midnight Fox*, *Stranded*, and *Shiloh*. Allow your students to choose the book they want to read and then organize students into literature circles. These groups can meet to set their reading pace and to decide whether they will read as partners, as a group, or alone. They can respond to the books in writing or through discussion. Many teachers include the choice of a culminating activity by offering responses such as designing a book jacket complete with the author's biography and recommendations by their peers or creating a commercial for the book that is taped à la the PBS series, *Reading Rainbow*.

by having students once again meet as a whole class, this time to pose their wonderings and questions. An instructional strategy such as K-W-L (Ogle, 1986) can be used at this point. In the first phase of K-W-L (what I know), students brainstorm all that they have learned about the topic at hand (for example, immigration) while the teacher records what students know. In the next phase (what I want to know), students pose questions they still have about the topic under study, and the teacher records their questions on a chart. The final phase of K-W-L (what I learned) occurs once the students have completed their research.

Inquiry charts can also be used to launch Phase 3 of literature-based inquiry units (Hoffman, 1992). An inquiry chart lists students' questions in columns, with spaces in which they can later record answers they obtain from different sources (see Figure 15.2). Once students have posed questions they want to explore, they can join small inquiry groups to research the questions that are of greatest interest to them.

In this final phase of a literature-based inquiry unit, students turn to a variety of sources to find answers to their questions. Certainly informational trade books are likely to be an especially important resource. However, other sources might include the Internet, old newspapers, outside experts, and individuals who have personal experience with the topic at hand.

Children's literature holds great potential for nurturing children's learning across the curriculum. Writers of diverse genres open the world for children, and as teachers integrate these treasures across the curriculum, they will motivate children to explore their world.

	Where do immigrants come from today?	Why do people come to America today?	Where do today's immigrants settle in America?	What work do immigrants do today?	How do immigrants become American citizens?
Immigrants by Martin Sandler					
Immigrant Kids by Russell Freedman					
Quilted Landscapes by Yale Strom					
From Exiles to Immigrants by Ronald Takaki					

FIGURE 15.2 Students' questions can be organized in an inquiry chart on which they record the answers they find in the various sources used for research.

Experiences for Further Learning

1. Author units are designed to help children discover what characterizes the work of a particular author or illustrator. While the primary means of achieving this end is by immersing children in the works of the writer or illustrator, sometimes it is helpful to also pull certain types of biographical information into the unit. Biographical "facts" such as where or when the author was born are usually less pertinent than information that helps students see how the author's life experiences may have influenced his or her writing. Choose a writer and read a number of that person's books. Then, gather information about the writer's life by turning to a book such as *Children's Books and Their Creators* (Silvey, 1995) or *Something about the Author* (Nakamura, 1998), or by going on the Internet to the author's own web site or to a site such as teachingbooks.net, which features video interviews with authors and illustrators of children's books. Many authors have written books in which they reflect on their writing process and acknowledge the people, books, and events that have influenced them. For example, in two volumes, Beverly Cleary describes her life as she evolved into an author: **A Girl from Yamhill** and **My Own Two Feet**. What links (if any) can you discover between the writer's life story and his or her writing? Teachers often find inspiration for understanding themselves as writers when they discover the motivations for published writers.

2. Teachers typically initiate literary study with at least some ideas about the types of links they want children to discover among the books featured in the unit. However, children are very capable of discovering connections on their own—sometimes connections their teachers have not seen. Gather together a set of related books and share them with children. For example, you might choose Cinderella variants such as **Sootface, The Egyptian Cinderella**, **Cendrillon**, and **Mufaro's Beautiful Daughters**. After reading the books to the children, ask them to brainstorm ways in which the stories are similar and ways in which they are different. In what ways did the children extend your own thinking about the books? Following the literary study of cultural variants of Cinderella, read several versions that parody Cinderella. Humorous versions, like **Bigfoot Cinderrrrrella** and **Cinder Edna** maintain the elements unique to Cinderella—but with a twist.

3. Units in which books are only loosely linked are less likely to evoke children's most insightful thinking. One way of helping to ensure that the books you have selected for a unit are linked in meaningful ways is by creating a Language Chart that might be used with the books. Working with a group of peers, select a theme that could be explored through literature. Themes such as "Celebrations" or "Journeys" or "Courage" offer rich opportunities for thematic study. Gather books that you believe might be appropriate for use in a unit and design a Language Chart to use with the books. Are the connections you identified significant ones? Go ahead and complete the chart with your peers. This is a good way of checking to make sure the questions you posed on the chart are likely to elicit the kinds of responses you envision.

Recommended Books

* indicates a picture book; **I** indicates interest level (P = preschool, YA = young adult)

Books about Imagination

Holm, Jennifer L. *Babymouse Beach Babe*. Illustrated by Matthew Holm. Random House, 2006. This graphic novel features Babymouse, a spunky grade school mouse with plenty of imagination. (**I:** 5–9)

*Houghton, Eric. *The Crooked Apple Tree*. Illustrated by Caroline Gold. Barefoot Books, 1999. When two siblings move to a new home, a crooked apple tree provides the backdrop for their imaginative play. (**I:** P–8)

*Keats, Ezra Jack. *Regards to the Man in the Moon*. Macmillan, 1981. Louie shows his friends how, with a little imagination, junk can turn into a great adventure. (**I:** P–8)

*Norman, Philip Ross. *A Mammoth Imagination*. Little, Brown, 1992. Little Bonbon discovers that he can have more fun playing and using his imagination than spending his time eating like the other wild boars. (**I:** P–8)

Portis, Antoinette. *Not a Box*. HarperCollins, 2006. While "it" may look like a box to others, an imaginative little rabbit sees things quite differently. (**I:** 4–7)

*Reynolds, Peter H. *The Dot*. Candlewick, 2003. A little girl is convinced she can't draw—until a perceptive teacher helps her discover her own potential. (**I:** 5–8)

*Schaefer, Carole Lexa. *The Squiggle*. Illustrated by Pierr Morgan. Crown, 1996. With a simple string, a little girl transforms her class's walk to the park. (**I:** P–7)

*Schotter, Roni. *Captain Bob Takes Flight*. Illustrated by Joe Cepeda. Atheneum, 2003. When Bob has to clean his room, an empty box soon becomes an airplane, and Bob becomes a fierce flyer. (**I:** P–7)

*Stadler, John. *Catilda*. Catilda has been put to bed, and this story's narrative consists of a quiet exchange between Catilda's parents who fancy their daughter spending quiet time before falling asleep. The illustrations tell another story all together, as Catilda journeys around the world in search of her lost toy. (**I:** P)

Books about Celebrations

*Ancona, George. *Powwow*. Harcourt, 1993. This informational book highlights the largest Native American powwow in the United States, which is held annually in Crow Agency, Montana. (**I:** 7–11)

*Goldin, Barbara Diamond. *The World's Birthday: A Rosh Hashanah Story*. Illustrated by Jeanette Winter. Harcourt, 1990. When his sister tells him that Rosh Hashanah is the time to celebrate the world's birthday, Daniel is determined to find a way to throw a birthday party for the whole world. (**I:** P–8)

*Johnston, Tony. *Day of the Dead*. Illustrated by Jeanette Winter. Harcourt, 1997. A family in a small Mexican town honors their dead loved ones on the Day of the Dead. (**I:** 5–9)

*Joseph, Lynn. *An Island Christmas*. Illustrated by Catherine Stock. Clarion, 1992. Preparations for Christmas on the island of Trinidad include picking red petals for the sorrel drink, mixing up the black currant cake, and singing along with the parang band. (**I:** 6–9)

*Livingston, Myra Cohn. *Festivals*. Illustrated by Leonard Everett Fisher. Holiday House, 1996. This collection of poetry features celebrations around the world. (**I:** 6 and up)

*Polacco, Patricia. *When Lightning Comes in a Jar*. Philomel, 2002. Through a wealth of details, Polacco brings to life the delight of a family reunion and the joy that comes with passing family traditions from one generation to the next. (**I:** 6–12)

*Rael, Elsa Okon. *Rivka's First Thanksgiving*. Illustrated by Maryann Kovalski. Margaret K. McElderry, 2001. When Rivka learns about Thanksgiving, she sets out to convince her Jewish immigrant family that this is a holiday for all Americans. When her family balks, Rivka faces the daunting task of winning over the rabbi to her view. (**I:** 6–9)

*Russell, Ching Yeung. *Moon Festival*. Illustrated by Christopher Zhong-Yuan Zhang. Boyds Mill, 1997. Ying and her grandmother prepare for their family's autumn celebration of the Moon Festival. (**I:** 6–10)

Books Featuring Special People in Our Lives

*Bercaw, Edna Coe. *Halmoni's Day*. Illustrated by Robert Hunt. Dial, 2000. Jennifer is embarrassed to take her Korean-speaking grandmother to the school's Grandparents' Day until Halmoni shares a story with the class that shows how love can reach over generational and language barriers. (**I:** 7–10)

*Cooke, Trish. *Full, Full, Full of Love*. Illustrated by Paul Howard. As Jay Jay waits for Sunday dinner to be ready, he finds that grandma's house is full of wonderful things, especially love. (**I:** P–6)

Creech, Sharon. *Granny Torrelli Makes Soup*. HarperCollins, 2003. When Rosie and her best friend Bailey have a "falling out," Granny Torrelli makes things right through her storytelling and family recipes. (**I:** 9–12)

*Grifalconi, Ann. *Osa's Pride*. Little, Brown, 1990. When Osa becomes a little too proud, her grandmother creates a story cloth that gently teaches Osa a lesson. (**I:** 6–10)

*Grimes, Nikki. *Meet Danitra Brown*. Illustrated by Floyd Cooper. Morrow, 1994. Through a series of poems, Zuri Jackson tells about her life, herself, and her best friend Danitra Brown. (**I:** 7–10)

*———. *My Man Blue*. Illustrated by Jerome Lagarrigue. Dial, 1999. This story of Blue and the boy he is determined to save from the inner-city streets is told through a collection of poems. (**I:** 8–12)

*Houston, Gloria. *My Great-Aunt Arizona*. Illustrated by Susan Condie Lamb. HarperCollins, 1997. Arizona was born in a small community in the Blue Ridge Mountains, where she dreamed of traveling to faraway places. She never left the area but became a teacher who touched the lives of many children by teaching them about the world. (**I:** 6 and up)

*Lorbiecki, Marybeth. *Sister Anne's Hands*. Illustrated by K. Wendy Popp. Dial, 1998. When Sister Anne, an African American nun, goes to teach in a small Southern town in the 1960s, she helps her students to discover the joy of learning and the hatefulness of racism. (**I:** 6–10)

*Martin, Jacqueline Briggs. *The Water Gift and the Pig of the Pig*. Illustrated by Linda S. Wingerter. Houghton Mifflin, 2003. When a grandfather with the gift of dousing loses faith in his ability, his granddaughter helps to restore his self confidence by convincing him to use his gift to find a lost pig. (**I:** 7–10)

*Mitchell, Margaree King. *Uncle Jed's Barbershop*. Illustrated by James Ransome. Simon & Schuster, 1993. Despite all the adversity he encounters in the segregated South of the 1920s, Uncle Jed never gives up his dream of opening his own barbershop. (**I:** 9–12)

*Polacco, Patricia. *Thank You, Mr. Falker*. Philomel, 1998. Trisha's self-esteem plummets as each year of school passes and she fails to learn to read. Then her fifth-grade teacher discovers the secret that Trisha has struggled to hide and helps her become a reader. (**I:** 7–11)

*Rosen, Michael J. *Elijah's Angel*. Illustrated by Aminah Brenda Lynn Robinson. Harcourt, 1992. A boy's parents help him to reach across cultural boundaries when his friend Elijah gives him a special carving. (**I:** 8–YA)

*Wild, Margaret. *Our Granny*. Illustrated by Julie Vivas. Ticknor & Fields, 1994. A celebration of all kinds of grannies. (**I:** P–8)

Books by Lois Ehlert

*Ehlert, Lois. *Color Zoo*. HarperCollins, 1989. As they turn the pages, children see various shapes that unlayer to reveal different animal faces. Shape names and animal names are included. A related title is *Color Farm* (1990). (**I:** P)

*———. *Cuckoo: Cucú*. Harcourt, 1997. Cuckoo may be beautiful, but the other birds believe that she doesn't do her share of the work—until a fire threatens the seed crop. (**I:** P–8)

*———. *Feathers for Lunch*. Harcourt, 1990. A housecat hopes to catch one of the birds in the backyard for lunch, but all get away safely and the cat ends up with only feathers. Bird descriptions are included. (**I:** P–7)

*———. *Fish Eyes: A Book You Can Count On*. Harcourt, 1990. The text is narrated in the voice of a young child who imagines touring the underwater world and seeing brightly colored fish. This counting book includes the concept of "one more," as the guide fish is added to the count on each page. (**I:** P–6)

*———. *Market Day*. Harcourt, 2000. The reader is taken on a tour of the market in this tale told through folk art from Latin America. (**I:** P–7)

*———. *Moon Rope: A Peruvian Folktale/Un lazo a la luna: Una leyenda Peruana*. Harcourt, 1992. A pourquoi tale in English and Spanish that explains why Mole lives in the ground and why we see Fox's likeness in the moon. (**I:** 6–10)

*———. *Nuts to You!* Harcourt, 1993. This is the simple story of the antics of a squirrel. (**I:** P–6)

*———. *Pie in the Sky*. Harcourt, 2004. Readers get to watch the tree's cycle as it moves from flower, to bud, to fruit—which in turn becomes pie. (**I:** P–7)

*———. *Snowballs*. Harcourt, 1995. It's snowing and time to create and decorate snow people with all sorts of odds and ends. (**I:** P–6)

*———. *Top Cat*. Harcourt, 1998. When Top Cat's space is invaded by a new kitten, Top Cat decides to initiate the kitten into all his naughty ways. (**I:** P–6)

Folktale Spin-Offs

*Ada, Alma Flor. *Yours Truly, Goldilocks*. Illustrated by Leslie Tryon. Atheneum, 1998. The house warming for the three little pigs is threatened when two ferocious wolves show up. This spin-off is told through the exchange of a series of letters written by some familiar characters, including Goldilocks, Peter Rabbit, and Little Red Riding Hood. (**I:** 6–9)

*———. *With Love, Little Red Hen*. Illustrated by Leslie Tryon. Atheneum, 2001. When Little Red Hen moves into Hidden Forest and starts to grow corn for her chicks, she finds some of her neighbors unwilling to help out. However, others—including Goldilocks and Little Red Riding Hood—generously lend a helping hand. Readers will enjoy this exchange of letters among familiar folklore characters. (**I:** 5–8)

*Ahlberg, Janet, and Allan Ahlberg. *The Jolly Postman or Other People's Letters*. Little, Brown, 1986. The jolly postman has mail—of all sorts, even junk mail—for some famous characters from folktales. (**I:** 6–10)

*Dealey, Erin. *Goldie Locks Has Chicken Pox*. Illustrated by Hanako Wakiyama. Atheneum, 2002. Goldie Locks has chicken pox. She is teased unmercifully by her little brother, and all the while friends from familiar tales drop in to see their ailing friend—Henny Penny, Little Red, and many others. (**I:** P–8)

*Emberley, Michael. *Ruby*. Little, Brown, 1990. Ruby, a small mouse in a red cloak, sets out through the city streets to take her granny a batch of pies. Forgetting her mother's advice, Ruby talks to a smooth-talking cat that threatens to turn her grandmother into a meal. (**I:** 6–9)

*Emberley, Rebecca. *Three Cool Kids*. Little, Brown, 1995. These three goats live in an empty lot in the city. Their lot is overgrazed, and they long to move to the one across the street. But in the sewer under that street lives a fierce rat. (**I:** 6–9)

*Lasky, Kathryn. *The Emperor's Old Clothes*. Illustrated by David Catrow. Harcourt Brace, 1999. When Farmer Henry stumbles across new finery cast off (by the emperor who wore no clothes), his new attire causes an uproar in the barnyard. (**I:** 6–10)

*Meddaugh, Susan. *Cinderella's Rat*. Houghton Mifflin, 1997. Readers learn of the misadventures of the rat that was turned into Cinderella's coachboy and of how the experience changed his life. (**I:** 6–10)

*Prater, John. *Once Upon a Time*. Candlewick, 1993. A little boy bemoans what promises to be an ordinary day—until a series of folktale characters appear on the landscape. (**I:** 6–9)

*Scieszka, Jon. *The Frog Prince Continued*. Illustrated by Steve Johnson. Viking, 1991. The Frog Prince isn't too happy in his marriage to the princess. So he sets off to find a witch who will turn him back into a frog. (**I:** 6–10)

*———. *The True Story of the 3 Little Pigs!* Illustrated by Lane Smith. Viking, 1989. The wolf tells his side of the story in this spin-off of "The Three Little Pigs." (**I:** All ages)

*Sierra, Judy. *The House That Drac Built*. Illustrated by Will Hillenbrand. Harcourt, 1995. Using the pattern of "The House That Jack Built," the author describes the house that Dracula built. (**I:** 6–9)

*Tolhurst, Marilyn. *Somebody and the Three Blairs*. Illustrated by Simone Abel. Orchard, 1990. In this upside down spin-off of "The Three Bears," Mr. and Mrs. Blair and Baby Blair go for a walk one morning, only to return home to find their home ransacked by Somebody—a bear, of course. (**I:** 5–8)

Trickster Tales

*Aardema, Verna. *Borreguita and the Coyote*. Illustrated by Petra Mathers. Knopf, 1991. Coyote is determined to have Borreguita for lunch, but the little lamb proves too clever for Coyote. (**I:** 5–9)

*Campoy, F. Isabel. *Rosa Raposa*. Illustrated by Jose Aruego and Ariane Dewey. Jaguar may be dangerous, but in this contemporary trickster tale, Rosa Raposa, the fox, manages to outsmart him every time. (**I:** 5–8)

*Galdone, Paul. *The Monkey and the Crocodile: A Jataka Tale from India*. Houghton Mifflin, 1969/1987. Monkey convinces crocodile that he shouldn't eat him until he returns to the tree to get his heart, which is, after all, the tastiest part of him. (**I:** 5–8)

*Goble, Paul. *Iktomi and the Coyote*. Orchard, 1998. The prairie dogs think that Iktomi is their friend, but Iktomi has a different idea: baked prairie dog for lunch. (**I:** 5–9)

*Kimmel, Eric A. *Anansi Goes Fishing*. Illustrated by Janet Stevens. Holiday, 1992. The tables are turned when Anansi sets out to trick his friend into doing all the work. (**I:** P–8)

*McDermott, Gerald. *Coyote: A Trickster Tale from the American Southwest*. Harcourt, 1994. Coyote convinces the crows to teach him how to fly, and the crows agree. But when the crows grow tired of Coyote's boasting, they decide to teach him a lesson. (**I:** 5–8)

*———. *Zomo the Rabbit: A Trickster Tale from West Africa*. Harcourt, 1992. Zomo the Rabbit is portrayed here wearing an African dashiki. (**I:** 5–8)

*McKissack, Patricia. *Flossie and the Fox*. Illustrated by Rachel Isadora. Dial, 1986. Flossie turns the tables on Mr. Fox when he tries to get her basket of eggs. (**I:** 5–10)

*Paye, Won-Ldy, and Margaret H. Lippert. *Mrs. Chicken and the Hungry Crocodile*. Illustrated by Julie Paschkis. In this folktale from Liberia, Mrs. Chicken uses her wits to trick Crocodile into freeing her rather than eating her. (**I:** 4–8)

*Souhami, Jessica. *The Leopard's Drum: An Asante Tale from West Africa*. Little, Brown, 1995. Humble tortoise outwits the boastful leopard to obtain the leopard's drum for the Sky-God. (**I:** 5–8)

*Stevens, Janet. *Tops and Bottoms*. Harcourt, 1995. Industrious and clever, Hare tricks lazy Bear by wheeling and dealing in the tops and bottoms of vegetables. (**I:** P–8)

Cinderella Variants

*Climo, Shirley. *The Egyptian Cinderella*. Illustrated by Ruth Heller. HarperTrophy, 1989. Rhodopis, a princess snatched from her home in Greece, is sold into slavery in Egypt. There she is befriended by a falcon and chosen by the Pharaoh to be his wife. This is one of the world's oldest Cinderella tales. (**I:** 8–12)

*Greaves, Margaret. *Tattercoats*. Illustrated by Margaret Chamberlain. Clarkson N. Potter, 1990. In this English version of the Cinderella story, Tattercoats sets out to the king's ball with the gooseboy. (**I:** 7–10)

*Hooks, William. *Moss Gown*. Illustrated by Donald Carrick. Clarion, 1987. A Cinderella story from the author's native eastern North Carolina. (**I:** 7–10)

*Pollock, Penny. *The Turkey Girl: A Zuni Cinderella Story*. Illustrated by Ed Young. Little, Brown, 1996. This rich pourquoi tale with a moral about keeping one's word is also a valuable take on the Cinderella story, with breathtaking illustrations. (**I:** 7–9)

*San Souci, Robert D. *Cendrillon: A Caribbean Cinderella*. Illustrated by Brian Pinkney. Simon & Schuster, 1998. When Cendrillon's godmother discovers how much her goddaughter longs to go to the ball, she uses her magic to make the dream come true. (**I:** 9–12).

*———. *Sootface: An Ojibwa Cinderella Story*. Illustrated by Daniel San Souci. Doubleday, 1994. A mighty warrior with the power to make himself invisible decides to marry the woman who can see him. Only Sootface, the youngest of three sisters, is able to see the warrior. (**I:** 8–11)

*———. *The Talking Eggs*. Illustrated by Jerry Pinkney. Dial, 1989. An African American variant of Cinderella. (**I:** 5–10)

*Steptoe, John. *Mufaro's Beautiful Daughters*. Lothrop, 1987. The humblest and kindest daughter gets the reward in this Caldecott winner. (**I:** 6–10)

Tomie dePaola Family Stories

*dePaola, Tomie. *The Art Lesson*. Putnam, 1989. Tommy loves to draw and is encouraged by his family to pursue his passion. But at school he encounters frustration until an understanding art teacher lends a helping hand. (**I:** P–8)

*———. *The Baby Sitter*. Putnam, 1996. Tommy is excited about the new baby sister who is coming, but he is not ready for the stern nana who comes to stay with him when his mother goes to the hospital. (**I:** P–8)

*———. *Nana Upstairs & Nana Downstairs*. Putnam, 1998. For young Tommy, Sundays were special, for that was when he visited his Nana Upstairs and Nana Downstairs. This is a story about family and remembering family. (**I:** 5–9)

*———. *Tom*. Putnam, 1993. Tommy is named after his grandfather Tom, and together the two share memorable times. (**I:** P–8)

———. *26 Fairmount Avenue*. Putnam, 1999. Memorable moments from a year in Tomie dePaola's boyhood fill the pages of this first chapter book. (**I:** 6–9)

*———. *Watch Out for the Chicken Feet in Your Soup*. Little Simon, 1985. His old-fashioned Italian grandmother embarrasses Joey—until he begins to see her through the eyes of his friend. (**I:** P–8)

Books about Courage

*Andrews, Jan. *Very Last First Time*. Illustrated by Ian Wallace. Margaret K. McElderry, 1985. The first time Eva goes under the ocean's ice to find mussels for her family, she must call on reserves of courage she never realized she had. (**I:** 6–10)

*Arnold, Marsha Diane. *The Bravest of Us All*. Illustrated by Brad Sneed. Dial, 2000. Ruby Jane is sure that her big sister, Velma Jean, is the bravest person in the world. But when a tornado threatens their farm, Ruby Jane discovers there are many kinds of courage. (**I:** 6–9)

*Gerstein, Mordicai. *The Man Who Walked between the Towers*. Roaring Brook Press, 2003. In 1974, a young French aerialist, with the help of friends, stretched a cable between the towers of the World Trade Center and walked that cable from one tower to the next, as free as a bird. (**I:** 6 and up)

*James, Simon. *Little One Step*. Candlewick, 2003. Little One Step (a duckling) is away from home and feels all wobbly, but his siblings convince him to take "one step" each time he falters. (**I:** P–7)

*Luenn, Nancy. *Nessa's Fish*. Illustrated by Neil Waldman. Atheneum, 1990. A brave Inuit girl defends her ailing grandmother and a cache of fish from marauding animals on the desolate ice. (**I:** 7–10)

*Scott, Ann H. *Brave as a Mountain Lion*. Illustrated by Glo Coalson. Clarion, 1996. Frightened at the idea of participating in the school spelling bee, Spider finds courage by seeking advice from his family and listening to his own spirit. (**I:** 6–10)

Books Featuring Exaggeration and Outlandish Situations

*Barrett, Judi. *Cloudy with a Chance of Meatballs*. Illustrated by Ron Barrett. Atheneum, 1978. Storms of food fall from the sky in the town of Chew-and-Swallow. (**I:** P–8)

*Birdseye, Tom. *A Regular Flood of Mishap*. Illustrated by Megan Lloyd. Holiday House, 1994. Ima Bean is only trying to help when she borrows Grandpa's fishing pole, but instead she starts a regular flood of mishap. (**I:** P–8)

*Darrow, Sharon. *Old Thunder and Miss Raney*. Dorling Kindersley, 2000. After Raney and her horse are caught up in a tornado, their ambitions for winning a blue ribbon at the county fair take an unexpected turn. This tale is filled with exaggeration and folksy language. (**I:** 5–8)

*Johnson, Paul Brett. *The Pig Who Ran a Red Light*. Orchard, 1999. When Miss Rosemary's pig starts doing everything the cow does, she is challenged to find a way to make the pig act like a pig. (**I:** P–7)

Lindgren, Astrid. *Pippi Longstocking*. Translated by Florence Lamborn. Illustrated by Louis S. Glanzman. Viking, 1950/1997. Living all alone, Pippi—the strongest girl in the world—is free to engage in hilarious antics. (**I:** 5–9)

*McKissack, Patricia. *A Million Fish . . . More or Less*. Illustrated by Dena Schutzer. Knopf, 1992. Visits to the bayou inspire unforgettable yarns. (**I:** 6–10)

*Nolen, Jerdine. *Thunder Rose*. Illustrated by Kadir Nelson. It soon becomes apparent that Thunder Rose, an African American child born on a stormy night, is no ordinary person as she engages in exploits like facing down tornadoes. (**I:** 5–9)

*Stanley, Diane. *Raising Sweetness*. Illustrated by G. Brian Karas. Putnam, 1999. Sweetness and the other children know that they are lucky to have been adopted by the sheriff; still, the sheriff's cooking and housekeeping leave something to be desired. So Sweetness sets out to find a solution to their problems. (**I:** P–8)

*———. *Saving Sweetness*. Illustrated by G. Brian Karas. Putnam, 1996. When the orphan Sweetness runs away from the orphanage, the sheriff sets out to save her, but Sweetness doesn't want to have anything to do with being saved. (**I:** P–8)

*White, Linda Arms. *Comes a Wind*. Illustrated by Tom Curry. Dorling Kindersley, 2000. Clement and Clyde's sibling rivalry reaches new heights as they exchange tales about windy days—until a wind they'll never forget blows up on their mother's birthday. (**I:** P–8)

Foxy Books

*Auch, Mary Jane. *Peeping Beauty*. Holiday House, 1993. Poulette, the hen, dreams of becoming a famous ballerina. So when a fox claiming to be a talent scout comes to the farm, Poulette is naively convinced that her dreams are about to come true. (**I:** 5–8)

*Marshall, James. *Wings: A Tale of Two Chickens*. Viking, 1995. Winnie, a hen who never reads, is lured away by a fox who promises to alleviate her boredom. (**I:** P–8)

*Steig, William. *Doctor De Soto*. Farrar, 1982. A fox visits a mouse dentist with the hope of having the dentist for dinner after his tooth has been fixed. (**I:** P–8)

*———. *A Flea in the Ear*. Illustrated by Ken Brown. Dutton, 1995. A big spotted hound, the faithful guardian of the chicken coop, is tricked by a wily fox. (**I:** P–8)

Books about Medieval Times

*Aliki. *A Medieval Feast*. HarperCollins, 1983. When the lord and lady of the manor learn that the king and his party will soon arrive for a short stay, they begin elaborate preparations for a feast. (**I:** 6–10)

Avi. *Crispin: The Cross of Lead*. Hyperion, 2002. Accused of a crime he did not commit and having lost his mother—his only living relative—Crispin must flee his village, the only home he has ever known. Pursued by unknown enemies, Crispin joins up with a juggler named Bear and finds himself swept up in the political forces of medieval England. (**I:** 10 and up)

Biesty, Stephen. *Stephen Biesty's Cross-Sections Castle*. Dorling Kindersley, 1994. This book contains various cross-sections of a medieval castle. Each cross-section is accompanied by text that highlights some facet of life during this period. (**I:** 10 and up)

Clare, John D. *Fourteenth-Century Towns*. Harcourt, 1993. This informational book covers many facets of life in medieval towns and is accompanied by photographs of reenactments of the period. (**I:** 10 and up)

Cushman, Karen. *Catherine, Called Birdy*. Clarion, 1994. Through her journal, a young girl chronicles her daily life in medieval England. (**I:** 11–YA)

———. *The Midwife's Apprentice*. Clarion, 1995. A homeless waif in medieval England is given the opportunity to become a midwife's apprentice. (**I:** 9–12)

de Angeli, Marguerite. *The Door in the Wall*. Doubleday, 1949/1989. A young boy loses the use of his legs and is still able to save the town and serve the king. (**I:** 8–12)

Ellis, Deborah. *A Company of Fools*. Fitzhenry & Whiteside, 2002. Henre's quiet life behind the abbey walls changes when street urchin Micah arrives at the abbey. Together the boys face unfathomable despair when the plague sweeps through Paris and their abbey. (**I:** 10 and up)

Love, D. Anne. *The Puppeteer's Apprentice*. McElderry/Simon & Schuster, 2003. After running away from the drudgery of manor life, Mouse sees a puppet show and determines to become a puppeteer. (**I:** 9–12)

Schlitz, Laura Amy. *Good Masters! Sweet Ladies!: Voices from a Medieval Village*. Candlewick, 2007. In this series of monologues set in the Middle Ages, children and young adults from various stations in life step forward to tell their tales. (**I:** 10 and up)

Temple, Frances. *The Ramsay Scallop*. Orchard, 1994. A young couple's pilgrimage from England to Spain transforms their views of the world and each other. (**I:** 11–YA)

Williams, Laura E. *The Executioner's Daughter*. Holt, 2000. Born into the family of an executioner, Lily is faced with becoming her father's assistant when her mother dies. Yet Lily is determined to change her fate and instead become a healer. (**I:** 10–YA)

Books about Slavery in America

*Adler, David. *A Picture Book of Frederick Douglass*. Illustrated by Samuel Byrd. Holiday House, 1993. This is a biography of Frederick Douglass, who escaped from slavery and became a leading abolitionist. (**I:** 8–11)

*————. *A Picture Book of Harriet Tubman*. Illustrated by Samuel Byrd. Holiday House, 1992. This is a biography of Harriet Tubman, who escaped from slavery and returned to the South to lead more than 300 slaves to freedom. (**I:** 8–11)

Curtis, Christopher Paul. *Elijah of Buxton*. Scholastic, 2007. Elijah, the first free born child in Buxton, Canada, discovers the horrors of slavery when he journeys to America in pursuit of a thief. (**I:** 10–14)

Hamilton, Virginia. *Anthony Burns: The Defeat and Triumph of a Fugitive Slave*. Knopf, 1988. In 1854, Anthony Burns escaped from a Virginia plantation and came to Boston, where he was arrested and tried under the Fugitive Slave Act. (**I:** 10–YA)

*Hopkinson, Deborah. *Sweet Clara and the Freedom Quilt*. Illustrated by James Ransome. Knopf, 1993. Determined to escape from slavery, Clara sews a quilt that maps the way to freedom. (**I:** 8–12)

Levine, Ellen. *Henry's Freedom Box* Illustrated by Kadir Nelson. Scholastic, 2007. This is the true story of Henry Brown, a slave who mailed himself to freedom. (**I:** 9–12)

Paterson, Katherine. *Jip: His Story*. Dutton, 1996. Jip, who has grown up in an orphanage, wonders why no one ever returned for him when he tumbled out of a wagon on West Hill Road. Then he discovers the secret of his ancestry and the horrible consequences it may bring. (**I:** 10–14)

Pinkney, Andrea Davis. *Silent Thunder*. Hyperion, 1999. Both Summer and her brother Rosco have their own "silent thunder"—deep-seated longings that roar within them. Summer dreams of learning to read, while Rosco longs to join the Union army. But these are dangerous dreams for children born into slavery. (**I:** 9–12)

*Polacco, Patricia. *Pink and Say*. Philomel, 1994. During the Civil War, an African American Union soldier befriends a white one. (**I:** 8–12)

Rinaldi, Ann. *Mine Eyes Have Seen*. Scholastic, 1998. Annie Brown, the daughter of John Brown, bears witness to the events leading up to her father's attempt to foster a slave insurrection by raiding the federal armory at Harper's Ferry, West Virginia. (**I:** 11–YA)

Rosen, Michael J. *A School for Pompey Walker*. Illustrated by Aminah Brenda Lynn Robinson. Harcourt, 1995. A former slave remembers how he raised money to build a school for all children. (**I:** 9–12)

*Schroeder, Alan. *Minty: A Story of Young Harriet Tubman*. Illustrated by Jerry Pinkney. Dial, 1996. This is a fictional account of Harriet Tubman's childhood. (**I:** 9–12)

*Smalls, Irene. *Irene Jennie and the Christmas Masquerade: The Johnkankus*. Illustrated by Melodye Rosales. Little, Brown, 1996. All the slaves look forward to Christmas Day and the celebration called the Johnkankus. Irene Jennie wants to be joyful, but how can she be when her parents have been loaned to another plantation for Christmas? (**I:** 8–11)

*————. *A Strawbeater's Thanksgiving*. Illustrated by Melodye Benson Rosales. Little, Brown, 1998. The harvest is in, and the slaves are given one night to celebrate. Jess is determined to be chosen as the special boy who helps the fiddler on this special night. (**I:** 8–10)

*Vaughan, Marcia. *The Secret to Freedom*. Illustrated by Larry Johnson. Lee & Low, 2001. Using quilts as part of a secret code, a young slave girl and her brother help their fellow slaves escape on the Underground Railroad. (**I:** 8–10)

*Weatherford, Carole Boston. *Moses: When Harriet Tubman Led Her People to Freedom*. Illustrated by Kadir Nelson. Jump at the Sun, 2006. This book highlights the strong religious convictions that inspired Harriet Tubman to lead fellow slaves to freedom. (**I:** 10 and up)

*Winter, Jeanette. *Follow the Drinking Gourd*. Knopf, 1988. This is the story of how one slave family escaped to freedom by following the drinking gourd. (**I:** 8–11)

*Wright, Courtni C. *Journey to Freedom: A Story of the Underground Railroad*. Illustrated by Gershom Griffith. Holiday House, 1994. This is the story of one slave family's journey to freedom with Harriet Tubman. (**I:** 9–12)

Books about Immigration

Applegate, Katherine. *Home of the Brave*. Feiwel and Friends, 2007. This novel in verse format features the story of a young Sudanese immigrant struggling to find a place for himself in America. (**I:** 10 and up)

*Avi. *Silent Movie*. Atheneum, 2003. An immigrant boy and his mother are unable to find his father on their arrival to America. Eventually the silent movies lead to their reunion. (**I:** 7–10)

*Bierman, Carol. *Journey to Ellis Island*. Illustrated by Laurie McGaw. Hyperion, 1998. Yehuda has journeyed across the ocean with his family but must now prove to the officials at Ellis Island that they should let a boy with a damaged hand enter America. (**I:** 8–11)

*Bunting, Eve. *A Day's Work*. Illustrated by Ronald Himler. Clarion, 1994. Francisco is supposed to help his grandfather, who speaks no English, get a job as a day laborer. In the long run, it is Francisco who learns important life lessons from his grandfather. (**I:** 8–11)

*————. *Going Home*. Illustrated by David Diaz. HarperCollins, 1996. Mexico is not home to Carlos and his sisters, but Carlos's parents are excited about their first trip home since they moved to the United States. Carlos and his sisters soon discover the magic of their roots and realize how much their parents left behind so that they might have a better future. (**I:** 8–12)

*————. *How Many Days to America?* Illustrated by Beth Peck. Clarion, 1988. A Latin American family escapes political persecution and survives the dangerous journey across the sea, arriving in America on Thanksgiving Day. (**I:** 7–10)

Buss, Fran Leeper. *Journey of the Sparrow*. Puffin, 2002. As undocumented immigrants from El Salvador, Maria and her siblings struggle to adjust to their new life in Chicago. (**I:** 12 and up)

Freedman, Russell. *Immigrant Kids*. Puffin, 1995. Through photographs and text, this book explores the experiences in America of immigrant children from Europe from the late nineteenth century through the early twentieth century. (**I:** 8–12)

Giff, Patricia Reilly. *Maggie's Door*. Wendy Lamb Books/Random House, 2003. In this sequel to *Nory Ryan's Song,* Nory and Sean leave Ireland and survive a harrowing trip across the Atlantic to finally be reunited with surviving members of their families. (**I:** 9–12)

Gunning, Monica. *America, My New Home*. Illustrated by Ken Condon. Boyds Mill Press, 2004. In this collection of poems, readers will see America through the eyes of a young Caribbean immigrant. (**I:** 7–11)

Hesse, Karen. *Letters from Rifka*. Holt, 1992/1995. Rifka writes about fleeing Russia and having to stay behind in Belgium when her family travels on to the United States. (**I:** 9–12)

*Hest, Amy. *When Jessie Came across the Sea*. Illustrated by P. J. Lynch. Candlewick, 1997. Jessie feels that her heart will break when she leaves her grandmother behind in eastern Europe. Her new life in America is complete only when her grandmother finally joins her. (**I:** 8–12)

*Hewett, Joan. *Hector Lives in the United States Now*. Photographs by Richard Hewett. Lippincott, 1990. Through text and photographs, this biography explores the life of a young Mexican immigrant and his family in the United States. (**I:** 8–11)

Hopkinson, Deborah. *Shutting Out the Sky*. Orchard, 2003. This is an historical account of life in the tenements of New York between 1880–1924. (**I:** 10 and up)

*Hoyt-Goldsmith, Diane. *Hoang Anh: A Vietnamese-American Boy*. Photographs by Lawrence Migdale. Holiday House, 1992. This biography of a young Vietnamese immigrant explores his family's life in the United States and ways in which they maintain their cultural ties to Vietnam. (**I:** 8–12)

Lasky, Kathryn. *A Journey to the New World: The Diary of Remember Patience Whipple*. Scholastic, 1996. Twelve-year-old Mem records in diary format her journey across the Atlantic in the Mayflower and her family's first year in Plimoth. (**I:** 9–12)

*Lawlor, Veronica. *I Was Dreaming to Come to America*. Puffin, 1995. This is a collection of excerpts from the oral histories of children and young adults that were collected as part of the Ellis Island Oral History Project. (**I:** 8–12)

*Leighton, Maxinne Rhea. *An Ellis Island Christmas*. Illustrated by Dennis Nolan. Viking, 1994. Krysia, her mother, and brothers arrive at Ellis Island on Christmas. Will Krysia's family be allowed to enter the United States? (**I:** 6–10)

Levine, Ellen. *If Your Name Was Changed at Ellis Island*. Illustrated by Wayne Parmenter. Scholastic, 1993. This informational book covers topics ranging from why immigrants came to America to how they came, what happened on their arrival at Ellis Island, and what happened beyond Ellis Island. (**I:** 8–11)

*Levinson, Riki. *Watch the Stars Come Out*. Illustrated by Diane Goode. Puffin, 1985. A brother and sister cross the Atlantic to America, where their parents await them in their new home. (**I:** 5–9)

Lord, Bette Bao. *In the Year of the Boar and Jackie Robinson*. Illustrated by Marc Simont. Harper & Row, 1984. An autobiographical novel about a Chinese girl who learns to love baseball as she adjusts to her new life in the United States. (**I:** 9–12)

*Medina, Jane. *My Name Is Jorge: On Both Sides of the River*. Illustrated by Fabricio Vanden Broeck. Boyds Mill, 1999. These bilingual poems are packed with poignant moments in the life of a Mexican immigrant child. (**I:** 9–12)

*Moss, Marissa. *Hannah's Journal: The Story of an Immigrant Girl*. Harcourt, 2000. Told in journal format, this is the story of a young European girl who journeys with her cousin to America. (**I:** 8–11)

Murphy, Jim. *Across America on an Emigrant Train*. Clarion, 2004. The author integrates descriptions written by Robert Louis Stevenson when he crossed America on an emigrant train with historical information about the building of the transcontinental railroad. (**I:** 9 and up)

Recorvits, Helen. *Goodbye, Walter Malinski*. Illustrated by Lloyd Bloom. Farrar, 1999. It is 1934, and Wanda's immigrant family struggles to make it in America in the midst of the Great Depression. (**I:** 9–12)

Sandler, Martin W. *Immigrants*. HarperCollins, 1995. Through text and photographs, this book explores immigration to the United States in the late nineteenth century and early twentieth century, with a particular focus on European immigrants. (**I:** 9–12)

*Say, Allen. *Grandfather's Journey*. Houghton Mifflin, 1993. A Japanese man emigrates to the United States and learns to love his new home, but he misses his homeland. When he visits Japan, the war keeps him from returning to the United States. (**I:** 6–9)

Son, John. *Finding My Hat*. Orchard, 2003. Jin-Han Park tells of his Korean family's search for a place in America and of his own years growing up. (**I:** 9–12)

Takaki, Ronald, Rebecca Stefoff, and Carol Takaki. *From Exiles to Immigrants: The Refugees from Southeast Asia*. Chelsea House, 1995. This book explores Asian immigration to the United States. (**I:** 9–12)

Tan, Shaun. *The Arrival*. Scholastic, 2006. This fantasy in graphic novel format explores two facets of the immigration experience—the journey to the new land and experiences in the new land. (**I:** 9 and up)

*Van Leeuwen, Jean. *Across the Wide Dark Sea*. Illustrated by Thomas B. Allen. Dial, 1995. A young boy and his family journey on the Mayflower to build a new life in America. (**I:** 6–10)

Wolf, Bernard. *Coming to America: A Muslim Family's Story*. Lee & Low, 2003. Readers meet the Madmoud family, a Muslim immigrant family from Egypt. Readers will be able to connect with this family on many levels. (**I:** 7–10)

*Wong, Janet S. *The Trip Back Home*. Illustrated by Bo Jia. Harcourt, 2000. A little girl and her mother travel from America to Korea to see the grandparents the girl has never met. (**I:** 6–9)

Yep, Laurence. *Dragon's Gate*. HarperCollins, 1993. In 1837, Chinese men came to the United States and found work digging and dynamiting tunnels through the Sierra Mountains in order for the railroad to cross the nation. (**I:** 11–YA)

*Yezerski, Thomas F. *Together in Pinecone Patch*. Farrar, 1998. In Pinecone Patch, Pennsylvania, Keara's family clings to their Irish roots while Stefan's family clings to their Polish roots. Only as adults do Keara and Stefan dare to reach across ethnic barriers to build a life together. (**I:** 8–11)

*Yin. *Brothers*. Illustrated by Chris Soentpiet. Philomel, 2006. Ming is lonely after his arrival from China until he is befriended by an Irish boy. (**I:** 9–12)

*———. *Coolies*. Illustrated by Chris Soentpiet. Philomel, 2001. Shek and Little Wong have come to America to help build the railroad across the West. Only the love and loyalty between the two brothers enables them to endure the bigotry and harsh treatment they find on the railroad. (**I:** 9–12)

Books by Kevin Henkes

Henkes, Kevin. *Chrysanthemum*. Greenwillow, 1991. Chrysanthemum always loved her name, until she started school and the other kids made fun of it. (**I:** 4–8)

———. *Julius, the Baby of the World*. Greenwillow, 1990. When Lilly's baby brother arrives, she launches an active rejection campaign. (**I:** 4–8)

———. *Lilly's Purple Plastic Purse*. Greenwillow, 1996. Lilly adores her teacher, until he says she can't share her new purse with the class. (**I:** 4–8)

———. *A Weekend with Wendell*. Greenwillow, 1986. The weekend Wendell spent with Sophie was unbearable, until Sophie found a way to get the upper hand. (**I:** 4–8)

———. *Wemberly Worried*. Greenwillow, 2000. Wemberly worries about everything, especially going to school. (**I:** 4–8)

Other Books

*Bash, Barbara. *Tree of Life: The World of the African Baobab*. Sierra Club, 1989. With lyrical language, the author documents the rich ecosystem of the African baobab tree. Other titles in this series include *Ancient Ones* (1994), *Desert Giant* (1990), and *In the Heart of the Village* (1996). (**I:** 6 and up)

*———. *Urban Roosts*. Sierra Club, 1990. The author explores how birds that live in the city have adapted their nest-building habits to their urban environment. (**I:** 6–10)

Cleary, Beverly. *A Girl from Yamhill*. HarperCollins, 1996. In this memoir about growing up in Portland, Oregon, during the Great Depression, Cleary details experiences that launched her into a writing career. The sequel is *My Own Two Feet*. (**I:** 9 and up)

Conrad, Pam. *Pedro's Journal: A Voyage with Christopher Columbus August 3, 1492–February 14, 1493*. Illustrated by Peter Koeppen. Scholastic, 1992. Pedro, the ship's boy on the Santa Maria, documents in his journal the trip across the Atlantic on Columbus's ship and the subsequent exploration of the newly discovered islands. (**I:** 9–12)

*Dewdney, Anna. *Llama Llama Mad at Mama*. Viking, 2007. When Mama pulls baby llama away from his toys and takes him shopping, the frustrated baby creates a "llama drama." (**I:** 4–7)

DiCamillo, Kate. *Because of Winn-Dixie*. Candlewick, 2000. Opal's new dog, Winn-Dixie, helps the 10-year-old come to terms with her mother's abandonment of her seven years before. (**I:** 9–12)

Forbes, Esther. *Johnny Tremain*. Houghton Mifflin, 1943. A silversmith's apprentice becomes part of the Sons of Liberty. (**I:** 10–YA)

Gardiner, John Reynolds. *Stone Fox*. HarperCollins, 1980. The story of a boy determined to win a dog sled race to save his grandfather's farm. (**I:** 9–12).

*George, Kristine O. *Hummingbird Nest*. Illustrated by Barry Moser. Harcourt, 2004. A journal of poems serves as a way to document the arrival of hummingbirds and all their subsequent activities during the spring. (**I:** 7–10)

*Hulpach, Vladimir. *Ahaiyute and Cloud Eater*. Illustrated by Marek Zawadzk. Harcourt, 1996. To become a warrior, Ahaiyute must accomplish a great deed, so he sets out to slay the giant monster and bring rain back to his people. (**I:** 8–11)

*Hutchins, Pat. *The Doorbell Rang*. Greenwillow, 1986. Two children see their portions of mom's freshly baked cookies dwindle as the doorbell rings and guests continue to arrive. (**I:** 5–8)

*Jackson, Ellen. *Cinder Edna*. HarperCollins, 1994. This is the tale of Cinderella's very practical neighbor, Cinder Edna, who approached the ball in a very different manner than did Cinderella. (**I:** 5–8)

*Johnston, Tony. *Bigfoot Cinderrrrella*. Illustrated by James Warhola. Scholastic, 1998. In this humorous parody of "Cinderella," Bigfoot Prince is looking for a wife. (**I:** 5–8)

*Long, Melinda. *How I Became a Pirate*. Illustrated by David Shannon. Harcourt, 2003. When Braid Beard extends an invitation, Jeremy quickly joins the pirate crew and is in for rollicking adventures. But when Jeremy finds out what pirates don't do, home soon begins to look much better. (**I:** 4–8)

Lunge-Larsen, Lise. *The Troll with No Heart in His Body and Other Tales of Trolls from Norway*. Illustrated by Betsy Bowen. Houghton Mifflin, 1999. This is a varied collection of troll tales from Norway. Accompanying illustrations are woodcuts. (**I:** 7–11)

*Martin, Bill. *A Beasty Story*. Illustrated by Steven Kellogg. Harcourt, 1999. Four brave little mice cautiously enter a haunted house in pursuit of what *may* be a scary beast. (**I:** 4–7)

*Martin, Claire. *Boots and the Glass Mountain*. Illustrated by Gennady Spirin. Dial, 1992. Boots, the youngest of three brothers, sets out to be the first to ride his horse to the top of a slippery glass mountain and win the hand of the princess. (**I:** 7–11)

*McNaughton, Colin. *Boo!* Harcourt, 1996. Preston Pig, a.k.a. as the Masked Avenger, successfully spreads terror through the neighborhood, until he encounters the greatest villain of all—his dad. (**I:** 4–7)

Mikaelsen, Ben. *Stranded*. Hyperion, 1995. Twelve-year-old Koby saves the lives of two injured pilot whales in the Florida Keys. In doing so, she confronts her feelings about her own injury that resulted in an artificial foot. (**I:** 10–YA).

Naylor, Phyllis Reynolds. *Shiloh*. Atheneum, 1991. A boy determines to save the dog he loves from further abuse by its owner. (**I:** 8–11)

Paterson, Katherine. *Preacher's Boy*. Clarion, 1999. Robbie's high-spirited ways often land him in trouble with his preacher father, but when one of his schemes endangers the life of someone else, Robbie finds the courage to face up to the consequences of his actions. (**I:** 9–12)

*Sendak, Maurice. *In the Night Kitchen*. Harper, 1970. Mickey awakens to the noise of the night kitchen and embarks on a fantastic trip in which he becomes the hero of the night kitchen. (**I:** P–6)

*———. *Outside Over There*. Harper, 1981. When her baby sister is stolen by the goblins, Ida goes "outside over there" to confront the goblins and rescue her sister. (**I:** P–8)

*———. *Where the Wild Things Are*. HarperCollins, 1963/1989. Sent to his room, Max travels to where the Wild Things are and becomes king of all Wild Things. (**I:** P–8)

*Stevens, Janet Crummel, Susan Stevens. *The Great Fuzz Frenzy*. Illustrated by Janet Stevens. Harcourt, 2005. A tennis ball that lands in the middle of a prairie-dog town causes quite a commotion. (**I:** 5–9)

*Van Allsburg, Chris. *The Polar Express*. Houghton Mifflin, 1985. A young boy boards a train that takes him to the North Pole, where Santa offers him any gift he would like. (**I:** P–8)

*Wells, Rosemary. *Timothy Goes to School*. Puffin, 2000. Timothy's first day at school is nearly ruined by perfect Claude. (**I:** P–8)

*Yorinks, Arthur. *Hey, Al!* Illustrated by Richard Egielski. Farrar, 1986. The paradise promised by a bird does not live up to the expectations of Al and his dog. (**I:** 6–12)

 ## Resources

Buss, K., and L. Karnowski. *Reading and Writing Literary Genres*. International Reading Association, 2000.

Cordier, Mary H., and Maria A. Perez-Stable. "Living in America, 1900–1950." *Book Links 9.3* (2000): 33–38.

Cullinan, Bernice E. *Fact and Fiction: Literature across the Curriculum*. International Reading Association, 1993.

Freeman, Evelyn B., and Diane Goetz Person. *Connecting Informational Children's Books with Content Area Learning*. Allyn & Bacon, 1998.

———. *Using Nonfiction Trade Books in the Elementary Classroom: From Ants to Zeppelins*. National Council of Teachers of English, 1992.

Lattimer, H. *Thinking through Genre: Units of Study in Reading and Writing Workshops 4–12*. Stenhouse, 2003.

McClure, A. A., and Kristo, J. V. *Adventuring with Books: A Booklist for Pre-K–Grade 6*. National Council of Teachers of English, 2002.

Moss, Joy F. *Focus on Literature: A Context for Literacy Learning*. Richard C. Owen, 1990.

———. *Using Literature in the Middle Grades: A Thematic Approach*. Christopher-Gordon, 1994.

Smith, J. Lea, and Holly Johnson. "Models for Implementing Literature in Content Studies." *The Reading Teacher 48* (1994): 198–208.

Tunnell, Michael O., and Richard Ammon. *The Story of Ourselves: Teaching History through Children's Literature*. Heinemann, 1993.

Zarnowski, Myra, and Arlene F. Gallagher. *Children's Literature and Social Studies: Selecting and Using Notable Books in the Classroom*. Kendall/Hunt, 1993.

 ## References

Alvermann, Donna E., and David W. Moore. "Secondary School Reading." Ed. Rebecca Barr, Michael Kamil, Peter Mosenthal, and P. David Pearson. *Handbook of Reading Research,* vol. II. Longman, 1991, pp. 951–983.

Baumann, James F., James V. Hoffman, Jennifer Moon, and Ann M. Duffy-Hester. "Where Are Teachers' Voices in the Phonics/Whole Language Debate? Results from a Survey of U.S. Elementary Classroom Teachers." *The Reading Teacher 51* (1998): 636–650.

Bloem, Patricia L., and Anthony L. Manna. "A Chorus of Questions: Readers Respond to Patricia Polacco." *The Reading Teacher 52* (1999): 802–808.

Bowker Staff. *Children's Books in Print: An Author, Title, and Illustrator Index to Books for Children and Young Adults*. Bowker Publishing, 2003.

Carle, Eric. *The Art of Eric Carle*. Philomel, 1996.

———. *You Can Make a Collage*. Klutz, 1998.

Chall, Jeanne S., and Sue S. Conard. *Should Textbooks Challenge Students?: The Case for Easier or Harder Textbooks*. Teachers College Press, 1991.

Eric Carle: Picture Writer. Directed by Rawn Fulton. Produced by Searchlight Films. Philomel, 1993.

Farest, Cindy, and Carolyn Miller. "Children's Insights into Literature: Using Dialogue Journals to Invite Literary Response." *Examining Central Issues in Literacy Research, Theory, and Practice*. Forty-Second Yearbook of the National Reading Conference. Ed. Donald J. Leu and Charles K. Kinzer. National Reading Conference, 1993, pp. 271–278.

Hoffman, James V. "Critical Reading/Thinking across the Curriculum: Using I-Charts to Support Learning." *Language Arts 69* (1992): 121–127.

Levstik, Linda. "A Gift of Time: Children's Historical Fiction." *Children's Literature in the Classroom: Weaving Charlotte's Web*. Ed. Janet Hickman and Bernice E. Cullinan. Christopher-Gordon, 1989, pp. 135–145.

Martinez, Miriam G., and Nancy L. Roser. (2003). "Children's Responses to Literature." In James Flood, Diane Lapp, Julie Jensen & James Squire. *Handbook of Research in Teaching the English Language Arts*. 2nd ed. (pp. 799–813). Mahwah, NJ: Lawrence Erlbaum.

Moss, Joy. *Focus Units in Literature: A Handbook for Elementary School Teachers*. National Council of Teachers of English, 1984.

———. "Using the Focus Unit to Enhance Children's Response to Literature." *Language Arts 55* (1978): 482–488.

———. *Using Literature in the Middle Grades: A Thematic Approach*. Christopher-Gordon, 1994.

Nakamura, Joyce, ed. *Something about the Author*. Gale Group, 1998.

Ogle, Donna. "K-W-L: A Teaching Model That Develops Active Reading of Expository Text." *The Reading Teacher 39* (1986): 564–570.

Peterson, Ralph, and Maryann Eeds. *Grand Conversations: Literature Groups in Action*. Scholastic-TAB, 1990.

Roser, Nancy, James V. Hoffman, and Cindy Farest. "Language, Literature, and At-Risk Children." *The Reading Teacher 43* (1990): 554–559.

Roser, Nancy L., James V. Hoffman, Cindy Farest, and Linda D. Labbo. "Language Charts: A Record of Story Time Talk." *Language Arts 69* (1992): 44–52.

Roser, Nancy, and Susan Keehn. "Fostering Thought, Talk, and Inquiry by Linking Literature with Social Studies." *The Reading Teacher,* 2002, pp. 416–427.

Short, Kathy G. "Intertextuality: Searching for Patterns That Connect." *Literacy Research, Theory, and Practice: Views from Many Perspectives: Forty-First Yearbook of the National Reading Conference.* Ed. Charles K. Kinzer and Donald J. Leu. National Reading Conference, 1992, pp. 187–197.

Silvey, Anita, ed. *Children's Books and Their Creators.* Houghton Mifflin, 1995.

Sipe, Lawrence R. "Individual Literary Response Styles of First and Second Graders." *Forty-Seventh Yearbook of the National Reading Conference.* Ed. Timothy Shanahan and Flora V. Rodriguez-Brown. National Reading Conference, 1998, pp. 76–89.

Tomlinson, Carl M., Michael O. Tunnell, and Donald J. Richgels. "The Content and Writing in Textbooks and Trade Books." *The Story of Ourselves: Teaching History through Children's Literature.* Ed. Michael O. Tunnell and Richard Ammon. Heinemann, 1993, pp. 51–62.

Tyson-Bernstein, Harriet, and Arthur Woodward. "Why Students Aren't Learning Very Much from Textbooks." *Educational Leadership 47* (1989): 14–17.

Walmsley, Sean A. "Reflections on the State of Elementary Literature Instruction." *Language Arts 69* (1992): 508–514.

Yolen, Jane. "How Basic Is SHAZAM?" *Language Arts 54* (1977): 645–651.

Zarnowski, Myra. "Using Literature Sets to Promote Conversation about Social Studies Topics." *Children's Literature and Social Studies.* Ed. Myra Zarnowski and Arlene F. Gallagher. Kendall/Hunt, 1993, pp. 35–41.

Children's Book Awards

There are many more awards and prizes for children's books than are described in this appendix. In some states, children vote for books that are nominated for awards. Information about awards from children can be obtained from various state libraries. Other awards are given in specific genres, such as the Nebula Award for science fiction and the Edgar Allan Poe Award for mystery. Many cultural and ethnic organizations give awards to authors of children's books that contribute to understanding and appreciation of the many cultures within the United States.

Jane Addams Book Award

The Jane Addams Children's Book Award has been presented annually since 1953 by the Women's International League for Peace and Freedom and the Jane Addams Peace Association to the children's book of the preceding year that most effectively promotes the cause of peace, social justice, and world community.

1953 *People Are Important* by Eva Knox Evans (Capital)

1954 *Stick-in-the-Mud* by Jean Ketchum (Cadmus Books, E. M. Hale)

1955 *Rainbow Round the World* by Elizabeth Yates (Bobbs-Merrill)

1956 *Story of the Negro* by Arna Bontemps (Knopf)

1957 *Blue Mystery* by Margot Benary-Isbert (Harcourt Brace)

1958 *The Perilous Road* by William O. Steele (Harcourt Brace)

1959 No award given

1960 *Champions of Peace* by Edith Patterson Meyer (Little, Brown)

1961 *What Then, Raman?* by Shirley L. Arora (Follett)

1962 *The Road to Agra* by Aimee Sommerfelt (Criterion)

1963 *The Monkey and the Wild, Wild Wind* by Ryerson Johnson (Abelard-Schuman)

1964 *Profiles in Courage: Young Readers Memorial Edition* by John F. Kennedy (Harper & Row)

1965 *Meeting with a Stranger* by Duane Bradley (Lippincott)

1966 *Berries Goodman* by Emily Cheney Neville (Harper & Row)

1967 *Queenie Peavy* by Robert Burch (Viking)

1968 *The Little Fishes* by Erik Christian Haugaard (Houghton Mifflin)

1969 *The Endless Steppe: Growing Up in Siberia* by Esther Hautzig (Crowell)

1970 *The Cay* by Theodore Taylor (Doubleday)

1971 *Jane Addams: Pioneer of Social Justice* by Cornelia Meigs (Little, Brown)

1972 *The Tamarack Tree* by Betty Underwood (Houghton Mifflin)

1973 *The Riddle of Racism* by S. Carl Hirsch (Viking)

Honor Book

The Upstairs Room by Johanna Reiss (Crowell)

1974 *Nilda* by Nicholasa Mohr (Harper & Row)

Honor Books

A Hero Ain't Nothin' but a Sandwich by Alice Childress (Coward, McCann & Geoghegan)

Men Against War by Barbara Habenstreit (Doubleday)

A Pocket Full of Seeds by Marilyn Sachs (Doubleday)

1975 *The Princess and the Admiral* by Charlotte Pomerantz (Addison-Wesley)

Honor Books

The Eye of Conscience by Milton Meltzer and Bernard Cole (Follett)

My Brother Sam Is Dead by James Lincoln Collier and Christopher Collier (Four Winds)

Viva la Raza! by Elizabeth Sutherland Martinez and Enrigueta Longeaux y Vasquez (Doubleday)

1976 *Paul Robeson* by Eloise Greenfield (Crowell)

Honor Books

Dragonwings by Laurence Yep (Harper & Row)

Song of the Trees by Mildred D. Taylor (Dial)

Z for Zachariah by Robert C. O'Brian (Atheneum)

1977 *Never to Forget: The Jews of the Holocaust* by Milton Meltzer (Harper & Row)

Honor Book

Roll of Thunder, Hear My Cry by Mildred D. Taylor (Dial)

1978 *Child of the Owl* by Laurence Yep (Harper & Row)

Honor Books

Alan and Naomi by Myron Levoy (Harper & Row)

Mischling, Second Degree: My Childhood in Nazi Germany by Ilse Koehn (Greenwillow)

Special Recognition

Amifika by Lucille Clifton (Dutton)

The Wheel of King Asoka by Ashok Davar (Follett)

1979 *Many Smokes, Many Moons: A Chronology of American History through Indian Art* by Jamake Highwater (Lippincott)

Honor Books

Escape to Freedom by Ossie Davis (Viking)

The Great Gilly Hopkins by Katherine Paterson (Crowell)

1980 *The Road from Home: The Story of an Armenian Girl* by David Kherdian (Greenwillow)

West Coast Honor Book: **Woman from Hiroshima** by Toshio Mori (Isthmus)

Special Recognition

Natural History by M. B. Goffstein (Farrar, Straus, & Giroux)

1981 *First Woman in Congress: Jeannette Rankin* by Florence Meiman White (Julian Messner)

Honor Books

Chase Me, Catch Nobody! by Erik Haugaard (Houghton Mifflin)

Doing Time: A Look at Crime and Prisons by Phyllis Clark and Robert Lehrman (Hastings House)

We Are Mesquakie, We Are One by Hadley Irwin (Feminist Press)

1982 *A Spirit to Ride the Whirlwind* by Athena V. Lord (Macmillan)

Honor Books

Let the Circle Be Unbroken by Mildred D. Taylor (Dial)

Lupita Mañana by Patricia Beatty (Morrow)

1983 *Hiroshima no pika* by Toshi Maruki, translated from Japanese (Lothrop, Lee & Shepard)

Honor Books

The Bomb by Sidney Lenz (Lodestar/Dutton)

If I Had a Paka: Poems in Eleven Languages by Charlotte Pomerantz (Greenwillow)

West Coast Honor Book: **People at the Edge of the World: The Ohlone of Central California** by Betty Morrow (Bacon)

Special Recognition

All the Colors of the Race by Arnold Adoff (Lothrop, Lee & Shepard)

Children as Teachers of Peace by Our Children (Celestial Press)

1984 *Rain of Fire* by Marion Dane Bauer (Clarion/Houghton Mifflin)

1985 *The Short Life of Sophie Scholl* by Hermann Vinke, with an interview with Ilse Aichinger, translated from German by Hedvig Pachter (Harper & Row)

Honor Books

The Island on Bird Street by Uri Orlev, translated from Hebrew by Hillel Halkin (Houghton Mifflin)

Music, Music for Everyone by Vera B. Williams (Greenwillow)

1986 *Ain't Gonna Study War No More: The Story of America's Peace Seekers* by Milton Meltzer (Harper & Row)

Honor Book

Journey to the Soviet Union by Samantha Smith (Little, Brown)

1987 *Nobody Wants a Nuclear War* by Judith Vigna (Albert Whitman)

Honor Books

All in a Day by Mitsumasa Anno (Philomel)

Children of the Maya: A Guatemalan Indian Odyssey by Brent Ashabranner, photographs by Paul Conklin (Dodd, Mead)

1988 *Waiting for the Rain: A Novel of South Africa* by Sheila Gordon (Orchard/Franklin Watts)

Honor Books

Nicolas, Where Have You Been? by Leo Lionni (Knopf)

Trouble at the Mines by Doreen Rappaport (Crowell)

1989 (tie)

Anthony Burns: The Defeat and Triumph of a Fugitive Slave by Virginia Hamilton (Knopf)

Looking Out by Victoria Boutis (Four Winds Press)

Honor Books

December Stillness by Mary Downing Hahn (Clarion)

The Most Beautiful Place in the World by Ann Cameron (Knopf)

Rescue: The Story of How Gentiles Saved Jews in the Holocaust by Milton Meltzer (Harper & Row)

1990 *A Long Hard Journey: The Story of the Pullman Porter* by Patricia and Fredrick McKissack (Walker)

Honor Books

Number the Stars by Lois Lowry (Houghton Mifflin)

Shades of Gray by Carolyn Reeder (Macmillan)

The Wednesday Surprise by Eve Bunting (Clarion)

1991 *The Big Book for Peace* edited by Ann Durell and Marilyn Sachs (Dutton)

Honor Books

The Journey: Japanese Americans, Racism and Renewal by Sheila Hamanaka (Richard Jackson/Orchard)

The Middle of Somewhere: A Story of South Africa by Sheila Gordon (Orchard)

1992 *Journey of the Sparrows* by Fran Leeper Buss with the assistance of Daisy Cubias (Lodestar)

Honor Book: **Now Is Your Time! The African-American Struggle for Freedom** by Walter Dean Myers (HarperCollins)

1993

Longer Book: **A Taste of Salt: A Story of Modern Haiti** by Frances Temple (Orchard)

Picture Book: **Aunt Harriet's Underground Railroad in the Sky** by Faith Ringgold (Crown)

Longer Book: **Letters from a Slave Girl: The Story of Harriet Jacobs** by Mary E. Lyons (Scribners)

Picture Book: **Mrs. Katz and Tush** by Patricia Polacco (Bantam)

1994

Longer Book: **Freedom's Children: Young Civil Rights Activists Tell Their Stories** by Ellen Levine (Putnam)

Picture Book: **This Land Is My Land** by George Littlechild (Children's Book Press)

Honor Books

Longer Book: **Eleanor Roosevelt: A Life of Discovery** by Russell Freedman (Clarion)

Picture Book: **Soul Looks Back in Wonder** by Tom Feelings (Dial)

1995

Longer Book: **Kids at Work: Lewis Hine and the Crusade against Child Labor** by Russell Freedman (Clarion)

Picture Book: **Sitti's Secrets** by Naomi Shihab Nye, illustrated by Nancy Carpenter (Four Winds Press)

Honor Books

Longer Books: **Cezanne Pinto** by Mary Stolz (Knopf)

I Hadn't Meant to Tell You This by Jacqueline Woodson (Delacorte)

Picture Book: **Bein' with You This Way** by W. Nikola-Lisa, illustrated by Michael Bryant (Lee & Low)

1996

Longer Book: **The Well** by Mildred D. Taylor (Dial)

Picture Book: No award given

Honor Books

Longer Books: **From the Notebooks of Melanin Sun** by Jacqueline Woodson (Blue Sky/Scholastic)

On the Wings of Peace: Writers and Illustrators Speak Out for Peace in Memory of Hiroshima and Nagasaki (Clarion)

The Watsons Go to Birmingham—1963 by Christopher Paul Curtis (Delacorte)

Special Commendation: **The Middle Passage** by Tom Feelings (Dial)

1997

Longer Book: **Growing Up in Coal Country** by Susan Campbell Bartoletti (Houghton Mifflin)

Picture Book: **Wilma Unlimited** by Kathleen Krull, illustrated by David Diaz (Harcourt Brace)

Honor Books

Longer Books: **Behind the Bedroom Wall** by Laura E. Williams (Milkweed)

Second Daughter: The Story of a Slave Girl by Mildred Pitts Walter (Scholastic)

Picture Book: **The Day Gogo Went to Vote** by Elinor Batezat Sisulu (Little, Brown)

1998

Longer Book: **Habibi** by Naomi Shihab Nye (Simon & Schuster)

Picture Book: **Seven Brave Women** by Betsy Hearne, illustrated by Bethanne Andersen (Greenwillow)

Honor Books

Longer Books: **The Circuit: Stories from the Life of a Migrant Child** by Francisco Jiménez (University of New Mexico Press)

Seedfolks by Paul Fleischman (HarperCollins)

Picture Books: **Celebrating Families** by Rosemarie Hausherr (Scholastic)

Passage to Freedom: The Sugihara Story by Ken Mochizuki, illustrated by Dom Lee (Lee & Low)

1999

Longer Book: **Bat 6** by Virginia Euwer Wolff (Scholastic)

Picture Book: **Painted Words/Spoken Memories: Marianthe's Story** by Aliki (Greenwillow)

Honor Books

Longer Books: **The Heart of a Chief** by Joseph Bruchac (Dial)

No More Strangers Now by Tim McKee, photographs by Anne Blackshaw (A Melanie Kroupa Book/DK Ink)

Restless Spirit: The Life and Work of Dorothea Lange by Elizabeth Partridge (Viking)

Picture Books: **Hey Little Ant** by Phillip and Hannah Hoose, illustrated by Debbie Tilley (Tricycle Press)

i see the rhythm by Toyomi Igus, illustrated by Michele Wood (Children's Book Press)

This Land Is Your Land words and music by Woodie Guthrie, illustrated by Kathy Jakobsen (Little, Brown)

2000

Longer Book: **Through My Eyes** by Ruby Bridges (Scholastic)

Picture Book: **Molly Bannaky** by Alice McGill, illustrated by Chris K. Soentpiet (Houghton Mifflin)

Honor Books

Longer Books: **The Birchbark House** by Louise Erdrich (Hyperion)

Kids on Strike! by Susan Campbell Bartoletti (Houghton Mifflin)

Picture Books

A Band of Angels: A Story Inspired by the Jubilee Singers by Deborah Hopkinson, illustrated by Racel Colón (Atheneum)

When Sophie Gets Angry—Really, Really Angry . . . by Molly Bang (The Blue Sky Press/Scholastic)

2001

Longer Book: **Esperanza Rising** by Pam Muñoz Ryan (Scholastic)

Honor Books

The Color of My Words by Lynn Joseph (Joanna Cotler/HarperCollins)

Darkness over Denmark: The Danish Resistance and the Rescue of the Jews by Ellen Levine (Holiday House)

Walking to the Bus-Rider Blues by Harriette Gillem Robinet (Jean Karl/ Atheneum/ Simon & Schuster)

Picture Book: The Composition by Antonio Skármeta, illustrated by Alfonso Ruano (Groundwood Books)

Honor Book: The Yellow Star: The Legend of King Christian X of Denmark by Carmen Agra Deedy, illustrated by Henri Sorensen (Peachtree)

2002

Book for Older Children: The Other Side of Truth by Beverley Naidoo (HarperCollins)

Honor Books: A Group of One by Rachna Gilmore (Henry Holt)

True Believer by Virginia Euwer Wolff (Atheneum/Simon & Schuster)

Picture Book: Martin's Big Words: The Life of Dr. Martin Luther King, Jr. by Doreen Rappaport, illustrated by Bryan Collier (Jump at the Sun/Hyperion)

Honor Book: Amber Was Brave, Essie Was Smart, written and illustrated by Vera B. Williams (Greenwillow/ HarperCollins)

2003

Book for Older Children: Parvana's Journey by Deborah Ellis (Groundwood Books/Douglas & McIntyre)

Honor Books: The Same Stuff as Stars by Katherine Paterson (Clarion)

When My Name Was Keoko by Linda Sue Park (Clarion)

Picture Book: Patrol: An American Soldier in Vietnam by Walter Dean Myers, illustrated by Ann Grifalconi (HarperCollins)

¡Si, Se Puede! Yes We Can! Janitor Strike in L.A. by Diana Cohn, illustrated by Francisco Delgado (Cinco Puntos Press)

The Village That Vanished by Ann Grifalconi, illustrated by Kadir Nelson (Dial)

2004

Book for Older Children: Out of Bounds: Seven Stories of Conflict and Hope by Beverly Naidoo (HarperCollins)

Honor Books

Getting Away with Murder: The True Story of the Emmett Till Case by Chris Crowe (Phyllis Fogelman Books)

Shutting Out the Sky: Life in the Tenements of New York, 1880–1924 by Deborah Hopkinson (Orchard Books)

Picture Book: Harvesting Hope: The Story of Cesar Chavez by Kathleen Krull, illustrated by Yuyi Morales (Harcourt)

Honor Books

Girl Wonder: A Baseball Story in Nine Innings by Deborah Hopkinson, illustrated by Terry Widener (Anne Schwartz Book/Atheneum).

Luba: Angel of Bergen-Belsen, told to Michell R. McCann by Luba Tryszynska-Frederick, illustrated by Ann Marshall (Tricycle Press)

2005

Books for Older Children: With Courage and Cloth: Winning the Fight for a Woman's Right to Vote, by Ann Bausum (National Geographic Society)

Honor Book: The Heaven Shop by Deborah Ellis (Fitzhenry & Whiteside)

Book for Younger Children: Sélavi, That is Life: A Haitian Story of Hope, written and illustrated by Youme Landowne (Cinco Puntos Press)

Honor Books: Hot Day on Abbott Avenue by Karen English, with collage art of Javaka Steptoe (Clarion Books)

Henry and the Kite Dragon, by Bruce Edward Hall, with paintings of William Low (Philomel Books/Penguin Young Readers Group)

Sequoyah: The Cherokee Man Who Gave His People Writing, by James Rumford and translated into Cherokee by Anna Sixkiller Huckaby (Houghton Mifflin Books for Children)

2006

Book for Older Children: Let Me Play: The Story of Title IX, the Law that Changed the Future of Girls in America, by Karen Blumenthal (Atheneum Books for Young Readers, an imprint of Simon & Schuster)

Honor Books: The Crazy Man, by Pamela Porter (Groundwood Books/House of Anansi Press)

Sweetgrass Basket, by Marlene Carvell (Dutton Children's Books, a Division of Penguin Young Readers Group)

Book for Younger Children: Delivering Justice: W. W. Law and the Fight for Civil Rights by Jim Haskins, illustrated by Benny Andrews (Candlewick Press)

Honor Book: Poems to Dream Together=Poemas Para Soñar Juntos by Francisco X. Alarcón, illustrated by Paula Barragán (Lee and Low Books, Inc.)

2007

Book for Older Children: Weedflower by Cynthia Kadohata, (Atheneum Books for Young Readers, an imprint of Simon & Schuster Children's Publishing)

Honor Book: Freedom Walkers by Russell Freedman (Holiday House)

Counting on Grace by Elizabeth Winthrop (Wendy Lamb Books)

Book for Younger Children: A Place Where Sunflowers Grow by Amy Lee-Tai, illustrated by Felicia Hoshino (Children's Book Press)

Honor Books: Night Boat to Freedom, written by Margot Theis Raven with pictures by E. B. Lewis (Melanie Kroupa Books)

Crossing Bok Chitto, told in written form by Choctaw storyteller, Tim Tingle, illustrated by Jeanne Rorex Bridges (Cinco Puntos Press)

2008

Book for Older Children: We Are One: The Story of Bayard Rustin by Larry Dane Brimner (Calkins Creek, an imprint of Boyds Mills Press, Inc.)

Honor Books: Rickshaw Girl by Mitali Perkins, with illustrations by Jamie Hogan (Charlesbridge)

Elijah of Buxton by Christopher Paul Curtis (Scholastic Press, an imprint of Scholastic, Inc.)

Birmingham, 1963 by Carole Boston Weatherford (Wordsong, an imprint of Boyds Mills Press)

Book for Younger Children: The Escape of Oney Judge: Martha Washington's Slave Finds Freedom, written and illustrated by Emily Arnold McCully (Farrar, Straus, & Giroux)

Honor Book: One Thousand Tracings: Healing the Wounds of World War II, written and illustrated by Lita Judge (Hyperion Books for Children)

2009

Book for Older Children: The Surrender Tree: Poems of Cuba's Struggle for Freedom by Margarita Engle (Henry Holt Books for Young Readers, an imprint of Macmillan Children's Publishing Group)

Honor Books: *The Shepherd's Granddaughter* by Anne Laurel Carter (Groundwood Books/House of Anansi Press)

Ain't Nothing But a Man: My Quest to Find the Real John Henry by Scott Reynolds Nelson with Marc Aronson (National Geographic)

Book for Younger Children: Planting the Trees of Kenya: The Story of Wangari Maathai, written and illustrated by Claire A. Nivola (Frances Foster Books/Farrar, Straus, & Giroux, an imprint of Macmillan Children's Publishing Group)

Honor Books: The Storyteller's Candle/La velita de los cuentos, by Story/Cuento Lucía González, Illustrations/Illustraciones Lulu Delacre (Children's Book Press)

Silent Music: A Story of Baghdad written and illustrated by James Rumford (Neal Porter Book/Roaring Brook Press, an imprint of Macmillan Children's Publishing Group)

Américas Award for Children's and Young Adult Literature

The Américas Award is given in recognition of U.S. works of fiction, poetry, folklore, or nonfiction (from picture books to works for young adults) published in the previous year in English or Spanish that authentically and engagingly portray Latin America, the Caribbean, or Latinos in the United States. By combining both languages and linking the Americas, the award reaches beyond geographic borders as well as multicultural boundaries, focusing instead on cultural heritages within the hemisphere. The award is sponsored by the national Consortium of Latin American Studies Programs (CLASP). The commended list is available at *http://www.uwm.edu/dept/cla/outreach_americas.*

1993 *Vejigante Masquerader* by Lulu Delacre (Scholastic)

1994 *The Mermaid's Twin Sister* by Lynn Joseph (Clarion)

1995 *Tonight, by Sea* by Frances Temple (Orchard)

1996 *In My Family/En mi familia* by Carmen Lomas Garza (Children's Book Press)

Parrot in the Oven by Victor Mart'nez (HarperCollins)

1997 *The Circuit* by Francisco Jiménez (University of New Mexico Press)

The Face at the Window by Regina Hanson, illustrated by Linda Saport (Clarion)

1998 *Barrio: José's Neighborhood* by George Ancona (Harcourt Brace)

Mama and Papa Have a Store by Amelia Lau Carling (Dial)

1999 *Crashboomlove* by Juan Felipe Herrera (University of New Mexico Press)

2000 *The Composition* by Antonio Skármeta, illustrated by Alfonso Ruano (Groundwood)

The Color of My Words by Lynn Joseph (HarperCollins)

2001 *A Movie in My Pillow* by Jorge Argueta, illustrated by Elizabeth Gómez (Children's Book Press)

Breaking Through by Francisco Jiménez (Houghton Mifflin Company)

2002 *Before We Were Free* by Julia Alvarez (Knopf)

2003 *Just A Minute: A Trickster Tale and Counting Book* by Yuyi Morales (Chronicle Books)

The Meaning of Consuelo by Judith Ortiz Cofer (Farrar, Straus, & Giroux)

2004 *My Name is Celia/Me llamo Celia* by Monica Brown; illustrated by Rafael López (Luna Rising)

Sammy & Juliana in Hollywood by Benjamin Alire Sáenz (Cinco Puntos)

2005 *Cinnamon Girl: letters found inside a cereal box* by Juan Felipe Herrera (HarperCollins, Joanna Cotler Books)

2006 *Josias, Hold the Book* by Jennifer Elvgren; illustrated by Nicole Tadgell (Boyds Mill)

The Poet Slave of Cuba by Margarita Engle; illustrated by Sean Qualls (Holt)

2007 *Red Glass* by Laura Resau (Delacorte)

YUM! ¡MMMM! ¡QUE RICO!: America's Sproutings by Pat Mora. Pictures by Rafael López (Lee & Low)

2008 *Just in Case: A Trickster Tale and Spanish Alphabet Book* by Yuyi Morales (Roaring Brook Press)

The Surrender Tree: Poems of Cuba's Struggle for Freedom by Margarita Engle (Holt)

Hans Christian Andersen Award

The International Board on Books for Young People has given the Hans Christian Andersen Award biennially since 1956 (since 1966 for the illustrator award). It is awarded to one author and one illustrator in recognition of his or her entire body of work.

1956 Eleanor Farjeon, Great Britain

1958 Astrid Lindgren, Sweden

1960 Erich Kästner, Federal Republic of Germany

1962 Meindert DeJong, United States

1964 René Guillot, France

1966 *Author:* Tove Jansson, Finland

Illustrator: Alois Carigiet, Switzerland

1968 *Authors:* James Krüss, Federal Republic of Germany

José Maria Sanchez-Silva, Spain

Illustrator: Juří Trnka, Czechoslovakia

1970 *Author:* Gianni Rodari, Italy

Illustrator: Maurice Sendak, United States

1972 *Author:* Scott O'Dell, United States

Illustrator: Ib Spang Olsen, Denmark

1974 *Author:* Maria Gripe, Sweden

Illustrator: Farshid Mesghali, Iran

1976 *Author:* Cecil Bødker, Denmark

Illustrator: Tatjana Mawrina, Soviet Union

1978 *Author:* Paula Fox, United States

Illustrator: Otto S. Svend, Denmark

1980 *Author:* Bohumil R'ha, Czechoslovakia

Illustrator: Suekichi Akaba, Japan

1982 *Author:* Lygia Bojunga Nunes, Brazil

Illustrator: Zbigniew Rychlicki, Poland

1984 *Author:* Christine Nöstlinger, Austria

Illustrator: Mitsumasa Anno, Japan

1986 *Author:* Patricia Wrightson, Australia

Illustrator: Robert Ingpen, Australia

1988 *Author:* Annie M. G. Schmidt, Netherlands

Illustrator: Duŭsan Kállay, Czechoslovakia

1990 *Author:* Tormod Haugen, Norway

Illustrator: Lisbeth Zwerger, Austria

1992 *Author:* Virginia Hamilton, United States

Illustrator: Kvuětá Pacovska, Czechoslovakia

1994 *Author:* Michio Mado, Japan

Illustrator: Jorg Müller, Switzerland

1996 *Author:* Uri Orlev, Israel

Illustrator: Klaus Ensikat, Germany

1998 *Author:* Katherine Paterson, United States

Illustrator: Tomi Ungerer, France

2000 *Author:* Ana Maria Machado, Brazil

Illustrator: Anthony Browne, United Kingdom

2002 *Author:* Aidan Chambers, UK

Illustrator: Quentin Blake, UK

2004 *Author:* Martin Waddell, Ireland

Illustrator: Max Velthuijs, the Netherlands

2006 *Author:* Margaret Mahy (New Zealand)

Illustrator: Wolf Erlbruch (Germany)

2008 *Author:* Jürg Schubiger (Switzerland)

Illustrator: Roberto Innocenti (Italy)

Mildred L. Batchelder Award

This award honors the former executive director of the Association for Library Service to Children (ALSC), a division of the American Library Association (ALA). The citation is given annually to a U.S. publisher for a children's book (defined as any trade book for children from pre-nursery school age through eighth grade) deemed the most outstanding book originally published in a foreign language in a foreign country, and then published in the United States. (From 1968 through 1977, the award was given for a book published in the previous two years; since 1979, the award has been given to a book published in the preceding year.)

1968 *The Little Man* by Erich Kästner, translated from German by James Krikup (Knopf)

1969 *Don't Take Teddy* by Babbis Friis-Baastad, translated from Norwegian by Lise Sømme McKinnon (Scribner's)

1970 *Wildcat under Glass* by Alki Zei, translated from Greek by Edward Fenton (Holt)

1971 *In the Land of Ur, the Discovery of Ancient Mesopotamia* by Hans Baumann, translated from German by Stella Humphries (Pantheon)

1972 *Friedrich* by Hans Peter Richter, translated from German by Edite Kroll (Holt)

1973 *Pulga* by S. R. Van Iterson, translated from Dutch by Alexander and Alison Gode (Morrow)

1974 *Petro's War* by Alki Zei, translated from Greek by Edward Fenton (Dutton)

1975 *An Old Tale Carved Out of Stone* by A. Linevski, translated from Russian by Maria Polushkin (Crown)

1976 *The Cat and Mouse Who Shared a House* by Ruth Hürlimann, translated from German by Anthea Bell (Walck)

1977 *The Leopard* by Cecil Bødker, translated from Danish by Gunnar Poulsen (Atheneum)

1978 No award given

1979 *Konrad* by Christine Nöstlinger (published 1977), translated from German by Anthea Bell (Watts)

Rabbit Island by Jörg Steiner (published 1978), translated from German by Ann Conrad Lammers (Harcourt)

1980 *The Sound of the Dragon's Feet* by Alki Zei, translated from Greek by Edward Fenton (Dutton)

1981 *The Winter When Time Was Frozen* by Els Pelgrom, translated from Dutch by Maryka and Raphael Rudnik (Morrow)

1982 *The Battle Horse* by Harry Kullman, translated from Swedish by George Blecher and Lone Thygesen Blecher (Bradbury)

1983 *Hiroshima no pika* by Toshi Maruki, translated from Japanese through Kurita-Bando Literary Agency (Lothrop)

1984 *Ronia, the Robber's Daughter* by Astrid Lindgren, translated from Swedish by Patricia Crampton (Viking)

1985 *The Island on Bird Street* by Uri Orlev, translated from Hebrew by Hillel Halkin (Houghton Mifflin)

1986 *Rose Blanche* by Christophe Gallaz and Robert Innocenti, translated from Italian by Martha Coventry and Richard Craglia (Creative Education)

1987 *No Hero for the Kaiser* by Rudolf Frank, translated from German by Patricia Crampton (Lothrop)

1988 *If You Didn't Have Me* by Ulf Nilsson, translated from Swedish by Lone Thygesen Blecher and George Blecher (McElderry)

1989 *Crutches* by Peter Härtling, translated from German by Elizabeth D. Crawford (Lothrop)

1990 *Buster's World* by Bjarne Reuter, translated from Danish by Anthea Bell (Dutton)

1991 *A Hand Full of Stars* by Rafik Schami, translated from German by Rika Lesser (Dutton)

1992 *The Man from the Other Side* by Uri Orlev, translated from Hebrew by Hillel Halkin (Houghton Mifflin)

1993 No award given

1994 *The Apprentice* by Pilar M. Llorente, translated from Spanish by Robin Longshaw (Farrar)

Honor Books

The Princess in the Kitchen Garden by Annemie and Margaret Heymans, translated from Dutch by Johanna H. Prins and Johanna W. Prins (Farrar)

Anne Frank Beyond the Diary: A Photographic Remembrance by Ruud van der Rol and Rian Verhoeven, translated from Dutch by Tony Langham and Plym Peters (Viking)

1995 *Boys from St. Petri* by Bjarne Reuter, translated from Danish by Anthea Bell (Dutton)

Honor Book: Sister Shako and Kolo the Goat: Memories of My Childhood in Turkey by Vedat Dalokay, translated from Turkish by Gÿner Ener (Lothrop)

1996 *The Lady with the Hat* by Uri Orlev, translated from Hebrew by Hillel Halkin (Houghton Mifflin)

Honor Books

Star of Fear, Star of Hope by Jo Hoestlandt, translated from French by Mark Polizzotti (Walker)

Damned Strong Love: The True Story of Willi G. and Stephan K. by Lutz van Dijk, translated from German by Elizabeth D. Crawford (Holt)

1997 *The Friends* by Kazumi Yumoto, translated from Japanese by Cathy Hirano (Farrar)

1998 *The Robber and Me* by Josef Holub, translated from German by Elizabeth D. Crawford (Holt)

Honor Books

Hostage to War: A True Story by Tatjana Wassiljewa, translated from German by Anna Trenter (Scholastic)

Nero Corleone: A Cat's Story by Elke Heidenrich, translated from German by Doris Orgel (Viking)

1999 *Thanks to My Mother* by Schoschana Rabinovici, translated from German by James Skofield (Dial)

Honor Book: Secret Letters from 0 to 10 by Susie Morgenstern, translated from French by Gill Rosner (Viking)

2000 *The Baboon King* by Anton Quintana, translated from Dutch by John Nieuwenhuizen (Walker and Company)

Honor Books

Collector of Moments by Quint Buchholz, translated from German by Peter F. Neumeyer (Farrar)

Asphalt Angels by Ineke Holtwijk, translated from Dutch by Wanda Boeke (Front Street)

Vendela in Venice by Christina Björk, illustrated by Inga-Karin Eriksson, translated from Swedish by Patricia Crampton (R&S Books)

2001 *Samir and Yonatan* by Daniella Carmi, translated from Hebrew by Yael Lotan (Arthur A. Levine/Scholastic)

Honor Book: Ultimate Game by Christian Lehmann, translated from French by William Rodarmor (David R. Godine)

2002 *How I Became an American* by Karin Gündisch, translated by James Skofield (Cricket Books/Carus Publishing)

Honor Book: A Book of Coupons by Susie Morgenstern with illustrations by Serge Bloch, translated from the French by Gill Rosner (Viking Press)

2003 *The Thief Lord* by Cornelia Funke, translated by Oliver Latsch (The Chicken House/Scholastic Publishing)

Honor Book: Henrietta and the Golden Eggs by Hanna Johansen, illustrated by Käthi Bhend, and translated by John Barrett (David R. Godine)

2004 *Run, Boy, Run* by Uri Orlev, translated Hillel Halkin (Walter Lorraine Books/Houghton Mifflin)

Honor Book: The Man Who Went to the Far Side of the Moon: The Story of Apollo 11 Astronaut Michael Collins by Bea Uusma Schyffert, translated by Emi Guner (Chronicle Books)

2005 *Shadows of Ghadames* by Joelle Stolz, translated by Catherine Temerson (Delacorte Press/Random House)

Honor Books

The Crow-Girl: The Children of Crow Cove by Bodil Bredsdorff, translated by Faith Ingwersen (Farrar, Straus, & Giroux)

Daniel Half Human and the Good Nazi by David Chotjewitz, translated by Doris Orgel (A Richard Jackson Book, Atheneum Books for Young Readers/ Simon & Schuster)

2006 *An Innocent Soldier* by Josef Holub, translated by Michael Hofmann (German) (Arthur A. Levine Books)

Honor Books

Nicholas by Rene Goscinny, translated by Anthea Bell (French) (Phaidon Press Limited)

When I Was a Soldier by Valerie Zenatti, translated by Adriana Hunter (French) (Bloomsbury Children's Books)

2007 *The Pull of the Ocean* by Jean-Claude Mourlevat, translated by Ymaudet (French) (Delacorte Press)

Honor Books

The Killer's Tears by Anne-Laure Bondoux, translated by Y. Maudet (French) (Delacorte Press)

The Last Dragon by Silvana De Mari, translated by Shaun Whiteside (Italian) (Hyperion/Miramax)

2008 *Brave Story* by Miyuki Miyabe, translated by Alexander O. Smith (Japanese) (VIZ Media)

Honor Books

The Cat: Or, How I Lost Eternity by Jutta Richter, translated by Anna brailovsky (German) (Milkweed Editions)

Nicholas and the Gang by Rene Goscinny, translated by Anthea Bell (French) (Phaidon Press)

2009 *Moribito: Guardian of the Spirit* by Nahoko Uehashi, translated by Cathy Hirano (Japanese) (Arthur A. Levine Books)

Honor Books

Garmann's Summer by Stian Hole, translated by Don Bartlett (Norwegian) (Eerdmans Books for Young Readers)

Tiger Moon by Antonia Michaelis, translated by Anthea Bell (German) (Amulet Books)

2010 *A Faraway Island* by Annika Thor, translated by Linda Schenck (Swedish) (Delacorte Press, an imprint of Random House Children's Books)

Honor Books

Big Wolf and Little Wolf by Nadine Brun-Cosme, illustrated by Olivier Tallec, translated by Claudia Bedrick (Enchanted Lion Books)

Eidi by Bodil Bredsdorff, translated by Kathryn Mahaffy (Farrar, Straus, & Giroux)

Moribito II: Guardian of the Darkness by Nahoko Uehashi, illustrated by Yuko Shimizu, translated by Cathy Hirano (Arthur A. Levine Books, an imprint of Scholastic)

The Pura Belpré Award

The Pura Belpré Award, established in 1996, is presented to a Latino/Latina writer and illustrator whose work best portrays, affirms, and celebrates the Latino cultural experience in an outstanding work of literature for children and youth. It is co-sponsored by the Association for Library Service to Children (ALSC), a division of the American Library Association (ALA), and the National Association to Promote Library Services to the Spanish Speaking (REFORMA), an ALA affiliate.

1996

Narrative: **An Island like You: Stories of the Barrio** by Judith Ortiz Cofer (Melanie Kroupa/Orchard)

Illustration: **Chato's Kitchen** by Gary Soto, illustrated by Susan Guevara (Putnam)

Honor Books

Narrative: **The Bossy Gallito/El gallo de bodas: A Traditional Cuban Folktale** by Lucía González, illustrated by Lulu Delacre (Scholastic)

Baseball in April, and Other Stories by Gary Soto (Harcourt)

Illustration: **Pablo Remembers: The Fiesta of the Day of the Dead**, illustrated by George Ancona (also published in a Spanish language edition: *Pablo recuenta: La fiesta de d'a de los muertos)* (Lothrop)

The Bossy Gallito/El gallo de bodas: A Traditional Cuban Folktale by Lucía González, illustrated by Lulu Delacre (Scholastic)

Family Pictures/Cuadros de familia by Carmen Lomas Garza, Spanish language text by Rosalma Zubizaretta, illustrated by Carmen Lomas Garza (Children's Book Press)

1998

Narrative: **Parrot in the Oven: Mi vida** by Victor Martinez (Joanna Cotler/HarperCollins)

Illustration: **Snapshots from the Wedding** by Gary Soto, illustrated by Stephanie Garcia (Putnam)

Honor Books

Narrative: **Laughing Tomatoes and Other Spring Poems/Jitomates risueños y otros poemas de primavera** by Francisco Alarcón, illustrated by Maya Christina Gonzalez (Children's Book Press)

Spirits of the High Mesa by Floyd Martinez (Arte Público)

Illustration: **In My Family/En mi familia** by Carmen Lomas Garza (Children's Book Press)

The Golden Flower: A Taino Myth from Puerto Rico by Nina Jaffe, illustrated by Enrique O. Sánchez (Simon & Schuster)

Gathering the Sun: An Alphabet in Spanish and English by Alma Flor Ada, English translation by Rosa Zubizarreta, illustrated by Simón Silva (Lothrop)

2000

Narrative: **Under the Royal Palms: A Childhood in Cuba** by Alma Flor Ada (Atheneum)

Illustration: **Magic Windows** by Carmen Lomas Garza (Children's Book Press)

Honor Books

Narrative: **From the Bellybutton of the Moon and Other Summer Poems/Del ombligo de la luna y otro poemas de verano** by Francisco X. Alarcón, illustrated by Maya Christina Gonzalez (Children's Book Press)

Laughing Out Loud, I Fly: Poems in English and Spanish by Juan Felipe Herrera, illustrated by Karen Barbour (HarperCollins)

Illustration: **Barrio: José's Neighborhood** by George Ancona (Harcourt Brace)

The Secret Stars by Joseph Slate, illustrated by Felipe Dávalos (Marshall Cavendish)

Mama and Papa Have a Store by Amelia Lau Carling (Dial)

2002

Narrative: **Esperanza Rising** by Pam Munoz Ryan (Scholastic Press)

Illustration: **Chato and the Party Animals** by Gary Soto, illustrated by Susan Guevara (G.P. Putnam's Sons)

Honor Books

Narrative: **Breaking Through** by Francisco Jiménez (Houghton Mifflin Company)

Iguanas in the Snow by Francisco X. Alarcón and illustrated by Maya Christina Gonzalez (Children's Book Press)

Illustration: **Juan Bobo Goes to Work** retold by Marisa Montes, illustrated by Joe Cepeda (HarperCollins)

2004

Narrative: **Before We Were Free** by Julia Alverez (Alfred A. Knopf)

Illustration: **Just a Minute: A Trickster Tale and Counting Book** by Yuyi Morales (Chronicle Books)

Honor Books

Narrative: **Cuba 15** by Nancy Osa (Delacorte Press)

My Diary from Here to There/Mi Diario de Aquí Hasta Allá by Amada Irma Pérez (Children's Book Press)

Illustration: **First Day in Grapes** by L. King Pérez, illustrated by Robert Casilla (Lee & Low Books)

The Pot That Juan Built by Nancy Andrews-Goebel, illustrated by David Diaz (Lee & Low Books)

Harvesting Hope: The Story of Cesar Chavez by Kathleen Krull, illustrated by Yuyi Morales (Harcourt)

2006

Narrative: **The Tequila Worm** by Viola Canales (New York: Wendy Lamb Books)

Illustration: **Doña Flor: a Tall Tale About a Giant Woman with a Great Big Heart** by Pat Mora, illustrated by Raul Colón (Knopf)

Honor Books

Narrative: **César: ¡Sí, Se Puede! Yes, We Can!** by Carmen T. Bernier-Grand (Marshall Cavendish)

Doña Flor: a Tall Tale About a Giant Woman with a Great Big Heart by Pat Mora (Knopf)

Becoming Naomi León, by Pam Muñoz Ryan *(Scholastic)*

Illustration: **Arrorró, Mi Niño: Latino Lullabies and Gentle Games** selected and illustrated by Lulu Delacre (Lee & Low Books)

César: ¡Sí, Se Puede! Yes, We Can! by Carmen T. Bernier-Grand, illustrated by David Diaz (Marshall Cavendish)

My Name Is Celia/ Me Llamo Celia: The Life of Celia Cruz by Monica Brown, illustrated by Rafael López (Rising Moon)

2008

Narrative: **The Poet Slave of Cuba: A Biography of Juan Francisco Manzano** by Margarita Engle, illustrated by Sean Qualls (Holt)

Illustration: **Los Gatos Black on Halloween** by Marisa Montes, illustrated by Yuyi Morales (Holt)

Honor Books

Narrative: Frida: **¡Viva la vida! Long Live Life!** by Carmen T. Bernier-Grand (Marshall Cavendish)

Martina the Beautiful Cockroach: A Cuban Folktale by Carmen Agra Deedy, illustrated by Michael Austin (Peachtree)

Los Gatos Black on Halloween by Marisa Montes, illustrated by Yuyi Morales (Holt)

Illustration: **My Name is Gabito: The Life of Gabriel García Márquez/Me llamo Gabito: la vida de Gabriel García Márquez** by Monica Brown, illustrated by Raul Colón (Luna Rising)

My Colors, My World/Mis colores, mi mundo by Maya Christina Gonzales (Children's Book Press)

2009

Narrative: **The Surrender Tree: Poems of Cuba's Struggle for Freedom** by Margarita Engle (Holt)

Illustration: **Just In Case** by Yuyi Morales (Roaring Brook Press)

Honor Books

Narrative: **Just In Case** by Yuyi Morales (Roaring Brook Press)

The Storyteller's Candle/La Velita de los Cuentos by Lucía González (Children's Book Press)

Reaching Out by Francisco Jiménez (Houghton Mifflin Company)

Illustration: **Papá and Me** by Arthur Dorros, illustrated by Rudy Gutierrez (Rayo/HarperCollinsPublishers)

The Storyteller's Candle/La Velita de los Cuentos by Lucía González, illustrated by Lulu Delacre (Children's Book Press)

What Can You Do With a Rebozo? by Carmen Tafolla, illustrated by Amy Córdova (Tricycle Press)

2010

Narrative: **Return to Sender** by Julia Alvarez (Alfred A. Knopf)

Illustration: **Fiesta!: Celebrate Children's Day/Book Day; Celebremos El día de los niños/El día de los libros** by Pat Mora, illustrated by Rafael López (Rayo, an imprint of HarperCollins Publishers)

Honor Books

Narrative: **Diego: Bigger Than Life** by Carmen T. Bernier-Grand, illustrated by David Diaz (Marshall Cavendish Children)

Federico García Lorca by Georgina Lázaro, illustrated by Enrique S. Moreiro (Lectorum Publications, Inc., a subsidiary of Scholastic Inc.)

Illustration: **Diego: Bigger Than Life** by Carmen T. Bernier-Grand, illustrated by David Diaz (Marshall Cavendish Children)

My Abuelita by Tony Johnston, illustrated by Yuyi Morales (Harcourt Children's Books, Houghton Mifflin Harcourt)

Gracias Thanks by Pat Mora, illustrated by John Parra (Lee & Low Books Inc.)

Boston Globe-Horn Book Award

This award, which was established in 1967, is cosponsored by the *Boston Globe* and the *Horn Book Magazine*. Originally, the award was given for text and illustration, but in 1976, the categories were changed. Currently, the award goes to one outstanding example of fiction, nonfiction, and illustration each year. The recipients of the awards need not be U.S. citizens; however, the books must have been published in the United States.

1967 *Text:* **The Little Fishes** by Erik Christian Haugaard (Houghton Mifflin)

Illustration: **London Bridge Is Falling Down** by Peter Spier (Doubleday)

1968 *Text:* **The Spring Rider** by John Lawson (Crowell)

Illustration: **Tikki Tikki Tembo** by Arlene Mosel, illustrated by Blair Lent (Holt)

1969 *Text:* **A Wizard of Earthsea** by Ursula K. Le Guin (Houghton Mifflin)

Illustration: **The Adventures of Paddy Pork** by John S. Goodall (Harcourt)

1970 *Text:* **The Intruder** by John Rowe Townsend (Lippincott)

Illustration: **Hi, Cat!** by Erza Jack Keats (Macmillan)

1971 *Text:* **A Room Made of Windows** by Eleanor Cameron (Atlantic/Little, Brown)

Illustration: **If I Built a Village** by Kazue Mizumura (Crowell)

1972 *Text:* **Tristan and Iseult** by Rosemary Sutcliff (Dutton)

Illustration: **Mr. Gumpy's Outing** by John Burningham (Holt)

1973 *Text:* **The Dark Is Rising** by Susan Cooper (Atheneum/McElderry)

Illustration: **King Stork** by Trina Schart Hyman (Little, Brown)

1974 *Text: **M. C. Higgins, the Great*** by Virginia Hamilton (Macmillan)

*Illustration: **Jambo Means Hello*** by Muriel Feelings, illustrated by Tom Feelings (Dial)

1975 *Text: **Transport 7-41-R*** by T. Degens (Viking)

*Illustration: **Anno's Alphabet*** by Mitsumasa Anno (Crowell)

1976 *Fiction: **Unleaving*** by Jill Paton Walsh (Farrar)

*Nonfiction: **Voyaging to Cathay: Americans in the China Trade*** by Alfred Tamarin and Shirley Glubok (Viking)

*Illustration: **Thirteen*** by Remy Charlip and Jerry Joyner (Parents)

1977 *Fiction: **Child of the Owl*** by Laurence Yep (Harper)

*Nonfiction: **Chance, Luck and Density*** by Peter Dickinson (Atlantic/Little, Brown)

*Illustration: **Granfa' Grig Had a Pig and Other Rhymes*** by Wallace Tripp (Little, Brown)

1978 *Fiction: **The Westing Game*** by Ellen Raskin (Dutton)

*Nonfiction: **Mischling, Second Degree: My Childhood in Nazi Germany*** by Ilse Koehn (Greenwillow)

*Illustration: **Anno's Journey*** by Mitsumasa Anno (Philomel)

1979 *Fiction: **Humbug Mountain*** by Sid Fleischman (Atlantic/Little, Brown)

*Nonfiction: **The Road from Home: The Story of an Armenian Girl*** by David Kherdian (Greenwillow)

*Illustration: **The Snowman*** by Raymond Briggs (Random House)

1980 *Fiction: **Conrad's War*** by Andrew Davies (Crown)

*Nonfiction: **Building: The Fight against Gravity*** by Mario Salvadori (Atheneum/McElderry)

*Illustration: **The Garden of Abdul Gasazi*** by Chris Van Allsburg (Houghton Mifflin)

1981 *Fiction: **The Leaving*** by Lynn Hall (Scribner's)

*Nonfiction: **The Weaver's Gift*** by Kathryn Lasky (Warne)

*Illustration: **Outside Over There*** by Maurice Sendak (Harper)

1982 *Fiction: **Playing Beatie Bow*** by Ruth Park (Atheneum)

*Nonfiction: **Upon the Head of the Goat: A Childhood in Hungary, 1939–1944*** by Aranka Siegal (Farrar)

*Illustration: **A Visit to William Blake's Inn: Poems for Innocent and Experienced Travelers*** by Nancy Willard, illustrated by Alice and Martin Provensen (Harcourt)

1983 *Fiction: **Sweet Whispers, Brother Rush*** by Virginia Hamilton (Philomel)

*Nonfiction: **Behind Barbed Wire: The Imprisonment of Japanese Americans During World War II*** by Daniel S. Davis (Dutton)

*Illustration: **A Chair for My Mother*** by Vera B. Williams (Greenwillow)

1984 *Fiction: **A Little Fear*** by Patricia Wrightson (McElderry/Atheneum)

*Nonfiction: **The Double Life of Pocahontas*** by Jean Fritz (Putnam)

*Illustration: **Jonah and the Great Fish*** retold and illustrated by Warwick Hutton (McElderry/Atheneum)

1985 *Fiction: **The Moves Make the Man*** by Bruce Brooks (Harper)

*Nonfiction: **Commodore Perry in the Land of the Shogun*** by Rhoda Blumberg (Lothrop)

*Illustration: **Mama Don't Allow*** by Thatcher Hurd (Harper)

1986 *Fiction: **In Summer Light*** by Zibby O'Neal (Viking)

*Nonfiction: **Auks, Rocks, and the Odd Dinosaur: Inside Stories from the Smithsonian Museum of Natural History*** by Peggy Thomson (Crowell)

*Illustration: **Paper Crane*** by Molly Bang (Greenwillow)

1987 *Fiction: **Rabble Starkey*** by Lois Lowry (Houghton Mifflin)

*Nonfiction: **Pilgrims of Plimoth*** by Marcia Sewall (Atheneum)

*Illustration: **Mufaro's Beautiful Daughters: An African Tale*** by John Steptoe (Lothrop)

1988 *Fiction: **The Friendship*** by Mildred D. Taylor (Dial)

*Nonfiction: **Anthony Burns: The Defeat and Triumph of a Fugitive Slave*** by Virginia Hamilton (Knopf)

*Illustration: **The Boy of the Three-Year Nap*** by Dianne Snyder, illustrated by Allen Say (Houghton Mifflin)

1989 *Fiction: **Village by the Sea*** by Paula Fox (Orchard)

*Nonfiction: **The Way Things Work*** by David Macaulay (Houghton Mifflin)

*Illustration: **Shy Charles*** by Rosemary Wells (Dial)

1990 *Fiction: **Maniac Magee*** by Jerry Spinelli (Little, Brown)

*Nonfiction: **Great Little Madison*** by Jean Fritz (Putnam)

*Picture Book: **Lon Po Po: A Red Riding Hood Story from China*** by Ed Young (Philomel)

Honor Books

*Fiction: **Saturnalia*** by Paul Fleischman (Harper)

Stonewords by Pam Conrad (Harper)

*Nonfiction: **Insect Metamorphosis: From Egg to Adult*** by Ron and Nancy Goor, illustrated with photographs by Ron Goor (Atheneum)

*Picture Book: **Chicka Chicka Boom Boom*** by Bill Martin, Jr. and John Archambault, illustrated by Lois Ehlert (Simon)

1991 *Fiction: **True Confessions of Charlotte Doyle*** by Avi (Orchard)

*Nonfiction: **Appalachia: The Voices of Sleeping Birds*** by Cynthia Rylant (Harcourt)

*Picture Book: **Tale of the Mandarin Ducks*** by Katherine Paterson, illustrated by Leo and Diane Dillon (Lodestar)

Honor Books

*Fiction: **Paradise Cafe and Other Stories*** by Martha Brooks (Joy Street)

Judy Scuppernong by Brenda Seabrooke (Cobblehill)

*Nonfiction: **The Wright Brothers: How They Invented the Airplane*** by Russell Freedman (Holiday House)

Good Queen Bess: The Story of Elizabeth I of England by Diane Stanley and Peter Vennema, illustrated by Diane Stanley (Four Winds)

*Picture Books: **Aardvarks, Disembark!*** by Ann Jonas
(Greenwillow)

Sophie and Lou by Petra Mathers (Harper)

1992 *Fiction: **Missing May*** by Cynthia Rylant (Orchard)

*Nonfiction: **Talking with Artists*** by Pat Cummings (Bradbury)

*Picture Book: **Seven Blind Mice*** by Ed Young (Philomel)

Honor Books

*Fiction: **Nothing but the Truth*** by Avi (Jackson/Orchard)

Somewhere in the Darkness by Walter Dean Myers (Scholastic)

*Nonfiction: **Red Leaf, Yellow Leaf*** by Lois Ehlert (Harcourt)

The Handmade Alphabet by Laura Rankin (Dial)

*Picture Book: **In the Tall, Tall Grass*** by Denise Fleming (Holt)

1993 *Fiction: **Ajeemah and His Son*** by James Berry (Harper)

*Nonfiction: **Sojourner Truth: Ain't I a Woman?*** by Patricia and
Fredrick McKissack (Scholastic)

*Picture Book: **Fortune Tellers*** by Lloyd Alexander, illustrated by
Trina Schart Hyman (Dutton)

Honor Books

*Fiction: **The Giver*** by Lois Lowry (Houghton)

*Nonfiction: **Lives of the Musicians: Good Times, Bad Times
(And What the Neighbors Thought)*** by Kathleen Krull,
illustrated by Kathryn Hewitt (Harcourt)

*Picture Books: **Komodo!*** by Peter Sis (Greenwillow)

Raven: A Trickster Tale from the Pacific Northwest by Gerald
McDermott (Harcourt)

1994 *Fiction: **Scooter*** by Vera Williams (Greenwillow)

*Nonfiction: **Eleanor Roosevelt: A Life of Discovery*** by Russell
Freedman (Houghton Mifflin)

*Picture Book: **Grandfather's Journey*** by Allen Say (Houghton
Mifflin)

Honor Books

*Fiction: **Flour Babies*** by Anne Fine (Little)

Western Wind by Paula Fox (Orchard)

*Nonfiction: **Unconditional Surrender: U.S. Grant and the Civil
War*** by Albert Marrin (Atheneum)

A Tree Place and Other Poems by Constance Levy, illustrated by
Robert Sabuda (McElderry)

*Picture Books: **Owen*** by Kevin Henkes (Greenwillow)

A Small Tall Tale from the Far Far North by Peter Sis (Knopf)

1995 *Fiction: **Some of the Kinder Planets*** by Tim Wynne-Jones
(Orchard)

*Nonfiction: **Abigail Adams: Witness to a Revolution*** by Natalie
S. Bober (Atheneum)

*Picture Book: **John Henry*** by Julius Lester, illustrated by Jerry
Pinkney (Dial)

Honor Books

*Fiction: **Jericho*** by Janet Hickman (Greenwillow)

Earthshine by Theresa Nelson (Jackson/Orchard)

*Nonfiction: **It's Perfectly Normal: Changing Bodies, Growing
Up, Sex, and Sexual Health*** by Robie H. Harris,
illustrated by Michael Emberley (Candlewick)

The Great Fire by Jim Murphy (Scholastic)

*Picture Book: **Swamp Angel*** by Anne Isaacs, illustrated by Paul
O. Zelinsky (Dutton)

1996 *Fiction: **Poppy*** by Avi, illustrated by Brian Floca (Jackson/
Orchard)

*Nonfiction: **Orphan Train Rider: One Boy's True Story*** by
Andrea Warren (Houghton Mifflin)

*Picture Book: **In the Rain with Baby Duck*** by Amy Hest,
illustrated by Jill Barton (Candlewick)

Honor Books

*Fiction: **The Moorchild*** by Eloise McGraw (McElderry)

Belle Prater's Boy by Ruth White (Farrar)

*Nonfiction: **The Boy Who Lived with the Bears: And Other
Iroquois Stories*** by Joseph Bruchac, illustrated by Murv
Jacob (Harper)

Haystack by Bonnie and Arthur Geisert, illustrated by Arthur
Geisert (Houghton)

*Picture Books: **Fanny's Dream*** by Caralyn Buehner, illustrated
by Mark Buehner (Dial)

Home Lovely by Lynne Rae Perkins (Greenwillow)

1997 *Fiction and Poetry: **The Friends*** by Kazumi Yumoto (Farrar)

*Nonfiction: **A Drop of Water: A Book of Science and Wonder*** by
Walter Wick (Scholastic)

*Picture Book: **The Adventures of Sparrowboy*** by Brian Pinkney
(Simon & Schuster)

Honor Books

*Fiction and Poetry: **Lily's Crossing*** by Patricia Reilly Giff
(Delacorte)

Harlem by Walter Dean Myers, illustrated by Christopher Myers
(Scholastic Press)

*Nonfiction: **Lou Gehrig: The Luckiest Man*** by David A. Adler,
illustrated by Terry Widener (Gulliver/Harcourt)

Leonardo da Vinci written and illustrated by Diane Stanley
(Morrow)

*Picture Books: **Home on the Bayou: A Cowboy's Story*** written
and illustrated by G. Brian Karas (Simon)

Potato: A Tale from the Great Depression by Kate Lied,
illustrated by Lisa Campbell Ernst (National Geographic)

1998 *Fiction and Poetry: **The Circuit: Stories from the Life of
a Migrant Child*** by Francisco Jiménez (University of New
Mexico Press)

*Nonfiction: **Leon's Story*** by Leon Walter Tillage, illustrated by
Susan L. Roth (Farrar)

*Picture Book: **And If the Moon Could Talk*** by Kate Banks,
illustrated by Georg Hallensleben (Foster/Farrar)

Honor Books

*Fiction and Poetry: **While No One Was Watching*** by Jane Leslie
Conly (Holt)

My Louisiana Sky by Kimberly Willis Holt (Holt)

Nonfiction: **Martha Graham: A Dancer's Life** by Russell Freedman (Clarion)

Chuck Close Up Close by Jan Greenberg and Sandra Jordan (DK Ink)

Picture Books: **Seven Brave Women** by Betsy Hearne, illustrated by Bethanne Andersen (Greenwillow)

Popcorn: Poems written and illustrated by James Stevenson (Greenwillow)

1999   *Fiction:* **Holes** by Louis Sachar (Foster/Farrar)

Nonfiction: **The Top of the World: Climbing Mount Everest** written and illustrated by Steve Jenkins (Houghton Mifflin)

Picture Book: **Red-Eyed Tree Frog** by Joy Cowley, illustrated with photographs by Nic Bishop (Scholastic Press)

Honor Books

Fiction: **The Trolls** by Polly Horvath (Farrar, Straus, & Giroux)

Monster by Walter Dean Myers, illustrated by Christopher Myers (HarperCollins)

Nonfiction: **Shipwreck at the Bottom of the World: The Extraordinary True Story of Shackleton and the Endurance** by Jennifer Armstrong (Crown)

William Shakespeare & the Globe written and illustrated by Aliki (HarperCollins)

Picture Books: **Dance** by Bill T. Jones and Susan Kuklin, illustrated with photographs by Susan Kuklin (Hyperion)

The Owl and the Pussycat by Edward Lear, illustrated by James Marshall (di Capua/HarperCollins)

Special Citation: **Tibet: Through the Red Box** written and illustrated by Peter Sis (Foster/Farrar)

2000   *Fiction:* **The Folk Keeper** by Franny Billingsley (Atheneum)

Nonfiction: **Sir Walter Ralegh and the Quest for El Dorado** by Marc Aronson (Clarion)

Picture Book: **Henry Hikes to Fitchburg** written and illustrated by D. B. Johnson (Houghton)

Honor Books

Fiction: **King of Shadows** by Susan Cooper (McElderry)

145th Street: Short Stories by Walter Dean Myers (Delacorte)

Nonfiction: **Osceola: Memories of a Sharecropper's Daughter** collected and edited by Alan Govenar, illustrated by Shane W. Evans (Jump at the Sun/Hyperion)

Sitting Bull and His World by Albert Marrin (Farrar, Straus, & Giroux)

Picture Books: **Buttons** written and illustrated by Brock Cole (Farrar, Straus, & Giroux)

a day, a dog illustrated by Gabrielle Vincent (Front Street)

2001   *Fiction and Poetry:* **Carver: A Life in Poems** by Marilyn Nelson (Front Street)

Nonfiction: **The Longitude Prize** by Joan Dash, illustrated by Dusan Petricic (Foster/Farrar)

Picture Book: **Cold Feet** by Cynthia DeFelice, illustrated by Robert Andrew Parker (DK Ink)

Honor Books

Fiction: **Everything on a Waffle** by Polly Horvath (Farrar)

Troy by Adèle Geras (Harcourt)

Nonfiction: **Rocks in His Head** by Carol Otis Hurst, illustrated by James Stevenson (Greenwillow)

Uncommon Traveler: Mary Kingsley in Africa written and illustrated by Tomek Bogacki (Foster/Farrar)

The Stray Dog retold and illustrated by Marc Simont (HarperCollins)

2002   *Fiction:* **The Lord of the Deep** by Graham Salisbury (Delacorte)

Nonfiction: **This Land Was Made for You and Me: The Life Songs of Woody Guthrie** by Elizabeth Partridge (Viking)

Picture Book: **"Let's Get a Pup!" Said Kate** written and illustrated by Bob Graham (Candlewick)

Honor Books

Fiction: **Amber Was Brave, Essie Was Smart** written and illustrated by Vera B. Williams (Greenwillow)

Saffy's Angel by Hilary McKay (McElderry)

Nonfiction: **Handel, Who Knew What He Liked** by M. T. Anderson (Candlewick)

Woody Guthrie: Poet of the People written and illustrated by Bonnie Christensen (Knopf)

Picture Book: **I Stink!** by Kate McMullen, illustrated by Jim McMullen (Cotler/HarperCollins)

Little Rat Sets Sail by Monica Bang-Campbell, illustrated by Molly Bang (Harcourt)

2003   *Fiction:* **The Jamie and Angus Stories** by Ann Fine (Candlewick)

Nonfiction: **Fireboat: the Heroic Adventures of John J. Harvey** by Maira Kalman (Putnam)

Picture Book: **Big Momma Makes the World** by Phyllis Root, illustrated by Helen Oxenbury (Candlewick)

Honor Books

Fiction: **Feed** by M. T. Andersen (Candlewick)

Locomotion by Jacqueline Woodson (Putnam)

Nonfiction: **To Fly: The Story of the Wright Brothers** by Wendy C. Old (Clarion)

Revenge of the Whale: The True Story of the Whaleship Essex by Nathaniel Philbrick (Putnam)

Picture Book: **Dahlia** by Barbara McClintock (Foster/Farrar)

blue's journey by Walter Dean Myers, illustrated by Christopher A. Myers (Holiday)

2004   *Fiction:* **The Fire Eaters** by David Almond (Delacorte)

Nonfiction: **An American Plague: the True and Terrifying Story of the Yellow Fever Epidemic of 1793** by Jim Murphy (Clarion)

Picture Book: **The Man Who Walked Between the Towers** by Mordicai Gerstien (Roaring Book)

Honor Books

Fiction: **God Went to Beauty School** by Cynthia Rylant (HarperTempest)

The Amulet of Samarkand: The Bartimaeus Trilogy, Book One by Jonathan Stroud (Hyperion)

Nonfiction: Surprising Sharks by Nicola Davies (Candlewick)

The Man Who Went to the Far Side of the Moon: The Story of Apollo 11 *Astronaut Michael Collins* by Bea Uusma Schyffert (Chronicle)

Picture Book: The Shape Game by Anthony Browne (Farrar)

Snow Music by Lynne Rae Perkins (Greenwillow)

2005

Fiction and Poetry: The Schwa Was Here by Neal Schusterman (Dutton)

Honor Books

Fiction and Poetry: Kalpana's Dream by Judith Clarke (Front Street)

A Wreath for Emmett Till by Marilyn Nelson (Houghton)

Nonfiction: The Race to Save the Lord God Bird by Phillip Hoose (Kroupa/Farrar)

Honor Books

Good Brother, Bad Brother by James Cross Giblin (Clarion)

Michael Rosen's Sad Book by Michael Rosen, illustrated by Quentin Blake (Candlewick)

Picture Books: Traction Man Is Here! by Mini Grey (Knopf)

Honor Books

That New Animal by Emily Jenkins, illustrated by Pierre Pratt (Foster/Farrar)

The Hello, Goodbye Window by Norton Juster, illustrated by Chris Raschka (di Capua/Hyperion)

2006

Picture Book: Leaf Man by Lois Ehlert (Harcourt)

Honor Books

Mama: A True Story in Which a Baby Hippo Loses His Mama during a Tsunami, but Finds a New Home, and a New Mama by Jeanette Winter (Harcourt)

Sky Boys: How They Built the Empire State Building by Deborah Hopkinson, illustrated by James E. Ransome (Schwartz & Wade/Random)

Fiction and Poetry: The Miraculous Journey of Edward Tulane by Kate DiCamillo, illustrated by Bagram Ibatoulline (Candlewick)

Honor Books

Yellow Elephant: A Bright Bestiary by Julie Larios, illustrated by Julie Paschkis (Harcourt)

Yellow Star by Jennifer Roy (Marshall Cavendish)

Nonfiction: If You Decide to Go to the Moon by Faith McNulty, illustrated by Steven Kellogg (Scholastic)

Honor Books

A Mother's Journey by Sandra Markle, illustrated by Alan Marks (Charlesbridge)

Wildfire by Taylor Morrison (Lorraine/Houghton)

2007

Picture Book: Dog and Bear: Two Friends, Three Stories written and illustrated by Laura Vaccaro Seeger (Porter/Roaring Brook)

Honor Books

365 Penguins by Jean-Luc Fromental, illustrated by Joelle Jolivet (Abrams)

Wolves written and illustrated by Emily Gravett (Simon)

Fiction and Poetry: The Astonishing Life of Octavian Nothing, Traitor to the Nation, Volume I: The Pox Party by M. T. Anderson (Candlewick)

Honor Books

Clementine by Sara Pennypacker, illustrated by Marla Frazee (Hyperion)

Rex Zero and the End of the World by Tim Wynne-Jones (Kroupa/Farrar)

Nonfiction: The Strongest Man in the World: Louis Cyr written and illustrated by Nicolas Debon (Groundwood)

Honor Books

Tracking Trash: Flotsam, Jetsam, and the Science of Ocean Motion by Loree Griffin Burns (Houghton)

Escape! by Sid Fleischman (Greenwillow)

2008

Picture Book: At Night by Jonathan Bean (Farrar)

Honor Books

Fred Stays with Me! by Nancy Coffelt, illustrated by Tricia Tusa (Little)

A Couple of Boys Have the Best Week Ever by Marla Frazee (Harcourt)

Fiction and Poetry: The Absolutely True Diary of a Part-Time Indian by Sherman Alexie, illustrated by Ellen Forney (Little)

Honor Books

Shooting the Moon by Frances O'Roark Dowell (Atheneum)

Savvy by Ingrid Law (Walden/Dial)

Nonfiction: The Wall by Peter Sis (Foster/Farrar)

Honor Books

Frogs by Nic Bishop (Scholastic)

What to Do About Alice? by Barbara Kerley, illustrated by Edwin Fotheringham (Scholastic)

Special Citation: The Arrival by Shaun Tan (Levine/Scholastic)

2009

Picture Book: Bubble Trouble by Margaret Mahy, illustrated by Polly Dunbar (Clarion)

Honor Books

Old Bear by Kevin Henkes (Greenwillow/HarperCollins)

Higher! Higher! by Leslie Patricelli (Candlewick)

Fiction: Nation by Terry Pratchett (HarperCollins)

Honor Books

The Astonishing Life of Octavian Nothing, Traitor to the Nation, Volume II: The Kingdom on the Waves by M. T. Anderson (Candlewick)

The Graveyard Book by Neil Gaiman (HarperCollins)

Nonfiction: The Lincolns: A Scrapbook Look at Abraham and Mary by Candace Fleming (Schwartz & Wade/Random House)

Honor Books

The Way We Work by David Macaulay with Richard Walker, illustrated by David Macaulay (Lorraine/Houghton)

Almost Astronauts: 13 Women Who Dared to Dream by Tanya Lee Stone (Candlewick)

Randolph Caldecott Medal

The Randolph Caldecott Medal, named in honor of the nineteenth-century illustrator of children's books, is awarded annually under the supervision of the Association for Library Service to Children of the American Library Association. It is awarded to the illustrator of the most distinguished children's book published in the United States in the previous year. Usually, one or more Honor Books are also chosen. The award is limited to residents or citizens of the United States.

1938   *Animals of the Bible* by Helen Dean Fish, illustrated by Dorothy P. Lathrop (Lippincott)

Honor Books

Four and Twenty Blackbirds by Helen Dean Fish, illustrated by Robert Lawson (Stokes)

Seven Simeons by Boris Artzybasheff (Viking)

1939   *Mei Li* by Thomas Handforth (Doubleday)

Honor Books

Andy and the Lion by James Daugherty (Viking)

Barkis by Clare Newberry (Harper)

The Forest Pool by Laura Adams Armer (Longman)

Snow White and the Seven Dwarfs by Wanda Gág (Coward)

Wee Gillis by Munro Leaf, illustrated by Robert Lawson (Viking)

1940   *Abraham Lincoln* by Ingri and Edgar Parin D'Aulaire (Doubleday)

Honor Books

The Ageless Story by Lauren Ford (Dodd)

Cock-a-Doodle Doo by Berta and Elmer Hader (Macmillan)

Madeline by Ludwig Bemelmans (Viking)

1941   *They Were Strong and Good* by Robert Lawson (Viking)

Honor Book: April's Kittens by Clare Newberry (Harper)

1942   *Make Way for Ducklings* by Robert McCloskey (Viking)

Honor Books

An American ABC by Maud and Miska Petersham (Macmillan)

In My Mother's House by Ann Nolan Clark, illustrated by Velino Herrera (Viking)

Nothing at All by Wanda Gág (Coward)

Paddle-to-the-Sea by Holling C. Holling (Houghton Mifflin)

1943   *The Little House* by Virginia Lee Burton (Houghton Mifflin)

Honor Books

Dash and Dart by Mary and Conrad Buff (Viking)

Marshmallow by Clare Newberry (Harper)

1944   *Many Moons* by James Thurber, illustrated by Louis Slobodkin (Harcourt)

Honor Books

A Child's Good Night Book by Margaret Wise Brown, illustrated by Jean Charlot (Scott)

Good Luck Horse by Chin-Yi Chan, illustrated by Plao Chan (Whittlesey)

The Mighty Hunter by Berta and Elmer Hader (Macmillan)

Pierre Pigeon by Lee Kingman, illustrated by Arnold E. Bare (Houghton Mifflin)

Small Rain: Verses from the Bible selected by Jessie Orton Jones, illustrated by Elizabeth Orton Jones (Viking)

1945   *Prayer for a Child* by Rachel Field, illustrated by Elizabeth Orton Jones (Macmillan)

Honor Books

The Christmas Anna Angel by Ruth Sawyer, illustrated by Kate Seredy (Viking)

In the Forest by Marie Hall Ets (Viking)

Mother Goose illustrated by Tasha Tudor (Walck)

Yonie Wondernose by Marguerite de Angeli (Doubleday)

1946   *The Rooster Crows* (traditional Mother Goose) illustrated by Maud and Miska Petersham (Macmillan)

Honor Books

Little Lost Lamb by Golden MacDonald, illustrated by Leonard Weisgard (Doubleday)

My Mother Is the Most Beautiful Woman in the World by Becky Reyher, illustrated by Ruth C. Gannett (Lothrop)

Sing Mother Goose by Opal Wheeler, illustrated by Marjorie Torrey (Dutton)

You Can Write Chinese by Kurt Wiese (Viking)

1947   *The Little Island* by Golden MacDonald, illustrated by Leonard Weisgard (Doubleday)

Honor Books

Boats on the River by Marjorie Flack, illustrated by Jay Hyde Barnum (Viking)

Pedro, the Angel of Olvera Street by Leo Politi (Scribner's)

Rain Drop Splash by Alvin Tresselt, illustrated by Leonard Weisgard (Lothrop)

Sing in Praise: A Collection of the Best Loved Hymns by Opal Wheeler, illustrated by Marjorie Torrey (Dutton)

Timothy Turtle by Al Graham, illustrated by Tony Palazzo (Welch)

1948   *White Snow, Bright Snow* by Alvin Tresselt, illustrated by Roger Duvoisin (Lothrop)

Honor Books

Bambino the Clown by George Schreiber (Viking)

McElligot's Pool by Dr. Seuss (Random House)

Roger and the Fox by Lavinia Davis, illustrated by Hildegard Woodward (Doubleday)

Song of Robin Hood edited by Anne Malcolmson, illustrated by Virginia Lee Burton (Houghton Mifflin)

Stone Soup by Marcia Brown (Scribner's)

1949   *The Big Snow* by Berta and Elmer Hader (Macmillan)

Honor Books

All Around the Town by Phyllis McGinley, illustrated by Helen Stone (Lippincott)

Blueberries for Sal by Robert McCloskey (Viking)

Fish in the Air by Kurt Wiese (Viking)

Juanita by Leo Politi (Scribner's)

1950   *Song of the Swallows* by Leo Politi (Scribner's)

Honor Books

America's Ethan Allen by Stewart Holbrook, illustrated by Lynd Ward (Houghton Mifflin)

Bartholomew and the Oobleck by Dr. Seuss (Random House)

The Happy Day by Ruth Krauss, illustrated by Marc Simont (Harper)

Henry Fisherman by Marcia Brown (Scribner's)

The Wild Birthday Cake by Lavinia Davis, illustrated by Hildegard Woodward (Doubleday)

1951   *The Egg Tree* by Katherine Milhous (Scribner's)

Honor Books

Dick Whittington and His Cat by Marcia Brown (Scribner's)

If I Ran the Zoo by Dr. Seuss (Random House)

The Most Wonderful Doll in the World by Phyllis McGinley, illustrated by Helen Stone (Lippincott)

T-Bone, the Baby Sitter by Clare Newberry (Harper)

The Two Reds by Will, illustrated by Nicolas (Harcourt)

1952   *Finders Keepers* by Will, illustrated by Nicolas (Harcourt)

Honor Books

All Falling Down by Gene Zion, illustrated by Margaret Bloy Graham (Harper)

Bear Party by William Pe`ne du Bois (Viking)

Feather Mountain by Elizabeth Olds (Houghton Mifflin)

Mr. T. W. Anthony Woo by Marie Hall Ets (Viking)

Skipper John's Cook by Marcia Brown (Scribner's)

1953   *The Biggest Bear* by Lynd Ward (Houghton Mifflin)

Honor Books

Ape in a Cape by Fritz Eichenberg (Harcourt)

Five Little Monkeys by Juliet Kepes (Houghton Mifflin)

One Morning in Maine by Robert McCloskey (Viking)

Puss in Boots by Charles Perrault, illustrated by Marcia Brown (Scribner's)

The Storm Book by Charlotte Zolotow, illustrated by Margaret Bloy Graham (Harper)

1954   *Madeline's Rescue* by Ludwig Bemelmans (Viking)

Honor Books

A Very Special House by Ruth Krauss, illustrated by Maurice Sendak (Harper)

Green Eyes by A. Birnbaum (Capitol)

Journey Cake, Ho! by Ruth Sawyer, illustrated by Robert McCloskey (Viking)

The Steadfast Tin Soldier by Hans Christian Andersen, illustrated by Marcia Brown (Scribner's)

When Will the World Be Mine? by Miriam Schlein, illustrated by Jean Charlot (Scott)

1955   *Cinderella, or the Little Glass Slipper* by Charles Perrault, illustrated by Marcia Brown (Scribner's)

Honor Books

Book of Nursery and Mother Goose Rhymes illustrated by Marguerite de Angeli (Doubleday)

The Thanksgiving Story by Alice Dalgliesh, illustrated by Helen Sewell (Scribner's)

Wheel on the Chimney by Margaret Wise Brown, illustrated by Tibor Gergely (Lippincott)

1956   *Frog Went A-Courtin'* retold by John Langstaff, illustrated by Feodor Rojankovsky (Harcourt)

Honor Books

Crow Boy by Taro Yashima (Viking)

Play with Me by Marie Hall Ets (Viking)

1957   *A Tree Is Nice* by Janice May Udry, illustrated by Marc Simont (Harper)

Honor Books

Anatole by Eve Titus, illustrated by Paul Galdone (McGraw-Hill)

Gillespie and the Guards by Benjamin Elkin, illustrated by James Daugherty (Viking)

Lion by William Pe`ne du Bois (Viking)

Mr. Penny's Race Horse by Marie Hall Ets (Viking)

1 Is One by Tasha Tudor (Walck)

1958   *Time of Wonder* by Robert McCloskey (Viking)

Honor Books

Anatole and the Cat by Eve Titus, illustrated by Paul Galdone (McGraw-Hill)

Fly High, Fly Low by Don Freeman (Viking)

1959   *Chanticleer and the Fox* adapted from Chaucer, illustrated by Barbara Cooney (Crowell)

Honor Books

The House That Jack Built by Antonio Frasconi (Harcourt)

Umbrella by Taro Yashima (Viking)

What Do You Say, Dear? by Sesyle Joslin, illustrated by Maurice Sendak (Scott)

1960   *Nine Days to Christmas* by Marie Hall Ets and Aurora Labastida, illustrated by Marie Hall Ets (Viking)

Honor Books

Houses from the Sea by Alice E. Goudey, illustrated by Adrienne Adams (Scribner's)

The Moon Jumpers by Janice May Udry, illustrated by Maurice Sendak (Harper)

1961 *Baboushka and the Three Kings* by Ruth Robbins, illustrated by Nicholas Sidjakov (Parnassus)

Honor Book: Inch by Inch by Leo Lionni (Astor-Honor)

1962 *Once a Mouse* by Marcia Brown (Scribner's)

Honor Books

The Day We Saw the Sun Come Up by Alice E. Goudey, illustrated by Adrienne Adams (Scribner's)

The Fox Went Out on a Chilly Night illustrated by Peter Spier (Doubleday)

Little Bear's Visit by Else Holmelund Minarik, illustrated by Maurice Sendak (Harper)

1963 *The Snowy Day* by Ezra Jack Keats (Viking)

Honor Books

Mr. Rabbit and the Lovely Present by Charlotte Zolotow, illustrated by Maurice Sendak (Harper)

The Sun Is a Golden Earring by Natalia M. Belting, illustrated by Bernarda Bryson (Holt)

1964 *Where the Wild Things Are* by Maurice Sendak (Harper)

Honor Books

All in the Morning Early by Sorche Nic Leodhas, illustrated by Evaline Ness (Holt)

Mother Goose and Nursery Rhymes illustrated by Philip Reed (Atheneum)

Swimmy by Leo Lionni (Pantheon)

1965 *May I Bring a Friend?* by Beatrice Schenk de Regniers, illustrated by Beni Montresor (Atheneum)

Honor Books

A Pocketful of Cricket by Rebecca Caudill, illustrated by Evaline Ness (Holt)

Rain Makes Applesauce by Julian Scheer, illustrated by Marvin Bileck (Holiday House)

The Wave by Margaret Hodges, illustrated by Blair Lent (Houghton Mifflin)

1966 *Always Room for One More* by Sorche Nic Leodhas, illustrated by Nonny Hogrogian (Holt)

Honor Books

Hide and Seek Fog by Alvin Tresselt, illustrated by Roger Duvoisin (Lothrop)

Just Me by Marie Hall Ets (Viking)

Tom Tit Tot by Evaline Ness (Scribner's)

1967 *Sam, Bangs & Moonshine* by Evaline Ness (Holt)

Honor Book: One Wide River to Cross by Barbara Emberley, illustrated by Ed Emberley (Prentice-Hall)

1968 *Drummer Hoff* by Barbara Emberley, illustrated by Ed Emberley (Prentice-Hall)

Honor Books

The Emperor and the Kite by Jane Yolen, illustrated by Ed Young (World)

Frederick by Leo Lionni (Pantheon)

Seashore Story by Taro Yashima (Viking)

1969 *The Fool of the World and the Flying Ship* retold by Arthur Ransome, illustrated by Uri Shulevitz (Farrar)

Honor Book: Why the Sun and the Moon Live in the Sky by Elphinstone Dayrell, illustrated by Blair Lent (Houghton Mifflin)

1970 *Sylvester and the Magic Pebble* by William Steig (Windmill/Simon & Schuster)

Honor Books

Alexander and the Wind-Up Mouse by Leo Lionni (Pantheon)

Goggles! by Ezra Jack Keats (Macmillan)

The Judge by Harve Zemach, illustrated by Margot Zemach (Farrar)

Pop Corn & Ma Goodness by Edna Mitchell Preston, illustrated by Robert Andrew Parker (Viking)

Thy Friend, Obadiah by Brinton Turkle (Viking)

1971 *A Story, a Story* by Gail E. Haley (Atheneum)

Honor Books

The Angry Moon by William Sleator, illustrated by Blair Lent (Atlantic/Little, Brown)

Frog and Toad Are Friends by Arnold Lobel (Harper)

In the Night Kitchen by Maurice Sendak (Harper)

1972 *One Fine Day* by Nonny Hogrogian (Macmillan)

Honor Books

Hildilid's Night by Cheli Durán Ryan, illustrated by Arnold Lobel (Macmillan)

If All the Seas Were One Sea by Janina Domanska (Macmillan)

Moja Means One by Muriel Feelings, illustrated by Tom Feelings (Dial)

1973 *The Funny Little Woman* retold by Arlene Mosel, illustrated by Blair Lent (Dutton)

Honor Books

Anansi the Spider adapted and illustrated by Gerald McDermott (Holt)

Hosie's Alphabet by Hosea, Tobias, and Lisa Baskin, illustrated by Leonard Baskin (Viking)

Snow White and the Seven Dwarfs illustrated by Nancy Eckholm Burkert (Farrar)

When Clay Sings by Byrd Baylor, illustrated by Tom Bahti (Scribner's)

1974 *Duffy and the Devil* retold by Harve Zemach, illustrated by Margot Zemach (Farrar)

Honor Books

Cathedral by David Macaulay (Houghton Mifflin)

Three Jovial Huntsmen by Susan Jeffers (Bradbury)

1975 *Arrow to the Sun* by Gerald McDermott (Viking)

Honor Book: **Jambo Means Hello** by Muriel Feelings, illustrated by Tom Feelings (Dial)

1976   **Why Mosquitoes Buzz in People's Ears** by Verna Aardema, illustrated by Leo and Diane Dillon (Dial)

Honor Books

The Desert Is Theirs by Byrd Baylor, illustrated by Peter Parnall (Scribner's)

Strega Nona retold and illustrated by Tomie de Paola (Prentice)

1977   **Ashanti to Zulu: African Traditions** by Margaret Musgrove, illustrated by Leo and Diane Dillon (Dial)

Honor Books

The Amazing Bone by William Steig (Farrar)

The Contest retold and illustrated by Nonny Hogrogian (Greenwillow)

Fish for Supper by M. B. Goffstein (Dial)

The Golem by Beverly Brodsky McDermott (Lippincott)

Hawk, I'm Your Brother by Byrd Baylor, illustrated by Peter Parnall (Scribner's)

1978   **Noah's Ark** illustrated by Peter Spier (Doubleday)

Honor Books

Castle by David Macaulay (Houghton Mifflin)

It Could Always Be Worse by Margot Zemach (Farrar)

1979   **The Girl Who Loved Wild Horses** by Paul Goble (Bradbury)

Honor Books

Freight Train by Donald Crews (Greenwillow)

The Way to Start a Day by Byrd Baylor, illustrated by Peter Parnall (Scribner's)

1980   **Ox-Cart Man** by Donald Hall, illustrated by Barbara Cooney (Viking)

Honor Books

Ben's Trumpet by Rachel Isadora (Greenwillow)

The Garden of Abdul Gasazi by Chris Van Allsburg (Houghton Mifflin)

The Treasure by Uri Shulevitz (Farrar)

1981   **Fables** by Arnold Lobel (Harper)

Honor Books

The Bremen Town Musicians retold and illustrated by Ilse Plume (Doubleday)

The Grey Lady and the Strawberry Snatcher by Molly Bang (Four Winds)

Mice Twice by Joseph Low (McElderry)

Truck by Donald Crews (Greenwillow)

1982   **Jumanji** by Chris Van Allsburg (Houghton Mifflin)

Honor Books

On Market Street by Arnold Lobel, illustrated by Anita Lobel (Greenwillow)

Outside Over There by Maurice Sendak (Harper)

A Visit to William Blake's Inn: Poems for Innocent and Experienced Travelers by Nancy Willard, illustrated by Alice and Martin Provensen (Harcourt)

Where the Buffaloes Begin by Olaf Baker, illustrated by Stephen Gammell (Viking)

1983   **Shadow** by Blaise Cendrars, illustrated by Marcia Brown (Scribner's)

Honor Books

A Chair for My Mother by Vera B. Williams (Greenwillow)

When I Was Young in the Mountains by Cynthia Rylant, illustrated by Diane Goode (Dutton)

1984   **The Glorious Flight: Across the Channel with Louis Blériot** by Alice and Martin Provensen (Viking)

Honor Books

Little Red Riding Hood retold and illustrated by Trina Schart Hyman (Holiday House)

Ten, Nine, Eight by Molly Bang (Greenwillow)

1985   **Saint George and the Dragon** by Margaret Hodges, illustrated by Trina Schart Hyman (Little, Brown)

Honor Books

Hansel and Gretel retold by Rika Lesser, illustrated by Paul O. Zelinsky (Dodd)

Have You Seen My Duckling? by Nancy Tafuri (Greenwillow)

The Story of Jumping Mouse retold and illustrated by John Steptoe (Lothrop)

1986   **The Polar Express** by Chris Van Allsburg (Houghton Mifflin)

Honor Books

King Bidgood's in the Bathtub by Audrey Wood, illustrated by Don Wood (Harcourt)

The Relatives Came by Cynthia Rylant, illustrated by Stephen Gammell (Bradbury)

1987   **Hey, Al!** by Arthur Yorinks, illustrated by Richard Egielski (Farrar)

Honor Books

Alphabatics by Suse MacDonald (Bradbury)

Rumpelstiltskin by Paul O. Zelinsky (Dutton)

The Village of Round and Square Houses by Ann Grifalconi (Little, Brown)

1988   **Owl Moon** by Jane Yolen, illustrated by John Schoenherr (Philomel)

Honor Book: **Mufaro's Beautiful Daughters: An African Tale** by John Steptoe (Lothrop)

1989   **Song and Dance Man** by Karen Ackerman, illustrated by Stephen Gammell (Knopf)

Honor Books

The Boy of the Three-Year Nap by Dianne Snyder, illustrated by Allen Say (Houghton Mifflin)

Free-Fall by David Wiesner (Lothrop)

Goldilocks and the Three Bears by James Marshall (Dial)

Mirandy and Brother Wind by Patricia C. McKissack, illustrated by Jerry Pinkney (Knopf)

1990 *Lon Po Po: A Red-Riding Hood Story from China* by Ed Young (Philomel)

Honor Books

Bill Peet: An Autobiography by Bill Peet (Houghton Mifflin)

Color Zoo by Lois Ehlert (Lippincott)

Hershel and the Hanukkah Goblins by Eric Kimmel, illustrated by Trina Schart Hyman (Holiday House)

The Talking Eggs by Robert D. San Souci, illustrated by Jerry Pinkney (Dial)

1991 *Black and White* by David Macaulay (Houghton Mifflin)

Honor Books

"More More More," Said the Baby: 3 Love Stories by Vera B. Williams (Greenwillow)

Puss in Boots by Charles Perrault, translated by Malcolm Arthur, illustrated by Fred Marcellino (Farrar)

1992 *Tuesday* by David Wiesner (Clarion)

Honor Book: Tar Beach by Faith Ringgold (Crown)

1993 *Mirette on the High Wire* by Emily Arnold McCully (Putnam)

Honor Books

Seven Blind Mice by Ed Young (Philomel)

The Stinky Cheese Man and Other Fairly Stupid Tales by Jon Scieszka, illustrated by Lane Smith (Viking)

Working Cotton by Sherley Anne Williams, illustrated by Carole Byard (Harcourt)

1994 *Grandfather's Journey* by Allen Say (Houghton Mifflin)

Honor Books

Owen by Kevin Henkes (Greenwillow)

Peppe, the Lamplighter by Elisa Bartone, illustrated by Ted Lewin (Lothrop)

Raven by Gerald McDermott (Harcourt)

In the Small, Small Pond by Denise Fleming (Holt)

Yo! Yes? by Chris Raschka (Orchard)

1995 *Smoky Night* by Eve Bunting, illustrated by David Diaz (Harcourt)

Honor Books

Swamp Angel by Anne Isaacs, illustrated by Paul O. Zelinksy (Dutton)

John Henry by Julius Lester, illustrated by Jerry Pinkney (Dial)

Time Flies by Eric Rohmann (Crown)

1996 *Officer Buckle and Gloria* by Peggy Rathmann (Putnam)

Honor Books

Alphabet City by Stephen T. Johnson (Viking)

Zin! Zin! Zin! A Violin by Lloyd Moss, illustrated by Marjorie Priceman (Simon & Schuster)

The Faithful Friend by Robert D. San Souci, illustrated by Brian Pinkney (Simon & Schuster)

Tops & Bottoms by Janet Stevens (Harcourt)

1997 *Golem* by David Wisniewski (Clarion)

Honor Books

Hush! A Thai Lullaby by Minfong Ho, illustrated by Holly Meade (Kroupa/Orchard)

The Graphic Alphabet by David Pelletier (Orchard)

The Paperboy by Dav Pilkey (Jackson/Orchard)

Starry Messenger by Peter Sís (Foster/Farrar)

1998 *Rapunzel* by Paul O. Zelinsky (Dutton)

Honor Books

The Gardener by Sarah Stewart, illustrated by David Small (Farrar)

Harlem by Walter Dean Myers, illustrated by Christopher Myers (Scholastic)

There Was an Old Lady Who Swallowed a Fly by Simms Taback (Viking)

1999 *Snowflake Bentley* by Jacqueline Briggs Martin, illustrated by Mary Azarian (Houghton Mifflin)

Honor Books

Duke Ellington: The Piano Prince and the Orchestra by Andrea Davis Pinkney, illustrated by Brian Pinkney (Hyperion)

No, David! by David Shannon (Scholastic)

Snow by Uri Shulevitz (Farrar)

Tibet: Through the Red Box by Peter Sís (Foster/Farrar)

2000 *Joseph Had a Little Overcoat* by Simms Taback (Viking)

Honor Books

A Child's Calendar by John Updike, illustrated by Trina Schart Hyman (Holiday House)

Sector 7 by David Wiesner (Clarion)

When Sophie Gets Angry—Really, Really Angry . . . by Molly Bang (Scholastic)

The Ugly Duckling by Hans Christian Andersen, adapted by Jerry Pinkney, illustrated by Jerry Pinkney (Morrow)

2001 *So You Want to Be President?* by Judith St. George, illustrated by David Small (Philomel)

Honor Books

Casey at the Bat by Ernest Lawrence Thayer, illustrated by Christopher Bing (Handprint)

Click, Clack, Moo: Cows That Type by Doreen Cronin, illustrated by Betsy Lewin (Simon & Schuster)

Olivia by Ian Falconer (Atheneum)

2002 *The Three Pigs* by David Wiesner (Clarion/Houghton Mifflin)

Honor Books

The Dinosaurs of Waterhouse Hawkins illustrated by Brian Selznick, text, Barbara Kerley (Scholastic)

Martin's Big Words: the Life of Dr. Martin Luther King, Jr. illustrated by Bryan Collier, text, Doreen Rappaport (Jump at the Sun/Hyperion)

The Stray Dog by Marc Simont (HarperCollins)

2003 *My Friend Rabbit* illustrated and written by Eric Rohmann (Roaring Brook Press/ Millbrook Press)

Honor Books

The Spider and the Fly illustrated and written by Tony DiTerlizzi (Simon & Schuster)

Hondo & Fabian illustrated and written by Peter McCarty (Henry Holt)

Noah's Ark illustrated and written by Jerry Pinkney (Sea Star/North-South Books)

2004 *The Man Who Walked Between the Towers* illustrated and written by Mordicai Gerstein (Roaring Brook Press/ Millbrook Press)

Honor Books

Ella Sarah Gets Dressed illustrated and written by Margaret Chodos-Irvine (Harcourt, Inc.)

What Do You Do with a Tail Like This? illustrated by Steve Jenkins; written by Robin Page and Steve Jenkins (Houghton Mifflin Company)

Don't Let the Pigeon Drive the Bus illustrated and written by Mo Willems (Hyperion)

2005 *Kitten's First Full Moon* illustrated and written by Kevin Henkes (Greenwillow/HarperCollins)

Honor Books

The Red Book illustrated by Barbara Lehman (Houghton Mifflin)

Coming on Home illustrated by E. B. Lewis, written by Jacqueline Woodson (Putnam)

Knuffle Bunny: A Cautionary Tale illustrated and written by Mo Willems (Hyperion)

2006 *The Hello, Goodbye Window* illustrated by Chris Raschka, written by Norton Juster (Michael di Capua/Hyperion)

Honor Books

Rosa illustrated by Bryan Collier and written by Nikki Giovanni (Holt)

Zen Shorts illustrated and written by Jon J. Muth (Scholastic Press)

Hot Air: The (Mostly) True Story of the First Hot-Air Balloon Ride illustrated and written by Marjorie Priceman (an Anne Schwartz Book/Atheneum Books for Young Readers/Simon & Schuster)

Song of the Water Boatman and Other Pond Poems illustrated by Beckie Prange, written by Joyce Sidman (Houghton Mifflin Company)

2007 *Flotsam* by David Wiesner (Clarion)

Honor Books

Gone Wild: An Endangered Animal Alphabet by David McLimans (Walker)

Moses: When Harriet Tubman Led Her People to Freedom illustrated by Kadir Nelson, written by Carole Boston Weatherford (Hyperion/Jump at the Sun)

2008 *The Invention of Hugo Cabret* by Brian Selznick (Scholastic Press, an imprint of Scholastic)

Honor Books

Henry's Freedom Box: A True Story from the Underground Railroad illustrated by Kadir Nelson, written by Ellen Levine (Scholastic Press)

First the Egg by Laura Vaccaro Seeger (Roaring Brook/Neal Porter)

The Wall: Growing Up Behind the Iron Curtain by Peter Sís (Farrar/Frances Foster)

Knuffle Bunny Too: A Case of Mistaken Identity by Mo Willems (Hyperion)

2009 *The House in the Night* illustrated by Beth Krommes, written by Susan Marie Swanson (Houghton Mifflin Company)

Honor Books

A Couple of Boys Have the Best Week Ever by Marie Frazee (Harcourt)

How I Learned Geography by Uri Shulevitz (Farrar, Straus, & Giroux)

A River of Words: The Story of William Carlos Williams, illustrated by Melissa Sweet, written by Jen Bryant (Eerdmans Books for Young Readers, an imprint of Wm. B. Eerdmans Publishing Co.)

2010 *The Lion & the Mouse* illustrated and written by Jerry Pinkney (Little, Brown and Company Books for Young Readers)

Honor Books

All the World by Liz Garton, illustrated by Marla Frazee (Beach Lane Books)

Red Sings from Treetops: A Year in Colors by Joyce Sidman, illustrated by Pamela Zagarenski (Houghton Mifflin Books for Children, Houghton Mifflin Harcourt)

International Reading Association Children's Book Award

This award is given annually to honor new talent in children's literature. Publishers worldwide are invited to suggest candidates. Since 1987, an award has been given to one author who writes for older readers and one author who writes for younger readers. In 1995, a third award was added for an author of an informational book.

1975 *Transport 7-41-R* by T. Degens (Viking, United States)

1976 *Dragonwings* by Laurence Yep (Harper, United States)

1977 *A String in the Harp* by Nancy Bond (McElderry, United States)

1978 *A Summer to Die* by Lois Lowry (Houghton Mifflin, United States)

1979 *Reserved for Mark Anthony Crowder* by Alison Smith (Dutton, United States)

1980 *Words by Heart* by Ouida Sebestyen (Atlantic/Little, Brown, United States)

1981 *My Own Private Sky* by Delores Beckman (Dutton, United States)

1982 *Goodnight, Mister Tom* by Michelle Magorian (Kestrel, Great Britain)

1983 *The Darkangel* by Meredith Ann Pierce (Atlantic/Little, Brown, United States)

1984 *Ratha's Creature* by Clare Bell (McElderry, United States)

1985 *Badger on the Barge* by Janni Howker (Julia MacRae, Great Britain)

1986 *Prairie Songs* by Pam Conrad (Harper, United States)

1987 *Older Readers: After the Dancing Days* by Margaret I. Rostkowski (Harper, United States)

Younger Readers: The Line-Up Book by Marisabina Russo (Greenwillow, United States)

1988 *Older Readers: The Ruby in the Smoke and Shadow in the North* by Philip Pullman (Oxford, Great Britain)

Younger Readers: The Third-Story Cat by Leslie Baker (Little, Brown, United States)

1989 *Older Readers: Probably Still Nick Swansen* by Virginia Euwer Wolff (Holt, United States)

Younger Readers: Rechenka's Eggs by Patricia Polacco (Philomel, United States)

1990 *Older Readers: Children of the River* by Linda Crew (Delacorte, United States)

Younger Readers: No Star Nights by Anna Egan Smucker, illustrated by Steve Johnson (Knopf, United States)

1991 *Older Readers: Under the Hawthorn Tree* by Marita Conlon-McKenna (O'Brien Press, Ireland)

Younger Readers: Is This a House for Hermit Crab? by Megan McDonald, illustrated by S. D. Schindler (Orchard, United States)

1992 *Older Readers: Rescue Josh McGuire* by Ben Mikaelsen (Hyperion, United States)

Younger Readers: Ten Little Rabbits by Virginia Grossman, illustrated by Sylvia Long (Chronicle, United States)

1993 *Older Readers: Letters from Rifka* by Karen Hesse (Holt, United States)

Younger Readers: Old Turtle by Douglas Wood, illustrated by Cheng-Khee Chee (Pfeifer-Hamilton, United States)

1994 *Older Readers: Behind the Secret Window: A Memoir of a Hidden Childhood* by Nelly S. Toll (Dutton, United States)

Younger Readers: Sweet Clara and the Freedom Quilt by Deborah Hopkinson, illustrated by James E. Ransome (Knopf, United States)

1995 *Older Readers: Spite Fences* by Trudy Krisher (Bantam, United States)

Younger Readers: The Ledgerbook of Thomas Blue Eagle by Gay Matthaei and Jewel Grutman, illustrated by Adam Cvijanovic (Thomasson-Grant, United States)

Informational Book: Stranded at Plimouth Plantation 1626 by Gary Bowen (HarperCollins, United States)

1996 *Older Readers: The King's Shadow* by Elizabeth Alder (Farrar, United States)

Younger Readers: More Than Anything Else by Marie Bradby, illustrated by Chris K. Soentpiet (Orchard, United States)

Informational Book: The Case of the Mummified Pigs and Other Mysteries in Nature by Susan E. Quinlan (Boyds Mills, United States)

1997 *Older Readers: Don't You Dare Read This Mrs. Dunphrey* by Margaret Peterson Haddix (Simon & Schuster, United States)

Younger Readers: The Fabulous Flying Fandinis by Ingrid Slyder (Cobblehill, United States)

Informational Book: Brooklyn Bridge by Elizabeth Mann (Mikaya Press, United States)

1998 *Older Readers: Moving Mama to Town* by Ronder Thomas Young (Orchard, United States)

Younger Readers: Nim and the War Effort by Millie Lee and Yangsook Choi (Farrar, United States)

Informational Book: Just What the Doctor Ordered: The History of American Medicine by Brandon Marie Miller (Lerner, United States)

1999 *Older Readers: Choosing Up Sides* by John Ritter (Penguin Putnam, United States)

Younger Readers: My Freedom Trip: A Child's Escape from North Korea by Frances and Ginger Park (Boyds Mills, United States)

Informational Book: First in the Field, Baseball Hero Jackie Robinson by Derek T. Dingle (Hyperion, United States)

2000 *Older Fiction: Bud, Not Buddy* by Christopher Paul Curtis (Delacorte, United States)

Older Nonfiction: Eleanor's Story: An American Girl in Hitler's Germany by Eleanor Ramrath Garner (Peachtree Publishers, United States)

Younger Fiction: Molly Bannaky by Alice McGill (Houghton Mifflin, United States)

Younger Nonfiction: The Snake Scientist by Sy Montgomery (Houghton Mifflin, United States)

2001 *Younger Fiction: Stranger in the Woods* by Carl R. Sams II and Jean Stoick (Carl R. Sams II Photography)

Younger Nonfiction: My Season With Penguins by Sophie Webb (Houghton Mifflin

Older Fiction: Jake's Orphan by Peggy Brooke (Dorling Kindersley)

Older Nonfiction: Girls Think of Everything by Catherine Thimmesh and Melissa Sweet (Houghton Mifflin)

2002 *Primary Fiction: Silver Seeds* by Paolilli and Dan Brewer (Viking, Penguin Putnam Books)

Primary Nonfiction: Aero and Officer Mike by Joan Plummer Russell (Boyds Mills Press)

Intermediate Fiction: Coolies by Yin (Philomel, Penguin Putnam Books)

Intermediate Nonfiction: Pearl Harbor Warriors by Dorinda Makanaonalani Nicholson and Larry Nicholson (Woodson House)

Young Adult Fiction: A Step From Heaven by Ann Na (Front Street)

Young Adult Nonfiction: Meltdown: A Race Against Nuclear Disaster at Three Mile Island by Wilborn Hampton (Candlewick Press)

2003 *Primary Fiction: One Leaf Rides the Wind* by Celeste Davidson Mannis (Viking)

Primary Nonfiction: **The Pot That Juan Built** by Nancy Andrews-Goebel (Lee & Low Books)

Intermediate Fiction: **Who Will Tell My Brother?** by Marlene Carvell (Hyperion)

Intermediate Nonfiction: **If the World Were a Village: A Book About the World's People** by David J. Smith (Kids Can Press)

Young Adult Fiction: **Mississippi Trial, 1955** by Chris Crowe (Phyllis Fogelman Books)

Young Adult Nonfiction: **Headin' for Better Times: The Arts of the Great Depression** by Duane Damon (Lerner)

2004 *Primary Fiction:* **Mary Smith** by Andrea U'ren (Farrar, Straus, & Giroux)

Primary Nonfiction: **Uncle Andy's: A Faabbbulous Visit with Andy Warhol** by James Warhola (Penguin)

Intermediate Fiction: **Sahara Special** by Esmé Raji Codell (Hyperion Books)

Intermediate Nonfiction: **Carl Sandburg: Adventures of a Poet** by Penelope Niven (Harcourt)

Young Adult Fiction: **Buddha Boy** by Kathe Koja (Farrar, Straus, & Giroux)

Young Adult Nonfiction: **At the End of Words: A Daughter's Memoir** by Miriam Stone (Candlewick Press)

2005 *Primary Fiction:* **Miss Bridie Chose a Shovel** by Leslie Conner and illustrated by Mary Azarian (Houghton Mifflin)

Primary Nonfiction: **Eliza and the Dragonfly** by Susie Caldwell Rinehart and illustrated by Anisa Claire Hovemann (Dawn Publications)

Intermediate Fiction: **The Golden Hour** by Maiya Williams (Amulet Books)

Intermediate Nonfiction: **Buildings in Disguise** by Joan Mariea Arbogast (Amulet Books)

Young Adult Fiction: **Emako Blue** by Brenda Woods (Boyds Mill Press)

Young Adult Nonfiction: **The Burn Journals** by Brent Runyon (G.P. Putnam's Sons)

2006 *Primary Fiction:* **Russell the Sheep** by Rob Scotton (Harper Collins)

Primary Nonfiction: **Night Wonders** by Jane Ann Peddicord (Charlesbridge)

Intermediate Fiction: **The Bicycle Man** By David L. Dudley (Clarion Books)

Intermediate Nonfiction: **Americans Who Tell the Truth** by Robert Shetterly (Dutton)

Young Adult Fiction: **Black and White** by Paul Volponi (Viking Press)

Young Adult Nonfiction: **JAZZ ABZ: An A to Z Collection of Jazz Portraits** by Wynton Marsalis and Paul Rogers (Candlewick Press)

2007 *Primary Fiction:* **Tickets to Ride: An Alphabetical Amusement** by Mark Rogalski (Running Press Kids)

Primary Nonfiction: **Theodore** by Frank Keating (Paula Wiseman Book, Simon & Schuster)

Intermediate Fiction: **Blue** by Joyce Moyer Hostetter (Calkins Creek Books, Boyds Mills Press)

Intermediate Nonfiction: **Something Out of Nothing: Marie Curie and Radium** by Carla Killough McClafferty (Farrar, Straus, & Giroux)

Young Adult Fiction: **Leonardo's Shadow: Or, My Astonishing Life as Leonardo da Vinci's Servant** by Christopher Grey (Atheneum Books, Simon & Schuster)

Young Adult Nonfiction: **The Poet Slave of Cuba: A Biography of Juan Francisco Manzano** by Margarita Engle (Henry Holt)

2008 *Primary Fiction:* **One Thousand Tracings: Healing the Wounds of World War II** by Lita Judge (Hyperion)

Intermediate Fiction: **The Silver Cup** by Constance Leeds (Viking Penguin Group)

Young Adult Fiction: **Red Glass** by Laura Resau (Delacorte Random House)

Primary Nonfiction: **Louis Sockalexis: Native American Baseball Pioneer** by Bill Wise, illustrated by Bill Farnsworth (Lee & Low)

Intermediate Nonfiction: **Tracking Trash: Flotsam, Jetsam, and the Science of Ocean Motion** by Loree Griffin Burns (Houghton Mifflin)

Young Adult Nonfiction: **Tasting the Sky: A Palestinian Childhood** by Ibtisam Barakat (Melanie Kroupa Books, Farrar, Straus, & Giroux)

2009 *Primary Fiction:* **The Wheat Doll** by Alison L. Randall (Peachtree)

Intermediate Fiction: **The Leanin' Dog** by K. A. Nuzum (HarperCollins)

Young Adult Fiction: **Freeze Frame** by Heidi Ayarbe (HarperCollins)

Primary Nonfiction: **Manfish: The Story of Jacques Cousteau** by Jennifer Berne (Chronicle)

Intermediate Nonfiction: **The Raucous Royals** by Carlyn Beccia (Houghton Mifflin)

Young Adult Nonfiction: **Snow Falling in Spring** by Moying Li (Farrar, Straus, & Giroux)

Ezra Jack Keats New Writers Award

Ezra Jack Keats (1919–1983) was a prolific illustrator of children's picture books who won the Caldecott Medal in 1963 for *The Snowy Day*. The Ezra Jack Keats award is funded by the Ezra Jack Keats Foundation and is given to a promising writer who has had six or fewer children's books published. The writer need not be the illustrator. The books must "reflect the tradition of Ezra Jack Keats," whose books portrayed strong family relationships and universal qualities of childhood; the books must also appeal to children nine years old or younger. The award is administered by the Early Childhood Resources and Information Center of the New York Public Library.

1987 **The Patchwork Quilt** by Valerie Flournoy, illustrated by Jerry Pinkney (Dial)

1989 **Jamaica's Find** by Juanita Havill, illustrated by Anne Sibley O'Brien (Houghton Mifflin)

1991 **Tell Me A Story, Mama** by Angela Johnson (Orchard)

1993 **Tar Beach** by Faith Ringgold (Crown)

1995 *Taxi, Taxi* by Cari Best, illustrated by Dale Gottlieb (Little, Brown)

1997 *Calling the Doves/El canto de las palomas* by Juan Felipé Herrera (Children's Book Press)

1999 *Elizabeti's Doll* by Stephanie Stuve-Bodeen, illustrated by Christy Hale (Lee & Low)

2000 *Dear Juno* by Soyung Pak, illustrated by Susan Kathleen Hartung (Viking)

2001 *Henry Hikes to Fitchberg* by D. B. Johnson (Houghton)

2002 *Freedom Summer* by Deborah Wiles, illustrated by James Lagarrigue (Simon & Schuster)

2003 *Ruby's Wish* by Shirim Yim Bridges, illustrated by Sophie Blackall (Chronicle)

2004 *My Name is Yoon* illustrated by Gabi Swiatowska (Farrar, Straus, & Giroux)

2005 *Going North* by Janice N. Harrington (Farrar, Straus, & Giroux)

2006 *New Illustrator Award: Silly Chicken* illustrated by Yunmee Kyong, written by Rukhsana Khan (Viking)

New Writer Award: My Best Friend by Mary Ann Rodman, illustrated by E. B. Lewis (Viking)

2007 *New Illustrator Award: Mystery Bottle* illustrated by Kristen Balouch (Hyperion)

New Writer Award: For You Are A Kenyan Child by Kelly Cunnane, illustrated by Ana Juan (Atheneum)

2008 *New Illustrator Award: The Apple Pie that Papa Baked* illustrated by Jonathan Bean, written by Lauren Thompson (Simon & Schuster)

New Writer Award: Leaves by David Ezra Stein (G.P. Putnam's Sons)

2009 *New Illustrator Award: Bird* illustrated by Shadra Strickland, written by Zetta Elliot (Lee and Low)

New Writer Award: Garmann's Summer by Stian Hole, illustrated by Stian Hole. Translated by Don Bartlett (Eardmans)

Coretta Scott King Award

The Coretta Scott King Award is presented annually by the Coretta Scott King Task Force of the American Library Association's Social Responsibilities Round Table. It has been awarded to African American authors since 1970 and also to African American illustrators since 1974 for books that encourage understanding and appreciation of people of all cultures and their pursuit of the "American dream." The award celebrates the life of Martin Luther King, Jr., and honors his widow, Coretta Scott King, for her strength and dedication in continuing the fight for racial equity and universal peace. One or more Honor Books may also be chosen each year.

1970 *Author Award: Dr. Martin Luther King, Jr., Man of Peace* by Lillie Patterson (Garrard)

1971 *Author Award: Black Troubadour: Langston Hughes* by Charlemae Rollins (Rand McNally)

Honor Books

I Know Why the Caged Bird Sings by Maya Angelou (Random House)

Unbought and Unbossed by Shirley Chisholm (Houghton Mifflin)

I Am a Black Woman by Mari Evans (Morrow)

Every Man Heart Lay Down by Lorenz Graham (Crowell)

The Voice of the Children by June Jordan and Terri Bush (Holt)

Black Means by Gladys Groom and Bonnie Grossman (Hill & Wang)

Ebony Book of Black Achievement by Margaret W. Peters (Johnson)

Mary Jo's Grandmother by Janice May Udry (Whitman)

1972 *Author Award: 17 Black Artists* by Elton C. Fax (Dodd)

1973 *Author Award: I Never Had It Made: The Autobiography of Jackie Robinson* by Alfred Duckett (Putnam)

1974 *Author Award: Ray Charles* by Sharon Bell Mathis (Crowell)

Honor Books

A Hero Ain't Nothin' but a Sandwich by Alice Childress (Coward-McCann)

Don't You Remember? by Lucille Clifton (Dutton)

Ms. Africa: Profiles of Modern African Women by Louise Crane (Lippincott)

Guest in the Promised Land by Kristin Hunter (Scribner's)

Mukasa by John Nagenda (Macmillan)

Illustrator Award: Ray Charles by Sharon Bell Mathis, illustrated by George Ford (Crowell)

1975 *Author Award: The Legend of Africana* by Dorothy Robinson (Johnson)

1976 *Author Award: Duey's Tale* by Pearl Bailey (Harcourt)

Honor Books

Julius K. Nyerere: Teacher of Africa by Shirley Graham (Messner)

Paul Robeson by Eloise Greenfield (Crowell)

Fast Sam, Cool Clyde and Stuff by Walter Dean Myers (Viking)

Song of the Trees by Mildred Taylor (Dial)

1977 *Author Award: The Story of Stevie Wonder* by James Haskins (Lothrop)

Honor Books

Everett Anderson's Friend by Lucille Clifton (Holt)

Roll of Thunder, Hear My Cry by Mildred D. Taylor (Dial)

Quiz Book on Black America by Clarence N. Blake and Donald F. Martin (Houghton Mifflin)

1978 *Author Award: Africa Dreams* by Eloise Greenfield (Crowell)

Honor Books

The Days When the Animals Talked: Black Folk Tales and How They Came to Be by William J. Faulkner (Follett)

Marvin and Tige by Frankcina Glass (St. Martin's)

Mary McCleod Bethune by Eloise Greenfield (Crowell)

Barbara Jordan by James Haskins (Dial)

Coretta Scott King by Lillie Patterson (Garrard)

Portia: The Life of Portia Washington Pittman, the Daughter of Booker T. Washington by Ruth Ann Stewart (Doubleday)

1979 *Author Award:* **Escape to Freedom: A Play about Young Frederick Douglass** by Ossie Davis (Viking)

Honor Books

Skates of Uncle Richard by Carol Fenner (Random House)

Justice and Her Brothers by Virginia Hamilton (Greenwillow)

Benjamin Banneker by Lillie Patterson (Abingdon)

I Have a Sister, My Sister Is Deaf by Jeanne W. Peterson (Harper)

Illustrator Award: **Something on My Mind** by Nikkie Grimes, illustrated by Tom Feelings (Dial)

1980 *Author Award:* **The Young Landlords** by Walter Dean Myers (Viking)

Honor Books

Movin' Up by Berry Gordy (Harper)

Childtimes: A Three-Generation Memoir by Eloise Greenfield and Lessie Jones Little (Harper)

Andrew Young: Young Man with a Mission by James Haskins (Lothrop)

James Van Der Zee: The Picture Takin' Man by James Haskins (Dodd)

Let the Lion Eat Straw by Ellease Southerland (Scribner's)

Illustrator Award: **Cornrows** by Camille Yarbrough, illustrated by Carole Byard (Coward-McCann)

1981 *Author Award:* **This Life** by Sidney Poitier (Knopf)

Honor Books

Don't Explain: A Song of Billie Holiday by Alexis De Veaux (Harper)

Illustrator Award: **Beat the Story Drum, Pum-Pum** by Ashley Bryan (Atheneum)

Honor Books

Grandmama's Joy by Eloise Greenfield, illustrated by Carole Byard (Philomel)

Count on Your Fingers African Style by Claudia Zaslavsky, illustrated by Jerry Pinkney (Crowell)

1982 *Author Award:* **Let the Circle Be Unbroken** by Mildred D. Taylor (Dial)

Honor Books

Rainbow Jordan by Alice Childress (Coward-McCann)

Lou in the Limelight by Kristin Hunter (Scribner's)

Mary: An Autobiography by Mary E. Mebane (Viking)

Illustrator Award: **Mother Crocodile: An Uncle Amadou Tale from Senegal** translated by Rosa Guy, illustrated by John Steptoe (Delacorte)

Honor Book: **Daydreamers** by Eloise Greenfield, illustrated by Tom Feelings (Dial)

1983 *Author Award:* **Sweet Whispers, Brother Rush** by Virginia Hamilton (Philomel)

Honor Book: **This Strange New Feeling** by Julius Lester (Dial)

Illustrator Award: **Black Child** by Peter Magubane (Knopf)

Honor Books

All the Colors of the Race by Arnold Adoff, illustrated by John Steptoe (Lothrop)

Just Us Women by Jeannette Caines, illustrated by Pat Cummings (Harper)

1984 *Author Award:* **Everett Anderson's Goodbye** by Lucille Clifton (Holt)

Special Citation: **The Words of Martin Luther King, Jr**. compiled by Coretta Scott King (Newmarket)

Honor Books

The Magical Adventures of Pretty Pearl by Virginia Hamilton (Harper)

Lena Horne by James Haskins (Coward-McCann)

Bright Shadow by Joyce Carol Thomas (Avon)

Because We Are by Mildred Pitts Walter (Lothrop)

Illustrator Award: **My Mama Needs Me** by Mildred Pitts Walter, illustrated by Pat Cummings (Lothrop)

1985 *Author Award:* **Motown and Didi** by Walter Dean Myers (Viking)

Honor Books

Circle of Gold by Candy Dawson Boyd (Apple/Scholastic)

A Little Love by Virginia Hamilton (Philomel)

1986 *Author Award:* **The People Could Fly: American Black Folktales** by Virginia Hamilton (Knopf)

Honor Books

Junius Over Far by Virginia Hamilton (Harper)

Trouble's Child by Mildred Pitts Walter (Lothrop)

Illustrator Award: **The Patchword Quilt** by Valerie Flournoy, illustrated by Jerry Pinkney (Dial)

Honor Book: **The People Could Fly: American Black Folktales** retold by Virginia Hamilton, illustrated by Leo and Diane Dillon (Knopf)

1987 *Author Award:* **Justin and the Best Biscuits in the World** by Mildred Pitts Walter (Lothrop)

Honor Books

Lion and the Ostrich Chicks and Other African Folk Tales by Ashley Bryan (Atheneum)

Which Way Freedom? by Joyce Hansen (Walker)

Illustrator Award: **Half a Moon and One Whole Star** by Crescent Dragonwagon, illustrated by Jerry Pinkney (Macmillan)

Honor Books

Lion and the Ostrich Chicks and Other African Folk Tales by Ashley Bryan (Atheneum)

C.L.O.U.D.S. by Pat Cummings (Lothrop)

1988 *Author Award:* **The Friendship** by Mildred D. Taylor (Dial)

Honor Books

An Enchanted Hair Tale by Alexis De Veaux (Harper)

The Tales of Uncle Remus: The Adventures of Brer Rabbit by Julius Lester (Dial)

*Illustrator Award: **Mufaro's Beautiful Daughters*** by John Steptoe (Lothrop)

Honor Books

What a Morning! The Christmas Story in Black Spirituals selected by John Langstaff, illustrated by Ashley Bryan (Macmillan)

The Invisible Hunters: A Legend from the Miskito Indians of Nicaragua compiled by Harriet Rohmer et al., illustrated by Joe Sam (Children's Book Press)

1989   *Author Award: **Fallen Angels*** by Walter Dean Myers (Scholastic)

Honor Books

A Thief in the Village and Other Stories by James Berry (Orchard)

Anthony Burns: The Defeat and Triumph of a Fugitive Slave by Virginia Hamilton (Knopf)

*Illustrator Award: **Mirandy and Brother Wind*** by Patricia C. McKissack, illustrated by Jerry Pinkney (Knopf)

Honor Books

Under the Sunday Tree by Eloise Greenfield, illustrated by Amos Ferguson (Harper)

Storm in the Night by Mary Stolz, illustrated by Pat Cummings (Harper)

1990   *Author Award: **A Long Hard Journey: The Story of the Pullman Porter*** by Patricia C. McKissack and Fredrick McKissack (Walker)

Honor Books

Nathaniel Talking by Eloise Greenfield (Black Butterfly)

The Bells of Christmas by Virginia Hamilton (Harcourt)

Martin Luther King, Jr. & the Freedom Movement by Lillie Patterson (Facts on File)

*Illustrator Award: **Nathaniel Talking*** by Eloise Greenfield, illustrated by Jan Spivey Gilchrist (Black Butterfly)

Honor Book

The Talking Eggs by Robert D. San Souci, illustrated by Jerry Pinkney (Dial)

1991   *Author Award: **The Road to Memphis*** by Mildred D. Taylor (Dial)

Honor Books

Black Dance in America by James Haskins (Crowell)

When I Am Old with You by Angela Johnson (Orchard)

*Illustrator Award: **Aida*** by Leontyne Price, illustrated by Leo Dillon and Diane Dillon (Harcourt)

1992   *Author Award: **Now Is Your Time: The African American Struggle for Freedom*** by Walter Dean Myers (HarperCollins)

*Honor Book: **Night on Neighborhood Street*** by Eloise Greenfield (Dial)

*Illustrator Award: **Tar Beach*** by Faith Ringgold (Crown)

Honor Books

All Night, All Day! A Child's First Book of African American Spirituals selected by Ashley Bryan (Atheneum)

Night on Neighborhood Street by Eloise Greenfield, illustrated by Jan Spivey Gilchrist (Dial)

1993   *Author Award: **The Dark-Thirty: Southern Tales of the Supernatural*** by Patricia C. McKissack (Knopf)

Honor Books

Mississippi Challenge by Mildred Pitts Walter (Bradbury)

Sojourner Truth: Ain't I a Woman? by Patricia C. McKissack and Fredrick McKissack (Scholastic)

Somewhere in the Darkness by Walter Dean Myers (Scholastic)

*Illustrator Award: **The Origin of Life on Earth: An African Creation Myth*** retold by David A. Anderson, illustrated by Kathleen Atkins Wilson (Sights)

Honor Books

Little Eight John by Jan Wahl, illustrated by Wil Clay (Lodestar)

Sukey and the Mermaid by Robert D. San Souci, illustrated by Brian Pinkney (Four Winds)

Working Cotton by Sherley Anne Williams, illustrated by Carol Byard (Harcourt)

1994   *Author Award: **Toning the Sweep*** by Angela Johnson (Orchard)

Honor Books

Brown Honey in Broomwheat Tea by Joyce Carol Thomas (HarperCollins)

Malcolm X: By Any Means Necessary by Walter Dean Myers (Scholastic)

*Illustrator Award: **Soul Looks Back in Wonder: Collection of African American Poets*** edited by Phyllis Fogelman, illustrated by Tom Feelings (Dial)

Honor Books

Brown Honey in Broomwheat Tea by Joyce Carol Thomas, illustrated by Floyd Cooper (HarperCollins)

Uncle Jed's Barbershop by Margaree King Mitchell, illustrated by James Ransome (Simon & Schuster)

1995   *Author Award: **Christmas in the Big House, Christmas in the Quarters*** by Patricia C. and Fredrick L. McKissack (Scholastic)

Honor Books

Black Diamond: The Story of the Negro Baseball Leagues by Patricia C. and Fredrick L. McKissack (Scholastic)

I Hadn't Meant to Tell You This by Jacqueline Woodson (Delacorte)

The Captive by Joyce Hansen (Scholastic)

*Illustrator Award: **The Creation*** by James Weldon Johnson, illustrated by James Ransome (Holiday House)

Honor Books

Meet Danitra Brown by Nikki Grimes, illustrated by Floyd Cooper (Lothrop)

The Singing Man by Angela Shelf, illustrated by Terea Shaffer (Holiday House)

1996 *Author Award:* **Her Stories** by Virginia Hamilton (Blue Sky Press)

Honor Books

The Watsons Go to Birmingham—1963 by Christopher Paul Curtis (Delacorte)

Like Sisters on the Homefront by Rita Williams-Garcia (Lodestar)

From the Notebooks of Melanin Sun by Jacqueline Woodson (Blue Sky)

Illustrator Award: **The Middle Passage: White Ships, Black Cargo** by Tom Feelings (Dial)

Honor Books

Her Stories by Virginia Hamilton, illustrated by Leo and Diane Dillon (Blue Sky)

The Faithful Friend by Robert D. San Souci, illustrated by Brian Pinkney (Simon & Schuster)

1997 *Author Award:* **Slam!** by Walter Dean Myers (Scholastic)

Honor Book: **Rebels against Slavery: American Slave Revolts** by Patricia C. McKissack and Fredrick McKissack (Scholastic)

Illustrator Award: **Minty: A Story of Young Harriet Tubman** by Alan Schroeder, illustrated by Jerry Pinkney (Dial)

Honor Books

The Palm of My Heart: Poetry by African American Children by Davida Adedjouma, illustrated by Gregory Christie (Lee & Low)

Running the Road to ABC by Denize Lauture, illustrated by Reynold Ruffins (Simon & Schuster)

Neeny Coming, Neeny Going by Karen English, illustrated by Synthia Saint James (Bridgewater)

1998 *Author Award:* **Forged by Fire** by Sharon M. Draper (Atheneum)

I Thought My Soul Would Rise and Fly: The Diary of Patsy, a Freed Girl by Joyce Hansen (Scholastic)

Honor Book: **Bayard Rustin: Behind the Scenes of the Civil Rights Movement** by James Haskins (Hyperion)

Illustrator Award: **In Daddy's Arms I Am Tall: African Americans Celebrating Fathers**, illustrated by Javaka Steptoe (Lee & Low)

Honor Books

Ashley Bryan's ABC of African American Poetry by Ashley Bryan (Jean Karl/Atheneum)

Harlem by Walter Dean Myers, illustrated by Christopher Myers (Scholastic)

The Hunterman and the Crocodile by Baba Wagué Diakité (Scholastic)

1999 *Author Award:* **Heaven** by Angela Johnson (Simon & Schuster)

Honor Books

Jazmin's Notebook by Nikki Grimes (Dial)

Breaking Ground, Breaking Silence: The Story of New York's African Burial Ground by Joyce Hansen and Gary McGowan (Holt)

The Other Side: Shorter Poems by Angela Johnson (Orchard)

Illustrator Award: **i see the rhythm** by Toyomi Igus, illustrated by Michele Wood (Children's Book Press)

Honor Books

I Have Heard of a Land by Joyce Carol Thomas, illustrated by Floyd Cooper (Joanna Cotler/HarperCollins)

The Bat Boy and His Violin by Gavin Curtis, illustrated by E. B. Lewis (Simon & Schuster)

Duke Ellington: The Piano Prince and His Orchestra by Andrea Davis, illustrated by Brian Pinkney (Hyperion)

2000 *Author Award:* **Bud, Not Buddy** by Christopher Paul Curtis (Delacorte)

Honor Books

Francie by Karen English (Farrar, Straus, & Giroux)

Black Hands, White Sails: The Story of African-American Whalers by Patricia C. and Fredrick McKissack (Scholastic)

Monster by Walter Dean Myers (HarperCollins)

Illustrator Award: **In the Time of the Drums** by Kim L. Siegelson, illustrated by Brian Pinkney (Jump at the Sun/Hyperion)

Honor Books

My Rows and Piles of Coins by Tololwa M. Mollel, illustrated by E. B. Lewis (Clarion)

Black Cat by Christopher Myers (Scholastic)

2001 *Author Award:* **Miracle's Boys** by Jacqueline Woodson (Putnam)

Honor Book: **Let It Shine! Stories of Black Women Freedom Fighters** by Andrea Davis, illustrated by Stephen Alcorn (Gulliver/Harcourt)

Illustrator Award: **Uptown** by Bryan Collier (Holt)

Honor Books

Freedom River by Bryan Collier (Jump at the Sun/Hyperion)

Only Passing Through: The Story of Sojourner Truth by Anne Rockwell, illustrated by R. Gregory Christie (Random House)

Virgie Goes to School with Us Boys by Elizabeth Fitzgerald Howard, illustrated by E. B. Lewis (Simon & Schuster)

2002 *Author Award Winner:* **The Land** by Mildred Taylor (Phyllis Fogelman Books/Penguin Putnam)

Honor Books

Money-Hungry by Sharon G. Flake (Jump at the Sun/Hyperion)

Carver: A Life in Poems by Marilyn Nelson (Front Street)

Illustrator Award Winner: **Goin' Someplace Special** illustrated by Jerry Pinkney, text by Patricia McKissack (Anne Schwartz Book/Atheneum)

Honor Book: **Martin's Big Words** illustrated by Bryan Collier, text by Doreen Rappoport (Jump at the Sun/Hyperion)

2003 *Author Award Winner:* **Bronx Masquerade** by Nikki Grimes (Dial Books for Young Readers)

Honor Books

The Red Rose Box by Brenda Woods (G.P. Putnam's Sons)

Talkin' About Bessie: the Story of Aviator Elizabeth Coleman by Nikki Grimes (Orchard Books/Scholastic)

Illustrator Award: **Talkin' About Bessie: the Story of Aviator Elizabeth Coleman** by Nikki Grimes (Orchard Books/Scholastic)

Honor Books

Rap a Tap Tap: Here's Bojangles—Think of That illustrated by Leo and Diane Dillion (Blue Sky Press/Scholastic, Inc.)

Visiting Langston illustrated by Bryan Collier (Henry Holt & Co.)

2004 *Author Award Winner:* **The First Part Last** by Angela Johnson (Simon & Schuster Books for Young Readers)

Honor Books

Days of Jubilee: The End of Slavery in the United States by Patricia C. and Fredrick L. McKissack (Scholastic)

Locomotion by Jacqueline Woodson (G.P. Putnam's Sons/Penguin Young Readers Group)

The Battle of Jericho by Sharon M. Draper (Atheneum Books for Young Readers)

Illustrator Award Winner: **Beautiful Blackbird** by Ashley Bryan (Atheneum Books for Young Readers)

Honor Books

Almost to Freedom by Colin Bootman (Carolrhoda Books/Lerner Publishing Group)

Thunder Rose by Kadir Nelson (Silver Whistle/Harcourt)

2005 *Author Award Winner:* **Remember: The Journey to School Integration** by Toni Morrison (Houghton Mifflin)

Honor Books

The Legend of Buddy Bush by Shelia P. Moses (Margaret K. McElderry Books/Simon & Schuster)

Who Am I Without Him?: Short Stories About Girls and the Boys in Their Lives by Sharon G. Flake (Jump at the Sun/Hyperion Books for Children)

Fortune's Bones: The Manumission Requiem by Marilyn Nelson (Front Street)

Illustrator Award Winner: **Ellington Was Not a Street** by Kadir Nelson (Simon & Schuster)

Honor Books

God Bless the Child illustrated by Jerry Pinkney, written by Billie Holiday and Arthur Herzog, Jr. (Amistad/HarperCollins)

The People Could Fly: The Picture Book illustrated by Leo and Diane Dillon, written by Virginia Hamilton (Alfred A. Knopf/Random House)

2006 *Author Award Winner:* **Day of Tears: A Novel in Dialogue** by Julius Lester (Jump at the Sun; Reprint edition)

Honor Books

Maritcha: A Nineteenth-Century American Girl by Tonya Bolden (Harry N. Abrams)

Dark Sons by Nikki Grimes (Jump at the Sun)

A Wreath for Emmett Till by Marilyn Nelson, illustrated by Philippe Lardy(Houghton Mifflin)

Illustrator Awards

Rosa by Nikki Giovanni, illustrated by Bryan Collier (Henry Holt and Co. (BYR))

Brothers in Hope: The Story of the Lost Boys of Sudan written and illustrated by R. Gregory Christie (Lee & Low Books)

New Talent: **Jimi & Me** by Jaime Adoff (Jump At The Sun)

2007 *Author Winner:* **Copper Sun** by Sharon M. Draper (Atheneum)

Honor Book: **The Road to Paris** by Nikki Grimes (Putnam Juvenile)

Illustrator Award Winner: **Moses: When Harriet Tubman Led Her People to Freedom** illustrated by Kadir Nelson, written by Carole Boston Weatherford (Jump At The Sun)

Jazz illustrated by Christopher Myers, written by Walter Dean (Holiday House)

Poetry for Young People: Langston Hughes edited by David Roessel and Arnold Rampersad, illustrated by Benny Andrews (Sterling)

New Talent: **Standing Against the Wind** by Traci L. Jones (Farrar, Straus, & Giroux (BYR))

2008 *Author Award:* **Elijah of Buxton** by Christopher Paul Curtis (Scholastic Press)

Honor Books

November Blues by Sharon M. Draper (Atheneum)

Twelve Rounds to Glory: The Story of Muhammad Ali by Charles R. Smith Jr., illustrated by Bryan Collier (Candlewick)

Illustrator Award: **Let it Shine** by Ashley Bryan (Atheneum)

The Secret Olivia Told Me written by N. Joy, illustrated by Nancy Devard (Just Us Books, Inc.)

Jazz On A Saturday Night by Leo and Diane Dillon (The Blue Sky Press)

New Talent: **Brendan Buckley's Universe and Everything in It** by Sundee T. Frazier (Delacorte Books for Young Readers)

2009 *Author Award:* **We Are the Ship: The Story of Negro League Baseball** written and illustrated by Kadir Nelson (Hyperion Book CH)

Honor Books

The Blacker the Berry by Joyce Carol Thomas, illustrated by Floyd Cooper (Amistad)

Keeping the Night Watch by Hope Anita Smith, illustrated by E. B. Lewis (Henry Holt and Co.)

Becoming Billie Holiday by Carole Weatherford, illustrated by Floyd Cooper (Wordsong; Library Binding edition)

Illustrator Award: **The Blacker the Berry** by Joyce Carol Thomas, illustrated by Floyd Cooper (Amistad)

We Are the Ship: The Story of Negro League Baseball written and illustrated by Kadir Nelson (Hyperion Book CH)

Before John Was a Jazz Giant: A Song of John Coltrane by Carole Boston Weatherford, illustrated by Sean Qualls (Henry Holt and Co.)

The Moon Over Star by Dianna Hutts Aston, illustrated by Jerry Pinkney (Dial)

New Talent: Shadra Strickland, illustrator of **Bird** by Zetta Elliott (Lee & Low Books)

2010 *Author Award:* **Bad News for Outlaws: The Remarkable Life of Bass Reeves, Deputy U.S. Marshal** by Vaunda Micheaux Nelson, illustrated by R. Gregory Christie (Carolrhoda Books, a division of Lerner Publishing Group, Inc.)

Honor Book

Mare's War by tanita s. davis (Alfred A. Knopf, an imprint of Random House Children's Books, a division of Random House, Inc.)

Illustrator Award: **My People** by Langston Hughes, illustrated by Charles R. Smith Jr. (Ginee Seo Books, Atheneum Books for Young Readers)

Honor Book

The Negro Speaks of Rivers by Langston Hughes, illustrated by E. B. Lewis (Disney-Jump at the Sun Books, an imprint of Disney Book Group)

New Talent: **The Rock and the River** by Kekla Magoon (Aladdin, an imprint of Simon & Schuster Children's Publishing Division)

Coretta Scott King-Virginia Hamilton Award for Lifetime Achievement: Walter Dean Myers, whose books include: **Amiri & Odette: A Love Story**, published by Scholastic Press, an imprint of Scholastic; **Fallen Angels**, published by Scholastic Press; **Monster**, published by Amistad and HarperTeen, imprints of HarperCollins Publishers; and **Sunrise Over Fallujah**, published by Scholastic Press.

National Council of Teachers of English (NCTE) Award for Excellence in Poetry for Children

This award was given annually from 1977 to 1982 and every three years after that to a living American poet in recognition of his or her entire body of work for children ages three through thirteen.

1977 David McCord

1978 Aileen Fisher

1979 Karla Kushin

1980 Myra Cohn Livingston

1981 Eve Merriam

1982 John Ciardi

1985 Lilian Moore

1988 Arnold Adoff

1991 Valerie Worth

1994 Barbara Juster Esbensen

1997 Eloise Greenfield

2000 X. J. Kennedy

2003 Mary Ann Hoberman

2006 Nikki Grimes

2009 Lee Bennett Hopkins

John Newbery Medal

The John Newbery Medal has been awarded annually since 1922 under the supervision of the ALA's Association for Library Service to Children. It is presented to the author of the work judged to be the most distinguished contribution to literature for children published in the United States during the previous year. One or more Honor Books are also chosen. Winners must be residents or citizens of the United States.

1922 **The Story of Mankind** by Hendrik Willem van Loon (Liveright)

Honor Books

Cedric the Forester by Bernard Marshall (Appleton)

The Golden Fleece and the Heroes Who Lived before Achilles by Padraic Colum (Macmillan)

The Great Quest by Charles Hawes (Little, Brown)

The Old Tobacco Shop by William Bowen (Macmillan)

Windy Hill by Cornelia Meigs (Macmillan)

1923 **The Voyages of Doctor Dolittle** by Hugh Lofting (Lippincott)

Honor Book No record

1924 **The Dark Frigate** by Charles Hawes (Atlantic/Little, Brown)

Honor Book No record

1925 **Tales from Silver Lands** by Charles Finger (Doubleday)

Honor Books

Dream Coach by Anne Parrish (Macmillan)

Nicholas by Anne Carroll Moore (Putnam)

1926 **Shen of the Sea** by Arthur Bowie Chrisman (Dutton)

Honor Book: **Voyagers** by Padraic Colum (Macmillan)

1927 **Smoky, the Cowhorse** by Will James (Scribner's)

Honor Book No record

1928 **Gayneck, the Story of a Pigeon** by Dhan Gopal Mukerji (Dutton)

Honor Books

Downright Dencey by Caroline Snedeker (Doubleday)

The Wonder Smith and His Son by Ella Young (Longmans)

1929 **The Trumpeter of Krakow** by Eric P. Kelly (Macmillan)

Honor Books

The Boy Who Was by Grace Hallock (Dutton)

Clearing Weather by Cornelia Meigs (Little, Brown)

Millions of Cats by Wanda Gág (Coward)

Pigtail of Ah Lee Ben Loo by John Bennett (Longmans)

Runaway Papoose by Grace Moon (Doubleday)

Tod of the Fens by Elinor Whitney (Macmillan)

1930 *Hitty, Her First Hundred Years* by Rachel Field (Macmillan)

Honor Books

Daughter of the Seine by Jeanette Eaton (Harper)

Jumping-Off Place by Marian Hurd McNeely (Longmans)

Little Blacknose by Hildegarde Swift (Harcourt)

Pran of Albania by Elizabeth Miller (Doubleday)

Tangle-Coated Horse and Other Tales by Ella Young (Longmans)

Vaino by Julia Davis Adams (Dutton)

1931 *The Cat Who Went to Heaven* by Elizabeth Coatsworth (Macmillan)

Honor Books

The Dark Star of Itza by Alida Malkus (Harcourt)

Floating Island by Anne Parrish (Harper)

Garram the Hunter by Herbert Best (Doubleday)

Meggy Macintosh by Elizabeth Janet Gray (Doubleday)

Mountains Are Free by Julia Davis Adams (Dutton)

Ood-Le-Uk the Wanderer by Alice Lide and Margaret Johansen (Little, Brown)

Queer Person by Ralph Hubbard (Doubleday)

Spice and the Devil's Cake by Agnes Hewes (Knopf)

1932 *Waterless Mountain* by Laura Adams Armer (Longmans)

Honor Books

Boy of the South Seas by Eunice Tietjens (Coward)

Calico Bush by Rachel Field (Macmillan)

The Fairy Circus by Dorothy P. Lathrop (Macmillan)

Jane's Island by Marjorie Allee (Houghton Mifflin)

Out of the Flames by Eloise Lownsbery (Longmans)

Truce of the Wolf and Other Tales of Old Italy by Mary Gould Davis (Harcourt)

1933 *Young Fu of the Upper Yangtze* by Elizabeth Lewis (Winston)

Honor Books

Children of the Soil by Nora Burglon (Doubleday)

The Railroad to Freedom by Hildegarde Swift (Harcourt)

Swift Rivers by Cornelia Meigs (Little, Brown)

1934 *Invincible Louisa* by Cornelia Meigs (Little, Brown)

Honor Books

ABC Bunny by Wanda Gág (Coward)

Apprentice of Florence by Anne Kyle (Houghton Mifflin)

Big Tree of Bunlahy by Padraic Colum (Macmillan)

The Forgotten Daughter by Caroline Snedeker (Doubleday)

Glory of the Seas by Agnes Hewes (Knopf)

New Land by Sarah Schmidt (McBride)

Swords of Steel by Elsie Singmaster (Houghton Mifflin)

Winged Girl of Knossos by Erik Berry (Appleton)

1935 *Dobry* by Monica Shannon (Viking)

Honor Books

Davy Crockett by Constance Rourke (Harcourt)

Day on Skates by Hilda Van Stockum (Harper)

Pageant of Chinese History by Elizabeth Seeger (Longmans)

1936 *Caddie Woodlawn* by Carol Ryrie Brink (Macmillan)

Honor Books

All Sail Set by Armstrong Sperry (Winston)

The Good Master by Kate Seredy (Viking)

Honk, The Moose by Phil Strong (Dodd)

Young Walter Scott by Elizabeth Janet Gray (Viking)

1937 *Roller Skates* by Ruth Sawyer (Viking)

Honor Books

Audubon by Constance Rourke (Harcourt)

The Codfish Musket by Agnes Hewes (Doubleday)

Golden Basket by Ludwig Bemelmans (Viking)

Phebe Fairchild: Her Book by Lois Lenski (Stokes)

Whistler's Van by Idwal Jones (Viking)

Winterbound by Margery Bianco (Viking)

1938 *The White Stag* by Kate Seredy (Viking)

Honor Books

Bright Island by Mabel Robinson (Random House)

On the Banks of Plum Creek by Laura Ingalls Wilder (Harper)

Pecos Bill by James Cloyd Bowman (Little, Brown)

1939 *Thimble Summer* by Elizabeth Enright (Rinehart)

Honor Books

Hello the Boat! by Phyllis Crawford (Holt)

Leader by Destiny: George Washington, Man and Patriot by Jeanette Eaton (Harcourt)

Mr. Popper's Penguins by Richard and Florence Atwater (Little, Brown)

Nino by Valenti Angelo (Viking)

Penn by Elizabeth Janet Gray (Viking)

1940 *Daniel Boone* by James Daugherty (Viking)

Honor Books

Boy with a Pack by Stephen W. Meader (Harcourt)

By the Shores of Silver Lake by Laura Ingalls Wilder (Harper)

Runner of the Mountain Tops by Mabel Robinson (Random House)

The Singing Tree by Kate Seredy (Viking)

1941 *Call It Courage* by Armstrong Sperry (Macmillan)

Honor Books

Blue Willow by Doris Gates (Viking)

The Long Winter by Laura Ingalls Wilder (Harper)

Nansen by Anna Gertrude Hall (Viking)

Young Mac of Fort Vancouver by Mary Jane Carr (Crowell)

1942 *The Matchlock Gun* by Walter D. Edmonds (Dodd)

Honor Books

Down Ryton Water by Eva Roe Gaggin (Viking)

George Washington's World by Genevieve Foster (Scribner's)

Indian Captive: The Story of Mary Jemison by Lois Lenski (Lippincott)

Little Town on the Prairie by Laura Ingalls Wilder (Harper)

1943 *Adam of the Road* by Elizabeth Janet Gray (Viking)

Honor Books

Have You Seen Tom Thumb? by Mabel Leigh Hunt (Lippincott)

The Middle Moffat by Eleanor Estes (Harcourt)

1944 *Johnny Tremain* by Esther Forbes (Houghton Mifflin)

Honor Books

Fog Magic by Julia Sauer (Viking)

Mountain Born by Elizabeth Yates (Coward)

Rufus M. by Eleanor Estes (Harcourt)

These Happy Golden Years by Laura Ingalls Wilder (Harper)

1945 *Rabbit Hill* by Robert Lawson (Viking)

Honor Books

Abraham Lincoln's World by Genevieve Foster (Scribner's)

The Hundred Dresses by Eleanor Estes (Harcourt)

Lone Journey: The Life of Roger Williams by Jeanette Eaton (Harcourt)

The Silver Pencil by Alice Dalgliesh (Scribner's)

1946 *Strawberry Girl* by Lois Lenski (Lippincott)

Honor Books

Bhimsa, the Dancing Bear by Christine Weston (Scribner's)

Justin Morgan Had a Horse by Marguerite Henry (Rand McNally)

The Moved-Outers by Florence Crannell Means (Houghton Mifflin)

New Found World by Katherine Shippen (Viking)

1947 *Miss Hickory* by Carolyn Sherwin Bailey (Viking)

Honor Books

The Avion My Uncle Flew by Cyrus Fisher (Appleton)

Big Tree by Mary and Conrad Buff (Viking)

The Heavenly Tenants by William Maxwell (Harper)

The Hidden Treasure of Glaston by Eleanore Jewett (Viking)

Wonderful Year by Nancy Barnes (Messner)

1948 *The Twenty-One Balloons* by William Pène du Bois (Viking)

Honor Books

The Cow-Tail Switch and Other West African Stories by Harold Courlander (Holt)

Li Lun, Lad of Courage by Carolyn Treffinger (Abingdon)

Misty of Chincoteague by Marguerite Henry (Rand McNally)

Pancakes-Paris by Claire Huchet Bishop (Viking)

The Quaint and Curious Quest of Johnny Longfoot by Catherine Besterman (Bobbs)

1949 *King of the Wind* by Marguerite Henry (Rand McNally)

Honor Books

Daughter of the Mountains by Louise Rankin (Viking)

My Father's Dragon by Ruth S. Gannett (Random House)

Seabird by Holling C. Holling (Houghton Mifflin)

Story of the Negro by Arna Bontemps (Knopf)

1950 *A Door in the Wall* by Marguerite de Angeli (Doubleday)

Honor Books

The Blue Cat of Castle Town by Catherine Coblentz (Longmans)

George Washington by Genevieve Foster (Scribner's)

Kildee House by Rutherford Montgomery (Doubleday)

Song of the Pines by Walter and Marion Havighurst (Winston)

Tree of Freedom by Rebecca Caudill (Viking)

1951 *Amos Fortune, Free Man* by Elizabeth Yates (Dutton)

Honor Books

Abraham Lincoln, Friend of the People by Clara Ingram Judson (Follett)

Better Known as Johnny Appleseed by Mabel Leigh Hunt (Lippincott)

Gandhi, Fighter without a Sword by Jeanette Eaton (Morrow)

The Story of Appleby Capple by Anne Parrish (Harper)

1952 *Ginger Pye* by Eleanor Estes (Harcourt)

Honor Books

Americans before Columbus by Elizabeth Baity (Viking)

The Apple and the Arrow by Mary and Conrad Buff (Houghton Mifflin)

The Defender by Nicholas Kalashnikoff (Scribner's)

The Light at Tern Rocks by Julia Sauer (Viking)

Minn of the Mississippi by Holling C. Holling (Houghton Mifflin)

1953 *Secret of the Andes* by Ann Nolan Clark (Viking)

Honor Books

The Bears of Hemlock Mountain by Alice Dalgliesh (Scribner's)

Birthdays of Freedom, Vol. 1 by Genevieve Foster (Scribner's)

Charlotte's Web by E. B. White (Harper)

Moccasin Trail by Eloise McGraw (Coward)

Red Sails to Capri by Ann Weil (Viking)

1954 *. . . And Now Miguel* by Joseph Krumgold (Crowell)

Honor Books

All Alone by Claire Huchet Bishop (Viking)

Hurry Home Candy by Meindert DeJong (Harper)

Magic Maize by Mary and Conrad Buff (Houghton Mifflin)

Shadrach by Meindert DeJong (Harper)

Theodore Roosevelt, Fighting Patriot by Clara Ingram Judson (Follett)

1955   *The Wheel on the School* by Meindert DeJong (Harper)

Honor Books

Banner in the Sky by James Ullman (Lippincott)

Courage of Sarah Noble by Alice Dalgliesh (Scribner's)

1956   *Carry On, Mr. Bowditch* by Jean Lee Latham (Houghton Mifflin)

Honor Books

The Golden Name Day by Jennie Lindquist (Harper)

Men, Microscopes, and Living Things by Katherine Shippen (Viking)

The Secret River by Marjorie Kinnan Rawlings (Scribner's)

1957   *Miracles on Maple Hill* by Virginia Sorensen (Harcourt)

Honor Books

Black Fox of Lorne by Marguerite de Angeli (Doubleday)

The Corn Grows Ripe by Dorothy Rhoads (Viking)

The House of Sixty Fathers by Meindert DeJong (Harper)

Mr. Justice Holmes by Clara Ingram Judson (Follett)

Old Yeller by Fred Gipson (Harper)

1958   *Rifles for Watie* by Harold Keith (Crowell)

Honor Books

Gone-Away Lake by Elizabeth Enright (Harcourt)

The Great Wheel by Robert Lawson (Viking)

The Horse Catcher by Mari Sandoz (Westminster)

Tom Paine, Freedom's Apostle by Leo Gurko (Crowell)

1959   *The Witch of Blackbird Pond* by Elizabeth George Speare (Houghton Mifflin)

Honor Books

Along Came a Dog by Meindert DeJong (Harper)

Chucaro: Wild Pony of the Pampa by Francis Kalnay (Harcourt)

The Family under the Bridge by Natalie Savage Carlson (Harper)

The Perilous Road by William O. Steele (Harcourt)

1960   *Onion John* by Joseph Krumgold (Crowell)

Honor Books

America Is Born by Gerald W. Johnson (Morrow)

The Gammage Cup by Carol Kendall (Harcourt)

My Side of the Mountain by Jean Craighead George (Dutton)

1961   *Island of the Blue Dolphins* by Scott O'Dell (Houghton Mifflin)

Honor Books

America Moves Forward by Gerald W. Johnson (Morrow)

The Cricket in Times Square by George Selden (Farrar)

Old Ramon by Jack Schaefer (Houghton Mifflin)

1962   *The Bronze Bow* by Elizabeth George Speare (Houghton Mifflin)

Honor Books

Belling the Tiger by Mary Stolz (Harper)

Frontier Living by Edwin Tunis (World)

The Golden Goblet by Eloise McGraw (Coward)

1963   *A Wrinkle in Time* by Madeleine L'Engle (Farrar)

Honor Books

Men of Athens by Olivia Coolidge (Houghton Mifflin)

Thistle and Thyme by Sorche Nic Leodhas (Holt)

1964   *It's Like This, Cat* by Emily Cheney Neville (Harper)

Honor Books

The Loner by Ester Wier (McKay)

Rascal by Sterling North (Dutton)

1965   *Shadow of a Bull* by Maia Wojciechowska (Atheneum)

Honor Book: Across Five Aprils by Irene Hunt (Follett)

1966   *I, Juan de Pareja* by Elizabeth Borten de Trevino (Farrar)

Honor Books

The Animal Family by Randall Jarrell (Pantheon)

The Black Cauldron by Lloyd Alexander (Holt)

The Noonday Friends by Mary Stolz (Harper)

1967   *Up a Road Slowly* by Irene Hunt (Follett)

Honor Books

The Jazz Man by Mary H. Weik (Atheneum)

The King's Fifth by Scott O'Dell (Houghton)

Zlateh the Goat and Other Stories by Isaac Bashevis Singer (Harper)

1968   *From the Mixed-Up Files of Mrs. Basil E. Frankweiler* by E. L. Konigsburg (Atheneum)

Honor Books

The Black Pearl by Scott O'Dell (Houghton Mifflin)

The Egypt Game by Zilpha Keatley Snyder (Atheneum)

The Fearsome Inn by Isaac Bashevis Singer (Scribner's)

Jennifer, Hecate, Macbeth, William McKinley, and Me, Elizabeth by E. L. Konigsburg (Atheneum)

1969   *The High King* by Lloyd Alexander (Holt)

Honor Books

To Be a Slave by Julius Lester (Dial)

When Sheemiel Went to Warsaw and Other Stories by Isaac Bashevis Singer (Farrar)

1970   *Sounder* by William H. Armstrong (Harper)

Honor Books

Journey Outside by Mary Q. Steele (Viking)

The Many Ways of Seeing: An Introduction to the Pleasures of Art by Janet Gaylord Moore (World)

Our Eddie by Sulamith Ish-Kishor (Pantheon)

1971   *Summer of the Swans* by Betsy Byars (Viking)

Honor Books

Enchantress from the Stars by Sylvia Louise Engdahl (Atheneum)

Knee-Knock Rise by Natalie Babbitt (Farrar)

Sing Down the Moon by Scott O'Dell (Houghton Mifflin)

1972 *Mrs. Frisby and the Rats of NIMH* by Robert C. O'Brien (Atheneum)

Honor Books

Annie and the Old One by Miska Miles (Atlantic/Little, Brown)

The Headless Cupid by Zilpha Keatley Snyder (Atheneum)

Incident at Hawk's Hill by Allan W. Eckert (Little, Brown)

The Planet of Junior Brown by Virginia Hamilton (Macmillan)

The Tombs of Atuan by Ursula K. Le Guin (Atheneum)

1973 *Julie of the Wolves* by Jean Craighead George (Harper)

Honor Books

Frog and Toad Together by Arnold Lobel (Harper)

The Upstairs Room by Johanna Reiss (Crowell)

The Witches of Worm by Zilpha Keatley Snyder (Atheneum)

1974 *The Slave Dancer* by Paula Fox (Bradbury)

Honor Book: The Dark Is Rising by Susan Cooper (McElderry)

1975 *M. C. Higgins, the Great* by Virginia Hamilton (Macmillan)

Honor Books

Figgs and Phantoms by Ellen Raskin (Dutton)

My Brother Sam Is Dead by James Lincoln Collier and Christopher Collier (Four Winds)

The Perilous Gard by Elizabeth Marie Pope (Houghton Mifflin)

Philip Hall Likes Me, I Reckon Maybe by Bette Greene (Dial)

1976 *The Grey King* by Susan Cooper (McElderry)

Honor Books

Dragonwings by Laurence Yep (Harper)

The Hundred Penny Box by Sharon Bell Mathis (Viking)

1977 *Roll of Thunder, Hear My Cry* by Mildred D. Taylor (Dial)

Honor Books

Abel's Island by William Steig (Farrar)

A String in the Harp by Nancy Bond (McElderry)

1978 *Bridge to Terabithia* by Katherine Paterson (Crowell)

Honor Books

Anpao: An American Indian Odyssey by Jamake Highwater (Lippincott)

Ramona and Her Father by Beverly Cleary (Morrow)

1979 *The Westing Game* by Ellen Raskin (Dutton)

Honor Book: The Great Gilly Hopkins by Katherine Paterson (Crowell)

1980 *A Gathering of Days: A New England Girl's Journal, 1830–1832* by Joan W. Blos (Scribner's)

Honor Book: The Road from Home: The Story of an Armenian Girl by David Kherdian (Greenwillow)

1981 *Jacob Have I Loved* by Katherine Paterson (Crowell)

Honor Books

The Fledgling by Jane Langton (Harper)

A Ring of Endless Light by Madeleine L'Engle (Farrar)

1982 *A Visit to William Blake's Inn: Poems for Innocent and Experienced Travelers* by Nancy Willard, illustrated by Alice and Martin Provensen (Harcourt)

Honor Books

Ramona Quimby, Age 8 by Beverly Cleary (Morrow)

Upon the Head of the Goat: A Childhood in Hungary, 1939–1944 by Aranka Siegal (Farrar)

1983 *Dicey's Song* by Cynthia Voigt (Atheneum)

Honor Books

The Blue Sword by Robin McKinley (Greenwillow)

Doctor De Soto by William Steig (Farrar)

Graven Images by Paul Fleischman (Harper)

Homesick: My Own Story by Jean Fritz (Putnam)

Sweet Whispers, Brother Rush by Virginia Hamilton (Philomel)

1984 *Dear Mr. Henshaw* by Beverly Cleary (Morrow)

Honor Books

The Sign of the Beaver by Elizabeth George Speare (Houghton Mifflin)

A Solitary Blue by Cynthia Voigt (Atheneum)

Sugaring Time by Kathryn Lasky (Macmillan)

The Wish Giver by Bill Brittain (Harper)

1985 *The Hero and the Crown* by Robin McKinley (Greenwillow)

Honor Books

Like Jake and Me by Mavis Jukes (Knopf)

The Moves Make the Man by Bruce Brooks (Harper)

One-Eyed Cat by Paula Fox (Bradbury)

1986 *Sarah, Plain and Tall* by Patricia MacLachlan (Harper)

Honor Books

Commodore Perry in the Land of the Shogun by Rhoda Blumberg (Lothrop)

Dogsong by Gary Paulsen (Bradbury)

1987 *The Whipping Boy* by Sid Fleischman (Greenwillow)

Honor Books

A Fine White Dust by Cynthia Rylant (Bradbury)

On My Honor by Marion Dane Bauer (Clarion)

Volcano: The Eruption and Healing of Mount St. Helens by Patricia Lauber (Bradbury)

1988 *Lincoln: A Photobiography* by Russell Freedman (Clarion)

Honor Books

After the Rain by Norma Fox Mazer (Morrow)

Hatchet by Gary Paulsen (Bradbury)

1989 *Joyful Noise: Poems for Two Voices* by Paul Fleischman (Harper)

Honor Books

In the Beginning: Creation Stories from Around the World by Virginia Hamilton (Harcourt)

Scorpions by Walter Dean Myers (Harper)

1990   *Number the Stars* by Lois Lowry (Houghton Mifflin)

Honor Books

Afternoon of the Elves by Janet Taylor Lisle (Orchard)

Shabanu: Daughter of the Wind by Suzanne Fisher Staples (Knopf)

The Winter Room by Gary Paulsen (Orchard)

1991   *Maniac Magee* by Jerry Spinelli (Little, Brown)

Honor Book: The True Confessions of Charlotte Doyle by Avi (Orchard)

1992   *Shiloh* by Phyllis Reynolds Naylor (Atheneum)

Honor Books

Nothing but the Truth: A Documentary Novel by Avi (Orchard)

The Wright Brothers: How They Invented the Airplane by Russell Freedman (Holiday House)

1993   *Missing May* by Cynthia Rylant (Orchard)

Honor Books

The Dark-Thirty: Southern Tales of the Supernatural by Patricia McKissack (Knopf)

Somewhere in the Darkness by Walter Dean Myers (Scholastic)

What Hearts by Bruce Brooks (HarperCollins)

1994   *The Giver* by Lois Lowry (Houghton Mifflin)

Honor Books

Crazy Lady! by Jane Leslie Conly (HarperCollins)

Dragon's Gate by Laurence Yep (HarperCollins)

Eleanor Roosevelt: A Life of Discovery by Russell Freedman (Clarion)

1995   *Walk Two Moons* by Sharon Creech (HarperCollins)

Honor Books

Catherine, Called Birdy by Karen Cushman (Clarion)

The Ear, the Eye and the Arm by Nancy Farmer (Richard Jackson/Orchard)

1996   *The Midwife's Apprentice* by Karen Cushman (Clarion)

Honor Books

What Jamie Saw by Carolyn Coman (Front Street)

The Watsons Go to Birmingham—1963 by Christopher Paul Curtis (Delacorte)

Yolonda's Genius by Carol Fenner (McElderry/Simon & Schuster)

The Great Fire by Jim Murphy (Scholastic)

1997   *The View from Saturday* by E. L. Konigsburg (Jean Karl/Atheneum)

Honor Books

A Girl Named Disaster by Nancy Farmer (Richard Jackson/Orchard)

Moorchild by Elois McGraw (McElderry)

The Thief by Megan Whalen Turner (Greenwillow)

Belle Prater's Boy by Ruth White (Farrar)

1998   *Out of the Dust* by Karen Hesse (Scholastic)

Honor Books

Ella Enchanted by Gail Carson Levine (HarperCollins)

Lily's Crossing by Patricia Reilly Giff (Delacorte)

Wringer by Jerry Spinelli (HarperCollins)

1999   *Holes* by Louis Sachar (Foster/Farrar)

Honor Book: A Long Way from Chicago by Richard Peck (Dial)

2000   *Bud, Not Buddy* by Christopher Paul Curtis (Delacorte)

Honor Books

Getting Near to Baby by Audrey Couloumbis (Putnam)

Our Only May Amelia by Jennifer L. Holm (HarperCollins)

26 Fairmount Avenue by Tomie dePaola (Putnam)

2001   *A Year Down Yonder* by Richard Peck (Dial)

Honor Books

Because of Winn-Dixie by Kate DiCamillo (Candlewick Press)

Hope Was Here by Joan Bauer (Putnam)

Joey Pigza Loses Control by Jack Gantos (Farrar, Straus, & Giroux)

The Wanderer by Sharon Creech (Joanne Cotler/HarperCollins)

2002   *A Single Shard* by Linda Sue Park (Clarion Books/Houghton Mifflin)

Honor Books

Everything on a Waffle by Polly Horvath (Farrar, Straus, & Giroux)

Carver: A Life In Poems by Marilyn Nelson (Front Street)

2003   *Crispin: The Cross of Lead* by Avi (Hyperion Books for Children)

Honor Books

The House of the Scorpion by Nancy Farmer (Atheneum)

Pictures of Hollis Woods by Patricia Reilly Giff (Random House/Wendy Lamb Books)

Hoot by Carl Hiaasen (Knopf)

A Corner of The Universe by Ann M. Martin (Scholastic)

Surviving the Applewhites by Stephanie S. Tolan (HarperCollins)

2004   *The Tale of Despereaux: Being the Story of a Mouse, a Princess, Some Soup, and a Spool of Thread* by Kate DiCamillo, illustrated by Timothy Basil Ering (Candlewick Press)

Honor Books

Olive's Ocean by Kevin Henkes (Greenwillow Books)

An American Plague: The True and Terrifying Story of the Yellow Fever Epidemic of 1793 by Jim Murphy (Clarion Books)

2005   *Kira-Kira* by Cynthia Kadohota (Atheneum/Simon & Schuster)

Honor Books

Lizzie Bright and the Buckminster Boy by Gary D. Schmidt (Clarion/Houghton Mifflin)

Al Capone Does My Shirts by Gennifer Choldenko (Putnam)

The Voice that Challenged a Nation: Marian Anderson and the Struggle for Equal Rights by Russell Freedman (Clarion/Houghton Mifflin)

2006 *Criss Cross* by Lynne Rae Perkins (Greenwillow Books/HarperCollins)

Honor Books

Whittington by Alan Armstrong, illustrated by S. D. Schindler (Random House)

Hitler Youth: Growing Up in Hitler's Shadow by Susan Campbell Bartoletti (Scholastic)

Princess Academy by Shannon Hale (Bloomsbury Children's Books)

Show Way by Jacqueline Woodson, illustrated by Hudson Talbott (G.P. Putnam's Sons)

2007 *The Higher Power of Lucky* by Susan Patron, illustrated by Matt Phelan (Simon & Schuster/Richard Jackson)

Honor Books

Penny from Heaven by Jennifer L. Holm (Random House)

Hattie Big Sky by Kirby Larson (Delacorte Press)

Rules by Cynthia Lord (Scholastic)

2008 *Good Masters! Sweet Ladies! Voices from a Medieval Village* by Laura Amy Schlitz (Candlewick)

Honor Books

Elijah of Buxton by Christopher Paul Curtis (Scholastic)

The Wednesday Wars by Gary D. Schmidt (Clarion)

Feathers by Jacqueline Woodson (Putnam)

2009 *The Graveyard Book* by Neil Gaiman (HarperCollins)

Honor Books

The Underneath by Kathi Appelt (Atheneum Books for Young Readers, an imprint of Simon & Schuster)

The Surrender Tree: Poems of Cuba's Struggle for Freedom by Margarita Engle (Henry Holt)

Savvy by Ingrid Law (Dial Books for Young Readers, a division of Penguin Young Readers Group in partnership with Walden Media)

After Tupac & D Foster by Jacqueline Woodson (G.P. Putnam's Sons, a division of Penguin Books for Young Readers)

2010 *You Reach Me* by Rebecca Stead (Wendy Lamb Books, an imprint of Random House Children's Books)

Honor Books

Claudette Colvin: Twice Toward Justice by Phillip Hoose (Melanie Kroupa Books/Farrar, Straus, & Giroux, an imprint of Macmillan Children's Publishing Group)

The Evolution of Calpurnia Tate by Jacqueline Kelly (Henry Holt and Company)

Where the Mountain Meets the Moon by Grace Lin (Little, Brown and Company Books for Young Readers)

The Mostly True Adventures of Homer P. Figg by Rodman Philbrick (The Blue Sky Press, An Imprint of Scholastic Inc.)

Orbis Pictus Award for Outstanding Nonfiction for Children

The National Council of Teachers of English (NCTE) established the Orbis Pictus Award in 1990 to recognize outstanding nonfiction for children. The annual award is named for *Orbis Pictus* (*The World in Pictures*), a 1657 work by John Amos Comenius, believed to be the first book written expressly for children.

1990 *The Great Little Madison* by Jean Fritz (Putnam)

Honor Books

The Great American Gold Rush by Rhoda Blumberg (Bradbury)

The News about Dinosaurs by Patricia Lauber (Bradbury)

1991 *Franklin Delano Roosevelt* by Russell Freedman (Clarion)

Honor Books

Arctic Memories by Normee Ekoomiak (Holt)

Seeing Earth from Space by Patricia Lauber (Orchard)

1992 *Flight: The Journey of Charles Lindbergh* by Robert Burleigh and Mike Wimmer (Philomel)

Honor Books

Now Is Your Time! The African American Struggle for Freedom by Walter Dean Myers (HarperCollins)

Prairie Visions: The Life and Times of Solomon Butcher by Pam Conrad (HarperCollins)

1993 *Children of the Dust Bowl: The True Story of the School of Weedpatch Camp* by Jerry Stanley (Crown)

Honor Books

Talking with Artists by Pat Cummings (Bradbury)

Come Back, Salmon by Molly Cone (Sierra Club)

1994 *Across America on an Emigrant Train* by Jim Murphy (Clarion)

Honor Books

To the Top of the World: Adventures with Arctic Wolves by Jim Brandenburg (Walker)

Making Sense: Animal Perception and Communication by Bruce Brooks (Farrar)

1995 *Safari Beneath the Sea: The Wonder World of the North Pacific Coast* by Diane Swanson (Sierra Club)

Honor Books

Wildlife Rescue: The Work of Dr. Kathleen Ramsay by Jennifer Owings Dewey (Boyds Mills)

Kids at Work: Lewis Hine and the Crusade against Child Labor by Russell Freedman (Clarion)

Christmas in the Big House, Christmas in the Quarters by Patricia and Fredrick McKissack (Scholastic)

1996 *The Great Fire* by Jim Murphy (Scholastic)

Honor Books

Dolphin Man: Exploring the World of Dolphins by Laurence Pringle, photos by Randall S. Wells (Atheneum)

Rosie the Riveter: Women Working on the Home Front in World War II by Penny Colman (Crown)

1997 *Leonardo da Vinci* by Diane Stanley (Morrow)

Honor Books

Full Steam Ahead: The Race to Build a Transcontinental Railroad by Rhoda Blumberg (National Geographic)

The Life and Death of Crazy Horse by Russell Freedman (Holiday House)

One World, Many Religions: The Ways We Worship by Mary Pope Osborne (Knopf)

1998 *An Extraordinary Life: The Story of a Monarch Butterfly* by Laurence Pringle (Orchard Books)

Honor Books

A Drop of Water: A Book of Science and Wonder by Walter Wick (Scholastic)

A Tree Is Growing by Arthur Dorros, illustrated by S. D. Schnidler (Scholastic)

Charles Lindbergh: A Human Hero by James Cross Giblin (Clarion)

Kennedy Assassinated! The World Mourns: A Reporter's Story by Wilborn Hampton (Candlewick)

Digger: The Tragic Fate of the California Indians from the Missions to the Gold Rush by Jerry Stanley (Crown)

1999 *Shipwreck at the Bottom of the World: The Extraordinary True Story of Shackleton and the Endurance* by Jennifer Armstrong (Crown)

Honor Books

Black Whiteness: Admiral Byrd Alone in the Antarctic by Robert Burleigh, illustrated by Walter Lyon Krudop (Atheneum)

Fossil Feud: The Rivalry of the First American Dinosaur Hunters by Thom Holmes (Messner)

Hottest, Coldest, Highest, Deepest by Steve Jenkins (Houghton)

No Pretty Pictures: A Child of War by Anita Lobel (Greenwillow)

2000 *Through My Eyes* by Ruby Bridges (Scholastic)

Honor Books

At Her Majesty's Request: An African Princess in Victorian England by Walter Dean Myers (Scholastic)

Clara Schumann: Piano Virtuoso by Susanna Reich (Clarion Books)

Mapping the World by Sylvia A. Johnson (Atheneum)

The Top of the World: Climbing Mount Everest by Steve Jenkins (Houghton)

2001 *Hurry Freedom: African Americans in Gold Rush California* by Jerry Stanley (Crown)

Honor Books

The Amazing Life of Benjamin Franklin by James Cross Giblin, illustrated by Michael Dooling (Scholastic)

America's Champion Swimmer: Gertrude Ederle by David A. Adler, illustrated by Terry Widener (Gulliver Books)

Michelangelo by Diane Stanley (HarperCollins)

Osceola: Memories of a Sharecropper's Daughter by Alan B. Govenar, illustrated by Shane W. Evans (Jump at the Sun)

Wild & Swampy by Jim Amosky (HarperCollins)

2002 *Black Potatoes: The Story of the Great Irish Famine, 1845–1850* by Susan Campbell Bartoletti (Houghton)

Honor Books

The Cod's Tale by Mark Kurlansky, illustrated by S. D. Schindler (Penguin Putnam Books)

The Dinosaurs of Waterhouse Hawkins: An Illuminating History of Mr. Waterhouse Hawkins, Artist and Lecturer by Barbara Kerley, illustrated by Brian Selznick (Scholastic)

Martin's Big Words: The Life of Dr. Martin Luther King, Jr. by Doreen Rappaport, illustrated by Bryan Collier (Hyperion)

2003 *When Marian Sang: The True Recital of Marian Anderson: The Voice of a Century* by Pam Muñoz Ryan, illustrated by Brian Selznick (Scholastic)

Honor Books

Confucius: The Golden Rule by Russell Freedman, illustrated by Frederic Clement (Arthur A. Levine Books)

Emperor's Silent Army: Terracotta Warriors of Ancient China by Jane O'Connor (Viking)

Phineas Gage:A Gruesome but True Story About Brain Science by John Fleischman (Houghton)

Tenement: Immigrant Life on the Lower East Side by Raymond Bial (Houghton)

To Fly: The Story of the Wright Brothers by Wendie C. Old, illustrated by Robert Andrew Parker (Clarion)

2004 *An American Plague: The True and Terrifying Story of the Yellow Fever Epidemic of 1793* by Jim Murphy (Clarion)

Honor Books

Empire State Building: When New York Reached for the Skies by Elizabeth Mann, illustrated by Alan Witschonke (Mikaya Press)

In Defense of Liberty: The Story of America's Bill of Rights by Russell Freedman (Holiday House)

Leonardo: Beautiful Dreamer by Robert Byrd (Dutton)

The Man Who Made Time Travel by Kathryn Lasky, illustrated by Kevin Hawkes (Farrar, Straus, & Giroux)

Shutting Out the Sky: Life in the Tenements of New York, 1880–1924 by Deborah Hopkinson (Orchard Books)

2005 *York's Adventure with Lewis and Clark: An African-American's Part in the Great Expedition* by Rhoda Blumberg (HarperCollins)

Honor Books

Actual Size by Steve Jenkins (Houghton)

The Race to Save the Lord God Bird by Phillip Hoose (Farrar, Straus, & Giroux)

Secrets of the Sphinx by James Cross Giblin, illustrated by Bagram Ibatoulline (Scholastic)

Seurat and La Grande Jatte: Connecting the Dots by Robert Burleigh (Abrams Books for Young Readers)

The Voice That Challenged a Nation: Marian Anderson and the Struggle for Equal Rights by Russell Freedman (Clarion)

2006 *Children of the Great Depression* by Russell Freedman (Clarion Books)

Honor Books

ER Vets: Life in an Animal Emergency Room by Donna Jackson (Houghton Mifflin)

Forbidden Schoolhouse: The True and Dramatic Story of Prudence Crandall and Her Students by Suzanne Jurmain (Houghton Mifflin)

Genius: A Photobiography of Albert Einstein by Marfe Ferguson Delano (National Geographic)

Hitler Youth: Growing Up in Hitler's Shadow by Susan Campbell Bartoletti (Scholastic)

Mosquito Bite by Alexandra Siy and Dennis Kunkel (Charlesbridge Publishing)

2007 *Quest for the Tree Kangaroo: An Expedition to the Cloud Forest of New Guinea* by Sy Montgomery, photos by Nic Bishop (Houghton Mifflin)

Honor Books

Gregor Mendel: The Friar Who Grew Peas by Cheryl Bardoe, illustrated by Jos. A. Smith (Abrams Books for Young Readers)

Freedom Walkers: The Story of the Montgomery Bus Boycott by Russell Freedman (Holiday House)

John Muir: America's First Environmentalist by Kathryn Lasky, illustrated by Stan Fellows (Candlewick Press)

Something Out of Nothing: Marie Curie and Radium by Carla Killough McClafferty (Farrar, Straus, & Giroux)

Team Moon: How 400,000 People Landed Apollo 11 on the Moon by Catherine Thimmesh (Houghton Mifflin)

2008 *M.L.K. Journey of a King* by Tonya Bolden (Abrams Books for Children)

Honor Books

Black and White Airman: Their True History by John Fleischman (Houghton Mifflin)

Spiders by Nic Bishop (Scholastic)

Helen Keller: Her Life in Pictures by George Sullivan (Scholastic)

Muckrakers by Ann Bausum (National Geographic)

Venom by Marilyn Singer (Darby Creek Publishing)

2009 *Amelia Earhart: The Legend of the Lost Aviator* by Shelley Tanaka, llustrated by David Craig (Abrams Books for Young Readers)

Honor Books

George Washington Carver by Tonya Bolden (Abrams Books for Young Readers)

The Lincolns: A Scrapbook Look at Abraham and Mary by Candace Fleming (Schwartz & Wade Books)

Washington at Valley Forge by Russell Freedman (Holiday House)

We Are the Ship: The Story of Negro League Baseball by Kadir Nelson (Hyperion Books for Children)

When the Wolves Returned: Restoring Nature's Balance in Yellowstone by Dorothy Hinshaw Patent, illustrated by Dan and Cassie Hartman (Walker Books for Young Readers)

2010 *The Secret World of Walter Anderson* by Hester Bass, illustrated by E. B. Lewis (Candlewick Press)

Honor Books

Almost Astronauts: 13 Women Who Dared to Dream by Tanya Lee Stone (Candlewick Press)

Darwin: With Glimpses into His Private Journal and Letters by Alice B. McGinty (Houghton Mifflin Books for Children)

The Frog Scientist by Pamela S. Turner (Houghton Mifflin Books for Children)

How Many Baby Pandas? by Sandra Markle (Walker Books for Young Readers)

Noah Webster: Weaver of Words by Pegi Deitz Shea (Calkins Creek Books)

Scott O'Dell Historical Fiction Award

The Scott O'Dell Historical Fiction Award was established in 1981 and is administered by the Advisory Committee of the Bulletin of the Center for Children's Books. Books must be historical fiction, have unusual literary merit, be written by a citizen of the United States, and be set in the New World. They must have been published in the previous year by a United States publisher and must be written for children or young adults.

1984 *The Sign of the Beaver* by Elizabeth George Speare (Houghton)

1985 *The Fighting Ground* by Avi (Harper)

1986 *Sarah, Plain and Tall* by Patricia MacLachlan (Harper)

1987 *Streams to the River, River to the Sea: A Novel of Sacagawea* by Scott O'Dell (Houghton)

1988 *Charley Skedaddle* by Patricia Beatty (Morrow)

1989 *The Honorable Prison* by Lyll Becerra de Jenkins (Lodestar)

1990 *Shades of Gray* by Carolyn Reeder (Macmillan)

1991 *A Time of Troubles* by Pieter VanRaven (Atheneum)

1992 *Stepping on the Cracks* by Mary Downing Hahn (Clarion)

1993 *Morning Girl* by Michael A. Dorris (Hyperion)

1994 *Bull Run* by Paul Fleischman (HarperCollins)

1995 *Under the Blood-Red Sun* by Graham Salisbury (Harcourt)

1996 *The Bomb* by Theodore Taylor (Harcourt)

1997 *Jip: His Story* by Katherine Paterson (Clarion)

1998 *Out of the Dust* by Karen Hesse (Scholastic)

1999 *Forty Acres and Maybe a Mule* by Harriette Gillem Robinet (Atheneum)

2000 *The Art of Keeping Cool* by Janet Taylor Lisle (Simon & Schuster)

2002 *The Land* by Mildred D. Taylor (Phyllis Fogelman Books)

2003 *Trouble Don't Last* by Shelley Pearsall (Alfred A. Knopf)

2004 *A River Between Us* by Richard Peck (Dial Press)

2005 *Worth* by A. LaFaye (Simon & Schuster)

2006 *The Game of Silence* by Louise Erdrich (HarperCollins Children's Books)

2007 *The Green Glass Sea* by Ellen Klages (Viking Children's Books)

2008 *Elijah of Buxton* by Christopher Paul Curtis (Scholastic)

2009 *Chains* by Laurie Halse Anderson (Simon & Schuster)

Michael L. Printz Award for Excellence in Young Adult Literature

The Michael L. Printz Award is an award for a book that exemplifies literary excellence in young adult literature. It is named for a Topeka, Kansas, school librarian who was a long-time active member of the Young Adult Library Services Association.

2000 *Monster* by Walter Dean Myers (Scholastic)

Honor Books

Speak by Laurie Halse Anderson (Farrar, Straus, & Giroux)

Skellig by David Almond (Delacorte)

Hard Love by Ellen Wittlinger (Simon & Schuster)

2001 *Kit's Wilderness* by David Almond (Delacorte)

Honor Books

Many Stones by Carolyn Coman (Front Street)

The Body of Christopher Creed by Carol Plum-Ucci (Harcourt Brace)

Angus, Thongs, and Full Frontal Snogging: Confessions of Georgia Nicolson by Louise Rennison (HarperCollins)

Stuck in Neutral by Terry Trueman (HarperCollins)

2002 *A Step from Heaven* by An Na (Front Street)

Honor Books

The Ropemaker by Peter Dickinson (Delacorte)

Heart to Heart: New Poems Inspired by Twentieth-Century American Art by Jan Greenberg (Abrams)

Freewill by Chris Lynch (HarperCollins)

True Believer by Virginia Euwer Wolff (Atheneum)

2003 *Postcards from No Man's Land* by Aidan Chambers (Dutton/Penguin Putnam)

Honor Books

The House of the Scorpion by Nancy Farmer (Simon and Schuster/Richard Jackson)

My Heartbeat by Garret Freymann-Weyr (Houghton Mifflin Company)

Hole in My Life by Jack Gantos (Farrar, Straus, & Giroux)

2004 *The First Part Last* by Angela Johnson (Simon & Schuster Books for Young Readers)

Honor Books

A Northern Light by Jennifer Donnelly (Harcourt, Inc.)

Keesha's House by Helen Frost (Farrar, Straus, & Giroux/Frances Foster Books)

Fat Kid Rules the World by K. L. Going (G.P. Putnam's Sons/Penguin Young Readers Group)

The Earth, My Butt and Other Big Round Things by Carolyn Mackler (Candlewick Press)

2005 *How I Live Now* by Meg Rosoff (Wendy Lamb books/Random House)

Honor Books

Airborn by Kenneth Oppel (HarperCollins)

Chanda's Secret by Allan Stratton (Annick Press)

Lizzie Bright and the Buckminster Boy by Gary D. Schmidt (Clarion/Houghton Mifflin)

2006 *Looking for Alaska* by John Green (Dutton Books)

Honor Books

Black Juice by Margo Lanagan (EOS, an imprint of HarperCollins)

I Am the Messenger by Markus Zusak (Alfred A. Knopf, an imprint of Random House Children's Books)

John Lennon: All I Want Is the Truth, a Photographic Biography by Elizabeth Partridge (Viking, a member of Penguin Group (USA) Inc.)

A Wreath for Emmett Till by Marilyn Nelson (Houghton Mifflin Company)

2007 *American Born Chinese* by Gene Luen Yang (First Second, an imprint of Roaring Brook Press)

Honor Books

The Astonishing Life of Octavian Nothing, Traitor to the Nation; v. 1: The Pox Party by M. T. Anderson (Candlewick)

An Abundance of Katherines by John Green (Dutton)

Surrender by Sonya Hartnett (Candlewick Press)

The Book Thief by Markus Zusak (Alfred A. Knopf)

2008 *The White Darkness* by Geraldine McCaughrean (HarperTempest)

Honor Books

Dreamquake: Book Two of the Dreamhunter Duet by Elizabeth Knox (Frances Foster Books)

One Whole and Perfect Day by Judith Clarke (Front Street)

Repossessed by A. M. Jenkins (HarperTeen)

Your Own, Sylvia: A Verse Portrait of Sylvia Plath by Stephanie Hemphill (Alfred A. Knopf)

2009 *Jellicoe Road* by Melina Marchetta (HarperTeen, an imprint of HarperCollins Publishers)

Honor Books

The Astonishing Life of Octavian Nothing, Traitor to the Nation, Volume II, The Kingdom on the Waves by M. T. Anderson (Candlewick Press)

The Disreputable History of Frankie Landau-Banks by E. Lockhart (Disney-Hyperion, an imprint of Disney Book Group)

Nation by Terry Pratchett (HarperCollins Children's Books, a division of HarperCollins Publishers)

Tender Morsels by Margo Lanagan (Alfred A. Knopf, an imprint of Random House Children's Books)

2010 *Going Bovine* by Libba Bray (Delacorte Press, an imprint of Random House Children's Books)

Honor Books

Charles and Emma: The Darwins' Leap of Faith by Deborah Heiligman (Henry Holt Books for Young Readers, an imprint of Macmillan Children's Publishing Group)

The Monstrumologist by Rick Yancey (Simon & Schuster Books for Young Readers, an imprint of Simon & Schuster Children's Publishing Group)

Punkzilla by Adam Rapp (Candlewick Press)

Tales of the Madman Underground: An Historical Romance, 1973 by John Barnes (Viking Children's Books, a division of Penguin Young Readers Group)

The Tomás Rivera Mexican American Children's Book Award

The Tomás Rivera Mexican American Children's Book Award, established in 1995, was founded by the College of Education at Texas State University-San Marcos. It is awarded annually to honor the most distinguished book depicting the Mexican American experience. Both fiction and nonfiction selections are eligible, as are books appropriate for children ages 0 to 16 years old. Literary quality and authenticity in representation are criteria for consideration.

1996 *Chato's Kitchen* by Gary Soto, illustrated by Susan Guevara (Putnam)

1997 *The Farolitos of Christmas* by Rudolfo Anaya, illustrated by Edward Gonzalez (Hyperion)

1998 *In My Family/En Mi Familia* written and illustrated by Carmen Lomas Garza (Children's Book Press)

1999 *Tomás and the Library Lady* by Pat Mora, illustrated by Raúl Colón (Knopf)

2000 *The Three Pigs/Los Tres Cerdos: Nacho, Tito, and Miguel* written and illustrated by Bobbi Salinas (Pinata Books)

2001 *My Land Sings: Stories of the Río Grande* by Rudolfo Anaya, illustrated by Amy Cordova (Rayo Rayo Rayo)

2002 *My Very Own Room* by Amada Irma Pérez, illustrated by Maya Christina Gonzalez (Children's Book Press)

2003 *A Library for Juana* by Pat Mora, illustrated by Beatriz Vidal (Knopf)

2004 *Just a Minute: A Trickster Tale and Counting Book* written and illustrated by Yuyi Morales (Chronicle Books)

2005 *Becoming Naomi León* by Pam Muñoz Ryan

2006 *José! Born to Dance* by Susanna Reich, illustrated by Raúl Colón

2007 *Downtown Boy* by Juan Felipe Herrera

2008 *Los Gatos Black on Halloween* by Marisa Montes, illustrated by Yuyi Morales

2009 *He Forgot to Say Goodbye* by Benjamin Alire Sáenz

The Holy Tortilla and a Pot of Beans by Carmen Tafolla

Robert F. Sibert Informational Book Award

Established in 2001, the Robert F. Sibert Informational Book Award is given annually to the author of the most distinguished informational book published during the preceding year. The award is named in honor of Robert F. Sibert, the long-time president of Bound to Stay Bound Books of Jacksonville, Illinois, and is sponsored by the company. The Association for Library Service to Children, a division of the American Library Association, administers the award.

2001 *Sir Walter Ralegh and the Quest for El Dorado* by Marc Aronson (Clarion)

Honor Books

The Longitude Prize by Joan Dash, illustrated by Dusan Petricic (Frances Foster Books/Farrar, Straus, & Giroux)

Blizzard! The Storm That Changed America by Jim Murphy (Scholastic)

My Season with Penguins by Sophie Webb (Houghton Mifflin)

Pedro and Me: Friendship, Loss, and What I Learned by Judd Winick (Holt)

2002 *Black Potatoes: The Story of the Great Irish Famine, 1845–1850* by Susan Campbell Bartoletti (Houghton Mifflin)

Honor Books

Surviving Hitler: A Boy in the Nazi Death Camps by Andrea Warren (HarperCollins)

Vincent van Gogh: Portrait of an Artist by Jan Greenberg and Sandra Jordan (Delacorte)

Brooklyn Bridge by Lynn Curlee (Atheneum)

2003 *The Life and Death of Adolf Hitler* by James Cross Giblin (Clarion)

Honor Books

Six Days in October: The Stock Market Crash of 1929 by Karen Blumenthal (Atheneum Books for Young Readers)

Hole in My Life by Jack Gantos (Farrar, Straus, & Giroux)

Action Jackson by Jan Greenberg and Sandra Jordan (Roaring Brook Press)

When Marian Sang by Pam Munoz Ryan (Scholastic)

2004 *An American Plague: The True and Terrifying Story of the Yellow Fever Epidemic of 1793* by Jim Murphy (Clarion)

Honor Book: I Face the Wind by Vicki Cobb with illustrations by Julia Gorton (HarperCollins)

2005 *The Voice that Challenged a Nation: Marian Anderson and the Struggle for Equal Rights* by Russell Freedman (Clarion/Houghton Mifflin)

Honor Books

Sequoyah: The Cherokee Man Who Gave His People Writing by James Rumford, translated into Cherokee by Anna Sixkiller Huckaby (Houghton Mifflin)

The Tarantula Scientist by Sy Montgomery, photographs by Nic Bishop (Houghton Mifflin)

Walt Whitman: Words for America by Barbara Kerley, illustrated by Brian Selznick (Scholastic)

2006 *Secrets of a Civil War Submarine: Solving the Mysteries of the H. L. Hunley* by Sally M. Walker (Carolrhoda Books, Inc., a division of Lerner Publishing Group)

Honor Book: *Hitler Youth: Growing Up in Hitler's Shadow* by Susan Campbell Bartoletti (Scholastic Nonfiction, an imprint of Scholastic)

2007 *Team Moon: How 400,000 People Landed Apollo 11 on the Moon* by Catherine Thimmesh (Houghton Mifflin)

Honor Books

Freedom Riders: John Lewis and Jim Zwerg on the Front Lines of the Civil Rights Movement by Ann Bausum (National Geographic)

Quest for the Tree Kangaroo: An Expedition to the Cloud Forest of New Guinea by Sy Montgomery, photographs by Nic Bishop (Houghton Mifflin)

To Dance: A Ballerina's Graphic Novel by Siena Cherson Siegel, illustrated by Mark Siegel (Simon & Schuster/Richard Jackson and Simon & Schuster/Aladdin)

2008 *The Wall: Growing Up Behind the Iron Curtain* by Peter Sís (Farrar/Frances Foster)

Honor Books

Lightship, written and illustrated by Brian Floca (Simon & Schuster/Richard Jackson)

Nic Bishop Spiders, written and photographed by Nic Bishop (Scholastic Nonfiction, an imprint of Scholastic)

2009 *We Are the Ship: The Story of Negro League Baseball* by Kadir Nelson (Disney-Jump at the Sun, an imprint of the Disney Book Group)

Honor Books

Bodies from the Ice: Melting Glaciers and the Recovery of the Past by James M. Deem (Houghton Mifflin)

What to Do About Alice?: How Alice Roosevelt Broke the Rules, Charmed the World, and Drove Her Father Teddy Crazy! by Barbara Kerley, illustrated by Edwin Fotheringham (Scholastic Press)

2010 *Almost Astronauts: 13 Women Who Dared to Dream* by Tanya Lee Stone (Candlewick Press)

Honor Books

The Day-Glo Brothers: The True Story of Bob and Joe Switzer's Bright Ideas and Brand-New Colors by Chris Barton, illustrated by Tony Persiani (Charlesbridge)

Moonshot: The Flight of Apollo 11 written and illustrated by Brian Floca (Richard Jackson/Atheneum Books for Young Readers)

Claudette Colvin: Twice Toward Justice by Phillip Hoose (Melanie Kroupa/Farrar, Straus, & Giroux, an imprint of Macmillan Children's Publishing Group)

Laura Ingalls Wilder Award

The Laura Ingalls Wilder Award is presented to an author or an illustrator whose books are published in the United States and have made a substantial and lasting contribution to literature for children over a period of years. The award was first presented in 1954 and was given every five years from 1960 to 1980; since then, it has been given every three years.

1954 Laura Ingalls Wilder

1960 Clara Ingram Judson

1965 Ruth Sawyer

1970 E. B. White

1975 Beverly Cleary

1980 Dr. Seuss (Theodor Seuss Geisel)

1983 Maurice B. Sendak

1986 Jean Fritz

1989 Elizabeth George Speare

1992 Marcia Brown

1995 Virginia Hamilton

1998 Russell Freedman

2001 Milton Meltzer

2003 Eric Carle

2005 Laurence Yep

2007 James Marshall

2009 Ashley Bryan

Name / Title Index

Subject Index

Credits